THE OXFORD HANDBOOK OF

EARLY CHRISTIAN STUDIES

Edited by

SUSAN ASHBROOK HARVEY

and

DAVID G. HUNTER

D1543221

OXFORD

UNIVERSITY PRESS

OXFORD
UNIVERSITY PRESS

Great Clarendon Street, Oxford OX2 6DP

Oxford University Press is a department of the University of Oxford.
It furthers the University's objective of excellence in research, scholarship,
and education by publishing worldwide in

Oxford New York

Auckland Cape Town Dar es Salaam Hong Kong Karachi
Kuala Lumpur Madrid Melbourne Mexico City Nairobi
New Delhi Shanghai Taipei Toronto

With offices in

Argentina Austria Brazil Chile Czech Republic France Greece
Guatemala Hungary Italy Japan Poland Portugal Singapore
South Korea Switzerland Thailand Turkey Ukraine Vietnam

Oxford is a registered trade mark of Oxford University Press
in the UK and in certain other countries

Published in the United States
by Oxford University Press Inc., New York

© Oxford University Press 2008

The moral rights of the authors have been asserted
Database right Oxford University Press (maker)

First published 2008

British Library Cataloguing in Publication Data
Data available

Library of Congress Cataloging in Publication Data
Data available

Typeset by SPI Publisher Services, Pondicherry, India
Printed in Great Britain
on acid-free paper by
CPI Antony Rowe, Chippenham, Wiltshire

ISBN 978–0–19–927156–6

1 3 5 7 9 10 8 6 4 2

ACKNOWLEDGEMENTS

Many people have helped to bring this volume to press. We are grateful to our essayists for their generosity, their patience and efficiency, and for the consistent excellence that characterizes the writings of this Handbook. We are deeply indebted to Samantha Papaioannou, whose skillful editing wove the pieces into a well-integrated whole. Brown University, and especially Professor Mark Cladis, Chair of the Department of Religious Studies, provided critical support both material and moral at crucial stages of the process. We also thank Patrick Owens for his work on the indexes, supported by the Cottrill-Rolfes Chair of Catholic Studies at the University of Kentucky. At Oxford University Press we have been assisted by a splendid team of editors: Jean van Altena, Tanya Dean, Hilary O'Shea, Lucy Qureshi, Dorothy McCarthy, Tom Perridge, Lizzie Robottom, Maggie Shade, and Jennifer Wagstaffe. Our heartfelt thanks go to each and every one of these. It has been a pleasure and an honour to work with such colleagues at every stage of this effort. Finally, we thank our respective spouses and families who have graciously tolerated the distraction of yet another scholarly project.

S. A. H.

D. G. H.

January 2008

Contents

PART I. PROLEGOMENA

PART II. EVIDENCE: MATERIAL AND TEXTUAL

PART III. IDENTITIES

PART IV. REGIONS

PART V. STRUCTURES AND AUTHORITIES

PART VI. EXPRESSIONS OF CHRISTIAN CULTURE

PART VII. RITUAL, PIETY, AND PRACTICE

PART VIII. THEOLOGICAL THEMES

LIST OF MAPS

LIST OF ILLUSTRATIONS

ABBREVIATIONS

Periodicals, Series, and Reference Works

ABD	*Anchor Bible Dictionary*, ed. D. N. Freedman
ACO	*Acta conciliorum oecumenicorum*
ACW	Ancient Christian Writers
AE	*L'année épigraphique*
Aev	*Aevum: Rassegna de scienza, storiche, linguistiche, e filologiche*
AJA	*American Journal of Archeology*
ALMA	*Archivum Latinitas Medii Aevi*
AnBoll	*Analecta Bollandiana*
ANF	Ante-Nicene Fathers Series
ANRW	*Aufstieg und Niedergang der römischen Welt: Geschichte und Kultur Roms im Spiegel der neueren Forschung*, ed. H. Temporini and W. Haase. Berlin, 1972–
Aug	*Augustinianum*
AugStud	*Augustinian Studies*
Aug(L)	*Augustiniana*, Leuven
AugLex	*Augustinus-Lexikon*
BA	*Biblical Archaeologist*
BA	Bibliothèque Augustinienne
BAR	British Archaeological Reports
BETL	Bibliotheca Ephemeridum Theologicarum Lovaniensium
BHG	*Bibliotheca Hagiographica Graeca*
BHL	*Bibliotheca Hagiographica Latina*
BHO	*Bibliotheca Hagiographica Orientalis*
BLE	*Bulletin de littérature ecclésiastique*
BMCR	*Bryn Mawr Classical Review*
ByF	*Byzantinische Forschungen*
CA	*Classical Antiquity*
CAH	*Cambridge Ancient History*
CBQ	*Catholic Biblical Quarterly*
CC	Corpus Christianorum
CCCM	Corpus Christianorum, Continuatio Mediaevalis
CCSA	Corpus Christianorum, Series Apocryphorum

CCSG	Corpus Christianorum, Series Graeca
CCSL	Corpus Christianorum, Series Latina
CERP	Centre d'études et de recherches pastorales
CFM.A 1	Corpus Fontium Manichaeorum, Series Archaeologica 1
CH	*Church History*
Chiron	*Chiron: Mitteilungen der Kommission für alte Geschichte und Epigraphik des Deutschen Archäologischen Instituts*
CIG	*Corpus inscriptionum graecarum*, ed. A. Boeckh, 4 vols., Berlin: Deutsche Akademie der Wissenschaften, 1828–77
CII	*Corpus inscriptionum iudaicarum*, ed. J. B. Frey, 2 vols., Rome: Pontificio Istituto di Archeologia Cristiana, 1936–52
CIL	*Corpus inscriptionum latinarum*, ed. F. W. Ritschl *et al.*, Berlin: Reimer, 1862–1932; de Gruyter, 1932–
CPG	*Clavis Patrum Graecorum*, ed. M. Geerard, 5 vols., Turnhout: Brepols, 1974–87; *Supplementum*, ed. M. Geerard and J. Noret, Turnhout: Brepols, 1998
CPL	*Clavis Patrum Latinorum*, ed. E. Dekkers, 3rd edn., Turnhout: Brepols, 1995
CQ	*Classical Quarterly*
CRAI	*Comptes rendus des l'Académie des inscriptions et belles-lettres*
CS	Cistercian Studies Series
CSCO	Corpus Scriptorum Christianorum Orientalium
CSEL	Corpus Scriptorum Ecclesiasticorum Latinorum
CWE	Collected Works of Erasmus
CWS	Classics of Western Spirituality
DACL	*Dictionnaire d'archéologie chrétienne et de liturgie*, ed. F. Cabrol and H. Leclercq, 15 vols., Paris: Letouzey et Ané (1907–53)
DOP	*Dumbarton Oaks Papers*
DSp	*Dictionnaire de spiritualité, ascétique et mystique, histoire et doctrine*, ed. M. Viller, A. Derville, P. Lamarche, and A. Solignac, 22 vols., Paris: Beauchesne, 1932–95
EA	*Epigraphica Anatolica*
ECF	Early Church Fathers
ETL	*Ephemerides theologicae lovanienses*
FC	Fathers of the Church
FKDG	Forschungen zur Kirchen- und Dogmengeschichte, Göttingen: Vandenhoeck & Ruprecht
FZPhTh	*Freiburger Zeitschrift für Philosophie und Theologie*
GCS	Die griechischen christlichen Schriftsteller der ersten drei Jahrhunderte
GNO	Gregorii Nyssensi Opera
GRBS	*Greek, Roman, and Byzantine Studies*

HLL	*Handbuch der lateinischen Literatur der Antike*
HTR	*Harvard Theological Review*
HTS	Harvard Theological Studies
ICUR	*Inscriptiones christianae urbis Romae septimo saeculo antiquiores*, ed. J. B. de Rossi, J.-B. and G. Gatti, Rome: Libraria Pontificia and P. Cuggiani 1861–1915
ICUR²	*Inscriptiones christianae urbis Romae septimo saeculo antiquiores, nova series*, ed. A. Silvagni *et al.*, Rome: Pontificio Istituto di Archeologia Cristiana, 1922–92
IGOccidChr	*Inscriptiones graecae christianae veteres occidentis*, ed. C. Wessel, Inscriptiones Christianae Italiae 1, Bari: Edipuglia, 1989
ILCV	*Inscriptiones latinae christianae veteres*, vols. 1–3, ed. E. Diehl, Berlin: Weidmann, 1925–31; vol. 4, ed. J. Moreau and H. I. Marrou, Berlin: Weidmann, 1961
JAAR	*Journal of the American Academy of Religion*
JAC	*Jahrbuch für Antike und Christentum*
JBL	*Journal of Biblical Literature*
JDT	*Jahrbüch für deutsche Theologie*
JECS	*Journal of Early Christian Studies*
JFSR	*Journal of Feminist Studies in Religion*
JHSex	*Journal of the History of Sexuality*
JMEMS	*Journal of Medieval and Early Modern Studies*
JRA	*Journal of Roman Archaeology*
JRS	*Journal of Roman Studies*
JSNT	*Journal for the Study of the New Testament*
JSPSup	Journal for the Study of the Pseudepigrapha: Supplement Series
JTS	*Journal of Theological Studies*
LCC	Library of Christian Classics
LCL	Loeb Classical Library
LTK	*Lexikon für Theologie und Kirche*
MFC	Message of the Fathers of the Church
Mus	*Muséon: Revue d'études orientales*
NHMS	Nag Hammadi and Manichaean Studies
NHS	Nag Hammadi Studies
NPNF[1]	Nicene and Post-Nicene Fathers, Series 1
NPNF[2]	Nicene and Post-Nicene Fathers, Series 2
NTS	*New Testament Studies*
OCP	*Orientalia christiana periodica*
OECS	Oxford Early Christian Studies
OECT	Oxford Early Christian Texts
OHMS	Oxford Historical Monograph Series
OrChrAn	Orientalia Christiana Analecta

Par.	Paradosis: Beiträge zur Geschichte der altchristlichen Literatur und Theologie
PCBE	*Prosopographie chrétienne du Bas-Empire*, ed. H.-I. Marrou and J.-R. Palanque, i: Paris: Éditions du Centre National de la Recherche Scientifique; ii: Rome: École française de Rome, 1999–2000
PG	Patrologia Graeca, ed. J.-P. Migne
PL	Patrologia Latina, ed. J.-P. Migne
PLRE	*The Prosopography of the Later Roman Empire*, ed. A. H. M. Jones, J. R. Martindale, and J. Morris, 4 vols., Cambridge: Cambridge University Press, 1980–92
PLS	*Patrologiae Latinae Supplementum*, ed. A. Hamman, 5 vols., Paris: Garnier, 1958–74
PMS	Patristic Monograph Series
PO	Patrologia Orientalis
PTS	Patristische Texte und Studien
RAC	*Reallexikon für Antike und Christentum*
RB	*Revue biblique*
RBén	*Revue Bénédictine*
REA	*Revue des études anciennes*
REAug	*Revue des études augustiniennes*
RechAug	*Recherches augustiniennes*
RHE	*Revue d'histoire ecclésiastique*
RQ	*Römische Quartalschrift für christliche Altertumskunde und für Kirchengeschichte*
RSPT	*Revue des sciences philosophiques et théologiques*
RSR	*Recherches de science religieuse*
RTAM	*Recherches de théologie ancienne et médiévale*
SAC	Studies in Antiquity and Christianity
SacEr	*Sacris erudiri: Jaarboek voor Godsdienstwetenschappen*
SAEMO	Sancti Ambrosii Episcopi Mediolanensis Opera
SBL	Society for Biblical Literature
SBLTT	Society of Biblical Literature Texts and Translations
SC	Sources chrétiennes
SCH	Studies in Church History
ScrHier	Scripta Hierosolymitana
SEG	*Supplementum epigraphicum graecum*, ed. J. J. E. Hondius, Leiden: Nijhof; Amsterdam: J. C. Gieben, 1923–71, 1979–
SO	*Symbolae osloenses*
SPLi	*Studia Patristica et liturgica*
SR	*Sciences religieuses*
StPatr	*Studia Patristica*
StPB	Studia post-biblica

StStor	Studi storici
Suppl. VC	Vigiliae Christianae Supplement
TaS	Texts and Studies
TRE	Theologische Realenzyklopädie
TRu	Theologische Rundschau
TS	Theological Studies
TU	Texte und Untersuchungen zur Geschichte der altchristliche Literatur
USQR	Union Seminary Quarterly Review
VC	Vigiliae Christianae
VetChr	Vetera Christianorum
WSA	The Works of Saint Augustine: A Translation for the 21st Century, Hyde Park, NY: New City Press
WUNT	Wissenschaftliche Untersuchungen zum Neuen Testament
ZAC	Zeitschrift für Antikes Christentum
ZDMG	Zeitschrift der Deutschen Morgenländischen Gesellschaft
ZKG	Zeitschrift für Kirchengeschichte
ZPE	Zeitschrift für Papyrologie und Epigraphik

Ancient sources

Ambrose of Milan

Ep.	Epistulae
Fid.	De fide
Hex.	Hexaemeron
Off.	De officiis
Paen.	De paenitentia
Sacr.	De sacramentis
Ser. c. Aux.	Sermo contra Auxentium

Ambrosiaster

Comm. in Rom. (etc.)	Commentarius in xiii epistulas Paulinas: ad Romanos (etc.)
Quaest.	Quaestiones veteris et novi testamenti

Anonymous

Barn.	Epistula Barnabi
Did.	Didache xii apostolorum
Diog.	Epistula ad Diognetum

Aphrahat

Dem.	Demonstrations

Arator

Ep. ad Virg.	Epistula ad Virgilium

Aristotle

Phys.   *Physica*

Arnobius

Nat.   *Adversus nationes*

Athanasius of Alexandria

Ar.   *Orationes tres contra Arianos*
Ep. Marcell.   *Epistula ad Marcellinum*
Inc.   *De incarnatione*
Vit. Ant.   *Vita Antonii*

Augustine of Hippo

Cat. rud.   *De catechizandis rudibus*
Civ.   *De civitate dei*
Conf.   *Confessiones*
Doct. chr.   *De doctrina christiana*
Ep.   *Epistulae*
Gen. imp.   *De Genesi ad litteram liber imperfectus*
Gen. litt.   *De Genesi ad litteram*
Gen. Man.   *De Genesi contra Manichaeos*
Haer.   *De haeresibus*
Mor. eccl.   *De moribus ecclesiae catholicae*
Nupt.   *De nuptiis et concupiscentia*
Pecc. or.   *De peccato originali*
Pecc. mer.   *De peccatorum meritis et remissione et de baptismo parvulorum*
Persev.   *De dono perseverantiae*
Psal.   *Enarrationes in Psalmos*
Retract.   *Retractationes*
Serm.   *Sermones*
Trin.   *De trinitate*

Basil of Caesarea

Spir.   *De Spiritu Sancto*
Ep.   *Epistulae*
Hex.   *In Hexaemeron homiliae*

Basil of Seleucia

Pasch.   *In sanctum Pascha homilia*

Caesarius of Arles

Serm.   *Sermones*

Clement of Alexandria

Paed.	*Paedagogus*
Prot.	*Protrepticus*
Strom.	*Stromateis*

Clement of Rome

1 Clem.	*Epistula Clementis ad Corinthios*

Cyprian of Carthage

Ep.	*Epistulae*

Cyril of Jerusalem

Catech. 1–18	*Catecheses illuminandorum*
Catech. 19–23	*Catecheses mystagogicae*

Epiphanius of Salamis

Pan.	*Panarion (Adversus haereses)*

Eusebius of Caesarea

Dem.	*Demonstratio evangelica*
Hist. eccl.	*Historia ecclesiastica*
Praep.	*Praeparatio evangelica*
Vit. Const.	*Vita Constantini*

Evagrius of Pontus

Cap. pract.	*Capita practica (Praktikos)*
Keph. gnost.	*Kephalaia gnostica*
Schol. in Ps.	*Scholia in Psalmos*
Schol. in Eccl.	*Scholia in Ecclesiasten*

Gennadius

Vir. ill.	*De viris illustribus*

Gregory of Nazianzus

Carm.	*Carmina*
Ep.	*Epistulae*
Or.	*Orationes*
Poem. Ar.	*Poemata arcana*

Gregory of Nyssa

Anim. et res.	*De anima et resurrectione*
Ep.	*Epistulae*
Eun.	*Contra Eunomium*

Hex.	*Apologia in Hexaemeron*
Hom. in Eccl.	*In Ecclesiasten homiliae*
Hom. opif.	*De hominis opificio*
Or. catech.	*Oratio catechetica*
Sanct. Pascha	*In sanctum Pascha homilia*

Hermas

Mand.	*Mandata pastoris*
Sim.	*Similitudines pastoris*
Vis.	*Visiones pastoris*

Hippolytus of Rome

Antichr.	*De antichristo*
Ben. Iacob.	*De benedictione Iacobi*
Haer.	*Refutatio omnium haeresium*

Ignatius of Antioch

Eph.	*Epistula ad Ephesios*
Phil.	*Epistula ad Philadelphios*
Rom.	*Epistula ad Romanos*
Smyr.	*Epistula ad Smyrnaeos*
Trall.	*Epistula ad Trallianos*

Irenaeus of Lyons

Haer.	*Adversus haereses*

Isidore of Seville

Etym.	*Etymologiae*

Jerome

Dial.	*Dialogus contra Pelagianos*
Ep.	*Epistulae*
Qu. Heb. Gen.	*Quaestionum Hebraicorum liber in Genesim*
Vir. ill.	*De viris illustribus*

John Chrysostom

Hom. in Mt.	*In Mattheum homilia*
Hom. in Rom.	*In epistolam ad Romanos homilia*
Hom. in 2 Thess.	*In epistulam ad Thessalonicenses 2 homilia*
Laed.	*Quod nemo laeditur nisi a seipso*
Poenit.	*De poenitentia*
Sac.	*De sacerdotio*
Scand.	*Ad eos qui scandalizati sunt ob adversitates*

John of Damascus

F.o.	*De fide orthodoxa*

Josephus

C. Ap.	*Contra Apionem*

Julian of Aeclanum

Flo.	*Ad Florum*

Justin Martyr

1 Apol.	*1 Apologia*
2 Apol.	*2 Apologia*
Dial.	*Dialogus cum Trypho*

Lactantius

Inst.	*Divinae Institutiones*
Mort.	*De mortibus persecutorum*

Maximus the Confessor

Amb.	*Ambiguorum liber*
Cap. theol.	*Capita theologica et oecumenica*
Ep.	*Epistulae*
Thal.	*Quaestiones ad Thalassium*

Maximus of Turin

Serm.	*Sermones*

Melito of Sardis

Pass.	*Homilia in passionem Christi (Peri pascha)*

Methodius of Olympus

Creat.	*De creatis* (frags.)

Nemesius of Emesa

Nat. hom.	*De natura hominis*

Origen of Alexandria

Cels.	*Contra Celsum*
Comm. Gen.	*Commentarii in Genesin*
Comm. Jo.	*Commentarii in Johannem*
Comm. Matt.	*Commentarii in Matthaeum libri x–xi*
Comm. Rom.	*Commentarii in epistulam ad Romanos*
Comm. ser. in Mt.	*Commentariorum series in Mattheum*

Hom. in Gen.	*Homiliae in Genesin*
Hom. in Jer.	*Homiliae in Jeremiam*
Hom. in Lev.	*Homiliae in Leviticum*
Hom. in Num.	*Homiliae in Numeros*
Or.	*De oratione*
Princ.	*De principiis*

Orosius

Hist. adv. pag.	*Historiarum adversus paganos, libri VII*

Paulinus of Nola

Carm.	*Carmina*
Ep.	*Epistulae*

Philo of Alexandria

Conf.	*De confusione linguarum*
Opif.	*De opificio mundi*

Plato

Tim.	*Timaeus*

Polycarp of Smyrna

Phil.	*Epistula ad Philippenses*

Porphyry

V. Plot.	*Vita Plotini*

Pseudo-Clement

Ep.	*Epistula Clementis*

Pseudo-Dionysius the Areopagite

D. n.	*De divinis nominibus*
E. h.	*De ecclesiastica hierarchia*

Pseudo-Plutarch

Plac. phil.	*Placita philosophorum*

Salvian of Marseilles

Gub.	*De gubernatione Dei*

Socrates Scholasticus

Hist. eccl.	*Historia ecclesiastica*

Sozomen

Hist. eccl.   *Historia ecclesiastica*

Sulpicius Severus

Chron.   *Chronicorum libri ii*

Tatian

Orat.   *Oratio ad Graecos*

Tertullian

Ad. Iud.	*Adversus Iudaeos*
An.	*De anima*
Apol.	*Apologeticus*
Bapt.	*De baptismo*
Cor. mil.	*De corona militum*
Exh. cast.	*De exhortatione castitatis*
Fuga pers.	*De fuga in persecutione*
Herm.	*Adversus Hermogenem*
Idol.	*De idololatria*
Marc.	*Adversus Marcionem*
Nat.	*Ad Nationes*
Or.	*De oratione*
Paen.	*De paenitentia*
Pall.	*De pallio*
Praescr.	*De praescriptione haereticorum*
Prax.	*Adversus Praxean*
Pud.	*De pudicitia*
Scap.	*Ad Scapulam*
Virg.	*De virginibus velandis*

Theodoret of Cyrrhus

H. rel.	*Historia religiosa*
Hist. eccl.	*Historia ecclesiastica*
Provid.	*De providentia orationes*

Theophilus of Antioch

Autol.   *Ad Autolycum*

Zacharias of Mytilene

Hist. eccl.   *Historia ecclesiastica*

LIST OF CONTRIBUTORS

William Adler is Professor of Religion at North Carolina State University, Raleigh.

Lewis Ayres is Associate Professor of Historical Theology in the Candler School of Theology at Emory University, Atlanta, Georgia.

Paul M. Blowers is Dean E. Walker Professor of Church History at the Emmanuel School of Religion, Johnson City, Tennessee.

David Brakke is Professor of Religious Studies at Indiana University, Bloomington.

Sebastian P. Brock is Reader in Syriac Studies Emeritus at the Oriental Institute, Oxford University.

Francine Cardman is Associate Professor of Historical Theology and Church History at Weston Jesuit School of Theology in Cambridge, Massachusetts.

Elizabeth A. Clark is John Carlisle Kilgo Professor of Religion at Duke University, Durham, North Carolina.

Brian E. Daley, SJ, is Catherine F. Huisking Professor of Theology at the University of Notre Dame, Notre Dame, Indiana.

Harold A. Drake is Professor of History at the University of California, Santa Barbara.

Hubertus R. Drobner is Professor of Church History and Patrology at the Theologische Fakultät Paderborn, Germany.

Mark Edwards is Tutor in Theology at Christ Church and Lecturer in Patristics at Oxford University.

Everett Ferguson is Professor of Church History Emeritus at Abilene Christian University, Abilene, Texas.

Allan D. Fitzgerald, OSA, is Professor of Patristics at the Augustinian Patristic Institute, Rome.

Georgia Frank is Associate Professor of Religion at Colgate University, Hamilton, New York.

J. William Harmless, SJ, is Professor of Theology at Creighton University, Omaha, Nebraska.

Susan Ashbrook Harvey is Professor of Religious Studies at Brown University, Providence, Rhode Island.

Michael W. Holmes is Professor of Biblical Studies and Early Christianity at Bethel University, St. Paul, Minnesota.

Mark Humphries is Professor of Ancient History at Swansea University, Swansea, Wales.

David G. Hunter is Cottrill–Rolfes Professor of Catholic Studies at the University of Kentucky, Lexington.

Andrew S. Jacobs is Associate Professor of Religious Studies at the University of California, Riverside.

Robin M. Jensen is Luce Chancellor's Professor of the History of Christian Art and Worship at the Vanderbilt University Divinity School, Nashville, Tennessee.

Maxwell E. Johnson is Professor of Liturgical Studies at the University of Notre Dame, Notre Dame, Indiana.

Joseph F. Kelly is Professor of Religious Studies at John Carroll University, University Heights, Ohio.

Karen L. King is Winn Professor of Ecclesiastical History at the Harvard University Divinity School, Cambridge, Massachusetts.

Ross Shepard Kraemer is Professor of Religious Studies and Judaic Studies at Brown University, Providence, Rhode Island.

Rebecca Krawiec is Assistant Professor of Religious Studies and Theology at Canisius College, Buffalo, New York.

Mathijs Lamberigts is Professor of Church History and Theology at Katholieke Universiteit, Leuven, Belgium.

Samuel N. C. Lieu is Professor of Ancient History and Co-Director of the Ancient History Documentary Research Centre, Macquarie University, Sydney, Australia.

J. Rebecca Lyman is Garrett Professor of Church History Emerita at the Church Divinity School of the Pacific, Berkeley, California.

Antti Marjanen is Docent of New Testament Studies at the University of Helsinki.

Ralph W. Mathisen is Professor of History, Classics, and Medieval Studies at the University of Illinois, Urbana/Champaign.

Wendy Mayer is Research Associate in the Centre for Early Christian Studies, Australian Catholic University.

John A. McGuckin is Nielsen Professor of Late Antique and Byzantine Christian History at Union Theological Seminary, New York, and Professor of Byzantine Christianity at Columbia University, New York.

Richard M. Price is Senior Lecturer in the History of Christianity at Heythrop College, University of London.

Andrew Radde-Gallwitz is Assistant Professor of Theology at Loyola University, Chicago, Illinois.

Éric Rebillard is Professor of Classics and History at Cornell University, Ithaca, New York.

Michael J. Roberts is Robert Rich Professor of Latin at Wesleyan University, Middletown, Connecticut.

Jeanne-Nicole Saint-Laurent is a Ph.D. candidate in Early Christianity at Brown University, Providence, Rhode Island.

Michele R. Salzman is Professor of History at the University of California, Riverside.

Daniel Sheerin is Professor of Classics and Theology Emeritus at the University of Notre Dame, Notre Dame, Indiana.

Stephen J. Shoemaker is Associate Professor of Religious Studies at the University of Oregon, Eugene.

Columba Stewart, OSB, is Professor of Theology at St. John's School of Theology-Seminary, Collegeville, Minnesota.

William Tabbernee is President and Stephen J. England Professor of the History of Christianity at Phillips Theological Seminary, Tulsa, Oklahoma.

Karen Jo Torjesen is Margo L. Goldsmith Professor of Women's Studies and Dean of the School of Religion at Claremont Graduate University, Claremont, California.

Raymond Van Dam is Professor of History at the University of Michigan, Ann Arbor.

Lucas Van Rompay is Professor of Eastern Christianity at Duke University, Durham, North Carolina.

Mark Vessey is Professor of English at the University of British Columbia, Vancouver.

Frances M. Young is Edward Cadbury Professor of Theology Emerita at the University of Birmingham.

INTRODUCTION

SUSAN ASHBROOK HARVEY
DAVID G. HUNTER

Recent decades have seen an explosion of research in the area of 'early Christian studies'. This Handbook has been prepared, in large measure, as a response to that development. Early Christian studies examines the history, literature, thought, practices, and material culture of the Christian religion in late antiquity (*c.* 100–600 CE). Once pursued primarily as a sub-speciality within Ecclesiastical History or Theology (that is, as 'Patristics'), the study of early Christianity has recently emerged as a distinctive and fully interdisciplinary endeavour in its own right, embracing the fields of Classics, Ancient History, Theology, Religious Studies, Art History, and Archaeology, among others. New trends in historiography, critical theory, and the humanistic sciences have also made their mark on this academic discipline.

A number of events have fostered this development. In recent decades there have been discoveries of new documents (for example, the Nag Hammadi Library, the Divjak letters and Dolbeau sermons of Augustine, and the Turfan Manichaean texts). New journals and book series have appeared, as well as a steady stream of new critical editions and translations. 'Late antiquity' has increasingly been recognized as a historical period with its own distinctive features and significance.

This proliferation of scholarship on early Christianity has called forth the present volume. When the representatives of Oxford University Press approached us with the idea of editing a volume in the Oxford Handbook series, it seemed an ideal opportunity to provide a useful service to the field. Because of the increasing range and diversity of scholarly work in early Christian studies, it has become impossible for any one scholar to maintain expertise in every aspect of the discipline. Certain topics have provoked an extraordinary amount of discussion (early Christian asceticism, for example, or the fourth-century Trinitarian controversies); other areas have become highly specialized sub-disciplines (Manichaean studies, for example, or Gnostic studies). A scholar working in one branch of early Christianity might have little notion of developments in another area of the field. We hope this volume in the Oxford Handbook series will address this difficulty by introducing readers to the wide variety of ways in which 'early Christian studies' are conducted and have been conducted, especially within the past thirty years. We intend it to be an aid to research both for beginners and for more seasoned scholars entering an unfamiliar sub-speciality.

To accomplish this task, we invited contributors to address their topics with the aim of orienting readers to the current 'state of the question' in that area. Contributors were asked to reflect on the main questions or issues that have animated research, to provide an introduction to the relevant primary sources, and to offer some guidance on the directions in which future research might be profitably pursued. Depending on the topic, different contributors emphasized one or more of these tasks, but our intention has been to provide a useful starting point for further investigation in that increasingly disparate discipline of 'early Christian studies'.

This focus on the trajectory of research and the developments within the scholarship itself differentiate this volume from others aiming to provide cogent summary introductions to various topics, figures, or historical assessments (that is, encyclopaedias, dictionaries, or histories). Further, it is the categories, issues, and areas (whether spatial or intellectual) of these developments that have guided our structuring of the essays into broadly defined thematic sections. The structure as a whole is prefaced by a set of prolegomena: three essays surveying the intellectual and scholarly changes that have reframed our study of the early Christian past. We encourage readers to consider the specific discussions of individual chapters against the backdrop of these prefatory essays.

The section divisions offer broad ways of organizing early Christian studies. They also reflect how the changing agendas of scholarship have refocused how we consider even the best known of the ancient materials. Thus, following Part I, 'Prolegomena', Part II, 'Evidence: Material and Textual', considers types of evidence crucial for establishing early Christian history and for providing concrete assessment of the literary evidence that has long dominated historical reconstruction of ancient history. Part III, 'Identities', looks at specific religious identities that have long been the foils against which the meaning of the term 'Christian' took shape, both by and for its ancient advocates and by modern scholars (as well as adherents). These labels, common in usage but elusive in historical reality, gain further and more nuanced substance in Part IV, 'Regions', where the huge geographical expanse of early Christianity is brought into play. One of the most significant results of recent scholarship has been the realization of the extent to which geographical location affected the issues, concerns, and even forms of early Christianity. Consideration of Donatism in terms other than as a problem confronting Augustine, for example, or of the Cappadocian fathers within their regional context brings to light important but generally neglected features. Part V, 'Structures and Authorities', draws out fundamental social structures and ecclesiastical authorities by which ancient Christians organized their lives, whether institutionally, politically, or domestically. Part VI, 'Expressions of Christian Culture', looks at the array of literary forms by which Christians articulated their concerns, identities, interests, debates, memories, practices, and teachings. In Part VII, 'Ritual, Piety, and Practice', those expressions are considered through their implementation as activities both collective and individual. Part VIII, 'Theological Themes', takes up perennially vibrant areas of theological discussion that have been much affected by the scholarly shifts charted in the volume as a whole.

Careful review of the Table of Contents and use of the indexes will help readers find topics or key figures whose locations may not seem to be readily apparent under this organizational scheme. Each essay is followed by suggestions for further reading, as well as important bibliography for the topic. The final chapter of the volume, 'Instrumenta Studiorum: Tools of the Trade', provides an extensive guide to various scholarly tools critical to any study of the field: major journals, published series of critical editions and translations, dictionaries and handbooks of various sorts and foci, data bases, websites, and related research tools. Our hope is that the fruitfulness of recent decades can here be not only acknowledged, but also gathered together in a form that will promote rich inquiry for a long time to come.

This volume takes as its chronological duration the period from 100 to 600 CE: that is, the period roughly stretching from the end of the New Testament era to the eve of Islam's appearance on the historical horizon. New Testament studies is in itself a field of massive scholarly enterprise, and its work is handled in a separate volume of the Oxford Handbook series. There will inevitably be some essays in the current volume that require engagement with New Testament materials, just as—at the other end of the chronological spectrum—there will be some that consider trajectories extending into the medieval and Byzantine periods. However, our focus is on that period during which Christianity takes its shape specifically as a religion. The salient issues are not those involving the historical figure of Jesus or his immediate followers or the formation of the New Testament documents, but rather, how the movement around those persons and events became an established, institutionalized, differentiated religion: a body of self-identified adherents related (however loosely) by practices and beliefs.

PART I

PROLEGOMENA

CHAPTER 1

....

FROM PATRISTICS TO EARLY CHRISTIAN STUDIES

....

ELIZABETH A. CLARK

CHARLES Kannengiesser's presidential address to the North American Patristics Society in 1990 was a lament originally titled 'Bye, Bye Patristics'. Most of the classically-educated French scholars who had revitalized patristics as part of what Kannengiesser termed 'the spiritual and humanistic revival in Europe after World War II' were dead, and educational support for these studies in Europe was dwindling (Kannengiesser 1989: 655, 638, 642). Yet, as Kannengiesser conceded in a subsequent essay, these giants in the field had not engaged (as he put it) 'the new social dimension of patristics' (Kannengiesser 1991: 133)—the very characteristic that distinguishes 'early Christian studies'. The passage from 'patristics' to 'early Christian studies', however, is not the whole story that is sketched here: we must first ask, how did 'patristics' itself emerge as a discipline?[1]

Older scholarship discussed in this essay will be cited in the main text with the original publication date; but the Bibliography gives the publication date for the English edition, generally the most recent (or most accessible) edition.

1.1 CREATING PATRISTICS

To be sure, medieval and early modern scholars, Protestant Reformers, and the Caroline divines studied Augustine, Jerome, John Chrysostom, and other church fathers—from the late fifteenth century onward, in printed editions. Yet patristics did not truly become a discipline in the modern sense of the word until the nineteenth century: the English word 'patristic' was allegedly coined by Isaac Taylor (1787–1865).[2] Moreover, even in the nineteenth century, apologetics and polemics often dominated the discussion. For patristics to achieve disciplinary status, institutional arrangements (universities, seminaries, conferences) and scholarly apparatuses (critical editions of texts and professional journals) needed to be established.

Different circumstances attended the development of patristics in various countries. In nineteenth-century Germany, the world-acclaimed, government-supported (and largely Protestant) university system was decisive. In Catholic France, editions of patristic texts by the Benedictines of St Maur and J.-P. Migne's Patrologia Latina and Patrologia Graeca were central; while in later decades, the Modernist crisis and the disenchantment with Thomism revived interest in patristics. In England, the Oxford Movement and the reactions to it throughout the nineteenth century spurred scholarship on the fathers.

Scholars from many other European countries also contributed to the development of patristics. Belgium's Jean-Baptiste Malou was instrumental in the production of the Patrologia Graeca (Hamman 1985), while in the twentieth century, Belgium was the seat of production for the Corpus Christianorum, Series Latina (1954) and Series Graeca (1977). Louvain also became a renowned centre for the study of 'oriental' patristics, as is discussed below.

In the Netherlands, formally separated from Belgium in 1830, Protestant scholars were slow to develop an interest in patristic studies. In 1923, with the founding of the Catholic University of Nijmegen, patristics received stronger encouragement. Special mention should be made of Dom Eligius Dekkers, who created the Clavis Patrum Latinorum (1951) and was a driving force behind the establishment at mid-century of the Corpus Christianorum, Series Latina (Lamberigts 1998–9).[3] An important—and continuing—Dutch contribution to patristic studies is the journal Vigiliae Christianae, whose first issue appeared in 1947, and which for many years was edited chiefly by Christine Mohrmann and Jan Hendrik Waszink.

Eighteenth-century Italian scholars edited and reprinted patristic sources (Petitmengin 1985: 30); in the nineteenth century, Giovanni Battista de Rossi's research on Roman catacombs and inscriptions greatly advanced knowledge of early Christian material culture and practice. In Vienna, the Corpus Scriptorum Ecclesiasticorum Latinorum was begun in 1866. As is evident, contributions from scholars of various European nations have been important for the development of modern patristic studies. In this essay, however, a brief review of developments in Germany, France, and England must suffice.

Protestant scholars in Germany and England (outside the circle of the Oxford Movement) showed a decided preference for the fathers of the first two centuries, who, in their view, remained closer to the revealed truth of the Bible. In the following centuries, they claimed, 'decline' became rampant—as manifested in metaphysical speculation and conciliar débâcles, allegorical exegesis, 'unscriptural' asceticism, ecclesiastical hierarchy, and 'state-churchism'. Despite German scholars' alleged embrace of the new historical and critical methods, their sectarian and anti-Catholic prejudices, overlaid with a modified Hegelianism, obstructed the development of a more solidly 'historical' view of the early church. Such skewing, however, was by no means solely a 'German problem': as Maurice Wiles has pointedly observed, the entanglements of present concerns with scholarship on the past almost inevitably 'skew the way evidence is read and interpreted' (Wiles 2003: 153).

1.1.1 Germany

German universities led the way in creating the academic discipline of church history, the rubric under which patristics developed in the Protestant world. Before the era of readily available critical editions and monographs, the interest in patristics can be charted largely through its treatment in textbooks and general histories of the early church: Johann L. Mosheim's *Ecclesiastical History* (1750s); Johann Gieseler's *Text-Book of Church History* (1824); and at mid-century Augustus Neander's *General History of the Christian Religion and Church*. The lack of ready access to primary sources was a central obstacle to the development of the field. Mosheim, for example, believed that his contribution lay chiefly in his consultation—uncommon in his day—of the 'original records…the genuine sources of sacred history'. Many manuscripts were still unavailable to scholars, he complained, being shut up 'in the collections of the curious (or the opulent, who are willing to pass for such)'. Although Roman Catholic scholars had greater access to manuscripts (presumably in the Vatican Library and elsewhere), their advantage had not forestalled, in Mosheim's view, their massive errors of interpretation (Mosheim 1810: pp. xiii–xvi).

Evangelistic Christians, however, who considered Mosheim's text 'rationalistic' and devoid of Christian fervour, turned to Johann Gieseler's *Text-Book of Church History*, which provided both lengthy extracts from the primary sources and evangelical spirit. Most favoured by mid-nineteenth-century professors, however, were the works of Augustus Neander, who held the Professorship of Church History at Berlin. Those who deemed Gieseler's textbook too synoptic; Mosheim's, 'scanty, cold, and superficial'; and English works by Milman and Waddington 'diffuse, declamatory, partisan, ignorant, popular' and 'mislead[ing]', praised Neander's

General History of the Christian Religion and Church as the only one worthy of the name.[4] Yet his multi-volumed work was far too large and dense for classroom use (and too wedded to the notion of 'development' for the taste of some English-language scholars). Also much admired at the time were Neander's studies of John Chrysostom and of Julian 'the Apostate'.

Several decades later, Adolph von Harnack's *History of Dogma* and *Mission and Expansion of Christianity in the First Three Centuries* strongly influenced the developing conception of patristics on the Continent and in the United States. The production of critical editions and monographs received a further stimulus in 1882, when Harnack and Oscar von Gebhardt founded Texte und Untersuchungen zur Geschichte der altchristlichen Literatur. In 1890, the Prussian Academy, impelled by Harnack and Theodor Mommsen, established the Kirchenväter-Kommission that produced the series Die griechischen christlichen Schriftsteller der ersten drei Jahrhunderte—a bringing together of *Altertumswissenschaft* and *Kirchengeschichte* (Treu 1993; May 1993; Rebenich 1993). Mommsen's stimulation of prosopographical research also encouraged the creation of *The Prosopography of the Later Roman Empire* by British scholars A. H. M. Jones and associates (1971) and the *Prosopographie chrétienne du Bas-Empire* by Henri-Irénée Marrou and other French scholars (1982). Accompanying these endeavours was the establishment of journals, the numbers of which markedly increased in the years after 1870 (Fugmann and Pollmann 1995: 240, 254–7). Last, the translation of patristic texts into German was undertaken by the Bibliothek der Kirchenväter, established in 1869.

In the twentieth century, the first volume of Franz-Josef Dölger's *Antike und Christentum*: *Kultur und Religiongeschichtliche Studien* appeared in 1929. Dölger, like many scholars internationally, wished to ground early Christianity more firmly in its late ancient classical setting; the name change of his institute to Institut zur Erforschung der Spätantike underscored this point (Fontaine 1984: 456). And from Ulrich von Wilamowitz-Moellendorff's request that Werner Jaeger undertake the edition of Gregory of Nyssa's *Contra Eunomium* resulted the edition of *Gregorii Nyssensi opera* (Jaeger 1921–).[5]

More recently, in 1997, Hanns Christof Brennecke and Christoph Markshies launched the *Zeitschrift für Antikes Christentum* (*ZAC*) (*Journal of Ancient Christianity*). Linking German- and English-speaking scholars, *ZAC* aims to incorporate 'patristics' into the newer scholarship on late antiquity, methodologies of the history of religions, and material culture (Kessler 1998: 520). In their first editorial, Brennecke and Markshies noted that increasing specialization among late ancient studies scholars often left them unaware of important discoveries, editions, or debates in areas related to their own; *ZAC* would serve to communicate such information, as well as to offer both 'external' and 'inner-Christian' perspectives on early Christian history and theology (Brennecke and Markshies 1997). *ZAC* renders an important service to the international community of patristics scholars.

1.1.2 France

Even in the seventeenth century, French scholars were active in creating tools for patristic scholarship. Jean Mabillon's pioneering work on the principles of documentary criticism (*De re diplomatica*, 1681) was an impetus for later critical scholarship. The Benedictine Maurists at Saint-Germain-des-Prés undertook editions of patristic texts, starting with the works of Augustine in 1679; in the eighteenth century, they continued with editions of John Chrysostom, Basil, Tertullian, Cyril of Jerusalem, Cyprian, Origen, and Gregory of Nazianzus (Chaussy 1989: 91–4, 189–93; Petitmengin 1985: 27–9)—an enterprise, Gibbon pointedly remarked, that should have made scholars in England blush with shame.[6] Of special importance were the Maurist Bernard de Montfaucon's editions of Athanasius, Origen, and John Chrysostom, which were either reprinted or used as a base by Migne. In addition, Louis-Sébastien le Nain de Tillemont's multi-volumed *Mémoires pour servir à l'histoire ecclésiastique des six premiers siècles* (1693–1712) provided a detailed account of the early church. French scholarship on the fathers thus received an early and impressive start.

J.-P. Migne's publication of the 218 volumes of the Patrologia Latina (1844–64) and the 166 volumes of the Patrologia Graeca (1857–66) marked a major step in making patristic texts available to a wider public—although doubtless not as wide as the abbé himself desired (Bloch 1994; Mandouze and Fouilheron 1985).[7] Migne's patrologies were a truly 'international' collaboration, involving scholars, editors, and proofreaders from Greece, Germany, Spain, Holland, and Belgium, along with a large contingent of Frenchmen, among whom Dom Jean-Baptiste Pitra's (often unacknowledged) work was central to the enterprise (Catrice 1985: 218; Soltner 1985).

The fortunes of patristic studies in nineteenth-century France were adversely affected by anticlericalism, the Franco–Prussian War, and the distinctive organization of the state university system, which was sometimes inhospitable to theology (Fontaine 1984: 448). In contrast to Germany, the university was not decisive in the French development of patristic studies. Although the Catholic University of Paris was established in 1875, it acquired a faculty of theology only in 1889, after the suppression of the Sorbonne's. Yet, since a French law of 1880 had prohibited private institutions from granting degrees or using the title 'university', the Catholic University was reduced to an 'Institute', and the study of 'patristics' was, in effect, pushed outside a university setting (Bressolette 1993: 193–4; Fredouille 1993: 100). As Émile Poulat has expressed it, in France, 'the knowledge of the fathers thus appeared as a culture before becoming a specialty' (Poulat 1993: 24).

In late nineteenth-century France, the recovery of the patristic tradition provided an important counter to the narrow focus on Thomism fostered by Leo XIII's encyclical *Aeterni patris* (1879), while in the twentieth century, French theologians encouraged a renewed Christian spirituality through a return to the fathers.[8]

Moreover, the debate over Modernism in the early twentieth century, although largely concerned with biblical criticism, also became a *cause célèbre* within patristic studies: Alfred Loisy's *L'Evangile et l'église* (1902) stood as a pointed retort to Harnack's ahistorical, 'essentializing' approach to early Christianity in *Das Wesen des Christentums* (1899) (Fontaine 1993: p. xiii; Poulat 1993: 22; Savon 1993: 127).[9] In the same period, the French Benedictine Dom Germain Morin was editing works of Jerome, Augustine, and Caesarius of Arles (Vessey 1993a). Years later, amidst the gruelling hardships of the Second World War, French Jesuits established the Sources Chrétiennes series of patristic texts, now numbering around 500 volumes. A stirring story of Sources Chrétiennes' early years is given in Etienne Fouilloux's *La Collection 'Sources Chrétiennes': Editer les Pères de l'église au XXᵉ siècle* (1995). Augustinian studies in particular flourished, with the founding of the Institut d'Études Augustiniennes in 1956 and the convocation of the Congrès international augustinien in 1954.

Jacques Fontaine stresses the importance of the links between lay scholars and those in religious orders in creating a more 'scientific' patristics in France (Abbé Paul Lejay, Paul Monceaux, Pierre de Labriolle, followed by Jean Bayet, Pierre Courcelle, and Henri-Irénée Marrou). Through the work of these and other scholars, Christian studies were incorporated into the newly named 'late antiquity', a field created by classicists who sought to bridge the 'no man's land' between classical antiquity and the Middle Ages (Fontaine 1984: 454). The French development of patristics thus differed from that in countries where Protestantism dominated; in the latter, patristics was more tightly linked to New Testament studies, and the fathers of the first three centuries received pride of place. (For a helpful overview of the development of patristics on the Continent through the middle decades of the twentieth century, see Charles Kannengiesser's 'Fifty Years of Patristics' (Kannengiesser 1989).)

1.1.3 Great Britain

In England, the development of patristics was marked by the Church of England's dominant role in nineteenth-century university life: Anglicanism's 'self-definition'—unlike that of Lutheran and Calvinist churches on the Continent—involved a strong identification with the church fathers (Wiles 2003: 153). High-church Oxford Movement scholars, Edward Pusey and John Henry Newman in particular, spurred interest in patristic studies and collaborated in publishing the Oxford Library of the Fathers (1835–88).

An early 'warning' against the Tractarians' love affair with patristics was sounded by Isaac Taylor, who, though grateful for their uncovering of the alleged 'pretensions of the Romish church', was alarmed by the confidence that they placed in the fathers; Taylor set about 'to loosen a little that antiquarian enthusiasm which is putting every thing [sic] dear to us in peril' (I. Taylor 1840: pp. viii, xi, xiv).[10] That the high-church appropriation of the fathers was still hotly challenged in the late nineteenth century reveals that movement's powerful influence (Lefroy 1897). Perhaps to provide a more evangelically Protestant version of early Christian texts, the Ante-Nicene Christian Library series was begun by the Scotsmen Alexander Roberts and James Donaldson in 1864. Several of the most prominent English authorities on patristic Christianity—J. B. Lightfoot and F. J. A. Hort, better known as New Testament scholars—were primarily interested in the first three centuries of Christianity, in which territory they steered a mean between high-church Anglicanism (with its concentration on clerical hierarchy, doctrine, and liturgy) and a 'morbid' Puritanism (Lightfoot 1895: 56–7; Hort 1895: 2, 86).

At the turn to the twentieth century, two noteworthy publications were launched in England. The *Journal of Theological Studies* (*JTS*) was founded in 1899 under the editorship of Henry B. Swete. Swete claimed that until then no English journal had 'devoted itself exclusively to the furtherance of theological learning' among students and teachers of theology (Swete 1899). Although hoping for an international readership, the editors of *JTS* nonetheless believed that a more judicious embrace of the new critical scholarship suited Englishmen better than the more radical approaches emanating from Germany (Wiles 1999: 492 n. 1, 508). Another of Swete's contributions to the establishment of patristics in England was his small handbook *Patristic Study*, published in 1902. Although designed for busy clergymen, *Patristic Study* outlined an ambitious programme of guided reading in the Greek and Latin fathers, along with basic bibliography.

A second important undertaking was the *Patristic Greek Lexicon*. The *Lexicon*, begun in 1906, was completed only in 1961 under the editorship of G. W. H. Lampe. Along the way, the *Lexicon* became a supplement to the Liddell–Scott–Jones dictionary, whose editors in the early twentieth century chose to exclude references to Christian texts except for the New Testament (Chadwick 1982: 66; Burghardt 1950: 265–8; Souter 1903: 512).

Last but not least, Leslie Cross's establishment of the Oxford International Patristic Conference in 1951 was of signal importance for the encouragement of patristic scholarship in the later twentieth century. Meeting every four years, this conference now attracts more than 700 scholars, many of whose papers are published in *Studia Patristica*. In addition, the Oxford Conference spurred the development of more specialized symposia on Origen and on Gregory of Nyssa (Wiles 2003: 158, 161–3).

1.1.4 'Oriental' Patristics

One important—and trans-national—aspect of patristic studies from the nineteenth century onward has been scholarship on the 'oriental' fathers. To this end, the Corpus Scriptorum Christianorum Orientalium (CSCO) was founded in 1903 in Paris, and the Patrologia Orientalis (PO) in 1907. The CSCO has published several hundred volumes of Syriac, Coptic, Arabic, and Ethiopic texts, with the PO adding Armenian and Georgian to its repertoire. In mid-twentieth-century Belgium, Paulin Ladeuze and Louis Théophile Lefort promoted Coptic studies, while Joseph Lebon's work on Monophysite sources (especially Severus of Antioch) fostered Syriac patristics. Tracing the development of Syriac and other 'oriental' studies in Europe from the sixteenth century, Sebastian Brock stressed the importance of collaboration between scholars from the Middle East and India, for whom patristic traditions remained a living faith, and European scholars (British, Estonian, Dutch, French, German, Irish, Italian) trained in critical-historical methods (Brock 1994a, b).

In addition to critical editions of these 'oriental' fathers' writings, the proliferation of interpretive studies and translations—especially in the areas of asceticism, 'heresy', liturgy, hymnology, Mariology, and biblical exegesis—makes knowledge of these 'oriental' writers' works available to a wider audience (e.g. Brock 1984, 1992, 1997, 1998, 1999; Drijvers 1984; McVey 1989; Griffith 1992, 1995, 2002; Frishman and Van Rompay 1997; Shoemaker 2002). The study of eastern Christian texts now flourishes to the extent that younger students of late ancient Christianity routinely expect to acquire facility in the languages of ancient Christianity other than Greek and Latin.

1.2 FROM PATRISTICS TO EARLY CHRISTIAN STUDIES

How did 'patristics' become 'early Christian studies' in the late twentieth century, and how did 'early Christian studies' itself develop to adopt new modes of analysis? Several factors—most prominently exhibited in North America—fostered the change in conception and nomenclature. The term 'patristics' fell increasingly into disuse, taken as a sign of ecclesiasticism, maleness, and 'orthodoxy', from which some scholars wished to dissociate themselves. Yet the more traditional topics—philology, theology, exegesis, historical studies—continued to flourish, sometimes taking surprising turns.

1.2.1 Institutional Factors

For understanding changes in nomenclature and conception, institutional considerations claim first consideration. As 'patristics' was assimilated to Humanities departments in secular universities and colleges, the relevance of confessional alliance declined: polemics there might be, but they did not usually relate to issues of sectarian commitment, as was frequently the case in the nineteenth century.

Although graduate education was slow to develop in the United States (Veysey 1965; Oleson and Voss 1979; Storr 1953), fifty-two Ph.D. programmes in Religion were in operation by 1970, aided by a 1963 Supreme Court ruling that granted public educational institutions the right to teach 'about' religion. Between 1964 and 1968, the number of graduate students in Religion jumped from 7,383 to 12,620, a rate of growth exceeding that of any other academic discipline. From this time onward, graduate students in Religion frequently chose programmes in non-denominational departments of religious studies within university settings. This trend was also present in some of the newer British universities, such as Manchester and Bristol. Programmes at Columbia, Duke, Princeton, the University of Pennsylvania, Yale, among other universities, spurred change in the discipline through organizing special seminars and reading groups on late antiquity/early Christianity. As Conrad Cherry has put it, there was 'the birth of a new university discipline out of the womb of theological studies' (Cherry 1995: 90)—and 'early Christian studies' received the benefit of the field's overall growth.

Moreover, the fact that North American academic life (unlike that of some European institutions) is organized so that junior scholars—women in almost equal numbers with men—are installed in regular-rank academic positions, and have the chance (with appropriate scholarly productivity) to rise to the professoriate, provides greater opportunity for the younger cohort to explore their own research interests. In these settings, traditional conceptions of 'patristics' were rapidly modified. The organization of academia and the rapid growth of religious studies programmes are thus significant institutional factors in the shift to 'early Christian studies'.

Another institutional factor spurring new approaches was the formation of the North American Patristics Society (NAPS) in 1970, which now counts more than 1,500 members and hosts conferences attracting international audiences.[11] Although in the late 1980s and early 1990s, NAPS members heatedly debated a name change for the Society, they reached a tacit agreement that non-traditional approaches could be accommodated under the older rubric. The launching of the *Journal of Early Christian Studies* (*JECS*; a continuation of *Second Century*, 1981–92) by NAPS in 1993 provided a venue for scholarship from non-traditional standpoints—'a showcase for work in newer fields, such as women's studies and literary theory', the editors wrote in the first issue (Clark and Ferguson 1993: p. vi). Elizabeth Clark and Everett Ferguson (who had been editor of *Second Century*) were the founding editors, with J. Patout Burns assuming a co-editorship in 2000, and David Brakke the head editorship in 2005. *JECS* now counts more than 1,400 subscriptions worldwide.

Another institutional factor that encouraged new approaches was the establishment of book series. Of signal importance was Peter Brown's editorship of The Transformation of the Classical Heritage series at the University of California Press, which published its first volume in 1981 and now boasts more than thirty titles. Also important is the recently revived series, Oxford Early Christian Texts, edited by Gillian Clark and Andrew Louth, while Oxford Early Christian Studies, started in the early 1990s, has continued to flourish. A more theoretically oriented series, Divinations: Rereading Late Ancient Religion, now published by the University of Pennsylvania Press, is edited by Daniel Boyarin, Virginia Burrus, and Derek Kreuger. NAPS also sponsors a Patristic Monograph Series, presently published by the Catholic University of America Press and edited by Philip Rousseau. Scholars from the Catholic University of America also contributed The Fathers of the Church and Ancient Christian Writers series, which has provided scores of patristic texts in English translation (Kannengiesser 1989: 643). The development of publishing venues explicitly focused on late antiquity and early Christianity was of central importance in promoting a new conceptualization of the field.

Last, it is significant that some of the most influential scholars of late ancient Christian studies in the English-speaking world—including, but not limited to, Timothy Barnes, Peter Brown, Averil Cameron, Robin Lane Fox, Ramsay MacMullen, Robert Markus, and Mark Vessey—are by disciplinary training and academic placement situated entirely *outside* departments of theology or religious studies. Their contributions have immensely enriched the study of early Christianity by bringing (among other things) a strong historical and 'area studies' approach to the subject. 'Early Christian studies' is now conceptualized less often as a branch of 'church history' than as an aspect of late ancient history and literature (Brakke 2002: 475–6). *Neither* denominationally oriented institutions *nor* religious studies departments, in other words, can now claim a monopoly on the field. Institutional arrangements, it is clear, have been central to the development of 'early Christian studies', especially in North America.

1.2.2 Disciplinary Factors: Social History

Another factor influencing the development of 'early Christian studies' is disciplinary: social history's dominance of the historical profession in the second half of the twentieth century. More recently, social history absorbed some aspects of cultural history, including an older 'history of ideas'; Roger Chartier suggests the phrase 'the cultural history of the social' to describe this shift (Chartier 1989: 549, 552). In the English-speaking world, scholarship on the social history of the late Republic and early Empire by Sir Ronald Syme, Fergus Millar, Peter Brown, John Matthews, Keith Hopkins, Richard Saller, Peter Garnsey, and Roger Bagnall, among others, was eagerly assimilated by those working in early and late ancient Christian studies.

Within early Christian studies, the interest in social history was manifest in research on women, asceticism, law, slavery, writing, the family, children, and heresy. On the family, for example, we can note anthologies edited by Halvor Moxnes (1997) and by David Balch and Carolyn Osiek (2003) and studies by Raymond Van Dam (2003), Brent Shaw (1987) Andrew Jacobs (2003) and Rebecca Krawiec (2003). In law, books by Judith Evans Grubbs (1995), Antti Arjava (1996), and Jill Harries (1999) proved important, as have studies of children (Leyerle 1997; Bakke 2005). (Other topics will be discussed below.) In addition, new *Letters* and *Sermons* of Augustine, discovered and edited by (respectively) Johannes Divjak (1981) and François Dolbeau (1996), have added a valuable cache of texts relating to the social world of that church father. Last, computers have enabled social historians, including those of late Christian antiquity, to achieve a higher degree of precision and refinement in their work, as is evidenced by Michele Salzman's *The Making of a Christian Aristocracy: Social and Religious Change in the Western Roman Empire* (2002).

1.2.3 Social Science Influences

Still another impetus to the changed conception of 'patristics' was an interest, shared by many scholars of religion, in certain aspects of the social sciences, especially anthropology. In addition, social-scientific *theory* provided new 'mental tools' quite different from the theological approaches that had dominated traditional early Christian studies. In the late 1970s and early 1980s, the seminars sponsored by the National Endowment for the Humanities and organized by Wayne Meeks on 'the social world of Christianity' encouraged the social-historical and social-scientific approaches of (among others) William Countrymen (1980), Elizabeth Clark (1979), and Bruce Malina (1986). Likewise, groups meeting under the aegis of the American Academy of Religion and the Society of Biblical Literature ('The Social World of Early Christianity'; 'Ascetic Behavior in Greco-Roman Antiquity'; 'Early Christian Families'; 'Social History of Formative Judaism and Christianity'; 'Europe and the Mediterranean in Late Antiquity') spurred interest in social science, as well as social history, approaches. Scholars treating texts of the earlier patristic period (1 *Clement*, the *Shepherd of Hermas*, Ignatius, and the *Didache*) drew on theories derived from Max Weber, Bryan Wilson, Peter Berger, Thomas Luckman, Émile Durkheim, and Pierre Bourdieu to illumine their work. Slightly later, social network theory, with its analyses of power relationships and 'brokerage', enabled scholars of early Christianity to unravel the workings of patronage and social hierarchy in late antiquity; a special issue of the journal *Semeia* (56 (1992)), edited by L. Michael White, was devoted to the subject. Studies of the social mechanisms of resistance, ritual theory, cost–benefit analysis, and public policy have variously inspired writings by Brent Shaw (1996), Rodney Stark (1996), Hal Drake (2000), and Michael Penn (2005).

Cultural anthropology, however, was the branch of social science most frequently appropriated by scholars of early Christianity and late antiquity. The 'thick description' of interpretive anthropology (Geertz 1973) resonated with historians' efforts to explain via contextualization. In addition, the subject-matter of some anthropological studies—purity and impurity, symbols—seemed ready-made for religious studies scholars, as were such theoretical tools as Mary Douglas's 'grids and groups' for the study of social connections and power relations inside and outside various communities (Douglas 1970).

Peter Brown pioneered the introduction of anthropology to studies of late ancient Christianity. Reflecting on his intellectual development, Brown stressed the liberating effect of Mary Douglas's work on his early scholarship: books such as *Purity and Danger* 'did not circulate among ancient historians', he wrote, but only among those who studied 'small face-to-face societies' (Brown 1997: 10, 21). Brown's essay on sorcery (1972) provides a good example of his anthropological investment.

Once anthropology was acknowledged as a stimulating 'talking partner' for religious studies scholars, the latter appropriated the notion of 'liminality' from Arnold Van Gennep and Victor Turner for the analysis of early Christian rituals such as baptism. Anthropological studies of pilgrimage (e.g. by Victor Turner and Edith Turner (1978)) were put to good use in Georgia Frank's *The Memory of the Eyes: Pilgrims to Living Saints in Christian Late Antiquity* (2000) and David Frankfurter's edited volume, *Pilgrimage and Holy Space in Late Antique Egypt* (1998). Anthropological studies by Claude Lévi-Strauss and Mary Douglas of food practices (including cannibalism) informed articles and books by Andrew McGowan (1994, 1999), Blake Leyerle (1995), and Teresa Shaw (1998).

1.2.4 Social Justice and the Academy

Another important influence on the development of early Christian studies originated *outside* the academy in movements seeking social justice for minorities—the formerly colonized, women, and gays—but readily found expression *inside*. Scholars of early Christianity, like their counterparts across the Humanities and Social Sciences, analysed the topics of women, sexuality, gender, 'the body', power, and post-coloniality from historical, theoretical, and comparative standpoints.

The first scholarly manifestation of these interests within early Christian studies pertained to women (Ruether 1974, 1979; Kraemer 1980, 1988; E. A. Clark 1979, 1983, 1984, 1986; Brock and Harvey 1987; with further contributions by Torjesen 1993; G. Clark 1993; Power 1995; Cooper 1996; Brooten 1996; Miller 2005; and Johnson 2006; among others—the Virgin Mary not excepted, Limberis 1994). From beyond the English-speaking world, this new sub-field was enriched with studies by (for example) Franca Ela Consolino (1986, 1988), Ruth Albrecht (1986), Kari Elisabeth Børresen (1981, 1991), Cordula Nolte (1995), Ann Jensen (1996), and Ute Eisen (2000).

Linked to the interest in the social history of women was the investigation of gender, 'the body', and sexuality. Scholars of early Christianity were greatly influenced both by Michel Foucault's volumes on *The History of Sexuality* (1978–86), in which sexuality in the ancient world was treated as a social and historically situated category, and by Aline Rousselle's *Porneia: On Desire and the Body in Antiquity* (1983). Peter Brown's *The Body and Society: Men, Women, and Sexual Renunciation in Early Christianity* (1988) was an early and important contribution to this discussion for religion scholars. Interests in women, sexuality, the body, diet, ancient medicine, and power merged in studies by Elizabeth Castelli (1986), Gail Patterson Corrington (1986), Elizabeth Clark (1989), Virginia Burrus (1991, 1994), and Teresa Shaw (1998). 'Gender', however, was not left entirely to social historians of early Christianity; more theologically oriented studies also mined the theme (Miles 1992; Harrison 1990; Coakley 1996; Burrus 2000). Although these studies have preponderantly focused on the female and 'the feminine', a growing number treat masculinity, male homoerotic interest, and transvestism (e.g. S. Young 1994; Cooper and Leyser 2000; Brakke 1995b, 2001; Davis 2002).

Interest in 'the body' also emerged in scholarly work on suffering and martyrdom (Droge and Tabor 1992; Perkins 1995; Boyarin 1999; Castelli 2004). Significant essays from the *Journal of Early Christian Studies* on these topics—as well as on suicide and torture—include James Rives's 'The Piety of a Persecutor' (1996); Dennis Trout's 'Re-textualizing Lucretia: Cultural Subversion in the *City of God*' (1994); and Brent Shaw's 'Judicial Nightmares and Christian Memory' (2003).

Still a different approach to 'the body' is illustrated by Susan Ashbrook Harvey's *Scenting Salvation: Ancient Christianity and the Olfactory Imagination* (2006). While scholars of late ancient Christianity, often inspired by film theory, had for some years explored the role of vision, 'the gaze', in early Christian texts (Leyerle 1993; Frank 2000), Harvey turns to a different sense, that of smell. Smells, Harvey argues, served as powerful signifiers in that they were invisible and immaterial, yet viscerally experienced, transgressive and unstable, unable to be contained. Especially in the post-Constantinian era did Christians engage the olfactory sense in liturgical practice, and as associated with relics, asceticism, and pilgrimage. Here, bodily experience is seen to bear epistemological significance, as a means for humans to gain knowledge of their relation to the divine.

Interest in women, gender, sexuality, and 'the body' merged in the renewed interest in early Christian asceticism—a topic that had often been neglected by scholars coming from Protestant traditions. Now, however, quests for the 'origins' of asceticism and phenomenological approaches retreated, and greater attention was paid to differentiation by time and place: for Egypt, see Rousseau (1985), Elm (1994), Brakke (1995a, 2006), and Goehring (1999); for Cappadocia, see Elm (1994) and Rousseau (1994); for Gaul, see Klingshirn (1994) and Stewart (1998); for Italy, see Trout (1999) and Lizzi (1989; 1991); for Palestine, see Binns (1994) and Hirschfeld (1992); for Syria, see Brock (1984, 1992, 1998); and Griffith (1994, 1995). Philip

Rousseau's *Ascetics, Authority, and the Church in the Age of Jerome and Cassian* (1978) covered more than one area and author, as did Elizabeth Clark's *Jerome, Chrysostom, and Friends* (1979), Susan Ashbrook Harvey's *Asceticism and Society in Crisis: John of Ephesus and 'The Lives of the Eastern Saints'* (1990), and Conrad Leyser's *Authority and Asceticism from Augustine to Gregory the Great* (2000). The work of the Society of Biblical Literature's Group on Ascetic Behavior in Greco-Roman Antiquity resulted in two large volumes, *Ascetic Behavior in Greco-Roman Antiquity* (Wimbush 1990) and *Asceticism* (Wimbush and Valantasis 1995). Particular practices of asceticism, such as fasting (T. Shaw 1998) and 'spiritual marriage' (Leyerle 2001), received special attention. Jerome's contribution to the development of women's asceticism was given thorough treatment by Patrick Laurence (1997). Equally to be noted are late ancient Christians who stood *against* the (to them) excessive ascetic enthusiasm fostered by Jerome and others. Robert Markus memorably characterized Augustine's contribution to the debate as 'a defence of Christian mediocrity' (1990), while articles (1987, 1993) and a book by David Hunter (2007) have provided the fullest discussion in recent times of the opponents of ascetic fervour.

The traditional view that Egyptian ascetics were illiterate devotees was challenged by Samuel Rubenson's claims for the letters of Antony—letters which, if accepted as authentic, establish that 'desert father' as a sophisticated interpreter of Origenist theology (Rubenson 1990). Another area in Egyptian monasticism of burgeoning interest is Shenoute studies. Stephen Emmel heads an international team of scholars engaged in preparing the critical editions of Shenoute's *Canons* and *Discourses*. Books reflecting this interest include Rebecca Krawiec's *Shenoute and the Women of the White Monastery* (2002) and Caroline Schroeder's *Disciplining the Monastic Body: The Asceticism of Shenoute of Atripe* (2006).

That asceticism, in theory an expression of humility, might in practice provide ample opportunity for the exercise of power was a view stimulated by Peter Brown's now classic article, 'The Rise and Function of the Holy Man in Late Antiquity' (1971). This essay, revised several times, was feted on its twenty-fifth anniversary by a conference held at the University of California–Berkeley and by an issue of the *JECS* (1998).[12] The analysis of power was also at the forefront of Brown's *Power and Persuasion in Late Antiquity* (1992), Richard Lim's *Public Disputation, Power, and Social Order in Late Antiquity* (1995), and Elizabeth DePalma Digeser's *The Making of a Christian Empire: Lactantius and Rome* (2000). That bishops became significant wielders of power as well as community-builders was evident in Neil McLynn's *Ambrose of Milan: Church and Court in a Christian Capital* (1994) and McLynn's forthcoming 'Gregory of Nazianzus: Orthodoxy and Experiment in a Christian Empire', William Klingshirn's *Caesarius of Arles: The Making of a Christian Community in Late Antique Gaul* (1994), Philip Rousseau's *Basil of Caesarea* (1994), David Brakke's *Athanasius and the Politics of Asceticism* (1995a), Andrea Sterk's *Renouncing the World Yet Leading the Church: The Monk-Bishop in Late Antiquity*

(2004), Claudia Rapp's *Holy Bishops in Late Antiquity* (2005), and Susanna Elm's 'Sons of Hellenism, Fathers of the Church: Gregory of Nazianzus, Emperor Julian, and the Christianization of the Late Roman Elites' (forthcoming)—while James J. O'Donnell's *Augustine: A New Biography* (2005), with its focus on that bishop's battles with the Donatists (and others), sets its subject resolutely in the realm of 'power politics'.

1.2.5 'Others' and Neighbours

Another indication of changes within 'early Christian studies' itself is the integration of early Christianity into the larger study of 'late antiquity' and its placement alongside its Jewish and 'pagan' neighbours. Indeed, some—such as David Brakke—have argued that the term 'Christian' might well be dropped in descriptions of the field in favour of 'late ancient studies' or 'late antiquity', which accords no privileged place to Christianity. Such was the guiding plan of the American Academy of Religion programme unit organized in 1994 by Brakke and Kate Cooper, 'Europe and the Mediterranean in Late Antiquity' (Brakke 2002: 475–8). That the thirteenth volume of *The Cambridge Ancient History* (1998), devoted to the late Empire, positions 'orthodox' Christianity alongside its 'polytheist', Jewish, Manichaean, and alleged heretical neighbours signals that historians of late antiquity now recognize religion's central importance in the era's cultural history (Cameron and Garnsey 1998). The development of Manichaean studies in relation to the Roman Empire has brought that particular 'other' into clearer view (S. N. C. Lieu 1992; BeDuhn 2000)—and who might constitute 'neighbour' or 'other' continues to expand as scholars focus on the Roman frontier and beyond (Garsoïan, Mathews, and Thomson 1982; Cowe 1990–1; Blanchard and Darling Young 1998). Post-colonial theory has spurred new interest among scholars of Christian antiquity concerning notions of 'race' and 'ethnicity' (Buell 2002, 2005).

The study of late ancient Christianity's relations with Judaism has also gone on apace, with seminal works such as Wayne Meeks and Robert Wilken's *Jews and Christians in Antioch* (1978) and Wilken's *The Land Called Holy* (1992), followed by Miriam Taylor's *Anti-Judaism and Early Christian Identity* (1995), Judith Lieu's *Image and Reality: The Jews in the World of the Christians in the Second Century* (1996) and *Christian Identity in the Jewish and Graeco-Roman World* (2004), Andrew Jacobs's *Remains of the Jews: The Holy Land and Christian Empire in Late Antiquity* (2004), Daniel Boyarin's *Border Lines: The Partition of Judaeo-Christianity* (2004), and in essays and a book by Paula Fredriksen (1995, 1999, 2006). An issue of *JECS* (9/4 (2001)), edited by Daniel Boyarin, explored the topic 'Judaeo-Christianity Redivivus'. Studies of women in Judaism, Christianity, and paganism of the era include Ross Kraemer's *Her Share of the Blessings: Women's Religions among Pagans, Jews, and Christians in the Greco-Roman World* (1992).

A lively interest in the 'other' has also been exhibited in discussions of what was formerly labelled 'heresy'. In 1982, Patrick Henry rued that social challenges to 'authority' in the 1960s encouraged the view within early Christian studies that 'orthodoxy' was oppressive and its challengers ('heretics') more interesting and worthy of study. Scholarship, Henry claimed, had gone beyond an 'even-handed' treatment of the 'heretics', who were now seen as 'the true religious geniuses' (Henry 1982). While Henry appeared correct in his analysis of changing currents, some might applaud, rather than rue, the development he noted.

Texts that were once considered outside the purview of orthodoxy (Ehrman 2003; Koester 1965) are now well incorporated into early Christian studies. Especially prominent has been work on the apocryphal acts of the apostles, whose 'trajectory' from the New Testament offers a different vision of Christianity's development than do the Pastoral Epistles and 'mainstream' Christianity of the second and third centuries. In 1983, Corpus Christianorum established a Series Apocryphorum, which continues to produce new editions of these texts. Building on the work of François Bovon, Eric Junod, and others, scholars have analysed the ways in which women, gender, asceticism, and the family have been portrayed in these writings (Davies 1980; MacDonald 1983; Burrus 1987; Valantasis 1997; Jacobs 1999; Davis 2001). Of special interest has been the role assigned to Mary Magdalene in some of the apocryphal acts and Gnostic materials (King 2003a).

Among late ancient religions, 'Gnosticism' has in recent decades received ample and sympathetic treatment. The mid-twentieth-century finds at Nag Hammadi spurred an explosion of scholarship on the topic: during the 1970s, the journal *Vigiliae Christianae* devoted more space to Gnosticism than to any other single subject. From a quest for 'origins' and 'influences', and from a conceptualization of 'Gnosticism' as 'Christian heresy' that marked nineteenth- and much twentieth-century scholarship, newer treatments question whether the term 'Gnosticism' correctly categorizes the highly diverse Nag Hammadi texts (M. A. Williams 1996; King 2003b). Many studies of women and of female imagery in the Nag Hammadi texts were published, of which Karen King's edited volume, *Images of the Feminine in Gnosticism* (1988), remains central.

Among other so-called 'heresies' receiving reconsideration, Arianism takes pride of place. Robert Gregg and Dennis Groh's *Early Arianism: A View of Salvation* (1981), Gregg's edition of papers on Arianism from the 1983 Oxford International Patristics Conference (*Arianism: Historical and Theological Reassessments* (1985)), Rowan Williams's *Arius: Heresy and Tradition* (1987), Daniel Williams's *Ambrose of Milan and the End of the Nicene–Arian Conflicts* (1995), and the numerous essays of Christopher Stead and Maurice Wiles on the topic all signal a more sympathetic reception (Wiles 2003: 167)—while Lewis Ayres abandons the category of 'Arians' as an inadequate historical descriptor, considering it 'Athanasius' creation of a genealogical rhetoric' (Ayres 2004: 110). Studies of Priscillianism (Burrus 1995), Messalianism (Stewart 1991), and Origenism (E. A. Clark 1992) show how 'heresy' appears differently in varied social and cultural frameworks. A special issue of the *JECS* (4/4 (1996)), 'The Markings of Heresy: Body, Text, and Community in Late Ancient Christianity', edited by Virginia Burrus, was devoted to reconsidering 'heresy'. And Susanna Elm, Eric Rebillard, and Antonella Romano's edited volume, *Orthodoxie, christianisme, histoire* (2000), represents a lively contribution to the ongoing revision of traditional categories.

1.3 BRIDGES BETWEEN OLD AND NEW

1.3.1 Theology

Despite newer social and cultural approaches to the study of late ancient Christianity, it is not the case that theology has been abandoned. In some quarters, theology and history are being more satisfactorily integrated to construct a genuinely *historical* theology. Here, an instructive example is offered by J. Rebecca Lyman's *Christology and Cosmology: Models of Divine Activity in Origen, Eusebius, and Athanasius* (1993). Later constructions of 'orthodoxy', Lyman claims, provide no key to theological concerns of the second through mid-fourth centuries, and the imposition of such later models serves only to 'obscure the actual history of early Christianity' (Lyman 1993: 7, 161). Underscoring the diversity of early Christian theologies, Lyman invites readers to attend to how the varying cosmological models embraced by various early Christian writers correlate with the different communal settings in which they lived and worked, from urban study groups to an ascetically oriented, and imperially established, *ecclesia* (Lyman 1993: 9, 162–4). The *function* of religious language in its social-historical setting is Lyman's overall concern.

A second example of 'theology in a different mode' is Virginia Burrus's '*Begotten, Not Made': Conceiving Manhood in Late Antiquity* (2000). Far from abandoning the concept 'patristics', Burrus pursues it with vigour, borrowing 'mental tools' from French feminist theory. Here, the fathers 'masculine' Trinitarian language is interrogated with the tools of gender theory.

1.3.2 Biblical Interpretation

Another area that links traditional and newer scholarship is early Christian biblical interpretation. Customary distinctions, such as 'Alexandria vs. Antioch', have been modified (Schäublin 1974; O'Keefe 1997: 42; Louth 1983: 118; F. Young 1989), with stronger agreement that 'figural representation belonged to all forms of early Christian exegesis' (F. Young 1997: 259). Newer handbooks of patristic exegesis (Simonetti

1994; Kannengiesser 2004), while in a traditional mode, provide resources for students of biblical interpretation.

Of particular importance for studies of the fathers' biblical interpretation has been a renewed interest in allegory. In the nineteenth and early twentieth centuries, allegory was decried by many Protestant scholars, whose deaf ear for its intricacies and spiritual power left them unsympathetic to the exegesis of (for example) Origen and Gregory of Nyssa (Crouzel 1993: 104; E. A. Clark 1999: 70–8). Championed decades ago by scholars from the Catholic tradition—Henri de Lubac (1959), Henri Crouzel (1964), and Bertrand de Margerie (1980)—allegory has been restored to the forefront of discussion, assisted by recent literary theorists' interest in the topic. Allegory is now seen not as so much as an embellishing trope, but as an interpretive practice that accomplishes 'work' of its own, as has been argued in David Dawson's *Allegorical Readers and Cultural Revision in Ancient Alexandria* (1992), Douglas Burton-Christie's *The Word in the Desert: Scripture and the Quest for Holiness in Early Christian Monasticism* (1993), Maureen Tilley's *The Bible in Christian North Africa: The Donatist World* (1997), Elizabeth Clark's *Reading Renunciation: Asceticism and Scripture in Early Christianity* (1999), Richard Layton's *Didymus the Blind and His Circle in Late-Antique Alexandria* (2004), and some essays in J. Den Boeft and M. L. van Poll-van de Lisdonk's edited volume, *The Impact of Scripture in Early Christianity* (1999). The relationship between ancient Jewish and Christian interpretive techniques has also received renewed attention (Boyarin 1993).

1.3.3 Material Culture

Various forms and practices of material culture, such as early Christian art, archaeology, and inscriptions, have been the focus of recent study. Most students of early Christianity, not trained in art history or archaeology, have been largely 'borrowers' from scholars such as Thomas Mathews, Jas Elsner, Henry Maguire, Robert Nelson, Charles Barber, and Annabel Wharton. Archaeological explorations and the resulting epigraphical and other finds have yielded interesting results for early Christian studies: for example, William Tabbernee's study of 'Montanists' in Asia Minor (Tabbernee 1997, 2003). A group working on early North African Christianity, established in 1994–5, received funding from the National Endowment for the Humanities to support their project 'Devotion and Dissent: The Practice of Christianity in Roman Africa'. Headed by Robin Jensen and J. Patout Burns of Vanderbilt University, the group organizes conference sessions (soon to appear as a book) that explore how material culture, including attention to ritual practices, can illuminate the study of texts. Shrines and mosaics, amulets and relics, have come back 'into their own', as fascinating objects of study for scholars of late ancient Christianity (e.g. Brown 1981; Van Dam 1993; Frankfurter 1998; G. Clark 1999; Frank 2000; Constas 2002; Miller 1998, 2000, 2004, 2005). Through the 'corporeal imagination' of late ancient writers, the holy was understood as present in matter—a claim considered dubious by philosophers and theologians a few centuries earlier (Miller, forthcoming).

In the last decades, the material practices associated with reading and writing in Christian antiquity have been explored (Gamble 1995; Haines-Eitzen 2000). Reconsideration has been given to biography and hagiography, whose 'map onto' social reality has been critically scrutinized (Cox 1983; Hägg and Rousseau 2000; Krueger 2004). Moreover, recent scholars trace the intersection of textuality and 'materiality', especially in ascetic devotions and the writing of hagiography (Krueger 2004; Miller, forthcoming).

1.3.4 The New Cultural Theory

By the 1990s, some scholars of late ancient Christianity were borrowing 'mental tools' from literary (and other) theory and from cultural studies more frequently than from the social sciences. Post-structuralist analysis of category construction has attracted interest—although, to be sure, scholars could analyse the development of categories (such as 'religion') without explicit reference to theory (e.g. Smith 1990, 1992). The constructed quality of religious categories has been a focus of interest in Denise Kimber Buell's *Making Christians: Clement of Alexandria and the Rhetoric of Legitimacy* (1999) and her *Why This New Race?: Ethnic Reasoning in Early Christianity* (2005), as well as in Dale Martin's *Inventing Superstition: From the Hippocratics to the Christians* (2004). In these works, the tools of ideology critique and post-colonial theory are brought to bear on ancient texts.

Late ancient Christian studies in general, however, leapt from a theological to a social-historical orientation in the 1970s and 1980s; bypassing structuralism and other contemporary intellectual currents, the discipline was a late-comer to post-structuralist analysis. Overlooked in the rush for alignment with the social sciences was a point not then so obvious: that scholars of late ancient Christianity work, for the most part, on 'high' literary and philosophical texts that lend themselves well to theoretical analysis, not with native informants, nor with masses of data amenable to statistical analysis. Some representative essays suggesting these newer directions can be found in *The Cultural Turn in Late Ancient Studies*, edited by Dale Martin and Patricia Cox Miller (2005), and also in the essays and book (*Grammar and the Christian Imagination in Late Antiquity*) of Catherine Chin (2006, 2008).

The renewed interest in early Christian texts as forms of *literature* is well illustrated in the work of three scholars of late ancient Christianity: Averil Cameron, Mark Vessey, and Patricia Cox Miller. In contrast to Peter Brown's *Power and Persuasion in Late Antiquity* (1992), in which 'persuasion' is analysed as a social and political category, Averil Cameron's *Christianity and the Rhetoric of Empire: The Development of Christian Discourse* (1991) explores how texts link with social forms to form 'discourse': Foucault's presence is here effectively signalled. Puzzling why scholars have been reluctant to examine early Christian texts *as literature*, Cameron summons her readers to consider the roles of figuration, narration, metaphor, and paradox in early Christian writing (Cameron 1991). As she puts it elsewhere, Christian writings from late antiquity should be read first as literary productions before they are read as sources of social data (Cameron 1997: 145)—a thesis suggested by the very title of her edited volume, *History as Text: The Writing of Ancient History* (1989).

A similar theme informs the essays of Mark Vessey. Like Cameron, Vessey seeks to integrate the history of interpretation with social forms of reading, writing, and teaching. Vessey extends Brian Stock's notion of textual communities back into the early Christian period and invites scholars to explore 'the functions and ideology of writing in late antiquity' (Vessey 1991: 144, 158). In articles focusing on Augustine, Jerome, and Cassiodorus, Vessey elaborates how writers, texts, and audiences jointly produced competing modes of interpretation—and thus competing theologies— that enlisted different Christian clienteles (Vessey 1993b, 1998a, 2005).

In 'The Demise of the Christian Writer and the Remaking of "Late Antiquity": From H.-I. Marrou's Saint Augustine (1938) to Peter Brown's Holy Man (1983)', Vessey (1998a), offers a respectful critique of historians who, in his view, neglect the *textual* quality of their evidence. Vessey notes Peter Brown's 'tacit and tactical effacement, in the interests of a certain kind of vividness...of the products and procedures of ancient literacy'. Augustine's placement in an elite literary culture disappears from Brown's account in favour of the story of a man who lived his life 'among men' (Vessey 1998a: 382–3).[13] By interpreting biography as 'portraiture', Vessey argues, Brown bypasses the *literary* quality of ancient texts (Vessey 1998a: 405). Likewise, Brown's 'holy man' essay that appeared in *Representations* (1983), Vessey argues, vests 'the *repraesentatio Christi*...in the "vivid person" of the late antique holy man', thus 'circumvent[ing] one of the main challenges posed by such a "New Historicism" or "Cultural Poetics" [as undergirds the journal *Representations*], that of theorizing the interactions of text and society' (Vessey 1998a: 409). Vessey's argument challenges the assumption that readers in our time can be brought 'face-to-face' with the ancients; a consideration of their literary representation is always demanded.

Patricia Cox Miller's books and essays have provided elegant readings of late ancient texts. Informed by post-structuralist theory (primarily literary and psychoanalytical) and by deep reading in ancient and contemporary philosophy, her work itself enacts what reading patristic texts as *literature*, considered in social and historical context, might mean. From her exploration of dreams as an interpretive 'language' of late antiquity (Miller 1994), and her evocation of late ancient poetic images of bodies—bestial (Jerome's centaur), human and potentially blazing (Eustochium's), spectral (the witch of Endor's shade)—readers derive an enhanced appreciation of the patristic imaginary (Miller 2001).

Analysing the creation and development of 'patristics'—and then 'early Christian studies'—adds an instructive chapter in the study of the institutional and intellectual aspects of a discipline's formation.

NOTES

1. For 'disciplinarity' as an ancient as well as a modern concern, see discussions of Augustine's modification of the ancient disciplines in Pollman and Vessey (2005). We may note, with J. O'Donnell (2001: 203), that neither 'late ancient studies' nor 'patristics' is considered a 'discipline' by deans, provosts, and presidents of universities of our time; is the field in their eyes an 'undiscipline'?

2. Schnorrenberg (2004).

3. For scepticism regarding the enterprise, see Waszink (1949); for praise, Burghardt (1950: 259–61).

4. From an anonymous review in the *Christian Inquirer*, praising the English translation of Neander's *The History of the Christian Religion and Church, During the First Three Centuries*, trans. Henry John Rose (Philadelphia: James M. Campbell & Co.; New York: Saxton & Miles, 1843).

5. On Wilamowitz's contribution of funds (solicited for his eightieth birthday present) to support the project, see Burghardt (1950: 261–3).

6. Gibbon, *Autobiography*, ed. Sheffield (London, 1907), 39, cited by Vessey (1993a: 186).

7. Henri Marrou expressed his scorn for this 'grand captain of industry', whose editorship reveals 'more about business than about science' (Marrou 1961: 82).

8. *Aeterni patris* in effect raised the status of Thomas to that of the pre-eminent doctrinal authority for Roman Catholics.

9. Recall Loisy's famous line, 'Jesus foretold the Kingdom, and it was the Church that came' (Loisy 1988: 145). Scholars now problematize Harnack's influence on French scholarship: he over-read 'system' into patristic writings (Crouzel 1993: 102–3, 105; Savon 1993: 114–15, 119).

10. Taylor argues that English Protestants were at a disadvantage, since both Romanists and Oxford divines knew far more about the history of the early church than do Taylor's readers (I. Taylor 1840: 34, 59), but accuses the Tractarians of hoodwinking the English public by passing over early Christian teachings that would be shocking to uninformed and simple-minded Bible-Protestant Christians—such as the early Christian exultation of celibacy and lifelong virginity (pp. 99–102). Taylor declares that since he—independent of the established church, a married layman who is thoroughly exempt from 'antiquarian enthusiasm'—has the patristic texts in hand, he is in a good position to inform his fellow countrymen of the real dangers to religion and morals lurking in those texts (pp. xv–xvii). Taylor's knowledge of the patristic writings is remarkable for his time and circumstances.

11. See the website <http://moses.creighton.edu/NAPS/Other_Information/Presidents/presidents.html>.

12. Peter Brown, 'The Rise and Function of the Holy Man in Late Antiquity', *JRS* 61 (1971): 80–101; with some nuances and revisions in 'The Saint as Exemplar in Late

Antiquity', *Representations*, 1 (1983): 1–25, and 'Arbiters of the Holy: The Christian Holy Man in Late Antiquity', in Brown (1995). The conference, 'Charisma and Society: The 25th Anniversary of Peter Brown's Analysis of the Late Antique Holy Man', was held 13–16 March, 1997, some papers from which were published in *JECS* 6 (1998).

13. Vessey cites the final paragraph of Brown (1967: 433) which in turn cites Possidius's *Vita Augustini*, 31. 9.

BIBLIOGRAPHY

ALBRECHT, R. (1986), *Das Leben der heiligen Makrina auf dem Hintergrund der Thekla-Traditionen: Studien zu den Ursprüngen des weiblichen Mönchtums im 4. Jahrhundert in Kleinasien* (Göttingen: Vandenhoeck & Ruprecht).

ARJAVA, A. (1996), *Women and Law in Late Antiquity* (Oxford: Clarendon Press).

AYRES, L. (2004), *Nicaea and its Legacy: an Approach to Fourth-Century Trinitarian Theology* (Oxford: Oxford University Press).

BAKKE, O. M. (2005), *When Children Became People: The Birth of Childhood in Early Christianity*, trans. B. McNeil (Minneapolis: Fortress Press).

BALCH, D. L., and OSIEK, C. (2003) (eds.), *Early Christian Families in Context: An Interdisciplinary Dialogue* (Grand Rapids, Mich.: William B. Eerdmans Publishing Company).

BEDUHN, J. (2000), *The Manichean Body: In Discipline and Ritual* (Baltimore: Johns Hopkins University Press).

BINNS, J. (1994), *Ascetics and Ambassadors of Christ: The Monasteries of Palestine, 314–631*, OECS (Oxford: Clarendon Press).

BLANCHARD, M. J., and DARLING YOUNG, R. (1998), *Enik of Kolb: On God*, Eastern Christian Texts in Translation (Leuven: Peeters).

BLOCH, R. H. (1994), *God's Plagiarist: Being an Account of the Fabulous Industry and Irregular Commerce of the Abbé Migne* (Chicago: University of Chicago Press).

BØRRESEN, K. E. (1981), *Subordination and Equivalence: The Nature and Role of Woman in Augustine and Thomas Aquinas*, trans. C. H. Talbot (Washington D.C.: University Press of America; originally published 1968).

—— (1991) (ed.), *Image of God and Gender Models in Judaeo-Christian Tradition* (Oslo: Solum Forlag).

BOYARIN, D. (1993), *Carnal Israel: Reading Sex in Talmudic Culture*, New Historicism Series, 25 (Berkeley: University of California Press).

—— (1999), *Dying for God: Martyrdom and the Making of Christianity and Judaism*, Figurae: Reading Medieval Culture (Palo Alto, Calif.: Stanford University Press).

—— (2001) (ed.), 'Judaeo-Christianity Redivivus', *JECS* 9: 417–19.

—— (2004), *Border Lines: The Partition of Judaeo-Christianity*, Divinations: Rereading Late Ancient Religion (Philadelphia: University of Pennsylvania Press).

BRAKKE, D. (1995a), *Athanasius and the Politics of Asceticism*, OECS (Oxford: Clarendon Press).

—— (1995b), 'The Problematization of Nocturnal Emissions in Early Christian Egypt, Syria, and Gaul', *JECS* 3: 419–60.

—— (2001), 'Ethiopian Demons: Male Sexuality, the Black-Skinned Other, and the Monastic Self', *JHSex* 10: 501–35.

—— (2002), 'The Early Church in North America: Late Antiquity, Theory, and the History of Christianity', *CH* 71: 473–91.

—— (2006), *Demons and the Making of the Monk: Spiritual Combat in Early Christianity* (Cambridge, Mass.: Harvard University Press).

BRENNECKE, C., and MARKSHIES, C. (1997), 'Editorial', *ZAC*, 1: 10–16.

BRESSOLETTE, C. (1993), 'L'Institut Catholique de Paris et la "science Allemande" ', in Fontaine *et al.* (1993), 193–210.

BROCK, S. P. (1984), *Syriac Perspectives on Late Antiquity* (London: Variorum Reprints).

—— (1992), *Studies in Syriac Christianty: Collected Studies* (Aldershot: Variorum).

—— (1994*a*), 'The Development of Syriac Studies', in K. J. Cathcart (ed.), *The Edward Hincks Bicentenary Lectures* (Dublin: University College Department of Near Eastern Languages), 94–113.

—— (1994*b*), 'Syriac Studies in the Last Three Decades: Some Reflections', in *VI Symposium Syriacum 1992*; Proceedings from University of Cambridge, 30 August–2 September 1992, R. Lavenant (ed.), OrChrAn 247 (Rome: Institium Pontificium Orientalium Studiorum), 13–29.

—— (1997), *A Brief Outline of Syriac Literature* (Kottayam: St Ephrem Ecumenical Research Institute).

—— (1998), 'Le monachisme syriaque: histoire et spiriualité', in *Le monachisme syriaque aux premiers siècles de l'Eglise: II*ᵉ*–début VII*ᵉ *siècle*, Patrimoine Syriaque, Actes du Colloque, V (Antelias: CERP), 21–31.

—— (1999), *From Ephrem to Romanos: Interactions between Syriac and Greek in Late Antiquity* (Aldershot: Variorum).

—— and HARVEY, S. (1987), *Holy Women of the Syrian Orient*, Transformation of the Classical Heritage, 13 (Berkeley: University of California Press).

BROOTEN, B. (1996), *Love Between Women: Early Christian Responses to Female Homoeroticism* (Chicago: University of Chicago Press).

BROWN, P. (1967), *Augustine of Hippo: A Biography* (London: Faber & Faber).

—— (1971), 'The Rise and Function of the Holy Man in Late Antiquity', *JRS* 61: 80–101; repr. in *Society and the Holy in Late Antiquity* (Berkeley: University of California Press, 1982), 103–52.

—— (1972), 'Sorcery, Demons and the Rise of Christianity: From Late Antiquity into the Middle Ages', in *Religion and Society in the Age of Saint Augustine* (New York: Harper & Row), 119–46.

—— (1981), *The Cult of the Saints: Its Rise and Function in Latin Christianity*, The Haskell Lectures on History of Religions, NS 2 (Chicago: University of Chicago Press).

—— (1983), 'The Saint as Exemplar in Late Antiquity', *Representations*, 1: 1–25.

—— (1988), *The Body and Society: Men, Women and Sexual Renunciation in Early Christianity*, Lectures on the History of Religions, 13 (New York: Columbia University Press).

—— (1992), *Power and Persuasion in Late Antiquity: Towards a Christian Empire* (Madison: University of Wisconsin Press).

—— (1995), *Authority and the Sacred: Aspects of the Christianization of the Roman World* (Cambridge: Cambridge University Press).

—— (1997), 'The World of Late Antiquity Revisited', *SO* 72: 5–30.

—— (1998), 'The Rise and Function of the Holy Man in Late Antiquity, 1971–1997', *JECS* 6: 353–76.

BUELL, D. K. (1999), *Making Christians: Clement of Alexandria and the Rhetoric of Legitimacy* (Princeton: Princeton University Press).

—— (2002), 'Race and Universalism in Early Christianity', *JECS* 10: 429–68.

—— (2005), *Why This New Race?: Ethnic Reasoning in Early Christianity* (New York: Columbia University Press).

BURGHARDT, W. (1950), 'Current Theology: Current Patristic Projects', *TS* 11: 259–74.

BURRUS, V. (1987), *Chastity as Autonomy: Women in the Stories of Apocryphal Acts*, Studies in Women and Religion, 23 (Lewiston, NY: Edwin Mellen Press).

—— (1991), 'The Heretical Woman as Symbol in Alexander, Athanasius, Epiphanius, and Jerome', *HTR* 84: 229–48.

—— (1994), 'Word and Flesh: The Bodies and Sexuality of Ascetic Women in Christian Antiquity', *JFSR* 10: 27–51.

—— (1995), *The Making of a Heretic: Gender, Authority, and the Priscillianist Controversy*, Transformation of the Classical Heritage, 24 (Berkeley: University of California Press).

—— (1996) (ed.), 'The Markings of Heresy: Body, Text, and Community in Late Ancient Christianity', *JECS* 4/4: 403–513.

—— (2000), '*Begotten Not Made': Conceiving Manhood in Late Antiquity*, Figurae: Reading Medieval Culture (Palo Alto, Calif.: Stanford University Press).

—— (2004), *The Sex Lives of Saints: An Erotics of Ancient Hagiography*, Divinations: Rereading Late Ancient Religion (Philadelphia: University of Pennsylvania Press).

BURTON-CHRISTIE, D. (1993), *The Word in the Desert: Scripture and the Quest for Holiness in Early Christian Monasticism* (New York: Oxford University Press).

CAMERON, A. (1989) (ed.), *History as Text: The Writing of Ancient History* (Chapel Hill, NC: University of North Carolina Press).

—— (1991), *Christianity and the Rhetoric of Empire: The Development of Christian Discourse*, Sather Classical Lectures, 55 (Berkeley: University of California Press).

—— (1997), 'Eusebius' *Vita Constantini* and the Construction of Constantine', in M. J. Edwards and S. Swain (eds.), *Portraits: Biographical Representations in the Greek and Latin Literature of the Roman Empire* (Oxford: Clarendon Press), 145–74.

—— and GARNSEY, P. (1998) (eds.), *The Cambridge Ancient History*, xiii: *The Late Empire, A.D. 337–425* (Cambridge: Cambridge University Press).

CASTELLI, E. (1986), 'Virginity and Its Meaning for Women's Sexuality in Early Christianity', *JFSR* 2: 61–88.

—— (2004), *Martyrdom and Memory: Early Christian Culture Making*, Gender, Theory, and Religion (New York: Columbia University Press).

CATRICE, P. (1985), 'L'Orientaliste Paul Drach, Collaborateur de l'Abbé Migne', in Mandouze and Fouilheron (1985), 211–24.

CHADWICK, H. (1982), 'The Patristic Greek Lexicon', in C. F. D. Moule (ed.), *G. W. H. Lampe, Christian, Scholar, Churchman: A Memoir by Friends* (London: Mowbray), 66–72.

CHARTIER, R. (1995), 'The World as Representation' (1989), excerpted in J. Revel and L. Hunt (eds.), trans. A. Goldhammer *et al.*, *Histories: French Constructions of the Past*, The New Press Postwar French Thought, R. Naddaff (ser. ed.), i (New York: New Press), 544–58.

CHAUSSY, Y. (1989), *Les Bénédictines de Saint-Maur*, Tome i: *Aperçu historique sur la Congregation* (Paris: L'Institut d'études augustiniennes).

CHERRY, C. (1995), *Hurrying Toward Zion: Universities, Divinity Schools, and American Protestantism* (Bloomington, Ind.: Indiana University Press).

CHIN, C. M. (2008), *Grammar and the Christian Imagination in Late Antiquity*, Divinations: Rereading Late Ancient Religion (Philadelphia: University of Pennsylvania Press).

——(2006), 'Origen and Christian Naming: Textual Exhaustion and the Boundaries of Gentility in *Commentary on John 1*', *JECS* 14: 407–16.

CLARK, E. A. (1979), *Jerome, Chrysostom, and Friends: Essays and Translations*, Studies in Women and Religion, 1 (Lewiston, NY: Edwin Mellen Press).

——(1983) (ed.), *Women in the Early Church* (Wilmington, Del.: Michael Glazier).

——(1984), *The Life of Melania, the Younger: Introduction, translation, and commentary* (Lewiston, NY: Edwin Mellen Press).

——(1986), *Ascetic Piety and Women's Faith: Essays on Late Ancient Christianity* (Lewiston, NY: Edwin Mellen Press).

——(1989), 'Foucault, The Fathers, and Sex', *JAAR* 56: 619–41.

——(1992), *The Origenist Controversy: The Cultural Construction of an Early Christian Debate* (Princeton: Princeton University Press).

——(1999), *Reading Renunciation: Asceticism and Scripture in Early Christianity* (Princeton: Princeton University Press).

——and FERGUSON, E. (1993), 'Editors' Note', *JECS* 1: pp. v–vi.

CLARK, G. (1993), *Women in Late Antiquity: Pagan and Christian Lifestyles* (Oxford: Clarendon Press).

——(1999), 'Victricius of Rouen: Praising the Saints', *JECS* 7: 365–99.

COAKLEY, S. (1996), ' "Batter my heart…"? On Sexuality, Spirituality, and the Christian Doctrine of the Trinity', in G. Gilbert (ed.), *The Papers of the Henry Luce III Fellows in Theology* (Atlanta: Scholars Press), i. 49–68.

CONSOLINO, F. E. (1986), 'Modelli di comportamento e modi di santificazione per l'aristocrazia femminile d'Occidente', in A. Giardina (ed.), *Società romana e impero tardoantico* (Rome: Laterza), i. 273–306.

——(1988), 'Il Monachesimo femminile nella tarda Antichità', *Codex Aquilarensis*, 2: 33–45.

CONSTAS, N. (2002), 'An Apology for the Cult of Saints in Late Antiquity: Eustratius Presbyter of Constantinople, *On the State of Souls after Death* (*CPG* 7522)', *JECS* 10: 267–85.

COOPER, K. (1996), *The Virgin and the Bride: Idealized Womanhood in Late Antiquity* (Cambridge, Mass.: Harvard University Press).

——and LEYSER, C. (2000), 'The Gender of Grace: Impotence, Servitude, and Manliness in the Fifth-century West', *Gender & History*, 12: 536–51.

CORRINGTON, G. P. (1986), 'Anorexia, Asceticism, and Autonomy: Self-Control as Liberation and Transcendence', *JFSR* 2: 51–61.

COUNTRYMAN, L. W. (1980), *The Rich Christian in the Church of the Early Empire: Contradictions and Accommodations*, Texts and Studies in Religion, 7 (Lewiston, NY: Edwin Mellen Press).

COWE, S. P. (1990–1), 'Tendentious Translation and the Evangelical Imperative: Religious Polemic in the Early Armenian Church', *Revue des études arméeniennes*, NS 22: 97–114.

COX, P. (MILLER, P. COX) (1983) *Biography in Late Antiquity: A Quest for the Holy Man*, Transformation of the Classical Heritage, 5 (Berkeley: University of California Press).

CROUZEL, H. (1964), 'La Distinction de la "typologie" et l' "allégorie" ', *BLE* 65: 161–74.

——(1993), 'Les Influences Allemandes sur l'étude d' Origène en France entre 1880 et 1930', in Fontaine *et al.* (1993), 102–10.

DAVIES, S. L. (1980), *The Revolt of the Widows: The Social World of the Apocryphal Acts* (Carbondale, Ill.: Southern Illinois University Press).

DAVIS S. J. (2001), *The Cult of Saint Thecla: A Tradition of Women's Piety in Late Antiquity*, OECS (Oxford: Oxford University Press).

——(2002), 'Crossed Texts, Crossed Sex: Intertextuality and Gender in Early Christian Legends of Holy Women Disguised as Men', *JECS* 10: 1–36.

DAWSON, D. (1992), *Allegorical Readers and Cultural Revision in Ancient Alexandria* (Berkeley: University of California Press).

DEN BOEFT, J., and VAN POLL-VAN DE LISDONK, M. L. (1999), *The Impact of Scripture in Early Christianity*, in Suppl. *VC*: Texts and Studies of Early Christian Life and Language, 44 (Leiden: E. J. Brill).

DIGESER, E. D. (2000), *The Making of a Christian Empire: Lactantius and Rome* (Ithaca, NY: Cornell University Press).

DIVJAK, J. (1981) (ed.), *Sancti Aureli Augustini opera: Epistolae ex duobus codicibus nuper in lucem prolatae*, CSEL 88 (Vienna: Hoelder-Pichler-Tempsky).

DOLBEAU, F. (1996) (ed.), *Augustin d'Hippone, Vingt-six sermons au peuple d'Afrique, retrouvés à Mayence*, Études augustiniennes, série Antiquité, 147 (Paris: L'Institut d'études augustiniennes).

DÖLGER, F.-J. (1929–), *Antike und Christentum; Kultur- und Religionsgeschichtliche Studien* (Westfalen: Aschendroff).

DOUGLAS, M. (1970), *Natural Symbols: Explorations in Cosmology* (New York: Pantheon Books/Random House).

DRAKE, H. (2000), *Constantine and the Bishops: The Politics of Intolerance* (Baltimore: Johns Hopkins University Press).

DRIJVERS, H. J. W. (1984), *East of Antioch: Studies in Early Syriac Christianity* (London: Variorum Reprints).

DROGE, A. J., and TABOR, J. D. (1992), *A Noble Death: Suicide and Martyrdom among Christians and Jews in Antiquity* (San Francisco: HarperSanFrancisco).

EHRMAN, B. D. (2003), *Lost Christianities: The Battle for Scripture and the Faiths We Never Knew* (New York: Oxford University Press).

EISEN, U. E. (2000), *Women Officeholders in Early Christianity: Epigraphical and Literary Studies*, trans. L. M. Maloney (Collegeville, Minn.: Liturgical Press).

ELM, S. (1994), *'Virgins of God': The Making of Asceticism in Late Antiquity*, Oxford Classical Monographs (Oxford: Clarendon Press).

——(forthcoming), 'Sons of Hellenism, Fathers of the Church: Gregory of Nazianzus, Emperor Julian, and the Christianization of Late Roman Elites'.

——REBILLARD, E., and ROMANO, A. (2000) (eds.), *Orthodoxie, christianisme, histoire/Orthodoxy, Christianity, History* (Rome: École française de Rome).

FONTAINE, J. (1984), 'Les laïcs et les études patristiques latines dans l'université française au XXᵉ siècle', *RBen* 94: 444–61.

——(1993), 'Avant-propos', in Fontaine *et al.* (1993), pp. xi–xvi.

——HERZOG, R., and POLLMANN, K. (1993) (eds.), *Patristique et antiquité tardive en Allemagne et en France de 1870 à 1930: Influences et échanges*, Actes du Colloque franco-allemand de Chantilly; 25–7 octobre 1991, Études augustiniennes, série Moyen Age et temps modernes, 27 (Paris: L'Institut d'études augustiniennes).

FOUCAULT, M. (1978–86), *The History of Sexuality*, i: *An Introduction*; ii: *The Use of Pleasure*; iii: *The Care of the Self*, trans. R. Hurley (New York: Random House).

FOUILLOUX, E. (1995), *La Collection 'Sources Chrétiennes': Editer les Pères de l' église au XXe siècle* (Paris: Éditions du Cerf).

FOWDEN, G. (1993), *Empire to Commonwealth: Consequences of Monotheism in Late Antiquity* (Princeton: Princeton University Press).

FRANK, G. (2000), *The Memory of the Eyes: Pilgrims to Living Saints in Christian Late Antiquity*, Transformation of the Classical Heritage, 32 (Berkeley: University of California Press).

FRANKFURTER, D. (1998) (ed.), *Pilgrimage and Holy Space in Late Antique Egypt*, Religions in the Graeco-Roman World, 134 (Leiden: E. J. Brill).

FREDOUILLE, J. (1993), 'Tertullien en Allemagne et en France de 1870 à 1930', in Fontaine *et al.* (1993), 93–101.

FREDRIKSEN, P. (1995), '*Excaecati Occulta Justitia Dei*: Augustine on Jews and Judaism', *JECS* 3: 299–324.

——(1999), '*Secundum Carnem*: History and Israel in the Theology of St. Augustine', in W. E. Klingshirn and M. Vessey (eds.), *The Limits of Ancient Christianity: Essays on Late Antique Thought and Culture in Honor of R. A. Markus*, Recentiores: Later Latin Texts and Contexts (Ann Arbor: University of Michigan Press), 26–41.

——(2006), *Augustine and the Jews* (New York: Doubleday).

FRISHMAN, J., and VAN ROMPAY, L. (1997) (eds.), *The Book of Genesis in Jewish and Oriental Christian Interpretation* (Louvain: Peeters).

FUGMANN, J., and POLLMAN, K. (1993), 'Wissenschaftsgeschichtliche Tendenzen zwischen Frankreich und Deutschland in der Patristik von 1870–1930 am Beispiel von Rezensionen', in Fontaine *et al.* (1993), 239–71.

GAMBLE, H. Y. (1995), *Books and Readers in the Early Church: A History of Early Christian Texts* (New Haven: Yale University Press).

GARSOÏAN, N. G., MATHEWS, T., and THOMSON, R. (1982) (eds.), *East of Byzantium: Syria and Armenia in the Formative Period* (Washington D.C.: Dumbarton Oaks).

GEERTZ, C. (1973), 'Thick Description: Toward an Interpretive Theory of Culture', in *The Interpretation of Cultures* (New York: Basic Books), 3–30.

GIESELER, J. K. L. (1836), *Text-Book of Ecclesiastical History*, trans. F. Cunningham from the 3rd German edn., 3 vols. (Philadelphia: Carey, Lea, and Blanchard).

GOEHRING, J. (1999), *Ascetics, Society, and the Desert: Studies in Early Egyptian Monasticism*, SAC (Harrisburg, Pa.: Trinity Press International).

GREGG, R. C. (1985) (ed.), *Arianism: Historical and Theological Reassessments*, PMS 11 (Philadelphia: The Philadelphia Patristic Foundation).

——and GROH, D. E. (1981), *Early Arianism: A View of Salvation* (Philadelphia: Fortress Press).

GRIFFITH, S. H. (1992), *Arabic Christianity in the Monasteries of Ninth-Century Palestine* (Aldershot: Variorum).

——(1994), 'Julian Saba, "Father of the Monks" of Syria', *JECS* 2: 175–216.

——(1995), 'Asceticism in the Church of Syria: The Hermeneutics of Early Syrian Monasticism', in Wimbush (1995), 220–45.

——(2002), *The Beginnings of Christian Theology in Arabic: Muslim–Christian Encounters in the Early Islamic Period* (Aldershot: Ashgate).

GRUBBS, J. E. (1994), ' "Pagan" and "Christian" Marriage: The State of the Question', *JECS* 2: 361–412.

GRUBBS, J. E. (1995), *Law and Family in Late Antiquity: The Emperor Constantine's Marriage Legislation* (Oxford: Clarendon Press).

HÄGG, T., and ROUSSEAU, P. (2000) (eds.), *Greek Biography and Panegyric in Late Antiquity*, Transformation of the Classical Heritage, 31 (Berkeley: University of California Press).

HAINES-EITZEN, K. (2000), *Guardians of Letters: Literacy, Power, and the Transmitters of Early Christian Literature* (New York: Oxford University Press).

HAMMAN, A. (1985), 'Les Principaux Collaborateurs des deux patrologies de Migne', in Mandouze and Fouilheron (1985), 179–91.

HARNACK, ADOLPH VON (1896–9), *History of Dogma*, 3 vols. English trans. (London: Williams and Norgate; German original, Freiburg: Mohr, 1885–9).

—— (1901), *What is Christianity*, trans. T. B. Saunders (London: Williams & Norgate; New York: G. P. Putnam's Sons).

—— (1908), *Mission and Expansion of the Christianity in the First Three Centuries* (London: Williams & Norgate; German original, Leipzig: Hinrichs, 1902, 1904).

HARRIES, J. (1999), *Law and Empire in Late Antiquity* (Cambridge: Cambridge University Press).

HARRISON, V. (1990), 'Male and Female in Cappadocian Theology', *JTS* 41: 441–71.

—— (1993), 'A Gender Reversal in Gregory of Nyssa's *First Homily on the Song of Songs*', *SPLi* 27: 34–41.

HARVEY, S. A. (1990), *Asceticism and Society in Crisis: John of Ephesus and 'The Lives of the Eastern Saints'*, Transformation of the Classical Heritage, 18 (Berkeley: University of California Press).

—— (2006), *Scenting Salvation: Ancient Christianity and the Olfactory Imagination*, Transformation of the Classical Heritage, 42 (Berkeley: University of California Press).

HENRY, P. (1982), 'Why Is Contemporary Scholarship so Enamored of Ancient Heretics?', *StPatr* 17/1: 123–6.

HIRSCHFELD, Y. (1992), *The Judean Desert Monasteries in the Byzantine Period* (New Haven: Yale University Press).

HORT, F. J. A. (1895), *Six Lectures on the Ante-Nicene Fathers* (London: Macmillan and Company; repr. Freeport, NY: Books for Libraries Press, 1972).

HUNTER, D. G. (1987), 'Resistance to the Virginal Ideal in Late-Fourth-Century Rome: The Case of Jovinian', *TS* 48: 45–64.

—— (1992), 'The Paradise of Patriarchy: Ambrosiaster on Woman as (Not) God's Image', *JTS* NS 43: 447–69.

—— (1993), 'Helvidius, Jovinian, and the Virginity of Mary in Late Fourth-Century Rome', *JECS* 1: 47–71.

—— (2007), *Marriage, Celibacy, and Heresy in Ancient Christianity: The Jovinianist Controversy*, OECS (Oxford: Oxford University Press).

JACOBS, A. S. (1999), 'A Family Affair: Marriage, Class, and Ethics in the Apocryphal Acts of the Apostles', *JECS* 7: 105–38.

—— (2003), ' "Let Him Guard *Pietas*": Early Christian Exegesis and the Ascetic Family', *JECS* 11: 265–81.

—— (2004), *Remains of the Jews: The Holy Land and Christian Empire in Late Antiquity*, Divinations: Rereading Late Ancient Religion (Palo Alto, Calif.: Stanford University Press).

JAEGER, W. (1921–) (ed.), *Contra Eunomium libri*. In GNO, 1, 2 (Berlin: Weidmann).

JENSEN, A. (1996), *God's Self-Confident Daughters: Early Christianity and the Liberation of Women*, trans. O. C. Dean, Jr. (Louisville, Ky: Westminster/John Knox Press).

JOHNSON, S. F. (2006), *The Life and Miracles of Thekla: A Literary Study* (Cambridge, Mass.: Harvard University Press).

JONES, A. H. M., MARTINDALE, J. R., and MORRIS, J. (1980–92) (eds.), *PLRE*, 4 vols. (Cambridge: Cambridge University Press).

KANNENGIESSER, C. (1989), 'Fifty Years of Patristics', *TS* 50: 633–56.

—— (1991), 'The Future of Patristics', *TS* 52: 128–39.

—— et al. (2004), *Handbook of Patristic Exegesis: The Bible in Ancient Christianity* (Leiden: E. J. Brill).

KESSLER, S. CH. (1998), 'Alte Kirche heute: Standortbestimmung einer theologischen Disziplin', *Herder-Korrespondenz*, 10/52: 516–21.

KING, K. L. (1988) (ed.), *Images of the Feminine in Gnosticism*, SAC (Philadelphia: Fortress Press).

—— (2003*a*), *The Gospel of Mary of Magdala: Jesus and the First Woman Apostle* (Santa Rosa, Calif.: Polebridge Press).

—— (2003*b*), *What Is Gnosticism?* (Cambridge, Mass.: Belknap Press of Harvard University Press).

KLINGSHIRN, W. E. (1994), *Caesarius of Arles: The Making of a Christian Community in Late Antique Gaul*, Cambridge Studies in Medieval Life and Thought, 4th ser., 22 (Cambridge: Cambridge University Press).

KOESTER, H. (1965), '*Gnomai Diaphori*: The Origin and Nature of Early Christian Diversity', *HTR* 58: 279–318.

KRAEMER, R. S. (1980), 'The Conversion of Women to Ascetic Forms of Christianity', *Signs*, 6: 298–307.

—— (1988) (ed.), *Maenads, Martyrs, Matrons, Monastics: A Sourcebook on Women's Religions in the Greco-Roman World* (Philadelphia: Fortress Press).

—— (1992), *Her Share of the Blessings: Women's Religions among Pagans, Jews, and Christians in the Greco-Roman World* (New York: Oxford University Press).

KRAWIEC, R. (2002), *Shenoute and the Women of the White Monastery* (New York: Oxford University Press).

—— (2003), 'From the Womb of the Church: Monastic Families', *JECS* 11: 283–307.

KRUEGER, D. (2004), *Writing and Holiness: The Practice of Authorship in the Early Christian East*, Divinations: Rereading Late Ancient Religion (Philadelphia: University of Pennsylvania Press).

LAMBERIGTS, M. (1998–99), '*Corpus Christianorum* (1947–1955): The Laborious Journey from Dream to Reality', *SacEr* 38: 47–73.

LAURENCE, P. (1997), *Jérôme et le nouveau modèle féminin: La Conversion à la 'vie parfaite'*, Études augustiniennes, série Antiquité, 155 (Paris: L'Institut d'études augustiniennes).

LAYTON, R. A. (2004), *Didymus the Blind and His Circle in Late-Antique Alexandria: Virtue and Narrative in Biblical Scholarship* (Urbana, Ill.: University of Illinois Press).

LEFROY, W. (1897) (ed.), *Lectures on Ecclesiastical History Delivered in Norwich Cathedral* (New York: Thomas Whitaker).

LE NAIN DE TILLEMONT, L.-S. (1693–1712), *Mémories pour servir a l'histoire ecclesiastique des six premiers siècles: justifiez par les citations des auteurs originaux: avec une chronologie, ou l'on fait un abregeé de l'historie ecclesiastique & profane, & des notes pour éclaircir les difficultez des faits & de la chronologie* (Brussels: Eugene Henry Fricx).

LEYERLE, B. (1993), 'John Chrysostom on the Gaze', *JECS* 1: 159–74.

—— (1995), 'Clement of Alexandria on the Importance of Table Etiquette', *JECS* 3: 123–41.

LEYERLE, B. (1997), 'Appealing to Children,' *JECS* 5: 243–70.

—— (2001), *Theatrical Shows and Ascetic Lives: John Chrysostom's Attack on Spiritual Marriage* (Berkeley: University of California Press).

LEYSER, C. (2000), *Authority and Asceticism from Augustine to Gregory the Great*. OHMS (Oxford: Clarendon Press).

LIEU, J. M. (1996), *Image and Reality: The Jews in the World of the Christians in the Second Century* (Edinburgh: T & T Clark).

—— (2004), *Christian Identity in the Jewish and Graeco-Roman World* (Oxford: Oxford University Press).

LIEU, S. N. C. (1992), *Manichaeism in the Later Roman Empire and Medieval China*. WUNT 63 (Tübingen: J. C. B. Mohr, 2nd edn., rev. and expanded).

LIGHTFOOT, J. B. (1895), *Historical Essays* (London: Macmillan and Company).

LIM, R. (1995), *Public Disputation, Power, and Social Order in Late Antiquity*, Transformation of the Classical Heritage, 23 (Berkeley: University of California Press).

LIMBERIS, V. (1994), *Divine Heiress: The Virgin Mary and the Creation of Christian Constantinople* (London: Routledge).

LIZZI, R. (1989), 'Una società esortata all'ascetismo: misure legislative e motivazioni economiche nel IV–V secolo d.C.', *St Stor* 30: 129–53.

—— (1991), 'Ascetismo e monachesimo nell' Italia tardoantica', *Codex aquilarensis*, 5: 53–76.

LOISY, A. F. (1988), *L'Evangile et l'église* (Paris, 1902). English trans.: *The Gospel and the Church*, ed. R. Joseph Hoffmann (Buffalo, NY: Prometheus Books).

LOUTH, A. (1983), *Discerning the Mystery: An Essay on the Nature of Theology* (Oxford: Clarendon Press).

LUBAC, H. DE (1959), *Exégèse Médiévale: Les quatre sens de l'Ecriture*, Théologie, 41 (Paris: Aubier).

LYMAN, J. R. (1993), *Christology and Cosmology: Models of Divine Activity in Origen, Eusebius, and Athanasius*, Oxford Theological Monograph Series (Oxford: Clarendon Press).

MABILLON J. (1681), *De re diplomatica libri VI. in quibus quidquid ad veterum instrumentorum antiquitatem, materiam* (Paris: L. Billaine).

MACDONALD, D. R. (1983), *The Legend and the Apostle: The Battle for Paul in Story and Canon* (Philadelphia: Westminster Press).

—— (1986) (ed.), *The Apocryphal Acts of the Apostles*, Semeia, 38 (Decatur, Ga.: Scholars Press).

MALINA, B. J. (1986), *Christian Origins and Cultural Anthropology: Practical Models for Biblical Interpretation* (Atlanta: John Knox Press).

MANDOUZE, A., and FOUILHERON, J. (1985) (eds.), *Migne et le renouveau de études patristiques*, Actes du Colloque de Saint-Flour, 7–8 July 1975, Théologie Historique, 66 (Paris: Beauschesne).

MARGERIE, B. DE (1980), *Introduction à l'histoire de l'exégèse*, i: *Les pères grecs et orientaux* (Paris: Éditions du Cerf).

MARKUS, R. A. (1990), *The End of Ancient Christianity* (Cambridge: Cambridge University Press).

MARROU, H. I. (1961), 'Philologie et histoire dans la période du pontificat de Léon XIII', in Giuseppe Rossini (ed.), *Aspetti della cultura cattolica nell'età di Leone XIII: atti del convegno tenuto a Bologna il 27–28–29 dicembre 1960* (Rome: Edizioni 5 Lune), 71–106.

—— *et al.* (1982–), *Prosopographie chrétienne du Bas-Empire* (Paris: Éditions du Centre national de la recherche scientifique).

MARTIN, D. B. (2004), *Inventing Superstition: From the Hippocratics to the Christians* (Cambridge, Mass.: Harvard University Press).

——and MILLER, P. Cox (2005) (eds.), *The Cultural Turn in Late Ancient Studies: Gender, Asceticism, and Historiography* (Durham, NC: Duke University Press).

MATTIOLO, U. (1992) (ed.), *La donna nel pensiero cristiano antico* (Genova: Marietti).

MAY, G. (1993), 'Das Konzept *Antike und Christentum* in der Patristik von 1870 bis 1930', in Fontaine *et al.* (1993), 3–19.

McGOWAN, A. (1994), 'Eating People: Accusations against Christians in the Second Century', *JECS* 2: 413–42.

——(1999), *Ascetic Eucharists: Food and Drink in Early Christian Ritual Meals* (Oxford: Clarendon Press).

McGUCKIN, J. M. (2001), *Saint Gregory of Nazianzen: An Intellectual Biography* (Crestwood, NY: St Vladimir's Seminary Press).

McLYNN, N. B. (1994), *Ambrose of Milan: Church and Court in a Christian Capital*, Transformation of the Classical Heritage, 22 (Berkeley: University of California Press).

——(forthcoming), 'Gregory of Nazianzus: Orthodoxy and Experiment in a Christian Empire'.

McVEY, K. E. (1989), *Ephrem the Syrian: Hymns*, CWS (New York: Paulist Press).

MEEKS, W. A., and WILKEN, R. L. (1978), *Jews and Christians in Antioch in the First Four Centuries of the Common Era*, SBL Sources for Biblical Study, 13 (Missoula, Mont.: Scholars Press).

MILES, M. R. (1992), *Desire and Delight: A New Reading of Augustine's* Confessions (New York: Crossroad).

MILLER, P. Cox (1994), *Dreams in Late Antiquity: Studies in Imagination and Culture* (Princeton: Princeton University Press).

——(1998), ' "Differential Networks": Relics and Other Fragments in Late Antiquity', *JECS* 6: 113–38.

——(2000), ' "The Little Blue Flower is Red": Relics and the Poetizing of the Body', *JECS* 8: 213–36.

——(2001), *The Poetry of Thought in Late Antiquity: Essays in Imagination and Religion* (Aldershot: Ashgate).

——(2004), 'Visceral Seeing: The Holy Book in Late Ancient Christianity', *JECS* 12: 391–411.

——(2005), 'Relics, Rhetoric, and Mental Spectacles', in G. de Nie, K. F. Morrison, and M. Mostert (eds.), *Seeing the Invisible in Late Antiquity and the Early Middle Ages*, Utrecht Studies in Medieval Literacy, 14 (Turnhout: Brepols), 25–52.

——(forthcoming), *Signifying the Holy: The Corporeal Imagination of Late Antiquity*.

MOSHEIM, J. J. L. (1810), *An Ecclesiastical History, Ancient and Modern, from the Birth of Christ to the Beginning of the Fourth Century*, i, trans. A. Maclaine, 2nd edn. (London: J. Haddon).

MOXNES, H. (1997) (ed.), *Constructing Early Christian Families: Family as Social Reality and Metaphor* (London: Routledge).

NEANDER, A. (1872), *General History of the Christian Religion and Church*, 9 vols., trans. J. Torrey, 11th American edn.; rev., corrected, and enlarged (Boston: Crocker and Brewster; London: Wiley and Putnam; first pub. 1843).

NOLTE, C. (1995), *Conversio und Christianitas: Frauen in der Christianisierung vom 5. bis 8. Jahrhundert* (Stuttgart: Hiersemann).

O'DONNELL, J. J. (2001), 'The Strangeness of Augustine', *AugStud* 32: 201–6.

O'DONNELL, J. J. (2005), *Augustine: A New Biography* (New York: HarperCollins).

O'KEEFE, J. J. (1997), 'Impassible Suffering? Divine Passion and Fifth-Century Christology', *TS* 58: 39–60.

OLESON, A., and VOSS, J. (1979) (eds.), *The Organization of Knowledge in Modern America, 1860–1920* (Baltimore: Johns Hopkins University Press).

PENN, M. (2005), *Kissing Christians: Ritual and Community in the Late Ancient Church*, Divinations: Rereading Late Ancient Religion (Philadelphia: University of Pennsylvania Press).

PERKINS, J. (1995), *The Suffering Self: Pain and Narrative Representation in the Early Christian Era* (London: Routledge).

PETITMENGIN, P. (1985), 'Les Patrologies avant Migne', in Mandouze and Fouilheron (1985), 15–38.

POLLMAN, K., and VESSEY, M. (2005) (eds.), *Augustine and the Disciplines: From Cassiciacum to 'Confessions'* (Oxford: Oxford University Press).

POULAT, É. (1993), 'Le Renouveau des études patristique en France et la crise moderniste', in Fontaine *et al.* (1993), 20–9.

POWER, K. (1995), *Veiled Desire: Augustine's Writing on Women* (London: Darton, Longman and Todd).

RAPP, C. (2005), *Holy Bishops in Late Antiquity: The Nature of Christian Leadership in an Age of Transition*, Transformation of the Classical Heritage, 37 (Berkeley: University of California Press).

REBENICH, S. (1993), 'Theodor Mommsen und das Verhältnis von Alter Geschichte und Patristik', in Fontaine *et al.* (1993), 131–54.

RIVES, J. (1996), 'The Piety of a Persecutor', *JECS* 4: 1–25.

ROUSSELLE, A. (1988), *Porneia: On Desire and the Body in Antiquity*, trans. F. Pheasant (Oxford: Basil Blackwell; orig. in French, 1983).

ROUSSEAU, P. (1978), *Ascetics, Authority, and the Church in the Age of Jerome and Cassian* (New York: Oxford University Press).

—— (1985), *Pachomius: The Making of a Community in Fourth-Century Egypt*, Transformation of the Classical Heritage, 6 (Berkeley: University of California Press).

—— (1994), *Basil of Caesarea*, Transformation of the Classical Heritage, 20 (Berkeley: University of California Press).

RUBENSON, S. (1990), *The Letters of St Antony: Origenist Theology, Monastic Tradition and the Making of a Saint* (Lund: Lund University Press).

RUETHER, R. R. (1974), 'Misogynism and Virginal Feminism in the Fathers of the Church', in R. R. Ruether (ed.), *Religion and Sexism: Images of Women in the Jewish and Christian Traditions* (New York: Simon & Schuster), 150–83.

—— (1979), 'Mothers of the Church: Ascetic Women in the Late Patristic Age', in R. R. Ruether and E. McLaughlin (eds.), *Women of Spirit: Female Leadership in the Jewish and Christian Traditions* (New York: Simon & Schuster), 71–98.

SALZMAN, M. (2002), *The Making of a Christian Aristocracy: Social and Religious Change in the Western Roman Empire* (Cambridge, Mass.: Harvard University Press).

SAVON, H. (1993), 'Les Recherches sur Saint Ambroise en Allemagne et en France de 1870 à 1930', in Fontaine *et al.* (1993), 111–28.

SCHÄUBLIN, C. (1974), *Untersuchungen zu Methode und Herkunft der Antiochenischen Exegese*, Theophaneia, 23 (Cologne: Peter Hanstein Verlag).

SCHNORRENBERG, B. B. (2004), 'Taylor, Isaac', in *The Oxford Dictionary of National Biography* (Oxford: Oxford University Press), lii. 912.

SCHROEDER, C. (2006), *Disciplining the Monastic Body: The Asceticism of Shenoute of Atripe*, Divinations: Rereading Late Ancient Religion (Philadelphia: University of Pennsylvania Press).

SHAW, B. (1987), 'The Family in Antiquity: The Experience of Augustine', *Past & Present*, 115: 3–51.

——(1996), 'Body/Power/Identity: The Passion of the Martyrs', *JECS* 4: 269–312.

——(2003), 'Judicial Nightmares and Christian Memory', *JECS* 11: 533–63.

SHAW, T. (1998), *'The Burden of the Flesh': Fasting and Sexuality in Early Christianity* (Minneapolis: Fortress Press).

SHOEMAKER, S. J. (2002), *Ancient Traditions of the Virgin Mary's Dormition and Assumption*, OECS (Oxford: Oxford University Press).

SIMONETTI, M. (1994), *Biblical Interpretation in the Early Church: An Historical Introduction to Patristic Exegesis*, ed. A. Bergquist and M. Bockmuehl, trans. J. A. Hughes (Edinburgh: T & T Clark).

SMITH, J. Z. (1990), *Drudgery Divine: On the Comparison of Early Christianities and the Religions of Late Antiquity* (Chicago: University of Chicago Press).

——(1992), *Differential Equations: On Constructing the 'Other'* (Tempe, Ariz.: Arizona State University).

SOLTNER, L. (1985), 'Migne, Dom Guéranger et Dom Pitra: La collaboration solesmienne aux entreprises de Migne', in Mandouze and Fouilheron (1985), 193–209.

SOUTER, A. (1903), 'Palaeography and Its Uses', *JTS* 4: 506–16.

STARK, R. (1996), *The Rise of Christianity: The Sociologist Reconsiders History* (Princeton: Princeton University Press).

STERK, A. (2004), *Renouncing the World Yet Leading the Church: The Monk-Bishop in Late Antiquity* (Cambridge, Mass.: Harvard University Press).

STEWART, C. (1991), *'Working the Earth of the Heart': The Messalian Controversy in History, Texts, and Language to A.D. 431*, Oxford Theological Monographs (Oxford: Clarendon Press).

——(1998), *Cassian the Monk* (New York: Oxford University Press).

STORR, RICHARD J. (1953), *The Beginnings of Graduate Education in America* (Chicago: University of Chicago Press).

SWETE, H. B. (1899), Introductory statement for first issue of *JTS* 1: 1–2.

——(1902), *Patristic Study*, Handbooks for the Clergy (London: Longmans, Green, and Company).

TABBERNEE, W. (1997), *Montanist Inscriptions and Testimonia: Epigraphic Sources Illustrating the History of Montanism*, PMS 16 (Macon, Ga.: Mercer University Press).

——(2003), 'Portals of the Montanist New Jerusalem: The Discovery of Pepouza and Tymion', *JECS* 11: 87–93.

TAYLOR, I. (1840), *Ancient Christianity and the Doctrines of the Oxford Tracts* (Philadelphia: Herman Hooker).

TAYLOR, M. S. (1995), *Anti-Judaism and Early Christian Identity: A Critique of the Scholarly Consensus*, StPB 46 (Leiden: E. J. Brill).

TILLEY, M. (1997), *The Bible in Christian North Africa: The Donatist World* (Minneapolis: Fortress Press).

TORJESEN, K. J. (1993), *When Women Were Priests: Women's Leadership in the Early Church and the Scandal of Their Subordination in the Rise of Christianity* (San Francisco: Harper-SanFrancisco).

TREU, U. (1993), 'Die Kirchenväter-Kommission', in Fontaine *et al.* (1993), 227–35.

TROUT, D. (1994), 'Re-textualizing Lucretia: Cultural Subversion in the *City of God*', JECS 2: 53–70.

——(1999), *Paulinus of Nola: Life, Letters, and Poems*, Transformation of the Classical Heritage, 27 (Berkeley: University of California Press).

TURNER, V., and TURNER, E. (1978), *Image and Pilgrimage in Christian Culture: Anthropological Perspectives*, Lectures on the History of Religions, NS 11 (New York: Columbia University Press).

VALANTASIS, R. (1997), *The Gospel of Thomas* (London: Routledge).

VAN DAM, R. (1985), *Leadership and Community in Late Antique Gaul*, Transformation of the Classical Heritage, 8 (Berkeley: University of California Press).

——(1993), *Saints and Their Miracles in Late Antique Gaul* (Princeton: Princeton University Press).

——(2003), *Families and Friends in Late Roman Cappadocia* (Philadelphia: University of Pennsylvania Press).

VESSEY, M. (1991), 'Literacy and Litteratura, A.D. 200–800', *Studies in Medieval and Renaissance History*, 13: 139–60.

——(1993*a*), 'After the Maurists: The Oxford Correspondence of Dom Germain Morin, OSB', in Fontaine *et al.* (1993), 165–90.

——(1993*b*), 'Conference and Confession: Literary Pragmatics in Augustine's *Apologia contra Hieronymum*', JECS 1: 175–213.

——(1998*a*), 'The Demise of the Christian Writer and the Remaking of "Late Antiquity": From H.-I. Marrou's Saint Augustine (1938) to Peter Brown's Holy Man (1983)', JECS 6: 377–41.

——(1998*b*), '*Opus Imperfectum*: Augustine and His Readers, 426–435 A.D.', VC 52: 264–318.

——(2005), *Latin Christian Writers in Late Antiquity and their Texts*, Variorum Collected Studies Series (Aldershot: Ashgate Variorum).

VEYSEY, L. R. (1965), *The Emergence of the American University* (Chicago: University of Chicago Press).

WASZINK, J. H. (1949), 'A New Migne?', VC 3: 186–7.

WHITE, L. M. (1992) (ed.), *Social Networks in the Early Christian Environment: Issues and Methods for Social History*, Semeia, 56 (Atlanta: Scholars Press).

WILES, M. (1999), 'The Journal of Theological Studies: Centenary Reflections', JTS 50: 491–519.

——(2003), 'British Patristic Scholarship in the Twentieth Century', in E. Nicholson (ed.), *A Century of Theological and Religious Studies in Britain* (Oxford: Oxford University Press), 153–70.

WILKEN, R. L. (1992), *The Land Called Holy: Palestine in Christian History and Thought* (New Haven: Yale University Press).

WILLIAMS, D. H. (1995), *Ambrose of Milan and the End of the Nicene–Arian Conflicts*, OECS (Oxford: Clarendon Press).

WILLIAMS, M. A. (1996), *Rethinking 'Gnosticism': An Argument for Dismantling a Dubious Category* (Princeton: Princeton University Press).

WILLIAMS, R. (1987), *Arius: Heresy and Tradition* (London: Darton, Longman and Todd).

WIMBUSH, V. L. (1990) (ed.), *Ascetic Behavior in Greco-Roman Antiquity: A Sourcebook*, SAC (Minneapolis: Fortress Press).

——and VALANTASIS, R. (1995) (eds.), *Asceticism* (New York: Oxford University Press).

YOUNG, F. M. (1989), 'The Rhetorical Schools and their Influence on Patristic Exegesis', in R. Williams (ed.), *The Making of Orthodoxy: Essays in Honour of Henry Chadwick* (Cambridge: Cambridge University Press), 182–99.

——(1997), *Biblical Exegesis and the Formation of Christian Culture* (Cambridge: Cambridge University Press).

YOUNG, S. (1994), 'Being a Man: The Pursuit of Manliness in *The Shepherd of Hermas*', JECS 2: 237–55.

CHAPTER 2

LITERATURE, PATRISTICS, EARLY CHRISTIAN WRITING

MARK VESSEY

2.1 LITERARY METHODOLOGIES

ONE of the earliest appearances of the neo-Latin term *methodologia*, according to the *Oxford English Dictionary* (s.v. 'methodology'), is in a handbook of historical theology by J. F. Buddeus (1727). The same writer provides a classic definition of 'patristic theology' as a science of the consensual 'mind and opinion of the Fathers'—that is, of accredited teachers of the early church.[1] The source material for such a science was the body of written work attributed to the fathers as 'authors', by then extensively published and inventoried in print.

Among bibliographical catalogues familiar to Buddeus would have been William Cave's *Scriptorum ecclesiasticorum historia literaria*, or 'Literary History of Church Writers' (1688–98), a chronological directory of Christian authors and their works from the preaching of Jesus Christ to the publishing of the *opera omnia* of Martin Luther. For Cave's readers, ecclesiastical 'literary history' meant a traversal of the textual archive of Christian doctrine and practice of past centuries, informed by a present understanding of the church. Both the idea of *historia literaria* and the term itself were novelties of the late Renaissance, inspired in part by Reformation-era apologetics: disputes over the descent of the 'true' church had set a new premium on written testimony. Underpinning the new coinage, nonetheless, was the ordinary and ancient sense of the Latin adjective *lit(t)erarius*, 'pertaining to what is written and read'. There was no reference to what would now count for us as 'literary'.

Because it is cognate with 'literature', the adjective 'literary' nowadays typically signals a particular concern with a privileged subset of *literary*, as opposed to *non-literary*, texts. This more exclusive, implicitly canonical sense of the 'literary' is scarcely attested before the end of the eighteenth century and did not become widespread until the nineteenth. Its retrojection on to the writings of early Christianity poses immediate problems of definition and conceptualization. How do we distinguish more from less 'literary' texts of the early Christian centuries? Where or when is the line to be drawn? What do we take ourselves to mean by 'literary' in such contexts? The failure to address these basic questions of language and method is a weakness of many contemporary scholarly treatments of early Christian (so-called) literature and literary texts.

Rather than propose a single, generally applicable literary methodology for early Christian studies—which would be impractical—or describe the many and varied, more and less self-consciously 'literary' methodologies nowadays applied in the field—which, even if possible, would risk being largely uninstructive—this chapter attempts to bring some clarity to current discussions by supplying elements of a genealogy of terms and methods hitherto in use. By observing past approaches to the 'letter' of early Christian texts, we may come to see more sharply what is at stake in our own. We shall, in any case, be reminded of the substantial dependence of modern idioms of text-based, 'literary' knowledge—including, at the limit, the privileged idiom of 'literature' itself—on western, *Latin*, Christian institutions.

2.2 BEFORE LITERATURE: THE RISE OF CHRISTIAN LETTERS IN THE WEST

Texts of writers confessing Christ were subjected early on to what would now be called 'literary' analysis. Augustine's discernment of levels of rhetorical style in passages of the apostle Paul, Cyprian, and Ambrose (*Doctr. chr.* 4. 20. 39–21. 50) is a *locus classicus*. 'Literary' study of early Christian texts, in something like the modern sense, is thus at least as old as the idea of the 'fathers' as a distinct category of approved Christian *authors*, a classification first clearly formulated (*c.* 434) by the Gallo-Roman monk Vincent of Lérins in his *Commonitorium* (Madoz 1933; Sieben 1979: 149–70). Nothing, however, in the 'classical' (Graeco-Roman) or Christian formation of men like Vincent and Augustine could have led them to postulate the modern disciplinary category of 'literature', which we apply to their works at our peril. To appreciate the distinctions they made, we need to return to the vocabulary of 'letters' that they inherited, and that—their contributions aside—would remain largely unchanged in the West until the end of the eighteenth century.

2.2.1 The Roman Vocabulary of Letters

The discourse-critical practice of Augustine and his contemporaries, like that of Cicero or Quintilian, was rhetorical and formalist, learned as part of a lifestyle, applicable equally to the production and reception of texts. Artistic verbal expression across a range of oral and written genres was the badge of a well-educated citizen of the Graeco-Roman world. The fully 'literate' person (Lat. *litteratus,-a*) not only knew the alphabet; he or she was capable of persuasive speech and writing.[2] Poetry and history had special rules. Utilitarian forms (e.g. compendia, handbooks) had their own formal conventions. None of these observances rent the universe of respectable discourse asunder between the 'literary' and 'non-literary'. All kinds of transmissible knowledge worth the attention of freeborn individuals, not only those included in summary lists of the 'liberal' arts or disciplines, belonged in principle to the common stock of 'letters' (Gk. *grammata*, Lat. *litterae*), in the sense of 'learning', 'body of knowledge', 'intellectual culture'. This was 'literature' in the ancient understanding: the plenary resources of an elite literacy, or the personal possession of them (Quinn 1979: 2–3; Schadewaldt 1973). The Latin term *litteratura*, in place of the usual *litterae*, was very occasionally used to denote it.[3] The rest was mere writing or talk.

2.2.2 The New Christian Literacy: *De doctrina christiana*

Christians had writing and talk of their own, including special writings (Gk. *hai graphai*, Lat. *scripturae*) in a variety of genres—the Old and New Testaments—and edifying talks (Gk. *homiliai*, Lat. *sermones*) that commonly cited or echoed those prior 'scriptural' texts.[4] At the end of the fourth century, as Latin-reading Christians grew increasingly self-conscious in their application of such categories, Augustine began his handbook *De doctrina christiana* by announcing 'certain guidelines for dealing with (the) scriptures (*scripturae*)'. These guidelines were designed to assist Christians both in their reading of writers who had already uncovered the hidden sense of the 'divine letters' and in their own efforts to expound the same scriptures to others, in whatever medium.[5] In giving rules for a rhetorical style proper to Christian discourse, Augustine was notably sensitive to the settings in which 'scriptural' teaching and learning occurred. He insisted, for example, that the rule of favouring clear expression, even at the cost of correctness, applied 'not only in conversation ... but also and especially when one is to hold forth in public [i.e. deliver a sermon]' (4. 10. 25). The ideal Christian speaker and teacher would thus be ready on any occasion to appear *less* than a perfect master of the norms of classical eloquence, for the sake of a more powerful, ultimately divine persuasion. In Augustine's book, the handling of Christian canonical scripture in speech and writing constantly threatens or promises to breach the limits of 'letters' as a measure of elite Roman culture (Auerbach 1965: 27–66; Banniard 1992: 65–104).

De doctrina christiana (begun 396/7, completed *c.* 427) is not only the first true handbook of Christian studies, but also possibly the single most influential essay in literary methodology ever written (Schäublin 1995; Markus 1996). Though indebted to ancient philological, rhetorical, and philosophical models, it cannot be reduced to any combination of them (Pollmann 1996; 2005). Nor, despite prefatory appearances, was it simply a digest of received Christian wisdom. Other Christian thinkers before Augustine, Greek and Latin, had reflected on many of the same issues of hermeneutical theory and exegetical-rhetorical method and, at several points, come to similar conclusions. The shared property of ancient liberal learning virtually guaranteed as much (Young 1997; Eden 1997: 41–63). None, however, had attempted to conceive an entire programme of Christian learning and teaching in terms of individual and ultimately communal relationships to the sacred 'letters' of canonical scripture, on the one hand, and to the available resources of non-biblical or 'secular' disciplinary knowledge, on the other. Together, the *universality* of Augustine's prescriptions and the inherent *tension* within them between Christian and non-Christian disciplinarities distinguished his programme from those of any of his precursors.

Augustine's concern with 'letters' embraces far more than the two curricular disciplines seemingly most akin to 'literature' in the modern sense: namely, grammar (correct speech, interpretation of the poets) and rhetoric (composition, style, performance). Literacy in his understanding was the portal to an immense store of knowledge, of which all the more useful, less deceptive parts were henceforth to be committed to the task of scriptural interpretation. When he names those parts (*Doct. chr.* 2. 19. 29 ff.), he does so in the wake of the Roman polymath Marcus Terentius Varro (d. 27 BCE), whose scheme of the liberal arts as a unified system of knowledge was still standard in late antiquity and, despite Augustine's overwriting of it in *De doctrina christiana*, would survive largely intact in later centuries beside—or more often, embedded in—the alternative model of a Christian, scripture-centred universe of letters (Shanzer 2005).

Augustine's ordering of readerly relations to Christian *scripturae* and the generality of *litterae* was once described, with some misgivings, as 'the founding charter of a Christian culture' (Marrou 1938: 413). It merits that description, provided we recognize that it was only gradually so acclaimed, and that the 'Christian culture' in question was from the start, and long remained, specific to the Latin-reading West. Whatever measures of Greek philosophy and theology Augustine imbibed in translation, his intellectual culture, including his Hellenism, was of a fundamentally Latin-Roman cast. As Virgil was to him the Roman poet and Cicero the Roman philosopher-orator *par excellence,* so Varro (in *De civitate dei* and elsewhere) stood for the sum of previous Latin erudition across *all* disciplines, human and divine (O'Daly 1999: 236–8). Varro's prolific encyclopaedism was itself the product of a Roman will to encompass and surpass the achievements of the Greeks in the higher arts, the expression of a rising colonial power with a cultural inferiority complex (Rawson 1985; compare Marrou 1949: 696–9). When Augustine had to consider how the texts and teachings of Christianity could be articulated within the cultural institutions of the late Empire, it was to this politicized vision of Roman universal knowledge that he repeatedly returned. The Christian encyclopaedia that he promulgated in works such as *De doctrina christiana, Confessiones,* and *De civitate dei* was no less ambitious for being predicated on love of God and neighbour. It would shape the disciplinarity of Latin Christendom and its successor states down to the present day.

2.2.3 Divine and Human Letters, or the Great Schism

Like its purported universality, the underlying tension between 'scriptural' and 'liberal' learning that characterizes Augustine's literary methodology and much subsequent Western disciplinary thinking is originally *Latin*. Greek Christian readers of Augustine's time and earlier could make the same broad division, without feeling constrained to specify the limits of accommodation as scrupulously as he did. In giving advice *To the Young* on the positive value of Greek learning, Basil of Caesarea spoke for a comfortable consensus. Almost the only signs of friction, in the Greek sphere, between the disciplinary norms of late antique Hellenism and the profession of Christianity relate to the emperor Julian's bizarre endeavour, in 362, to ban Christians from the teaching of grammar and rhetoric, for which he was criticized even by the 'pagan' historian Ammianus Marcellinus (22. 10. 7; 25. 4. 20). Otherwise, traditionally educated Christians in the eastern part of the Empire distinguished hygienically between Greek 'literature [*sic*] and intellectual reflection', which they could safely adopt, and Greek 'mythology with its concomitant cults', which they naturally rejected (Bowersock 1990: 12). The modern scholarly notion of a generalized conflict between Christian and classical literary values in late antiquity has no support in the Byzantine tradition.

In fact, the only long-term repercussions of Julian's edict were in the West, where Jerome's hallucination of being flogged for following Cicero instead of Christ (*Ep.* 22. 30) melodramatically transposed the heroics of a bygone age of martyrs into the key of an artificial, Julianic separation of politico-religious cultures. Although Jerome echoed Tertullian, whose sometimes negative evaluation of the ordinary intellectual culture of his time provides a natural reference point for scholarship (e.g. Hagendahl 1983), his attempt to erect an imaginary firewall between divine and human readings was more than a little eccentric in a Christian writer of the post-Constantinian era. Eccentric, and extraordinarily successful. After Jerome, scenes and narratives of Christian 'literary conversion' proliferated, above all in ascetic—and, initially, aristocratic—milieux. Augustine, whose earlier writings betray an attitude closer to that of the Greeks (and to Jerome's actual practice), made a glittering addition to the company of reformed intellectuals with his *Confessions*, parts of which can be read as a silent *agon* with Jerome.

2.2.4 The Line of 'Scriptural' Writers: Church History as Bibliography

As well as adopting a toned-down version of Jerome's histrionic account of Christian literate choices, Augustine took wary note (*Ep.* 40. 2, 9; 75. 3) of his advocacy of a tradition of trans-generic Christian writing 'on the scriptures' that would extend from the New Testament to the present, as set forth in the catalogue *De scriptoribus ecclesiasticis* ('On Church Writers'), otherwise *De viris illustribus* ('On Famous Men'), of 392/3. In this chronological bio-bibliography, prototype for many later such compilations, Jerome drew on the *Ecclesiastical History* of Eusebius of Caesarea for the pre-Nicene period, but only in order to extract information on Christian *authors* from his predecessor's much broader historical narrative. In combination with his *Chronicle*, likewise adapted from Eusebius, Jerome's *Church Writers* would largely displace the full-dress, Eusebian kind of ecclesiastical historiography in the West until the Reformation. His most immediate formal models in this case were the Latin bio-bibliographies of Varro and Suetonius. As those earlier writers had taken stock of the intellectual resources of an ascendant, expansionist Roman polity, Jerome now asserted the monopoly of a new regime of Christian writing in, or rendered into, Latin. Henceforth, at least in theory, these texts would comprise the only 'letters' worth possessing for themselves. Like Augustine's *De doctrina christiana*, Jerome's *De scriptoribus ecclesiasticis* is a western initiative, as inalienably Latinophone in its way as the 'Vulgate' translation of the Bible. The only comparable Greek Christian bio-bibliography for several centuries to come would be a translation of Jerome's (Blum 1983: 42–52, 97, 132–6).

2.2.5 *Methodologia perennis*: The Afterlife of Handbooks

By the later sixth century in the West—the period of Benedict, Cassiodorus, and Gregory the Great—the scripturally oriented programme of Christian studies outlined by Jerome and Augustine had become normative (Markus 1990; Vessey 2004). Few works were more sedulously copied during the Middle Ages than the twin handbooks *De scriptoribus ecclesiasticis* (McKitterick 1989: 192–210; 2004: 221–6, 235–44) and *De doctrina christiana* (Gorman 1985; English 1995). As late as the heyday of Scholasticism, the most innovative students of Latin Christian hermeneutics and poetics still deferred to such authorities (Wawrykow 1995; Ocker 2002). The Renaissance discovery of 'Antiquity' in turn ensured that the same texts would enjoy a fresh vogue as documents of an authentically ancient Christian culture, even if Petrarch and his successors had to downplay the violence of Jerome's Ciceronian 'dream' (Rice 1985: 85–7) and exaggerate the scope of Augustine's advice on the proper use of pagan learning (*Doct. chr.* 2. 40. 60–42. 63: 'spoiling of the Egyptians'). Not surprisingly, Basil of Caesarea's serene counsel *To the Young* was used for want of better warrants from Latin fathers (Wilson 1992: 14–16). When the young Erasmus (1466–1536) began drafting an apology for humanist literary values, *The Antibarbarians*, he took his co-ordinates from *De doctrina christiana* and *De scriptoribus ecclesiasticis*. Later, Augustine's handbook served him as primary model for the treatise on biblical interpretation that he prefixed to the second edition (1519) of his epoch-making Greek and Latin New Testament, the *Ratio seu methodus verae theologiae* ('Theory or Method of True Theology') (Béné 1969: 59–91, 215–80, 434–6). With these Erasmian manifestos, so integrally related to the educational reforms of Renaissance humanism and the ensuing Reformations of the western church, we come to the threshold of the history of *patristics* as a modern theological discipline, as defined already by Buddeus in 1727 (see Backus 2003 on the immediate pre-history of patristics).

2.3 UNDER LITERATURE: EARLY CHRISTIAN WRITING BETWEEN THE ENLIGHTENMENT AND LATE MODERNISM

In the course of the later eighteenth and early nineteenth centuries, the vocabulary of letters in modern European languages registered three successive, related semantic shifts:

Activization. Besides denoting the accumulated intellectual resources of a culture or an individual's purported mastery of them (as in the Roman and post-Roman vocabulary of *litterae*), 'letters' and 'literature' now also came to be used for the *contemporary* production or profession of 'writing'. It was in this sense that Thomas Carlyle would single out Samuel Johnson, Robert Burns, and Jean-Jacques Rousseau as specimens of that new breed of heroes, the 'man of letters' (Carlyle 1841). The new man of letters, or *writer*, was paid in proportion to the commercial success of his published work.

Objectification. Without losing its inclusive reference to all reputable genres and disciplines, the word 'literature' began to specify, in particular, the total deposit of literary works of a given period or nation—that is, a clearly delimited *body of writings.* The later eighteenth century saw the first appearance in Europe of works of national bibliography and literary historiography composed in languages other than Latin and with 'literature' in their titles.

Specialization. Finally, as part of the movement of Romanticism, the scope of 'literature' narrowed in certain applications to a few highly artistic forms: poetry, drama, superior prose fiction, selected non-fictional prose. Thus we arrive at length at the familiar 'restricted sense' of the word, as 'applied to writing which has claim to consideration on the ground of beauty of form or emotional effect', a sense still qualified by English lexicographers in 1903 as 'of very recent emergence' (*Oxford English Dictionary*, s.v. 'literature'; see further Escarpit 1958: 1738–41; Williams 1976: 150–4; Widdowson 1999: 31–41).

For two centuries or so after the Reformation, the title 'literary history' (*historia lit[t]eraria*) was used to signal a historical inventory of the resources of one or more arts or sciences, howsoever defined (Cristin 1973: 96–109). Cave's *Scriptorum ecclesiasticorum historia literaria* or 'Literary History of Church Writers' is an example of the genre, delimited in that case by a sense of 'ecclesiastical writing' as old as Jerome's *De viris illustribus* or *De scriptoribus ecclesiasticis*. In the late eighteenth century, the European sense of 'literary history' began to shift towards the more aesthetically inflected definition of 'literature' just given. Samuel Taylor Coleridge's account of his own intellectual and artistic development, the *Biographia Literaria* (1817), plays on the contemporary awareness of innovation: as there could now be a history of literature (in the new sense), so there could be a biography of one of its exponents, himself a poet and critic. In fact, the commonest way of thinking about the history of literature was as a kind of biography with a 'suprapersonal entity' as its subject. In the wake of Romanticism, that entity was regularly construed as 'the character or "mind" of a race, region, people, or nation', corresponding 'to what Dilthey, with reference to historiography in general, call[ed] "ideal unities" or "logical subjects" ', among which Dilthey also counted religions (Perkins 1992: 2–3). If modern nation-states were henceforth to be the subjects of new-style literary histories, why not then too the self-proclaimed race of Christians (see already Chateaubriand 1802)? How would the earliest phases of Christianity appear in such a light?

2.3.1 Patristics as Literary History

The idea of reformulating *patristics* as a species of 'Christian literary history' was announced in the title of a posthumously published work by the Roman Catholic historian and theologian Johann Adam Möhler (1840), but it was an article published twenty-five years later by the Protestant Friedrich Nitzsch that first sparked serious interest in it. Nitzsch argued that the new (Protestant) science of *Dogmengeschichte* ('history of dogmas') had rendered patristics otiose as a theological discipline. What now went by the name of patristics was really 'patrology', which, lacking any true rationale of its own, offered only 'a conglomerate or aggregate of biographical and literary notices, arranged in chronological order' (Nitzsch 1865: 46; see also n. 1). The way to save patristics as an academic discipline was to redefine it clearly as 'ecclesiastical literary history'. Since the interest of early Christian writing, according to Nitzsch, lay chiefly in its *content*, the aim of this new discipline would still be to provide 'a history of theology [*sic*] in its foundation period' (p. 55).

Nitzsch's proposal was taken up and turned on its head by another German Protestant theologian, Franz Overbeck, in a famous article 'On the Beginnings of Patristic Literature'. Overbeck imagined someone contemplating the in-folio editions of the church fathers, wondering what this 'literature' was and how it came into being. 'In vain', he wrote, 'would such a person turn to any of the handbooks of patristics currently available' (Overbeck 1882: 417). What was lacking was a genuinely literary-historical account of the fathers. Since 'the history of literature lies in its *forms*', Overbeck continued, contradicting Nitzsch, the task of any reconstituted patristics would be to provide a *Formengeschichte*, or 'history of forms', of early Christian writing (p. 423, emphasis added). Not, however, of *all* early Christian writing. Against the bibliographical tradition of Jerome, Cave, and others, Overbeck distinguished sharply between 'Christian proto-literature' (*christliche Urliteratur*), meaning primarily the New Testament and Apostolic Fathers, and 'patristic literature' proper, beginning with the apologists. The difference, as he saw it, was that the latter, unlike the former, derived its character *as literature* from Hellenistic-Roman models of expression. Patristic literature began when Christian writers strategically adopted the rhetorical and formal-generic repertoire of 'pagan' culture, which they did for the sake of evangelization rather than out of any desire to appear as literary figures. 'The church fathers are writers (*Schriftsteller*) against their will,' asserted Overbeck, citing Clement of Alexandria's reprise (*Strom.* 1. 1) of Plato's doubts about the fitness of writing as a medium of philosophical instruction (p. 447). 'Setting aside the literature of Christian origins', he concluded, 'we are left with a definition of patristic literature as Graeco-Roman literature of Christian confession and Christian interest' (p. 444).

Overbeck's emphasis on artistic form and his apology for the fathers as authors despite themselves reflected the latest trends in European literary historiography. From being witnesses to Christian doctrine and institutions, the fathers had become, not merely 'writers', but producers of a reputed 'literature' that now filled several hundred volumes of J.-P. Migne's Patrologia (1844–66; Bloch 1994). It was around this time, too, that the hero of J. K. Huysmans's novel *À Rebours* (1884) picked his way fastidiously through the Latin fathers, as part of a larger selection of 'decadent' literary classics.

The idea that a history might be written of ancient Christian literature to set beside the latest histories of, say, French or English literature inspired several younger scholars, including Adolf Harnack, the third (unpublished) part of whose *Geschichte der altchristlichen Literatur bis Eusebius* (1893–1904) was to have made literary-historical sense of the vast documentation included in the first two. Although Overbeck had given no clear instructions, it was assumed that his projected 'history of forms' would be founded on a taxonomy of literary genres (*Gattungen*). The experiment was tried, without much success (Jordan 1911; see Tetz 1967: 25–6). Meanwhile, 'patrologies', or chronological bibliographies of early Christian writers, continued to appear, some of them optimistically styled 'literary histories'. Looking back on more than half a century of such productions in 1947, Joseph de Ghellinck had to concede that there had been little methodological advance since Overbeck (de Ghellinck 1947: 149–80, at 161).

De Ghellinck's harsh verdict covered not only the latest patrologies, but also sundry efforts by classical philologists to incorporate early Christian writings into their histories and handbooks of Greek and Roman literature. Overbeck's proposals had caught the spirit of a powerful movement of German ancient-historical scholarship, which—after Vico, Herder, and Hegel—called for the synoptic treatment of all cultural phenomena. As matter for the new *Altertumswissenschaft* promoted by the likes of Theodor Mommsen and Ulrich Wilamowitz-Moellendorf, early Christianity now fell within a general historical science of Mediterranean antiquity. Even as late as mid-century, however, it was still far from obvious what the most suitable methods might be for the study of Christian 'literature' of the later Graeco-Roman centuries.

2.3.2 The Literature(s) of Late Antiquity

As de Ghellinck cast a backward eye over recent failed experiments in patristics as literary history, a handful of books appeared that can now be seen to mark an epoch in historical research on 'Greco-Roman literature of Christian confession' (Overbeck). These books had two traits in common: a readiness to treat ancient Christian 'letters' as part of a history unconfined by the Church, and a deep sensitivity to the crisis of Christian and classically humanist values brought on by the horrors of Nazism and the Second World War.

Pierre Courcelle's *Histoire littéraire des grandes invasions germaniques* (1948) is 'literary history' in a revealingly anomalous sense: an account of the fifth- and sixth-century confrontations of Romans and 'barbarians' as related in contemporary texts, almost all of them Christian (and printed in Migne).[6] If readers saw parallels with more recent history, the author suggested in his preface, they would only be following in the footsteps of the fathers, who liked to find prefigurations of their own times in biblical accounts of past events. The allusion to patristic habits of 'literal' or 'historical' (re)interpretation of biblical narrative points to the mid-twentieth-century rediscovery of typological exegesis by French and other patristic scholars (e.g. Daniélou 1950; cf. Young 1994). It also recalls one of the leading motifs of Erich Auerbach's *Mimesis: The Representation of Reality in Western Literature* (1946, Eng. trans. 1953), another in this cluster of epoch-marking books. In Auerbach's conspectus of 'European' literature from Homer to James Joyce, the patristic doctrine of typological or 'figural' understanding emerged as one of the primary sources of modern or novelistic literary realism, alongside Augustine's doctrine of the ideal Christian 'plain style', or *sermo humilis*, itself modelled on the language of the gospels (Auerbach 1953: 72–6, 554–6; 1965: 27–66). For Auerbach, the way in which the Latin church fathers read history into and out of the letter of their texts, beginning with the scriptures, was foundational for a ('literary') culture that included Dante, Shakespeare, and Goethe, that had culminated in the latest experiments of Modernism, but whose future, in 1946, was beyond divining.

Auerbach and Courcelle were not alone in their figural readings. In wartime and immediately post-War Europe, the letter of patristic texts took on a sudden new weight of testimony, prophecy, and exemplarity. The series Sources Chrétiennes (1942–) was born at that hour (Bertrand 2002), in the same milieu—occupied Lyons—as Henri-Irénée Marrou's *History of Education in Antiquity* (1948, Eng. trans. 1956) and, coupled with it, the far-reaching 'Retractatio' (1949) to his thesis on *Saint Augustin et la fin de la culture antique* (1938).

A classically trained humanist and a Roman Catholic, Marrou wished to discern the process by which the intellectual culture of the ancient Greek and Roman cities had turned into the Christian, Bible-focused, clerical-monastic literacy of the medieval Latin West. At the heart of his enterprise was a reckoning with Augustine's *De doctrina christiana*, presented by him both as 'the founding charter of a Christian culture' (Marrou 1938: 413) and, upon further reflection, as the expression of a 'Byzantine' Christian-classical sensibility soon thereafter to be extinguished in the West (Marrou 1948: 328–9; 1949: 690–702). Was Augustine the first medieval man, or the last of the ancients? Resisting the dichotomy, while still keeping the Middle Ages at bay, Marrou finally adopted a German period-term for the later Roman centuries and called him a man of the *Spätantike* ('late antiquity'). Although he elsewhere closely identified the new Christian culture of late antiquity with 'The Golden Age of the Fathers of the Church', *c.* 350–430 (Daniélou and Marrou 1963: 341–8), the 'culture of late antiquity' was not specifically Christian. It was a form of the 'life of the mind' common to Christians and non-Christians alike. This was the doubly epoch-making claim of Marrou's 1949 'Retractatio', and one of the foundations for the later work in English of such scholars as Peter Brown and Robert Markus (Brown 1997; Vessey 1998; Markus, forthcoming.)

Marrou's researches on the structures of *paideia* and the liberal arts painstakingly respected the ancient vocabulary of letters. The essentially late modern, post-Romantic question 'What is literature?', posed by Jean-Paul Sartre in 1948 and

presupposed by the whole subsequent discourse of 'literary theory', never troubled his texts. The same is true of the last work on this shelf of wartime books,
Ernst Robert Curtius's *European Literature and the Latin Middle Ages* (1948, Eng.
trans. 1953), though for a different reason. Marrou's field of research was 'letters'
in the classical understanding of the word: the intellectual resources of the educated elite. Curtius's subject was 'literature' in the Romantic sense defined above—
active, objectified, specialized—but now made retroactively to englobe all that this
scholar held most vital to the cultural tradition of the West. Literature for him was
'the great intellectual and spiritual tradition of western culture as given form in
language' (Curtius 1953: p. x). It began with Homer, because the Greeks 'found
their past, their essential nature, and their world of deities ideally reflected in a
poet', rather than in a set of priestly books (p. 36). Quintilian, Curtius noted,
used *litteratura* to translate Greek *grammatikē*, grammar: 'Thus [the word] does
not at first mean literature in our sense; the *litteratus* is one who knows grammar and poetry ... but is not necessarily a writer' (p. 42; but see n. 2). Curtius
never explained how in fact 'literature' had acquired its current sense. The original
association of Latin *litteratura* with poetry was enough for his purpose. In his
eyes, literature *was* poetry. His book plots the survival and creative transformation of ancient poetics from Macrobius in the fourth century to Goethe in the
eighteenth.

Despite their influence in other domains of literary study, neither Curtius's book
nor Auerbach's elicited much response from students of early Christian texts. Instead, the great catalyst for future work in this domain was Marrou's choice of 'late
antiquity' (*Spätantike, antiquité tardive, tardo antico*, etc.) as the master concept for
a comprehensive cultural history. As *Spätaltertumswissenchaft* became the order of
the day for historians, classical philologists revised the terms on which they approached early Christian and later classical texts. Rather than the exclusively 'early
Christian' philology postulated at one point by Curtius (1953: 446), what emerged
in French and other Continental European scholarship of the second half of the
twentieth century was a newly inclusive science of the languages, works, authors,
styles, and genres of the 'literature' (or cognate 'literatures') of late antiquity, in
which the dividing line between Christian and non-Christian forms of expression
was never settled but always to seek. The chief exponents of that science have
been classical philologists with lay university appointments, though often working
closely with patristic scholars. The most influential of them have been Latinists.
A synopsis of their work may be found in the later volumes of the *Handbuch der
lateinischen Literatur der Antike* (1989– , hereafter *HLL*). Two names will serve to
mark the time and place in scholarship.

From the same academic milieu as Courcelle and Marrou, though neither's pupil,
Jacques Fontaine (b. 1922) was among the first to see how the discovery of 'late
antiquity' made possible new departures in literary analysis and historiography.[7]
Patristics approached the works of Christian authors 'as the treasure and deposit

of a homogeneous religious tradition'. Its focus was on the message rather than the media of transmission, on consensual mind rather than individual enunciation. Yet, insisted Fontaine, 'the works of Christian authors . . . are first of all literary works'. Every author performs an 'act of *style*', and it is at the level of style, therefore, that 'any properly literary analysis ought to be situated' (Fontaine 1970: 6–7). The philologist's or literary historian's task was to demonstrate how the expressive *forms* of a culture were adapted on each occasion to a particular expressive *intent*, in a given *setting*. Applying Marrou's intuition of a common 'late antique' sensibility to works of verbal art, Fontaine would relocate early Christian texts within their original aesthetic horizon, in order to reassert their singularity as literary acts. The 'literary conversion' narratives of Jerome and his kind were not to be taken at face value. Even in the Latin West of the later fourth and early fifth centuries 'a Christian writer remain[ed] a late antique author through and through' (Fontaine 1982: 19; see also Fontaine 1984). By the early 1980s, the evolution of 'forms' of early Christian writing in Latin had been reconceived as part of a unified history of the Latin literature of late antiquity, itself implicitly conceived as part of a universal literary history.[8]

When the project of such a history of late antique Latin literature came before the public in volume v of the *HLL*, its manifesto was written by Reinhart Herzog (in Herzog 1989: 1–44; see further Herzog 2002). A long outdated predecessor handbook of classical Latin literature had divided the materials for later centuries between 'national (i.e. Roman) literature' and 'Christian literature'. That barrier now came down: there was henceforth to be only one 'literature' of (Latin) late antiquity. The keynotes of Herzog's presentation of 'late antiquity' as a *literary-historiographical* period-concept were those already sounded by Fontaine and others: far-reaching community of 'forms' between Christian and non-Christian writers; prevalence of generic mixing and improvisation; decisiveness, for *Latin* literary history, of fourth-century *Christian* reflection on classical and biblical discursive norms. Whereas Fontaine, partly under the influence of Marrou, had favoured naturalistic metaphors for the relationship of Christian artistic forms to their larger cultural environment ('osmosis', 'symbiosis'), Herzog applied a term with distinct literary-historiographical and literary-theoretical resonance: *reception*. The whole Latin literature of late antiquity was one of 'productive reception' (p. 33), specifically of the 'reception of ancient literature' across a range of 'forms' or genres (*Gattungen*) (p. 24). Just as 'late antiquity' already understood *itself* as the 'reception of Rome' (p. 10), this literature could now be said to constitute 'the first post-Roman literature of Europe' (p. 1). Christians might extend, even at times exceed, the traditional formal and stylistic repertoire. From a literary-historiographical point of view, however, the first question to be asked was always: How do their artistic initiatives respect or modify the *status quo ante*? 'Literature' itself, Herzog (like Overbeck and Curtius) assumed, was something that late antique *litterati*, Christian and non-Christian alike, *received* from the (classical) tradition. Not even the most adventurous spirits of the Theodosian age were to be credited with a new 'theory of literature' (p. 18; but see above, pp. 44–7, on Jerome and Augustine).

'We are all German Romantics,' a French essayist quipped not long ago (Darras 2002). European literary-historical research on later ancient, especially Latin, Christian texts during the second half of the twentieth century reveals one way in which some (of us) have been. By continuing to treat 'literature'—in the post-Romantic sense—as if it were an invariant, trans-historical category at least as old as Homer and presumably common to all human cultures, such scholarship automatically precludes the diagnosis of historic shifts in the construction and differentiation of the 'literary', including any diagnosis that would attribute long-term significance to specifically (early) Christian developments. Classicists are now increasingly sensitive to the problematic status of 'literature' as a quasi-transcendent concept (e.g. Goldhill 1999), even if far from unanimous in their responses to the difficulties thereby created for would-be historians of ancient Greek or Latin 'literature'. By accident of birth, the new 'early Christian studies' may be less burdened from the start by the legacy of European Romanticism.

2.3.3 The End of European Literary History and the Advent of Early Christian Studies

HLL is still a work in progress. Like all handbooks, it is also already a thing of the past. Its late antique volumes, envisaged from the outset as the collegial enterprise of German and French scholars, conclude a process of post-War cultural reconstruction begun by Marrou, Curtius, and their contemporaries. Herzog's prolegomena to 'the first post-Roman literature of Europe' could be read in the early 1990s against the background of German and European reunification. Reconsidered from the other side of 2000, *a fortiori* from the other side of the Atlantic, they now savour distinctly of Old Europe. Such differences of time and place cannot be sidestepped. The likelihood that the best accredited recent 'literary methodology' for the study of early Christian texts will seem alien to the concerns of many readers of the present chapter is a sign of important disciplinary non- and realignments.

As Elizabeth Clark reminds us (above, p. 15), the 'early Christian studies' of this handbook have their institutional origins in the North American academy of the closing decades of the last century. The abbreviated disciplinary history has 'early Christian studies' supplanting 'patristics', assisted by the rise of 'late antiquity'. While similar plots could be adduced for other parts of the world, the North American context is peculiar. First of all, the science of late antiquity in North America has remained largely untouched by the philological, literary-historical tradition of Continental European scholarship since Marrou. Its models have instead been primarily social- and religious-historical, the work of Peter Brown exerting a decisive influence. It was Brown, following Marrou in his own fashion, who in the 1970s made the idea of 'late antiquity' current in anglophone scholarship. He did so as a self-professed historian of religion and society, and in the absence of any concerted attempt by either British or North American classicists to resituate the study of (later) early Christian texts within an expanded *classical* philology. The success of Brown's work has generalized the disciplinary orientation. Despite some distinguished exceptions, Anglo-American late antiquity has for the most part been resolutely *un*textual. With such a godparent, 'early Christian studies' was never likely to have any distinctive literary methodology of its own.

A second factor in the formation of North American early Christian studies is its special relation (or non-relation) to what was once known as '*literary* theory'. As Clark has also pointed out, patristic studies in North America and elsewhere were bound by their own disciplinarity *not* to respond to the provocation of post-structuralist theories of textuality and discursivity when these were initially disseminated, between the late 1960s and early 1980s (Clark 2004). Without exception, the French thinkers commonly saluted as masters of post-structuralism (e.g. Roland Barthes, Jacques Derrida, Michel Foucault) elaborated their doctrines of text and discourse in conscious relation or reaction to the most loaded terms of Christian theology and hermeneutics: *logos*, writing (*écriture*, scripture), letter/spirit, literal/allegorical, text/book, canon, tradition, author(ity), etc. As American critics fastened on the work of such writers and fashioned the curricular literary theory of the later 1970s and 1980s, their titles played the same gamut: *Saving the Text*, *Allegories of Reading*, and so on. Biblical scholars could not ignore the challenge presented by this quasi-religious turn in literary theorizing. Unless their subject was early Christian hermeneutics, however, patristic scholars could and for the most part did. Largely indifferent to the new European literary historiography of late antiquity, early Christian studies likewise began life largely innocent of literary theory.

If these were deficiencies, they virtually cancelled each other. Having no stake in over-long histories of (western) *literature*, early Christian studies had little immediately to gain or lose from *literary* theory as such. Post-structuralism, after all, was supposed to be an awakening from the structuralist dream of a total 'theory of literature'. When Barthes, Derrida, and Foucault—following Maurice Blanchot—dissented from 'theological' ways of understanding texts, their nearest reference was not usually the Bible, the fathers, or the Church, but a sacralized institution of 'literature'. The post-structuralist doctrine of endlessly fertile, writerly *textuality* tilted against the restrictive practices of a scholastic-professional exegesis of the canon(s) of 'literature' consecrated by European Romanticism and its heirs. This was the anti-canonical impulse that would prove so productively disruptive in North America in the 1980s and early 1990s, to the point of inspiring elegies for the 'Western canon' and laments for the 'death of literature'. Alarmist as such reactions were, they did not wholly misrepresent the tenor of the times. The charge that adepts of literary theory no longer cared for literature, or that they had given up on traditional literary history, contained important elements of truth. The academic disciplinarity of 'literature' in the modern sense had been undermined for ever. By the late 1980s, as anti-theories of *literature* gave way to post-post-structuralist theories of *culture*, Curtius's classic definition of literature as 'the great intellectual and spiritual tradition of western culture as given form in language' assumed a new kind of *anthropological* interest. The question was no longer 'What *is* literature?', but 'What sort of a culture *was* it that produced and named that thing (once) called literature?'

From the perspective of 'literary theory', then, the timeliness of the latest early Christian studies will have had much to do with their belatedness. As this new (un)discipline disaffiliated itself from long-standing genres of ecclesiastical, patristic, theological 'literary history', so by right of its late coming it assumed a licence to play upon ancient texts unhampered by any *modern* law of 'literature'. The results of these freedoms can be seen in the recent profusion of meticulously text-based studies that configure their early Christian, late antique subjects in terms that not only exclude the name of 'literature' but also frequently occlude the graphic literality of their texts—terms such as 'rhetoric', 'representation', 'figuration', 'imagination', 'visuality', 'performance', 'memory'. None of these choices of alternative register bespeaks a methodology specific to early Christian studies. All are equally characteristic of current research in other areas of the humanities and social sciences. To the extent that work on late ancient Christianity follows models validated by scholarship in more ostensibly 'literary' disciplines or academic departments, it may be said to participate in the disavowal of 'literature' that has ensued upon the mainstreaming of 'theory' in those milieux. If there is any common literary methodology in the humanities nowadays, it is that of cultural studies that take all cultures to be nearly readable (like texts) but ultimately irreducible to the sum of their written resources.

Yet the vocation of early Christian studies to the analysis and history of culture(s) has not come at the price of total renunciation of the *sensus lit(t)eralis*. The more or less strategic effacement of the letter that we find in much current work in the field is elsewhere matched by a sustained focus on the material dimensions of texts and on the physical, technological, and sociological contexts of their realization. Patterns and regimes of literacy; the forms, techniques, and personnel of book production, distribution, and collection; the functioning of textual, scriptural, or interpretative communities; textuality and intertextuality; modes and methods of reading; constructions of authorship—all these topics are now in the foreground of research, along with a range of others once left to the more tender care of palaeographers and codicologists. This reorientation, too, can be seen as part of a general trend in humanistic scholarship of the last two decades or so, epitomized by the ascendancy of an interdisciplinary 'book history'. In early Christian studies, as in other domains, the displacement of the literal—even more so of the 'literary'— has assisted, not precluded, a fresh emphasis on the materiality of letters in related contexts. The paradox is only apparent. For what these seemingly contradictory gestures alike resist, or so we may infer, is the *naturalization* of (certain kinds of) writing as the primary vehicle and expression of (high) culture or civilization: a principle that informed the western ideology of letters from the moment of its creation by Hellenized and Hellenizing Romans, that was selectively reinforced and extended by the 'scriptural' initiatives of late ancient Latin Christianity, and fatefully reasserted, albeit with further crucial differences and limitations by the prophets of 'literature' in post-Enlightenment Europe.

While granting the solidarity of early Christian studies with other kinds of contemporary academic research, we should not underestimate their originality—or advantage. Coming at the end, and from the transatlantic edge, of European literary history, they are blessed with a distance from their subject matter that other modern (un)disciplines of the 'literary' have had to win by laborious, even deconstructive, means.

2.4 AFTER LITERATURE: REHISTORICIZING EARLY CHRISTIAN WRITING

What, then, have early Christian studies still to *do* with early Christian 'letters' as such?

Without meaning to present anything like a programme, the previous paragraphs have hinted at a reply to that question that would also begin to answer Averil Cameron's summons to students of late antique texts to 'move [their] subject on from literary history to the history of culture' (Cameron 1998: 707). Here it is necessary to specify: the history of *a* culture. For, as we have seen, to speak of 'literary history' or 'literary methodology' is already (or still) to think occidentally. From Cicero and Varro to Jerome and Augustine, to Erasmus and the post-Reformation inventors of patristics, to the Romantic reinventors of literature and its Modernist proselytizers, to the 1960s French theorists and their anglophone disciples, the discourse of universal *literary* value has been at base a Latin-Roman, hence western, one. The implications of this fact are only just beginning to be considered.

A few years ago, in a lecture much concerned with the recent history of Europe, Jacques Derrida suggested that E. R. Curtius, along with many others before and after him, had been mistaken in treating Homer as the founding hero of European literature. In ancient Greece, Derrida pointed out, there was as yet 'no project, no social institution, no right, no concept, nor even a word corresponding to what we call, *stricto sensu,* literature' (likewise Goldhill 1999: 67–8). *Literature* was, and would forever remain, a Latinism. To speak of 'literature', in any language, was to seek to make oneself understood 'in the constraining hospitality or the violent reception of a latinity'. Roman and post-Roman history dictated, moreover, that this *reception* would in some vital sense also always be indebted to Christianity. '[T]o take account of the latinity of the modern institution of literature', Derrida argued, would be 'to take account of Christendom.' The impossible question 'What is literature?' then became a 'question of the *literality of literarity*, insofar as the latter is close in its destiny to the European heritage of Christian Rome' (Derrida 2000: 22–5).

This new and hardly less difficult 'question of literature' was broached by Derrida in his lecture and left open. Elsewhere he elaborated it in terms of all that literature could be supposed to owe to Abrahamic religion, highlighting its right 'to say anything and conceal anything' like the God of Abraham—or, we might add, the God of the Christian scriptures theorized by Augustine. 'For who will deny', Derrida asked, 'that literature remains one of the remains of religion (*reste un reste de religion*), a link to and substitute for sacrosanctity in a society without God?'.[9] Familiar as that premiss may be, it acquires new potential from Derrida's deeply pondered—if at best historically impressionistic—reflections on European cultural institutions and the fortunes of Abrahamic monotheism. His reopening of the vexed question of literature suggests a particular question for us to close on. What if, as well as appearing *before* literature, the 'project' of Christian writing in Latin late antiquity could be shown to be constitutive of what literature *became*—and hence of what it remains to this day, in its global attributions?

Notes

1. Buddeus (1727: 535): 'Per theologiam patristicam intelligimus complexum dogmatum sacrorum ex mente sententiaque patrum, inde ut cognoscatur, quo pacto veritas religionis christianae conservata semper sit in ecclesia ac propagata' ('By means of patristic theology we understand the ensemble of sacred dogmas according to the mind and opinion of the fathers, and thereby know how the truth of the Christian religion has at all times been preserved and disseminated in the church'). The attempt to distinguish 'patristics' (derived from *theologia patristica*) as a branch of theology from 'patrology' (formerly *patrologia*: Gerhard 1653) as a non-theological, philological, or literary-historical discipline can be traced to the nineteenth-century Protestant theologian F. Nitzsch, who cites this passage of Buddeus (Nitzsch 1865: 41). See further Quasten (1950–60: i. 1–22); Tetz (1967); Siniscalco (1980); Merkt (2001: 240–3); above, pp. 49–50.

2. See e.g. Suetonius, *De grammaticis*, 4. 1: 'litteratos...vulgo appellari...eos qui aliquid diligenter et acute scienterque possint aut dicere aut scribere' ('the title of *litteratus* is commonly applied to those who can speak or write carefully, pointedly, and knowledgeably'), with Kaster's commentary *ad loc.* and, more generally, Morgan (1998).

3. *Thesaurus linguae latinae*, s.v. 'litteratura', sense 2b: the examples are mainly post-classical. The more restricted sense 2a ('grammar', translating Gk. *grammatikē*) is

attested by Augustine among others, but seems already to have been obsolete by his time: Bower (1961); Burton (2005: 147–8).

4. This way of putting it already takes for granted a long process of canon formation, on which see M. Holmes, Ch. 20 below.

5. Augustine, *Doct. chr.*, pref. 1: 'ut non solum legendo alios, qui divinarum litterarum operta aperuerunt, sed etiam ipsi aperiendo proficiant'. Cf. ibid. 1. 1. 1: those who minister from their own scriptural understanding, however limited, will receive more in return—with a reference to the miracle of the loaves and fishes.

6. Courcelle's predilection for the 'letter' of ancient texts would also manifest itself in pathbreaking research on the survival of Greek culture in the later Latin West (Courcelle 1943) and a revolutionary approach to Augustine's *Confessions* (Courcelle 1950). Bibliography in Courcelle (1984).

7. Methodological statements: Fontaine (1982, 1984*b*). Institutional-disciplinary retrospect: Fontaine (1984*a*).

8. The case is even clearer for the volume of essays on late antique 'literature' edited by Engels and Hofmann (1997) as of one 25 vols. comprising the *Neues Handbuch der Literaturwissenschaft.*

9. Derrida (1999: 205–9), partially summarized by him in Caputo and Scanlon (2005: 208): '[I]t is as if the question of literature, modern literature…asks for forgiveness for having forgotten or betrayed the Christian origin of literature, of writing.'

SUGGESTED READING

CAMERON, ALAN (2004), 'Poetry and Literary Culture in Late Antiquity', in S. Swain and M. Edwards (eds.), *Approaching Late Antiquity: The Transformation from Early to Late Empire* (Oxford: Oxford University Press), 327–54.

CAMERON, AVERIL (1991), *Christianity and the Rhetoric of Empire: The Development of Christian Discourse* (Berkeley: University of California Press).

——(1998), 'Education and Literary Culture', in A. Cameron and P. Garnsey (eds.), *The Cambridge Ancient History*, xiii: *The Late Roman Empire, A.D. 337–425* (Cambridge: Cambridge University Press), 665–707.

CAVALLO, G., and CHARTIER, R. (1999) (eds.), *A History of Reading in the West*, trans. L. G. Cochrane (Cambridge: Polity).

CLARK, E. A. (2004), *History, Theory, Text: Historians and the Linguistic Turn* (Cambridge, Mass.: Harvard University Press).

DAWSON, J. D. (2002), *Christian Figural Reading and the Fashioning of Identity* (Berkeley: University of California Press).

DIHLE, A. (1994), *Greek and Latin Literature of the Roman Empire*, trans. M. Malzahn (London: Routledge).

FONTAINE, J. (1981), *Naissance de la poésie dans l'Occident chrétien: Esquisse d'une histoire de la poésie latine chrétienne du IIIᵉ au VIᵉ siècle* (Paris: L'Institut d'études augustiniennes).

GAMBLE, H. Y. (1995), *Books and Readers in the Early Church: A History of Early Christian Texts* (New Haven: Yale University Press).

HARRIS, W. V. (1989), *Ancient Literacy* (Cambridge, Mass.: Harvard University Press).

KASTER, R. A. (1988), *Guardians of Language: The Grammarian and Society in Late Antiquity* (Berkeley: University of California Press).

KLINGSHIRN, W. E., and SAFRAN, L. (2007) (eds.), *The Early Christian Book* (Washington D.C.: Catholic University of America Press).

MORESCHINI, C., and NORELLI, E. (2005) (eds.), *Early Christian Greek and Latin Literature: A Literary History*, trans. M. J. O'Connell (Peabody, Mass.: Hendrickson Publishers).

YOUNG, F. M. (1997), *Biblical Exegesis and the Formation of Christian Culture* (Cambridge: Cambridge University Press).

——AYRES, L., and LOUTH, A. (2004) (eds.), *The Cambridge History of Early Christian Literature* (Cambridge: Cambridge University Press).

BIBLIOGRAPHY

Primary sources

AMMIANUS MARCELLINUS, *Res gestae*, ed. and trans. J. C. Rolfe (Cambridge, Mass.: Harvard University Press, 1935–40).

AUGUSTINE, *De doctrina christiana*, ed. and trans. R. P. H. Green (Oxford: Oxford University Press, 1995).

——*Epistulae*, ed. A. Goldbacher, CSEL 34. 1–2, 44, 57, 58 (Vienna: Tempsky, 1895–1923); trans. J. C. Cunningham, NPNF[1], 219–593.

BASIL OF CAESAREA, *Ad adolescentes*, in N. G. Wilson (ed.), *Saint Basil on the Value of Greek Literature* (London: Duckworth, 1975); trans. R. J. Deferrari, *St. Basil: Letters*, LCL (Cambridge, Mass.: Harvard University Press, 1934), iv. 249–348.

CLEMENT OF ALEXANDRIA, *Stromateis* 1–6, ed. O. Stählin, GCS 15 (Berlin: Akademie Verlag, 1939); trans. W. Wilson, ANF 2 (1885), 299–567.

JEROME, *De viris illustribus*, ed. E. C. Richardson, TU 14. 1 (Leipzig: Hinrichs, 1896); trans. T. P. Halton, *On Illustrious Men*, FC 100 (Washington D.C.: Catholic University of America Press, 1999).

——*Epistulae*, ed. I. Hilberg, CSEL 54–6 (Vienna: Tempsky, 1910–18); trans. W. H. Fremantle, NPNF[2] 6 (1892), 1–295.

SUETONIUS, *De grammaticis et rhetoribus*, ed. and trans. R. A. Kaster (Oxford: Clarendon Press, 1995).

VINCENT OF LÉRINS, *Commonitorium*, ed. R. Demeulenaere, CCSL 64 (Turnhout: Brepols, 1985), 125–231; trans. C. A. Heurtley, NPNF[2] 11 (1884), 123–59.

Secondary sources

AUERBACH, E. (1953), *Mimesis: The Representation of Reality in Western Literature*, trans. W. R. Trask (Princeton: Princeton University Press; original German edn. 1946).

——(1965), *Literary Language and Its Public in Late Latin Antiquity and in the Middle Ages*, trans. R. Manheim (Princeton: Princeton University Press).

BACKUS, I. (2003), *Historical Method and Confessional Identity in the Era of the Reformation (1378–1615)* (Leiden: E. J. Brill).

BANNIARD, M. (1992), *Viva Voce: Communication écrite et communication orale du IVe au IXe siècle en Occident latin* (Paris: L'Institut d'études augustiniennes).

BÉNÉ, C. (1969), *Érasme et saint Augustin ou influence de saint Augustin sur l'humanisme d'Érasme* (Geneva: Droz).

BERTRAND, D. (2002), 'Der Aufschwung der Patristik in Frankreich in der Mitte des 20. Jahrhunderts (1942–1958)', in H. Duchhardt and G. May (eds.), *Geschichtswissenschaft um 1950* (Mainz am Rhein: Verlag Philipp von Zabern), 112–26.

BLOCH, R. HOWARD (1994), *God's Plagiarist: Being an Account of the Fabulous Industry and Irregular Commerce of the Abbé Migne* (Chicago: University of Chicago Press).

BLUM, R. (1983), 'Die Literaturverzeichnung im Altertum und Mittelalter', *Archiv für Geschichte des Buchwesens*, 24: 1–256.

BOWER, E. W. (1961), 'Some Technical Terms in Roman Education', *Hermes*, 89: 462–77.

BOWERSOCK, G. W. (1990), *Hellenism in Late Antiquity* (Ann Arbor: University of Michigan Press).

BROWN, P. (1997), 'The World of Late Antiquity Revisited', *SO* 72: 5–30.

BUDDEUS, J. F. (1727), *Isagoge historico-theologia ad theologiam universam* (Leipzig: T. Fritschius).

BURTON, P. (2005), 'The Vocabulary of the Liberal Arts in Augustine's *Confessions*', in Pollmann and Vessey (2005), 141–64.

CAMERON, A[VERIL] (1998), 'Education and Literary Culture', in A. Cameron and P. Garnsey (eds.), *The Cambridge Ancient History*, xiii: *The Late Roman Empire, A.D. 337–425* (Cambridge: Cambridge University Press), 665–707.

CAPUTO, J. D., and SCANLON, M. J. (2005) (eds.), *Augustine and Postmodernism: Confessions and Circumfession* (Bloomington, Ind.: Indiana University Press).

CARLYLE, T. (1841), *On Heroes, Hero-Worship and the Heroic in History* (London: Chapman and Hall).

CAVE, W. (1688–98), *Scriptorum ecclesiasticorum historia literaria* (London: R. Chiswell).

CHATEAUBRIAND, F.-R. DE (1802), *Le génie du christianisme ou beautés de la religion chrétienne* (Paris: Migneret).

CLARK, E. A. (2004), *History, Theory, Text: Historians and the Linguistic Turn* (Cambridge, Mass.: Harvard University Press).

COURCELLE, P. (1943), *Les lettres grecques en Occident, de Macrobe à Cassiodore* (Paris: Éditions de Boccard; 2nd edn. 1948); trans. H. E. Wedeck as *Late Latin Writers and their Greek Sources* (Cambridge, Mass.: Harvard University Press, 1969).

—— (1948), *Histoire littéraire des grandes invasions germaniques* (Paris: Hachette; 3rd edn. Paris: L'Institut d'études augustiniennes, 1964).

—— (1950), *Recherches sur les 'Confessions' de saint Augustin* (Paris: E. de Boccard; 2nd edn. 1968).

—— (1984), *Opuscula selecta: Bibliographie et recueil d'articles publiés entre 1938 et 1980* (Paris: L'Institut d'études augustiniennes).

CRISTIN, C. (1973), *Aux origines de l'histoire littéraire* (Grenoble: Presses universitaires de Grenoble).

CURTIUS, E. R. (1953), *European Literature and the Latin Middle Ages* (Princeton: Princeton University Press; original German edn. 1948).

DANIÉLOU, J. (1950), *Sacramentum futuri: Études sur les origines de la typologie biblique* (Paris: Beauchesne); trans. as *From Shadows to Reality: Studies in the Biblical Typology of the Fathers* (London: Burns & Oates, 1960).

—— and MARROU, H. (1963), *Nouvelle Histoire de l'Eglise*, ed. L.-J. Roger *et al.*, ii: *Des origines à saint Grégoire le Grand* (Paris: Seuil).

DARRAS, J. (2002), *Nous sommes tous des romantiques allemands: De Dante à Whitman en passant par Iéna* (Paris: Calmann-Lévy).

DE GHELLINCK, J. (1947), *Patristique et Moyen Âge: Études d'histoire littéraire et doctrinale*, ii: *Introduction et compléments à l'étude de la patristique* (Gembloux: J. Duculot).

DERRIDA, J. (1999), *Donner la mort* (Paris: Galilée).

—— (2000), *Demeure: Fiction and Testimony*, trans. E. Rottenberg (Palo Alto, Calif.: Stanford University Press; original French edn. 1998).

EDEN, K. (1997), *Hermeneutics and the Rhetorical Tradition: Chapters in the Ancient Legacy and its Humanist Reception* (New Haven: Yale University Press).

ENGELS, L. J., and HOFMANN, H. (1997) (eds.), *Spätantike*, Neues Handbuch der Literaturwissenschaft, 4 (Wiesbaden: AULA Verlag).

ENGLISH, E. D. (1995) (ed.), *Reading and Wisdom: The* De doctrina christiana *of Augustine in the Middle Ages* (Notre Dame, Ind.: University of Notre Dame Press).

ERASMUS, D. (1978), *Antibarbari* ['The Antibarbarians'] / *Parabolae*, trans. C. R. Thompson, *CWE* 23 (Toronto: University of Toronto Press).

ESCARPIT, R. (1958), 'Définitions de l'histoire et de la littérature', in R. Queneau (ed.), *Histoire des littératures*, iii: *Littératures françaises, connexes et marginales* (Paris: Gallimard), 1737–1811.

FONTAINE, J. (1970), *La littérature latine chrétienne* (Paris: Presses universitaires de France).

—— (1982), 'Christentum ist auch Antike: Einige Überlegungen zu Bildung und Literatur in der lateinischen Spätantike', *JAC* 25: 5–21.

—— (1984*a*) 'Les laïcs et les études patristique latines dans l'Université française au XXᵉ Siècle', *RBén* 94: 444–61.

—— (1984*b*), 'Postclassicisme, Antiquité tardive, latin des chrétiens: L'évolution de la problématique d'une histoire de la littérature romaine du IIIᵉ au VIᵉ siècle depuis Schanz', *Bulletin de l'Association Guillaume Budé*, 1984/2: 195–212.

GERHARD, J. (1653), *Patrologia sive de primitivae ecclesiae christianae doctorum vita ac lucubrationibus opusculum* (Iena: G. Sengenwaldius).

GOLDHILL, S. (1999), 'Literary History without Literature', *SubStance*, 88: 57–89.

GORMAN, M. (1985), 'The Diffusion of the Manuscripts of St Augustine's *De doctrina christiana* in the Early Middle Ages', *RBén* 95: 11–24.

HAGENDAHL, H. (1983), *Von Tertullian zu Cassiodor: Die profane literarische Tradition in dem lateinischen christlichen Schrifttum*, Studia Graeca et Latina Gothoburgensia (Göteborg: Acta Universitatis Gothoburgensis).

HARNACK, A. (1968), *Geschichte der altchristlichen Literatur bis Eusebius*, 2 vols. in 4 parts (Leipzig: Zentralantiquariat der Deutschen Demokratischen Republik; originally published, Leipzig: J. C. Hinrichs, 1893–1904).

HERZOG, R. (2002), *Spätantike: Studien zur römischen und lateinisch-christlichen Literatur*, ed. P. Habermehl, Hypomnemata: Untersuchungen zur Antike und zu ihrem Nachleben, Supplement-Reihe Bd. 3 (Göttingen: Vandenhoeck & Ruprecht).

—— (1989) (ed.), *Restauration und Erneuerung: die lateinische Literatur von 284 bis 374 n. Chr*, Handbuch der lateinischen Literatur der Antike, 5 (Munich: C. H. Beck).

HUYSMANS, J. K. (2003), *À Rebours*; trans. R. Baldick as *Against Nature* (London: Penguin) from *Œuvres complètes*, vii (Paris: Crès, 1929; original French publication, Paris: G. Charpentier, 1884).

JORDAN, H. (1911), *Geschichte der altchristlichen Literatur* (Leipzig: Quelle & Meyer).

MADOZ, J. (1933), *El concepto de la tradición en S. Vicente de Lerins*, Analecta Gregoriana, 5 (Rome: Pontificia Università Gregoriana).

MCKITTERICK, R. (1989), *The Carolingians and the Written Word* (Cambridge: Cambridge University Press).

——(2004), *History and Memory in the Carolingian World* (Cambridge: Cambridge University Press).

MARKUS, R. A. (1990), *The End of Ancient Christianity* (Cambridge: Cambridge University Press).

——(1996), *Signs and Meanings: World and Text in Ancient Christianity* (Liverpool: Liverpool University Press).

——(forthcoming), 'Between Marrou and Brown: Transformations of Late Antique Christianity', in P. Rousseau and M. Papoutsakis (eds.), *Transformations of Late Antiquity: Essays for Peter Brown* (Aldershot and Burlington, Vt.: Ashgate).

MARROU, H.-I. (1938), *Saint Augustin et la fin de la culture antique* (Paris: E. de Boccard; reissued with a 'Retractatio', 1949).

——(1948), *Histoire de l'éducation dans l'antiquité* (Paris: Seuil); trans. G. Lamb as *A History of Education in Antiquity* (London: Sheed and Ward, 1956).

——(1949), 'Retractatio' appended to reissue of Marrou 1938 (with continuous pagination).

MERKT, A. (2001), *Das patristische Prinzip: Eine Studie zur theologische Bedeutung der Kirchenväter* (Leiden: E. J. Brill).

MÖHLER, J. A. (1840), *Patrologie oder christliche literärgeschichte* (Regensburg: G. J. Manz).

MORGAN, T. (1998), *Literate Education in the Hellenistic and Roman Worlds* (Cambridge: Cambridge University Press).

NITZSCH, F. (1865), 'Geschichtliches und Methodologisches zur Patristik', *JDT* 10: 37–63.

OCKER, C. (2002), *Biblical Poetics before Humanism and Reformation* (Cambridge: Cambridge University Press).

O'DALY, G. J. P. (1999), *Augustine's 'City of God': A Reader's Guide* (Oxford: Clarendon Press).

OVERBECK, F. (1882), 'Über die Anfänge der patristischen Literatur', *Historische Zeitschrift*, NS 12: 417–72.

PERKINS, D. (1992), *Is Literary History Possible?* (Baltimore: Johns Hopkins University Press).

POLLMANN, K. (1996), *Doctrina Christiana: Untersuchungen zu den Anfängen der christlichen Hermeneutik unter besonderer Berücksichtigung von Augustinus, De doctrina christiana*, Par. 41 (Freiburg, Schweiz: Universitätsverlag Freiburg).

——(2005), 'Augustine's Hermeneutics as a Universal Discipline!?', in Pollmann and Vessey (2005), 206–31.

——and VESSEY, M. (2005) (eds.), *Augustine and the Disciplines: Cassiciacum to 'Confessions'* (Oxford: Oxford University Press).

QUASTEN, J. (1950–60), *Patrology*, 3 vols. (Westminster, Md.: Newman Press; Utrecht: Spectrum).

QUINN, K. (1979), *Texts and Contexts: The Roman Writers and their Audience* (London: Routledge & Kegan Paul).

RAWSON, E. (1985), *Intellectual Life in the Late Roman Republic* (London: Duckworth).

RICE, E. F. JUN. (1983), *Saint Jerome in the Renaissance* (Baltimore: Johns Hopkins University Press).

SARTRE, J.-P. (1948), *Qu'est-ce que la littérature?* (Paris: Gallimard); trans. B. Frechtman as *What is Literature?* (London: Methuen, 1950).

SCHADEWALDT, W. (1973), 'Der Umfang des Begriffs der Literatur in der Antike', in H. Rüdiger (ed.), *Literature und Dichtung: Versuch einer Begriffsbestimmung* (Stuttgart: W. Kohlhammer), 12–25.

SCHÄUBLIN, C. (1995), '*De doctrina christiana*: A Classic of Western Culture?', in D. W. H. Arnold and P. Bright (eds.), *De Doctrina Christiana: A Classic of Western Culture* (Notre Dame, Ind.: University of Notre Dame Press), 47–67.

SHANZER, D. (2005), 'Augustine's Disciplines: *Silent diutius Musae Varronis?*', in Pollmann and Vessey (2005), 69–112.

SIEBEN, H. J. (1979), *Die Konzilsidee der Alten Kirche* (Paderborn: F. Schöningh).

SINISCALCO, P. (1980), 'Patristica, patrologia e letteratura cristiana antica ieri e oggi: Postille storiche e metodologiche', *Aug* 20: 383–400.

TETZ, M. (1967), 'Altchristliche Literaturgeschichte—Patrologie', *TRu* 32: 1–42.

VESSEY, M. (1998), 'The Demise of the Christian Writer and the Remaking of "Late Antiquity": From H.-I. Marrou's Saint Augustine (1938) to Peter Brown's Holy Man (1983)', *JECS* 6: 377–411; repr. in *idem*., *Latin Christian Writers in Late Antiquity and their Texts* (Aldershot: Ashgate: 2005, item XI)

—— (2004), 'Introduction', in *Cassiodorus: 'Institutions of Divine and Secular Learning' and 'On the Soul'*, trans. J. W. Halporn, Translated Texts for Historians, 42 (Liverpool: Liverpool University Press), 1–101.

WAWRYKOW, J. (1995), 'Reflections on the Place of the *De doctrina christiana* in High Scholastic Discussions of Theology', in English (1995), 99–125.

WIDDOWSON, P. (1999), *Literature* (London: Routledge).

WILLIAMS, R. (1976), *Keywords* (London: Croom Helm).

WILSON, N. G. (1992), *From Byzantium to Italy: Greek Studies in the Italian Renaissance* (Baltimore: Johns Hopkins University Press).

YOUNG, F. (1994), 'Typology', in S. E. Porter, P. Joyce, and D. E. Orton (eds.), *Crossing the Boundaries: Essays in Biblical Interpretation in Honour of Michael D. Goulder* (Leiden: E. J. Brill), 29–48.

—— (1997), *Biblical Exegesis and the Formation of Christian Culture* (Cambridge: Cambridge University Press).

CHAPTER 3

WHICH EARLY CHRISTIANITY?

KAREN L. KING

'FOR it has been reported to me by Chloe's people that there is quarrelling among you, my brethren. What I mean is that each one of you says, "I belong to Paul", or "I belong to Apollos", or "I belong to Cephas", or "I belong to Christ".' Thus begins one of the very earliest surviving documents of Christianity, Paul's first letter to the Corinthians (1: 11–12). It would seem that the questions 'Which Christianity? Whose Christianity?' were posed very early, even before the gospels and most of the New Testament literature had been composed, and at a time when the number of believers must have been very small indeed. Throughout the history of Christianity, diverse beliefs and practices would ebb and flow on the tides of historical change and conflict, navigating and sometimes floundering with ever-shifting geographical, social-political, and cultural contexts as Christianity expanded from a tiny movement to a global religion. The issues, actors, and contexts would vary, but diversity would continue to characterize Christianity, even in the face of powerful claims to unity and uniformity.

The question is how to represent this ever-shifting diversity adequately. This problem has become increasingly urgent owing to several factors, prominent among them the rise of critical historical methodologies and new frameworks for the study of early Christianity; astonishing discoveries of previously unknown ancient texts from Egypt; and questions arising from new contexts, especially from ecumenism and the realities of local and global pluralisms.

3.1 HISTORICAL CRITICISM

Given that Christianity has never been a unified or uniform phenomenon, how has the problem of diversity been discussed? In ancient Christianity, it was generally posed in terms of unity and division. By the fourth century, Christian discussions of variety and difference settled into the tidy, bifurcating mode of orthodoxy and heresy, right and wrong, true and false. The master narrative of Christian origins and development claimed that the true path of orthodoxy inaugurated by Jesus had been passed on to twelve male apostles (plus Paul) and their successors, the bishops of the one true Church. Satan had later corrupted this original truth by the introduction of divisive heresy (Bauer 1971: pp. xxi–xxv; Le Boulluec 1985). The defenders of the true Church promulgated powerful rhetorical claims to the unity and harmony of the Church, combined with derisive denunciations of the heretics' factionalism. The heretics, they claimed, had contaminated the true faith by importing Greek philosophy or had fallen back into the clutches of an unredeemed religion of Jewish legalism. They deviated from the doctrinal prescriptions of the creed and the practices of the true Church, lacked true morality, were incapable of properly interpreting scripture, and were disobedient to the proper authority of the established leadership. This rhetorical discourse of orthodoxy and heresy has proved extremely powerful and persistent throughout the history of Christianity (King 2003*b*: 20–54).

Close examination by modern historians, however, has found much to criticize in this tidy portrait of the causes and character of early Christian diversity. In particular, the rise of historical criticism in New Testament scholarship introduced methodological principles that exposed fundamental disparities already in the supposed harmony of the earliest Christians. These historians assumed that the ancient authors all wrote with particular purposes in mind and directed their works at specific audiences. It followed, then, that the particular historical circumstances and theological tendencies of each work had to be elucidated in the context of the work's original composition within the broader framework of early Christian history. Prior to this time, scripture had been understood to express the single, unchanging voice of God; apparent differences were harmonized through reading practices that emphasized their conformity to established creed and doctrine. In this approach, differences were minimalized, while similarities were emphasized or even manufactured, often with great intellectual effort and ingenuity. But with the rise of historical criticism, the age-old practice of interpreting scripture as a unitary whole was discredited. With the ban on harmonization, theological and historical differences among the canonical texts began to appear quite forcefully.

Historical criticism has produced at least three durable (if not entirely unproblematic) effects. One effect was to categorize the earliest forms of Christianity into four basic types, each with subtypes or variants located along their spectra: Jewish Christianity, Gentile Christianity, Apocalyptic Christianity, and early Catholicism. Second, exposing authors' tendentious interests slowly worked to relativize the seemingly impartial historical value of the canonical books. History was no longer understood as the ground upon which Satan futilely opposed the inexorable, teleological movement of God's will; it became a place of human struggle, conflict, and constructive negotiation. Third, using the idea of authorial intentionality to ground a monological reading of each particular text or corpus of texts produced a set of homogeneous, self-enclosed types of Christianity, each increasingly identified with a well-bounded community. Eventually there would be studies of Matthew's or John's community, Pauline churches, Thomas Christianity, and the like. Variety came to dwell within the New Testament canon itself and spilled out beyond its edges.

The historical-critical approach is exemplified in the work of Ferdinand Christian Baur (1792–1860), who set out a number of fundamental oppositions that would reorient the writing of early Christian history (1878, 1879). Chief among them were the contrast between Jesus' proclamation of the kingdom of God and the Pauline kerygma of the crucified and exalted Christ; a sharp distinction between the theology of the Synoptic Gospels (Matthew, Mark, and Luke) and the Gospel of John; and conflict between the Gentile (Hellenistic) Christianity of Paul and the Jewish Christianity of Peter and the Jerusalem church. In Baur's view, later works, like the Acts of the Apostles and the Pastoral Epistles, needed to be read as attempts to unify the church by reconciling the disagreements between Jewish Christians and Hellenizers. Theologically, he argued that Paul's view of Christ was central to early Christian development because it provided a bridge between the human Jesus of the Synoptic Gospels and the pre-existent Logos of the Johannine Gospel (Baur 1878: 44–183; 1879: 65–72). The catholic (universal) Church developed its dogma and hierarchical institutions as the antithesis to Gnosticism and Montanism (1879: 1–61).

Later historians would nuance this picture considerably, insisting that rather than developing along a linear model of Hegelian dialectic as Baur had proposed (of thesis, antithesis, synthesis), conflicting forms of Christianity existed simultaneously. Historians also multiplied the types of early Christianities in conflict, most importantly adding Apocalyptic Christianity as a basic type (now distinct from Jewish Christianity). At the turn of the twentieth century, scholars such as Johannes Weiss and Albert Schweitzer emphasized the apocalyptic theology of Jesus and earliest Christianity, setting it in direct contrast to later forms of catholic Christianity (represented by Acts and the Pastoral Epistles) that were now considered to have been formed at least in part by 'the delay of the parousia' (Weiss 1985; Schweitzer 1954). Historians also increasingly linked doctrinal conflict with the historical development of different forms of social life. Describing the audiences addressed by the New Testament texts, as well as the groups out of which they arose, would come to be a central task of early Christian historiography. Texts were read as reflections of the historical situations of the communities that produced them. Theological differences in the texts frequently (and problematically) came to be read as ciphers for communities in conflict (e.g. Riley 1995; critique by Dunderberg 1997).

Another watershed in the representation of early Christian diversity came in 1932 with the publication of Walter Bauer's monograph *Rechtgläubigkeit und Ketzerei in ältesten Christentum* (*Orthodoxy and Heresy in Earliest Christianity*). Although Bauer kept the categories of orthodoxy and heresy intact, he argued that the earliest forms of Christianity were not always or everywhere 'orthodox'. Rather, Christianity initially developed different forms in different geographical areas, some of which were 'heretical' from the beginning. This position fundamentally challenged the supposition that the origin of Christianity was characterized by a 'pure orthodoxy' untainted by 'heresy'. Although scholars have challenged various aspects of Bauer's thesis, it was to have a decisive effect on subsequent representations of early Christian diversity (King 2003*b*: 110–15). James M. Robinson and Helmut Koester, for example, were building on Bauer's work when they proposed a model of development in terms of 'trajectories'. The term 'trajectory' was meant to capture the dynamics of historical movement through the Hellenistic world, rather than delineate a unique essence against its supposedly static 'background' (1971: 14–15). Trajectories would chart directionality and flow, rejecting the anachronistic distinctions between orthodoxy and heresy that Bauer had presupposed in favour of a theological approach tied to literary forms (1971: 186; critique by Janßen 1999). With varying success, others sought to establish the histories of particular streams of tradition under the names of particular apostles, notably Pauline, Johannine, and Thomas Christianities. The soundest developments of Bauer's work, however, have stemmed from his notion that the history of Christianity has to be written regionally. Koester, for example, organized much of his eminent *History and Literature of Early Christianity* by geographical regions (1982). Other studies have been undertaken of particular locales; an outstanding recent example is Peter Lampe's study of the diversity of Christianity at Rome (2003). Such studies have largely avoided creating homogeneous types of Christianity in each locale, but rather have demonstrated that even while Christianity developed differently in particular regions, each region also has its own complex story of early Christian diversity.

By stressing the diversity of early Christianity, such approaches simultaneously raised the urgent theological question of whether any discernible unity lay beneath all this division, and how to characterize it. In what sense may we speak of all this variety as Christianity? One kind of solution is exemplified by Adolph von Harnack, who located the essence of Christianity in a trans-historical religion characterized by inwardness and enthusiasm, expressed in the gospel teachings of Jesus. This essence was preserved intact despite changing historical dress or development. Indeed, he argued, it is precisely because the Gospel is not tied to any particular form of expression that it continues to signify (1957: esp. 54–6, 62–8, 149; King 2003*b*: 55–70).

Some, however, found this ahistorical essentializing unsatisfying and turned to a more thematic theological approach. A good example is found in James Dunn's monograph *Unity and Diversity in the New Testament* (1977). He agreed with Bauer that no foundational orthodoxy lay at the origin of Christianity; nonetheless, he argued that all the New Testament books provide evidence of a common theological core—the unity between the earthly (crucified) Jesus and the exalted Christ. Although he recognized that this thematic formulation is an abstraction that is nowhere to be found as such in the texts themselves, he insisted that each text offers an expression of this common kerygma or confessional formula appropriate to its own particular situation, despite the real differences and disagreements that resulted (1977: 30–1, 56–8). The lesson he drew is that the validity of the New Testament lies in its continuing ability to bear 'consistent testimony to the unifying centre' and simultaneously to recognize 'the validity of diversity', a view specifically crafted in the context of contemporary ecumenism (1977: 376–7).[1] He goes on to suggest that this common core also defined the limits of acceptable diversity, marking off true expressions of the proto-orthodox faith in Jewish Christianity, Hellenistic Christianity, Apocalypticism, and early Catholicism from their excesses in Ebionism, Gnosticism, Montanism, and (with less emphasis) later Catholicism (1977: 262–6, 306–8, 336–40, 376).

Although other theologians have defined the content of this core in other ways, the tendency has been to characterize variety within early Christianity as being of a single sort with a unitary core, increasingly referred to as 'proto-orthodoxy' (for example, Ehrman 2003). In this way, variety is presented as in some sense merely different versions of the same thing. Moreover, although this nomenclature implicitly acknowledges that 'orthodoxy' is a term of hindsight when applied to the earliest materials, the term 'proto-orthodoxy' functions to establish continuity with true orthodoxy defined by canon and creed. In contrast, other types of early Christianity are generally characterized in terms of their marginality or deviance from established norms, and are generally not referred to by a single term but by distinctive nomenclature, such as Montanism, Ebionism, and Gnosticism, or even 'lost Christianities'. The effect is to emphasize sameness and continuity among the works classified as 'proto-orthodox', while other forms of Christianity are characterized by their differences, both from 'the mainstream' and from each other. So in the end, despite widespread recognition of the enormous variety of early Christianity, in practice this diversity has been resolved back into the two basic categories of the ancient master narrative: orthodoxy and heresy.

One reason why this dual taxonomy continues to be reproduced has to do with the sources. Although the nineteenth- and twentieth-century views of early Christian diversity were formed on the basis of new historical-critical approaches, they were largely applied to well-known literature, and thus that literature continued to supply not only the data but also the framework for reconstruction. As a result, despite the methodological innovations of historical criticism, the twentieth-century classification of the varieties of Christianity largely reproduced the classificatory system and rhetorical strategies of early Christian polemicists.

In my opinion, we are now at the brink of another watershed in the representation of early Christian diversity. Building on the foundations established by historical criticism, numerous recent studies in New Testament and late antiquity have laid the groundwork for a reconsideration of early Christian notions of difference. These studies draw upon and contribute to work in social history, cultural anthropology, feminism, post-structuralism, and postmodern criticism, and are aided by work integrating archaeological materials, including the new textual discoveries from Qumran, Nag Hammadi, Oxyrhynchus, and elsewhere, into early Christian historiography. Owing to considerations of space, it is not possible to give an adequate account of the impact of this wide-ranging work here. Let me offer a summary of just one kind of approach: the analytical shift from essence to practice in considering early Christian 'identities'.

3.2 IDENTITIES

An adequate framework for historical descriptions of early Christian diversity needs to recognize that all religions contain ever-shifting, competing, and contradictory claims, plural possibilities, and alternative voices. '[B]oundedness, continuity, and homogeneity are not objective aspects of social life' (Handler, in van der Veer 1994: 208–9), but are rhetorical terms used in constructing shared religious identity. Yet typologies of the varieties of early Christianity instead frequently constitute attempts to define and categorize the unique and essential qualities of distinct theological systems or social groups. Essentializing categories tend to reify the complex, overlapping, multifarious clusters of material that constitute the continually shifting, interactive forms of early Christian meaning-making and social belonging into homogenous, stable, well-bounded theological or sociological formations.

There are at least two problems with this kind of approach. First, the data are not so tidy, and trying to fit them neatly into such categories has distorted the evidence to the point where they can serve no useful purpose (M. A. Williams 1996; King 2003b). New texts from discoveries in the modern period have served only to confound this situation, straining the categories to the breaking point. Second, this essentializing freezes the processes of historical and theological dynamics, misleading us into thinking that any religion is a homogeneous and fixed entity with a determinate essence or decisive moment of pure origination rather than properly apprehending that it encompasses multiform constructions that require assiduous, ongoing labour to maintain, both in the face of contested power relations within and porous, overlapping boundaries with traditions without. Social groups are constantly engaged in the processes of meaning-making and social formation, using the manifold valued resources at hand to think with. To understand these processes, it is critical to shift the perspective away from understanding 'religions as ready-made systems of meaning awaiting interpretation', as Ortner puts it, to the view that 'people are spinning what Geertz called "webs of meaning" all the time, with whatever cultural resources happen to be at hand'. The fundamental assumption we need to work with is that 'people are always trying to make sense of their lives, always weaving fabrics of meaning, however fragile and fragmentary' (Ortner 1997: 9). Viewed this way, the focus is not upon identifying the essential character-istics of various homogeneous types of Christianity, but upon analysing the variety of discourses, material and intellectual resources, processes, and practices by which people make sense of their lives in contexts of ancient pluralism, the governing regimes and institutions that further and constrain such practices, and the power relations that are at stake (King 2003b: 230–1). It is these that an adequate account of diversity would need to chart. Such analyses would necessarily contextualize the complex dynamics of social and intellectual life that are fully embedded in the ancient Mediterranean world. They would consider stability as well as change over time, and the processes that bind groups as well as what separates them.

Such analyses would also be fully aware of the limits as well as the possibilities of our access to this world through our (largely textual) historical evidence. Because any contexts exposed by such writings are themselves already textualized through the rhetorical aims and methods of the literary work, they cannot be read as mirrors onto social reality, but have to be understood as rhetorical constructions (Schüssler Fiorenza 1999; Clark 2004). What, then, are the surviving texts evidence of? Do they offer proof of the existence of well-bounded and distinct groups, or is that merely the effect of essentializing methods? Given that texts are always replete with alternative meanings because they are characterized by gaps, incongruity, and polyphony, we would expect to find multiple and competing voices even within individual texts. No composition is ever an act of pure creativity, in that all texts are dialogically composed of the 'already said', and because cultural codes constrain, as well as enable, literary production (King 2003b: 231–3). The task is to grasp the literary practices, cultural codes, discursive structures, hermeneutical strategies, and rhetorical ends that constitute the production of particular literary works. We need to ask not only what resource materials are being drawn upon but toward what ends and for whom.

Given that there are many ways to map difference, and given that any categoriza-tion of early Christian diversity will both illumine some things and distort or hide others, depending upon its aims (Smith 1982; 2004: 30–1, 208–9, 316), any resulting typologies would necessarily be positional and provisional; that is, they would be understood as scholarly constructs intended to do limited kinds of carefully specified intellectual work in order to serve some particular end. Such analyses would acknowledge that our systems of classification give us information not only about the data under consideration but also about the classifiers' intellectual interests, the power relations they desire to maintain, critique, or revise, and the values they hold implicitly or explicitly.

One of the most promising new approaches is the analysis of identity formation (Lieu 2004). Although the project of analysing Christianity in the framework of identity formation is broader than the question of 'Which Early Christianity?', its aims and methods lend themselves to the questions of diversity (see e.g. Lieu's discussion of the 'varieties of Judaism', 2004: 18–19). It aims to understand the discursive strategies and processes by which early Christians developed notions of themselves as distinct from others within the Mediterranean world (and were recognized as such by others), including the multiple ways in which Christians produced various constructions of what it meant to be Christian. Methodologically, it is oriented toward the critical analysis of practices, such as producing texts; constructing shared history through memory, selective appropriation, negotiation, and invention of tradition; developing ritual performances such as baptism and meals; writing and selectively privileging certain theological forms (e.g. creeds) and canons; forming bodies and gender; making place and marking time; assigning nomenclature and establishing categories; defining 'others'; and so on.

This approach has the advantage of considering symbolic and discursive activities as social-rhetorical practices fully embedded in social-material conditions, shaping as well as being shaped by them—especially in distinction from approaches that distinguish too sharply between ideology and material reality or that 'ignore the material, embodied, place-making dimensions of religion' by focusing exclusively 'on meaning and signification in religion' (Vasquez 2005: 224). Rather than reinscribe the discourse of orthodoxy and heresy, this framework requires analysis of the deployments and effects of this rhetoric as a discursive strategy by which borders could be constructed, patrolled, and maintained while simultaneously paying attention to the disjunctures and continuities that are constitutive of groups and that define their relations to each other and to the past. This analysis is also concerned with the mechanisms that bind groups together and that shape both local and trans-local affirmations of common identity. Identity formation does not take place in a vacuum, but groups define themselves in relation to each other, often using similar strategies. As a result, 'there is not any universal meaning that can be attributed to terms such as "Roman", "Greek", "Christian", "barbarian", "Jew" '; nor are they 'mutually exclusive categories, and so we can only expect to understand one term in its relations with the others' (Lieu 2004: 21). It would, for example, be impossible to understand Christian claims to be 'a third race' (as well as the limits of Christian claims to universalism) apart from ancient uses of ethnic reasoning by Greeks, Romans, and Jews (Buell 2005). This perspective requires shifting our notion of early Christian diversity from a catalogue of supposedly fixed, homogeneous entities to an analysis of the multifarious, fluid, and sometimes contradictory practices in which Christians engaged.

A brief consideration of Jewish Christianity will begin to illustrate the possibilities in shifting the discussion of early Christian diversity from essentializing reifications to the analysis of practices.

3.3 JEWISH CHRISTIANITY

The term 'Jewish Christianity' can refer to any of the following:

- Christianity as a variant type of Judaism, exemplified in the fact that Jesus and his earliest followers were Jews.
- Ethnic Jews who accepted Jesus as the Messiah.
- Christians who maintained Jewish practices, such as faithful adherence to the Law, Sabbath observance, dietary practices, male circumcision, festivals, or synagogue attendance.
- First-century members of the Jerusalem church who may have fled to Pella during the war with Rome (Acts 1: 12–8: 3; Eusebius of Caesarea, *Hist. eccl.* 3. 5. 3). Ebionites or Nazoreans, an alternative nomenclature for certain Jewish Christians found in second-century and later polemical literature, are sometimes understood to have derived from the Jerusalem church or from Peter's teaching, or to be a later group altogether (Jones 1997 [1990]).
- The influence of Jewish concepts and texts, including acceptance of the authority of Hebrew scriptures, reliance on Jewish theology (especially apocalypticism), or the use of Jewish modes of biblical interpretation.
- An adoptionist Christology (maintaining that Jesus was only a human being 'adopted' by God to be his Son; rejection of the virginal conception of Jesus).
- A denigration of Paul in favour of Peter and/or James.
- The exclusive use of Matthew's Gospel.

These items refer variously to ethnicity, religious beliefs or practices, historical events, sectarian groups, and literary or hermeneutical practices, making 'Jewish Christianity' a particularly exasperating case of classificatory imprecision.

To begin to grasp the difficulties of applying this category usefully, let us take a look at the apostle Paul. On the one hand, Paul was a Pharisaic Jew who believed in Christ; his theology was shaped by an acceptance of scriptural authority, various streams of Jewish theology, modes of biblical interpretation, messianic expectations, and much more. Does that make him a Jewish Christian? Is Pauline Christianity thus a type of Jewish Christianity? Or did Paul never think he had ceased being a Jew when he accepted Jesus as the Christ, so should we talk about Pauline theology as one of the many expressions of early Judaism? Or is the issue, rather, that it is too early to draw a clear line between Christians and Jews? And what about Paul's attitude toward Gentiles? Paul argued that Gentiles who believed in Christ did not need to follow the practices of Jewish table fellowship, and Gentile males did not need to be circumcised. In that sense he has been understood as the exemplary purveyor of Gentile Christianity. So is Pauline Christianity a kind of Gentile Christianity? Is this confirmed by his apparent tensions with the leadership of the Jerusalem church and Peter—also all Jews? Or should Paul's disputes with other Jews rather lead us to speak about intra-Jewish controversy here, rather than a conflict between Jewish and Gentile types of Christianity?

The problem of how to categorize Paul is yet further complicated by attempts to gain a clear picture of the churches to which Paul is writing. Far from portraying some homogeneous form of Pauline Christianity, the controversies in Paul's letters offer evidence of a variety of viewpoints among and within the churches he addressed, as well as diversity of ethnicity, gender, marital status, age, economic status, and social status, *inter alia*. The authorial voice of the letters offers a rhetorical representation of the inscribed author, opponents, audience, and various issues under debate from which some scholars have reconstructed a nuanced and reasonably consistent portrait of the basic contours of Pauline theology; but the dialogical character of the text continually lets us hear alternative voices as well. These voices disrupt the authorial voice's attempt to define the 'reality' of the situation, instead making space for alternative reconstructions of what was going on and what was at stake (see e.g. Schüssler Fiorenza 1985: 160–241; 1999: 105–28; Wire 1990; Martin 1995; Miller 2004).

Plenty of ink has been spilled in trying to fix the identity of these alternative voices by figuring them as 'Paul's opponents' or as factions that Paul is trying to reconcile. In Corinth, for example, they have been identified as Gentile Christians, Gnostics, spiritual enthusiasts, elites, disruptive women, and loquacious prophets, among others. In Galatians, Paul tells us that he had directly opposed Peter in Antioch when 'certain men came from James' and he feared 'the circumcision faction' (2: 11–12). This array of potential 'opponents' may have something to do with the profusion and diversity of the issues under debate, such as whether the faithful should eat meat offered to idols, whether women prophets should continue to pray in the congregation unveiled, whether one should pay taxes to Caesar or circumcise Gentile men who accept Jesus Christ, and so on. Paul's 'opponents' themselves may not have all been of one mind on these many issues or have consistently aligned themselves against his position. They most certainly would not always have defined the issues as he did or have considered the same things to be at stake. Nor is it clear that Paul's authority was always equally accepted everywhere; indeed, the Corinthian correspondence seems to indicate that Paul was unable to persuade very many there to accept his views. Clearly the churches Paul addressed were diverse, both internally and geographically, making it difficult, if not impossible, to divide either his 'opponents' (or his churches) neatly into examples of Gentile or Jewish Christianity.

The letters of Paul do not offer a well-bounded homogeneous entity or type of Christianity, but multiformity, polyphony, and dialogical engagement with select Graeco-Roman and Jewish materials in a variety of social contexts. We hear not only Paul's pleading and exhortation, but alternative voices in dialogue and conflict with him and each other, such as competing claims about the roles of women in the Spirit-filled community and plural possibilities for defining the relationship between Judaism and Christianity. To complicate the problem of categorization further, Paul's theology is rife with apocalyptic themes and images; his letters were highly influential among so-called heretics (Gnostics) like Valentinus and Heracleon; and the early catholic Pastoral Epistles are written in his name—suggesting possible connections with Apocalyptic Christianity, Gnosticism, or early Catholicism as well as Gentile or Jewish Christianity. In the end, these categories are not particularly helpful in understanding what was going on in the Pauline churches or the reception of Paul's letters, what was at stake, and for whom.

One might argue that Paul is an unusual case, but even if we turn to what might appear to be a more straightforward example of Jewish Christianity, the Ebionites, the situation is not much improved (Strecker 1971; Taylor 1990). Our information about Jewish Christian groups like the Ebionites is scant, and reconstructions have to take into account the rhetorical strategies of the polemicists who supply most of our information. It would seem that they wanted to construct clear boundaries in situations that were in fact ambiguous, given that at least some followers of Jesus continued to attend synagogue, to observe the commandments, including dietary laws and circumcision, and even to emphasize a common, non-supersessionist heritage well into the third and fourth centuries (Taylor 1990: 319–320). There is no evidence that these people understood following Jesus to imply a break with these Jewish practices. Taylor suggests that the patristic term 'Ebionites' functioned to mass together a variety of persons or groups 'who followed Jewish customs for various reasons and in various ways' in order to present 'a precise identifiable heresy.... It is by no means the case that they would have defined themselves as sectarian or given themselves a name' (1990: 324). The apparent existence of a monolithic movement of Ebionites is the effect of patristic discourse, not a sociological fact.

Attempts to imagine Jewish Christianity as an essential, homogeneous type of Christianity with a fixed set of characteristics result in imprecision, because the phenomena are multiform and fluid—and not only Christianity, but Judaism and practices of Jewish identity formation are diverse and complex in this period (Cohen 1999; Boyarin 2004). If instead we ask how early Christians variously construed 'Judaism' and 'Judaizing', how they defined their relationship to this 'Judaism', and why defining that relationship was at once so crucial to Christian identity and so hotly contested, then we get at one of the single most important foci of Christian practices of religious identity formation and boundary setting. Even a cursory look at texts that explicitly take up the issue of the relationship to Judaism not only reveals a wide range of positions, but also indicates the multiple ways in which early Christians mapped differences, both from Judaism (or 'paganism') and from each other (heresy). Those mappings did a variety of different kinds of work: setting boundaries, marking the limits of internal difference, and supplying intellectual materials for constructive theology and ethics. In each case we have to ask: What difference makes a difference? What work does it do? What is at stake?

For example, for Paul the difference that makes a difference is accepting Jesus as the Christ by receiving the Holy Spirit in baptism. He uses this difference to redefine the borders of Israel by including Gentiles who accepted Jesus Christ, while excluding Jews who did not (Rom 11: 17–24). At stake is not only the possibility of eternal life, but membership in the church of the saints, and all that entailed. In Paul's economy of salvation, circumcision and table purity were differences that ceased to matter—a point of considerable tension (Gal 2). Through the next two millennia, however, Paul's letters would be put to work that exceeded any intention of Paul's. Indeed, at some point in that history Paul ceased to be a Jew altogether and was refigured into one of the great Christian founders of orthodoxy. He became the apostle of Gentile Christianity, who defined the true Christianity of faith and love over against a dead Judaism of law and works—a distortion only slowly being corrected in the face of contemporary Jewish–Christian relations in a post-Holocaust world (Stendahl 1976; Boyarin 1994: 136–57). In fact, the meaning of Paul's letters has never been stable—even in their first reading—but shifts with the ways in which Christians (and Jews) define Judaism and its relationship to Christianity. This instability is apparent not only in ancient disputes about circumcision and table practices, but also in contemporary Christian theological and historical shifts from supersession to 'parting of the ways' or shifts in terminology from 'Late Judaism' to 'Early Judaism' (Becker and Reed 2003: 1–24). These moves coincide with shifts in the positionality of Christians: from a divided and persecuted minority to persecutors of Jews and heretics; from post-Holocaust ecumenism to post-colonialism's attention to the hybridity of Judaisms and Christianities. This complex history clearly shows that there was never one definitive 'parting of the ways' between Judaism and Christianity accomplished at one time once and for all (Lieu 2002: 11–29). Nor are processes of boundary setting one-sided (Boyarin 1999, 2004). Rather, the processes of mutual definition and self-definition never really ended, but had to be—and continue to be—constantly renegotiated. What is at stake in the ways that Christians define Judaism is the very nature of Christianity itself, because defining the appropriate relationship to Jews and Judaism was, and is, deeply implicated in basic aspects of Christian self-understanding, including the proper interpretation of scripture and the role of Jesus Christ in salvation.

If we turn now to non-Pauline Christian literature from the early centuries, we might attempt to illustrate early Christian diversity by mapping the strategic discourses defining the relationship of Christianity to Judaism on a continuum from identity and accommodation (Gospel of Matthew) to supersession (Hebrews) and even outright rejection (Marcion). That would usefully illustrate variety, but it would not adequately show that our early sources are not all speaking about the same thing when they talked about Jews, Judaism, and Judaizing; nor are the distinctions they are making all doing the same kind of work. For example, the *Testimony of Truth* (IX, 3) from Nag Hammadi states that the mission of Christ was to bring 'the dominion of carnal procreation to an end'. It condemns all those Christians who were bound by the 'old leaven of the Pharisees and the scribes of the Law', which leads them to marry and beget children according to the commands of Moses in Genesis (*Testimony of Truth*, 29. 6–30. 30). It goes on to vilify everyone who believed in the saving value of baptism, martyrdom, and the resurrection of the flesh. Ignatius of Antioch, on the other hand, identified Judaizing with circumcision and Sabbath observance (not procreation), and his advocacy of martyrdom strongly affirmed the bodily nature of Christ's death and the resurrection of the flesh. These differences are not primarily about affirming or denying the body, but illustrate different deployments of body symbolism to articulate different theological positions in support of different social projects. The concern of the *Testimony of Truth* is to authorize the abstemious practices of a developing ascetic tradition, while Ignatius is using his authority as an about-to-be martyr to restore unity under the authority of the monarchical episcopate in Antioch (Schoedel 1980). For both Ignatius and the *Testimony of Truth*, defining the nature of 'Judaism' simultaneously served to set borders with Judaism and to charge Christian 'heretics' with Judaizing. But note how they map 'Judaizing heresy' differently onto the social world of early Christianity. Ignatius is usually read as a proto-orthodox theologian opposed to Judaizers ('Jewish Christians') and docetists ('Gnostics'). The *Testimony of Truth* would regard as heretics not only the so-called proto-orthodox, but also Valentinus, Isidore, Simonians, and perhaps Basilides—central figures of so-called Gnosticism—even though modern scholars generally classify the *Testimony of Truth* as itself Gnostic!

Like 'Jewish Christianity', the category of 'Gnostic' is generally confusing *vis-à-vis* Christian relationships to Judaism, since texts classed under that rubric express a broad range of strategic relations to Jewish tradition. The *Gospel of Thomas* (II, 2) builds its Christology primarily from Jewish Wisdom literature, and interprets much of Jesus's teaching in the light of Genesis and Wisdom literature (Davies 1983; Pagels 1999). The *Gospel of Mary*, on the other hand, interprets the sayings tradition of Jesus without regard to Jewish thought at all; even Jesus's command not to set down laws 'like the lawgiver' is less a reference to Jewish Law than a caution against Christians themselves setting up rules and regulations beyond what Jesus commanded them: for example, in refusing to honour Mary Magdalene's teaching because she is a woman who received private instruction from the Lord (King 2003a). The *Apocryphon of John* offers yet another model, placing Hebrew scriptures at the centre of Christ's revelation—but in order to correct them; thus Jewish scriptures are fundamental to understanding the world, but only in the light of Christ's corrective revelation (King 2006). Implied here are very different ways of defining the relationship of Christianity to Jewish scripture and tradition. Additional examples only increase the confusion, further undermining the simplistic and misleading stereotype that 'Gnostics rejected Jewish scripture'. Some did, some didn't; those who did, did so differently.

The point here is that an account of early Christian diversity aimed at mapping the strategic construction of early Christian identities *vis-à-vis* constructions of Judaism would not result in the categories of Jewish Christianity, Hellenistic Christianity, Gnosticism, Apocalypticism, and early Catholicism. Nor can the multiformity of the early Christian phenomena be adequately represented by a bifurcating frame, whether orthodoxy versus heresy or the so-called 'parting of the ways'.

If we return to the initial list defining Jewish Christianity, we can now see that one reason why it is so imprecise is that a single category is trying to serve a variety of different purposes: notably, to chart continuities between Judaism and Christianity; to establish clear boundaries between them; to construct a usable Judaism against which to define Christianity; and to mark the limits of (un)acceptable difference within the group *vis-à-vis* Judaism (variously constructed). What the list does, then, is to illustrate several strategies of early Christian identity formation, strategies which do not necessarily reproduce the historical contours of distinct groups or persons, practices, and ideas that define the character and social make-up of a particular type of early Christianity.

Indeed, it is arguable that early Christian discourses of difference themselves produced certain effects, which modern scholarship tends to reproduce. They invented whole cloth groups that never existed, such as Epiphanius's 'Stratiotics' and 'Socratites' (*Pan.* 1. 35. 3, 5; F. Williams 1987: 236), turned multiform phenomena into monolithic entities (Ebionism and Gnosticism), and produced schismatic churches by exacerbating minor differences into intolerable otherness (Montanism; Tabbernee 1985; 1997: 23–4; Trevett 1996). Thomassen (2004) has suggested that the rhetoric of church unity itself may have led to division. Some Christians (such as Hermas, Marcion, and Valentinus) came to regard diversity as intolerable and attempted reforms that were intended to institute moral, ritual, and/or doctrinal uniformity, but had the concomitant effect of hardening internal differences. In practice, early Christian discourses of difference operated by treating differences differently: some are emphasized or even created; others are harmonized to make them disappear; others are simply ignored, never rising to the level of discursive employment. Constructing the impression of unity out of all this multiformity required emphasizing or even manufacturing similarities (often through harmonization) while ignoring differences. In contrast, excluding heretics meant emphasizing or even manufacturing differences while overlooking similarities. The result is that it becomes difficult for us to see the immense common territory that those who are labelled heretics shared with other Christians; where the real differences between them lie and what is at stake; and where there is (perhaps mutual) incomprehension, either because they simply had different theological interests or because they sidestepped, ignored, or simply failed to be cognizant of the interests of the other (King 2003b: 30; and forthcoming).

A more adequate analysis would replace the division of early Christianity into static and inaccurate types, which do little more than reproduce or (slightly) readjust the boundary-setting enterprises of ancient discourses of orthodoxy and heresy, with an analysis of the full range of early Christian practices of mapping difference and identity. While not all diversity is about identity formation or boundary setting, this approach would serve to illustrate the dynamics of early Christian practice, and it would simultaneously restore a fuller and more accurate portrait of early Christian diversity, including a place for those whose perspectives have been marginalized, silenced, or inadequately engaged critically.

3.4 New Contexts/New Questions

Why the urgency surrounding the question 'Which early Christianity?' Certainly as J. Z. Smith argues, consideration of difference is fundamental to constructions of both self and other (2004: 230–302). The old categories and assumptions are widely criticized as inadequate—both to a disciplined analysis of the evidence and to addressing the crucial questions of identity, belonging, hierarchies, and exclusions raised so poignantly in our current post-colonial and pluralistic world. The ancient discourse rhetorically linked sameness with right belief and unity (orthodoxy) and difference with error and schism (heresy); but contemporary theory recognizes that difference is not in itself a problem. Our differences are constitutive of who we are. The problems are injustice, suffering, and other forms of evil. A reproduction of difference solely as deviant divisiveness will not further religious understanding in pluralistic societies.

The analysis I propose here aims to get at practice (see esp. Bourdieu 1990; Schatzki 2002), not a fixed and essentialized categorization of early Christian multiformity. The results of this historiographical method would be to demonstrate where and how the 'textual' resources, cultural codes, literary themes, hermeneutical strategies, and social-political interests of various rhetorical acts of Christian literary production, theological reflection, ritual and ethical practices, and social construction simultaneously form multiple overlapping continuities, disjunctures, contradictions, and discontinuities, both locally and trans-locally. Such historio-graphical enterprises will result in more than one 'true and authentic' account of early Christian diversity, but not in a narrative of Christian triumph or a natu-ralization of the development of orthodoxy, since they would chart the ongoing processes of constructing 'orthodoxy' through rhetorical-political acts of erasure, harmonization, and fiat within the complex of identity practices in the ancient Mediterranean world.

And tradition is never the whole story of identity; it is only a part of the mix. As Homi K. Bhabha writes, '[R]estaging the past . . . introduces other, incommensu-rable cultural temporalities into the invention of tradition. This process estranges any immediate access to an originary identity or a "received" tradition.' Bhabha describes cultural change as a process in which breaking and joining occur simul-taneously, in which 'the terms of cultural engagement, whether antagonistic or affiliative, are produced performatively' (1994: 2). It eschews the identity politics of anti-syncretistic rhetoric by refusing to assume, construct, or reify essential-ist categories of religious identity. Hybridity, not purity, characterizes historical processes.

Such approaches would note throughout what was at stake, and for whom. Given the role of religion in constructing personal and national identities and the manifest involvement of religion in violence, such reflexivity is necessary. Current constructions of religious difference—including ecumenism, multiculturalism, and hybridity, affirmations of distinctiveness and programmes of separateness, sec-ularization, and fundamentalism—can all be found in academic discussions of diversity. For some, the affirmation of diversity supplies more complex resources to think about the complex issues of our time, as well as new perspectives for critical-constructive engagement with tradition. For others, the very idea of legitimate diversity undermines the authority and exclusive claims of scripture, dogma, and established structures of church leadership. For myself and others, the ethical point that follows from diversity is not relativism, but the need to take responsibility for how scripture and tradition are read and appropriated. Whatever the project, however, it is best served by historical reconstruction that is based in an adequate comprehension of the multifarious practices of early Christians, including their constructions of identity and difference.

Note

1. He twice cites Ernst Käsemann: 'the New Testament canon does not, as such, con-stitute the foundation for the unity of the church. On the contrary, as such (i.e. in its accessibility to the historian) it provides the basis for the multiplicity of the confessions' (Dunn 1977: 122, 376).

Suggested Reading

The following are recommended: Bauer (1971); Boyarin (2004); Buell (2005); Clark (2004); Cohen (1999); King (2003); Lieu (2004); Schüssler Fiorenza (1985); Taylor (1990).

Bibliography

BAUER, W. (1971), *Orthodoxy and Heresy in Earliest Christianity* (Philadelphia: Fortress Press); trans. from German, *Rechtgläubigkeit und Ketzerei in ältesten Christentum* (1932), by a team from the Philadelphia Seminar on Christian Origins, ed. R. A. Kraft and G. Krodel, new edn., with added appendices, by G. Strecker (Mifflintown, Pa.: Sigler Press, 1996).

BAUR, F. C. (1878, 1879), *The Church History of the First Three Centuries*, 2 vols., 3rd edn. (Edinburgh: Williams & Norgate).

BECKER, A. H., and REED, A. Y. (2003) (eds.), *The Ways that Never Parted: Jews and Christians in Late Antiquity and the Early Middle Ages* (Tübingen: J. C. B. Mohr/Paul Siebeck).

BHABHA, H. K. (2004), *The Location of Culture* (London: Routledge; originally published 1994).

BOURDIEU, P. (1990), *The Logic of Practice* (Stanford, Calif.: Stanford University Press).

BOYARIN, D. (1994), *A Radical Jew: Paul and the Politics of Identity* (Berkeley: University of California Press).

——(1999), *Dying for God: Martyrdom and the Making of Christianity and Judaism*, Figurae: Reading Medieval Culture (Palo Alto, Calif.: Stanford University Press).

——(2004), *Border Lines: The Partition of Judaeo-Christianity*, Divinations: Rereading Late Ancient Religion (Philadelphia: University of Pennsylvania Press).

BUELL, D. K. (2005), *Why This New Race? Ethnic Reasoning in Early Christianity* (New York: Columbia University Press).

CLARK, E. A. (2004), *History, Theory, Text: Historians and the Linguistic Turn* (Cambridge, Mass.: Harvard University Press).

COHEN, S. J. D. (1999), *The Beginnings of Jewishness: Boundaries, Varieties, Uncertainties* (Berkeley: University of California Press).

DAVIES, S. L. (1983), *The Gospel of Thomas and Christian Wisdom* (New York: Seabury Press).

DUNDERBERG, I. (1997), 'John and Thomas in Conflict?', in the Proceedings of the 1995 Society of Biblical Literature Commemoration, J. D. Turner and A. McGuire (eds.), *The Nag Hammadi Library after Fifty Years*, NHMS 44 (Leiden: E. J. Brill), 361–80.

DUNN, JAMES D. G. (1977), *Unity and Diversity in the New Testament: An Inquiry into the Character of Earliest Christianity* (Philadelphia: Westminster Press).

EHRMAN, B. D. (2003), *Lost Christianities: The Battles for Scripture and the Faiths We Never Knew* (Oxford: Oxford University Press).

HARNACK, A. (1957), *What is Christianity?* (New York: Harper Torchbooks).

JANßEN, M. (1999), 'Mystagogus Gnosticus? Zur Gattung der "gnostischen Gespräche des Auferstandenen"', in G. Lüdemann (ed.), *Studien zur Gnosis*, Arbeiten zur Religion und Geschichte des Urchristentums, 9 (Frankfurt am Main: Lang), 21–260.

JONES, F. S. (1997 [1990]), 'Ebionites', in E. Ferguson (ed.), M. McHugh and F. W. Norris (assoc. eds.), *Encyclopedia of Early Christianity*, 2nd edn. (New York: Garland Publishing), 287–88.

KING, K. L. (2003*a*), *The Gospel of Mary of Magdala: Jesus and the First Woman Apostle* (Santa Rosa, Calif.: Polebridge Press).

—— (2003*b*), *What Is Gnosticism?* (Cambridge, Mass.: Harvard University Press).

—— (2006), *The Secret Revelation of John* (Cambridge, Mass.: Harvard University Press).

—— (forthcoming), 'Social and Theological Effects of Heresiological Discourse', in E. Iricinschi and H. Zellentin (eds.), *Making Selves and Marking Others: Heresy and Self-Definition in Late Antiquity* (Tübingen: Mohr/Siebeck).

KOESTER, H. (1982), *Introduction to the New Testament: History and Literature of Early Christianity*, ii (Philadelphia: Fortress Press; originally published in German, 1980).

LAMPE, P. (2003), *From Paul to Valentinus: Christians at Rome in the First Two Centuries* (Minneapolis: Fortress Press).

LE BOULLUEC, A. (1985), *Le Notion d'hérésie dans la littérature grecque IIe–IIIe siècles* (Paris: Études augustiniennes).

LIEU, J. M. (2002), *Neither Jew Nor Greek? Constructing Early Christianity* (London: T & T Clark).

—— (2004), *Christian Identity in the Jewish and Graeco-Roman World* (Oxford: Oxford University Press).

MARTIN, D. B. (1995), *The Corinthian Body* (New Haven: Yale University Press).

MILLER, M. P. (2004), 'Antioch, Paul, and Jerusalem: Diaspora Myths of Origins in the Homeland', in R. Cameron and M. P. Miller (eds.), *Redescribing Christian Origins*, SBL symposium, 28 (Atlanta: SBL), 177–235.

ORTNER, S. B. (1997), 'Introduction', *Representations*, 59: 1–13.

PAGELS, E. P. (1999), 'Exegesis of Genesis 1 in the Gospels of Thomas and John', *JBL* 118/3: 477–96.

RILEY, G. (1995), *Resurrection Reconsidered: Thomas and John in Conflict* (Minneapolis: Fortress Press).

ROBINSON, J. M., and KOESTER, H. (1971), *Trajectories through Early Christianity* (Philadelphia: Fortress Press).

SCHATZKI, T. R. (2002), *The Site of the Social: A Philosophical Account of the Constitution of Social Life and Change* (University Park, Pa.: Pennsylvania State University Press).

SCHOEDEL, W. R. (1980), 'Theological Norms and Social Perspectives in Ignatius of Antioch', in E. P. Sanders (ed.), *Jewish and Christian Self-Definition*, i: *The Shaping of Christianity in the Second and Third Centuries*. (Philadelphia: Fortress Press), 30–56.

SCHÜSSLER FIORENZA, E. (1985), *In Memory of Her: A Feminist Theological Reconstruction of Christian Origins* (New York: Crossroad).

—— (1999), *Rhetoric and Ethic: The Politics of Biblical Studies* (Minneapolis: Fortress Press).

SCHWEITZER, A. (1954), *The Mystery of the Kingdom of God: The Secret of Jesus' Messiahship and Passion*, trans. W. Lowrie (New York: MacMillan).

SMITH, J. Z. (1982), 'Fences and Neighbors: Some Contours of Early Judaism', in *Imagining Religion: From Babylon to Jonestown*, Chicago Studies in the History of Judaism (Chicago: University of Chicago Press), 1–18.

—— (2004), *Relating Religion: Essays in the Study of Religion* (Chicago: University of Chicago Press).

STENDAHL, K. (1976), *Paul among Jews and Gentiles* (Philadelphia: Fortress Press).

STRECKER, G. (1971), 'On the Problem of Jewish Christianity', in Bauer (1971), 241–85.

TABBERNEE, W. (1985), 'Early Montanism and Voluntary Martyrdom', *Colloquium*, 17: 33–44.

—— (1997), *Montanist Inscriptions and Testimonia: Epigraphic Sources Illustrating the History of Montanist*, PMS 16 (Macon, Ga.: Mercer University Press).

TAYLOR, J. E. (1990), 'The Phenomenon of Early Jewish-Christianity: Reality or Scholarly Invention?', *VC* 44: 313–34.

THOMASSEN, E. (2004), 'Orthodoxy and Heresy in Second-Century Rome', *HTR* 97/3: 241–56.

TREVETT, D. (1996), *Montanism: Gender, Authority and the New Prophecy* (Cambridge: Cambridge University Press).

VAN DER VEER, P. (1994), 'Syncretism, Multiculturalism and the Discourse of Tolerance', in C. Stewart and R. Shaw (eds.), *Syncretism/Anti-syncretism: The Politics of Religious Synthesis*, European Association of Social Anthropologists (London: Routledge), 196–211.

VASQUEZ, M. A. (2005), 'Historicizing and Materializing the Study of Religion: The Contribution of Migration Studies', in K. I. Leonard, A. Stepick, M. A. Vasquez, and J. Holdaway (eds.), *Immigrant Faiths: Transforming Religious Life in America* (Walnut Creek, Calif.: AltaMira Press), 219–42.

WEISS, J. (1985), *Jesus' Proclamation of the Kingdom of God* (Chico, Calif.: Scholars Press).

WILLIAMS, F. (1987), *The Panarion of Epiphanius of Salamis: Book 1 (Sects 1–46)*, NHS 35 (Leiden: E. J. Brill).

WILLIAMS, M. A. (1996), *Rethinking 'Gnosticism': An Argument for Dismantling a Dubious Category* (Princeton: Princeton University Press).

WIRE, A. C. (1990), *The Corinthian Women Prophets: A Reconstruction through Paul's Rhetoric* (Minneapolis: Fortress Press).

PART II

EVIDENCE:
MATERIAL AND
TEXTUAL

CHAPTER 4

MATERIAL EVIDENCE (1): ARCHAEOLOGY

MARK HUMPHRIES

4.1 INTRODUCTION: THE TOMB OF ST PAUL?

ON 6 December 2006 Vatican officials announced to an excited world that excavations at the great basilica of San Paolo fuori le Mura (St Paul outside the Walls), located just south of Rome, had revealed a sarcophagus that might well have been the repository for the remains of the apostle Paul. In the international news media, the discovery was reported with breathless speculations as to whether the sarcophagus was indeed Paul's final resting place. By contrast, the official communiqué issued by archaeologist Giorgio Filippi on 11 December via the Vatican Press Office was more measured in tone, giving a detailed description of the materials and dimensions of the artefact unearthed. Whereas the media were mesmerized by the possibility that the bones of a biblical figure had been unearthed, Filippi was more concerned to locate the sarcophagus in the archaeological context presented by the church itself, particularly the two different phases of construction in the fourth century associated with the emperors Constantine (306–37) and Theodosius I (379–95).[1]

Filippi's discovery at San Paolo fuori le Mura and popular reactions to it are quite revealing of attitudes to the archaeology of early Christianity. The media hype generated by the prospect of the discovery of St Paul's remains is symptomatic of a general sensationalism that attaches to any 'scientific' discovery that might have a bearing on proving the veracity or otherwise of Christian scripture. In that respect, reaction to the discovery is not unique: similar lurid speculations have been provoked particularly by investigations into the supposed archaeological evidence for Jesus Christ himself. Famous recent examples are an ossuary (burial casket) that emerged on the Israeli antiquities market, and which was claimed to belong to James the brother of Jesus, and the tomb found in the Jerusalem suburb of Talpiot (sometimes spelled Talpiyot) that was claimed to be the family sepulchre of Jesus, his mother Mary, and Mary Magdalene; both contentions have garnered considerable attention in the media, but have been roundly rejected by professional biblical scholars (Scham 2003; Magness 2005, 2007). In the case of the December 2006 Vatican announcement, what is perhaps most striking about the popular response to it is the emphasis on the discovery as possibly providing a tangible link to a key personality from the New Testament; in stark contrast, scant attention was paid in media reports to the post-biblical archaeological context in which the discovery was made. At the same time, however much the excavations may have been reported in a clinical archaeological language that stressed contexts, dimensions, and materials, they were inspired by a similar concern to gain access to a biblical personality. The church of San Paolo fuori le Mura has long been a destination of pilgrims, and the search for the tomb of St Paul was initiated in order to make it more accessible to modern Christians wishing to venerate the apostle.

Perhaps it will seem overly sensationalist to begin an essay on material evidence for early Christianity with examples of the intersection of archaeology, pseudo-archaeology, and media attention. Yet such instances are revealing in themselves of some of the tensions that surround archaeological investigations of the early Christians. In particular, they demonstrate that, quite unlike most other branches of archaeological inquiry, the study of the early Christian material record frequently excites extraordinary emotions, with the attendant risk that sober analysis will suffer. While such concerns will be attached particularly to discoveries associated with the period of the New Testament, the study of early Christian archaeology as a whole has often been held in tension between what might be termed 'dogmatic concerns' and 'scientific archaeology'. Thus, although this chapter will survey the range of archaeological evidence for early Christianity and the potential avenues of inquiry that it opens up for modern scholars, it seems sensible to begin with a critical summary of how the study of early Christian archaeology has developed, and how interpretations have often been driven by interests extraneous to the evidence itself.

4.2 EARLY CHRISTIAN ARCHAEOLOGY BETWEEN DOGMA AND DISCIPLINE

If Bishop Eusebius of Caesarea merits the title 'father' of church history, then his contemporary Helena Augusta, mother of the emperor Constantine, could well deserve that of 'mother' of Christian archaeology (Frend 1996: 1–5). To be sure, Helena's quest for holy sites in Jerusalem such as Golgotha and the tomb of Christ was guided more by prayer than by anything that remotely resembles modern archaeological practice (cf. Eusebius, *Vit. Const.* 3. 28); but her desire to seek out places associated with the origins of Christianity is not entirely unlike efforts in our own day to uncover the tomb of the apostle Paul in Rome and make it accessible to pilgrims. Moreover, her pious search for material evidence sets the tone for much subsequent investigation of Christian archaeology, in that for centuries the discipline was associated above all with seeking proofs for particular beliefs.

This can be illustrated neatly by consideration of what are perhaps the most celebrated archaeological sites associated with early Christianity: the subterranean burial complexes in the catacombs of Rome. They are instructive not only for the variety of evidence that they present to the scholar (tomb complexes, inscriptions, frescoes, and so forth), but also of how dogmatic concerns have influenced the ways in which they have been interpreted. Visits to the catacombs today can—depending on the proclivities of one's guide—quickly turn into exercises in the imaginative reconstruction of the grim plight of the 'church of the martyrs', where the catacombs are cast as furtive places of sanctuary for 'good' Christians cruelly oppressed by 'wicked' pagans. This essentially emotional response is not just un-critical pious fancy, but is rooted in long-established traditions of interpreting the catacombs. They were in continuous use from the second century onwards, either for burial or as places where the tombs of martyrs could be venerated (Rutgers 2000: 53–81). Already in the fourth century, we find evidence of them being reno-vated to facilitate worship: many inscriptions attest the activity of Pope Damasus I (366–84) in restoring various catacombs to make accessible the resting places of martyrs (Grig 2004: 127–34). Such redevelopments of the catacombs continued into the early Middle Ages, as is attested, for instance, by the construction in the seventh century of the beautiful basilica of S. Agnese on the Via Nomentana, built over catacombs associated with that martyr (Crook 2000: 89). At the same time, however, many martyr relics were being removed from their original tombs and translated to churches both within Rome and further afield, so that by the end of the ninth century, the catacombs were no longer the resting places of the martyrs and came to be all but abandoned (Ghilardi 2002).

It was only in the sixteenth century that rediscovery of the catacombs began in earnest, when the first effort to catalogue them was undertaken by Antonio Bosio

(1575–1629). His *Roma Sotteranea* ('Subterranean Rome'), published posthumously in four volumes in 1634, established the catacombs once more as venerable monuments of Christian antiquity, particularly from the age of the martyrs (Rutgers 2000: 15–25). Yet Bosio's work, however foundational it might have been for subsequent study of the catacombs, was hardly scientific archaeology in the modern sense. His investigations were sponsored by the papacy and were not unrelated to the broader tides of religious history in the sixteenth and seventeenth centuries. In particular, the Protestant Reformation challenged papal authority, based on succession to St Peter, over western Christendom, to which the Roman Church responded by reaffirming its continuous history from apostolic times. In this enterprise, the evidence of the catacombs played a key role: here, it seemed, was proof that the Christian community at Rome, and with it the papacy, could trace its origins back to the age of Jesus's disciples. By contrast, Protestant scholars maintained that the catacombs in fact testified to the corruption of post-apostolic Christianity by pagan culture, and that as such they undermined the authority of the Roman Church (Frend 1996: 17).

With the advent of what might be termed more scientific approaches to archaeology in the nineteenth century, such explicitly theological interpretations of the evidence might be expected to have receded. In some respects they did: a new thorough study of the catacombs, *Roma sotteranea cristiana* ('Subterranean Christian Rome'), by Giovanni Battista de Rossi (1822–94) was guided by the author's insistence that he was 'an archaeologist, not a theologian' (quoted in Rutgers 2000: 34). Even so, a determination to view the material evidence of early Christianity through a confessional lens proved difficult to dislodge. For instance, as recently as 1929, the director of the Pontifical Commission for Christian Archaeology could publish a book that not only began with a diatribe against Protestant archaeologists but that also regarded evidence from the catacombs as 'confirming the present Catholic faith' (Marucchi 1929: 25). Similar concerns impelled Pope Pius XII (1939–58) to inaugurate his pontificate with a quest for the tomb of St Peter under the Vatican basilica (Toynbee and Ward-Perkins 1956). Only in the last 40 years has catacomb archaeology come into line with other branches of the discipline, in that new discoveries are laboriously investigated, and small finds, such as ceramics, meticulously catalogued, where once they might have been discarded in a mad scramble for the tombs of martyrs (Rutgers 2000: 39–41).

In some respects it is hardly surprising that the evidence of the Roman catacombs should have been interpreted in such an explicitly theological manner: the status and authority of the Roman Church often meant that there was more at stake for some scholars than simply matters of archaeological import. Yet similar tendencies have bedevilled the interpretation of archaeological evidence from other parts of the Mediterranean world. Excavations at Capernaum in Galilee, for example, have revealed an octagonal church structure which, according to the testimony of sixth-century pilgrims, was dedicated to the apostle Peter and associated with a house that scripture records him as occupying in the village (Mark 1: 29; White 1996–7: ii. 154–5). Modern investigation of the site was conducted by members of the Franciscan Order. They were most insistent on identifying a first-century house underneath the later church as *actually* belonging to Peter, and argued, in a way that is difficult (even impossible) to sustain from the evidence itself, that it quickly became a place of Christian worship (thus Hoppe 1994: 81–9; cf. Reed 2000: 142; White 1996–7: ii. 153).

This determination to read archaeological evidence through the prism of New Testament texts might be comprehensible in a case where, like Capernaum, a discovery was made at a place mentioned in scripture. Nevertheless, biblical texts have been used to interpret material data even when found in places far removed from the lands of the New Testament. In 1931, French and American archaeologists working at Dura Europos, a city on the Roman Empire's Euphrates frontier, excavated a Christian building of third-century date (Kraeling 1967). The structure is usually known as a 'house church', a term that derives ultimately from the descriptions in the letters of Paul of gatherings of the faithful in domestic settings (e.g. 1 Cor 16: 19; cf. White 1996–7: i. 4–9, 103–10). Moreover, at the time of the discovery, scholars regarded it as important precisely because it seemed to offer a window onto the experience of Christians in the apostolic age (Filson 1939), in spite of the fact that it dates from nearly two centuries after Paul's time and is located far outside the Palestinian and Aegean milieux of Paul's activities.

It is a regrettable fact that much Christian archaeology has been driven by interpretations generated within a framework informed above all by dogmatic concerns, while paying only scant attention to the broader socio-cultural context within which the material evidence survives. Happily, more recent work has begun to challenge this ideologically driven view and, far from regarding the archaeological evidence for early Christianity in isolation, has sought to examine it in a broader context, including evidence pertaining to other religious groups, such as Jews and worshippers of Mithras (White 1996–7). These analyses point to new possibilities in the study of early Christian archaeology, and to those we now turn.

4.3 CATEGORIES, EVIDENCE, AND INTERPRETATION

The archaeological evidence available for the study of early Christianity is extraordinarily diverse, even for the period before the religion was accorded toleration under Constantine (Snyder 2003). Scholars have traditionally prioritized the remains of church buildings, whether of small so-called house churches like that at

Dura Europos, or of large basilicas like those that appeared in cities throughout the Roman Empire between the fourth century and the sixth. Other artefacts that have commanded considerable attention are those that fall in the category of early Christian art, such as sculpted sarcophagi, elegantly wrought metalwork, and frescoes and mosaics. Such a concentration on art and architecture (e.g. Beckwith 1979; Brandenburg 2006; Kock 1996; Krautheimer 1986; Milburn 1988) might be regarded as having hindered a sensitive appreciation of what archaeology can tell us about early Christianity, just as much as dogmatic agendas have. Like the art-historical approach that once dominated classical archaeology, it tended to lay most emphasis on great works of elite production and consumption, and to interpret them primarily in aesthetic terms, rather than using the full range of evidence to suggest interpretations of early Christian history that go beyond what can be known from written sources alone. A number of examples will demonstrate both the pitfalls of that rigidly art-historical approach and the possibilities offered by a more holistic approach to the material evidence.

Among the most important archaeological discoveries pertaining to Christianity in the pre-Constantinian era is the aforementioned Christian building at Dura Europos. The significance of the find is enhanced by the fact that it can be dated with unusual precision. Dura Europos, a strategic fortress town on the Roman Empire's eastern frontier, was utterly destroyed in a Persian attack of 256, thus giving a terminal date for the building. Meanwhile, a graffito on a layer of plaster underneath that of the Christian structure means 'the year 544' in the local Seleucid era which began in 312/311 BCE, thus giving 231/2 CE as the date after which the building was remodelled for Christian use (White 1996–7: ii. 132 n. 6). Thus we have an early Christian building that was in use for, at most, about 25 years in the mid-third century. Moreover, it was converted for use by Christians from a pre-existing domestic structure. These renovations included knocking together two rooms to create an assembly hall with a speaker's platform at one end and the construction of a baptismal font in another room that was decorated with frescoes depicting scenes from scripture.

This is clearly an archaeological site of paramount importance. All too often, however, its various components are studied in isolation, with the paintings considered separately from the architecture, and the graffiti separately again (e.g. Snyder 2003: 70, 128–34, 263–5). At one level this approach is readily comprehensible: it often makes sense to distinguish different categories of evidence, both for detailed analysis and for ease of presentation in handbooks. Even so, this atomized treatment of the evidence can hinder a more nuanced interpretation of the archaeological assemblage as a whole. This would enable us to examine side by side the various elements that make up the building: to interpret its development from private house to church; to consider what bearing the subjects chosen for the fresco cycle in the baptistery might tell us about the attitudes of Dura Europos's Christians to initiation and scripture; and to speculate as to the social profile of the community that used the building (White 1996–7: ii. 123–34). We might go further too. The church building at Dura Europos's was one of several domestic structures in the city renovated to provide a cult space: elsewhere we find houses remodelled to serve as a Jewish synagogue and as temples of Mithras and the Palmyrene deity Gaddē (Wharton 1995: 27–9; White 1996–7: i. 40–4, ii. 261–300). If we bring these examples to bear on our analysis of the Christian building, then we can view it not only in terms of its uniqueness, as a well-preserved pre-Constantinian church, but also in the way in which it suggests that local Christians, by remodelling a pre-existing structure to serve their needs, were following a procedure of architectural adaptation already pursued by other religious groups in the city (White 1996–7: i. 144).

An analogous problem of contextualization is presented by the ecclesiastical buildings, ranging in date from the fifth century to the seventh, in the upland regions of Syria. Their spectacular remains, such as those of the monastery at Qal'at Si'man built around the pillar atop which the monk St Simeon Stylites (c. 390–459) famously spent many years, impress in large measure by their extraordinary condition of preservation. When they were first discovered by archaeologists in the mid-nineteenth century, they were often regarded as precursors of architectural forms that would reach their apogee in the Romanesque style of western Europe in the central Middle Ages. Such interpretations, it is now clear, reflect the imperfect knowledge base upon which nineteenth- and early twentieth-century architectural historians based their interpretations (Krautheimer 1986: 136–7). Even so, studies of the ecclesiastical buildings of Syria have continued to prioritize the notion that they can be analysed as examples of developmental trends in Christian architecture, such as the evolution of the so-called house church (White 1996–7: ii. 135–51). Only more recently have scholars sought to locate them in their specific regional context, and to elucidate their architectural peculiarities through comparison with the extensive ruins of fifth- to seventh-century villages with which they were associated (Kidner 2001).

Not all archaeological evidence for early Christianity is quite so spectacular as that unearthed at Dura Europos or preserved on the Syrian plateau. If we turn our attention to Britain at the opposite end of the Roman Empire, we find that the material record for early Christianity is very different. Evidence for church buildings from the period of Roman occupation (before c. 410) is slight, in stark contrast to the wealth of evidence from the sixth and later centuries (Blair 2005: 65–71). Moreover, the identification as churches of some Romano-British structures with halls and apses, such as those at Silchester and Colchester, has been vigorously disputed (Esmonde-Cleary 1989: 124). Apart from churches, most attention has focused on evidence from a number of villas that bear Christian symbols: for example, the frescoes from Lullingstone and the mosaic pavements from Hinton St Mary and Frampton (e.g. Cookson 1987). The attention lavished on such remains probably reflects the priorities of the art-historical approach to Christian archaeology noted above. Yet the bulk of Christian material from Britain is much less spectacular, consisting mainly of small finds—such as lead tanks and small metal, bone, or ceramic objects—marked with Christian symbols. Nevertheless, careful study of such artefacts—for example, by plotting their provenances on distribution maps—can allow speculative conclusions to be drawn about the nature and extent of Romano-British Christianity (Thomas 1981; Mawer 1995).

The differences between the archaeological evidence provided by the buildings in Dura Europos and Syria, on the one hand, and the predominantly small finds from Britain, on the other, should warn us that we ought not to presume that the material record for early Christianity will conform to monolithic expectations. Similarly, we ought to be wary of efforts to force the archaeological material to fit narratives of early Christian history derived from literary sources. Recent work on the city of Rome in late antiquity highlights the pitfalls of such an approach. Only a quarter of a century ago, it was possible to envisage the history of Rome between the reign of Constantine and the pontificate of Gregory the Great as witnessing an eclipse of imperial power by the rising authority of the Roman church. Archaeological evidence was marshalled in support of this thesis, as attention was drawn to such awe-inspiring structures as basilicas like Santa Sabina, Santa Maria Maggiore, San Giovanni in Laterano, and so forth. This evidence, it was argued, demonstrated that control of space within the city was quickly monopolized by the church to the detriment of secular powers such as the emperor and the senate (e.g. Krautheimer 1980). In recent decades, however, new excavations have revealed a wealth of new data for this period that has led scholars to reappraise the urban evolution of Rome between antiquity and the Middle Ages (Marazzi 2000). Thus, where once the fifth century was regarded as a period when Rome was dominated by papal building projects, we now have evidence of secular building, including a large new imperial palace on the Pincian hill (Broise, Dewailly, and Jolivet 2000). Consequently, fifth-century Rome is no longer regarded as a city increasingly in thrall to the papacy, but one where established secular grandees like emperors and senators continued to play an active role in determining the shape of the urban landscape (Humphries 2007; Machado, forthcoming). At the same time, these new discoveries have prompted careful reconsideration of older archaeological evidence, so that the construction of Christian basilicas can be seen within a broader context of building activity in the city at this time (Cecchelli 2001).

The example of fifth-century Rome is a reminder that the archaeological evidence for early Christianity needs to be interpreted in a manner that is sensitive to other forces in the matrix of society. To these might be added other religious groups. Attention was drawn earlier to the Christian catacombs of Rome. While study of these tomb complexes has tended to focus on Christian material, it ought to be borne in mind that they have also produced evidence for pagan and Jewish burials, and that these suggest that the same workshops produced such items as sarcophagi, gold glass, and ceramic lamps for pagans and Jews as well as Christians (Rutgers 1995: 50–99; cf. Elsner 2003). As a consequence, our interpretation of the archaeological material from Rome's Christian catacombs must allow for interaction between religious groups rather than see them evolving in isolation from—or in opposition to—one another. Other instances are indicative of the same trend. If late antiquity is often regarded as the era in which Palestine developed into a Christian Holy Land (Parker 1999b), it must also account for evidence such as that from Capernaum which shows that the church associated with St Peter was first constructed around the same time as a large synagogue complex that lay only some 20 metres away (Hoppe 1994: 33–40). Indeed, the late antique period saw the construction of numerous synagogues throughout Galilee, meaning that any view of the 'Christianization' of this landscape must be tempered by recognition of the continued vitality of Judaism in the region (Stemberger 2000: 121–60), together with an acknowledgement that Judaism and Christianity, far from being diametrically opposed to one another, probably interacted dynamically with each other (Boyarin 2004).

If evidence for Judaism is, relatively speaking, plentiful, the same cannot be said for late paganism. One instance will suffice to demonstrate the complexity of the issues. The cult of Mithras has often, if erroneously (Clauss 2000: 168–72), been seen as representing a serious challenge to Christianity, and it has been speculated on the basis of literary notices (e.g. Jerome, *Ep.* 107. 2) that it was the victim of a deliberate campaign of suppression by Christians in the fourth century. Others have argued that the cult was already defunct by the end of the fourth century, and simply faded out of existence (Martin 1989). Reassessment of the archaeological evidence for Mithraism in late antiquity suggests, however, that neither interpretation adequately explains the end of the cult. In some instances, the deliberate concealment of Mithraic cult objects could suggest precautions were being taken against Christian attacks; but elsewhere, such as along the Rhine frontier, coin sequences suggest that Mithraic shrines were abandoned in the context of upheavals resulting from barbarian invasions, and that purely religious considerations cannot explain the end of Mithraism in that region (Sauer 1996).

In short, then, the archaeological evidence for early Christianity must be interpreted in ways that take account of these multiple contexts and interpretations. It is all too easy to allow Christian buildings and artefacts to dominate our archaeological vision of the period 100–600, especially after the fourth century, and hence to lend support to an essentially teleological narrative of a culture that was becoming increasingly 'Christianized'. In some respects, of course, that account contains an element of truth: the Mediterranean and adjacent regions were clearly more Christian at the end of the sixth century than at the beginning of the second. Nevertheless, we must not forget that Christianity existed for much of this period cheek by jowl with other religions, and archaeological evidence for them must be adduced if we are not to end up with an unbalanced and simplistic interpretation of the processes by which 'Christianization' occurred.

Thus far, the analysis offered in this chapter has perhaps been rather cautious in its appraisal of the scope of archaeological evidence to inform our understanding of early Christianity. To conclude, therefore, I want to suggest a number of more positive avenues of inquiry, showing how archaeological data can assist our understanding of the early Christian period. It will hardly surprise readers if at the same time I utter caveats on the limits we must impose on our interpretations of that evidence.

4.4 TOWARDS AN ARCHAEOLOGY OF EARLY CHRISTIANITY

In baldly quantifiable terms, the sheer volume of Christian material increases enormously from the fourth century onwards. Remains of church buildings can help us to gauge how Christianity came to dominate not only urban topography, but also the activities of social elites engaged in architectural patronage (Ward-Perkins 1984: 51–84; Caillet 1993). As always, it is important to see such developments in context. For example, the proliferation of church buildings on the Syrian plateau after 400 needs to be understood as part of a general flourishing of villages in the region in the same period, which occurred in the context of an economic boom (MacAdam 1994). Indeed, socio-economic factors played as significant a role in the transformation of cities in this period as did church building (Ward-Perkins 1998). Nevertheless, the dominant presence of churches in archaeological landscapes essentially supports the picture derived from literary sources that, throughout the Mediterranean region, ecclesiastical hierarchies were coming to exercise important functions of social leadership (Liebeschuetz 2001: 137–68). Sometimes archaeology allows us to examine this process in detail. Recent excavations of a sixth-century church at Petra have revealed not only a well-preserved building decorated with exquisite mosaics, but also a cache of papyrus documents in a room adjoining one of the aisles (Fiema, Kanellopoulos, Waliszewski, and Schick 2001). The contents of the archive suggest that ecclesiastical officials were playing a major role in local administration, and the presence of such a dossier provides us with an opportunity to examine how the growing social dominance of the church in local society worked at a practical level (Frösén, Arjava, and Lehtinen 2002).

While the archaeological evidence is often very telling of the processes of social transformation, it is more difficult than historians might wish to link it with precise chronological markers drawn from literary data. At late antique Milan, for instance, the enormous suburban basilica of San Lorenzo was built on a platform carefully assembled from some 6,000 stones robbed from the nearby amphitheatre (Kinney

1972: 98–9). Thus the structure neatly encapsulates the process by which the secular entertainments of the Roman past disappeared under the new Christian dispensation (cf. Ward-Perkins 1984: 92–118). Yet, in spite of its importance, no secure date can be offered for the church (McLynn 1994: 176–8), in spite of efforts to associate it with well-attested historical figures such as Bishop Ambrose of Milan (374–97) or the emperor Theodosius I (Lewis 1973). The difficulty of dating San Lorenzo with precision highlights the problems of seeking to make the archaeological data fit neatly with narratives drawn from literary evidence.

In addition to helping us chart the growing social dominance of the church, archaeology can also shed light on the developing cultural profile of early Christianity. Artefacts such as sarcophagi, mosaics, and metalwork reveal how the early Christians were able to adapt the artistic heritage of classical antiquity to their needs. Furthermore, the use of classical iconographic devices, such as elements drawn from classical mythology, in such Christian works allows us to study the way in which Christianity intersected with the classical cultural heritage, and as such neatly complements what can be known from literary sources (Bowersock 2006: 31–63). Similarly, examination of the development of church buildings can demonstrate the extent to which the construction of such edifices was driven by concerns of social status as much as piety. The prominent positions granted in such buildings to inscriptions recording lay elite patronage is particularly revealing of this trend (Caillet 1993).

Archaeology can also be revelatory of aspects of the internal life of Christian communities. It is possible, for instance, to elucidate from church buildings something of the liturgies performed within them. That such rituals became more ostentatious is suggested by the growing monumentality of churches, with colonnaded porticoes and processional routes that would have facilitated the performance of grand public ceremonial (Stringer 2005: 26–88). Nevertheless, it is difficult to elucidate exact details of liturgies from the archaeology alone, and it is usually necessary to appeal to texts, such as liturgical manuals, to make sense of the physical evidence (Baldovin 1987; Mathews 1962; Xydis 1949). Even so, archaeological data offer clear support for the considerable variety in liturgical practices in the early Christian world, both from region to region and over time. At the same time, the multiplicity of church types excavated implies that different reasons may explain the choice of a particular form. Analysis of the distribution of *bēmata* (curved platforms for the delivery of prayers) in Syrian churches suggests that the decision to include such structures may have been driven by the influence of the Antiochene church on local patrons (Loosley 2001). Similarly, a large five-aisled basilica recently excavated at Abila in Jordan may have been built as a local imitation of the Church of the Nativity in Bethlehem (Menninga 2004: 43).

The scope of archaeology to shed light on the multitudinous variety of early Christianity works best when the material evidence is read side by side with other data, whether literary, epigraphic, or papyrological, and when interpretations are sensitive to local cultural, economic, and social contexts. From such considerations it is possible to mark out an agenda for the future development of the archaeology of early Christianity. In order to gauge more astutely the broader profile of Christianity in the period 100–600, we plainly need more studies of individual centres and regions, from which a better-informed general picture can be drawn. These have been appearing with ever more frequency in recent years, ranging from detailed examinations of individual cities to broader surveys of larger regions (see the examples cited below in the list of Suggested Reading). While such careful studies undoubtedly contribute to a more subtle appreciation of the general contours of early Christian history, we must also be aware that the archaeological landscape is a mutable one, and that new discoveries can at any time force us to reappraise our general picture. The recent discovery at Aila (modern Aqaba in Jordan) of a building that the excavators believe to be a church dating from before *c.* 320 provides an example (Parker 1999*a*). Identification of the structure as a church awaits confirmation, and its implications for our understanding of early Christianity have barely begun to be made: yet this current uncertainty over a new discovery is an exciting reminder of the scope of archaeological evidence to prompt reassessments of how we interpret the world of the early Christians.

NOTE

1. Filippi's communiqué (in Italian) can be found on the Vatican news website at <http://212.77.1.245/news_services/bulletin/news/19405.php?index=19405&po_date=11.12.2006>, consulted March 2007.

SUGGESTED READING

A number of manuals provide an introduction to the various types of evidence: Deichmann (1993), Snyder (2003), and White (1996–7). Beginners should also consult the various syntheses on early Christian art and architecture: Koch (1996) and Milburn (1988) are convenient single-volume surveys, while separate aspects are dealt with in (e.g.) Beckwith (1979) and Krautheimer (1986). In addition, there are two major reference encyclopaedias: the fifteen volumes of the *Dictionnaire d'archéologie chrétienne et de liturgie* (Paris: Letouzey et Ané, 1907–53) can still be consulted with profit in spite of their age; but they can now be supplemented with the *Reallexikon für Antike und Christentum* ('Specialist Dictionary for Antiquity and Christianity') (Stuttgart: Hieresmann, 1950–), which is still in progress. For the history of the discipline, Frend (1996) provides a good survey; the works of Rutgers (1995 and 2000) on the catacombs are unusually well informed by reflections on the history of Christian archaeology, while Elsner (2003) demonstrates how the categorization of evidence can often be (mis)informed by confessional concerns. Reed (2000), though dealing mainly with matters related to the New Testament, provides an instructive guide to the problems of reading archaeological data in the light of paradigms derived from religious texts.

A number of recent studies provide suggestive and instructive ways of reading the archaeological record for early Christianity. The first volume of White (1996–7) examines Christian architecture side by side with that of Mithraism and Judaism, but places excessive emphasis on the evolution of building types, while not paying enough attention to local contexts (see above, p. 93). The Christianization of urban space has attracted considerable attention. Wharton (1995) is an imaginative (and self-confessedly idiosyncratic) attempt to read the evidence in the light of literary texts and critical theory, but is not entirely reliable on details; for a more comprehensive treatment, Liebeschuetz (2001), whatever view one takes of his insistence on late antiquity as a period of 'decline', must be the starting point. The collections of essays edited by Burns and Eadie (2001), Christie and Loseby (1996), and Rich (1992) also contain many useful analyses of the archaeological evidence for Christianity and the late ancient city. By contrast, the place of Christianity in the countryside is still understudied. Tchalenko (1953–8) was a pioneering study of the villages on the limestone plateaux of Syria, but his conclusions have been revised by much recent work, such as the essays in King and Cameron (1994) and, with specific relevance to Christian archaeology, Kidner (2001); for comparative purposes, Bowes (2001) is suggestive on Christianity in rural Spain.

As noted in my discussion, numerous excellent studies integrating the material and documentary evidence for individual sites and regions have appeared in recent years: these include cities and towns such as Aquileia in northern Italy (Sotinel 2005), Ephesus (Koester 1995), and Rusafa in Syria (Key Fowden 1999). Inevitably, Rome has attracted a great deal of attention: Curran (2000) provides a convenient synthesis for the fourth century; for the later period, a comprehensive survey of the data from recent excavations is provided by Meneghini and Santangeli Valenzani (2004); on churches, Brandenburg (2006) is the most up-to-date survey, albeit one that prioritizes an essentially evolutionary model of ecclesiastical architectural development; among older works, Krautheimer (1980), if treated with caution, can be read with profit. There are too many regional surveys to list all of them here, but the following give some idea of the scope of archaeology to shed light on early Christianity in its local context: the second volume of Mitchell (1993) provides an incisive analysis of the rise of Christianity in Asia Minor that deftly synthesizes archaeological and documentary evidence; Kulikowski (2004) examines the impact of Christianity in Spain; Italy is well served with, for instance, Christie (2006: 73–192) surveying the whole region, and Campione (2000) reviewing southern Italian material; Parker (1999b) provides a comprehensive survey of archaeological material from Palestine, and gives an instructive example of how to view the development of Christianity in a broader context. The complexities of interpreting archaeological evidence for early Christianity are perhaps best appreciated by reading excavation reports: again, there are too many to list comprehensively, but Kraeling (1967) (on Dura Europos) and Fiema et al. (2001) (on the Petra basilica) give an idea of the processes involved. Finally, it should be noted that regular perusal of journals will yield much of value. For instance, a special issue of World Archaeology in 1987 was devoted to Christian archaeology and included useful surveys of excavations at Geneva (Bonnet 1987) and Carthage (Ennabli 1987). The Rivista di Archeologia cristiana is entirely devoted to the topic, albeit with a Roman focus; Near Eastern Archaeology (formerly Biblical Archaeology) often contains sumptuously illustrated articles on Christian archaeology in the Middle East. Many excavation reports appear first in local journals, among which Vetera Christianorum, edited at the University of Bari, provides unrivalled coverage of archaeological work on Jewish and Christian sites throughout southern Italy.

BIBLIOGRAPHY

BALDOVIN, J. F. (1987), *The Urban Character of Christian Worship: The Origins, Development and Meaning of Stational Liturgy*, OrChrAn 228 (Rome: Pontificium Institutum Orientalium Studiorum).

BECKWITH, J. (1979), *Early Christian and Byzantine Art*, 2nd edn. (Harmondsworth: Penguin).

BLAIR, J. (2005), *The Church in Anglo-Saxon Society* (Oxford: Oxford University Press).

BONNET, C. (1987), 'The Archaeological Site of the Cathedral of Saint Peter (Saint-Pierre), Geneva', *World Archaeology*, 18: 330–40.

BOYARIN, D. (2004), *Borderlines: The Partition of Judaeo-Christianity* (Philadelphia: University of Pennsylvania Press).

BOWERSOCK, G. W. (2006), *Mosaics as History: The Near East from Late Antiquity to Islam* (Cambridge, Mass.: Belknap Press of Harvard University Press).

BOWES, K. (2001), ' "…Nec sedere in villam": Villa Churches, Rural Piety and the Priscillianist Controversy', in Burns and Eadie (2001), 323–48.

BRANDENBURG, H. (2006), *Ancient Churches of Rome from the Fourth to the Seventh Century*, Bibliothèque de l'Antiquité Tardive, 8 (Turnhout: Brepols).

BROISE, H., DEWAILLY, M., and JOLIVET, V. (2000), '*Horti Luculliani*: un palazzo tardoantico a Villa Medici', in S. Ensoli and E. La Rocca (eds.), *Aurea Roma: Dalla città pagana alla città cristiana* (Rome: L'Erma di Bretschneider), 113–15.

BURNS, T. S., and EADIE, J. W. (2001) (eds.), *Urban Centres and Rural Contexts in Late Antiquity* (East Lansing, Mich.: Michigan State University Press).

CAILLET, J.-P. (1993), *L'évergétisme monumental chrétien en Italie et à ses marges* (Rome: École française de Rome).

CAMPIONE, A. (2000), *La Basilicata paleocristiana: diocesi e culti*, Scavi e ricerche, 13 (Bari: Edipuglia).

CECCHELLI, M. (2001), *Materiali e techniche dell'edilizia paleocristiana a Roma*, Materiali della cultura artistica, 4 (Rome: Edizioni De Luca).

CHRISTIE, N. (2006), *From Constantine to Charlemagne: An Archaeology of Italy, AD 300–800* (Aldershot: Ashgate).

CHRISTIE, N., and LOSEBY, S. T. (1996) (eds.), *Towns in Transition: Urban Evolution in Late Antiquity and the Early Middle Ages* (Aldershot: Ashgate).

CLAUSS, M. (2000), *The Roman Cult of Mithras* (Edinburgh: Edinburgh University Press).

COOKSON, N. (1987), 'The Christian Church in Roman Britain: A Synthesis of Archaeology', *World Archaeology*, 18: 426–33.

CROOK, J. (2000), *The Architectural Setting of the Cult of Saints in the Early Christian West, c. 300–c. 1200* (Oxford: Oxford University Press).

CURRAN, J. R. (2000), *Pagan City and Christian Capital: Rome in the Fourth Century* (Oxford: Oxford University Press).

DEICHMANN, F. W. (1993), *Archeologia Cristiana*, Studia Archaeologica, 63 (Rome: L'Erma di Bretschneider).

ELSNER, J. (2003), 'Archaeologies and Agendas: Reflections on Late Ancient Jewish Art and Early Christian Art', *JRS* 93: 114–28.

ENNABLI, L. (1987), 'Results of the International Save Carthage Campaign: The Christian Monuments', *World Archaeology*, 18: 291–311.

ESMONDE-CLEARY, A. S. (1989), *The Ending of Roman Britain* (London: Batsford; Savage, Md.: Barnes and Noble, 1990).

FIEMA, Z. T., KANELLOPOULOS, K., WALISZEWSKI, T., and SCHICK, R. (2001), *The Petra Church*, American Centre for Oriental Research Publications, 3 (Amman: American Center for Oriental Research).

FILSON, F. V. (1939), 'The Significance of the Early House Churches', *JBL* 58: 105–12.

FREND, W. H. C. (1996), *The Archaeology of Early Christianity: A History* (London: Geoffrey Chapman).

FRÖSÉN, J., ARJAVA, A., and LEHTINEN, M. (2002), *The Petra Papyri*, American Centre for Oriental Research Publications, 4 (Amman: American Center for Oriental Research).

GHILARDI, M. (2002), 'Le catacombe di Roma tra la tarda antichità e l'alto medioevo', *Aug* 42: 205–36.

GRIG, L. (2004), *Making Martyrs in Late Antiquity* (London: Duckworth).

HOPPE, L. J. (1994), *The Synagogues and Churches of Ancient Palestine* (Collegeville, Minn.: Michael Glazier).

HUMPHRIES, M. (2007), 'From Emperor to Pope? Ceremonial, Space, and Authority in Rome from Constantine to Gregory the Great', in K. Cooper and J. Hillner (eds.), *Dynasty, Patronage, and Authority in a Christian Capital: Rome, c. 350–850* (Cambridge: Cambridge University Press), 21–58.

KEY FOWDEN, E. (1999), *The Barbarian Plain: Saint Sergius Between Rome and Iran* (Berkeley: University of California Press).

KIDNER, F. L. (2001), 'Christianizing the Syrian Countryside: An Archaeological and Architectural Approach', in Burns and Eadie (2001), 349–79.

KING, G. R. D., and CAMERON, AVERIL (1994) (eds.), *The Byzantine and Early Islamic Near East*, ii: *Land Use and Settlement Patterns* (Princeton: Darwin Press).

KINNEY, D. (1972), 'The Evidence for the Dating of S. Lorenzo in Milan', *Journal of the Society of Architectural Historians*, 31: 92–107.

KOCH, G. (1996), *Early Christian Art and Architecture* (London: SCM Press).

KOESTER, H. (1995) (ed.), *Ephesos, Metropolis of Asia: An Interdisciplinary Approach to its Archaeology, Religion, and Culture* (Valley Forge, Pa.: Trinity Press International).

KRAELING, C. H. (1967), *The Christian Building* (*Excavations at Dura Europus, Final Report* VIII, 2) (New Haven: Yale University Press).

KRAUTHEIMER, R. (1980), *Rome, Profile of a City 312–1308* (Princeton: Princeton University Press).

——(1986), *Early Christian and Byzantine Arrchitecture*, 4th edn. (Harmondsworth: Penguin).

KULIKOWSKI, M. (2004), *Late Roman Spain and its Cities* (Baltimore: Johns Hopkins University Press).

LEWIS, S. (1973), 'San Lorenzo Revisited: A Theodosian Palace Church at Milan', *Journal of the Society of Architectural Historians*, 32: 197–222.

LIEBESCHUETZ, J. H. W. G. (2001), *The Decline and Fall of the Roman City* (Oxford: Oxford University Press).

LOOSLEY, E. (2001), 'The Early Christian *bema* Churches of Syria Revisited', *Antiquity*, 75: 509–10.

MACADAM, H. I. (1994), 'Settlements and Settlement Patterns in Northern and Central Transjordania, *ca* 550–*ca* 750', in King and Cameron (1994), 49–93.

McLYNN, N. B. (1994), *Ambrose of Milan: Church and Court in a Christian Capital* (Berkeley: University of California Press).

MACHADO, C. (forthcoming), 'Building the Past: Monuments and Memory in the Forum Romanum', *Late Antique Archaeology*.

MAGNESS, J. (2005), 'Ossuaries and the Burials of Jesus and James', *JBL* 124: 121–54.

—— (2007), 'Has the Tomb of Jesus been Discovered?', *SBL Forum* online <http://www.sbl-site.org/Article.aspx?ArticleId=640>, consulted June 2007.

MARAZZI, F. (2000), 'Rome in Transition: Economic and Political Change in the Fourth and Fifth Centuries', in J. M. H. Smith (ed.), *Early Medieval Rome and the Christian West: Essays in Honour of Donald A. Bullough* (Leiden: E. J. Brill), 21–41.

MARTIN, L. H. (1989), 'Roman Mithraism and Christianity', *Numen*, 36: 2–15.

MARUCCHI, O. (1929), *The Evidence of the Catacombs for the Doctrines and Organisation of the Primitive Church* (London: Sheed and Ward).

MATHEWS, T. F. (1962), 'An Early Roman Chancel Arrangement and its Liturgical Function', *Rivistà di Archeologia Cristiana*, 38: 73–95.

MAWER, C. F. (1995), *Evidence for Christianity in Roman Britain: The Small Finds*, BAR: British Series, 243 (Oxford: Tempus Reparatum).

MENEGHINI, R., and SANTANGELI VALENZANI, R. (2004), *Roma nell'Altomedioevo: topografia e urbanistica della città dal V al X secolo* (Rome: Istituto Poligrafico dello Stato).

MENNINGA, C. (2004), 'The Unique Church at Abila in the Decapolis', *Near Eastern Archaeology*, 67: 40–9.

MILBURN, R. (1988), *Early Christian Art and Architecture* (Aldershot: Scolar; Berkeley: University of California Press).

MITCHELL, S. (1993), *Anatolia: Land, Men, and Gods in Asia Minor*, 2 Vols. (Oxford: Clarendon Press).

PARKER, S. T. (1999a), 'Brief Notice on a Possible Early 4th-c. Church at Aqaba, Jordan', *JRA* 12: 372–6.

—— (1999b), 'An Empire's New Holy Land: The Byzantine Period', *Near Eastern Archaeology*, 62: 134–80.

REED, J. L. (2000), *Archaeology and the Galilean Jesus* (Harrisburg, Pa.: Trinity Press International).

RICH, J. (1992) (ed.), *The City in Late Antiquity* (London: Routledge).

RUTGERS, L. V. (1995), *The Jews of Late Ancient Rome: Evidence for Cultural Interaction in the Roman Diaspora* (Leiden: E. J. Brill).

—— (2000), *Subterranean Rome: In Search of the Roots of Christianity in the Catacombs of the Eternal City* (Leuven: Peeters).

SAUER, E. (1996), *The End of Paganism in the North-Western Provinces of the Roman Empire: The Example of the Mithras Cult*, BAR: International Series, 634, (Oxford: Tempus Reparatum).

SCHAM, S. (2003), 'The Archaeology of the "The Passion"', *Near Eastern Archaeology*, 66: 143.

SNYDER, G. F. (2003), *Ante Pacem: Archaeological Evidence of Church Life before Constantine*, 2nd edn. (Macon, Ga.: Mercer University Press).

SOTINEL, C. (2005), *Identité civique et christianisme: Aquile/e du IVe au VIe siècle* (Rome: École française de Rome).

STEMBERGER, G. (2000), *Jews and Christians in the Holy Land: Palestine in the Fourth Century* (Edinburgh: T & T Clark).

STRINGER, M. (2005), *A Sociological History of Christian Worship* (Cambridge: Cambridge University Press).

TCHALENKO, G. (1953–8), *Villages antiques de la Syrie du Nord: le massif du Bélus à l'époque romaine*, 3 vols. (Paris: P. Geunther).

THOMAS, C. (1981), *Christianity in Roman Britain to AD 500* (London: Batsford; Berkeley: University of California Press).

TOYNBEE, J., and WARD-PERKINS, J. (1956), *The Shrine of St Peter and the Vatican Excavations* (London: Longmans, Green, and Co).

WARD-PERKINS, B. (1984), *From Classical Antiquity to the Middle Ages: Urban Public Building in Northern and Central Italy AD 300–850* (Oxford: Oxford University Press).

——— (1998), 'The cities', in Averil Cameron and P. Garnsey (eds.), *The Cambridge Ancient History*, xiii: *The Late Empire AD 337–425* (Cambridge: Cambridge University Press), 371–410.

WHARTON, A. J. (1995), *Refiguring the Post Classical City: Dura Europos, Jerash, Jerusalem and Ravenna* (Cambridge: Cambridge University Press).

WHITE, L. M. (1996–7), *The Social Origins of Christian Architecture*, 2 vols. (Valley Forge, Pa.: Trinity Press International).

XYDIS, S. G. (1949), 'The Chancel Barrier, Solea, and Ambo of Hagia Sophia', *Art Bulletin*, 29: 1–24.

CHAPTER 5

MATERIAL EVIDENCE (2): VISUAL CULTURE

ROBIN M. JENSEN

5.1 INTRODUCTION: DEFINITIONS AND METHODOLOGICAL CONSIDERATIONS

LIKE other students of culture, historians of ancient Christianity deem the visual art, artefacts, and architecture of the early church as resources indispensable to discerning how various early Christian communities expressed and transmitted their religious beliefs. Far more than mere illustration of the ideas or teachings articulated in surviving written documents, visual and material artefacts add depth and perspective to the analysis of a particular Christian group. The study of visual images, moreover, not only supplements and balances documentary research, but often affords scholars access to objects of great beauty as well as powerful agents of message and meaning. Furthermore, it opens the question of how vision itself functioned in religious practice. For this reason, material evidence should not be subordinated to the study of texts, but regarded as an invaluable and independent source of historical data. The insights gained from the study of visual culture are achieved not only from comparing textual evidence with material evidence, but also from the appreciation of the interpretive role, expressive power, and aesthetic qualities of physical remains in their own right, along with the analysis of the visual experience itself (both production and reception) as a meaning-constructive activity.

The term 'visual culture' encompasses images and artefacts produced by artists or artisans that reflect aspects of civilization which may or may not be evident in other cultural artefacts such as written documents. In its broadest sense, a study of early Christian visual culture considers all kinds of human-made material remains, including everyday objects (e.g. decorated lamps, bowls, coins, etc.), as well as those products that we locate within the designation 'fine arts' (e.g. sculpture, painting, and mosaic). It also includes the study of the built spaces (architecture) that not only housed these artefacts but also reflect the patterns and values of daily life, religious practices, and special ceremonies (e.g. domestic, ecclesial, and funerary structures). Those objects most likely to be the focus of historians of Christianity are those with obvious religious associations, as evident in their content (iconography), context (religious settings), or function (ritual use).

Despite the almost undisputed value accorded to the study of visual culture, historians of early Christianity often confront certain obstacles that make them reluctant to engage such data. First, the traditional text-focused training leaves many unprepared to evaluate artefacts or art objects with any confidence. Lacking expertise, they must rely upon the analyses of scholars trained in the fields of art history and archaeology. Such reliance sometimes leads to fruitful collaboration, but may also be compromised by the divergent methods, questions, or priorities of these different academic fields. On the other hand, careful and conscious integration of these different perspectives can result in useful insights about the evidence itself and inhibit inclinations either simply to equate texts and artefacts or to interpret the one through the other. At the same time, text scholars may profitably bring documentary evidence to the table, helping to foster inclusive and integrated historical research with added dimension and texture.

Generally, the first step in the study of visual culture is the attentive observation, careful description, provisional identification, and preliminary classification of the artefacts or objects under consideration. This includes efforts to date and establish provenance, as well as to note material, stylistic details or potential models. But the study of visual culture goes many steps beyond describing and classifying or categorizing evidence. Assessing the appearance and geographical placement of an object, including its specific imagery, inscriptions, fabrication, apparent function, condition, and physical context is essential, but not sufficient or conclusive. The scholar of visual culture uses this arguably factual material to begin to theorize about the object's role in transmitting certain socio-religious convictions, ideas, or values, but also sees it in the context of and relationship to other cultural artefacts or products, including written documents. Finally, the analyst may ask how the object might have been regarded in the act of seeing and the nature of the relationship between subject (viewer/maker) and object (artefact/product).

Texts, however, are to be used not as definitive guides to establishing the meaning or function of an object, but rather as parallel forms of communication and
comparable modes of interpretation. Incorporating available and relevant documentary evidence into the analysis of visual data produces a synthetic approach
that not only identifies common motifs, concepts, or preoccupations, but also notes
contradictions or discontinuity between material and textual artefacts. So long as
neither form of evidence is automatically privileged, such a dialectical approach is
mutually illuminating. One does not interpret the other, but both are understood as
works of interpretation in their own terms. At the same time, they are not altogether
independent and unrelated.

The study of visual culture has much in common with the discipline of art
history, but is also distinct from it in significant respects. In the past, art historians
were often concerned principally with formal stylistic and technical analyses of
artworks and in establishing their dates, origins, and influences. The art object was
appreciated for its aesthetic qualities as well as its place in the evolution of a style.
Art historians also studied the cultural and historical context of a work—as well
as its placement within a particular artist's (or movement's) œuvre or trajectory—
although these issues were not always their sole preoccupation. In the past century,
however, the field of art history has directed much attention to the problem of
interpretation—in discerning what objects signified to their makers or viewers—or
even to modern scholars themselves. Newer studies have considered the significance
of narrative themes or symbolic motifs, and have evaluated the ways in which an
object's appearance projects its message or reveals its function—in other words,
finding meaning in external form.

By contrast, scholars of visual culture typically expend less energy on extensive
formal or stylistic analysis of those objects under examination and concentrate on
assessing their significance and function within their social, conceptual, and religious context. They also choose to consider evidence that would not be widely regarded as 'fine art'. They are also more interested in the study of visualization itself,
as an activity that constructs meaning and affects the nature of perception as well
as representation. In other words, these researchers share many of preoccupations
of art historians, but not all of them, or to the same degree—and they also examine
a wider array of objects. Additionally, they tend to place the art object into a larger
frame that includes other cultural artefacts, especially documentary evidence, and
draw upon the work of social historians, intellectual historians, ritual theorists, and
anthropologists, as well as art historians. Because they view material evidence as
an expression and means of transmission of particular socially constructed ideas
or values, students of visual culture are less interested in or even appreciative of
their aesthetic values (or lack thereof). In other words, these artefacts are valued
more for their communicative function than for their intrinsic beauty or value. In
this respect, they are not ends in themselves, but means toward a different goal.
The differences between the two fields are not always so easy to grasp, however,

partly because the field of art history has become more diverse in its theory and methodology in the past half century, and partly because the study of visual culture, to a great degree, emerged out of this 'sibling field'.

5.1.1 Brief Overview of the History of the Field

Several foundational thinkers profoundly influenced the development of the study of visual culture. Among them, Erwin Panofsky (1892–1968) is generally regarded as the founder of the study of iconography in the early part of the twentieth century. In his influential (retrospective) volume of essays, *Meaning in the Visual Arts: Papers in and on Art History* (1955), Panofsky defined not only the field but also its methodology. He considered iconography as that branch of art history particularly concerned with subject matter or meaning, in contrast to form— with images more than with discrete works of art. Panofsky's method required the incorporation of supplementary evidence as illuminatory and essential for understanding the images within their specific contexts. His method drew upon theological treatises, poetry, philosophy, histories, and other cultural artefacts, in order to arrive at synthetic hypotheses to contextualize and synthetically in-terpret the meaning of certain images. For Panofsky, a work of art pointed far beyond itself as it participated in or reflected upon a civilization's foundational symbols.

Panofsky, however, was interested not only in a synthetic and culturally sensitive interpretation of images, but also in the transmission of meaning within a single culture, and from one time and place to another. He referred to this kind of discursive interpretation as 'iconology', rather than 'iconography', since it was far more than the mere decoding of a visual language. In his view, all aspects of a visual image, including its basic design elements (colour, pattern, shape, etc.), its content (imagery), its religious significance (secular or sacred), and its aesthetic percep-tion (beautiful, ugly) are culturally mediated qualities or perceptions. Viewers— whether ancient or modern—are likewise thoroughly influenced by their cultural or social locations. Thus, for Panofsky, the work of interpretation was as much influenced by the mindset of the interpreter as it drew upon congruent data. This means, of course, that interpretations vary from viewer to viewer, and that visual evidence has no single, established meaning.

Panofsky's work, although not aimed specifically at early Christian art or visual culture in general, influenced many who followed him, including Emile Mâle (1862–1954), Charles Rufus Morey (1877–1955), and Otto von Simson (1912–), all of whom studied Christian art within its broader liturgical, theological, social, and political contexts. Morey (who founded the Index of Christian Art at Princeton University in 1917) was interested less in the cultural or social implications of Christian art and more in establishing a way of classifying different objects according to their iconographic themes. Within this structure, however, Morey also attended to variations in the ways in which the same subjects were depicted. A similar, but distinct, taxonomic effort was undertaken by the Dutch scholar Henri van de Waal (1919–72), who developed the now universally used system known as Iconclass, which categorizes images almost entirely according to subject-matter, with far less attention to their compositional distinctions.

Although Panofsky is usually credited as the founder of the field, his mentor, Aby Warburg (1866–1929), had actually pioneered the study of iconology in Europe, calling for the examination of art objects as part of a larger social milieu and with reference to other cultural products. Warburg in turn influenced important thinkers in Germany, including Fritz Saxl (1890–1948), who founded the Warburg Institute in 1921. Saxl was interested in the intersections of the history of art and religion and emphasized the continuity between Christian and Graeco-Roman art. This idea was embraced by many German scholars, including Franz Joseph Dölger (1879–1940), who criticized earlier art historians as being too narrowly dogmatic or Christian in their orientation. Many of those earlier scholars worked under the auspices of the Pontifical Commission for Sacred Archaeology, and were actually the principal investigators of early Christian painting and sculpture in Rome: Giovanni Battista de Rossi (1822–94), Raffaele Garucci (1812–85), Giuseppe Marchi (1795–1860), and Josef Wilpert (1857–1944). Against their supposed Christian or doctrinal bias, the German school claimed interpretive strategies that were more objective and scientific, drawing upon methodologies developed by the social sciences and the history of religions schools as these were framed in the mid-twentieth century. They also promoted their view of Christian art as being more contextualized and attentive to the distinctions between official and popular religion.

Perhaps the most widely known student of early Christian iconography, however, was André Grabar (1896–1990), whose influence on the field has been unmatched. Taking up the cause of integrating the study of culture, politics, and theology in the analysis of early Christian visual art, Grabar believed that images constituted a special type of language. He claimed to be uninterested in creating a manual of Christian images that would classify them according to their themes or attend to their nuances of style, provenance, or workshop. Instead, Grabar approached the study of Christian iconography with two overriding questions: why early Christian images looked the way they did, and what religious purpose they served (Grabar 1968: p. xli). Grabar's key work, *Christian Iconography: A Study of its Origins*, attended particularly to the political and theological contexts of the objects he examined and saw them both as representing theological ideas and as implicitly political.

Like many of his contemporaries who rejected the notion that Christian art could have arisen *de novo*, Grabar regarded Christian art as originating in Roman secular and religious iconography, first assimilating, then adapting and extending, its visual vocabulary. At the same time, he posited the emergence of Jewish art as prior to and influential on Christian art, asserting that it was more iconographically evolved. The intersection of culture and art resulted in a transformation of Christian imagery in the fourth century, according to Grabar, as scenes of military victory or posthumous apotheosis were reformed into an iconography that expressed the dynamism (and political character) of the triumphant Church. Thus art both served and transmitted the ideology or agenda of the Empire as much as the contents of the faith.

In general, the scholarship of the twentieth century sought to place early Christian visual culture in the context of a larger political, social, and religious milieu. Some scholars retained an affinity for formal, stylistic analysis, among them Ernst Kitzinger (1912–2003), who also extended the range of 'early Christian' to include monuments from the Byzantine world. In the meantime, some important reference works appeared, including the monumental, multi-volumed *Dictionnaire d'archéologie chrétienne et de liturgie*, edited by Fernand Cabrol and Henri Leclercq (1907–53), which provided a non-methodologically driven treasure trove to students interested in the intersections of liturgy, architecture, and visual art. In mid-century the *Reallexikon für Antike und Christentum* appeared, edited by Theodor Klauser in collaboration with scholars from the 'German School', Franz Joseph Dölger, Hans Lietzmann, and Ernst Dassman (1950–). This was followed by more iconographically and thematically focused reference works, including Louis Réau's *Iconographie de l'art chrétien*; Engelbert Kirschbaum's, *Lexikon der christlichen Ikonographie*, and the two-volume *Iconography of Christian Art*, by Gertrude Schiller (translated from the German edition of 1969).

5.1.2 More Recent Trends

The emphasis on continuity between Graeco-Roman and Christian visual culture continued to be pressed in scholarship toward the end of the twentieth century. The exhibition titled 'The Age of Spirituality: Late Antique and Early Christian Art, Third to Seventh Century', held at the Metropolitan Museum in 1977–8, produced an extensive catalogue edited by Kurt Weitzmann that identified the categories of monuments according to their 'realms' (imperial, classical, secular, Jewish, Christian), and further broke down the entries according to their content (portraits, scenic representations, mythological figures, architecture). The extensive range of objects, as well its significant contributors (including Herbert Kessler, James Breckenridge, Richard Brilliant, and Erich Dinkler), made the catalogue for that exhibition a landmark publication. This catalogue's Christian section also classed artworks as having abbreviated, narrative, or iconic compositions, despite considerable overlap in their visual content. Such categorization implies evolution in the composition of Christian art, as well as allowing for discussion of the theological significance of the works themselves, an aspect that was even more developed in an accompanying symposium volume with articles by Peter Brown, Beat Brenk, Massey Shepherd, Richard Krautheimer, George M. A. Hanfmann, and Ernst Kitzinger on the intersections of art, culture, and religion in late antiquity.

Along with the question of cultural continuity, some scholars of the late twentieth century began to challenge the view that art necessarily reflects the ideology or values of the social elite, and emphasized the social function of images across a wider cultural spectrum as a means to overcome the 'invisibility' of the non-literate classes. In the 1980s and 1990s several studies appeared that revisited the questions and conclusions drawn by the earlier generations, and which also exemplify these different interpretive trajectories. In the mid-1980s Graydon Snyder published his first edition of *Ante Pacem: Archaeological Evidence of Church Life before Constantine*. In an effort to identify a particular quality that distinguished post-Constantinian Christian remains from those of the period *ante pacem*, Snyder took the side of the German school (e.g. Dölger, Klauser, and Dinkler), whom he refers to as 'contextualists', and criticized the work of the old 'Roman school' (along with some of its later representatives—Aldo Nestori, Orazio Marucchi, Margherita Guarducci, Antonio Ferrua, and Fabrizio Bisconti) for taking a particularly Catholic confessional and apologetic approach to the material and reading later theological or doctrinal developments back into much earlier evidence. Snyder was much influenced by contemporary scholars studying the socio-cultural matrix of the emergent Church (e.g. Gerd Theissen and Wayne Meeks), when he argued that early Christian art should be viewed as especially representative of a house-church community of disenfranchised and egalitarian Christians who eschewed images of sacrifice and instead represented Christ as social and personal deliverer (Snyder 1985: 165–6).

In the early 1990s, Thomas Mathews's *The Clash of Gods: A Reinterpretation of Early Christian Art* (1993) offered a different critique of earlier scholarship, as Mathews disparaged the tendency to subsume early Christian art into the category of 'Late Antique' and to view Christian art as inferior or aberrant—a factor in the general 'decline of Roman art' (Mathews 1993: 11–12). He also attacked the theory espoused by Grabar and others that Christian art after Constantine was infused with imperial motifs, even modelling images of Christ himself after portrayals of the Emperor. Mathews argued that this more or less unchallenged theory ('The Emperor Mystique') arose from personal ideological agendas of its principle instigators (Ernst Kantorowicz, Andreas Alföldi, and Grabar), who nurtured a nostalgic longing for lost empires in the years between the two World Wars. He also noted that scholars who held a less positive view of imperialism still clung to the characterization of post-Constantinian art as its visual prop (e.g. von Simson and Karl Lehmann-Hartleben). Identifying the 'Emperor Mystique' as 'the real problem facing the study of Early Christian art', Mathews proposed instead to see the artistic representation of the triumph of Christianity as not the manipulation of religion by a winning political party, but rather the iconographic record of Christ's victory in a 'clash of gods'. Thus, rather than being modelled on an enthroned emperor, the image of Christ in his glory was drawn from depictions of a regnant Jupiter (Mathews 1993: 21).

Finally, such late twentieth-century philosophical movements as semiotics, postmodern literary criticism, and reader response theory have influenced the way in which students of visual culture interpret their data. These approaches undermine all claims to interpretive certitude or established conclusions and challenge the choices which historians make about the objects for their study. Moreover, because it is presumably impossible to establish a single correct answer, instead of asking 'what' an image signifies, scholars have become more interested in 'how' it communicates. In this case the study of visual culture becomes more focused on the way that images shape reality in a dialectical relationship with viewers, rather than viewing them as bits of historical data that almost accidentally reflect reality. Thus the field has moved from attention to iconography as a part of intellectual history toward more critical social and ideological analysis. At the same time, it called for attention to objects or cultural products that were often overlooked. Semiotic theorists, in particular, assert that all textual and material artefacts (visual culture) function as a semantic system, consisting of signs and symbols that are dynamic and multifaceted. No particular group of objects or single interpretation is sufficient or representative, as it represents only one of a myriad of viewpoints. One important example of this type of scholarship is Tonio Hölscher's 1987 work, translated into English as *The Language of Images in Roman Art* (2004). Another important contributor to the discussion about the subjective nature of selecting and interpreting ancient objects and monuments is Annabelle Wharton, who not only incorporated a close study of texts into her study of archaeological remains but also addressed the gap between historical artefact and a contemporary viewer by recognizing the unavoidable presumptions and biases of any individual, modern analysis. Her 1995 book, *Refiguring the Post-Classical City: Dura Europos, Jerash, Jerusalem and Ravenna*, not only examines these spaces in light of relevant documents, but also draws upon comparable encounters with buildings of the present era.

A foreword to Hölscher's above-mentioned work was written by Jas Elsner, himself one of the most important contemporary theorists of visual culture. Like many of his predecessors, Elsner contextualizes early Christian art, regarding it as a subcategory of Roman visual culture generally. In two books published in the late 1990s, *Art and the Roman Viewer* (1995) and *Imperial Rome and Christian Triumph* (1998), Elsner avoids making clear distinctions between Roman and Christian material remains. Nevertheless, he also tracks the changes wrought by the advent of Christianity. He argues that even though Christian iconography was rooted in both the secular and religious imagery of Graeco-Roman culture, it was able to adapt it and infuse it with new religious content. In other words, it did not break with the past, but rather transformed or redefined it (Elser 1998: 3). Thus Christian art remains Roman art—with biblical characters dressed in Roman garb and inhabiting a Roman social world. Against Mathews, therefore, Elsner deems the iconographic developments of the fourth century as exemplifying this cultural and religious evolution, rather than as the visual expression of religious competition. Imperial iconography after the time of Constantine was not intended to make Christ into the Emperor (or vice versa), but to put 'iconic stress on the emperor's office and its relationship to the economy of earth and heaven' (Elsner 1995: 189). Finally, out of his emphasis on continuity with Roman culture, Elsner favours classical litera-ture as his textual backdrop and pays scant attention to early Christian literature (theological treatises or biblical commentaries) or liturgical texts. At the same time, Elsner considers small objects as well as large monuments for the ways in which they create, reflect, and transmit a religious worldview; the way that image and space together construct a socio-political topography.

These various theories and approaches to the incorporation of visual evidence into the study of the history of Christianity inevitably raise the problem of scholarly objectivity or detachment. Although analysis of any type of data is undoubtedly in-fluenced by the intellectual, political, or even theological biases and preconceptions of the interpreter, the study of Christian artefacts presents a challenge to researchers accustomed to examining written documents. In large part the consequence of aca-demic training and general familiarity, images seem more ambiguous than words, and thus vulnerable to being manipulated to serve different scholarly or theolog-ical agendas. For example, while some scholars might assume early Christian art to reflect mainstream or orthodox practices and teachings, others argue that it demonstrates a diversity of theological views and attitudes toward authority, or it represents only a particular segment of the Christian populace. Some scholars see an evolution and separation of Christian art out of its Roman milieu; others empha-size its cultural continuity and regard it as a subcategory of Roman art—far from unambiguously Christian in its meaning. Where some historians see a progressive march toward uniformity, others find continuing evidence of religious syncretism and the survival of 'popular religion' versus 'official' forms of Christianity. Some scholars posit a class distinction between people who read books and those who looked at images, while others note that art was often produced for a society's elite or materially secure members. Drawing upon disciplinary specialities and expertise, some interpreters will consider visual culture in light of social history, others in terms of intellectual movements, still others in the context of religious practices. Depending on where they stand on these issues, some historians (including this author) will turn to contemporary Christian documents for illumination, seeing early Christian art as a related form of theological or scriptural exposition, while others will draw more from the broader themes of late classical (religious and secular) literature.

5.2 Evidence and Issues Pertaining to the Nature of the Data

As demonstrated above, early Christian visual culture has been studied, sorted, and interpreted in many different ways, depending on the examiner's purposes, questions, intentions, or assumptions. Some scholars are most interested in coming up with a reasonable chronology, and perhaps look for key influences and an evolution of style. They may be interested in the ways in which different workshops in different parts of the Roman Empire constructed their images, or perhaps in the commonalities among these different workshops. Other scholars are less interested in the formal aspects of the art and more intent on discerning the way in which the art communicates aspects or tenets of a system of belief or values. Different scholars have different ways of approaching the material, all of them mediated by their academic training, different purposes or goals, and even their personal, religious, or scholarly biases. Some will be more likely to assert the provisional nature of their conclusions, others more concerned with forging an interdisciplinary methodology. These differences are critically important in the selection as well as the analysis of evidence.

However, whatever the goals, methods, or assumptions of the researcher or scholar, certain limitations of the evidence apply to them all. The first of these limitations is chronological. Little evidence of what we might call recognizably Christian art can be dated prior to the third century. Such art can be identified as Christian primarily by its content rather than its context, since very little of it comes from specifically Christian settings. Its iconography is, then, the means by which it is identified as 'Christian'; it includes symbols commonly found next to Christian inscriptions and known to have Christian significance (e.g. dove, boat, shepherd) or scenes based upon biblical narratives (e.g. Noah, Jonah, the three youths in the fiery furnace). Prior to the late second or early third century, either Christians produced no distinguishable art of their own, or what they produced has been lost. Although either option is possible, the likelihood that early Christians created no new iconography but rather saw Christian significance in widely popular decorative floral, bucolic, or maritime motifs is supported by textual references to the form of the cross as apparent in the world, Christian interpretations of common figures (boat, vineyard), or the appropriate symbol for a Christian signet ring (dove, fish, ship, lyre, anchor).[1] Certain other standard types (praying figure, seated philosopher reading from a scroll) may have taken on a specific Christian meaning (Christianity as true wisdom, for example).[2]

Nevertheless, the relative lateness of distinctively Christian art has led many historians to conclude that first- and second-century Christians were aniconic or even iconophobic—due either to the influence of Jewish injunctions against figurative visual images or to universal Christian adherence to the second commandment. Such a conclusion thus implies a separation from Judaism in the third century or, alternatively, a loss of distinctively Christian identity and values as the religion began to become assimilated into Graeco-Roman culture at that time. Within the last 30 years, however, partly due to the work of Mary Charles Murray and Paul Corby Finney, historians have tended to view the emergence of Christian art as the result of a gradual evolution, rather than a change in practice, theology, or culture. In the meantime, discoveries such as the synagogue at Dura Europos also demolished the perception that Judaism itself was universally aniconic.

A second limitation of the earlier evidence is its context. The majority of the earliest available remains come not from churches or specifically Christian settings but from funereal contexts which were not exclusively Christian. These artefacts—paintings on the walls of the Roman catacombs and carvings on sarcophagi—survived in large measure because they were underground, and thus not subject to the vicissitudes of urban renewal or the destruction of war. Even those terra cotta lamps, manufactured for domestic use, were largely discovered in tombs. However, the fact that so much of early Christian visual culture comes from a sepulchral setting bears consideration in their interpretation. Very little comparable material evidence can be accessed before the early fourth century, apart from such exceptional monuments as the Dura Europos house church. Along with this limited setting for early Christian remains is their provenance. Most of the first and most significant examples come from Rome and its environs, again with certain possible exceptions such as a late third-century sarcophagus from Gaul. A final characteristic of the earliest remains is that for the most part they consist of wall paintings in tombs, inscriptions and carved images on burial plaques, or relief carvings on sarcophagi. A few mosaics again are the exception, one famous example discovered beneath St Peter's basilica in Rome showing Christ in the guise of Sol or Apollo and dating to the turn of the fourth century.

The repertoire of images found on these early Christian monuments is fairly limited. The oldest group includes those decorative or symbolic motifs described above (birds, garlands, the shepherd, orante, banquet scene) as well as abbreviated references to particular biblical narrative scenes. Stock representations of Adam and Eve, Noah in his ark, Jonah being cast overboard and thrown back up on dry land, Abraham offering Isaac, Moses striking the rock in the wilderness, Daniel with his lions, and the three youths in the fiery furnace show some variations, but share enough standardizing characteristics to make them easily identifiable. Scenes from the Christian New Testament, including the adoration of the magi and of Jesus healing or working wonders also appear after the middle of the third century. The repetition (popularity), variability, and evolution over time of these images are significant factors in their interpretation.

The frequency of motifs based upon stories in the Hebrew scriptures led many scholars to posit a Jewish source for early Christian art. Beginning with Joseph

Stzygowsky (1923) in the early twentieth century, and continuing with C. R. Morey (1942) and Pierre du Bourguet (1971), some historians concluded that early Christian biblical images must have been derived from Jewish prototypes. Perhaps most influential was Kurt Weitzmann's hypothesis that a lost Jewish prototype—perhaps an illustrated Septuagint produced by a Hellenistic Jewish community—provided many of the models for early Christian iconography (1990). Among the critics of this position was Joseph Gutmann (1971), who also rejected the idea that Jews in late antiquity could be so clearly distinguished into normative and non-normative communities.

Beginning in the mid-fourth century, this situation changed considerably. The identification of Christian visual culture was no longer based solely on its content, but was also denoted by its context. The building programme of Constantine was a signal beginning to the monumental shift in the amount and variety, as well as the quality and scale, of the material remains. Pilgrimage shrines and cemetery churches were constructed and decorated with figurative mosaic programmes along their nave walls and in their apses. Illuminated manuscripts of the scriptures began to be produced. Precious metal and ivory objects were manufactured for ritual use, to adorn churches, or for private devotion. Gemstones and amulets were incised with Christian symbols and inscriptions. Smaller, more commonplace objects also appear, and constitute a special category of Christian visual culture. Pilgrimage tokens were mass-produced as souvenirs. Ceramic bowls, lamps, tiles, glassware, and textiles were fabricated for domestic or personal use.

Along with this extensive shift in the type, quality, and quantity of Christian visual culture beginning in the Constantinian era was a change in its content. By the middle of the fourth century most of the popular motifs of earlier generations began to disappear from both catacomb painting and sarcophagus reliefs. Jonah and Noah almost completely vanish. Meanwhile, a new repertoire of images, including Moses receiving the Law, the crossing of the Red Sea, and portraits of the saints, apostles, the Virgin Mary, and Christ emerge to take their place. Images of Jesus enthroned or ascendant giving the new law to Peter and Paul appear along with the earliest visual depictions of scenes from the passion and crucifixion. Biblical narrative images continued, but were now moved on to the nave walls of churches or appeared on the pages of illustrated Bibles. Funeral monuments, by contrast, tended to be adorned with more symbolic and stylized depictions of peacocks, sheep, twining vines, chalices, doves, and christograms.

How historians view these changes in the context, content, style, and scale of Christian material evidence from the third through the sixth centuries will generally vary according to whether they see it as the Christianization of Roman culture, the Romanization (or imperialization) of the Christian religion, or the final consolidation of something essentially and distinctively Christian, no matter how much influenced by Roman or even Jewish prototypes and parallels. These different viewpoints will depend, to a large degree, on the preconceptions each scholar brings to the material itself. The question of whether Christian visual culture is best understood as rooted in and related to its Roman past or as an innovation arising out of and responding to the values and teachings of a new religious movement will not be easily resolved. The most useful conclusion probably incorporates both of those perspectives and sees visual culture as dynamically preserving the old and cautiously inventing the new; interlacing the past with the present in almost constantly varying and subtle proportions.

NOTES

1. Justin Martyr, *1 Apol.* 55. 3–8; *Dial.* 86. 6; Hippolytus of Rome, *Antichr.* 59; *Ben. Iacob.* 25; Clement of Alexandria, *Paed.* 3. 11.
2. See Tertullian, *Nat.* 1. 4; Justin Martyr, *1 Apol.* 5. 44, 46; *2 Apol.* 10, 13; Clement of Alexandria, *Prot.* 6. 11; *Strom.* 1. 28. 3.

SUGGESTED READING

Some of the most significant recent studies of Christian iconography are mentioned in the essay and reference list, including Finney (1994), Elsner (1998), Mathews (1999), and Snyder (2003). Other important summaries and ground-breaking theoretical works from the past three to four decades include the following:

BELTING, H. (1994), *Likeness and Presence: A History of the Image before the Era of Art*, trans. E. Jephcott (Chicago: University of Chicago Press).

BRENK, B., and BRANDENBURG, H. (1977), *Spätantike und frühes Christentum* (Frankfurt am Main: Propyläen-Verlag).

CARTLIDGE, D. R., and ELLIOTT, J. K. (2001), *Art and the Christian Apocrypha* (London: Routledge).

JENSEN, R. (2000), *Understanding Early Christian Art* (London: Routledge).

——(2005), *Face to Face: Portraits of the Divine in Early Christianity* (Minneapolis: Fortress Press).

KOCH, G. (2003), *Early Christian Art and Architecture* (London: SCM Press).

LOWDEN, J. (1997), *Early Christian and Byzantine Art* (London: Phaidon).

MILBURN, R. (1988), *Early Christian Art and Architecture* (Berkeley: University of California Press).

MILES, M. (1985), *Image as Insight: Visual Understanding in Western Christianity and Secular Culture* (Boston: Beacon Press).

SPIER, J. (2007), *Picturing the Bible: The Earliest Christian Art* (New York: Oxford University Press).

TRONZO, W. (1986), *The Via Latina Catacomb* (University Park, Pa.: Pennsylvania State University Press).

Principle resources or tools for research mentioned in the above essay and reference list include the *Dictionnaire d'archéologie chrétienne et de liturgie* (Cabrol and Leclercq 1924–53); *Iconographie de l'art chrétien* (Réau 1955–9); *Iconography of Christian Art* (Schiller 1971–2); *Lexikon der Christlichen Iconographie* (Kirschbaum, 1968–76); and the *Reallexikon für Antike und Christentum* (Klauser *et al.* 1968–76). To these the following important collections should be added:

BISCONTI, F. (2000), (ed.), *Temi di iconografia paleocristiana* (Vatican City: Pontificio istituto di archeologia cristiana).

DEICHMANN, F. W. (1967–2003), *Repertorium der christlich-antiken Sarkophage*, 3 vols. (Wiesbaden: F. Steiner).

KRAUTHEIMER, R. *et al.* (1937–), *Corpus Basilicarum Christianarum Romae: The Early Christian Basilicas of Rome* (Vatican City: Pontificio istituto di archeologia cristiana).

Major works by authors cited in the essay are included in the Bibliography below.

BIBLIOGRAPHY

ALFÖLDI, A. (1970), *Die monarchisch Repräsentation im römischen Kaiserreiche* (Darmstadt: Wissenschaftliche Buchges).

BISCONTI, F., with NICOLAI, V., and MAZZOLENI, D. (2002), *The Christian Catacombs of Rome: History, Decoration, Inscriptions*, trans. C. C. Stella and L. Touchette (Regensberg: Verlag Schnell and Steiner GmbH).

BRENK, B. (1980), 'The Imperial Heritage of Early Christian Art', in K. Weitzmann (1980), 39–52.

BRECKRENRIDGE, J. (1979), 'The Imperial Realm: Portraiture', in K. Weitzmann (1979), 2–7.

BRILLIANT, R. (1979), 'The Classical Realm: Mythology', in K. Weitzmann (1979), 126–31.

BROWN, P. (1980), 'Art and Society in Late Antiquity', in K. Weitzmann (1980), 17–27.

CABROL, F., and LECLERCQ, H. (1907–53), *Dictionnaire d'archéologie chrétienne et de liturgie* (Paris: Letouzey et Ané).

DASSMAN, E. (1973), *Sündenvergebung durch Taufe, Busse und Martyrerfürbitte in den Zeugnissen früchristlicher Frömmigkeit und Kunst* (Münster: Verlag Aschendorff).

——(1982), *Paulus in früchristlicher Frömmigkeit und Kunst* (Opladen: Westdeutscher Verlag).

DINKLER, E. (1964), *Das Apsismosaik von S. Apollinare in Classe* (Cologne: Westdeutscher Verlag).

——(1979), 'The Christian Realm: Abbreviated Representations', in K. Weitzmann (1979), 396–403.

DÖLGER, F. J. (1943), *IXΘYC [Ichthys]: Das Fisch-symbol in der früchristlicher Zeit* (Münster in Westfalen: Aschendorff).

DU BOURGUET, P. (1971), *Early Christian Art*, trans. T. Burton (New York: Reynal).

ELSNER, J. (1995), *Art and the Roman Viewer: The Transformation of Art from the Pagan World to Christianity* (Cambridge: Cambridge University Press).

——(1998), *Imperial Rome and Christian Triumph: The Art of the Roman Empire A.D. 100–450* (Oxford: Oxford University Press).

FERRUA, A. (1960), *Le pitture della nuova catacomba di Via Latina* (Vatican City: Pontificio istituto di archeologia cristiana).

——(1990), *The Unknown Catacomb: A Unique Discovery of Early Christian Art*, trans. I. Inglis (New Lanark, Scotland: Geddes and Grosset Ltd.).

FINNEY, P. C. (1994), *The Invisible God: The Earliest Christians on Art* (New York: Oxford University Press).

GARUCCI, R. (1873–81), *Storia dell'arte cristiana nei primi otto secoli della Chiesa* (Prato: Gaetano Guasti).

GRABAR, A. (1968), *Christian Iconography: A Study of Its Origins*, trans. T. Grabar (Princeton: Princeton University Press).

——(1969), *Early Christian Art: From the Rise of Christianity to the Death of Theodosius*, trans. S. Gilbert and J. Emmons (New York: Odyssey Press).

GUARDUCCI, M. (1963), *The Tradition of Peter in the Vatican: In the Light of History and Archaeology* (Vatican City: Vatican Polyglot Press).

GUTMANN, J. (1971) (ed.), *No Graven Images: Studies in Art and the Hebrew Bible* (New York: KTAV).

HANFMANN, G. M. A. (1980), 'The Continuity of Classical Art: Culture, Myth, and Faith', in K. Weitzmann (1980), 75–99.

HÖLSCHER, T. (2004), *The Language of Images in Roman Art*, trans. A. Snodgrass and A.-M. Künzl-Snodgrass (Cambridge: Cambridge University Press).

KANTOROWICZ, E. (1957), *The King's Two Bodies: A Study in Medieval Political Theology* (Princeton: Princeton University Press).

——(1965), *Selected Studies* (Locust Valley, NY: J. J. Augustin).

KESSLER, H. L. (1979), 'The Christian Realm: Narrative Representations', in K. Weitzmann (1979), 39–52.

KIRSCHBAUM, E. (1968–76), *Lexikon der Christlichen Ikonographie* (Rome: Herder).

KITZINGER, E. (1980a), *Byzantine Art in the Making* (Cambridge, Mass.: Harvard University Press).

——(1980b), 'Christian Imagery: Growth and Impact', in K. Weitzmann (1980), 141–63.

KLAUSER, T., with DASSMAN, E., DÖLGER, F.-J., and LIETZMANN, H. (1950–), *Reallexikon für Antiké und Christentum: Sachwörterbuch zur Auseinandersetzung des Christentums mit der antiken Welt* (Stuttgart: Hiersemann).

KRAUTHEIMER, R. (1980), 'Success and Failure in Late Antique Church Planning', in K. Weitzmann (1980), 121–39.

LIETZMANN, H. (1927), *Petrus und Paulus in Rom: liturgische und archaeologische Studien*, 2nd edn. (Berlin: de Gruyter).

MÂLE, E. (1960), *The Early Churches of Rome*, trans. D. Buxton (London: E. Benn).

MARCHI, G. (1844), *Monumenti delle arti cristiane primitive nella metropoli del cristianesimo* (Rome: Tip. di C. Puccinelli).

MARUCCHI, O. (1932), *Le catacombe romane* (Rome: La Libreria dello stato).

——(1935), *Manual of Christian archaeology*, trans. Hubert Vecchierello (Paterson, NJ: St. Anthony Guild Press).

MATHEWS, T. (1993), *The Clash of Gods: A Reinterpretation of Early Christian Art* (Princeton: Princeton University Press; rev. edn. 1999).

MEEKS, W. (1983), *The First Urban Christians* (New Haven: Yale University Press).

MOREY, C. R. (1942), *Early Christian Art* (Princeton: Princeton University Press).

MURRAY, SR M. C. (1977), 'Art and the Early Church', *JTS* NS 28/2: 304–5.

——(1981), *Rebirth and Afterlife: A Study of the Transmutation of Some Pagan Imagery in Early Christian Art*, BAR International Series, 100 (Oxford: BAR).

PANOFSKY, E. (1955), *Meaning in the Visual Arts: Papers in and on Art History* (Garden City, NY: Doubleday).

RÉAU, L. (1955–9), *Iconographie de l'art chrétien* (Paris: Presses universitaires de France).

ROSSI, G. DE (1864–77), *La Roma sotterranea* (Rome: Cromo-litografia pontificia).

SAXL, F. (1957), *Lectures*, 2 vols. (London: University of London, Warburg Institute).

SCHILLER, G. (1971–2), *Iconography of Christian Art*, trans. J. Seligman (Greenwich, Conn.: New York Graphic Society).

SHEPHERD, M. H. (1980), 'Christology: A Central Problem of Early Christian Theology and Art', in K. Weitzmann (1980), 101–20.

SIMSON, OTTO VON (1948), *Sacred Fortress: Art and Statecraft in Ravenna* (Chicago: University of Chicago Press).

SNYDER, G. (2003), *Ante Pacem: Archaeological Evidence of Church Life before Constantine*, rev. edn. (Macon, Ga.: Mercer University Press).

STRZYGOWSKI, J. (1923), *The Origin of Christian Church Art: New Facts and Principles of Research* (Oxford: Clarendon Press).

THEISSEN, G. (1982), *Social Setting of Pauline Christianity* (Philadelphia: Fortress Press).

WEITZMANN, K. (1979) (ed.), *Age of Spirituality: Catalogue of the Exhibition at the Metropolitan Museum of Art, November 19, 1977–February 12, 1978* (New York: Metropolitan Museum of Art).

——(1980), *Age of Spirituality: A Symposium* (New York: Metropolitan Museum of Art).

——and KESSLER, H. L. (1990), *The Frescoes of the Dura Synagogue and Christian Art* (Washington D.C.: Dumbarton Oaks).

WHARTON, A. J. (1995), *Refiguring the Post-Classical City: Dura Europos, Jerash, Jerusalem and Ravenna* (New York: Cambridge University Press).

WILPERT, J. (1901), *Die Malerein der Katakomben Roms* (Freiburg i. B.: Herder).

——(1916), *Die römischen Mosaiken und Maleriien der kirchlichen Bauten vom IV. bis XIII. Jahrhundert*, 4 vols., 2nd edn. (Freiburg i. B.: Herder).

——(1929–36), *I sarcofagi cristiani antichi*, 4 vols. (Rome: Pontificio istituto di archeologia cristiana).

——(1938), *La fede della chiesa nascente: secondo i monumenti dell'arte funeraria antica* (Vatican City: Pontificio istituto di archeologia cristiana).

CHAPTER 6

EPIGRAPHY

WILLIAM TABBERNEE

DISPLAYED prominently on a large wall of the National Museum in Carthage, Tunisia, are the carefully reassembled remains of what was once a rectangular marble slab approximately 1.13 meters wide and 0.80 meters high. The thirty-four extant fragments of the slab were meticulously pieced together during 1906–7 by Father Alfred-Louis Delattre, soon after he had discovered these fragments in the ruins of the Basilica majorum on the outskirts of Carthage.

The text of the inscription carved on the marble slab reveals that it was a commemorative plaque honouring North Africa's most famous early Christian martyrs:

	[+	Hic] sunt marty[res]
2	+	Saturus, Satu[r]n[inus],
	+	Rebocatus, S[e]c[undulus],
4	+	Felicit(as), Per[pe]t(ua), pas(si) n[on(as) Mart(ias)].
	[+]	Maiulu[s – – – ᶜ·¹⁶ – – –]
	+	Here are the martyrs
2	+	Saturus, Saturninus,
	+	Revocatus, Secundulus,
4	+	Felicitas (and) Perpetua, who suffered on March 7.
	+	Mavilus....

Perpetua was a young Roman matron who, according to the *Passio sanctarum Perpetuae et Felicitatis* (7. 9; 16. 3), was put to death in the amphitheatre in Carthage during public spectacles celebrating the birthday of Geta Caesar (Tabbernee 2005). Publius Septimius Geta, the son of the Roman emperor Lucius Septimius Severus (193–211), was born on the *nones* of March (= 7 March), enabling the restoration at the end of line 4. The restored letters in lines 1–3 are also based on the *passio*,

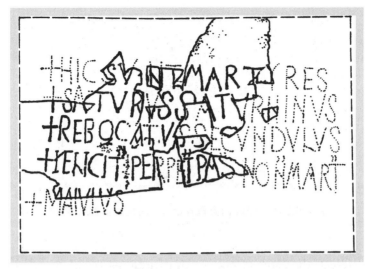

Fig. 6.1 Inscription commemorating Perpetua and other North African martyrs.

which records that a slave girl named Felicitas and four men (Saturus, Saturninus, Revocatus, and Secundulus) died in the amphitheatre at the same time as Perpetua. The spelling REBOCATUS (Fig. 6.1, line 3) with a B rather than a V is not unusual in Latin inscriptions and reflects local pronunciation. Similarly, letters were also often transposed by careless, even illiterate, stonecutters, as at the beginning of line 5, which should have been carved as MAVILVS not MAIVLVS.

The year in which Perpetua and her companions were martyred is not reported by the inscription, but is almost certainly 203 (Leclercq 1939: col. 420). The style of the lettering on the extant fragments of the slab, however, reveals that the plaque was made and erected centuries after the martyrs' deaths and, therefore, is not even a close contemporary of the martyrs whom it honours. The elegantly carved letters are in a style popular when the Vandal kings ruled North Africa. This particular plaque was probably made during the reign of Hilderic (523–30), presumably re-placing an earlier plaque installed in the crypt during the fourth century at the time the Basilica majorum was constructed (Ennabli 1986: 191).

The Basilica majorum appears to have been built on the site of an even earlier martyrium containing the relics of Perpetua and other martyrs. Whether or not such an earlier martyrium had any connection with the actual burial place of Perpetua (as assumed by Dunn 2005: 445 and n. 88) is, however, uncertain. Although another inscription (*CIL* 8, 4. 25272) also found at the Basilica majorum bearing the text *Perpetue filie dulcissimae* (Fig. 6.2) was claimed by Delattre (1908: 61–3) as Perpetua's original tombstone, this is highly doubtful (Tabbernee 1997: 110–12).

The fourth-century Basilica majorum, and presumably the earlier martyrium, also contained the bones of martyrs other than those who died in 203. Line 5 of

Fig. 6.2 Epitaph of a Perpetua, sweetest daughter.

the plaque reveals the name of one North African martyr whose relics had been transferred, at some time, to the Basilica majorum or its predecessor. The martyr was probably Mavilus of Hadrumetum (Tertullian, *Scap.* 3. 5), who was put to death between 184 and 188 or 191 and 193 when Caecilius Capella was governor of Africa Proconsularis (Birley 1991: 87–90, esp. 89 n. 28; Dunn 2005: 445–6). After Mavilus's name there is space for approximately sixteen more letters (or symbols) in line 5, which may have contained either a date for Mavilus's martyrdom or the names of other martyrs.

The sixth-century plaque, originally from the crypt of the Basilica majorum but now in the Carthage National Museum, illustrates both the meticulous work which epigraphers (also known as epigraphists) have to undertake to publish accurate editions of inscriptions and the crucial importance of this painstaking work. Put simply: epigraphy is the academic study of texts which are normally inscribed rather than produced by calligraphy. Inscriptions were usually (but not invariably) produced professionally, frequently in workshops consisting of master stonemasons and other artisans. The master stonemasons, at least theoretically, checked the work carried out by less experienced stonecutters. Inscriptions were carved on a number of different hard surfaces (stone, brick, wall stucco, pottery, metal)—although by far the most common materials were marble and (less expensive) limestone. Professionally prepared inscriptions were generally painted as well as inscribed, the colour red being particularly popular for highlighting the indented letters. Sometimes inscribed letters, especially those on ossuaries ('bone boxes'), were filled in with charcoal. Epigraphy also studies ancient texts which take the form of 'inscriptions' but were painted rather than inscribed (e.g. on wood) or made from letters cut out from metal such as bronze and mounted on other surfaces. Mosaics often include 'inscriptions' made, like the rest of the mosaic, of tesserae (small coloured pieces of stone or glass). Ancient graffiti, scratched into rocks or walls, are also epigraphic texts.

The academic discipline of epigraphy includes the search for and discovery of hitherto unknown (or unpublished) inscriptions, the publication of accurate editions and translations of and commentaries on inscriptions, and the scholarly discussion and dissemination of the data provided by inscriptions.

6.1 FIELD-WORK

Epigraphy as a 'science' (like its related discipline archaeology) has come a long way with respect to handling responsibly the extant material evidence of the past. No longer are inscriptions haphazardly extracted from the ground or cut from ancient walls and carried off to museums or private collections. The governments of most countries now have stringent controls in place regarding who can (and cannot) have access to archaeological sites and how these sites are to be excavated under government supervision. Archaeological teams normally include epigraphers who measure, photograph, take squeezes (paper 'casts'), make transcriptions, provisional restorations, and translations of the texts of any inscriptions (including graffiti) found on the site.

Professional epigraphers also examine inscriptions which are still *in situ* at sites other than those related to archaeological digs. This is the case especially in countries like Turkey, where countless early Christian inscriptions are still to be seen in and around rural villages (e.g. *IMont* 17, 21, 24, 33, 69).

When the stone on which an inscription is carved is no longer in the place where it was originally erected, it is sometimes possible to locate the 'find-spot' through 'ethno-archaeology', that is, interviewing locals, especially elderly villagers, about the original location of inscribed stones in their area; for example, see Tabbernee (2003: 87–9) and Lampe and Tabbernee (2004). The information provided by ethno-archaeology, however, needs to be treated with a great deal of caution—as archaeologists and epigraphers may be told what the villagers think they want to hear. Multiple and independent attestation of oral data is required before the data can be considered reliable.

Sometimes the stones on which inscriptions are carved have been reused in walls of more recent buildings or as 'water fountains' (e.g. *IMont* 9, 48), with the inscriptions and/or Christian symbols still clearly visible. Such reused stones are called *spolia*. *Spolia* can be sources of important epigraphic data (Saradi 1997; Yasin 2000); but the value of these data is enhanced, as with inscriptions now in museums or private collections, if there is information available about provenance (sometimes referred to as 'provenience'), that is, regarding exactly where the stones were before their reuse or transfer to a museum or other type of collection.

Recording the *current* provenance (as well as the original find-spot) where an inscription is located is important—even if all that can be recorded is the name of the modern village and a comment such as 'in the wall of a house', 'in the grounds of the mosque', or 'in a field'.

6.2 EDITIONS

Following his field-work at the ruins of Basilica majorum, Delattre wrote a number of papers publishing his findings. The first of these (Delattre 1907*b*) contains the *editio princeps* (i.e. the first, or primary, edition) of the inscription honouring Perpetua, her co-martyrs, and Mavilus. An *editio princeps*, however, is not necessarily the best edition, as subsequent editions have the benefit of more extensive examination both of the inscription itself and of other data which may supply (or suggest) restoration of missing letters or symbols. Delattre's *editio princeps*, for example, does not restore NON MART at the end of line 4, whereas in the edition which Delattre published only a few months later (1907*a*: 405–6), these words *are* restored. In both editions a Latin-style cross rather than a Greek-style cross is printed before each of the five lines, even though the photograph of the reassembled pieces of the commemorative plaque, published along with Delattre's *editio princeps*, clearly shows Greek, not Latin, crosses at lines 3–4 and the lower half of a Greek cross at line 2. A 'Greek cross' (*crux quadrata*) has equilateral horizontal bars, whereas in a 'Latin cross' (*crux immissa*), the horizontal bar cuts across the vertical approximately one-third from the top. Neither of Delattre's 1907 editions indicates that the crosses in lines 1 and 2 are restorations, or that some of the non-restored letters and symbols are only partially visible.

Delattre should not be blamed for what today would be judged as editorial shortcomings in his publications of the commemorative plaque he had discovered at the Basilica majorum. It was not until 1931 that an international standardized method of publishing inscriptions was agreed upon by epigraphers at Leiden, the Netherlands, and slightly amended subsequently (Dow 1969). One of the most important aspects of 'the Leiden system' is the use of standard *sigla* ('signs') to denote exactly how the text of an inscription has been edited. Some of the most frequently used *sigla* are shown in Table 6.1.

The term 'ligature' in Table 6.1 refers to the epigraphic result of carving two or more letters together by using part of the previous letter to form the subsequent letter in order to conserve space on the stone. For example, the first word of

Table 6.1 Standard epigraphic *sigla*

AB	Individual letters are legible but do not make sense in their context.
α<u>β</u>	Letters are no longer extant but were still visible when copied by an earlier editor.
α̣β̣	'Underdots' indicate that letters are not completely legible, although the accuracy of the reading is deemed certain.
----	Four letters are missing.
[-- $^{c.\,8}$ --]	About eight letters are missing.
[αβ]	Letters are missing but restored by the editor.
<αβ>	Letters originally omitted are added by the editor.
«αβ»	The editor has corrected wrong letters in the text.
(αβ)	The editor has resolved an abbreviation in the text.
{αβ}	Erroneous letters are cancelled by the editor.
⟦αβ⟧	A (still legible) original erasure.
`αβ′	Letters are written above the line.
a͡β	A ligature.
a̅β̅	An abbreviation is indicated by the original text.
α′	The letter stands for a numerical equivalent.
(v.), (vv.), (vac.)	One, two, or several letter spaces are left blank.

the phrase μνήμης χαρίν ('in memory') was frequently carved on tombstones as ΜΝΗΜΗ, that is, the letters *M*, *N*, *H*, *M*, *H*, and *Σ* (utilizing a quadratic sigma). In editions using the standardized Leiden system, the word would be printed μνήμης.

In Greek inscriptions, alphabetic numerals following the words for year, month, and/or day are often placed at the beginning of epigraphic texts. The resultant date, of course, needs to be converted to its modern equivalent, as the alphabetic numerals refer to regional or local 'eras', months, and days.

Greek and Latin inscriptions were carved in capital letters, normally without breaks between words, although some inscriptions contain small marks (e.g. dots, triangles, leaves), called *interpuncts*, to separate words or to indicate that the previous letters stand for an abbreviation. Because in editions words are printed separately, *interpuncts* are normally included only if they originally signified a separation between groups of words. Abbreviations may also be indicated by marks above letters, such as the double curved vertical lines resembling quotation marks in line 4 of the Perpetua plaque (Fig. 6.1). More common indicators of intentional abbreviations in epigraphic texts are horizontal lines called macrons. In Christian inscriptions, macrons are frequently used to designate *nomina sacra* ('sacred names'); for example, $\overline{IC}\ \overline{XC}$ stands for Ἰ(ησοῦ)ς Χ(ριστό)ς, that is, 'Jesus Christ'. Quadratic sigmas, especially in the Byzantine period, were frequently carved (or painted) in the shape of a C.

6.3 GENERAL EPIGRAPHIC GUIDES, HANDBOOKS, AND INTERNET SOURCES

A list of Latin epigraphic abbreviations is contained in Gordon (1983: 207–25), which remains a helpful, practical guide to reading Latin inscriptions, as are Susini (1973) and Keppie (1991). Capelli (1961) contains more than 1,400 Latin abbreviations and ligatures. Useful introductions to studying Greek inscriptions are Pfohl (1977), Woodhead (1981), and Cook (1987). Regarding epigraphy as a source for ancient historians, see Woodhead (1977), Millar (1983), and Bodel (2001).

The most recent and most comprehensive guide to epigraphy is Bérard *et al.* (2000), which publishes annual supplements, which may be downloaded from the internet. Since the 1980s, digitalization of inscriptions has enabled the production of electronic epigraphic data bases, available via CD-ROM and/or the internet; see Bérard *et al.* (2000) and Fonti epigrafiche, which has links to all the other most relevant sites on epigraphy.

6.4 PUBLISHED INSCRIPTIONS

Other than for professional epigraphers, *published* inscriptions are far more accessible than those still *in situ* or even in museums. Many universities possess the *Corpus inscriptionum latinarum (CIL)* (1862–), the *Corpus inscriptionum graecarum (CIG)* (1828–77), its geographically organized successor *Inscriptiones graecae (IG)* (1924–), the *Corpus inscriptionum iudaicarum (CII;* frequently abbreviated as *CIJ)* (1936–52), and more recently published collections such as the various volumes of the series Inschriften griechischer Städte aus Kleinasien (1972–). Annuals, such as *L'année épigraphique (AE)* (1888–) and the *Supplementum epigraphicum graecum (SEG)* (1923–71; 1979–), are intended to keep scholars informed about the publication of newly discovered inscriptions and about new editions of already published inscriptions. Similarly, the lists of the epigraphic texts of various cities published by McCabe *et al.* (e.g. *IEphMcCabe* (1991)) are helpful in quickly gaining a comprehensive overview of the range of inscriptions from a particular location. The *Actes des congrès internationaux d'épigraphie grecque et latine*, published since 1952, contain a wealth of information about the latest in epigraphic scholarship. See Bérard *et al.* (2000) for lists of standardized abbreviations of *corpora* and other epigraphic works. Horsley and Lee (1994) provide a checklist of abbreviations for Greek epigraphic volumes.

6.5 Identifying *Christian* Inscriptions

Identifying inscriptions, especially pre-Constantinian inscriptions, as Christian is not as simple as some of the early handbooks on Christian epigraphy have assumed—especially when examining inscriptions which may be Jewish rather than Christian (Kraemer 1991). The earliest Christians, even if they were sufficiently wealthy to participate in the 'epigraphic habit' of the Roman Empire (MacMullen 1982), did not distinguish their tombstones with specifically Christian symbols, formulae, or words. Claims of identifiably Christian inscriptions from the first or early second centuries (*ICUR* 1. 1–4; *EG* 4: 440–4 no. 1; compare Guarducci (1992: 279–80)) are overly optimistic. Only from the second half of the second century onward do we see clear evidence of Christianity on *stelai* (grave-markers) and, of course, on or near Christian graves in the catacombs at Rome or elsewhere.

6.5.1 Symbols

The earliest dated recognizably Christian tombstone is probably that of a man named Eutyches (Calder 1955: 33–5 no. 2). The object which the deceased is shown holding in his right hand appears to be eucharistic bread (the *panis quadratus*; compare *IMont* 3, 5–7), and the bunch of grapes in his left hand presumably represents eucharistic wine. Other (non-Christian) interpretations of these symbols, however, are possible. As with other Christian art on public display (Clement of Alexandria, *Paed.* 3. 59 .2–60. 1), it seems that Christians for the first three centuries chose symbols which were part of the wider culture but which also had special Christian significance (Finney 1994: 108–14). The presence of such symbols (e.g. dove, palm branch, anchor, fish) often help to identify as Christian otherwise religiously neutral inscriptions. However, symbols, even those popular among Christians, because they were shared with people from other cultures and religions, are not infallible indicators of Christianity.

The earliest extant epigraphic use of the now well-known *ΙΧΘΥΣ* ('FISH') acrostic, standing for the words Ἰ(ησοῦς) Χ(ριστὸς) Θ(εοῦ) Υ(ιὸς) Σ(ωτήρ), that is, 'Jesus Christ, God's Son, Saviour', is not in the form of a decorative symbol but as part of the text of the tombstone of Aberkios, bishop of Hierapolis in Phrygia, *c.* 180 (Ramsay 1897: 722–9; compare Hirschmann 2000, 2003; Tabbernee, forthcoming). Lines 17–22 read: 'Having Paul in the carriage, Faith led the way everywhere and set before me as nourishment everywhere a fish from a spring, immense, spotless, which a holy virgin caught.' Aberkios's epitaph also contains a number of other purposely ambiguous allusions to Christianity, such as to

Christ (lines 3–6), baptism (lines 11–12), and the eucharist (lines 23–6). Given the precarious legal status of Christians prior to Constantine, ambiguous epigraphic expressions on monuments erected in places where they could be seen by anyone is not surprising. From *c.* 200, however, Christian communities were able to own their own cemeteries (Tertullian, *Scap.* 3. 1; Origen, *Hom. in Jer.* 4. 13. 6). The most famous of these are the catacombs in Rome (Fiocchi Nicolai, Bisconti, and Mazzoleni, 1999). Therefore, from the beginning of the third century, open expressions of Christianity in 'secure' burial locations were not only possible but became common—although not every extant epitaph in Christian cemeteries is necessarily Christian.

6.5.2 Formulae

Gradually during the third century, even tombstones erected by Christians in public places became more openly Christian, depending on the level of security Christians felt at particular times and in particular locations. For example, in the area around Eumeneia in Phrygia, Christians began to adopt and adapt an originally non-Christian funerary curse formula. This curse formula, directed at potential grave violators (e.g. *IMont* 20, 33, 35), reads: ἔσται αὐτῷ πρὸς τὸν Θεόν ('He [or she] will have to reckon with God'). Christian adaptations of this formula reveal progressively more openly that, for them, *TON ΘEON* was a reference to the God of the Christians (Tabbernee 1983: 136–9; 1997: 144–7). Jews, however, also adopted the ἔσται αὐτῷ πρὸς τὸν Θεόν formula, so not every adaptation of the formula is automatically to be deemed Christian. Similarly, not every inscription which includes seemingly traditional 'pagan' formulae need be non-Christian. For example, the common 'pagan' abbreviation D·M·S (*Dis manibus sacrae*; i.e. 'Sacred to the Divine Spirits of the Lower World') was frequently retained by Christians on their tombstones—especially if they bought stones from a workshop which had pre-carved these abbreviations at the top of the stone. The Christians simply reinterpreted the abbreviation to stand for *Deo magno sacrum* ('Sacred to the Great God') (Grossi Gondi 1920: 480).

The so-called 'Christians for Christians' (Χριστιανοί Χριστιανοῖς) formula (e.g. *IMont* 24–9, 31, 38–52) is the most openly Christian expression on pre-Constantinian tombstones. Formerly commonly classified as Montanist, the sectarian designation of the 'Christians for Christians' inscriptions is no longer viable (Tabbernee 1997: 147–50, 405–6, 553–6). Similarly, the formula ἐνθάδε κεῖται ('here lies'), or one of its variants (e.g. *IMont* 59–62, 72–4, 80, 93–5), popular among Christians from the fourth century onward, can no longer be held to be exclusively Christian.

6.5.3 Specific Words, Phrases, or Designations

The most obvious single epigraphic indicator of Christianity, of course, is the word 'Christian' or 'Christians', whether in a formula or by itself. One of the earliest dated examples of the use of the word 'Christian' to mark a grave other than in the catacombs is *IMont* 17, which has a date which equates to either 24 May or 16 July, 243. The grave altar on which this inscription was carved also contains one of the earliest extant Latin crosses on a publicly displayed Christian tombstone. In the catacombs, descriptions of the deceased as *fidelis* ('one of the faithful') or *neophytus/a* ('novice', i.e. 'recently baptized') often substitute for the word 'Christian'.

The presence of the word κοιμητήριον (e.g. *IMont* 68), that is, 'sleeping place' for the deceased ('cemetery') or the word κοιμάω ('to sleep'), especially when part of the formula ἐνθάδε καθεύδη ('here sleeps'; e.g. *IMont* 87), still provides a reasonably reliable indication of Christianity. Phrases such as *depositum/a est* ('is buried'), *in Deo* ('in God'), *in pace* ('in peace'), and titles such as πρεσβύτερος, however, were commonly shared at least with Jews, and hence are not as indicative of Christianity as was once thought (Kraemer 1991). References to martyrs, such as Perpetua and Felicitas; to apostles, bishops, abbots, or abbesses; to archdeacons, deacons (male and female); to lesser clergy with designations like subdeacon, acolyte, exorcist, lector (reader), notarius, steward, and doorkeeper; or to monks, anchorites, virgins, and widows, are usually positive indicators of the Christian nature of an inscription.

6.5.4 Alleged 'crypto-Christian' indicators of Christianity

Great caution needs to be exercised with regard to inscriptions sometimes designated 'crypto-Christian': for example, those allegedly using palindromes, acronym-acrostics, isopsephisms, or cryptograms. A palindrome is a word square

R	O	T	A	S
O	P	E	R	A
T	E	N	E	T
A	R	E	P	O
S	A	T	O	R

Fig. 6.3 *Rotas/sator* palindrome.

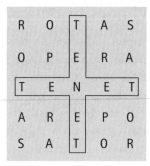

Fig. 6.4 *Rotas/sator* palindrome with *tenet* forming cross.

which reads the same in four directions. The central word of the pre-Constantinian *rotas/sator* palindrome (Fig. 6.3) is *tenet* ('he/she holds fast to'), which when read downwards and across forms a cross (Fig. 6.4), at each point commenced and concluded with a T (symbol for cross?) flanked by AO (=AΩ?). The letters can also be rearranged (Fig. 6.5) to twice form the word *paternoster* ('Our Father') with the AO (Grosser 1926). *Christian* use of this (probably originally Mithraic) palindrome, however, may be as late as 500 CE (Tabbernee 1997: 24–5).

The letters XMΓ which are inscribed prominently on some third-century as well as later (definitely Christian) inscriptions used to be interpreted as a cryptic-Christian acronym-acrostic for $X(ριστὸν)$ $M(αρία)$ $Γ(εννᾷ)$ ['Mary gives birth to Christ'] (e.g. Tjäder 1970). It has recently been shown, however, that the letters XMΓ form an isopsephism (Llewelyn 1997): that is, an alphabetic numeral having the same numeric value as the word or phrase for which it stands. XMΓ stands for $Θεὸς$ $Βοηθός$ (the letters of which equal $9 + 5 + 70 + 200 + 2 + 70 + 8 + 9 + 70 + 200 = 643$, i.e. XMΓ). The term $Θεὸς$ $Βοηθός$ ('God the Helper') is not exclusively Christian, but certainly became popular among Christians, especially as part of imprecations, including those inscribed on amulets or on door lintels.

Guarducci's theory (1978*b*) that, in the pre-Constantinian era, there was extensive use by Christians of 'mystical cryptology' has not won widespread support. The examples she cites come mainly from the Christian catacombs, where the need for secrecy would have been irrelevant. Rather than comprising an esoteric language made up of 'cryptograms' (e.g. P = Peter; T = Cross; S = Salvation), as Guarducci claims, it seems best to view the juxtaposition of letters and symbols as the creative (or careless) use of ligatures and/or a kind of epigraphic shorthand (Tabbernee, forthcoming).

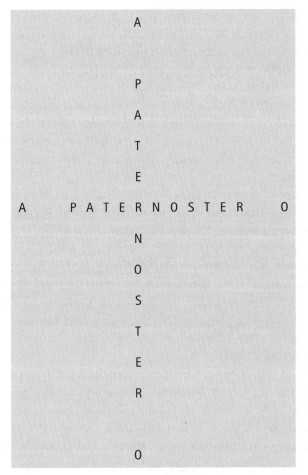

Fig. 6.5 *Rotas/sator* palindrome rearranged to form *paternoster*.

6.6 PUBLISHED COLLECTIONS OF SPECIFICALLY CHRISTIAN INSCRIPTIONS

One of the earliest and most extensive printed collections of exclusively Christian inscriptions is *Inscriptiones christianae urbis Romae* (*ICUR*; also *ICVR*) (1861–1915; new series 1922–92 (*ICUR²*; *ICVR²*)). Volume 2, 1 of *ICUR* contains the texts of no longer extant Christian inscriptions from Rome known from the *testimonia* of pilgrims and other travellers who, from the late antique period onward, copied and recorded the inscriptions they saw in manuscripts or early printed works in collections known as *syllogae*. In accordance with standard epigraphic practice, collections of inscriptions or *testimonia* are cited, in this chapter, not by editor but by standardized abbreviations. For the sake of convenience, cross-references from the particular abbreviation to the editor is provided below.

Christian inscriptions from Italy as a whole are published in the series Inscriptiones Christianae Italiae (1989–). The first in this series, *Inscriptiones graecae christianae veteres occidentis* (*IGOccidChr*) (1989), contains many significant inscriptions from elsewhere in Italy as well as from Rome. The series also includes a useful concordance (Felle 1991), cross-referencing the inscriptions published in *IGOccidChr* with their publication in earlier *corpora* or journals. Other volumes are devoted to specific Italian cities.

A great number of *corpora* of the Christian inscriptions from other geographic regions exist. Three illustrative examples of these are the *Recueil des inscriptions chrétiennes de Macédoine du IIIᵉ au VIᵉ siècle* (*IMakedChr*) (1983), *The Greek Christian Inscriptions of Crete* (*IKretChr*) (1970), and the *Recueil des inscriptions grecques chrétiennes d'Asie Mineure* (*IAsMinChr*) (1922). Sometimes *corpora*, including regionally based ones, concentrate on particular types of inscriptions; for example, *Les inscriptions funéraires chrétiennes de Carthage* (*ICKarth*) (1975–91) (*ICKarth* 2. 1 = Perpetua plaque); *The 'Christians for Christians' Inscriptions of Phrygia* (*IPhrygChr*) (1978); *Montanist Inscriptions and Testimonia* (*IMont*) (1997) (*IMont* 14 = Perpetua plaque).

Some published collections of Christian inscriptions feature representative samples, rather than all the known inscriptions from a particular region or category. The most comprehensive collection of sample Christian inscriptions is *Inscriptiones latinae christianae veteres* (*ILCV*) (1961–85) (*ILCV* 1. 2041 = Perpetua plaque), but see also Nunn (1920), Wischmeyer (1982), Johnson (1995), and Snyder (2003: 209–66). Perhaps the most beautifully carved Christian inscriptions are the metrical epitaphs composed by Pope Damasus (366–84), and crafted by Furius Dionysius Philocalus, to commemorate the martyrs buried in the catacombs and elsewhere in Rome. The Damasus epigrams have been collected, edited, and published by Ferrua (1942); see also Kaufmann (1917: 338–65) and Mazzoleni (1999: 174–9).

6.7 OTHER PUBLISHED CHRISTIAN INSCRIPTIONS

Scattered throughout the major *corpora* are numerous early Christian inscriptions, easily located via the indexes of individual volumes or separately published indexes covering multiple volumes. For example, *CIL* 8, 4. 25038 is the Perpetua plaque and *CIG* 4. 8606–9595a are all Christian inscriptions. The indexes of *L'année épigraphique* and the *Supplementum epigraphicum graecum* are extremely helpful for locating inscriptions relevant to the study of early Christianity. Especially useful are the *Bulletin épigraphique* (1888–1984; 1987–), published in the *Revue des études grecques*, and *L'année philologique*, both of which have extensive sections specifically about Christian inscriptions.

Early Christian inscriptions are also published in monographs and/or discussed in journals devoted to epigraphy in general, such as *Epigraphica Anatolica* or the *Zeitschrift für Papyrologie und Epigraphik*. Notices on new inscriptions also appear regularly in the *Journal of Roman Studies*, the *Classical Review*, and the *American Journal of Archaeology*. *Repertoria*, that is detailed catalogues describing and giving preliminary texts rather than definitive editions of epigraphic texts, often provide early access to inscriptions—including Christian ones (e.g. Pilhofer 2000).

6.8 HANDBOOKS ON AND INTRODUCTIONS TO CHRISTIAN EPIGRAPHY

The fourth volume of *Epigrafia greca* (Guarducci 1978a), includes the best introduction to early (Greek) Christian inscriptions. Marucchi (1912), Kaufmann (1917), and Grossi Gondi (1920), while superseded in terms of epigraphic methodology and editions of epigraphic texts, are still helpful introductions to Christian epigraphy as a whole. Each of these handbooks contains numerous illustrative examples of early Christian inscriptions. Similar examples, often with beautiful line drawings, also abound in the *Dictionnaire d'archéologie chrétienne et de liturgie* (1920–53). For survey articles on Christian epigraphy, see Guarducci (1992) and McHugh (1997). Keppie (1991: 119–24) and Markschies (1995: 32–6) also give a helpful brief introduction to the field.

6.9 SCHOLARSHIP

Inscriptions provide unique glimpses into the lives (and deaths) of early Christian women and men, prophets and prophetesses, clergy and laity, 'orthodox' and 'heretics', martyrs and monks. Such unfiltered epigraphic glimpses, devoid of much of the editorial bias inherent in extant literary historical documents mainly written from the perspective of 'the winners', often provide new, or hitherto not noticed, data regarding the 'losers' (e.g. the Montanists) or the 'powerless' (e.g. women).

These, until now mainly overlooked, data have enabled recent scholars to provide a more accurate account of the social identity of early Christians (Schöllgen 1984; Lampe 2003), including those deemed heretical (Tabbernee 1997: 556–69), and of the role of women in the early church (Eisen 2000; Madigan and Osiek 2005).

Particularly revealing have been the epigraphic data regarding ordained women and women who, even if not ordained, carried out significant ecclesiastical functions in the early church. Female presbyters are attested epigraphically in the context of Montanism (*IMont* 4) and, most likely, also in the context of proto-Catholic and Catholic Christianity, although some of the relevant *presbutera* inscriptions have been interpreted by some scholars to refer to 'old women', 'wives of male presbyters', or considered to be Jewish rather than Christian. For the case that at least some of the extant *presbutera* inscriptions refer to 'mainstream' Christian, ordained women ecclesiastical office-bearers, see Tabbernee (1997: 67–70), Eisen (2000: 116–32), and Madigan and Osiek (2005: 169–71, 193–8). A fifth-century Christian sarcophagus inscription (*CIL* 3. 14900) from ancient Salona (modern Solin, Croatia), contains the word [*sace*]*rdotae*, indicating that the sarcophagus was that of a woman with priestly (*sacerdotal*) responsibilities. As 'sacerdotess', she was at least a woman presbyter, but may even have been a bishop.

The title *episcopa* occurs in three extant inscriptions, but it is difficult to know exactly what the term signifies in those inscriptions. *CIL* 11. 4339 (originally from Interamna Nahars (modern Terni, Italy) but now at St Paul's Outside the Walls in Rome) refers to a *venerabilis fem*[*ina*] *episcopa*. The name of this 'venerable woman' with the title *episcopa* most likely commenced with a Q, although the Q may be part of a phrase giving her age at death (*ILCV* 1. 121: *qa*[*e vix.* |*a* ...]). In the past, the Interamna Nahars inscription has usually been interpreted as the epitaph of the *wife* of a bishop. It may be, however, that 'Q'(?) was the *mother* of a bishop (Madigan and Osiek 2005: 193): namely, Pope Siricius (384–99). Similarly, the designation *episcopa* in the other two extant inscriptions with the term (Eisen 2000: 200–5) may also have been honorific references: namely, to Theodora, the mother of Pope Paschal I (817–24). Both Theodora inscriptions, one on a mosaic and the other on a commemorative plaque, are in the chapel of St Zeno in the church of Santa Prassede in Rome, dedicated by Paschal I. Perhaps 'Q'(?) and Theodora held actual, rather than honorific, episcopal roles; but this is neither proven nor ruled out by the extant epigraphic (or literary) data. Overwhelming epigraphic confirmation of the existence of women who held the actual ecclesiastical office of *deacon*, however, does exist (Eisen 2000: 158–98; Madigan and Osiek 2005: 67–96, 143–5).

There are also numerous inscriptions of ecclesiastically designated women commemorated epigraphically as prophets/prophetesses, theological teachers, financial administrators, members of the order of widows, virgins, and heads of religious communities (Eisen 2000; Madigan and Osiek 2005).

6.10 Conclusion

Well over 50,000 early Christian inscriptions have been published thus far, and more are being discovered every day. Most of these are in Greek or Latin, but early Christian inscriptions or testimonia to such inscriptions exist also in many other languages, including Syriac, Coptic, and even Chinese. The historical data provided by the huge number of early Christian inscriptions are indispensable to the non-specialist as well as the specialist student of early Christianity. Understanding and interpreting such data correctly demands at least a rudimentary knowledge of the methodology, resources, and results of the academic discipline called epigraphy—such as that provided by this chapter.

Nothing, of course, is a substitute for seeing actual inscriptions—ideally with a published edition (and, if necessary, translation) in hand. Catalogues are available to guide one to the specific location of particular inscriptions in museums and in the catacombs, although some inscriptions may not be on public display or have been moved since the catalogue was published. Visiting museums such as Carthage's National Museum to see the Perpetua plaque, the Vatican's Museo Pio Cristiani to see Aberkios's gravestone, or the catacombs to see Damasus's metrical inscriptions honouring the Roman martyrs are memorable experiences. Turning over the pages of the large leather-bound volumes of the great *corpora* of published inscriptions, commenced in the nineteenth century, can be almost as rewarding. These magnificent large-print volumes often include beautiful line drawings of the inscriptions and of the monuments on which they were inscribed. More recent collections often publish excellent photographs of, and commentaries about, the inscriptions with which they deal. A good way to become familiar with the range of early Christian inscriptions is to start with the following resources.

Suggested Reading

The following are recommended: Eisen (2000); Finegan (1992); Fiocchi Nicolai, Bisconti, and Mazzoleni (1999); Horsley *et al.* (1981–); Keppie (1991); Kraemer (1991, 2004); Madigan and Osiek (2005); Marucchi (1912); Snyder (2003); and Tabbernee (1997).

Abbreviations used in text which are not included in the Abbreviations section on pp. xiv–xxiv.

EG: see Guarducci (1967–78)
IAsMinChr: see Grégoire (1922)
ICKarth: see Ennabli (1975–91)
IEphMcCabe: see McCabe *et al.* (1991)
IG: see Hiller de Gaertringen *et al.* (1924–)

IKretChr: see Bandy (1970)
IMakedChr: see Feissel (1983)
IMont: see Tabbernee (1997)
IPhrygChr: see Gibson (1978)

BIBLIOGRAPHY

BANDY, A. C. (1970), *The Greek Inscriptions of Crete*, Christianikai Epigraphai tēs Hellados, 10 (Athens: Christian Archaeological Society).

BÉRARD, F., *et al.* (2000) (eds.), *Guide de l'épigraphiste: Bibliographie choisie des épigraphies antiques et médiévales*, 3rd edn. (Paris: Éditions rue d'Ulm).

BIRLEY, A. R. (1991), 'Caecilius Capella: Persecutor of Christians, Defender of Byzantium', *GRBS* 32: 81–98.

BODEL, J. (2001) (ed.), *Epigraphic Evidence: Ancient History from Inscriptions* (London: Routledge).

BOECKH, A., *et al.* (1827–77) (eds.), *Corpus inscriptionum graecarum*, i–iv plus Index (Berlin: Reimer; repr. Hildesheim: Georg Olms, 1977).

CABROL, F., and LECLERCQ, H. (1920–53) (eds.), *Dictionnaire d'archéologie chrétienne et de liturgie* (Paris: Letouzey et Ané).

CAGNAT, R., *et al.* (1888–) (eds.), *L'année épigraphique* (Paris: Presses universitaires de France).

CALDER, W. M. (1955), 'Early Christian Epitaphs from Phrygia', *Anatolian Studies*, 5: 25–38.

CAPELLI, A. (1961), *Lexicon abbreviaturarum: Dizionario di abbreviature latine ed italiane*, 6th edn. (Milan: Ulrico Hoepli; repr., 1994).

COOK, B. F. (1987), *Greek Inscriptions* (Berkeley: University of California Press).

DELATTRE, A.-L. (1907*a*), 'Inscriptions chrétiennes de Carthage', *Revue Tunisien*, 14: 405–19.

—— (1907*b*), 'Lettre du R. P. Delattre à M. Héron de Villefosse sur l'inscription des Martyrs de Carthage, Sainte Perpétue, Sainte Félicité et leur compagnons', *CRAI*, 5th ser. 8: 193–5.

—— (1908), 'La basilica majorum', *CRAI*, 5th ser. 9: 59–69.

DE ROSSI, J.-B., and GATTI, G. (1861–1915) (eds.), *Inscriptiones christianae urbis Romae septimo saeculo antiquiores*, i; ii, 1 and *Supplementum* fascicle 1 (Rome: Officina Libraria Pontificia, P. Cuggiani).

DIEHL, E. (1961–85) (ed.), *Inscriptiones latinae christianae veteres*, i–iii, 2nd edn.; iv: *Supplementum*; v: *Nuove correzione allo Silloge del Diehl* (Zürich: Weidmann; Vatican City: Istituto di archeologia cristiana).

DOW, S. (1969), *Conventions in Editing: A Suggested Reformulation of the Leiden System*, Greek, Roman, and Byzantine Scholarly Aids, 2, 2nd edn. (Durham, NC: Duke University Press).

DUNN, G. D. (2005), 'Mavilus of Hadrumetum, African Proconsuls and Mediaeval Martyrologies', in C. Deroux (ed.), *Studies in Latin Literature and Roman History*, xii, Collection Latomus, 27 (Brussels: Latomus), 433–46.

EISEN, U. E. (2000), *Women Office Holders in Early Christianity: Epigraphical and Literary Studies*, trans. L. M. Maloney (Collegeville, Minn.: Liturgical Press).

ENNABLI, L. (1975–91), *Les inscriptions funéraries chrétiennes de Carthage*, i–iii, Collection de l'École française de Rome, 25, 62, 151 (Rome: École française de Rome).

—— (1986), 'Les inscriptions chrétiennes de Carthage et leur apport pour la connaissance de la Carthage chrétienne', in A. Mastino (ed.), *L'Africa romana: Atti del III convegno di studio Sassari, 13–15 dicembre 1985* (Sassari: Edizioni Gallizzi), 189–203.

FEISSEL, D. (1983), *Recueil des inscriptions chrétiennes de Macédoine du IIIe au VIe siècle*, Bulletin de Correspondence Hellenique, Suppl. 8 (Paris: de Boccard).

FELLE, A. E. (1991), *Concordanze della inscriptions graecae christianae veteres occidentis*, Inscriptiones Christianae Italiae, 2 (Bari: Edipuglia).

FERRUA, A. (1942), *Epigrammata Damasiana* (Rome: Pontificio istituto di archeologia cristiana).

FINEGAN, J. (1992), *The Archaeology of the New Testament: The Life of Jesus and the Beginning of the Early Church*, rev. edn. (Princeton: Princeton University Press).

FINNEY, P. C. (1994), *The Invisible God: The Earliest Christians on Art* (Oxford: Oxford University Press).

FIOCCHI NICOLAI, V., BISCONTI F. F., and MAZZOLENI, D. (1999), *The Christian Catacombs of Rome: History, Decoration, Inscriptions*, trans. C. C. Stella and L.-A. Touchette (Regensburg: Schnell & Steiner).

FONTI EPIGRAFICHE (<www.rassegna.unibo.it/epigrafi.html>), 19 September 2006.

FREY, J.-B. (1936–52) (ed.), *Corpus inscriptionum iudicarum: Recueil des inscriptions juives qui vont du IIIe siècle avant Jésus-Christ au VIIe siècle de notre ère*, i–ii, Sussidi allo Studio della antichità Cristiane, 1, 3 (Vatican City: Pontificio istituto di archeologia cristiana; vol. i repr. with corrections and additions, New York: KTAV, 1975).

GIBSON, E. (1978), *The 'Christians for Christians' Inscriptions of Phrygia: Greek Texts, Translations and Commentary*, HTS 32 (Missoula, Mont.: Scholars Press).

GORDON, A. E. (1983), *Illustrated Introduction to Latin Epigraphy* (Berkeley: University of California Press).

GRÉGOIRE, H. (1922), *Recueil des inscriptions grecques chrétiennes d'Asie Mineure*, fasc. 1 (the only one published) (Paris: Ernest Leroux; repr. Chicago: Ares, 1980).

GROSSER, F. (1926), 'Ein neuer Vorschlag zur Deuting der Sator-Formel: Pater noster', *Archiv für Religionswissenschaft*, 24: 165–9.

GROSSI GONDI, F. (1920), *Trattato di epigrafia cristiana: Latina e greca del mondo romano occidentale*, I monumenti cristiani dei primi sei secoli, 1 (Rome: Università Gregoriana; repr. Rome: L'Erma di Bretschneider, 1968).

GUARDUCCI, M. (1967–78), *Epigrafia greca*, i–iv (Rome: Istituto della Stato).

—— (1978), 'Dal gioco letterale alle crittografia mistica', *ANRW* 2. 16. 2: 1736–73.

—— (1992), 'Epigraphy, Christian', in A. Di Berardino (ed.), *Encyclopedia of the Early Church*, trans. A. Walford (Oxford: Oxford University Press), i. 279–81.

HILLER DE GAERTRINGEN, F., *et al.* (1924–) (eds.), *Inscriptiones graeca* (Berlin: Reimer, de Gruyter).

HIRSCHMANN, V. (2000), 'Untersuchungen zur Grabschrift des Aberkios', *ZPE* 129: 109–16.

—— (2003), 'Ungelöste Rätsel?: Nochmals zur Grabschrift des Aberkios', *ZPE* 145: 133–9.

HONDIUS, J. J. E., *et al.* (1923–71, 1979–) (eds.), *Supplementum epigraphicum graecum* (Leiden: Nijhof; Amsterdam: J. C. Gieben). Consolidated indexes also published separately.

HORSLEY, G. H. R., and LEE, J. A. L. (1994), 'A Preliminary Checklist of Abbreviations of Greek Epigraphic, Volumes', *Epigraphica*, 56: 129–69.

HORSLEY, G. H. R., *et al.* (1981–) (eds.), *New Documents Illustrating Early Christianity* (North Ryde, New South Wales: Macquarie University Ancient History Documentary Research Centre; Grand Rapids, Mich.: William B. Eerdmans).

HOUSSOLIER, B., *et al.* (1888–1984, 1987–) (eds.), *Bulletin épigraphique*, published in the *Revue des études grecques*. The issues edited by J. and L. Robert between 1938 and 1984 have been published separately in 10 vols. There are also five separately published indexes.

JOHNSON, G. J. (1995), *Early-Christian Epitaphs from Anatolia*, SBLTT 35; Early Christian Literature Series, 8 (Atlanta: Scholars Press).

KAUFMANN, C. M. (1917), *Handbuch der altchristlichen Epigraphik* (Freiburg: Herder).

KEPPIE, L. J. F. (1991), *Understanding Roman Inscriptions* (Baltimore: Johns Hopkins University Press).

KRAEMER, R. S. (1991), 'Jewish Tuna and Christian Fish: Identifying Religious Affiliation in Epigraphic Sources', *HTR* 84: 141–62.

——(2004) (ed.), *Women's Religions in the Greco-Roman World: A Sourcebook* (Oxford: Oxford University Press).

LAMPE, P. (2003), *From Paul to Valentinus: Christians at Rome in the First Two Centuries*, ed. M. D. Johnson, trans. M. Steinhauer (Minneapolis: Fortress Press).

——and TABBERNEE, W. (2004), 'Das Reskript von Septimius Severus und Caracalla an die Kolonen der kaiserlichen Domäne von Tymion und Simoe', *EA* 37: 169–78.

LECLERCQ, H. (1939), 'Perpétue et Félicité (Saintes)', in *DACL* xiv. 1, cols. 393–444.

LLEWELYN, S. R. (1997), 'The Christian Symbol XMΓ, an Acrostic or an Isopsephism?', in G. H. R. Horsley, *et al.* (eds.), *New Documents Illustrating Early Christianity*, viii: *A Review of the Greek Inscriptions and Papyri Published 1984–85* (North Ryde, New South Wales: Macquarie University Ancient History Documentary Research Centre; Grand Rapids, Mich.: William B. Eerdmans), 156–68.

MacMULLEN, R. (1982), 'The Epigraphic Habit in the Roman Empire', *American Journal of Philology*, 103: 233–46.

MADIGAN, K., and OSIEK, C. (2005) (eds. and trans.), *Ordained Women in the Early Church: A Documentary History* (Baltimore: Johns Hopkins University Press).

MARKSCHIES, C. (1995), *Arbeitsbuch Kirchengeschichte* (Tübingen: J. C. B. Mohr/Paul Siebeck).

MARUCCHI, O. (1912), *Christian Epigraphy: An Elementary Treatise with a Collection of Ancient Christian Inscriptions mainly of Roman Origin*, trans. J. A. Willis (Cambridge: Cambridge University Press; repr. Chicago: Ares, 1974).

MAZZOLENI, D. (1999), 'Inscriptions in Roman Catacombs', in Fiocchi Nicolai *et al.* (1999), 146–85.

McCABE, D. F., *et al.* (1991) (eds.), *Ephesos Inscriptions: Texts and Lists*, i–ii, texts; iii: lists (Princeton: Princeton University Institute for Advanced Studies).

McHUGH, M. P. (1997), 'Inscriptions', in E. Ferguson, *et al.* (eds.), *Encyclopedia of Early Christianity*, 2nd edn. (New York: Garland), 574–6.

MILLAR, F. (1983), 'Epigraphy', in M. Crawford (ed.), *Sources for Ancient History* (Cambridge: Cambridge University Press), 80–136.

NUNN, H. P. V. (1920), *Christian Inscriptions* (London: S.P.C.K.; New York: Macmillan; repr. New York: Philosophical Library, 1952).

PFOHL, G. (1977) (ed.), *Das Studium der griechischen Epigraphik* (Darmstadt: Wissenschaftliche Buchgesellschaft).

PILHOFER, P. (2000), *Philippi*, ii: *Katalog der Inschriften von Philippi*, WUNT 119 (Tübingen: J. B. C. Mohr/Paul Siebeck).

RAMSAY, W. M. (1897), *The Cities and Bishoprics of Phrygia: Being an Essay of the Local History of Phrygia from the Earliest Times to the Turkish Conquest*, i. Part 2: *West and West-Central Phrygia* (Oxford: Clarendon Press; repr. New York: Arno, 1975).

RITSCHL, F. W., *et al.* (1862–) (eds.), *Corpus inscriptionum latinarum* (Berlin: Reimer, 1862–1932, de Gruyter, 1932–).

SARADI, H. (1997), 'The Use of Spolia in Byzantine Monuments: The Archeological and Literary Evidence', *International Journal of the Classical Tradition*, 3: 395–423.

SCHÖLLGEN, G. (1984), *Ecclesia Sordida?: Zur Frage der socialen Schichtung frühchristlicher Gemeinden am Beispiel Karthagos zur zeit Tertullians*, *JAC*, Ergänzungsband 12 (Münster: Aschendorff).

SILVAGNI, A., *et al.* (1922–92) (eds.), *Inscriptiones christianae urbis Romae septimo saeculo antiquiores, nova series* (Vatican City: Pontificio istituto di archeologia cristiana).

SNYDER, G. F. (2003), *Ante Pacem: Archaeological Evidence of Church Life before Constantine*, rev. edn. (Macon, Ga.: Mercer University Press).

SUSINI, G. (1973), *The Roman Stonecutter: An Introduction to Latin Epigraphy*, ed. E. Badian, trans. A. M. Dabrowski (Oxford: Blackwell).

TABBERNEE, W. (1983), 'Christian Inscriptions from Phrygia', in G. H. R. Horsley, *et al.* (eds.), *New Documents Illustrating Early Christianity*, iii: *A Review of the Greek Inscriptions and Papyri Published in 1978* (North Ryde, New South Wales: Macquarie University Ancient History Documentary Research Centre; Grand Rapids, Mich.: William B. Eerdmans), 128–39.

—— (1997), *Montanist Inscriptions and Testimonia: Epigraphic Sources Illustrating the History of Montanism*, PMS, 16 (Macon, Ga.: Mercer University Press; Washington: Catholic University of America Press). [*IMont*]

—— (2003), 'Portals of the New Jerusalem: The Discovery of Pepouza and Tymion', *JECS* 11: 87–94.

—— (2005), 'Perpetua, Montanism, and Christian Ministry in Carthage c. 203 C.E.', *Perspectives in Religious Studies*, 32: 421–41.

—— (forthcoming), 'Inscriptions: Clandestine/Crypto-Christian', in P. C. Finney (ed.), *Encyclopedia of Early Christian Art and Architecture* (Grand Rapids, Mich.: William B. Eerdmans).

TJÄDER, J.-O. (1970), 'Christ, Our Lord, Born of the Virgin Mary (XMΓ and VDN), *Eranos*, 68: 148–90.

WESSEL, C. (1989) (ed.), *Inscriptiones graecae christianae veteres occidentis*, Inscriptiones Christianae Italiae, 1 (Bari: Edipuglia).

WISCHMEYER, W. (1982), *Griechische und lateinische Inschriften zur Sozialgeschichte der Alten Kirche*, Texte zur Kirchen- und Theologiegeschichte, 28 (Gütersloh: Gerd Mohn).

WOODHEAD, A. G. (1977), 'Epigraphik und Geschichte', in Pfohl (1977), 73–93.

—— (1981), *The Study of Greek Inscriptions*, 2nd edn. (Cambridge: Cambridge University Press; repr. 1992).

YASIN, A. M. (2000), 'Displaying the Sacred Past: Ancient Inscriptions in Early Modern Rome', *International Journal of the Classical Tradition*, 7: 39–57.

CHAPTER 7

PALAEOGRAPHY AND CODICOLOGY

RALPH W. MATHISEN

7.1 INTRODUCTION: TERMINOLOGY AND HISTORY

THE world of early Christianity was a world of texts, ranging from scriptural and patristic to calendars, charters, private letters, and even graffiti. Documents were written on many different kinds of materials in several different languages, primarily Greek, Hebrew, and Latin, but others as well. The study of ancient and medieval texts comprises several different scholarly disciplines. For example, texts written on durable materials such as stone, bone, metal (such as bronze and lead), pottery, or clay are subsumed under the field of epigraphy, whereas numismatics deals with the specialized category of the inscriptions and iconography of coins and medals. Characteristically, epigraphic and numismatic documents are rather short, often just several lines, as in the case of epitaphs, legal documents, or graffiti. Longer documents, such as books, were written on more perishable materials, such as papyrus, parchment, vellum, and even wax tablets. The study of these documents, including identifying their dates, classifying their different types of scripts, and reading their texts, is known generically as palaeography, from the Greek words for 'ancient writing'. All of the palaeographic documents written in antiquity and the Middle Ages were written by hand, the Latin for which, '*manu scripta*', gives its name to manuscripts. The discipline of Latin palaeography was established by Jean Mabillon and the Benedictine monks of St Maur in the late seventeenth century for the purpose of establishing the age of Latin manuscripts based on their hand-writing and other internal considerations (Mabillon 1681; Metzger 1981: 3). Shortly thereafter, the first to study Greek palaeography was the Benedictine monk Bernard de Montfaucon (1708). The study of both Greek and Latin palaeography was greatly furthered by the publication of many manuscript facsimiles beginning in the mid-nineteenth century, and of indexes of manuscript catalogues and microfilm catalogues in the twentieth century. The study of papyrus documents has its own sub-discipline, papyrology. Codicology (from *codex*, the name for a manuscript book), on the other hand, studies the materials from which books were constructed, the way in which books were assembled, and the manner in which texts were laid out on the page (Metzger 1981: 3; Thompson 1894: *passim*). And diplomatics studies the provenance (origin) of charters and archival documents. Taken together, codicology and palaeography have much to tell us about how early Christian writings were preserved from antiquity until the modern day.

7.2 PALAEOGRAPHIC MATERIALS

Some ancient documents, such as charters or personal letters, required but a page or two. But longer documents, such as books of scripture or biblical commentaries, could occupy hundreds of pages, and required some means of connecting pages together to create a *liber* (Greek *biblion* or *biblos*) or book. Materials that were used for bookmaking included papyrus, wax tablets, parchment, and vellum. They were fabricated into books in two formats: the scroll and the codex.

7.2.1 Writing Surfaces and their Formats

(i) *Papyrus*

The earliest form of perishable writing material was papyrus, made as early as 3,000 BCE from a species of sedge, also known as bulrush or paper reed, that grew along the banks of the Nile. In order to create writing material, the outer skin of the hollow papyrus stem was peeled off, and the inner pith was split, flattened, and cut into strips up to 15 inches long. The strips were laid side by side vertically, slightly overlapping, with another layer of strips laid horizontally, edge-to-edge on top. The two layers were moistened, pounded together, and then dried under pressure in the sun. The gum released by the fibres helped to fuse the strips into a uniform sheet. The sheets were smoothed with pumice dust and trimmed. A standard papyrus sheet, or *charta*, therefore, was square, the length and width, often around 10 inches, being a bit less than the length of the original strips.

(ii) *The scroll*

The earliest form of book, the papyrus scroll, Greek *tomos* or Latin *volumen* ('rolled up'), was created by gluing many papyrus sheets together, with the horizontal layers on the same side, to create rolls up to 35 feet long, the maximum manageable length. The *volumen* was wound around an *omphalos* (dowel) made of wood, metal, or bone. The side with the horizontal layer of strips, being smoother, became the writing side, or recto. The back, or verso, was usually left blank, although it too could be used if writing material ran short. The text on Greek papyrus scrolls was written with a reed pen and arranged in columns generally 2–3.5 inches wide with half-inch margins, about 18–25 letters per line and anywhere from 25 to 50 lines per column. The horizontal plant fibres provided guide lines. When a scroll was unrolled, left to right, only about four columns of text would be visible at a time. The standard size of the *volumen* determined the standard length of the individual sections (or 'books') of lengthy literary works. Multi-volume books were kept together in *capsae* (cylindrical containers) (Thompson 1894: 183 ff.).

(iii) *Wax tablets*

A ubiquitous writing surface was a tablet, usually wooden but sometimes ivory, with its surface covered with wax, often black or green. Tablets were usually strung together in pairs (diptychs) or triplets (triptychs). The wax was inscribed with a metal stylus that had a sharp point for writing on one end and a knob or flattened spatula on the other end that could be used for smoothing the wax for erasures or reuse. Tablets, being less expensive to manufacture than papyrus, were useful for rough drafts, letters, copies of documents, account books, and a multitude of other daily purposes. The satirist Horace referred to the use of tablets to write rough drafts when he commented (*Satires*, 1. 10. 72–3), 'Turn your stylus often, again and again, if you are going to write anything worthy of being read.' For lengthy documents, several diptychs could be bound together with leather thongs, creating a book-like document called a *codex* (or *caudex*), a word meaning 'tree trunk'.

(iv) *Parchment and vellum*

The most expensive kinds of writing material were parchment and vellum, which were made from the treated skins of animals such as sheep, cattle, and goats. According to Pliny the Elder (*Natural History*, 13. 21), this kind of material originated when one of the Ptolemaic kings of Egypt refused to supply papyrus for the library of Pergamum. A king Eumenes, probably Eumenes II (197–160 BCE), developed writing material made from animal skins known as *membrana* (Latin for animal skin) or *charta Pergamena* (whence the word 'parchment'). Technically, parchment was made from sheepskin, and vellum (from the Latin word *vitellus*, or calf) from rather tougher materials such as calf or goat skin. But both terms are often used generically to refer to all types of writing materials made from animal skins, ranging from paper-thin uterine lambskin to board-hard cow skin. For the sake of convenience, the term 'parchment' will be used in this discussion to refer to both parchment and vellum.

The production of parchment began by soaking the skins in a lime bath to remove fat and loose flesh and to loosen the hair. A skin then was stretched on a wooden frame and scraped with a *lunellum*, a crescent-shaped knife, to smooth it, to remove the hair and any other adherences, and to keep the skin supple as it dried. Once the skin was dry, the two sides, and especially the hair side, were rubbed smooth with pumice. The same process could make the skin thinner and stretch it out farther. The flesh side, which was more absorbent, then was dressed with pounce (from *pumex*, or pumice), gum sandarac mixed with pumice, to make it less absorbent so that the ink would not run. The hair side, on the other hand, was pounced with chalk and pumice to whiten it. Pounce was also used to reduce greasiness. In spite of this treatment, the hair and flesh sides often could be differentiated: the flesh side tended to be white and a bit concave (it shrank more), whereas the hair side often was yellowish and showed traces of the hair follicles. The treated skins were then trimmed to make large rectangular sheets, or *folia*, with the leftover scraps being used for labels, ties, or even tiny pages. Thick skins could even be split into two layers, and folia also could be dyed for special purposes.

(v) *The codex*

Parchment books were constructed differently from papyrus books. Parchment sheets were stacked in layers, folded in two, and sewn together along the fold, creating a codex with four times as many pages (front and back) as original parchment sheets. The word codex gives its name to codicology, which is the study of books in codex form. Codex also gives its name to 'codification', for this was the book format that eventually was used for large collections of written texts. By the first century BCE, parchment codex notebooks were being used, like codices made from wax tablets, for rough drafts, keeping accounts, and so on. In the following century, the codex came into increasing use as a means of copying literary works. Each group of folded pages with a common internal fold is known as a 'quire' or 'gathering'. Early codices were of a single-quire format, but the bigger the book, the more clumsy this method was; fatter books were liable to crack at the spine, and the outer pages had to be much wider than the inner ones. Thus, it was eventually found more practical to bind several quires into books of whatever length one desired. The sixteen-page length, the 'quaternion' (*tetradēs* in Greek), made from four folded sheets, became standard; although one also encounters quires of other sizes, ranging from binions (two sheets) and ternions (three sheets) on up. Beginning in late antiquity, the bottom of the last page of each quire was often marked with a sequential quire number, or 'signature', for example, 'Q III', or 'the third quaternion'. These numbers facilitated binding, and also are very helpful in reassembling books that have come apart or survive only in a fragmentary state.

Each page in a codex has a front (top) side, the 'recto' (on the right side of a pair of pages) and a back (bottom) side, the 'verso' (on the left of a pair of pages). Sheets were initially numbered by folia, often in the upper right corner of the recto side. Thus, the pages on the front and back of each leaf have the same folio number: the recto page is given the superscript 'r' and the verso the superscript 'v'. Only later did it become common to number individual pages. The pages of parchment codices were organized so that each spread (a set of facing pages) consisted of flesh or hair sides of the parchment sheets, so that like-tinted pages faced each other.

(vi) *Paper*

Paper was not used at all during the early Christian period. The Arabs learned to manufacture paper from cotton, linen, or even silk fibres from the Chinese by the mid-eighth century, but it did not begin to be used in Europe until the late eleventh century, in Spain. Thence its use passed gradually into the rest of Europe, where it began to be used for books as of about 1400 CE. Paper books were almost invariably in the codex format. After the spread of printing and the need for bulk quantities of writing material, parchment was largely replaced by paper, remaining in use only for high-quality books or other specialized uses, such as modern 'sheepskins', a word still applied to school diplomas.

7.2.2 Predominance of Parchment and the Codex Format

(i) *Choice of writing material*

Papyrus remained the writing material of choice until into the fourth century. It was relatively inexpensive, produced in large quantities, and readily available thanks to the freely functioning Roman trade networks. But the utility of parchment became increasingly clear for several reasons. Papyrus was available only from Egypt, and, while initially very sturdy, it became very friable with age. It did not stand up to damp climates or hard use. For example, in the late fifth century a friend of Ruricius of Limoges wrote to him: 'As you directed, I have found the saint Augustine … It is a papyrus book and insufficiently strong to bear mistreatment, because, as you know, papyrus is quickly consumed by age. Read it, if you wish, and copy it (*Ep. Litterae sanctitatis*). As a consequence of its perishable nature, most extant papyrus documents come from the sands of Egypt; only a very few survive from elsewhere. Parchment, on the other hand, could be made anywhere, was rewritable, and was very durable. Although liable to fire, mildew, and mice, it was otherwise virtually indestructible. As of the fourth century, there began a transition from the use of papyrus to that of parchment, especially for documents that would receive heavy use. Some resisted the change. Galen, for example, claimed that parchment's glare caused eye-strain (*Opera* 3, 18). But, gradually, parchment replaced papyrus as the writing material of choice, especially in the western world. Availability considerations also came into play. By the fifth century, with the *de facto* split of the Roman Empire into eastern and western halves and a rise in Mediterranean piracy, papyrus was less and less available in the West. As a result, an increasingly large number of original parchment documents survive from the fifth century and later. The vast majority of these are church-related.

(ii) *Choice of book format*

At the same time that parchment was superseding papyrus, the codex format was also gaining in popularity. The codex had several advantages over the scroll: it could be written on both sides and still have the pages stay in sequence; it made cross-referencing and paging back and forth easier; it was more portable, and it was easier to store on shelves. Whereas the scroll was well suited to accessing a sequential group of pages, the codex was better for random access among passages scattered throughout a book. For Christian purposes, the codex was clearly superior. In the church, the codex facilitated flipping easily from one scriptural passage to another, a process that would have necessitated a clumsy and time-consuming rolling and unrolling of a 35-foot scroll. It has also been suggested that a desire to distance themselves from the Jewish scroll also may have been a reason why early Christians preferred the codex format: in Christian iconography, the Hebrew prophets are represented holding scrolls and the evangelists holding codices. By the second century CE the codex had replaced the scroll in Christian circles. During the fourth century the triumph of Christianity also encouraged the general replacement of the scroll by the codex. The emperor Constantine, for example, requested Eusebius of Caesarea 'to order fifty copies of the sacred Scriptures, to be written on prepared parchment in a legible manner, and in a convenient, portable form, by professional transcribers' (*Vit. Const.* 4. 36).

(iii) *Exceptions*

The papyrus codex and parchment rotulus

Generally speaking, papyrus was used in scroll format, and parchment in codex format, but there were exceptions. Parchment was also used for scrolls, as in the Pergamum Library and in the Dead Sea Scrolls. And papyrus was adapted to the codex format, although its loss of suppleness over time made it increasingly difficult to turn the pages. In papyrus codices, horizontally and vertically oriented pages were organized to face each other.

The use of the scroll, meanwhile, did not die out completely, but survived, as the *rotulus*, into the Middle Ages. Rather than being made of sheets glued side by side, the *rotulus* was created by gluing or sewing parchment sheets top to bottom, and was unrolled vertically rather than horizontally. It was used primarily for storing records that were suited to this kind of format, such as genealogies and pedigrees, year-by-year chronicles, or lists of saints. *Exultet* rolls contained liturgical texts on one side and illustrations, upside down, on the other, so that when the texts were read in church, the congregation would be able to see the illustration on the other side.

Exotic materials

In addition to the use of papyrus, wax tablets, and parchment, other, more exotic materials were used for documents that palaeographers occasionally have to deal with. These include wood, as manifested in the Vindolanda tablets and the *Tablettes Albertini*, and slate, as seen in documents originating in Visigothic Spain.

7.3 PRODUCING A CODEX

Most manuscripts produced in the early Christian period and later were not original works but rather copies of earlier works, such as books of scripture or works of esteemed patristic authors. Creating a manuscript from scratch was a time-, labour-, and resource-intensive business.

7.3.1 Personnel

During the early Christian centuries, documents could be written either by professional copyists (scribes) or, very often, by the person who intended to use the document. Until the third century, it was common for Christians to copy their own documents. According to Eusebius of Caesarea (*Hist. eccl.* 6. 23; Haines-Eitzen 2000, ch. 2), for example, Origen used as copyists 'girls who were skilled in elegant writing'. There was a great demand for copies of Christian texts, exacerbated by spates of persecutions when scriptures were confiscated by government authorities, resulting in the need to re-create, re-copy, and re-circulate new copies. But once Christianity became politically acceptable in the fourth century, and increasingly large numbers of well-to-do individuals converted, the production and reproduction of Christian texts became a major occupation of professional and amateur scribes alike. A professional scribe (*scriba, notarius,* or *amanuensis*) was paid according to the quality of the work and by the number of lines. During the Middle Ages, much of the copying of Christian texts took place in the *scriptoria* (writing rooms) of monasteries and episcopal chanceries, and was performed by ecclesiastical scribes skilled in manuscript production. The production of an entire codex was a time-consuming affair requiring personnel with many different skills, including not only scribes, but also rubricators (heading-makers), illuminators, binders, lectors (readers), correctors, and librarians.

7.3.2 Pre-production Issues

When a codex book was created, several considerations had to be borne in mind before the copying process could begin. How large would the pages be? How many pages of writing material would be required? The number of pages would be determined both by the size of the page and by the size of the margins on each page (wide margins would leave room for comments and additions, small margins would make most efficient use of the parchment). The gatherings were arranged ahead of time, but were not actually sewn together until after the pages had been written, meaning that much planning had to be given to how the pages would be laid out. Decisions had to be made about the placement of text, headings, and illustrations, and about the number of columns, lines per page, and characters per line.

(i) *Size considerations*

Parchment codices were made in standardized sizes that were based upon the size of a sheep. A single sheet created from an average-sized sheepskin was a folio. Folding a folio in half created a bi-folium of four pages, front and back. Gatherings made from bi-folia are said to be in 'folio' format. Smaller-sized books could be created from cutting folia in half, and then folding these half-folia. This created books in 'quarto' format (four leaves from each folio sheet). Likewise, quarto sheets could be cut in half and folded to create books in 'octavo' format (eight leaves per folio sheet). Because, on average, all sheep were a standard size, 'folio' (roughly 12 by 19 inches), 'quarto' (9 1/2 by 12 inches), and 'octavo' (6 by 9 1/2 inches) formats likewise were (and continue to be) of similar sizes everywhere. Even smaller page sizes could be created by making additional folds, or just by using parchment scraps.

The choice of which size to use was often determined by the type of document being copied. Books considered to be of greater importance, or for public use, usually merited a larger format. For example, the largest extant early biblical manuscript, the fourth-century Greek *Codex Sinaiticus*, weighs in at a whopping 43 by 38 cm (17.2 by 15.2 inches). Other extant fifth- and sixth-century biblical manuscripts average about 27 by 20 cm (11 by 8 inches). Pocket editions for private use, on the other hand, could be tiny: a fifth-century Greek gospel measures only 67 mm (2.6 inches) on a side, and the written space of a small Latin copy of the gospel of John of *c.* 500 CE measures only 71 by 51 mm (2.8 by 2.0 inches) (McGurk 1994: 7–9).

(ii) *Availability of writing material*

The actual production of a manuscript book began with the collection of a sufficient amount of writing material. A large book in folio format, such as a complete Bible, could require 1,000 pages, or 250 folia, that is, the skins of 250 sheep. This made book production a very expensive business.

Palimpsests

If fresh parchment was not available, as was often the case, then obsolete or worn-out books could be recycled. The existing writing was laboriously washed (with a mixture of oat bran and milk) or scraped (with powdered pumice) off the pages, and a new layer of writing laid down atop the old. This created a 'palimpsest' (from the Greek, meaning 'scraped again'). During the sixth and seventh centuries in particular, there was a great trade in reused parchment in the Latin West. The cannibalization of old manuscripts for writing material became so endemic that Byzantine church councils forbade the destruction of good copies of scriptural or patristic documents for this purpose. But the practice continued. Many of the literary works of classical antiquity survive only as palimpsests, such as a fourth-century copy of Cicero's *De republica*, written over in the seventh century by Augustine's *On the Psalms* (*Vaticanus Latinus* 5757; See Fig. 7.1). Some documents even survive as double palimpsests, as in the case of a fifth-century (or later) copy of Granius Licinianus which was overwritten in the sixth century (or later) with a Latin grammatical treatise and then overwritten in the eleventh century with a Syriac translation of the sermons of John Chrysostom (British Library, Add. MS 17212). In the nineteenth century, scholars seeking to read palimpsests attacked (and often destroyed) them with chemicals such as tincture of gall or ammonium hydrosulphate. More recently, non-destructive methods, such as ultraviolet light or digital imaging, have proved more successful in reading the underwriting.

(iii) *Surface preparation: ruling*

To enable a scribe to align the text, a parchment sheet was ruled horizontally (ruling lines) and vertically (bounding lines) with impressed lines made with a blunt metal or bone stylus drawn along a rule, a method known as 'hardpoint'. In order to duplicate ruling lines within a manuscript and avoid re-measuring every leaf, it was common to place pin-pricks through a stack of leaves and then to 'connect the dots' on each leaf. As of the twelfth century, ruling lines were also made with a metal point, a writing implement with a metal tip (such as lead) that left trace marks on a document. Ink was also used for ruling later in the Middle Ages.

Fig. 7.1 Palimpsest of Cicero, *De Republica*. The large fourth-century uncial letters of the Cicero text, the primary script, lie underneath the seventh-century letters of the secondary script, Augustine's *On the Psalms*.

Source: Steffens 1903: pl. 13.

7.3.3 Writing the Text

(i) *Writing implements and inks*

In antiquity, the writing implements for both papyrus and parchment were a reed pen (Greek *kalamos*, Latin *calamus*) and black ink. In the sixth century the reed was generally replaced, especially for writing on parchment, by the quill pen. The quill was taken from the long flight feather of a bird, often a goose. Indeed, the word pen derives from *penna*, Latin for feather. The nib, or point of the pen, could be cut with a knife to produce different kinds of lines for different kinds of writing: thin points were generally better for informal cursive scripts, and thicker ones for formal book hands. Black ink was initially made from a mixture of carbon (often obtained from soot), gum, and water. After about 300 CE, black ink made by adding green vitriol (ferrous sulfate) to tannin obtained from gall nuts (often oak galls) and carbon came into use. The sometimes corrosive action caused by the tannic acid and the oxidation of the iron gave ink its Latin name, *encaustum* ('burnt in'), a reference also to its indelibility. This permanent, water-resistant ink, which over time faded to a rust brown colour, became the standard European black ink until the nineteenth

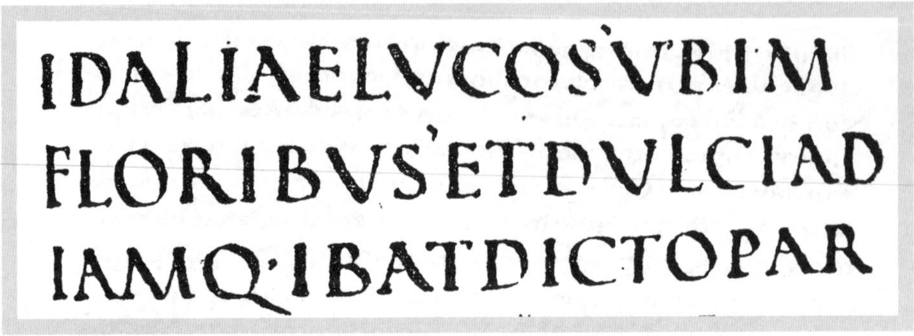

IDALIAELVCOSVBIM
FLORIBVS'ETDVLCIAD
IAMQ·IBATDICTOPAR

Fig. 7.2 *Capitalis quadrata* used in a fourth- or fifth-century copy of Vergil's *Aeneid.*

Source: Thompson 1894: 185.

century. Red ink, made from cinnabar (mercury sulphide) or minium (lead oxide, or 'red lead'), was used for titles and headings, which had the generic name 'rubrics' (from Latin *rubrica*, or red earth). For deluxe documents, purple (from the shell of the murex), gold, or silver ink could be used on purple-dyed parchment to create a *codex purpureus*, such as the sixth-century Rossano Gospels, or the *Codex Argenteus*, a sixth-century Gothic Bible.

Painted illuminations and historiated initials (large initial letters containing a painting) could be applied with brushes made from frayed reeds or animal hairs. Paints were made from animal, vegetable, and mineral compounds mixed with a binding medium such as egg white. Along with red, made from the minerals discussed above, blue could be made from azurite, and green from malachite (both forms of copper carbonate), yellow from saffron, and white from white lead (lead carbonate). Some of these compounds were quite toxic, and great care had to be taken in their use.

(ii) *Sections of a codex*

The contents of a codex had several sections in addition to the actual text. Some manuscripts were preceded by a table of contents, either of different works in a single manuscript or of the sections of a single work. Individual documents and sections within works were often preceded by a heading (title) and descriptive lemma, often written in red letters (rubrics). The first words of a text proper are known as the *incipit*, and the concluding words as the *explicit*. After the *explicit* sometimes comes a colophon, or subscription, personal comments of the scribe perhaps giving his or her name, the date, or expressing relief at having finally completed the task: e.g. 'Finit. Gratias Deo'. Marginal or intertextual notes known as *scholia* (or *marginalia*) could be added at any time during or after the initial writing process.

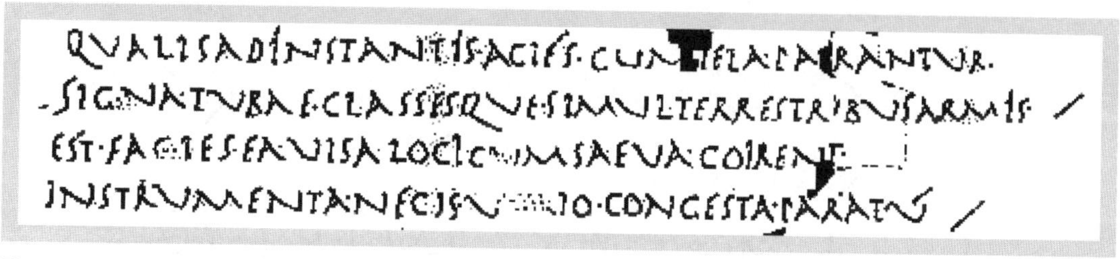

Fig. 7.3 Rustic capitals used in the *Carmen de bello Actiaco*, pre–79 CE from Herculaneum. Note the slashes used as paragraph punctuation.

Source: Steffens 1910: pl. 3.

(iii) *Writing the text*

Scripts

One of the primary activities of palaeographers is the identification of different types of scripts, which not only allows a text to be read, but also, very often, helps a text to be dated and localized. In Greek and Latin antiquity, there were initially two basic types of script: block capital and cursive. Capitals (or maiuscules, or 'upper case') were derived from the block letters used in inscriptions, and were used for formal documents, such as literary texts, intended to be permanent. They were thus the first 'book hands'. Capital letters were inscribed (with few exceptions) as separate letters between two actual or imaginary parallel lines so that all the letters are the same height. The most severe style of capital script, known as *capitalis quadrata*, *monumentalis*, or *elegans*, was modelled directly on lapidary capitals, and used curved lines only where the letter form requires them (as in Latin O or S), often with serifs. *Quadrata* was used for the most deluxe editions (Fig. 7.2). *Capitalis rustica*, or rustic capital, on the other hand, could be written rather more quickly, with rather slender, wavy strokes (Fig. 7.3; Thompson 1894: 183).

Cursive, or 'running', style, on the other hand, was a shorthand way of writing the capital letters, and was used for everyday, non-literary documents, such as letters, accounts, and receipts (Fig. 7.4). It used ascenders that extended above the bodies of the letters and descenders that fell below. It was varied in style and notoriously illegible, as attested in a passage from Plautus's play the *Pseudolus* (1. 25–30) from the late third century BCE:

PSEUDOLUS. By Pollux, I believe that no one but the Sibyl could read these letters; no one else could interpret them.

CALIDORUS. Why do you speak negatively about these lovely letters and lovely tablets written with a lovely hand?

PSEUDOLUS. Or, I beg you by Hercules, do they reflect the hands of a chicken? For certainly a chicken has written them.

Cursive capitals developed into miniscule letters (lower case) called 'new Roman cursive' during the Roman imperial period (Fig. 7.5). Miniscule cursive made use

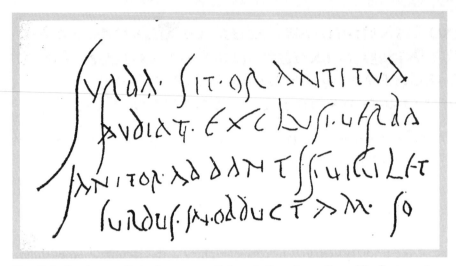

Fig. 7.4 Cursive capitals from a wall inscription from Pompeii, first century CE, with lines from Ovid (*Amores*, 1. 8. 97) and Propertius (4. 47), beginning 'SVRDA SIT ORANTI TVA'.

Source: Thompson 1894: 206.

of ligatures (connected letters), and can be even more difficult to read than cursive capitals.

Around the third century CE, a new form of book hand, uncial, developed (Fig. 7.6). It was comprised primarily of maiuscules that made greater use of rounded forms (as seen in the m) along with some rather miniscule forms (as with e, h, and q), both of which made the writing process quicker and more efficient.

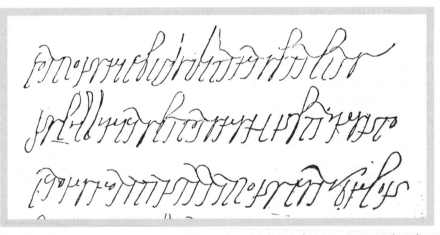

Fig. 7.5 New Roman cursive used in an imperial rescript on papyrus dated to the fifth century, beginning 'portionem ipsi debitam resarcire'.

Source: Thompson 1894: 212.

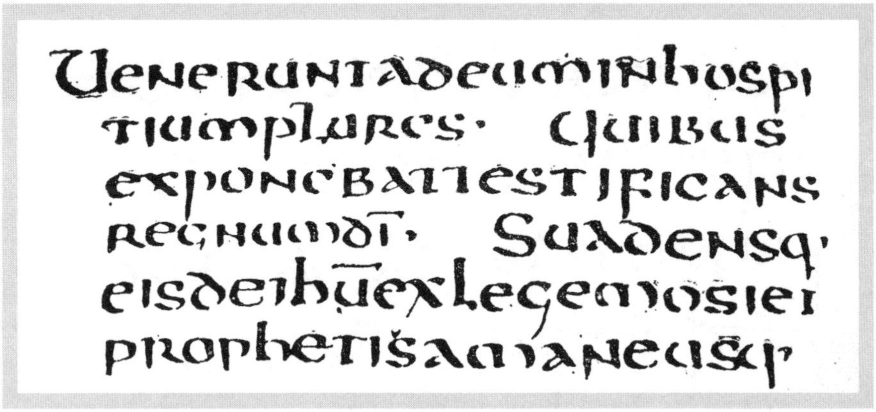

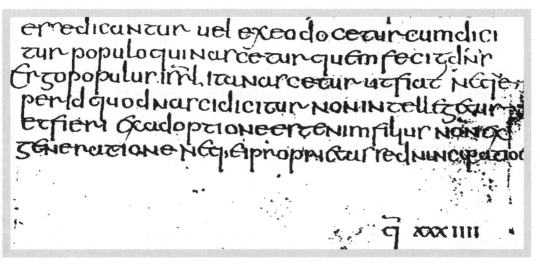

Fig. 7.6 An uncial copy of the book of Acts, chapter 28, from the mid-sixth century.

Source: Thompson 1894: 194.

Uncial then remained a standard Latin book hand until the eighth century CE and even later.

Toward the end of the fifth century, another book hand, known either as half-uncial or semi-uncial, developed (Fig. 7.7). It retained some uncial characteristics, such as rounded letter forms, the capital letters F, N, and T, and the uncial forms for E, H, and U/V. But the other letters were minuscules, drawn from the cursive tradition, with ascenders and descenders. There was also greater use of ligatures, such as N-T or L-I combinations, all of which made for greater writing speed.

Fig. 7.7 Half-uncial copy of the *In Constantium imperatorem* of Hilary of Poitiers, dating to 509/510 CE, with quaternion marking at bottom right.

Source: Steffens 1903: no. 17.

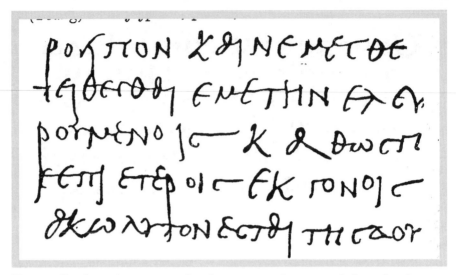

Fig. 7.8 Greek cursive papyrus dated to 355 CE; the manumission of a slave.

Source: Thompson 1894: 142.

Greek scripts developed similarly to Latin. The same capital (maiuscule) letters used in inscriptions were also used on papyrus, although not to nearly as great an extent as in Latin. With a few exceptions, Greek cursive used the Greek maiuscule letters, making use of ligatures that allowed the pen to remain on the page (Fig. 7.8). A few letters, such as alpha, took a miniscule form. Greek cursive was used not only for administrative documents, but also for literary texts to a greater extent than in Latin.

Greek uncial, with rounded letters, was introduced during the Hellenistic period (third century BCE and later), the most characteristic forms being the lower-case alpha, delta, epsilon, mu, xi, lunate sigma, and omega (Fig. 7.9). Uncial then served as the primary Greek book hand until the appearance of Greek miniscule in the ninth century, which also used the characteristic Greek accents and breathing marks (Fig. 7.10).

The weight of tradition and authority of the Roman Empire created a uniformity of scripts throughout the Greek and Latin worlds. But after the fall of the Roman Empire, a great diversity of scripts appeared in the Latin West. Although uncial and semi-uncial remained the standard book hands, various kinds of cursive evolved in the different national areas, including Visigothic in Spain, Merovingian in France, Insular in Anglo-Saxon England, and Beneventan in Lombard Italy. In the Carolingian period (eighth–ninth centuries), a standardized miniscule emerged, Caroline miniscule, which then replaced uncial as the standard book hand, although uncial continued to be used as a display hand for headings and titles (Fig. 7.11). Subsequently, in the late eleventh century, a group of scripts generically referred to as 'Gothic' (a term also used to refer to a new architectural style)

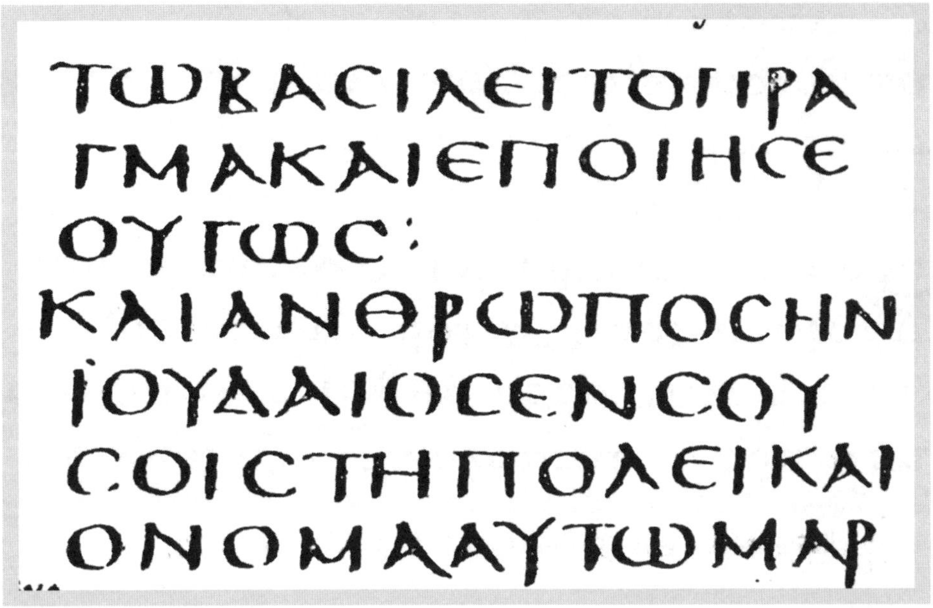

TⲱⲔⲀⲤⲒⲖⲈⲒⲦⲞⲅⲒⲢⲀ
ⲅⲘⲀⲔⲀⲒⲈⲠⲞⲒⲎⲤⲈ
ⲞⲨⲅⲱⲤ·
ⲔⲀⲒⲀⲚⲐⲢⲱⲠⲞⲤⲎⲚ
ⲒⲞⲨⲆⲀⲒⲞⲤⲈⲚⲤⲞⲨ
ⲤⲞⲒⲤⲦⲎⲠⲞⲖⲈⲒⲔⲀⲒ
ⲞⲚⲞⲘⲀⲀⲨⲦⲱⲘⲀⲢ

Fig. 7.9 Greek uncial from the *Codex Sinaiticus*, a copy of the Septuagint dating to the fourth century CE and one of the two oldest surviving copies of the Greek Bible.

Source: Thompson 1894: 150.

emerged in northern France. And even later, during the Renaissance, a rounded 'humanistic' script also was used as a book hand. It eventually developed into the modern 'roman' typeface, whereas the angular cursive used for business documents developed into modern 'italic' type.

Writing and reading aids

The writing and reading of manuscripts was facilitated by the use of stichometry, colometry, punctuation, and abbreviations.

a. Stichometry and colometry Greek and Latin manuscripts were written in *scripta continua*, without any spaces between the words. Various methods were introduced that permitted texts to be broken down into smaller units, in order to create smaller logical units, to facilitate a more euphonius delivery, and simply to count lines and navigate through the text. In antiquity, the length of literary works was measured by a unit called the 'stichos', the length of an average Homeric or Vergilian hexameter line, about 16 syllables or 36 letters. The total number of *stichoi* was often noted at the end of a work. The count of *stichoi* was used to determine a scribe's wages and the price of a book; to allow referencing of different sections of books (which were numbered in the margin in units of 50 or 100); and to help ensure against later additions or deletions (rather like a computer parity check). Josephus, for example, claimed that his *Antiquities of the Jews* contained 60,000 *stichoi*. The use of the

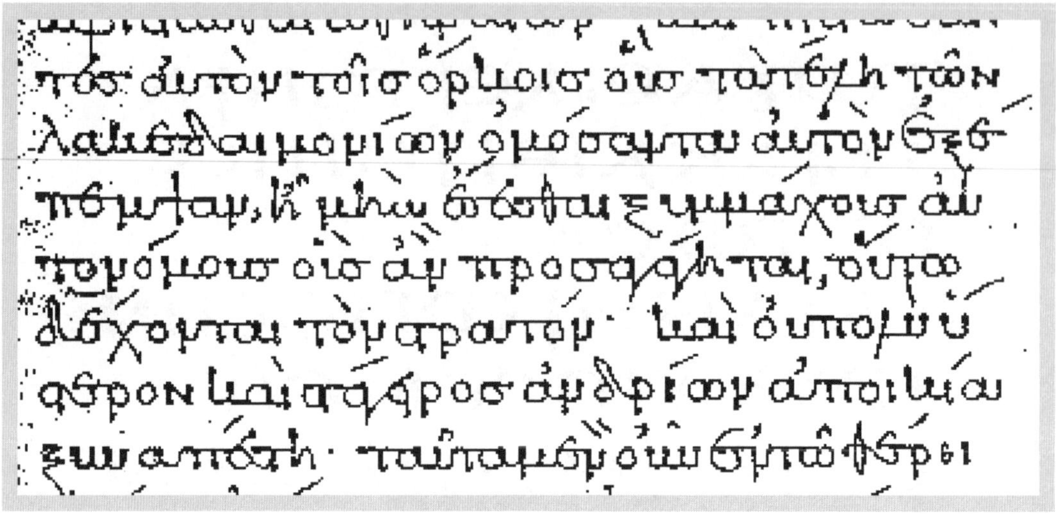

Fig. 7.10 Greek miniscule, a tenth-century copy of Thucydides.

Source: Thompson 1912: pl. 57.

stichos (Latin *versus*) in the marketplace is attested in Diocletian's Edict on Max-imum Prices of 302 CE that also gave the respective values of book hand and cursive (*Edictum de pretiis* 6. 41–3): 'For a copyist, for a hundred lines (*versus*) of best writ-ing, 25 *denarii*; for a hundred lines of next-quality writing, 20 *denarii*; for a tablet-writer, for the writing of a letter or of account books, for a hundred lines, 10 *denarii*.'

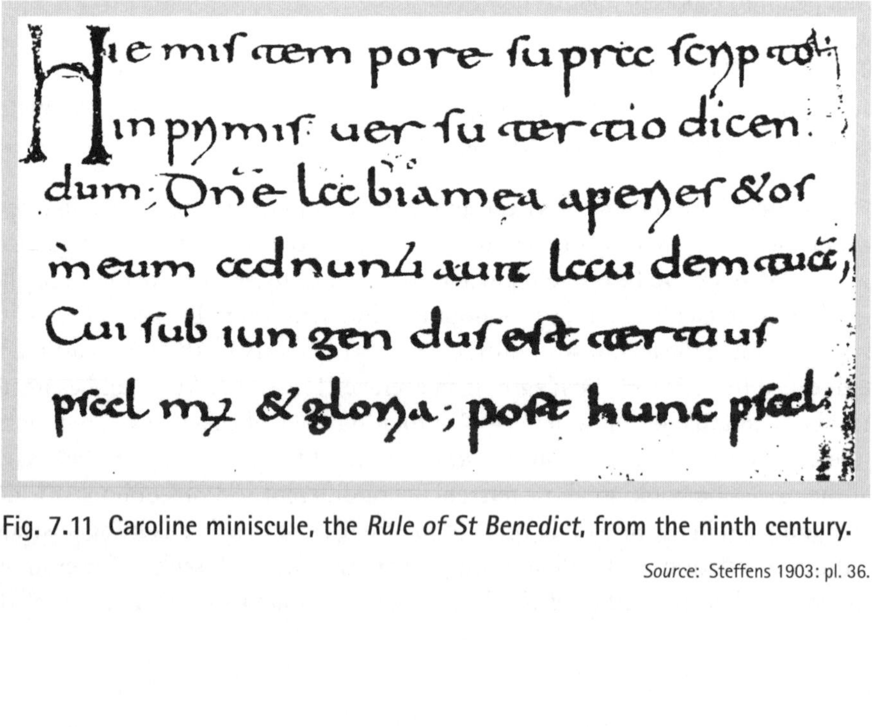

Fig. 7.11 Caroline miniscule, the *Rule of St Benedict*, from the ninth century.

Source: Steffens 1903: pl. 36.

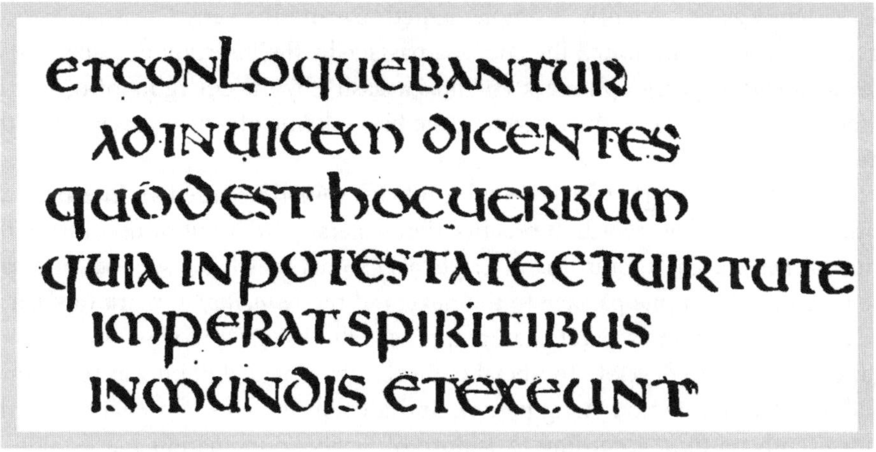

ETCONLoQUEBANTUR
ADINUICEM DICENTES
quoDEST hocuERBUM
quia INPOTESTATEETUIRTUTE
IMPERAT SPIRITIBUS
INMUNDIS ETEXEUNT

Fig. 7.12 A section of the seventh-century uncial *Codex Amiatinus,* the best extant example of the Vulgate, showing divisions into *cola* and *commata.*

Source: Thompson 1894: 195.

When copying verse texts, it was common to begin stanzas or lines with a capital letter and often on a separate line, a practice that was also used in the biblical poetic books (Job, Psalms, Proverbs, Ecclesiastes, and Song of Solomon). A related system of parsing lengthy texts into smaller units, and an alternative to using punctuation marks, is known as colometry, which consisted of breaking texts up into *cola* and *commata,* sense-lines of clauses and phrases that assisted the reader not only in understanding a text but also in inserting pauses and inflections in the appropriate places (Fig. 7.12). This system was utilized in the Vulgate by Jerome, who observed:

No one seeing the Prophets set out in meter would think that they were constrained by the Hebrew language, and he would have a rather similar opinion about the Psalms, or the works of Solomon, but one would see that which generally happens in Demosthenes and Cicero, who surely wrote in prose and not in verses, that they are written in cola and commata. We, likewise, planning for the utility of readers, have defined a new interpretation with a new kind of writing.

(*Praefatio in Isaiam,* PL 28. 771)

On a manuscript page, *cola* began at the left margin and *commata* were indented a space or two. The disadvantage of this system is that it was rather wasteful of manuscript space.

b. Punctuation Another way of breaking up a continuous text involved the use of punctuation marks. Said to have been invented by Aristophanes of Byzantium (*c.* 200 BCE) as an aid for barbarians trying to learn Greek, they were intended to assist readers in parsing a text during oral delivery. His marks consisted of a point inserted at different levels of a text line to represent the length of a pause. But this system was not extensively implemented. During the early Christian period, Greek manuscripts indicated the end of a passage by the insertion of a space or of a *paragraphos* or paragraph mark (such as a slash), by the enlarging of the initial letter of a new passage, or by extending the first full line of a new passage into the left margin.

Early Latin texts, especially epigraphical texts, sometimes used an interpunct, a raised dot, to separate words, a practice that generally went out of use during the imperial period. Early Latin manuscripts also sometimes left a space to indicate the transition from one passage to the next, and the *paragraphos* mark (a slash in the *De bello Actiaco*) to separate paragraphs was also used. Otherwise, punctuation marks were slow to develop. In uncial manuscripts, a medial point was sometimes used to indicate a period (long pause), and a colon the end of a chapter. In the mid-seventh century, according to Isidore of Seville, punctuation marks akin to those of Aristophanes were used by Latin writers to mark out the *cola* and *commata*: 'Punctuation is a form for distinguishing meaning through the use of *cola*, *commata*, and periods. . . . The first mark is called the *subdistinctio*, the same as the *comma*. The *media distinctio* follows it, the same as the *cola*. The *ultima distinctio*, which closes the entire thought, is the same as the period' (*Etym.* 1. 20). The *comma* marked a place to take a breath, the *cola* a logical division of a thought, and the period the end of a thought (sentence). The marks were indicated by a *punctus* (point) placed at the bottom, middle, and top of the line respectively. By the same time other marks also were in use, such as a semicolon for a longer pause, and a virgule ('⌐') for a period, or full stop. The question mark appeared in the ninth century in both Greek and Latin texts (Thompson 1894: 70–1). These methods for parsing texts ultimately gave rise to the modern division of scripture into verses.

c. **Abbreviations and shorthand** Several methods were used to save space in a manuscript. In Greek manuscripts, for example, letters were sometimes superposed one above the other. Nearly all Greek and Latin scripts made use of some degree of abbreviation. In Christian texts, the earliest and most commonly abbreviated words were the *nomina sacra*, or sacred words, which were contracted so that only the initial and final letter or letters were printed. In Greek, for example, *theos* was abbreviated *ths*, whereas in Latin, *dominus* was abbreviated *dns*. A special sign was the Tetragrammaton, an abbreviation of the name of God based on the four Hebrew letters spelling the name of God. For marginal notations in particular, Tironian notes, a form of tachygraphy (shorthand) used in the Roman period, continued to be used in the Middle Ages. Tironian notes were a form of linked, compressed cursive combined with abbreviations (such as *p* for *primus*).

7.4 Post-production Issues

Once a manuscript had been produced, its history was only beginning. It then had to be preserved, used, and its contents transmitted to future generations.

7.4.1 Binding

Once a lengthy document had been copied, the gatherings were usually bound together, often but not always with boards on the front and back for protective purposes. The gatherings were sewn on to leather cords perpendicular to the spine of the book. For a permanent binding, the loose ends of these cords were then threaded through holes drilled into boards on front and back and secured by pegs. The boards and spine were then covered by damp leather, folded and glued over the edges of the boards (the 'turn-ins'), that dried to a tight fit, with the cords showing through on the spine. A pastedown leaf, often made from fragments of discarded manuscripts, could be pasted on the inside of the boards for cosmetic purposes. It was also common to insert a guard leaf, often cannibalized from a discarded manuscript, between the boards and the manuscript, and to use discarded manuscript scraps in other parts of the binding as well. A simpler 'limp binding' of parchment or fabric could also be used, but did not protect the volume nearly as well.

7.4.2 Storage and preservation

Books represented wealth, not only because they were very labour-intensive but also because of the material resources used in their construction. As treasures, books were often stored with the other valuables of a church, monastery, or household. In antiquity, the great libraries of Alexandria and Pergamum assembled myriads of papyrus scrolls. Many of these works eventually made their way, in one form or another, to Constantinople during the Byzantine period. Greek patristic and classical manuscripts were also preserved in libraries such as those of Mt Sinai and Mt Athos. In the fifteenth century many works of Greek antiquity and Christianity then travelled to the West before and after the capture of Constantinople by the Turks in 1453 CE. The primary repositories of books during the western Middle Ages were monastic libraries, the largest of which could contain more than a thousand volumes. Some of the most significant early monastic and cathedral libraries, which served both as copying centres and repositories, included Vivarium, Nonantola, Monte Cassino, and Bobbio in Italy; St Gallen in Switzerland; Luxeuil, Fleury, Cluny, Lyon, St-Riquier, Tours, and Corbie in France; Fulda, Reichenau, Corvey, Lorsch, and Sponheim in Germany; and Iona, Lindesfarne, and Jarrow in the British

Isles. Were it not for these scriptoria and libraries, most of the literature of classical antiquity and the early Christian period would not have survived.

7.5 THE PURPOSE OF PALAEOGRAPHY AND CODICOLOGY

Not a single ancient or early Christian text survives in an original (or 'autograph') copy. Even papyrus documents are copies. Except for the case of a *codex unicus*, a copy of an ancient work that survives only in a single copy, ancient works survive in multiple manuscript copies. Different manuscript copies of the same text invariably have different readings for some of the same words or passages. How is the scholar to know which reading is the 'correct' one? The primary purpose of palaeography and codicology as disciplines is to assist in establishing the earliest and most authoritative versions of ancient texts.

7.5.1 Technical Considerations

Much of a palaeographer's work is very technical. A knowledge of scripts and abbreviations can do much to help to transcribe (establish a full, unabbreviated text) and date a manuscript, for even scripts with a long lifetime, such as uncial, exhibit different characteristics at different times. The date of a manuscript can also be established by patterns of abbreviation and punctuation, by folio and quaternion markings, by binding type, and by a multitude of other considerations. Palaeographers also identify changes of hands in manuscript copying or the later appearance of new hands, as by later correctors or commentators, for each scribe had his or her own unique style of handwriting. Even from fragmentary pages, a codicologist can often estimate the length of the line and number of lines per page in a manuscript, especially if margins are preserved, and this in turn can help to reconstruct the length of a lost text. A palaeographer can also help to identify forged documents.

7.5.2 Textual Analysis and Criticism

The actual work of creating modern editions of ancient works lies in the sphere of textual analysis and criticism. Textual critics attempt to re-create, as much as possible, the original texts that lie behind the surviving manuscripts, and can take different approaches in doing so. One school of thought attempts to reconstruct the original 'edition' of a work, however that is defined (ancient works were not 'published' in the modern sense, and from the moment of their composition most ancient texts were in a constant state of revision); another school of thought attempts to establish what the author intended to be the authoritative text.

The primary problem that confronts textual critics is that surviving manuscripts almost certainly contain words or passages that were not in the original text (known as the 'archetype'). In the case where there are many manuscript versions of the same document (the New Testament, for example, survives in more than 5,300 Greek manuscripts alone dating from the third to the sixteenth century), textual critics attempt to classify manuscripts in order to determine which are the most reliable. One method for assigning manuscripts to the same class is by noting common errors that appear in all of them and must have originated in a single exemplar (original copy). Textual critics then create a stemma, or family, of manuscript classes that allows them to postulate an archetype from which all of the surviving manuscripts of a text have descended. Sometimes, or even often, the oldest manuscript does not preserve the most authoritative text, for a much later manuscript might in fact preserve a copy of a very early manuscript. The archetype is not necessarily the 'original' edition, but is the closest that editors can get to it based on the manuscript evidence. Textual critics also often suggest emendations to a surviving text that are not preserved in any of the manuscript readings, but which seem to an editor to fit the literary, grammatical, or historical context of the text better than the manuscript readings.

(i) *Transmission and errors*

Palaeographers can assist textual critics not only by deciphering manuscript scripts, but also by identifying ways in which errors can creep into manuscript copies. The very copying process introduced many opportunities for error, and the proliferation of copies over the centuries created opportunities for the propagation of erroneous readings.

Unintentional or accidental errors could occur in many ways. There were several kinds of sight errors. Letters with a similar appearance (e.g. in Greek uncial, epsilon, theta, omicron, and lunate sigma; or gamma, tau, and pi) could be confused. In 'permutation', a scribe transposed letters, syllables, or words because of bad light, bad eyesight, or a hard-to-read copy. *Parablepsis* ('glancing to the side') occurred when the scribe's eye did not return to the correct place on the page. This could lead to the error of haplography (omission) resulting from homoteleuton (two adjacent lines ending with the same word or letters). On the other hand, 'dittography' (duplication) occurred when a scribe re-copied the same section of a manuscript. Memory lapses during the split second between reading and copying could result in the substitution of synonyms or variations in the sequence of words. Other unintentional errors resulted from hearing errors, when a text was being dictated by a lector or when a scribe was reading it aloud. Both Greek and Latin had many homophones, different letters or combinations of letters that, when read, sounded alike, such as (in Greek) omega and omicron or omicron-upsilon and upsilon. The error of 'itacism' resulted in Greek because, as of the fourth century, the vowels eta, iota, and upsilon, and the diphtongs ei, oi, and ui, were all pronounced like long e in English.

Changes to an original text could also be intentional or purposeful, introduced by a scribe who wanted to improve a text. Scribes sometimes attempted to correct spelling or grammar. Doing so could result in hypercorrection, the 'correcting' of non-existent mistakes, such as adding an 'h' to the beginning of a word on the assumption that an unpronounced 'h' had dropped out. This kind of error was mentioned by Jerome in a letter to a friend who had sent several scribes to copy Jerome's works: 'If you encounter any errors, you ought to blame the copyists, who write not what they see but what they understand, and when they attempt to emend the errors of others they display their own' (*Ep.* 71. 5). In Christian manuscripts, another kind of intentional alteration could involve making doctrinal or theological 'corrections' to an objectionable passage.

(ii) *Additional aids to textual critics*

Documents in other languages

Documents were also copied in a multitude of other scripts in many other languages, too numerous to be considered in detail here, but which include Syriac, Samaritan, Coptic, Old Nubian, Meroitic, Ethiopic, Aramaic, Georgian, Armenian, Arabic, Persian, and Gothic, whose testimony can often augment the evidence of the Greek, Hebrew, and Latin manuscripts. Syriac, Coptic, and Samaritan manuscripts, for example, can preserve alternative scriptural traditions. And Arabic manuscripts, in particular, preserve translations of Greek documents that no longer survive.

New discoveries

One of the most exciting aspects of the palaeographer's work is the possibility of the discovery of new texts to study. Previously unknown texts can be found in the bindings of medieval manuscripts (such as part of the second book of *De reditu suo* of Rutilius Namatianus); in palimpsests (such as the new letters of Augustine); preserved in Renaissance or early modern copies of now-lost documents (such as the new Augustinian sermons); or as ancient texts, usually papyri (such as the Dead Sea Scrolls), preserved in the desiccated climates of Egypt and Palestine.

(iii) *Future directions*

Many opportunities for new work in palaeography and codicology as related to the history of early Christianity are offered by the application of computer and scientific technology. Potentially exciting use of scientific analyses has shed light on the development of early biblical and patristic texts. Modern scientific methods permit the evaluation and processing of existing and newly discovered texts that are in a bad state of preservation—the recently, processed Judas Gospel, which had disintegrated into more than 1,000 fragments and for which radiocarbon dating was used to prove that the papyrus on which it was written dated to between 220 and 340 CE, being a good case in point. Another example of the results that can follow from meticulous detective work and restoration is provided by the recent edition of Philodemus's 'On Piety', re-created from a carbonized papyrus scroll found in Pompeii. New techniques of restoring and preserving ancient documents promise to make other biblical and patristic texts available to the scholarly community as well.

Manuscript pages and fragments can now be preserved using ultra-high resolution digital images that can also be made available on the internet, so as to make documents much more accessible than in the past. Once texts have been digitized, they can be categorized and analysed in any number of ways. Computer software can be used to identify similar scripts used in different manuscripts. Manuscript tables of contents can be collated and compared to identify similar transmission processes. Thousands of texts can be compared electronically for use in studies of authorship. Electronic publication venues, such as the 'Digital Medievalist', <http://www.digitalmedievalist.org/>, permit the dissemination of information about new advances in digital techniques to a worldwide audience.

Techniques of biological research are also beginning to be used to provide new insights into ancient and medieval texts. Computer programs used to chart the evolution of changes in DNA structure can also be applied to creating evolutionary trees of manuscript text transmission. And, most recently, it has even been suggested that DNA analysis can be applied to identify the source of and interrelationships among ancient manuscript materials derived from animal hides.

BIBLIOGRAPHY

ALAND, J., and ALAND, B. (1989), *Der Text des Neuen Testaments: Einführung in die wissenschaftlichen Ausgaben sowie in Theorie und Praxis der modernen Textkritik*, 2nd edn. (Stuttgart: Deutsche Bibelgesellschaft); 1st edn., trans. E. F. Rhodes, *The Text of the New Testament: An Introduction to the Critical Editions and to the Theory and Practice of Modern Textual Criticism* (Grand Rapids, Mich: Eerdmans, 1987).

BARBOUR, R. (1981), *Greek Literary Hands, A.D. 400–1600* (Oxford: Clarendon Press).

BEIT-ARIE, M. (1993), *The Makings of the Medieval Hebrew Book: Studies in Palaeography and Codicology* (Jerusalem: Magnes Press).

BISCHOFF, B. (1986), *Paläographie des römischen Altertums und des abendlandischen Mittelalters*, 2nd edn. (Berlin: E. Schmidt; first published 1979); trans. Daibhi o Croinin and

D. Ganz, *Latin Palaeography: Antiquity and the Middle Ages* (Cambridge: Cambridge University Press, 1990).

BOYLE, L. (1984), *Medieval Latin Palaeography: A Bibliographical Introduction* (Toronto: University of Toronto Press).

BRASWELL, L. NICHOLS (1981), *Western Manuscripts from Classical Antiquity to the Renaissance: A Handbook* (New York: Garland Publishing Co.).

BROWN, M. P. (1990), *A Guide to Western Historical Scripts from Antiquity to 1600* (Toronto: University of Toronto Press).

CAPPELLI, A. (1985), *Lexicon abbreviaturarum* (Milan: Hoepli, 1912); trans. D. Heimann and R. Kay as *The Elements of Abbreviations in Medieval Latin Palaeography* (Milan: Hoepli).

CAVALLO, G. (1967), *Ricerche sulla maiuscola biblica* (Florence: Le Monnier).

—— and MAEHLER, H. (1987), *Greek Bookhands of the Early Byzantine Period, A.D. 300–800* (London: University of London, Institute of Classical Studies).

DE MONTFAUCON, B. (1708), *Palaeographia Graeca* (Paris).

DEROLEZ, A. (1979), *Les catalogues de bibliotheques* (Turnhout: Brepols).

DILLER, A. (1983), *Studies in Greek Manuscript Tradition* (Amsterdam: Hakkert).

GRONINGEN, B. A. VAN (1963), *Short Manual of Greek Palaeography*, 3rd rev. edn. (Leiden: Sijthoff).

HAINES-EITZEN, K. (2000), *Guardians of Letters: Literacy, Power, and the Transmitters of Early Christian Literature* (New York: Oxford University Press).

HARLFINGER, D. (1980) (ed.), *Griechische Kodikologie und Textüberlieferung* (Darmstadt: Wissenschaftliche Buchgesellschaft).

HUNGER, H. (1954), *Studien zur griechischen Paläographie* (Vienna: Hollinek).

LEWIS, N. (1974), *Papyrus in Classical Antiquity* (Oxford: Oxford University Press).

LOWE, E. A. (1934–66) (eds.), *Codices latini antiquiores: A Palaeographical Guide to Latin Manuscripts prior to the Ninth Century* (Oxford: Clarendon Press).

MABILLON, J. (1681), *De re diplomatica* (Paris).

MCGURK, P. (1994), 'The Oldest Manuscripts of the Latin Bible', in R. Gameson (ed.), *The Early Medieval Bible: Its Production, Decoration and Use* (Cambridge: Cambridge University Press), 1–23.

METZGER, B. (1968), *The Text of the New Testament: Its Transmission, Corruption, and Restoration* (New York: Oxford University Press).

—— (1981), *Manuscripts of the Greek Bible: An Introduction to Greek Palaeography* (New York: Oxford University Press).

OBBINK, D. (1996) (ed.), *Philodemus, On Piety Part I* (Oxford: Clarendon Press).

PESTMAN, P. W. (1994), *The New Papyrological Primer*, 2nd edn. (Leiden: E. J. Brill).

REYNOLDS, L. D., and WILSON, N. G. (1991), *Scribes and Scholars: A Guide to the Transmission of Greek and Latin Literature*, 3rd edn. (Oxford: Clarendon Press).

RICHARD, M. (1995), *Repertoire des bibliothèques et des catalogues de manuscrits grecs*, 3rd edn. (Turnhout: Brepols).

ROBERTS, C. H. (1956), *Greek Literary Hands, 350 B.C.–400 A.D.* (Oxford: Clarendon Press).

SEIDER, R. (1967–90), *Paläographie der griechischen Papyri* (Stuttgart: Hiersemann).

STEFFENS, F. (1903), *Lateinische Paläographie: Hundert Tafeln in Lichtdruck mit genübersthender Transscription nebst Erläuterungen und einer systematischen Darstellung der Entwicklung der lateinischen Schrift* (Freiburg: Veith).

—— (1910), *Paléographie latine: 125 facsimilés en phototypie accompagnés de transcriptions et d'explications avec un exposé systématique de l'histoire de l'écriture latine* (Trier: Schaar & Dathe; Paris: H. Champion).

THOMPSON, E. M. (1894), *Handbook of Greek and Latin Palaeography* (London: Kegan Paul, Trench, Trübner & Co. repr., Chicago: Ares, 1980).

—— (1912), *An Introduction to Greek and Latin Palaeography* (Oxford: Clarendon Press; repr., New York: Burt Franklin, 1973).

THORPE, J. E. (1972), *Principles of Textual Criticism* (San Marino, Calif.: Huntington Library).

TRAUBE, L. (1907), *Nomina sacra: Versuch einer Geschichte der christlichen Kurzung* (Munich: Beck; repr., Darmstadt: Wissenschaftliche Buchgesellschaft, 1967).

TURNER, E. G. (1968), *Greek Papyri: An Introduction* (Princeton: Princeton University Press).

WEST, M. L. (1973), *Textual Criticism and Editorial Technique Applicable to Greek and Latin Texts* (Stuttgart: Teubner).

Websites

'Biblical Manuscripts Project', T. J. Finney, Manning, Australia: <http://alpha.reltech.org/BibleMSS.html>, 1 October 2006.

The Codex Sinaiticus Project, University of Birmingham: <http://www.itsee.bham.ac.uk/projects/sinaiticus/>, 1 October 2006.

'Codices Electronici Sangallenses,' Stiftsbibliothek, Sankt Gallen: <http://www.cesg.unifr.ch/virt_bib/handschriften.htm>, 1 October 2006.

'Digital Medievalist': <http://www.digitalmedievalist.org>, 1 October 2006.

Electronic Access to Medieval Manuscripts Project, Hill Monastic Manuscript Library and Vatican Film Library: <http://www.hmml.org/eamms/index.html>, 1 October 2006.

Hill Museum and Manuscript Library, St John's University, over 75,000 records: <http://www.hmml.org/>, 1 October 2006.

Institut de recherche et d'histoire des textes (IRHT), Paris, microfilm of 55,000 manuscripts: <http://www.irht.cnrs.fr>, 1 October 2006; with a glossary at <http://vocabulaire.irht.cnrs.fr/pages/vocab1.htm>, 1 October 2006.

Manuscript Libraries, John Rawlings, Stanford University: <http://www-sul.stanford.edu/depts/ssrg/medieval/mss/manind.html>, 1 October 2006.

'Medieval Manuscript Manual' (Dept. of Medieval Studies, Central European University): <http://www.ceu.hu/medstud/manual/MMM/>, 1 October 2006.

'Medieval Writing', Dianne and John Tillotson, Canberra: <http://medievalwriting.50megs.com/writing.htm>, 1 October 2006.

'Palaeography,' The Schoyen Collection, Oslo and London: <http://www.nb.no/baser/schoyen/4/4.4/index.html>, 1 October 2006.

'Paleografia Latina,' Fernando de Lasala, Rome: <http://www.unigre.it/pubblicazioni/lasala/WEB/>, 1 October 2006.

'POxy: Oxyrhynchus Online', Oxford University, the Oxyrhynchus papyri: <http://www.papyrology.ox.ac.uk/POxy/>, 1 October 2006.

Vatican Film Library, St Louis University, over 30,000 Vatican manuscripts: <http://www.slu.edu/libraries/vfl/>, 1 October 2006.

PART III

IDENTITIES

CHAPTER 8

....

JEWS AND CHRISTIANS

....

ANDREW S. JACOBS

8.1 APPROACHES

....

A concise narrative of the 'split' between ancient Judaism and Christianity persists in modern scholarship. This narrative has its roots in a theologically conditioned, supersessionist reading of the New Testament, in which the messianic salvation rejected by the Jews was taken up by Gentile believers and became the distinct religion of 'the Christians' (Acts 11: 26). A less overtly theological permutation of this narrative endures in secular academia (although note Lieu 1994). Commonly, and somewhat romantically, referred to as the 'parting of the ways' (Dunn 1991 and 1992; Lieu 1994; Becker and Reed 2003b), this account describes how inner-sectarian debate over Jesus's messiahship, combined with the trauma of Jewish revolts in the first and second centuries, led those more universalist members of the Jesus movement to splinter off from 'mainstream' Judaism (solidifying, according to many followers of this model, into nascent rabbinism during the same period) (Segal 1986). Students of this 'parting of the ways' attend to various 'moments' as important way-stations on this path to definitive division: the expulsion of Jesus-believing Jews from the synagogues;[1] the repercussions of the first and second Jewish Wars (Goodman 1989); even the fourth-century legalization and institutionalization of 'orthodox' Christianity following Constantine the Great and the Council of Nicaea

I would like to thank Annette Yoshiko Reed and Rebecca Krawiec for reading through a draft of this chapter and offering valuable comments and suggestions.

have been identified as 'points of no return' on the parting of the ways (Ruether 1972; Boyarin 2003: 66). From that point on (whatever point is identified), this view teaches, relations between the distinctive religions of Jews and Christians were rare and usually competitive in nature.

As Adam Becker and Annette Yoshiko Reed have recently explained, both historically and theologically minded students of early Christianity find common cause in subscribing to this 'parting of the ways' model:

> [T]he metaphor of 'parted ways' allows for both Judaism and Christianity to be approached as authentic religions in their own right, with equally strong links to the biblical and Second Temple Jewish heritage they share. . . . Moreover, the notion of the 'Parting of the Ways' fits well with contemporary ecumenical concerns, providing a foundation for inter-religious dialogue and buttressing popular appeals to a common 'Judeo-Christian' ethic.
>
> (Becker and Reed 2003b: 15–16)

That is, the 'parting of the ways' is a clear yet benign metaphor that allows each religion to maintain a robust history and a common genealogy, just connected enough to justify ongoing, friendly relations, but not so connected that the distinctive tradition of each religion becomes too blurred. This amicable model, however, rests on several contestable presuppositions.

In order to be sure that the ways have parted, we must be able to recognize a twin set of distinctive ideological destinations called 'Judaism' and 'Christianity'. Yet how do we, at a remove of several centuries, determine who was a Jew and who was a Christian? One option is to rely on such authoritative (and, ultimately, triumphant) sources as 'the rabbis' and 'the fathers'. Such reliance, however, risks reifying normative discourses that were by no means universally acknowledged in the first centuries CE. Another option is to take the word of anyone claiming the identity 'Jew' and 'Christian' and reconstruct more expansive 'Judaisms' and 'Christianities'; in this case, though, we risk ending up with categories so broad and amorphous as to be ultimately unhelpful. What would it mean to speak of a non-Jewish Christianity that embraces both Marcionites and Ebionites? How do we envision the boundaries of a non-Gentile Judaism whose members might be substantively indistinguishable from their Gentile neighbours (S. J. D. Cohen 1993)? And how do we locate those groups that seem to confound any boundary-making, such as Gentile 'Godfearers' frequenting synagogues, or those groups that scholars dub 'Jewish Christians' who stubbornly resist classification (Fredriksen 2003: 49–51; Reed 2003: 188–96, 219–21)? Without secure, historically identifiable groups, the parting ways could lead us off a conceptual cliff.

This historiographic uncertainty leads directly to a methodological quandary facing, to some degree, all students of the history of religions. To imagine 'parting ways' is to envision religions as stable entities developing coherently over time, occasionally shedding unsuccessful 'mutations' (heresies) like so many exotic, extinct religious Neanderthals. This kind of evolutionary view of religions emerged in the nineteenth century, 'scientifically' rewriting what were at root colonialist discourses of theological self-description (Chidester 2000). The sources at hand in the study of ancient Judaism and Christianity, insisting as they do on the providentially guided triumph of 'true' religion (orthodoxy), make this evolutionary model, while historiographically perilous, also especially tempting. Yet, since the work of Walter Bauer (1971; German original 1934), students of early Christianity especially have learned to mistrust overly monolithic models of orthodox development.

An additional problematic assumption of the 'parting of the ways' is the relative rarity and enmity of 'Jewish–Christian relations' in antiquity. This downplaying of ongoing and complex interactions between Jews and Christians is ultimately the result of centuries-long debates over how to balance the rhetorical and historical aspects of our ancient sources.[2] These debates have serious historiographic and ethical implications. In the late nineteenth and early twentieth centuries, there was no attempt to reconstruct 'Jewish–Christian relations', because most prominent historians believed that there were no such relations. Judaism, following the advent of Christ and the destruction of the Temple, was a failed world religion withering on the vine (Harnack 1965: 70–1). For scholars such as Adolf von Harnack, the 'parting of the ways' had Christians taking the only open road, while *Spätjudentum* ('late Judaism') ran off the rails into a ditch (Harnack 1883: 59–91; S. J. D. Cohen 1991). Furthermore, the listless failure of Judaism meant that Christians must have been focused rather on their more vibrant 'pagan' rivals. Any Christian writings about Jews, therefore, were a literary smokescreen: there was nothing to be learned about Jews and Christians from the writings of the early church.

While some of Harnack's contemporaries protested against the overtly supersessionist vision of lively Christianity leaving a crippled Judaism in the dust (see Jacobs 2003: 100), it took the shattering events of the Second World War, and the traumatized aftermath of the Holocaust, to bring a sea change to the study of Jews and Christians (Gager 1985: 13). Scholars realized that the assertion of ancient Judaism's spiritual vacuity might have been motivated by more than impartial scholarship, and might further have licensed violence—both theological and literal—against contemporary Jews. A new study of 'Jewish–Christian relations' emerged to rectify this historiographic and ethical lapse. Soon after the War appeared Marcel Simon's *Verus Israel*, reversing the terms of Harnack's sceptical supersessionism (Simon 1986; Baumgarten 1999). Judaism was no longer moribund, but vigorous; Christian writings about Jews were no longer rhetorical ciphers, but realistic reflections of an ongoing and spirited confrontation between the two religions (Simon 1986: 369). Simon and his fellow travellers reimagined a 'parting of the ways' that set Judaism and Christianity on equally broad boulevards of development, with the roads frequently, and spectacularly, crossing. In recent decades, this hopeful scholarship of recovery and reinvigoration of Judaism has coincided with a broader ethical concern for multiculturalism.

Miriam Taylor's *Anti-Judaism and Early Christian Identity* (1995) challenged Simon's 'conflict theory' (her characterization of Simon's especially dynamic vision of Jewish–Christian relations): could not such a reading, she asked, be used to blame Jews for the violence perpetrated against them throughout history? Could any Jewish provocation possibly justify the virulence of Christian rhetoric and animus toward the Jews? She proposed, instead, a return to reading Christian literature on Jews as rhetorical devices that conveyed symbolic information about Christian theology. The lives and minds of the Jews themselves perforce remained a mystery (although she did not return to Harnack's historical pessimism with regard to Jewish vitality), but Christians must maintain responsibility for their own rhetorical violence (Taylor 1995: 195). While the ways certainly parted, only the rocky and troubling Christian road remained visible from our historical vantage point.

Taylor's claims have crystallized an ongoing debate among a variety of scholars committed both ethically and historiographically to the recovery of real, vivacious Jews coexisting with Christians (Carleton Paget 1997; Shoemaker 1999). Few scholars assert that all of our sources can be read as positive evidence for the messy, but ultimately 'real', experience of early Jews and Christians (see Fredriksen 2003); rather, most try to steer a middle ground between 'image' and 'reality' in order to bracket off clearly hyperbolic Christian rhetoric from the kernels of historical interaction embedded within our sources (De Lange 1976; Wilken 1983; Lieu 1996). Throughout the course of this debate, the intersection of historiographic and ethical claims in the studies of ancient Jews and Christians becomes apparent: the robustness of Judaism in the first centuries CE is linked directly with our interpretations of the reality of Jews encoded in the early Christian writings. To read Jews in Christian texts as 'mere rhetoric' is either to claim the triumph of Christian supersession and the fallibility of ancient Judaism (so Harnack) or to privilege the deeply encoded 'symbolic anti-Judaism' that pervades all such Christian writings (so Taylor). Conversely, to read Christian evidence for Jews as reflective of a 'real situation' is both to posit the vitality of ancient Judaism and possibly to concede a concrete basis for Christian vitriol (see Cameron 1994 and Horowitz 1998).

8.2 SOURCES

The tangle of historiographic and ethical issues embedded in the study of Jewish–Christian relations must be confronted by any student hoping to do productive work in this area. It is rare to find an early Christian text that does *not* speak about Jews and Judaism, and usually in a highly charged (although multifaceted) manner. The present challenge for the historian of early Jewish–Christian relations is to juggle the rhetorical bias of our sources and the academic desire for an unbiased analysis of history. A fair-minded student of early Christianity might seek to avoid unduly internalizing early Christian prejudice by turning to non-Christian sources for balance: surely any anti-Jewish sting of our Christian texts might be tempered by gaining perspective from the 'other side'? Some early studies have sought to 'fact check' Christian sources in this manner (e.g. Bardy 1925; Ginzberg 1935), but caution is still warranted (Baskin 1985: 56–9). First, the quantity and quality of Jewish sources in the first five centuries CE are monumentally dwarfed by what we have from the Christian side: after the textual riches of first-century Judaism (the Dead Sea Scrolls, Philo, Josephus) comes a sudden quiet from Mediterranean Jewry. Historians of Judaism have made valiant efforts to fill in that lacuna with lesser-known texts, epigraphic and other inscriptional remains, and archaeological witnesses (Rutgers 1992, 1995; Braun 1998), but the rising crescendo of Christian voices still risks drowning out these Jewish remains.

One significant body of Jewish texts surviving from this period is, of course, the rabbinic corpus: the Mishnah and Tosefta from the third centuries, early midrashim, the Talmudic compilations from Palestine and Mesopotamia, as well as scattered, related liturgical, poetic, and apocalyptic texts from the pre-Islamic period (Strack and Stemberger 1992; Neusner 1999). These sources present their own obstacles to 'balancing' out the Christian voice (but see Segal 1991). In the first place, while we might imagine the slow interpenetration of rabbinic Jewish authority into the synagogues of the Mediterranean and Near Eastern diaspora, there is no clear evidence that rabbinic Judaism was the norm outside of the circle of sages and disciples before the Islamic period (Schwartz 2001: 103–28; Boyarin 2004: 151–201). To make rabbinism the voice of ancient Judaism, therefore, is to slip into an anachronistic essentialism that uncritically takes up the normative discourse of the rabbis themselves.

Even when we can reasonably theorize some form of contact between the sages of Palestine and Christians (as in the case of Origen of Alexandria, Eusebius of Caesarea, and Jerome: Urbach 1971; Kimelman 1980; Blowers 1988; Lapin 1996; Hollerich 1999: 147–53), rabbinic texts do not treat Christianity with the same obsessiveness as Christians speak of Judaism (the scandalous tales about Jesus compiled in the *Sefer toldot Yeshu* represent a much later crystallization of scattered rabbinic folklore: Biale 1999: 131–6). When Christianity appears in the rabbinic writings, or in poetical or apocalyptic texts, it is thickly veiled and coded, or lumped together with the panoply of 'heresies' (*minim*) that serve for the theoretical and rhetorical construction of rabbinism (Kalmin 1994; Himmelfarb 1990; Wheeler 1991; Biale 1999). It is, of course, interesting to find this compounded, even deliberate silence on the rabbinic side in late antiquity, but interpreting that silence can prove frustrating.

Lacking any significant narrative discussion of Christians by Jews, some scholars have turned to more oblique modes of 'contact' that might be gauged from both sides, such as very promising recent work on the possibilities of competitive biblical interpretation (e.g. Baskin 1985; Visotzky 1995; Hirshman 1996). These studies not only demonstrate the likelihood of intellectual interaction (both adversarial and, it has been suggested, co-operative), they also provide a useful corrective to the segregated paths depicted by the 'parting of the ways'. Yet, even as these valuable contributions to intellectual and cultural histories provide us with new, broad-brush views of the exegetical contacts between elite Jews and Christians, they still do not provide a full-blooded social history of Jewish–Christian relations.

Some students of late antiquity have turned to material remains as a way of ameliorating the partiality of Christian sources and the paucity of Jewish sources. Historians have made strides in reconstructing varieties of ancient Judaism from the wealth of late ancient evidence from synagogues across the Mediterranean and ancient Near East (Rutgers 1995; Schwartz 2001: 203–89). The physical remains of Jews and Christians, often discovered in tantalizing proximity, suggest contacts and relations between the two groups throughout the late ancient Mediterranean. Certainly the thick material presence of Jews in the ancient Mediterranean and Near East (some estimates calculate Jews comprising as much as 7–8 per cent of the population of the Roman Empire; Hopkins 1998: 212–16) belies the notion that Jews and Christians walked on parted ways that only rarely crossed (Meyers 1988; North 1992). Yet, as critical histories of archaeology demonstrate, even the analysis of stones and bones often entangles the analyst in questions of bias, presupposition, and hermeneutical uncertainty (so argue the proponents of 'postprocessual archaeology'). Usually, material remains can establish only the bare fact of proximity or coexistence, leaving the analyst to fill in the quality of such spatial relations, often with highly contradictory conclusions.[3] Stones can only tell so much of the story, and, eventually, the historian will find herself turning to the fraught literary remains of Christians.[4]

It is difficult to catalogue the number and contents of Christian writings that deal with Jews and Judaism, because the topic is so ubiquitous. From the second century onward, many Christians (who so self-identify) used the category of 'Jews', along with its conceptual double, 'the Greeks' or 'the Gentiles', as totalizing rubrics by which to shape a new world-view. Among early examples are the *Epistle to Diognetus* 5 and Aristides's *Apology* 2. Pauline universalizing language of 'neither Jew nor Greek' by the fourth century had become a classificatory lens through which to fashion a global religious topography (Eusebius, *Praep.* 1. 5. 12 and *Dem.* 1. 2. 1). Within this Christian totalizing discourse, the 'Jew' appears with such frequency as to risk blurring any historical focus. In order to sharpen our angle of approach, it is perhaps worth attempting some classification of our sources.

First, it is important to distinguish between pre-Constantinian and post-Constantinian sources. By the end of the fourth century, the interests of Christian institutions had begun to merge—fitfully and not without drama, to be sure—with the political interests of the Roman Empire. (A similar merging of religious and political interests also took place in the Persian Sasanian Empire, with comparable effects on relations between Zoroastrians and Jews (Neusner 1970).) Briefly, a Christian thinking and writing about Jews in the second century operated from a very different political and social position than his counterpart three centuries later, when the full weight of Roman imperial authority potentially lay behind his words and ideas. A student of early Jewish–Christian relations must attend differently to texts such as the *Epistle of Barnabas*, Justin Martyr's *Dialogue with Trypho*, or Tertullian's *Against the Jews* than she would Ephrem's anti-Jewish hymns or the biblical commentaries of Jerome or Cyril of Alexandria.

Next, we can begin to ask how Jews function in various Christian texts. Some of the earliest Christian writings posit Jews as religious adversaries. This apologetic literature, supposedly written in 'defence' of the new faith of the Christians, constructs a spiritual world under siege, both literal and metaphorical. Jews appear aligned in a sinister fashion with Rome in second-century martyrologies (see the Martyrdoms of Polycarp and Pionius, and Gibson 2001, 2003) and as a source of the ill-informed rumours and slanders necessitating response in apologetic texts (e.g. Tertullian, *Apol.* 7). An apologetic subgenre of texts 'in response to Jews' (*adversus Iudaeos*) emerged in the third century in the Latin West (e.g. Tertullian, *Ad Iud.*; Lukyn 1935), and compilations of biblical *testimonia* allegedly written to answer Jewish debates proliferated across the Mediterranean (e.g. Cyprian, *Testimonies for Quirinus*; Albl 2004).

For more positivist historians, the representation of Jews as adversaries encodes a social reality: that Jews, who enjoyed official public status in the Roman Empire, were on the attack against Christians (although not with the literal violence conveyed in martyr texts). They prayed against Christians, met them acrimoniously in the marketplace of religious ideas, and even cheered as they were tortured and executed by unsympathetic Roman authorities (Gibson 2001, 2003; North 1992). A different historical reading finds in all of these texts rhetorical construction with little or no basis in reality: Christians projected their own fears and dissatisfactions on to the Jews (already encoded as 'the bad guys' by a particular reading of the gospels), and we learn nothing of historical interest from these highly literary constructions.

Even accepting the latter, more pessimistic view, however, the historian of Jewish–Christian relations should not despair of attaining some glimpse into ancient lives and ideas. We can shift our focus away from reconstructing the immediate motives for the creation and consumption of these texts, and look instead to their 'afterlife': how would Christians, instructed by these adversarial accounts of Jews, potentially interact with 'real' Jews the next time they left the house? Patterned on real conflicts, or concocted from a stew of unfair stereotypes, the adversarial and apologetic literature of the first Christian centuries constituted formative texts, scripting world-views and even future interactions and, in this sense, they can tell us something historically 'real' about Jewish–Christian relations.

We can use the same approach with even more literary narrative sources, in which Jews function as 'characters' patently crafted to convey Christian ideas. Beginning in the second century, Christians wrote about their 'dialogues' with Jews (Justin Martyr's *Dial.* is the earliest complete text; on later texts see Varner 2005 and Lahey 2006). Although some Christians do mention holding public and private debates with Jews (Tertullian, *Ad Iud.* 1; Origen, *Letter to Africanus*, 1. 9, and *Cels.* 1. 44; Jerome, *Preface to the Book of Psalms*), scholars debate how much we can distil the perspective of actual Jews from such Christian texts (Harnack 1883; Olster 1994; Horner 2001). Nonetheless, these texts may provide a window into the evolving parameters within which Jews and Christians might plausibly interact. Even the most highly literary and fantastic of creations in which Jews figure as characters, such as the hagiographic literature of the fourth and fifth centuries, may be read not as direct windows into what specific Jews did, but how Jews in general might be perceived by their Christian neighbours. A host of texts, for instance, related to the discovery (*inventio*) of relics portray Jewish characters as integral to the recovery of a sacred past (Drijvers and Drijvers 1997; Limor 1996; Jacobs 2004: 174–91); few scholars credit the existence of these convenient Jewish figures at the discovery of the True Cross or Mary's robe, but we can appreciate the degree to which hagiography gave Christians a lens through which to bring their own world, and the Jews within it, into focus. We can even begin to consider the ways in which Jews—otherwise falling into historical silence—might likewise have taken up and played with the roles scripted for them in Christian texts.

As part of this rich textual mosaic we can even include those texts in which Jews appear as a cipher: homilies and biblical commentaries in which Jews function as the metaphorical symbol of wilful unbelief (Wilken 1971) and heresiological sources in which 'Judaizing' signals inappropriate beliefs about the full divinity of Christ (Lorenz 1980; Burrus 2002). Even when 'the Jew' stands as a Christian metaphor, we can sense the patterns of the manner in which Christians defined their place in a newly Christian world, and the solidifying role they constructed for Jews in that world. Even from the most rhetorical of Christian literature, we can still hope to gain a sense of the possibilities of historical relations between Jews and Christians.

Just as we might derive from these metaphorical depictions of Jews rough contours of social history, so too we must endeavour to recall that even the most mundane and 'realistic' of Christian texts are ideological and rhetorical products. For instance, Jews figure significantly in the narrative of the first Christian histories. Eusebius enshrines the supersessionist 'parting of the ways' in his *Ecclesiastical History*; and his successors in the Latin West and Greek East (Rufinus of Aquileia, Socrates Scholasticus, Sozomen, Theodoret of Cyrrhus) continue to integrate Jews into their heavily theological historical narratives of the dovetailing of orthodoxy and empire, with Jews cast as the impious and politically disloyal 'others'. These authors carefully frame Christian communal identity through a re-conceptualization of 'the past', and so should not be read as simple factual accounts. Though we should carefully weigh the historical details of these accounts, their broad, prescriptive framing of Jewish–Christian relations can be understood, along with our other sources, as producing, as opposed to recording, a particular brand of reality. We can likewise approach the legislation regarding Jews from the post-Constantinian period, particularly those laws contained in the codes of the arch-orthodox emperors Theodosius II and Justinian I. Historians continue to debate the historical value of imperial legislation, which was often repetitious, contradictory, and difficult to enforce. The 'matter-of-fact' quality of legislation on Jews (see e.g. various laws concerning Jews in *Theodosian Code*, book 16, and *Justinianic Code*, book 1, as well as Theodosius II's Novella 3 and Justinian's Novella 146) presents us, again, with an opportunity to parse the subtle ways in which Christian rhetoric constructed a real world for its Christian, as well as its Jewish, subjects (Bachrach 1985; Linder 1987).

We can achieve a further sense of how this constructed worldview could shape both Christian and Jewish reality through those writings in which Jews function as the subject of debate between Christians: for instance, in the homilies of John Chrysostom (usually referred to as 'Against the Jews' but ostensibly directed against Judaizing Christians), who rails against Christians who frequent the local synagogue for festivals and oath-taking (Wilken 1983); or in the controversy between Jerome and Rufinus and, a little later, the correspondence between Jerome and Augustine in which Jerome is taken to task for consulting with and learning Hebrew and midrash from Palestinian Jews (Jacobs 2004: 83–96). In the course of Jerome's defence, he utters the memorable line that may very well encapsulate the multifaceted ways in which Christians constructed Jews into their world-view: 'If it is expedient to hate any people and to detest any nation, I have a notable hatred for the circumcised; even now they persecute our Lord Jesus Christ in the synagogues of Satan. Yet can anyone object to me for having had a Jew as a teacher?' (*Ep.* 84. 3. 3) The contradictions of desire and loathing that mark Jerome's peculiar—and yet, increasingly, representative—view of 'Jewish–Christian relations' is also visible in a cautionary tale told to Jerome by his peevish correspondent Augustine.

Jerome's new translation of the book of Jonah, executed *iuxta Hebraeos* ('according to the Hebrews' or 'according to the Jews'), was read out in a small North African village. Upon reaching Jerome's new translation of a single word—'ivy' instead of 'gourd' (Jonah 4: 6)—the assembled congregation burst out in anger, accusing the translation of being impiously 'Judaized' and thus inappropriate for church reading. At that point the beleaguered bishop brought in a group of local Jews, who treacherously sided with the rabble-rousers against Jerome's more authentic Jewish retranslation (Augustine, *Ep.* 71. 3. 5; see Fürst 1999). How should the student of Jewish–Christian relations interpret this group of North African Jews summoned by a small-town bishop? Do they represent a casual and amicable détente between the two communities, or the fearful minority serving at the pleasure of Christian masters? Is their response genuine and helpful, or sly and deliberately subversive? Any single answer that seeks definitively to pin down historical details would drain this anecdote of its richer cultural significance: the inscription of complex, even contradictory, motives, fears, and desires at the core of these tangled inter-religious contacts. It is worth noting that the teller of this story, Augustine of Hippo Regius, would leave as his own legacy in western 'Jewish–Christian relations' the dubious 'witness theology': Jews remain in this Christian world to bear witness both to the truth of scriptures (as, perhaps, in this little story) and to the suffering inflicted on those who hear and reject the salvation of Christ (J. Cohen 1998; 1999: 19–67).

Despite the productive multiplicity of our sources, scholars are often tempted to distil Jewish–Christian relations to a single theme: 'rhetorical excess' or 'real-life conflict' or 'parted ways'. Such irresoluble anxieties emerge out of a scholarly tension that haunts much of the project of history writing: the desire for certainty about the past combined with a suspicion of the truth-claims of our primary sources (Clark 2004). The study of Jews and Christians in late antiquity makes this tense longing even more acute, conditioned as it has been by ideological, theological, and philosophical insistence on separation, segregation, and self-definition reaching all the way back to the early Jews and Christians themselves. Yet the particular circumstances of this sub-discipline of early Christian (and, in perhaps another Handbook, early Jewish) studies also provide an opportunity for the scholar critically and productively to engage with this persistent academic anxiety. Over the course of the first Christian centuries, as the political and cultural positions of Christians fluctuated and transmuted, Christians constructed a complex series of relationships with their Jewish neighbours. They scripted these complexities through a variety of texts, ranging from the fanciful to the mundane, resulting in a mutable and unstable matrix of the possibilities of 'Jewish–Christian relations'.

If any observation could be said to define the cultural, intellectual, and social contexts of late antiquity, it is that the various discourses of stability ('Hellenism', 'imperium', 'Romanitas') frequently masked deep-rooted and complex fluidities (Bowersock 1990; Cameron 1991; Ando 2000). The implications of this observation are slowly beginning to take hold in the study of Jews and Christians in this period, as much recent, engaging work on ancient Jews and Christians has moved to overcome facile assumptions of stable religious and inter-religious identities (S. J. D. Cohen 1999; Fonrobert 2000, 2001; Boyarin 2004). Even as we take seriously the desire of many ancient Christian and Jews for secure self-definition and differentiation from 'others', we must also understand these desires as a species of self-fashioning rhetoric: 'true' in the sense that they work materially to shape the worldview of Jews and Christians, even if they are not 'factual' in the sense that we directly recover from such historical remains an unmediated past.

Notes

1. The debated theory of an 'expulsion' of the Jesus movement from first- or second-century synagogues rests on a confluence of interpretations of the Gospel of John (see Jn 9: 22, 12: 42, and 16: 2); ambiguous references in Justin Martyr, Origen, Epiphanius, and Jerome; and speculation on the origins and functions of the rabbinic *birkat ha-minim* (Kimelman 1981; Horbury 1982).

2. For more detail on this material, see Becker and Reed (2003*b*) and Jacobs (2003).

3. Take, for example, the long, strange history of interpretation of the monumental synagogue of Capernaum built 'down the street' from the church of St Peter (Jacobs 1999: 363–5).

4. Even the identification of literary remains as 'Christian' is fraught (see above on essentialism). For the purposes of approaching 'Jewish–Christian relations', we can focus on written sources operating from a self-consciously Christian and non-Jewish perspective. The question of so-called Jewish Christians who (according to Christian sources, at least) claimed to be *both* Jewish and Christian, (see Jerome, *Ep.* 112. 13) is left aside for now, but see Reed (2003: 189–96).

Suggested Reading

Primary sources

It is difficult to find an early Christian text that does *not* mention Jews or Judaism. Williams (1935) remains a helpful collection of texts written explicitly *adversus Judaeos* (against Judaism), balanced by the critical survey of Baskin (1985). In addition, some primary sources repeatedly surface in the study of early Jewish–Christian relations and provide important touchstones for any work in the discipline (sources found below in the references are listed only by title; for all others, date and publisher of a good, recent translation are given where available): Melito of Sardis's *Paschal Homily* in *On Pascha*, trans. and ed. Alistair Stewart-Sykes (Crestwood, NY: St Vladimir's Press, 1999); Justin Martyr's *Dialogue*; much discussion of Jews and Judaism is found in Origen's *Cels.*, as well as his *Letter to Africanus* and his homilies and commentaries (many translated in ANF); Tertullian's *Against the Jews*, which laid groundwork for much of the Latin genre, up to Augustine's treatise of the same name; Eusebius of Caesarea's *Praep.*, as well as his *Hist. eccl.*; the Syriac author Aphrahat's select *Demonstrations* against Judaism, trans. and commented on by Jacob Neusner, *Aphrahat and Judaism: The Christian–Jewish Argument in Fourth-Century Iran* (Leiden: E. J. Brill, 1971); John Chrysostom's homilies *Against the Judaizers*; Jerome's various translations, commentaries, and correspondence; and Augustine's development of the 'witness-theology' in *City of God*, 18, trans. Henry Bettenson (London: Penguin, 2003).

Secondary sources

Many modern secondary sources continue to be influential—in terms of both historical content and methodological criticism—and should provide ample groundwork for the student of early Christianity. As most of these works are found in the references below, I give them only by author and year. Baskin (1985) provides a still useful analysis of important work that has been done, and remains to be done, in the field; Becker and Reed (2003*a*, *b*) contains both a helpful overview and several important, individual studies on the topic. Important general and specific studies to begin with are Boyarin (2004); De Lange (1976); Fredriksen (2003); Gager (1983); Lieu (1992, 1994, 1996); Simon (1986); Wilken (1971, 1983).

Bibliography

Primary sources

Recent English translations are given where available; otherwise, the reader is directed to older translations or critical editions with translations into other modern languages.

Aristides, *Apologia*, ed. J. Armitage Robison, TaS 1. 1 (Cambridge, 1893). Text and Eng. trans. in J. Rendel Harris (2004) (ed.), *The Apology of Aristides on Behalf of the Christians* (Piscataway, NJ: Gorgias Press).

Cyprian of Carthage, *Testimonia ad Quirinum*. Latin text ed. R. Weber and M. Beveuot, in CCSL 3 (Turnhout: Brepols, 1972). The only modern Eng. trans. is in the ANF 5P.

Epistle of Barnabas. Text and Eng. trans. in B. Ehrman (2003) (ed.), *The Apostolic Fathers*: *Epistle of Barnabas, Papias and Quadratus, Epistle to Diognetus, The Shepherd of Hermas*, ii, LCL (Cambridge, Mass.: Harvard University Press).

Epistle to Diognetus. Text and Eng. trans. in (2003) B. Ehrman (ed.), *The Apostolic Fathers*, containing *Epistle of Barnabas, Papias and Quadratus, Diogn., The Shepherd of Hermas*, ii, LCL (Cambridge, Mass.: Harvard University Press).

Eusebius of Caesarea, *Ecclesiastical History*. Rev. Eng. trans. in A. Louth (1989) (ed.), *The History of the Church from Christ to Constantine*, trans. G. A. Williamson (London: Penguin).

—— *Demonstratio evangelica*. The 1920 Eng. trans. by W. J. Ferrar was reprinted in *The Proof of the Gospel: Being the* Demonstratio evangelica *of Eusebius of Cæsarea* (Eugene, Ore.: Wipf & Stock, 2001).

—— *Praeparatio evangelica*. The 1903 Eng. trans. by E. Hamilton Gifford was reprinted in *De evangelica praeparatione* (Grand Rapids, Mich.: Baker Books, 1981). A French trans. and critical edition, ed. J. Sirinelli *et al.*, has been published in SC 206, 215, 228, 262, 266, 292, 307, 338, and 369 (Paris: Éditions du Cerf, 1974–91).

Jerome, *Letters*. Trans. of some letters are in NPNF[2] 6; Latin text ed. I. Hilberg in *Epistulae*, CSEL 54–6 (Vienna: Tempsky, 1910–18). Correspondence with Augustine is in C. White (1990) (ed. and trans.), *The Correspondence (394–419) between Jerome and Augustine of Hippo* (Lewiston, NY: Edwin Mellen Press).

—— *Preface to the book of Psalms*. For Eng. trans. NPNF[2] 6.

John Chrysostom, *Adversus Iudaeos*. Eng. trans. in P. W. Harkins (1979) (trans.), *Discourses against Judaizing Christians* (Washington D.C.: Catholic University of America Press).

Justin Martyr, *Dialogue with Trypho*, ed. M. Marcovich, PTS 47 (Berlin: de Gruyter, 1997). Revised Eng. trans. in T. B. Falls (2003), rev. T. P. Halton (Washington D.C.: Catholic University of America Press).

Justinianic Code and *Novellae*. The entire *Corpus Iuris Civilis* of Justinian is in P. Krueger, W. Kunkel, and R. Schoell (1872–1988) (eds.), 3 vols. (Dublin: Weidmann; Berlin: de

Gruyter, 1915). An Eng. trans. of many of these sources is found in *The Digest of Justinian*, ed. A. Watson (Philadelphia: University of Pennsylvania Press, 1998).

Martyrdom of Pionius. In H. Musurillo (2000) (ed.), *The Acts of the Christian Martyrs*, with introduction, texts, and trans., 2 vols., OECT (Oxford: Clarendon Press, repr. from the 1972 edn.)

Martyrdom of Polycarp. Text and Eng. trans. in B. Ehrman (2003) (ed.), *The Apostolic Fathers*, contains *I Clement, II Clement, Ignatius, Polycarp, Didache et al.*, i, LCL (Cambridge, Mass.: Harvard University Press).

ORIGEN, *Against Celsus*. Eng. trans. in H. Chadwick (1952), *Origen: Contra Celsum* (Cambridge: Cambridge University Press).

—— *Letter to Africanus*, *Ep.* 1. Eng. trans. of this correspondence is in ANF 4. A French trans, ed. N. de Lange, in SC 30 (Paris: Éditions du Cerf, 1983).

TERTULLIAN, *Adversus Iudaeos*. Eng. trans. in G. Dunn (2004) (trans.), *Tertullian: The Early Church Father* (London: Routledge), 63–104.

—— *Apology*. Text and Eng. trans. in T. R. Glover (1998) (ed.), *Apology; De Spectaculis*, repr. LCL (Cambridge, Mass.: Harvard University Press); ed. J. W. Ph. Borleffs *et al.*, CCSL 1 (Turnhout: Brepols, 1954); ed. H. Hoppe, CSEL 69 (Vienna: Tempsky, 1939).

The Theodosian Code and Novels, in C. Pharr (1950) (trans.) (Princeton: Princeton University Press). Latin text in *Codex Theodosianus*, ed. P. Krüger (Berlin: T. Mommsen & P. M. Meyer, 1895, 1923).

Secondary sources

ALBL, M. C. (2004), *Pseudo-Gregory of Nyssa: Testimonies Against the Jews* (Leiden: E. J. Brill).

ANDO, C. (2000), *Imperial Ideology and Provincial Loyalty in the Roman Empire* (Berkeley: University of California Press).

BACHRACH, B. S. (1985), 'The Jewish Community of the Later Roman Empire as Seen in the *Codex Theodosianus*', in J. Neusner and E. Frerichs (eds.), *'To See Ourselves as Others See Us': Christians, Jews, 'Others' in Late Antiquity* (Chico, Calif.: Scholars Press), 399–421.

BARDY, G. (1925), 'Les traditions juives dans l'oeuvre d'Origène', *RB* 34: 217–52.

BASKIN, J. (1985), 'Rabbinic–Patristic Exegetical Contacts in Late Antiquity: A Bibliographical Reappraisal', in W. S. Green (ed.), *Approaches to Ancient Judaism*, v: *Studies in Judaism in its Greco-Roman Context* (Atlanta: Scholars Press), 53–80.

BAUER, W. (1971), *Orthodoxy and Heresy in Earliest Christianity* (Philadelphia: Fortress Press). Trans. from German, *Rechtgläubigkeit und Ketzerei in ältesten Christentum* (1934), by a team from the Philadelphia Seminar on Christian Origins, ed. R. A. Kraft and G. Krodel, new edn., with added appendices by G. Strecker (Mifflintown, Pa.: Sigler Press, 1996).

BAUMGARTEN, A. I. (1999), 'Marcel Simon's *Verus Israel* as a Contribution to Jewish History', *HTR* 92: 465–78.

BECKER, A., and REED, A. Y. (2003*a*) (eds.), *The Ways that Never Parted: Jews and Christians in Late Antiquity and the Early Middle Ages* (Tübingen: J. C. B. Mohr/Paul Siebeck).

—— (2003*b*), 'Introduction: Traditional Models and New Directions', in Becker and Reed (2003*a*), 1–33.

BIALE, D. (1999), 'Counter-History and Jewish Polemics against Christianity: The *Sefer toldot yeshu* and the *Sefer zerubavel*', *Jewish Social Studies*, 6/1: 130–45.

BLOWERS, P. (1988), 'Origen, the Rabbis, and the Bible: Towards a Picture of Judaism and Christianity in Third-Century Caesarea', in C. Kannengeisser and W. L. Petersen (eds.), *Origen of Alexandria: His World and Legacy* (Notre Dame, Ind.: University of Notre Dame Press), 96–116.

BOWERSOCK, G. (1990), *Hellenism in Late Antiquity* (Cambridge: Cambridge University Press).

BOYARIN, D. (2003), 'Semantic Differences; or, "Judaism/Christianity" ', in Becker and Reed (2003a), 66–85.

—— (2004), *Border Lines: The Partition of Judaeo-Christianity*, Divinations: Rereading Late Ancient Religion (Philadelphia: University of Pennsylvania Press).

BRAUN, T. (1998), 'The Jews in the Late Roman Empire', *Scripta Classica Israelica*, 17: 142–71.

BURRUS, V. (2002), 'Hailing Zenobia: Anti-Judaism, Trinitarianism, and John Henry Newman', *Culture and Religion*, 3: 163–77.

CAMERON, A. (1991), *Christianity and the Rhetoric of Empire: The Development of Christian Discourse*, Sather Classical Lectures, 55 (Berkeley: University of California Press).

—— (1994), 'The Jews in Seventh-Century Palestine', *Scripta Classica Israelica*, 13: 75–93.

CARLETON PAGET, J. (1997), 'Anti-Judaism and Early Christian Identity', *ZAC* 1: 195–225.

CHIDESTER, D. (2000), 'Colonialism', in W. Braun and R. T. McCutcheon (eds.), *Guide to the Study of Religion* (London: Cassell), 423–37.

CLARK, E. A. (2004), *History, Theory, Text: Historians and the Linguistic Turn* (Cambridge, Mass.: Harvard University Press).

COHEN, J. (1998), ' "Slay Them Not": Augustine and the Jews in Modern Scholarship', *Medieval Encounters*, 4: 78–92.

—— (1999), *Living Letters of the Law: Ideas of the Jew in Medieval Christianity* (Berkeley: University of California Press).

COHEN, S. J. D. (1991), 'Adolf Harnack's "The Mission and Expansion of Judaism": Christianity Succeeds Where Judaism Fails', in B. A. Pearson (ed.), *The Future of Early Christianity: Essays in Honor of Helmut Koester* (Minneapolis: Fortress Press), 163–9.

—— (1993), ' "Those Who Say They Are Jews But Are Not": How Do You Know a Jew in Antiquity When You See One?', in S. J. D. Cohen and E. Frerichs (eds.), *Diasporas in Antiquity* (Atlanta: Scholars Press), 1–45.

—— (1999), *The Beginnings of Jewishness: Boundaries, Varieties, Uncertainties* (Berkeley: University of California Press).

DE LANGE, N. (1976), *Origen and the Jews: Studies in Jewish–Christian Relations in Third-Century Palestine* (Cambridge: Cambridge University Press).

DRIJVERS, H. J. W., and DRIJVERS, J. W. (1997), *The Finding of the True Cross: The Judas Kyriakos Legend in Syriac: Introduction, Text, and Translation* (Leuven: Peeters).

DUNN, J. J. D. (1991), *The Parting of the Ways between Christianity and Judaism and their Significance for the Character of Christianity* (London: SCM Press).

—— (1992), *Jews and Christians: The Parting of the Ways, A.D. 70 to 135* (Grand Rapids, Mich.: Eerdmans).

FONROBERT, C. E. (2000), *Menstrual Purity: Rabbinic and Christian Reconstructions of Biblical Gender* (Stanford, Calif.: Stanford University Press).

—— (2001), 'The *Didascalia Apostolorum*: A Mishnah for the Followers of Jesus', *JECS* 9: 483–509.

FREDRIKSEN, P. (2003), 'What "Parting of the Ways"? Jews, Gentiles, and the Ancient Mediterranean City', in Becker and Reed (2003a), 35–63.

FÜRST, ALFONS (1999), *Augustins Briefwechsel mit Hieronymus* (Münster: Aschendorff Verlagsbuchhandlung).

GAGER, J. (1983), *The Origins of Anti-Semitism: Attitudes toward Judaism in Pagan and Christian Antiquity* (Oxford: Oxford University Press).

GIBSON, E. L. (2001), 'Jewish Antagonism or Christian Polemic: The Case of the *Martyrdom of Pionius*', *JECS* 9: 339–58.

—— (2003), 'The Jews and Christians in the Martyrdom of Polycarp: Entangled or Parted Ways?', in Becker and Reed (2003*a*), 145–58.

GINZBERG, L. (1935), 'Die Haggada bei den Kirchenvätern, VI.: Der Kommentar des Hieronymus zu Jesaja', in S. Baron and A. Marx (eds.), *Jewish Studies in Memory of George A. Kohut* (New York: Alexander Kohut Memorial Foundation), 279–314.

GOODMAN, MARTIN (1989), 'Nerva, the *Fiscus Iudaicus*, and Jewish Identity', *JRS* 79: 40–4.

HARNACK, A. VON (1883), *Die Altercatio Simonis Iudaei et Theophilii Christiani: nebst Untersuchungen über die antijüdische Polemik in der alten Kirche; und Die Acta Archelai und das Diatessaron Tatians*, TU 1.3a (Leipzig: J. C. Hinrichs).

—— (1965), *Die Mission und Ausbreitung des Christentums in den ersten drei Jahrhunderten*, 4th edn. (Leipzig: Zentral-Antiquariat de Deutschen Demokratischen Republick; originally J. C. Hinrichs, 1924).

HIMMELFARB, M. (1990), 'Sefer Zerubbabel', in D. Stern and M. J. Mirsky (eds.), *Rabbinic Fantasies: Imaginative Narratives from Classical Hebrew Literature* (New Haven: Yale University Press), 67–90.

HIRSHMAN, M. (1996), *A Rivalry of Genius: Jewish and Christian Biblical Interpretation in Late Antiquity* (Albany, NY: SUNY Press).

HOLLERICH, M. J. (1999), *Eusebius of Caesarea's 'Commentary on Isaiah': Christian Exegesis in the Age of Constantine*. OECS (Oxford: Clarendon Press).

HOPKINS, K. (1998), 'Christian Number and its Implications', *JECS* 6: 185–226.

HORBURY, W. (1982), 'The Benediction of the Minim and Early Jewish–Christian Controversy', *JTS*, NS 33: 19–61.

HORNER, T. J. (2001), *Listening to Trypho: Justin Martyr's Dialogue Reconsidered* (Leuven: Peeters).

HOROWITZ, E. (1998), ' "The Vengeance of the Jews Was Stronger than their Avarice": Modern Historians and the Persian Conquest of Jerusalem in 614', *Jewish Social Studies*, 4/2: 1–39.

JACOBS, A. S. (1999), 'Visible Ghosts and Invisible Demons: The Place of Jews in Early Christian *Terra Sancta*', in E. M. Meyers (ed.), *Galilee Through the Centuries: Confluence of Cultures* (Winona Lake, Ind.: Eisenbrauns), 359–75.

—— (2003), 'The Lion and the Lamb: Reconsidering Jewish–Christian Relations in Antiquity', in Becker and Reed (2003*a*), 94–118.

—— (2004), *Remains of the Jews: The Holy Land and Christian Empire in Late Antiquity* (Palo Alto, Calif.: Stanford University Press).

KALMIN, R. (1994), 'Christians and Heretics in Rabbinic Literature of Late Antiquity', *HTR* 87: 155–69.

KIMELMAN, R. (1980), 'Rabbi Yohanan and Origen on the Song of Songs: A Third-Century Jewish–Christian Debate', *HTR* 73: 567–95.

—— (1981), '*Birkat Ha-Minim* and the Lack of Evidence for an Anti-Christian Jewish Prayer in Late Antiquity', in E. P. Sanders, A. I. Baumgarten, and A. Mendelson (eds.), *Jewish and*

Christian Self-Definition, ii: *Aspects of Judaism in the Graeco-Roman Period* (Philadelphia: Fortress Press), 226–44, 391–403.

LAHEY, L. (2006), 'The Christian–Jewish Dialogues through the Sixth Century (Excluding Justin)', in O. Skarsaune and R. Hvalvik (eds.), *Jewish Believers in Jesus: A History from Antiquity to the Present* (Peabody, Mass.: Hendrickson Press), i. 581–639.

LAPIN, H. (1996), 'Jewish and Christian Academics in Roman Palestine: Some Preliminary Observations', in A. Raban and K. G. Holum (eds.), *Caesarea Maritima: A Retrospective after Two Millennia* (Leiden: E. J. Brill), 496–512.

LIEU, J. (1992), 'History and Theology in Christian Views of Judaism', in J. Lieu, J. North, and T. Rajak (eds.), *The Jews among Pagans and Christians in the Roman Empire* (London: Routledge), 79–96.

—— (1994), ' "The Parting of the Ways": Theological Construct or Historical Reality?', *JSNT* 56: 101–19.

—— (1996), *Image and Reality: The Jews in the World of the Christians in the Second Century* (Edinburgh: T & T Clark).

LIMOR, O. (1996), 'Christian Sacred Space and the Jews', in J. Cohen (ed.), *From Witness to Witchcraft: Jews and Judaism in Medieval Christian Thought* (Wiesbaden: Harrassowitz Verlag), 55–77.

LINDER, A. (1987), *The Jews in Roman Imperial Legislation* (Detroit: Wayne State University Press).

LORENZ, R. (1980), *Arius Judaizans? Untersuchung zur dogmengeschichtlichen Einordnung des Arius*, FKDG 31 (Göttingen: Vandenhoeck & Ruprecht).

MEYERS, E. M. (1988), 'Early Judaism and Christianity in the Light of Archaeology', *BA* 51: 69–79.

NEUSNER, J. (1970), *A History of the Jews of Babylonia*, v: *Later Sasanian Times* (Leiden: E. J. Brill).

—— (1999), *Introduction to Rabbinic Literature* (New York: Doubleday).

NORTH, J. (1992), 'The Development of Religious Pluralism', in J. Lieu, J. North, and T. Rajak (eds.), *The Jews among Pagans and Christians in the Roman Empire* (London: Routledge), 174–93.

OLSTER, D. M. (1994), *Roman Defeat, Christian Response, and the Literary Construction of the Jew* (Philadelphia: University of Pennsylvania Press).

REED, A. Y. (2003), ' "Jewish Christianity" after the "Parting of the Ways": Approaches to Historiography and Self-Definition in the Pseudo-Clementines', in Becker and Reed (2003*a*), 189–231.

RUETHER, R. RADFORD (1972), 'Judaism and Christianity: Two Fourth-Century Religions', *SR* 2: 1–10.

RUTGERS, L. V. (1992), 'Archaeological Evidence for the Interaction of Jews and Non-Jews in Antiquity', *AJA* 96: 101–18.

—— (1995), *The Jews in Late Ancient Rome* (Leiden: E. J. Brill).

SCHWARTZ, S. (2001), *Imperialism and Jewish Society, 200 B.C.E. to 640 C.E.* (Princeton: Princeton University Press).

SEGAL, A. (1986), *Rebecca's Children: Judaism and Christianity in the Roman World* (Cambridge, Mass.: Harvard University Press).

—— (1991), 'Studying Judaism with Christian Sources', *USQR* 44: 267–86.

SHOEMAKER, S. J. (1999), ' "Let Us Go and Burn Her Body": The Image of the Jews in the Early Dormition Traditions', *CH* 68: 775–823.

SIMON, M. (1986), *Verus Israel: A Study in the Relations between Christians and Jews in the Roman Empire (135–425)*, trans. H. McKeating (Oxford: Oxford University Press).

STRACK, H. L., and STEMBERGER, G. (1992), *Introduction to the Talmud and Midrash*, trans. M. Bockmuehl (Minneapolis: Fortress Press).

TAYLOR, M. S. (1995), *Anti-Judaism and Early Christian Identity: A Critique of the Scholarly Consensus* (Leiden: E. J. Brill).

URBACH, E. E. (1971), 'The Homiletical Interpretation of the Sages and the Expositions of Origen on Canticles, and the Jewish Christian Disputation', in J. Heinemann and D. Noy (eds.), *Studies in Aggadah and Folk Literature*, ScrHier 22 (Jerusalem: Magnes Press), 247–75.

VARNER, W. (2005), *Ancient Jewish–Christian Dialogues: Athanasius and Zacchaeus, Simon and Theophilus, Timothy and Aquila: Introductions, Texts, and Translations* (Lewiston, NY: Edwin Mellen Press).

VISOTZKY, B. L. (1995), *Fathers of the World: Essays in Rabbinic and Patristic Literatures*, WUNT 80 (Tübingen: J. C. B. Mohr/Paul Siebeck).

WHEELER, B. M. (1991), 'Imagining the Sasanian Capture of Jerusalem: The "Prophecy and Dream of Zerubabel" and Antiochus Strategos' "Capture of Jerusalem" ', *OCP* 57: 69–85.

WILKEN, R. (1971), *Judaism and the Early Christian Mind: A Study of Cyril of Alexandria's Exegesis and Theology* (New Haven: Yale University Press).

—— (1983), *John Chrysostom and the Jews: Rhetoric and Reality in the Late 4th Century* (Berkeley: University of California Press).

WILLIAMS, A. LUKYN (1935), *Adversus Judaeos: A Bird's-Eye View of Christian 'Apologiae' until the Renaissance* (Cambridge: Cambridge University Press).

CHAPTER 9

PAGANS AND CHRISTIANS

MICHELE R. SALZMAN

9.1 APPROACHES

TRADITIONAL narratives on pagans and Christians in the Roman Empire focus on political conflict and end with the triumph of Christianity. In these, the death of Christ opened the way to three centuries of coercion and sporadic outbursts against Christians, precipitated largely by pagans who pressured the state to take action (Frend 1981; Lane Fox 1987: 423–92; Sherwin-White 1964; Ste. Croix 1963, 1964). The emperor Trajan's letter to Pliny is seen as setting the precedent for state policy; Trajan stipulated the pardoning of Christians who proved by worshipping 'our gods' that they were no longer 'atheists'. But those who refused to recant were to be killed, with the imperial caveat that Christians were not be hunted down (Pliny, *Ep.* 10. 96, to Trajan; 10. 97 is Trajan's response). In response to this threatening state policy and to hostility from their suspicious neighbours, Christians sought to explain their religion; Christian apologetic literature flourished.

Only in the middle of the third century did the emperor Decius, in an apparent attempt to unify the Empire, initiate the first Empire-wide religious test that forced the persecution of Christians. Subsequent persecutions by Valerian (257 CE) and Diocletian (303–11) failed miserably as state policy. The conversion of Constantine to Christianity, conventionally dated to his defeat of Maxentius in 312 CE, changed pagan–Christian relations for ever; in 313 CE Constantine and Licinius issued the Edict of Milan which stipulated that the Roman state adopt a position of neutrality and allow religious freedom to all. Constantine soon took the opportunity to favour his new religion with gifts and privileges. But as Christianity 'triumphed' over the course of the fourth century, so too did Christians' growing intolerance for pagans, and also Jews and 'heretical Christians' (Drake 1996; 2000: 20–4). So, in the traditional narrative, Christians end the fourth century by persecuting pagans and coercing their conversion.

The constant element in this traditional narrative is the political conflict between pagans—most often represented by the Roman state before Constantine—and Christians; only the balance of power shifted after Constantine as Christians came to persecute pagans in the new Christian empire. This clear, simple model of pagan–Christian political conflict leading, in the first three centuries, to persecution and martyrdom, and ending, in the fourth century with Christianity triumphant, has been challenged, if not displaced, by nuanced studies of the interactions of pagans and Christians in Roman society. While it is true that politics is still a component in understanding relations between pagans and Christians, social and cultural as well as ideological factors have received greater attention, and the results of these researches have called into question this simple political top-down model of pagan–Christian relations. Even the terms of analysis have been reconsidered.

9.1.1 Terms

There is a growing realization among scholars that the categories—pagans and Christians—are the result of the 'triumph of Christianity narrative'. The category of 'pagan' is a Christian construction, and a rather late one at that; it has been argued that the earliest written usage of the term to signify non-Christians occurs in the writings of Tertullian (*Pall.* 4; *Cor. mil.* 11), but it is not until the fourth century that we find Christian inscriptions using it with some frequency to refer to persons who had not been baptized (O'Donnell 1977; Lane Fox 1987: 30–1; King 2003: 48). Christians before this date used a varied language to refer to their non-Jewish, non-Christian neighbours. They could call them 'Gentile', 'the heathens', 'the nations'; or they could merge them with Greek terminology ('Greek', 'Hellene'). As King observed, 'Jews and Christians were the constants in this triadic grouping, with the pagans designated depending on who was speaking or who was being addressed' (King 2003: 48). From this Christian usage classical historians 'invented' the term 'paganism' to bring together a wide range of traditional religions and cultic practices in the Mediterranean world (Lane Fox 1987: 31).

Given the derogatory and essentially Christian perception of 'paganism' as a rival religious system, some scholars have argued that simply using the term 'pagan' is to assent to the 'Christian view of the division in society' (O'Donnell 2002). But then how to describe the non-Christian, non-Jewish religionists in the Roman Empire?

The term 'polytheist', derived from the usage of anthropology, has been advanced as a more neutral alternative which also focuses on the multiplicity of cults, 'highly discontinuous with one another, highly dissimilar' (O'Donnell 2002; Fowden 1993: 119; Kirsch 2004). However, not all pagans were polytheists; a growing number of scholars see monotheistic tendencies among non-Christians and non-Jews in the early Empire, and have argued that pagans approaching monotheism not only through philosophy but through non-elite cults like *Theos Hypsistos* represent one of the most important innovations in the second- through to the third-century Roman Empire (Athanassiadi and Frede 1999: 1–20; for *Theos Hypsistos*, see Mitchell 1999). So pagans are, arguably, monotheists, much as Jews were, insofar as they focused on one god; but this does not mean that they thought that there was only one god (Fredriksen 2005). So, when Christians call non-Christians polytheists, they are denigrating them just as if they were calling them 'pagans'; in this way, too, they could turn the strong tradition of philosophical monotheism against non-Christians (North 2005: 142).

Trombley attempted to avoid the term 'pagan' entirely. Hence, his book, entitled *Hellenic Religion and Christianization. c. 370–529 CE* (1993–4), translates literally the word used by Christian apologists for non-Christians. Using the adjective 'Hellenic', however, as a general term to describe all non-Christian and native religious elements tends to give everything an Attic patina and obscures the fact that the religion under consideration entailed also Roman, Egyptian, and native cults that were venerated by Roman citizens.

Given the problems in finding new terminology, most scholars have fallen back on using the term 'pagan', but are careful to explain 'pagan' as meaning 'upholders of the ancient or traditional religions' of the Mediterranean. In this regard, Chuvin, for one, focused on the etymology of *pagani*, or pagans, as simply 'people of the place', town or country, who preserved their local customs, whereas the *alieni*, the people from elsewhere, were increasingly 'Christian'; thus, for Chuvin, paganism is the 'religion of the homeland in its narrowest sense: the city and its outlying countryside, characterized by diversity of practices and beliefs' (Chuvin 1990: 9). Moreover, throughout antiquity, paganism was a 'mosaic of established religions linked to the political order' (Chuvin 1990: 9). This focus on native religious traditions coming in contact with outside ideas—that is, Christianity—infuses more recent regional studies of religion in the Empire, such as Frankfurter's important study of religion in Roman Egypt (1998); this book's subtitle, 'Assimilation and Resistance', is meant to 'challenge the simplistic notion of "pagans" deliberately fighting off Christian encroachment' (Frankfurter 1998: 6). Thus Frankfurter, like most ancient historians and religionists, still uses the term 'pagan', but he strips it of its derogatory meaning and uses it with greater sensitivity to its origins (see also Bowersock, 1990: 6; Salzman 2002: 270–1).

For some scholars, the notion that the term 'pagan' was, itself, a construction as a social category is attractive; Hedrick has willingly constructed 'pagans' as the

Christians did, because, he argues, in part, this is what happened in late antiquity: 'Paganism (as everyone agrees) comes into existence in late antiquity, precisely with the rise of Christianity to a position of political dominance. It is a creation of the dialectical opposition of two groups, but it is nonetheless socially real, and any account of the period must consider it' (Hedrick 2000: 52). For North, 'pagan' has the advantage of being a known term; to introduce another term might well create even further confusion (North 2005: 135).

Similarly problematic is the notion that there was one kind of Christian or one kind of Christianity (Mack 1995: 43–96). The numerous varieties of Christians in the Roman Empire, just as the numerous varieties of 'pagans', as well as those who fell between the two or shared in both cultic worlds, or in Judaism (that is, God-fearers; pagan Christians), should make scholars aware of the limits of assuming a deep divide in Roman society along clear-cut fault lines and speaking only in terms of the 'conflict between pagans and Christians'. Moreover, scholars are more and more in agreement that 'the church' was little more than an abstraction in the first three centuries, 'symbolizing a loosely linked confederation of local traditions that, by later standards, were exceptionally diverse in the concepts of correct practice and belief' (Drake 2002: 363). Hence, 'the church' before Constantine was little able to draw such boundaries, and even after this emperor, neither it nor the state was easily able or willing to do so either.

9.1.2 Conflict or Accommodation and Assimilation in the First Three Centuries

Perhaps the most disputed element in the traditional narrative is the central notion of conflict in characterizing pagan–Christian relations in the centuries before Constantine. Focusing on conflict reflects, first and foremost, the nature of our sources. There is little anti-Christian polemic that survives, but the Christian apologetic tradition provides a skewed picture of pagan–Christian relations, suggesting, as it does, Christians facing persecution and conflict without end. Indeed, pagans of the early Empire who mention Christians—notably Pliny the Younger, Suetonius, and Tacitus—allege the sorts of vices associated with many groups deemed deviant: arson, antisocial behaviour, cannibalism, and sexual irregularities like incest. Yet, such hostility and intolerance need not translate into political conflict on a daily basis. (For more on the bias in pre-Constantinian sources, see section 9.3.1 below and G. Clark 2005: 16–37.)

Second, traditional scholarly narratives focus on religious conflict precipitated by the Roman state or its emperor in explaining pagan–Christian relations. This simple top-down political conflict model of religious interaction and change does not take into account the complexity of social and cultural ties that existed between pagans, Christians, Jews, God-fearers, and the like in the Roman Empire. In a world in which these groups lived side by side and interacted on a daily basis and with far less violence than the apologetic sources would suggest, scholars have seen it as increasingly important to consider religion within its social and local contexts, and to take into account how Christians and pagans influenced each other. This approach has been in part inspired by the social sciences, especially anthropology. W. Meeks's study *The First Urban Christians* (1983) was paradigmatic of this new approach and highly influential. His book examined the 'Social World of the Apostle Paul' and the spread of Christianity in the early Empire against the backdrop of an ordinary person's life in specific Roman cities through the lens of social theory and 'moderate functionalism' (1983: 1–8). E. A. Clark (1992) used social network theory to explain the spread of Origen's ideas in the Roman Empire. Lane Fox's book, *Pagans and Christians* (1987), examined the interactions of these two groups within local, historical contexts, although he too devoted much of his analysis of pagan–Christian relations to moments of conflict represented by the spectacular martyrdoms of Christians (Lane Fox 1987: 419–92). Indeed, the impact of martyrdom on pagans and Christians remains a central focus of study in analysing the interaction of these two groups, although the approaches to martyrdom have similarly benefited from more nuanced social and literary theory (Barton 1993; Bowersock 1995; Castelli 2004).

Dissatisfaction with a top-down view of pagan–Christian relations that focuses on conflict has led scholars to re-examine the link between the emperors and these religions. The limits of imperial power have been emphasized in this area, as in others (Salzman 2002: 178–99; compare Millar 1977: 3–12). So, in a groundbreaking article, Rives has argued that the third century saw a new emphasis on universalizing religiosity, represented by Decius's edict (Rives 1999). New notions of the role of religion in Roman society had, in his view, taken hold over the course of the third century. Decius's persecution was, consequently, not an arbitrary top-down policy, as Christian authors have tended to view it, but rather, a response to pre-existing changed notions. Hence, imperial law followed a more general shift in society and religion. Rives's argument reflects, too, the growing emphasis on what pagans and Christians shared concerning Roman culture. The limits of explaining religious change and pagan–Christian relations solely in terms of imperial influence are highlighted by Rives's work and his shift of perspective on the persecution of Christians in the third century.

9.1.3 Constantine's Reign as a Turning Point in Pagan–Christian Relations

Constantine's reign looms large still; but while most scholars can agree that his reign represents a turning point in any narrative of pagan–Christian relations, the direction in which he turned, his point of departure, and his impact have been much contested. Even the terms of the scholarly debate surrounding Constantine have noticeably shifted. In the late nineteenth and into the middle of the twentieth century, the focus was on Constantine's motives for conversion. J. Burckhardt's biography depicted a politically savvy Constantine, playing to the masses of Christians and cynically employing them for his own ends (Burckhardt 1880; 2nd edn. 1949). Early twentieth-century scholars argued over Constantine as a confused pagan syncretist (Piganiol 1932) or an evolving Christian syncretist (J. R. Palanque 1949; Alföldi 1948).

While some scholars may still argue about Constantine's motives, most have increasingly moved away from the fruitless debate about Constantine's sincerity to ask more productive questions concerning the kind of Christianity that Constantine embraced and his impact on pagan–Christian relations. On this, however, there is no consensus. Two recent biographies of Constantine exemplify the divergence in scholarship. According to C. M. Odahl, Constantine was an earnest religious reformer, intent on converting the Empire (2004). H. A. Drake, however, sees Constantine more as a pragmatic politician, searching for religious equilibrium in his laws and in his attempts at mediating between Christians; for Drake, Constantine unleashed religious forces outside his control unwittingly, as he was aiming to unify the Empire, not divide it along pagan–Christian lines (2000). These two scholars differ, too, on their use of the key source for Constantine: namely, Eusebius's *Life of Constantine*. Odahl takes Eusebius more or less at his word; Drake, however, sees Eusebius's *Life* as shaped by his polemical and political intentions, and these, in turn, colour his reporting. Depending, then, on how one reads Eusebius, scholars reach differing conclusions about how effective and aggressive Constantine was in repressing pagans as he advanced Christians. The issue is not his support for Christians—of that there is certainty—but how much his policies set pagans and Christians at odds with one another, and how aggressively the Emperor attacked pagans and their institutions.

9.1.4 After Constantine: Conflict or Accommodation and Assimilation?

It remains a disputed question how best to characterize pagan–Christian relations in the century after Constantine. A. Momigliano's seminal collection of essays emphasized conflict even in its title: *The Conflict between Paganism and Christianity in the Fourth Century* (1963). In an influential paper expanding on his 1945 essay, H. Bloch argued for a pagan reaction and revival in the West at the end of the fourth century (Bloch 1963). Bloch made his argument based on a wide range of evidence, much of it now familiar—that is, the documents on the Altar of Victory controversy, texts written against pagans, most notably the *Carmen contra paganos*, epigraphy, subscriptions to Livy, the *Saturnalia* of Macrobius, the Nicomachorum/Symmachorum diptychs, and the usurpation of Eugenius and Arbogastes—but it all pointed to a party of Roman aristocrats leading a pagan revival in reaction to increasingly hostile Christian imperial pressures.

This interpretation of the late fourth century as one of sharp pagan–Christian conflict sat well with Bloch's generation of scholars who had lived through the Second World War. Bloch's position has been undermined by a new generation of scholars, influenced in large measure by Peter Brown's important 1961 article 'Aspects of the Christianization of the Roman Aristocracy', and by a series of articles by Alan Cameron, beginning with his innovative 1966 article that re-dated the *Saturnalia* of Macrobius to the 430s rather than the 390s (Cameron 1966); both Brown and Cameron advanced a revisionist view of the fourth century that focused on the processes of accommodation and assimilation, rather than conflict, in explaining, among other things, the Christianization of the Roman Empire.

Inspired by this revisionist perspective, scholars re-examined and reinterpreted many of the same events, texts, and artefacts advanced by Bloch as evidence for conflict. For example, in a series of articles, O'Donnell has argued that the rebellion of Eugenius and Arbogast (392–4 CE) that ended in their defeat at the battle at the river Frigidus in 394 was a conflict about dynastic legitimacy, not religious difference; Eugenius (nominally a Christian) had fought for recognition from Theodosius as Emperor in the West (O'Donnell 1979).[1] Reassessing the religious dimension of the usurpation of Eugenius and Arbogastes also highlights one of our best-documented instances of fourth-century pagan–Christian conflict: namely, the controversy concerning the removal of the Altar of Victory from the Roman senate house. For Bloch, the alleged return of this altar by Eugenius at the request of the pagan aristocrat Flavianus was a clear sign that religion was at the heart of the usurpation (Bloch 1963: 195–7; Paulinus of Milan, *Life of Ambrose*, 26). But McLynn, for one, has argued *contra* that the return of the altar was a political move, granted by Eugenius only after he entered Italy and abandoned all hopes of winning Theodosius's support (McLynn 1994: 344–6). And Cameron has argued that even the initial request to return the altar, preserved in Symmachus's famous *Third State Paper* and countered in *Letters* 17 and 18 by the bishop Ambrose, was motivated not so much by religious concerns as by the preservation of Roman traditions of tolerance, a position that suggests a pagan side intent on coexistence and accommodation, not conflict (Alan Cameron 1984). As Cameron sees it, the Christians, not the pagans, turned the altar into a religious *cause célèbre*. Religious conflict, such as it was, according to Cameron, was one-sided; we do not have pagan voices raised in opposition, not because these voices were suppressed, but because pagans in general were too apathetic to write in opposition (Alan Cameron 1984: 45).

A reaction to Cameron's accommodationist view of late Roman pagans' position has emerged among scholars who have come to question the passivity of pagans and this binary vision of pagan–Christian relations as either conflict *or* accommodation and assimilation; C. Hedrick, jun., for one, has argued that 'Religious assimilation and conflict are not mutually exclusive, but are two faces of the same coin. Both are a reaction to a social tension, a religious differentiation, and it is necessary to read each in light of the other, not to choose one over the other' (Hedrick 2000: 50). Similarly, I have argued that religion was part of a late Roman aristocrat's status, culture, and social identity; separating out religion from that identity was a prolonged task, requiring negotiation and reformulation of elite values over the course of the fourth century (Salzman 2002: 61–5). These are but two works that reflect the importance of taking into account the ways in which religion was entwined in all elements of social and political life in the Roman world; to try to remove it entirely from understanding the history and movements of this period is anachronistic.

But scholars dispute—and where Hedrick and I disagree—the degree to which they see religion as the key motivating factor in events. So, for example, Hedrick has argued for religious motivation in the events leading up to the battle at the Frigidus (Hedrick 2000: 42–6, 50–1, 85). Indeed, for Hedrick, this is true, since 'cultural behaviour of all kinds is coherent' (p. 50); even the act of emending pagan texts is part of the broader cultural discourse and hence holds significance as part of a 'pagan' ideology, albeit indirectly (p. 202). While I would agree that religion is embedded in late Roman life, this does not mean that religion should always be taken as the primary, causal factor in all events; emperors, for example, chose military leaders for a host of reasons, not necessarily having to do with religion (Salzman 2002: 192–3).

Assessing the impact of religious motivation is especially difficult, since the Christians controlled the media; in the case of Eugenius's rebellion, no pagan texts survive. Only after the event do we have interpretations, almost entirely from Christians, and these texts are often biased and hence unreliable (Hedrick 2000: 49). For some scholars, like Hedrick, what is key is the way in which these texts control the construction of the past. So, Hedrick claims, even if 'Flavianus, Eugenius, and Arbogast did not see themselves as leading a pagan revolt against Christianity in 394, the usurpation was constructed as a religious rebellion in the years following their demise' (Hedrick 2000: 71–2). Hence Hedrick would elide religious motivation with religious reconstruction; such an elision is not satisfying to historians who see it still as their task to assess the causes of events.

Recent scholarship has moved away from the simple binary model of social relations and political religious conflict that characterized traditional narratives on pagan–Christian relations. Most fruitful have been recent re-examinations of the most extreme forms of alleged pagan–Christian conflict: namely, those involving violence. The sources—mostly Christian—from the post-Constantinian world offer many instances of violence motivated by religion. This evidence has led some scholars, like MacMullen, to argue that violence and coercion were necessary and significant factors in converting pagans to Christianity in the fourth and early fifth centuries (MacMullen 1986: 86–101; 1997: 1–73). Violence was essential since, by most estimates, Christians were no more than a 10 per cent minority in the Empire at the beginning of the reign of Constantine (MacMullen 1986; Stark 1996: 6).

Other scholars have been hesitant to place so much emphasis on violence as the predominant factor in the conversion of pagans; they underscore a wider range of social and cultural factors in explaining religious change, and in pagan–Christian relations in general (compare Gaddis 2005; Mc Lynn 1992; Salzman 2006; Trombley 1993–4). One of the most promising examples of this approach that breaks away from a strictly binary model of social relations is J. Hahn's source-critical analysis of alleged religious violence that occurred in four cities from the years 312–425 CE: Alexandria, Antioch, Gaza, and Panopolis. His main conclusion is, I think, important; he finds that religious violence is not the norm, but rather the exception in late antiquity; religious conflicts were nearly always mingled with other problems— economic, social, political, generational (Hahn 2004: 292). In most cities, pagans, Christians, and Jews lived side by side in relatively peaceful coexistence. Hahn arrived at this through a careful analysis of the sources, which, in his view, indicate a Christian tradition that focuses on religious violence and conflict, but which is, essentially a '*reduktionistische . . . Perspektive*' (Hahn 2004: 275). Studies such as Hahn's indicate the necessity of detailed, source-critical research; but his work also underscores the importance of integrating social and cultural factors along with the political and theological issues in explaining pagan–Christian relations in a local context.

Finally, the traditional view of Christianity triumphant by the late fourth century can no longer be accepted at face value. Trombley, for one (1993–4: 1–97, 380–6), has demonstrated in abundant detail the resilience of paganism and how differently pagan cults were Christianized in various parts of the eastern empire at different times. Moreover, this process unfolded through to the early sixth century.

9.2 NEW DIRECTIONS

Scholars in search of a more nuanced understanding of pagans and Christians in the Roman Empire have re-examined not only the sources, but also their reliance on the conflict model. More and more, scholars have turned their attention to what pagans and Christians shared in religion and society. Consequently, scholars have studied such areas of ancient life as friendship networks, patronage ties, education, commerce, family bonds, and artefacts in assessing the nature of pagan–Christian relations. This focus on shared social and cultural elements represents to me an undeniable advance over previous generations of scholars who focused almost exclusively on political conflict to chart the relations between pagans and Christians.

The incorporation of social and cultural factors alongside political and theological issues to gain a more balanced perspective is one of the key shifts in the study of pagan–Christian relations in the past 35 years. Many of the studies noted above exemplify this approach (e.g. Frankfurter 1998; MacMullen 1986; McLynn 1994), but much work remains to be done. To mention but one area, the texts of Gnostics, Chaldaean oracles, and Neoplatonic thinkers show quite clearly that there was much common ground between pagans and Christians (Athanassiadi 1999; Frede 1999). Scholars who have studied late Platonism in relation to Christian theology have discussed this connection particularly well (Armstrong 1990; O'Daly 2001). But mapping out common ground between pagans and Christians on specific issues—such as attitudes toward deity, death, monotheism, rituals, festivals, to name but a few—remains a desideratum.

Finally, the social and cultural elements shared by pagans and Christians need to be studied within specific geographic and chronological parameters. So, for example, expectations for women likely affected pagan–Christian relations in the East differently from those in the West. And civic structures affected the role of the bishop in the East differently from those in the West, and varied too between large and small cities. Only through nuanced studies that locate pagan–Christian relations within specific historical contexts will we be able to understand the forces that mediated the vertical, political forces for religious conflict and change.

9.3 Sources

9.3.1 Textual Sources before Constantine

Given the growing awareness of the limits on categories of 'pagan' and 'Christian' and the fluidity of religious identity in the first three centuries of the Empire, scholars have become increasingly sensitive to the ways in which they interpret the sources for pagans and Christians. Here, dates do matter; Christian apologists in the centuries before Constantine were writing in a world in which they could be martyred for their faith. In defence of their religion, Christians in the East, like Justin Martyr and Tatian, and in the West, Minucius Felix, defended their practices even though, as Edwards has argued, we cannot know if the defence they offered responded to specific attacks (Edwards, Goodman, and Price 1999: 1–14). Indeed, we do not even know whether or how many other works, now lost, attacked Christianity. And, as King has argued, one of the principal aims of the apologists was the construction of Christian identity and the spreading of their religion (King 2003: 22–40).

In sharp contrast, non-Christians—that is, pagans—did not consider Christians and Christianity as key factors in constructing their social identity in the first and second centuries. Only a small group of early second-century texts by pagans mention Christians. Suetonius, who served in the administration of the emperor

Hadrian, included two references to Christians in his *Lives of the Emperors Claudius* (24. 5) and *Nero* (16. 2). In the latter, he notes that Christians were 'followers of a new and wicked superstition' (*superstitio nova ac malefica*). The early second-century historian Tacitus, governor of the province of Asia under Trajan, describes the Christians who were scapegoated for Nero's fire in 64 CE as members of a deadly cult (*exitiabilis superstitio*) and adds the intriguing note that the Christians were 'hated for their crimes' (*flagitia*; *Annals* 15. 44). Similarly, the younger Pliny, who wrote to the emperor Trajan in 112 CE, called Christianity a 'perverse and excessive superstition' (*superstitio prava et immodica*; *Ep.* 10. 96). To these second-century pagans, Christianity was a *superstitio*, an excessive and unacceptable new cult, barely worth noting except as a potential threat to public safety (Beard, Price, and North 1998: i. 217–28).

The first pagan author we know of who took Christianity seriously enough to write a philosophical polemic against it is Celsus. *The True Doctrine*, written probably between 175 and 181 CE, is primarily known through Origen's *Contra Celsum*, itself written *c.* 240 CE. Similarly, the Neoplatonist Porphyry, writing at the end of the third century, directed some fifteen books against Christians (perhaps part of a longer work); since these were burned under Constantine, what we know of his argument is through Christian writers, especially Eusebius and Augustine, who quoted Porphyry to attack him. Hence, scholars have had to reconstruct pagan attitudes toward Christians in the first through the third centuries largely as refracted through Christian apologetic works. This fact has certain important implications: for one, scholars cannot assume that the Christian apologists' depiction of relations between pagans and Christians represents simple historical reality. Indeed, the rhetorical ends of these texts need to be considered, and, as Edwards (Edwards, Goodman, and Price 1999) has well argued, the connection of Christian apologetic to the contemporary world needs further examination. One way to address the limitations of the texts is to turn to non-textual sources, notably art and architecture. This is also true in the later centuries (see section 9.3.3).

9.3.2 Textual Sources from the Age of Constantine and After

One of the key elements in the shift in the scholarship on Constantine has been an awareness of the fruitlessness of trying to reconstruct Constantine's original religious intent based on our sources; our best text for these intentions, Eusebius's *Life of Constantine*, was written as a panegyric, then revised by Eusebius into a biography intended to highlight Constantine's religious role, including citations of the Emperor's laws and letters on behalf of the Church but written in such a way as to avoid offending his successors. Yet, Eusebius's personal contact with the Emperor was limited to four public occasions (Barnes 1981: 265–7). After Eusebius died in 339 CE, the *Life* was published by a redactor who did little to change its content

(Pasquali 1910). Given the circumstances of its composition and posthumous publication for hagiographic reasons and to influence Constantine's successor, the veracity of the *Life* as a source has been very differently interpreted (see section 9.1.3).

In order to balance the views of Eusebius, scholars have turned to a wide variety of textual documents. Constantine's *Letters*, many of them included in Eusebius's *Life*, have at times been the focus of attention (e.g. Baynes 1972). Other scholars have focused on the law codes of Constantine and his successors that survive in the Code of Theodosius and in the Code and Novels of Justinian. Yet, these laws, as recent studies have shown, were shaped both by their original collectors and by the nature of their transmission and reconstruction (Harries and Wood 1993; Matthews 2000). Hence, scholars who use these laws for pagan–Christian relations need to be aware of the ways in which the complex transmission of these codes shaped the modern texts they use. Moreover, scholars must also acknowledge the prescriptive nature of Roman law; laws do not necessarily indicate lived reality and often lag behind it (Salzman 1993). The same caveats apply to scholars who turn to the canons of the church councils that bear on pagan–Christian relations.

For the age of Constantine and continuing into the fifth century, there survive many textual sources to reconstruct pagan–Christian relations. Most of these sources were written by Christians. They include a wide range of documents, ranging from the private letter collections of key Christian figures—such as Jerome, Augustine of Hippo, Ambrose of Milan, Gregory of Nazianzus, Basil of Caesarea—to the public pronouncements of prominent people, as preserved by their sermons and theological tracts. Christian apologists continued to write into the fifth century; even though pagan sacrifice and cult rituals were outlawed, Christian writers still felt that they had to defend Christianity by explaining, as did Augustine in his *City of God*, why disasters befell a now Christian empire.

It is from the fourth century that we have, understandably, our clearest pagan responses to the growing number of Christians in their midst. In addition to the *Third State Paper* (*Relatio*) by Symmachus, written in response to the removal of the Altar of Victory from the Roman senate house in 384 CE, we also have the pagan emperor Julian's work *Against the Galilaeans*. These are central texts for examining the pagan view of Christianity. Indeed, the fourth century saw a revival of Latin literature and history, much of it of use in examining pagan and Christian relations (Alan Cameron 1984).

9.3.3 Non-textual Sources

To assess pagan–Christian relations, scholars have been willing to look beyond texts to incorporate epigraphic and numismatic as well as archaeological evidence. For the age of Constantine and after, this is rich indeed. The discussion of the usurpation of Eugenius as pagan–Christian conflict above is exemplary; the scholarship revolved around a wide range of sources, including inscriptions and the Nicomachorum/Symmachorum diptychs as well as the letters of Ambrose and the State Papers of the pagan Symmachus on the Altar of Victory controversy. Artefacts, such as the *Codex-Calendar of 354* and the *Esquiline Treasury* help to reconstruct the daily lives of pagans and Christians and show how much they indeed shared one world (Salzman 1990; Elsner 1998). In dealing with this wealth of information, historians have to be aware of the genres and traditions of the material evidence; yet the richness of these and of the textual remains allow for creative scholarship not possible in dealing with other periods of ancient religion.

NOTE

1. O'Donnell (1979) also pointed out several other problems with the revolt when viewed as a conflict narrative, including the fact that the number of pagans involved in this revolt is unattested, and no pagan aristocrat other than Flavianus is named; after the defeat, only Flavianus appears to have chosen suicide over surrender (Rufinus, *Hist. eccl.* 2. 33).

SUGGESTED READING

Primary sources

Many of the key primary sources for pagan–Christian relations both before and after Constantine have noted in this chapter. There is an abundance of texts by Christian authors that mention pagans, and of special note are the works by Christian apologists in Greek and Latin (for a useful bibliography, see Edwards, Goodman, and Price 1999: 277–81). Far fewer pagans mention Christians. The early second-century writers Suetonius, Tacitus, and Pliny have already been noted (see section 9.3.1). For the pre-Constantinian period, the pagan attack on Christianity is preserved via Origen's *Against Celsus*. For the third century, the fragments of Porphyry's work *Against the Christians* are of special note.

The reign of Constantine is a turning point for our sources. The *Life of Constantine* by Eusebius, now conveniently edited by A. Cameron and S. Hall (1999), is essential reading. Christian apologists continue to write through the fourth and fifth centuries, as evidenced, for instance, by Eusebius's *Against Hierocles* and Cyril of Alexandria's *Against Julian*. Pagan voices that are preserved and are of special import in this regard include Julian's *Against the Galilaeans* (fragmentary) and Symmachus's *Third State Paper*. For a good survey of the primary sources for the fourth century, see Averil Cameron (1993: 199–207). For an English translation of the *Theodosian Code*, see Pharr (1952). For the *Novels* and *Code of Justinian*, there is an unreliable English translation by S. P. Scott (1973; first pub. 1932).

There are several good collections of primary sources in translation that bear on pagans and Christians. Of special note is Croke and Harries (1982); Hillgarth (1986); Lee (2000); Maas (2000); and Valantasis (2000).

Secondary sources

Many of the key secondary works have been noted in the discussion. For an excellent entrée into the study of pagans and Christians, see Lane Fox (1987). For a good survey of the evidence for the pagan persecution of Christians, but outdated in terms of analysis, see Frend (1981 repr.). For the Christian apologists, see Edwards, Goodman, and Price (1999). For the nature of late Roman paganism, see MacMullen (1983); Athanassiadi and Frede (1999); and Beard, North, and Price (1998). For the study of Christianity in the Roman Empire, G. Clark (2005) is an excellent guide; see too Markus (1990). For the reign of Constantine, Drake (2000) and Odahl (2004) are the most recent and useful guides to the major issues involved, but Barnes (1981) is also invaluable for detailed chronological and textual matters especially. For the conversion of pagans to Christianity in the post-Constantine period, see G. Clark (2005); Fowden (1993); Frankfurter (1998); MacMullen (1986, 1997); Salzman (2002); Trombley (1993–4).

BIBLIOGRAPHY

ALFÖLDI, A. (1948), *The Conversion of Constantine and Pagan Rome*, trans. H. Mattingly (Oxford: Clarendon Press).

ARMSTRONG, A. H. (1990), *Hellenic and Christian Studies* (Aldershot: Variorum; Brookfield, Vt.: Gower Publishers).

ATHANASSIADI, P. (1999), 'The Chaldaean Oracles: Theology and Theurgy', in Athanassiadi and Frede (1999), 149–84.

——and FREDE, M. (1999) (eds.), *Pagan Monotheism in Late Antiquity* (Oxford: Oxford University Press).

BARNES, T. D. (1981), *Constantine and Eusebius* (Cambridge, Mass.: Harvard University Press).

BARTON, CARLIN A. (1993), *The Sorrows of the Ancient Romans: The Gladiator and the Monster* (Princeton: Princeton University Press).

BEARD, M., NORTH, J., and PRICE, S. (1998), *Religions of Rome*, 2 vols. (Cambridge: Cambridge University Press).

BAYNES, N. H. (1972), *Constantine the Great and the Christian Church*, with a preface by H. Chadwick. Originally published as *Proceedings of the British Academy, 1929* (London: Oxford University Press for the British Academy, 2nd edn. (1st edn. repr.)), 341–442.

BLOCH, H. (1945), 'A New Document of the Last Pagan Revival in the West', *HTR* 38: 199–244.

——(1963), 'The Pagan Revival in the West at the End of the Fourth Century', in Momigliano (1963), 193–217.

BOWERSOCK, G. W. (1990), *Hellenism in Late Antiquity* (Ann Arbor: University of Michigan Press).

——(1995), *Martyrdom and Rome* (Cambridge: Cambridge University Press).

BROWN, P. (1961), 'Aspects of the Christianization of the Roman Aristocracy', *JRS* 51: 1–11.

BURCKHARDT, J. (1880), *Die Zeit Konstantins des Grossen*, trans. M. Hadas, *The Age of Constantine the Great* (New York: Dorset Press, 1989, orig. 1949).

CAMERON, ALAN (1966), 'The Date and Identity of Macrobius', *JRS* 54: 25–38.

CAMERON, ALAN (1984), 'The Latin Revival of the Fourth Century', in W. Treadgold (ed.), *Renaissances before the Renaissance: Cultural Revivals of Late Antiquity and the Middle Ages* (Stanford, Calif.: Stanford University Press), 42–58.

CAMERON, AVERIL (1993), *The Later Roman Empire* (Cambridge, Mass.: Harvard University Press).

——and HALL, S. (1999), *Eusebius: Life of Constantine* (Oxford: Oxford University Press).

CASTELLI, E. (2004), *Martyrdom and Memory: Early Christian Culture Making* (New York: Columbia University Press).

CHUVIN, PIERRE (1990), *A Chronicle of the Last Pagans*, trans. B. A. Archer (Cambridge, Mass.: Harvard University Press).

CLARK, E. A. (1992), *The Origenist Controversy: The Cultural Construction of an Early Christian Debate* (Princeton: Princeton University Press).

CLARK, G. (2005), *Christianity and Roman Society* (Cambridge: Cambridge University Press).

CROKE, B., and HARRIES, J. (1982), *Religious Conflict in Fourth Century Rome* (Sydney: Sydney University Press).

DRAKE, H. (1996), 'Lambs into Lions: Explaining Early Christian Intolerance', *Past and Present*, 153: 3–36.

——(2000), *Constantine and the Bishops: The Politics of Intolerance* (Baltimore: Johns Hopkins University Press).

——(2002), 'A Response to Liz Clark', *Scottish Journal of Theology*, 55: 363–8.

EDWARDS, M., GOODMAN, M., and PRICE, S. (1999) (editors in association with Christopher Rowland), *Apologetics in the Roman Empire: Pagans, Jews and Christians* (Oxford: Oxford University Press).

ELSNER, J. (1998), *Imperial Rome and Christian Triumph* (Oxford: Oxford University Press).

FOWDEN, G. (1993), *Empire to Commonwealth: Consequences of Monotheism in Late Antiquity* (Princeton: Princeton University Press).

FRANKFURTER, D. (1998), *Religion in Roman Egypt: Assimilation and Resistance* (Princeton: Princeton University Press).

FREDE, M. (1999), 'Monotheism and Pagan Philosophy in Later Antiquity', in Athanassiadi and Frede (1999), 41–68.

FREDRIKSEN, P. (2005), Review of G. Clark (2005), *JECS* 13: 532.

FREND, W. H. C. (1981), *Martyrdom and Persecution in the Early Church: A Study of a Conflict from Maccabees to Donatus* (Grand Rapids, Mich.: Baker Book House; originally Oxford: Basil Blackwell, 1965).

GADDIS, M. (2005), *There is No Crime for Those who have Christ: Religious Violence in the Christian Roman Empire* (Berkeley: University of California Press).

HAHN, J. (2004), *Gewalt und religiöser Konflikt: Studien zu den Auseinandersetzungen zwischen Christen, Heiden und Juden im Osten des Römischen Reiches (von Konstantin bis Theodosius II)*, Beiträge zur Alten Geschichte, Beihefte. NS 8 (Berlin: Akademie Verlag).

HARRIES, J., and WOOD, I. (1993) (eds.), *The Theodosian Code* (Ithaca, NY: Cornell University Press).

HEDRICK, C. JR. (2000), *History and Silence: Purge and Rehabilitation of Memory in Late Antiquity* (Austin, Tex.: University of Texas Press).

HILLGARTH, J. N. (1986), *Christianity and Paganism, 350–750* (Philadelphia: University of Pennsylvania Press).

KING, K. (2003), *What is Gnosticism?* (Cambridge, Mass.: Harvard University Press).

KIRSCH, J. (2004), *God against the Gods: The History of the War between Monotheism and Polytheism* (New York: Viking Press).

LANE FOX, R. (1987), *Pagans and Christians* (New York: Alfred A. Knopf).

LEE, D. (2000), *Pagans and Christians in Late Antiquity* (London: Routledge).

MAAS, M. (2000), *Readings in Late Antiquity* (London: Routledge).

MACK, B. (1995), *Who Wrote the New Testament?: The Making of the Christian Myth* (San Francisco: Harper San Francisco).

MACMULLEN, R. (1983), *Paganism in the Roman Empire* (New Haven: Yale University Press).

—— (1986), *Christianizing the Roman Empire, A.D. 100–400* (New Haven: Yale University Press).

—— (1997), *Christianity and Paganism in the Fourth to Eighth Centuries* (New Haven: Yale University Press).

MARKUS, R. A. (1990), *The End of Ancient Christianity* (Cambridge: Cambridge University Press).

MATTHEWS, J. F. (2000), *Laying down the Law: A Study of the Theodosian Code* (New Haven: Yale University Press).

MCLYNN, N. (1992), 'Christian Controversy and Violence in the Fourth Century', *Kodai*, 2: 15–44.

—— (1994), *Ambrose of Milan: Church and Court in a Christian Capital* (Berkeley: University of California Press).

MEEKS, W. (2003), *The First Urban Christians: The Social World of the Apostle Paul*, 2nd edn. (New Haven: Yale University Press).

MILLAR, F. (1977), *The Emperor in the Roman World* (Ithaca, NY: Cornell University Press).

MITCHELL, S. (1999), 'The Cult of *Theos Hypsistos* between Pagans, Jews and Christians', in Athanassiadi and Frede (1999), 81–148.

MOMIGLIANO, A. (1963) (ed.), *The Conflict between Paganism and Christianity in the Fourth Century* (Oxford: Oxford University Press).

NORTH, J. (2005), 'Pagans, Polytheists, and the Pendulum', in W. V. Harris (ed.), *The Spread of Christianity in the First Four Centuries: Essays in Explanation* (Leiden: E. J. Brill), 125–43.

ODAHL, C. M. (2004), *Constantine and the Christian Empire* (New York: Routledge).

O'DALY, G. (2001), *Platonism Pagan and Christian: Studies in Plotinus and Augustine* (Aldershot: Ashgate).

O'DONNELL, J. J. (1977), 'Paganus', *Classical Folia*, 31: 163–9.

—— (1979), 'The Demise of Paganism', *Traditio*, 35: 43–88.

—— (2002), A review of Salzman (2002), *BMCR* 2002.06.04; <http://ccat.sas.upenn.edu/bmcr/2002–06–04.html>.

PASQUALI, G. (1910), 'Die composition der *Vita Constantini* des Eusebius', *Hermes*, 45: 368–86.

PHARR, C. (1952), *The Theodosian Code and Novels and the Sirmondian Constitiutions: Translation, with Commentary* (Princeton: Princeton University Press).

PIGANIOL, A. (1932), *L'Empereur Constantin* (Paris: Rieder).

RIVES, J. (1999), 'The Decree of Decius and the Religion of the Empire', *JRS* 89: 135–54.

SALZMAN, M. R. (1990), *On Roman Time: The Codex-Calendar of 354 and the Rhythms of Urban Life in Late Antiquity* (Berkeley: University of California Press).

—— (1993), 'The Evidence for the Conversion of the Roman Empire to Christianity in the Theodosian Code', *Historia*, 42: 362–78.

SALZMAN, M. R. (2002), *The Making of a Christian Aristocracy: Social and Religious Change in Late Antiquity* (Cambridge, Mass.: Harvard University Press).

—— (2006), 'Re-thinking Pagan–Christian Religious Violence', in H. A. Drake (ed.), *Violence in Late Antiquity: Perceptions and Practices* [based on papers presented at the fifth biennial Conference on Shifting Frontiers in Late Antiquity, held at the University of California, Santa Barbara, 20–3 March 2003] (Aldershot: Ashgate), 265–85.

SCOTT, S. P. (1973), *The Civil Law, including the Twelve Tables, the Institutes of Gaius, the Rules of Ulpian, the Opinions of Paulus, the Enactments of Justinian, and the Constitutions of Leo: Translated from the Original Latin, Edited, and Compared with all Accessible Systems of Jurisprudence Ancient and Modern* (New York: AMS Press; originally published in 1932 by The Central Trust Company, Cincinnati, Ohio).

SHERWIN-WHITE, A. N. (1964), 'Why were the Early Christians Persecuted?—An Amendment', *Past and Present*, 27: 23–7.

STARK, R. (1996), *The Rise of Christianity* (Princeton: Princeton University Press).

STE. CROIX, G. E. M. DE (1963), 'Why were the Early Christians Persecuted?', *Past and Present*, 26: 6–31.

—— (1964), 'Why were the Christians Persecuted?—A Rejoinder', *Past and Present*, 27: 28–33.

TROMBLEY, F. R. (1993–4), *Hellenic Religion and Christianization c. 370–529 CE*, Religions in the Graeco-Roman World, 115, 2 vols. (Leiden: E. J. Brill).

VALANTASIS, R. (2000) (ed.), *Religions of Late Antiquity in Practice*, Princeton Readings in Religions (Princeton: Princeton University Press).

CHAPTER 10

··

'GNOSTICISM'

··

ANTTI MARJANEN

10.1 APPROACHES TO 'GNOSTICISM'

··

THE state of research into what is traditionally called 'Gnosticism', a religious phenomenon of late antiquity,[1] is opaque or even confusing at the moment. In a recent collection of essays on the topic, two prominent scholars approach the topic of 'Gnosticism' in very different ways. Birger Pearson states: 'in answer to the question posed by the theme of this [volume], "Was There a Gnostic Religion?" my reply is: Yes there was, and it still exists' (Pearson 2005b: 101).

Michael Williams, in turn, concludes with the comment: 'Louis Painchaud recently expressed the opinion that it is increasingly apparent that full advantage of the study of Nag Hammadi and related texts will be realized only when one "dims the switch" (*mettre en veilleuse*) on the category Gnosticism. I would say we should at least consider turning it off completely, to see what might only then be visible in the natural light of the sources themselves' (Williams 2005b: 79). In a footnote Williams specifies his view even more pointedly: 'I only allude with the metaphor to a position that I do hold strongly, that the most common current framework—the category 'Gnosticism' in its conventional forms—has indeed become very obstructive to our reading of the actual content of our sources. Whether it can ever adequately be reshaped by new analysis of these sources, or whether at this stage it is merely in the way, is one of the important issues in debate here.'

The major part of research for this article was carried out during a period of study at Yale Divinity School in the spring of 2006. The opportunity was made possible by a grant from the Academy of Finland.

The two views presented above well illustrate that in the current scholarly discussion no consensus prevails as to how the religious category or phenomenon 'Gnosticism' is to be conceived or even employed. Therefore, every treatment or usage of the term 'Gnosticism' has to be accompanied by a definition of its content and some clarification of the purpose for which the term is being used. However, before suggesting parameters for a modern study of 'Gnosticism', it will be helpful to see how the phenomenon has been perceived in the past. In the history of the study of 'Gnosticism', there have basically been three ways to approach this religious phenomenon. The first represents an ancient view, contemporary with the assumed genesis of 'Gnosticism'. The other two are later scholarly products.

10.1.1 Heresiological Approach

Although the early Christian theologians of the second, third, and fourth centuries, most notably Irenaeus, Clement of Alexandria, Tertullian, Hippolytus, and Epiphanius, did not use the term 'Gnosticism',[2] they referred to contemporary religious thinkers and groups that they called 'gnostics' or that, according to them, gave themselves this title (Marjanen 2005: 10–24). In their presentations, these church fathers do provide excerpts of the mythological accounts as well as information on doctrines and religious practices of various religious groups they regard as 'gnostics'. Common to these groups is at least a separation between the Highest God and the creator, a dichotomy between the human body and the divine soul embedded in it, and an idea of saving knowledge (*gnōsis*). Nonetheless, the primary purpose of the descriptions of the church fathers is not to give an analytical and systematic—let alone unbiased—picture of the 'gnostics'. On the contrary, they serve to point out the heretical character of the teachings and practices of these religious opponents. Thus, the writings of the church fathers tend to depict such features—real, caricatured, or even imaginary—which make 'gnostics' appear to be both ridiculous and dangerous.

Irenaeus wrote the first extant heresiological work, *Refutation and Overthrow of What is Falsely Called Gnosis*, commonly known as *Against Heresies* (c. 180 CE). He laid out the basic strategy against 'gnostics' which some of the later heresiologists would also use in their polemics. First of all, it was important to Irenaeus to show that the origin of all heresies could be ascribed to a single figure of dubious reputation. Irenaeus's candidate for that role was Simon Magus, who was known to be a Christian convert but whose attempt to buy the authority to impart the gift of the Holy Spirit rendered him suspect in the eyes of the readers, especially when Irenaeus failed to say anything about his repentance, mentioned by Luke in Acts 8 (*Haer.* 1. 23. 1). Simon's position as an arch-heretic was further corroborated by the fact that Irenaeus informed his readers that Simon Magus had followers in Rome who regarded him as a god.

Second, Irenaeus argued for a clearly observable genealogy of heretical movements, starting with Simon, continuing with various 'gnostic' teachers and groups, and ending up with his main adversaries, the Valentinians (King 2003: 31–2). The use of the genealogy metaphor gave Irenaeus and his later fellow heresiologists a powerful weapon in their struggle against their opponents. As John Henderson has pointed out, the genealogy of heresy 'gave order and coherence to a very puzzling and diverse set of phenomena by linking them together in a chain of succession. . . . The genealogy of heresy having been established, later heresiologists found it both effective and economical to attack later heresies by linking them with already refuted and discredited earlier ones' (1998: 151–2).

Irenaeus's third strategical move was to place all important heresies under the same umbrella by calling them by the same name. This made it easier to refute their views, because it could be done collectively. The name Irenaeus chose for this purpose was 'gnostics'. Although he seemed to know a particular heretical group which he called by this name (*Haer*. 1. 29–30), in the course of his writing he could also expand the scope of the term to include other religious groups and persons, such as the Basilideans, the Carpocratians, the adherents of Saturninus, and finally even Marcion, Valentinus, Simon Magus himself, as well as Menander (Marjanen 2005: 11–12).

Fourth, Irenaeus wanted to emphasize the mutual divergences of various 'gnostic' groups. This served to demonstrate that the heretics lacked any kind of social and doctrinal unity (King 2003: 31). It was no problem, for example, to say that some 'gnostics' believed that the world was created by angels (*Haer*. 3. 11. 2), whereas others insisted that the false father was the maker of heaven and earth (*Haer*. 4. 6. 4).

Irenaeus's heresiological approach to 'Gnosticism' was thus 'to show that the gnostics had a common origin and name, they formed a chain of heretical succession, but in reality they were a quarrelling bunch of people who, above all, did not share the apostolic origin and teaching' (Marjanen 2005: 13). Irenaeus's followers, Hippolytus, Tertullian, and Epiphanius, added to this characterization an additional polemical note. They argued that the real inspiration of the 'gnostics' lay in pagan philosophy. Not even Clement of Alexandria, who could use the term 'gnostic' for a spiritually advanced Christian, saw anything positive in a false 'gnostic'. For him, like his predecessors and fellow heresiologists, this kind of gnostic was nothing but a heretic *par excellence*.

10.1.2 Typological Approach

Along with the Enlightenment, the scope of the study of 'Gnosticism' changed. Although the heresiological concerns did not entirely vanish, as emphatically pointed out by Karen King (2003, 2005), scientifically more acceptable approaches began to develop. The first scientific studies of 'Gnosticism' were mostly interested in its origins. These genealogical approaches could see 'Gnosticism' either as part of the intra-Christian development or as a non- or extra-Christian phenomenon which eventually infiltrated or affected the Christian religion. For example, they could demonstrate that the conversion of Jesus' uncomplicated and genuine faith into a philosophical and ascetic 'gnostic' religion was due to the influence of the Hellenistic spirit (Harnack) or that 'Gnosticism' was a pre-Christian religious movement which had its roots in ancient Persian religion and which also underlay many early Christian conceptions (Bousset, Reitzenstein). The genealogical approaches were a necessary forerunner of the typological characterizations which became the most important twentieth-century approach to 'Gnosticism'.

The typological approach to 'Gnosticism' considers it an independent religion or religious movement with definable doctrinal and social characteristics. Although typological definitions are reached by making observations on a certain set of ancient religious texts, they serve as overarching theoretical models which are assigned to understand and explain individual features in various 'gnostic' texts and groups representing the 'gnostic' religion.

A thorough characterization of the basic features of 'Gnosticism' was presented already by Adolf Harnack (1961: i. 257–62; King 2003: 62–3; Marjanen 2005: 34), but it was some 50 years ago when the most influential typology of 'Gnosticism' was produced. When Hans Jonas wrote his seminal overall presentation of 'Gnosticism', he styled his work *The Gnostic Religion* (1963), thus suggesting that, in addition to Christianity and Judaism, the Hellenistic world became a matrix of a third religion which utilized traditions of the Hebrew Bible. Although Jonas recognized that the 'gnostic religion' consisted of various factions and currents, he insisted not only that they could be brought together under a common heading but also that they shared main religious tenets typical of them all.

According to Jonas, 'Gnosticism' was characterized by eight basic features (Jonas 1963, 1967; Marjanen 2005: 42–4):[3] (1) the idea of *saving knowledge* (*gnōsis*), the content of which consists of transcendent history, including the events that led to the origin of the lower world; (2) the dynamic, emanative nature of the divine self which led to a *history of devolution*; (3) the *mythical character* of the gnostic thought presented not in a philosophical discourse but in a story; (4) a *radically dualistic world-view* manifesting itself in the sharp differentiation between the true God of the transcendent realm and the ignorant or evil creator of the lower world, as well as in the dichotomy between the human body and the divine self embedded in it; (5) the *aggressive polemics* it displays against other religious traditions, for example the Jewish conception of God; (6) the *artificiality* and *non-originality* of its myth; (7) the syncretistic character of its religious views; (8) the *pneumatic morality*, which may lead to either asceticism or libertinism.

Jonas's typological approach to 'Gnosticism' has found a large following (Rudolph 1983; Markschies 2003; Meyer 2003; Pearson 2005*b*), although the nature and number of characteristics attached to the phenomenon may vary. Some advocates of the typological approach may also accept that a 'gnostic' text, group, or thinker need not necessarily embrace all the features typical of 'Gnosticism'. Therefore, some definitions of 'Gnosticism' may regard as 'gnostic', for example, the *Gospel of Thomas*, Marcion, and Hermetic writings, while others exclude them.

10.1.3 Self-Designation Approach

Rather than concentrating on a set of typological features, Bentley Layton (1995) begins his approach to 'Gnosticism' with an observation that some ancient religious groups are said to have identified themselves as 'gnostics'. Based on this, Layton suggests that, in the first centuries of the common era, there were historically and socially definable groups that not only were called 'gnostics' by their adversaries but that also used the term as a proper noun to characterize themselves. Thus, he starts his approach to 'Gnosticism' with the study of the testimonia about the use of this self-designation.[4] By the aid of these testimonia, Layton identifies as 'gnostics' the 'so-called "Knowledge-Supplying" school of thought' mentioned by Irenaeus in *Haer*. 1. 11. 1, as well as the Carpocratians in *Haer*. 1. 25. 6 and the 'Barbelognostics' in *Haer*. 1. 29, the 'gnostics' referred to by the Neoplatonist philosopher Porphyry (*V. Plot.* 16) and a non-Christian Middle Platonist Celsus (*Origen, Cels*. 5. 61), as well as Prodicus mentioned by Clement of Alexandria in *Strom*. 2. 117. 5 (Layton 1995: 338).

After having established the basic set of testimonia about the 'gnostics', Layton uses the mythological material found in them, especially in that of the 'Barbelognostics' imparted by Irenaeus in *Haer*. 1. 29, to reconstruct the principal content of the 'gnostic' mythological teaching. By comparing it with the corresponding mythological data found in other relevant sources, Layton can expand his 'gnostic' evidence to include the *Apocryphon of John*, a Sethian or 'Barbelognostic' text found in three exemplars in the Nag Hammadi library and in one in the so-called Berlin Codex. Layton also points out that Porphyry refers to three Sethian texts: *Zostrianos*, the *Book of Zoroaster* (excerpted in the longer version of the *Apocryphon of John*), and *Allogenes* (discovered not long ago in the Nag Hammadi library), texts which the 'gnostics' in Rome used during the time of Plotinus. On the basis of these observations, Layton concludes that the so-called Sethian sources in the Nag Hammadi library and related documents, fourteen in number, and the Sethian system, identified and described for the first time by Hans-Martin Schenke (1974, 1981), should be considered 'gnostic'.

According to Layton, the fourteen 'Sethian gnostic' texts include the *Apocryphon of John*, the *Book of Zoroaster* (excerpted in the longer version of the *Apocryphon of John*), the *Apocalypse of Adam*, the *Hypostasis of the Archons*, the *Trimorphic Protennoia*, *Thunder: Perfect Mind*, the *Gospel of the Egyptians*, *Zostrianos*, *Allogenes*, the *Three Steles of Seth*, *Marsanes*, *Melchizedek*, the *Thought of Norea*, and the *Untitled Text* in the Bruce Codex (Layton 1995: 342–3).

A further step in Layton's approach is to trace additional material, comparable to the testimonia about the 'gnostics' and the fourteen Sethian texts, in order to increase 'gnostic' evidence, although that data may be ascribed to other religious mythmakers in the sources. In this way, Layton adds to his corpus of 'Gnosticism' Saturninus of Antioch, Epiphanius's 'Gnostics', Sethians, and Archontics, as well as the group called Audians by Theodore bar Koni.[5]

In its starting point, Layton's approach clearly disagrees with the typological approach. It is worth noting, however, that Layton and some modern representatives of the typological approach, such as Birger Pearson (2005b), end up with a similar understanding of 'Gnosticism', with Sethian texts and the Sethian system at its core. To be sure, Pearson's typological categorization of 'Gnosticism' allows him to expand the phenomenon wider than Layton; therefore, he also includes in his definition of 'Gnosticism' at least Simon Magus, Menander, the Valentinians, the Mandeans (Pearson 2005b), and Basilides (Pearson 2005a).

10.1.4 What Can Ancient 'Gnosticism' Mean Today?

It is clear that of the three approaches sketched above, the heresiological one can no longer be legitimately adopted by modern 'Gnosticism' scholarship. In order to elevate one Christian tradition above all the others, the nascent 'orthodoxy' denigrated others by calling them heretical. In this process, the term 'gnostic' became practically synonymous with a 'heretic'. In the Christian polemics of the first centuries, this kind of approach served survival needs. In modern scholarship, however, there is no justification for this sort of strategy. On the contrary, ancient alternative Christian movements need to be heard in their own right, both for their own sake and for a better understanding of the overall development of early Christianity.

Not even the two modern approaches to 'Gnosticism', typological and self-designation, have escaped criticism. In his influential book, *Rethinking 'Gnosticism': An Argument for Dismantling a Dubious Category* (1996), and in his later article (2005b), Michael Williams sets out to challenge both approaches. The basic problem he sees with any typological definitions of 'Gnosticism' is that they do not do 'justice to the diverse data that by scholarly convention have come to be lumped into this category' (Williams 1996: 51). Williams provides many examples of the texts, usually thought to represent 'Gnosticism' or a 'gnostic' religion, which at one or several points deviate from what is usually called 'gnostic' according to typological definitions. For instance, a so-called Sethian text, *Marsanes* 41. 30–42. 11, can contain an exhortation to contemplate the order of the cosmos and thus diverge from a radical anti-cosmism, a feature supposedly very typical of the so-called 'gnostic' attitude (Williams 2005b: 69).

In his criticism of Layton's approach, Williams points out that, given the important role that the self-designation 'gnostics' has in Layton's understanding of

'Gnosticism' as an ancient historical phenomenon, it is astonishing that this self-designation appears only in heresiological testimonia, but nowhere in Nag Hammadi or other original sources. Layton defends his thesis by stressing that in the texts, which do not speak of second- and third-century school controversies but rather of primordial, eschatological, and metaphysical events and relationships, there is 'no context in which a second-century school name such as Gnostikos might naturally occur' (Layton 1995: 344). Layton's counter-argument is not very convincing, however, since in the 'gnostic' data base identified by him there are several other self-designations, such as 'race of Seth', 'children of light', 'the immovable race', which, despite Layton's objections, are hardly qualitatively different from 'gnostikoi'.

Based on his critical observations of typological and Layton's self-designation approaches, Michael Williams has suggested that the categories 'Gnosticism' or 'a gnostic religion' be abandoned altogether. Instead, one should accept that in the first centuries of the Common Era there developed various new religious movements which underlie the sources that scholars have customarily treated under the heading 'Gnosticism'. Although some of these religious movements reveal common features and may even represent social continuity, many of them are so different from each other that to lump them together in one category 'Gnosticism' is more harmful than helpful for understanding them. Therefore, Williams recommends that rather than defining a single religion into which one must fit all available data, a more flexible and useful approach might be to identify common significant phenomenological features which various writings and traditions share and subject them to study. For Williams, a good example of this kind of feature is the notion of 'demiurgy', a motif that many scholars have regarded as a central hallmark of 'Gnosticism' in their typological definitions. Yet, the term 'biblical demiurgical', which for Williams is the characterization of 'a teaching that ascribes the creation and management of the cosmos to some lower entity or entities, distinct from the highest divinity, and in the process incorporates or adapts traditions from Jewish or Christian scripture' (Williams 2005b: 78), should not be considered just another label for 'Gnosticism'. Rather, it is a heuristic category which functions as 'a simple typology for organizing several religious innovations and new religious movements' (Williams 1996: 265–6) without necessarily assuming other specific doctrinal or sociological connections between them.

Williams's rejection of 'Gnosticism' as a label for an ancient religion is confirmed by Karen King, who also insists that there was no such thing as 'Gnosticism', 'if we mean by that some kind of ancient religious entity with a single origin and distinct set of characteristics' (King 2004: 653). For her, the term 'belongs to the discourse of normative identity formation'. In this discourse—especially in its initial phase, but also later, including modern times—'Gnosticism' refers to all varieties of early Christianity that are characterized by too little or too negative an appropriation of Judaism, to any outside, non-Jewish contamination of pure

Christianity or its pre-Christian roots, as well as to any tradition said to be closely related to this contaminated Christianity, whether or not they contain explicitly Christian elements (e.g. Hermeticism, Platonizing Sethianism, Mandaeism, and Manichaeism). 'Gnosticism' has thus become a problematic term, since 'a rhetorical term has been confused with a historical entity' (King 2003: 1). Behind the term there is nonetheless a variety of mostly unrelated individuals and groups, the study of whom and whose writings is of course possible and desirable, whether or not they are called 'gnostic'.

What kind of conclusions should one draw from Williams's and King's critical comments on the previous use and content of the term 'Gnosticism' for the future study of the texts traditionally called 'gnostic'? Should the term 'Gnosticism' be dropped altogether as a misleading generalization which only hampers the genuine character of the individual texts from becoming evident? Or could the term be employed as a means of general classification, if its use and content were redefined?

To be sure, Williams's proposal to turn '[the category "Gnosticism"] off completely, to see what might only then be visible in the natural light of the sources themselves' (Williams 2005b: 79), is a valid alternative. Detailed analyses and inter-textual comparisons of the texts, which contribute to our overall understanding of early Christianity as well as its components and development, are possible without making too hasty conclusions about their general theological character and perspective.

Yet, although Michael Williams has expressed serious doubts about the possibility of defining the term 'Gnosticism' in such a manner that it could still be used in a meaningful and precise way, I will make a suggestion to that effect here. Even Williams admits that, in spite of remarkable differences, there are common characteristics among various texts and currents traditionally called 'gnostic'. The fact that Williams can place a large number of texts normally called 'gnostic' in the category 'biblical demiurgical' on the basis that they contain a notion of (an) evil or ignorant world creator(s) separate from the highest divinity most clearly proves the point. In addition, he points out that many of the texts share another common feature; they presuppose that the human soul or spirit originates from a transcendental world and, having become aware of that, has the potential of returning there after life in this world (Williams 2005b: 78). I suggest that the combination of these two features found together in or presupposed by numerous texts and myths creates the prerequisite for classifying these texts and myths under the same heading. Without positing the existence of a distinct 'gnostic' religion or a common social context which would account for the origin of the texts, the texts can still be classified as 'gnostic'. When this term is used, it should indeed be seen as a heuristic scholarly construct comprising the two main characteristics presented above. Understood in this bipolar way, 'Gnosticism' can be employed as a typologically defined category but, compared to previous typologies, in a minimalistic and more controllable sense. It is also important to emphasize that 'Gnosticism' cannot be used as an analytical tool by which one interprets individual texts and their features. Rather, it is to be seen as a means by which one can group ancient religious texts and thinkers for closer analysis and comparison.

Delineated in this bipolar manner, 'Gnosticism' is to be seen as a broader concept than in Layton's self-designation approach, but as a narrower term than in many traditional typological approaches. 'Gnosticism' can, for example, include Valentinian mythography, since that contains both a notion of an ignorant world creator and a pre-existent soul that has the potential of returning to a transcendent realm after having received the gnosis of its divine origin. On the other hand, the *Gospel of Thomas* cannot be regarded as 'gnostic', since it lacks the idea of a distinct creator. Marcion, in turn, made a clear distinction between the true God and the demiurge, but did not accept the 'gnostic' notion of the divine element within a human being; hence Marcion cannot be considered 'gnostic'.

10.2 SOURCES

Until the middle of the eighteenth century, when the first original 'gnostic' sources were discovered, the view of 'Gnosticism' was based solely on heresiological writings. Although highly polemical and not always trustworthy by nature, they still provide important complementary source material for the study of 'Gnosticism'. The most important heresiological writers are Irenaeus of Lyons (*c.* 115–*c.* 202), Clement of Alexandria (*c.* 160–215), Tertullian (*c.* 160–*c.* 225), Origen (*c.* 185–*c.* 253), Hippolytus of Rome (*c.* 170–236), Pseudo-Tertullian (3rd century), and Epiphanius (*c.* 315–403). Irenaeus, Hippolytus, and Epiphanius have composed multi-volume, systematic refutations of contemporary 'heresies', and Pseudo-Tertullian presents a concise summary of heretical teachers and movements from Simon Magus to Praxeas. Apart from Pseudo-Tertullian, the others also quote some important original sources. Irenaeus, for example, summarizes a 'gnostic' text resembling the *Apocryphon of John* (*Haer.* 1. 29). In his *Refutation of All Heresies.* Hippolytus cites, among other things, the so-called *Naassene Hymn* (*Haer.* 5. 10. 2), and Epiphanius has preserved a famous Valentinian text, *Ptolemy's Letter to Flora* (*Pan.* 33. 3. 1–7. 10).

Although Tertullian has not written a systematic refutation of heresies, in his apologetic and theological texts he nevertheless provides much useful information on Christian movements he considers 'heretical'. Usually he deals with 'heretical' opinions in connection with certain theological themes (flesh of Christ, resurrection of the dead), but he has also composed a special refutation against one 'gnostic' movement, the Valentinians. Clement of Alexandria and Origen are important authors, since they quote original 'gnostic' sources which are otherwise unknown. Clement of Alexandria is the only source for a Valentinian teacher, Theodotus. Origen, for his part, cites the Valentinian Heracleon in his *Commentary on the Gospel of John*.

The first 'gnostic' original sources surfaced in the second half of the eighteenth century. Codex Askewianus, a Coptic manuscript which contained *Pistis Sophia*, was purchased by a British collector, Dr Askew, in London in 1773, later transferred to the British Museum, and first published in 1851. *Pistis Sophia* consists of four books, the fourth being only secondarily attached to the first three. The texts can be dated to the third century. Both *Pistis Sophia I–III* and *Pistis Sophia IV* are revelation dialogues in which the risen Saviour converses with his disciples. The topics vary from the destiny of the fallen Sophia, here called Pistis Sophia, and the human souls to the ultimate fate of various sinners. The other eighteenth-century Coptic 'gnostic' manuscript was Codex Brucianus, comprising three texts: *First* and *Second Book of Jeu*, containing teachings of Jesus to his disciples, and a Sethian *Untitled Text*, presenting a theogony and cosmogony.

The following two 'gnostic' original sources came to light when another Coptic manuscript, discovered in Egypt, was acquired for the Berlin Museum in 1896. After its initial introduction in the same year, unfortunately it took nearly 60 years before the codex, Papyrus Berolinensis 8502, was published. Hence, the texts of the codex, the 'gnostic' *Apocryphon of John* and *Sophia of Jesus Christ*, as well as the 'non-gnostic' *Gospel of Mary* and *Act of Peter*, did not receive the attention they deserved. In fact, even when finally published, the manuscript tended to be eclipsed by a fabulous new manuscript find, the Nag Hammadi library, especially since this discovery also contained both 'gnostic' texts found in Papyrus Berolinensis 8502.

The year 1945 was a turning point in the study of 'Gnosticism'. In December of that year, approximately 10 kilometres from the town of Nag Hammadi, some Egyptian fellahs accidentally came upon a jar which contained twelve Coptic codices. Eventually, after many dramatic events involving blood revenge, some papyrus leaves being used as kindling, and smuggling, the codices arrived at the Coptic Museum in Cairo (Robinson 1988: 22–5). Already the first inspections of the texts assured scholars that the number of 'gnostic' original sources had increased manifold. In fact, initially many of the scholars who had access to the manuscripts assumed almost uncritically that practically all of the fifty-two texts of the library were 'gnostic'.

It was only after more careful study that it began to become evident that the composition of the library was very diverse, and it was not necessarily the 'gnostic' character of the texts—according to any definition of 'Gnosticism'—which had led them to be part of the same collection. There were also other features in the texts which united many of them, such as an emphasis on asceticism and a fascination with the esoteric and the mystical. Still, it is clear that the Nag Hammadi library contains more 'gnostic' original sources than all the other manuscript finds until

now. In the following pages, I shall briefly introduce those Nag Hammadi documents which can be characterized as 'gnostic' according to the bipolar definition
presented above.

In the Nag Hammadi library there are two major sets of 'gnostic' literature
which are generally recognized, although the exact boundaries of the two sets
can be debated. The core of the first set, the Valentinian texts, is usually seen to
consist of the following eight works: the *Prayer of the Apostle Paul*, *Gospel of Truth*,
Treatise on the Resurrection, *Tripartite Tractate*, *Gospel of Philip*, *First Apocalypse
of James*, *Interpretation of Knowledge*, and *A Valentinian Exposition*. A borderline
case, characterized as Valentinian by some scholars, not by others, is the *Second
Apocalypse of James*.

Among the Valentinian Nag Hammadi texts, the two which rise above others
as far as their general interest and significance is concerned are the *Gospel of
Truth* and the *Tripartite Tractate*. Despite its name, the *Gospel of Truth* is not a
gospel but rather a homily, in which knowledge is proclaimed as the way to the
Father and to eternal rest. Unlike the description of a Valentinian theology by
Irenaeus, the *Gospel of Truth* does not posit a primal dyad but regards the Father
as a sole source of the transcendental totality. In this way, the *Gospel of Truth* is
clearly part of that branch of Valentinian theology, represented by the *Tripartite
Tractate*, *A Valentinian Exposition*, and the Valentinians depicted by Hippolytus,
which is characterized by monadic ontology. Another unusual feature of the *Gospel
of Truth* is the fact that the text does not make any explicit mention of the fall of
Sophia or of the creation by the demiurge. This dearth has caused some scholars
to conclude that the *Gospel of Truth* is not Valentinian at all. Yet the references to
'the totality searching for the one from whom they had come forth' (*Gos. Truth* 17.
5–6; translation by Attridge and MacRae) and to error who 'became powerful' and
who 'set about with a creation' (*Gos. Truth* 17. 14–15, 18) may be hidden allusions
to a Valentinian myth, although the role of error is more negative than that of the
Valentinian demiurge in other texts. Since Irenaeus knows about a text called the
Gospel of Truth which the Valentinians used (*Haer.* 3. 11. 9), it has been suggested
that the work could date from the middle or even the first part of the second
century. This early dating combined with a rather uncomplicated theology and
a beautiful style has likewise led some scholars to think that the *Gospel of Truth*
was written by Valentinus himself. This thesis, however, has not been generally
accepted.

The *Tripartite Tractate* is a lengthy theological treatise which 'gives an account
of the whole process of devolution from and reintegration into the primordial
Godhead' (Attridge and Pagels 1985: 176). Like the *Gospel of Truth*, the *Tripartite
Tractate* also represents monadic Valentinian theology. This is illustrated by the
fact that Sige ('silence'), Nous ('mind'), and Aletheia ('truth') are not co-workers
of the Father in producing other transcendental aeons, but are qualities which
describe the state of his being (Attridge and Pagels 1985: 180). In its account of the

devolution of the divine, the *Tripartite Tractate* contains a surprising feature. Unlike other Valentinian (or other 'gnostic') cosmogonies, the *Tripartite Tractate* does not attribute the fall to the activity of Sophia but to the Logos. The Logos, whose choice for this task is possibly suggested by the Johannine prologue (Attridge and Pagels 1985: 181), initiates the unfortunate process of creation, but does not act out of ill will but out of love, although his inability prevents him from accomplishing what he wishes. The whole description tries to emphasize that, in the final analysis, even the creation of the world is something which happens according to the divine plan. The Logos repents of his action, and this repentance leads to a process of restoration and salvation not only to Valentinians but to all Christians.

The second set of 'gnostic' literature which scholars have found in the Nag Hammadi library is the Sethian texts. Some of the ancient heresiologists had indeed referred to a 'gnostic' group they styled Sethians, but it was only the Nag Hammadi find which made it possible to speak about a Sethian text corpus. Hans-Martin Schenke (1974, 1981) was the first to realize that certain Nag Hammadi documents, although quite varied, disclose a common set of mythological themes, such as a primordial divine triad consisting of Father (Invisible Spirit), Mother (Barbelo), and Son (Autogenes–Christ); four aeons and illuminators called Armozel, Oroiael, Daveithe, and Eleleth, constituting the final place of rest for Adam, Seth, the seed of Seth ('gnostics'), and those who repent late; the emergence from Sophia of lower entities, including Yaldabaoth (Sakla, Samael), who become rulers of the material world situated under the divine realm; Yaldabaoth and his companions, who create humans in the image of the divine Adam and imprison them in the material body; and a distinctive periodization of history: the age of Adam, the age of Seth, the age of the original Sethians, and the present time.

Since all the above-mentioned characteristics do not all necessarily occur in the same text or exactly in the same form, there have been some differences of opinion as to which Nag Hammadi texts should be included in the Sethian corpus. A fairly common view among those who subscribe to the Sethian thesis is that, apart from *Thunder: Perfect Mind*, all the texts found in the list broached by Layton (see above) should be classified as Sethian. Recently, some suspicions about the homogeneity of the Sethian corpus, have been raised. In his dissertation, Tuomas Rasimus (2006) has suggested that instead of one Sethian corpus, one should talk about a wider 'classic gnostic' trajectory which consists of three clusters of material, 'Ophite', 'Barbeloite', and 'Sethite'. Rasimus's three-branched 'Classic Gnosticism' partly overlaps with Schenke's notion of Sethian Gnosticism, but it also expands the number of available sources (e.g. *Eugnostos the Blessed*, *Sophia of Jesus Christ*, and *On the Origin of the World* are included), and, above all, its point of departure is that the three mythologies underlying 'Classic Gnosticism' originally formed independent traditions. Only later were they interconnected when individual authors utilized and linked them in various combinations. Rasimus argues that only in one writing, the *Apocryphon of John*, are all three traditions brought together, whereas in others two of them are interfused. Some documents even represent only one particular mythological tradition.

In addition to Valentinian and so-called Sethian works, the Nag Hammadi library comprises several 'gnostic' texts which defy classification. Among them, one can mention the *Apocalypse of Paul, Concept of Our Great Power, Second Treatise of Great Seth, Apocalypse of Peter, Letter of Peter to Philip*, and the *Testimony of Truth*. The *Apocalypse of Paul* is a description of the apostle's ascent through the heavens. During his journey through the heavens he meets both ascending souls and gatekeepers. Having resisted the attempt of a demiurgical figure to prevent him from proceeding to the seventh heaven, Paul joins with the twelve apostles in the eighth heaven, and they all go up to the tenth, which is the goal of the ascent. The *Concept of Our Great Power* is a 'gnostic' explication of salvation history in apocalyptic form. Time is divided into several periods. The fleshly aeon ends with the Flood, and the Saviour appears during the psychic aeon. The final aeon is unchangeable and characterized by beauty.

The *Second Treatise of Great Seth* contains a revelation discourse delivered by Jesus to the 'perfect and incorruptible ones', and the *Apocalypse of Peter* is an account of a revelation imparted to Peter and explicated by Jesus. Both texts are polemical. The *Second Treatise of Great Seth* describes the true understanding of Jesus and his teachings over against false Christians who think 'they are advancing the name of Christ' (59. 25–6) while persecuting those liberated by Christ. In the *Apocalypse of Peter* the Christians are seen as split into several factions, who attack and persecute the 'gnostic-Christian' group represented by Peter. One interesting detail appears in both texts when they describe the crucifixion. In docetic fashion, Jesus is portrayed as watching and laughing when somebody else is nailed on the cross instead of him.

Despite its title, the *Letter of Peter to Philip* is not a letter but a revelation dialogue between the risen Saviour and his disciples. The basic thrust of the text is to advise Christians how to fight evil powers, and to explain why they have to suffer. The *Testimony of Truth* is a polemical text. The first part is written to support Christians who are in danger of following the commandments of the Law, placing false hopes in martyrdom and bodily resurrection, and yielding to carnal temptations. The latter part, which is unfortunately badly damaged, strongly criticizes other Christians and their views. It is interesting that the criticism is directed not only against representatives of the nascent 'orthodoxy' but also against Valentinians, Basilideans, and Simonians.

The latest addition to the 'gnostic' text corpus is provided by the famous Codex Tchacos which, after many exciting events, was finally acquired for restoration and is now being edited. The Coptic manuscript is comprised of four texts (Kasser *et al.* 2006: 49–50). Two of them, the *First Apocalypse of James* and the *Letter of Peter to Philip*, are versions of texts already known from the Nag Hammadi library. The two others, the *Gospel of Judas* and the *Book of Allogenes*, were previously unknown.

For the time being, only the *Gospel of Judas* has been published. It is a revelation dialogue between Jesus and his disciples. Jesus' most perceptive interlocutor is Judas Iscariot, who not only understands his master best, but who also agrees to fulfil his last request—to hand him over and to free him from the body which fettered him to the earth. The *Gospel of Judas* seems to derive much of its material from Sethian and/or 'Barbelognostic' mythology. It contains a notion of the divine triad (Invisible Spirit, Barbelo, Autogenes) and the four primary luminaries, as well as 360 other luminaries, a reference to the incorruptible race of Seth, and a mention of Yaldabaoth as the creator of humanity (Meyer in Kasser *et al.* 2006: 137–69).

10.3 CHALLENGES FOR THE STUDY OF 'GNOSTICISM'

As the first section of this chapter paradoxically demonstrates, during the last 20 years the definition of 'Gnosticism' has become the most difficult issue in the study of 'Gnosticism'. Future research will have to show whether a new, working definition, which does justice to the sources and which can gain general acceptance, can be reached, or whether the category has become so meaningless and confusing that it has to be rejected altogether, and the texts which used to be called 'gnostic' should be classified exclusively under other labels, such as Valentinian, Sethian, Ophite, Christian, or 'biblical demiurgical'.

In the nineteenth and twentieth centuries, another crucial issue in the study of 'Gnosticism' was the question of its origins. There were several competing theories, the most important ones situating the beginnings of 'Gnosticism' in Hellenistic, Jewish, Persian, or Christian milieux. The purpose of this search was mainly an attempt to explain the phenomenon itself, to ascertain a kind of 'gnostic' identity, with the understanding that if one knows the roots one can determine the content and the further development. Although the quest for the origins of 'Gnosticism' has not completely vanished from the research agenda of 'Gnosticism' scholars, it has lost its significance and at the same time become more difficult. We have become more and more aware that various cultural phenomena do not generally have clearly definable beginnings; they are always part of a continuum—or actually continua, which meet and cross each other. They do not begin, but they develop, change, give and receive impulses, and form new combinations. Therefore, a new challenge in understanding a phenomenon such as 'Gnosticism' is to trace trajectories and to study the innovations which take place in them.

Heresiologists refer to numerous 'gnostic' groups and thinkers. A good example is Epiphanius, who introduces eighty 'heresies' in his *Panarion*. Among them are those of 'non-gnostic' groups and teachers and also those which he invents in order to come up to the round figure presupposed by his Old Testament proof-text. Still, there remains a plethora of different 'gnostic' groups he claims to know. The same is true with Irenaeus and Hippolytus. The picture one seems to get based on the extant authentic 'gnostic' sources is different. The only names of 'gnostic' groups and teachers which are explicitly mentioned by the Nag Hammadi documents are Valentinus, Basilides, Isidore, and Simonians in the polemical statements of the *Testimony of Truth*. In fact, practically none of the 'gnostic' Nag Hammadi texts is connected with any group or teacher. This is even true with those texts which scholars have later identified as Valentinian or Sethian. What is the reason for this discrepancy? Have we really lost all the writings that formed the basis for heresiologists writing their accounts of various 'gnostic' groups? Or have they fabricated all their descriptions? Or can some of the extant original sources be connected with some 'gnostic' groups or teachers based on a closer analysis of both the original sources and the reports of the heresiologists?

Since the discovery of the Nag Hammadi library, much time and energy has been used for the study of the texts. Nevertheless, most of the effort has still been invested in the editing and translating of the documents. Only a few 'gnostic' texts, such as the *Gospel of Truth*, the *Apocryphon of John*, the *Gospel of Philip*, and the *Hypostasis of Archons*, have really become the object of thorough and versatile investigations. In order that the Nag Hammadi texts can really make a contribution to our overall understanding of early Christianity, detailed studies of both the text and symbolic world of all Nag Hammadi writings are needed. To combat stereotypical views of 'Gnosticism', it is also crucial that the questions of 'gnostic' ethics, social history, power politics, and gender be included in the future research agenda of the Nag Hammadi texts.

Notes

1. The term is also used in connection with medieval or even modern phenomena (see Smith 1988; van den Broek and Hanegraaff 1998; Hanegraaff 2006), but since the present study is confined to the period of late antiquity, the later use of the term is beyond the scope of the article.
2. As pointed out by Bentley Layton (1995: 348–9), the term 'Gnosticism' was coined by a seventeenth-century English theologian, Henry More.
3. The presentation of Jonas's typological definition of 'Gnosticism' is a combination of the characteristic 'gnostic' features presented by him in *The Gnostic Religion* (1963: 34–7, 42–7) and in his article from 1968.
4. The name 'Self-Designation Approach' is not invented by Bentley Layton himself but by me (see also Williams 1996: 31–43). I choose to use this rather cumbersome title since it nevertheless indicates in a shorthand fashion that the starting point of Layton's

approach is to trace those texts which contain a reference to the self-designation 'gnostic' and which thus provides the basis for creating a 'gnostic' data base. Karen King (2003: 14) describes Layton's methodology as 'a nominalist approach to defining Gnosticism'.

5. Layton's characterization of 'Gnosticism' in his 1995 article corresponds to what he called 'Classic Gnostic Scripture' in his earlier work *The Gnostic Scriptures* (1987). In addition to the 'Classic Gnostic Scripture', the latter work includes other related texts: the writings of Valentinus, the school of Valentinus, the school of St Thomas, and other early currents. Nevertheless, these texts are not for Layton 'gnostic' in the strict technical sense of the word. According to him, 'Valentinus and his followers', for example, 'can best be kept apart as a distinct mutation, or reformed offshoot, of the original Gnostics' (Layton 1995: 343).

SUGGESTED READING

Primary sources

BARNSTONE, W., and MEYER, M. (2003) (eds.), *The Gnostic Bible* (Boston: Shambhala).

HOLL, K. (1915–33) (ed.), *Epiphanius: Panarion und Anchoratus*, 3 vols., GCS 25, 31, 37 (Leipzig: J. C. Hinrichs; vols. ii and iii rev. J. Dummer 1980–5; Berlin: Akademie Verlag).

MARKOVICH, M. (1986) (ed.), *Hippolytus: Refutatio omnium haeresium*, PTS 25 (Berlin: de Gruyter).

ROBERTS, A., and DONALDSON, J. (1885–7) (eds.), *Ante-Nicene Fathers*, rev. A. Cleveland Coxe, 10 vols. (repr. Peabody, Mass.: Hendrickson, 1995).

ROBINSON, J. M. (1988) (ed.), *The Nag Hammadi Library in English*. 3rd rev. edn. (Leiden: E. J. Brill).

ROUSSEAU, A., DOUTRELEAU, L., and MERCIER, C. (1952–82) (eds.), *Irénée de Lyon: Contre les hérésies*, 9 vols., SC 100, 152–3, 210–11, 263–4, 293–4 (Paris: Éditions du Cerf).

WILLIAMS, F. (1987) (trans.), *The Panarion of Epiphanius of Salamis: Book I (Sects 1–46)*, NHS 35 (Leiden: E. J. Brill).

——(1994) (trans.), *The Panarion of Epiphanius of Salamis: Books II and III (Sects 47–80, De Fide)*, NHMS 36 (Leiden: E. J. Brill).

See also Kasser *et al.* (2006); Layton (1987).

Secondary literature

DUNDERBERG, I. (2005), 'The School of Valentinus', in A. Marjanen and P. Luomanen (eds.), *A Companion to Second-Century Christian 'Heretics'*, Suppl. VC 76 (Leiden: E. J. Brill), 64–99.

FILORAMO, G. (1990), *A History Gnosticism*, trans. A. Alcock (Oxford: Blackwell).

KING, K. L. (2006), *The Secret Revelation of John* (Cambridge, Mass.: Harvard University Press).

LEBOULLUEC, A. (1985), *La notion d'hérésie dans la littérature grecque IIe–IIIe siècles*, 2 vols. (Paris: L'Institut d'études augustiniennes).

MARJANEN, A. (2005) (ed.), *Was There a Gnostic Religion?*, Publications of the Finnish Exegetical Society, 87 (Helsinki: The Finnish Exegetical Society; Göttingen: Vandenhoeck & Ruprecht).

PAGELS, E. (1979), *The Gnostic Gospels* (New York: Random House).

THOMASSEN, E. (2006), *The Spiritual Seed: The Church of the 'Valentinians'*, NHMS 60 (Leiden: E. J. Brill).

TURNER, J. D. (2001), *Sethian Gnosticism and the Platonic Tradition*, Bibliothèque copte de Nag Hammadi, 'Études', 6 (Quebec: Les Presses de l'Université Laval; Louvain: Peeters).

—— and MAJERCIK, R. (2000) (eds.), *Gnosticism and Later Platonism: Themes, Figures, and Texts*, Symposium Series, 12 (Atlanta: SBL).

WILLIAMS, M. A. (2005a), 'Sethianism', in A. Marjanen and P. Luomanen (eds.), *A Companion to Second-Century Christian 'Heretics'*, Suppl. *VC* 76 (Leiden: E. J. Brill), 32–63.

See also King (2003); Markschies (2003); Rudolph (1983); Williams (1996).

BIBLIOGRAPHY

ATTRIDGE, H. W., and MACRAE, G. W. (1985), 'NHC I,3: The Gospel of Truth', in H. W. Attridge (ed.), *Nag Hammadi Codex I (The Jung Codex): Introductions, Texts, Translations, Indices*, NHS 22 (Leiden: E. J. Brill), 55–117.

—— and PAGELS, E. (1985), 'NHC I,5: The Tripartite Tractate', in H. W. Attridge (ed.), *Nag Hammadi Codex I (The Jung Codex): Introductions, Texts, Translations, Indices*, NHS 22 (Leiden: E. J. Brill), 159–337.

BROEK, R. VAN DEN, and HANEGRAAFF, W. J. (1998) (eds.), *Gnosis and Hermeticism: From Antiquity to Modern Times* (Albany, NY: SUNY Press).

HANEGRAAFF, W. J. (2006), 'Gnosticism', in K. von Stuckard (ed.), *The Brill Dictionary of Religion*, ii: E–L (Leiden: E. J. Brill), 790–8.

HARNACK, A. (1961), *History of Dogma*, trans. from 3rd German edn. by Neil Buchanan, 4 vols. (New York: Dover).

HENDERSON, J. B. (1998), *The Construction of Orthodoxy and Heresy: Neo-Confucian, Islamic, Jewish, and Early Christian Patterns* (Albany, NY: SUNY Press).

JONAS, H. (1963), *The Gnostic Religion: The Message of the Alien God and the Beginnings of Christianity*, 2nd edn. rev. (London: Routledge).

—— (1967), 'The Delimitation of the Gnostic Phenomenon—Typological and Historical', in U. Bianchi (ed.), *Le origini dello gnosticismo: Colloquio di Messina, 13–18 Aprile 1966*, Studies in the History of Religions (Supplements to *Numen*), 12 (Leiden: E. J. Brill), 90–108.

KASSER, R., MEYER, M., and WURST, G. (2006) (eds.), *The Gospel of Judas from Codex Tchacos* (Washington D.C.: National Geographic).

KING, K. L. (2003), *What Is Gnosticism?* (Cambridge, Mass.: Belknap Press of Harvard University Press).

—— (2004), 'Esotericism and Mysticism: Gnosticism', in S. I. Johnston (ed.), *Religions of the Ancient World: A Guide* (Cambridge, Mass.: Belknap Press of Harvard University Press), 652–6.

KING, K. L. (2005), 'The Origins of Gnosticism and the Identity of Christianity', in A. Marjanen (ed.), *Was There a Gnostic Religion?*, Publications of the Finnish Exegetical Society, 87 (Helsinki: The Finnish Exegetical Society; Göttingen: Vandenhoeck & Ruprecht), 103–20.

LAYTON, B. (1987), *The Gnostic Scriptures*, The Anchor Bible Reference Library (New York: Doubleday).

—— (1995), 'Prolegomena to the Study of Ancient Gnosticism', in L. M. White and O. L. Yarbrough (eds.), *The Social World of the First Christians: Essays in Honor of Wayne A. Meeks* (Minneapolis: Fortress Press), 334–50.

MARJANEN, A. (2005), 'What Is Gnosticism? From the Pastorals to Rudolph', in A. Marjanen (ed.), *Was There a Gnostic Religion?*, Publications of the Finnish Exegetical Society, 87 (Helsinki: The Finnish Exegetical Society; Göttingen: Vandenhoeck & Ruprecht), 1–53.

MARKSCHIES, C. (2003), *Gnosis: An Introduction*, trans. J. Bowden (Edinburgh: T & T Clark).

MEYER, M. (2003), 'Gnosticism, Gnostics, and the Gnostic Bible', in W. Barnstone and M. Meyer (eds.), *The Gnostic Bible* (Boston: Shambhala), 1–19.

PEARSON, B. A. (2005*a*), 'Basilides the Gnostic', in A. Marjanen and P. Luomanen (eds.), *A Companion to Second-Century Christian 'Heretics'*, Suppl. *VC* 76 (Leiden: E. J. Brill), 1–31.

—— (2005*b*), 'Gnosticism as a Religion', in A. Marjanen (ed.), *Was There a Gnostic Religion?*, Publications of the Finnish Exegetical Society, 87 (Helsinki: The Finnish Exegetical Society; Göttingen: Vandenhoeck & Ruprecht), 81–101.

RASIMUS, T. (2006), 'Paradise Reconsidered: A Study of the Ophite Myth and Ritual and their Relationship to Sethianism' (Diss. Université Laval, Quebec; University of Helsinki).

ROBINSON, J. M. (1988) (ed.), 'Introduction', in J. M. Robinson (ed.), *The Nag Hammadi Library in English*, 3rd rev. edn. (Leiden: E. J. Brill), 1–26.

RUDOLPH, K. (1983), *Gnosis: The Nature and History of Gnosticism*, trans. R. McLachlan Wilson (San Francisco: Harper & Row).

SCHENKE, H.-M. (1974), 'Das sethianische System nach Nag-Hammadi-Handschriften', in P. Nagel (ed.), *Studia Coptica* (Berlin: Akademie Verlag), 165–74.

—— (1981), 'The Phenomenon and Significance of Gnostic Sethianism', in B. Layton (ed.), *The Rediscovery of Gnosticism: Proceedings of the International Conference on Gnosticism at Yale, New Haven, Connecticut, March 28–31, 1978*, 2 vols. (Leiden: E. J. Brill), ii. 588–616.

SMITH, R. (1988), 'Afterword: The Modern Relevance of Gnosticism', in J. M. Robinson (ed.), *The Nag Hammadi Library in English*, 3rd rev. edn. (Leiden: E. J. Brill), 532–49.

WILLIAMS, M. A. (1996), *Rethinking 'Gnosticism': An Argument for Dismantling a Dubious Category* (Princeton: Princeton University Press).

—— (2005*b*), 'Was There a Gnostic Religion? Strategies for a Clearer Analysis', in A. Marjanen (ed.), *Was There a Gnostic Religion?*, Publications of the Finnish Exegetical Society, 87 (Helsinki: The Finnish Exegetical Society; Göttingen: Vandenhoeck & Ruprecht), 55–79.

CHAPTER 11

MANICHAEISM

SAMUEL N.C. LIEU

11.1 ORIGINS

Of all the heresies which threatened the unity of the early church, the followers of Mani occupied an exceptional position, as they were devotees not of Jesus but first and foremost of a prophet from Mesopotamia who claimed to be a later-day 'Apostle of Jesus Christ' and possessor of 'the seal of the prophet'. Mani, the founder of the sect, was born of Parthian parents (c. 216 CE) in or near Ctesiphon, the winter capital of the Parthian Empire, to which his parents had migrated from Hamadan. While in Ctesiphon, his father Patticius was converted to the teachings of an ascetic baptizing sect, whose followers lived in communities in southern Babylonia. Mani entered such a community as an infant, and later as a young man rebelled against the strict teachings of the sect on self-ablution and the ritual washing of food, especially fruit and vegetables, which was said to be founded upon the teaching of a Jewish-Christian leader Elchasaios. Mani gave a more gnostic interpretation to the rituals, but his views were held to be dangerous by the elders of the sect, who subsequently expelled Mani. His father Patticius and a small number of sectarians followed him, and Mani travelled to Mesene on the Persian Gulf (c. 240 CE), where he sailed for India.

It was probably in India that he encountered Buddhist asceticism and monasticism as well as the doctrine of metempsychosis—all of which exercised strong influence on his teaching. On his return to Mesopotamia, he converted the Shah of Mesene to his teaching, and through him Mani was able to have an audience with Shapur I, the second Shahanshah (King of Kings) of the new Sasanian dynasty which had replaced Parthian rule in the Near East. Shapur was sufficiently impressed by Mani to permit him to disseminate his religion throughout his empire, and as the Sasanians then controlled a considerable part of the Roman Near East, the religion quickly diffused into the Roman Empire. Mani also actively propagated his religion in Iran and Parthia and in adjacent central Asia. He acquired a considerable reputation as a faith-healer and as a book-illustrator. His religion was well established on all the major trade routes between China and the Mediterranean by the time of his death (c. 276 CE). Although he was not executed, but died of torture in prison under an unsympathetic Shahanshah Bahram I, his followers regarded his martyrdom as a form of 'crucifixion' (Pedersen 2006: 42–85), and in spring each year the sect celebrated the feast of the Bema in which a portrait of Mani was placed on a platform of five steps (Lieu 1992: 35–85; Gardner and Lieu 2004: 3–8, 46–108).

11.2 MANICHAEAN SCRIPTURES

Manichaeism was a religion of the book. Mani's main teaching was contained in a canon of seven scriptures. They are: (1) Living Gospel; (2) Treasure of Life; (3) Pragmateia; (4) the Book of Mysteries; (5) the Book of the Giants; (6) the Letters; (7) Psalms and Prayers. These he wrote in an Aramaic dialect akin to Syriac. However, the need to acquaint his patron Shapur I with his teaching led to the compilation or composition in Middle Persian (the official language of the Sasanian court) of a summary of his teaching in which extensive use was made of Zoroastrian religious terminology. In Mar Ammo, Mani had a disciple who was fluent in Syriac and in Parthian, and he inaugurated the systematic translation of Manichaean texts into Parthian. These were later translated into both Middle Persian and Sogdian— the latter being the predominant commercial language of the Silk Road—and from Sogdian into Old Turkish and Chinese. In the Roman Empire, the Syriac writings of Mani were translated into Greek and Coptic, and from them into Latin. Systematic and severe persecution by Roman authorities in the West and Muslim authorities in the East led to the complete disappearance of genuine Manichaean writings until a large number of fragments of Manichaean writings in a distinctive script adapted from Syriac was found by German explorers in Turfan between 1904 and 1914 (Klimkeit 1993: pp. vii–xx). These consisted of texts in Middle Iranian and Old Turkish. More Old Turkish and a number of Chinese Manichaean texts were found in nearby Dunhuang by Aurel Stein and by Chinese scholars. However, the importance of the texts from central Asia for the study of the relationship between Manichaeism and early Christianity was completely overshadowed by the discovery of a sizeable collection of Manichaean texts from Egypt which were much older in date and were found in a predominantly Christian milieu.

The texts were discovered in 1929 by workmen digging for fertilizer among the ruins of Medinet Madi; a small village situated in a large depression in the south-west of the Fayyum to the north-west of modern Gharak (Ptolemaic Kerkeosiris). The chest which contained the texts was found in a cellar, and because of the high humidity of the soil (the entire region was swampy and was subject to flooding by the nearby Lake Moeris), the texts would almost certainly have perished had they not been placed inside a chest. The pages of the papyrus codices, however, acted as a kind of filter for the highly saline flood water, with the result that they were encrusted in salt. The encrustation was particularly dense at the edges of the pages. This, together with the fine quality of the papyrus, made separation into individual pages extremely difficult.

The find at Medinet Madi was estimated to have totalled 2,000 leaves, but the cache was broken up by the first dealer: some parts went to Cairo, and some remained in the provinces. A substantial part of the find was purchased by Chester Beatty and is now in Dublin, but the bulk of the find went to Berlin. Reassigning the separated quires to their original codices was far from easy. By 1933 seven codices were identified. In the Berlin collection: (1) Letters of Mani (P 15998); (2) *Kephalaia of the Teacher* (i.e. Mani) (P 15996) (Gardner 1995); (3) Synaxes codex, which appears to be a commentary (?) on the Living Gospel, a canonical work of Mani (P 15995); (4) the so-called Acta Codex (P 15997), a historical work which gave a life of Mani and the early history of the sect; in the Chester Beatty Collection, then in London and now in Dublin: (5) Homilies (Codex D) (Pedersen 2006); (6) Psalm-Book (Codex A) (Allberry 1938); (7) *Kephalaia of the Wisdom of my Lord Mani* (Codex C). Sadly, some of the codices housed in Berlin were taken by rail to the then Soviet Union after the Second World War, and among those which were not subsequently returned to Berlin (and are presumed lost) were the Letters of Mani and most of the volume containing the Acta Codex (see Gardner and Lieu 2004: 35–40).

In 1970 a miniature parchment codex from Egypt containing a semi-autobiographical account in Greek of Mani's early life was successfully deciphered and conserved. Known as the Cologne Mani-Codex—so-called because it is now housed in the Papyrussammlung of the University of Cologne—the text has given a massive boost to the study of the origin of Manichaeism. The Cologne Mani-Codex itself might have once formed the early part of the Acta Codex (P 15997) from Medinet Madi, lost since the end of the Second World War (see Gardner and Lieu 2004: 41–3).

It is from the Cologne Mani-Codex that scholars came to know of Mani's involvement with a Jewish-Christian 'baptist' sect which Mani claimed to have been founded by a certain 'Alchasaios'. This has prompted debate among scholars on the exact link between them and the Jewish-Christian Elchasaites, a sect known to us from the writings of heresiologists like Hippolytus and Epiphanius. While we know of the existence of an apocalyptic work known as the *Book of Elxai*, the actual existence of a heretical Jewish-Christian sect under the leadership of Elchasaios is less certain. In the Greek Mani-Codex, a leader or the actual founder (*archēgos*) of the sect is called Alchasaios (*sic*). Moreover, there is such dissimilarity between the teaching of the *Book of Elxai* and the 'Baptists' of the Mani-Codex that the two might not have been historically related (Luttikhuizen 1985: 210–20, 225–6), or the connection might have been invented to link Manichaeism with an earlier phase of Christian history by his followers. The discovery, however, of the name 'lxs' in a biographical text of Mani in a Parthian text (see Sundermann 1981: 19) suggests that the Alchasaios of the Mani-Codex was not just an ordinary leader of the sect, and the fact that the text was in a dialect of Middle Iranian rules out the possibility of Manichaean missionaries active in the more Christianized parts of Mesopotamia and the Roman Empire 'inventing' the 'Alchasaios' anecdotes to strengthen the sect's link with Christianity (Merkelbach 1988).

A second controversy concerns the date of the Mani-Codex itself. When it was first deciphered in 1970, it was believed that this miniature codex was produced in the fourth century at the height of the Manichaean mission in the Roman Empire. However, two scholars (Fonkic and Poljakov 1990) have suggested that the codex should be dated to the seventh century CE on palaeographical grounds, as the script it uses is unique to Greek texts translated from Syriac. Others have noted that the New Testament citations in the Mani-Codex appear to have been based on late versions and standardized versions of the Greek Bible. A direct translation from Syriac in the seventh century is hard to imagine, because translation is a missionary activity which one would associate with the sect's first entry into the Roman Empire. On the other hand, the late date of the codex and of the translation would explain why a number of accurate details including the Greek versions of the names of some of the tradents of the Codex were found in an early Byzantine anathema text and not in earlier Greek anti-Manichaean polemical writings. The call for re-dating has been little heeded, as the study of the subject is subdivided largely along linguistic lines (see below) with too few scholars within each linguistic area to generate an informed debate.

The announcement in 1992 of yet another discovery of Manichaean documents from Australian excavations at Kellis in the Dakhleh Oasis in Egypt sheds considerable new light on the diffusion of the sect from the Nile Valley. The first major find was made at House 3; but in 1993 a Manichaean psalm inscribed on wooden board was also found in House 4 (A/6), which is a substantial distance from the earlier sites. This strongly indicates that the inhabitants of House 3 were not an isolated group of Manichaeans. The geographical isolation of the oasis was an ideal haven for the sect from its persecutors. The texts so far discovered are unique, in that they were found in an archaeological context and not merely as a hidden cache, and were found together with some private letters of the sect (on this see below). The latter clearly showed that in a corner of the Empire where it was free from religious persecution (pagan or Christian), the sect was able to perceive itself as the true followers of Christ, as presented by Mani (Gardner and Lieu 2004: 43–5, 272–8).

11.3 THE GNOSIS OF MANI

The teaching of Mani is often seen as the last manifestation of Gnosticism. Many features of Gnosticism, especially of Valentinianism, are certainly encountered in Manichaean teaching. It shares with most gnostic systems the inherent anguish Man(kind) feels being enslaved to time, to the body, and to the physical world. The Manichaean is taught that God is nothing but truth and goodness, and therefore could not have willed suffering and evil in the physical world. Human souls share in the very nature of God; they are particles of the Light coming from the transcendent world. How they have fallen and become entrapped in evil Matter is explained by Mani in a cosmogonic drama which is played out in three acts or moments: Former, Present, and Future. In the Former Moment, Light and Darkness are separate principles. The former is the epitome of all that is good, beautiful, and honourable—its climate is always temperate, and it is insulated from the horrors of war and suffering; its inhabitants are not afflicted with such common ailments as stomach complaints and toothache. It is composed of five elements: Air, Wind, Light, Water, and Fire, and has also five dwellings: Intelligence, Knowledge, Reason, Thought, and Deliberation. The Kingdom of Darkness, which is situated to the south, is ruled by the Prince of Darkness in his infernal kingdom and dominated by concupiscence and strife. He is depicted as a multi-formed monster: his head is like the head of a lion, his rump like the rump of a dragon, his wings like the wings of a bird, his tail like the tail of a great fish, his feet like the feet of crawling animals.

In the Middle Moment, forces from the Kingdom of Darkness (usually described as Archons) accidentally entered the Kingdom of Light. They liked what they saw and decided to remain there. As the Kingdom of Light is not equipped for war, not even for its own self-defence, its ruler, the Father of Greatness, has to call forth other deities to fulfil this new role. He evokes from within himself the Mother of Life, who is also called the Great Spirit, and she in turn evokes the Primal Man whom she arms with the five Light Elements of air, wind, light, water, and fire. The Living Spirit and the Mother of Life go down into the realm of darkness. They defeat the Archons of the realm of darkness, out of whose bodies the cosmos is constructed by another deity known as the Demiurge. It is significant that the Demiurge, the shaper of the world, is valued positively in Manichaeism.

Ten heavens and eight earths are created by the Demiurge to imprison the evil Archons. But for the cosmos to remain in its correct order, five sons are evoked by the Living Spirit: Splenditenens, the great King of Honour, the Light-Adamas, the King of Glory, and Atlas. The first one holds the cosmos, while the last one carries it; so the universal fire comes to pass when, at the end of the world, both of them cease their activities. The Living Spirit attacks the powers of darkness in various different ways. If they have not been used in the making of the world, he pins them to the heavens. By means of the Three Garments of wind, water, and fire, he sweeps the evil water, darkness, and the evil fire (i.e. the three evil ferries) on to the earth. When the corresponding elements of the earth have joined them, he sweeps them out of the world and into ditches which have been prepared for this purpose. Splenditenens, the first of the five sons, is given oversight of the eighth, ninth, and tenth heavens, while the great King of Honour, who sits in the seventh heaven, oversees the rest of the heavens. The King of Glory is put in charge of the three wheels of wind, water, and fire, but the Living Spirit then takes off the Three Garments of the wind, water, and fire and places them below all things. From there, in the Third or Final Moment (see below), they will rise up above the earths to their place of rest. While the Living Spirit forms the sun and moon out of purified light, the stars—both the planets and the signs of the zodiac—are Archons. The fact that they are hostile to each other is, of itself, an indication of their evil origin. They are fastened to the 'wheel of the sphere'.

A new evocation, the hermaphroditic (Third) Envoy, then seduces the male and female Archons with his/her good looks and induces them to ejaculate and abort the Light-Particles held captive in them. These fall on the earth and bring forth plant and animal life. An elaborate system involving a set of Three Wheels and the main planetary and stellar bodies is then set in motion to return the Light-Particles to their original abode. The redeemed Light-Particles are transported via the Column of Glory, whose visible appearance is the Milky Way. When the Three Wheels are set in motion, the Light-Particles or souls are drawn up, refined, and sublimated, and at the same time conveyed along the Milky Way from the moon to the sun. The two stellar bodies are both receiving stations for Light-Particles as well as vessels for their conveyance. The periodic waxing and waning of the moon are therefore caused by the migration of these Light-Particles. From the sun the Light-Particles eventually go to a New Earth which is created by the Great Builder. This New Earth or Paradise ruled by the Primal Man is not the same as the Kingdom of Light, but is made of the same substance. Its main function is to be a home for the deities which have been evoked and the Light which they have redeemed, so that the Kingdom of Light may stay aloof from the turmoil.

Smarted by this apparent defeat, the Prince of Darkness creates a pair of male and female demons. The former devours the offspring of the abortions, and thereby ingests their Light-Particles within them and copulates with his partner, who gives birth to the First Man (Adam) and the First Woman (Eve) who are microcosms—exact miniatures of the universe (macrocosm), since both possess a mixture of Light and Matter. Adam is made to forget his distant divine origin by his slavery to Matter. His soul, firmly bound to the accursed body, has literally lost consciousness. It is at this moment that the transcendent Jesus whom the Manichaeans called 'Jesus the Splendour' comes to his aid. Jesus, who for the Manichaeans and also for some Gnostic sects plays a cosmic role, here fulfils his more usual function of teacher and exorcizer of demons. He shows him the Father in the heights and his own self which is cast down before the teeth of wild beasts, devoured by dogs, mingled with and imprisoned in everything that exists, shackled in the corruption of darkness. Jesus also raises Adam and makes him eat of the Tree of Life through which he comes to full realization of the imprisonment of his divine soul by his sinful body. The revelation by Jesus the Splendour to Adam sets the example for all future human redemption. To achieve this liberation, Jesus the Splendour evokes the Light-Mind, and in turn summons forth the Apostle of Light who becomes incarnate in the great religious leaders throughout history and the world. The Light Mind (an important figure in genuine Manichaean literature, but never mentioned in the writings of the sect's Christian opponents) is the first emanation of Jesus the Splendour, and is also the symbol of the Manichaean church. He dwells in the human body, and deals with the propensity of the Old Man—a concept Mani borrowed from St Paul—to sin, as the evil Archons still lie bound within the macrocosm, and their periodic rebellions are reflected on a microcosmic level through sinning, as the human body is constructed from evil Matter. Yet, the human soul is divine, being formed from the unsoiled parts of five sons of the First Man. The five intellectual qualities they represent are bound in the body and overlaid by corresponding evil qualities. This led the soul into error and forgetfulness of its divine origin. When the Light-Mind, whose personification is the Apostle Mani, comes, it liberates the divine qualities, binds the evil ones, and subjugates sin and thereby transforms the believer by divine knowledge (*gnōsis*) into a New Man. Nevertheless, sin can still occur and cloud the intellectual qualities, leading the believer once again into forgetfulness and error. The love and support of church leaders and friends are needed to help to nurture a believer to gradually turn to the true faith. This 'New Man'—also a Pauline concept—will now display the five virtues of love, faith, perfection, patience, and wisdom (see esp. Gardner 1995: 93–105; Heuser and Klimkeit 1998: 74–6, 123–41).

Manichaeism offers a powerful image of how everywhere in the cosmos light and darkness are mixed, and of the channels which shelter light and separate off the darkness. To achieve this separation, the Third Envoy calls up the Column of Glory, up which the parts of light can ascend. First they take their place in the moon, and when the moon wanes, they are transported to the sun and from there on to Paradise. Eventually, in the final of the three episodes, the Final Moment, a new Paradise is constructed for the gods who originated from the Kingdom of Light. When the Light-Particles in the world have been purified out enough for them to come together in the form of the 'Last Statue', then the end of the world starts. This will be signalled by the Great War which will come upon human beings unannounced. The Manichaean church will then be severely persecuted, but in the end the church will triumph over every danger and attempt to disperse its believers. The teaching of Mani will win a splendid victory, resulting in the conversion of all humankind. A collective liberation of the Light which has remained in the world until then will accompany this triumph. Jesus the Splendour then appears as the Last Judge and separates good from evil. While the Elect are transformed into angels, the faithful

Hearers are labelled as 'sheep', while the non-believers will be stigmatized as 'goats'. Mani taught that the first death, viz. the end of human life, is the abandonment of the soul which is composed of Light-Elements into a mixture with evil Matter. A second death is suffered by those who do not believe; in this death they are refused the return of their souls to the Kingdom of Light and therefore condemned to an eternal mixing with Matter. A Universal Fire of 1,468 years will take place, and finally the darkness will be compressed into a lump (Gk *bōlos*), in which certain sinful souls remain. The two principles will now have returned to their original separate existence. Evil, which is now captured and divided into male and female elements entombed in separate areas in the *bōlos*, is now incapable of invading the Kingdom of Light (see Lieu 1992: 7–32; Klimkeit 1993: 8–24; Puech 1951, 1968).

11.4 MANICHAEAN WRITINGS AND EARLY CHRISTIAN LITERATURE

Mani's Jewish-Christian upbringing accounts for his familiarity with Christian writings. His canonical writings owe their titles to the New Testament and the writings of Marcion and of Bardaisan. Even the summary of his teaching which he presented to his patron Shapur I and composed in Middle Persian in the style of Zoroastrian writings contains a lengthy pericope on Matthew 25: 31–46. His pastoral letters are clearly modelled on those of St Paul. The Syriac version of the *Diatessaron* of Tatian was probably his main source of gospel history, and the work is frequently used by his disciples to equate his 'martyrdom' with that of Jesus. Manichaean writings on asceticism drew heavily on the apocryphal *Acts of Thomas*. On the other hand, Mani's Gospel, which has survived only in fragments, contains clearly polytheistic elements amidst abundant echoes of Christian writings. Besides the Jesus of Splendour, who plays a major soteriological role, the Manichaeans also honour the historical Jesus. In Mani's teaching he is essentially a prophet rather than a redeemer-figure, and his suffering on the cross was purely a feint or similitude. On the other hand, the 'suffering Jesus' (*Jesus patibilis*) in the Manichaean system is a separate deity who personifies the crucifixion of Light-Particles in Matter, and is more highly revered by the sect (Franzmann 2003: 99–118). Mani's debt to Marcion is particularly strong, and in a Manichaean text in Parthian the God who sent Jesus to the cross was referred to as 'the God of Marcion'. Like Marcion, Mani rejected the teaching of the Old Testament except for the prophetic roles of the patriarchs. His disciple Adda (Latin *Adimantus*) would later compose a refutation of the Old Testament modelled on the *Antitheses* of Marcion.

11.5 MANICHAEAN ETHICS AND HIERARCHY

The long-term imprisonment of Light by Matter in the physical universe, which the Manichaeans see as a form of crucifixion, has important practical consequences for those who have been illumined by Mani's gnosis. Their duty is to be instruments for the liberation of this Light. To do this requires both a conscious effort for virtue by the individual and the avoidance of any action which might harm the Light or prolong its captivity. The Manichaeans are therefore enjoined to observe the 'Five Commandments' (fasting, almsgiving, no killing, no flesh-eating, and poverty) and the 'Three Seals': i.e. those of 'mouth, hands and breast'. The Seal of the Mouth forbids an Elect from eating meat and drinking wine, while the Seal of the Breast prevents fornication and marriage, and therefore physical procreation, which prolongs the captivity of Light. The Seal of the Hands is the command to avoid injury to water, fire, trees, and living things, and hence bans the procurement of food. Strict observance of these rules is of course possible only for a select few, and the sect therefore consists of a dyarchy of Elect, who endeavour to keep all the laws, and the Hearers, who are allowed to marry and to procreate and generate wealth as long as they serve the daily needs of the Elect. Mani preached a form of metempsychosis in which a person who violated plant and animal life would be reincarnated in those forms of life as an additional warning to avoid killing and harvesting. One can understand why Augustine was sufficiently outraged to create a popular image of the Hearers as enjoying maximum indulgence for their vices provided they kept their Elect well supplied! However, according to the seminal study of BeDuhn (2000: 126–233), Manichaean asceticism for the Elect was motivated not purely by a negative view of the material world or a form of social and hierarchical dominance over the Hearers, but by a positive cosmic plan, as envisaged by Mani, to use the body of the Elect as a means of refining the Light-Particles and the liberation of the Living Self, the sum total of the Light-Elements enslaved in Matter and the cosmos. The Manichaean ritual meal was, according to BeDuhn, an essential part of the religious life of a Manichaean community, or cell. The Manichaeans belonged to a cultic community, and the community was identified in historical sources primarily as revolving round the cultic meal. Conducted daily, the Hearers delivered the food as alms to the place of consumption and the table on which the food is placed is a ritual locale. In BeDuhn's words (2000: 164–5): 'Manichaeans participated in a templeless and altarless tradition. While other religious communities carried their offerings into temples, where their priests burned them on altars, the Manichaeans bore their alms to the Elect, who cooked them in their own stomachs.'

Though the Manichaean cosmogony is highly complex, and replete with a multitude of deities and demons, the Manichaeans were expert in reducing their main ethical teachings to 'The Three Seals', 'The Five Commandments' (for the Elect) and 'The Ten Commandments' (for the Hearers). Important to our understanding of the cultic meal as a focus of community ritual is a set of Manichaean texts commonly known as the 'Sermon of the Light-Mind' preserved in Coptic, Parthian, Sogdian, Old Turkish, and Chinese. The sermon places the redemptive role of the Light-Mind in both a cosmogonic and an ethical context. It shows how the cosmic process of redemption of Light was temporarily shackled by Greed and Lust congenital to the Old Man. But through adhesion to the commandments of the sect and the intervention of the Light Mind, the Old Man is refashioned into a New Man ruled by the Light-Mind. Combat between the Old and the New Man is frequent and the Light-Particles which are 'transient guests' in the body of the Elect would thus suffer periodically, had not the Light-Mind in its redemptive role planted in the body the twelve cardinal virtues. BeDuhn makes the important observation that the Manichaean concept of the Twelve Hours of the Second Light Day represent the Twelve Forms of the Beneficent Light in the Elect, the possession of which became the ultimate moral goal of the Manichaean ritual meal. These Twelve Hours (or Twelve Maidens in some sources) are: (1) Sovereignty; (2) Wisdom; (3) Victory; (4) Persuasion; (5) Chastity; (6) Truth; (7) Faith; (8) Long-suffering; (9) Integrity; (10) Grace; (11) Justice; (12) Light. It is the need for the Elect to put these virtues into practice to assist in the liberation of the Living Self, and not a negative world-view, which lies at the heart of Manichaean asceticism and food taboos. The perfected bodies of the Elect pass through the corresponding stages of cosmic perfection and actively help the liberated Living Self or Soul to establish dominion over the body, not through detachment or self-focused meditation (BeDuhn 2000: 226–33). In this respect the meal is not unlike the Christian eucharist in that in most Christian liturgical expositions the sacred meal is not purely an act of remembrance but also one of contrition, confession, and forgiveness of sins as well as fostering the moral and spiritual uplifting of the participants. Not surprisingly, the sacred meal was widely regarded within the Christian Roman Empire as the Manichaean (and perverted) version of the eucharist.

In addition to the dyarchy of Elect and Hearers, the Elect themselves are further divided into five grades: (1) the leader (Gk *archēgos*) who is the successor of Mani; (2) twelve apostles or teachers; (3) seventy-two bishops; (4) 360 elders. After the death of Mani, the first *archēgos* was Sisinnios, but he soon suffered martyrdom and was succeeded by Innaios. Subsequent *archēgoi* remained in Ctesiphon until the archdiocese was moved to the outskirts of Baghdad in the Islamic period. Later (*c.* 908 CE) the seat of the *archēgos* was moved to Chorasan in central Asia as the religion attracted increasing numbers of followers on the Silk Road (BeDuhn 2000: 25–208; Gardner and Lieu 2004: 21–5). Unlike the Manichaean manuscripts produced in the Roman West, which are extremely plain, those produced in central Asia are beautifully illuminated, and they clearly had a major impact on Islamic book production (Gulácsi 2001, 2005). The high quality of calligraphy is a boon to the reconstruction of often heavily mutilated texts, and has resulted in the leading expert on Manichaean texts, Professor Werner Sundermann, remarking that the Manichaean *textus unicus* is often the *textus optimus*.

11.6 THE GREEK FATHERS AND MANICHAEISM

The oldest surviving Christian anti-Manichaean work is the *Acta Archelai* attributed to Hegemonius (trans. Vermes 2001: 35–153). Originally composed in Greek, this work has survived in a complete form only in a Latin translation made no later than the beginning of the fourth century. Important parts of the original Greek version of the work have survived in the major anti-heretical work, the *Panarion* of Epiphanius. In this Mani is depicted as a failed prophet and miracle-worker who was imprisoned by the Shahanshah of Persia for failing to cure the Crown Prince from a fatal illness. Mani, however, managed to escape across the border, and tried to convert Marcellus, the leading citizen of Carchar (= Roman Carrhae?) to his new religion. His efforts were thwarted by Archelaus, the Christian bishop of the city, who engaged Mani in a public debate adjudicated by pagan sophists. Crestfallen, Mani returned to Persian-held territory, where he was immediately re-arrested and tortured to death (Coyle 2007: 68–73). This anti-hagiographical version of the life of Mani was widely circulated in the Christian East and formed the basis of the anti-Manichaean writings of Epiphanius and Cyril of Jerusalem. Other Greek fathers, such as Serapion of Thmuis and Titus of Bostra, tried to tackle the philosophical implications of dualism, but their works reveal little detailed knowledge of Manichaean writings. The only Greek father to cite verbatim from a genuine Manichaean work is Severus of Antioch, but his cathedral homily against the Manichaeans (*Cathedral Homilies* 123) has survived only in two Syriac translations. The usual objection to the Manichaean solution to the problem of evil by supposing that its appearance in human life is due to the mixture of two dissimilar substances is an ethical one. Evil for the Christian Platonist is not a substance but the negation of reality and a failure to grasp the latent possibilities of the good in life. The primary cause of evil in the world is human sin, which is the direct result of free will and can be combated by ascetical living and charity. Such an idealistic view of human suffering probably succeeded only in making Manichaeism more popular (Klein 1991: 16–50; Pedersen 2004: 177–54).

11.7 AUGUSTINE AND MANICHAEISM

Augustine of Thagaste (354–430 CE, later bishop of Hippo Regius) was undoubtedly the most famous convert to Manichaeism. He encountered the sect when he was a student and later a teacher of rhetoric in Carthage, and was a Hearer for nine years (*c.* 373–382 CE) between the ages of 19 and 28. He was attracted to the sect by its comradeship and hospitality, as well as by its claim to possession of a rational faith. The solution which a dualist faith could offer to the problem concerning the origins of evil was certainly appealing to a thinking young man dissatisfied with Judaeo-Christian monotheism. Like many Christians who came to Christianity from a predominantly pagan cultural background, Augustine was offended by the crude language and seemingly barbaric stories contained in the Old Testament. The rejection by the Manichaeans of the relevance of Jewish scriptures to their gnostic form of redemption was certainly a blessed relief. Augustine formed a close friendship with Faustus of Milevis, one of the most eloquent and effective Manichaean teachers of his time, and virtually became his literary assistant. He was impressed by the ability of the Manichaeans to underscore the apostleship of Mani by subverting the Christian scriptures through pointing out the numerous inconsistencies and contradictions they contain. It appears that he still had Manichaean friends when he moved to Rome, as he convalesced in the house of a member of the sect after a severe illness (c. 384 CE), and it was with their support that he was appointed rhetor at Milan. Later, thanks to his involvement with the Neoplatonists at Milan and to Ambrose's preaching on the allegorical interpretation of the Old Testament, he gradually moved away intellectually from Manichaeism prior to his famous conversion in 387 CE. While the story of his Manichaean years is famously told in his *Confessions* (3. 6–5. 13), his intellectual odyssey has to be pieced together from his earlier writings, especially the *De moribus Manichaeorum* (c. 388 CE) and the *De utilitate credendi* (391 CE). His most substantial work against the sect—*Contra Faustum Manichaeum*—was published in 397, shortly before his famous *Confessions*. The only substantial reply he received to this popular publishing success was a letter from a Manichaean called Secundinus (399 CE), who remembered Augustine from his short stay in Rome. Secundinus strongly urged Augustine to distance himself from a barbaric and non-Roman religion like Catholicism and return to Mani's true gnosis (trans. Vermes in Gardner and Lieu 2004: 136–42).

One of the most influential of Augustine's works against Manichaeism is *De natura boni* published around 399 (and not 404 as traditionally suggested), which is more influenced by Neoplatonic thinking on the problem of evil than his other works. The Manichaean concept of an independent evil principle is refuted by the Neoplatonic argument that evil is a privation of Good and cannot therefore exist without Good. Every nature possesses three basic perfections—limit, form, and order (*modus, species, ordo*)—and is therefore by nature good. God is the supreme Good, and visible nature, including human nature, is created not out of the substance of God but out of nothing (*ex nihilo*). Because all things which are created out of nothing participate not only in being but also in non-being, there is an original lack which gives rise to change. Change or mutability can be for better or for worse, hence the possibility of evil. While the supreme godhead, like the Plotinian Monad, radiates goodness, Darkness exists not in its own right but where the radiated light peters out. Because man is created out of nothing, he is vulnerable to suffering by being a sentient creature. This is not due to his natural limitation as a creature, but is a consequence of the sin of Adam, and is experienced as a punishment. It also deprives mankind of preternatural gifts which had been gratuitously conferred upon him by the creator. Adam's disobedience symbolizes mankind's desertion of the creator for the creature. However, human volition for good or evil is part of God's goodness, and it is a divine mystery why God did not create man without the proclivity to sin.

Augustine's response to the Manichaean solution to the problem of evil would become standard throughout the Middle Ages. Revised by Thomas Aquinas, it still remains at the fountainhead of Augustinian and Catholic theology (Moon 1955: 14–41; Evans 1982: 11–40, 12–36).

11.8 FUTURE DIRECTIONS IN RESEARCH

Few subjects in the study of early Christianity are as heavily dominated by linguists as Manichaeism. Manichaean texts recovered from within the confines of the former Roman Empire and testimonia on the beliefs of the sect preserved by church fathers exist in Coptic, Greek, Latin, and Syriac. Those preserved in the writings of Christian and Islamic writers in Iraq and Iran are in Syriac, Arabic, and New Persian, while those recovered from the Turfan Oasis and from Dunhuang in central Asia are in an even wider range of exotic languages: Middle Persian, Parthian, Sogdian, Old Turkish (Uighur), Tocharian B, Bactrian, and Chinese. As some of these languages were little known prior to the discovery of fragmentary Manichaean texts and codices from Turfan at the beginning of the last century, a great deal of ongoing research is still focused on the decipherment of the languages and the reconstruction and conservation of the fragmentary manuscripts and codices. The scholars best qualified to undertake this work are trained in Oriental or Coptic studies, and their primary interest is often in linguistic problems and in textual reconstruction, with only secondary interest in the teaching and history of the sect. As a result, the discipline may appear to be singularly lacking in major controversies, even though a major international conference has been held every four years since the early 1990s. The difficulty of working with a plethora of often unrelated ancient and medieval languages makes its own scholarly demands and often requires international collaboration at the highest level. Moreover, the compilation of specialist dictionaries of under-studied central Asian languages, such as Sogdian and Uighur, as well as rarer dialects of Coptic is a sub-discipline in itself. The successful launch of the UNESCO-sponsored Corpus Fontium Manichaeorum project in 1992 has made the editing and translation of genuine Manichaean texts and of patristic and oriental sources on Manichaeism the primary focus of international scholarly effort for the next half-century. Nine volumes of the Corpus have appeared so far, including three volumes of the *Dictionary of Manichaean Texts*. The ongoing need for international funding for the continuation of collaborative research on the texts has tended to encourage scholars to stress agreements rather than disagreements, for pragmatic reasons. A valuable forum of contribution and debate over the last years, especially by scholars based in North America, has been the Society of Biblical Literature's Manichaean Studies Seminar (BeDuhn and Mirecki 2007: vii–viii.

A major focus of new research is likely to be the Manichaean material from Kellis in the Darkhleh Oasis in Egypt, which was discovered *in situ*. The texts, mainly in Coptic and some in Greek and Syriac, were found written on both papyri and wooden boards, and are mainly fourth century in date. Among them are a dozen letters of Mani in Coptic which greatly augment our knowledge of the canonical work known as the Epistles (Gardner and Lieu 2004: 166–8; Gardner 2006). Among the texts recovered is a well-preserved hymn to the pantheon of Manichaean deities inscribed on a wooden board which was composed originally in Greek and not translated from Syriac or Coptic. Known by its original title as 'The Hymn (or Prayer) of the Emanations', the work underlines the polytheistic elements of Manichaeism, which would certainly have been an attraction to a pagan audience. More significant still is the personal correspondence of the Manichaean community, which is highly informative on a number of aspects of the social and religious life of the sect. These letters employ almost all the standard conventions of Christian epistolography and the use of the *nomina sacra* (Choat 2006: 26–7, 74–100). A particularly important example is the letter by a certain Makarios to his 'longed-for' son Matheos (Gardner *et al.* 1999: 160), which was written probably in the 350s, or soon after, in which he urges the young man to be diligent in his reading of scriptures both Manichaean and apocryphal Christian:

Before everything: I greet you. I remember your gentleness and your calm, and the example of your... propriety; for all this time I have been without you, I have been asking after you and hearing of your good reputation. Also, when I came to you, I found you correct as you have always been. This too is the (right) way. Now, be in worthy matters; just as the Paraclete has said: 'The disciple of righteousness is found with the fear of his teacher upon him (even) while he is far from him.' Like guardians (?). Do likewise, my loved one; so that I may be grateful for you and God too may be grateful for you, and you will be glorified by a multitude of people. Do not acquire fault or mockery for your good conduct.

Study [your] psalms, whether Greek or Coptic, <every> day (?)...Do not abandon your vow. Here, the Judgement of Peter is with you. [Do the] Apostolos; or else master the Great Prayers and the Greek Psalms. Here too, the Sayings are with you: study them! Here are the Prostrations. Write a little from time to time, more and more. Write a daily example, for I need you to write books here. Do not be like the other one who came to question (?) when he was about to receive instruction about...everything.

(trans. Gardner in Gardner and Lieu 2004: 273–4)

While almost all the texts listed are well-known Manichaean works, the *Judgment of Peter* is clearly not Manichaean, as the figure of Peter hardly features in any genuine Manichaean texts. That the Manichaean community in Kellis saw itself as both

Manichaean and Christian is startlingly confirmed by these letters. One could see why the orthodox-minded Christian leaders saw the religion both as an external rival and as a major internal threat to the Christian church.

SUGGESTED READING

A useful collection of sources on Manichaeism in the Christian Roman Empire in translation is Gardner and Lieu (2004) with full introduction and notes. For a fuller account of the history of Manichaeism from its origins in Mesopotamia to its final demise in China, see Lieu (1992). BeDuhn (2000) is a stimulating and controversial work on Manichaean ethics and rituals. Gardner (1995, 1996, 2007) presents many important Manichaean texts from both Medinet Madi and Kellis in Egypt. For those interested in the passage of Manichaeism to the East, Klimkeit (1993) remains essential, and the works of Gulácsi (2001 and 2005) provide balanced and well-illustrated studies of Manichaean art, especially of illuminated books recovered from Turfan. Franzmann (2003) is one of the few studies in English on the complex subject of Manichaean Christology.

BIBLIOGRAPHY

ALLBERRY, C. R. C. (1938), *A Manichaean Psalm-Book*: Part II (Stuttgart: Kohlhammer).

BeDUHN, J. (2000), *The Manichaean Body in Discipline and Ritual* (Baltimore: Johns Hopkins University Press).

——and MIRECKI, P. (2007) (eds.), *Frontiers of Faith: The Christian Encounter with Manichaeism in the Acts of Archelaus*, NHMS 61 (Leiden: E. J. Brill).

BRYDER, P. (1988) (ed.), *Manichaean Studies*, Proceedings of the First International Conference on Manichaeism, Lund Studies in African and Asian Religions, 1 (Lund: Plus Ultra).

CHOAT, M. (2006), *Belief and Cult in Fourth Century Papyri*, Studia Antiqua Australiensia, 1 (Turnhout: Brepols).

COYLE, J. K. (2007), 'A Clash of Portraits: Contrasts between Archelaus and Mani in the *Acta Archelai*', in BeDuhn and Mirecki (2007), 67–76.

EVANS, G. R. (1982), *Augustine on Evil* (Cambridge: Cambridge University Press).

FONKIC, B. L., and POLJAKOV, B. L. (1990), 'Paläographische Grundlagen der Datierung des Kölner Mani-Kodex', *Byzantinische Zeitschrift*, 83/1: 22–30.

FRANZMANN, M. (2003), *Jesus in the Manichaean Writings* (London: T & T Clark).

GARDNER, I. M. F. (1995) (trans.), *The Kephalaia of the Teacher* (Leiden: E. J. Brill).

——(1996) (ed. and trans.), *Kellis Literary Texts I* (Oxford: Oxbow Books).

——(2007) (ed. and trans.), *Kellis Literary Texts II* (Oxford: Oxbow Books).

——and Lieu, S. N. C. (2004), *Manichaean Texts from the Roman Empire* (Cambridge: Cambridge University Press).

——et al. (1999) (eds. and trans.), *Coptic Documentary Texts from Kellis*, i (Oxford: Oxbow Books).

GULÁCSI, Z. (2001), *Manichaean Art in Berlin Collections*, CFM.A1 (Turnhout: Brepols).

——(2005), *Medieval Manichaean Book Art*, NHMS 57 (Leiden: E. J. Brill).

HEUSER, M., and KLIMKEIT, H.-J. (1998), *Studies in Manichaean Literature and Art*, trans. M. Franzmann (Leiden: E. J. Brill).

KLEIN, W. W. (1991), *Die Argumentation in den griechisech-christlichen Antimanichaica*, Studies in Oriental Religions, 19 (Wiesbaden: Harrassowitz).

KLIMKEIT, H.-J. (1993), *Gnosis on the Silk Road—Gnostic Texts from Central Asia* (San Francisco: HarperCollins).

LIEU, S. N. C. (1992), *Manichaeism in the Later Roman Empire and Medieval China*, 2nd edn. (Tübingen: Mohr/Siebeck).

LUTTIKHUIZEN, G. (1985), *The Revelation of Elchasai: Investigations into the Evidence of a Mesopotamian Jewish Apocalypse of the Second Century and its Reception by Judaeo-Christian Propagandists*, Texte und Studien zum Antiken Judentum, 8. (Tübingen: Mohr/Siebeck).

MERKELBACH, R. (1988), 'Die Täufer, bei denen Mani aufwuchs', in Bryder (1988), 105–33.

MOON, A. A. (1955), *The De Natura Boni of Saint Augustine—A Translation with an Introduction and Commentary* (Washington D.C.: Catholic University of America Press).

PEDERSEN, N. A. (2004), *Demonstrative Proof in Defence of God—A Study of Titus of Bostra's Contra Manichaeos: The Work's Sources, Aims and Relation to its Contemporary Theology*, NHMS 56 (Leiden: E. J. Brill).

—— (2006), *Manichaean Homilies*, CFM Series Coptica (Turnhout: Brespols).

PUECH, C.-H. (1951), 'The Prince of Darkness and his Kingdom', in *Satan* (London and New York: Sheed & Ward), 127–57; originally in French, 'Le Prince des Ténèbres en son royaume', in *Satan*, ed. B. de Jesus-Marie (Paris: Desclée de Brouwer, 1948), 136–74.

—— (1968), 'The Concept of Redemption in Manichaeism', in J. Campbell (ed.), *The Mystic Vision: Papers from the Eranos Yearbooks*, 6; Bollingen, 30, 6 (Princeton: Princeton University Press), 247–314.

SUNDERMANN, W. (1981), *Mitteliranische manichäische Texte kirchengeschichtlichen Inhalts*, Berliner Turfantexte, XI (Berlin: Akademie Verlag).

VERMES, M. (2001) (trans.), [Hegemonius], *Acta Archelai (The Acts of Archelaus)*, Manichaean Studies, 4 (Turnhout: Brepols).

CHAPTER 12

....

ARIUS AND ARIANS

....

J. REBECCA LYMAN

12.1 INTRODUCTION

....

ALTHOUGH the teachings of Arius of Alexandria sparked a series of theological debates and church councils in the fourth century concerning the nature and redemptive activity of God, scholars share a slim consensus as to the origins and content of his teaching. For the first time in 325 the adjudication of Christian controversy took the form of a council including the Roman emperor Constantine at the lakeside town of Nicaea close to the imperial capital of Nicomedia. In the decades that followed, the statements of the Nicene Council slowly took on venerable, if not sacred, weight, especially as defined by the often embattled bishop of Alexandria, Athanasius. Many of those who opposed the theology of Nicaea or Athanasius were polemically grouped together and labelled as 'Arians' in spite of significant theological differences from Arius or each other, and indeed doctrinal differences existed among those who accepted Nicaea. Although the statement of the Council of Constantinople in 381 reflected conceptual shifts developed over the course of the century, the council and Emperor Theodosius evoked Nicaea as a theological precedent which established its authority as a definitive rule of orthodox identity. The theological conflicts of the fourth century thus achieved unprecedented authority within Christianity because of the crucial function of 'conciliar' creeds to define and cement multiple geographical centres and theological traditions into a unified Christian identity. As discussed by Maurice Wiles (1996), Arius, as the theologian condemned at Nicaea, became the archetypal heretic; 'Arianism' thus became the archetypal heresy, which denied the saving divinity of Christ, and therefore essential

Christian identity. By its rejection of Arius and Arianism, the orthodox tradition past and present has defined its own belief and practice.

Historically, this polarized theological tradition has made the origins and significance of Arius and the later opponents of Nicaea difficult to reconstruct. First, we have only three letters and fragments from a theological poem, the *Thalia*, from Arius himself, so much of the information about his theology exists through the mediation of hostile sources. Such heresiological sources are notoriously difficult to interpret. By the fourth century ancient controversialists followed a polemical form which emphasized sectarian, disobedient, and demonic behaviour. Opponents were excluded from Christian tradition by labelling in accordance with previous heresies and association with external beliefs such as Judaism or Hellenism. Any retrieval of theological argument must therefore be filtered through these forms of speech as well as compared to other contemporary documents. Second, scholars have begun to unravel the assumed theological ties between Arius and those later called 'Arians'. They now reject a coherent movement called 'Arianism', but rather study the variety of doctrines and alliances of those opposed to Nicaea, i.e. 'non-Nicenes'. Third, if Christian religious identity is defined according to spiritual and theological principles of Nicene orthodoxy, it may be difficult to retrieve or comprehend alternatives as vital forms of Christian belief and practice. The broadening of the study of 'Arianism' to examine questions of asceticism, spirituality, and liturgy, as well as soteriology and cosmology, reflects these historiographical concerns. Finally, the controversy spans a period of significant change in Christian institutional structures, public roles, and theological authority. These shifts, with their opportunities and anxieties, are woven into the texture of the debates, so that a strictly theological account is inevitably an impoverished one. This essay will review recent studies of Arius and non-Nicenes from the outbreak of the controversy to the conversions of the tribal peoples in the western empire.

12.2 THE QUEST FOR THE HISTORICAL ARIUS

In an interesting echo of the methodological scepticism eventually voiced by scholars in the nineteenth century seeking the historical Jesus, the recent focus on recovering the historical Arius in the last 25 years has accorded similar charges of distorting interpretive lenses: Arius as recently reconstructed is too 'modern' or too 'Barthian' (Vaggione 1989: 77; Löhr 2005, 2006). These evaluations, besides continuing the ancient practice of labelling opposing opinions, reflect the paucity of historical evidence, the continuing strength of the traditional paradigm, and the freshness of the scholarly revisions. To date, most reconstructions of Arius have not been able to make conclusive sense of the origins of the controversy, though they have begun to illuminate various possibilities of re-charting the conflict. Ironically, the increasing separation of Arius from later 'Arianism' has worked to make him less important in the reinterpretation of the history of the subsequent theological struggles. He is currently viewed more as a catalyst for conflict than as the founder of a movement.

Given the intellectual liveliness and seminal apostolic traditions of the Christian communities in the large cities along the eastern rim of the Mediterranean, it is not surprising that a major theological controversy should originate there, especially in Alexandria, known for its ethnic and civic divisions as well as its intellectual energy. Arius was the presbyter of a community in a suburb in Alexandria, Baucalis, and originally from Libya. In this location his church would have included local herders; it may have been close to the tomb of St Mark and other martyrs, and perhaps a gathering place for early ascetics. Given his later popularity among ascetics— a number of virgins shared his excommunication—and comments on his drawn appearance, Arius may well have been an early ascetic (Haas 1997: 272). From his extant writings he appears to have been well educated in traditional theology and philosophy. From his appeal to Eusebius of Nicomedia as a 'co-Lucianist', he probably studied with Lucian of Antioch, a famous teacher and martyr, although he does not appear on any list of students (Parvis 2006: 40 f.). He was ordained after the persecution of Diocletian, possibly around 311. Different policies concerning the treatment of the lapsed had divided the Alexandrian church and clergy, as they had done in North Africa and other parts of the Empire. Although Arius was accused of being a member of the schismatic Meletian party, recent scholarship discounts this (Hanson 1988: 5).

According to the extant literary sources, the initial conflict began as a theological disagreement on the relation of the Father and the Son between Alexander, the bishop of Alexandria, and Arius. The exact chronology remains disputed, but it is generally thought to have begun in the period from 318 to 323 (Parvis 2006: 68–73). According to the later church historian Socrates, and implied in a letter of Constantine, Alexander initiated a discussion of scripture among the clergy, and Arius's reply was unacceptable (*Hist. eccl.* 1. 5, 7). Arius complained in a letter to Eusebius, bishop of Nicomedia, that he had been unjustly persecuted since he had disagreed with Alexander's teaching. He characterized the bishop's views as portraying the Father and Son as eternally coexistent and the Son as without beginning. This, he claimed, would make a number of eastern bishops anathema since they all teach that God has an existence without beginning prior to the Son. Arius insisted that the Son was not 'unbegotten' (*agennētos*) nor a part of unbegotten being, but by will and counsel before time came into being 'only-begotten' and unchangeable. Before he was begotten, the Son did not exist. Therefore they are being persecuted because they teach that the Son has a beginning (*archē*), but God does not; he is made from nothing (*ek ouk ontōn*) rather than a part of God or pre-existing material.

Arius appealed to the bishop as a 'co-Lucianist' to remember his suffering (*Urk.* 1 = Epiphanius, *Pan.* 69. 6; Theodoret, *Hist. eccl.* 1. 4).[1]

A second letter from Arius and others sets out their faith seemingly in response to Alexander's objections. They claim that they have learned this theology from their forefathers and from him. They affirm one God as the only unbegotten, and his begetting of his only begotten Son by his will, unchangeable, a perfect creature, but not as other creatures. They then list unacceptable alternatives to understand the beginning of the Son: neither an emanation as Valentinus, nor a consubstantial (*homoousios*) part as Mani, nor a divided torch as Sabellius. Rather, he is a Son created by the will of the Father, and subsists with him, receiving from him his life, glory, and being without depriving the Father. Three hypostases exist: God alone is the cause of everything and without beginning, the Son begotten alone by the Father before time, though not co-eternal or co-uncreated with the Father, and God is one (*monas*) and first principle. God cannot be composite, divisible, or mutable, so generation should not be understood as corporeal. In this letter the claim that the Son came from non-existence was no longer included, and an emphasis on the Son as unchangeable even as a creature was affirmed (*Urk.* 6 = Epiphanius, *Pan.* 69. 7).

These two letters may then be compared to fragments of the theological poem, the *Thalia*, which Athanasius claimed that Arius wrote for propaganda, and which he preserves in two polemical works. The poetic form does appear to invite broad participation in theological discussion, but the reconstruction of its content and structure as retrieved solely from an admittedly hostile source remains contested (Stead 1978; R. Williams 2001: 256). Arius began by affirming his own spiritual and intellectual lineage from the wise. The theology then expressed was profoundly apophatic in affirming God's unbegotten essence as ineffable, so that worship and knowledge of him came only through 'the one in nature begotten', the 'one who has a beginning', the 'one born in time'. The Son is 'appointed' and 'born', but has nothing proper to God in his essence, being neither equal to nor consubstantial with him. The Son cannot see God, but sees only the invisible through the power given to him. The Son thus existed by the paternal will as only begotten God, and becomes 'wisdom' by the will of God who retains the original faculty of wisdom in himself. So, the Son is conceived by means of many concepts (*epinoia*) including spirit, power, wisdom, glory, truth, and light. He praises the supreme God, but he cannot by comprehension know the ingenerate one who begot him. These fragments seem to be a theological hymn on the transcendence of God as creator and the unique revelatory agency of the subordinate Son.

Two letters from Alexander set out his response to this theology, although the authorship and chronology of both are disputed (Parvis 2006: 69–72). In *Henos Sōmatos* Alexander defended his disciplining of Arius and criticized the support of Eusebius of Nicomedia in a letter addressed to fellow ministers (*Urk.* 4b = Socrates, *Hist. eccl.* 1. 6). He listed twelve clergy and two bishops who were teaching contrary to scripture. He summarized their teaching as rejecting the eternity of

God's fatherhood: God as being itself created the Son out of nothing, so the Son does not share God's nature, nor is the Son the essential Word or Wisdom of God. He is one of the things created. Therefore, he was mutable by nature, and does not fully know or see the Father. In an echo of Origen's debate about the nature of the devil, Alexander claims that they also agree that theoretically the Word can change, since it is begotten. Given its vocabulary and theological emphasis, the letter may in fact have been written by Athanasius (Stead 1988).

The other letter attributed to Alexander, *Hē Philarchos* (*Urk.* 14 = Theodoret, *Hist. eccl.* 1. 3), is a longer account of conspiracy, madness, and association with Jews and Greeks. There certainly appears to be a broader social problem of separate meetings, involvement of women ascetics, lawsuits, and persuasion of other clergy to their theological opinion. Theologically, the focus of the letter's description was on their absurd doctrine of the created Son. Alexander's opponents claim that there was a time when the Son was not. God created all things from non-existence, so the Son is of a mutable nature. Therefore, humans can become sons of God just like he did; for God knew through foresight that the Son would not break faith, and singled him out for his discipline (*askēsis*). They therefore ignore the scriptural passages on the immutability of Wisdom and focus on the passages of the Saviour's obedience (Ps 14: 7). Alexander refuted, first, creation from nothing as inappropriate to the eternal Word of God. The Son as God's essential Wisdom and Image was always with God. He has therefore an immutable nature, and is a Son by nature not capable of progress or change. Thus, he could reveal the Father to Philip (Jn 14: 8–9). The author denies that this implies two unbegottens; even if the generation is mysterious and beyond comprehension, the Son is the immutable and precise image of the Father.

In the initial years of the conflict, the church of Alexandria became deeply divided. Both sides of the argument described their opponents in polemical terms as unfaithful, unjust, and doctrinally heretical. The confrontation seems to have involved literary exchanges as well as physical demonstrations, involving other clergy, laity, and ascetics. Rowan Williams has suggested that the fierce tone of the controversy represents a conflict between public episcopal Christianity and private academic Christianity within the 'spectacularly fissiparous' world of Alexandrian Christianity with its independent presbyters and Gnostic traditions. Arius therefore represented the older 'school' form of speculative Christianity which was now in conflict with the public, sacramental, and communal authority of Alexander emerging in the early fourth century. The allies of Arius, such as Eusebius of Caesarea, were therefore part of the 'school' tradition which elsewhere had given way to the authority of the monarchical bishop (2001: 46–85).

Several factors should caution us about this explanation of the initial Alexandrian crisis. First, Alexandria was a divided church in the early fourth century due to persecution and theological disputes, but the fault lines probably do not break so clearly between public episcopal and private teaching authorities. Epiphanius remains a foundational text for seeing Alexandrian presbyters as rival teachers, but this is clearly a heresiological explanation for the creation of sects: Arius creates Arians and Colluthus creates Colluthians (Haas 1997: 270; Brakke 1995: 64; Davis 2004: 52). In fact, Alexandria may have had more unity at this period between teaching and episcopal offices. In the third century Demetrius had created ties between the bishop and a school for the catechesis of converts by appointing Origen as its teacher; this unity continued, as seen in the many bishops emerging from the school over the course of the third century, and portraying themselves as theological authorities (Davis 2004: 27). Bishops in Alexandria were elected from presbyters rooted in the divisions of the city, and this custom seemed to persist in Alexandria until Peter and Alexander in the early fourth century began a tradition of appointing their successors (Kemp 1955). This departure from the earlier pattern might be significant, but for all Alexandrian presbyters, not merely 'teachers'. Philostorgius and Theodoret suggest that Arius was a possible competitor to Alexander for the episcopacy, although episcopal rivals are as heresiologically stereotypical as 'bishops and teachers' (Parvis 2006: 73).

Second, as recently argued by Claudia Rapp, Weber's opposition of charismatic and institutional authority which underlies this analysis does not entirely fit the ancient Christian communities, in which all leaders were bearers of the Spirit (2005: 17). Unlike Origen, a teacher at the time of his conflict with Demetrius, Arius was a presbyter in charge of a local congregation. Throughout the controversy the majority of participants were all clergy, indeed were bishops, but controversialists regularly labelled their opponents as 'intellectuals' or outsiders, as part of the rhetorical construction of a heresy. Unfortunately, these labels continue to stick. Williams underlines Arius's claim to be *theodidaktos* ('God-taught') as an indication of a primary teaching identity, when in fact it was a commonplace from 1 Thessalonians 4: 9 defending sacred rather than secular teaching and also used by Alexander in *Hē Philarchos* 35 (R. Williams 2001: 85–7). The fact that this acrimonious debate spread rapidly beyond Alexandria to include other clerics, as well as ascetics and laity at home, suggests that the issues involved struck religious chords much broader than those of an esoteric teacher.

Returning to the possible doctrinal issues, scholars have struggled to understand the significance of the theological positions outlined in the brief letters of Arius and Alexander. Both men are on new ground theologically, but why they occupy this space remains puzzling. The problem of the causality of the Son was inextricable from Christian claims to be monotheists who also affirmed the divinity of the Son. Following scriptural images which described Christ as the Son, Wisdom, Word, image, or glory, and philosophical models of a mediating cosmic agent, earlier theologians could portray a pre-existent being who necessarily shared divinity with the Father, yet was subordinate in his creating or saving actions. As the Word or Wisdom of God, the Son could be described as eternally pre-existent with the Father. In Alexandria, Origen had defended a model of eternal generation of the

Son as a separate, pre-existent hypostasis along the lines of a Wisdom theology; this refuted both an improper blurring of the Father and Son (modalism), who were evidently distinguished as separate persons in scripture by such verses as Mark 10: 18, and the promotion of a human being (adoptionism), which was obviously against the testimony to the Son's divinity such as the prologue to the Gospel of John. Scripture conveyed a range of meanings concerning the relation of the Father and the Son which theologians struggled to reconcile. In the fourth century this Logos model of a subordinate or secondary divinity, however traditional or even biblical, was increasingly seen as inadequate to express divine unity.

Equally important, theologians struggled to find categories which conveyed the obedience and suffering of the incarnate Son recorded in ancient Christian writings. Origen described the union of a pre-existent human soul with the Word; the incarnate Word could then be seen through divine and human natures as both obedient image of humanity and the divine revelation of the Father. For Origen, titles such as 'Jesus' or 'Christ' were used to describe the human life of the incarnate Word, and exegetes needed to understand the multiple titles of scripture. In Alexandria, Alexander and Arius shared an important modification of Origen's theology: neither made room for a human soul in the model of the Incarnation, and both applied all scripture to the one subject of the Logos. This could create problems of docetism, in which the divine Word did not seem to share truly in human experience, or adoptionism, in which the human experiences of the Word seemed to indicate his necessary separation from the Father. Thus, in the ensuing debates, Alexander complained that Arius applied passages of 'humiliation' and 'weakness' inappropriately to the divine Son, and later non-Nicenes complained that a Son who was of the same divine nature could not be the authentic subject of suffering and obedience. The problem of scriptural titles and actions is clearly an issue. Is the Son the very Wisdom or Word of God, or does he receive this title as a gift from the Father? Causality, exegesis, and soteriology were intertwined.

The modern investigation of Arius began by questioning his traditional reputation as merely a speculative philosopher and granting some respect to his theological questions about the generation of the Son, including the ambiguity of scripture and earlier tradition on such matters (Wiles 1962). In 1981 Robert Gregg and Dennis Groh directly challenged the traditional interpretation of Arius by asserting that the centre of his thought was indeed a process of salvation; this reversed the commonplace which portrayed Athanasius as defending soteriology through divinization (God became man, so that man could become divine), in contrast to Arius's arcane focus on cosmological causality. According to Gregg and Groh, the essential distinction of the Son's nature from the Father's enabled the created Son to be a true moral exemplar for the life of the believer. As brought into being, he was changeable, though he remained unchangeable by will. The portrayal of the Son was therefore based on Luke–Acts and Hebrews as a model of faithfulness and spiritual progress. They placed this into the contemporary situation of asceticism as well as the traditional high demands of Christian ethics.

This presentation provoked a number of criticisms. Although they used material from Asterius as well as Arius to portray 'early Arianism', critics noted the diversity, if not disagreement, of opinions in the texts, so questioning the existence of a coherent movement. Equally important, the centrality of the soteriology of the advancing Son rested heavily on the reports by hostile sources: namely, the letters of Alexander and later passages in Athanasius. If this were a main theme, it should have been more evident in the *Thalia* or explicitly condemned by later 'conciliar' decrees (R. Williams 2001: 258; Stead 1994: 26). However, their attention to Athanasius's polemics in asceticism and the social context of Arius pushed the evaluation of the controversy out of purely cosmological models and sparked a re-examination.

Other scholars also pursued links between the generation of the Son and the meaning of the Incarnation. Rudolf Lorenz portrayed Arius as indebted to the thought of Origen concerning the human soul of Christ. Lorenz argued that by modifying Origen's claim of eternal generation of the Logos, Arius reframed Origen's process of incarnation. The created Logos now functioned as the obedient human soul and the site of foreseen virtue and exemplary behaviour (Lorenz 1979, 1983). Scholars were again reluctant to see a positive use of 'adoptionism' by a theologian and felt that Arianism was being explained through polemical charges rather than on its own terms (Stead 1994: 36). Richard Hanson also emphasized incarnation as central to Arius's concern. He argued that the distinction of the Son from the Father allowed the incarnate Son to be the subject of suffering, a concern evident in later fourth-century arguments of non-Nicenes. He remained more sympathetic to the arguments of Gregg and Groh and Lorenz, but was criticized for the breadth of his category of 'Arian' (Hanson 1988). Simonetti made a connection between the emphasis on divine will, exact image, and non-existence in Lucian of Antioch; but the paucity of Lucian's extant works, as well as those of Arius, can easily make this a circular argument (Simonetti 1975).

Scholars have also tried to link Arius to larger cosmological shifts at this time. Rowan Williams located the origins of Arius's concern in the shifting Platonic models of the fourth century. Not only did Arius deny eternal generation; he also denied the knowledge of the Father by the Son as well as any participation in essence. Williams argued that this shift reflected changes in contemporary Platonism: namely, the increased transcendence of Plotinian thought and the rejection of analogy. Arius was therefore a philosophical radical, if a theological conservative. His focus on the Son as mediator and worshipper of the Father might also be linked to Alexandrian traditions concerning worship and the angel liturgy (R. Williams 2001). Although this is a highly suggestive account, the verbal parallels with Plotinian philosophy are contested (Stead 1997). The portrayal of Arius as fundamentally philosophical also seems to hark back to polemical stereotypes (Vaggione 1989: 75; Wiles 1996: 178). Finally, Arius's rejection of coexistent principles could also be linked to the growing presence in Egypt of Manichees, who were identified as Christians and taught two eternal principles of Good and Evil. The appearance of two coexistent principles in a concept of eternal generation could be a sensitive charge given the local strength of the Manichees (Lyman 1989; Heil 2002).

Because of the ancient Christian love of letter writing and networking, especially during controversy, the dispute rapidly involved a number of prominent eastern bishops. For the most part the supporters of Arius seem to have been drawn together by the theology of Lucian of Antioch and geography, including Libya and Palestine (Parvis 2006: 39–50). Eusebius of Nicomedia, whose see was the eastern imperial capital and who was linked to the family of Constantine, was appealed to by Arius as a 'co-Lucianist'. He received Arius after his excommunication in Alexandria, wrote letters in his defence (*Urk.* 8 = Theodoret, *Hist. eccl.* 1. 5), and was one of the leading opponents of Nicaea, as well as sponsoring missions to India and to the Goths. His few extant letters emphasize the singularity of divine essence as unoriginated and the creation of the Son as a complete likeness by will (Hanson 1988: 28–30). Asterius was also a pupil of Lucian, and wrote a *Syntagmation* in defence of Arius. He emphasized the Son's separate hypostasis, especially for incarnation, as well as the generation of the Son by the will of the Father as 'exact image' (Kinzig 1990; Vinzent 1993). Eusebius of Caesarea defended the transcendence of the Father and the creation of the Son as the image of the true God. Early in the controversy he wrote to Alexander wondering how anyone could suppose that the Father as first cause could share his nature with a product (*Urk.* 7). After being condemned at the Council of Antioch in 324, Eusebius accepted the creed of Nicaea. However, he interpreted it to his congregation in such a way as to continue to emphasize the power of the Father as the cause of the Son (*Urk.* 22 = Socrates, *Hist. eccl.* 1. 8). Other early supporters included Paulinus of Tyre and Athanasius of Anazarbus.

Though Arius was condemned at local synods in Egypt and Antioch, and defended at synods in Bithynia and Caesarea, the Council of Nicaea was eventually organized by Constantine to sort out the problem. In his letter to the disputants in 324, Constantine rebuked them for public quarrelling like philosophers about obscure theological points, and encouraged them to make peace for the sake of the Church (*Urk.* 17 = Eusebius, *Vit. Const.* 2. 64). The Council may have been originally organized by Alexander and his supporters to meet at Ancyra, but was changed by Constantine to a place nearer his capital of Nicomedia. The bishop of Ancyra, Marcellus, was a controversial ally of Alexander and Athanasius. Following a tradition of theology from Asia Minor, he affirmed that God was a monad, and 'Son' only a temporary title for divine action in incarnation; no distinction existed in God eternally (Lienhard 1999; Parvis 2006). If Arius was present at Nicaea, he was a minor figure as a presbyter, as was Athanasius as a deacon, since the bishops were the official representatives and voting members. We have no official account of the council and several conflicting accounts. The term *homoousios* seems to have been included, perhaps at the suggestion of Constantine, because it was rejected by Eusebius of Nicomedia and others (Drake 2000: 250–8). Two bishops from Libya refused to sign and were exiled, as was Arius. Although Eusebius of Nicomedia signed the creed, he was exiled shortly after because he gave hospitality to followers of Arius from Alexandria.

After Nicaea we have only limited evidence about Arius's activities. Evidence suggests that Arius was recalled from exile around 327/8 through a small council at Nicaea. He had written to the emperor asking to put arguments aside and be returned (*Urk.* 30 = Socrates, *Hist. eccl.* 1. 26). Constantine wrote to Alexander asking him to reinstate Arius in Alexandria, but Alexander died shortly thereafter, and his successor, Athanasius, refused to accept Arius (*Urk.* 32). Over the next years Arius seems to have been in Egypt or Libya. Around 333 Constantine replied to yet another letter from Arius asking for help in being reinstated, as well as discussing issues of incarnation. Wishing to maintain peace, the emperor criticized his separatism, his theology, and his ascetic appearance; an edict was issued which compared him to Porphyry, and ordered his works to be burned (*Urk.* 34; *Urk.* 33 = Socrates, *Hist. eccl.* 1. 9). However, Constantine later invited him to answer his charges, and Arius successfully did so at a synod in Jerusalem in 335. However, when he returned to Alexandria, rioting occurred, and the emperor summoned him to Constantinople. At another synod in 336 Arius accepted the Nicene statement of faith, and the bishop of Constantinople was ordered to admit him to communion. According to Athanasius' sensational account, on the eve of this event, Arius died suddenly in a public lavatory. Eusebius of Nicomedia saw to his burial (Hanson 1988: 264–5).

12.3 Theologies and Alliances after Nicaea

The immediate result of the Nicene Council was not the stabilizing consensus hoped for by Constantine, but the hardening of certain theological alliances and the creation of others. Recent scholarship has argued that the focus after the council was not Arius, but rather the theology of Marcellus of Ancyra, who was a supporter of Nicaea, but was suspected of modalism, and therefore offered a target for those who opposed Nicaea (Lienhard 1999; Parvis 2006). The excluding term *homoousios* remained unpopular due to its novelty and past use by Gnostics together with the anathemas which condemned the use of 'three hypostases'. Lienhard (1987) suggested that one could chart the shifting theological alliances by attention to categories of one hypostasis (Marcellus) or two (Eusebius of Caesarea). More recently, Ayres has argued for a configuration of Homoiousians, Heterousians, etc., but also emphasizing the diversity of opinion and networking as alliances rather than coherent theological parties (2004: 13). As Vaggione suggested, the battles became increasingly heated and technical, not because of profound differences, but rather because in fact so much was shared in common and progress occurred only incrementally (2000: 104). Institutionally, the often confusing series of imperial councils and creeds together with the continually shifting political alliances was a new phenomenon in Christianity. Some groupings remained alliances, whereas others developed into separate churches (Löhr 1986).

For the most part Arius became irrelevant to later controversy except as a heretical category to be attached to opponents of Nicaea (Wiles 1993). Those who had supported him initially, including Eusebius of Nicomedia and Eusebius of Caesarea, did not wholly share his views; those non-Nicenes who later saw themselves as followers of Lucian of Antioch criticized Arius for his lack of theological acuity on certain points (Ferguson 2005). In his *Orations Against the Arians* (c. 339/40), Athanasius in exile in Rome, perhaps in the company of Marcellus of Ancyra, created 'Arian' as the heretical label to apply to any one who opposed him as bishop of Alexandria or the doctrine of Nicaea (Parvis 2006: 180–1). Using conventional heresiological tactics, a 'school' was created based on a 'teacher', Arius, and diverse sets of opinions could be melded into a coherent sect relentlessly opposed to the apostolic truth of the Church. If one held similar opinions, one was thus part of this movement and an 'Arian', not a 'Christian'. Athanasius also associated Arian theology with ideas outside Christianity such as those of Jews, philosophers, or Manichees (Burrus 1991; Lyman 1993*a*; Gwynn 2007). He created a demonic succession to explain Arius's teaching, and showed how his thought echoed other condemned thinkers such as Paul of Samosata. However, as doctrinal questions and political alliances shifted, so did his categories. By 359 he reserved the term 'Arian' for only the most extreme non-Nicenes, the 'Neo-Arians', and upholders of the Homoian creed (T. D. Barnes 1993: 135).

If we discard the label 'Arian' as a collective for those who opposed Nicaea or Athanasius, we are returned to the complex theological negotiations of varied authors. In the East, the polemical title of 'Arian' did not even figure in all controversies or was used as a theoretical boundary in contradistinction to modalism (Lyman 1993*a*; M. Barnes 1998). As mentioned above, the powerful alliance of churchmen who were the earliest supporters of Arius seemed to share a theological legacy from Lucian of Antioch, a martyr and teacher (d. 312). Lucian had taught the singleness of God as creator, the power of divine will, and the full revelation of God through the Son, his perfect and unchanging image; God consisted of three hypostases in one will. A council at Antioch in 341, 'the Dedication Council', echoed this theology. The Son was the 'exact image' of the Father (Brennecke 1993). This insistence on separate hypostases and the priority of the Father was supported by

Eusebius of Caesarea against Marcellus; he emphasized the will of the Father and the separate agency of the Son as the secondary, if exact, image.

The church in Rome accepted the account and orthodoxy of the exiled Marcellus and Athanasius, but others of course had different views. In the West the conflict came alive only after the series of councils under Constantius, especially the Council of Sirmium in 357. This council rejected the use of *ousia* language altogether as unscriptural and controversial; it affirmed the superiority of the Father, and asserted that the Son was begotten and subordinate. This led to the 'Dated' creed of Sirmium in 359, in which the Son was affirmed to be simply 'like the Father in all things'. The emperor Constantius found this to be theologically acute and supported the decisions of this council. The alliance which affirmed that the Son was 'like the Father' and 'like according to the scriptures' has been called the 'Homoians'. Examining the bishops who supported this council, we find a diversity of views as well as changing theological positions which should encourage us again to think of alliances rather than dogmatic parties. The successor and follower of Eusebius of Caesarea, Acacius of Caesarea, taught that the Son was the image of the *ousia* of the Father, and therefore distinct and subordinate; like many, he attempted to weather the successive councils by compromise and silence, accepting at times Nicaea and at other times a more radical Homoian position (Hanson 1988: 581–3). Eudoxius was allied with the Heterousians or radical Homoians, Aetius and Eunomius, but eventually adopted a more moderate course. He was alleged by opponents to have made many provocative, and even humorous, assertions to show the transcendence and distinction of the Father; to the radical Homoians, he was a traitor by his later failure to defend Eunomius. As bishop of Constantinople, he became the advisor of Valens and the supporter of Ulfilas and his mission to Christianize the Goths (Hanson 1988: 581–8).

Another series of councils shows the work of Basil of Ancyra, the leader of a network often called the Homoiousians, who affirmed a 'like substance' between the Father and the Son, if maintaining a hierarchy of being and action. This position was developed in reaction to both Nicene thought and the increasing radicalism and politics of some Homoians, namely Eudoxius and Aetius. Condemning the 'modalism' of Marcellus and the unscriptural theology of Aetius, they presented themselves as true heirs of Lucian of Antioch (Steenson 1983; Löhr 1986; Brennecke 1988). They protested against both the theology and the tactics of Eudoxius in becoming bishop of Antioch. Emperor Constantius became convinced of the orthodoxy of their position and encouraged their presence at the Council of Sirmium in 359. Constantius banished the extreme Homoians and convened yet another gathering in December 359 which seemed to affirm the Homoiousian position. Local Homoians, however, legislated against them in Constantinople, and refused to accept the statement. The party split into those who eventually accepted Nicaea and those who continued a non-Nicene position.

The complex politics of the new imperial councils, as well as the increasing local power of bishops, sparked debates concerning proper clerical behaviour and public theological discourse. Non-Nicenes were accused of being too close to the court, not practising asceticism, and exhibiting inappropriate disclosure of theological concepts. Eudoxius and, later, Eunomius were in fact well connected to the court, and perhaps exemplified a style of civic moderation as well as learned theology (Vaggione 1993; Van Dam 2003). Nicene apologetics focused on the necessary link between orthodoxy, divinization, and asceticism, especially as interpreted by bishops (Brakke 1995; Lim 1995). In Alexandria those opposed to Athanasius and Nicaea embraced different facets of urban community (Haas 1997: 274 f.). Resistant to imperial coercion, large numbers of the urban aristocracy followed this cause. In 356 young men of this class were accused of both heretical ordinations and violence against opposing churches. Given the tradition of urban violence, these groups of those receiving office and others engaging in supportive violence could be explained by class and civic pride rather than theology (Haas 1997: 276). In part this group is a response to the violence of Athanasius. However, the repressive rule of George of Cappadocia, who persecuted Jews, Christians, and pagans, broke the non-Nicene alliance of ascetics, aristocrats, and imperial officials in the city (Haas 1997: 274 f.).

The most strenuous opponents of *homoousios* were Aetius and Eunomius, often called 'Neo-Arians' or Anomoeans (or more recently in Ayres (2004) 'Heterousians'), to distinguish them from their Homoian allies. The wealth of polemical literature from Gregory Nazianzus and Basil provides a social history for this portion of the controversy which has only begun to be explored. For example, Aetius's social mobility from goldsmith to deacon in Antioch, as well as his intimidating dialectical skill, was exploited by the Cappadocians, who contrasted their own nobility of birth and ascetic philosophy with the supposedly crude marketplace antics of their rivals. Their contrast of those who were 'made' as opposed to those 'born' may have theological implications in the midst of a debate about 'begotten' versus 'created' Sons (Burrus 2000; Van Dam 2003: 17). The Anomoeans claimed that the nature of the Son must be different from that of the unbegotten Father (*heterousion*) or dissimilar (*anomoios*). Also linked to Lucian of Antioch, their relationship to Arius is an interesting one, since they seem to have embraced his focus on the singularity of the unbegotten Father, but rejected his negative epistemology. In his *Syntagmation* of 359 Aetius defined the divine essence as 'ingenerate' (*agenētos*), and insisted that this description was fully revelatory of God and the basis of all theological teaching, which he expressed in thirty-seven propositions (Wickham 1968). Since for him names expressed realities, 'ingenerate' was not merely a title, but expressed the very essence of God.

Descended from a merchant family in northern Cappadocia, Eunomius met Aetius in Antioch and became his pupil. When Aetius moved to Alexandria, Eunomius acquired Eudoxius of Constantinople as a patron, and eventually became bishop of Cyzicus. However, in loyally supporting his teacher Aetius, he ran afoul of Eudoxius and the court, and returned to Cappadocia. He thus went into exile several times depending on the theological position of the Emperor, lastly at the request of Theodosius (Van Dam 2003: 15–43). From extant portions of his two *Apologies* and *Confession*, we have a good account of his teaching, which emphasized the full revelation of the ingenerate Father through the subordinate Son. Because of this precise revelation, theologians must be exact (*akribeia*) in their interpretation, and this theological ability was linked to their spiritual power as teachers. This central claim that God was knowable in essence was of course in direct contradiction to Arius's earlier claims; paradoxically, the Cappadocians defended divine incomprehensibility in response to these teachings. As shown in the *Apostolic Constitutions*, Eunomius practised a Christocentric baptism in which believers were baptized into the death of Christ and emerged as adopted sons and daughters (Kopecek 1985; Vaggione 2000: 336–40). Philostorgius wrote a Eunomian history in which he outlined an authentic theological succession from Eusebius of Nicomedia to Eunomius. He criticized Arius for his negative theology, and Asterius for his theology of the image of the Son; *akribeia* in theology, and not merely ecclesiastical office, was important (Ferguson 2005; Marasco 2005). Eunomius and his followers were condemned by name at the Council of Constantinople, and their rights increasingly curtailed by imperial legislation. Ironically, their devotion to tradition and *akribeia* left them unable to negotiate with regard to theological terminology, and therefore increasingly isolated (Vaggione 2000: 381).

In the West, theological debates also continued between those who accepted the developing Trinitarian theology of *homoousios* and those who did not. Ambrose in 374 succeeded a Homoian bishop, Auxentius. With the death of Valens, Ambrose moved to enforce Nicene orthodoxy in his area by condemning several local bishops. Refusing to be labeled as 'Arian', Palladius, the venerable bishop of Ratiaria, claimed to teach an inherited and biblical theology of a subordinate and suffering Son. Their several literary exchanges in *De fide* and *Apologia*, as well as the recorded debate at the Council of Aquileia, reflected their mutual theological, personal, and political contempt, as well as the power of emperors in religious policy (Meslin 1967: 85–92; McLynn 1991, 1994). The local enforcement of Nicene orthodoxy by Ambrose escalated tensions, and indeed a revival of the Homoian theology (D. Williams 1995). Another Auxentius of Milan, this one being a pupil of the bishop to the Goths, Ulfilas, came to Milan during Ambrose's tenure as an evangelist for the non-Nicene gospel and rebaptized converts. Valentinian legislated tolerance for Homoians, and a conflict developed over the main basilica. In the later fourth century theological power was increasingly expressed by who occupied public space and who needed to meet privately (Maier 1994; Colish 2002). The eventual change of emperor with the military success of Maximus, together with the discovery of the relics of martyrs whom Ambrose claimed as defenders of Nicaea, ended the Homoian revival. When Theodosius enforced the heresy laws in the West, the only non-Nicenes publicly acknowledged seem to have been the Goths (Duval 1998). However, from the evidence of the *Opus imperfectum in Matthaeum*, dated to the fifth century, we learn that non-Nicenes continued to meet privately (Maier 2005).

Throughout these debates we may trace a commitment of non-Nicenes to a separate and subordinate model of divinity which made them deny the equality of the Father and Son or a unity of *ousia*. The incomparable sovereign and creative power of the Father was consistently affirmed as an essential doctrine expressed in scripture, revealed by the Son, and logically consistent in reflections on causality: the Father is 'incomparably greater than all' in Julian's *Commentary on Job*, 9 (Hanson 1988: 101). According to the *Letter of Auxentius* 'this God... in order to show his goodness and power by force of will alone, impassive and free from passion, incorruptible... made and established the only begotten God' (Heather and Matthews 1991: 147). This subordinate Son could then be the single subject of his cosmological and earthly activity; his essential separation from the transcendent Father ensured the reality of his obedience and suffering. Thus, many authors, including Palladius and the author of the Latin *Opus imperfectum*, insisted that the Son as the lesser divinity must be subject to suffering. Eudoxius noted: 'He was passible by the Incarnation; for if only soul and body had suffered, he could not have changed the world. Let them answer then how this one... could be consubstantial with God who is beyond these things: suffering and death?' (Hanson 1988: 112). As succinctly expressed by Vaggione, 'Their attempt to safeguard exegesis through metaphysics made the traditional descending hierarchy a dogmatic as well as dramatic necessity' (2000: 128). The biblical accounts of the obedient, suffering, and worshipping Christ were ensured by the hierarchical cosmology. Liturgy affirmed the saving revelation of the ingenerate God through the life and death of the Son. The strength of the non-Nicene position was thus the unity of the story of the creation and the appointment of the Son as saviour from the beginning of time (Vaggione 2000: 143–8).

12.4 CHRISTIANITY AND TRIBAL PEOPLES

The actions and legislation of Theodosius had curtailed non-Nicene liturgical and theological life within the Roman Empire, but non-Nicene Christianity persisted until the sixth century among tribal peoples who eventually migrated into and controlled parts of the former western empire. The second canon of the Council of Constantinople in 381 had allowed the churches among the barbarians to be governed according to the rule of their fathers. Ironically, if these peoples adopted Christianity as a political courtesy to the Empire, they eventually found that their version, mainly taught by Ulfilas in 360, was no longer considered to be orthodox. The prototype of this form of conversion was the Goths. After initial resistance to and persecution of Christians, Goths adopted Christianity in 376 when they crossed into the Roman Empire. Scholars concur that the Goths then maintained their non-Nicene Christianity in part as a means of distinguishing themselves as a people from the Romans; their eventual conversion to Nicene Christianity in the sixth century is therefore linked to increasing cultural assimilation (Heather 1996: 313). The Christianization of tribes through the decisions of their rulers is echoed in the non-Nicene conversions of the Suevi, Vandals, Lombards, and Burgundians, although the exact historical process or reason for these religious changes often remains unclear (Thompson 1983; Schwarcz 1999; Pohl 2000).

Although we have references to Nicene Goths, such as the martyr Saba, whose relics were brought to Cappadocia, the majority of Gothic Christians were shaped by the theological inheritance of Christianity before Theodosius, including especially, but not exclusively, Ulfilas. According to his disciple, Auxentius, Ulfilas rejected the substance language of most other fourth-century theologies, preferring to describe not separate identities but rather different dispositions (*adfectus*). The Son was the only-begotten God created by the unbegotten Father. He therefore supported the theology of Euxodius of Constantinople in 360 concerning the 'likeness' of the Father and the Son, though his own theology focused on the separate functions of the Father, Son, and Holy Spirit. In 383 he tried to persuade Theodosius of his error in accepting *homoousios* (*Letter of Auxentius* in Heather and Matthews 1991: 145–53; Wiles 1996: 43–5). He translated the Bible into Gothic, though Philostorgius claimed that he omitted the book of Kings so as not to encourage their aggression. Salvian argued a century later that the Goths remained 'Arian' because of the poor translation of their scripture, which was riddled with errors (Heather and Matthews 1991: 167–9). The Gothic translation of scripture appears at critical points to emphasize likeness between the Father and Son rather than equality or identity (Wiles 1996: 50).

In the next several centuries the two forms of Christianity coexisted largely as descriptive of distinct ethnic groups. In a sixth-century manuscript Arianism was described as *lex Gothorum* (Heather and Matthews 1991: 245). The use of Gothic in liturgy and scripture, as well as a separate cup for aristocrats, did not encourage conversions, and the majority of local inhabitants remained Nicene. The Ostrogothic ruler Theodoric in northern Italy seemed intentionally to encourage peaceful coexistence, and intervened helpfully in a Catholic schism in Rome. His capital, Ravenna, preserves the best visual evidence of Gothic Christianity in the churches dedicated to St Apollinaris and the baptistery. In spite of much debate, most scholars conclude that little theological difference can be discerned in the images of Christ in the mosaics (Jensen 2000: 118–19; Ward-Perkins 2007).

In Spain, Nicenes were 'the Roman religion', and Goths spoke of themselves as 'catholic'. Some kings enjoyed theological debate about *homoousios*, but for the most part theological conflict was expressed in competing miracles or success in battle; for example, Gregory of Tour outlined the unsuccessful healings of Arian bishops and the conversion of a king based on the miraculous power of Nicene Christianity (Van Dam 1993: 187–9). However, in North Africa the Vandal rulers pursued at times a violent policy in the interest of social unity. Nicenes were persecuted in 484, and again after a Council of Carthage in 522. Bishop Victor of Vita wrote an account of the earlier persecution modelled on the traditional genre of martyrdom which also revealed significant exchange and interaction between populations (Shanzer 2004). Their Christianity disappeared with the reconquest of North Africa by Justinian. In Visigothic Spain, Leovigild attempted to unite his kingdom in 580 by declaring the full divinity of the Son, but the inferiority of the Spirit; he also outlawed rebaptism of Nicene converts and allowed intermarriage. After his death in 587 his son Reccared ascended the throne and became a Nicene. At the Council of Toledo in 589 Nicene Christianity was formally adopted by the kingdom and its clergy, ending the ethnic division of religion; several revolts followed, as well as the unfortunate destruction of many Visigothic Christian texts. Whether or not this period may contribute only a theology 'characterized by a ponderous and earthbound reliance on the text of the Bible' (Thompson 1966: 123) may rest on future study of tribal peoples.

12.5 DIRECTIONS FOR FURTHER STUDY

The fourth century with its theological controversies, institutional inventions, expansion of asceticism, and gradual Christianization of Roman society was a religious and social watershed in late antiquity. Studies of Arius and 'Arianism' therefore must continue to take into account the ever increasing resources on the history of spirituality, liturgy, and ecclesiology as well as theology to deepen our understanding of the course of the controversy. The complexity and diversity of devotional practice or the use of philosophy and scripture encourages a less binary approach to the development of Nicene orthodoxy. Attention has been shifting from Arius and the origins of the controversy to later figures, which promises to illuminate our understanding of particular theologies, as well as eventually shift our overall account of the development of the conflict. Many of these controversial texts would profit from readings with more attention to rhetorical or sociological models of conflict as well as theological nuance. Equally important, as the fourth-century histories of Hellenism and Judaism are revised, the polemical links in Christian theology must also be reconsidered. The cumulative weight of these particular and diverse studies therefore promise new insights into, and perhaps a new configuration of, one of the most important theological conflicts of Christian history.

NOTE

1. References to the documents of the early controversy (*Urk.*) refer to a collection of Greek texts by Opitz (1935).

SUGGESTED READING

The best historical survey which encompasses both East and West remains Hanson (1988). Vaggione (2000), Ayres (2004), and Parvis (2006) offer recent outlines of revised chronologies and scholarly debate. The best introductions to the new scholarship on Arius are Vaggione (1989, 2000), with Wiles (1996) presenting a historical and theological overview of 'Arianism' as a theological category. Readers must then evaluate Gregg and Groh (1981), Lorenz (1979), Simonetti (1975), and R. Williams (2001). Important essay collections include Barnes and Williams (1993) and Gregg (1985). The later eastern non-Nicene movements are discussed by Kopecek (1979) and Vaggione (2000). Thompson (1966, 1969), Heather and Matthews (1991), and Wiles (1996) discuss the evidence concerning the Goths.

The best primary source collection in Greek is Opitz (1935). The fragments of Asterius are collected by M. Vinzent in *Asterius von Kappadokien: Die Theologischen Fragmente* (Leiden: E. J. Brill, 1993). The fragments of Eunomius are collected in *Eunomius: The Extant Works*, ed. and trans. R. Vaggione (Oxford: Clarendon Press, 1987). R. Gryson has collected the fragments of many western non-Nicenes in *Scripta Arriana Latina* (Turnhout: Brepols, 1982) and also *Scolies ariennes sur le Concile d' Aquilée*, SC 267 (Paris: Éditions du Cerf, 1980). The *Opus Imperfectum in Matthaeum* is edited by J. van Banning in CCSL 87B (Turnhout: Brepols, 1988). Selections from Ulfilas and other Gothic documents are translated in Heather and Matthews (1991).

BIBLIOGRAPHY

AYRES, L. (2004), *Nicaea and its Legacy: An Approach to Fourth-Century Trinitarian Theology* (Oxford: Oxford University Press).

BARNES, M. (1998), 'The Fourth Century as Trinitarian Canon', in L. Ayres and G. Jones (eds.), *Christian Origins: Theology, Rhetoric and Community* (London: Routledge), 47–67.

——and WILLIAMS, D. (1993) (eds.), *Arianism after Arius: Essays on the Development of the Fourth-Century Trinitarian Conflicts* (Edinburgh: T & T Clark).

BARNES, T. D. (1993), *Athanasius and Constantius* (Cambridge, Mass.: Harvard University Press).

BRAKKE, D. (1995), *Athanasius and the Politics of Asceticism* (Oxford: Clarendon Press).

BRENNECKE, H. (1988), *Studien zur Geschichte der Homöer: Der Osten bis zum Ende der homöischen Reichskirche* (Tübingen: Mohr).

——(1993), 'Lukian von Antiochien in der Geschichte arianischen Streites', in *idem*, E. L. Grusmück and C. Markschies (eds.), *Logos: Festschrift für Luise Abramowski* (Berlin: de Gruyter), 170–92.

Burrus, V. (1991), 'The Heretical Woman as Symbol in Alexander, Athanasius, Epiphanius, and Jerome', *HTR* 84: 229–48.

—— (2000), *'Begotten not Made': Conceiving Manhood in Late Antiquity* (Palo Alto, Calif.: Stanford University Press).

Colish, M. (2002), 'Why the Portiana? Reflections on the Milanese Basilica Crisis of 386', *JECS* 10: 361–72.

Davis, S. (2004), *The Early Coptic Papacy: The Egyptian Church and its Leadership in Late Antiquity* (Cairo: The American University in Cairo Press).

Drake, H. (2000), *Constantine and the Bishops: The Politics of Intolerance* (Baltimore: Johns Hopkins University Press).

Duval, Y.-M. (1998), *L'extirpation de l'Arianisme en Italie du Nord et en Occident*, Variorum Collected Studies Series (Aldershot: Ashgate).

Ferguson, T. (2005), *The Past is Prologue: The Revolution of Nicene Historiography* (Leiden: E. J. Brill).

Gregg, R. (1985) (ed.), *Arianism: Historical and Theological Reassessments* (Philadelphia: The Philadelphia Patristic Foundation, Ltd.).

—— and Groh, D. (1981), *Early Arianism: A View of Salvation* (Philadelphia: Fortress Press).

Gwynn, D. (2007), *The Eusebians: The Polemic of Athanasius and the Construction of the 'Arian Controversy'* (Oxford: Oxford University Press).

Haas, C. (1997), *Alexandria in Late Antiquity: Topography and Social Conflict* (Baltimore: Johns Hopkins University Press).

Hanson, R. P. C. (1988), *The Search for the Christian Doctrine of God: The Arian Controversy 318–381* (Edinburgh: T & T Clark).

Heather, P. (1996), *The Goths* (Oxford: Blackwell).

—— and Matthews, J. (1991) (eds. and trans.), *The Goths of the Fourth Century* (Liverpool: Liverpool University Press).

Heil, U. (2002), ' "…blossnicht wie die Manichäer!" Ein Verschlag zu den Hintergründen des arianischen Streites', *ZAC* 6: 299–319.

Jensen, R. M. (2000), *Understanding Early Christian Art* (London: Routledge).

Kemp, E. (1955), 'Bishops and Presbyters in Alexandria', *JEH* 6: 125–42.

Kinzig, W. (1990), *In Search of Asterius: Studies on the Authorship of the Psalms* (Göttingen: Vandenhoeck & Ruprecht).

Kopecek, T. (1979), *A History of Neo-Arianism*, 2 vols. (Philadelphia: Philadelphia Patristic Foundation).

—— (1985), 'Neo-Arian Religion: The Evidence of the *Apostolic Constitutions*', in R. Gregg (1985), 153–80.

Lienhard, J. (1987), 'The Arian Controversy: Some Categories Reconsidered', *TS* 48: 415–36.

—— (1999), *Contra Marcellum: Marcellus of Ancyra and Fourth-Century Theology* (Washington D.C.: Catholic University of America Press).

Lim, R. (1995), *Public Disputation, Power and Social Order in Late Antiquity* (Berkeley: University of California Press).

Löhr, W. A. (1986), *Die Entstehung der homöischen und homöusianischen Kirchenparteien: Studien zur Synodalgeschichte des 4. Jahrhunderts* (Bonn: Wehle).

—— (2005), 'Arius Reconsidered: Part One', *ZAC* 9: 524–60.

—— (2006), 'Arius Reconsidered: Part Two', *ZAC* 10: 121–37.

Lorenz, R. (1979), *Arius judaizans? Untersuchungen zur dogmengeschichtlichen Einordnung des Arius* (Göttingen: Vandenboeck & Ruprecht).

LORENZ, R. (1983), 'Die Christusseele im arianischen Streit: nebst einigen Bemerkungen zur Quellenkritik des Arius und zur Glaubwürdigkeit des Athanasius', *ZKG* 94: 1–51.

LYMAN, R. (1989), 'Arians and Manichees on Christ', *JTS* 40: 493–503.

—— (1993a), *Christology and Cosmology: Models of Divine Activity in Origen, Eusebius, and Athanasius* (Oxford: Clarendon Press).

—— (1993b), 'A Topography of Heresy: Mapping the Rhetorical Creation of Arianism', in Barnes and Williams (1993), 45–62.

MAIER, H. (1994), 'Private Space as the Social Context of Arianism in Milan', *JTS* 45: 72–92.

—— (2005), 'Heresy, Households, and the Disciplining of Diversity', in V. Burrus (ed.), *Late Ancient Christianity: The People's History of Christianity*, ii (Minneapolis: Fortress Press), 213–33.

MARASCO, G. (2005), *Filostorgio: Cultura, fede et politica in uno storico ecclesiastico del V secolo* (Rome: Institutum patristicum Augustinianum).

McLYNN, N. (1991), 'The " Apology" of Palladius: Nature and Purpose', *JTS* 42: 52–76.

—— (1994), *Ambrose of Milan: Church and Court in a Christian Capital* (Berkeley: University of California Press).

MERILLS, A. H. (2004) (ed.), *Vandals, Romans and Berbers: New Perspectives on Late Antique North Africa* (Aldershot: Ashgate).

MESLIN, M. (1967), *Les Ariens d' Occident* (Paris: Éditions du Seuil).

OPITZ, H. G. (1935), *Athanasius Werke, iii/1: Urkunden zur Geschichte des Arianischen Streites* (Berlin: de Gruyter).

PARVIS, S. (2006), *Marcellus of Ancyra and the Lost Years of the Arian Controversy 325–343* (Oxford: Oxford University Press).

POHL, W. (2000), 'Deliberate Ambiguity—the Lombards and Christianity', in G. Armstrong and I. N. Wood (eds.), *Christianizing Peoples and Converting Individuals* (Turnhout: Brepols), 47–58.

RAPP, C. (2005), *Holy Bishops in Late Antiquity: The Nature of Christian Leadership in an Age of Transition* (Berkeley: University of California Press).

SCHWARCZ, A. (1999), 'Cult and Religion among the Tervingi and the Visigoths and their Conversion to Christianity', in P. Heather (ed.), *The Visigoths: From the Migration Period to the Seventh Century, An Ethnographic Perspective* (San Marino, Calif.: Boydell Press).

SHANZER, D. (2004), 'Intentions and Audiences: History, Hagiography, Martyrdom and Confession in Victor of Vita's *Historia Persecutionis*', in Merills (2004), 271–90.

SIMONETTI, M. (1975), *La crisi ariana nel IV secolo* (Rome: Institutum Patristicum Augustinianum).

STEAD, C. (1978), 'The *Thalia* of Arius and the Testimony of Athanasius', *JTS* 29: 20–52.

—— (1988), 'Athanasius's Earliest Written Work?', *JTS* 39: 76–91.

—— (1994), 'Arius in Modern Research', *JTS* 45: 24–36.

—— (1997), 'Was Arius a Neo-Platonist?', *St Patr* 32: 39–52.

STEENSON, J. N. (1983), 'Basil of Ancyra and the Course of Nicene Orthodoxy' (D. Phil. thesis, Oxford).

THOMPSON, E. A. (1966), *The Visigoths in the Time of Ulfila* (Oxford: Clarendon Press).

—— (1969), *The Goths in Spain* (Oxford: Clarendon Press).

VAGGIONE, R. (1989), ' "Arius, Heresy and Tradition" by Rowan Williams: A Review Article', *Toronto Journal of Theology*, 5/1: 63–87.

—— (1993), 'Of Monks and Lounge Lizards: "Arians", Polemics and Asceticism in the Roman East', in Barnes and Williams (1993), 181–214.

—— (2000), *Eunomius of Cyzicus and the Nicene Revolution* (Oxford: Oxford University Press).

VAN DAM, R. (1993), *Saints and Their Miracles in Late Antique Gaul* (Princeton: Princeton University Press).

—— (2003), *Becoming Christian: The Conversion of Roman Cappadocia* (Philadelphia: University of Pennsylvania Press).

VINZENT, M. (1993), 'Gottes Wesen, Logos, Weisheit und Kraft bei Asterius von Kappadokien und Markell von Ankyra', *VC* 47: 170–91.

WARD-PERKINS, B. (2007), 'Where is the Archaeology and Iconography of Arianism?', in D. W. Gwynn and S. Bangert (eds.), *Late Antique Archaeology*, V.I: *Religious Diversity in Late Antiquity* (Leiden: E. J. Brill).

WICKHAM, L. (1968), 'The Syntagmation of Aetius the Anomean', *JTS* 19: 532–69.

WILES, M. (1962), 'In Defense of Arius', *JTS* 13: 339–47.

—— (1993), 'Attitudes to Arius in the Arian Controversy', in Barnes and Williams (1993), 31–44.

—— (1996), *Archetypal Heresy: Arianism through the Centuries* (Oxford: Clarendon Press).

WILLIAMS, D. (1995), *Ambrose of Milan and the End of the Arian–Nicene Conflicts* (Oxford: Clarendon Press).

WILLIAMS, R. (2001), *Arius: Heresy and Tradition*, 2nd. edn. (London: SCM; 1st edn. London: Darton, Longman, and Todd, 1987).

CHAPTER 13

PELAGIUS AND PELAGIANS

MATHIJS LAMBERIGTS

13.1 INTRODUCTION

THE Pelagian controversy is generally considered to have been the first *western* theological controversy. The debate between Pelagius and his followers, on the one hand, and Augustine, Jerome, Paulus Orosius, and the bishops of Rome (Innocent I, Boniface I, Celestine I, Sixtus I, Leo the Great), on the other hand, deeply influenced theological developments in the West. One may think here of Gottschalck of Orbais, Luther, Calvin, and Jansenius, who clearly took Augustine's side in the dispute about the relation between creation and salvation, nature and grace, freedom and grace, Adam versus Christ, predestination, etc. At the same time, one should remember that several of these authors, who, to a certain degree, wanted to be faithful to Augustine, were condemned by the Roman Catholic Church. Furthermore, they became the cause and object of many disputes in the Protestant communities. It should also be remembered that, from the beginning, not all of Augustine's positions in the controversy were accepted and received by tradition. To give one example, the Council of Orange (529) clearly did not follow Augustine's predestinarian ideas.

With regard to the presentation of Pelagius and Pelagians as heretics, systematic theologians especially often took Augustine's presentation of these people for granted. In his extensive writings against the Pelagians, the *doctor gratiae* presented his opponents as enemies of grace (Bonner 1993). Excellent polemicist that he was,

Augustine often offered the positions of his opponents in a concise and pointed summary (Wermelinger 1975). In line with Augustine, systematic theologians transformed Pelagianism into a coherent system (for a good survey, see Garcia-Sanchez 1978). The main features of such generalizing presentation were praise of human persons and their capacity to do what they were expected to do by God; praise of the potentialities of the free will; exclusion of a prevenient grace; reduction of grace to an external help, whereby the Law and the example of Christ were offered to human beings, who were completely free to accept or reject this help. Pelagians were accused of denying the doctrine of original sin and its consequences for human nature. At best, Pelagians were described as 'humanists', at worse, as naturalists (for a survey, see Lamberigts 2002).

Recent historical studies not only offer a good survey of the developments in the research on Pelagius and Pelagianism (Garcia-Sanchez 1978; Nuvolone-Solignac 1986; Wermelinger 1989; Bonner 1996b), but also contribute to an outspoken (Greshake 1972) or a more prudent rehabilitation of at least Pelagius himself (Wermelinger 1975; Lamberigts 2000). In any case, it has become clear that a doctrine of original sin, as held by Augustine and his African colleagues, was not present in the teachings of their predecessors, either in the West or in the East.

Although the Pelagian controversy took place mainly in the West, one should also pay attention to the fact that Pelagians had many contacts with the East. Pelagius, Caelestius, and Julian stayed for a longer or a shorter while in the East. Pelagian circles showed much interest in the work of Chrysostom. Some have linked the Pelagian *exemplum* idea to the Greek concept of *paideia* (Greshake 1972). With regard to the work of the Greek fathers, one might also think of Annianus of Celada (Nuvolone 1986; Pietri and Pietri 1999). Annianus, together with Pelagius, had to defend himself at the Synod of Diospolis (415). He criticized Jerome for his attack on Pelagius (Lamberigts 2002). He extensively translated work of Chrysostom in order to refute the 'Manichaeans' (Musurillo 1970; Skalitzky 1971). His translation of the sermons of Chrysostom on the Gospel of Matthew was dedicated to Bishop Orontius (Primmer 1972), one of the bishops who was eventually sent into exile by Zosimus. He is considered to be the translator of another collection of texts of Chrysostom (Pietri and Pietri 1999). His translation of the sermon of Chrysostom, *Ad neophytos* (Bouhot 1971), served Julian in his controversy with Augustine. In order to refute the allegedly Manichaean ideas in Augustine's writings, Julian made use of a translation of a work of Serapion of Thmuis against the Manichaeans (Cipriani 1987). Augustine received the acts of the Synod of Diospolis from Cyril of Alexandria (Augustine, *Ep.* 4*).

In the context of relations between East and West, one must mention the intriguing Rufinus the Syrian. During the lawsuit at Carthage against Caelestius (411), Caelestius mentioned this Rufinus as being opposed to the idea of original sin (cf. Augustine, *Pecc. or.* 2. 3), a position which is indeed present in Rufinus's *Libellus fidei* and known to Augustine (cf. *Pecc. mer.* 1. 23). As a result of much scholarly discussion, specialists seemed to agree that this Rufinus could be identified with the monk who lived with Jerome in Bethlehem and came to Rome about 399 (de Veer 1975). Recently, however, it was suggested that one might identify this Rufinus with Rufinus of Aquileia (Dunphy 2000). In any case, it is clear that a satisfying identification of this Rufinus would be of great help with regard to the non-eastern roots of the beginning of Pelagianism.

13.2 THE 'CORPUS PELAGIANUM': A PROBLEM

Due to many discoveries, the body of 'Pelagian' writings very much increased over the last 100 years or so, mainly due to the discovery of Pelagius's commentary on the letters of Paul, the attribution of several commentaries to Julian of Aeclanum, and the discovery of the Corpus Caspari (Caspari 1890). The Corpus Caspari consisted of the following treatises: *Epistula honorificentiae tuae*, *Epistula humanae referent litterae* (also known as *Epistula ad adolescentem*), *Epistula de possibilitate non peccandi* (also known as *Epistula qualiter*), *Epistula sancti Sixti episcopi et martyris de divitiis*, *Epistula sancti Sixti episcopi et martyris de malis doctoribus et operibus fidei et de iudicio futuro*, and *Epistula sancti Sixti episcopi et martyris de castitate*.

It is rather difficult to find helpful criteria to define what belongs to Pelagian literature and what does not. As long as scholars disagree about the extent of the corpus of treatises written by Pelagius himself, it will remain difficult to do justice to Pelagius and the ideas he might have held. In an article published in 1934, G. de Plinval attributed about thirty-four 'Pelagian' writings (books, letters, smaller treatises) to Pelagius himself. As a result, Pelagius suddenly could be considered as one of the most fruitful writers of the fifth century. However, de Plinval's attributions, mostly based on vocabulary and stylistic arguments, were soon criticized by J. Kirmer (1938), J. Morris (1965), and especially R. F. Evans (1968b). According to Evans, only the following works could be safely attributed to Pelagius: his commentary on the letters of Paul, *Ad Demetriadem*, *De virginitate*, *De lege divina*, *De vita christiana*, and *Ad Celantiam*. Evans came to this conclusion on the basis of similarity in themes and the use of the same biblical quotations (Evans 1968a). It should be emphasized that both the commentary and the letters did not really concern the key issues in the Pelagian debate. Indeed, of works which were at stake during the controversy, *De natura* (Löhr 1999), *Pro libero arbitrio*, and, to a lesser degree, *De trinitate*, only fragments have been preserved, mostly thanks to Augustine, who quoted from these works in order to refute Pelagius. It goes without saying that often the critical reader misses the context within which such fragments can be found.

Moreover, Wermelinger (1989) suggested that Evans might have attributed too many letters to Pelagius. Especially the attribution of *Ad Celantiam*, *De divina lege*, and *Ad Claudiam* to Pelagius was difficult to accept. Wermelinger's main argument was that Pelagius explicitly denied the authorship of some of these works, and that one has to accept that he thus lied. Further, Wermelinger hesitated about the possibility of proving authorship on the basis of philological and literary-critical arguments alone. Finally, he suggested that the content of these three letters could hardly be qualified as the doctrine of Pelagius. Other scholars, however, have continued to maintain Pelagius's authorship of these three letters (Rees 1988: 133–4; Duval 2003; Hunter 2007).

The attribution of the remaining treatises of the Caspari Corpus to a specific author or authors is still a matter of debate, and it is impossible to give an exhaustive survey of all the positions taken in this regard. We limit ourselves to the essential. Evans (1968*a*) suggested that the author of this corpus might be a Sicilian Breton, but without success (Nuvolone 1986). The prudent attribution of the works *De divitiis*, *De malis doctoribus*, and *De castitate* to Sixtus, the later bishop of Rome (Nuvolone 1986; Wermelinger 1989) was, with regard to *De divitiis*, rejected by Kessler (1999). Nuvolone and Wermelinger had suggested this attribution on the basis of the manuscript tradition and on the fact that Sixtus was described by Augustine as a patron of Pelagius (*Ep.* 191. 1). Kessler rejected this attribution, however, and suggested that *De divitiis* was written by a spiritual author who did not belong to a Pelagian milieu. In line with Kessler, I would suggest that one should not immediately relate all kinds of ascetical ideals and societal critiques with Pelagius and Pelagianism. I am well aware of the fact that many authors, in line with Augustine, considered the promotion of such ideals as an expression of self-confidence and as a clear proof that these people exaggerated human nature's capacities. At the same time, one cannot deny that ascetical lifestyles were developing everywhere, and that the number of ascetic communities was growing; in other words, asceticism was in the air. The writings of the Caspari Corpus also promote virginity and celibacy in widowhood, and clearly prefer virginity over marriage. They highly appreciate willingness to sell everything to give it to the poor. The writings aim at a morally perfect life. They promote the reading of the Bible and Christian literature, and invite the reader to imitate Christ by searching for eternal values instead of riches, honour, and secular roles. The treatises give evidence of a strong belief in God's goodness, human beings' responsibilities, etc. Qualifying these treatises as Pelagian (with its 'heretical' connotation) seems to be an exaggeration. In that case, much ascetic literature, written before and after the Pelagian controversy, has to be labelled as 'Pelagian heresy'. Jerome, certainly not a Pelagian, is a good example of a promoter of ascetic life in Rome. In passing, it should be mentioned that there is still a broad range of treatises, dealing with ascetic ideals, that, for better or worse, were described as Pelagian; but, again, promoting ascetic ideals does not necessarily mean that one is a Pelagian (in this regard, Nuvolone 1986, s.v. 'Fastidius', gives a very convincing example).

Further, it would be unwise to qualify Pelagius's or Pelagians' works as heretical because they were written by them. The following example can probably clarify this. The authorship of Pelagius's *Epistula ad Demetriadem* was, for centuries, attributed to Jerome or to Augustine because of its highly ascetic content. Once it became clear that this letter was written by Pelagius, it suddenly received epithets such as 'un-evangelical' and 'non-Pauline' (de Plinval 1943; Valero 1980), a somewhat surprising change of perspective if one takes into account that Pelagius paid much attention to Paul's letters (Souter 1926; see now also Frede 1973–4; de Bruyn 1993; Tauer 1994). Frede's studies made clear that many of the 'Pelagian' ideas in the commentary were later additions, not Pelagius's own opinion (also Wermelinger 1989), and that Pelagius's approach to Paul was in line with what was at the time the custom in the Latin world (Tauer 1994). Indeed, in his commentary Pelagius was influenced by a Latin, mostly North African, anti-Jewish and anti-pagan tradition (de Bruyn 1993, Tauer 1994). He was also influenced by commentaries of predecessors such as Lactantius, Hilary, Ambrose, Jerome, to mention a few (Tauer 1994). At least in his commentary, Pelagius showed a great familiarity with scripture, and the often-heard critique that he was deeply influenced by Stoic philosophy has, in recent times, clearly been nuanced (cf. Tauer 1994).

In passing, it must be said that already in 1516 the humanist Erasmus considered Jerome to be the author of Pelagius's commentary on Paul (PL 33. 646–909). It remains surprising that simply because the letter to Demetrias—through the ages a real success—could be attributed to Pelagius, scholars changed their qualification of the work and that it became subject to critique.

While the debate on Pelagius's authorship continues, there is, at least in the twentieth century, common agreement about the attribution of a series of exegetical commentaries to Julian of Aeclanum. Because history attributed these commentaries to other, more 'orthodox' authors, they were preserved, again a proof that orthodoxy or heterodoxy often depend upon what we know about the author. In any case, Julian was recognized as the author of the *Tractatus prophetarum Osee, Iohel et Amos*, the *Expositio libri Job*, and the translator of Theodore of Mopsuestia's commentary on the Psalms (at least for Ps 1–16) (CCSL 88–88A). The authorship with regard to the summary of the rest (the so-called *Epitomē*) is more problematic (De Coninck and D'Hont 1977).

Less consensus is found with regard to the *Libellus fidei*. Bouwman (1957) at-tributed this work to Julian, and Cipriani (2004) thinks such attribution is prob-able. Julian's authorship is denied by Bruckner (1897), Nuvolone (1986), and Lössl (2001a). For a hesitant option, see Lamberigts (2002). While pros and cons regard-ing Pelagius's authorship have been well examined, one still awaits an extensive philological, literary, and theological study of the relationship between Julian's œuvre and the *Libellus*, which is often assigned to a northern Italian milieu. If this opinion is correct, it would be proof that the opposition to the African perspectives was much greater than most of the surveys on the controversy suggest.

13.3 PELAGIUS

13.3.1 A Short Biography

Pelagius was born in Brittany (Augustine, *Ep.* 186. 1), a fact which has led some Anglo-Saxon authors to conclude that Pelagianism might have British roots (Myres 1960; Morris 1965), although such a position is rather questionable (Liebeschuetz 1963, 1967). Pelagius went to Rome, where he received a classical education, as is evident in his commentary on the letters of Paul (Tauer 1994), and where from 380 to 410 he gained fame as a Christian ascetic and teacher, as had been the case with Jerome (Brown 1972). He was highly respected in Roman aristocratic milieux (Brown 1967, 1972). In a period when many embraced Christianity for opportunistic reasons but did not take into account the demands of this religion, Pelagius reacted against these nominal Christians and promoted a genuine Christian ascetical way of life. Because of such a plea for a true Christian life, Pelagius has often been presented as a moral theologian, promoting a church of perfect people. Such an evaluation, however, does not do justice to him and is still deeply influenced by the positions of Pelagius's opponents at the time of the controversy (Bonner 1966; Wermelinger 1989).

Pelagius really wanted to be a (critical) theologian and an exegete. Already at an early stage, he criticized theological ideas of Augustine—he probably read work of Augustine in the library of Paulinus of Nola (Brown 1972)—about the dominance of grace over free will (Augustine, *Persev.* 20. 53) and in about 405/6 wrote a treatise on nature (Duval 1990). Before 410 he also wrote his commentary on the letters of Paul. After the invasion of the Goths in 410, Pelagius, together with Caelestius, left Italy and went to North Africa, where he arrived in Hippo and stayed for a short period in Carthage. During this stay in Carthage he twice met Augustine, to whom he had sent a letter of courtesy (den Boeft 1987; Duval 1999). Soon he left Africa and went to the East, where he lived in Palestine under the protection of Bishop John of Jerusalem and ran into trouble with Jerome (Evans 1964; 1968*a, b*). He remained a respected person: together with Innocent, Augustine, and Jerome, he was invited to write a treatise for Demetrias, daughter of Juliana Anicia and granddaughter of Proba, members of the aristocratic family of the Anicii. In 415 he was accused of heresy by the bishops Heros and Lazarus, both exiled in Gaul. The main inspirer of the accusations was Jerome (Nuvolone 1986). During meetings held in Jerusalem and Diospolis, Pelagius was acquitted by oriental bishops, proof that there did not yet exist a kind of universal 'orthodoxy' on the questions of Adam's fall, original sin, free will, and grace. Augustine's accusation that this acquittal was the result of dishonesty and lies remains a matter of scholarly discussion (Evans 1964; Wermelinger 1989).

The acquittal caused much unrest in Africa, where Augustine wrote a series of works directed against the 'heresy'. The Africans condemned 'Pelagian' ideas at synods in Carthage and Milevis (416)—it is still unclear whether what was condemned was in fact held by Pelagius—and alarmed the bishop of Rome (Innocent I) and the emperor Honorius at Ravenna. Innocent deprived Pelagius and Caelestius of ecclesial communion, but gave them the possibility to appeal and to justify their positions. Both did so. Their appeals arrived in Rome after Innocent's death. Innocent's successor, Zosimus, first regarded Pelagius and Caelestius as orthodox. Both had shown their willingness to obey the Church by going in person to Rome (Caelestius) or by sending a letter and a *Libellus fidei* (Pelagius). It was on the basis of their oral and written testimony that Zosimus first set them free (Lamberigts 1992). However, under pressure from Africa and the court in Ravenna—Pelagius and Caelestius were both condemned at the Synod of Carthage, 1 May 418, and by a prescript of Honorius, 30 April 418—Zosimus finally condemned Pelagius and his allies with a letter, *Epistula tractoria*, in the summer of 418 (Lamberigts 1992). It remains a mystery why this letter, which was sent to bishops all over the empire, has been preserved only in fragments (Wermelinger 1979). What is preserved makes clear that one cannot qualify this letter as being 'clearly Augustinian' (Floëri 1955). Pelagius had to leave Palestine and probably took refuge in Egypt, where he died at an unknown date. Like Caelestius, Julian, and others, he was condemned at Ephesus in 431.

13.3.2 Pelagius's Basic Intuitions

Because it is hard to determine exactly what can be considered Pelagius's own writings, I will present Pelagius's basic ideas on the basis of the works which are undoubtedly considered to be his own writings. Certitude and unanimity exist only with respect to the commentary on Paul, the letter to Demetrias, the *Libellus fidei*, and a number of fragments, including *De natura* and *Pro libero arbitrio* (Evans 1968*a*,*b*; Wermelinger 1975, 1979, 1989; Kessler 1999).

Pelagius really wanted to be a man of the Church, an orthodox writer. In his writings he distanced himself explicitly from the heterodox movements of his time, including Arianism, Manichaeism, and the positions adopted by Jovinian (Bohlin 1957; Bonner 1963; Greshake 1972). Mainly because he rejected Manichaean determinism, he emphasized the existence and value of human beings' free will. He considered Manichaeism as a threat to an authentic Christian life, for its

deterministic view would annihilate human freedom and thus ethical responsibility. His Christology has been evaluated as orthodox (Rivière 1946; Dewart
1982).

Pelagius's emphasis on human beings' freedom and responsibility was closely
related to his view of God as creator. According to Pelagius, God has given human
beings the ability (*posse*) to do what they are expected to do. The gift of the *posse*
is the gift *par excellence*. Our freedom depends upon God's gift of it. God enables
us to do what we must do. In other words, what is often described as a sign of
Pelagian arrogance, in fact must be seen as a divine gift. What we will (*velle*) or
actually do (*facere*) belongs to our responsibility; that we are enabled to will and to
act belongs to God's creative activity (Greshake 1972). Does this mean that Pelagius
held that human beings *de facto* could live a sinless life, as Jerome suggested (*Dial.*
1. 26)? Not at all! Pelagius did not believe that human beings could live a sinless
life. A careful reading of *De natura*, written in about 405/6 (Duval 1990), reveals
that already at this relatively early stage, Pelagius had reacted against the charge
that he had neglected God's grace. In Diospolis (415), he explicitly stated that one
constantly needs this gift of grace (cf. Augustine, *Pecc. or.* 2. 2). Also Pelagius had
a theology of grace, and this on the level of creation, revelation, and forgiveness
(Bohlin 1957; Greshake 1972; Garcia-Sanchez 1978).

In line with Augustine, it is often suggested that Pelagius considered Christ to
be an external example, a person one should imitate. Pedagogy has made clear that
imitating someone influences the one who wants to imitate. It is also a process
of inner development and being influenced. This is also the case with Pelagius.
Christ's example is not simply a mere external example. Imitating Christ is the
result of a conscious process, of interiorization of Christ's precepts, and thus has
to do with adults (Geerlings 1978). Whereas Augustine put so much emphasis on
original sin and, in that context, time and again pleaded in favour of infant baptism,
Pelagius first and foremost addressed himself to adults. For Pelagius, as for many
of his predecessors, baptism was a break with the old, the beginning of new life,
unification with Christ, enlightenment (Garcia-Sanchez 1978). The gift of baptism
is more than remission of sins or a defeat of the weaknesses of the flesh. Through
this gift, mediated by the Church, human beings become the image of God, enter
into the community of the saints, and are invited to obedience to God under the
guidance of the Holy Spirit. Salvation in Christ is offered through the Church.
Pelagius was a strong promoter of the sanctity of the Church and its members, but
he would never accept the Novatianist idea of Christians as perfect people. Also for
Pelagius, the Church consisted of saints and sinners. This explains why ideas such
as humility play an important role in his writings. The emphasis on the need for
repentance is to be understood not simply as a reaction against the Novatianists or
Jovinianists, but as essentially part of his concern for the Church and a longing for
Christian sanctity (Wermelinger 1989, rightly referring to Pelagius's commentary
on the letter of Paul to the Ephesians). Christian sanctity is a task and a duty for

the faithful, but it is a task and duty that requires the help of Christ's grace (Garcia-Sanchez 1978; Wermelinger 1989; Thier 1999).

A final remark: whether or not one shows sympathy for Pelagius and his allies, one must admit that at least some of the accusations against them are not present in their preserved writings. This is the case for the often repeated accusation that the Pelagians held a theologically indefensible distinction between the kingdom of God and eternal life (Refoulé 1963). The same must be said about the accusation that he defended an idea of sinlessness (*impeccantia*), an accusation formulated by Jerome (Annecchino 2004).

13.4 CAELESTIUS

In line with Augustine and Jerome, people tend to refer to Pelagius and Caelestius in one and the same breath. Augustine himself spoke in this regard of *Pelagiani et Coelestiani* (or *Caelestiani*; *Nupt.* 2. 8), presenting their (eventual) followers as belonging to a coherent group. Jerome explicitly describes Caelestius as a disciple of Pelagius and as the leader of the group (Jerome, *Ep.* 133. 5). Caelestius lived an ascetic life. He seems to have been attracted by Pelagius's teachings and way of life. In Rome, he met Rufinus, who openly rejected the idea of a transmission of sin. Caelestius himself wrote a (now lost) treatise against the *tradux peccati* idea (*Praedestinatus*, 88). After the fall of Rome (410), Caelestius joined Pelagius in Africa. Caelestius wanted to become a priest in the church of Carthage. However, his orthodoxy was questioned by the Italian deacon Paulinus of Milan. Whether Paulinus intervened because he knew Caelestius's ideas or because he was asked to by the Africans remains unclear (Nuvolone 1986). In any case, the minutes of the meeting in Carthage (411) (Wermelinger 1975), a meeting held in the absence of Augustine, make clear that the theological positions under discussion could not be accepted by the Africans (to a large extent, the issues under discussion, up to 418, are the same: Adam's fall and the consequence for himself and his progeny, the presence of original sin in babies and the need for baptism, the value of the Law, sinlessness).

At Carthage, Caelestius stated that the idea of a transmission of sin was considered to be a matter of discussion. In this regard, he explicitly mentioned Rufinus (Augustine, *Pecc. or.* 2. 3). Although he admitted the need for infant baptism, he did not accept that such baptism was intended for the remission of original sin (Augustine, *Pecc. or.* 2. 3). He was not admitted to the priesthood, and left Africa for the East, where he was ordained a priest at Ephesus. Although several theses, submitted to meetings in Jerusalem and Diospolis, were attributed to Caelestius, it is hard to prove whether Caelestius really held these positions. In any case, for a short while Pelagius distanced himself from Caelestius; but a reconciliation must have taken place shortly after Diospolis (Wermelinger 1975). Like Pelagius, Caelestius was the subject of condemnations in Africa (Carthage 416, Milevis 416) and in Rome (417). Under Zosimus, Caelestius again defended his case in Rome. First he was set free conditionally—Africa was requested to prove his (and Pelagius's) heterodoxy—again a proof that 'orthodoxy' in this matter was still a flexible concept.

Finally, because of pressure from Africa and the court at Ravenna, on the one hand, and his refusal to present himself before Zosimus for a more detailed examination of his positions, on the other hand, he was condemned by Zosimus and sent into exile. He tried to have his case be re-examined under the bishops Boniface and Celestine, but failed (Bonner 1992). In any case, a comparison of the *Libellus fidei* of Pelagius and Caelestius makes clear that their ideas were very near to each other (Bonner 1992). In about 428–9 Caelestius took refuge in Constantinople, but, at the instigation of Marius Mercator, was again expelled and finally condemned at the Council of Ephesus, together with Julian and his companions. Given the fact that most of his writings are lost, and attributions of preserved writings and/or fragments to Caelestius are problematic, it is rather difficult to have a clear view of his positions. But he must have been critical of the idea of a transmission of original sin. In this regard it should be repeated that Pelagius himself had also been critical of works of Augustine long before the outbreak of the controversy. It seems reasonable to suggest that Caelestius, more than Pelagius, emphasized the importance of the freedom of the will and thus paid less attention to hamartiology and soteriology (Nuvolone 1986; Wermelinger 1989; Honnay 1994; Lamberigts 2002). In any case, it may be unfair to minimize Pelagius's role at the expense of Caelestius (Honnay 1994).

13.5 JULIAN OF AECLANUM

13.5.1 A Short Biography

Julian of Aeclanum was born in Apulia in about 380. He was the son of Memor, or Memorius, who may also have been the bishop of Aeclanum and predecessor of Julian (Lössl 2001a), and his wife, Juliana. Julian had two sisters. He received a good literary, rhetorical, and theological education (Gennadius, *Vir. ill.* 46; Cipriani 1975; Lamberigts 1999; Lössl 2001a; Moreschini 2004; Santorelli 2004). In about 400 he married Titia (or Ia), the daughter of Aemilius, the bishop of Beneventum. Bishop Aemilius was sent by Innocent, bishop of Rome, to the East in order to intervene in favour of John Chrysostom during the bishop's dispute with the emperor. It should be remembered that the Pelagians showed much sympathy for this Greek moral theologian.

At the occasion of Julian's wedding, Paulinus of Nola, friend of Aemilius, Augustine, and Pelagius, wrote a wedding song, or *epithalamium* (Paulinus, *Carm.* 25; Lössl (2001a) offers a detailed presentation of this wedding song). During his controversy with Augustine, Julian, like Pelagius, shows a certain familiarity with some of Augustine's early works. Julian must have been a promising man, for in about 408–9 Augustine asked his father to send Julian to Hippo (Augustine, *Ep.* 101). Julian indeed visited Carthage, where he met the Manichaean Honoratus (*Flo.* 5. 26), who in 411–12 would be warned by Augustine against the adversaries of grace (Bochet 2001); but whether Julian ever met Augustine is unknown. It is worth mentioning that Julian only twice mentioned the name of Pelagius in his works against Augustine (*Flo.* 4. 88, 112). In both cases he explicitly expressed his sympathy for Pelagius, but literal quotations from Pelagius's work are not present in Julian's writings.

Julian was really a man of the Church: when he married, he was a lector; at the time of the epistolary contacts between his father and Augustine, he was a deacon, and *c.* 415/16 he became bishop of Aeclanum. He took care of the poor by distributing his possessions during a period of famine (Gennadius, *Vir. ill.* 46).

From 418 onwards, Julian was the main Pelagian player in the controversy. Together with eighteen colleagues, he refused to sign Zosimus's *Epistula tractoria*, for people were urged to sign this letter without discussion and under pressure (Lamberigts 1992). Julian defended his position in a letter to Count Valerius at the court of Ravenna in two letters to Zosimus during a public discussion and in a letter to the bishop of Thessalonica, Rufus; but it was all in vain, for Zosimus condemned Julian. In his writings Julian showed his disappointment about the change in the pope's position. After a new condemnation of the Pelagians by the emperor (summer 419), Julian had to leave Italy (Wermelinger 1975). He regarded his controversy with Augustine as a fight against Punic and Manichaean invaders, who wanted to destroy the church in Italy. He extensively criticized the first book of Augustine's *De nuptiis et concupiscentia* in a work addressed to his confrère Turbantius (*Ad Turbantium*). Later, in eight books written to his colleague Florus (six are preserved thanks to Augustine's reply, *Contra Julianum opus imperfectum*), Julian responded to the second book of *De nuptiis et concupiscentia* (the latter was Augustine's response to a summary of Julian's *Ad Turbantium*; Augustine's full reply is found in *Contra Julianum*). Julian probably wrote his eight books *Ad Florum* in the East, while taking refuge with Theodore of Mopsuestia (Nuvolone 1986). The work seems to have been intended for the West, for Alypius received it during his visit to Italy (427). It is possible that Julian also wrote a treatise *De bono constantiae* while in the East. Of this work, which clearly refers to John Chrysostom's *Quod nemo laeditur nisi a seipso* (translated by Annianus), only fragments are preserved. It is suggested that Julian was also condemned by Theodore (Marius Mercator, *Versio symboli Theodori, ACO* I, V, p. 23), but Marius Mercator is not always trustworthy in his information. In 429 Julian, together with Caelestius and some of his colleagues, stayed in Constantinople. Here they asked Nestorius, bishop of Constantinople, for a review of their case. Although Nestorius made serious efforts to obtain information from Pope Celestine, he was not successful. Moreover, due to the interventions of Marius Mercator, Julian and his friends and Caelestius were exiled by the emperor (for details, see Lössl 2001a). The Council of Ephesus explicitly condemned the Pelagians (Lamberigts 1985). During the whole controversy, Julian had asked for an objective and open forum for discussion, but such opportunity was never given to him or any of his companions. This, too, belongs to the history of Pelagianism. Under Bishop Sixtus, Julian attempted to get a review of his case, but did not succeed. He died sometime before 455 (Lössl 2001a).

13.5.2 Julian the Exegete

As mentioned above, the list of writings attributed to Julian was substantially enlarged during the twentieth century. Although his exegetical works did not play an important role in the controversy, they greatly contributed to a better understanding of this polemicist, whom Augustine described as his most intelligent opponent. Research on Julian's exegesis started only in recent times (Strobl 1991; Lössl 2001a, b, c; 2003; 2004; Pennacchio 2004). The studies of Lössl especially have opened new perspectives, for they make clear that Julian's exegetical works should not be considered merely as the work of a 'western' exegete—although Julian owed an important part of his exegetical ideas and approaches to Jerome (see De Coninck and D'Hont 1977: *Indices*; Lössl 2001a; Canellis 2004)—but that one should also take into account the exegetical work of Theodore of Mopsuestia. In any case, Julian's exegetical approach can no longer be evaluated as merely rationalist and strictly literalist. His exegesis was driven by particular theological concerns, especially those derived from Christian tradition and spirituality (Lössl 2003). In his exegesis, he was, generally speaking, in line with the approach of the Antiochene school. Julian was very much in favour of a historical understanding of scripture. However, he accepted that a biblical text could also have a typological meaning, though he was of the opinion that this kind of exegesis always should remain within well-defined limits. In any case, Julian could not accept that the truth of reason and the truth of scripture were in contradiction with each other: results of sane rational reasoning will be confirmed by scripture (*Flo.* 4. 136; Lössl 2003). The rationale behind this position is, of course, that scripture and reason are both gifts of God. The one who speaks in scripture is the same as the one who created rational human beings.

Whether Julian in his controversy with Augustine was influenced by eastern ideas remains an open question. An answer to that question depends upon the chronology of Julian's work: if one assigns Julian's exegetical works to the period before the controversy with Augustine, then such influence is possible. Unfortunately, Julian seldom shows a thorough knowledge of Greek in his works against Augustine. In the debate on Romans 5 (*Flo.* 2) Julian does not make use of the Greek text in order to refute Augustine. Further, he mentions Theodore only once, in a vague and general way (*Flo.* 3. 111). When referring to Greek literature, Julian seems to make use of translations (see Cipriani 1987). One also has to take into account that Julian visited Theodore only in the period when he was in exile in the East, i.e. after 422. Therefore, it seems not unreasonable to assign the exegetical works chronologically after Julian's controversial literature against Augustine (Nuvolone 1986; Canellis 2004; Pennacchio 2004). However, it is possible that, at the time he wrote his *Ad Florum,* Julian lived in the neighbourhood of Theodore (Cipriani 1994). In any case, Julian's exegesis of Genesis shows similarities to that of Theodore, if not influences by Theodore (Cipriani 1993). Since the exegetical works as such did not play a role in the controversy, I will not discuss them here, but it should be remembered that Julian's exegesis as present in the controversy with Augustine is described as 'well integrated in the traditional ecclesiastical context of his time' (Lössl 2003).

13.5.3 Julian the Theologian and Polemicist

Within the context of the Pelagian controversy, it is one of Julian's merits that he urged Augustine constantly to defend and explain his positions. Augustine's *De nuptiis et concupiscentia, Contra duas epistulas Pelagianorum, Contra Julianum,* and *Contra Julianum opus imperfectum,* together an impressive *œuvre,* contain not only citations but a complete version of the books I–VI of Julian's *Ad Florum,* a unique phenomenon in ancient Christian polemical literature.

In his works against Augustine, Julian reveals himself as a scholar with a good classical background (Lamberigts 1999; Lössl 2001a; Weber 2001). He is a sharp debater, very familiar with all the techniques that one should use in a controversy (Weber 2001, 2003; Lamberigts 2003). However, his arguments in the controversy seem to be mainly theological in nature (Lamberigts 1988; for another opinion, see Smalbrugge 2004; on possible Greek influences in Julian's theology, see Cipriani 2004). His basic axiom was the following: the good God is the creator of a good nature. This goodness of creation is a contingent one: people are created mutable and mortal. Pain and suffering do not have 'ethical' connotations, but belong to nature as it is created (Lössl 2002b). Evil is not considered to be a substance, a position which explains Julian's outspoken critique of Manichaeism and the way in which he links Augustine to Manichaeans (Cipriani 1994). Both soul and body must be qualified as good. As a supporter of the creationist view with regard to the soul, he was of the opinion that God gives to every newborn a newly created soul, probably the best argument one can bring against Augustine's idea of original sin. Indeed, when the ethical behaviour of the human person must be situated on the level of the soul, the presence of an inherited sin in newborn infants—sin considered to be the result of an ethical act of an adult person—must be rejected. Any acceptance of sin and guilt on that level would be a criticism of God's creative activity: God himself would be responsible for this guilt, a view unacceptable to Julian (Lamberigts 1996). The conviction that God creates a new soul for every newborn also explains why, for Julian, the sin of Adam was not as dramatic as it was for Augustine. In fact, for Julian, Adam was a *homo olim defunctus* (*Flo.* 2. 163; Lamberigts 1990). All human beings are born with a free will. All are gifted with innate virtues. Therefore, all know what they have to do, and they are created by God as free human beings who can thus do what they have to do. Since Julian is convinced that God is also the creator of the body, everything that belongs to the body must be considered as good. In the context of the debate, this means that for Julian, in opposition to Augustine, concupiscence is to be qualified as good, for it is a necessary instrument for procreation. This is not to say that Julian is a promoter of sexual lust. For him, just as for Augustine, sexual concupiscence should be used only within the context of a legitimate marriage with the purpose of procreation. He simply considers this to be a necessary instrument to be used in order to fulfil God's command in Genesis 1: 28, 'Increase and multiply and fill the earth'. Julian appreciated the corporeality of human beings and their sexual desires as a prerequisite for bringing the natural good of marriage, procreation, to completion (Clark 1986a, b). With regard to Julian's view on sexuality, one should also take into account that Julian's medical knowledge had a role to play: concupiscence of both man and woman was considered as necessary for procreation (Brown 1983). Julian is a good example of a thinker who, in his theological reflection, integrates and elaborates what the sciences have to offer. He certainly tries to respect what is present in scripture and in Christian teaching, but does so while at the same time accepting scientific insights.

Julian thus clearly presents himself as a promoter of the goodness of human beings. At the same time, he is well aware of the sinfulness of human beings. He rejects the idea that such sinfulness is the result of human nature. He considers sin to be the result of an act of a free human being. All people sin, and all are responsible for their sins (Barclift 1991). On this level, Julian presents a plea for a just God: God punishes human beings justly because of their sins, for all know what to do and thus deserve punishment. It is also on this level that he emphasizes the need to be saved by Christ. Christ forgives our sins and inspires us by his example. Within this context, it should be noted that for Julian, in opposition to Augustine,

Christ possessed the same human nature as all other human beings. Julian did not worry about an eventual presence of concupiscence in Christ. Christ's function as an *exemplum* could only make sense insofar as he was, as human being, like all other human beings. The greatness of the human being Christ lay in the fact that he, a human being like us, surpasses all of us, but at the same time inspires us with his magnificent example. He invites us to imitate him (Lamberigts 2005). Membership in the Church is a way to salvation. The gift of saving grace is the offer of a loving God. As such, this grace can never force people. It can never be described as opposed to human beings' freedom. On this level, Julian seems to be a defender of a balanced, synergetic interaction between human beings' freedom and God's saving and helping grace (Lamberigts 1993).

For Julian, such a position was also related to God's justice. In Julian's view, justice meant restoring to each person what is due without fraud or preferential treatment (*Flo.* 1. 35; McGrath 1983). This idea was not only present in Roman law, but could also be found in scripture: 'The child will not suffer for the injustice of his parents, nor will the parents suffer for the injustice of their child. The justice of the just will be upon themselves, and the sinfulness of the sinful will be upon themselves' (Ezek 18: 20) (see e.g. *Flo.* 3. 49), again a proof that Julian combined secular knowledge and scriptural material. According to Julian, God was not only a good God, but also a just God, which means that he gives every human being what he merits. In the case of original sin—which, for Julian, was synonymous with innate sin—human beings are already guilty before they are able to act properly and autonomously. As a result, they are already condemned before having acted themselves. Moreover, they are condemned by God, the good creator of both body and soul, simply because they are the result of his work. In a sense, God condemns his own work. Therefore, Julian could not accept the doctrine of original sin, not only because he believed in God as a good creator, but also because he considered this God to be a just judge of human beings, created as rational and responsible human beings, with a free will, able to choose good and evil.

Although Julian did not accept the doctrine of original sin, he strongly promoted the baptism of children, for he considered this to be a gateway to heaven, the way to become a member of the Church, and a means of sanctifying the newly born. Needless to say, the idea of baptizing children because of original sin (i.e. because of the sin of another person) could be considered a position that was accepted in Africa at the time of the controversy. The theological motivation for this practice, however, was not universally accepted prior to the beginning of the fifth century (Lamberigts 2000).

By way of conclusion, it should be stressed that Julian's role in the controversy is different from that of Pelagius. During the controversy, Pelagius had to defend himself. Julian chose to attack. He also paid much more attention to issues such as concupiscence and marriage. The overall impression remains that Julian, more than Pelagius, presented himself as a dogmatic theologian.

13.6 CONCLUSION

Due to intense research over the last 50 years or so, it has become clear that Pelagianism as a well-organized movement never existed. The authors, labelled as 'Pelagians', took different positions and discussed quite a broad range of topics. The attribution of the writings to specific authors remains, for a large part, a *crux interpretum*. This makes evaluation of individuals a difficult, if not impossible, task. Pelagianism as a consistent doctrine is a construction of its opponents, and Pelagius himself probably did not always recognize his own views in this construction. Such a construction does not do justice to the theological pluralism that existed at the beginning of the fifth century.

The history of Pelagius and the so-called Pelagians is something of a drama. Pelagius and the Pelagians wanted to be, first and foremost, honest and genuine Christians. They wanted to take their faith seriously, and this on the level of both orthodoxy and orthopraxis. At least up to 410, their positions were not openly questioned, and their way of living was highly admired by the Roman nobility. Only in the confrontation with the African positions with regard to Adam, his fall and the consequences for his progeny, vitiated nature, the primacy of grace over human beings' free will, the uniqueness of Christ as Saviour, and the baptism of children because of original sin, did their own intuitions become suspected of heresy, although it should be admitted that several of the so-called Pelagian writings did not develop clear positions on these topics.

Further, one should not forget that, at least before 410, the idea of the transmission of sin was still a matter of discussion, not a fixed doctrine. Moreover, in 415 the Synod of Diospolis acquitted Pelagius of the charges of which he was accused, and in 417 Bishop Zosimus of Rome was still convinced of Pelagius's and Caelestius's orthodoxy. Pelagius's and Caelestius's condemnations were the result of a well-organized action of the African episcopacy and of Augustine's involvement in it. Through these actions, resulting in condemnations at synods in Carthage and at Milevis (416)—decisions confirmed in a rather vague way by Innocent—and their influence at the court at Ravenna, the Africans finally succeeded in their efforts to have Pelagius and Caelestius condemned by both the western emperor and the bishop of Rome (418).

The way in which Julian of Aeclanum criticized Augustine and the sometimes excellent arguments that he used in his controversy with Augustine made clear that the Augustinian positions themselves were not unproblematic, especially with regard to the creation of the soul, the human nature of Christ, and the baptism of children because of original sin. However, the critique was no longer taken into account, and a final condemnation of the Pelagians took place in Ephesus (431), although it is still unclear whether people there really knew what exactly they were condemning. History has made clear that, despite the official condemnation of the Pelagians, western Christianity continued to struggle with issues such as the relationship between grace and free will. Too rapid condemnations seldom, if ever, are of benefit to Christianity.

In any case, further research is needed. We still lack a detailed comparison of the theological positions present in the different 'Pelagian' writings. Do Pelagius and Julian of Aeclanum take the same positions with regard to freedom and free will, the fall of Adam, and the need of grace? There is still a need for such comparative studies. Further, it would be instructive to search for possible links between 'Pelagian' ideas and eastern theologies. Pelagian sympathy for John Chrysostom and Theodore's hospitality to Julian offer good reasons for such a search. It would also be interesting to compare the so-called Pelagian writings with non-Pelagian ascetic writings. This might well contribute to a redefinition of what is 'orthodox' or 'heterodox'. Indeed, one has the feeling that there is a large distance between the content of a condemnation and the specific views of the condemned one. Do we really find the canons as condemned at Carthage in 418 in the works of Pelagius? I have my doubts.

When Julian of Aeclanum speaks about justice, he refers to both Cicero and the Bible (Ezek 18: 20). Both references are legitimate, although they speak about concept of justice other than the one we find in Paul and Augustine. Is it not an urgent *desideratum* to show the complexity of the biblical language and messages, in order to do better justice to positions such as those of Julian? Does historical research not require that one take into account all elements of a dossier before formulating an evaluation? On this level, much work remains to be done.

In any case, a systematic comparison of the different theologies in the West might reveal that quite a large number of non-African authors did not share all details of the African positions with regard to topics such as grace and free will, the fall of Adam, and original sin. In fact, how can authors who hold a creationist view of the soul accept the existence of original sin?

SUGGESTED READING

Most of the primary sources on the controversy between Augustine and the Pelagians are now available in The Works of Saint Augustine: A Translation for the 21st Century. A substantial part of the Pelagian corpus is translated by Rees (1991).

Bonner (1993) and Nuvolone (1986) offer very good introductory surveys, while Brown's many interesting insights about the broader context (1972) are still worth reading. In-depth studies in English on individual persons such as Pelagius and Caelestius are Rees (1988), de Bruyn (1993), and Honnay (1994). For Julian of Aeclanum one is expected to consult studies in other languages.

Bibliography

In this bibliography, I mostly limit myself to secondary literature. I refer as much as possible to the most recent literature. On the basis of that literature, the reader can easily discover the older studies.

For the primary sources, one should simply look under the names of the authors under discussion in the excellent work of E. Deckers, *Clavis patrum latinorum*, 3rd augmented edn. (Turnhout: Brepols, 1995).

ANNECCHINO, M. (2004), 'La nozione di impeccantia negli scritti pelagiani', in A. V. Nazzaro (ed.), *Giuliano d'Eclano e l'Hirpinia Christiana: Atti del Convegno 4–6 giugno 2003* (Naples: Arte tipografica), 73–86.

BARCLIFT, P. L. (1991), 'In Controversy with Saint Augustine: Julian of Eclanum on the Nature of Sin', *RTAM* 58: 5–20.

BOCHET, I. (2001), 'Honoratus: le destinaire de la Lettre 140 est-il l'ancien ami manichéen d'Augustin', *StPatr* 38: 8–15.

BOHLIN, T. (1957), *Die Theologie des Pelagius und ihre Genesis* (Uppsala: Lundequistska bokhandeln).

BONNER, G. (1963), *St Augustine of Hippo: Life and Controversies*, The Library of History and Doctrine (London: SCM Press).

—— (1966), 'How Pelagian was Pelagius? An Examination of the Contentions of Torgny Bohlin', *StPatr* 9: 350–8; repr. Bonner (1996a), ch. 3.

—— (1992), 'Caelestius', *Aug(L)* i, 5/6: 693–8.

—— (1993), 'Augustine and Pelagianism', *AugStud* 24: 27–47.

—— (1996a), *Church and Faith in the Patristic Tradition: Augustine, Pelagianism, and Early Christian Northumbria*, Collected Studies Series, 7 (Aldershot: Variorum).

—— (1996b), 'Pelagius/Pelagianischer Streit', in *TRE* xxvi. 176–85.

BOUHOT, J.-P. (1971), 'Version inédite du sermon Ad Neophytos de saint Jean Chrysostome utilisée par saint Augustin', *REA* 17: 27–41.

BOUWMAN, G. (1957), 'Zum Wortschatz des Julian von Aeclanum', *ALMA* 27: 141–64.

—— (1958), *Des Julian von Aeclanum Kommentar zu den Propheten Osee, Joël und Amos: Ein Beitrag zur Geschichte der Exegese* (Rome: Pontificio Istituto Biblico).

BROWN, P. (1967), *Augustine of Hippo: A Biography* (Berkeley: University of California Press).

—— (1972), *Religion and Society in the Age of Saint Augustine* (London: Faber & Faber).

—— (1983), 'Sexuality and Society in the Fifth Century A.D.: Augustine and Julian of Eclanum', in E. Gabba (ed.), *Tria Corda: Scritti in on ore di Arnaldo Momigliano* (Como: Edizioni New Press), 49–70.

BRUCKNER, A. (1897), *Julian von Eclanum, sein Leben and seine Lehre: Ein Beitrag zur Geschichte des Pelagianismus* (Leipzig: J. C. Hinrichs).

CANELLIS, A. (2004), 'Julien d'Éclane et l'In Ioel de saint Jérôme', in B. Gain, P. Jay, G. Nauroy (eds.), *Chartae caritatis: Études de patristique et d'antiquité tardive en hommage à Yves-Marie Duval*, Collection des Études Augustiniennes, Série Antiquité, 173 (Turnhout: Brepols), 359–75.

CASPARI, C. P. (1890), *Briefe, Abhandlungen und Predigten aus dem zwei letzten Jahrhunderten des kirchlichen Altertums* (Christiana [Oslo]: Mallingsche Buchdruckevei; repr. Brussells: Culture et Civilisation, 1964).

CIPRIANI, N. (1975), 'Aspetti letterari dell' Ad Florum di Giuliano d'Edano', *Aug* 15: 125–67.

—— (1987), 'L'Autore dei testi pseudobasiliani riportati nel C. Iulianum (I, 16–17) e la polemica agostiniana di Giuliano d'Eclano', in *Congresso internazionale su S. Agostino nel XVI centenario della conversione, Roma, 15–20 settembre 1986, Atti I: Cronaca del Congresso, Sessioni generali, Sezione di Studi I*, Studia Ephemeridis 'Augustinianum', 24 (Rome: Institutum Patristicum Augustinianum), 439–49.

—— (1993), 'La presenza di Teodoro di Mopsuestia nella teologia di Giuliano d'Eclano', in *Cristianesimo Latino e cultura Greca sino al sec. IV: XXI Incontro di studiosi dell'antichità cristiana, Roma, 7–9 maggio 1992*, Studia Ephemeridis "Augustinianum", 42 (Rome: Institutum Patristicum Augustinianum), 364–78.

—— (1994), 'La polemica antiafricana di Giuliano d'Eclano: artificio letterario o scontro di tradizioni teologiche?', in *Cristianesimo e specificità regionali nel Mediterraneo latino (sec. IV–VI): XXII Incontro di studiosi dell'antichità cristiana, Roma, 6–8 maggio 1993*, Studia Ephemeridis "Augustinianum", 46 (Rome: Institutum Patristicum Augustinianum), 147–60.

—— (2004), 'Sulle fonti orientali della teologia di Giuliano d'Eclano', in A. V. Nazzaro (ed.), *Giuliano d'Eclano e l'Hirpinia Christiana: Atti del Convegno 4–6 giugno 2003* (Naples: Arte tipografica), 157–70.

CLARK, E. A. (1986a), 'Adam's Only Companion: Augustine and the Early Christian Debate on Marriage', *RechAug* 21: 139–62.

—— (1986b), 'Vitiated Seeds and Holy Vessels: Augustine's Manichaean Past', in E. A. Clark (ed.), *Ascetic Piety and Woman's Faith: Essays on Late Ancient Christianity* (Lewiston, NY: Mellen), 291–349.

DE CONINCK, L., and D'HONT, M. J. (1977) (eds.), *Iuliani Aeclanensis expositio libri Iob, tractatus prophetarum Osee, Iohel et Amos, accedunt operum deperditorum fragmenta post Albertum Bruckner denuo collecta aucta ordinata: Theodori Mopsuesteni expositiones in Psalmos Iuliano Aeclanensi interprete in Latinum versae quae supersunt*, CCSL 88–88A (Turnhout: Brepols).

DE BRUYN, TH. (1993), *Pelagius' Commentary on St. Paul's Epistle to the Romans* (Oxford: Clarendon Press).

DEN BOEFT, J. (1987), 'Augustine's Letter to Pelagius', in J. den Boeft and J. van Oort (éds.), *Augustiniana Traiectina: Communications présentées au Colloque International d'Utrecht, 13–14 novembre 1986*, Études Augustiniennes (Paris: L'Institut d'études augustiniennes), 73–84.

DE PLINVAL, G. (1934), 'Recherches sur l'oeuvre littéraire de Pélage', *Revue de Philologie*, 60: 9–42.

—— (1943), *Pélage, ses écrits, sa vie et sa réforme* (Lausanne: Payot).

—— (1959), 'Julien d'Eclane devant la Bible', *RSR* 47: 345–66.

DEWART, J. McW. (1982), 'The Christology of the Pelagian Controversy', *StPatr* 17/3: 1221–44.

DUNPHY, W. (2000), 'An Unlisted Profession of Faith (Pseudo-Rufinus, *De Fide*)', *SacEr* 39: 37–53.

DUVAL, Y.-M. (1990), 'La date du "De natura" de Pélage: les premières étapes de la controverse sur la nature de la grâce', *REAug* 36: 257–83.

—— (1999), 'La correspondance entre Augustin et Pélage', *REAug* 45: 363–84.

—— (2001), 'Pélage en son temps: Données chronologiques nouvelles pour une présentation nouvelle', *StPatr* 38: 95–118.

—— (2003), *L'affaire Jovinien: D'une crise de la société romaine à une crise de la pensée chrétienne à la fin de IVe et au début de Ve siècle* (Rome: Institutum Patristicum Augustinianum).

EVANS, R. F. (1964), 'Pelagius' Veracity at the Synod of Diospolis', in J. Sommerfeldt (ed.), *Studies in Medieval Culture* (Kalamazoo, Mich.: Western Michigan University Press), 21–30.

—— (1968a), *Four Letters of Pelagius* (London: Black).

—— (1968b), *Pelagius: Inquiries and Reappraisals* (London: Black).

FLOËRI, F. (1955), 'Le péché originel d'après Zosime et Augustin', in *Augustinus Magister: Congrès international augustinien, Paris, 21–24 septembre 1954*, (Paris: L'Institut d'études augustiniennes), 755–61.

FREDE, H. J. (1973–4), *Ein neuer Paulustext und Kommentar*, Vetus Latina, Aus der Geschichte der lateinischen Bibel, 7–8 (Freiburg: Herder).

GARCIA-SANCHEZ, C. (1978), *Pelagius and Christian Initiation: A Study in Historical Theology* (Washington D.C.: Catholic University of America Press).

GEERLINGS, W. (1978), *Christus Exemplum: Studien zur Christologie und Christusverkündigung Augustins*, Tübinger theologische Studien, 13 (Mainz: Matthias-Grünewald).

GRESHAKE, G. (1972), *Gnade als konkrete Freiheit: Eine Untersuchung zur Gnadenlehre des Pelagius* (Mainz: Matthias-Grünewald).

HONNAY, G. (1994), 'Caelestius, discipulus Pelagii', *Aug(L)* 44: 271–302.

HUNTER, D. G. (2007), *Marriage, Celibacy, and Heresy in Ancient Christianity: The Jovinianist Controversy* (Oxford: Oxford University Press).

KESSLER, A. (1999), *Reichtumskritik und Pelagianismus: Die pelagianische Diatribe de divitiis: Situierung, Lesetext, Übersetzung, Kommentar*, Par. 43 (Freiburg (Schweiz): Universität Verlag).

KIRMER, I. (1938), *Das Eigentum des Fastidius in Pelagianischen Schriften* (St Ottilien: Oberbayern).

LAMBERIGTS, M. (1985), 'Les évêques pélagiens déposés, Nestorius et Ephèse', *Aug(L)* 35: 264–80.

—— (1988), 'Julian of Aeclanum: A Plea for a Good Creator', *Aug(L)* 38: 5–24.

—— (1990), 'Julien d'Eclane et Augustin d'Hippone: deux conceptions d'Adam', *Aug(L)* 40: 393–435.

—— (1992), 'Augustine and Julian of Aeclanum on Zosimus', *Aug(L)* 42: 311–30.

—— (1993), 'Julian of Aeclanum on Grace: Some Considerations', *StPatr* 27: 342–9.

—— (1996), 'Julian of Eclanum and Augustine on the Origin of the Soul', *Aug(L)* 46: 243–60.

—— (1999), 'Iulianus IV (Iulianus von Aeclanum)', in *RAC* xix. 483–505.

—— (2000), 'Pélage: la réhabilitation d'un hérétique', in J. Pirotte and E. Louchez (eds.), *Deux mille ans d'histoire de l'Eglise: Bilan et perspectives historiographiques*, RHE 95/3 (Louvain: Université catholique de Louvain), 97–111.

—— (2002), 'Recent Research into Pelagianism with Particular Emphasis on the Role of Julian of Aeclanum', *Aug* 52: 175–98.

—— (2003), 'The Italian Julian of Aeclanum about the African Augustine of Hippo', in P.-Y. Fux, J.-M. Roessli and O. Wermelinger (eds.), *Augustinus Afer: Saint Augustin: africanité et universalité, Actes du colloque international Alger-Annaba, 1–7 avril 2001*, Par. 45/1 (Fribourg: Éditions universitaires), 83–93.

LAMBERIGTS, M. (2005), 'In Defence of Jesus Christ: Augustine on Christ in the Pelagian Controversy', *AugStud* 36: 159–94.

LIEBESCHUETZ, W. (1963), 'Did the Pelagian Movement have Social Aims?', *Historia*, 12: 227–41.

—— (1967), 'Pelagian Evidence on the Last Period of Roman Britain?', *Latomus*, 26: 436–47.

LÖHR, W. (1999), 'Pelagius' Schrift *De natura*: Rekonstruktion und Analyse', *RechAug* 31: 135–94.

LÖSSL, J. (2001a), *Julian von Aeclanum: Studien zu seinem Leben, seinem Werk, seiner Lehre und ihrer Überlieferung*, Suppl. *VC*, 60 (Leiden: E. J. Brill).

—— (2001b), 'Julian of Aeclanum's Tractatus in Osee, Iohel, Amos', *Aug* 51: 5–31.

—— (2001c), 'A Shift in Patristic Exegesis: Hebrew Clarity and Historical Verity in Augustine, Jerome, Julian of Aeclanum and Theodore of Mopsuestia', *AugStud* 32: 157–75.

—— (2002a), 'Amos 6:1: Its Text and Ancient Translations', *Journal of Northwest Semitic Languages*, 28: 43–67.

—— (2002b), 'Julian of Aeclanum on Pain', *JECS* 10: 203–43.

—— (2003), 'Julian of Aeclanum's "Rationalist" Exegesis: Albert Bruckner Revisited', *Aug* 53: 77–106.

—— (2004), 'Teodoro di Mopsuestia e Giuliano di Eclano sulle cause naturali dei terremoti', in A. V. Nazzaro (ed.), *Giuliano d'Eclano e l'Hirpinia Christiana: Atti del Convegno 4–6 giugno 2003* (Naples: Arte tipografica), 103–11.

McGRATH, A. E. (1983), 'Divine Justice and Divine Equity in the Controversy between Augustine and Julian of Eclanum', *Downside Review*, 101: 312–19.

MORESCHINI, C. (2004), 'Natura e peccatum in Giuliano d'Eclano', in A. V. Nazzaro (ed.), *Giuliano d'Eclano e l'Hirpinia Christiana: Atti del Convegno 4–6 giugno 2003* (Naples: Arte tipografica), 55–72.

MORRIS, J. (1965), 'Pelagian Literature', *JTS* NS 16: 26–60.

MUSURILLO, H. (1970), 'John Chrysostom's Homilies on Matthew and the Version of Annianus', in *Kyriakon: Festschrift Johannes Quasten*, i (Münster: Aschendorff), 452–60.

MYRES, J. N. L. (1960), 'Pelagius and the End of Roman Rule in Britain', *JRS* 50: 21–36.

NUVOLONE, F. G. (1986), 'Pélage et Pélagianisme, I: Les écrivains', in *DSp* xii/2. 2889–2923 (with an impressive bibliography on the issue).

PENNACCHIO, M. C. (2004), 'Cum sermo propheticus absolute utrumque promiserit: l'interpretazione Giulianea del concetto di Theoria', in A. V. Nazzaro (ed.), *Giuliano d'Eclano e l'Hirpinia Christiana: Atti del Convegno 4–6 giugno 2003* (Naples: Arte tipografica), 171–89.

PIETRI, CH., and PIETRI, L. (1999), *Prosopographie chrétienne du Bas-Empire*, ii: *Prosopographie de l'Italie chrétienne (313–604)* (Rome: École française de Rome).

PRIMMER, A. (1972), 'Die Originalverfassung von Anianus' Epistula ad Orontium', in *Antidosis: Festschrift für Walther Kraus* (Vienna: Böhlau), 278–89.

RACKETT, MICHAEL R. (1997), 'Anxious for Worldly Things: The Critique of Marriage in the Anonymous Pelagian Treatise *De castitate*', *StPatr* 33: 229–35.

—— (2002), 'What's Wrong with Pelagianism: Augustine and Jerome on the Dangers of Pelagius and his Followers', *AugStud* 33: 223–37.

REES, B. R. (1988), *Pelagius: A Reluctant Heretic* (Woodbridge: Boydell and Brewer).

—— (1991), *The Letters of Pelagius and his Followers* (Woodbridge: Boydell Press).

REFOULÉ, F. (1963), 'La distinction "Royaume de Dieu-vie éternelle", est elle pélagienne?', *RSR* 51: 247–54.

RIVIÈRE, J. (1946), 'Hétérodoxie des pélagiens en fait de rédemption?', *RHE* 41: 5–43.

SANTORELLI, P. (2004), 'Note sulla terminologia retorica in Giuliano d'Eclano', in A. V. Nazzaro (ed.), *Giuliano d'Eclano e l'Hirpinia Christiana: Atti del Convegno 4–6 giugno 2003* (Naples: Arte tipografica), 73–86.

SKALITZKY, R. (1971), 'Annianus of Celeda: His Text of Chrysostom's Homilies on Matthew', *Aev* 45: 208–33.

SMALBRUGGE, M. (2004), 'L'identification interdite et imposée avec Dieu: Sur le moralisme de Julien d'Éclane', *Aug(L)* 54: 307–23.

SOLIGNAC, A. (1986), 'Pélage et Pélagianisme, II: Le mouvement et sa doctrine', in *DSp* xii/2. 2923–36.

SOUTER, A. (1926), *Pelagius's Expositions of Thirteen Epistles of St Paul*, TaS 9 (Cambridge: Cambridge University Press).

STROBL, I. (1991), 'Eine Untersuchung zum Verständnis alttestamentlicher Prophetie anhand des Julian von Aeclanum zugeschriebenen Kommentars zum propheten Joel' (unpublished M. A. thesis, Vienna).

TAUER, J. (1994), 'Neue Orientierungen zur Paulusexegese des Pelagius', *Aug* 34: 313–58.

THIER, S. (1999), *Kirche bei Pelagius*, PTS 50 (Berlin: de Gruyter).

VALERO, J. B. (1980), *Las bases antropologicas de Pelagio en su tratado de las Expositiones* (Madrid: Universidad Pontificia Comillas).

VEER, A. DE (1975), 'Le prêtre Rufinus' (note complémentaire 11), in *Œuvres de Saint Augustin 22: La crise pélagienne*, ii: Introduction, traduction et notes par J. Plagnieux and F.-J. Thonnard, BA 22 (Paris: L'Institut d'études augustiniennes), 704–11.

WEBER, D. (2001), 'Klassische Literatur im Dienst theologischer Polemik: Julian von Eclanum, Ad Florum', *StPatr* 38: 503–9.

—— (2003), 'For What is so Monstrous as What the Punic Fellow Says?', in P.-Y. Fux, J.-M. Roessli, and O. Wermelinger (eds.), *Augustinus Afer: Saint Augustin: africanité et universalité, Actes du colloque international Alger-Annaba, 1–7 avril 2001*, Par. 45/1 (Fribourg: Éditions universitaires), 75–82.

WERMELINGER, O. (1975), *Rom und Pelagius*, Päpste und Papsttum, 7 (Stuttgart: Hiersemann).

—— (1979), 'Das Pelagiusdossier in der Tractoria des Zosimus', *FZPhTh* 26: 336–68.

—— (1989), 'Neuere Forschungskontroversen um Augustinus und Pelagius', in C. Mayer, and K. H. Chelius (eds.), *Internationales Symposion über den Stand der Augustinus-Forschung vom 12. bis 16. April 1987 im Schloss Rauischholzhausen der Justus-Liebig-Universität Giessen*, Cassiciacum, 39/1 (Würzburg: Augustinus Verlag), 189–217.

PART IV

REGIONS

Map 14.1 Latin West

CHAPTER 14

THE WEST (1): ITALY, GAUL, AND SPAIN

MARK HUMPHRIES

14.1 INTRODUCTION: GREGORY OF TOURS AND THE EARLY CHRISTIAN WEST

SOMETIME around the year 576, a Gallic noble began writing what was to become his *magnum opus*. This aristocratic author was named Georgius Florentius Gregorius, but is better known today as Gregory of Tours, after the city in which he served as bishop from 573 until his death in 594. The work upon which he embarked was entitled *Historiae* (Goffart 1989). Much of the work is concerned with the Franks, a Germanic people who had taken control of much of the former Roman provinces of Gaul, Belgica, and Germania; but Gregory's conception of this work was couched primarily in religious terms. At the outset of the first of ten books, he explained that his subject would encompass the deeds of martyrs and struggles against heresy as well as the activities of kings; and he followed this with a statement of his own beliefs, through which he sought to present himself as unimpeachably orthodox— that is, to adopt his own terminology, a Catholic who believed in the unity of the Trinity. Moreover, he began his narrative with the creation of the world as it is described in scripture, and followed this with a selected account of Old and New Testament events, before proceeding to the early history of the Church in Gaul.

Indeed, it is not until the second book of the *Historiae* that the Franks actually appear in Gregory's pages.

This religious framework is equally explicit in Gregory's other writings. The majority of these were concerned with the deeds of martyrs and other saints who had made sacrifices on behalf of the true faith (Van Dam 1993). In the case of the *Historiae*, however, we see how Gregory explicitly conceived of all history—political as well as ecclesiastical—as having a place in God's creation (Heinzelmann 2001). For him, the history of Gaul, and of Christianity there, followed a particular trajectory that united the sacred history narrated in the books of the Bible with the events of his own day. This was emphasized further in the final chapter of the last book of the *Historiae*, where Gregory calculated in which year since the world's creation he was completing his narrative. Throughout the work, Gregory's portrait of the kings of the Franks conformed to this religious scheme. Thus he described the victory of Clovis over the Visigothic king Alaric II at the Battle of Vouillé (507) in terms of the support an orthodox Christian king could expect to receive from God; the defeated Alaric, by contrast, paid for his heretical beliefs by losing 'his kingship, his subjects, and, what is more important, the life hereafter' (*Historiae*, 3, pref.).

Of course, Gregory was not the first Christian writer to conceive of history in these terms. He owed a considerable debt to a long line of precursors stretching back to the beginning of the fourth century, when Eusebius of Caesarea, confronted by the conversion of Constantine to Christianity, sought out a providential role for the Roman Empire in the history of humankind. Eusebius had written in the eastern empire, but his ideas were readily imported to the West through the translation into Latin, with appended continuations, of his most important historical works, the *Chronicle* and the *Ecclesiastical History*. Hence the Eusebian conception of history came to be the dominant one in western Christian late antiquity. The struggles between orthodoxy and heresy and the triumphs of the martyrs for their faith were two themes that Eusebius had decreed to be central to the history of the Church and which Gregory picked up. Eusebius had also devoted considerable space to setting out the successions of bishops in major cities (Jerusalem, Antioch, Alexandria, and Rome), which, he held, guaranteed the preservation of pristine orthodoxy in the Church, handed down in an unbroken line since apostolic times. This too was a theme that Gregory developed for Gaul. The final chapter of the *Historiae* described the succession of bishops at Tours from the foundation of the see in the third century down to his own incumbency (*Hist.* 10. 31). Furthermore, by making the first bishop an appointee of the bishop of Rome, Gregory was able to link Catholic Christianity at Tours back to the foundation of the Christian community at Rome under the apostle Peter.

For centuries, this historiographical model has dominated efforts to trace the history of Christianity in western Europe. The focus on topics such as the development of bishoprics, the cults of saints (particularly as organized under episcopal patronage), and the struggle of orthodoxy against heresy has meant that such accounts have focused on the institutional history of the Church. This has tended to regard the contributions of groups that lay outside the central ecclesiastical hierarchy, such as 'heretics', women, or even the laity as a whole, as marginal (or, worse, deviant). It also led to a propensity—which grew more pronounced when 'church history' became a discipline distinct from political and social history (see Brakke 2002)—to see the development of Christianity as following its own logic, almost as if it evolved separately from society more generally. Furthermore, the traditional investigation of Christian history as church history has tended to privilege the study of written sources that tell us most about the institution and its definition of its beliefs. Even where archaeological evidence was admitted, it tended to be considered within a theological framework (e.g. Marucchi 1929). These days our approach to the evidence is altogether more sophisticated: all forms of evidence are considered as much as possible in the context of the societies in which they were produced (see Marazzi 2000). The purpose of this chapter is to capitalize on these new approaches and challenge traditional accounts of the development of Christianity in western Europe that emphasize ecclesiastical structures for their own sake. It aims to locate the history of early western Christianity—and not just the Church—in the social contexts in which it evolved and to illuminate its development by appealing to the widest range of sources possible.

14.2 FROM MYTH TO HISTORY: THE ORIGINS OF CHRISTIANITY IN THE WEST

The emphasis on tradition, especially ecclesiastical tradition, has had a profound influence on the study of Christian origins in the West. Gregory, as we have seen, was confident that he could trace the church at Tours back to its origins. Also in the sixth century, various compilers at Rome were putting together an account that traced the origins of the church there to the very earliest days of Christianity. The *Liber Pontificalis* (*Book of Pontiffs*) contains biographies of Roman bishops beginning with the apostle Peter, after whom came a succession of 'popes' in an unbroken line (Davis 2000). Even today, there are some who would subscribe to this account of Christian origins at Rome and would maintain, moreover, that it justifies the claim of the Roman Church to be the most authentic representative of Christ's teaching on earth (e.g. Guarducci 2003).

Other examples of such texts exist, many of them, however, only of ninth-century or later date. We have detailed episcopal histories for Ravenna and Naples as well as Rome, and for Gallic sees such as Metz and Le Mans (Sot 1981). In addition, by the high Middle Ages there existed for many bishoprics throughout the West lists of their incumbents stretching back into the dim mists of antiquity (Duchesne 1907–15; Picard 1988). Such documents, together with the hagiographical accounts of local saints (many of them clergy), have often formed the basis even for modern historical investigations of the origins of Christianity in particular regions in the West (e.g. Lanzoni 1923). Yet, for various reasons, they are an unsatisfactory foundation for the study of the Christian West.

The chief flaw of these accounts is that many of them were demonstrably concocted or manipulated to conform to ideological statements of ecclesiastical authority in the medieval period, as a number of Italian examples show. Already by the fifth century, for instance, we find bishops of Rome asserting their headship of Christianity throughout the world on the basis of the foundation of the Roman church by the apostle Peter. Yet Rome's primatial authority was frequently contested, even within the West. A tradition at Milan, for example, which traced its Christian origins to another apostle, Barnabas, a companion of Paul in the Acts of the Apostles, was elaborated in the eleventh century when the Milanese church found itself locked in a bitter struggle over authority with the papacy (Humphries 1999: 61–3). Similarly, the church of Ravenna claimed to have been founded by an early bishop, Apollinaris, who was a contemporary of the apostles; by the mid-seventh century, this tradition was seemingly linked to notions that Ravenna possessed an apostolic authority independent of Rome (T. S. Brown 1979).

It is possible, of course, that some of these traditional episcopal histories contain a core of accurate historical information shrouded in a fog of legend; in most cases, however, it is practically impossible to distinguish one from the other. For that reason, such texts should be treated with extreme caution, and perhaps even ignored as sources for the earliest Christianity in the West. But that too presents problems: without them, our knowledge of the origins of Christianity in western Europe loses the comfortable narrative structures that such sources provide. Contemporary accounts of the arrival of Christianity in Italy, Gaul, and Spain are lacking. For instance, none of these regions is particularly prominent in the New Testament documents, with the exception of Rome. The apostle Paul wrote his Letter to the Romans describing his plan to visit the city and, moreover, his intention to travel onwards to Spain (Rom 15: 22–8). While Paul did travel to the imperial capital, albeit under compulsion to stand trial, there is no compelling evidence that he travelled further west (*contra* Murphy-O'Connor 1996: 359–63).

The sources for later periods similarly highlight the fragmentary nature of our knowledge. A church council held at Carthage *c.* 256 addressed a letter to clergy and laity in the Spanish cities of Legio (León), Asturica (Astorga), and Emerita (Mérida) (Cyprian, *Ep.* 67). This is our first glimpse of Christianity in Spain: how (and when) these congregations originated is not explained; nor can we tell very much about how large they were (Clarke 1984–9: iv. 141–5). By the end of the fourth century, it would appear that the presence of Christianity in Spain had increased considerably. Lists of clergy attending various Spanish councils in this period show the existence of Christian communities in about fifty towns and cities (Vilella 2002: esp. fig. 14.1). On the face of it, this might suggest that Christianity in Spain expanded enormously over a short period. Such a hypothesis would correspond neatly with recent sociological analyses of the growth of Christianity in the Roman world that have suggested that the third and fourth centuries were a period of considerable growth, with Christian numbers rocketing from 200,000 c. 200 to perhaps as many as thirty million by the second half of the fourth century (Stark 1996; see Hopkins 1998). Looked at more closely, however, the picture is not so clear, especially for the third-century data. We have no way of knowing if the three Christian communities mentioned by the Carthaginian council were the only ones in existence in Spain at that time and must entertain the possibility (even probability) that there were others not addressed by the council. Similarly, for the congregations mentioned in fourth-century records, we have no explicit testimony of how long they had existed. Hence the growth between the mid-third and late fourth centuries might be less momentous than at first appears from a simple juxtaposition of raw data from church councils.

Indeed, evidence from elsewhere suggests that evidence from conciliar records provides only a rough indication of the development of Christianity in a given region. The list of subscriptions to the Council of Arles in 314 records Aquileia in north-eastern Italy being represented by its bishop Theodore and a deacon. This is the first documentary reference to Christianity at Aquileia, but there is reason to suppose that it had been firmly established in the city for some time already. The same Bishop Theodore is recorded in inscriptions in the mosaic pavements of a church built in the city in the early fourth century. The size of this church (comprising two halls, each measuring approximately 630m^2) and the lavishness of its decoration suggest that the Christian community at Aquileia was already numerous and prosperous by the time of its first appearance in the written sources (Humphries 1999: 73–9). As with the Spanish examples mentioned above, it is clear that our documentary sources provide little explanation of the processes by which Christianity arrived and developed in western Europe.

Does this mean that we can recover nothing about the dynamics of early Christian expansion in the West? That, I think, would be too pessimistic. Several other considerations allow us to make some reasonable speculations. The Christian faith originated, of course, in the eastern Mediterranean, and much of the evidence shows that the earliest western communities were strongly Hellenic in character. Our earliest Christian authors from Gaul (Irenaeus of Lyons) and Italy (such as Hermas and Hippolytus) wrote in Greek. Close connections between western and eastern Churches are suggested by Eusebius's account of the persecution of Christians from Lyons and Vienne in Gaul in 177, which is cited from a description of these events in a letter sent by Christians in the two cities 'to the brethren in Asia and Phrygia' (*Hist. eccl.* 5. 1. 3). Such factors imply a strong immigrant presence in the earliest Christian communities in the West.

This in turn has prompted various suggestions about who was responsible for spreading the faith. One category that has attracted attention is traders (Frend 1964). Some evidence might seem to support this thesis. It is clear that areas with strong trading links to the wider Mediterranean world seem to have boasted the earliest Christian presences in the West. The aforementioned Aquileia was a major port city. Similarly, a map plotting the distribution of Christian communities in Spain before *c.* 350 shows a notable concentration in southern Iberia, a region that boasted a lively export trade in olive oil and wine. Yet, for all that, precise references to Christian traders spreading the gospel in the West are lacking. The shipowner Marcion from Asia Minor taught a brand of Christianity (later denounced as heresy) at Rome in the late second century—but it is not certain if it was maritime trade that brought him west (Lampe 2003: 241–4). It may make more sense, then, to think in terms of a variety of networks, of which trade is certainly one, that caused movements of people around the Empire and along which Christianity spread (Humphries 1998). For example, Rome attracted a diverse migrant population for various reasons, such as trade, employment, slavery, and service in the imperial administration. As a result, the city hosted a range of foreign religious traditions, including Christianity (Noy 2000; Lampe 2003).

If the mechanisms by which Christianity spread to the West are unknown, they also seem to have been haphazard, in sharp contrast to the picture of organized missionary activities favoured by Christian tradition. This is apparent already in the first century. When Paul was dispatched to Rome, he found that there were already Christians in the imperial capital and at Puteoli on the Bay of Naples, his landfall in Italy (Acts 28: 14–15). The uncoordinated nature of early Christian expansion to the West is also suggested by the patchiness of its distribution there. We have already seen that it was prevalent in southern Spain while it was less common in other parts of the Iberian peninsula. In Gaul, Christian communities clustered around the valley of the river Rhône, but were sparse elsewhere. In Italy, to judge from the lists of bishoprics mentioned at third- and fourth-century church councils, there seem to have been concentrations of Christian groups in the centre of the peninsula, around Rome, and in the Po valley in the north; but elsewhere, such as in the south and in Sicily, there is no compelling evidence for Christianity before the fourth or even fifth century.

That the spread of Christianity in the West was uneven is perhaps unsurprising. It should be noted also that the processes involved were by no means straight-forwardly cumulative or linear. In Britain, for example, there was a Christian presence already by the time of Constantine, when bishops from London, York, and (probably) Lincoln attended the Council of Arles in 314. That such evidence provides only a very sketchy portrait of the earliest British Christianity is clear from archaeological evidence, which shows the presence of Christian buildings of fourth and fifth-century date at a variety of sites, ranging from urban centres to rural villas. This not only allows us to confirm that Christianity was more widespread than the evidence of church councils would suggest, but also to speculate (in a limited fashion) about the size and socio-economic profile of individual Christian groups. In general, the evidence suggests that the profile of Christianity in fourth-century Britain was comparable to that in the north-western provinces of the Empire at that time (Thomas 1981). Even so, it seems that the presence of Christianity in Britain declined, particularly in the south-east of the island, with the demise of Roman rule. By the end of the sixth century, Christianity in southern Britain had been undermined to such an extent that the island was the focus for renewed missionary activity by Irish monks and clergy from Rome. Ireland provides another example of the random, disorganized patterns of Christian expansion. In 431, one Palladius (not to be confused with the author of the *Lausiac History*) was appointed bishop over pre-existing Christian communities there; later, an apparently independent mission was established (perhaps in another part of the island) under the leadership of Patrick (Charles-Edwards 2003).

The earliest history of Christianity in western Europe defies easy categorization. Diversity of experience is everywhere, and this is most probably to be explained by the different contexts within which the faith spread in different regions. In other words, it is absolutely crucial to see the spread of Christianity in the West in terms of the human environments that might have favoured—or hindered—its progress. Furthermore, the uneven pace at which the expansion of Christianity occurred can be paralleled when we look at its further development and institutionalization in these areas.

14.3 The Formation of Christian Societies in the West

In several respects, the history of Christianity in western Europe was broadly comparable to that in other parts of the Mediterranean world. From the fourth century onwards there was a gradual eclipse of paganism and the establishment of Christianity as the region's main religion. Similarly, the western church generally came to be structured around dioceses centred on cities and administered by bishops and lesser clergy. As Christianity became more entrenched, it evolved in ways that proclaimed its increased confidence and dominance. A series of decisions made at synods in Spain about the admission of catechumens to the church provides a neat summary of this process. The fourth-century canons ascribed to the Council of Elvira demanded a catechumenate of two years for men, five for women, and stringent regulations were to be enforced on those seeking admission to the Christian community. By the late sixth century, however, the Council of Braga required a catechumenate of only 20 days. This remarkable change should perhaps be interpreted as reflecting the transformed circumstances of Christianity in Spain over the course of late antiquity. The stern rules laid down at Elvira presuppose a society in which Christians formed a quite exclusive minority, and where the threat of pagan, worldly temptation lay everywhere. The drastically foreshortened catechumenate described at Braga implies a society in which Christianity was the dominant religion and threats from non-Christian social mores had diminished correspondingly (Fernández Ubiña 2002: 164–5). While such processes can be paralleled in other regions, it would be erroneous to assume that the development of Christianity in the West followed an identical trajectory in all respects and could thus be considered as part of some sort of grand teleological narrative of inexorable Christian triumph. Rather, there was considerable regional variation, not only between western Europe and other parts of the Mediterranean world, but also within the West itself.

The place of Christianity in cities provides some striking examples. It is clear that the pace of development varied from city to city. Once more, our evidence is very fragmentary for the period before Constantine. The Christian communities in Spain addressed by the third-century Carthaginian council, for example, are described as comprising bishops, clergy, and laity. This hierarchy presupposes organized congregations, but precisely how organized they were remains unknown. At other times, we need to be wary of extrapolating too much from scattered details. Eusebius quotes from a letter of Pope Cornelius (251–3) which tells us that the Roman church in the mid-third century comprised a bishop, forty-six presbyters, seven deacons, seven subdeacons, forty-two acolytes, and fifty-two exorcists, readers, and doorkeepers, as well as supporting more than 1,500 widows and paupers (*Hist. eccl.* 6. 43. 11). Impressive though this is, it should not be taken as typical of the organization of western churches more broadly: the very particular circumstances of Rome, the largest metropolis in the ancient Mediterranean, almost certainly mean that this level of complexity is exceptional.

If we turn to the fourth and later centuries, a similarly diverse picture presents itself. Across the Mediterranean, there was a general trend for cities to become increasingly dominated by the church, both physically, in that ecclesiastical buildings often became the most prominent structures in the urban landscape, and institutionally, with bishops often taking on important roles as community leaders (Bowersock 1986; Liebeschuetz 2001: 136–67). Such trends were certainly visible in the West; but again, change occurred at a pace specific not only to each region but also to individual centres.

Consider the encroachment of Christianity on the physical fabric of the city. By *c.* 600, most urban centres in Spain, Gaul, and Italy will have boasted at least one substantial church building. Their scale and elaborate decoration are suggestive of the degree to which Christianity became enmeshed in the society in which it developed. Inscriptions in stone and mosaic recording the patronage of church construction and embellishment by members of local elites attest how Christianity became a new outlet for the public display of social hierarchies (Caillet 1993; Ward-Perkins 1984). Yet it is difficult to generalize the processes by which this situation was achieved. Already by the mid-fourth century, some cities in western Europe boasted large churches, such as that in Aquileia; other examples can be found in Milan, Rome, and Trier. Significant differences between these cities mean that it is hard to find a typical pattern in such constructions. At Rome, the earliest large churches were built with imperial patronage (Curran 2000: 90–114; see Bowersock 2002), and subvention by the Emperor very likely explains the churches in Milan and Trier also. At Aquileia, however, there is no clear evidence of imperial benefaction. Similarly, while the churches in Trier and Milan were built in the heart of each city, the imperial foundations at Rome, such as St Peter's and St John Lateran, were built only on the margins of the urban centre.

Although monumental churches appeared in some centres before the end of the fourth century, elsewhere the encroachment of Christian buildings on urban space was a later development. Many centres in Spain, for instance, had no sizeable churches before the fifth century, and in most places they seem to have been located outside city walls (Kulikowski 2004: 220–40). We have to allow, of course, for the unevenness of the archaeological record here, and the fact that even where we have no material record for church buildings, they are known from literary sources: such is the case for Tarraco, where there are no material remains pre-dating the mid-fifth century, but where an elaborate Christian building is implied by a description in a letter of Augustine written c. 400 (Keay 1996: 33). Moreover, the pattern of church building varied so markedly from centre to centre across the West that even within particular regions there could be considerable variety (Humphries 1999: 202–7; Loseby 1992).

A similarly complex picture is presented by the development of the western episcopate. There are certainly many notable western examples of the bishop as a community leader. Thus the position of Martin of Tours (c. 361–97) as monk-bishop, of Ambrose of Milan (374–97) as a Christian leader confronting imperial authority, and of Gregory the Great of Rome (590–602) providing urban leadership at a time of political and social upheaval can be regarded as emblematic of general trends in late antique Christian society. In no small measure, the attention lavished on such figures reflects the importance that they have assumed in the Christian historical consciousness either as a result of their portraits of themselves in their writings (as is the case with Ambrose and Gregory) or because their reputation was the focus of literary endeavours by followers and admirers (as with Martin, whose achievements were celebrated by Sulpicius Severus, Venantius Fortunatus, and Gregory of Tours).

The very fact that we depend on self-conscious literary portraits for our under-standing of such bishops should warn us that what we are dealing with is not an objective portrait but a calculated one (see McLynn 1994 and Liebeschuetz 2005 on Ambrose). Moreover, it is clear that the achievements of one particularly dynamic bishop might not be replicated by his successors. Thus, while Ambrose achieved, in large measure through his forceful personality, a considerable influence over other bishops in northern Italy (and in surrounding territories such as southern Gaul and the north-western Balkans), this did not translate into a lasting authority for the church of Milan, which began to be eroded, for example by the church of Turin, after Ambrose's death (Lizzi 1989: 209).

Moreover, we should be wary of regarding expression of episcopal authority as part of some cumulative, teleological process. For instance, appeals by bishops of Rome to the apostles Peter and Paul might be perceived as reflecting a straightforward growth in the authority of the Roman see, beginning with Damasus (366–84) and reaching a crescendo under Leo I (440–61) (e.g. Ullmann 1972: 13–27). Viewed in context, however, the reality was more complex. Damasus's fostering of the cult of the Roman martyrs was probably aimed at achieving harmony in a Christian community at Rome which had been bitterly divided at the time of his election (Curran 2000: 137–55; Sághy 2000). Meanwhile, Leo's trenchant assertions of Rome's Petrine supremacy depended on the support of the emperor Valentinian III (425–55) for them to be enforced on the church in southern Gaul (*Novellae Valentiniani*, 17).

A wider perspective on the development of the western episcopate suggests a more diverse history than a concentration on 'heroic' figures like Martin, Ambrose, and Gregory would suggest. Not all bishops were dynamically forceful characters. Jerome, for example, excoriated the feeble leadership of Lupicinus, bishop of his hometown of Stridon, not far from Aquileia (*Ep. 7. 5*). Similarly, whereas Gregory the Great might be taken as a paradigm of dynamic papal leadership at the dawn of the Middle Ages, some of his immediate predecessors (and, indeed, successors) found themselves bullied and cajoled by emperors at Constantinople who regarded the bishop of Rome as some sort of subordinate (Sotinel 2005).

An equally diverse picture is presented by that corollary of the rise of Christianity in late antiquity, the demise of paganism. It is always difficult to gauge the nature and extent of pagan survivals, not least because we are at the mercy of ecclesiastical sources when it comes to formulating a picture of the processes involved. Christian writers tend to emphasize the conflict with paganism—but pagans themselves are much less vocal. Thus, while many fourth-century Roman senators were members of old pagan priesthoods (Salzman 2002), we should be wary of regarding them as extremists battling to defend their traditions in opposition to Christianity. That the relationship between the senator Symmachus and Ambrose of Milan encompassed both the debate on the Altar of Victory in 384 and a friendly correspondence is a reminder that pagans and Christians were not always locked in relentless struggle (Cameron 1999). Furthermore, Christian writers often condemned *any* manifestation of old-style pagan culture as threatening, even if those involved in maintaining such traditions were themselves Christian and did not view their actions as particularly problematic (Markus 1990). Thus, in the early fifth century, bishop Peter Chrysologus of Ravenna thundered against the display of pagan images in circus processions in his city (*Sermo* 155). Later, Gelasius of Rome (492–6) condemned the continued participation of members of his flock in the ancient Lupercalia festival (Pomarès 1959). It is important to remember, however, that bishops' imprecations about lapses of piety have much to do with efforts to define episcopal power. Gelasius's condemnation of the Lupercalia was but one statement of authority made by him: he also criticized Christians who read popular literature, not sanctioned by the Church, about martyrs; more broadly, he was a determined advocate of Roman ecclesial supremacy (Llewellyn 1993: 38–40).

Nevertheless, it is clear that paganism did survive for a considerable period beyond Constantine (MacMullen 1997). For instance, even as it acquired church buildings of grand proportions, Rome (and nearby Ostia) was also embellished through the agency of senatorial patronage with new or restored pagan temples until the 390s (Ward-Perkins 1984: 88–9). In other parts of Italy, however, the pace of change was different. Already by *c.* 380, the temple of Jupiter in Verona seems to have been in a ruinous state, if we are to judge from an inscription recording the re-erection in the city's forum of a statue from the temple that had lain fallen for a considerable time (Humphries 1999: 210). It is similarly difficult to quantify the displacement of paganism by Christianity in rural areas, even if excavation of many rural sites, notably villas, has yielded evidence of Christian cult rooms and small churches (Bowes 2001). The theme of the backwardness of country folk, and the responsibility of urban Christians to take the lead in securing their conversion, echoes throughout the fourth, fifth, and sixth centuries in the writings of bishops such as Vigilius of Trent, Maximus of Turin, Caesarius of Arles, and Martin of Braga (Trout 1996). Once again, however, penetrating the episcopal rhetoric is far from easy.

The evidence for the creation of Christian societies in western Europe presents a picture that, like that for the spread of the faith there, is characterized above all by local variation. Other examples could be marshalled in support of this argument. The spread of asceticism, for example, proceeded at different rates in different places and took manifold forms (Dunn 2000: 82–137). At times, moreover, asceticism could provoke conflicts within the Church that could seep into society more broadly, as was notably the case with the Spaniard Priscillian in the late fourth century, whose teachings prompted debates about the role of lay women in the Christian community (Burrus 1996; Chadwick 1976; Escribano Paño 2002). So too, the involvement of social elites in the running of their local churches occurred in different ways. In Spain and Gaul, local aristocrats were entering the episcopate in increasing numbers by the fifth century (Van Dam 1985: 141–56), but in Italy secular career paths continued to dominate aristocratic ambitions well into the sixth century (Bartlett 2001). Equally, the veneration of saints and relics, perhaps one of the salient characteristics of early medieval Christianity, manifested itself differently between, and within, regions, making casual generalizations about *the* cult of saints unwise (Van Dam 1993). Thus, while western Europe was substantially Christian by the end of the sixth century, it is crucial not to lose sight of either the varied processes through which this situation was achieved or the diverse character of the end result.

14.4 POLITICS AND THE IDENTITY OF WESTERN CHRISTENDOM

None of this is to say that Christianity in western Europe developed in isolation from the rest of the Christian world. Awareness of broader currents in the development of the religion throughout the Mediterranean world can be demonstrated from very early on. We have already seen Christians in Lyons and Vienne writing about their experience of persecution in 177 to their brethren in Asia Minor. Not much later, Irenaeus of Lyons wrote a detailed refutation of a brand of Christianity that he denounced as heresy and termed 'Gnostic'. Manuscripts discovered at Nag Hammadi in Egypt in 1945 included a number of texts that Irenaeus apparently had in mind when composing his polemic, thus confirming that he was well versed in heterodox beliefs popular far beyond his own province of Gaul.

Nevertheless, western involvement in wider Christian affairs often followed a peculiarly western trajectory. For example, traditional histories of the church in the fourth century are often dominated by the dispute about the Trinity that raged between the Councils of Nicaea (325) and Constantinople (381). The theological debates of this conflict were largely played out in the eastern Mediterranean, however, and western involvement was tardy. Only when the emperor Constantius II, in the process of imposing his authority over the West after defeating the usurper Magnentius in 353, sought to achieve ecclesiastical uniformity throughout the Roman Empire were bishops in western Europe confronted with doctrinal formulations about which, at first, many of them were plainly ill-informed. Thereafter, western bishops such as Hilary of Poitiers, Eusebius of Vercelli, and Ambrose of Milan were compelled to reach a more sophisticated understanding of Trinitarian theology (Williams 1995). Even so, certain westerners' grasp of the theological issues remained idiosyncratic. Thus when Filastrius of Brescia (c. 380) composed a handbook on heresy, he gave a misleading account of the teachings of the Alexandrian priest Arius; his portrait of 'Arian' theology seems to owe more to doctrinal opinions held by contemporary bishops in the western Balkans, against whom Filastrius and other western churchmen found themselves opposed (Humphries 1999: 133–5).

That western engagement with debates in the wider Christian world should hinge on so apparently haphazard an event as an emperor's campaigns against a usurper reminds us not to underestimate the extent to which the political history of Western Europe has influenced the development of Christianity there. This can be seen, for instance, in the way in which particular cities became important episcopal sees. The dominance of Milan under Ambrose was in no small measure related to the presence there of the imperial court. Later, when the emperors moved to Ravenna, it grew in ecclesiastical stature (Markus 1997: 143–7). Similarly, the move of the headquarters of the praetorian prefect of Gaul from Trier to Arles sometime around 400 led to an increase in the influence of the latter city's bishop (Mathisen 1989: 18–26; see Loseby 1996).

In broader terms, the period between 100 and 600 saw in western Europe the displacement of Roman power by a number of barbarian kingdoms. For the Christians of Gaul, this meant living under Franks who espoused Catholic Christianity, a factor that may have assisted the transition from Roman to barbarian rule. In Spain and Italy, pre-existing Christian populations found themselves living under Gothic overlords whose Christianity was of a heterodox, Arian variety. In stark contrast to the experience of their brethren living under Vandal rule in Africa, however, Spanish and Italian Catholics did not suffer any systematic persecution. Indeed, in Spain Catholics and Arians existed side by side, with many communities having not one, but two, bishops. Furthermore, at the Fourth Council of Toledo in 590, King Reccared opted to abandon Arianism in favour of Catholicism, a decision that very probably reflected a tendency towards integration between Hispano-Romans and Goths across doctrinal boundaries (Stocking 2000). Paradoxically, greater trauma was unleashed on Italian Christians by the Byzantine reconquest launched by the emperor Justinian in 535. Once Italy was brought back into the imperial orbit, its bishops were expected to acquiesce in doctrinal rulings emanating from Constantinople. When Justinian ordered the condemnation of the 'Three Chapters', and secured, under duress, the acquiescence of Pope Vigilius and his successor Pelagius, a number of north Italian churches broke off communion with Rome, thus undoing much of the work of fourth- and fifth-century bishops of Rome in seeking to establish the primacy of the Roman church (Markus 1997: 125–40). If Gregory the Great was able to secure some recovery in papal fortunes, this owed much to contemporary political upheavals: in the face of Lombard conquests in Italy, the church of Rome was able to provide an element of social leadership that filled a gap left by the beleaguered Byzantine military administration (Humphries 2000).

14.5 PROSPECTS

This chapter has argued that the early history of Christianity in western Europe, however much it was marked by trends observable elsewhere in the Mediterranean, was profoundly influenced by the social, political, and cultural circumstances of the region within which it evolved. It is important to keep these regional (and local) horizons in view at all times, rather than attempt to squeeze what is known about early Christianity in the West into a framework of pan-Mediterranean ecclesiastical history derived from Eusebius of Caesarea and his successors. In terms of approach, this requires a nuanced reading of the literary and documentary sources—a reading that almost goes against the grain of such writings, since, by their very nature, they often support the thrust of the ecclesiastical historiographical model. Equally, it is important to take account of non-traditional sources, notably archaeology, that sometimes confound expectations derived from written documents. Moreover, this fund of material evidence is constantly increasing, and continually requires us to re-evaluate our interpretations. Just 10 years ago, it could be written of Spain that 'little is known about the advent and broader impact of the church as a focus for a new form of urban spirit' (Keay 1996: 19). Since then, a major synthesis of the development of late antique Iberia has exploited a rich seam of archaeological evidence to examine the ways in which Christianity was deeply influenced by the society in which it was embedded (Kulikowski 2004). From this example, it is clear that much has been done to elucidate the history and character of early Christianity in western Europe; equally, however, there remains much to be done.

SUGGESTED READING

Many of the primary sources for the early Christian West are increasingly available in English translation. For Gregory of Tours, see Thorpe (1974) for the *Histories*, and, for the minor works, James (1991) and Van Dam (1988*a, b*; 1993). See Klingshirn (1994) for Caesarius of Arles. Among the Spanish sources now available, note especially the chronicles in Wolf (1999) and the saints' lives in Fear (1997). Italian bishops are well represented: see Liebeschuetz (2005) and Ramsay (1997) for Ambrose, Ramsay (1989) for Maximus of Turin, Ganss (1953) for Peter Chrysologus, and Martyn (2004) and Moorhead (2005) for Gregory the Great; while Davis (2000) provides a comprehensible access to the difficult *Liber Pontificalis*. Lives of some important western bishops are contained in Hoare (1954). Hillgarth (1969) and Peters (1975) are useful anthologies.

For the problems presented by the sources, Mathisen and Shanzer (2001) provide a collection of recent case-studies. Gregory of Tours is best approached via Heinzelmann (2001) and Van Dam (1993). On episcopal lists, Picard (1988) is magnificent; those who do not read French will find plenty that is useful in Pizarro (1995). For individual regions, Griffe (1964–6) remains valuable on Gaul, but should be supplemented by Harries (1992, 1994), Mathisen (1989), and Van Dam (1985). For Italy, there are many recent studies (in Italian) of particular regions: Campione (2000), Greco (1999), Lizzi (1989), Otranto (1990); on Rome, Pietri (1976, in French) is still fundamental. Up-to-date material in English is more rare. There are useful essays on the church and the papacy in La Rocca (2002). On Rome, Krautheimer (1980) is the classic study, although some of his assumptions are challenged by new archaeological discoveries: see Curran (2000) and Humphries (2001, 2007).

On the Po valley, see Humphries (1999) and Lizzi (1990). Wilson (1990: ch. 8) surveys early Christianity in Sicily. For Spain there is now the synthesis of Kulikowski (2004), but those who can read Spanish will find Teja (2002) valuable. Numerous western bishops have been the focus of some recent valuable studies: Klingshirn (1993), McLynn (1994), Markus (1997), and Stancliffe (1983). For the whole subject, P. Brown (2003) and Smith (2005) provide masterly surveys.

BIBLIOGRAPHY

BARTLETT, R. (2001), 'Aristocracy and Asceticism: The Letters of Ennodius and the Gallic and Italian Churches', in Mathisen and Shanzer (2001), 201–16.

BOWERSOCK, G. W. (1986), 'From Emperor to Bishop: The Self-conscious Transformation of Political Power in the Fourth Century AD', *Classical Philology*, 81: 298–307.

——(2002), 'Peter and Constantine', in J.-M. Carrié and R. Lizzi Testa (eds.), *"Humana Sapit": Études d'antiquité tardive offertes à Lellia Cracco Ruggini*, Bibliothèque de L'Antiquité Tardive, 3 (Turnhout: Brepols), 209–17.

BOWES, K. (2001), ' "... Nec sedere in villam": Villa Churches, Rural Piety and the Priscillianist Controversy', in T. S. Burns and J. W. Eadie (eds.), *Urban Centres and Rural Contexts in Late Antiquity* (East Lansing, Mich.: Michigan State University Press), 323–48.

BRAKKE, D. (2002), 'The Early Church in North America: Late Antiquity, Theory, and Early Christianity', *CH* 71: 473–91.

BROWN, P. (2003), *The Rise of Western Christendom: Triumph and Diversity AD 200–1000*, 2nd edn. (Malden, Mass.: Blackwell).

BROWN, T. S. (1979), 'The Church of Ravenna and the Imperial Administration in the Seventh Century', *English Historical Review*, 94: 1–28.

BURRUS, V. (1996), *The Making of a Heretic: Gender, Authority, and the Priscillianist Controversy* (Berkeley: University of California Press).

CAILLET, J.-P. (1993), *L'évergétisme monumental chrétien en Italie et à ses marges* (Rome: École française de Rome).

CAMERON, A. (1999), 'The Last Pagans of Rome', in W. V. Harris (ed.), *The Transformation of Vrbs Roma in Late Antiquity*, JRA Suppl. 33 (Portsmonth, RI: Journal of Roman Archaeology), 109–22.

CAMPIONE, A. (2000), *La Basilicata paleocristiana: diocesi e culti*, Scavi e ricerche, 13 (Bari: Edipuglia).

CHADWICK, H. (1976), *Priscillian of Avila: The Occult and the Charismatic in the Early Church* (Oxford: Clarendon Press).

CHARLES-EDWARDS, T. (2003), 'Conversion to Christianity', in idem (ed.), *After Rome* (Oxford: Oxford University Press), 103–39.

CHRISTIE, N., and LOSEBY, S. T. (1996) (eds.), *Towns in Transition: Urban Evolution in Late Antiquity and the Early Middle Ages* (Aldershot: Ashgate).

CLARKE, G. W. (1984–9), *The Letters of St Cyprian of Carthage* ACW 43, 44, 46, 47 (New York: Newman Press/Paulist Press).

CURRAN, J. R. (2000), *Pagan City and Christian Capital: Rome in the Fourth Century* (Oxford: Oxford University Press).

DAVIS, R. (2000), *The Book of Pontiffs (Liber Pontificalis)*, rev. edn. (Liverpool: Liverpool University Press).

DUCHESNE, L. (1907–15), *Fastes épiscopaux de l'ancienne Gaule*, 3 vols. (Paris: A. Fontemoing).

DUNN, M. (2000), *The Emergence of Monasticism: From the Desert Fathers to the Early Middle Ages* (Oxford: Blackwell).

ESCRIBANO PAÑO, M. V. (2002), 'La disputa priscilianista', in Teja (2002), 205–30.

FEAR, A. T. (1997), *Lives of the Visigothic Fathers* (Liverpool: Liverpool University Press).

FERNÁNDEZ UBIÑA, J. (2002), 'La iglesia y la formacíon de la jerarquía ecclesiástica', in Teja (2002), 161–203.

FREND, W. H. C. (1964), 'A Note on the Influence of Greek Immigrants on the Spread of Christianity to the West', in A. Stuiber (ed), *Mullus: Festschrift für Theodor Klauser, JAC*, Ergänzungsband 1 (Münster: Aschendorff), 125–9.

GANSS, G. E. (1953), *St Peter Chrysologus, Sermons; St Valerian, Homilies* (Washington D.C.: Catholic University of America Press).

GOFFART, W. (1989), 'From Historiae to Historia Francorum and Back Again: Aspects of the Textual History of Gregory of Tours', in *idem, Rome's Fall and After* (London: Hambledon Press), 255–74.

GRECO, R. (1999), *Pagani e Cristiani a Siracusa tra il III e il IV secolo d.C.*, Supplementi a Kokalos, 16 (Rome: Giorgio Bretschneider).

GRIFFE, E. (1964–6), *La Gaule chrétienne à l'epoque romaine*, 3 vols. (Paris: Letouzey et Ané).

GUARDUCCI, M. (2003), *The Primacy of the Church of Rome: Documents, Reflections, Proofs* (San Francisco: Ignatius Press).

HARRIES, J. D. (1992), 'Christianity and the City in Late Roman Gaul', in J. Rich (ed.), *The City in Late Antiquity* (London: Routledge), 77–98.

—— (1994), *Sidonius Apollinaris and the Fall of Rome* (Oxford: Clarendon Press).

HEINZELMANN, M. (2001), *Gregory of Tours: History and Society in the Sixth Century* (Cambridge: Cambridge University Press).

HILLGARTH, J. N. (1969), *The Conversion of Western Europe, 350–750* (Englewood Cliffs, NJ: Prentice-Hall).

HOARE, F. J. (1954), *The Western Fathers* (London: Sheed and Ward).

HOPKINS, K. (1998), 'Christian Number and its Implications', *JECS* 6: 185–226.

HUMPHRIES, M. (1998), 'Trading Gods in Northern Italy', in H. Parkins and C. Smith (eds.), *Trade, Traders and the Ancient City* (London: Routledge), 203–24.

—— (1999), *Communities of the Blessed: Social Environment and Religious Change in Northern Italy, AD 200–400* (Oxford: Oxford University Press).

—— (2000), 'Italy, AD 425–605', in A. Cameron, B. Ward-Perkins, and M. Whitby (eds.), *CAH*, xiv: *Late Antiquity: Empire and Successors AD 425–600* (Cambridge: Cambridge University Press), 525–51.

—— (2001), 'Constantine, Christianity, and Rome', *Hermathena*, 171: 47–63.

—— (2007), 'From Emperor to Pope? Ceremonial, space, and authority in Rome from Constantine to Gregory the Great', in K. Cooper and J. Hillner (eds.), *Dynasty, Patronage, and Authority in a Christian Capital: Rome, c. 350–850* (Cambridge: Cambridge University Press), 21–58.

JAMES, E. (1991), *Gregory of Tours: Life of the Fathers* (Liverpool: Liverpool University Press).

KEAY, S. J. (1996), 'Tarraco in Late Antiquity', in Christie and Loseby (1996), 18–44.

KLINGSHIRN, W. (1993), *Caesarius of Arles: The Making of a Christian Community in Late Antique Gaul* (Cambridge: Cambridge University Press).

——(1994), *Caesarius of Arles: Life, Testament, Letters* (Liverpool: Liverpool University Press).

KRAUTHEIMER, R. (1980), *Rome, Profile of a City, 312–1308* (Princeton: Princeton University Press).

KULIKOWSKI, M. (2004), *Late Roman Spain and its Cities* (Baltimore: Johns Hopkins University Press).

LAMPE, P. (2003), *From Paul to Valentinus: Christians at Rome in the First Two Centuries* (Minneapolis: Fortress Press).

LANZONI, F. (1923), *Le orgini delle diocesi antiche d'Italia*, Studi e Testi, 35 (Rome: Biblioteca Apostolica Vaticana).

LA ROCCA, C. (2002) (ed.), *Italy in the Early Middle Ages, 476–1000* (Oxford: Oxford University Press).

LIEBESCHUETZ, J. H. W. G. (2001), *The Decline and Fall of the Roman City* (Oxford: Oxford University Press).

——(2005), *Ambrose of Milan: Political Letters and Speeches* (Liverpool: Liverpool University Press).

LIZZI, R. (1989), *Vescovi e strutture ecclesiastiche nella città tardoantica: L'Italia Annonaria nel IV–V secolo d.C.* (Como: New Press).

——(1990), 'Ambrose's Contemporaries and the Christianisation of Northern Italy', *JRS* 80: 156–73.

LLEWELLYN, P. (1993), *Rome in the Dark Ages*, 2nd edn. (London: Constable & Robinson Ltd.).

LOSEBY, S. T. (1992), 'Bishops and Cathedrals: Order and Diversity in the Fifth-Century Urban Landscape of Southern Gaul', in J. Drinkwater and H. Elton (eds.), *Fifth-century Gaul: A Crisis of Identity?* (Cambridge: Cambridge University Press), 144–55.

——(1996), 'Arles in Late Antiquity: *Gallula Roma Arelas* and *Urbs Genesii*', in Christie and Loseby (1996), 45–70.

McLYNN, N. B. (1994), *Ambrose of Milan: Church and Court in a Christian Capital* (Berkeley: University of California Press).

MacMULLEN, R. (1997), *Christianity and Paganism in the Fourth to Eighth Centuries*. (New Haven: Yale University Press).

MARAZZI, F. (2000), 'Rome in Transition: Economic and Political Change in the Fourth and Fifth Centuries', in J. M. H. Smith (ed.), *Early Medieval Rome and the Christian West: Essays in honour of Donald A. Bullough* (Leiden: E. J. Brill), 21–41.

MARKUS, R. A. (1990), *The End of Ancient Christianity* (Cambridge: Cambridge University Press).

——(1997), *Gregory the Great and his World* (Cambridge: Cambridge University Press).

MARTYN, J. R. C. (2004), *The Letters of Gregory the Great*, Mediaeval Sources in Translation, 40 (Turnhout: Brepols).

MARUCCHI, O. (1929), *The Evidence of the Catacombs for the Doctrines and Organisation of the Primitive Church* (London: Sheed and Ward).

MATHISEN, R. W. (1989), *Ecclesiastical Factionalism and Religious Controversy in Fifth Century Gaul* (Washington D.C.: Catholic University of America Press).

——and SHANZER, D. (eds.) (2001), *Society and Culture in Late Antique Gaul: Revisiting the Sources* (Aldershot: Ashgate).

MOORHEAD, J. (2005), *Gregory the Great* (London: Routledge).

MURPHY-O'CONNOR, J. (1996), *Paul: A Critical Life* (Oxford: Oxford University Press).

NOY, D. (2000), *Foreigners at Rome: Citizens and Strangers* (London: Duckworth; Swansea: Classical Press of Wales).

OTRANTO, G. (1990), *Italia meridionale e puglia paleocristiana: saggi storici*, Scavi e ricerche, 5 (Bari: Edipuglia).

PETERS, E. (1975), *Monks, Bishops, and Pagans: Christian Culture in Gaul and Italy, 500–700* (Philadelphia: University of Pennsylvania Press).

PICARD, J.-C. (1988), *Le souvenir des évêques: sépultures, listes épiscopales et culte des évêques en Italie du Nord des origines au Xe siècle* (Rome: École française de Rome).

PIETRI, C. (1976), *Roma christiana: recherches sur l'Église de Rome, son organisation, sa politique, son idéologie de Miltiade à Sixte III (311–440)* (Rome: École française de Rome).

PIZARRO, J. M. (1995) *Writing Ravenna: The* Liber Pontificalis *of Andreas Agnellus* (Ann Arbor: University of Michigan Press).

POMARÈS, G. (1959), *Lettre contre les Lupercales et Dix-huit messes du Sacramentaire léonien*, SC 65 (Paris: Éditions du Cerf).

RAMSAY, B. (1989), *The Sermons of Maximus of Turin*, ACW 50 (New York: Newman Press/Paulist Press).

—— (1997), *Ambrose* (London: Routledge).

SÁGHY, M. (2000), 'Scinditur in partes populus: Pope Damasus and the Martyrs of Rome', *Early Medieval Europe*, 9: 273–87.

SALZMAN, M. R. (2002), *The Making of a Christian Aristocracy: Social and Religious Change in the Western Roman Empire* (Cambridge, Mass.: Harvard University Press).

SMITH, J. M. H. (2005), *Europe after Rome: A New Cultural History 500–1000* (Oxford: Oxford University Press).

SOT, M. (1981), 'Arguments hagiographiques et historiographiques dans les "Gesta episcoporum" ', in *Hagiographies: Culture et sociétés, IVe–XIIe siècles* (Paris: L'Institutd' études augustiniennes), 95–104.

SOTINEL, C. (2005), 'Emperors and Popes in the Sixth Century: The Western View', in M. Maas (ed.), *The Cambridge Companion to the Age of Justinian* (Cambridge: Cambridge University Press), 267–315.

STANCLIFFE, C. (1983), *St Martin and his Hagiographer: History and Miracle in Sulpicius Severus* (Oxford: Clarendon Press).

STARK, R. (1996), *The Rise of Christianity: A Sociologist Reconsiders History* (Princeton: Princeton University Press).

STOCKING, R. L. (2000), *Bishops, Councils, and Consensus in the Visigothic Kingdom, 589–633* (Ann Arbor: University of Michigan Press).

TEJA, R. (2002) (ed.), *La Hispania del siglo IV: administración, economía, sociedad, cristianización*, Munera, 19 (Bari: Edipuglia).

THOMAS, C. (1981), *Christianily in Roman Britain to AD 500* (London: Batsford).

THORPE, L. (1974), *Gregory of Tours: The History of the Franks* (Harmondsworth: Penguin).

TROUT, D. E. (1996), 'Town, Country, and Christianization at Paulinus' Nola', in R. W. Mathisen and H. Sivan (eds.), *Shifting Frontiers in Late Antiquity* (Aldershot: Ashgate), 175–86.

ULLMANN, W. (1972), *A Short History of the Papacy in the Middle Ages* (London: Methuen).

VAN DAM, R. (1985), *Leadership and Community in Late Antique Gaul* (Berkeley: University of California Press).

—— (1988a), *Gregory of Tours: Glory of the Confessors* (Liverpool: Liverpool University Press).

—— (1988b), *Gregory of Tours: Glory of the Martyrs* (Liverpool: Liverpool University Press).

—— (1993), *Saints and their Miracles in Late Antique Gaul* (Princeton: Princeton University Press).

VILELLA, J. (2002), 'Las iglesias y las cristiandades hispanas: panorama prosopográfico', in Teja (2002), 117–59.

WARD-PERKINS, B. (1984), *From Classical Antiquity to the Middle Ages: Urban Public Building in Northern and Central Italy AD 300–850* (Oxford: Oxford University Press).

WILLIAMS, D. H. (1995), *Ambrose of Milan and the End of the Arian–Nicene Conflicts* (Oxford: Clarendon Press).

WILSON, R. J. A. (1990), *Sicily under the Roman Empire* (Warminster: Aris and Phillips).

WOLF, K. B. (1999), *Conquerors and Chroniclers of Early Medieval Spain*, 2nd edn. (Liverpool: Liverpool University Press).

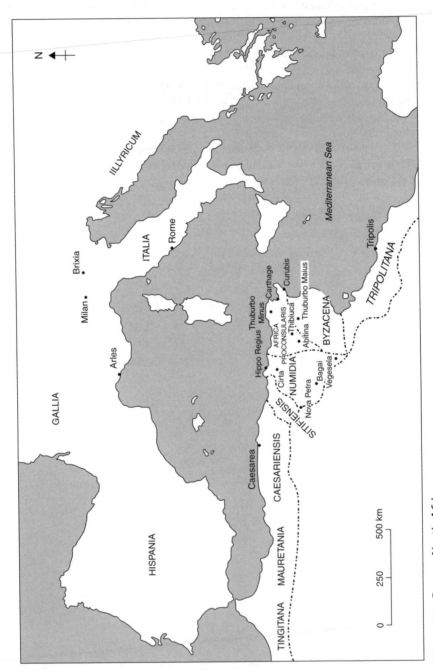

Map 15.1 Roman North Africa

CHAPTER 15

THE WEST (2): NORTH AFRICA

ÉRIC REBILLARD

RATHER than provide a continuous narrative, this chapter tries to bring to the fore some exceptional documents that allow the historian to go beyond the received view of the history of Christianity in North Africa. It also deliberately focuses on the literary sources, although the archaeological and epigraphic evidence is abundant. This choice is justified only insofar as it would be difficult to deal with both the literary and the non-literary evidence on their own terms within the limits of a chapter, which wants to be an invitation to read afresh some documents known for a long time and to discover documents recently made available to scholars.

15.1 THE ORIGINS OF CHRISTIANITY IN NORTH AFRICA

The origins of Christianity in North Africa is a vexed question, and already in antiquity very little seems to have been known. Tertullian implies the existence of very strong ties between Rome and Carthage (*Praescr.* 36. 2, 4), but never explicitly says that the North African church was first settled by Rome (Barnes 1985: 67; but see Dunn 2001: 408–10). The hypothesis of a Jewish origin has no better ground (Barnes 1985: 273–5). Interestingly, in Augustine's debate with the Donatists, who argued for a form of African isolationism (at least according to Augustine) by mentioning the late arrival of Christianity in Africa, he cannot oppose them with a more precise answer than that Africa had an 'apostolic origin' (for example, *Psal.* 44. 23). In a letter, he mentions the strong links with Rome and with 'all the other regions from where the gospel came to Africa' (*Ep.* 43. 7). A multiple origin for African Christianity seems a very reasonable hypothesis (Telfer 1961). It is not before the Byzantine period that legends attributing the evangelization of Africa to Peter and other apostles appeared.

The first African Christians we know about are the Scillitan martyrs executed by the proconsul Saturninus in 180 (Musurillo 1972; Ruggiero 1991). Scilli, the hometown of the martyrs, cannot be located, but the involvement of the proconsul implies that it was in the province of Africa Proconsularis. Since we have a fairly good knowledge of African cities, we can assume that Scilli was a (very) small one, which attests that already in 180 Christianity was present in the African countryside.

15.2 TERTULLIAN AND THE CHRISTIANS IN CARTHAGE AT THE END OF THE SECOND CENTURY

If the beginnings of Christianity in Africa are rather obscure, its development at the turn of the second to the third century is well documented thanks to the exceptional testimony of Tertullian. Little is known about Tertullian himself (Barnes 1985; Dunn 2004*b*). His dates of birth and death are uncertain, but he wrote during the reigns of Septimius Severus (193–211) and Caracalla (211–17). His writings attest a good education; nowadays the identification with the jurist Tertullianus is not retained. Jerome says that Tertullian was a presbyter of the church of Carthage (*Vir. ill.* 53), but there is no external evidence to either confirm or deny his statement. The old hypothesis of the existence of a catechetical school in Carthage on the model of the Alexandrian one, whose head would have been Tertullian, has been definitively abandoned. In the context of what we now know of the organization of Christian groups at the end of the second century, the question of the status of Tertullian is less relevant than was earlier believed. We will come back to this when we will consider the question of his separation from the Catholics.

Several hints in Tertullian's works let us see that at least some Christians were known as such by their fellow citizens in Carthage. First, it was easy to identify the Christians as groups. In *Ad Nationes* 1. 7. 19 Tertullian says that the Roman officials knew when and where they gathered for their rites, and in several other texts he suggests that it was there that they were usually arrested (*Apol.* 7. 4; *Fuga pers.* 3. 2; see White 1997: 54–62). The meeting place or places of the Christians in Carthage at that time have not been identified or located (Ennabli 1997), but they were known to the non-Christians, a fact that invites us to qualify the 'private' status usually granted to them.

Second, as Tertullian ironically suggests by saying in *De spectaculis* 27. 2 that a Christian who goes to the games must not fear anything from the pagans, it was not possible to identify a Christian from outside. However, in interpersonal relations it was difficult, if not impossible, to hide one's Christian identity. In the *Apologeticus* 3. 1, Tertullian argues that pagans' hatred drives them to ignore the personal qualities of Christians because of their faith; to support his position, he invents comments made by pagans about some of their fellow citizens who converted to Christianity: ' "A good man, they say, this Caius Seius, only that he is a Christian." Then another says: "I am surprised that that wise man, Lucius Titius, has suddenly become a Christian." ' The names are fictitious, but it is very likely that conversions to Christianity engendered comments among neighbours, friends, and relations. In the *De idololatria*, Tertullian depicts the 'world full of gods' (Hopkins 1999) in which Christians were living, and he uses the word *timiditas* three times to describe the fear of being identified as a Christian in personal interactions: in 13. 1 about the participation in public feasts, in 20. 1 about the reluctance to pronounce the name of the pagan gods, and in 21. 1 about oaths and maledictions. It was in daily life and in normal interactions that their religious affiliation could singularize the Christians and therefore expose them to denunciations in periods of persecution.

Third, according to Tertullian, the Christians had become so numerous and belonged to so many different social classes that it was impossible to avoid them in any kind of social interaction (*Apol.* 37. 4–8; see also *Scap.* 2 and 5; *Ad. Iud.* 7. 5; *Cor. mil.* 12). These affirmations have of course no numerical value, but the great social variety of the Christians has been amply confirmed by modern historians (Schöllgen 1984). Tertullian's exact social status might be difficult to recover, but he certainly belonged to the upper literary circle of Carthage (Barnes 1985: 69; Schöllgen 1984: 176–89). In his works there are allusions to Christians from the three orders of senators, equestrians, and decurions, even if it is impossible to evaluate their number (Schöllgen 1984: 223). The majority of Christians belonged, however, to the urban *plebs*, a mix of highly qualified workers, small shopkeepers, and occasional workers in the harbour, not usually mentioned with much precision in our sources as their integration into the church did not present any problem (Schöllgen 1984: 267).

What was the attitude of these Christians toward contemporary society? They were obviously more integrated than Tertullian would have liked them to be. The *De idololatria* is a very interesting text in this regard. It has too often been read as if Tertullian's attitude was representative of all Christians, when in fact it is possible to find in the text clear echoes of different points of view. Tertullian criticizes

Christians for improper use of scripture to defend their choices. The passage, 1 Corinthians 7: 20, 'Each one should remain in the situation which he was in when God called him', was thus mentioned by artists who did not intend to stop working for pagan temples (*Idol.* 5. 1), and Romans 12: 15, 'Rejoice with those who rejoice', by Christians who wished to take part in public festivals (*Idol.* 13. 2). Even Tertullian is more nuanced than is sometimes recognized. He would rather see Christians not be teachers of literature, but he insists on the need for Christians to be instructed in literature (*Idol.* 10). Such a discussion reveals that, on the one hand, some converted schoolteachers did not want to renounce their profession, while, on the other hand, there were Christian parents who were not inclined to send their children to the 'pagan' school. This is a rare example of the subtle negotiations that took place on the limits of the interactions between Christians and the institutions of the city in which they were living. As we have seen with the use of Romans 12: 15, there were also discussions about the participation in holidays and other public festivals. Tertullian rejects participation in the spectacles of the circus or the hippodrome, as he did in the *De spectaculis*. He also rejects celebrating in pagan public festivities (*Idol.* 13–14). Christians may, however, take part in family festivals like marriages and name-giving ceremonies: in this case, even if the feast is tainted by idolatry, the events concerned are good, and participation can be regarded as a normal social duty (*Idol.* 16). Here again the negotiation of the limits of interaction is subtle (Stroumsa 1998).

Too often Tertullian's forceful expression of his point of view has obscured the glimpses of a wider range of social experience that we can find in his texts. Careful attention to what is implied or rejected, and some reading against the grain, allow the historian to develop a richer and more nuanced picture of the Christian groups at the turn of the second to the third century. We will not be offered such rich glimpses before the turn of the fourth to the fifth century in the works of Augustine.

We find very little detail on the organization of the African church in Tertullian. In the *Apologeticus*, Tertullian offers a description of Christian groups for a pagan audience and compares them to voluntary associations (*collegia*), a familiar feature in any city of the Roman Empire. Like the members of an association, the Christians meet regularly, but for prayers and readings; their common meals are also very different from the drinking parties of the associations; their contributions are made on a voluntary basis and are used for the care of the poor (*Apol.* 39). This text does not prove that Christian groups constituted associations in order to have a legal status in the Roman Empire (Rebillard 2003: 55–61); the comparison is intended only to make the Christian groups, whose meetings generated all sort of rumours, look familiar to the pagans.

Tertullian's works offer no clear indication of the organization of the clergy, and this might be the key to understanding a vexed question associated with the name of Tertullian: his separation from the Catholics, sometimes described as a schism. At some point, Tertullian became an adept of what he calls the 'New Prophecy', the prophetic movement initiated in Asia Minor by Montanus, known as Montanism in the anti-heretical sources. African (Tertullian's?) Montanism was mainly characterized by exceptionally rigorous practices: longer and stricter fasting, a ban on remarriage, longer and harder penance (Trevett 1996). Tertullian is very careful to state that only disciplinary issues are at stake, and that the 'rule of faith' is not concerned. However, he expresses rather harshly his dissent from the Christians he calls the 'Psychici', or the carnally minded, whom the later tradition calls the Catholics, and goes so far as to say that on account of his acknowledgement and defence of the Paraclete he separated from them (*Prax.* 1. 7). In the light of the later testimonies of both Jerome (*Vir. ill.* 53) and Augustine (*Haer.* 1. 86), it has been a commonplace to state that Tertullian then joined a schismatic group of adherents of the New Prophecy. Nowhere in his writings does Tertullian make a clear allusion to such a schismatic group, and in several passages he continues to refer to all Christians as 'us', as opposed to Jews or pagans. Cyprian also claims him as his 'Master', a name which he would hardly give to a known schismatic (Powell 1975; Mattei 1990; van der Lof 1991; Rankin 1995). The problem with considering Tertullian a schismatic arises partially from the fact that the category of schism has been applied by later writers (and modern historians) to a period when the relationships between groups within the Church were much more fluid and able to accommodate different schools (van der Lof 1991: 361; Brent 1995: 535–40). The situation is already different by the middle of the third century, as the testimony of Cyprian on the organization of the African church makes clear: by then the bishop had become the indisputable locus of ecclesiastical power.

15.3 CYPRIAN AND THE ORGANIZATION OF THE AFRICAN CHURCH IN THE THIRD CENTURY

Cyprian was bishop of Carthage from 248/9 to his martyrdom in 258. He was born into a well-established family of Carthage and had won renown for his oratorical skills before his conversion to Christianity. From his baptism to his election as bishop, only a few years passed, and some older priests opposed his appointment. It seems that Cyprian was an unusually *socially* high-standing figure in the Carthaginian clergy, and that this explains the choice made by the *plebs* (Sage 1975: 95–143). Cyprian's treatises, and especially his letters, are a very rich source on the organization of the African churches, but also more generally on the period, since the 250s are particularly badly documented in our extant sources.

At the time when Cyprian was writing, the distinction between the clergy and the laity seems to have been well established: Cyprian sometimes uses the words *clerus* and *plebs* for designating two distinct groups of addressees in his letters (Duval 2005). The *plebs* contributes to the church by its almsgiving, but also by its participation in the election of the bishop. The actual way in which the *plebs* voted is not known, but its vote was the final, decisive step in the election. The *plebs* can also be associated, though in a very limited and strictly controlled way, with some judicial decisions of the bishop (Duval 2005).

The *Letters* provide the names of three to six deacons and of six to eight subdeacons for the decade of Cyprian's episcopate. It is therefore likely that the Carthaginian clergy counted the maximum number of seven deacons fixed by Acts 6: 1–6 and the same number of subdeacons. The deacons were the bishop's deputies in the works of assistance and in handling the church finances; the subdeacons were their assistants. Up to twelve Carthaginian presbyters are known in the *Letters*, not all of them being in charge at the same time. This number can be compared to the forty-six presbyters of Rome at the same period (Eusebius, *Hist. eccl.* 6. 43. 11). The main function of the presbyters was to teach the catechumens; it appears that in the absence of the bishop they could act as his deputies for the administration of penance and even the celebration of the eucharist. Six acolytes appear as letter-carriers and distributors of alms: they were the assistants of the presbyters. A reasonable conjecture is that the Carthaginian staff numbered one-eighth of the Roman staff (Clarke 1984: i. 39–44).

As the *Letters* amply document, Cyprian was at the head of all the African churches, but it is difficult to determine if this was the result of his own authority or if this was *ex officio* as bishop of Carthage (Dunn 2002a). The churches do not seem to have been divided yet into provinces following the administrative divisions: bishops from Africa Proconsularis, but also from Numidia and the Mauretanias, participated in the councils gathered under the authority of Cyprian in Carthage (Duval 2005: 30–4 and 51 ff.). It appears that the custom was to schedule a council once a year with a flexible agenda (Dunn 2003). The bishops were invited to attend, but their participation remained on a voluntary basis out of respect for the principle of local autonomy and independence. The decisions reached at a council, which were published in a letter signed by all the bishops present, sometimes called a synodal letter, were sent around to the other bishops in the hope that they would implement them in their own sees (Dunn 2004a). The principle of local autonomy was combined with a strong commitment to the unity of the Church. The relationships between Cyprian and the other African bishops have been analysed in terms of patronage (Dunn 2003), but our only example of such is Cyprian once sending money to some Numidian bishops in order to help them ransom brethren captured by barbarians (*Ep.* 62).

Cyprian's *Letters* also attest his relationships with bishops outside Africa. He exchanged letters with bishops from Spain (*Ep.* 67), Gaul (*Ep.* 68), Cappadocia

(*Ep.* 75) and especially Rome (*Ep.* 9, 20, 27, etc.). Cyprian was trying to enforce at this level of communication the same principles of the independence of the local churches and of the unity of the Church. The baptismal controversy of 254–6 between Cyprian and Stephen, bishop of Rome, is worth considering, even briefly, from this point of view (Sage 1975: 295–335). The issue at stake was how to receive converts baptized in schism: Cyprian thought that their baptism was invalid, and that they must be baptized in the true Church, while Stephen accepted the validity of their baptism and thought that it was enough to receive them by the imposition of hands alone. An African council held in Carthage in 256 reached a decision conforming to Cyprian's position. Stephen then reacted by threatening to break communion with all bishops who would rebaptize converts from schism. Cyprian was ready to concede some prominence to the church of Rome, but denied Stephen the right to impose his views on other local churches. Cyprian defended the same position in a letter addressed to two Spanish churches in which he offered support, even though he knew that Stephen took a different stance (Dunn 2002*b*).

15.4 THE PERSECUTIONS IN NORTH AFRICA

Cyprian is also a major source of information for the persecution of Decius in 249/50 and then the persecution of Valerian in 257/8. Since at least 180 there had been executions of Christians in Africa, but it was not systematic; Christians were denounced by private individuals to the Roman authorities and then executed (Barnes 1968). We have already mentioned the Scillitan Martyrs, and several texts of Tertullian attest such sporadic outbursts of violence (Barnes 1985: 143–63). The most famous case is the martyrdom of Perpetua and her companions, all condemned to death at Carthage in 203. Even the persecution of Decius became a persecution of Christians only because they did not comply with the general call to sacrifice to the gods of the Empire (Rives 1999; Selinger 1994 and 2002). In a letter preserved among Cyprian's, Lucianus, himself imprisoned and expecting to die of hunger rather than by execution, gives the names of seventeen victims in Carthage (*Ep.* 22). Some Christians fled, as Cyprian himself did; others bought false certificates of sacrifice; others just sacrificed. Even if few Christians died, the edict of Decius caused a major disruption in the Carthaginian church, especially as dissension arose regarding the way to deal with the lapsed (Burns 2002).

The persecution of Valerian was of a different nature: the first law (August 257) singled out the high clergy and forbade holding assemblies; the second law (August 258) prescribed immediate execution of bishops, presbyters, and deacons, and execution of all the *honestiores* who would persevere in remaining Christians

(Selinger 2002: 83 ff.). It was the first explicit persecution of Christianity, even if short-lived. Gallienus issued an edict of tolerance as soon as the news of the death of Valerian was known in 260 (Selinger 2002: 94–5). There were, however, a few martyrs, especially in Africa, where the laws of Valerian had been zealously implemented. Cyprian was beheaded on 14 September, 258, after having been relegated for a year to Curubis, some 60 miles from Carthage. His martyrdom, as well as his two trials, are narrated in the eponymous *Acts* (Musurillo 1972). Two other African texts document the persecution: the *Acts of Montanus and Lucius* for Africa Proconsularis and the *Acts of Marian and James* for Numidia. The period of relative peace for the Christians that followed the edict of Gallienus and lasted some 40 years is unfortunately not documented for Africa.[1] At the end of this period, the soldiers Maximilian in 295 and Marcellus in 298 were executed not because they were Christian, but because as Christians they did not submit to military discipline. Even if, as Eusebius mentions, there were some earlier purges in the army, the 'Great Persecution' did not start before 303.

The edict of 23 February, 303 ordered churches to be razed to the ground, the scriptures destroyed by fire, and the Christians among the *honestiores* to be deprived of their liberty. City officials were in charge locally of inventorying the places of worship and the copies of the scriptures; they were also to refer to the governor the members of the clergy who would not comply. This is what happened at Thibiuca in Africa Proconsularis, where the bishop Felix refused to surrender the scriptures and was thus sent to Carthage to be tried (Musurillo 1972). At Abitinae, also in Africa Proconsularis, despite the surrendering of the scriptures by the bishop Fundanus, the officials arrested forty-two people who were celebrating the Sunday liturgy in a private household. The zeal of the local magistrates there can be explained by the presence among the Christians of Dativus, who had been accused of the kidnapping of a young Christian woman who fled her pagan family (Maier 1987; Lepelley 1979: 335–6). The *Acts of Gallonius*, recently discovered, show that the local authorities at Thimida Regia also arrested a group of Christians who gathered for the Sunday liturgy despite the edict (Chiesa 1996; Lancel 1999; Lepelley 1999).

The implementation of the edicts of Diocletian in Africa is also documented by two texts that are major pieces in the dossier concerning the origins of Donatism; they are not hagiographical, but rather authentic local proceedings. The case of Abthugni, a little city 50 miles south-west of Carthage, is known thanks to the later involvement of its bishop, Felix, in the Donatist controversy. According to the proceedings of the trial, when Felix was tried in 313–14 for his participation in the election of Caecilianus to the see of Carthage, the local magistrate in charge of the implementation of the edict of 303 testified as to his own conduct at that time. The issue at stake in 313/14 was whether Felix surrendered any copy of the scriptures himself. It appears that he was in fact absent from Abthugni when the officials came to seize the scriptures, and that the local officials were content with the destruction of a throne and the doors of the church. No further measure of persecution was taken in the city against any of the Christians. The Christians and their bishop seem to have been on friendly terms with the magistrate, and indeed the Christians themselves, as it is reported, sent people to ask him about the measures he wanted to take to implement the edict of the Emperor (Edwards 1997: 170–80; Lepelley 1984 = Lepelley 2001: 321–8; Duval 2000).

It was also during a later trial (320) involving Donatists and Catholics that the official acts of what was done at Cirta in 303 were produced and thus preserved for us among the Donatist dossier. Although the governor of Numidia was residing in Cirta, the local officials performed the searches and confiscations. It appears that the bishop Paulus did not offer any resistance and handed over most of the objects and goods kept in the church with the help of his clergy. Among them was Silvanus, a subdeacon in 303, who was later elected bishop by the Donatists and whom the Catholics had on trial in 320. The document is precious, as it shows how the 'persecution' at a local level was mainly a police matter without any religious zeal being involved (Edwards 1997: 150–69; Lepelley 1981: 391–4; Duval 2000).

The attitude of the bishop Paulus, who rather quickly complied with the edicts, was not isolated; some found ways of saving their lives without betraying their faith, like Mensurius, the bishop of Carthage, who handed over heretical writings (Augustine, *Breviculus Collationis*, 3. 13. 25); but in many places Christians heroically resisted, and some died. When the persecution ended, problems arose, as some Christians denied legitimacy to those whom they called *traditores* ('surrenderers'). In the 250s Cyprian managed to maintain the unity of the African churches when a similar problem occurred, but these quarrels engendered a schism that lasted for more than a century.

15.5 THE ORIGINS OF DONATISM

Our main source for the origins of the schism is the pamphlet written by the 'Catholic' bishop Optatus of Milevis, *Against the Donatists*. It was important to trace the origins of the schism in order to make a claim for legitimacy. Optatus had access to a dossier of original documents, and this dossier, although incomplete, was copied in one manuscript as an appendix to his treatise. With the two proceedings we already mentioned, the dossier includes several letters of Constantine, whose involvement in the beginnings of the schism was decisive. The dossier seems to have been compiled towards the end of his reign.

Upon the death of Mensurius, one of his deacons, Caecilianus, was elected without the customary participation of the Numidian primate. One of the bishops who consecrated him, Felix of Abthugni, was accused of being a *traditor*, and thus the Numidian primate convened a meeting in Carthage to depose Caecilianus and elect one Majorinus in his place, but Caecilianus did not accept this decision. Thus by 307/8 there were two rival bishops for the see of Carthage. In April 313, the supporters of Majorinus appealed to Constantine, even though he had given his support to Caecilianus after taking control of Africa late in 312. Constantine handed the case over to the bishop of Rome, who gathered a few Italian bishops in a council. In October 313, they acquitted Caecilianus and condemned Donatus, who had by that time replaced Majorinus. It is after his name that the schism was called Donatism. When he saw that this decision did not end the conflict, Constantine gathered a larger council with bishops from all over the West. In Arles in August 314 the council again condemned the Donatists. When they brought new documents establishing their case, the Emperor charged the *vicarius* of Africa to investigate. Felix of Abthugni was found innocent, and therefore the election of Caecilianus was declared valid. The *vicarius* of Africa did not conclude his inquiry before February 315, and it took another 16 months, during which time Constantine contemplated the possibility of dealing with the issue in person, before in November 316 he finally ordered the confiscation of the churches belonging to the Donatists and exiled their bishops.

Repression followed and lasted until 321, when Constantine recalled all Donatists from exile. He could not appear to persecute Christians, even schismatics, and still present himself as the champion of Christianity against Licinius. The Donatist church prospered quickly, and in 336 Donatus could hold a council in Carthage attended by 270 bishops (Barnes 1981: 54 ff. and 1982: 238 ff.; Birley 1987).

I cannot give here a complete, or even brief, outline of the following history of the relations of the two churches in Africa between the end of the reign of Constantine and the Conference of Carthage in 411 (see Frend 1952; Crespin 1965). I will instead give some information on documents that allow the historian direct access to the Donatists.[2] Augustine in his anti-Donatist treatises quotes large extracts from the writings of his opponents, but this does not constitute a reliable and unbiased source. This is not the case with a little group of Donatist martyr stories.

15.6 DONATIST MARTYR STORIES

It is important first to make a clear distinction between texts which record the martyrdom of Donatists and those which record the memory of martyrs from the pagan persecutions and have been in use in the Donatist church.[3] Like the Catholics, the Donatists commemorated the martyrs by the reading of their *Acts* during the liturgy on the day of the anniversary of their martyrdom (de Gaiffier 1954). We thus have evidence of their use of the *Acts of Cyprian* and the *Acts of Crispina*, an African woman martyr from the 'Great Persecution'. In each case, one version in the manuscript tradition contains the distinctive Donatist formula 'Praise God/Christ'.

The *Acts of Saturninus, Dativus, Felix and Companions* mentioned above are known to us only in a Donatist version (Dolbeau 2003: 276–7, *contra* Tilley 1996: 24–5). The case of the *Acts of Maxima, Donatilla and Secunda*, also executed during the Great Persecution, is more complicated: it is difficult to decide whether the only version we have is a Donatist version modified by the Catholics or a Catholic version modified by the Donatists (Maier 1987: 92–105).

Three martyr stories record the memory of Donatist martyrs and have been used in the polemic against the Catholics. The first one is a testimony on the persecution that followed the edict of 316: it mentions a Donatus and an Advocatus in its title, but commemorates in fact the heroic resistance of Donatists expelled from their church (Dolbeau 1992). The other two commemorate martyrs from the 'days of Macarius'. Macarius is one of the two commissioners sent by the emperor Constans in order to distribute money officially to both churches and thus to encourage their reunification. The commissioners, however, quickly showed their sympathy for the Catholics, and Donatus ordered his bishops to refuse their gifts. Violent incidents marked Macarius's tour of Numidia, where the Donatists were especially well established. On 15 August 346 an imperial decree proclaimed unity between the two churches under Bishop Gratus, the successor of Caecilianus, and then systematic repression started. Donatus and many other leaders of his church were sent into exile, and churches were confiscated all over North Africa (Frend 1952: 177–82; Cecconi 1990; Mastandrea 1991). Even if it did not bring a total collapse, the 'days of Macarius' were later to be remembered by the Donatists as an event as important as the 'Great Persecution'. They considered the victims of the repression as martyrs and commemorated them in martyr stories. The *Passion of Maximian and Isaac* records how the eponymous heroes tore down the edict imposing unity in Carthage and how they were imprisoned, tortured, and put to death. The *Passion of Marculus* narrates an episode of Macarius's tour in Numidia. When ten bishops with Marculus at their head met with Macarius at Vegesela, discussions deteriorated, and Marculus was arrested and then executed at Nova Petra (Mastandrea 1995). The *Passion* says that he was thrown from a cliff by Roman soldiers, while the Catholics asserted that he had jumped himself (for example, Augustine, *Contra litteras Petiliani*, 2. 20. 46). This group of texts is all the more interesting because they are among the few Donatist texts that have been preserved.[4]

15.7 THE CONFERENCE OF CARTHAGE IN 411

The second document that deserves some attention is the *Proceedings of the Conference of Carthage* that brought together Donatists and Catholics in 411. Here, too, the historian can hear the Donatist voice unfiltered through Catholic biases. When the emperor Honorius appointed the count Marcellinus to preside over the conference, the Catholics, thanks to the action of Aurelius, bishop of Carthage, and Augustine, bishop of Hippo, had already obtained that the Donatists be assimilated to heretics and therefore liable to the anti-heretical legislation. It was nevertheless symbolically important to hold a conference in order to force the Donatists to recognize publicly that there was only one Church (Frend 1952: 244–73). What makes the document's historical value exceptional is that the actual verbal content of what the participants said has been preserved. Part of the first session was dedicated to establishing the protocol for recording the minutes of the conference: the words of each speaker were to be recorded in shorthand, transcribed, checked by members of both parties, and finally authenticated and notarized by the speaker himself. Procedural matters in general were widely discussed. It was, however, more than a dilatory tactic adopted by the Donatists. They were thus able, for instance, to demonstrate that they had at least as many representatives as the Catholics. Thanks to the long and painful checking of numbers and identities of bishops of the two sides, we thus have a rather extensive idea of the respective strength of the Catholics and the Donatists in the different provinces of North Africa, with a stronger presence of Donatists in Numidia and of Catholics in Africa Proconsularis (Lancel 1972; Tilley 1991; Shaw 1992). The discussions recorded in the *Proceedings* also allow us a more nuanced view of their ecclesiology than the one offered by Augustine through the refutation of their arguments, especially regarding the Donatist view of the Catholic Church outside Africa (Eno 1972).

15.8 INTERPRETATIONS OF DONATISM

A few words must be said about modern interpretations of two related issues: What is 'African' about Donatism? And who were the Circumcellions? W. H. C. Frend in his 1952 book *The Donatist Church* sought to explain Donatism as 'a movement of protest in Roman North Africa', and considered Donatism as the true expression of African Christianity. His thorough knowledge of the geography, the ethnology, and the archaeology of North Africa allowed him to emphasize that the cradle of Donatism was the rural Numidia of the Berbers, while the Catholics were stronger in the cities of Africa Proconsularis. Donatists would thus be motivated more by nationalist and social than by religious concerns. The inherent danger in such a search for a local explanation is that it presupposes, rather than demonstrates, continuity in the history of Africa (Brown 1961, 1968; Congar 1963: 25–48). Donatism must be studied both in its local context and in the larger context of late antique Mediterranean Christianity. Donatists represent those Christians in North Africa who remained committed to a sharp division between the world and the Church (Markus 1990).

The Circumcellions are known as Donatism's militant wing. I made a quick allusion to them when I mentioned the violence which accompanied the mission of Paulus and Macarius in 347; this is when they appear for the first time in our sources. Optatus describes how the bishop of Bagai in Numidia, another Donatus, called them in order to harass the imperial commissioners. He also records how these same Circumcellions had terrorized the countryside some years before (Optatus, *Against the Donatists*, 3. 4). This is what led some scholars to see them as social revolutionaries and to understand their association with the Donatists as an opportunity to give a religious dimension to a primarily social movement. It seems implausible, however, to assume too strong a continuity between the members of the peasant revolt of the 340s and the religious activists of the Donatist church still operating in the 410s (Birley 1987: 32–4; Lepelley 1992). To consider them as a religious phenomenon that presents an analogy with phenomena from other parts of the Roman world is very likely a fruitful method, but more work needs to be done on the primary sources.[5]

15.9 AUGUSTINE AND THE LIMITS OF CHRISTIANIZATION OF NORTH AFRICA

The name of Augustine has been mentioned with that of Aurelius, the bishop of Carthage from 391/2 to 427. Augustine had been ordained priest of Hippo in 391, and would be elected bishop in 395. The two men worked together to revitalize the Catholic Church of Africa, in particular through the planning of regular councils. It is in Hippo that in 393 the first plenary council of Africa summoned by Aurelius was held. Its decisions formed the basis of the conciliar legislation for the church of Africa, especially in matters of ecclesiastical discipline. To ensure unity before the schismatics, they inaugurated the holding of an annual general council, to which each province would send three legates. Aurelius and Augustine also used this institution to defend their positions *vis-à-vis* the Roman see. Augustine, though he was only a presbyter, delivered a speech in the presence of all the bishops, 'On faith and the symbol', a synthesis of Catholic doctrine, which would establish him as the spokesman of the African church for the next 40 years (Cross 1961; Munier 1968, 2003).

It is not possible here to trace the career of Augustine, or to evoke his role as controversialist (Brown 2000; Lancel 2002; O'Donnell 2005). I will instead focus on his sermons, as they shed an unusual light on his daily life as a bishop. New evidence considerably renewed interest in his preaching, especially when François Dolbeau discovered some twenty-six new sermons in 1990.[6] Preaching was the duty and privilege of the bishop.[7] The most regular day for preaching was Sunday, but we know that Augustine also preached regularly on Saturday. The liturgical calendar could, however, impose other rhythms: a sermon every day during Lent or a week with several sermons a day for Easter, for instance. Augustine preached in the different churches of Hippo, but he also delivered sermons in many other places. Every time he was in Carthage, Bishop Aurelius invited him to preach, and so did other bishops when he was travelling through the province. His sermons were delivered extemporaneously for the most part, and they are filled with evidence of spontaneity like a conversational tone and irregularities of syntax. Augustine's sermons were recorded by stenographers who took notes in shorthand as they were being delivered and then transcribed them in longhand. Not all the sermons delivered by Augustine were recorded: a likely estimate is that only one out of ten sermons has been preserved. The recorded discourses were then archived in the bishop's library. Augustine never completed the revised edition of his sermons that he was preparing in 428 (*Ep.* 224.2; *Retract.* 2. 67. 23), and we thus depend on collections gathered already during his lifetime and after his death in Africa, Italy, and the south of Gaul. During the process of their transmission, many sermons have been truncated by the copyists, who deleted in particular every concrete allusion to the circumstances of preaching (Dolbeau 1996: 521–3). The great value of the collections discovered by F. Dolbeau is that they contain some sermons which were known before only in a shortened version. We are thus able now to determine with a reasonable certainty which sermons are 'complete'. These are the most precious sermons for historians, as they contain a great deal of information about the context of the delivery and the audience.

One aspect that these sermons document firsthand are the limits of the Christianization of North Africa in the age of Augustine. A century or so after the conversion of Constantine and after the recent mission of special imperial agents to close pagan shrines in Africa (399), the pagans, especially the educated ones, were still very much present in Augustine's preaching (Chadwick 1998). In a very long sermon preached for the Calends of January 404, he tried to prevent his fellow Christians from being impressed by men who could boast: 'And am I going to be what my janitress, and not rather what Plato was, or Pythagoras?' (*Serm. Dolbeau* 26. 59). Many of these educated pagans were still leading the local municipalities around Hippo (Lepelley 1998). As the letters show, some of these pagan aristocrats were ready to consider Augustine as one of them, regardless of his religion (Rebillard 1998). Historians have pointed out that Augustine was living in a world in which the Christians were very likely a majority, but in which public life, and in particular the administration of the city, remained largely untouched by Christianity (Lepelley 1975: 32–7; 1979: 371–6). The calendar itself was still very much the same, despite the new rhythms imposed on it by the Christian liturgy. If Augustine preached for more than two hours on the Calends of January 404, it was in part to keep in church those of the Christians who wanted very much to join their neighbours and friends for the festivities of the Calends (Scheid 1998). Even if it was an issue of authority for Augustine to determine what was and was not 'pagan' in the religious practices of his flock (Brown 1995: 24), and if, as a consequence, his labels should not be taken at face value, his sermons allow us to picture a society in which the boundaries were not as strictly drawn as the Christian bishop would have liked, a society in which Christians and non-Christians were sharing a lot, a society in which the limits of what was religious were still the object of constant and subtle negotiations.

15.10 THE END OF CHRISTIANITY IN NORTH AFRICA?

In 430, Augustine died in a city surrounded by the Vandals, who had recently invaded Numidia. One year later Hippo was evacuated and partially burned. Sometime before 436, the Vandal king Gaiseric settled the capital of his newly conquered kingdom there. When he took Carthage in 439, it was the end of Roman Africa. The history of the African churches during the Vandal (429–533) and Byzantine (533–698) period is usually written as one of a long and irremediable decline before the Arab conquest, achieved in 711, put an end to African Christianity. This scheme has undergone a drastic revision thanks to some new and very good scholarship in the last few years.[8] The African churches had a long history after the end of Roman Africa, as evinced by Arab sources and even epitaphs of Christians dated to the tenth and eleventh centuries. This newly documented vitality of Christianity as late as the tenth and eleventh centuries, even if relative, invites us to look afresh at the intermediary periods of Vandal and Byzantine Africa and to leave aside the discourse on the decline and end of Christianity which has pervaded most of the bibliography (Handley 2004).

NOTES

1. A contemporary of Cyprian, who wrote in Africa if not an African, is Commodianus. His *Instructions* give some interesting vignettes on the daily life of Christians in the third century.
2. For an interesting attempt to read the Donatist texts and a reconstruction of their world, see Tilley (1997).

3. Tilley (1996) provides an English translation of most of the Donatist martyr stories. Her introductory notes on the manuscript tradition and on the different versions of the texts are not always reliable: see Dolbeau (2003: 276–7).

4. Some sixty sermons have recently been attributed to a Donatist bishop preaching between 411 and 429 (Leroy 1994, 1997, 1999; see Schindler 2003). I did not mention the name of the Donatist writer Tyconius (c.330–c.390), as only part of his exegetical works is known (see Tilley 1997: 112 ff.).

5. See recently Caner (2002: 223–35) and Gaddis (2005: 103–30), who both tend, however, to sidestep the previous scholarly debate. Shaw (2004) considers the non-African tradition on the Circumcellions and gives already an idea of 'who [the Circumcellions] were *not*' (p. 258),

6. The Dolbeau sermons have been published from 1990 (see now Dolbeau 1996 and 2005) and an English translation appeared in 1997 (Hill). Brown (2000: 441–81) gives a very thorough analysis of these two sets of texts. See also Chadwick (1996), Madec (1998).

7. On this and the following description of Augustine's preaching, see Rebillard (1999) with references to the texts and bibliography.

8. For the traditional narrative, see Frend (1952), and a vigorous critic of it in Handley (2004). On the Vandals, Courtois (1955) is still fundamental, but see Ben Abed and Duval (2002 and 2003), and Merrils (2004); on the Moors, see Modéran (2003); on African Christians after the Arab conquest, Handley (2004 with bibliography).

Suggested Reading

The primary sources for North African Christianity are numerous, and the ones listed below are only an attempt to guide the very first steps of readers who want to start working in this field. Dunn (2004b) in the series of The Early Church Fathers is a good introduction to Tertullian and his works. The *Letters* of Cyprian are available in English translation with the precious commentary of G. W. Clarke (1984–9). Augustine (2001) provides a good selection of letters and sermons of Augustine.

A lot of the secondary literature is not available in English, but here are a few titles that can stimulate further the curiosity of the reader. Frend (1952), despite the reservations made in the chapter, gives a good survey of the period. Brown (2000) is much more than a biography of Augustine. Brown (1972) collects several essays on North Africa; so does Shaw (1995).

Bibliography

AUGUSTINE (1997), *The Works of Saint Augustine*, Part III: *Sermons*, xi: *Newly Discovered Sermons*, trans. E. Hill (Hyde Park, NY: New City Press).

—— (2001), *Political Writings*, ed. E. M. Atkins and R. J. Dodaro (Cambridge: Cambridge University Press).

BARNES, T. D. (1968), 'Legislation against the Christians', *JRS* 58/1–2: 32–50.

—— (1981), *Constantine and Eusebius* (Cambridge, Mass.: Harvard University Press).

——(1982), *The New Empire of Diocletian and Constantine* (Cambridge, Mass.: Harvard University Press).

——(1985), *Tertullian: A Historical and Literary Study*, new edn. with corrections and a postscript (Oxford: Oxford University Press).

BEN ABED, A., and DUVAL, N. (2002) (eds.), 'L'Afrique vandale et byzantine', *Antiquité tardive*, 10: 21–290.

——(2003) (eds.), 'L'Afrique vandale et byzantine, 2', *Antiquité tardive*, 11: 13–179.

BIRLEY, A. R. (1987), 'Some Notes on the Donatist Schism', *Libyan Studies*, 18: 29–41.

BRENT, A. (1995), *Hippolytus and the Roman Church in the Third Century: Communities in Tension before the Emergence of a Monarch-bishop* (Leiden: E. J. Brill).

BROWN, P. (1961), 'Religious Dissent in the Later Roman Empire: The Case of North Africa', *History*, 46: 83–101.

——(1968), 'Christianity and Local Culture in Late Roman Africa', *JRS* 58: 85–95.

——(1972), *Religion and Society in the Age of Saint Augustine* (New York: Harper & Row).

——(1995), *Authority and the Sacred: Aspects of the Christianisation of the Roman World* (Cambridge: Cambridge University Press).

——(2000), *Augustine of Hippo: A Biography*, new edn. with an epilogue (Berkeley: University of California Press).

BURNS, J. PATOUT (2002), *Cyprian the Bishop* (London: Routledge).

CANER, D. (2002), *Wandering, Begging Monks: Spiritual Authority and the Promotion of Monasticism in Late Antiquity* (Berkeley: University of California Press).

CECCONI, G. A. (1990), 'Elemosina e propaganda: un analisi della "Macariana persecutio" nel libro III di Ottato di Milevi', *REAug* 36: 42–66.

CHADWICK, H. (1996), 'New Sermons of Saint Augustine', *JTS* 47: 69–91.

——(1998), 'Augustin et les païens', in Madec (1998), 323–6.

CHIESA, P. (1996), 'Un testo agiografico africano ad Aquileia: gli Acta di Gallonio e dei martiri di Timida Regia', *AnBoll* 114: 241–38.

CLARKE, G. W. (1984–9), *The Letters of St. Cyprian of Carthage*, ACW 43, 44, 46, 47 (New York: Newman Press).

CONGAR, Y. M. (1963), 'Introduction générale', in Augustin, *Traités antidonatistes*, i (Paris: Desclée de Brouwer), 7–133.

COURTOIS, C. (1955), *Les Vandales et l'Afrique* (Paris: Arts & Métiers).

CRESPIN, R. (1965), *Ministère et sainteté: pastorale du clergé et solution de la crise donatiste dans la vie et la doctrine de saint Augustin* (Paris: Institut d'études augustiniennes).

CROSS, F. L. (1961), 'History and Fiction in the African Canons', *JTS* 12: 227–47.

DOLBEAU, F. (1992), 'La Passio sancti Donati (BHL 2303 b): une tentative d'édition critique', in *Memoriam sanctorum venerantes: Miscellanea in onore di Monsignor Victor Saxer* (Rome: Pontificio Istituto di archeologia cristiana), 251–67.

——(1996), *Vingt-six sermons au peuple d'Afrique* (Paris: Institut d'études augustiniennes).

——(2003), 'La Passion des martyrs d'Abitina: remarques sur l'établissement du texte', *AnBoll* 121: 273–96.

——(2005), *Augustin et la prédication en Afrique: recherches sur divers sermons authentiques, apocryphes ou anonymes* (Paris: L'Institut d'études augustiniennes).

DUNN, G. D. (2001), 'Peter and Paul in Rome: The Perspective of the North African Church', in *Pietro e Paolo: Il loro rapporto con Roma nelle testimonianze antiche: xxix Incontro di studiosi dell'antichità cristiana, Roma 4–6 maggio 2000* (Rome: Institutum Patristicum Augustinianum), 405–13.

DUNN, G. D. (2002*a*), 'The Carthaginian Synod of 251: Cyprian's Model of Pastoral Ministry', in *I concili della cristianità occidentale secoli III–V: xxx Incontro di studiosi dell'antichità cristiana, Roma 3–5 maggio 2001* (Rome: Institutum Patristicum Augustinianum), 235–57.

—— (2002*b*), 'Cyprian of Carthage and the Episcopal Synod of Late 254', *REAug* 48: 229–47.

—— (2003), 'Cyprian and His Collegae: Patronage and the Episcopal Synod of 252', *Journal of Religious History*, 27/1: 1–13.

—— (2004*a*), 'Censuimus: Cyprian and the Episcopal Synod of 253', *Latomus*, 63: 672–88.

—— (2004*b*), *Tertullian*, ECF (London: Routledge).

DUVAL, Y. (2000), *Chrétiens d'Afrique à l'aube de la paix constantinienne: les premiers échos de la grande persécution* (Paris: Institut d'études augustiniennes).

—— (2005), *Les chrétientés d'Occident et leur évêque au III*^e *siècle: plebs in ecclesia constituta (Cyprien, Ep. 63)* (Paris: Institut d'études augustiniennes).

EDWARDS, M. (1997), *Optatus, Against the Donatists* (Liverpool: Liverpool University Press).

ENNABLI, L. (1997), *Carthage: une métropole chrétienne du IV*^e *à la fin du VII*^e *siècle* (Paris: CNRS Editions).

ENO, R. B. (1972), 'Some Nuances in the Ecclesiology of the Donatists', *REAug* 17: 46–50.

FREND, W. H. C. (1952), *The Donatist Church: A Movement of Protest in Roman North Africa* (Oxford: Clarendon Press).

GADDIS, M. (2005), *There is No Crime for Those who have Christ: Religious Violence in the Christian Roman Empire* (Berkeley: University of California Press).

GAIFFIER, B. DE (1954), 'La lecture des Actes de martyrs dans la prière liturgique en Occident: à propos du passionnaire hispannique', *AnBoll* 73: 134–66.

HANDLEY, M. A. (2004), 'Disputing the End of African Christianity', in Merrils (2004), 291–310.

HOPKINS, K. (1999), *A World Full of Gods: Pagans, Jews, and Christians in the Roman Empire* (London: Weidenfeld & Nicolson).

LANCEL, S. (1972), *Actes de la Conférence de Carthage en 411* (Paris: Éditions du Cerf).

—— (1999), 'Le proconsul Anullinus et la grande persécution en Afrique en 303–304 ap. J.-C.: nouveaux documents', *CRAI* 1999 (3): 1013–22.

—— (2002), *Saint Augustine* (London: SCM Press).

LEPELLEY, C. (1975), 'Saint Augustin et la cité romano-africaine', in C. Kannengiesser (ed.), *Jean Chrysostome et Augustin: actes du colloque de Chantilly (1974)* (Paris: Beauchesne), 13–39.

—— (1979), *Les cités de l'Afrique romaine au Bas-Empire* (Paris: Institut d'études augustiniennes).

—— (1981), *Les cités de l'Afrique romaine au Bas-Empire*, ii: *Notices d'histoire municipale* (Paris: L'Institut d'études augustiniennes).

—— (1984), 'Chrétiens et païens au temps de la persécution de Dioclétien: le cas d'Abthugnî', *StPatr* 15: 226–32.

—— (1992), 'Circumcelliones', in C. Mayer (ed.), *AugLex*, i, facs. 5–6 (Basel: Schwabe), 930–6.

—— (1998), 'L'aristocratie lettrée païenne: une menace aux yeux d'Augustin (à propos du sermon Dolbeau 26–Mayence 62)', in Madec (1998), 327–42.

—— (1999), 'L'apport d'actes des martyrs nouvellement découverts à la connaissance de la géographie historique de l'Afrique proconsulaire', *Bulletin de la Société nationale des antiquaires de France*, 205–21.

—— (2001), *Aspects de l'Afrique romaine: les cités, la vie rurale, le Christianisme* (Bari: Edipuglia).

LEROY, F.-J. (1994), 'Vingt-deux homélies africaines nouvelles attribuables à l'un des anonymes du Chrysostome latin (PLS 4)', *RBén* 104: 123–47.

—— (1997), 'L'homélie donatiste ignorée du corpus Escorial (Chrysostomus Latinus, PLS IV, sermon 18)', *RBén* 107: 250–62.

—— (1999), 'Les 22 inédits de la catéchèse donatiste de Vienne: une édition provisoire', *RechAug* 31: 149–234.

MADEC, G. (1998) (ed.), *Augustin Prédicateur (395–411): actes du Colloque International de Chantilly, 5–7 septembre 1996* (Paris: L'Institut d'études augustiniennes).

MAIER, J. L. (1987), *Le dossier du donatisme* (Berlin: Akademie Verlag).

MARKUS, ROBERT A. (1990), *The End of Ancient Christianity* (Cambridge: Cambridge University Press).

MASTANDREA, P. (1991), 'Per la cronologia dei tempora Macariana', *Koinonia*, 15: 19–39.

—— (1995), 'Passioni di martiri donatisti (BHL 4473 e 5271), *AnBoll* 113/N_2: 39–88.

MATTEI, P. (1990), 'Le schisme de Tertullien: essai de mise au point biographique et ecclé-siologique', in J. Granarolo (ed.), *Hommage à René Braun*, ii: *Autour de Tertullien* (Paris: Les Belles Lettres), 129–49.

MERRILS, A. H. (2004) (ed.), *Vandals, Romans and Berbers: New Perspectives on Late Antique North Africa* (Aldershot: Ashgate).

MODÉRAN, Y. (2003), *Les Maures et l'Afrique romaine (IVe–VIIe siècle)* (Rome: École française de Rome).

MUNIER, C. (1968), 'Cinq canons inédits du Concile d'Hippone', *Revue de droit canonique*, 18: 16–29.

—— (2003), 'L'influence de saint Augustin sur la législation ecclésiastique de son temps', in P. Fux, J. Roessli, and O. Wermelinger (eds.), *Augustinus Afer: Saint Augustin: africanité et universalité: actes du colloque international, Alger-Annaba, 1–7 avril 2001*, 2 vols. (Fribourg: Éditions Universitaires), i. 109–23.

MUSURILLO, H. (1972), *The Acts of the Christian Martyrs* (Oxford: Clarendon Press).

O'DONNELL, J. J. (2005), *Augustine: A New Biography*(New York: Ecco).

POWELL, D. (1975), 'Tertullianists and Cataphrygians', *VC* 29: 33–54.

RANKIN, D. I. (1995), *Tertullian and the Church* (Cambridge: Cambridge University Press).

REBILLARD, É. (1998), 'Augustin et le rituel épistolaire de l'élite sociale et culturelle de son temps: éléments pour une analyse processuelle des relations de l'évêque et de la cité dans l'Antiquité tardive', in É. Rebillard and C. Sotinel (eds.), *L'évêque dans la cité du IVe au Ve siècle: image et autorité: actes de la table ronde organisée par l'Istituto Patristico Augustinianum et l'École française de Rome, 1er et 2 décembre 1995* (Rome: École française de Rome), 127–52.

—— (1999), 'Sermones', in A. Fitzgerald (ed.), *Augustine through the Ages: An Encyclopedia* (Grand Rapids, Mich.: Eerdmans), 773–92.

—— (2003), *Religion et sépulture: l'église, les vivants et les morts dans l'antiquité tardive* (Paris: École des hautes études en sciences sociales).

RIVES, J. (1999), 'The Decree of Decius and the Religion of Empire', *JRS* 89: 135–54.

Ruggiero, F. (1991), *Atti dei Martiri scilitani* (Rome: Accademia Nazionale dei Lincei).

Sage, M. M. (1975), *Cyprian* (Cambridge, Mass.: Philadelphia Patristic Foundation).

Scheid, J. (1998), 'Les rejouissances des calendes de janvier d'après le *sermon* Dolbeau 26: nouvelles lumières sur une fête mal connue', in Madec (1998), 354–65.

Schindler, A. (2003), 'Du nouveau sur les donatistes au temps de saint Augustin?', in P. Fux, J. Roessli, and O. Wermelinger (eds.), *Augustinus Afer: Saint Augustin: africanité et universalité: actes du colloque international, Alger-Annaba, 1–7 avril 2001*, 2 vols. (Fribourg: Éditions Universitaires), i. 149–52.

Schöllgen, G. (1984), *Ecclesia sordida?: zur Frage der sozialen Schichtung frühchristlicher Gemeinden am Beispiel Karthagos zur Zeit Tertullians* (Münster: Aschendorff).

Selinger, R. (1994), *Die Religionspolitik des Kaisers Decius: Anatomie einer Christenverfolgung* (Frankfurt am Main: P. Lang).

——(2002), *The Mid-Third Century Persecutions of Decius and Valerian* (Frankfurt am Main: P. Lang).

Shaw, B. D. (1992), 'African Christianity: Disputes, Definitions, and Donatists', in M. R. Greenshields and T. A. Robinson (eds.), *Orthodoxy and Heresy in Religious Movements: Discipline and Dissent* (Lewiston, NY: Mellen), 4–342.

——(1995), *Rulers, Nomads, and Christians in Roman North Africa* (Aldershot: Variorum).

——(2004), 'Who were the Circumcellions?', in Merrils (2004), 227–58.

Stroumsa, G. G. (1998), 'Tertullian on Idolatry and the Limits of Tolerance', in G. N. Stanton and G. G. Stroumsa (eds.), *Tolerance and Intolerance in Early Judaism and Christianity* (Cambridge, Mass.: Harvard University Press), 173–84.

Telfer, W. (1961), 'The Origins of Christianity in Africa', in F. L. Cross (ed.), *StPatr 4*: 512–17.

Tilley, M. A. (1991), 'Dilatory Donatists or Procrastinating Catholics: The Trial at the Conference of Carthage', *CH* 60/1: 7–19.

——(1996), *Donatist Martyr Stories: The Church in Conflict in Roman North Africa* (Liverpool: Liverpool University Press).

——(1997), *The Bible in Christian North Africa: The Donatist World* (Minneapolis: Fortress Press).

Trevett, C. (1996), *Montanism: Gender, Authority and the New Prophecy* (New York: Cambridge University Press).

van der Lof, Johan L. (1991), 'The Plebs of the Psychici: Are the Psychici of De monogamia Fellow-Catholics of Tertullian?', in Gerard J. M. Bartelink, A. Hilhorst, and C. H. Kneepkens (eds.), *Eulogia: mélanges offers à Antoon A. R. Bastiaensen à l'occasion de son soixante-cinquième anniversaire* (Steenbrugge: Sint-Pieters Abdij), 353–63.

White, L. M. (1997), *The Social Origins of Christian Architecture*, ii: *Texts and Monuments for the Christian Domus Ecclesiae in its Environment* (Valley Forge, Pa.: Trinity Press).

CHAPTER 16

THE EAST (1): GREECE AND ASIA MINOR

RAYMOND VAN DAM

THE apostle Paul was primarily responsible for the initial introduction of Christianity in western, central, and southern Asia Minor and in the Greek peninsula. During the mid-first century his evangelism had taken him from the first communities of Christians in Palestine and Syria as far as the northern frontier regions in the Balkans, 'from Jerusalem and round about as far as Illyricum' (Rom 5: 19). Paul's writings were even more influential, in particular the letters addressed collectively or individually to the churches he had helped found in these regions. Eventually his letters were included in the canon of the New Testament, along with the Gospels and Acts of the Apostles. As a result, while the Gospels of course highlighted Jesus' ministry in Palestine, much of the rest of the New Testament represented the concerns of early Christian communities in Asia Minor and Greece. Asia Minor in particular retained its vital importance in eastern Christianity for centuries, producing several of the major theologians of late antiquity. From the fifth century, however, the eastern Roman Empire began to fragment because of theological controversies and pressure on the frontiers. By the seventh century the heartlands of a Christian Greek Roman Empire were Asia Minor and the eastern coastal regions of the Greek peninsula. The scope of Paul's journeys had been a prescient preview of the contours of the medieval Byzantine Empire.

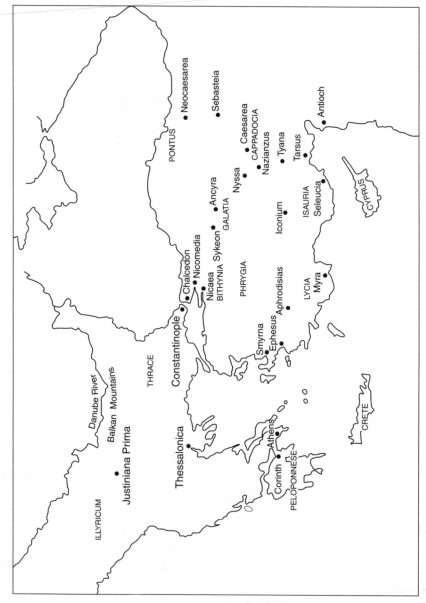

Map 16.1 Greece and Asia Minor

16.1 GREEKNESS AND ROMANNESS

Despite Paul's activities, in the early Roman Empire Christian communities were not widespread in Asia Minor, and were even less common in the Greek peninsula. When Ignatius, bishop of Antioch, travelled to Rome in the early second century, he visited a few communities in south central and western Asia Minor. Since at the time there were quite likely fewer than 10,000 Christians in the entire Roman world (Hopkins 1998), these were probably still the only Christian communities in Asia Minor.

Two centuries later, Christianity was prominent enough that when the emperor Diocletian initiated persecution of the Christians at Nicomedia in 303, he could watch the destruction of the cathedral, 'which was visible from the palace' (Lactantius, *Mort.* 12. 3). The fundamental ancient narrative of the gradual rise of early Christianity in the eastern provinces is the *Ecclesiastical History* by Eusebius, bishop of Caesarea in Palestine. Eusebius's *History* started with Jesus and concluded with the emperor Constantine's establishment of his rule over the eastern provinces in 324. Because he organized the history of early Christianity around distinct themes, and because he cited important documents verbatim, many modern accounts of early Christianity continue to follow his lead. As a result, the greatest challenge for writing the history of early Christianity (and not just in Asia Minor and Greece) is to escape Eusebius's confessional viewpoint.

One way of emending Eusebius's perspective is by incorporating additional evidence. For this early period archaeology offers little: there are few material remains for early Christianity in Greece and Asia Minor (Frend 1996). In contrast, epigraphy, the study of inscriptions, has been very rewarding. Under Roman rule cities and villages in Greece and Asia Minor were littered with thousands of inscriptions, including records of municipal decisions, lists of honours for local notables, dedications to gods, tombstone epitaphs, and copies of imperial edicts and rescripts. Christians also erected dedications and epitaphs, and almost every epigraphical catalogue includes Christian inscriptions. Over the past century the scholarship on these inscriptions in Asia Minor and Greece has been magnificent. Louis Robert, the greatest epigrapher of the twentieth century, focused on the Greek East, and scholars have edited extensive catalogues for cities and regions (Lane Fox 1987). For enhancing our understanding of early Christianity in Asia Minor the rewards of sorting through these collections can be impressive; the best example is the outstanding synthesis in Mitchell (1993: ii. 37–51). In Asia Minor some rural Christian communities are known only through their inscriptions. In the region south of Iconium the number of inscriptions using Christian formulae and images, and presumably the number of Christians, increased dramatically during the third century. In southern Phrygia one group used the 'Eumeneian formula' that left grave-robbers to God's judgement. In western Phrygia another sect distinguished its dedications with the phrase 'Christians for Christians' (Gibson 1978), and by the later third century a majority of people commissioning gravestones from the local workshops professed to be Christians.

A second tactic for modifying Eusebius's narrative starts with recognizing his use of rhetorical strategies. Like other authors, Eusebius constructed a narrative of the past that reinforced his own notions of theology and ecclesiastical order, while trying to convince his audience of their correctness. Understanding historical narratives as literary texts that used rhetorical strategies can help reinterpret one of Eusebius's favourite themes, the linear development of orthodoxy. The rugged topography of Asia Minor, especially in the interior, encouraged the appearance of isolated local varieties of Christianity that jostled for recognition and support. Under Roman rule Asia Minor was an innovative laboratory of Christian diversity and a nursery of conflicting theologies, disparate lifestyles, and new institutions. Well into late antiquity heresiologists were stunned at the 'numerous heresies' that continued to flourish in the central highlands (Epiphanius, *Pan.* 47. 1). Too often modern narratives internalize these categories by likewise disparaging such local Christianities as 'heresies', outdated or exotic sidelines to the inevitable emergence of an institutionalized Church. The most notorious was the 'New Prophecy' of Montanus, who began preaching in the highlands of north-western Phrygia during the later second century. Even though his teachings clearly challenged the emerging ecclesiastical hierarchy of bishops and clerics, Montanist communities were soon widespread throughout central Asia Minor. Different approaches can help illuminate Montanist Christianity. Strobel (1980) focused on topography and the archaeology of various sites; Tabbernee (1997) compiled an excellent collection of Montanist inscriptions; Trevett (1996) closely critiqued and synthesized the largely hostile literary sources. The most promising interpretive approach is by Nasrallah (2003), who evaluates the accusations against this sect as attempts to demarcate proper Christian behaviour and beliefs by imagining the unacceptable behaviour and beliefs of heretical others. Since Montanist Christians were of course engaged in the same process of boundary formation, each variant of Christianity should be defined as a strategy for people to discover individual identities, articulate meaning in ordinary life, and represent both themselves and their communities (King 2003). We can then evaluate these Christianities without prejudging the outcome of disputes over the formation of a sanctioned orthodox version.

This appreciation of the varieties of early Christianity in Asia Minor suggests a final way of reorienting traditional perspectives. Defining Christianity in terms of meanings and representations, rather than simply religious beliefs and doctrines, allows us to compare it with other strategies of constructing identities in the early Roman Empire, and hence to locate Christianity properly in larger social and cultural trends. Christianity was competing not only with other religious cults; its rivals also included political and cultural formulations of identity.

In Asia Minor and Greece two influential options were available in the early Roman Empire. One was in terms of Romanness. Many cities openly acknowledged Roman rule by founding cults and constructing temples in honour of emperors (Price 1984), while some provincial notables held offices in the imperial administration. Another option for finding an identity was in terms of Greekness. Cities had long been the hallmarks of classical Greek culture, and Roman rule encouraged the public life of cities. Cities were the arenas in which local notables would compete for prestige by holding municipal offices and displaying their generosity. Cities often defined their municipal citizenship in terms of participation in traditional cults and religious festivals. Roman emperors and their administrators hence promoted the beneficial ideology of living in cities. In return, learned Greeks inserted Roman emperors and Roman rule into classical mythology and Greek history, in particular during the renaissance of Greek culture known as the Second Sophistic. During the past decade modern historians have rediscovered the significance of this emphasis on language purism and an association with the classical past for creating 'a coherent and recognizable identity for the Greek elite at this time' (Swain 1996: 410).

Christianity in Asia Minor and Greece needs to be evaluated in the context of this Second Sophistic. In comparison to the political activities included in Romanness and the cultural and religious aspects included in Greekness, early Christianity was not an attractive option as a form of self-presentation. This concession has two important implications. One is that Christianity, in all its many local varieties, was readily defined as the opposite of the conventional norms and expectations of Romanness and Greekness. This marginalization was most apparent in sporadic outbreaks of hostility. In the early second century the provincial governor Pliny supported those communities in Bithynia and Pontus that were enforcing their religious boundaries by executing Christians. At Smyrna, Bishop Polycarp was martyred in part because he refused to show any respect for the traditional gods or devotion to the Emperor. The citizens of Smyrna labelled him 'the destroyer of gods', and Christians in general as 'atheists'. In the mid-third century the priest Pionius was executed at Smyrna after an imperial edict ordered everyone to sacrifice. The crowd in the marketplace agreed with this punitive assessment of Christians as outsiders: 'if they do not sacrifice, they are to be punished' (Musurillo 1972; Robert 1994). The conclusion to be drawn from these examples is not that Christianity already had a significant and growing presence in the Roman society of Asia Minor. Instead, in most cases this hostility toward Christians was simply an incidental by-product of boundary maintenance, attempts by cities to continue to define themselves in terms of Romanness and Greekness. As a result, Christianity seemed fated to remain insignificant in Asia Minor, fragmented into many local sects.

The second implication affects how we explain the eventual success of Christianity. As a medium for constructing identities, it could not become more attractive until alternative strategies such as Romanness and Greekness became less appealing. The rise of Constantine as a Christian emperor in the early fourth century was

certainly an important factor for assisting the expansion of Christianity, both geographically into more peripheral regions and socially among municipal notables.
But Constantine's reign itself coincided with a fundamental transformation of the
role and structures of cities in the Greek world. Diocletian and his fellow emperors
had increased the size of the imperial administration and the standing army. To
finance this larger administration and army, they confiscated some of the revenues
of cities. Local Greek notables now faced a dilemma. For centuries they had been
proud to serve as municipal magistrates and priests in their home towns and to
use their own resources to fund games and monuments. In return, their fellow
citizens had commemorated their benefactions in dedications and acclamations.
But after the emperors appropriated municipal resources for imperial expenses,
the responsibilities of municipal service became a financial burden. From the early
fourth century many local notables were looking to avoid municipal offices (Jones
1964: 712–66).

Emperors now offered opportunities to evade these obligations. Local aristocrats
could make careers by holding offices in the inflated imperial administration; others
could become secretaries in the civil ministries. Constantine's inauguration of Constantinople was an invitation for thousands of provincial elites in each generation to
become senators in the new capital. Holding high office and acquiring membership
in the senate of Constantinople conferred immunity from municipal service. So did
service as a bishop or a cleric. As a result, from the fourth century in Asia Minor,
most of the known bishops with known backgrounds were local notables who
would otherwise have been expected to serve as municipal magistrates and private
benefactors (Jones 1964: 920–9; Eck 1978). Both pagan emperors like Diocletian
and his colleagues, with their structural changes in the imperial administration,
and Christian emperors like Constantine and his successors, with their extension
of immunities to bishops and clerics, contributed to the transformation of classical
cities into Christian cities (Liebeschuetz 2001). In comparison to both Romanness
and Greekness, political and social changes had helped make Christianity more
attractive as a strategy of self-representation.

16.2 BISHOPS

During the fourth century bishops assumed increasingly more prominent roles in
their cities. In Asia Minor the best-known examples are the famous Cappadocian
fathers, whose careers pointedly indicate that ecclesiastical service had now become
a viable option for young men from aristocratic families. Basil and his younger
brother Gregory of Nyssa were descendants of local notables in Pontus. Their

grandparents had had to go into hiding during the persecutions in the early fourth century; their father was a grammarian at Neocaesarea; they themselves were thoroughly educated in classical culture. After studying at Constantinople and Athens, Basil had devoted himself to theological studies and ecclesiastical affairs, and eventually became metropolitan bishop at Caesarea in Cappadocia during the 370s. Gregory served as bishop at Nyssa in Cappadocia for more than 20 years until his death in the mid-390s, and Peter, another brother from this family, served as bishop at Sebasteia (Fedwick 1979, 1981; Rousseau 1994; McLynn 2001; Van Dam 2003b).

Gregory of Nazianzus's father had been a municipal magistrate at Nazianzus and a member of a local cult. But once he observed all the bishops who travelled across Asia Minor at the summons of the emperor Constantine to attend the Council of Nicaea, he converted to Christianity and in 329 became bishop of his home town. His son Gregory of Nazianzus studied classical culture abroad at Alexandria and Athens. Even though at first Gregory seems to have preferred a career as a scholar, he soon became a priest, assisting his father at Nazianzus. His brother had meanwhile finessed his education in medicine into a position at the imperial court in Constantinople and then a career in the imperial administration. Gregory himself eventually served for a few months in 381 as bishop of Constantinople. After his return to Cappadocia he served briefly as acting bishop at Nazianzus (Bernardi 1995; McGuckin 2001; Van Dam 2003b).

The careers of Basil of Caesarea, his brother Gregory of Nyssa, their friend Gregory of Nazianzus, his cousin Bishop Amphilochius of Iconium, and their heterodox rivals Aetius and Eunomius are uncommonly well documented through their own extensive writings. Even without including the sermons and treatises of John Chrysostom at Constantinople, more than one-quarter of the surviving Greek patristic texts from the fourth century were written by these churchmen from central and eastern Asia Minor. Modern scholarship on the Cappadocian fathers is outstanding. Recent editions of the letters, orations, and autobiographical poems of Gregory of Nazianzus, typically with comprehensive introductions and notes, are available in Sources chrétiennes and the Budé series (Gallay 1964–7; Bernardi 1968; Meehan 1987; Van Dam 1995). Excellent editions of most of the writings of Gregory of Nyssa are available in Gregorii Nysseni Opera; in Sources chrétiennes, the introductions by M. Aubineau to Gregory's *On Virginity* (Aubineau 1966) and by P. Maraval to Gregory's *Life of Macrina* and *Letters* are superb (Maraval 1971, 1990a). Basil of Caesarea has been served less well. The basic edition for most of his homilies is still PG 29, 31. The editions and translations of his letters in the Budé and Loeb series are often unreliable; in contrast, the translation and notes by W.-D. Hauschild (1973–93) and the studies by Gain (1985) and Pouchet (1992) are excellent on the letters. Perhaps the extraordinarily thorough examination of the manuscript traditions by Fedwick (1993–2004) will inspire more new editions.

The writings of the Cappadocian fathers and their peers are the basis for all sorts of studies of Christianity in Asia Minor or, more generally, about the development of theology, spirituality, and monasticism during the fourth century (Meredith 1995). In studies of bishops (for example, most recently, Sterk 2004; Hübner 2005; Rapp 2005) they appear as prominent representatives of larger trends about the rise of monk-bishops and their combination of secular duties and spiritual authority. In fact, the availability of so much information focused on these regions for only a few decades poses several problems of historical interpretation.

One concern in evaluating these careers is not to take their prominence for granted. Churchmen had many powerful competitors. Emperors and their court magistrates visited Cappadocia frequently as they journeyed between Constantinople and Antioch. But before Theodosius most eastern emperors did not support Nicene Christianity, and their meetings with local bishops such as Basil and Gregory of Nazianzus's father were consistently confrontational (Van Dam 1986). Provincial governors were often more concerned about their reputations at court than with local affairs, and bishops constantly prodded them on behalf of local citizens (Van Dam 2002; Slootjes 2006). Grammarians and rhetoricians retained their prestige as guardians of classical culture (Kaster 1988), while wealthy local landowners might take advantage of food shortages to enhance their own reputations as generous benefactors (Coulie 1985; Daley 1999; Holman 2001). In response, although bishops could appeal to a moral high ground, most did not have adequate resources, either grain or accumulated wealth, to compete with these powerful regional patrons. As long as Roman rule was effective, as long as Greek culture remained attractive, as long as local aristocrats could deploy their wealth in benefactions, bishops struggled to assert their authority.

A second interpretive issue is the possibility of generalization. How typical were the careers and experiences of the Cappadocian fathers? During the entire fourth century only a few men actually served as bishops in each city. Unlike the imperial administration, in which provincial governors and other magistrates might serve for only a year or two, bishops had lifetime tenure. Between the death of Constantine in 337 and the accession of Theodosius in 379 only three or four bishops served at Caesarea. At Nazianzus, Gregory's father was bishop for 45 years and was eventually succeeded by a relative. Since particular families might dominate sees for decades, service as a bishop was not a particularly realistic goal (Van Dam 2003a: 53–71). In addition, bishops faced competition from alternative ecclesiastical hierarchies. In some cities, most notably Constantinople and Antioch, there were sometimes two or three rival bishops representing different theological communities; the supporters of the heresiarch Eunomius appointed regional bishops in Asia Minor (Kopecek 1979; Vaggione 2000). Lifetime tenure and competition between rival bishops, furthermore, restricted any smooth expansion of episcopal authority.

A final interpretive concern is the impact of Christianity on Greek and Roman society. Even though the transition was gradual, the relentless spread of Christianization was powerfully disruptive in traditional society. One good example is the invention of new legends and new histories. In previous centuries cities in

Asia Minor and Greece had promoted foundation stories and traditional rituals that provided links to the famous myths and historical events associated with Greekness and Romanness. Many had claimed gods like Zeus or Hercules or mythological heroes like Jason and the Argonauts as their founders. Other cities would commemorate their ties to conquerors like Alexander the Great or more recent Roman emperors (Harl 1987). Well into the later Roman Empire, Athens prided itself as a citadel of Greek classical culture. Even Jerome stopped to see the famous statue of Athena on the Acropolis.

During the fourth century, however, many Greek cities wanted to become part of a Christian history. Gregory of Nyssa claimed that the centurion who had stood at the foot of Jesus' cross later introduced Christianity to Cappadocia. He also described the activities of Gregory Thaumaturgus ('the Wonder-worker'), a student of the famous theologian Origen, who had returned to convert the region of Pontus and serve as bishop of Neocaesarea in the mid-third century. In this case a legend about a popular saint also conveniently bolstered the prominence of his own family, since one of his grandmothers had memorized the sayings of Gregory Thaumaturgus and passed on the stories to her descendants (Van Dam 1982; Mitchell 1999). Cities also commemorated martyrs, in particular those who had suffered during the persecutions under Diocletian and his successors, such as the famous Forty Martyrs of Sebasteia. Heterodox Christian communities likewise invented legends. At Ancyra in the mid-fourth century Montanist Christians commemorated their own martyrs (Mitchell 1982); in the early sixth century Novatianist Christians accounted for their prominence in north-western and central Asia Minor by composing a *Life* of a local martyr (Foss 1987). During late antiquity the making of so many new Christian histories, for families, cities, and the Church in general, contributed to the loss of many older Greek and Roman traditions, legends, and shrines (Van Dam 2003a: 72–97).

This new sense of history was also apparent in the building of churches. Many were overt commentaries on the rise of a Christian society. At Ephesus a market basilica was rebuilt as a large church dedicated to the Virgin Mary, and a huge church dedicated to St John overshadowed a relic of the past, the famous temple of Artemis (Foss 1979; Karwiese 1995). At Athens a new church was constructed in the courtyard of the library of Hadrian, north of the Acropolis. At about the same time in the mid-fifth century Christians removed the celebrated statue of Athena from the Parthenon (Frantz 1988; Fowden 1990). At Thessalonica the rotunda that had once been intended as the mausoleum of the emperor Galerius, a noted persecutor of Christianity, was converted into a large church in the mid-fifth century. At Aphrodisias at about the same time, the pagan temple of Aphrodite was rebuilt into a cathedral dedicated to the archangel Michael (Cormack 1990). In Asia Minor and Greece modern scholars can examine the construction of new Christian histories, in literary texts and in monumental shrines, from the rubble of old memories of paganism, persecution, and martyrdom.

After Constantine's reign Christianity became the dominant religion in Asia Minor and Greece, in large part because it now comprised more than beliefs, doctrines, and liturgy. It also offered careers as bishops or clerics, an outlet for local charity, and a sense of tradition and history for cities. These were impressive accomplishments. But to temper any overstatement, we modern historians still need to acknowledge the alternatives to, the limits on, and the outright disruptive impact of Christianity. We need to forget the future and again hold our breath about the outcome of the process. We need to appreciate the ambitions of the emperor Julian, who was certainly not convinced that the reign of his uncle Constantine had changed everything. Julian was a contemporary of the Cappadocian fathers, and had even grown up in Cappadocia. But as emperor he rejected the Christianity of his boyhood. As he travelled through central Asia Minor in 362, he hoped to enhance the effectiveness of Roman rule and the vitality of Greek cities by reviving traditional cults and funding municipal priesthoods. At Ancyra he would have seen the new church, the crowds of poor people in its courtyard waiting to receive daily rations, and the patients in a hospital staffed by monks (Foss 1977). Perhaps as a reaction to these signs of the manifest success of Christians, Julian now encouraged the local priests in Galatia to construct hostels for the assistance of strangers and the poor, and he offered to contribute grain and wine. But precisely at that moment of extravagance Julian seems to have sensed that he could not return to the past, because as a model for their generosity he encouraged these priests to imitate the charity of Christians (Van Dam 2002: 159–80). As a cultural system of identity and meaning, Christianity had now trumped both Romanness and Greekness.

16.3 New Rome but Greek Empire

One of Constantine's most durable innovations was the inauguration of Constantinople in 330. As a residence for emperors who were concerned about both the Balkans and the eastern frontier, as the centre for many departments of imperial administrators, the foundation of Constantinople suggested the possibility of forming an eastern empire that combined Romanness, Greekness, and Christianity (Dagron 1974).

The presence of Constantinople soon became the most important factor in shaping Christianity in the Greek East. Contemporaries already noticed its detrimental impact as it siphoned away the resources of the eastern Mediterranean. Notables from the provinces moved to the new capital to serve in its senate, monuments in the provinces were scavenged for building supplies, and much of the grain from Egypt that had been sent to Rome was now diverted to Constantinople. The excellent studies of Dagron (1984), Mango (1985), and Bassett (2004) have furthermore shown how this new capital appropriated a suitable history. The importation of numerous statues and celebratory monuments located Constantinople in classical Greek mythology and history and associated it with the foundation legends of Rome itself. Once a small garrison, Constantinople now became a leading Roman and Greek city.

It also became a leading ecclesiastical city. The Council that met at Constantinople in 381 pointedly acknowledged the new capital as 'New Rome', and designated a 'seniority of honour' for its bishop, 'second only to the bishop of Rome'. The bishops of other great cities in the eastern Mediterranean, in particular Alexandria and Antioch, had to swallow their pride, because this council furthermore limited their authority while leaving the bishops of Constantinople with priority in Asia Minor and much of the Greek peninsula. A canon of the Council of Chalcedon in 451 reaffirmed this priority by bestowing upon the 'archbishop' of Constantinople the formal power to consecrate the metropolitan bishops in Thrace and most of Asia Minor.

Churches in Asia Minor and the Greek peninsula now had to deal with the influence of Constantinople. One issue was meddling by its bishops, for which the formidable tenure of John Chrysostom in the late fourth and early fifth centuries set the tone (Liebeschuetz 1990; Kelly 1995). A related issue was the seductiveness of the big city, as bishops and clerics often travelled to the capital to attend councils, meet the archbishop and his clerics, and greet the Emperor and his magistrates at court. Just as local notables from the provinces moved to the capital to serve in the senate or imperial ministries, so many provincial churchmen took up permanent residence at or in the vicinity of Constantinople. In the early fifth century, Philostorgius, a native of Cappadocia (Van Dam 2003a), and Sozomen, a native of Palestine, moved to the capital, where each wrote a continuation of Eusebius's *Ecclesiastical History* (Urbainczyk 1997). At about the same time, Hypatius, a native of Phrygia, founded a monastery near Chalcedon (Dagron 1970; Bartelink 1971). Alexander, a native of an Aegean island, first lived as a monk in the borderlands on the eastern frontier before he returned to found a monastery in the middle of Constantinople (Caner 2002). Daniel was born in a village near Samosata on the eastern frontier. In the mid-fifth century he moved to Constantinople and took up residence on top of a column, in imitation of the famous Symeon the Stylite (Lane Fox 1997). Many relics were also imported from the provinces, including the remains of the prophet Samuel, the apostle Andrew, the evangelist Luke, and the missionary Timothy, and the head of John the Baptist. Eventually Constantinople acquired so many relics and shrines that it seemed to have become the capital of a biblical and ecclesiastical holy land, even 'Second Jerusalem' (*Life of Daniel the Stylite*, 10). With the support of the resident emperors, the bishops of Constantinople imposed their ecclesiastical leadership by vacuuming up resources, including young men and relics, from the eastern provinces.

But not everyone admired the growth of Constantinople as New Rome and New Jerusalem. The most notable characteristic of Christianity in Asia Minor and

Greece during the fifth and sixth centuries was the tension between Constantinople and outlying regions and cities. This tension was especially apparent in the great doctrinal controversies over Christology. Just as earlier arguments over orthodoxy and heresy had been disputes over identity and authority, so these new controversies should be interpreted as idioms for articulating the ecclesiastical role of emperors and the relative power of bishops. Through a discourse over Christology, people tried to imagine the contours of a distinctively eastern empire.

First, the bishops of Constantinople soon learned the limits of their influence. John Chrysostom was sent into exile, in part because of hostility from Bishop Theophilus of Alexandria, many bishops in Asia Minor, and monks at Constantinople. A generation later, Bishop Cyril of Alexandria engineered the deposition of Bishop Nestorius of Constantinople, ostensibly over disagreements about Christological doctrines. At the Council of Ephesus in 449, Bishop Dioscorus of Alexandria presided over the deposition of Bishop Flavianus of Constantinople. These confrontations split bishops and their communities in Asia Minor. In Cappadocia the bishop of Caesarea, who had supported Cyril, tried to depose the neighbouring bishop of Tyana, who had supported Nestorius (Calvet-Sebasti and Gatier 1989). The Council of Chalcedon in 451 attempted to find a suitable doctrinal accommodation. Predictably, this compromise was itself contested. When the bishop of Side hesitated to sign, a deacon punched him repeatedly in the head (Zacharias of Mytilene, *Hist. eccl.* 3. 1).

Second, both Asia Minor and the Greek peninsula were caught in the doctrinal crossfire. After 451 emperors were typically associated with Chalcedonian theology, and sometimes tried to impose a uniform orthodoxy by proposing accommodation with anti-Chalcedonian (Monophysite) Christians. But some of the loudest opponents of the authority of Constantinople were churchmen from Syria, Palestine, and Egypt. Because of their influence, many bishops in central and western Asia Minor, most notably at Ephesus, were likewise often anti-Chalcedonian (Frend 1972). During the sixth century, churchmen were very active in promoting Monophysite doctrines throughout Asia Minor and even at Constantinople. At Tralles the Egyptian bishop John of Hephaestopolis once ordained fifty priests in the upper gallery of a church during the celebration of a Chalcedonian service in the nave below. During the mid-sixth century Jacob Baradaeus was more often on the road than in his see of Edessa, visiting much of Asia Minor and some of the Aegean islands. John of Ephesus, whom Jacob consecrated as bishop, in turn claimed to have transformed seven synagogues into churches and converted 80,000 pagans throughout western and central Asia Minor; he also recorded all these examples (Brooks 1923–5). As a result of these initiatives, more bishops and congregations in Asia Minor adopted the anti-Chalcedonian cause (Honigmann 1951; Métivier 2005). The communities of Asia Minor hence had to choose between an alignment with Constantinople to the north and alignment with centres like Antioch and Alexandria to the south.

The Greek peninsula was likewise caught in the middle. Since the Council of Chalcedon had also evaluated the doctrines of Pope Leo, it highlighted the tension over the ecclesiastical jurisdiction of Rome and New Rome. After the Council, the bishops of Rome often objected to attempts by eastern emperors to accommodate anti-Chalcedonian churchmen. In 535 Pope Agapetus tried to assert authority over cities in the Balkan region, including Justiniana Prima, the home town of the emperor Justinian. At the end of the sixth century, Pope Gregory still claimed jurisdiction over several metropolitan sees in Greece (including Corinth and Thessalonica), and even over Crete. The bishops and congregations of the Greek peninsula hence had to choose between alignment with Constantinople to the east and alignment with Rome to the west.

A third manifestation of this discourse over the role of Constantinople and the identity of an eastern empire concerned the authority of emperors in these doctrinal controversies, and also in general ecclesiastical affairs. Even though he made some theological concessions to the anti-Chalcedonian position, the emperor Justinian was especially forceful in promoting Chalcedonian unity during his long reign in the mid-sixth century. In particular, Justinian tried to reassert both his imperial authority and the centrality of Constantinople through his patronage for building projects. Outside Myra in Lycia he contributed to the reconstruction of the church of St Nicholas (Ševčenko and Ševčenko 1984; Foss 1991). At Ephesus he replaced the dilapidated church in honour of St John with an enormous church that included a large enclosed courtyard. This new church was as much a tribute to the Emperor as a memorial to the Evangelist, since inside one fresco depicted the Emperor receiving his crown from the Saint (Foss 1979: 88–94). Justinian's most notable constructions were of course at Constantinople, which he hardly ever left during his long reign. Here his crowning achievement was the great church of Hagia Sophia ('Holy Wisdom'). With its soaring dome and exquisite decoration, this glorious church was such an architectural masterpiece that it seemed to symbolize the uncontested eminence of Constantinople. In reality, however, doctrinal disputes had alienated many regions of the eastern empire from the emperors and their courts. In the perspective of dissident churchmen, New Rome was still just an upstart see well into the sixth century.

Modern scholarship has been inadequate in investigating these dynamics of ecclesiastical life in Asia Minor and the Greek peninsula. Because theological controversies dominated church history after the Council of Chalcedon, modern studies tend to focus on Constantinople at the centre, as well as Rome, Syria, and Egypt. We need more new research on the local varieties of Christianity in Asia Minor and Greece during the fifth and sixth centuries. The archaeology of various cities can be one important source. The volumes in *Tabula Imperii Byzantini* provide encyclopaedic coverage of regions in Greece and Asia Minor; the best synthetic studies are by Foss (1990, 1996). Literary sources are scattered, and there is regrettably no narrative equivalent to Eusebius's *Ecclesiastical History* or concentration of prominent bishops like the Cappadocian fathers. But one of the intriguing characteristics of the stray surviving texts about local communities is their apparent lack of interest in the grand theological controversies. Theodore of Sykeon, a bishop in Galatia, visited Constantinople and Jerusalem several times before his death in 613; but according to his *Life*, he seemed blissfully unaware of current doctrinal disputes (Festugière 1970; Mitchell 1993: ii. 122–50).

Just as scholars should correlate the rise of early Christianity with structural changes in classical cities, likewise they need to investigate the impact of pressure on the frontiers in resolving these tensions about the prominence of Constantinople and the authority of Christian emperors in ecclesiastical affairs. In the East, invasions by Persian armies threatened cities in eastern, central, and even western Asia Minor. By defending the eastern frontier in the early seventh century, the emperor Heraclius also extended the influence of imperial Christianity, and anti-Chalcedonian Christianity seems to have lost much of its appeal in Asia Minor. On the northern frontier the Slavs and Avars were infiltrating the Balkans and the Greek peninsula, even as far south as the Peloponnese. Only divine assistance protected some cities. According to tradition, Thessalonica owed its defence to its patron St Demetrius, 'who rode a white horse and wore a white cloak. Everyone recognized him as the commander of a heavenly army' (Lemerle 1981; Skedros 1999). By the beginning of the seventh century, the settlements of the Slavs and Avars had diminished the influence of the popes in the Balkans. Constantinople was now the uncontested capital, political and ecclesiastical, of the cities in Asia Minor and Greece still under Roman control.

16.4 PAUL'S SHOES

After his journeys throughout the Greek world, the apostle Paul had sailed off into the sunset, where tradition claimed he was martyred in Rome. Over the centuries he was known primarily as a western saint, associated in particular with the prestige of the popes. In the Greek world, in contrast, there were few memorials of Paul's significance as an early evangelist. At Seleucia, in Isauria, a beautiful shrine commemorated Thecla, a young girl whom legends had turned into Paul's disciple (Dagron 1978; Davis 2001). But Paul himself was largely forgotten. When the pilgrim Egeria stopped at this shrine in the early 380s, she wanted to read only about St Thecla. Having just visited the Holy Land in Palestine, she discovered no comparable holy land of pilgrimage shrines that commemorated the footsteps of Paul in the Greek world.

In the early fifth century, a marble box was unearthed at Paul's home-town of Tarsus. This box contained the shoes 'in which Paul had walked as he preached the word of God' (Silverstein and Hilhorst 1997: 68). Paul's journeys had in fact been unexpectedly successful, and under Roman rule Asia Minor and Greece had become strongholds of Christianity. But modern scholars should ponder why, over the centuries, communities did not claim Paul as a founder or patron saint. As an evangelist who was also a Roman citizen and a Greek intellectual, Paul would have been a natural model for later Christians in Asia Minor and Greece who were still trying to incorporate Romanness and Greekness into a Christian eastern empire.

SUGGESTED READING

For the history of Christianity in Greece and Asia Minor before Constantine, the most important source is Eusebius's *Ecclesiastical History*, available in several English translations. His narrative can be supplemented with more or less contemporary texts, such as the letters of Pliny and accounts of martyrdoms, and various retrospective accounts, such as Gregory of Nyssa's *Life of Gregory Thaumaturgus*.

The voluminous writings of the three Cappadocian fathers dominate the fourth century. NPNF has assigned a volume each to Basil of Caesarea, Gregory of Nyssa, and Gregory of Nazianzus; other English translations of various treatises are available in ACW, FC, and LCL. The French translations in SC and Budé and the German translations in Bibliothek der griechischen Literatur include excellent introductions and are typically well annotated.

For Constantinople in the late fourth century the extensive writings of John Chrysostom are essential. Socrates, Sozomen, and Theodoret of Cyrrhus wrote continuations of Eusebius's *Ecclesiastical History* into the early fifth century. Thereafter the literary sources are sporadic. They include the letters of Bishop Firmus of Caesarea in the first half of the fifth century, the Acts of the ecumenical councils, the imperial laws collected in the *Justinian Code*, and the Novels, the new edicts, of the emperor Justinian. The *Lives* of various saints, including Hypatius at Chalcedon, Alexander and Daniel at Constantinople (Dawes and Baynes 1948), Athenogenes at Pedachthoe (Maraval 1990*b*), Theodore at Sykeon, and the Monophysite heroes memorialized by John of Ephesus, are especially useful as regional narratives.

Ecclesiastical history needs to be better integrated with scholarship on Greek and Roman society. Outstanding examples of such a more comprehensive perspective include Mitchell (1993), on Christianity in central Asia Minor, and Dagron (1974), on the impact of Constantinople. Van Dam (2002, 2003*a*, *b*) uses the writings of the Cappadocian Fathers and their peers to discuss not only the place of Roman rule and Greek culture in a newly Christian society, but also the personal dynamics of families and friendships. Jones (1964) remains the most important and most durable overview of the administration and institutions of the later Roman Empire, including the Church.

BIBLIOGRAPHY

Tabula Imperii Byzantini = volumes in Österreichischen Akademie der Wissenschaften, philosophisch-historische Klass, Denkschriften (Vienna: Verlag der Österreichischen Akademie der Wissenschaften):

Vol. 1: J. Koder and F. Hild, *Hellas und Thessalia*, Bd. 125 (1976).

Vol. 2: F. Hild and M. Restle, *Kappadokien (Kappadokia, Charsianon, Sebasteia und Lykandos)*, Bd. 149 (1981).

Vol. 3: P. Soustal, *Nikopolis und Kephallenia*, Bd. 150 (1981).

Vol. 4: K. Belke, *Galatien und Lykaonien*, Bd. 172 (1984).

Vol. 5: F. Hild and H. Hellenkemper, *Kilikien und Isaurien*, 2 vols., Bd. 215 (1990).

Vol. 6. P. Soustal, *Thrakien (Thrake, Rodope und Haimimontos)*, Bd. 221 (1991).

Vol. 7: K. Belke and N. Mersich, *Phrygien und Pisidien*, Bd. 211 (1990).

Vol. 8: H. Hellenkemper and F. Hild, *Lydien und Pamphylien*, Bd. 320 (2004).

Vol. 9: K. Belke, *Paphlagonien und Honorias*, Bd. 249 (1996).

AUBINEAU, M. (1966) (ed. and trans.), *Grégoire de Nysse: Traité de la virginité*, SC 119 (Paris: Éditions du Cerf).

BARTELINK, G. J. M. (1971) (ed. and trans.), *Callinicos: Vie d'Hypatios*, SC 177 (Paris: Éditions du Cerf).

BASSETT, S. (2004), *The Urban Image of Late Antique Constantinople* (Cambridge: Cambridge University Press).

BERNARDI, J. (1968), *La prédication des Pères Cappadociens: le prédicateur et son auditoire* (Paris: Presses universitaires de France).

—— (1995), *Saint Grégoire de Nazianze: le théologien et son temps (330–390)* (Paris: Éditions du Cerf).

BROOKS, E. W. (1923–25) (ed. and trans.), *John of Ephesus: Lives of the Eastern Saints*, PO 17. 1, 18. 4, 19. 2 (Paris: Firmin-Didot).

CALVET-SEBASTI, M.-A., and GATIER, P.-L. (1989) (ed. and trans.), *Firmus de Césarée: Lettres*, SC 350 (Paris: Éditions du Cerf).

CANER, D. (2002), *Wandering, Begging Monks: Spiritual Authority and the Promotion of Monasticism in Late Antiquity*, The Transformation of the Classical Heritage, 33 (Berkeley: University of California Press).

CORMACK, R. (1990), 'Byzantine Aprodisias: Changing the Symbolic Map of a City', *Proceedings of the Cambridge Philological Society*, 216 NS 36: 26–41.

COULIE, B. (1985), *Les richesses dans l'oeuvre de Saint Grégoire de Nazianze: étude littéraire et historique*, Publications de l'Institut orientaliste de Louvain, 32 (Louvain: Peeters).

DAGRON, G. (1970), 'Les moines et la ville: le monachisme à Constantinople jusqu'au concile de Chalcédoine (451)', *Travaux et Mémoires*, 4: 229–76.

—— (1974), *Naissance d'une capitale: Constantinople et ses institutions de 330 à 451*, Bibliothèque byzantine, Études, 7 (Paris: Presses universitaires de France).

—— (1978) (ed. and trans.), *Vie et miracles de sainte Thècle: texte grec, traduction et commentaire*, Subsidia Hagiographica, 62 (Brussels: Société des Bollandistes).

—— (1984), *Constantinople imaginaire: études sur le recueil des Patria*, Bibliothèque byzantine, Études, 8 (Paris: Presses universitaires de France).

DALEY, B. E. (1999), 'Building a New City: The Cappadocian Fathers and the Rhetoric of Philanthropy', *JECS* 7: 431–61.

DAVIS, S. J. (2001), *The Cult of Saint Thecla: A Tradition of Women's Piety in Late Antiquity* (Oxford: Oxford University Press).

DAWES, E., and BAYNES, N. H. (1948), *Three Byzantine Saints: Contemporary Biographies of St Daniel the Stylite, St Theodore of Sykeon and St John the Almsgiver Translated from the Greek* (London: Basil Blackwell).

ECK, W. (1978), 'Der Einfluß der konstantinischen Wende auf die Auswahl der Bischöfe im 4. u. 5. Jahrhundert', *Chiron* 8: 561–85.

FEDWICK, P. J. (1979), *The Church and the Charisma of Leadership in Basil of Caesarea* (Toronto: Pontifical Institute of Medieval Studies).

—— (1981) (ed.), *Basil of Caesarea: Christian, Humanist, Ascetic: A Sixteen-Hundredth Anniversary Symposium*, 2 vols. (Toronto: Pontifical Institute of Medieval Studies).

—— (1993–2004), *Bibliotheca Basiliana Universalis: A Study of the Manuscript Tradition of the Works of Basil of Caesarea*, 5 vols. (Turnhout: Brepols).

FESTUGIÈRE, A.-J. (1970), *Vie de Théodore de Sykéon*, 2 vols., Subsidia Hagiographica, 48 (Brussels: Société des Bollandistes).

FOSS, C. (1977), 'Late Antique and Byzantine Ankara', *DOP* 31: 29–87.

—— (1979), *Ephesus After Antiquity: A Late Antique Byzantine and Turkish City* (Cambridge: Cambridge University Press).

—— (1987), 'St. Autonomus and His Church in Bithynia', *DOP* 41: 187–98.

—— (1990), *History and Archaeology of Byzantine Asia Minor* (Aldershot: Variorum).

—— (1991), 'Cities and Villages of Lycia in the Life of Saint Nicholas of Holy Zion', *Greek Orthodox Theological Review*, 36: 303–39.

—— (1996), *Cities, Fortresses and Villages of Byzantine Asia Minor* (Aldershot: Variorum).

FOWDEN, G. (1990), 'The Athenian Agora and the Progress of Christianity', *JRA* 3: 494–501.

FRANTZ, A. (1988), *The Athenian Agora: Results of Excavations Conducted by the American School of Classical Studies at Athens*, xxiv: *Late Antiquity: A.D. 267–700* (Princeton: American School of Classical Studies at Athens).

FREND, W. H. C. (1972), *The Rise of the Monophysite Movement* (Cambridge: Cambridge University Press).

—— (1996), *The Archaeology of Early Christianity: A History* (Minneapolis: Fortress Press).

GAIN, B. (1985), *L'église de Cappadoce au IVe siècle d'après la correspondance de Basile de Césarée (330–379)*, OrChrAn 225 (Rome: Pontificium Institutum Orientale).

GALLAY, P. (1964–7) (ed. and trans.), *Saint Grégoire de Nazianze: Lettres*, 2 vols. (Paris: Les Belles Lettres).

GIBSON, E. (1978), *The 'Christians for Christians' Inscriptions of Phrygia: Greek Texts, Translation and Commentary*, HTS 32 (Missoula, Mont.: Scholars Press).

HARL, K. (1987), *Civic Coins and Civic Politics in the Roman East A.D. 180–275* (Berkeley: University of California Press).

HAUSCHILD, W.-D. (1973–93) (trans.), *Basilius von Caesarea: Briefe*, Bibliothek der griechischen Literatur, 3 vols., Abteilung Patristik 3, 32, 37 (Stuttgart: A. Hiersemann).

HOLMAN, S. R. (2001), *The Hungry are Dying: Beggars and Bishops in Roman Cappadocia* (Oxford: Oxford University Press).

HONIGMANN, E. (1951), *Evêques et évêchés monophysites d'Asie anterieure au VIe siècle*, CSCO 127, Subsidia 2 (Louvain: L. Durbecq).

HOPKINS, K. (1998), 'Christian Number and Its Implications', *JECS* 6: 185–226.

HÜBNER, S. (2005), *Der Klerus in der Gesellschaft des spätantiken Kleinasiens*, Altertumswissenschaftliches Kolloquium, 15 (Stuttgart: Steiner).

JONES, A. H. M. (1964), *The Later Roman Empire 284–602: A Social, Economic and Administrative Survey* (Oxford: Basil Blackwell; Norman, Okla.: University of Oklahoma Press).

KARWIESE, S. (1995), 'The Church of Mary and the Temple of Hadrian Olympius', in H. Koester (ed.), *Ephesos: Metropolis of Asia: An Interdisciplinary Approach to Its Archaeology, Religion, and Culture*, HTS 41 (Valley Forge, Pa.: Trinity Press International), 311–19.

KASTER, R. A. (1988), *Guardians of Language: The Grammarian and Society in Late Antiquity* (Berkeley: University of California Press).

KELLY, J. N. D. (1995), *Golden Mouth: The Story of John Chrysostom—Ascetic, Preacher, Bishop* (London: Duckworth).

KING, K. L. (2003), *What is Gnosticism?* (Cambridge, Mass.: Harvard University Press).

KOPECEK, T. A. (1979), *A History of Neo-Arianism*, 2 vols., PMS 8 (Cambridge, Mass.: Philadelphia Patristic Foundation).

LANE FOX, R. (1987), *Pagans and Christians* (New York: Knopf).

—— (1997), 'The *Life of Daniel*', in M. J. Edwards and S. Swain (eds.), *Portraits: Biographical Representation in the Greek and Latin Literature of the Roman Empire* (Oxford: Clarendon Press), 175–225.

LEMERLE, P. (1981) (ed.), *Les plus anciens recueils des miracles de saint Démétrius et la pénétration des Slaves dans les Balkans*, 2 vols. (Paris: Centre National de la Recherche Scientifique).

LIEBESCHUETZ, J. H. W. G. (1990), *Barbarians and Bishops: Army, Church, and State in the Age of Arcadius and Chrysostom* (Oxford: Clarendon Press).

—— (2001), *Decline and Fall of the Roman City* (Oxford: Oxford University Press).

MANGO, C. (1985), *Le développement urbain de Constantinople (IVe–VIIe siècles)*, Travaux et Mémoires du Centre de recherche d'histoire et civilisation de Byzance, Collège de France, Monographies, 2 (Paris: Diffusion de Boccard).

MARAVAL, P. (1971) (ed. and trans.), *Grégoire de Nysse: Vie de sainte Macrine*, SC 178 (Paris: Éditions du Cerf).

—— (1990*a*) (ed. and trans.), *Grégoire de Nysse: Lettres*, SC 363 (Paris: Éditions du Cerf).

—— (1990*b*) (ed. and trans.), *La passion inédite de S. Athénogène de Pédachthoé en Cappadoce*, BHG 197b, Subsidia Hagiographica, 75 (Brussels: Société des Bollandistes).

McGUCKIN, J. A. (2001), *St. Gregory of Nazianzus: An Intellectual Biography* (Crestwood, NY: St Vladimir's Seminary Press).

McLYNN, N. (2001), 'Gregory Nazianzen's Basil: The Literary Construction of a Christian Friendship', StPatr 37: 178–93.

MEEHAN, D. M. (1987) (trans.), *Saint Gregory of Nazianzus: Three Poems, Concerning His Own Affairs, Concerning Himself and the Bishops, Concerning His Own Life*, FC 75 (Washington: Catholic University of America Press).

MEREDITH, A. (1995), *The Cappadocians* (London: Geoffrey Chapman; Crestwood, NY: St Vladimir's Seminary Press).

MÉTIVIER, S. (2005), *La Cappadoce (IVe–VIe siècle): une histoire provinciale de l'empire romain d'Orient*, Byzantina Sorbonensia, 22 (Paris: Publications de la Sorbonne).

MITCHELL, S. (1982), 'The Life of Saint Theodotus of Ancyra', *Anatolian Studies*, 32: 93–113.

—— (1993), *Anatolia: Land, Men, and Gods in Asia Minor*, 2 vols. (Oxford: Clarendon Press).

—— (1999), 'The Life and *Lives* of Gregory Thaumaturgus', in J. W. Drijvers and J. W. Watt (eds.), *Portraits of Spiritual Authority: Religious Power in Early Christianity, Byzantium and the Christian Orient*, Religions in the Graeco-Roman World, 137 (Leiden: Brill), 99–138.

MUSURILLO, H. (1972), *The Acts of the Christian Martyrs*, OECT (Oxford: Clarendon Press).

NASRALLAH, L. S. (2003), *'An Ecstasy of Folly': Prophecy and Authority in Early Christianity*, HTS 52 (Cambridge, Mass.: distributed by Harvard University Press).

POUCHET, R. (1992), *Basile le Grand et son univers d'amis d'après sa correspondance: une stratégie de communion*, Studia Ephemeridis 'Augustinianum', 36 (Rome: Institutum Patristicum Augustinianum).

PRICE, S. R. F. (1984), *Rituals and Power: The Roman Imperial Cult in Asia Minor* (Cambridge: Cambridge University Press).

RAPP, C. (2005), *Holy Bishops in Late Antiquity: The Nature of Christian Leadership in an Age of Transition*, The Transformation of the Classical Heritage, 37 (Berkeley: University of California Press).

ROBERT, L. (1994), *Le martyre de Pionios prêtre de Smyrne*, ed. G. W. Bowersock and C. P. Jones (Washington D.C.: Dumbarton Oaks Research Library and Collection).

ROUSSEAU, P. (1994), *Basil of Caesarea*, The Transformation of the Classical Heritage, 20 (Berkeley: University of California Press).

ŠEVČENKO, I., and ŠEVČENKO, N. P. (1984) (eds. and trans.), *The Life of Saint Nicholas of Sion*, The Archbishop Iakovos Library of Ecclesiastical and Historical Sources, 10 (Brookline, Mass.: Hellenic College Press).

SILVERSTEIN, T., and HILHORST, A., (1997), *Apocalypse of Paul: A New Critical Edition of Three Long Latin Versions*, Cahiers d'Orientalisme, 21 (Geneva: P. Cramer).

SKEDROS, J. C. (1999), *Saint Demetrios of Thessaloniki: Civic Patron and Divine Protector 4th–7th Centuries CE*, HTS 47 (Harrisburg, Pa.: Trinity Press International).

SLOOTJES, D. (2006), *The Governor and His Subjects in the Later Roman Empire*, Mnemosyne, Supplements, 275 (Leiden: Brill).

STERK, A. (2004), *Renouncing the World Yet Leading the Church: The Monk-Bishop in Late Antiquity* (Cambridge, Mass.: Harvard University Press).

STROBEL, A. (1980), *Das heilige Land der Montanisten: Eine religionsgeographische Untersuchung*, Religionsgeschichtliche Versuche und Vorarbeiten, 37 (Berlin: de Gruyter).

SWAIN, S. (1996), *Hellenism and Empire: Language, Classicism, and Power in the Greek World AD 50–250* (Oxford: Clarendon Press).

TABBERNEE, W. (1997), *Montanist Inscriptions and Testimonia: Epigraphic Sources Illustrating the History of Montanism*, PMS 16 (Macon, Ga.: Mercer University Press).

TREVETT, C. (1996), *Montanism: Gender, Authority and the New Prophecy* (Cambridge: Cambridge University Press).

URBAINCZYK, T. (1997), *Socrates of Constantinople: Historian of Church and State* (Ann Arbor: University of Michigan Press).

VAGGIONE, R. P. (2000), *Eunomius of Cyzicus and the Nicene Revolution* (Oxford: Oxford University Press).

VAN DAM, R. (1982), 'Hagiography and History: The Life of Gregory Thaumaturgus', *CA* 1: 272–308.

—— (1986), 'Emperor, Bishops, and Friends in Late Antique Cappadocia', *JTS* NS 37: 53–76.

—— (1995), 'Self-Representation in the Will of Gregory of Nazianzus', *JTS* NS 46: 118–48.

—— (2002), *Kingdom of Snow: Roman Rule and Greek Culture in Cappadocia* (Philadelphia: University of Pennsylvania Press).

—— (2003a), *Becoming Christian: The Conversion of Roman Cappadocia* (Philadelphia: University of Pennsylvania Press).

—— (2003b), *Families and Friends in Late Roman Cappadocia* (Philadelphia: University of Pennsylvania Press).

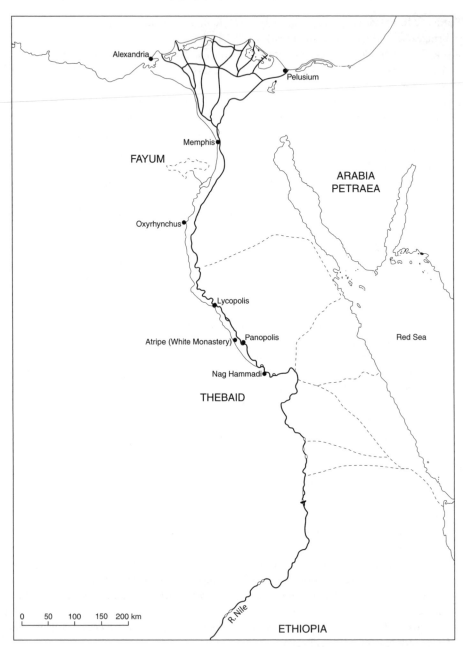

Map 17.1 Egypt

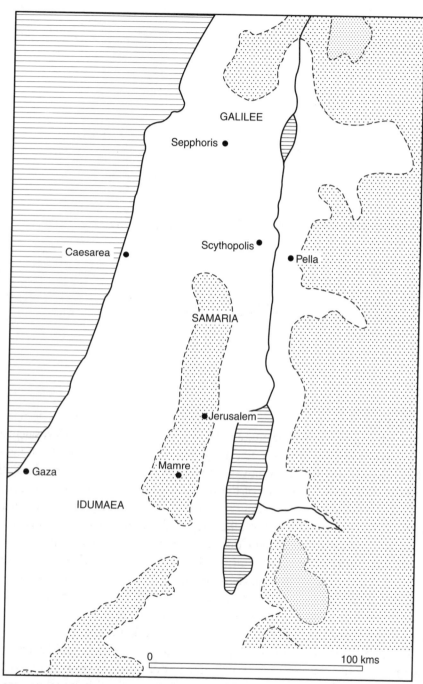

GALILEE

Sepphoris ●

Caesarea ─● Scythopolis ● ● Pella

SAMARIA

●Jerusalem

● Mamre ●

● Gaza

IDUMAEA

0   100 kms

Map 17.2 Palestine

CHAPTER 17

THE EAST (2): EGYPT AND PALESTINE

DAVID BRAKKE

FEW if any regions in which ancient Christianity thrived capture the modern imagination in the same way as Palestine and Egypt, whose famous cities (Jerusalem and Alexandria) and equally famous desert regions provided the settings for Jesus and his first followers and later for innovative theologians and legendary monks. Rather than attempt a thorough survey of the issues in, and sources for, the histories of Christianity in Egypt and Palestine, this chapter focuses on problems or themes that shape the current study of both these regional varieties of ancient Christianity. Despite the numerous significant differences between Egypt and Palestine and between the courses that Christianity took in them, the churches in these areas shared common features. In both cases, forms of Christianity originated as forms of Judaism, but scholars continue to debate how Christianity emerged from local Judaisms and how Jews and Christians continued to interact throughout the early period. The formidable Origen spent his career and left his mark in both Egypt and Palestine, which were later troubled by disputes over 'Origenism'. Monasticism took root in both areas, where it contributed in different ways to reconfigurations of sacred space and to processes of Christianization. Finally, although both regional churches initially opposed the Council of Chalcedon of 451, in the end Palestine became Chalcedonian and Egypt emerged as a centre of anti-Chalcedonian theology.

17.1 CHRISTIAN ORIGINS AND JUDAISM

The origins of Christianity in Palestine may seem simple enough: it was here that, around 30 CE, the Jews who had followed Jesus of Nazareth first believed that the crucified Jesus had risen from the dead as God's messiah ('anointed one'). But our earliest account of Christianity's birth comes from Paul, more than 20 years after the event: c. 55 CE he describes for his followers in Corinth a series of appearances of the risen Jesus that began with an appearance to Cephas (Peter?) and concluded with one to Paul himself (1 Cor 15: 3–11). The Gospels and the Acts of the Apostles, which date to the last three decades of the first century, present contradictory accounts of the discovery of the empty tomb and the appearances of Jesus to his followers in Judaea and Galilee (Mt 28: 1–20; Mk 16: 1–8; Lk 24: 1–53; Jn 20: 1–21: 25; Acts 1: 1–11): their reports reflect differences among early Christian groups about which founding figures carried the greatest authority (Peter, Mary Magdalene, the 'Beloved Disciple' of the Fourth Gospel). The authors of these works looked back at the early days and at Jesus' own ministry from a time when the distance between the believers of Jesus ('Christians') and their fellow Jews was much greater than it had been in the preceding decades.

Despite these problems, scholars continue to mine the Gospels especially for information about the earliest Christian communities in Palestine and for their relationships and eventual break with other Jewish groups. The Gospel of Matthew is often seen as the product of a Jewish–Christian community in Palestine or Syria engaged in debate with other Jewish groups over how to follow the Torah in the aftermath of the Temple's destruction in 70 CE (Saldarini 1994; Meeks 2002: 127–31). In an influential study, Theissen (1978) sifted through traditions in the Synoptic Gospels, including those associated with the hypothetical sayings source Q, to develop a picture of earliest Palestinian Christianity as centred around wandering charismatics who preached the approaching judgement in imitation of Jesus the Son of Man and were supported by more settled, household-based groups. Because Q, if it existed, likely originated before 70, it is a crucial source for reconstructing earliest Christianity in Palestine, but scholars debate intensely what they learn from it. Some find in its eschatological orientation and emphasis on Jesus as Son of Man evidence that the early Christians resembled other Palestinian Jews who looked forward to an imminent and dramatic intervention by God and the establishment of a new 'kingdom of God' ('apocalyptic eschatology'); but other scholars claim to be able to discern earlier strata in Q that indicate an originally non-apocalyptic movement, which focused on Jesus as a manifestation of God's Wisdom (Mack 1993; Tuckett 1992, 1996). This debate centres in large part on the extent of Hellenized urbanism in first-century Galilee and its effects on Jesus and his followers (Batey 1991; Chancey 2002).

The Gospel of John, if it originated in Palestine, as many scholars believe, appears to present a clear and compelling picture of one Christian community's origination in and separation from a Jewish community. Anachronistic references to followers of Jesus being 'expelled from the synagogue' (Jn 9: 22; 16: 2) have suggested that a story like that of the blind man in chapter 9, although it purports to relate an incident from the ministry of Jesus, in fact shows that early acclamations of Jesus as a miracle worker and prophet became increasingly radical (Jesus is 'equal to God'; Jn 5: 18) as Jewish leaders pressured their followers to choose between their teaching of Torah ('Moses') or adherence to Jesus. Such conflicts in the emerging (not yet normative) synagogues of Palestine led to breaks between believers in Jesus and other Jews (Martyn 2003; Meeks 2002: 91–105, 116–23). Although few scholars now believe that the so-called benediction against the heretics can be used to support a scenario in which 'the synagogue' expelled the Christians in the last decade of the first century, the general case that the Johannine community broke with a Jewish group has been widely accepted (see D. M. Smith in Martyn 2003: 20–2). Boyarin (2002, 2004) challenges parts of this theory and uses John's understanding of Jesus in terms of Word and Wisdom to argue against any definitive separation between 'Christians' and 'Jews' before the fourth century. In general, how theological motifs and social indicators in our sources should affect our picture of emerging Judaism and Christianity in Palestine and other regions remains an important area for scholarly investigation (Wilson 1995).

Our knowledge of Christianity in Palestine through the end of the second century remains sketchy (Wilken 1992: 84–5). Eusebius reports that during the First Jewish Revolt (66–70) Christians in Jerusalem fled to Pella on the eastern side of the Jordan (*Hist. eccl.* 3. 5. 3; Wehnert 1991; Murphy-O'Connor 1995). At the end of the Bar Kochba Revolt in 135, Hadrian levelled Jerusalem, expelled Jews from it, and founded a new city, Aelia Capitolina. Christians, especially Jewish ones, must have been affected by these events, but they were, of course, not confined to Jerusalem. When controversy broke out toward the end of the second century over the date of Easter, the bishop of Caesarea Maritima, Palestine's leading city in the post-70 era (Levine 1975), presided along with his colleague from Aelia Capitolina over a synod on this question (Eusebius, *Hist. eccl.* 5. 23. 3). Otherwise, our sources provide little information about Palestinian Christians before Origen's arrival in Caesarea around 234.

Origen came to Palestine from Alexandria in Egypt; ancient sources provide little information about the advent of Christianity in this major city. Eusebius claims that Mark was the apostle who first preached in Alexandria (*Hist. eccl.* 2. 16), but his report has problems, and Eusebius otherwise knows little about the Christian community there before the emergence of Clement of Alexandria (c. 180) (Davis 2004: 2–17). Clement himself tells us nothing about how Christianity came to his city. Walter Bauer, in a landmark book (1971; German original 1934), explained this silence simply: the earliest Christian community in Alexandria was Gnostic in character, and later proto-orthodox writers like Clement and Eusebius either do not know about these early Gnostic Christians or purposefully fail to mention them. The 1945 discovery in Egypt of the Nag Hammadi codices, which contain many writings that scholars consider Gnostic, appeared to support Bauer's hypothesis.

But Roberts (1977) presented scholars with a powerful argument against Bauer's view: Egyptian Christianity's earliest surviving papyri and manuscript fragments do not show a greater proclivity for 'heterodox' theology than in other regions, and he instead argued that an interest in divine names (*nomina sacra*) suggest a connection to Palestinian Judaism. Nearly all scholars now agree that Alexandrian Christianity originated in a mission from Palestinian Jewish Christianity, and that the earliest Christians there may not have differed too much from Alexandrian Jews like Philo (d. 45 CE). Many point to the devastating Roman repression of a Jewish revolt in 115–17, after which evidence for Alexandrian Jewry disappears until the fourth century, as the moment when Christians took on an identity clearly separate from Jews. The anti-Jewish polemics in a work like the *Epistle of Barnabas*, hypothetically assigned an Alexandrian provenance, and aspects of the thought of the Christian teacher Basilides (*c.* 130) may have resulted from Christians' effort to differentiate themselves from non-Christian Jews (Dawson 1992: 171–6; Pearson 1986; 2004: 82–99; Layton 1989).

Even if one accepts the hypothesis of Jewish origins for Alexandrian Christianity, questions still remain. Was the revolt of 115–17 as decisive a moment as scholars have believed? How did the works of Philo exert their obvious influence on Christians like Clement and Origen? Did they only read his books, or did some Jewish-Christian tradition continue from the first into the second and even third centuries? Even if Bauer was incorrect about a Gnostic origin for Alexandrian Christianity, many of the earliest Alexandrian Christians about whom we have information (Basilides, Theudas, Valentinus) appear to have been learned scholars who had contact with Gnostics or at least with their ideas (if one accepts the existence of Gnostics in antiquity, itself a vexed question) (Layton 1989). How, then, do these Christian philosophers and their study circles fit into a picture of Christianity originating in Judaism?

However one imagines the origins of Christianity in Palestine and Egypt in relationship to the Judaisms of those regions, 'Jewish–Christian relations' surfaces as a significant issue in the study of both of these areas in later centuries. In Egypt the paucity of evidence for Jewish life after 115–17 makes it difficult to contextualize references to Jews in Christian sources (Haas 1997: 91–127). During the fourth century, anti-Jewish rhetoric appears frequently in the writings of Bishop Athanasius of Alexandria (bishop 328–73), and sources report that Jews participated in the violent clashes that marred this controversial bishop's tenure (Brakke 2001). Bishop Cyril of Alexandria (bishop 412–44) engages in even more heated polemic against Jews (Wilken 1971), and the church historian Socrates reports that in 415 he led a violent campaign against Jewish synagogues in the city, forcing many Jews to leave (*Hist.*

eccl. 7. 13). Without much evidence from the Jewish side, scholars vigorously debate whether to understand these Christian attacks on Jews as serving merely rhetorical ends, with 'Jews' meaning primarily biblical characters or imagined enemies, or as indicating real interchange between Christians and a revived Jewish community.

In Palestine the situation is clearer and more complex. Unlike Alexandria, Palestine provides plenty of evidence for the persistence of a large and lively Jewish community throughout our period, led by an official patriarch (Avi-Yonah 1976; Schwartz 2001). After the Christian scholar Origen moved from Alexandria to Palestinian Caesarea in 234, he refers to his contact with Jewish intellectuals and the knowledge he gained from local Jews in his scholarship and disputes with other Christians. Origen's writings provide scholars with information about real social contact between Jews and Christians in the third century (Bietenhard 1974; De Lange 1976). Origen interacted with Jews from what he perceived as a position of weakness: Christians like him were an oppressed minority, ruled by the Romans and fewer and less respected than the Jews (at least in his context) (Jacobs 2004: 60–7). Conditions changed dramatically in the fourth century, when Constantine converted to Christianity and initiated imperial support for the construction of churches and other buildings at the holy places in Jerusalem and elsewhere in Palestine. Christians now sought to remake Palestine as a Christian Holy Land and so to displace Jews from their ancient land both on the ground and in religious ideology, but Jewish life and institutions remained vibrant (Stemberger 2000). As Christians like Jerome wrote about local Jews, they now did so from positions of power that conflated Christian and imperial interests. Jacobs (2004) uses insights from post-colonial criticism to gain new leverage on the question of whether Christian literature from this period provides accurate representations of relations between Jews and Christians: by taking seriously the power imbalance in the new Christian Empire, Jacobs argues that Christian anti-Jewish rhetoric created a reality that both constrained Palestinian Jews and gave them openings for resistance. Because scholarship on Jews and Christians in late ancient Palestine requires extensive linguistic and archaeological skills, many studies focus primarily on one community or the other. Scholars in Israel have emerged as pioneers in developing a more comprehensive view of religious life in ancient and Byzantine Palestine (Kofsky and Stroumsa 1998).

17.2 ORIGEN AND 'ORIGENISM'

During the ancient period no figure dominates the theology and politics of Christianity in both Egypt and Palestine more than Origen (*c.* 185–*c.* 253) (Crouzel 1989; Trigg 1983, 1998). This brilliant Christian scholar set the agenda for theological discussion and became the focus of bitter conflicts in both regions. Historians typically see Origen as the quintessential Alexandrian, embodying that city's long tradition of scholarship and intellectual creativity. This view is true enough, but perhaps historians of Christianity have not appreciated sufficiently that the bishop of Alexandria expelled Origen from that city, while he received ordination and support (as well as continued criticism) in the Palestinian city of Caesarea Maritima.

In its Alexandrian context Origen's career raises questions about the character of institutional Christianity there. Eusebius reports that Bishop Demetrius appointed Origen the head of an official catechetical school, an auxiliary of the episcopate that Eusebius traces back to the middle of the second century. The historicity and character of this catechetical school have been subject to much scholarly discussion in the modern period. Eusebius identifies Pantaenus as the first head of the school, and claims that he was succeeded by Clement and then by Origen (*Hist. eccl.* 6. 6). Most scholars doubt this scenario: they are uncertain what to say about the shadowy Pantaenus, and most agree that Clement did not head an official school operating under episcopal sanction, but guided small groups of interested Christians as a fully independent teacher. On this view, second-century Alexandrian Christianity would have been characterized by a number of Christian study circles representing a variety of theological perspectives and directed by philosophers like Clement, who had to legitimate his teaching activities (Dawson 1992: 219–22; Buell 1999). Although there must have also been communities led by what we would call clergy, a monarchical bishop with city-wide authority did not emerge until Demetrius in the last decades of the century.

According to this reconstruction, Demetrius actually established a school with more formal ties to the bishop and appointed Origen as its first leader, in order to secure some episcopal control over Christianity's intellectual life. The clash between Demetrius and Origen, which resulted in Origen leaving the city, reflected not only a dispute over doctrine but also a conflict between two Christian cultures, academic and episcopal, and their values. Some scholars see this tension as never quite resolved in Alexandria's Christian community, surfacing again in the conflict between Bishop Alexander and the presbyter-teacher Arius in the early fourth century (Williams 2002; Brakke 1994). Still, many scholars accept only portions or even none of this view of early Christian Alexandria and Origen's place in it. Some scholars continue to think that Clement may have headed a formal Christian school, if not precisely what Eusebius describes (van den Hoek 1997), and others challenge the distinction between academic and episcopal modes of spirituality (Gregg 1989). Clement's position within Alexandrian Christianity and the character of groups like the Gnostics and the Valentinians remain fertile areas of study, which provide the context out of which the remarkable Origen emerged.

When he left Alexandria, Origen found an intellectual and spiritual home among the Christians of Caesarea Maritima (Crouzel 1989: 24–33). There, even as he preached regularly as a presbyter (his many sermons come from this period), Origen established a new school, and that institution, along with Origen's vast library, helped Caesarea to emerge as a major Christian intellectual centre to rival Alexandria. Gregory the Wonder-worker's *Address of Thanksgiving to Origen*, delivered when Gregory finished his studies under Origen in 238, suggests that Origen's school was not a catechetical school or any other official auxiliary of the Church, but an independent competitor for students of all religious stripes in a multicultural city, although Origen's curriculum intended to lead the student to the ultimate truth in Christ (Gregory Thaumaturgus, *Panegyric on Origen*; Knauber 1968; Crouzel 1970). The career of Bishop Eusebius of Caesarea (*c.* 260–339) represents the Palestinian city and Origen's influence at their height: heir to Origen's thought, as well as his library, Eusebius became a prodigious scholar, influential theologian, and formidable politician (Barnes 1981: 81–188). His *Martyrs of Palestine* provides crucial information about Christian communities in pre-Nicene Palestine, as does his *Onomasticon*, which also lists known biblical sites that pre-date Constantine's building programme and marks a significant step toward the conception of Palestine as a Christian Holy Land (Groh 1983).

In his own day and ever since, Origen's theology has been controversial. Origen's tendency to float ideas without really committing to them and the incomplete transmission of his works sometimes make it difficult to be precise about what Origen taught, and thus scholars continue to debate, for example, how Origen envisioned the resurrection and whether he taught that the final return of all creatures to God could be followed by another fall (Armantage 1970; Scott 1991). Some of these differences reflect the degree to which scholars are willing to trust the Latin translations of works that do not survive in the original Greek: did translators like Rufinus of Aquileia spin Origen's texts in a more 'orthodox' direction (e.g. Rist 1975)? Origen also serves as a flashpoint for discussing the relationship between the Christian gospel and Hellenistic culture, especially Platonism. Construing these two things as essentially different can lead to the charge that Origen was more a Platonist than a Christian or was *a*—if not *the*—primary agent of Christianity's 'Hellenization'. Recent scholarship has worked hard to undermine these rigid categories, and so to place Origen in a more complex intellectual setting in which neither Christianity nor Platonism ever existed in a pure, unmixed form (Lyman 1993: 10–81; Edwards 2002).

Such modern debates often echo ancient conflicts over 'Origenism', which flared in both Egypt and Palestine. The so-called first Origenist controversy arose in the late fourth century and persisted into the early fifth: its major players included the bishops of Jerusalem and Alexandria as well as prominent ascetics in the monastic communities in and near those cities. Charging that someone taught 'Origenist' doctrines such as the pre-existence of souls and a non-physical resurrection became a way to discredit an opponent and even to have him excommunicated. Clark (1992) stresses both theological and social factors in the controversy's origin and persistence. On the one hand, she shows that persons in the conflict tended to divide based on already formed social ties, suggesting that the conflict had as much to do with competing networks of friendship and patronage as with theological convictions. On the other hand, she argues that, although the precise meaning of 'Origenism' shifted over decades of controversy, authors did focus on real disagreements over the status of the physical body, the nature of God's image in humanity, and the relative weight of human free will and God's grace. Still, the motives of many players in the early conflict remain murky, especially those of Bishop Theophilus of Alexandria, who first supported and then opposed so-called Origenist monks in their dispute with so-called anthropomorphite monks (Lazzati 1935; Favale 1958; Clark 1992: 44–58, 105–21). Golitzin (2002, 2003) has tried to uncover the exegetical and spiritual roots of both 'Origenist' and 'anthropomorphite' views, with important implications for what the conflict reveals about the nature of early monastic spirituality in Egypt and Palestine. In particular, scholars consider the possibility that the teachings of Evagrius Ponticus (d. 399) lay behind much of this first controversy, even though his name is not mentioned by anti-Origenists (Clark 1992: 61–84).

It seems clear that Evagrius's works did play a role in the second Origenist controversy, which arose among monasteries in Palestine, and culminated in the condemnations of Origen and Evagrius at the Council of Constantinople in 553 (Diekamp 1899; Guillaumont 1962). Correspondence of the sixth-century monastic teachers Barsanuphius and John reveals that Palestinian monks differed on how and even whether the monk could read Evagrius, who had developed the most sophisticated theory of the monastic life in late antiquity, one highly indebted to the thought of Origen (Binns 1994: 201–2). Although several of the early monasteries in Jerusalem and its immediate suburbs had been founded by Christian intellectuals for whom scriptural study and theological inquiry were valued activities (e.g. Jerome, Rufinus, Melania the Elder), the laura monasteries in the nearby desert appear to have been divided from their early years between monks with and without such scholarly proclivities. Precisely why the conflict arose and became as virulent as it did may never be fully known, but it seems likely that a failure of the leadership in the Great Laura resulted in the formation of a group of intellectually inclined monks at the New Laura. Attracted to the theologies of Origen and Evagrius but, even more, simply interested in theological work as such, these monks coalesced into a genuine faction under the intellectual leadership of Nonnus and Leontius of Byzantium. A power struggle ensued, which was resolved by the Council of 553 (Binns 1994: 201–17). Origen was still a prominent name in Palestinian Christianity some three centuries after his death.

17.3 A CHRISTIAN LAND: MONASTICISM, SACRED SPACE, AND CHRISTIANIZATION

When the emperor Constantine began to direct imperial support toward the Christian churches in the early fourth century, he helped to accelerate a process of remaking the territories of Egypt and Palestine into Christian space. In both of these regions monasticism and pilgrimage played important roles in creating sacred space and in converting worship sites and people from traditional religion to Christianity ('Christianization'), and similar problems of sources and methodology attend the study of these phenomena. On the other hand, differences in topography and Palestine's unique status as the site of biblical events gave these processes different characters.

The sources for and problems in studying monasticism in general are discussed in Chapter 24, but students of Egyptian and Palestinian Christianities will want to attend to the specific ways in which monastic movements emerged and interacted with other forms of Christian life in the two regions (Chitty 1966). The ideology of Egyptian monasticism was shaped by the stark difference between the arable land along the Nile and in the Delta, on the one hand, and the inhospitable desert, on the other. Even though many monks lived in and alongside cities and villages, the stark visual contrast between 'world' and 'desert' gave monastic groups an aura of distance that bishops and monastic leaders tried hard to bridge. Recent scholarship has undermined any simple scenario that would trace distinct forms of monastic life to individual founders; rather, beginning in the second half of the third century, Christians experimented with a variety of forms of 'withdrawal', which evolved, solidified, or disappeared in the centuries that followed (Goehring 1999). It was not clear at first how monastic groups should relate to local episcopally led communities and to the bishop of Alexandria, Egypt's patriarch. Scholars now study how monastic and episcopal authorities negotiated their relationships in the fourth and following centuries, a process in which Athanasius played a key role. The situation was complicated by the Melitian Schism, which in part expressed a gap between Alexandria and southern Egypt (Brakke 1995; Martin 1996). The Alexandrian patriarchate established and maintained its authority in the face of monastic challenges and Melitian opposition by presenting itself as ascetic in character and patronizing monastic groups (Davis 2004: 43–84).

In Palestine too, monastic life took diverse forms and had no single point of origin. Although numerous monks in Egypt came there from elsewhere, in Palestine ascetic Christians from other regions played a much more significant role in founding monasteries and shaping their characters. Latin-speaking Christians from the West such as Rufinus, Melania, Jerome, and Paula created and led large monastic communities in and around Jerusalem: their extensive literary and political contacts throughout the Mediterranean situated their ascetic endeavours within theological and ecclesiastical politics from the start (Kelly 1975: 129–40). Starting at the turn of the fifth century, a wave of migration from monastic communities in Egypt brought Egyptian monastic traditions to Gaza and other areas of southern Palestine, which became the centre for the transmission and consolidation of the *Apophthegmata Patrum*, or *Sayings of the Desert Fathers* (Regnault 1981; Bitton-Ashkelony and Kofsky 2000). In comparison to the Egyptian scene, the relative proximity to Jerusalem of major monasteries in the desert region between the hills of Judaea and the Dead Sea meant that traffic between 'desert' and 'city' was constant. And unlike the bishop of Alexandria, the bishop of Jerusalem had in his counterpart in Caesarea a formidable rival to his claims of primacy within his region. The holy city of Jerusalem, its bishop, and the nearby monasteries rose in prominence together and in relationship to one another (Sivan 1990).

In both Egypt and Palestine, then, monastic communities helped to create a new sacred topography. In Egypt the desert provided a contrast with 'the world', rendering 'the city' (whether Alexandria or Panopolis or any other city) morally ambiguous, and generating a myth of 'the desert' that granted great moral prestige to the monk and naturalized certain Christian notions of virtue by planting them in the landscape (Goehring 2003). Monastic sources, however, often refer to the Judaean desert in which vast numbers of Palestinian monks lived as 'the desert of the Holy City', configuring Jerusalem not as the desert's natural opposite but as its political and spiritual centre (Hirschfeld 1992: 10). These different monastic views of space help to explain the distinct ways in which controversies such as conflicts over Chalcedon proceeded in these two regions, and they must have had a range of effects still awaiting scholarly exploration.

Pilgrimage to holy sites in Jerusalem and elsewhere provided Palestinian monasticism with a significant mission and organizing principle, as well as a constant stream of new recruits. Many factors contributed to the rise of holy sites and pilgrimage in Christian piety during the fourth century (Bitton-Ashkelony 2005: 17–29), but Constantine's decision to fund the building of churches at caves associated with the nativity, crucifixion, and ascension of Jesus accelerated the creation of a Christian Holy Land in Palestine, which rapidly drew pilgrims from all over the Christian world (Hunt 1982; Wilken 1992: 101–25; see Chapter 40). Christian sources appear to indicate that already before Constantine's conversion a few Jews and Christians had identified some locations of biblical events and visited them for pious reasons (Wilken 1992: 108–11), although controversy surrounds this point (Taylor 1993; Bitton-Ashkelony 2005: 17–29). Yet any such pre-Constantinian holy sites were few in comparison with the numerous foundations of the fourth and fifth centuries. The impact of large-scale pilgrimage on Palestinian Christianity must have been extensive, and provides many areas for further study. In ecclesiastical politics, the stature of Jerusalem's bishop increased dramatically, making him a rival to the bishop of Caesarea Maritima, previously the dominant see in Palestine (Walker 1990: 52–7; Rubin 1996, 1999). Bishop Cyril of Jerusalem (bishop 350–87) clashed repeatedly with Bishop Acacius of Caesarea and vigorously promoted the special status of Jerusalem, exploiting the emerging cult of the Cross in particular (Drijvers 2004: 35–41, 153–76). Pilgrims brought with them not only their prayers and devotion, but also their money, providing a ready source of income for churches and monasteries alike (Avi-Yonah 1958). The emperor Julian's aborted plan to rebuild the Jewish Temple in the early 360s must have caused Jerusalem's Christians great anxiety, but sources are lacking; scholars debate the authenticity of a newly discovered letter on this topic that purports to be from Cyril himself (Brock 1977; Wainwright 1986; Drijvers 2004: 127–52). Although it could not match the prestige of the Holy Land, Egypt developed its own network of holy places and pilgrimage destinations, rooted in the veneration of martyrs and inclusive of living and deceased monks (Frankfurter 1994, 1998a; Frank 2000; Davis 2001).

Christian holy places—and the monks who staffed them and hosted their pilgrims (Hirschfeld 1992: 196–200)—proved to be engines of Christianization, especially by giving a new Christian focus to previously pagan or Jewish sites or by providing a new Christian idiom for traditional religious practices. For example, in southern Palestine, Mamre, associated with Abraham (Gen 13–18), functioned as a regional cult centre whose festival attracted Jews, Christians, and pagans. The evidence for Mamre's multi-religious appeal may be unique, but literary hints as well as evidence of archaeological continuity suggest that, although many of the new holy sites were new discoveries, others had long been revered by Jews or pagans or both. Thus the creation of a Christian Holy Land was not so much the imposition of a foreign topography on a previously 'secular' landscape as the creation of a new network of locative piety through the transformation of pre-existing regional cults as well as the foundation of new centres (Kofsky 1998). Scholars increasingly recognize the persistence of traditional religions ('paganism') at the local level even in the Christian 'Holy Land' (Geiger 1998).

An emphasis on the local dimension of late ancient religion characterizes the most recent innovative work on what scholars have called 'Christianization' in Egypt and Palestine. Trombley (1993–4) looks at the big picture and tends to treat traditional non-Jewish and non-Christian religion as a single entity ('Hellenic religion'), co-opted by a single Christianity; it contains authoritative analysis of anti-pagan legislation and studies Christianization in Palestine and Egypt through such major sources as Mark the Deacon's *Life of St. Porphyry of Gaza* and Eunapius of Sardis's *Lives of the Sophists*. Frankfurter (1998b), on the other hand, examines local and regional religious practices as settings in which people received, adapted, and transformed larger religious ideologies ('Hellenism' and 'Christianity') and makes use of anthropological models of cultural interaction and change. Wipszycka (1988) likewise emphasizes the local and uneven character of Christianization. Recent studies of Christianization in Caesarea and Scythopolis in Palestine make use of both literary and archaeological evidence to describe local change (Holum 2003; Tsafrir 2003). Scholars will most likely always need to move back and forth between comprehensive and local perspectives, but the regional approach gives a better sense of how late ancient religiosity was always regionally distinctive. There continued to be 'Egyptian' ways of addressing divine powers, rooted in long habits of mind and specific local concerns, even as those ways increasingly expressed themselves in Christian terms.

In both contexts monks played important roles in Christianization and have gained a reputation for violently destroying temples and attacking people. Holy men and monks doubtless both led and participated in violence against non-Christians and their worship sites (Gaddis 2005: 151–250), but scholars point out that Palestinian monks at times participated also in more peaceful religious interaction (Perrone 1998), and that Egyptian monks displayed a range of attitudes toward pagan temples (Brakke 2006: 216–26). In fact, although the violent desecration of non-Christian temples and cult objects is readily documented (Caseau 2001), it is difficult to discern precisely how many pagan worship structures were destroyed or dramatically converted to Christian use; most likely fell into neglect before they were torn down or renovated for new purposes (Hahn *et al.*, in press). The monastic prophet or holy man might violently confront traditional religion, but he could also act as a facilitator of more gradual religious change (Brown 1995; Frankfurter 2000, 2003). The dossier of the monastic archimandrite Shenoute of Atripe (*c.* 350–465) provides rare firsthand documentation of a monk's often violent campaign against traditional religion in his context (Emmel 2002, in press). Shenoute's writings are so valuable because most studies of holy space, monasticism, and Christianization must rely on hagiographic accounts like Mark the Deacon's *Life of St. Porphyry of Gaza* (Van Dam 1985; Rubin 1998). Hagiography's penchant for stereotypes and biblical typologies and its didactic purposes pose numerous challenges to the historian who wishes to reconstruct actual events, while it may still serve as a rich source for the values of monks and their admirers (Bagnall 1993: 7–8; Gaddis 2005: 153–60; Brakke 2006: 222–3; Frankfurter 2007: forthcoming).

17.4 CHRISTOLOGY AND EMPIRE

As in all the regions of the eastern Mediterranean, the histories of Christianity in Egypt and Palestine in the fifth and sixth centuries are dominated by the controversies over Christology, and in particular over the Council of Chalcedon in 451. Scholars continue to debate how to understand the theological conflict and to account for the enduring schism that it produced, and the reader should turn to Chapter 43 for a fuller treatment of these issues. Here, however, the salient point is that Palestine and Egypt ended up on opposite sides of the schism over Chalcedon. Although in the decades after Chalcedon most Palestinian Christians rejected the council, and anti-Chalcedonian groups never disappeared, Palestine eventually accepted Chalcedon. The Egyptian church, in contrast, remained solidly anti-Chalcedonian, despite enduring pockets of support for the council and several Chalcedonian or 'wobbly' patriarchs. Few scholars now consider anti-Chalcedonianism to have been primarily a function of emerging 'nationalist' sentiments in regions such as Syria and Egypt (Jones 1959), but significant regional differences in the character and history of Christianity must be considered as factors in understanding the differing outcomes of the Chalcedonian conflict in Egypt and Palestine (Frend 1972: 66–79).

The steadfast rejection of Chalcedon in Egypt appears to have been predictable in terms of theological tradition and monastic solidarity. The Christology of 'one nature' that Chalcedon rejected had deep roots in the teachings of the Alexandrian bishops Athanasius and Cyril, which emphasized the dramatic salvific results of the Word of God's incarnation in the flesh (Roldanus 1968; McGuckin 1994; Keating 2004). Cyril's success at wrapping himself in the mantle of Athanasian orthodoxy made him an icon for Egyptian Christians (Wessel 2004). Although advocates of the Chalcedonian Definition argued that their theology was faithful to the thought of both Athanasius and Cyril, Egyptians were not convinced; rather, they saw the Definition as a rejection of their theological heritage and spirituality of divination through contact with the incarnate Word. With a few exceptions, the large and powerful monastic communities, their immense prestige enhanced by the Egyptian myth of the desert, supported the anti-Chalcedonian cause and provided rallying points for Egyptian Christians (Frend 1972: 79–83 and *passim*). A minority of monks in the Pachomian federation, based primarily at the northern monastery at Canopus, supported Chalcedon and provided an opening for the emperor Justinian to remove their leader and replace him with a pro-Chalcedonian, leading to the federation's dissolution. The resolutely anti-Chalcedonian White Monastery federation led by Shenoute of Atripe consequently replaced the Pachomian koinonia in the imagination of subsequent Coptic Christianity (Goehring 2006).

On the other hand, the often bewildering history of the Egyptian church and the frequently divided Alexandrian patriarchate up to the Arab conquest should not be seen simply as the attempt of an external imperial power to force its will on a uniformly resistant Coptic church. Stephen Davis (2004: 85–128) persuasively describes intervention by the imperial pro-Chalcedonian church in Egyptian Christianity as 'a form of ecclesiastical colonialism'. Borrowing insights from studies of modern colonialism, Davis argues that Coptic resistance to Chalcedonian imperial authority was a 'multi-faceted process of cultural negotiation', involving forms of compromise and complicity, and shaping new elite systems and lines of communal identity along ethnic, linguistic, and religious lines. This interpretive approach keeps theological and non-theological dimensions to the conflict in play, and even ties them more closely together, and it provides a fresh perspective on how Coptic Christians dealt with rival imperial powers such as the Persians and the Muslims when they appeared on the scene.

Precisely why the Palestinian church, in contrast, eventually embraced the Chalcedonian position has been less fully explored (Perrone 1980). The immediate reaction to Chalcedon in Palestine was overwhelmingly negative, and the Jerusalem patriarchate suffered the same kinds of exiles, forced candidates, and rival claimants as plagued Alexandria. The patriarch of Jerusalem enjoyed his primacy only after a long period of rivalry with another see, Caesarea (Rubin 1996), and thus did not function as the symbol for an entire region as did his Alexandrian counterpart. Certainly another factor was the enormous imperial investment in the network of holy places—not simply wealth (although that was significant) but also prestige or cultural capital. Funded by imperial patronage and built at imperial initiative, the holy places broadcast the emperor's Christian piety and generosity. (The pro-Chalcedonian Chitty (1966: 114) opined that 'the power of the Holy Places' helped Palestinian Christians maintain 'a sober historical Faith'.) Unlike Egypt, the church in Palestine did not have the same theological stake in the conflict. Although pro- and anti-Chalcedonian beliefs were genuinely held and debated, there was no core Palestinian theological tradition embodied in iconic figures (like Cyril of Alexandria in Egypt) that Chalcedon appeared to endanger. Also in contrast to Egypt, at least one highly prestigious monastic leader immediately supported Chalcedon: Euthymius the Great (377–473), who had founded two monastic communities, withdrew to live as a hermit when most of his fellow monks opposed the council. His tomb was venerated after his death, and even posthumously he provided the basis for a tradition of pro-Chalcedonian monasticism in Palestine (Binns 1994: 184–8).

Binns (1994: 191–9) argues that Palestinian topography and the resulting character of its monasticism helped to make Palestinian Christianity more receptive to imperial promotion of Chalcedonian beliefs. The rugged cliffs of the Judaean desert did not lend themselves to the tight-knit cenobitic communities found especially in southern Egypt; the more decentralized character of Palestinian monasteries fostered theological diversity and inhibited united opposition to imperial authority. More monks in Palestine came from other regions, bringing with them a variety of theological and liturgical traditions and maintaining personal ties to other Chalcedonian areas. Finally, the tradition of a strong connection between the monastic communities and the Jerusalem patriarchate encouraged the monks to move in a Chalcedonian direction once a Chalcedonian bishop was firmly established there.

Although the concept of 'nationalism' may not be a fruitful way to understand the fate of the Council of Chalcedon in various regions, attention to the Chalcedonian struggle in terms of imperial interaction with local cultures, as in the case of Jewish–Christian relations discussed earlier, may provide a promising approach to this period of Christianity in Egypt and Palestine. These regions had experienced different histories of relating to the imperial centre, and thus, despite their shared history, monastic traditions, and initial opposition to Chalcedon, in the end these two venerable and closely connected branches of Christianity took opposing paths.

SUGGESTED READING

The primary sources for ancient Christianity in Egypt and Palestine are too numerous to list here, and the student should consult the *Instrumenta Studiorum* at the end of this book. Still, a good way to access the writings of and bibliography for some of the key figures are the volumes in the series of The Early Church Fathers. Relevant volumes for Egypt and Palestine published thus far include those on Origen (Trigg 1998), Athanasius (Anatolios 2004), Cyril of Alexandria (Russell 2000), Jerome (Rebenich 2002), and Cyril of Jerusalem (Yarnold 2000).

Secondary literature on Alexandrian and Egyptian Christianity is abundant, and many of the best works are in English. Griggs (1990) provides a useful survey of church history in Egypt, but Davis (2004), although focused on the Alexandrian patriarchate, is more up to date. For the early period in Alexandria, Dawson (1992) investigates the key issues, and for the third and later centuries in Alexandria and Egypt three works are essential: Bagnall (1993), Haas (1997), and Frankfurter (1998b). Biographies of Origen (Crouzel 1989 and Trigg 1983) provide good entries into Christianity in both Egypt and Palestine. In comparison to Egypt, Palestine is less well served by secondary literature in English, most of which focuses on the holy places, pilgrimage, and monasticism. Heyer (1984) provides an overall survey in German; such is lacking in English, but Wilken (1992) comes close. Other basic works include Barnes (1981) and Stemberger (2000). Kofsky and Stroumsa (1998) gathers essays that reflect the new sophisticated study of religious interaction in Palestine, and Drijvers (2004) provides a study of Cyril of Jerusalem that goes beyond the usual focus on liturgy and theology.

REFERENCES

ANATOLIOS, K. (2004), *Athanasius* (London: Routledge).

ARMANTAGE, J. W. (1970), 'Will the Body Be Raised? Origen and the Origenist Controversies' (Ph.D. dissertation, Yale University).

AVI-YONAH, M. (1958), 'The Economics of Byzantine Palestine', *Israel Exploration Journal*, 8: 39–51.

——(1976), *The Jews of Palestine: A Political History from the Bar Kokhba War to the Arab Conquest* (New York: Schocken Books).

BAGNALL, R. (1993), *Egypt in Late Antiquity* (Princeton: Princeton University Press).

BARNES, T. D. (1981), *Constantine and Eusebius* (Cambridge, Mass.: Harvard University Press).

BATEY, R. A. (1991), *Jesus and the Forgotten City: New Light on Sepphoris and the Urban World of Jesus* (Grand Rapids, Mich.: Baker Book House).

BAUER, W. (1971), *Orthodoxy and Heresy in Earliest Christianity* (Philadelphia: Fortress Press).

BIETENHARD, H. (1974), *Caesarea, Origenes und die Juden* (Stuttgart: W. Kohlhammer).

BINNS, J. (1994), *Ascetics and Ambassadors of Christ: The Monasteries of Palestine, 314–631* (Oxford: Clarendon Press).

BITTON-ASHKELONY, B. (2005), *Encountering the Sacred: The Debate on Christian Pilgrimage in Late Antiquity* (Berkeley: University of California Press).

—— and KOFSKY, A. (2000), 'Gazan Monasticism in the Fourth–Sixth Centuries: From Anchoritic to Cenobitic', *Proche-Orient Chrétien*, 50: 14–62.

BOYARIN, D. (2002), 'The *Ioudaioi* in John and the Prehistory of "Judaism"', in J. C. Anderson, P. Sellew, and C. Setzer (eds.), *Pauline Conversations in Context: Essays in Honor of Calvin J. Roetzel* (Sheffield: Sheffield Academic Press), 216–39.

—— (2004), *Border Lines: The Partition of Judaeo-Christianity* (Philadelphia: University of Pennsylvania Press).

BRAKKE, D. (1994), 'Canon Formation and Social Conflict in Fourth-Century Egypt: Athanasius of Alexandria's Thirty-Ninth *Festal Letter*', *HTR* 87: 395–419.

—— (1995), *Athanasius and the Politics of Asceticism* (Oxford: Oxford University Press).

—— (2001), 'Jewish Flesh and Christian Spirit in Athanasius of Alexandria', *JECS* 9: 453–81.

—— (2006), *Demons and the Making of the Monk: Spiritual Combat in Early Christianity* (Cambridge, Mass.: Harvard University Press).

—— (in press), 'From Temple to Cell, From Gods to Demons: Pagan Temples in the Monastic Topography of Fourth-Century Egypt', in Hahn *et al.* (in press).

BROCK, S. (1977), 'A Letter Attributed to Cyril of Jerusalem on the Rebuilding of the Temple', *Bulletin of the School of Oriental and African Studies*, 40: 267–86.

BROWN, P. (1995), *Authority and the Sacred: Aspects of the Christianisation of the Roman World* (Cambridge: Cambridge University Press).

BUELL, D. K. (1999), *Making Christians: Clement of Alexandria and the Rhetoric of Legitimacy* (Princeton: Princeton University Press).

CASEAU, B. (2001), '*Polemein Lithois*: La désacralisation des espaces et des objets religieux païens durant l'antiquité tardive', in M. Kaplan (ed.), *Le sacré et son inscription dans l'espace à Byzance et en Occident* (Paris: Publications de la Sorbonne), 61–123.

CHANCEY, M. A. (2002), *The Myth of a Gentile Galilee* (Cambridge: Cambridge University Press).

CHITTY, D. J. (1966), *The Desert a City: An Introduction to the Study of Egyptian and Palestinian Monasticism under the Christian Empire* (London: Mowbrays).

CLARK, E. A. (1992), *The Origenist Controversy: The Cultural Construction of an Early Christian Debate* (Princeton: Princeton University Press).

CROUZEL, H. (1970), 'L'école d'Origène à Césarée: Postscriptum à une édition de Grégoire le Thaumaturge', *BLE* 71: 15–27.

—— (1989), *Origen* (San Francisco: Harper & Row).

DAVIS, S. J. (2001), *The Cult of Saint Thecla: A Tradition of Women's Piety in Late Antiquity* (Oxford: Clarendon Press).

—— (2004), *The Early Coptic Papacy: The Egyptian Church and its Leadership in Late Antiquity* (Cairo: American University in Cairo Press).

DAWSON, D. (1992), *Allegorical Readers and Cultural Revision in Ancient Alexandria* (Berkeley: University of California Press).

DE LANGE, N. (1976), *Origen and the Jews: Studies in Jewish–Christian Relations in Third-Century Palestine* (Cambridge: Cambridge University Press).

DIEKAMP, F. (1899), *Die origenistischen Streitgkeiten im sechsten Jarhhundert und das fünfte allgemeine Konzil* (Münster: Aschendorff).

DRIJVERS, J. W. (2004), *Cyril of Jerusalem: Bishop and City* (Leiden: E. J. Brill).

EDWARDS, M. J. (2002), *Origen against Plato* (Aldershot: Ashgate).

EMMEL, S. (2002), 'From the Other Side of the Nile: Shenoute and Panopolis', in A. Egberts, B. P. Muhs, and J. van der Vliet (eds.), *Perspectives on Panopolis: An Egyptian Town from Alexander the Great to the Arab Conquest; Acts of an International Symposium Held in Leiden on 16, 17, and 18 December 1998* (Leiden: E. J. Brill), 95–113.

——(in press), 'Shenoute of Atripe and the Christian Destruction of Temples in Egypt: Rhetoric and Reality', in Hahn *et al.* (in press).

FAVALE, A. (1958), *Teolfilo d'Alessandria (345c.–412): Scritti, vita e dottrina* (Turin: Societa Editrice Internazionale).

FRANK, G. (2000), *The Memory of the Eyes: Pilgrims to Living Saints in Christian Late Antiquity* (Berkeley: University of California Press).

FRANKFURTER, D. (1994), 'The Cult of the Martyrs in Egypt before Constantine: The Evidence of the Coptic *Apocalypse of Elijah*', VC 48: 25–47.

——(1998a) (ed.), *Pilgrimage and Holy Space in Late Antique Egypt* (Leiden: E. J. Brill).

——(1998b), *Religion in Roman Egypt: Assimilation and Resistance* (Princeton: Princeton University Press).

——(2000), ' "Things Unbefitting Christians": Violence and Christianization in Fifth-Century Panopolis', JECS 8: 273–95.

——(2003), 'Syncretism and the Holy Man in Late Antique Egypt', JECS 11: 339–85.

——(2007), 'Illuminating the Cult of Kothos: The *Panegyric on Macarius* and Local Religion in Fifth-Century Egypt', in J. E. Goehring and J. A. Timbie (eds.), *The World of Early Egyptian Christianity: Language, Literature, and Social Context; Essays in Honor of David W. Johnson* (Washington D.C.: Catholic University of America Press).

——(forthcoming), 'Hagiography and the Reconstruction of Local Religion in Late Antique Egypt: Memories, Inventions, and Landscapes', *Dutch Review of Church History*, 86.

FREND, W. H. C. (1972), *The Rise of the Monophysite Movement: Chapters in the History of the Church in the Fifth and Sixth Centuries* (Cambridge: Cambridge University Press).

GADDIS, M. (2005), *There is No Crime for Those Who Have Christ: Religious Violence in the Christian Roman Empire* (Berkeley: University of California Press).

GEIGER, J. (1998), 'Aspects of Palestinian Paganism in Late Antiquity', in Kofsky and Stroumsa (1998), 3–17.

GOEHRING, J. E. (1999), *Ascetics, Society, and the Desert: Studies in Early Egyptian Monasticism* (Harrisburg, Pa.: Trinity Press International).

——(2003), 'The Dark Side of Landscape: Ideology and Power in the Christian Myth of the Desert', JMEMS 33: 437–51.

——(2006), 'Remembering Abraham of Farshut: History, Hagiography, and the Fate of the Pachomian Tradition', JECS 14: 1–26.

GOLITZIN, A. (2002), ' "The Demons Suggest an Illusion of God's Glory in a Form": Controversy over the Divine Body in Some Late Fourth, Early Fifth Century Monastic Literature', *Studia Monastica*, 44: 13–43.

—— (2003), 'The Vision of God and the Form of Glory: More Reflections on the Anthropomorphite Controversy of AD 399', in J. Behr, A. Louth, and D. Conomos (eds.), *Abba: The Tradition of Orthodoxy in the West; Festschrift for Bishop Kallistos (Ware) of Diokleia* (Crestwood, NY: St Vladimir's Seminary Press), 273–97.

GREGG, R. C. (1989), review of Rowan Williams, *Arius: Heresy and Tradition*, JTS NS 40: 247–54.

GRIGGS, C. W. (1990), *Early Egyptian Christianity: From its Origins to 451 C.E.* (Leiden: E. J. Brill).

GROH, D. (1983), 'The Onomastikon of Eusebius and the Rise of Christian Palestine', *St Patr* 18: 23–31.

GUILLAUMONT, A. (1962), *Les 'Kephalaia Gnostica' d'Evagre le Pontique et l'histoire de l'Origénisma chez les Grecs et les Syriens* (Paris: Éditions du Seuil).

HAAS, C. (1997), *Alexandria in Late Antiquity: Topography and Social Conflict* (Baltimore: Johns Hopkins University Press).

HAHN, J., EMMEL, S., and GOTTER, U. (in press) (eds.), *From Temple to Church: Destruction and Renewal of Local Cultic Topography in Late Antiquity* (Leiden: E. J. Brill).

HEYER, F. (1984), *Kirchengeschichte des heiligen Landes* (Stuttgart: W. Kohlhammer).

HIRSCHFELD, Y. (1992), *The Judean Desert Monasteries in the Byzantine Period* (New Haven: Yale University Press).

HOLUM, K. G. (2003), 'The Christianizing of Caesarea Paleastinae', in G. Brands and H.-G. Severin (eds.), *Die spätantike Stadt und ihre Christianisierung: Symposion vom 14. bis 16. Februar 2000 in Halle/Saale* (Wiesbaden: Reichert), 151–64.

HUNT, E. D. (1982), *Holy Land Pilgrimage in the Later Roman Empire, AD 312–460* (Oxford: Clarendon Press).

JACOBS, A. S. (2004), *The Remains of the Jews: The Holy Land and Christian Empire in Late Antiquity* (Palo Alto, Calif.: Stanford University Press).

JONES, A. H. M. (1959), 'Were the Ancient Heresies National or Social Movements in Disguise?', JTS NS 10: 280–98.

KEATING, D. A. (2004), *The Appropriation of Divine Life in Cyril of Alexandria* (Oxford: Oxford University Press).

KELLY, J. N. D. (1975), *Jerome: His Life, Writings, and Controversies* (London: Duckworth).

KNAUBER, A. (1968), 'Das Anliegen der Schule des Origenes zu Cäsarea', *Münchener theologische Zeitsohrift*, 19: 182–203.

KOFSKY, A. (1998), 'Mamre: A Case of a Regional Cult?', in Kofsky and Stroumsa (1998*b*), 19–30.

—— and STROUMSA, G. G. (1998) (eds.), *Sharing the Sacred: Religious Contacts and Conflicts in the Holy Land* (Jerusalem: Yad Izhak ben Zvi).

LAYTON, B. (1989), 'The Significance of Basilides in Ancient Christian Thought', *Representations*, 28: 135–51.

LAZZATI, G. (1935), *Teofilo d'Alessandria*, Scienze filologiche, 19 (Milan: Società editrice 'Vita e Pensiero').

LEVINE, L. I. (1975), *Caesarea under Roman Rule* (Leiden: E. J. Brill).

LYMAN, J. R. (1993), *Christology and Cosmology: Models of Divine Activity in Origen, Eusebius, and Athanasius* (Oxford: Clarendon Press).

MACK, B. (1993), *The Lost Gospel: The Book of Q and Christian Origins* (San Francisco: HarperSanFrancisco).

MARTIN, A. (1996), *Athanase d'Alexandrie et l'église d'Égypte au IVe siècle (328–373)* (Rome: École française de Rome).

MARTYN, J. L. (2003), *History and Theology in the Fourth Gospel*, 3rd edn. (Louisville, Ky.: Westminster John Knox Press).

McGUCKIN, J. A. (1994), *St. Cyril of Alexandria: The Christological Controversy* (Leiden: E. J. Brill).

MEEKS, W. A. (2002), *In Search of the Early Christians* (New Haven: Yale University Press).

MURPHY-O'CONNOR, J. (1995), 'Pre-Constantinian Christian Jerusalem', in A. O'Mahony, G. Gunner, and K. Hintlian (eds.), *The Christian Heritage in the Holy Land* (London: Scorpion Cavendish), 13–21.

PEARSON, B. A. (1986), 'Earliest Christianity in Egypt: Some Observations', in B. A. Pearson and J. E. Goehring (eds.), *The Roots of Egyptian Christianity* (Philadelphia: Fortress Press), 132–59.

——— (2004), *Gnosticism and Christianity in Roman and Coptic Egypt* (New York: T & T Clark International).

PERRONE, L. (1980), *La chiesa di Palestina e le controversie cristologiche: dal concilio di Efeso (431) al secondo concilio di Costantinopoli (553)* (Brescia: Paideia Editrice).

——— (1998), 'Monasticism as a Factor of Religious Interaction in the Holy Land during the Byzantine Period', in Kofsky and Stroumsa (1998), 67–95.

REBENICH, S. (2002), *Jerome* (London: Routledge).

REGNAULT, L. (1981), 'Les apophthegmes en Palestine aux Ve–VIe siècles', *Irénikon*, 54: 320–30.

RIST, J. (1975), 'The Greek and Latin Texts of the Discussion of Free Will in *De Principiis*, Book III', in H. Crouzel, G. Lomiento, and J. Rius-Camps (eds.), *Origeniana: Premier colloque international des études origéniennes* (Bari: Instituto di Letteratura Cristiana Antica, Università di Bari), 97–111.

ROBERTS C. H. (1977), *Manuscript, Society, and Belief in Early Christian Egypt* (Oxford: Oxford University Press).

ROLDANUS, J. R. (1968), *Le Christ et l'homme dans le théologie d'Athanase d'Alexandrie* (Leiden: E. J. Brill).

RUBIN, Z. (1996), 'The See of Caesaria in Conflict with Jerusalem from Nicaea (325) to Chalcedon (451)', in A. Raban and K. G. Holum (eds.), *Caesarea Maritima: Retrospective after Two Millenia* (Leiden: E. J. Brill), 562–7.

——— (1998), 'Porphyrius of Gaza and the Conflict between Christianity and Paganism in Southern Palestine', in Kofsky and Stroumsa (1998), 31–66.

——— (1999), 'The Cult of the Holy Land and Christian Politics in Byzantine Jerusalem', in L. I. Levine (ed.), *Jerusalem: Its Sanctity and Centrality to Judaism, Christianity, and Islam* (New York: Continuum), 151–62.

RUSSELL, N. (2000), *Cyril of Alexandria* (London: Routledge).

SALDARINI, A. J. (1994), *Matthew's Christian-Jewish Community* (Chicago: University of Chicago Press).

Schwartz, S. (2001), *Imperialism and Jewish Society, 200 B.C.E. to 640 C.E.* (Princeton: Princeton University Press).

Scott, A. (1991), *Origen and the Life of the Stars: A History of an Idea* (Oxford: Clarendon Press).

Sivan, H. (1990), 'Pilgrimage, Monasticism, and the Emergence of Christian Palestine in the 4th Century', in R. Ousterhout (ed.), *The Blessings of Pilgrimage* (Urbana, Ill.: University of Illinois Press), 54–65.

Stemberger, G. (2000), *Jews and Christians in the Holy Land: Palestine in the Fourth Century* (Edinburgh: T & T Clark).

Taylor, J. E. (1993), *Christians and the Holy Places: The Myth of Jewish-Christian Origins* (Oxford: Clarendon Press).

Theissen, G. (1978), *Sociology of Early Palestinian Christianity* (Philadelphia: Fortress Press).

Trigg, J. W. (1983), *Origen: The Bible and Philosophy in the Third-Century Church* (Atlanta: John Knox Press).

—— (1998), *Origen* (London: Routledge).

Trombley, F. R. (1993–4), *Hellenic Religion and Christianization, c.370–529* (Leiden: E. J. Brill).

Tsafrir, Y. (2003), 'The Christianization of Bet Shean (Scythopolis) and its Social-Cultural Influence on the City', in G. Brands and H.-G. Severin (eds.), *Die spätantike Stadt und ihre Christianisierung: Symposion vom 14. bis 16. Februar 2000 in Halle/Saale* (Wiesbaden: Reichert), 275–84.

Tuckett, C. M. (1992), 'Q (Gospel Source)', in *ABD* v. 567–72.

—— (1996), *Q and the History of Early Christianity: Studies on Q* (Edinburgh: T & T Clark).

Van Dam, R. (1985), 'From Paganism to Christianity in Late Antique Gaza', *Viator*, 16: 1–20.

van den Hoek, A. (1997), 'The "Catechetical" School of Early Christian Alexandria and its Philonic Heritage', *HTR* 90: 59–87.

Wainwright, P. (1986), 'The Authenticity of the Recently Discovered Letter Attributed to Cyril of Jerusalem', *VC* 40: 286–93.

Walker, P. W. L. (1990), *Holy City, Holy Places? Christian Attitudes to Jerusalem and the Holy Land in the Fourth Century* (Oxford: Clarendon Press).

Wehnert, J. (1991), 'Die Auswanderung der Jerusalemer Christen nach Pella—Historisches Faktum oder theologische Konstruktion?', *ZKG* 102: 231–55.

Wessel, S. (2004), *Cyril of Alexandria and the Nestorian Controversy: The Making of a Saint and of a Heretic* (Oxford: Oxford University Press).

Wilken, R. L. (1971), *Judaism and the Early Christian Mind: A Study of Cyril of Alexandria's Exegesis and Theology* (New Haven: Yale University Press).

—— (1992), *The Land Called Holy: Palestine in Christian History and Thought* (New Haven: Yale University Press).

Williams, R. (2002), *Arius: Heresy and Tradition*, rev. edn. (Grand Rapids, Mich.: Eerdmans).

Wilson, S. G. (1995), *Related Strangers: Jews and Christians, 70–170 C.E.* (Minneapolis: Fortress Press).

Wipszycka, E. (1988), 'La christianisation de l'Égypte aux IVe–VIe siècles', *Aegyptus*, 68: 117–65.

Yarnold, E. J. (2000), *Cyril of Jerusalem* (London: Routledge).

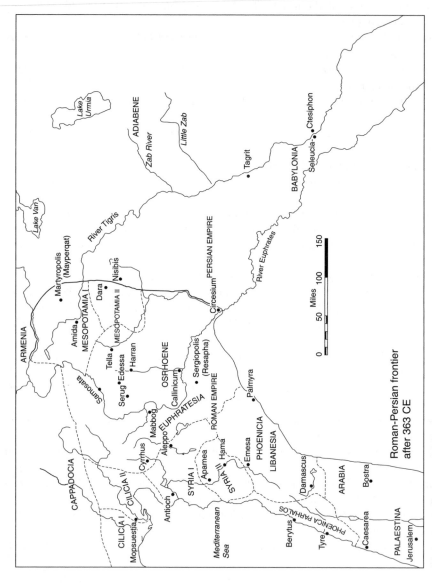

Map 18.1 Syria and Mesopotamia

CHAPTER 18

....

THE EAST (3): SYRIA AND MESOPOTAMIA

....

LUCAS VAN ROMPAY

In contrast to other Christian traditions emerging and flourishing in the eastern Mediterranean, Syriac Christianity does not derive its main scriptural texts exclusively from the Greek world. Most notably in the translation of the Syriac Old Testament from the Hebrew Bible, rather than from the Greek Septuagint, Syriac Christianity shows its independent position *vis-à-vis* Greek Christianity. The question, then, as to whether Syriac Christianity might give us some insights into non-Greek, Semitic, or Jewish forms of early Christianity has often been in the mind of scholars. Whatever the answer to this question may be, in the course of the fourth and fifth centuries, Syriac Christianity, which developed and expanded in close contact with the imperial church, became increasingly influenced by the paradigms of Greek Christianity and thoroughly Hellenized. But in spite of this far-reaching adaptation to Greek modes of theology and praxis, the majority of Syriac Christians in the next period of their history, the sixth and seventh centuries, gradually dissociated themselves from the imperial church and created their own communities in Syria and in Mesopotamia—communities which were doctrinally distinct from Roman and Byzantine Christianity. These independent communities exist to the present day in the Middle East and in the world-wide diaspora of the Middle Eastern Christian churches.

Given the position of Syriac Christianity at the intersection of the Semitic and Greek worlds, it is no surprise that questions of linguistic and cultural transformation of Christian traditions, along with issues of religious identity and community building, have been at the forefront of Syriac studies in recent decades.[1]

The term 'Syriac Christianity' is understood here as Christian culture expressed in Syriac, one of the East-Aramaic languages. Syriac Christianity emerged in northern Mesopotamia, an area of encounter between various peoples and civilizations, in which Aramean settlement began as early as the end of the second millennium BCE. In the first Christian centuries, this area was a buffer between the Roman and Parthian Empires. When, in the course of the third century, Rome extended its rule eastward and the Sasanids reorganized and centralized the Persian Empire, Syriac Christians became divided between two empires. From the fourth century onwards, Syriac Christian communities existed in the eastern provinces of the Roman Empire (particularly in Mesopotamia Prima and Secunda, Osrhoene, Euphratesia, Syria Prima and Secunda, and Phoenicia Libanesia) as well as in the Persian–Sasanid Empire (mainly in north and central Mesopotamia). While Edessa, the capital of Osrhoene, is often seen as its main centre, the geographical area of Syriac Christianity in its heyday was quite vast, extending from the hinterland of the Hellenized city of Antioch in the west to the political heartland of the Persian Sasanids, around Seleucia-Ctesiphon, in the east. In the eastern provinces of the Roman Empire, Syriac coexisted with Greek, which was the dominant language of the imperial church (Millar 1998). Connections with Greek Christianity, therefore, should always be considered in the study of Syriac Christianity; on the other hand, Greek writing authors of the Syrian area—Eusebius of Emesa, John Chrysostom, Theodoret of Cyrrhus, and many others—deserve to be studied against their Syriac background. The focus of the present essay will be on the *Syriac* expression of Christianity in Syria and Mesopotamia up to the sixth century.

The origins of Syriac Christianity can be traced back to the second century, when Christians began to use the Aramaic of Edessa as their literary language. The Edessene language itself goes back to an earlier period, as is evidenced by pagan Syriac inscriptions (the earliest dated inscription is from 6 CE), and it continued in a pagan or non-Christian context well into the third century (Drijvers and Healey 1999). But it was Christian use that made the language popular over a wide area and a convenient vehicle for the spread of Christianity wherever there was a substrate of spoken Aramaic.[2]

18.1 Scriptural Foundations: Old and New Testament

The Syriac translation of the Old Testament (commonly known under its later name 'Peshitta') and some version of the four Gospels must be among the earliest products of Syriac literature. In both cases, there is evidence for a second-century date.

Scholars have long been divided over the question of whether the Old Testament Peshitta, translated from the Hebrew Bible, is of Jewish or Christian origin. In 1999, Michael Weitzman made a very important contribution to this discussion with his posthumously published monograph, *The Syriac Version of the Old Testament*. He situated the Peshitta translators as a team of Jewish intellectuals, working for a generation or two, in the second half of the second century, perhaps in Edessa (Weitzman 1999). They were non-rabbinic Jews, whose emphasis on prayer over against ritual brought them close to Christianity. They subsequently converted and passed on to Syriac Christianity their newly translated Aramaic Bible, written in a form of the language close to the new literary language of Edessene Christians. While this historical reconstruction leaves a number of questions unanswered, Weitzman's philological groundwork is solid and impressive. It shows beyond a doubt that the translators had an excellent knowledge of Hebrew and were steeped in the Jewish tradition. They may have been Jews moving towards Christianity, as Weitzman would have it, or alternatively, as others have suggested, recent Christian converts from Judaism who stood somewhere between the two faiths (ter Haar Romeny 2005: 29–31). Whatever the case may be, the Old Testament Peshitta constitutes a major point of contact, or an avenue of interaction, between (one type of Aramaic-speaking) Judaism and nascent Syriac Christianity. It exemplified and reaffirmed the close connection between Judaism and Syriac Christianity at a time when elsewhere in the ancient world Judaism and Christianity were rapidly and irrevocably parting ways.

Syriac Christians in the second century shared with Jews the literary tradition of Aramaic, which in the same period, along with Hebrew, began to be used to redact and transmit rabbinic texts, both in Palestine and in Mesopotamia, including the Aramaic translations of the Hebrew Bible, i.e. the Targumim. Some of the phraseology characteristic of the Targumim also exists in Syriac,[3] both within and outside the Peshitta. Occasionally, such phrases found their way into the language of the liturgy, in which these frozen archaic elements subsisted as silent witnesses to a period of close proximity between Judaism and Syriac Christianity.

Apart from language and phraseology, Syriac liturgical tradition has preserved other elements reminiscent of the Jewish past as well. In his 1997 study, Gerard Rouwhorst discussed five features that he considered to be indicative of Syriac Christianity's unique relationship to Judaism: (1) the presence of the *bēma*, a raised platform on which the liturgy of the Word was performed in the churches of Mesopotamia and North Syria, which has its parallels in synagogue architecture; (2) the preservation of two Old Testament pericopes among the readings of the eucharist, reminiscent of the use in the synagogue; (3) the structure of the earliest eucharistic prayer, which parallels the *Birkat ha-mazon*; (4) traces of a positive attitude towards the Sabbath, found particularly in the *Apostolic Constitutions*; (5)

the Syriac Christians' adherence, until the early fourth century, to the celebration of Passover on the night of the 14th of Nisan, in accordance with Jewish practice (Rouwhorst 1997). Most of these features cannot be explained as later borrowings, and must go back to the roots of Syriac Christianity itself. While some of them gradually disappeared and gave way to practices that conformed to mainstream Christianity, others survived. The conclusion must be that the Jewish impact on Syriac Christianity right from the beginning was significant, even if it was only one among several constituent traditions, as we will see.

Along with the beginnings of the Syriac Old Testament, the second century also saw the first Syriac translation of the Gospels. There has been much discussion among scholars about the question of whether Syriac Christians first knew the four Gospels separately or harmonized together into a single Gospel known as the *Diatessaron*, a work that is attributed to Tatian, who describes himself as being 'born in the land of the Assyrians'.[4] Tatian was a disciple of Justin Martyr in Rome, and after Justin's death (between 163 and 167), he returned to the East.[5] Regardless of whether the *Diatessaron* was originally written in Greek or in Syriac (the majority view tends towards Syriac, even though Tatian worked on the basis of the Greek Gospels), the Syriac version enjoyed great popularity well into the fourth and fifth centuries. The *Diatessaron* has not survived in its original redaction in either Greek or Syriac, and can be only partly reconstructed from quotations in later works. It is clear, however, that Tatian, in selecting, combining, and rewriting passages from the four Gospels, conveyed his message of *enkrateia* ('self-control'), which included a negative view of the world and a rejection of humanity's enslavement to food and sexuality.[6] Tatian further elaborated these ideas in the *Oration to the Greeks*, his only work preserved in Greek, and they became widespread in early Syriac Christianity. Some scholars, therefore, are inclined to see Tatian as a typical representative of the Syriac Christianity of his day, or even to assume that he played a major role in shaping early Syriac Christianity, with its proclivity towards rigorous asceticism (Hunt 2003: 144–75). We do not know, however, how far Tatian's influence went beyond the popularity of the *Diatessaron*. He remains an elusive figure, and there is no evidence of any activity by him in the East following his return from Rome.

If the *Diatessaron*, datable to around 170 CE, preceded the earliest version of the four separate Gospels in Syriac known as the 'Old Syriac' (or *Vetus Syra*)— a view that is now prevalent—then the translators of the Old Syriac, perhaps working in the early third century, were certainly influenced by the *Diatessaron*. In their rather free rendering of the Greek Gospels, they often adopted Tatian's readings. The two incomplete fifth-century manuscripts, known as Curetonianus and Sinaiticus, present slightly divergent texts, indicating the fluidity of the earliest textual tradition, which only after a thorough revision in the fifth century led to the Peshitta, the standard text of the Syriac Gospels and New Testament, much more in line with the Greek text.

There can be no doubt that the Syriac Gospel texts of both the *Diatessaron* and the Old Syriac derived from Greek. A question then remains as to whether the translators, who were speakers and writers of Aramaic, were also familiar with written or oral accounts of Jesus' message in Aramaic or with some Aramaic phrases from the earliest Palestinian ministry, which they occasionally may have woven into their translation work. This assumption has found enthusiastic defenders for over a century (Joosten 1997). While the suggestion of a written account cannot be substantiated, the case for isolated oral reminiscences is more convincing, even though the evidence is slim and rarely unequivocal.[7]

18.2 SYRIAC CHRISTIANITY AROUND 200: THE WIDER CONTEXT

With these few major texts—the Old Testament, the *Diatessaron*, the four separate Gospels—situated in the late second to third centuries, how do other early Syriac texts fit into this picture?[8]

The message of *enkrateia* is illustrated most vividly in the *Acts of Judas Thomas* (Drijvers 1992). In his preaching to the Indians, Thomas strongly advocates a Christ-like life, renunciation of this world, and abstention from sexual activity (even within marriage), in an attempt to regain the original purity of Paradise prior to the Fall. This rebirth can be achieved through man's free will; Christ's incarnation, crucifixion, and resurrection are notably absent from the salvation process. Thomas allegedly died as a martyr in India, and his bones were brought to Edessa, where he was particularly venerated. Most scholars assume that the *Acts* were originally written in Syriac, even though the preserved Syriac text may represent a later rewriting, and the Greek version may occasionally reflect the original more faithfully. Given the prominent position of Thomas in Edessa, which is evidenced at least from the fourth century onwards, several scholars have suggested that the *Acts* were written in that city. There is little evidence for this, however, and an origin to the east of Edessa would be equally conceivable. One branch of the textual tradition inserts the charming *Hymn of the Pearl*, which reveals a quite different religious background and exhibits linguistic features pointing to a type of Aramaic more eastern than Edessene Syriac (Beyer 1991).[9] The *Acts* must have been quite popular in Mesopotamia, as they were adopted by Mani and his followers, which suggests the early third century as the *terminus ante quem* for their origin.

Another text associated with Thomas, and in modern scholarship often connected with Edessa, is the *Gospel of Thomas*, one of the Coptic texts found at Nag Hammadi. The name 'Judas Thomas', the dualistic-encratite message of many of the sayings, the textual links with the *Diatessaron*, and a number of 'Aramaisms' or 'Syriacisms' have lent appeal to the hypothesis of a Syriac origin, in Edessa, somewhere in the second century. The evidence, however, is sketchy, without a coherent picture emerging. If, as several scholars believe, the *Gospel of Thomas* dates from the first half of the second century, then it would be the earliest known representative of Syriac Christianity—without clear links to any of the later texts! A recent attempt to situate the original *Gospel of Thomas* in late-second-century Edessa, and to uncover the alleged Syriac profile of the Coptic text remains problematic in a number of ways (Perrin 2002). Given the lack of consensus on the date and on the literary and historical contexts, it is uncertain at present to what extent, if at all, the *Gospel of Thomas* can inform our knowledge of early Syriac Christianity.[10]

A historical person who definitely belongs to Syriac Christianity around the year 200 is the theologian-philosopher Bardaisan. He lived and worked at the royal court of Edessa—in his day still an autonomous kingdom situated between the Roman and Parthian worlds—and his mere presence there shows how far Christianity had penetrated into the social fabric of the city. Bardaisan presents a picture of Christianity quite different from what the other sources seem to tell us. He is a man of the world, not an ascetic or encratite, and his main interest is in the philosophical questions of his day, which he approaches with the tools of the Greek philosophical tradition. Although he is well informed about Judaism, his primary involvement is with pagan Hellenistic culture, not with Judaism. Should we then posit Bardaisan, rather than Tatian, as the main spokesperson for Edessene Christianity around 200? Here, as in the case of Tatian, we should proceed with great caution. Later generations of Syriac Christians explicitly rejected Bardaisan's heritage, and Ephrem condemned and cursed him as one of the arch-heretics. His many works were not copied by later generations and entirely disappeared, with the exception of the fascinating *Book of the Laws of the Countries*,[11] which assesses the role of nature, fate, and human free will, and was written down by Bardaisan's disciple Philippus.

There are thus competing and seemingly conflicting images of early Syriac Christianity: the Jewish Peshitta translators, Tatian the encratite, and Bardaisan the court philosopher. One should add the Marcionites to this list. They certainly had a strong presence in Syria, and most of the other groups responded to them. These various strands originated perhaps independently of one another in different areas and at different times, before a more unified picture of Syriac Christianity emerged. Many of the obvious categories of the later period, such as orthodoxy versus heresy, centre versus periphery, and Judaism versus Christianity cannot be applied to the earlier period without resulting in historical distortions.[12] Moreover, such questions as to whether Christianity was brought to northern Mesopotamia from Greek-speaking Antioch or from Jewish Palestine, and to what extent Edessene Christianity retained its Aramaic or Semitic stamp rather than being absorbed by Graeco-Roman culture, cannot be given simple answers. We should also realize that most of the earliest texts have disappeared. The few texts that for specific reasons were incorporated into the later literary tradition were detached from their original context and given new layers of meaning. For example, such texts as the *Odes of Solomon* are very hard to imagine in their original context. Some scholars have emphasized the proximity of these hymns to Jewish thanksgiving hymns, such as those known from the Dead Sea Scrolls, and have considered the possibility of an early Palestinian and possibly Jewish-Christian origin. Others have explored the connections of the *Odes* with second- or third-century Edessene Christianity (Charlesworth 1998; Lattke 1999–2005, with further references).

18.3 Syriac Christianity at the Beginning of the Fourth Century: The Witness of Eusebius of Caesarea

It is only around 300 that Syriac Christianity fully emerges on the historical scene. From this time on, there is a historiography complete with events and names of places and persons that are part of the uninterrupted Christian history, which later generations of Syriac Christians recognized as their own. With most of northern Mesopotamia fully integrated within the Roman Empire, Syriac Christianity from this time on developed within the framework of expanding imperial Christianity, the foundations of which were laid by Constantine's conversion and the Council of Nicaea (325).

In the early fourth century, the West heard about Christianity in Mesopotamia through Eusebius of Caesarea, who included in his *Ecclesiastical History* the story of Edessa's conversion to Christianity in the days of King Abgar, a contemporary of Jesus (I, 13). The text of Abgar's letter to Jesus and of Jesus's reply was added as evidence, translated into Greek from the Syriac originals which, Eusebius asserts, were preserved in the archives of Edessa (Brock 1992). This legend must have been created around, or shortly before, 300 by one group of Edessene Christians wanting to boost their position, using the most powerful tools: Jesus's authorship of the letter, the mission of one of the seventy apostles, the prestige of the royal house (which most likely never was Christian), and the renown of the Aramaic language. The legend was expanded in the early fifth-century *Teaching of Addai* and became very popular throughout the Christian world (Griffith 2003). Its notable absence from some important Syriac sources, including Ephrem, may indicate that it was not universally endorsed or given credence by fourth-century Syriac Christians.

Eusebius certainly contributed to granting Syriac Christianity its rightful—albeit somewhat peripheral—place within Christianity as it developed in the Roman

Empire. The position of Syriac Christian communities outside the Roman Empire, especially those living under the Sasanid Persians, Rome's eternal enemies, was more problematic. In northern Mesopotamia, the frontier between the Roman and Persian Empires became a real dividing line between the Christian and Zoroastrian worlds, cutting across the homelands of the Aramaic-speaking population. Syriac Christians were a minority in the Zoroastrian state. In times of peace, they enjoyed freedom and some sort of official protection. In times of war with the Roman neighbours, however, their position was vulnerable, and persecution occurred regularly (Rist 1996).

18.4 APHRAHAT AND EPHREM

Two of the most important Syriac authors, Aphrahat and Ephrem, lived in the fourth century. Together they are the most eloquent and distinctive spokespersons of Syriac Christianity, on the two sides of the Roman–Persian frontier.[13] Aphrahat's modest literary corpus consists of twenty-three *Demonstrations*, or treatises, written in epistolary form and dated to the years 337–45. Ephrem worked in Nisibis until 363, when, following Julian's death, the Romans surrendered the city to the Persians, and many Christians, Ephrem among them, moved westwards to Edessa. He lived the last 10 years of his life in that city, where he died in 373. Ephrem's *œuvre* is much more voluminous than that of Aphrahat and includes biblical commentaries, prose treatises, and above all poetical compositions. In spite of the geographical distance and the different political worlds in which they operated, Aphrahat and Ephrem had a great deal in common. Heirs to the Aramaic cultural heritage of Mesopotamia, they expressed themselves in a high form of literary Syriac, of which both were skilled masters. While the Old Testament occupies a prominent place in their thought (Van Rompay 1996: 619–28), their theological views and expressions show some marked differences. Ephrem wholeheartedly espoused Nicene Christianity, of which he became a staunch defender (Griffith 1986). Aphrahat, on the other hand, does not betray any knowledge of the Nicene Creed and exhibits a theology which in both its Trinitarian and its Christological concepts is unique.[14]

Ephrem fully believed in the Christian Empire under the protection of the God-appointed emperor Constantine and his successors (he saw Julian's short-lived reign in the 360s as a lamentable intermezzo). Aphrahat's position is much more complicated. Viewing contemporary history through the lens of Daniel's prophetic visions, he awaits the eschatological kingdom of Christ. The Roman Empire for him is the fourth kingdom, represented by the fourth beast, which is 'dreadful, mighty, and exceedingly strong' (Dan 7: 7; *Dem.* 5. 19).[15] It will be killed at the inauguration of the eternal kingdom, and its body will perish, but until then it will last. The Persians, symbolized by the ram (Dan 8: 4–8), therefore, will not prevail against it. This interpretation does not imply Aphrahat's full sympathy with the Roman Christian Empire, but the Empire does have a clear place in his view of history, a place not challenged by Persian aggression.

While Ephrem often polemicizes against perceived enemies of Christianity, open polemic is much rarer in Aphrahat. Ephrem focuses his invective on the Marcionites, the followers of Bardaisan, and the Manichaeans. Each of these groups, which Ephrem sees as genealogically related, must have held their appeal for many Christians in northern Mesopotamia. Aphrahat, on the other hand, occasionally refers to Marcion and Mani, but never mentions Bardaisan. A further distinction is Ephrem's rebuttal of Arius and Arianism, which has no parallel in Aphrahat, who, as we have seen, had no part in the discussions surrounding Nicaea.

An area in which Aphrahat and Ephrem have similarities while also being clearly distinctive is their attitude towards Judaism. Both authors are familiar with Jewish traditions, Jewish interpretations of the Hebrew Bible, and Jewish hermeneutical principles. The ease and frequency with which they incorporate such interpretations and motifs in their work is very revealing, not only about their own intellectual background, but also about that of their audiences. While some of this shared heritage may have entered Syriac Christianity along with the Old Testament Peshitta, other elements seem to reflect later contacts, or even to respond to contemporary discussions.[16] We must conclude, therefore, that in fourth-century central Mesopotamia, as well as in Nisibis and Edessa, there was still a shared discourse connecting Judaism and Syriac Christianity.

In spite of this obvious proximity (or, should one say, because of it?), there is also strong antagonism toward Judaism. Ephrem, following the rhetorical lead of the Hebrew Bible prophets, speaks extremely negatively not only about the Israel of the Old Testament, but also about contemporary Judaism. Aphrahat, while sharing several of the themes of Christian anti-Jewish literature of his day, is much more restrained in his critique, and tries to persuade his alleged Jewish interlocutor with arguments taken primarily from the Old Testament, searching for Old Testament precedents—not just types—for the main tenets of Christianity.

Much work has been done in the past decades both on the parallels that Aphrahat and Ephrem share with Jewish tradition and on their anti-Judaism.[17] How exactly these two aspects should be brought together is not yet clear. To what extent does the anti-Jewish discourse reflect the historical realities in the Persian and the Roman Empires? Why is the anti-Jewish rhetoric of these two Syriac authors, who speak with voices so distinct from those of western Christianity, often so similar to the anti-Judaism of western church fathers?

The writings of Aphrahat and Ephrem, created in central Mesopotamia under Persian rule and in north Mesopotamia under Roman rule, display the essential unity of Syriac literary tradition in the fourth century. There is, however, very little evidence of direct links between the two literary corpora.[18] It is only a hundred years after Ephrem's death that we know for sure that Aphrahat's work circulated in Edessa, Ephrem's second home town, when the scribe of what is now the first part of London, British Library, Add. MS 17, 182 (fos. 1–99) copied the first ten of the *Demonstrations*, in Edessa, in September 474 (Wright 1871: 403a–404a).

Aphrahat and Ephrem have received more attention from Syriac scholars than any other authors. In the past decades, many of their works, critically edited from manuscripts as early as the fifth and sixth centuries, have become available in modern translations. Both the literary qualities and the symbolic theology of their works have been explored.[19] Although both authors are still seen as having been affected only a little by Greek philosophical and theological thinking, in an important recent publication (1999) Ute Possekel has convincingly shown Ephrem's familiarity with the Greek philosophical concepts of his day.

18.5 The Beginnings of Syriac Ascetic Literature

Aphrahat and Ephrem, ascetics themselves, are important witnesses to the concepts and institutions of fourth-century Syriac asceticism. Particularly intriguing, and much studied, is the institution of the *bnay/bnāt qyāmā*, usually translated as 'sons/daughters of the covenant'.[20] Standing between the clergy and the lay people, these ascetics had a specific role within the community at large. Aphrahat's and Ephrem's works are aimed not at a separate body of ascetics, but at the broader Christian community. The idea of ascetic withdrawal from society seems first to appear in the Syrian area around the middle of the fourth century (Griffith 1994), and it is around 400 that we first hear about communities of ascetics deliberately conceived as distinct from lay society. The *Book of Steps* (*Liber graduum*) is a collection of thirty treatises addressed to a Christian community in which ordinary Christians (called 'the Upright') lived side by side with 'the Perfect'. The Perfect were enjoined to keep the 'major commandments' of radical asceticism, which included rejection of possessions, marriage, and manual labour, as well as total 'self-emptying' (cf. Phil 2: 7), while the 'minor commandments' were assigned to the Upright, who in addition were expected to provide for the Perfect (Kitchen and Parmentier 2004). Geographically, the *Book of Steps* belongs to the Persian part of northern Mesopotamia, probably to the region known as Adiabene. The spiritual instructions that the *Book* imparts are put into the mouth of an anonymous visionary leader, whom the alleged editor of the work (who may or may not be the real author) introduces as 'one of the first teachers who wrote in Syriac' and as the peer of fathers like 'Gregory the Great (i.e. of Nazianzus), Basil the Great, and blessed Evagrius' (Syriac Editor's Preface). The radical asceticism of the Perfect seems to echo the rigorous practices advocated by Tatian and in the *Acts of Thomas*, while there are also intriguing parallels with the Greek homilies attributed to Macarius as well as with Manichaean asceticism (Caner 2002).

Perhaps a decade or two after the *Book of Steps*, a different voice of Syriac asceticism expressed itself in the works of John the Solitary (Lavenant 1984). He lived near Apamea, in Syria Secunda (an important centre of Middle Platonist and Neoplatonist philosophy), and was among the first Syriac authors working that far west of the Euphrates (Brock 1998b: 715). John's focus was not community life, but the individual ascetic's spiritual progress, which he analysed in philosophical and psychological terms. There is general agreement nowadays that John originally wrote in Syriac. His familiarity with Greek philosophy certainly did not place him outside the mainstream tradition of Syriac asceticism, which he marked profoundly with his imprint.

Prior to the popularity in Syriac of writings associated with Egyptian asceticism, such as the corpus attributed to Evagrius Ponticus (which became available in Syriac no later than *c.* 500), the *Book of Steps* and John the Solitary's *œuvre* indicate that the early fifth century was an important period in the formative process of Syriac Christianity. The significance of this period is marked in other ways as well.

18.6 THE EARLY FIFTH CENTURY AND THE INCREASING HELLENIZATION OF SYRIAC CHRISTIANITY

An important manuscript was completed at Edessa in November 411. It survived and is actually the earliest dated Syriac manuscript: London, British Library, Add. Ms 12, 150 (Wright 1871: 631a–633b). It contains the following texts: (1) selections from the Pseudo-Clementine *Recognitions*; (2) Titus of Bostra's work against the Manichaeans; (3) Eusebius of Caesarea's *Theophany*; (4) Eusebius's *On the Martyrs of Palestine*; (5) Eusebius's *Praise of the Martyrs*; (6) a martyrology, arranged according to the Syriac months, with the names of martyrs in Persia added at the end (unfortunately damaged and incomplete).

Texts 1–5 are translations from Greek. Eusebius's earlier interest in things Edessene seems to be reciprocated here with a full Syriac translation of three of his works (one of them, the *Theophany*, is not otherwise preserved). The *Recognitions*, exhibiting traces of a more Jewish type of Christianity, probably originated in Greek in fourth-century Syria (Jones 1995, 2003), while Titus's work, only partly preserved in Greek, was one of the most systematic refutations of Manichaeism—written around 370 by the bishop of Bostra in Arabia (Pedersen 2004). These major Greek works, products of the neighbouring provinces of Syria, Palaestina, and Arabia, must have been deliberately incorporated in the literary tradition of Edessene Christianity, which was in the process of redefining its place within imperial Christianity. At the same time, there was a sense of attachment to Syriac Christians in Persia, indicated by the inclusion of their martyrs in the manuscript. Contacts with Persian Christians became more frequent, as the local Synod of Seleucia-Ctesiphon of 410, held under the auspices of the Persian Emperor, declared Christianity in Persia in agreement with the church of the Roman Empire. Among the protagonists of the synod was Maruta, bishop of Mayperqat (Martyropolis), who travelled back and forth as an envoy between the two empires (Winkler 2003: 25–8, 55–8). The relief in the situation of the Christians of Persia, which was inaugurated by the 410 synod, was only temporary, for by the year 419 political tension with the Roman Empire increased, and persecution resumed (Van Rompay 1995; Rist 1996: 31–3).

18.7 THE FIFTH-CENTURY CHRISTOLOGICAL DISCUSSIONS AND THEIR AFTERMATH

Developments in Edessa were marked decisively by the long tenure of the energetic Bishop Rabbula (411/12–435). Rules for monks, priests, and *bnay* and *bnāt qyāmā*, which he issued, show him as a committed organizer, keen to increase discipline and to regulate religious life. There is also evidence that he energetically set up programmes for the poor and the sick (Harvey 1994; Drijvers 1996),[21] while his dealings with pagans, heretics, and Jews (many of whom he allegedly succeeded in converting) have been variously interpreted. He promoted the use of the four separate Gospels, over against the *Diatessaron* (Petersen 1994: 42–3), and it is generally agreed that he had some involvement in the standardization of the New Testament text, although his exact role in creating and introducing the New Testament Peshitta remains debated.

During Rabbula's tenure, theological conflict broke out between Cyril of Alexandria and Nestorius of Constantinople, leading to the condemnation of Nestorius at the Council of Ephesus (431). Rabbula eventually became a staunch defender of Cyril's Christology. Whether he turned to it for political reasons, or whether this was his deepest conviction from the outset, will always remain a mystery.[22] In the campaign that Rabbula subsequently launched against the opponents of Alexandrian Christology, it was not so much Nestorius who was the target, but Theodore of Mopsuestia, who had died in peace in 428 and was now branded as one of the initiators of Nestorius's two-nature Christology. Many of Theodore's Greek works at this point already existed in Syriac translations and enjoyed great popularity in the School of Edessa, an academic institution with connections to the ecclesiastical authorities. By linking Theodore's name to the struggle against Nestorianism and by condemning Theodore's works to be burnt in Edessa (432), Rabbula contributed to dividing Edessene and Syriac Christianity into two opposing camps, which would never again be reconciled. At the same time, Syriac Christianity was thrown into the midst of the Christological controversy that pervaded the imperial church for more than a century and led up to the ecumenical councils of Chalcedon (451) and Constantinople (553).

Many in Edessa remained faithful to Theodore's legacy, to his Christology and biblical interpretation. While they continued studying his works and reinterpreting them in Syriac, they succeeded in creating a synthesis between the new Antiochene theology and the earlier Syriac tradition. One of the promoters of this process of adaptation and transformation of Theodore's works was Narsai, a gifted poet from Persian Mesopotamia. As a student at the School of Edessa and later, from the middle of the fifth century, as the school's director, he expressed the Antiochene views on Christ, human history, and salvation in metrical homilies, the language and style of which are often reminiscent of the earlier Syriac literary tradition. Just as in his exposition of the two-nature Christology Narsai emphasized Christ's full humanity (Frishman 1995–6), so too in his biblical interpretation he highlighted the human measure of God's dealings with man throughout history. The story of Paradise, for example, was seen not as the account of man's revolt and rejection that for ever changed human nature, but as the first step in the learning process through which God, according to his plan, led man to perfection (Frishman 1997; Becker 2006: 98–125).

This Antiochene, Theodorean line of thought met with increasing opposition in Edessa, so that, somewhere in the second half of the fifth century, Narsai, along with his followers and his books, left the city and established a new school in the city of Nisibis, which was within Persian territory. Narsai was the director of this new school until his death in 502/3. The School of Nisibis quickly became the intellectual centre of Persian Christianity, which adopted Theodore's two-nature Christology as its official doctrine at synods held in 484 and 486 (Winkler 2003: 66–9; Becker 2006). The East Syriac church, which is often infelicitously and incorrectly called 'Nestorian' (whereas its theology is in fact much closer to Theodore than to Nestorius), was henceforth seen as heretical by the imperial church.

Those in Edessa and elsewhere in Syria, who did not identify with Antiochene theology and exegesis as interpreted by Theodore of Mopsuestia, instead embraced Cyril of Alexandria's concepts and thoughts. Rabbula himself was one of the first interpreters of Cyril in Syriac. A process parallel to what happened to Theodore took place with regard to Cyril and Alexandrian theology. One of its main representatives in the late fifth and early sixth century was Jacob of Serug, who, just like Narsai, though probably slightly later than him, had been a student at the School of Edessa. In contrast with Narsai, he belonged to those in the school who opposed Theodore's influence.[23]

The demise of Antiochene theology within the Roman Empire and the exodus from Edessa to Nisibis did not imply that the Cyrillian opponents, who followed in the footsteps of Rabbula and Jacob of Serug, emerged as the winners. For 20 years after Ephesus, at the Council of Chalcedon (451), the imperial church endorsed a moderate form of the two-nature Christology. Intent on steering a middle course, the Council of Chalcedon condemned at the same time (what it saw as) extreme Dyophysitism, which was associated with the name of Nestorius, and Monophysitism, which was associated with the name of Eutyches. Chalcedon's sanctioning of the two-nature Christology, which became the doctrinal foundation for the whole of western Christianity, however, was unacceptable to many Christians, even those who were not willing to follow Eutyches (according to whom Christ's human nature was entirely absorbed within, and thus erased by, his divinity). Many Christians in Syria and Mesopotamia—as well as in Egypt, and later in Armenia and Ethiopia—thought that God-becoming-man could not exist in two natures, but had to be envisioned in one new nature of the God-man Christ. This was not, in their view, a particular expression of their type of eastern Christianity; rather, they were fully convinced that Miaphysitism, the one-nature doctrine,[24] was fully consonant with the teaching of the earlier orthodox church fathers, including Athanasius of Alexandria, the Cappadocians, Cyril, and all those who were universally recognized as the pillars of (imperial) orthodoxy.

It is in this spirit that the main theologians of the Miaphysite tradition, Philoxenus of Mabbog in Syriac and Severus of Antioch in Greek, defended the orthodoxy of their views. In the late fifth and early sixth century, they had the emperors' ears and occasionally their support, especially between 512 and 518, when Severus occupied the patriarchate of Antioch. In those years, Miaphysitism held sway all over the eastern empire, in Antioch, Alexandria, and even in Constantinople, while with Rome a schism existed between 482 and 518. At the accession of Justin I, in 518, however, Chalcedonian orthodoxy was restored as the basis of the Empire's religious policy. Severus was deposed and fled to Egypt, while the Miaphysites became the target of the emperors' assiduous attempts to bring them back to normative Chalcedonianism, either by persuasion or by force (Van Rompay 2005).

18.8 A SCATTERED LEGACY AND A DIVIDED TRADITION: THE SIXTH CENTURY AND BEYOND

These attempts failed. Instead, anti-Chalcedonians within the Roman Empire gradually shaped their own identity and their own ecclesiastical structures. Towards the end of the sixth century, the resistance against the imperial Church—which the Miaphysites saw as heretical—expressed itself predominantly in Syriac (mirroring the role of Coptic in the same period in Egypt), and the foundations were laid for a self-conscious, anti-Chalcedonian, Syrian Orthodox community. The sixth century in many ways was a very creative period. Earlier works by Ephrem and others were copied, while new texts—theological, hagiographical, historical, and philosophical—were authored. Churches and monasteries were built or expanded (Van Rompay 2005: 256–7). In the same period, Dyophysite Christianity had its formative period in the Persian-Sasanid Empire (Reinink 1995). These two Syriac churches were further consolidated under Islamic rule, while Syriac Christians of Chalcedonian allegiance found their way either into the Maronite Church, with its original centre in the region of Apamea, or into the Melkite (i.e. Byzantine Orthodox) Church of the patriarchate of Antioch.

Each of these traditions in its own way continues to the present day the religious and cultural heritage of Syriac Christianity. The Greek interpretation of Christianity in the course of history may have left a strong imprint on Syriac Christianity, even transforming it in a number of ways. Yet the historian should not see these developments as a move away from the early indigenous roots of Syriac Christian culture. Each period should be studied in its own right, with its own historical and cultural complexities, as an authentic expression of Syriac Christianity.

NOTES

1. For surveys of Syriac scholarship, see Brock (1994); De Halleux (1996); Murray (2004: 1–38).
2. With the exception of the surroundings of Jerusalem and some areas in Palestine, where there was a modest development of a different, West-Aramaic literary language, i.e. Christian Palestinian Aramaic.
3. Examples are the use of 'distancing' techniques when God is addressed or spoken about (in an attempt to emphasize God's transcendence); the introduction of prayer language where this is absent from the biblical text; the use of the term 'Shekintâ', denoting the Divine Presence. See Brock (1995b, 1998a: 489–93).
4. This may refer to any place in Syria or Mesopotamia, see Millar (1993: 227); *contra* Hunt (2003: 181 n. 1).

5. A critical survey of scholarship on the *Diatessaron* is available in Petersen (1994).

6. The term *enkrateia* is used here in its general sense, rather than as the specific designation of a sect, constructed by later heresiologists; see Hunt (2003: 145–50).

7. For a cautious and methodologically important study of some terms related to the incarnation, each having its own Jewish-Aramaic background, see Brock (1989); see also Brock (2001: 388 and 391–5).

8. Murray (2004) and Drijvers (1984) should be singled out among the scholars who have been most successful in depicting coherent pictures of pre-fourth-century Syriac Christianity.

9. For scholarship on the *Hymn of the Pearl*, see Poirier (1981) and Ferreira (2002).

10. For the state of the research, see Uro (2003: esp. 26–30 and 134–8). According to Uro, 'it has been almost universally acknowledged that [the *Gospel of*] *Thomas* should be seen as a product of east Syrian Christianity' (p. 137). He regards the period between *c.*100 and 140 CE as 'the best conjecture' for the date. DeConick (2005) suggests a mid-first-century origin for the 'kernel' text in a Palestinian-Aramaic context, while the complete Gospel, to be dated no later than 120 CE, might reflect adaptation and modification in Syriac (esp. pp. 240–4). Quispel (2006), agreeing with DeConick, asserts that the *Gospel of Thomas* was written in Edessa before 140 CE.

11. The most accessible English translation is Drijvers (1965). For a recent German translation, with some notes, see Krannich and Stein (2004). A recent analysis of Bardaisan's view on the resurrection can be found in Possekel (2004).

12. Another categorization which is not helpful in the study of early Syriac Christianity is that of Gnosticism. While some texts have been understood as Gnostic by ancient readers or by modern scholars, the distinction makes sense only from the perspective of a (later) non-Gnostic orthodox standard. Attempts to group together certain Gnostic texts of alleged Syrian origin have remained problematic. See King (2003: 162–5) and Uro (2003: 20–4).

13. Introductions to Ephrem's world and writings can be found in McVey (1989) and Brock (1990); for Aphrahat, see Baarda (1975: 1–10); Pierre (1988); Bruns (1990, 1991).

14. An excellent treatment of Aphrahat's Christology is Bruns (1990). On the possible connection between this Christology and Jewish Christianity, see the author's nuanced observations on pp. 214–16.

15. References are to Valavanolickal (2005).

16. For Ephrem, see Kronholm (1978); for Aphrahat, see Koltun-Fromm (1996).

17. For Ephrem, see Shepardson (2001) and Kuhlmann (2004); for Aphrahat, see Becker (2002, 2003).

18. Brock (1995a: 77) identified a passage in Ephrem's *Commentary on the Diatessaron* that mirrors, and may have been borrowed from, Aphrahat's *Demonstration* 23.

19. Murray (2004) focuses on Aphrahat and Ephrem while taking other early texts into consideration as well. On Ephrem, see also Bou Mansour (1988). For an exploration of Ephrem's poetic language and style within the broader Aramaic literary tradition, see Rodrigues Pereira (1997).

20. Griffith (1995: 229–34). For a possible connection between the *qyāmā* and the Jewish institution of the *maʿamad*, see Pierre (1988: 99 n. 84); de Halleux (1996: 161 with n. 78); Murray (2004: 14 n. 65). For further possible layers of meaning, see Murray (1999, 2004: 16–17). For a recent study on the *bnāt qyāmā*, see Harvey (2005).

21. Doran (2006) conveniently brings together English translations of the most relevant Syriac texts, with introductions and notes.

22. For a recent discussion of some of the theological implications of Rabbula's position, see Doran (2006: 61–4), while the possible social dimension of the conflict in Edessa is indicated (pp. 115–19).

23. On Jacob's Christology, see Bou Mansour (2002). The parallelism between Jacob and Narsai may not be complete, as Jacob does not seem not to have followed Cyril as radically as Narsai followed Theodore. Both in his theology and in his biblical interpretation Jacob was closer to Ephrem than was Narsai. See Bou Mansour (2002: 497–9); Van Rompay (1996: 637–9).

24. There is a tendency in recent scholarship to use the term 'Miaphysite', which reflects Cyril of Alexandria's Christological terminology, and to avoid other terms that in the past were used to designate the anti-Chalcedonians, such as 'Monophysite' and 'Jacobite'. The latter names, coined by the anti-Chalcedonians' opponents, are seen by the present-day non-Chalcedonian communities as inadequate descriptions of their tradition. The term 'Monophysite' is associated with Eutyches, whose Christology is rejected by all later Miaphysite theologians.

Suggested Reading

Many of the works referred to in the Bibliography will serve as introductions to important themes and as stepping stones towards further explorations and research. The following titles are additional.

Atallah, M. et al. (2005) (eds.), Sources syriaques, i: Nos sources: Arts et littérature syriaques (Antélias: Centre d'Études et de Recherches Orientales).

Brock, S. (1997), A Brief Outline of Syriac Literature, Moran 'Etho, 9 (Baker Hill, Kottayam: St Ephrem Ecumenical Research Institute).

—— and Harvey, S. A. (1987), Holy Women of the Syrian Orient, The Transformation of the Classical Heritage, 13 (Berkeley: University of California Press).

Camplani, A. (1998), 'Rivisitando Bardesane: Note sulle fonti siriache del bardesanismo e sulla sua collocazione storico-religiosa', Cristianesimo nella Storia, 19: 519–96.

—— (2005), 'Bardesane et les bardesanites', Annuaire de l'École pratique des hautes études: Section des sciences religieuses: Résumé des conférences et travaux 112: 29–50.

Donceel-Voûte, P. (1988), Les pavements des églises byzantines de Syrie et du Liban: Décor, archéologie et liturgie, Publications d'histoire de l'art et d'archéologie de l'Université de Louvain, 69 (Louvain-la-Neuve: Département d'archéologie et d'histoire de l'art).

Garsoïan, N., Mathews, T., and Thomson R. W. (1982) (eds.), East of Byzantium: Syria and Armenia in the Formative Period (Washington D.C.: Dumbarton Oaks).

Harvey, S. A. (1990), Asceticism and Society in Crisis: John of Ephesus and the Lives of the Eastern Saints, The Transformation of the Classical Heritage, 18 (Berkeley: University of California Press).

Ross, S. K. (2001), Roman Edessa: Politics and Culture on the Eastern Fringes of the Roman Empire, 114–242 CE (London: Routledge).

WALKER, J. T. (2006), *The Legend of Mar Qardagh: Narrative and Christian Heroism in Late Antique Iraq*, Transformation of the Classical Heritage, 40 (Berkeley: University of California Press).

BIBLIOGRAPHY

BAARDA, T. (1975), *The Gospel Quotations of Aphrahat the Persian Sage*, i: *Aphrahat's Text of the Fourth Gospel* (Amsterdam: Vrije Universiteit Amsterdam).

BECKER, A. H. (2002), 'Anti-Judaism and Care for the Poor in Aphrahat's *Demonstration 20*', *JECS* 10: 305–27.

—— (2003), 'Beyond the Spatial and Temporal *Limes*: Questioning the "Parting of the Ways" Outside the Roman Empire', in A. H. Becker and A. Y. Reed (eds.), *The Ways that Never Parted: Jews and Christians in Late Antiquity and the Early Middle Ages*, Texte und Studien zum antiken Judentum, 95 (Tübingen: Mohr/Paul Siebeck), 373–92.

—— (2006), *Fear of God and the Beginning of Wisdom: The School of Nisibis and Christian Scholastic Culture in Late Antique Mesopotamia*, Divinations: Rereading Late Ancient Religion (Philadelphia: University of Pennsylvania Press).

BEYER, K. (1991), 'Das syrische Perlenlied: ein Erlösungsmythos als Märchengedicht', *ZDMG* 140: 234–59.

BOU MANSOUR, T. (1988), *La pensée symbolique de Saint Éphrem le Syrien*, Bibliothèque de l'Université Saint Esprit, 16 (Kaslik: Université Saint-Esprit).

—— (2002), 'Die Christologie des Jakob von Sarug', in A. Grillmeier (ed.), *Jesus der Christus im Glauben der Kirche*, Band 2/3: *Die Kirchen von Jerusalem und Antiochien nach 451 bis 600*, mit Beiträgen von A. Grillmeier, Th. Hainthaler, T. Bou Mansour, L. Abramowski, herausgegeben von Th. Hainthaler (Freiburg: Herder), 449–99.

BROCK, S. (1989), 'The Lost Old Syriac at Luke 1:35 and the Earliest Syriac Terms for the Incarnation', in W. L. Petersen (ed.), *Gospel Traditions in the Second Century: Origins, Recensions, Text, and Transmission*, Christianity and Judaism in Antiquity, 3 (Notre Dame, Ind.: University of Notre Dame Press), 117–31.

—— (1990), *Saint Ephrem: Hymns on Paradise* (Crestwood, NY: St Vladimir's Seminary Press).

—— (1992), 'Eusebius and Syriac Christianity', in H. W. Attridge and G. Hata (eds.), *Eusebius, Christianity, and Judaism* (Detroit: Wayne State University Press), 212–34.

—— (1994), 'Syriac Studies in the Last Three Decades', in R. Lavenant (ed.), *VI Symposium Syriacum* 1992, OrChrAn 247 (Rome: Pontificium Institutum Orientalium Studiorum), 13–29.

—— (1995*a*), '*Notulae Syriacae*: Some Miscellaneous Identifications', *Mus* 108: 69–78.

—— (1995*b*), 'A Palestinian Targum Feature in Syriac', *Journal of Jewish Studies*, 46: 271–82.

—— (1998*a*), 'The Peshitta Old Testament: Between Judaism and Christianity', *Cristianesimo nella Storia*, 19: 483–502.

—— (1998*b*), 'Syriac Culture, 337–425', in A. Cameron and P. Garnsey (eds.), *CAH Ancient History*, xiii: *The Late Empire*, A.D. *337–425* (Cambridge: Cambridge University Press), 708–19.

BROCK, S. (2001), 'Invocations to/for the Holy Spirit in Syriac Liturgical Texts: Some Comparative Approaches', in R. F. Taft and G. Winkler (eds.), *Comparative Liturgy Fifty Years after Anton Baumstark (1872–1948)*, OrChrAn 265 (Rome: Pontificium Institutum Orientalium Studiorum), 377–406.

BRUNS, P. (1990), *Das Christusbild Aphrahats des Persischen Weisen*, Hereditas: Studien zur Alten Kirchengeschichte, 4 (Bonn: Borengässer).

—— (1991), *Aphrahat: Unterweisungen*, Fontes Christiani, 5/1–2 (Freiburg: Herder).

CANER, D. (2002), *Wandering, Begging Monks: Spiritual Authority and the Promotion of Monasticism in Late Antiquity*, The Transformation of the Classical Heritage, 33 (Berkeley: University of California Press).

CHARLESWORTH, J. H. (1998), *Critical Reflections on the Odes of Solomon*, i: *Literary Setting, Textual Studies, Gnosticism, the Dead Sea Scrolls and the Gospel of John*, JSPSup 22 (Sheffield: Sheffield Academic Press).

DECONICK, A. D. (2005), *Recovering the Original* Gospel of Thomas: *A History of the Gospel and its Growth*, Early Christianity in Context—Library of New Testament Studies, 286 (London: T & T Clark).

DORAN, R. (2006), *Stewards of the Poor: The Man of God, Rabbula, and Hiba in Fifth-Century Edessa*, CS 208 (Kalamazoo, Mich.: Cistercian Publications).

DRIJVERS, H. J. W. (1965), *The Book of the Laws of Countries: Dialogue on Fate of Bardaisan of Edessa*, Semitic Texts with Translations (Assen: Van Gorcum).

—— (1984), 'East of Antioch: Forces and Structures in the Development of Early Syriac Theology', in H. J. W. Drijvers, *East of Antioch: Studies in Early Syriac Christianity* (London: Variorum Reprints), 1–27.

—— (1992), 'The Acts of Thomas', in W. Schneemelcher (ed.), *New Testament Apocrypha*, rev. ed., ii.: *Writings Relating to the Apostles: Apocalypses and Related Subjects* (Louisville, Ky.: Westminster/John Knox Press), 322–411.

—— (1996), 'The Man of God of Edessa, Bishop Rabbula, and the Urban Poor: Church and Society in the Fifth Century', *JECS* 4: 235–48.

—— and HEALEY, J. F. (1999), *The Old Syriac Inscriptions of Edessa and Osrhoene*, Handbuch der Orientalistik, i, 42 (Leiden: E. J. Brill).

FERREIRA, J. (2002), *The Hymn of the Pearl: The Syriac and Greek Texts with Introduction, Translations, and Notes*, Early Christian Studies, 3 (Sydney: St Paul's Publications).

FRISHMAN, J. (1995–6), 'Narsai's Christology according to his Homily "On the Word Became Flesh"', *The Harp: A Review of Syriac and Oriental Ecumenical Studies*, 8–9: 289–303.

—— (1997), 'Themes on Genesis 1–5 in Early East-Syrian Exegesis', in J. Frishman and L. Van Rompay (eds.), *The Book of Genesis in Jewish and Oriental Christian Interpretation: A Collection of Essays*, Traditio Exegetica Graeca, 5 (Louvain: Peeters), 171–86.

GRIFFITH, S. H. (1986), 'Ephraem, the Deacon of Edessa, and the Church of the Empire', in Th. Halton and J. P. Williman (eds.), *Diakonia: Studies in Honor of Robert T. Meyer* (Washington: The Catholic University of America Press), 22–52.

—— (1994), 'Julian Saba, "Father of the Monks" of Syria', *JECS* 2: 185–216.

—— (1995), 'Asceticism in the Church of Syria: The Hermeneutics of Early Syrian Monasticism', in V. L. Wimbush and R. Valantasis (eds.), *Asceticism* (New York: Oxford University Press), 220–45.

—— (2003), 'The Doctrina Addai as a Paradigm of Christian Thought in Edessa in the Fifth Century', *Hugoye: Journal of Syriac Studies*, <http://syrcom.cua.edu/syrcom/Hugoye>, 6/2.

HAAR ROMENY, B. TER (2005), 'Hypotheses on the Development of Judaism and Christianity in Syria in the Period after 70 C.E.', in H. van de Sandt (ed.), *Matthew and the Didache: Two Documents from the Same Jewish-Christian Milieu?* (Assen: Van Gorcum; Minneapolis: Fortress Press), 13–33.

HALLEUX, A. DE (1996), 'Vingt ans d'étude critique des Églises syriaques', in R. F. Taft (ed.), *The Christian East: Its Institutions and Its Thoughts: A Critical Reflection*, OrChrAn 252 (Rome: Pontificium Institutum Orientalium Studiorum), 145–79.

HARVEY, S. A. (1994), 'The Holy and the Poor: Models from Early Syriac Christianity', in E. A. Hanawalt and C. Lindberg (eds.), *'Through the Eye of the Needle': Judeo-Christian Roots of Social Welfare* (Kirksville, Mo.: The Thomas Jefferson University Press), 43–66.

—— (2005), 'Revisiting the Daughters of the Covenant: Women's Choirs and Sacred Song in Ancient Syriac Christianity', *Hugoye: Journal of Syriac Studies*, <http://syrcom.cua.edu/syrcom/Hugoye>, 8/2.

HUNT, E. J. (2003), *Christianity in the Second Century: The Case of Tatian* (London: Routledge).

JONES, F. S. (1995), *An Ancient Jewish Christian Source on the History of Christianity: Pseudo-Clementine Recognitions 1, 27–71*, SBLTT, Christian Apocrypha Series, 37/2 (Atlanta: Scholars Press).

—— (2003), 'Clement of Rome and the *Pseudo-Clementines*: History and/or Fiction', in Ph. Luisier (ed.), *Studi su Clemente Romano*, OrChrAn 268 (Rome: Pontificium Institutum Orientalium Studiorum), 139–61.

JOOSTEN, J. (1997), 'La tradition syriaque des évangiles et la question du «substrat araméen»', *Revue d'histoire et de philosophie religieuses*, 77: 257–72.

KING, K. L. (2003), *What is Gnosticism?* (Cambridge, Mass.: Harvard University Press).

KITCHEN, R. A., and PARMENTIER, M. F. G. (2004), *The Book of Steps: The Syriac Liber Graduum*, CS 196 (Kalamazoo, Mich.: Cistercian Publications).

KOLTUN-FROMM, N. (1996), 'A Jewish–Christian Conversation in Fourth-Century Persian Mesopotamia', *Journal of Jewish Studies*, 47: 45–63.

KRANNICH, T., and STEIN, P. (2004), 'Das "Buch der Gesetze der Länder" des Bardesanes von Edessa', *ZAC* 8: 203–29.

KRONHOLM, T. (1978), *Motifs from Genesis 1–11 in the Genuine Hymns of Ephrem the Syrian: With Particular Reference to the Influence of Jewish Exegetical Tradition*, Coniectanea Biblica, Old Testament Series, 11 (Lund: Gleerup).

KUHLMANN, K. H. (2004), 'The Harp out of Tune: The Anti-Judaism/Anti-Semitism of St. Ephrem', *The Harp: A Review of Syriac and Oriental Ecumenical Studies*, 17: 177–83.

LATTKE, M. (1999–2005), *Oden Salomos: Text, Übersetzung, Kommentar*, Novum Testamentum et Orbis Antiquus, 41/1–3 (Freiburg: Universitätsverlag; Göttingen: Vandenhoeck & Ruprecht).

LAVENANT, R. (1984), *Jean d'Apamée: Dialogues et traités*, SC 311 (Paris: Éditions du Cerf).

McVEY, K. E. (1989), *Ephrem the Syrian: Hymns*, CWS (Mahwah, NJ: Paulist Press).

MILLAR, F. (1993), *The Roman Near East 31 BC–AD 337* (Cambridge, Mass.: Harvard University Press).

—— (1998), 'Ethnic Identity in the Roman Near East, 325–450: Language, Religion, and Culture', *Mediterranean Archaeology*, 11: 159–76.

MURRAY, R. (2004), *Symbols of Church and Kingdom: A Study in Early Syriac Tradition* (Cambridge: Cambridge University Press, 1975; repr. Gorgias Press).

Murray, R. (1999), ' "Circumcision of Heart" and the Origins of the *Qyâmâ*', in G. J. Reinink and A. C. Klugkist (eds.), *After Bardaisan: Studies on Continuity and Change in Honour of Professor Han J.W. Drijvers*, Orientalia Lovaniensia Analecta, 89 (Leuven: Peeters), 201–11.

Pedersen, N. A. (2004), *Demonstrative Proof in Defence of God: A Study of Titus of Bostra's Contra Manichaeos—The Work's Sources, Aims and Relation to its Contemporary Theology*, NHMS 56 (Leiden: E. J. Brill).

Perrin, N. (2002), *Thomas and Tatian: The Relationship between the Gospel of Thomas and the Diatessaron*, SBL, Academia Biblica, 5 (Atlanta: SBL).

Petersen, W. L. (1994), *Tatian's Diatessaron: Its Creation, Dissemination, Significance, and History in Scholarship*, Suppl. *VC* 25 (Leiden: E. J. Brill).

Pierre, M.-J. (1988), *Aphraate, le Sage persan: Les Exposés*, SC 249–50 (Paris: Éditions du Cerf).

Poirier, P. H. (1981), *L'Hymne de la Perle des Actes de Thomas*, Homo Religiosus, 8 (Louvain-la-Neuve: Centre d'histoire des religions).

Possekel, U. (1999), *Evidence of Greek Philosophical Concepts in the Writings of Ephrem the Syrian*, CSCO 580, Subsidia, 102 (Louvain: Peeters).

——(2004), 'Bardaisan of Edessa on the Resurrection: Early Syriac Eschatology in its Religious-Historical Context', *Oriens Christianus*, 88: 1–28.

Quispel, G. (2006), review of DeConick (2005), *VC* 60: 231–3.

Reinink, G. J. (1995), '«Edessa Grew Dim and Nisibis Shone Forth»: The School of Nisibis at the Transition of the Sixth-Seventh Century', in J. W. Drijvers and A. A. MacDonald (eds.), *Centres of Learning: Learning and Location in Pre-Modern Europe and the Near East* (Leiden: E. J. Brill), 77–90.

Rist, J. (1996), 'Die Verfolgung der Christen im spätantiken Sasanidenreich: Ursachen, Verlauf und Folgen', *Oriens Christianus*, 80: 17–42.

Rodrigues Pereira, A. S. (1997), *Studies in Aramaic Poetry (c. 100 B.C.E.–c. 600 C.E.): Selected Jewish, Christian and Samaritan Poems*, Studia Semitica Neerlandica (Assen: Van Gorcum).

Rouwhorst, G. (1997), 'Jewish Liturgical Traditions in Early Syriac Christianity', *VC* 51: 72–93.

Shepardson, C. (2001), 'Anti-Jewish Rhetoric and Intra-Christian Conflict in the Sermons of Ephrem Syrus', in M. F. Wiles and E. J. Yarnold (eds.), *StPatr* 35 (Leuven: Peeters), 502–7.

Uro, R. (2003), *Thomas: Seeking the Historical Context of the Gospel of Thomas* (London: T & T Clark).

Valavanolickal, K. (2005), *Aphrahat: Demonstrationes*, i–ii: *Moran 'Etho*, 23–24 (Baker Hill, Kottayam: St Ephrem Ecumenical Research Institute).

Van Rompay, L. (1995), 'Impetuous Martyrs? The Situation of the Persian Christians in the Last Years of Yazdgard I (419–420)', in M. Lamberigts and P. Van Deun (eds.), *Martyrium in Multidisciplinary Perspective: Memorial L. Reekmans*, BETL 117 (Leuven: Leuven University Press and Peeters), 363–75.

——(1996), 'The Christian Syriac Tradition of Interpretation', in M. Sæbø (ed.), *Hebrew Bible / Old Testament: The History of Its Interpretation*, i, 1: *Antiquity* (Göttingen: Vandenhoeck & Ruprecht), 612–41.

——(2005), 'Society and Community in the Christian East', in M. Maas (ed.), *The Cambridge Companion to the Age of Justinian* (Cambridge: Cambridge University Press), 239–66.

WEITZMAN, M. P. (1999), *The Syriac Version of the Old Testament: An Introduction*, University of Cambridge Oriental Publications, 56 (Cambridge: Cambridge University Press).

WINKLER, D. W. (2003), *Ostsyrisches Christentum: Untersuchungen zu Christologie, Ekklesiologie und zu den ökumenischen Beziehungen der Assyrischen Kirche des Ostens*, Studien zur Orientalischen Kirchengeschichte, 26 (Münster: LIT Verlag).

WRIGHT, W. (1870–2), *Catalogue of Syriac Manuscripts in the British Museum Acquired since the Year 1838*, 3 vols. (London: Trustees of the British Museum).

PART V

STRUCTURES AND AUTHORITIES

CHAPTER 19

CLERGY AND LAITY

KAREN JO TORJESEN

19.1 INTRODUCTION

THE distinction between clergy and laity in its most elemental form is a way of creating and setting apart an elite. The societies around the Mediterranean constituted their elites in a variety of ways. Within the philosophical schools there were master teachers and seekers, to train and form the young there were pedagogues, in civic life there were rulers and people, in social relations there were patrons and clients, and in religious life there were priests and worshippers; finally, there were ascetics, a spiritual elite spawned within Christianity. Pierre Bourdieu summarizes this formation of elites as a sociological process, explaining that when a group of religious specialists become socially recognized as possessing an exclusive and necessary expertise, they monopolize the cult through the exclusion of those who are constituted as laity, those unskilled in the doctrines and removed from the sacred (Bourdieu 1971: 304). Clergy and laity form a dyad; they are categories that emerge only in terms of their relationship to each other.

The question about the clergy and the laity then becomes a fascinating historical question about how the unity of the Church—symbolic, organizational, and political—comes to rest on the constitution of these two classes and the relationship between them. Why did early Christian churches create a distinction and division between clergy and laity? Joseph Blenkinsopp puts the question poignantly: 'Why the sacralization (and hierarchicalization) of office in what began clearly as a lay movement?' (Blenkinsopp 1967: 436). How did new organizational models adopted by an expanding Christian community reshape the boundaries between clergy and laity?

The use of the term *laikos* in the first three centuries is sporadic, and when it is used, it is used in different senses. The first appearance of the term *laikos* is in the *First Letter to the Corinthians* of Clement of Rome (40. 5). Here it is used in the context of evoking the image of the Israelite priesthood to give a special status to the presbyters and bishops, distinct from that of the 'laity'. It was more than a hundred years before the term was used again, this time by Clement of Alexandria, who used it in discussing the monogamy required of presbyters, deacons, and laymen. In this context *laikos* represents a status above what later becomes a non-clerical status. Attila Jakab argues that distinguishing the *laikoi* from women, children, and perhaps even twice-married men implies that the *laikos* serves the *ekklēsia* in some fashion (Jakab 2004: 186). Interestingly, in Alexandria both Clement and Heracleon deploy the term *laikos* to designate unbelievers or carnal Christians by appropriating temple imagery of the holy place and those who stand outside it. In fact, Greek translations of the Hebrew Bible used the term *laikos* for what was profane, not holy.

The term *laikos* comes from the word *laos*, meaning people. Hence it came to mean of or from the people, unofficial, civilian, or common. In contrast, the word *klēros* as the origin of the Christian term 'clergy' is more perplexing. It begins as the term for casting lots; what is assigned by lot refers to a piece of land, then to a legacy or inheritance or a body of inheritors. The LXX uses the term *klēros* for the Levites in Deuteronomy 18: 4: 'they do not receive a portion of the land, but the Lord is their *klēros*'. Originally the notion of *klēros* applied to all Christians, who were *klēronomoi* (inheritors) of divine promises. In 1 Peter 5: 3 *klēros* applies to all the people. The *Pontificale Romanum* makes this passage the basis for the meaning of the term *klēros* applied to the upper hierarchy of church leadership. After the notion of the holiness of the clergy evolved, the term for cleric was extended in canon law to include monastics, for their being set apart from the world and consequent holiness.

Contemporary interpretations of the terms 'laity' and 'clergy' vary widely, but draw on seeds of meanings that lie within the historical usage. The *Catholic Encyclopedia* of 1910 explains the relationship of clergy and laity within a juridical framework of rights and duties of rulers and ruled. To the clergy belongs the triple aspect of spiritual authority: government, teaching, and worship. The laity are those who are 'not depositaries of spiritual power', are excluded from it and subjugated to it (Mugnier 1910). The duties of the laity are respect and deference to the clergy and financial maintenance; their rights are to direction, protection, and instruction from the clergy. On the other hand, Yves Congar, writing in 1976 for the *Dictionnaire de Spiritualité* explains the term laity within the framework of spirituality by referring back to the period when all Christians were considered *klēronomoi*; consequently, the laity also bear responsibility for much of the work of the Church. Through baptism all are members of Christ, the High Priest, and therefore set apart. Together they participate in the divine mysteries as holy people. Further, teaching is the work of all; the whole community participates in theological debate. Esteemed teachers are recognized by reputation rather than installation in office. The models of holiness for the laity are the martyrs and the ascetics. Through these models the whole of the Christian community sees itself as living from an eschatological perspective, leading the heavenly life (Congar 1976: 81–2).

19.2 PAST SCHOLARSHIP

The premiss of much of the earlier scholarship held that development of the ecclesiastical hierarchy and the clergy/laity dyad was evolutionary, an organic unfolding of an embryonic distinction between clergy and laity into a fully elaborated polarity based on the priestly functions of the clergy and the sacrality of the liturgy. To establish the continuity between the present and an apostolic past, histories were constructed by reading backward from later, fully developed forms of clerical organization to earlier, simpler versions. The theological notion of the unity of the Church also framed the research on the clergy and the laity that sought to reconstruct a single master narrative for the stages through which the clergy/laity dyad developed. The master narrative tracked two distinct trajectories: a process of increasing hierarchicalization and a process of growing sacralization. Consequently, the scholarship of this era drew heavily on ecclesiastical and theological sources to show the internal dynamics of the evolution of the clergy/laity dyad and considered external influences only tangentially.

Textual evidence for a clear divide between clergy and laity, the bishop's monarchical authority, and the connections between church office and the liturgy does not appear until the third century. In fact, the leading scholar of the clergy/laity dyad insists that such a distinction was completely unknown; higher church offices are not treated as a collective over against the laity (Faivre 1983: 195). The challenge for traditional scholarship was to show how these elements were in place, at least implicitly, in the second and third century. Hans von Campenhausen's *Ecclesiastical Authority and Spiritual Power*, which established that the model for leadership in the second century was charismatic, nonetheless located an embryonic form of episcopal office (the power of the keys in the primitive church) in the practice of correction and the offering of forgiveness (Campenhausen 1969: 124–48). The letters of Ignatius figure in this debate; clearly Ignatius is arguing for the mono-episcopacy in a way that implies a sharper divide between leaders and people. The question of whether Ignatius's new vision for the bishop's role found support among second-century Christians is debated by scholars.

Issues of orthodoxy and heresy also shaped the reconstruction of the relationships between leaders and people. Relationships between clergy and laity among groups labelled Gnostic, Montanist, or Donatist have not been incorporated into historical reconstructions of the evolution of the clergy and the laity, even though their ecclesiastical organizations were well documented. When included, these groups function as the foils against which an orthodox Christianity defines itself. Consequently, the Montanists and the Gnostics are presented by Campenhausen as precipitating the crisis of Christian unity and authority that necessitated a doctrine of apostolic succession to link contemporary bishops with the apostles.

As the clergy gained ascendancy, Christian leaders sought to demonstrate that even their present form of church organization was based on apostolic authority. The production of the church orders in the second, third, and fourth centuries, asserting apostolic authorship and regulating liturgy, church office, and moral conduct, reflected the need to provide the same normative basis for the relationships between clergy and laity as that established for Christian teachings.

19.3 NEW APPROACHES

Scholarship on the institutionalization of Christianity that in an earlier era had been primarily ecclesiastical and theological is now increasingly cross-disciplinary, drawing on work in sociology, politics, economics, archaeology, gender, and religion. The theological and ecclesiastical concerns of the earlier generation of scholars are still present in recent scholarship, but these concerns are related to the cultural, political, and religious milieux in which the churches evolved. What is emerging is a new interest in social change, in the social, cultural, political, and economic factors involved in the process of institutionalization, and the way in which those factors shaped the notions of clergy and laity.

19.3.1 Sociology

Social class and patronage were the key identifiers of the Roman elites. As members of these elites were drawn into church leadership, their status and their social roles shaped the formation of the clergy, and in turn the relationship between clergy, and laity as that between patrons and clients. Studies of Roman systems of patronage and the extensive work of Roman historians on imperial interests in Christianization have provided the next generation of scholars with new models for analysing the formation of a Christian elite. Patrons were members of a higher social class, who provided protection and support to clients of the lower classes, who reciprocated through honour and loyalty. Wealth was effective only when converted to social power, and patronage was the prime mode for doing so. Charles Bobertz (1990) used a model of patronage to interpret Cyprian's rapid ascendancy to the episcopacy. With this model he was able to illuminate how the recently converted aristocrat, elected by acclamation to the episcopacy at Carthage, consolidated his power through gifts to individuals, appointments to office, and support for the poor. The wealth of patrons allowed them to provide financial support, their social networks to secure appointments to office. During the third century bishops were chosen more frequently from the curial class, the municipal elites, whose political power rested on patronage. For the post-Constantinian era Roman historians like Michele Salzman (2002) have shown how Christian emperors showered status on bishops, creating a new Christian aristocracy that could be integrated into the Roman elites who functioned as their clients.

19.3.2 Politics

As early as 1930, Alexander Beck demonstrated that Tertullian of Carthage was one of the first Christian intellectuals to use the language, metaphors, and paradigms of public life to interpret the Church (Beck 1930: 39 ff.). In Tertullian's ideology of the Church, the Church is a legal body (*corpus* or *societas*) unified by a common law (*lex fidei*) and a common moral discipline (*disciplina*). Elizabeth Herrmann, in *Ecclesia in Re Publica* (1980) expanded on the idea of the influence of Roman public life on Christian institutions by demonstrating how Roman civic institutions (city councils) served as models for church organization. Her study further revealed significant regional differences in the development of the clerical office corresponding to regional differences among city councils. The political models shaped the relationships between clergy and laity as those between rulers and the ruled. The influence of Roman political organization on church office is even more obvious for the period after Constantine. As Hal Drake shows in *Constantine and the Bishops*, the emperors' strategy of incorporating the bishops into their power base had the unintended consequences of giving the bishops new political authority (Drake 2000: 441–83).

19.3.3 Economics

Georg Schöllgen analysed the evolution of the clergy/laity dyad, or what he calls 'the professionalization of the clergy', from the standpoint of the degree and kind of financial support that church leaders could claim. The official priesthoods of the Greek and Roman cities form the baseline for his assessment—priests had rights to the offerings (*sportula*) made to the gods. By the third century, clergy were receiving not only gifts, *sportula*, but also a monthly allotment. Even more significant is the fact that this remuneration was pro-rated to reflect clerical rank—bishops receiving more than presbyters, presbyters more than widows. Schöllgen sees this financial recognition of rank and the later inclusion of the lower clergy as evidence for an incipient clerical *cursus honorum* (Schöllgen 1998: 67).

19.3.4 Archaeology

Archaeology opens an entirely new perspective on the relationships between leaders and people. The social meanings of the domestic space in the house churches and those of the monumental basilicas framed relationships between people and leaders differently. Michael White's *The Social Origins of Christian Architecture* (1997) not only provides a valuable periodization for the transition from house churches to basilicas, but also collects all the relevant documentation into one easily usable volume. Archaeological reports, art, inscriptions on the site, and descriptions in early Christian literature are the sources from which he constructs the periods of early Christian development. His attention to the inscriptions reveals that bishops and presbyters were frequently the donors of house churches or paid for expensive renovations within them. The commemoration of these donors by dedicatory inscriptions reveals that social status and financial resources could be a conduit to church office.

The evidence of documentary sources, epitaphs, and dedicatory inscriptions is especially useful, for these sources record information about the activities of individuals in the ordinary routines of life captured for ever in stone. General statements about church office-holders and their functions and qualifications provided by literary sources can be tested against these documentary sources.

Even more surprising is the inscriptional evidence for women holding church offices. In *Women Office Holders in Early Christianity* (2000), Ute Eisen has assembled considerable epigraphic evidence that women were prophets, teachers, presbyters, deacons, and widows. Her work followed on the ground-breaking study of Bernadette Brooten in 1982, showing on the basis of epigraphic evidence that women were elders, rulers, and mothers in Jewish synagogues. This archaeological evidence of the activities of individual women raises questions about how to interpret literary sources that declare women unfit for church office.

19.3.5 Gender

Contemporary controversies over the ordination of women have introduced gender as a mode of analysis in studying the shifting frontiers between clergy and laity. On the one hand, classification of widows and virgins as part of the clergy signals a high value placed on female asceticism. On the other hand, debates over the legitimacy of women leaders indicate a masculinization of leadership. Historical and anthropological studies on gender and sexuality provide new tools for understanding the role of gender in the process of institutionalization. Several scholars have explored the religious and social authority of women as leaders and office-holders: Antoinette Clark Wire, *Corinthian Women Prophets* (1990), Anne Jensen, *God's Self-Confident Daughters* (1992), and Christine Trevett, *Montanism: Gender, Authority and the New Prophecy* (1996) examine the way in which prophetic authority underwrites women's leadership and the translation of that authority into church office. Antoinette Wire uses a rhetorical analysis to discern the voices of the groups resisting Paul's model of authority for house churches. Their Christology emphasizing the transformation into a new identity opened the way to challenge the cultural norms of women's inferiority and subordination. Anne Jensen traces women's leadership from the Pauline churches of the first century through the fourth.

Christine Trevett's study brings the excluded 'heretic' into the discussion of leadership. Although the Montanists began as a revival of the spirit of prophecy in the second century, they evolved the same organizational structure as the 'orthodox' churches. Consequently, women held episcopal office and exercised the same authority as other bishops. The attempts of 'orthodox' bishops to exorcize a female bishop mark the growing cultural conviction that church office is an exclusively male prerogative. In my *When Women Were Priests* (Torjesen 1993), I analyse the social sources for women's authority as office-holders. The patronage exercised by Christian leaders was not gendered. According to the cultural norms of Roman antiquity, women as well as men could be patrons. Furthermore, as long as Christian groups met in house churches, they were operating in the private sphere, a domain in which women's leadership was expected and respected. At the same time, I examine the cultural forces that resisted women's leadership. The construction of gender roles among the elites reserved the political sphere of office holding, public speaking, and military command to men; the domestic sphere was women's domain. As the organization models imitated public life, women's leadership became increasingly controversial.

19.3.6 Asceticism

Like gender studies, the burgeoning field of studies of early Christian asceticism has added a new dimension to the analysis of the hierarchicalization and sacralization of the clergy. The third-century Syrian church order, the *Didascalia*, reveals the bishops' struggles to bring the ascetic order of widows more firmly under episcopal control. In Alexandria, the power base of the ascetic teacher and priest, Arius, was a large and powerful contingent of virgins. As ascetics gathered in larger communities at the edges of town or in the deserts beyond, they constituted centres of power that rivalled episcopal Christianity. Ascetic authority was based not on office but on practice—disciplines of the body, a life of prayer, and separation from the world. But by its very nature it existed as a critique of the wealth, power, and enmeshment in the world of fourth-century bishops; consequently, bishops worked in a variety of ways to incorporate ascetic power.

Athanasius was actively consolidating the power of the Alexandrian episcopacy, extending it throughout the province of Egypt, while he promulgated Nicene orthodoxy. He was even prepared to oppose the Emperor's authority, though such acts of courage sent him into exile on several occasions. The years he spent in exile among the monks inspired him to assimilate the ascetic authority of the desert monks into the episcopal Christianity of the city. David Brakke's *Athanasius and Asceticism* (1995) uncovers several strategies: integrating fasting into liturgical practice, affiliating monastic communities with the episcopacy, upholding an episcopal version of the monk as the prototype for all Christians, and, above all, bringing the virgins under episcopal control. For Claudia Rapp (2005), the integration of ascetic authority into the office of bishop was so complete that it constituted one of the three sources of episcopal authority—pragmatic, spiritual, and ascetic. The assimilation of ascetic authority to clerical office created a new divide between clergy and laity—holy and secular.

19.3.7 Religion

One of the most significant changes in recent approaches is the interest in the influence of Roman state religion in the emergence of the monarchical episcopacy. The insistence on a Christianity set over against paganism suppressed potential interest in the influence of Roman religious institutions on the formation of the episcopacy. In *The Imperial Cult and the Development of Church Order* (1999), Allen Brent interprets Callistus's attempt to unify all the Roman presbyters under his authority as a response to and imitation of Elagabal's attempt to unite all cults under the imperial cult in the third century. Both employed the concept of *monarchia* (a single rule) to articulate their new vision for cultic organization. In *Religion and Authority in Roman Carthage from Augustus to Constantine* (1995), J. B. Rives finds compelling parallels between the interests of the civic elites in establishing the *sacra publica*, and thereby enhancing their own honour, and that of the city and the interests of the new Christian elites in establishing visibility and prestige for the Carthaginian churches. Like their counterparts, the priests of the *sacra publica*, Christian clergy held their offices for life and thus formed a powerful interest group in civic life. These studies illuminate the extent to which religious roles in the Roman cult influenced the formation of the clergy/laity dyad.

19.4 PERIODIZATION

Crucial to the question of what constitutes the clergy/laity dyad is the larger problem of defining the stages of development from primitive Christianity to imperial Christianity. Any scholar's exposition of the demarcation between clergy and laity will depend on his or her dating of several key transformations in models of leadership: When does the transition from collegial models to episcopal models take place? When does the consolidation of other church offices under the bishop occur? When does the office of bishop take on priestly functions? When are lower clergy excluded from priestly functions?

19.4.1 House Churches: Leadership as Ministry

While there is agreement over the variegated forms of leadership in the house churches of the first and second centuries, there is considerable controversy over the meanings of these roles for claiming a division within the church between clergy and laity. The vitality of the house churches was generated by the multiple roles and ministries that their members undertook. Those with some social status and a modicum of wealth took on the roles of patrons by hosting meals, writing letters of recommendation, giving to leaders, and sending contributions to other churches. Patrons were often acknowledged by giving them leadership roles. Debate centres on whether these leaders were early versions of bishops. Others took on administrative ministries, caring for the sick, overseeing the poor, and securing training for orphans. Those exercising these ministries were designated as administrator or overseer (*episkopos*) and manager (*diakonos*). Those with responsibility for the group were designated elders (*presbyteros*). The question posed by such titles is: do these terms in the second century mean the same thing as they do in the fourth?

  House churches recognized the ministries of revelation in the work of travelling prophets or of prophets in residence, and developed criteria for testing their authenticity. Scholars debate over how and when the functions of the prophets become assimilated to those of the clergy. Was the role of the bishops in the New Prophecy movement an example of that assimilation, or was the persistence of the role of prophet the reason for the condemnation of the Montanist churches? Teachers, also, were recognized as leaders, and were given similar standing as prophets, leading to the question of when and how their functions became assimilated to those of the clergy. Fasting and praying were disciplines encouraged for all Christians, but these ascetic ministries made the widows significant leaders. The presence of widows among the ranks of the clergy has challenged scholars to probe not only the significance of ascetic practices for clerical authority, but also the roles of women within the clergy. The ministries of correction and rebuke were responsibilities of the community as a whole, as well as of the leaders. Interestingly, the *Apostolic Tradition* attempts to distinguish the ministries of widows from those of presbyters and bishops by insisting that they are not ordained to office, but rather installed in their office.

Christians in house churches considered themselves members of a spiritual elite. They had committed themselves to a demanding moral discipline that set them apart. Further, as recipients of divine teachings and participants in ongoing revelation, they had unmediated access to the divine. Scholars are divided on the question of whether this meant that all Christians were laity or that they were all part of an elite—priests and prophets?

19.4.2 Hierarchicalization: Rulers and People

Scholars distinguish between two phases in the development of the episcopacy. The first is the emergence of a mono-episcopacy reflected most strongly in the letters of Ignatius, the second, the mono-episcopacy's full flowering into the monarchical episcopacy (Dassmann 1974: 74). Debate has focused more on the dating of the mono-episcopacy than on the reasons for its emergence. One interesting theory is that the presiding elder achieved city-wide recognition through collecting food, clothing, and gifts, providing for burials, and caring for the poor (Volp 2000: 208). Nevertheless, sometime in the third century Christians in cities with more than one house church felt the need for a presiding bishop who would represent the Christians in all the house churches within the city. Those ambitious Christian leaders who assumed this responsibility soon felt that they could not carry out their work without having direct control over the multiple ministries carried on within the house churches. Their new vision for the consolidation of house-church ministries under their control led to power struggles with teachers, widows, confessors, and the laity. Their claims to authority precipitated debates over who had the right to baptize, catechize, evangelize, preach, and even give financial support to ministries. During this restructuring, house churches were welded into a single socio-political body within a city, unified under the authority of the bishop who co-ordinated the ministries within the city through a hierarchy of clerical offices.

While bishops did their work of consolidating their authority, Christian intellectuals created the rationale for these changes. Tertullian in Romanized Africa conceived the society of the Church as analogous to Roman society, divided into distinct classes or ranks, which were distinguished from one another in terms of honour and authority. The clergy (*ordo ecclesiasticus*) form a rank similar to the *ordo senatorius* (the ruling senatorial class); the laity formed the *ordo plebius* (the subject plebeian class). By virtue of their rank, clergy, like their counterparts the senators, possessed certain rights: the right to baptize (*ius dandi baptismi*), the right to teach (*ius docendi*), the right to offer the eucharist (*ius offerendi*), and the right to restore to fellowship after penance (*ius delicta donandi*) (*Exh. cast.* 7, 17; *Bapt.* 1; *Pud.* 21). The clergy as the *ordo ecclesiasticus* represented, as well as manifested, the honour and authority of the Church; therefore, it was imperative that it exemplify the moral discipline of the Church (Torjesen 1989). What is not evident from the discussion of Tertullian's novel views of the Church is that in asserting that the Church was a body politic, he was also asserting that it was a male domain and that leadership was a masculine prerogative. Each of the three treatises named above in which he elaborates his views on the Church also deals with women's place in the Church. The constitution of the clergy/laity dyad is inextricably bound up with issues of gender.

During the third century the churches structured the relations between clergy and laity by adapting a Roman political model. This new organization prepared the way for the clergy to be incorporated into the imperial administration in the fourth century, when the Christian churches were granted imperial patronage. Constantine granted the clergy the same privileges (financial support and tax exemptions) enjoyed by the Roman priests who officiated in state cult. Later, bishops' courts were granted the same standing as imperial courts. The integration of clerical office into the imperial bureaucracy made church office attractive to the Roman elites, and reshaped the hierarchy of clerical offices as a *cursus honorum*.

The innovative incorporation of the Roman *cursus honorum* begins, not surprisingly, with the bishop of Rome, who had assumed the role of consultant and arbiter for other bishops, especially in the West. Pope Siricius laid out five stages in the progression to the office of bishop: lector, acolyte or subdeacon, deacon, presbyter, and bishop, with set years of service required for each one. This insistence on a clerical *cursus honorum* was intended to strengthen each office and to prevent the election by acclamation of bishops whose qualifications were secular (wealth or power). Aristocrats, with the ability to be patrons, and high-ranking individuals were often chosen by the laity through spontaneous acclamation. As in the case of Cyprian, such appointments created tensions with the presbyters, the collegial body governing the Church.

19.4.3 Sacralization: Priests and People

Christians did not use the term 'priest', *sacerdos*, for their leaders until the third century. The earliest usage is found in Cyprian, applied to the bishop as a representative of Christ, the High Priest (Laurance 1984: 200). In their critique of pagan polytheism with its images of deities and sacred precincts, Christians distanced themselves from a sacralization of place (God was everywhere, not just in temples) and sacred persons (all Christians were sacred persons, set apart, ministering to God with their prayers). Most sources in the first two centuries do not mention bishops in connection with liturgy. Scholars disagree on when and how the authority of church office was tied to liturgy, when the priestly functions of leaders set them apart from the laity. Some place it in the early second century, arguing for 'presidency' over the eucharistic meal (Volp 2000: 189). Alexandre Faivre identifies a process of sacralization between 180 and 260 (Faivre 1992: 80). The clearest evidence is provided by an early third-century church order, the *Apostolic Tradition*, which contains a fully elaborated eucharistic liturgy and rituals for the ordination of bishop, presbyter, and deacon that set them apart for liturgical ministry. During Cyprian's struggle to bring the clergy and the confessors under strict episcopal control, he invoked a new world of symbolism for church office, that of the priesthood. When dealing with administrative issues, he used *sacerdos/sacerdotium* in preference to *episcopus/episcopatus*, in order to create a sacral and hierophantic aura to the priesthood. Even though Cyprian did not connect the 'sacralized' office of bishop to the liturgy, he nonetheless laid the foundation for that connection (Torjesen 1989).

The clearest marker of the sacralization of the clergy was the imposition of celibacy, or sexual continence, on married clergy. Although the process extended over ten centuries, the Synod of Elvira marks a starting point for episcopal legislation on continence, to be followed by councils at Ancyra, Neo-Caesarea, and Nicaea in the fourth century. Pope Siricius embedded the requirement for sexual continence on the part of the clergy in his *cursus honorum*. This included married priests, who would practice continence after ordination. Above the office of lector, married clergy were expected to practice sexual continence. Like the Levitical priesthood, the Christian priesthood was likewise required to maintain ritual purity. However, unlike the Levitical service to the Temple, which was cyclical, married Christian priests must be prepared to offer the eucharist daily and baptism when required; hence they were bound to perpetual continence. This new formulation of church office as a priesthood that requires ritual purity also influenced how Christian ritual was understood. Eventually celibacy, the renunciation of marriage, rather than continence, was imposed on western clergy; however, the eastern churches insisted only on temporary sexual continence for the celebration of the eucharist. Roger Gryson argues that because the eucharistic liturgy was performed daily in the Roman church, celibacy was necessary (Gryson 1968: 197). Consequently, the celibacy of the clergy translates into a sacrality of the ritual from which the laity is excluded. 'While clerical celibacy helped to elevate the clergy above the married laity, the link with ritual purity served to distinguish clerical celibacy from the celibacy practiced by monastics' (Hunter 2007: 218).

By the fifth century, the symbolic markers that distinguished clergy from laity had been borrowed from every domain of Roman life, political, priestly, civic, educational, and ascetic. The seating for the clergy on the circular bench that lined the apse of what had once been the Roman basilica signalled that the clergy were rulers over the laity. The position of the bishop's throne at the centre established his authority over the rest of the clergy. The mosaic of the Pantocrator (the enthroned Christ) directly above the bishop's throne affirmed the bishop's role as the *vicarius Christi*. Clerical vestments, borrowed from both civic and religious life, identified clergy as members of the ruling elites, as the Roman toga did, and indicated as well their priestly roles. The *sportula* that clergy received in the third century became the equivalent under Constantine of the stipend and tax exemptions given to the Roman priesthood, whose ritual work was done for the benefit of the Roman state. The retinue of the bishops who moved with them as they crossed the city demonstrated their power as patrons; the accompanying virgins or lower clergy would be understood as their clients. The bishop's palace in the major cities would further establish the bishops as powerful patrons, as would the large crowds congregating in the atrium seeking help, favours, or recommendations. The literacy of the clergy, their sole right to teach and preach, and their roles as catechists and interpreters of scripture were markers of an elite drawn from the schools. The expectation that the clergy should be moral exemplars, and the importance of celibacy or marital continence, helped to underwrite the authority of the clergy in the face of the challenge of growing communities of monks and nuns whose spiritual authority threatened to eclipse that of the clergy.

The twin trajectories of hierarchicalization and sacralization do not reach their apotheosis by the sixth century. Rather, these trajectories continue to arc across the centuries. Bernard Cook, in *The Distancing of God: The Ambiguity of Symbol in History and Theology* (1990), posits three critical moments: the new legal standing with which Constantine endowed the clergy of our period, the Carolingian reform of the eighth century, when the clergy alone was declared the active participant in the Mass, and the Gregorian reform of the twelfth century, when theologians asserted that a priest receives a power that cannot be lost. What is crucial here is not so much the historical moments, but the clear trajectory that renders the laity ever more passive and gives ever higher standing to the clergy. Nonetheless, within this framework scholars have identified a theology of the laity drawing on two sources: the model of the monk and the work of Christ's kingdom (Congar 1954: 1–158). Lay persons, like monastics, are identified by their way of life, practices of sanctity, moral life, and good deeds. Christ as prophet, priest, and king defines the work of the Church. The work of establishing the kingdom, the work of Christ in the world, is the ministry of the laity.

19.5 New Directions: Cultural Regions of the Mediterranean

While the move to centralize the administration of the Christian community within cities occurred across Mediterranean cultures, the forms that it took reflected those regional cultures, and so the ways in which the clergy/laity dyad formed differed from region to region. The evolutionary model for the clergy/laity dyad emphasizes a diachronic progression in the form of twin trajectories of hierarchialization and sacralization. Scholars who operate out of this model draw on sources for all regions of the Mediterranean to map a series of stages in the evolution of the clergy/lay relations. A social change model has a synchronic focus, analysing the multiple forces of change that operate within the same time frame in a particular cultural region. With a heightened awareness of the differences in linguistic worlds, cultural values, and political institutions among the cultures of the Mediterranean, some scholars are focusing on the regional development of the clergy/laity dyad.

(i) Rome

Several scholars have focused on the early processes of institutionalization in Rome: Allen Brent (1999), Harry O. Maier (2001), and James Jeffers (1991). The lack of legal standing for Roman Christians meant that they could either meet in secret or declare themselves to be a private association. Private associations such as professional guilds, religious associations (*collegia sodalicia*), burial societies, and household associations (*collegia domestica*) were guaranteed legal rights to convene. James Jeffers (1991) analyses two fascinating documents that survive from the earliest period: a revelation given to a freedman, Hermas (*The Shepherd*), and a letter of Clement, a leader of a Roman house church, to the churches in Corinth (*First Letter to the Corinthians*). Jeffers's study shows that social class differences among the house churches within the same city produced different conceptions of the relationships of Christians to their leaders.

In the revelation of the freedman, the criteria by which leadership is judged is service: bishops are praised for offering the hospitality of their homes; prophets are welcomed; all participate in correcting each other and their leaders (Jeffers 1991: 106–20). In Clement's letter to Corinth, the distinction between leaders and other Christians is stronger. The writer demands obedience and respect for leaders; they may not be critiqued, and certainly not deposed. The writer of this letter reflects the values of the Roman elites that office is sacrosanct, that peace and concord are created through submission to authorities.

(ii) Alexandria

Alexandria was the vibrant intellectual centre of the Hellenistic world, gathering scholars, scientists, and seekers from East and West to its famous library, Museum, and Serapeum. Not surprisingly, the major figures of second-century Alexandrian Christianity were independent teachers, like Valentinus, Carpocrates, Basilides, and Pantaenus, seeking answers to the perennial questions, 'Who are we? Where have we come from? How do we attain the divine?' Attila Jakab's (2004) study of the process of institutionalization in Alexandria begins with the pluralism of Alexandrian

Christianity (including the Gnostic groups) and illuminates the importance of the master teacher/seeker in shaping the clergy/laity dyad.

In keeping with the intellectual culture of the city, a Christian school was founded with a succession of teachers who led eager students deeper into the mysteries of an emerging Christian Platonism (Jakab 2004: 91–106). Within such schools the distinctions between Christians were framed by a Platonic world-view that divided an intelligible (real) unchanging realm from the sensible, temporal world. The cultivation of Christian morality and the inculcation of Christian doctrines were the new means for progressing from the sensible to the spiritual. Clement uses the term *laikos* for those who are beginners and novices in this spiritual practice (*Strom.* 5.33.2–4). In Alexandria the eventual division between clergy and laity began as the divide between the spiritual or perfect (*gnōstikoi*) and the simple believers, sometimes called 'fleshly' for their inability to grasp spiritual realities.

19.6 SOURCES

The sources for the first three centuries are few and somewhat eclectic. All reconstructions of the clergy/laity dyad for this period rely on letters of church leaders dealing with organizational issues—Clement's letter to the Corinthians (Rome), Ignatius's letters to the seven churches (Asia Minor)—and writings and sermons of teachers—Clement and Origen (Alexandria)—as well as church orders, the *Didache* (Syria or Egypt), the *Apostolic Tradition* (Rome), *Didascalia* (Syria), theological, apologetic, and polemical writings, such as Justin's apology (Rome) and Tertullian's polemical treatises (Carthage) and bishops' letters—those of Cyprian (Carthage), Demetrios (Alexandria). From the third century onward, the sources are more plentiful: the letters of bishops of the important sees (Rome, Milan, Carthage, Alexandria, Antioch, and Jerusalem), resolutions of regional councils and canons of the ecumenical councils and the later church orders, the *Apostolic Constitutions* and the *Testament of the Lord*.

The church orders require additional commentary. With respect to their content, they are extremely valuable for researching the clergy/laity dyad. They contain instructions on church organization, delineate responsibilities for the various church offices, describe the activities of the laity, prescribe the liturgies for baptism, eucharist, and agapē, and set out rituals of ordination for all ranks of church leaders. With respect to their authorship they are more problematic. Since their authors remain anonymous, in order to assert apostolic authority for their writings, their own local context and historical moment remain murky. Their authority is not tied to a particular see, nor do they represent the deliberations of synods or councils.

Although written by anonymous individuals, they circulated widely, and early ones were incorporated into later ones.

SUGGESTED READING

The following are recommended: Brent (1999); Brakke (1995); Campenhausen (1969); Cook (1990); Eisen (2000); Gryson (1970); Jakab (2004); Rapp (2005); and Schöllgen (1998). Also:

FAIVRE, A. (1977), *Naissance d'une hiérarchie: Les premières étapes du cursus clerical* (Paris: Beauchesene).
—— (1990), *The Emergence of the Laity in the Early Church*, trans. D. Smith (New York: Paulist Press).
GRYSON, R. (1968), *Le Prêtre selon saint Ambroise* (Louvain: Éditions Orientalistes).

BIBLIOGRAPHY

BECK, A. (1930), *Romisches Recht bei Tertullian und Cyprian* (Halle: Max Niemeyer).
BLENKINSOPP, J. (1967), 'Ministry in the Early Church', *Worship*, 41/7: 428–38.
BOBERTZ, C. (1990), 'Cyprian of Carthage as Patron: A Social Historical Study of the Role of Bishop in Ancient Christian Communities'. (Yale University dissertation; Ann Arbor: UMI).
BOURDIEU, PIERRE (1971), 'Genèse et structure du champ religieux', *Revue française de sociologie*, 12: 295–334. English trans.: 'Genesis and Structure of the Religious Field', in C. Calhoun (ed.), *Comparative Social Research: A Research Annual*, 13 (1991): 1–44.
BRAKKE, D. (1995), *Athanasius and Asceticism* (Baltimore: Johns Hopkins University Press).
BRENT, A. (1999), *The Imperial Cult and the Development of Church Order: Concepts and Images of Authority in Paganism and Early Christianity before the Age of Cyprian*, Suppl. VC 45 (Leiden: E. J. Brill).
BROOTEN, B. (1982), *Women Leaders in the Ancient Synagogue: Inscriptional Evidence and Background Issues* (Chico, Calif.: Scholars Press).
CAMPENHAUSEN, H. VON (1969), *Ecclesiastical Authority and Spiritual Power* (Palo Alto, Calif.: Stanford University Press).
CONGAR, Y. (1954), *Jalons pour une théologie du laïcat* (Paris: Éditions du Cerf).
—— (1976), 'Laïc et laicat', in *DSP* ix. 79–93.
COOK, B. J. (1990), *The Distancing of God: The Ambiguity of Symbol in History and Theology* (Minneapolis: Fortress Press).
DASSMANN, E. (1974), 'Zur Enstehung des Monoepiskopats', *JAC* 17: 74–90.
DRAKE, H. (2000), *Constantine and the Bishops: The Politics of Intolerance* (Baltimore: Johns Hopkins University Press).
EISEN, U. (2000), *Women Office Holders in Early Christianity* (Collegeville, Minn.: Liturgical Press).
FAIVRE, A. (1983), 'Clerc/laic: historie d'une frontière', *Université des Sciences Humaines de Strasbourg*, 57, Année nr 3 (July): 195–220.

—— (1992), *Ordonner la fraternité: Pourvoir d'innover et retour à l'ordre dans la Église ancienne* (Paris: Éditions du Cerf).

GRYSON, R. (1968), *Les origines du célibat ecclésiastique* (Gembloux: Éditions J. Duculot, S.A.).

HERRMANN, E. (1980), *Ecclesia in Re Publica: Die Entwicklung der Kirche von pseudostaatlicher zu staatlich inkorporierte Existenz* (Frankfurt: Peter D. Lang).

HUNTER, D. G. (2007), *Marriage, Celibacy, and Heresy in Ancient Christianity: The Jovinianist Controversy* (Oxford: Oxford University Press).

JAKAB, A. (2004), *Ecclesia Alexandria: Evolution social et institutionnelle du christianisme alexandrine (IIe et IIIe siècles)* (Bern: Peter Lang).

JEFFERS, J. S. (1991), *Conflict at Rome: Social Order and Hierarchy in Early Christianity* (Minneapolis: Fortress Press).

JENSEN, A. (1992), *God's Self-Confident Daughter: Early Christianity and the Liberation of Women* (Louisville, Ky.: Westminster/John Knox).

LAURANCE, J. D. (1984), *'Priest' as Type of Christ* (New York: Peter Lang).

MAIER, H. O. (2001), *The Social Setting of the Ministry as Reflected in the Writings of Hermas, Clement and Ignatius*, Dissertation Sr, i (Waterloo, Ont.: Wilfred Laurier University Press, for the Canadian Corporation for Studies in Religion).

MUGNIER, F. (1910), 'laity', in *The Catholic Encyclopedia*, ii/2. 748–9.

RAPP, C. (2005), *Holy Bishops in Late Antiquity: The Nature of Christian Leadership in an Age of Transition* (Berkeley: University of California Press).

RIVES, J. B. (1995), *Religion and Authority in Roman Carthage from Augustus to Constantine* (Oxford: Clarendon Press).

SALZMAN, M. (2002), *The Making of a Christian Aristocracy: Social and Religion Change in the Western Roman Empire* (Cambridge, Mass.: Harvard University Press).

SCHÖLLGEN, G. (1998), *Die Anfänge der professionaliserung des Klerus und das Kirchliche Amt in der Syrischen Didaskalie*, JAC, Ergänzungsband 26 (Münster: Aschendorff Verlagsbuchhandlung).

TORJESEN, K. J. (1989), 'Tertullian's Political Ecclesiology and Women's Leadership', *StPatr* 21: 277–82.

—— (1993), *When Women Were Priests: Women's Leadership in the Early Church and the Scandal of their Subordination in the Rise of Christianity* (San Francisco: HarperCollins).

—— (2001), 'The Episcopacy—Sacerdotal or Monarchial? Cyprian and the Didascalia's Appeal to Old Testament Institutions', *StPatr* 36: 387–406.

TREVETT, C. (1996), *Montanism: Gender, Authority and New Prophecy* (Cambridge: Cambridge University Press).

VOLP, U. (2000), 'Liturgical Authority Reconsidered: Remarks on the Bishop's Role in Pre-Constantinian Worship', in B. Neil, G. D. Dunn, and L. Cross (eds.), *Prayer and Spirituality in the Early Church* (Sydney, Australia: St Paul's Publications), iii. 189–210.

WHITE, M. (1997), *The Social Origins of Christian Architecture* (Valley Forge, Pa.: Trinity Press).

WIRE, A. C. (1990), *Corinthian Women Prophets: A Reconstruction Through Paul's Rhetoric* (Minneapolis: Fortress Press).

CHAPTER 20

THE BIBLICAL CANON

MICHAEL W. HOLMES

20.1 DEFINITIONS

20.1.1 'Scripture' versus 'Canon'

CHRISTIANITY has, for much of its history, worked with a closed canon of scripture, 'canon' in the sense of a clearly defined and authoritative list of writings considered to be scripture. In such circumstances, every document that is viewed as 'scripture' is at the same time also considered to be 'canonical'. Thus formal and material aspects coincide: the 'canon of scripture' becomes 'equivalent to the contents of the writings included in such a list' (Metzger 1987: 293). One common consequence— and a characteristic of many investigations of the early history of the canon—is the treatment of 'scripture' and 'canon' as nearly synonymous terms.

The two terms, however, are not synonymous, and such indiscriminate usage obscures the multivalency of the term 'canon'. A fundamental feature of recent research is the differentiation between these terms and the attempt to define more precisely what is meant by 'canon'. Path setting in this respect is an essay by Sundberg (1968; see Campenhausen 1972: 103), who distinguished sharply between 'scripture' (i.e. 'religiously authoritative writings') and 'canon' (defined, for the moment, as a 'list' or 'catalogue' of writings considered to be scripture).

When the two terms are distinguished in this way, it is clear that 'canon' presumes the existence of 'scripture', but 'scripture' does not require a 'canon'. There can be scripture without a canon, but no canon without scripture—no 'list' or 'catalogue', because there would be nothing to put on the list. Canonicity is a matter of list-making, not scriptural status.

20.1.2 The Meaning of 'Canon'

Of the many meanings of this term (at least eleven; see Metzger 1987: 289–93), two require attention in the present context, one because it is a frequent source of confusion, and the other because the issues and problems attending its definition lead to the heart of contemporary discussion (see Sheppard 1987).

The first meaning of interest is (1) 'canon' as a rule, norm, or guide—'the ideal norm according to which the Christian's life and teaching must be conformed' (Metzger 1987: 291, with examples). The second is (2) 'canon' as a list, register, or catalogue (examples in Metzger 1987: 291–2); indeed, *katalogos*, 'catalogue', is a close synonym for this sense of *kanōn*.

In the early Christian movement there is no doubt that scripture functioned as a 'norm' or 'guide' for a particular way of living, but early Christian writers do not use *kanōn* to express this idea. Moreover, that scripture functions as a rule or norm (*kanōn*) does not mean that it is necessarily 'canonical', in the sense of being part of a list or catalogue of items. In short, the idea of scripture as a 'norm' (canon 1) must be carefully distinguished from the idea of a 'list' (canon 2) of scriptures (see Sheppard 1987).

Exploring further the case of 'canon 2', we may ask: Is it 'a list of authoritative books', or 'an authoritative list of books' (Metzger 1987: 282)? In the former, the emphasis is on the intrinsic authority of the books, whereas in the latter the focus is on the ascribed authority of the list.

Some have argued that only the latter properly catches the meaning of 'canon', in the sense of a closed official list, incapable of alteration, that consciously both includes and excludes (e.g. Sundberg 1976: 137; Ulrich 2002: 30–3; Stroumsa 1994: 313). Indeed, in Smith's opinion, 'closure remains the sole discriminator of canon in contradistinction to list or catalogue' (1998: 304). Others, however, have challenged this privileging of a particular definition. Brakke argues that such a formal definition 'assumes a canon of only one type—the Christian Protestant canon—and so obscures other kinds of scriptural collections' (1994: 409), or other ways of categorizing 'canons'. For example, one could classify a canon as either dependent (one that finds significance only in the context of some other religious activity or authority) or primary (one that precedes and grounds other religious activities) (Brakke 1994: 408–9, building on Folkert 1989; cf. Stroumsa 1994: 315–16).

This matter of definition is not without effect. For Zahn (1904, 1908), 'canonical' meant 'authoritative', and so he located the formation of the New Testament canon near the end of the first century. For Harnack (1925), 'canonical' meant 'regarded as scripture', and so he placed it a century later, while for Sundberg (1968), it means a closed authoritative list, and consequently he dates it to the fourth century.

For all their definitional differences, however, none of the three really disagrees about the basic facts or evidence (Metzger 1987: 24; with Barton 1997: 12–13). Thus the disagreement regarding a formal definition of the specific term 'canon' may be to some degree beside the point. As Smith himself acknowledges, 'for the purposes of understanding a particular historical tradition, closure may well need to be understood as a relative category' (Smith 1998: 306; similarly Ulrich 2002: 33; for a much different approach to the issue, Wyrick 2004: 185–90).

In short, the legitimate concern to define 'canon' should not be permitted to overshadow the fundamental significance of the distinction between 'scripture' and 'canon'. Nor should it distract from the larger and more interesting questions attending the phenomenon of canon formation in early Christianity, and it is to these questions we now turn. If no comprehensive explanation yet commands assent, nonetheless we may take note of where matters currently stand.

20.2 THE JEWISH SCRIPTURES IN EARLY CHRISTIANITY

A significant portion of the Christian scriptures was taken over from the Jewish milieu out of which the Christian movement emerged. Therefore, study of the 'biblical canon' in early Christianity must start by attempting to determine exactly what the early Christian movement took over as its founding scriptures.

The regnant answer given to this question for much of the nineteenth and twentieth centuries was relatively uncomplicated: the Christian movement received from 'Judaism' a closed and textually stable canon of scripture, whose contents and text were essentially identical to the Masoretic Hebrew Bible. This, it was widely thought, was the 'Bible' of Jesus, Paul, and Jerome, to which the Protestant Reformers returned, and upon which nearly all modern translations of the Hebrew scriptures are based. The Pentateuch had been closed or 'canonized' by c. 400 BCE, the Prophets by c. 200 BCE, and the Writings achieved near final form by around the turn of the eras. Lingering doubts about some books in the Writings (e.g. Song of Songs or Ecclesiastes) were resolved at a rabbinic council held at Jamnia (Yavneh) sometime around 90 CE, at which the canonical status of these books was affirmed—a way of putting the matter which implies that the contents and form of this final section were already essentially established (cf. Chapman 2000: 3–70; 2003: 30–2; Lewis 2002: 146–51; Sanders 2002: 252–4).

The consensus supporting this view (still defended in various forms: see Leiman 1976; Beckwith 1985; with modifications, van der Kooij 1998) has largely collapsed, undermined primarily by (a) the recognition that the idea of an authoritative 'council' dealing with matters of canon at Jamnia is largely a myth (Lewis 1964, 2002) and (b) the evidence and implications arising out of the discovery of the Qumran Scrolls (surveys in VanderKam 2002; Ulrich 2003), which revealed that the Pharisaic/rabbinic/Masoretic textual tradition represented only one of the textual streams available to Second Temple Judaism (Barthélemy 1984). Increasingly it appears that the boundaries of the third section were still fluid in the first century CE, as was the text of virtually the entire collection (overviews in Sanders 2002; Ulrich 2003). Thus, during the Christian movement's early years, there apparently did not exist a 'closed' canon of Hebrew scriptures for it to take over.[1]

Another factor further complicates the situation: the early Christian movement took over the Jewish scriptures in their Greek form. The Septuagint (using the term in its popular, not technical, sense), not the Hebrew, became the scriptures of early Christianity. To be sure, notable figures—Melito of Sardis, Origen, and Jerome—would voice support for a Hebrew canon and/or text, and the Peshitta Old Testament read by Syriac-speaking Christians (a significant strand of Christianity in the second and subsequent centuries) was largely translated from Hebrew. Nonetheless, for most early Christians the Septuagint (or daughter translations into Latin and Coptic) served as their scriptures. Consequently, the story of the Septuagint canon, rather than the Hebrew scriptures, is more relevant to our question.

That story begins in the third century BCE with the translation of the Torah into Greek (on Septuagintal origins and history, consult Jobes and Silva 2000; Fernández Marcos 2000; Dorival and Munnich 1995; Jellicoe 1968). The translations of the historical and prophetic books were probably made during the following century, with the translation (and, in a few instances, composition) of the other books completed by about the middle of the first century CE (Jobes and Silva 2000: 34, 45). In its modern form (e.g. Rahlfs 1935) it contains a number of writings not found in the Masoretic Hebrew Bible, including Tobit, Judith, additions to Esther, 1–3 Maccabees, Psalm 151, Wisdom, Sirach, Baruch, the Letter of Jeremiah, Susannah, and additions to Daniel.

That the LXX represented an 'Alexandrian' canon (different from the collection of Hebrew writings in Palestine), as once thought, is a hypothesis without evidence (Sundberg 1964). It was simply the scriptures of Hellenistic Judaism (Sundberg 2002), used wherever Jews spoke Greek (including Palestine, where some of the books were translated). Virtually nothing is known about either the arrangement or contents of the Jewish LXX, because after its adoption by early Christianity, Judaism basically abandoned the LXX in the second century CE, creating instead new translations (e.g. Aquilla, Symmachus, Theodotion) for its own use (on Jewish reaction to Christian appropriation of the LXX, see Hengel 2002: 43–7). Virtually all the available evidence regarding the contents and order of the LXX comes from

Christian sources (McDonald 2002a: 581–2, 585–8), and the process of defining the limits (canon 2) of the LXX was essentially a Christian enterprise.

20.2.1 The Canon of the Septuagint in Early Christianity

If the question of canon was not settled prior to the rise of Christianity, when did the process of defining the boundaries of the LXX get under way? While the early Christians unquestionably sought to live by scripture, viewing it as a guide or rule for life (canon 1), there is no evidence that Jesus or his followers ever discussed or attempted to determine its boundaries (canon 2) during the first century or so of the Christian movement (Stuhlmacher 1991: 2, 3; cf. Hengel 2002: 105), and the same may be said of the Apostolic Fathers. Furthermore, while it is a matter of debate whether Jesus and his immediate followers ever used as scripture documents not found in the Hebrew Bible (cf. Sundberg 1964: 53–5, updated in McDonald 1995: 259–67, versus Beckwith 1985: 387; 1993: 102; Ellis 1991: 36; Skarsaune 1996: 445), it is widely agreed that their second-century successors certainly cited as authoritative or in some way 'normative' (canon 1) a range of writings and documents considerably more extensive than what eventually came to comprise the contents of either the Hebrew Bible or the Septuagint (Hengel 2002: 114–22; Oepke and Meyer 1965: 992–7 (Oepke); McDonald 1995: 102–3, 128–31). This phenomenon in turn is taken as fairly clear evidence that a fixed canon did not yet exist in early Christianity (Aland 1962: 4; cf. Stuhlmacher 1991: 2–3). The early Christians made extensive use of 'scripture', but did not, apparently, discuss its boundaries.

In fact, the matter of how properly to interpret the LXX seems to have been a more pressing concern than defining the boundaries of its contents. Three contemporaries, Justin Martyr, Marcion, and Ptolemy—of whom the first two were certainly in Rome in the middle of the second century, and the last may have been (Lampe 2003: 239–40)—each wrestled with this matter.

Marcion, of course, is (in)famous for having tossed out *in toto* the Jewish scriptures. What is important to note is that his action was not motivated by a concern about the canon (canon 2), but rather was 'theologically conditioned' (Campenhausen 1972: 149; Barton 2002: 344–8), a logical consequence of a prior hermeneutical insight. On the basis of his reading of the Pauline letters, Marcion made a fundamental differentiation between law and faith. The Pauline tension between these two concepts became for Marcion a simple contradiction, which he resolved by rejecting the Jewish scriptures as the work of a lesser god (Campenhausen 1972: 87, 148–67).

Though Marcion's solution was almost universally rejected, the problem with which he wrestled—in essence, the relationship between Law and Gospel—could not be so easily ignored. Ptolemy, a Valentinian teacher, in his *Letter to Flora* (text in Layton 1987: 308–15), resolved it by differentiating in the Jewish scriptures between human and divine contributions, the latter of which required further differentiation between obsolete and still relevant elements. For Ptolemy, 'the Law is to be assessed by the words of Jesus'; all of it is 'scripture', but only that which Jesus affirmed is binding (Campenhausen 1972: 82–7, here 84; Perkins 2002: 357).

Justin Martyr solved the hermeneutical problem by viewing the Jewish scriptures primarily as 'prophecy' rather than 'law', which enabled him to affirm a 'prophecy and fulfilment' relationship between the Jewish scriptures and the gospel about Jesus. He further argued for the divine inspiration of the entire LXX by taking up and reworking the Jewish legend about its origins. Whereas the Letter of Aristeas spoke of the translation of the Torah alone, Justin (1 Apol. 31) speaks of the translation of the entire collection of 'prophetic writings' (even Moses is stereotyped as a prophet). Thus the LXX becomes for Justin the 'authorized' form of the Jewish scriptures, whose textual detail—important, when the Christological exegesis of a prophetic text such as Isaiah 7: 14 can turn on a single word—is thereby guaranteed (see Campenhausen 1972: 88–102, 167; Hengel 2002: 26–8, 36–41; Wyrick 2004: 315–43).

Justin nowhere specifies precisely which books comprised this 'authorized' translation. It appears from his writings that he quoted only from those books now found in the Masoretic canon. The significance of this phenomenon is unclear, however, since this apparent restriction may well have been voluntary in view of his putative 'Jewish' conversation partners in the Dialogue (Hengel 2002: 29). Thus the evidence of Justin is ambiguous with regard to the limits of his scriptures.

A decade or two after Justin, Melito of Sardis (d. c. 190 CE) presents two important 'firsts': the first known Christian list of the contents of the 'Jewish' scriptures and the first occurrence of the phrase 'Old Testament'. In a passage preserved by Eusebius (Hist. eccl. 4. 26. 13–14), Melito speaks of travelling 'to the east' on behalf of his brother Onesimus, who desired to know 'the accurate facts' about both the number and order of 'the ancient writings'. There he 'learned accurately' the 'books of the Old Testament' (on this phrase see Campenhausen 1972: 262–8): Genesis, Exodus, Numbers, Leviticus, Deuteronomy, Joshua, Judges, Ruth, 1–4 Kingdoms (= 1–2 Samuel, 1–2 Kings), 1–2 Chronicles, Psalms, Proverbs (or Wisdom), Ecclesiastes, Song of Songs, Job, Isaiah, Jeremiah, the Twelve, Daniel, Ezekiel, Esdras (= Ezra/Nehemiah?).

Numerous questions arise: to where did Melito travel? (Palestine? So Hengel 2002: 61). From whom did he learn this information, Jewish Christians or Jews? In particular, is this concern about the limits of scripture a 'new' or a 'continuing' issue, and in either case, what prompted it? Unfortunately, we simply don't know.

As for the 'accurate facts' about the number and order: the reversal of Numbers and Leviticus is likely a simple error. Esther is missing. The overall arrangement is clearly Septuagintal, not Masoretic (e.g. 1–2 Chronicles is among the historical books, rather than grouped with the 'Writings'), but has its own quirks: the

Twelve in the middle of the other prophets (rather than at the head), and 'Esdras' as the last entry. Also, does the reference to 'Jeremiah' include (as it does in some LXX MSS) Baruch and/or Lamentations and/or the Letter of Jeremiah? This first witness, rather than settling matters, instead raises additional questions (on Melito, see Campenhausen 1972: 65; Hengel 2002: 60–1; Sundberg 1964: 133–4).

Even though Melito does not use the term 'canon'—Eusebius labels Melito's list a *katalogos*—it is evident from his concern for accurate information about the number and order (*taxis*) of the books that the concept or idea of a defined list of scriptures (canon 2) is clearly in mind. Moreover, only a few years later (the last decade or so of the second century) we find, in a comment by an anonymous anti-Montanist writer (perhaps Polycrates of Ephesus; cf. Campenhausen 1972: 231) preserved by Eusebius (*Hist. eccl.* 5. 16. 3) the earliest known occurrence in Christian literature of what would become a widely disseminated phrase: the concern 'neither to add nor take away' anything from what is considered to be 'scripture' (Unnik 1949; for the idea cf. Josephus, *C. Ap.* 1. 42). Hengel rightly observes that the LXX was 'not yet strictly defined nor universally accepted at the beginning of the third century' (2002: 56); nonetheless, an interest in ascertaining its boundaries is clearly evident.

From this time on, primary evidence of concern for boundaries comes in the form of lists of, reports about, or manuscripts containing the books of what is now termed, with increasing frequency, the 'Old Testament'. Eusebius (*Hist. eccl.* 6. 13. 5–7), for example, reports about Clement of Alexandria's use of certain books: namely, the Wisdom of Solomon and Sirach (along with Hebrews, *Barnabas*, 1 *Clement*, and Jude). Eusebius does so, however, in a manner that tells us more about his perspective—he labels them 'disputed writings' (*antilegomenōn graphōn*; on Eusebius's terminology see Kalin 2002: 393–7)—than it does about Clement's views the contents on the LXX.

Origen, well known for his work on the LXX text that resulted in the *Hexapla*, presents an ambiguous picture with respect to its canon. Sometimes he seems to have preferred a 'shorter' canon similar in content (but not arrangement) to the Masoretic Jewish canon (e.g. in his commentary on Psalm 1, cited by Eusebius, *Hist. eccl.* 6. 25. 1–2). In other places, however (e.g. his *Letter to Julius Africanus*, a contemporary who rejected the story of Susannah found in the LXX), he indicates, in explicit contrast to the Jewish scriptures, a clear preference for 'our bible' (i.e. the LXX), including additions such as Susannah. Unfortunately, he never specifies in full what he thinks the contents of the LXX are (or should be). Indubitably there are tensions regarding this point in his writings (see Carleton Paget 1996: 503); indeed, Hengel thinks the problem of Origen's canon is 'insoluble' (2002: 11; see further Campenhausen 1972: 317; Sundberg 1964: 134–8; and Oikonomos 1991: 20, who thinks that Origen viewed the Septuagintal 'extras' as canonical).

After Origen, available evidence comes from the fourth century, primarily in the form of lists (from both individuals and councils), no two of which agree completely (Junod 1984: 135–51; McDonald 1995: 268–73; 2002*a*: 585–8). There is also some important manuscript testimony (discussed below). Moreover, insofar as we have evidence, the first instance of the term 'canon' as a 'list of books' (canon 2) occurs shortly after 350, in Athanasius (details in Metzger 1987: 292). This makes Athanasius's later list, in which he speaks of the 'canonical books' (*biblia kanōnizomena*), of particular interest.

In his *Festal* (Easter) *Letter* of 367 CE Athanasius opposes two influential groups, the Melitians and the Homoeans, on the grounds that they do not follow the ancient traditions. Athanasius and his followers, on the other hand, 'celebrate the feast according to the traditions of our forefathers, because we have the holy scriptures; they are sufficient to instruct us perfectly'. The possibility that opponents may mislead some believers on the basis of other books, 'so-called apocryphal writings', motivates Athanasius, who has 'investigated the matter from the beginning', to enumerate precisely and 'in order the writings that have been put in the canon, that have been handed down and confirmed as divine'. Then, after giving the list, Athanasius adds: 'In these books alone the teaching of piety is proclaimed. Let no one add to them or take away from them anything' (Markschies 2003: 189–91 for the preceding paragraph; also Brakke 1994).

Clearly Athanasius is promulgating, in a polemical context, a 'closed canon' of the LXX, which in his estimation represents the inherited tradition of the Church. It is also evident that the context of this list implies (a) the existence of competing 'canons' utilized by his opponents, and (b) that Athanasius—if the allusion to the Lucan prologue is not merely a rhetorical flourish—may have had to research the matter himself before compiling the list.

In the course of setting out his list, Athanasius specifies three categories of books: canonical books, non-canonical books to be read by new converts, and apocryphal writings (whose titles he carefully avoids mentioning). In the first are 'twenty two' books: Genesis, Exodus, Leviticus, Numbers, Deuteronomy, Joshua, Judges, Ruth, 1–2 Kings, 3–4 Kings, 1–2 Chronicles, 1–2 Esdras,[2] Psalms, Proverbs, Ecclesiastes, Song of Songs, Job, the Twelve, Isaiah, Jeremiah + Baruch + Lamentations + Letter of Jeremiah, Ezekiel, and Daniel. 'Books to be read' include Wisdom of Solomon, Sirach, Esther, Judith, and Tobit.

In view of the forcefulness with which Athanasius promotes his canon, it is interesting to compare it with the contents of the two earliest extant (and originally complete) manuscripts of the LXX: namely, Codex Vaticanus and Codex Sinaiticus, which were copied within a few years before or after Athanasius's letter. Vaticanus presents in a single codex exactly the books that Athanasius names in his first two categories. The order and arrangement differ, however: the 'books to be read' that Athanasius places 'outside' his canon appear in Vaticanus interspersed among and undifferentiated from his 'canonical' books.

Codex Sinaiticus, though incomplete today, agrees (to the extent that we can infer its original contents) with Athanasius and Vaticanus through 1–2 Esdras, after which it offers an independent order and includes two additional books (1 and 4 Maccabees). (The fifth-century Codex Alexandrinus, the third of the major codices, matches Athanasius and Vaticanus through Chronicles; it then presents yet another independent order and adds five additional books: 1, 2, 3, 4, Maccabees and Psalms of Solomon.)[3]

A comparison of lists promulgated by various church councils held between 363 and 397 (see McDonald 1995: 270–2) reveals a situation similar to that found in the manuscripts. There is a central core, a variable fringe, and differences in arrangement.

In the late fourth century, the LXX (together with its daughter translations) is clearly and unquestionably the 'Old Testament' of the Christian movement (as it has been virtually from the movement's earliest days). Jerome's efforts at the end of the fourth century to return to the *hebraica veritas*, though somewhat successful on a textual level, would prove futile on the canonical level.

But if it is clear that the LXX is the Church's 'bible' (technological improvements with regard to the codex having by now made it possible to inscribe all the writings in a single volume), it is equally clear that the question of the boundaries of that 'bible' are still fluid. Despite multiple efforts (on the part of individuals and councils), there is no single 'definitive' canon of the LXX. Indeed, the three 'canons' (i.e. lists) of Athanasius, Vaticanus, and Sinaiticus are paradigmatic of the overall situation in the late fourth century in at least three respects. First, there is wide agreement as to a 'central core' of writings, which (with the occasional exception of Esther) corresponds closely to the contents of the Masoretic Hebrew canon. Second, the order and arrangement of this 'core canon' in the LXX (a) differ significantly from the Masoretic arrangement (which has slight variations within its own tradition), and (b), within the Septuagintal lists themselves, differ significantly in the second half of the core collection. Third, there is persistent disagreement as to the status, size, and arrangement of a smaller 'variable fringe' of 'Septuagintal extras' around this central core. For example, Athanasius's canon list includes three additional books (1 Esdras, Baruch, and Letter of Jeremiah) but leaves out Esther, while Vaticanus has seven additional writings, and Sinaiticus nine (not counting the additions to Daniel or Esther).

Hengel observes that 'at the Synod of Carthage in 397, a relatively but by no means definitively closed scripture collection was *gradually* nearing more definite delimitation' (2002: 57). Yet a 'clear decision on the extent of the Septuagint has never been taken. On the contrary, the Second Trullan Synod of 692 recognizes no less than six different canonical lists, . . . which in places vary considerably among themselves' (Rüger 1991: 153; cf. Oikonomos 1991: 21). The relative uniformity characteristic of the New Testament canon was never achieved for the Septuagintal canon.

20.3 THE FORMATION OF A SECOND TESTAMENT IN EARLY CHRISTIANITY

In addition to 'canonizing' selected Jewish scriptures, the early Christian movement also canonized selected writings composed by early Christians. The basic narrative of 'how' this happened is relatively non-controversial. A brief sketch will provide a canvas against which to consider the more difficult questions of 'why' or 'for what reason' the New Testament canon took the shape it did.

From Christianity's earliest days two categories of authoritative traditions gave it shape and direction: the Jewish scriptures and the 'gospel' (the teachings of and narratives about Jesus), the latter providing the hermeneutical key to the former. At first transmitted orally, some of these teachings and narratives were committed to writing sometime during the second half of the first century, and for some decades both forms of transmission continued side by side. By the middle of the second century CE, however, the traditions survived largely in written form, primarily (but not exclusively) in documents known as 'gospels'.

Even before there were written gospels, there were already other authoritative writings in circulation, mostly letters to fellow believers composed by followers of Jesus in the course of carrying on his mission. Thus, by the early second century, the emerging Christian movement possessed two kinds of 'normative' (canon 1) documents: Jewish scriptures and Christian writings composed by (or attributed to) early followers of Jesus (primarily gospels and letters, but also a book of 'Acts' and an apocalypse).

In other Christian writings composed during the last decade of the first century or in the first half of the second—roughly from Clement of Rome to Justin Martyr of Rome—we find these earlier Christian documents utilized in the same manner as the Jewish scriptures. Both categories of documents are treated as authoritative guides for how Christians are to conduct themselves, for answering moral questions, and for explaining why Christians are the way they are. Furthermore, writings from both categories are read and expounded when congregations gather for worship (Justin, *1 Apol.* 67. 3). In short, the latter category of writings comes to function in the same way as the former. It is perhaps unsurprising, therefore, that the descriptor of the former group—'scripture'—is being applied as well to the latter group by the middle of the second century, or that common usage increasingly links the 'Law and Prophets' with the 'Gospels and Apostles' (Ferguson 2002: 304–7).

The first hints of 'collections' of early Christian writings are also evident by this time. Clement of Rome certainly knew 1 Corinthians, and very probably Romans and Hebrews (Gregory 2005), and Polycarp's *Letter to the Philippians* (*c.* 120–35) reveals knowledge of at least four (and possibly seven) Pauline letters, as well as 1 Peter and 1 John. But whether these groupings represent deliberate collections (like

Polycarp's collection of seven Ignatian letters) or merely circumstantial accumulations is unclear (Holmes 2005). The same question hangs over early collections of gospels. The use by Christians of the codex format (a late first-century innovation) meant that the technology to gather multiple gospels into one volume was available, but it is not clear when such collections first appeared (discussion and bibliography in Gamble 2002: 276–82, with Head 2005). The apparent use of a gospel harmony by Justin presupposes the use of more than one gospel, but does not prove there was yet a 'collection' of them.

In short, by the mid-second century or so, Christians were according an increasing but still indeterminate number of Christian writings the status of scripture. A widely used 'core group', consisting of about twenty documents—four gospels (Matthew, Mark, Luke, John), Acts, thirteen Pauline letters, plus 1 John and 1 Peter—is beginning to emerge, but these are only the core of a larger unbounded group. Furthermore, believers continued to pen documents in increasing numbers (letters, gospels, acts, instruction manuals, sermons, treatises, an apocalypse or two), evidence of the flourishing diversity within the Church. There are ambiguous glimpses of efforts to collect or consolidate smaller subgroups, but—as was the case with the Septuagint at this time—no hint of any concerted effort to specify the precise contents or boundaries of any collection.

At this point it may be useful to pause to survey the traditional description of the rise of the New Testament canon. Typically three key stages are sketched: (1) the rise of Christian writings to the status of scripture, mid-first through mid-second century (described above); (2) the informal acknowledgement, in response to the appearance of Marcion's 'canon' of edited versions of ten letters of Paul and the gospel of Luke, of a core group of about twenty documents (see previous paragraph), around which floated a penumbra of an indeterminate number of books whose status as 'scripture' was subject to debate or uncertainty (mid-second into early third century); and (3) in the late third and especially fourth centuries the formal canonization of the NT, as authoritative decisions are made regarding which books to include and which to exclude (e.g. Sundberg 1976: 137–40; Du Toit 1993; Gamble 2002: 272; Metzger 1987: 7).

Barton has observed that while the three major formulations of the history of the NT canon—exemplified by Zahn (1904, 1908) and Kümmel (1975); Harnack (1925) and Campenhausen (1972); and Sundberg (1968)—disagree as to which of the three periods is to be emphasized (respectively, the first, the second, or the third), they (and most researchers since) nonetheless agree regarding this basic pattern. He further notes that each position is simultaneously right and wrong in its particular emphasis. (1) Some early Christian writings 'did have considerable authority' early on (as Zahn thought), but no one was yet thinking of anything like a 'New Testament'; (2) while other books were raised to this same authoritative status during what Harnack considered the key second-century 'formative period', a central core was already well established by then; and (3) authoritative rulings appear only in the fourth century, but they essentially codify what was already a matter of widespread practice. Thus Barton suggests that something is amiss (1997: 14–15; cf. 15–24).

Barton's own thoughtful proposal—that the history of the canon involves two simultaneous and interacting processes, one of growth and one of limitation (1997: 24–31)—leaves unmentioned what may be a critical weakness of the typical three-stage description: its teleological perspective. It conceptualizes the story of the New Testament canon from the perspective of its outcome: it knows how the story ends and works from there back to its beginning. This leads to the tracing of a single line of development as though it were somehow natural and inevitable, and no notice is taken of the many other possible directions in which the whole process might have gone. When Marcion and the Montanist movement can be categorized as 'external factors' shaping the development of the canon (Ferguson 2002: 309–16), the pernicious effect of this teleological perspective is evident, for Marcion and the Montanists, at the time they first arose, were very much part and parcel of the Christian movement. Thus it may be worth asking: What would it be like to look at the matter from the middle of the second century forward, rather than backward from the fourth?

In the preceding survey of the Septuagintal canon, I observed that a key is-sue in the mid-second century was not boundaries but interpretation—in short, hermeneutics. Marcion's treatment of the Jewish scriptures, for example, was the logical outworking of his basic hermeneutical insight—and the same may be said of his handling of early Christian writings. His hermeneutics led him to accept as authoritative only a limited number of Christian documents (and only in a revised form), a 'collection' that is widely considered the first 'canon' of Christian writings (e.g. Campenhausen 1972).

In short, Marcion was arguing for a particular definition of what it means to be a follower of Jesus—a definition shaped by claims about both a hermeneutical perspective and a body of authoritative writings. If we look at the 'canon ques-tion' in this light, it becomes possible to understand it as part of a larger issue with which early Christianity, like rabbinic Judaism, was concerned: namely, that of self-definition. At the heart of this effort, in both rabbinic Judaism and early Christianity, was the question of which traditions to accept as normative and how they ought to be interpreted (similarly Stroumsa 1994: 314–16).

During (approximately) the third quarter of the second century, Marcion is only one of a number of individuals or groups proposing answers to this ques-tion. The Montanist movement, for example, worked with a pneumatologically oriented hermeneutic, and argued that new revelations should be accorded as much (or more) authority as existing traditions. Tatian's hermeneutic had a def-inite encratite slant, and he created a single continuous gospel (the *Diatessaron*) to serve as his authoritative form of gospel tradition, in place of the 'standard four' (plus possibly a fifth) from which he compiled his gospel. Similarly Irenaeus (*Haer.* 3. 11. 7) reports that other Christians used a single gospel. Clearly, Marcion was not alone in proposing a group of authoritative writings smaller than the emerging 'core'.

Nor were the Montanists the only ones proposing an expanded group of authoritative revelations or traditions. The individuals or groups associated with the *Gospel of Thomas* or the *Apocryphon of James*, for example, proposed to define themselves not only in terms of a dualistic or 'gnostic' hermeneutic, but also in terms of documents claiming to embody secret traditions that go beyond (but do not replace) the emergent 'core' group. Indeed, Perkins observes that 'esoteric gnostic teaching has been cast in literary forms which presume general agreement concerning the authority of the "four gospels and Acts" ' (2002: 360).

Valentinus, on the other hand, seems to have been content to work with the basic 'core group' of authoritative documents (Layton 1987: pp. xxii–xxiii); his particular 'self-identity' derives not from a variant or distinctive group of authorities, but from his distinctive hermeneutical perspective. As Perkins has noted, 'Hermeneutics, not canon formation, is the central point at issue' between Valentinus and Irenaeus (2002: 371).

For his part, Irenaeus—who may stand as representative of the 'proto-orthodox' strand of early Christianity—serves as a reminder that the boundaries of the 'core group' (for which he is a key witness) are still very much undefined. His polemic in favour of a closed four-gospel collection (*Haer.* 3. 11. 8) reveals how far from settled were opinions on this major point; further, his own 'core group' included, in addition to the twenty documents named above, Revelation and *The Shepherd of Hermas* (*Haer.* 4. 20. 2).

In addition to authoritative writings, Irenaeus had a defining hermeneutic: the 'rule of faith' (*kanōn tēs pisteōs*). Essentially an oral summary of the common inherited foundational beliefs of the Christian movement, received from the apostles and transmitted from generation to generation ever since (cf. *Haer.* 1. 10. 1–2), it provided an apostolic norm (canon 1) by which to interpret the written form of apostolic tradition (Donovan 1997: 11–17; cf. Stroumsa 1994: 309–11).

If by 175 CE or so there was as yet no 'canon' in the sense of a closed collection of scriptures (Sundberg's definition), there were, without question, emerging 'proto-canons', different groupings of authoritative writings by which different strands of the Christian movement defined themselves—virtually always, it would seem, in conjunction with an accompanying hermeneutical perspective that shaped their interpretation. Each strand offered its own 'take' on what it meant to be a Christian, its own perspective on what the essence of Christianity was—often accompanied by a different sense of which writings counted as 'scripture'.

Which of these options would thrive and prosper, which would not? Around 175, the answer was not obvious. Perhaps that is the point of this effort to look at the canon from the beginning forward, rather than from the end back: to realize that there was nothing particularly inevitable about how matters turned out. This in turn leads to a different question: instead of 'how' did a twenty-seven-book canon eventually emerge in the fourth century from the amorphous collection of writings visible two centuries earlier, perhaps the more interesting question becomes 'why' did this particular proposal carry the day?

Whatever a full answer to that question may look like,[4] one part of the answer is clear: Irenaeus. The case that Irenaeus made (in his major work, *Against Heresies*) for seeing the 'rule of faith' and his core group of writings as the authentic and reliable transmitters of the teachings of Jesus and his 'true disciples' (*Haer.* 2. 32. 4) proved to be widely persuasive. Irenaeus was 'but the pioneering representative of a method and approach which everywhere met an urgent need', and Clement, Tertullian, and Hippolytus, among others, picked up and developed further his ideas concerning the central role of authoritative tradition (Campenhausen 1972: 210; also 208–9). With the support of such an able group of advocates, Irenaeus's 'answer' eventually became the 'mainstream' answer.

With Irenaeus, however, the story is, chronologically, only about half over. During the period between Irenaeus and Athanasius at least nineteen books formed a part of the floating penumbra around the relatively stable core group: not just 2–3 John, 2 Peter, Jude, James, Hebrews, and Revelation, but also the *Gospel of the Hebrews, Gospel of the Egyptians, Acts of Paul, Acts of Peter, 3 Corinthians, Letter to the Laodiceans, Apocalypse of Peter, Didache, 1 Clement, 2 Clement, Letter of Barnabas,* and *Shepherd of Hermas*—all of which were considered by someone sometime as scripture (see further Metzger 1987: 165–89).

How this number was eventually reduced and agreement reached regarding the twenty-seven books that came to comprise the New Testament canon is uncertain (primarily due to an absence of evidence). Most of the available information consists of lists that, as in the case of the LXX, reveal more of the 'what' than the 'why' (lists in Metzger 1987: 305–15).

Possibly the earliest extant list of early Christian writings, and certainly the most controversial, is the *Muratorian Canon*. The tenuousness of the traditional dating, to *c.* 180–200, has been exposed by Sundberg (1973) and Hahneman (1992, 2002), who propose (unconvincingly: see Holmes 1994) a fourth-century date. Current opinion on the matter remains deeply divided (Verheyden 2003). Various features of the document make it something of an anomaly in either period, and in any case its evidentiary worth has probably been over-valued (but Verheyden 2003: 556 offers a more positive assessment).

By the end of the second century (as noted in discussing the LXX) the idea of a collection of writings concerning which nothing could be added or taken away was circulating, even if such a collection did not yet exist. From the mid-third century, Origen, partly in his own writings and partly in material recorded by Eusebius (*Hist. eccl.* 6. 25. 3–14), who may have shaped it (Kalin 1990), offers an overview. His categories of 'acknowledged' (four gospels, fourteen Pauline letters, Acts, 1 Peter, 1 John, Jude, Revelation) and 'disputed' books (James, 2 Peter, 2–3 John) embody the concept of a canon (canon 2), even as they reveal that the question of boundaries was still fluid—especially in light of Origen's apparent treatment of *1 Clement*, *Barnabas*, and *Shepherd of Hermas* as scripture (McDonald 1995: 201–5; Metzger 1987: 135–41).

In the early fourth century (*c*. 325–30) Eusebius's well-known comments (*Hist. eccl.* 3. 25. 1–7, 3. 3. 1–7; see Kalin 2002) employ categories similar to Origen's and reveal a continuing fluidity with regard to certain books. The shape of the core group of twenty from the time of Irenaeus remains stable, while debate continues within the Church about seven others (Hebrews, James, 2 Peter, 2–3 John, Jude, and Revelation). What is notable about Eusebius's report, as compared to Origen, is the absence of debate about additional books (such as *1 Clement* or *Shepherd of Hermas*).

As was the case with the Septuagint, Athanasius (whose emphasis on the importance and centrality of tradition echoes the arguments of Irenaeus) marks the beginning of the end of the process. His *Festal Letter* of 367 (whose social context was discussed above) is the first known list to catalogue as 'canonical' exactly the twenty-seven books that today comprise the New Testament. The same list was later ratified by the Council of Carthage (397) and subsequent councils.

Even after such formal action, however, not all variation disappeared, not even in Alexandria (Ehrman 1983), and especially not in the East. In particular, Hebrews (in the West) and Revelation (in the East) remained under a cloud of suspicion in many quarters; additional books appear in major early manuscripts such as Sinaiticus (fourth century: *Barnabas* and *Shepherd of Hermas*) and Alexandrinus (fifth century: *1–2 Clement*); and the Syriac Peshitta New Testament (late fourth–early fifth century) lacked the minor Catholic epistles (Siker 1987) and Revelation. 'Closure', it seems, was a relative matter.

Notes

1. The earliest reference to a 'closed' list of scriptures is in Josephus (*C. Ap.* 1. 37–43, written *c*. 93–5 CE (discussion in Mason 1996, 2002); Josephus does not, however, specify the precise contents of the list. The earliest list of specific scriptures comes from a Christian source, Melito of Sardis, *c*. 180 CE (as cited by Eusebius, *Hist. eccl.* 4. 26. 13–14; discussed below). Other key references regarding the 'canon' of the Hebrew scriptures include the Prologue to Sirach, 4QMMT (on which see esp. Ulrich 2003: 67–71), Lk 24: 44, and *b. Baba Bathra* 14b–15a (possibly second century CE, more probably third century or later: Lightstone 2002: 178). For a full list see McDonald 2002a: 580–2 (with brief discussions in McDonald 1995).

2. In the LXX, '2 Esdras' = the canonical Ezra–Nehemiah. '1 Esdras' is an alternative account of the Israel's captivity and return that combines material borrowed from 2 Chronicles and Ezra-Nehemiah with some original material (= 3. 1–5. 6).

3. The significant differences in both content and arrangement so evident in Vaticanus, Sinaiticus, and Alexandrinus constitute strong evidence against the hypothesis of D. Trobisch that the mid-second century editors of what he terms a 'Canonical Edition' standardized features of the LXX and placed the books in a specific order (2000: 62–5).

4. One may suggest, as a start, that in a social context that valued tradition and stability, the 'proto-orthodox' proposal was apparently a more attractive 'product' with a more compelling rationale. Also, the proto-orthodox appear to have had a more effective and broadly based organization. Moreover, whatever factors led to the victory of Nicene Christianity over competing formulations likely assisted the closure of a New Testament canon favoured by the Nicene proponents.

SUGGESTED READING

The volumes edited by McDonald and Sanders (2002) and Auwers and de Jonge (2003) offer excellent points of entry for both testaments, and Snoek (1998) provides an outstanding annotated bibliography. For the Septuagint, consult Hengel (2002) and Dorival and Munnich (1995). For the New Testament canon, consult Gamble (2002), de Jonge (2003), and Metzger (1987); for recent German literature see Markschies (2001) and Lips (2004).

Gamble (2002) and Metzger (1987) typically offer, respectively, brief and more detailed starting points for some traditional *topoi* only alluded to above, such as the 'criteria of selection' (e.g. antiquity, catholicity, or agreement with the rule of faith; cf. also McDonald 2002b and Ludlow 2003), or the extent to which various factors (e.g. persecution and martyrdom, growth and expansion, or various 'heresies') contributed to the shaping and closing of the canon (see also Ferguson 2002; Perkins 2002).

On the socio-historical context of canon formation, and circumstances that shaped, influenced, or gave rise to particular lists, consult Brakke (1994), Schaper (1998), Davies (2002), Chapman (2003), and Markschies (2003); for sociological and anthropological perspectives on canon formation (e.g. canon formation as an exercise of power), Chapman (2003). Regarding the significance of textual criticism and codicology to canon history and formation, see Epp (2002); on the impact of the shift from roll to codex, Kraft (2002), Schmidt (2002), and, more broadly, Gamble (1995). For canon formation and Christian attitudes towards Judaism, see Simon (1997) and Tomson (1998); for possible Jewish influence on the Christian canon (was it perhaps 'benignly imitative' of Jewish developments?), Zevit (1998: 158).

Ripe for further research are issues such as the extent of regional and chronological variation, and the associated methodological problems of properly utilizing scattered reports from different regions and times to write a single narrative (how does one avoid the temptation to generalize about 'the church' or 'the early Christian movement' when the only evidence is a sparse collection of 'snapshots' from various regions?); selection and use of models or metaphors to characterize canon history (might other metaphors better serve than the common 'conflict' or 'crisis' ones? See Markschies (2003: 175–82) and Chapman (2003)); and the role and impact of liturgical usage and practice.

Bibliography

ALAND, K. (1962), *The Problem of the New Testament Canon* (London: Mowbray).

AUWERS, J.-M., and JONGE, H. J. DE (2003), *The Biblical Canons*, BETL 163 (Leuven: Peeters).

BARTHÉLEMY, D. (1984), 'L'état de la Bible Juive depuis le début de notre ère jusqu'a la deux-ième révolte contre Rome (131–135)', in S. Amsler, J.-D. Kaestli and O. Wermelinger (eds.), *Le canon de l'Ancien Testament: Sa formation et son histoire* (Geneva: Labor et Fides), 9–45.

BARTON, J. (1997), *Holy Writings, Sacred Text: The Canon in Early Christianity* (Louisville, Ky.: Westminster/John Knox).

—— (2002), 'Marcion Revisited', in McDonald and Sanders (2002), 341–54.

—— and WOLTER, M. (2003) (eds.), *Die Einheit der Schrift und die Vielfalt des Kanons* (*The Unity of Scripture and the Diversity of the Canon*) (Berlin: de Gruyter).

BECKWITH, R. (1985), *The Old Testament Canon of the New Testament Church* (Grand Rapids, Mich.: Eerdmans).

—— (1993), 'Canon of the Hebrew Bible and the Old Testament', in B. M. Metzger and M. D. Coogan (eds.), *The Oxford Companion to the Bible* (New York: Oxford University Press), 100–2.

BRAKKE, D. (1994), 'Canon Formation and Social Conflict in Fourth-Century Egypt: Athanasius of Alexandria's Thirty-Ninth *Festal Letter*', HTR 87/4: 395–419.

CAMPENHAUSEN, H. VON (1972), *The Formation of the Christian Bible* (Philadelphia: Fortress Press).

CARLETON PAGET, J. N. B. (1996), 'The Christian Exegesis of the Old Testament in the Alexandrian Tradition', in Magne Sæbø (ed.), *Hebrew Bible/Old Testament: The History of Its Interpretation*, i: *From the Beginnings to the Middle Ages (until 1300)* (Gottingen: Vandenhoeck & Ruprecht), 478–542.

CHAPMAN, S. B. (2000), *The Law and the Prophets: A Study in Old Testament Canon Formation* (Tübingen: Mohr/Siebeck).

—— (2003), 'How the Biblical Canon Began: Working Models and Open Questions', in M. Finkelberg and G. Stroumsa (eds.), *Homer, the Bible, and Beyond: Literary and Religious Canons in the Ancient World*, Jerusalem Studies in Religion and Culture, 2 (Leiden: E. J. Brill), 29–51.

DAVIES, P. R. (2002), 'The Jewish Scriptural Canon in Cultural Perspective', in McDonald and Sanders (2002), 36–52.

DONOVAN, M. A. (1997), *One Right Reading? A Guide to Irenaeus* (Collegeville, Minn.: Michael Glazier).

DORIVAL, G., and MUNNICH, O. (1995), (eds.), *«Selon les Septante»: Trente études sur la Bible grecque des Septante: en hommage à Marguerite Harl* (Paris: Cerf).

DU TOIT, A. B. (1993), 'Canon: New Testament', in B. M. Metzger and M. D. Coogan (eds.), *The Oxford Companion to the Bible* (New York: Oxford University Press), 102–4.

EHRMAN, BART D. (1983), 'The New Testament Canon of Didymus the Blind', VC 37: 1–21.

ELLIS, E. E. (1991), *The Old Testament in Early Christianity: Canon and Interpretation in the Light of Modern Research*, WUNT 54 (repr. Grand Rapids, Mich.: Baker, 1992).

EPP, E. J. (2002), 'Issues in the Interrelation of New Testament Textual Criticism and Canon', in McDonald and Sanders (2002), 485–515.

FERGUSON, E. (2002), 'Factors Leading to the Selection and Closure of the New Testament Canon: A Survey of Some Recent Studies', in McDonald and Sanders (2002), 295–320.

FERNÁNDEZ MARCOS, N. (2000), *The Septuagint in Context: Introduction to the Greek Versions of the Bible* (Leiden: E. J. Brill).

FOLKERT, K. W. (1989), 'The "Canons" of "Scripture"', in M. Levering (ed.), *Rethinking Scripture: Essays from a Comparative Perspective* (Albany, NY: SUNY Press), 170–9.

GAMBLE, H. Y. (1995), *Books and Readers in the Early Church: A History of Early Christian Texts* (New Haven: Yale University Press).

—— (2002), 'The New Testament Canon: Recent Research and the Status Quaestionis', in McDonald and Sanders (2002), 267–94.

GREGORY, A. (2005), '*1 Clement* and the Writings that Later Formed the New Testament', in A. Gregory and C. Tuckett (eds.), *The Reception of the New Testament in the Apostolic Fathers* (Oxford: Oxford University Press), 129–57.

HAHNEMAN, G. M. (1992), *The Muratorian Fragment and the Development of the Canon* (Oxford: Clarendon Press).

—— (2002), 'The Muratorian Fragment and the Origins of the New Testament Canon', in McDonald and Sanders (2002), 405–15.

HARNACK, A. VON (1925), *The Origin of the New Testament and the Most Important Consequences of the New Creation*, 2nd edn. (London: Williams & Norgate).

HEAD, P. M. (2005), 'Is P^4, P^{64}, and P^{67} the Oldest Manuscript of the Four Gospels? A Response to T. C. Skeat', *NTS* 51: 450–7.

HENGEL, M. (2002), *The Septuagint as Christian Scripture: Its Prehistory and the Problem of Its Canon* (Grand Rapids, Mich.: Baker Academic).

HOLMES, M. W. (1994), review of Hahneman (1992), *CBQ*, 56: 594–5.

—— (2005), 'Polycarp's *Letter to the Philippians* and the Writings that Later Formed the New Testament', in A. Gregory and C. Tuckett (eds.), *The Reception of the New Testament in the Apostolic Fathers* (Oxford: Oxford University Press), 187–227.

JELLICOE, S. (1968), *The Septuagint and Modern Study* (Oxford: Clarendon Press).

JOBES, K. H., and SILVA, M. (2000), *Invitation to the Septuagint* (Grand Rapids, Mich.: Baker Academic).

JONGE, H. J. DE (2003), 'Introduction: The New Testament Canon', in Auwers and de Jonge (2003), 309–19.

JUNOD, E. (1984), 'La formation et la composition de l'Ancien Testament dans l'Église grecque des quatre premiers siècles', in S. Amsler, J.-D. Kaestli and O. Wermelinger (eds.), *Le canon de L'Ancien Testament: Sa formation et son histoire* (Geneva: Labor et Fides), 105–51.

KALIN, E. R. (1990), 'Re-examining New Testament Canon History: 1. The Canon of Origen', *Currents in Theology and Mission*, 17: 274–82.

—— (2002), 'The New Testament Canon of Eusebius', in McDonald and Sanders (2002), 386–404.

KOOIJ, A. VAN DER (1998), 'The Canonization of Ancient Books Kept in the Temple of Jerusalem', in A. van der Kooij and K. van der Toorn (eds.), *Canonization and Decanonization* (Leiden: E. J. Brill), 17–40.

KRAFT, R. A. (2002), 'The Codex and Canon Consciousness', in McDonald and Sanders (2002), 229–33.

KÜMMEL, W. G. (1975), *Introduction to the New Testament*, rev. ed. (Nashville, Ky: Abingdon).

LAMPE, P. (2003), *From Paul to Valentinus: Christians at Rome in the First Two Centuries* (Minneapolis: Fortress Press).

LAYTON, B. (1987), *The Gnostic Scriptures* (New York: Doubleday).

LEIMAN, S. Z. (1976), *The Canonization of the Hebrew Scripture: The Talmudic and Midrashic Evidence* (Hamden, Conn.: Archon Books).

LEWIS, J. P. (1964), 'What Do We Mean by Jabneh?', *Journal of Bible and Religion*, 32: 125–32.

—— (2002), 'Jamnia Revisited', in McDonald and Sanders (2002), 146–62.

LIGHTSTONE, J. N. (2002), 'The Rabbis' Bible: The Canon of the Hebrew Bible and the Early Rabbinic Guild', in McDonald and Sanders (2002), 163–84.

LIPS, HERMANN VON (2004), *Der neutestamentliche Kanon: Seine Geschichte und Bedeutung*, Zürcher Grundrisse zur Bibel (Zürich: Theologischer Verlag).

LUDLOW, M. (2003), ' "Criteria of canonicity" and the Early Church', in Barton and Wolter (2003), 69–93.

MARKSCHIES, C. (2001), 'Neue Forschungen zur Kanonisierung des Neuen Testaments', *Apocrypha*, 12: 237–63.

—— (2003), 'The Canon of the New Testament in Antiquity: Some New Horizons for Future Research', in M. Finkelberg and G. Stroumsa (eds.), *Homer, the Bible, and Beyond: Literary and Religious Canons in the Ancient World*, Jerusalem Studies in Religion and Culture, 2 (Leiden: E. J. Brill), 175–94.

MASON, S. (1996), 'Josephus on Canon and Scriptures', in Magne Sæbø (ed.), *Hebrew Bible / Old Testament: The History of Its Interpretation*, i: *From the Beginnings to the Middle Ages (until 1300)* (Göttingen: Vandenhoeck & Ruprecht), 217–35.

—— (2002), 'Josephus and His Twenty-Two Book Canon', in McDonald and Sanders (2002), 110–27.

McDONALD, L. M. (1995), *The Formation of the Christian Biblical Canon*, rev. and expanded edn. (Peabody, Mass.: Hendrickson).

—— (2002a), 'Appendixes', in McDonald and Sanders (2002), 580–97.

—— (2002b), 'Identifying Scripture and Canon in the Early Church: The Criteria Question', in McDonald and Sanders (2002), 416–39.

—— and SANDERS, J. A. (2002) (eds.), *The Canon Debate* (Peabody, Mass.: Hendrickson).

METZGER, B. M. (1987), *The Canon of the New Testament: Its Origin, Development, and Significance* (Oxford: Clarendon Press).

OEPKE, A., and MEYER, R. (1965), 'Κρύπτω, etc.', in *Theological Dictionary of the New Testament* (Grand Rapids, Mich.: Eerdmans), iii. 957–1000.

OIKONOMOS, E. (1991), 'The Significance of the Deuterocanonical Writings in the Orthodox Church', in S. Meurer (ed.), *The Apocrypha in Ecumenical Perspective* (New York: United Bible Societies), 16–32.

PERKINS, P. (2002), 'Gnosticism and the Christian Bible', in McDonald and Sanders (2002), 355–71.

RAHLFS, A. (1935), *Septuaginta*, 2 vols. (Stuttgart: Württembergische Bibelanstalt).

RÜGER, H. P. (1991), 'The Extent of the Old Testament Canon', in S. Meurer (ed.), *The Apocrypha in Ecumenical Perspective* (New York: United Bible Societies), 151–60.

SANDERS, J. A. (2002), 'The Issue of Closure in the Canonical Process', in McDonald and Sanders (2002), 252–63.

SCHAPER, J. (1998), 'The Rabbinic Canon and the Old Testament of the Early Church: A Social-Historical View', in A. van der Kooij and K. van der Toorn (eds.), *Canonization and Decanonization*, Studies in the History of Religions, 82 (Leiden: E. J. Brill), 93–106.

SCHMIDT, D. D. (2002), 'The Greek New Testament as a Codex', in McDonald and Sanders (2002), 469–84.

SHEPPARD, G. T. (1987), 'Canon', in M. Eliade (ed.), *Encyclopedia of Religion* (New York: Macmillan), iii.: 62–9.

SIKER, JEFFREY S. (1987), 'The Canonical Status of the Catholic Epistles in the Syriac New Testament', *JTS* 38/2: 311–40.

SIMON, M. (1997), 'The Bible in the Earliest Controversies between Jews and Christians', in P. Blowers (ed.), *The Bible in Greek Christian Antiquity* (Notre Dame, Ind.: University of Notre Dame Press), 49–68.

SKARSAUNE, OSKAR (1996), 'Canon and Text in the Early Greek Church', in Magne Sæbø (ed.), *Hebrew Bible / Old Testament: The History of Its Interpretation*, i.: *From the Beginnings to the Middle Ages (until 1300)* (Göttingen: Vandenhoeck & Ruprecht), 443–50.

SMITH, J. Z. (1998), 'Canons, Catalogues and Classics', in A. van der Kooij and K. van der Toorn (eds.), *Canonization and Decanonization*, Studies in the History of Religions, 82 (Leiden: E. J. Brill), 295–311.

SNOEK, J. A. M. (1998), 'Canonization and Decanonization: An Annotated Bibliography', in A. van der Kooij and K. van der Toorn (eds.), *Canonization and Decanonization*, Studies in the History of Religions, 82 (Leiden: E. J. Brill), 435–506.

STROUMSA, GUY G. (1994), 'The Body of Truth and its Measures: New Testament Canonization in Context', in H. Preissler and H. Seiwert (eds.), *Gnosisforschung und Religionsgeschichte*: *Festschrift für Kurt Rudolph zum 65. Geburtstag.* (Marburg: Diagonal Verlag), 307–16.

STUHLMACHER, P. (1991), 'The Significance of the Old Testament Apocrypha and Pseudepigrapha for the Understanding of Jesus and Christology', in S. Meurer (ed.), *The Apocrypha in Ecumenical Perspective* (New York: United Bible Societies), 1–15.

SUNDBERG, A. C. (1964), *The Old Testament of the Early Church*, HTS, 20. (Cambridge, Mass: Harvard University Press; London: Oxford University Press).

—— (1968), 'Toward a Revised History of the New Testament Canon', in F. L. Cross (ed.), *Studia Evangelica*, iv/1 (Berlin: Akademie Verlag), 452–61.

—— (1973), 'Canon Muratori: A Fourth-Century List', *HTR* 66: 1–41.

—— (1976), 'Canon of the NT', in *Interpreter's Dictionary of the Bible: Supplementary Volume* (Nashville, Tenn.: Abingdon), 136–40.

—— (2002), 'The Septuagint: The Bible of Hellenistic Judaism', in McDonald and Sanders (2002), 68–90.

TOMSON, P. J. (1998), 'The New Testament Canon as the Embodiment of Evolving Christian Attitudes towards the Jews', in A. van der Kooij and K. van der Toorn (eds.), *Canonization and Decanonization*, Studies in the History of Religions, 82 (Leiden: E. J. Brill), 107–31.

TROBISCH, D. (2000), *The First Edition of the New Testament* (New York: Oxford University Press).

ULRICH, E. (2002), 'The Notion and Definition of Canon', in McDonald and Sanders (2002), 21–35.

—— (2003), 'Qumran and the Canon of the Old Testament', in Auwers and de Jonge (2003), 57–80.

UNNIK, W. C. VAN (1949), 'De la règle μήτε προσθεῖναι μήτε ἀφελεῖν dans l'histoire du canon', *VC* 3: 1–36.

VANDERKAM, J. C. (2002), 'Questions of Canon Viewed through the Dead Sea Scrolls', in McDonald and Sanders (2002), 91–109.

VERHEYDEN, J. (2003), 'The Canon Muratori: A Matter of Dispute', in Auwers and de Jonge (2003), 487–556.

WYRICK, J. (2004), *The Ascension of Authorship: Attribution and Canon Formation in Jewish, Hellenistic, and Christian Traditions* (Cambridge, Mass.: Harvard University Press).

ZAHN, T. (1904), *Grundriss der Geschichte des neutestamentlichen Kanons* (Leipzig: A. Deichert).

——(1908), 'Canon of Scripture', in S. M. Jackson (ed.), *New Schaff-Herzog Encyclopedia of Religious Knowledge* (New York: Funk and Wagnalls), ii.: 388–400.

ZEVIT, Z. (1998), 'The Second-Third Century Canonization of the Hebrew Bible and Its Influence on Christian Canonizing', in A. van der Kooij and K. van der Toorn (eds.), *Canonization and Decanonization*, Studies in the History of Religions, 82 (Leiden: E. J. Brill), 133–60.

CHAPTER 21

···

CREEDS, COUNCILS, AND CANONS

···

EVERETT FERGUSON

CREEDS, councils, and canons are interrelated topics. Disputes over beliefs and practices prompted the meeting of church councils, which defined acceptable statements of belief (creeds) and drew up rules (canons) governing conduct, discipline, organization, and worship. Nonetheless, the three topics are distinct phenomena and may best be treated separately.

21.1 CREEDS

···

The two most widely used and ecumenically acceptable creeds are also historically the most problematic: the Apostles' Creed in the western churches and the Nicene Creed, originating in the East and accepted in the West. The classic work of J. N. D. Kelly (1972) was the nodal point in twentieth-century study of the creeds, and his conclusions may be taken as the starting point for this survey.

21.1.1 The Synthesis of J. N. D. Kelly

Various confessions of faith or confessional-like statements may be found in the New Testament (e.g. Rom 1: 3–4; 1 Cor 8: 6; 1 Tim 2: 5–6; 1 Pet 3: 18–21) and in other early Christian literature (Ignatius, *Trall.* 9; Polycarp, *Phil.*. 2). There were also summaries of apostolic preaching (the *kerygma*—like 1 Cor 15: 3–8) and the important Trinitarian baptismal formula of Matthew 28: 19. These materials formed the pre-history of creeds. Earlier studies failed to distinguish the *regula*, the 'rule of faith', which was a summary of essential doctrine, from creeds proper (the confessions of faith). The *regula* was a summary of the apostolic preaching, fixed in outline but flexible in detail and wording.

Catechesis and baptism constituted the principal setting in which creeds developed. Declaratory creeds (fourth century) were 'summaries of Christian doctrine compiled for the benefit of converts undergoing instruction' (Kelly 1972: 50). The earliest form of baptismal creed, however, was interrogatory: 'Do you believe ...?' to which the candidate replied, 'I believe'. Why the word 'symbol' (*symbolon*, *symbolum*), meaning a sign or token, was adopted as the word for the baptismal questions and answers and, later, for declaratory creeds remains unclear.

The Old Roman Creed (R) was one of the earliest local creeds to take shape, and it is the direct ancestor of the Apostles' Creed. The text is derived from the Latin commentary on the *Symbolorum apostolorum* by Rufinus (400; Eng. trans. in Kelly 1955) and the Greek profession of faith by Marcellus of Ancyra addressed to Bishop Julius of Rome (340; text in Epiphanius, *Pan.* 72. 2. 3). Their wording is the declaratory form of the three questions asked of baptismal candidates according to the *Apostolic Tradition* (chapter 21) attributed to Hippolytus of Rome in the early third century. The structure is a Trinitarian outline enlarged in its second article by an 'originally independent Christological summary' (Kelly 1972: 122). The article on the Holy Spirit in R was expanded to include the Church, remission of sins, and the resurrection of the flesh.

Rome took the lead in giving a fairly stable wording to confessions. R was one of several credal summaries in use, but all western creeds, as known from many places in the fourth through sixth centuries, are directly descended from it. The Received Text (T) that emerged served as the declaratory creed at baptism and found a place in the divine office also. It originated in southern Gaul in the sixth or seventh century, and from the eighth and ninth centuries as part of Charlemagne's efforts at liturgical uniformity it became the sole baptismal creed of the western church.

Eastern churches too used baptismal interrogations in the third century, and from the fourth and fifth centuries local declaratory creeds, probably of earlier origin, are known for several cities and in several writings. There was 'no one original stock from which all creeds derived', but they had common features because of being 'embedded in the act of baptism and the catechetical rule of faith' (Kelly 1972: 204).

The Council of Nicaea (325) marked a new era in the history of creeds, with the introduction of synodal creeds of wider than local authority and to be used as tests of orthodoxy for all Christians. Antecedents to the use of confessions to prove orthodoxy may be seen in the statement by Heraclides, cited in Origen's *Dialogue with Heraclides* (Eng. trans. by Chadwick in Oulton and Chadwick 1954: 437–55), and the letter addressed to Paul of Samosata by the bishops at Antioch in 268. The Council at Antioch in early 325 condemned Eusebius of Caesarea and two other bishops for not signing the council's creed, which anathematized those who said that the Son of God is a creature (English trans. in Kelly 1972: 209–10; corrections in Abramowski 1975: 356–60).

This action at Antioch (325) prompted Eusebius to submit a statement of his beliefs to the Council of Nicaea. Some had argued that the creed of Caesarea was the basis of the creed adopted at Nicaea (N), but Kelly refutes this (1972: 221–6). Rather, it seems that N was a local baptismal creed from Syria or Palestine enlarged to meet the issues confronting the council on the relationship of Christ to God the Father. The purpose of the creed in general, and especially the introduction of the word *homoousios*, was not to establish a particular wording but to exclude the views of Arius that Christ was a creature. This is made explicit in the anathemas at the end, signalling the change from a confession of faith to a standard of orthodoxy.

The many creeds adopted by councils in the half-century after Nicaea show that it was not immediately accepted as the one creed of Christendom. It had excluded the views of Arius, but *homoousios* was not sacrosanct, and many other formulations were attempted.

The fortunes of N became entwined in modern study with its problematic relationship to the Council of Constantinope (381). The creed now recited as the Nicene Creed in most churches of the East and West is another creed, which, since the Council of Chalcedon (451), has been ascribed to the Council of Constantinople (381). That council claimed to uphold the faith of Nicaea, and the creed associated with it was said to be the Nicene Creed with some additions to counter heresies after 325; hence this creed is sometimes termed the Niceno-Constantinopolitan Creed (C).

Although N and C are different documents, Kelly argued that most church fathers were not so concerned about precise, exact words, and by 'the faith of Nicaea' referred to any creed that agreed with its doctrine even if differing in language. Against views that C did not originate at the Council of Constantinople, Kelly adopted the position that the council accepted a creed already in liturgical use, touched it up, and promulgated it as confirming the Nicene faith. Only later was the pure text of N clearly distinguished from C, but C established itself as a more adequate statement. C was the official baptismal creed at Constantinople and in the surrounding region, came to be used in the eucharist (by around 500), and after Chalcedon spread through East and West.

The ecumenical acceptability of C was ruptured when the West added to the article about the Holy Spirit a double procession, from the Father 'and the Son' (*filioque*). This was part of Augustine's doctrine of the Trinity (*Trin.* 2. 4. 7; 4. 20. 29), and was incorporated into C at the Council of Toledo in 589. The addition only slowly gained acceptance in Rome and was never accepted by the Greek churches.

21.1.2 The Apostles' Creed

Subsequent studies have challenged key points in the reconstruction of the Apostles' Creed and reopened the discussion of the connection of C with the Council of Constantinople. An alternative reconstruction of the history of the Apostles' Creed has been presented by three German scholars (Kinzig, Markschies, and Vinzent 1999; summarized in Kinzig and Vinzent 1999). Their reconstruction combines elements from Kelly (1972) and A. M. Ritter (1984 and 1991), who developed views of Hans von Campenhausen. That a Christological summary and Trinitarian formula were originally independent of each other, they say, is universally accepted, and they agree that we must distinguish the *regula* from confessions of faith. They further affirm the new consensus that there is no evidence of a declaratory creed, including the Old Roman Creed, before the fourth century.

The connection of the so-called *Apostolic Tradition* with Hippolytus has been under heavy attack (Markschies in Kinzig, Markschies, and Vinzent 1999: 1–74; Brent 1995: 184–96). The name of Hippolytus entered the transmission of the church order literature only at the end of the fourth century. There is no example in the witnesses to the reconstructed *Apostolic Tradition* of a title corresponding to 'The Apostolic Tradition Concerning Gifts' listed on the statue in Rome assigned to Hippolytus. The *Apostolic Tradition* belongs to church-use literature, or 'living' literature, so it has no one author but is a collection of materials from different periods (see also Bradshaw, Johnson, and Phillips 2002: 1–6, 13–16, following Metzger 1988, 1992*a*, 1992*b*). Hence, the baptismal questions (ch. 21) may in their present form be dependent on the old Roman symbol of the fourth century, and cannot be used to reconstruct the baptismal questions of the third century or as an early witness to what became the Roman symbol.

Apart from documents associated with the *Apostolic Tradition*, the oldest liturgical document with an interrogatory creed is the *Old Gelasian Sacramentary*; nevertheless, literary documents allow for the use of an interrogatory creed from the late second century. The question with regard to Christ in the *Gelasian* is the short form, 'born and suffered' (*natum et passum*). Kinzig (in Kinzig, Markschies, and Vinzent 1999: 75–183) argues that this is the original form of the second article (second or third century) and assembles a considerable number of examples of this form of confession. The declaratory creed of R influenced the baptismal questions in some documents after the fourth century.

The genus 'confession' belongs to the time of the imperial Church, in spite of Rufinus's unfounded assertion of an unchanging Roman confession (Vinzent, in Kinzig, Markschies, and Vinzent 1999: 185–409, 195). The declaratory creeds of the fourth century were not initially liturgical but doctrinal, to safeguard Christian truth against heresy. Marcellus's confession of faith submitted to Rome draws on traditional and liturgical material but is not a quotation of the confession in use at Rome. His creed was a personal reply to other creeds drawn up in the context of the debate over Arius's views. Rome accepted it as orthodox, and with his name deleted took it over for catechetical and baptismal use.

The model in the formulation of the creeds was that of building blocks: elements were taken over from traditional and liturgical material and from opponents' work, correcting the latter. Some of the creeds thus 'assembled' became points of reference in liturgy and catechesis (Kinzig and Vinzent 1999: 552, 557; Kinzig, Markschies, and Vinzent 1999: 238–9).

Liuwe H. Westra (2002) produced a major study with a comprehensive survey of the evidence that responded to Kinzig et al. and reaffirmed key points in the consensus of Kelly and Ritter with modifications to form a new hypothesis. Agreeing with Vinzent that Marcellus's creed was a private creed, of which we have many in the fourth century, and was not a borrowing of R, for it excellently fitted his theological position, Westra also rejects the interpretation that Marcellus's creed became R. Vinzent's arguments are unconvincing: Augustine, Rufinus, and Ambrose testify that the creed was a venerable tradition in Rome, and western echoes of R are closer to it than are the echoes in eastern sources (all creeds necessarily covered much of the same ground) (Westra 2002: 33–7). As Kelly showed, the *regula fidei* was different from creeds (a distinction blurred by Vinzent) and was always flexible in formulation. The interrogations at baptism were different from declaratory creeds, which had their origin in the different practice that arose in the fourth century of delivering a summary of the faith to the candidates, who learned it and repeated it back (*traditio et redditio symboli*). The earliest certain evidence of this practice, and so of a declaratory creed, is Cyril of Jerusalem (*Catech.* 5.12). The *regula* was a forerunner of the baptismal questions and of creeds.

Against Kinzig, Westra argues that 'born and suffered' of the *Old Gelasian Sacramentary* was not the model for R, for the Christological sequence was already set as early as the second century. R was never intended to draw the line against heresies; that was the function of the *regula*, not of the baptismal questions and declaratory creeds before the synodal and private creeds in the fourth century took over the function of the *regula* (Westra 2002: 49–54).

In this context Westra offers a new hypothesis: that there was a proto-R. R, the baptismal questions in *Veronensis* (the Latin version of the *Apostolic Tradition*), and later western forms of the creed point in the direction of an original form to which all known forms hark back (Westra 2002: 65–7). This hypothesis prompts the counter question: May the variety be original, and there have been no one common form until later? There continued to be many regional types of the Apostles' Creed before the spread of T.

21.1.3 The Nicene Creed

Two topics may be highlighted for comment: the word *homoousios* in the creed of 325 and the origin of C. The exact meaning and intent of *homoousios* ('of the same substance') have been controversial from the beginning. Beyond the propriety of the introduction of a non-scriptural word into the creed, there was the question of its precise sense. The major study in English of the Greek word *ousia* (substance) in the Christian doctrine of God is by Christopher Stead (1977). In summarizing his study, Stead (1975) recognized twenty-eight theoretically possible senses of *ousia*, and found early Christian theologians employing many of these senses and not always with consistency, even in the same author. As clarified in the Trinitarian debates of the fourth century, *ousia* referred to the divine nature, what God is (Norris 1997). In an earlier study criticizing previous efforts to define *homoousios*, Stead (1961) opted for a broad, flexible sense, 'identity-in-difference', as light and ray (*phōs* and *apaugasma*) or mind and thought (*nous* and *logos*) are the same in essence but distinguishable.

Eusebius reported that the emperor Constantine proposed the word *homoousios* to the Council of Nicaea (quoted by Athanasius, *De decretis*, 33. 4). Most students have doubted that Constantine had the philosophical and theological sophistication to have originated the use of the word and have thought that someone else suggested the term to him—most likely Ossius of Cordoba, his religious advisor, or possibly Eustathius of Antioch or Alexander of Alexandria. It has now been argued on the basis of the use of *homoousios* in the Hermetic tractate *Poimandres* for the common nature of Nous and his Son the Logos and of Constantine's knowledge of Hermeticism that Constantine himself was indeed the source for introducing this term into the Nicene Creed (Beatrice 2002: 257–60, 264–9).

The absence of clear contemporary evidence continues to make the connection of C with the Council of Constantinople (381) controversial. A plausible and influential reconstruction of the setting for C was advanced by A. M. Ritter in his published dissertation (1965). Ritter affirms that there is no valid reason not to accept a connection of C with the Council of 381. It was a creed of the Nicene type, but drafted as a basis for peacemaking (unsuccessful) between the orthodox (repeating the *homoousios* and opposing Marcellus of Ancyra) and moderate Macedonians (who accepted the deity of the Son but not of the Spirit); hence the third article was carefully worded. He reiterated his position in a standard reference work (Ritter 1989). Without calling the Holy Spirit God or using *homoousios* for the Spirit, the creed of Constantinople uses biblical language to call the Spirit 'Lord', to assign to him the divine functions of giving life and inspiring the prophets, to attribute his origin to the Father by procession, and to affirm worship and glory to him together with the Father and the Son.

Against alternative views by Luis Abrammowski (1992)—that C is a version of the Nicene Creed expanded with regard to the Holy Spirit by a synod at Rome (probably in 378) and presented to the Synod of Antioch in 379—and by Rudolf Staats (1990)—that C originated as a unity confession between Rome and the East, developed in Antioch in 379, combining elements from R, the Jerusalem confession, and N—Ritter defended his position on C (Ritter 1993). That Theodore of Mopsuestia's *Catechetical Homilies* reflect the expanded wording on the Holy Spirit that was used in Antioch in the 380s says nothing in favour of its derivation from C and against his position, and the confession cited and explained by Theodore does not exactly correspond to C. The other explanations offered do not explain why C lacks an explicit confession of the deity and *homoousia* of the Holy Spirit. Abramowski and Staats avoid the important and abundant testimony of Gregory of Nazianzus.

Another important suggestion about how C came to be associated with the Council of 381 is that it was the creed used at the baptism and consecration of Nectarius as bishop of Constantinople during the council (Davis 1990: 121).

21.1.4 Other Confessional Statements

The Definition of Faith approved at Chalcedon (451) on the two natures of Christ in one person has not had the ecumenical acceptance of the Nicene Creed (being rejected by the Henophysite churches of the East) or its liturgical use.

Whereas earlier confessional statements had been more concerned with the doctrine expressed than with the wording itself, in the fifth and subsequent centuries there was an emphasis on scrupulous adhesion to exact wording. This was manifested in the West in the so-called Athanasian Creed (*Quicunque vult*), deriving from Spain or southern Gaul in the fifth or sixth century and enshrining the theology of Augustine, which required belief in its statements as necessary for salvation.

21.1.5 Recent Collections

Jaroslav Pelikan, assisted by V. Hotchkiss, is responsible for a comprehensive collection of *Creeds and Confessions of Faith in the Christian Tradition* (2003). Volume i includes 'Biblical and Primitive Rules of Faith', 'Ante-Nicene Creeds and Confessional Statements', 'Regional, Synodal, and Personal Symbols', and 'Conciliar and Ecumenical Decrees: From Nicaea I to II'. An introduction, the Greek and Latin texts, and an English translation accompany each document.

Pelikan wrote an accompanying volume, *Credo*, in which he argues for the necessity and usefulness of creeds and downplays their negative, condemnatory aspect. He identifies four factors in the genesis of creeds: exegesis of scripture, prayer, polemics, and politics. Pelikan takes from the early centuries many of his examples to illustrate his analysis of the important features of the creeds. For instance, he notes that the items appended to the third article on the Holy Spirit in C are actions by the Holy Spirit (Pelikan 2003: 53). Furthermore, Augustine quotes C in at least three variations of wording: Do these differences reflect Augustine's personal creeds, or that the wording for him was still not sacrosanct? (Pelikan 2003: 369).

At the time of writing there is announced as in preparation for the series Oxford Early Christian Texts a volume on *Early Christian Creeds* by Wolfram Kinzig.

21.2 COUNCILS

21.2.1 The Work of H. J. Sieben

Vatican II (1962–5) prompted considerable interest in the history and concept of councils, particularly ecumenical councils. In the early centuries the words 'synod' and 'council' were used interchangeably. The work of H. J. Sieben (1979) is the benchmark for late twentieth-century studies of the idea of councils.

The gathering of apostles and elders in Acts 15 (understood by Sieben as described on the analogy of the Jewish Sanhedrin) became the scriptural precedent for church councils; but this was a late development, for only in the fifth and sixth centuries was it invoked as a model. The statement, 'For it seemed good to the Holy Spirit and to us' (Acts 15: 28) became the basis for a claim to inspiration guiding the decisions of councils. (The statement, however, may not be a claim to the guidance of the Spirit in framing the decree, but a reference to the Spirit's role in Peter's and Paul's work of bringing Gentiles into the Church.)

The local councils of the third century in which Origen participated were dominated by a teacher and not by bishops, and unity was achieved by argument and not by official authority. The councils at which Cyprian presided, by way of contrast, followed the procedures of the Roman senate (but see below) with the president stating the question and each participant giving his opinion. Some councils in the fourth century followed Roman judicial processes. Councils of the Roman church were councils not so much of individuals as of an office (the Petrine office). In the Germanic kingdoms of the fifth and sixth centuries the councils had the characteristics of the ruling body of the Germanic peoples.

Sieben concentrated on the concept of councils, rather than on the history of individual councils. Athanasius argued for the superiority of Nicaea (325) over the subsequent councils on the grounds of its relative universality and freedom and the legitimacy of its participants, as contrasted with the limited numbers, state manipulation, and illegitimacy of some participants in the other gatherings. Athanasius initially argued for the authority of the Nicene symbol with scriptural and rational proofs; then he identified the council's faith with tradition (transmitted not in identical formulae but in the same unchangeable spirit); finally he affirmed that the council, as mediating scriptural truth, taught the inspired word of God. Thus Athanasius contributed to making Nicaea not only a recipient of tradition but also creative of tradition.

Augustine's doctrine of councils emphasized the difference between scripture and the decrees of councils, for all councils are capable of being amended, yet he upheld the authority of a universal council as the voice of the Catholic Church.

Leo the Great saw councils as confirming the peace and harmony of the Church. In his time it was still necessary to argue for the authority of councils. He did so on the basis of their inspiration, conformity with scripture, and witness to ecumenical and traditional consensus, with the added contention of the papacy as the essential witness to tradition and the principle of unity.

Vincent of Lérins identified tradition with a fixed, written norm: the decrees of councils and the writings of the fathers. The ecumenical councils realized the idea of a consensus with antiquity and with the universal church.

The impetus for the development of conciliar theory came from arguments over the reception of particular councils. Some defenders of the *homoousios* did not acknowledge that the Nicene symbol had any authority. The first arguments for its authority were non-theological; but increasingly, the affirmation was made of divine help in its formulation. With the success of the arguments of Athanasius and the Roman see for Nicaea, its symbol became an important subject in the Christological debates of the fifth century. Defenders of Chalcedon had to justify the place of other councils as independent moments in the Church's tradition and not simply as confirmations of the faith of Nicaea. New formulae were necessary, it was argued, to answer heretical novelties, and not because of a lack in the creed itself.

The holding of multiple councils required that there be norms for determining which councils were to be followed. Pope Gelasius expressed these criteria: agreement with scripture, agreement with tradition, observance of the canons of church law, reception by the whole Church, and confirmation by the Apostolic See (Rome). Sieben saw consent to the councils as involving agreement both vertically (with scripture and tradition) and horizontally (general assent of the faithful). It is notable that originally the authority of papal decretals (see below) was advanced by linking them with the authority of the decrees of ancient councils.

The Frankish church developed a new conciliar theory in opposition to Nicaea II (787). The theologians of Charlemagne's realm contended that the consensus of the Church is represented not by the five patriarchs (as advocated by the Greeks) but by the majority of all the churches. Consensus with tradition must be established by critical reading of the texts, not by simple citation.

21.2.2 Local and Regional Councils

Regional meetings of bishops occurred in the latter half of the second century in
Asia Minor to decide on policy with regard to the Montanist movement (Eusebius,
Hist. eccl. 5.16.9–10) and in several regions later in the century in regard to the
celebration of the Pasch (Eusebius, *Hist. eccl.* 5.23). Tertullian refers to councils in
Greece (*De ieiunio*, 13); his reference to 'every council of the churches' (*Pud.* 10)
refers to meetings of local churches (Brent 1995: 293).

During the third century, meetings of bishops in a province became a regular feature of church life in many regions. Cyprian, bishop of Carthage (248–
58), refers to synods in North Africa before his time (*Ep.* 71.4; 59.10). Firmil-
ian, bishop of Caesarea in Cappadocia (d. 268), in writing to Cyprian refers to
annual meetings of elders and bishops in his area (Cyprian, *Ep.* 75.4.3). When
Cyprian reported the results of synods at which he presided, he wrote in the
plural for all the bishops, unlike the bishop of Rome, who wrote in his own
name, for Roman synods were enlarged sessions of his advisory college. In Alexandria the presbyters were more independent of their bishop than they were in
Rome.

From the writings of Cyprian we know something of procedures at councils
in North Africa, which have much in common with those of the Roman senate:
convocare as the verb for convening the meeting, the meeting open to the public,
a *relatio* setting forth the matter for discussion, *censere* as the verb for the roll-
call at which each member stated his *sententia*, equality of the bishops present
in their voting, and the resolution which was approved put in written form for
the interested parties and put into archives. These similarities lead to the conclusion of conscious imitation. However, these procedures were also to be found in
town councils, private associations, and provincial assemblies, so they formed the
common 'Roman parliamentary procedure'. It is more likely that, rather than consciously borrowing senatorial practice, church synods in the West simply followed
normal custom, especially as known from municipal councils (Amidon 1983: 329,
331–3, 336).

In the synods in which Cyprian and Origen participated, they looked upon
their opponents as still members of the Church even if they judged their opinions
erroneous. Before Cyprian and Paul of Samosata we know of no councils that
excommunicated schismatics and heretics or ordained their replacements (Brent
1995: 440–5). This practice became frequent in the fourth-century theological
conflicts.

The Council of Arles (314), called by Constantine to deal with the Donatist
controversy and related matters, brought bishops from the western provinces ruled
by Constantine and set a precedent for councils beyond one province or region to
represent the area controlled by one political authority.

21.2.3 Ecumenical Councils

Understandably, most attention to the study of the councils has been directed to those that became recognized as ecumenical: that is, having authority for the universal Church. On the ecumenical councils we are now fortunate in having an accessible edition of the text and English translation of the *Decrees of the Ecumenical Councils* (Tanner, Alberigo, *et al.* 1990). The Greek and Latin texts are from *Conciliorum Oecumenicorum Decreta* (ed. Alberigo *et al.* 1973). There is a brief introduction and bibliography for each council. The purpose is to provide a collection of sources, not an exposition of the teachings and laws of the councils. The work contains all the decrees (doctrinal and canonical) of the ecumenical councils, but only these decrees. The acts (proceedings or 'minutes') of the councils, even where they are available, are not included.

Complementing Tanner and Alberigo's collection of pronouncements by the councils is Leo Donald Davis's (1990) popular treatment of the history and theology of the seven ecumenical councils. He aims not to be original but to put together in convenient form the political tumult and theological speculation that occasioned these councils. The main value of his survey is in setting the historical context of the councils. He does not document the sources, but attempts to represent the current state of knowledge.

On Nicaea (325) Davis includes the importance of the synod at Antioch (325) as an innovation in issuing a credal statement for bishops (not catechumens) accompanied by anathemas. He sees conciliar procedures as modelled on the Roman senate. The third article in the Niceno-Constantinopolitan Creed gives divine functions to the Holy Spirit without making a direct claim for his deity. The party claiming to follow Cyril of Alexandria in the controversies surrounding the Council of Chalcedon (451) adhered to his slogan, 'One incarnate nature of the divine Word', and claimed that there is no nature without hypostasis and no hypostasis without person. Chalcedon instead adopted the wording of two natures in one hypostasis to define the relation of the divine and human in the one person of Jesus Christ. The condemnation of Origen preceded the Council of Constantinople II (553). Those interested in the treatment of the Neo-Chalcedonians should take account of the work by Brian Daley (e.g. 1993).

Nicaea was a significant turning point not only for its authoritative creed with anathemas, but also for the degree of imperial involvement. The emperor called it, financed it, published some of its decisions, and added secular penalties to its ecclesiastical anathemas. All of the first seven ecumenical councils were called by the emperor, as representing the universality of Church and Empire. Indeed, the term 'ecumenical' as first applied to councils probably referred to their being 'general' or broader than a civil diocese, and was not a technical term for a particular kind of council—Eusebius was the first to call Nicaea 'ecumenical' (*Vit. Const.* 3. 6;

for the background to this usage, see Chadwick 1972). The first four ecumenical councils held a special place of honour. From the sixth century in Palestine they were likened to the four Gospels, and this analogy entered the medieval tradition through Gregory the Great (*Epistle* 1. 24). The seven councils were likened to the seven pillars of wisdom (Prov 9: 1) and the seven gifts of the Spirit (Isa 11: 2).

The papal theory of what constituted a council as ecumenical was approval by the pope; the eastern theory involved imperial convocation. Both views involved inconsistencies. What was really decisive, both practically and theologically, was reception by the Church at large. The councils were not institutions, but events; they were representations of the Church, and their authority was not canonical but 'charismatic'. The consensus of the mind of the Church was decisive (Florovsky 1967: 177, 186–8).

Number symbolism played an important role in the historical tradition about councils. Despite earlier reports that would put the number of bishops at Nicaea around 250, the standard number came to be 318 under the influence of the symbolic interpretation of the 318 circumcised servants of Abraham (Gen 14: 14; 17: 23) as standing for Jesus and the cross (Aubineau 1966). The number 630 for the bishops at Chalcedon, although the actual number was probably nearer 450, came from the numerical equivalent of the first two consonants in Greek of Chalcedon (L'Huillier 1996: 187).

One of the many who had unpleasant experiences with councils pronounced a negative judgement on their usefulness: 'For my part, if I am to write the truth, my inclination is to avoid all assemblies of bishops, because I have never seen any council come to a good end, nor turn out to be a solution of evils. On the contrary, it usually increases them. You always find there love of contention and love of power' (Gregory of Nazianzus, *Ep.* 130). For all of the importance of councils in doctrinal and institutional history, these words are a reminder of the negative aspects of the atmosphere surrounding them and their proceedings.

21.3 CANONS

The bishops in council felt that in doctrinal matters they could only transmit the apostolic teaching, so they said, 'We confess'; but in details of organization, discipline, and liturgy they felt that they could make their own decisions. Hence, the canons were in principle amenable to change, but here too the appeal to tradition and ancient customs had its influence.

Heinz Ohme (1998) has provided a major and comprehensive study of the variety of uses of *kanōn* (Latin *canon*, *regula*)—from what is standard or normative to refer to individual church laws, the collection of biblical writings, and summaries of fundamental beliefs. The word was used (as in the following treatment) for synodal decrees in the Greek East from *c.* 330, but in the West not until the sixth century.

21.3.1 The Contributions of Jean Gaudemet

Major contributions to the study of the development of the canon law of the early church were made in the late twentieth century by Jean Gaudemet (1979, 1985, 1989). We take his popular introduction (with good bibliographies) to the history of the sources (not of canon law itself), *Les sources du droit de l'église en occident du II*ᵉ *au VII*ᵉ *siècle* (1985), as the basis of our survey.

Many of the eastern canons were received in the West, but the reverse is not the case. Isidore of Seville gave the definition: 'Canon, a Greek word, signifies in Latin *regula* [rule]' (*Etym.* 6.16.1). In the early church one of the usages of *kanōn* was a designation of the disciplinary prescriptions of councils. Only in the fourth century do the two types of sources for later canon law appear: decisions of councils (from the beginning of the century) and decretals of popes (from its last decades).

The conciliar legislation of the fourth and fifth centuries is known only from later collections. The canons of councils (regional and ecumenical) in Greek before the council in Trullo (691) are known only in the recension by patriarch John Scholasticus (565–77), *Synagogē*. The canons of Nicaea and Sardica (342/3) had a separate and complicated history in Latin translation (important is the *Vetus Romana*); their combination in a continuous numeration led to the mistake of assigning canons from Sardica to the authority of Nicaea. Conciliar legislation touched on all sectors of ecclesiastical life; unanimity was often claimed for decisions because it was inconceivable that the Holy Spirit did not lead all participants to the same conclusions.

The medieval canonists defined a decretal as a response by the pope to a question posed to him by an individual or an ecclesiastical authority. The word comes from *decretum*, a decision. Comparable to the imperial rescripts, papal decretals had a wider currency than the particular question addressed because of the authority recognized in the pope. The decretals from the early period also survive only in later canonical collections. The oldest decretal may be a letter to the bishops of Gaul attributed to Damasus, or perhaps a letter sent by Siricius to Himerius of Tarragon in 385. The legislative activity of the popes became important with the decretals of Innocent I (401–17). Although formulating a new law, the pontifical legislation presented itself as supported by scripture, tradition, and decisions of predecessors.

A collection of canons from the councils at Ancyra (314), Neocaesarea (314/19), Antioch (341), Gangra (343), and Laodicea (?), to which was later added the canons of Nicaea, was made at Antioch. It was translated into Syriac *c.* 400 and used by the church in Persia. Enlarged by the canons of Constantinople I and Chalcedon, a new Syriac translation was made *c.* 500.

Among African collections may be mentioned the *Breviary of Hippo*, containing the acts of councils at Hippo in 393 and 397, and the *Codex canonum ecclesiae Africanae*, made by a priest at Carthage concerning African councils between 393 and 418. In Gaul a compilation of fifty-six canons from Arles (314), Nicaea (325), Orange (441), and Vaison (442) was made between 442 and 506. The *Statuta ecclesiae antiqua* from the second half of the fifth century (perhaps by Gennadius) collected 102 canons.

The *Collectio Avellana*, a little after 553, has letters of popes and imperial constitutions. During the sixth and seventh centuries the only outstanding pope was Gregory the Great, but his numerous letters address canonical questions.

Conciliar activity in the sixth and seventh centuries in the West now occurred in the context of the new Germanic kingdoms. Numerous councils met in Merovingian Gaul; repetition of the same prescriptions in regard to organization, discipline, cult, liturgy, and conduct indicates their poor observation in the churches. In Visigothic Spain a particularly influential compilation was composed *c.* 634, the *Hispana*, which cited 67 councils and 105 decretals; the unknown author was more concerned with practical ends than rigorous respect for texts. In North Africa the *Breviatio canonum* of Fulgentius Ferrand, deacon at Carthage in the middle of the sixth century, introduced the innovation of organizing the canons topically instead of chronologically.

Another source of canonical regulations was the penitential literature that appeared in Celtic Christianity and spread in the sixth and seventh centuries, lasting until the twelfth century. The oldest well-developed representative is the *Irish Penitential of Finnian* (Finnian of Clonard, d. *c.* 559), containing fifty canons. The most important of the Irish penitentials is the *Penitential of Cummean* (bishop of Clofert, d. 662), which orders sins and their punishments according to the classification of eight grave sins made by John Cassian. A major collection was the *Penitential of Theodore* from the end of the seventh or the beginning of the eighth century.

The most important collection for the future was the *Dionysiana*, begun by Dionysius Exiguus *c.* 500. He added to the conciliar series of canons a series of papal decretals, and in the second version gave a continuous numeration of the eastern canons. The third redaction in 527 eliminated canons not universally accepted. Since his work provided a better translation than earlier collections and included an index, it had great success. It was sent by Pope Hadrian to Charlemagne in 774. The combination of the *Dionysio-Hadriana* and the *Hispana*, the two great collections of the first millennium, became influential in Gaul.

For students working on the early history of canon law in the West, the works of Gaudemet can be supplemented by the bibliographical guide prepared by Lotte Kéry (1999). For each collection (she lists sixty-one for the period before the end of the eighth century, arranged chronologically and geographically) she describes its type and contents, date and place of compilation, and author (if known), and lists editions and manuscripts with a full bibliography.

21.3.2 Other Sources in the East

Besides the canons of councils, some private collections attained a place in the canon law of the eastern churches. An important source of regulations for ecclesiastical life (known also in the West) was the *Apostolic Canons*. The compiler-author of the *Apostolic Constitutions* in the late fourth century appended to his work eighty-five canons (forty-seven canons plus thirty-eight from councils), which because of the fiction of apostolic origin had a wide recognition.

The so-called *Canons of Hippolytus* put in the form of thirty-eight canons material based on the *Apostolic Tradition* ascribed to Hippolytus. The work probably originated in lower Egypt around the middle of the fourth century, but survives only in an Arabic translation of a Coptic version of the original Greek.

Basil the Great's letters often dealt with matters of canon law. Three in particular acquired legal status in the Greek church: *Epistles* 188, 199, and 217, addressed to Amphilochius, bishop of Iconium.

21.3.3 Disciplinary Work of the Ecumenical Councils

Peter L'Huillier (1996) prepared a detailed commentary on the individual canons of the first four ecumenical councils. He provided voluminous notes to a translation and a commentary that seeks to discern the significance of the canons for the life of the Church today, as well as demonstrating the value of the canons for historical research by showing the evolution in structures of the Church, its discipline, and relations with society. The work was written two decades earlier in French, as a doctoral dissertation in canon law for the Theological Academy of Moscow, and then translated into Russian before this English version.

L'Huillier's discussions add nuance to the interpretation of the canons throughout, notably the long treatment of the controversial so-called canon 28 of Chalcedon that gave Constantinople as the new capital of the Empire a position next to Rome, taking into account the history of interpretation (pp. 267–96). The commentary on the Nicene canons (especially canons 8 and 19) needs a fuller perspective on the meaning of ordination in the fourth century (Ferguson 1972). The following paragraphs, instead of treating further his particular commentary, will highlight his comments of broader relevance.

The legislation at Nicaea was treated with as much or more respect as the dogmatic decisions (canon 1). Not only doctrine, but also the fundamental norms of church order, were part and parcel of the tradition of the Church (canon 7). Nevertheless, there was more reserve about appeals to custom than is often recognized (canon 2). Justinian confirmed the juridical validity of the canons of the four ecumenical councils and of the local councils accepted by them (*Novellae* 131, pref.). The ancient canons were considered to have been issued under divine inspiration (canon 10). The canons at Nicaea reflect 'the territorial principle [that] is inherent in Orthodox ecclesiology' (canon 62), the change of presbyters from counsellors of the bishop to his delegates (canon 71), and the concern for liturgical uniformity (canon 81–3).

A council at Constantinople in 382, with most of the bishops present in 381 participating, adopted two decrees that were later joined to the four canons of 381 to make six, but the West never accepted these two. The Council of Ephesus called itself 'ecumenical' (canons 7, 8). The canons of the ecumenical councils represent a shift from the varied customary law of earlier centuries toward a written law universally applicable.

21.4 FOR THE FUTURE

It is to be expected that the Apostles Creed will draw continued discussion, despite (or in part because of) the extensive collections of material assembled in recent studies. Clarification of how the creed of Nicaea (325) became the Nicene Creed (381) appears to be dependent on the (unlikely?) discovery of new source material. Work needs to be done on other confessional statements that have not attracted the attention of those with liturgical and ecumenical use—the Chalcedonian Definition of Faith, the Athanasian Creed.

Why were other important doctrines—notably the atonement, eschatology, and the eucharist—not addressed in the credal statements? Was this because they were not as foundational as the nature of God, Christ, and the Holy Spirit? Or did they not become major occasions of controversy (although there were clearly differences of formulation on these matters) in the formative period of the Church? Or was the situation that confessions on these matters did not have occasion to enter liturgical use at baptism or the eucharistic assembly?

The history of the councils and the contents of canonical legislation can be profitably studied further in relation to the developing structures of the Church and to the often unstated views of ecclesiology that they imply. The canons have been exploited mostly in relation to constitutional and liturgical questions. More can be done in the way of examining differences in regions that have not been studied as closely as France and North Africa. Such examinations could tell us more about social conditions, the lives of individuals in the churches, and the Christianization of society.

SUGGESTED READING

AYRES, L. (2004), *Nicaea and its Legacy* (Oxford: Oxford University Press).

BRUNDAGE, J. A. (1995), *Medieval Canon Law* (London: Longmans), chs. 1–2.

FERGUSON, E. (1997), 'Councils' and 'Creeds', in E. Ferguson, M. P. McHugh, and F. W. Norris (eds.), *Encyclopedia of Early Christianity*, 2nd edn. (New York: Garland [Taylor & Francis]), 296–7, 300–2.

HANSON, R. P. C. (1992), 'Creeds and Confessions of Faith', in A. Di Berardino (ed.), *Encyclopedia of the Early Church* (New York: Oxford University Press), i.: 206–8.

HEIM, S. M. (1991) (ed.), *Faith to Creed: Ecumenical Perspectives on the Affirmation of the Apostolic Faith in the Fourth Century* (Grand Rapids, Mich.: Eerdmans).

KRETSCHMAR, G. (1966), 'The Councils of the Ancient Church', in H. J. Margull (ed.), *The Councils of the Church: History and Analysis* (Philadelphia: Fortress Press), 1–81.

LYNCH, J. E. (1997), 'Canons, Canon Law', in E. Ferguson, M. P. McHugh, and F. W. Norris (eds.), *Encyclopedia of Early Christianity*, 2nd edn. (New York: Garland [Taylor & Francis]), i.: 211–12.

VAN DE WIEL, C. (1991), *History of Canon Law* (Louvain: Peeters), First Period.

YOUNG, F. (1991), *The Making of the Creeds* (Philadelphia: Trinity Press International).

The following are also recommended: Davis (1990) and Ritter (1991).

BIBLIOGRAPHY

ABRAMOWSKI, L. (1975), 'Die Synode von Antiochien 324/25 und ihr Symbol', *ZKG*, 86: 356–66.

—— (1992), 'Was hat das Nicaeno-Constantinopolitanum [C] mit dem Konzil von Konstantinopel 381 zu tun?', *Theologie und Philosophie*, 67: 451–513.

ALBERIGO, G., *et al.* (1973) (eds.), *Conciliorum Oecumenicorum Decreta*, 3rd edn. (Bologna: Istituto per le Scienze Religiose).

AMIDON, P. R. (1983), 'The Procedure of St. Cyprian's Synods', *VC* 37: 328–39; repr. in E. Ferguson (ed.), *Church, Ministry, and Organization in the Early Church Era*, Studies in Early Christianity, 13 (New York: Garland [Taylor & Francis], 1993), 224–35.

AUBINEAU, M. (1965), 'Les 318 serviteurs d'Abraham (Gen., XIV, 14) et le nombre des pères au Concile de Nicée (325)', *RHE*, 61: 5–43.

BEATRICE, P. F. (2002), 'The Word "Homoousios" from Hellenism to Christianity', *CH* 71: 243–72.

BRADSHAW, P., JOHNSON, M. E., and PHILLIPS, L. E. (2002), *The Apostolic Tradition*, Hermeneia (Minneapolis: Fortress Press).

BRENT, A. (1995), *Hippolytus and the Roman Church in the Third Century: Communities in Tension before the Emergence of a Monarch-Bishop* (Leiden: E. J. Brill).

CHADWICK, H. (1972), 'The Origin of the Title "Oecumenical Council"', *JTS* NS 23: 132–5.

DALEY, B. E. (1993), ' "A Richer Union": Leontius of Byzantium and the Relationship of Human and Divine in Christ', *StPatr* 24: 239–65.

DAVIS, L. D. (1990), *The First Seven Ecumenical Councils (325–787): Their History and Theology* (Collegeville, Minn.: Liturgical Press).

FERGUSON, E. (1972), 'Attitudes to Schism at the Council of Nicaea', in D. Baker (ed.), *Schism, Heresy and Religious Protest*, SCH 9 (Cambridge: Cambridge University Press), 57–63.

FLOROVSKY, G. (1967), 'The Authority of the Ancient Councils and the Tradition of the Fathers', in G. Müller and W. Zeller (eds.), *Glaube, Geist, Geschichte: Festschrift für Ernst Benz* (Leiden: E. J. Brill), 177–88; repr. in E. Ferguson (ed.), *Church, Ministry, and Organization in the Early Church Era*, Studies in Early Christianity, 13 (New York: Garland [Taylor & Francis], 1993), 211–22.

GAUDEMET, J. (1979), *La formation du droit séculier et du droit de l'église au IVᵉ et Vᵉ siècles*, 2nd edn. (Paris: Sirey).

—— (1985), *Les sources du droit de l'église en occident du IIᵉ au VIIᵉ siècle* (Paris: Cerf).

—— (1989), *L'église dans l'empire romain (IVᵉ–Vᵉ) siècles*, 2nd edn. (Paris: Sirey).

HESS, H. (2002), *The Early Development of Canon Law and the Council of Serdica*, OECS (Oxford: Oxford University Press).

KELLY, J. N. D. (1955), *Rufinus: A Commentary on the Apostles Creed*, ACW 20 (New York: Newman).

—— (1972), *Early Christian Creeds*, 3rd edn. (London: Longman; orig. pub. 1950).

KÉRY, L. (1999), *Canonical Collections of the Early Middle Ages (ca. 400–1140): A Bibliographical Guide to the Manuscripts and Literature* (Washington: Catholic University of America Press).

KINZIG, W. and M. VINZENT (1999), 'Recent Research on the Origin of the Creed', *JTS* NS 50: 535–59.

——MARKSCHIES, CHRISTOPH, and VINZENT, MARKUS (1999), *Tauffragen und Bekenntnis* (Berlin: de Gruyter).

L'HUILLIER, P. (1996), *The Church of the Ancient Councils: The Disciplinary Work of the First Four Ecumenical Councils* (Crestwood, NY: St Vladimir's Seminary Press).

METZGER, M. (1988), 'Nouvelles perspectives pour le prétendue *Tradition apostolique*', *Ecclesia Orans*, 5: 241–59.

—— (1992a), 'Enquêtes autour de la prétendue *Tradition apostolique*', *Ecclesia Orans*, 9: 7–36.

—— (1992b), 'A propos des règlements écclesiastiques et de la prétendue *Tradition apostolique*', *RSR* 66: 249–61.

NORRIS, R. A. (1997), 'Substance', in E. Ferguson, M. P. McHugh, and F. W. Norris (eds.), *Encyclopedia of Early Christianity*, 2nd edn. (New York: Garland [Taylor & Francis]), 1092–4.

OHME, HEINZ (1998), *Kanon ekklesiastikos: Die Bedeutung des altkirchlichen Kanonbegriffs*, Arbeiten zur Kirchengeschichte, 67 (Berlin: de Gruyter).

OULTON, J. E. L., and CHADWICK, H. (1954), *Alexandrian Christianity*, LCC 2 (Philadelphia: Westminster Press).

PELIKAN, J. (2003), *Credo: Historical and Theological Guide to Creeds and Confessions of Faith in the Christian Tradition* (New Haven: Yale University Press).

—— and HOTCHKISS, V. (2003), *Creeds and Confessions of Faith in the Christian Tradition*, i (New Haven: Yale University Press).

RITTER, A. M. (1965), *Das Konzil von Konstantinopel und sein Symbol: Studien zur Geschichte und Theologie des II. Ökumenischen Konzils* (Göttingen: Vandenhoeck & Ruprecht).

—— (1984), 'Glaubensbekenntnis(se) V. Alte Kirche', in *TRE* xiii. 399–412.

—— (1989), 'Konstantinopel. Ökumenische Synoden (I)', in *TRE* xix. 518–24.

—— (1991), 'Creeds', in Ian Hazlett (ed.), *Early Christian Origins and Evolution to AD 600: In Honour of W. H. C. Frend* (Nashville, Tenn.: Abingdon Press), 92–100.

—— (1993), 'Noch einmal: "Was hat das Nicaeno-Constantinopolitanum (C) mit dem Konzil von Konstantinopel zu tun?" ' *Theologie und Philosophie*, 68: 553–60.

SIEBEN, H. J. (1979), *Die Konzilsidee der alten Kirche* (Munich: Schöningh).

STAATS, R. (1990), 'Die römische Tradition im Symbol von 381 [NC] und seine Entstehung auf der Synode von Antiochien 379', *VC* 44: 209–21.

STEAD, G. C. (1961), 'The Significance of the Homoousios', *StPatr* 3: 397–412.

—— (1975), 'The Concept of Divine Substance', *VC* 29: 1–14; repr. in E. Ferguson (ed.), *Doctrines of God and Christ in the Early Church*, Studies in Early Christianity, 9 (New York: Garland [Taylor & Francis], 1993), 29–42.

—— (1977), *Divine Substance* (Oxford: Clarendon Press).

TANNER, N. P., ALBERIGO, G., *et al.* (1990) (eds.), *Decrees of the Ecumenical Councils*, i: *Nicaea I to Lateran V* (London: Sheed and Ward; Washington D.C.: Georgetown University Press).

WESTRA, L. H. (2002), *The Apostles' Creed: Origin, History, and Some Early Commentaries* (Turnhout: Brepols).

CHURCH AND EMPIRE

HAROLD A. DRAKE

On the walls of the old triclinium of the Lateran palace in Rome once stood a mosaic of Christ and the apostles (Fig. 22.1) that neatly encapsulates the concept of Church and Empire that is the subject of this chapter, while at the same time illustrating the problem that this relationship poses for modern scholars.[1] Arrayed on either side of this central scene were a pair of matching images. On the left, a seated Christ was displayed handing keys to St Peter and a banner to the emperor Constantine. The parallel scene on the right showed Peter conferring the papal pallium on the ninth-century Pope Leo III and handing a slightly different banner to his contemporary, Charlemagne. The hierarchy is firmly underscored by the inferior position assigned to the recipients, who are shown performing obeisance to their benefactors.

The agenda of the mosaic is obvious. The items being transferred were meant to symbolize the source of the recipient's power, and thus the basis of his legitimacy. The keys that Peter receives stand for the authority to bind and loose souls that Jesus gave him (Mt 16: 19). The banner handed to Constantine must be the labarum, talisman of the new Christian empire he created by virtue of his vision of the Cross. Similar symbols pass to Leo and Charlemagne. The bishops and emperors are meant to personify two separate institutions—'Church' and 'Empire', respectively. They are configured in such a way as to emphasize that pope and emperor share the receipt of power, thereby confirming the theory of government asserted by Roman bishops as early as Gelasius I, who wrote to the eastern emperor Anastasius in 494 that 'two forces rule this world—the sacred authority of the

Fig. 22.1 Mosaic of Christ and the apostles that once adorned the walls of the old triclinium of the Lateran palace in Rome.

bishops and the royal power' (*Ep.* 6; PL 59. 42). The mosaic visibly confirms this concept of the 'two powers'. And that is precisely the problem. The categories of 'Church' and 'Empire' (or, more broadly, 'church' and 'state') are so firmly ingrained in modern thought that they pose significant obstacles to a full understanding of the relationship between Christian and imperial rulers that began in late antiquity. To unravel that relationship and get at its true meaning, some cherished notions that have guided scholarship for a century and more will have to be discarded.

Like the Lateran mosaic, this story begins with Constantine. Prior to that emperor's adoption of Christianity—traditionally, *en route* to his decisive battle for Rome in 312—Christians had given little thought to how they might share in Rome's rule. Their spokesmen responded to sporadic persecution by professing allegiance to the Emperor, citing Paul's teaching that all government comes from God (Rom 13: 1). In the second century, Melito of Sardis went further, using the chronological coincidence of Augustus and Jesus to argue that from the start God had intended a joint role for Church and Empire. His message would be picked up and fine-tuned by Eusebius of Caesarea into a rationale for a Christian empire (Baynes 1934), while the Christian rhetorician Lactantius used his *Divine Institutes* to speculate on the creation of a Christian state (Digeser 2000). But it is significant that both of these advances took place during the reign of Constantine. In practical terms, prior to that time, Christian thinking had proceeded little beyond the succinct advice of the author of 1 Peter to 'fear God, honour the emperor' (2: 17).

However sporadic, persecution contributed to the development of Church and Empire in two fateful ways. First, it made opposition to Rome an important aspect of Christian identity, embedding the heroic role of the martyrs in both literature and liturgy. Second, it solidified communities around the person of their bishop. By the time of Constantine, these local leaders had developed mechanisms for periodic provincial meetings to resolve issues of discipline and doctrine, and for communicating the results of these sessions to their peers in other provinces. While nothing like the strict hierarchy that later developed in the medieval West, this degree of extra-governmental organization was impressive by ancient standards, creating the notion of a 'universal church', a body distinct from that of the state, without which there would be no need to discuss the relationship between the two.

Constantine's alliance with Christian bishops set that relationship in motion. Because scholarship on this pivotal reign has long focused on religious issues, such as the 'sincerity' of Constantine's conversion (Baynes 1929; Barnes 1981), the following section will concentrate on the political implications of his reign. It will move on to the way in which a newly muscular Christianity used that relationship to suppress variant means of understanding divinity, and the analytical tools that scholars have used to explain that phenomenon. With this air cleared, the final sections will consider the implications of these developments for the concepts of Church and Empire.

22.1 CONSTANTINE

'And Constantine opened the churches throughout the whole world; he threw open the prison doors; he manifested forth the Cross, he confirmed the orthodox faith; he built the Church of the Resurrection of our Lord in Jerusalem.' This account of Constantine's victory comes from an encomium on the martyr George of Cappadocia (Budge 1888: 325), but the joy it reflects could easily be replicated with only slight variation in literally hundreds of late antique legends and hagiographies that sprang up in the wake of the dramatic reversal of fortune that Christians experienced with Constantine's victory. Under Diocletian and his immediate successors, Christians had endured an official persecution aimed at forcing them to abandon their faith and honour the traditional gods of Rome. Even a deathbed reversal by his erstwhile lieutenant Galerius had failed to put an end to Diocletian's persecution in the eastern provinces, where Christians were most heavily concentrated. Word that a new emperor in the West had experienced divine intervention in his successful effort to oust a rival was soon followed by the similar overthrow of their most relentless foe, Maximinus Daia, by Constantine's eastern colleague Licinius.[2]

As these events unfolded, governors in the East received a letter from Licinius informing them of decisions that he and Constantine had taken in Milan while cementing their alliance. The document, traditionally known as the 'Edict of Milan',

ordered the release of all imprisoned Christians and the restitution of their property, guaranteeing them and all other citizens freedom to worship as they pleased.[3]
The year was 313, a good 10 years since the first edict of persecution had been posted
in Nicomedia. No wonder Christians in the East could be heard to heave a collective
sigh of relief.

The Edict of Milan was a reversal in more ways than one. Whereas Diocletian
and his colleagues had been very specific about the names of deities who were
to be worshipped, the Edict professed a refreshing neutrality, speaking only of a
'supreme divinity' (*summa divinitas*) and 'whatever divinity there is in the seat of
heaven'. Where the tetrarchs recognized only one form of worship (sacrifice), the
Edict encouraged each citizen to devote himself 'to that religion which he felt was
most fitting to himself', being concerned only to 'ensure that no cult or religion may
seem to have been impaired by us' (*Mort.* 48. 2–3, 6). These and similar passages
make the Edict the first guarantee of the freedom of worship in western history
(Dörries 1960).

The Edict will play an important role in the discussion of Church and Empire,
but a more immediate issue came from the province of Africa (roughly, modern
Tunisia), where the breakaway sect of the Donatists appealed for Constantine's
support in their struggle against Caecilian and his party.[4] There was precedent
for Christians to petition for imperial relief—eastern bishops had done so almost
half a century earlier in their dispute with Paul of Samosata. Aurelian, the emperor
who received this petition, set another precedent by turning the matter over to the
bishop of Rome and committing himself to enforce that decision (Millar 1971). Constantine, therefore, was on familiar ground when he made similar arrangements
with Bishop Miltiades in 313. But when the Donatists protested their treatment
at Miltiades' hands, Constantine took the unprecedented step of referring that
decision to a council at Arles (314) to be composed of all the bishops under his
dominion. Not only did he take the initiative to summon the council, but he made
the further unprecedented decision to fund it out of his treasury, in particular by
arranging for bishops to travel via the public post. It is no exaggeration to say that
the formal relationship between Christianity and the Roman Empire traces directly
to the steps that Constantine took to resolve this controversy.

For this reason, Constantine's reign is frequently identified as the origin of 'Caesaropapism', a situation in which the secular ruler, or Caesar, asserts the authority
of a spiritual ruler, or pope. But Caesaropapism is a modern term, developed
in the nineteenth century; its application to the ancient world is dangerously
anachronistic (Dagron 1996). The Edict of Milan provides a simpler answer for
Constantine's actions: by legalizing the Christian god, it also opened the door for
Constantine as *pontifex maximus* to assume responsibility for the correct functioning of that god's cult. This much Roman emperors had always done. But the Donatist issue shows that Constantine did not intend to be a passive partner. The same
willingness to intervene exhibited itself a decade later, when Constantine seized the

eastern empire from Licinius in 324. Immediately, he found himself embroiled in the Arian controversy. After failing to settle the dispute through personal diplomacy, Constantine fell back on the lesson learned at Arles, and summoned a council of bishops to resolve the issue. Since he now controlled both halves of the Empire, this council would be ecumenical, or world-wide—the first of its sort in Christian history.

Originally, the council was set to be held in Ancyra in central Anatolia. But amid signs that the organizers of this meeting had already prejudged the issue, Constantine relocated it to Nicaea, a site that he said would be more accessible to bishops from the West; although he did not say so, it was also a site more accessible to himself. Attending this council and serving as a *de facto* moderator of the debates, he overawed the assembly through a calculated combination of personal modesty and the splendour of late Roman imperial ceremony.[5] More substantively, once the council achieved virtual consensus on a common profession of faith, Constantine undertook to enforce the decision, putting the coercive power of the state firmly behind the majority party.

This intervention was far more extensive than anything Aurelian might have conceived; it is the new thing in Christian relations with the Empire that emerged during Constantine's reign. From this time, emperors became increasingly involved in theological questions. The historian Ammianus Marcellinus mocked the frequent councils called by Constantine's son, Constantius II, giving posterity the image of 'throngs of bishops [who] hastened hither and thither on the public post-horses to the various synods', in such great numbers as to create imperial gridlock.[6] These theological disputes are frequently cited as a reason for the fall of the Roman Empire in the West, by distracting emperors from more serious tasks, splintering the eastern empire, and leading to an irreparable breach between East and West.

To cement this baleful legacy, scholars also point to the zeal with which Christians went about suppressing the traditional beliefs of the ancient Mediterranean, a phenomenon which, according to an even longer tradition, inevitably resulted from the intolerance that characterizes that faith. Together, 'Caesaropapism' and 'intolerance' sum up the negative influences of the Church on the Empire. Both of these terms, however, need to be rethought.

22.2 THE COERCIVE TURN

'If God helps those who help themselves', Peter Brown observed in his path-breaking *The World of Late Antiquity*, 'then no group better deserved the miracle of the "conversion" of Constantine in 312 than did the Christians'

(Brown 1971: 86). Brown had in mind the speed with which church leaders turned imperial power to their own agenda—an agenda that began with the suppression of deviant belief within the Church, but expanded fairly rapidly to the suppression of the traditional religions of the Graeco-Roman world—those religions now lumped together into the single category of 'paganism' (Fowden 1993: 38). This is a story traditionally studied under the rubric of Christian 'intolerance'. For the English-speaking world, Edward Gibbon set the tone with his analysis of Christianity's rise in the famous fifteenth chapter of his *Decline and Fall of the Roman Empire* (1909–14), where 'intolerant zeal' heads his list of five causes for Christian success. It is a powerful thesis that has fuelled much of modern scholarship, including the once-dominant conflict model of pagan–Christian relations, in which the two systems were assumed to be in a 'life-and-death struggle' (see the essays in Momigliano 1963). Its influence can still be seen in definitions that equate 'paganism' with 'toleration' and 'Christianity' with 'intolerance' (O'Donnell 1977) and in portraits of Constantine as a fire-breathing 'reformer' (Barnes 1984). With this stereotype as a guide, it was all too easy to conclude that, prior to Constantine, Christians had lacked only the means, not the will, to impose their singular beliefs on others. Once this emperor put the means into their hands, the outcome was predetermined.

There is certainly some truth to this proposition. As the previous section showed, Constantine was by no means reluctant to enter the fray created by the Donatists and Arius. Indeed, he took the initiative in sponsoring meetings of bishops to resolve these disputes, and his decision to use the coercive powers of the state to compel acceptance of the Nicene Creed proved to be a dangerous precedent. But Constantine's record in dealing with traditional religion is more problematic. While he closed down some famous sites and looted others, the motivation for these actions does not appear to have been religious competition, despite the spin that his biographer, Eusebius of Caesarea, puts on them (Mango 1963; Cameron 1997). On the contrary, the Edict of Milan's guarantee of religious liberty for all worshippers continued to underpin Constantine's policy, as two documents from the period of his sole control of the Empire (after Licinius was put down in 324) show.

The first is an open letter addressed to his new subjects in the East. Echoing the Edict of Milan, Constantine asks the Supreme God (to whom he addressed these prayers) to '[l]et mankind, all of us, take advantage of the common heritage of good bequeathed to us, that is the blessing of peace'. Warning that 'inner conviction' is no excuse for harming others, Constantine lays out a policy: 'What each has seen and understood, he must use, if possible, to help the other; but if that is impossible, the matter should be dropped. It is one thing to take on willingly the contest for immortality, quite another to enforce it with sanctions.'[7] Because Diocletian's persecution was still a fresh memory, these words could be one more signal of Constantine's intention to protect Christians from further abuse. But the subsequent sentence shows that Constantine had Christians as well as pagans in his sights. 'I have said these things and explained them at greater length than the purpose of my clemency requires', Constantine states, 'because I did not wish to conceal my belief in the truth; especially since (so I hear) some persons are saying that the customs of the temples and the agency of darkness have been removed altogether.' Constantine does not say whether Christians or pagans were making these claims, but only Christians could have been pressing for dismantling the state religion. This means, in turn, that Constantine's motive in circulating this statement of his policy was to disavow any such action.

The same sentiment can be derived from the second document, a lengthy oration that Constantine delivered to a Christian audience. In the form we have it, the speech, entitled 'Oration to the Saints', appears to have been delivered in Nicomedia during Easter season of 325, although this date does not preclude the possibility of at least some parts of it having been delivered earlier.[8] The aim of this speech appears to have been threefold: to demonstrate Constantine's Christian credentials, the workings of divine Providence, and the support of that Providence for his rule. In the course of this exposition, however, Constantine finds several occasions to reassert his position that any religious change must take place through peaceful means—persuasion, not coercion. Thus at one point he mocks certain unnamed individuals for failing to recognize that diversity is part of God's plan (ch. 13), and at another he praises as 'the greatest victory' Christ's restraint in the exercise of his power (11. 4–7). Finally, he uses the moment of Jesus's arrest to affirm that, by rebuking the apostle who drew his sword (Mt 26: 51–2), Jesus laid down the rule that force must not be used even in a just cause (15. 3). This indeed, Constantine exclaims, 'is heavenly wisdom, to choose to be injured rather than to injure, and when it is necessary, to suffer evil rather than to do it' (15. 4).

The moderate tone of these statements does not accord well with the intolerance model, and scholars have accordingly had two options, neither entirely satisfactory: either to question the sincerity of Constantine's conversion (Burckhardt 1880) or to flip these documents into aggressive calls for an end to pagan sacrifice (Barnes 1981: 210). But the flaw lies in the model itself: its weakness is that it constructs intolerant Christians—those chafing with 'a mood of resentment and vengeance', in the words of one important scholar(Momigliano 1963: 79)—as the normative Christians of this age, dismissing all others as 'semi-Christians'—Christians whose conversion, like Constantine's, did not completely take (see Armstrong 1984). In this way, it ignores those Christians who had obviously made their peace with classical culture and society, as well as the central and most revolutionary message of Jesus's ministry to return hatred with love.

Hindsight certainly encourages such sentiments. But newer scholarship has been taking a broader view that makes much of this old argument irrelevant. It now appears, for instance, that communities had been replacing sacrifices with cheaper and more popular entertainments for some time (Bradbury 1995), and traits previously considered uniquely Christian were in fact part of a vibrant religious 'marketplace' (North 1992; Athanassiadi and Frede 1999). At the time when Constantine formulated his policy, he was on more solid ground than the conflict model would lead one to believe. As Peter Garnsey (1984) has observed, for well over a century Christians had argued that true belief could not be coerced, for the simple reason that God could tell the difference between true and feigned love. Constantine himself probably heard Lactantius argue that persuasion was preferable to coercion (Digeser 1994), and a council of Spanish bishops meeting at Elvira sometime early in the fourth century had even made such sentiments canonical. Ruling that Christians killed for attacks on idol temples should not be considered martyrs, the bishops explained: 'for we find [such acts] nowhere in the Gospels nor ever committed by the Apostles' (Jonkers 1954: 18).

Constantine's religious policy makes a lot more sense when the presence of a broad range of Christians is acknowledged. His biographer Eusebius testifies to the type of Christian that Constantine chose. 'Then such as he saw able to be prevailed upon by argument and adopting a calm and conciliatory attitude', he tells us, 'he commended most warmly, showing how he favoured general unanimity, but the obstinate he rejected' (*Vit. Const.* 1. 44. 3). Because of the nature of the field, the broader implication of such statements for Constantine's policy has rarely been explored, despite abundant evidence that Constantine's own agenda was not identical to that of Eusebius and other Christian writers. Much can be learned by letting Constantine speak for his own interests.

An example is a letter that he wrote to Bishop Alexander of Alexandria and his renegade priest Arius, in an early attempt to settle their dispute over the relationship of the Father and Son in the Trinity (*Vit. Const.* 2. 64–72). Here Constantine dismisses the issue as 'extremely trivial', 'quite unworthy of so much controversy', calling these 'small and utterly unimportant matters', that were 'not suitable to the intelligence of priests and informed men'. Scholarly reaction has ranged from embarrassment to derision, and from the standpoint of theology and Christian belief, such responses are fully merited. But other parts of the letter show that Constantine had matters other than Christian theology on his mind. From the very start, he laid out a much wider agenda, to create a common attitude towards 'the Divinity' throughout the Empire, and to 'restore and heal the body of the republic which lay severely wounded'. This is the reason why he finds their dispute troubling— not because it is theologically insignificant, but because it is not a dispute that involves the law; therefore, it need not be conducted in public. These thoughts lead Constantine to make a very explicit distinction between the public and private role of religion:

On the subject of divine Providence therefore let there be one faith among you, one understanding, one agreement about the Supreme; the precise details about these minimal disputes among yourselves, even if you cannot bring yourselves to a single point of view, ought to remain in the mind, guarded in the hidden recesses of thought.

This letter reveals not only a different set of goals, but also the way in which Constantine thought about Christianity, and the role he expected it to play in his Empire. Constantine's primary concerns were for the safety, stability, and security of the Empire. As he said repeatedly here and elsewhere, there is simply too much diversity in human nature to expect unanimity on every detail of divine worship. Seen in the context of Diocletian's persecution, such comments show that Constantine had learned the lesson that coercion of belief would not work. Diocletian had tried to insist on one, specific form of worship for the entire Empire, and Constantine saw how divisive such a policy could be—he constantly likened the persecution not to a conflict between pagans and Christians but, as in the passage just cited, to a civil war that divided all Romans. His message to Alexander and Arius was that the Roman state did not need the fine definition that Christian devotion might require. Such inquiries were perfectly acceptable as part of the private sphere. The public religion that he envisioned for the Empire would be generally monotheistic; beyond that, definition *in public* was unnecessary. All that the state required was a religiously neutral public space built around a policy of vague monotheism. Beyond that, he would pray, teach, and exhort; but he would not coerce.

The biggest objection to this interpretation of Constantine's religious policy is that this is not the way things turned out. Christian emperors increasingly supported, or in any case did not punish, the destruction of temples and sanctuaries, and by the end of the fourth century Theodosius I discontinued support for the state cults and declared Christianity the only licit religion of the Empire. Even Constantine had to use coercion, first against Arius, then against other dissenters. But policies do not always work as they are intended; serious analysis requires that intent and outcome be studied separately. At the very least, the fact that Constantine thought that there was a viable alternative to coercion, and that he was attentive to a strain of Christian thought that condemned such aggression, should call into question the easy assumption that the Christian turn to coercion was inevitable.

Intolerance certainly played a role in the failure of Constantine's plans, but it is not in itself a sufficient explanation. Save for the way in which the question has been formulated, it would be easy to see that Diocletian's persecution was based just as much on intolerance as later Christian acts would be. A common denominator is needed that explains the actions of polytheists as well as monotheists. That common denominator is not intolerance, but the particular way in which power came to be constructed in late antiquity.

22.3 CHURCH AND EMPIRE

Ironically, an accurate assessment of the relationship between religion and coercion in the later Roman Empire needs to begin with the Edict of Milan. As indicated above, this document's most innovative aspects are the guarantees of freedom of worship for all, which stood in deliberate contrast to the policy of the tetrarchs. But the reason that Constantine and Licinius gave for making these guarantees reflects a much older and more traditional concept of imperial responsibility. The emperors say that they are acting so that 'whatever divinity there is in the seat of heaven may be appeased and made propitious towards us and towards all who have been set under our power', so as to insure that this divinity will 'be able to show in all matters His accustomed favour and benevolence towards us', and 'will continue for all time to prosper our achievements along with the public wellbeing' (*Mort.* 48. 2–3).

This connection that the emperors draw between the favour of divinity and the security and prosperity of the state had been a vital part of ancient political thought from the earliest days of organized government, and it took the longest to disappear. More than two centuries after the Edict of Milan, the emperor Justinian used virtually the same language to explain his concern for the Christian priesthood. Nothing, he wrote, required the Emperor's attention more than the clergy, because 'if the priesthood is everywhere free from blame, and the Empire full of confidence in God is administered equitably and judiciously, general good will result'.[9] The Edict of Milan thus serves as a reminder of the important connection in ancient thinking between the good will of divinity and the well-being of the state. In the Roman Empire, the person recognized as having the authority to maintain that tie was the Emperor—the person who was last among gods and first among men, as Isis put it in one of the Hermetic tracts.[10] Christians could not pay homage to the Emperor through what were in their eyes false gods, but this idea that the Emperor had religious responsibilities, even that he was himself a holy being, was too deeply embedded in ancient thought even for Christians to think of challenging it, and once the Emperor himself became Christian, the transition to a similar role in the Church was remarkably smooth. Few, for instance, challenged Constantine's right to summon councils or even to participate in their proceedings, even though he was until his dying days little more than a catechumen, and thus officially not eligible even to attend, much less participate in, the eucharist. This assumption about the religious role of the Emperor needs to be emphasized because it differs so greatly from modern thinking.

Another difference needs to be taken into account. At least since the Enlightenment, the western world has thought of deity as a 'Master Clockmaker', one who set the laws of the universe in motion and now does not intervene in the normal operation of those laws. In the ancient world, Christians and pagans alike believed that deity intervened in human affairs on a regular basis, in ways that could be decisive, and often catastrophic. With such a world-view, it was obviously the primary duty of leaders to do everything they could to make sure that these interventions would occur in ways that were beneficial to the state. Thus every public official had duties that today fall in the religious sphere, even those whose office now would be considered 'secular'.

For reasons that are not completely clear, but that certainly include the example set by the revived and suddenly very dangerous empire of Sasanian Persia, Roman emperors in the third century started to make this divine tie their pre-eminent claim to legitimacy. For the first time, something that might be called a Roman state religion emerged (Rives 1999), creating a politically volatile situation in which failure on the part of subjects to acknowledge this divine tie threatened an emperor's right to rule and thereby undermined his ability to get the job done. It is therefore hardly a coincidence that the first state-sponsored and empire-wide persecutions—those of Decius in 250 and Valerian in 257—occurred at precisely this time.

With such a world-view, it becomes exceptionally difficult to separate political from religious activity, as the concept of Caesaropapism requires. In the preface to his Novel cited above, for instance, Justinian distinguished between the roles of Emperor and clergy in a way that accorded completely with Gelasius's thinking:

The priesthood and the empire are the two greatest gifts which God, in His infinite clemency, has bestowed upon mortals; the former has reference to divine matters, the latter presides over and directs human affairs, and both, proceeding from the same principle, adorn the life of mankind.

Yet the conclusion Justinian drew from this distinction was diametrically opposed to that of Gelasius: not that regulation of the Church should be left to the bishops, but that it was all the more imperative for him, as Emperor, to undertake it. Since clergy are part of the same whole, since they play such an important role in cultivating divine favour, and since he was the person supremely responsible for maintaining the good will that was so essential to the prosperity of the state, it was the Emperor's most important duty to ensure that the people who discharged this office did so correctly. Like episcopal spokesmen, Justinian recognized the dual roles of Emperor and priest; but according to his reasoning, primary responsibility was the Emperor's, as it always had been. The fact that Justinian continued to think that his writ extended to Christian clergy is a sign that the new Christian order continued to be developed within ancient modes of thought. Distinct they may have been, but Church and Empire continued to be conjoined.

This blurring of the lines of authority is at the heart of the problem, for in a certain sense it put emperors and priests in competition with each other in a way that they would not have been had Constantine not assumed responsibility for enforcing Christian doctrine.

An episode in the *Life of St Daniel the Stylite*—one of that generation of exotic fifth-century holy men who demonstrated their indifference to things of this world by living their lives perched atop pillars that soared as high as 40 feet above the ground—illustrates the point. When the emperor Leo sent Titus, a rising military star, to be blessed by the saint, the officer was so impressed by what he saw that he resigned his commission in order to live as an ascetic himself. Initially furious with the saint for abetting the loss of a talented field commander, Leo is brought up short by Daniel's reply. The holy man rebukes the Emperor for not realizing that his perfect faith is worth more than any number of military officers. Reminded of the efficacy of prayer (or smart enough to know when he is in a fight he cannot win), Leo replies, 'To crown all your good deeds there yet remained this good thing for you to do. Let the man, then, remain under your authority, and may God accept his good purpose' (Dawes and Baynes 1948: 43–4).

In a world that believed in the direct intervention of deity in day-to-day affairs, this was no theoretical proclamation; whoever was recognized as having the right to negotiate with and speak for that deity instantly became an arbiter of earthly power, which meant that persons like Daniel, who today are classified strictly in a religious register, intervened in 'secular' matters as regularly as emperors did in 'religious' ones.

For this reason, the title of this chapter—'Church and Empire'—like the more familiar antithesis of 'church' and 'state'—can be dangerously and profoundly misleading. In this world there was no such division of authority. It is impossible to re-create this unity in the modern mind, on which these categories are so firmly imprinted that 'church' and 'state' will always be two separate circles, with larger or smaller degrees of overlap. Perhaps the best way is to borrow language from contemporary theological disputes: to all the participants in this competition, 'Church' and 'Empire' were not separate substances, but two natures of the same substance. This is why the term 'Caesaropapism' is not helpful for understanding the relation of church and empire in this period. In the ancient state, it was taken for granted that 'caesar' would also be 'pope'. The new thing in the Christian empire was the intrusion of people like Daniel and Gelasius who contested that authority. To understand this confusion is to put the Christian turn to coercion in an entirely new and far more revealing light.

22.4 STATE CHURCH OR CHURCH STATE?

In the Gospel of Matthew, Jesus is asked by the Pharisees whether Jews should pay taxes to Rome—a politically tricky question to which there was seemingly no good answer. Replying in the affirmative would alienate supporters looking for someone to deliver them from Rome, whereas encouraging Jews not to pay would brand

Jesus a rebel. According to Matthew, Jesus knew that this was a loaded question, being put to him for mischievous purposes. He replied, as he so frequently did, in a way that moved the topic into an entirely different realm. Asking his interrogators to show him a coin, Jesus answered with a question of his own: 'Whose likeness and inscription is this?' When they responded, 'Caesar's', Jesus told them, 'Render therefore to Caesar the things that are Caesar's, and to God the things that are God's' (Mt 22: 17–21).

The story now suggests that the binary opposition of church and state personified in the Lateran mosaic by parallel images of emperors and bishops has deep roots in Christian thought. But this is not the lesson that the earliest Christian commentators drew from this text. To them, the lesson was one of priorities: it taught that the model Christian, like Jesus, should be indifferent to the demands of this earthly realm (viz. Paul; Rom 13: 1–7). The first use of this story to signify a division between religion and the state occurred, suggestively enough, in 356, when Bishop Ossius of Cordoba upbraided Constantine's son, the emperor Constantius II, for attempting to dictate a solution to the ongoing controversy over the relationship between Father and Son. 'It is written', Ossius observed, ' "Render unto Caesar the things that are Caesar's, and unto God the things that are God's." Neither therefore is it permitted unto us to exercise an earthly rule, nor have you, Sire, any authority to burn incense' (Atkinson and Robinson 1891: 285–6).

From here, a direct line seemingly runs through Gelasius I's distinction between the 'two powers' to the images in the Lateran mosaic. But if the aim of this mosaic was to underscore the concept of 'two powers', then something is decidedly amiss. In such a case, Christ should be shown giving power to the first emperor, Augustus, as the earliest apologists did when they postulated a joint purpose for Church and Empire. The use of Constantine is meant to call attention to a different moment— not the founding of the Empire, but the founding of the Christian Empire. It is the same with the second set of figures: since Leo III is the Pope who crowned Charlemagne Roman Emperor on Christmas Day of the year 800, this scene commemorates another specific moment, the creation of the Holy Roman Empire. Even more significant is the use of Peter to confer power in this second grouping. For a proper parallel with the 'two powers' motif of the Constantine scene, Leo and Charlemagne should also be shown receiving their power from Christ. By the simple substitution of Peter, parallel lines of authority have been replaced by a single line flowing through Rome's first bishop. The mosaic is, thus, as much a political as a religious statement. Its message is that secular authority and ecclesiastical authority both proceed from the Church. The Lateran mosaic is not arguing for the equality of Church and Empire, much less for the separation of the two. On the contrary, it asserts the priority of the priesthood over imperial power.

In the ninth century, this was hardly a new claim. Four hundred years earlier, a youthful John Chrysostom asserted that even imperial souls rested in priestly hands, and his counterpart in the West, Ambrose of Milan, lectured the youthful emperor

Valentinian II that 'the emperor is in the Church, not above it'.[11] Yet by the time of Leo III this position was being asserted in the West with a new confidence. To this same period belongs the 'Donation of Constantine', a forgery that purported to show that, before he departed for the East, Constantine gave suzerainty over the West to none other than Pope Sylvester (314–35), the bishop of Rome who by this time Western Christianity believed to have baptized him. Frescos in the thirteenth-century chapel of St Sylvester convey the same message by depicting Constantine, on foot, holding the reins of a white horse on which a regal Sylvester is firmly seated (Kantorowicz 1964; Lieu 2006). The significance of the Lateran mosaic for present purposes is thus that it shows why it is so dangerous to read modern concepts of the separation of church and state back into earlier periods of Christian thought. Not the separation of Church and Empire, but their continued unity, is the fullest message of the Lateran mosaic.

22.5 CONCLUSION

Like a mosaic, the pieces of Church and Empire may be assembled to tell many stories. One might show a virgin Church submitting to the blandishments of power and thereby losing its former innocence. Another could just as easily show an Empire distracted and drained by the power struggles of contentious bishops. While either would be pleasing to the modern eye, neither of these patterns can serve as an accurate reflection of the early Christian world. In the modern world, the only thing that 'politics' and 'religion' have in common is that neither is an appropriate topic for dinner party conversation. In the ancient world, they had everything in common, and the search for an accurate picture of Church and Empire must begin with that inseparable mixture.

Nor would either of these presentations illuminate the important question of why Christians abandoned the principled stand against compulsory belief that they had taken for centuries and increasingly used the tools of state to suppress traditional religions. Gibbon made a brilliant assemblage by using intolerance to hold the pieces together, but there are several missing from that picture, the most important of which for present purposes is that it has no satisfactory explanation for the outbreak of government-sponsored efforts to coerce Christian adherence to the traditional gods, beginning in the mid-third century.

To explain both Christian and pagan persecutions, to add depth and texture to the mosaic, two age-old ingredients of political thought that came together in a unique and volatile way in late antiquity need to be brought into the picture. The first of these is the belief that deity actively intervenes in human affairs; the second, that it was a primary duty of the state's leadership to ensure that this intervention happened in ways that benefited the state. Once emperors in the third century came to believe that enforcing uniform worship was the way to achieve that outcome, the mixture exploded. To put the issue in terms that might be easier to grasp for a world that no longer conceives of deity in this way, perhaps the concept of 'national security' may serve: when deity is the most important weapon in a state's arsenal, doing everything possible to maintain the potency of that weapon becomes a matter of national security. Individuals who interfere with its function are guilty of sabotaging the national interest.

That is the missing piece, the common denominator. Since Christians were the first to feel the effects of this shift in thought, it is doubly unfair to cite their intolerance as its cause. What Christians did bring that was new was not intolerance, which is as old as history itself, but a means of interceding with deity that had developed independent of the traditional institutions of the Roman state. Well established by the fourth century and represented by the figure of the bishop, this separate hierarchy could not be seamlessly blended with the traditional prerogatives of the Emperor. In a world where the right to intercede with deity on behalf of the state amounted to political power, conflict was, if not inevitable, at least highly probable. But the conflict in the new Christian empire that was taking shape was not between 'church' and 'state'; that is a retrospective reading. The problem was due not to the separate identity of these two spheres, but to the difficulty that bishops and emperors had in seeing the difference. To the extent that Christian bishops and holy men like Daniel were essential to achieving positive results for the state from their god, to that extent, their problems and concerns perforce became the Emperor's as well. This is the change that Ammianus Marcellinus failed to grasp with his lament about the burden that bishops placed on imperial resources: their activities were now vital to state security. In such an environment, it became increasingly difficult for Christian emperors to distinguish between the needs of the Empire and the needs of the Church as clearly as Constantine once had.

Their conflict, in other words, was not over independence, but over priority. The same Ambrose of Milan famous for placing the Emperor within rather than above the Church also provides an example of the deleterious effects that can follow from such confusion. In 388, while the emperor Theodosius I was residing in Milan, word arrived that an overly zealous bishop on the eastern frontier had caused the destruction of a local synagogue. Not about to let this clear violation of public order go unpunished, Theodosius ordered the bishop to make restitution, which today seems a modest enough penalty. Ambrose, however, saw it differently. Equating this simple act of equity with homage to false gods and support of the Church's enemies, Ambrose demanded that Theodosius choose between his duty as Emperor and his duty as a Christian: 'Which is of more importance', he asked, 'a demonstration of discipline or the cause of religion?' His own answer: 'The maintenance of civil law should be secondary to religion.'[12] This was a breathtakingly audacious claim, tantamount to saying that, where the interests of Church and Empire collide, a Christian emperor must obey the Church.

Ambrose has come down in the tradition of the western church as a champion of the independence of Church from state, but as these words make clear, the struggle in his eyes was not to separate the two. Like all other Christians, he accepted the joint role that was the nature of the ancient state; what he wanted to do was to reverse the polarity, so to speak: from a state that was the Church to a Church that was the state.

The Lateran mosaic thus encapsulates centuries of struggle between bishops and emperors. It shows that, by the end of antiquity, 'Church' and 'Empire' had emerged as distinct concepts, but the idea of a separation of Church and Empire had not. Despite the theoretical groundwork laid by Augustine in *City of God*, the fruition of that idea would have to wait for the Enlightenment and the American Revolution.

Notes

1. The banquet hall was destroyed during renovations in the sixteenth century, and the identity of the bishop who receives authority from Jesus is conjectural (it may have been Sylvester, the bishop ultimately credited with Constantine's baptism). A reconstruction of the mosaic is on display in the Piazza di Porta San Giovanni, to the right of the basilica. The original dates to the reign of Pope Leo III (795–816), as indicated by the square nimbus with which he is wreathed, a round nimbus being assigned only after a saint's death. See Noble (2001: 68–9).

2. Two contemporary sources, both Christian, are Lactantius, *Mort.* (Creed 1984); and Eusebius of Caesarea, *Vit. Const.* (Winkelmann 1975), trans. Cameron and Hall (1999).

3. Text and translation in Lactantius, *Mort.* 48. 2–12 (Creed 1984). A Greek translation with slight variants is in Eusebius, *Hist. eccl.* 10. 5. 2–14 (Schwartz 1903–9).

4. A dossier of documents dealing with this controversy was put together later in the fourth century by Bishop Optatus of Milevis (Maier 1987–9); Eng. trans. Edwards (1997). Frend (1952) remains the standard work. See also Girardet (1989).

5. Eusebius, *Vit. Const.* 3. 6–15, is an eyewitness, though disingenuous, account. See Hanson (1988).

6. 21. 16. 18, trans. Rolfe (1940): ii. 185.

7. Letter to provincials, in *Vit. Const.* 2. 48–60, trans. Cameron and Hall (1999). The passages cited are 2. 59–60.

8. For the text, Heikel (1902); translations are from Edwards (2003). On the date, see Bleckmann (1997); Barnes (2001); Edwards (1999).

9. Novel VI; trans. Scott (1932): xvi. 31. For the text, Schoell and Kroll (1912): 35–6.

10. *Kore kosmu*, in Stobaeus i. 49. 45.

11. *Ser. c. Aux.* 37 (PL 15. 1018): for Chrysostom, see *Homiliae de statuis ad populum Antiochenum habitae*, iii. 3. 2 (PG 49. 49).

12. *Ep.* 40.11, trans. Beyenka 1954: 11.

Suggested Reading

Not much has been written directly on political thought in late antiquity. Two staples by Ernest Barker—*From Alexander to Constantine: Passages and Documents Illustrating the History of Social and Political Ideas, 336 BC–AD 337* (Oxford: Oxford University Press, 1956) and *Social and Political Thought in Byzantium from Justinian to the Last Palaeologus* (Oxford: Oxford University Press, 1957)—remain useful collections of primary documents in English translation, thoughtfully introduced. Francis Dvornik, *Early Christian and Byzantine Political Philosophy*, 2 vols. (Washington D.C.: Dumbarton Oaks, 1966) is a gold-mine, but severely dated in its outlook. A stimulating essay on the joint effect of Christianity and Islam is provided by Garth Fowden (1993). John Meyendorff surveys church and empire from the perspective of the Orthodox Church in *Imperial Unity and Christian Divisions: The Church 450–680 A.D.* (Crestwood, NY: St Vladimir's Seminary Press, 1989), while Dominic O'Meara takes the philosophical perspective in *Platonopolis: Platonic Political Philosophy in Late Antiquity* (Oxford: Oxford University Press, 2003). Peter I. Kaufman, *Redeeming Politics* (Princeton: Princeton University Press, 1990) takes a fresh look at the relationship between religion and power from Constantine to the Reformation. Claudia Rapp, *Holy Bishops in Late Antiquity: The Nature of Christian Leadership in an Age of Transition*, The Transformation of the Classical Heritage, 37 (Berkeley: University of California Press, 2005) is a sophisticated study of the bases of power in this period. Neil McLynn, *Ambrose of Milan: Church and Court in a Christian Capital* (Berkeley: University of California Press, 1994) reappraises a pivotal relationship. I have made the case for a political understanding of Constantine and Christian coercion in *Constantine and the Bishops: The Politics of Intolerance* (Baltimore: Johns Hopkins University Press, 2000).

Bibliography

Armstrong, A. H. (1984), 'The Way and the Ways: Religious Tolerance and Intolerance in the Fourth Century A.D.', *VC* 38: 1–17.

Atkinson, M., and Robinson, M. (1891) (trans.), Athanasius of Alexandria, 'History of the Arians', in NPNF 4: 270–302.

Athanassiadi, P., and Frede, M. (1999) (eds.), *Pagan Monotheism in Late Antiquity* (Oxford: Oxford University Press).

Barnes, T. D. (1981), *Constantine and Eusebius* (Cambridge, Mass.: Harvard University Press).

—— (1984), 'The Constantinian Reformation', in *The Crake Lectures* (Sackville, New Brunswick: Crake Institute), 39–57.

—— (2001), 'Constantine's Speech to the Assembly of the Saints: Place and Date of Delivery', *JTS* NS 52: 26–33.

Baynes, N. H. (1929), 'Constantine the Great and the Christian Church', *Proceedings of the British Academy*, 15: 341–442; issued separately in 1931; 2nd edn. London, 1972.

—— (1934), 'Eusebius and the Christian Empire', *Annuaire de l'Institut de Philologie et d'Histoire Orientale* (Mélanges Bidez), 2: 13–18.

BEYENKA, M. (1954) (trans.), *Ambrose, Letters 1–91*, FC 26 (Washington: Catholic University of America Press).

BLECKMANN, B. (1997), 'Ein Kaiser als Prediger: zur Datierung der Konstantinischen Rede an die Versammlung der Heiligen', *Hermes*, 125: 183–202.

BRADBURY, S. (1995), 'Julian's Pagan Revival and the Decline of Blood Sacrifice', *Phoenix*, 49: 331–56.

BROWN, P. R. L. (1971), *The World of Late Antiquity, AD 150–750* (New York: Harcourt Brace Jovanovich).

BUDGE, E. A. W. (1888), *The Martyrdom and Miracles of St. George of Cappadocia* (London: D. Nutt).

BURCKHARDT, J. (1880), *The Age of Constantine the Great.* 2ed (1880) (trans.) M. Hadas. New York: Pantheon Books, 1949; repr. 1967. [Orig. pub.: *Die Zeit Constantin's des Grossen* (Basel, 1853).]

CAMERON, A. (1997), 'Eusebius' Vita Constantini and the Construction of Constantine', in M. J. Edwards and S. Swain (eds.), *Portraits: Biographical Representation in the Greek and Latin Literature of the Roman Empire* (Oxford: Clarendon Press), 145–74.

—— and HALL, S. (1999) (trans.), *Eusebius of Caesarea, Life of Constantine* (Oxford: Clarendon Press).

CREED, J. L. (1984) (ed. and trans.), *Lactantius, De mortibus persecutorum* (Oxford: Clarendon Press).

DAGRON, G. (1996), *Empereur et prêtre: étude sur le 'cesaropapisme' byzantin*, Bibliothèque des histoires (Paris: Gallimard).

DAWES, E., and BAYNES, N. (1948) (trans.), *Three Byzantine Saints: Contemporary Biographies of St Daniel the Stylite, St Theodore of Sykeon and St John the Almsgiver* (Oxford: Blackwell).

DIGESER, E. (1994), 'Lactantius and Constantine's Letter to Arles: Dating the Divine Institutes', *JECS* 2: 33–52.

—— (2000), *The Making of a Christian Empire: Lactantius and Rome* (Ithaca, NY: Cornell University Press).

DÖRRIES, H. (1960), *Constantine and Religious Liberty*, trans. R. Bainton (New Haven: Yale University Press).

EDWARDS, M. (1997) (trans. and ed.), *Against the Donatists*, Translated Texts for Historians, 27 (Liverpool: Liverpool University Press).

—— (1999), 'The Constantinian Circle and the Oration to the Saints', in M. Edwards *et al.* (eds.), *Apologetics in the Roman Empire: Pagans, Jews, and Christians* (Oxford: Oxford University Press), 251–75.

—— (2003), *Constantine and Christendom: The Oration to the Saints, the Greek and Latin Accounts of the Discovery of the Cross, the Edict of Constantine to Pope Silvester*, Translated Texts for Historians, 39 (Liverpool: Liverpool University Press).

FOWDEN, G. (1993), *Empire to Commonwealth: Consequences of Monotheism in Late Antiquity* (Princeton: Princeton University Press).

FREND, W. H. C. (1952), *The Donatist Church: A Movement of Protest in Roman North Africa* (Oxford: Clarendon Press).

GARNSEY, P. (1984), 'Religious Toleration in Classical Antiquity', in W. J. Shiels (ed.), *Persecution and Toleration*, SCH 21 (Oxford: Blackwell), 1–27.

GIBBON, E. (1909–14), *The History of the Decline and Fall of the Roman Empire*, ed. J. B. Bury, 7 vols. (London: Methuen).

GIRARDET, K. M. (1989), 'Die Petition der Donatisten an Kaiser Konstantin (Frühjahr 313)—historische Voraussetzungen und Folgen', *Chiron*, 19: 185–206.

HANSON, R. P. C. (1988), *The Search for the Christian Doctrine of God: The Arian Controversy, 318–381* (Edinburgh: T & T Clark).

HEIKEL, I. A. (1902) (ed.), 'Constantins Rede an die heilige Versammlung', in *Eusebius Werke*, i, GCS 7 (Leipzig: J. C. Hinrichs), 149–92.

JONKERS, E. J. (1954) (ed.), *Acta et symbola conciliorum quae saeculo quarto habita sunt*, Textus minores, 29 (Leiden: E. J. Brill).

KANTOROWICZ, E. (1964), 'Constantinus Strator, Marginalien zum Constitutum Constantini', in A. Hermann and A. Stuiber (eds.), *Mullus: Festschrift Theodor Klauser*, JAC Ergänzungsband i (Münster: Aschendorff), 181–9.

LIEU, S. N. C. (2006), 'Constantine in Legendary Literature', in N. Lenski (ed.), *The Cambridge Companion to the Age of Constantine* (Cambridge: Cambridge University Press), 298–303.

MAIER, J.-L. (1987–9) (ed. and trans.), *Optatus, Le dossier du Donatisme*, 2 vols., TU 134, 135 (Berlin: Akademie Verlag).

MANGO, C. (1963), 'Antique Statuary and the Byzantine Beholder', *DOP* 17: 53–75.

MILLAR, F. (1971), 'Paul of Samosata, Zenobia and Aurelian: The Church, Local Culture and Political Allegiance in Third Century Syria', *JRS* 61: 1–17.

MOMIGLIANO, A. D. (1963) (ed.), *The Conflict between Paganism and Christianity in the Fourth Century* (Oxford: Clarendon Press).

NOBLE, T. F. (2001), 'Topography, Celebration, and Power: The Making of a Papal Rome in the Eighth and Ninth Centuries', in M. de Jong and F. Theuws (eds.), *Topographies of Power in the Early Middle Ages*, The Transformation of the Roman World, vi (Leiden: E. J. Brill), 45–71.

NOCK, A. D. (1947), 'The Emperor's Divine *Comes*', *JRS* 37: 102–16.

NORTH, J. (1992), 'The Development of Religious Pluralism', in J. Lieu, T. Rajak, and J. North (eds.), *The Jews among Pagans and Christians in the Roman Empire* (London: Routledge), 174–93.

O'DONNELL, J. J. (1977), 'Paganus', *Classical Folia*, 31: 163–9.

RIVES, J. B. (1999), 'The Decree of Decius and the Religion of Empire', *JRS* 89: 135–54.

ROLFE, J. C. (1940) (trans.), *Ammianus Marcellinus*, LCL, 3 vols. (Cambridge, Mass.: Harvard University Press).

SCHOELL, R., and KROLL, G. (1912) (eds.), *Corpus Iuris Civilis*, iii: *Novellae* (Berlin: Weidmann).

SCHWARTZ, E. (1903–9) (ed.), *Eusebius of Caesarea, Die Kirchengeschichte*, 3 vols. GCS 9 (Leipzig: J. C. Hinrichs).

SCOTT, S. P. (1932) (ed. and trans.), *The Civil Law*, 17 vols. (Cincinnati: Central Trust Co.).

WINKELMANN, F. (1975) (ed.), *Über das Leben des Kaisers Konstantins*, GCS 1 (Leipzig: J. C. Hinrichs).

CHAPTER 23

....

WOMEN AND GENDER

....

ROSS SHEPARD KRAEMER

23.1 GENERAL ORIENTATION
....

ONLY 30 years ago, the design of a handbook such as this would very likely not have
included a piece titled 'Women and Gender'. Nevertheless, had the editors for such
a handbook had the unusual foresight to commission such an entry, its contours
would have been significantly different. Emerging scholarship in the late 1970s was
beginning, if still only gingerly, to inquire about the reliability of ancient male depictions of women, and about how male interests might shape their representations
of female experience. A few scholars were beginning to apply models drawn from
twentieth-century social-scientific theories to account for both the descriptions of
women's lives and the attitudes toward women they discerned in the sources (Slater
1968; Doyle 1974) The section on the history of scholarship would thus have been
relatively brief, particularly if the emphasis was on scholarship of the last several
decades.

The present essay is concerned with several overlapping issues, including prosopographic work (the identification of particular actual ancient Christian women);
the reconstruction of the activities and beliefs of Christian women, an analysis of those activities and beliefs from the perspective of the study of religions
more broadly and theoretically, and a consideration of specifically Christian constructions of gender within the broader discourses of gender in the ancient
world.

23.2 PARAMETERS

The chronological, geographic, and linguistic parameters of this topic are coterminous with those of the volume as a whole. Still, a starting point of the late first or early second century CE poses certain dilemmas. Some of the richest early Christian texts for questions of women and gender are precisely those which some scholars would date to the first century (e.g. Luke–Acts and the Pastorals) but which others (myself included) think more likely to be second-century productions (Koester 1990).

Further, the very category of (ancient) Christian women that this entry presumes is itself somewhat problematic. In privileging the overarching categories of 'Christian', and 'women' we risk erasing, or at least obscuring, almost all other operative ancient social categories, including those of ethnicity and regionality, rank and social status and/or class, and even varieties of 'Christian' identity. Not only is it often difficult to know precisely when one can begin to speak of persons as Christians, it also sometimes remains ambiguous whether identifying persons, texts, or practices as Christian makes them distinct from and in opposition to Jews and Judaism (Dunn 1991; Lieu 1994; Frankfurter 2001; Marshall 2001; Reed and Becker 2004).

The key terms 'women' and 'gender' require some definitional observations. While cognizant of contemporary debates about gender identity and the imperfect mapping of gender categories onto actual persons, whether in modernity or in antiquity, I utilize the term 'women' here as broadly and inclusively as possible to encompass those persons in antiquity whom we would recognize as such by twenty-first-century methods of discerning anatomical and genetic difference. Further, I intend the term 'women' to signal adult status, while recognizing that such status is itself culturally determined.

Yet in the Graeco-Roman Mediterranean, the terms we generally translate as woman or women usually encode numerous and complex elements of social identity, including distinctions of physical and social maturity, of rank and class, of licit marriage and so forth (Hanson 1990, 1999). The Latin term *matrona*, for instance, often translated with the cognate 'matron', connotes adulthood, free status, and licit marriage. Parker has even proposed that the definition of a *femina/puella* is precisely a person who is sexually penetrated in the vagina (Parker 1997, using somewhat coarser language). Persons liable to such penetration who refuse or renounce it may then no be longer female, but 'male'. These ancient connotations have ramifications for early Christian studies. For instance, the possibility that virgins constitute a separate category distinct from 'women' undergirds certain early Christian discourse about 'women' holding office and exercising masculine authority.

While scholars both inside and outside ancient studies continue to debate definitions of gender (Bynum *et al.* 1986; Scott 1986; J. Butler 1993, 2004; Castelli

2001; Bourdieu 2001, Kuefler 2001), most discussions share the view that gender is a culturally constructed system of difference mapped onto perceived biological/anatomical difference. Three decades of feminist scholarship, particularly in classics, has greatly illuminated the prevailing constructions of gender in the ancient world, and associated constructions of sexuality, as well as the centrality of gender in the organization and structure of ancient social life (Foucault 1976; Halperin 1990; Winkler 1990; Gleason 1990, 1999; Boyarin 1998; Hanson 1999; Ringrose 2003). Central to these constructions is the notion that men are properly active (and penetrating); women are properly passive (and penetrated); gender is always hierarchical and is an overarching means of expressing hierarchy in other domains (e.g. slavery, human/divine relations, etc.). Constructions of masculinity, if not also femininity, varied according to social class (Glancy 2003). Gender difference permeated all aspects of ancient social life: meals and foods, dress, sexual practices, bodily comportment, war, education, politics, commerce, and those practices we categorize under the label of religion.

23.3 SOURCES

The sources relevant for this entry, too, are in many ways coterminous with the sources for the study of ancient Christianity as a whole. Nevertheless, certain sources seem far richer for these purposes, and have been the subject of extensive study in recent years.

The list of works attributed to ancient Christian women authors, let alone securely so, is quite short (Wilson-Kastner 1981). It consists of the first-person prison narrative in the *Martyrdom of Saints Perpetua and Felicitas*, which the text itself ascribes to Perpetua; a cento attributed to a fourth-century Roman Christian matron, Faltonia Betitia Proba (Clark and Hatch 1981); a first-person narrative of a fourth-century traveller to holy sites and holy persons, probably named Egeria (Dietz 2005: 43–51); and several works composed by the fifth-century Christian empress Eudokia, including a *Life of St. Cyprian of Antioch*, a cento, and a poem commemorating the opening of a spa complex at Hammat-Gadar. Often overlooked is a letter that claims to be from Jerome's 'disciple' Paula and her daughter, Eustochium, to Marcella (Jerome, *Ep.* 46). Usually attributed to Jerome himself, some scholars now argue that its authorship should be taken at face value (Dietz 2005: 129 n. 82; Dronke 1984: 17).

Why so few writings survive that are attributed to ancient women has been discussed extensively (Wilson-Kastner 1981; Snyder 1989; Kraemer 1991; Lefkowitz 1991). Suggested explanations range from low literacy rates for women, to the lack of time and resources necessary for literary composition, to deliberate male suppression of women's writings, and the failure of subsequent male tradents to transmit women's writings to modernity. In part, the problem may be one not just of actual composition, but of attribution. Many ancient Christian (and Jewish) texts are either anonymous, lacking any attribution of authorship, or pseudonymous, claiming an author that at least to modern sensibilities is clearly artificial (such as an ancient authority from the Hebrew Bible). Christian women might have had their own particular reasons for writing under the cloak of anonymity or pseudonymity. At least in proto-orthodox and orthodox circles, there may have been explicit opposition to women writing books in their own names, opposition that was supported by, if not grounded in, interpretations of the (pseudo-) Pauline prohibition of women teaching (Kraemer 1991, 1992). Women composers or authors have been suggested for a number of early Christian texts, especially some of the apocryphal acts (Davies 1980; D. R. MacDonald 1983; Burrus 1987; but see also Kaestli 1989, 1990; Kraemer 1991).

The absence of literary sources and other writings known to have been authored by women clearly hampers our access to Christian women's own self-representations and limits our knowledge of activities familiar to women but largely obscured to men when the degree of gender segregation in daily life was quite high. Yet even a plethora of sources by women themselves would alleviate only some of our difficulties, given the immersion of women, particularly elite, educated women, in ancient systems of gender.

The literary sources for the study of women, gender, and religion in ancient Christianity take about as many forms as the literary evidence for Christianity as a whole. The so-called Apocryphal Acts of the Apostles are rich in narratives about women: e.g. Thecla in the Acts of (Paul and) Thecla; Mygdonia and Tertia in the Acts of Thomas; Maximilla in the Acts of Andrew; Drusiana in the Acts of John; Mariamme in the Acts of Philip. So-called gnostic texts like Thunder: Perfect Mind, The Hypostasis of the Archons, or The Thought of Norea, are rich in female cosmological figures. Several gospels feature women as mediators of divine revelation, such as Mary in the Gospel of Mary, the Dialogue of the Saviour, the Gospel of the Egyptians, and others. Eusebius of Caesarea's Ecclesiastical History is filled with references to specific women and steeped in ancient gender constructions, as are the heresiological catalogues of Hippolytus and Epiphanius. (By comparison, the later Ecclesiastical History of Sozomen, preoccupied with bishops, councils, and doctrinal disputes, and that of Socrates, contain far fewer such references.) The homilies of preachers like Chrysostom and Augustine regularly refer to women's lives and practices (Chrysostom in particular is noteworthy for his accounts of weddings, nursing and weaning practices, marital conflicts, and so forth). Hymns sometimes utilize feminine imagery for the divine, like the references to the breasts and milk of Christ in the Odes of Solomon, and hymns to the Virgin Mary eventually proliferate.

Authors like Jerome and John Chrysostom conducted extensive correspondence with female patrons, disciples, and others in the fourth and fifth centuries, as did the abbot Shenoute with female monastics at the White Monastery. Roughly a third of Jerome's extant correspondence is to women, although, perhaps unsurprisingly, none of the women's letters survive (with the possible exception of Jerome, *Ep.* 46, as noted above). Many other individual letters are intriguing: that of a second-century gnostic teacher, Ptolemaeus, to his female disciple, Flora, or the scattered references to various women in the undisputed letters of Ignatius of Antioch, or the correspondence between pseudo-Ignatius and one Mary of Cassabola (or even the short exchange of letters between pseudo-Ignatius and the Blessed Virgin Mary).

Although the number of ancient Christian *Lives* of exemplary men is far greater, a significant number of women are praised in works explicitly called *Lives*: (Gregory of Nyssa's *Life of Macrina* (his sister); an anonymous *Life of Olympias* (Chrysostom's patron); Gerontius's *Life of Melania the Younger*; the *Life and Regimen of the Blessed and Holy Teacher, Syncletica* attributed to the fourth-century Athanasius of Alexandria, but probably actually fifth-century; as well as the Syriac *Life of Saint Mary the Harlot*, the *Life of Saint Pelagia the Harlot* (attributed to a deacon named Jacob), the *Life of Saint Eugenia*, and shorter accounts in writers like Palladius (*Lausiac History*) and Theodoret (*History of the Monks of Syria*). In the same general category are funeral orations such as that of Gregory of Nazianzus for his sister Gorgonia, or Jerome's famous encomium for Paula, written as a letter to her daughter, Eustochium. The earlier *Acts of (Paul and) Thecla* is reworked in a fifth-century *Life and Miracles of Saint Thecla*.

Narratives of martyred Christian women appear as early as the *Acts of the Scilitan Martyrs*, which takes the form of a court transcript dated to 17 July, 180 CE, or the *Letter of the Churches of Lyon and Vienne*, transmitted in Eusebius (*Hist. eccl.* 5. 1. 3–63), on the death of Blandina and several male companions. Eusebius also preserves additional accounts of the martyrdom of Christian women. Lengthier, free-standing martyrdom accounts include the most famous *Martyrdom of Saints Perpetua and Felicitas*, as well as the elaborate early Byzantine martyrdoms of saints Barbara, Irene, and Christine, among others.

Regulations and rules for women's practices appear in works like the fourth-century *Constitutions of the Holy Apostles*, with its extensive prescriptions for women generally and widows in particular, as well as in the formal rules of monastic communities.

Numerous theological treatises pertain explicitly to women's practices, such as the works of Tertullian: *On the Veiling of Virgins, On the Apparel of Women, On Modesty*, and others. The extensive Christian interest in virginity and celibacy, and the attendant debates, produced numerous treatises on virginity, marriage, and related subjects by authors ranging from Tertullian, to Jerome, Rufinus, and Augustine, to John Chrysostom, to the Cappadocian Gregory of Nyssa and Basil of Ancyra. At least one writer, Methodius, in the third century, drew on Plato's *Symposium* for a Christian version, known sometimes as the *Banquet of the Ten Virgins*, in defence of chastity, whose ten speakers were all women, including Thecla.

Like that for Christian men, identifiable non-literary evidence for Christian women is rare before the third century and increases significantly and unsurprisingly in the fourth century. A few Christian inscriptions are explicitly dated to the late third century, such as the so-called 'Christians for Christians' inscriptions from the region of Phrygia (modern Turkey), several of which include women (Gibson 1978; Tabbernee 1997; Kraemer 2004: nos. 66E, 66G). Particularly striking is a Roman inscription for a woman named Flavia Sophe whose rich imagery may have gnostic associations (Ferrua 1944/5; McGuire 1999) or the fourth-century inscription of Sophia the Deacon (Alt 1921: no. 17; Kraemer 2004: no. 91A). It is not always easy to determine which inscriptions are Christian, however, as in the case of a particularly striking epitaph for a woman prophet named Nanas from the Phrygian highlands (Haspels 1971: 107; Eisen 2000; Tabbernee 1997; Kraemer 2004: no. 97). Papyri from the fourth century on document the lives of Christian women, primarily in Egypt. Early Christian catacombs in Rome are associated with women, such as the famous Catacomb of Priscilla, while the spatial arrangements of early Christian churches suggest gendered liturgical practices (Mayer 1997; Schroeder 2004). Amulets and other objects testify to Christian women's engagement in those practices often classed as 'magic'. Female figures appear early in Christian painting and mosaic, such as the wall paintings in the church at Dura-Europos, or the numerous early Byzantine representations of Mary and other female saints.

The kinds of questions these sources pose may be illustrated by four examples: the figure of Thecla, Origen of Alexandria, *The Martyrdom of Saints Perpetua and Felicitas*, and the Virgin Mary.

23.3.1 Thecla

The *Acts of Thecla* (as I prefer to call it), a staple for discussions of women in early Christian texts, tells the story of a young elite woman in the city of Iconium in Asia Minor (modern Konya) who converts to an ascetic form of Christianity preached by the apostle Paul in her native Iconium. Dazzled by Paul, Thecla reneges on her engagement to a prominent citizen, is denounced by her own mother, escapes various trials and temptations, and baptizes herself in a pool of voracious seals. Ultimately commissioned by Paul to 'go forth and teach the word of God', Thecla is said to have 'enlightened many' before an unremarkable death. Some versions of the text contain additional endings that narrate more of a martyr's death, and Thecla eventually acquires the epithet 'proto-martyr'.

Although virtually no modern scholars consider Thecla to have been a disciple of the historical Paul, there is little consensus beyond this as to how to account for the tale, which was probably composed in Greek in the second century, and subsequently translated into Latin, Syriac, and numerous other languages. Early work on the *Acts of Thecla*, including my own, saw the heroine's renunciation of the traditional roles of wife and mother for the life of an autonomous, wandering Christian teacher as a thinly fictionalized window into the actual practices and motivations of female converts to ascetic forms of Christianity in the second century (Kraemer 1976, 1980; Davies 1980; D. R. MacDonald 1983, Burrus 1987). Several scholars even argued that the highly favourable representations of women in the story and the relatively negative portraits of male apostles in the *Acts of Thecla* and other comparable tales in the apocryphal acts pointed to female authorship or composition (Davies 1980; D. R. MacDonald 1983; Burrus 1987; see also Matthews 2002), although these arguments have been heavily critiqued on a variety of grounds (Kraemer 1991; Kaestli 1989; 1990; Matthews 2002). D. R. MacDonald suggested that the story of Thecla might be related to the emergence of a prophetic Christian movement arising in Asia Minor in the late second century (Trevett 1996). Its proponents called it the 'New Prophecy': its opponents called it 'Montanism', after one of its three founding prophets, a man named Montanus (the other two being women named Priscilla and Maximilla).

The story of Thecla clearly had implications for contemporary Christian feminist concerns. The view of some early scholars that the *Acts of Thecla* was indicative of something like a women's movement in early Christianity, ultimately repressed, drew harsh critique from conservative scholars (see Matthews 2002; also Bremmer 2003). Still, the participants in these debates differed mostly in their willingness to see the practices and beliefs attributed to Paul and to Thecla as reflections of widely held, authoritative positions.

The most substantial challenge to all these readings has come from Kate Cooper, whose interests were not in debates about contemporary Christian practice, but rather in the articulation and analysis of ancient Christian rhetoric about virginity in particular. She argues that the story of Thecla (and others like it) has little to do with actual Christian women, and everything to do with male disputes about masculine identity, expressed in the conflict between the male Christian apostle on the one hand and the elite male fiancé or husband on the other (Cooper 1996). Yet the matter is complex. A story of Thecla is denounced by Tertullian (*Bapt.* 17), who claims that some people (perhaps more accurately some women (Hilhorst 1996)), were using it to support their views that women were authorized to baptize and teach. In fact, Tertullian claims, it was written by an anonymous presbyter in Asia Minor who subsequently confessed to the forgery and left his office (a claim some scholars accept (D. R. MacDonald 1983; Bremmer 1996), while others (myself included) are more sceptical). Regardless of who wrote the *Acts of Thecla* and why,

Tertullian's report points to a crucial issue: namely, ancient contestations over the legitimacy of Christian women exercising authority in various forms, contestations that appear grounded not merely in debates about gender, but in arguments over actual practices.

Despite Tertullian's denunciation, Thecla was the object of extensive veneration by both women and men, although subsequent versions of her story appear to have been sanitized, removing some of the elements most objectionable to subsequent orthodox positions. Egeria describes a visit to the shrine of Thecla, while Thecla was apparently the 'secret' name of Gregory's sister Macrina, and later evidence for devotion to Thecla is extensive (Davis 2001; Johnson 2006). Devotion to Thecla continues to this day, especially in Syria. Thus, the study of Thecla traditions engages virtually the entire panoply of issues with which this piece is concerned.

23.3.2 Origen

The figure of Origen raises comparable, but not entirely identical, questions. This prolific, deeply controversial scholar, theologian, and apologist for Christianity is responsible for preserving one of the most intriguing accusations of ancient Christians in the second-century anti-Christian work of Celsus, *The True Doctrine*. Celsus alleges that only 'the foolish, the dishonourable and stupid, and only slaves, women, and little children' are attracted to the deficient doctrines of Christianity (cited in *Cels.* 3. 44).

Not least because Origen does not deny it, the question of whether Celsus was accurate in his social description has engaged scholars at least since von Harnack (1904–5; Lieu 1998; M. Y. MacDonald 1996, 2003), whose claim that women were the majority of converts to earliest Christianity may be based on little more than Celsus (and which, if true, nevertheless failed to have a significant impact on his analysis). Origen responds that the gospel calls not only these persons, but also those much superior to them (*Cels.* 3. 49). Both Celsus's accusation and Origen's response raise questions about how to read the gendered rhetoric of ancient male authors and how much, if any, access such rhetoric provides to the realities of ancient (Christian) women's lives.

According to Eusebius, Origen was supported by an unnamed wealthy woman, obtained his copies of the works of Symmachus, an important translator and commentator on scripture, from a woman named Juliana, taught both women and men, and utilized the services of girls trained in calligraphic arts (*Hist. eccl.* 6. 2. 12–14; 6. 17. 1; 6. 8. 1–3; 6. 23. 1–2). Eusebius's portrait of Origen points, however problematically, to the complexities of ancient Christian social realia, even while how these bits of description function in Eusebius requires further work (E. Clark 1992).

23.3.3 Perpetua

The martyrdom of Perpetua similarly exemplifies the possibilities and the problems. Probably because it professes to contain Perpetua's own first-person narrative,
it has been the subject of extensive scholarly investigation (e.g. B. Shaw 1993; Tilley
1994; Perkins 1995: 104–23; Kraemer 1992; Kraemer and Lander 2000; Bremmer
2003; also Salisbury 1997). Whether it in fact contains the writing of Perpetua herself
is by no means clear (Heffernan 1995; Kraemer and Lander 2000): if so, it is almost
certainly the earliest writing by a Christian woman and clearly of major importance
not only for documenting the experiences of a young Christian catechumen and
martyr, but also for providing at least potential access to the self-understanding
and/or self-fashioning of a young Christian matron in the early third century.

Both the narrative portion ascribed to Perpetua, and the larger account point
beyond Perpetua to the New Prophecy (R. D. Butler 2006): the opening lines of the
Martyrdom quote a biblical text beloved of the movement: Joel 2: 28–9/Acts 2: 17–18.
Tertullian was for a time a member of the movement, and his eventual disaffection
may have had something to do with the movement's views of women prophets and
leaders (Klawiter 1980; Wypustek 1997). The evidence for the New Prophecy is itself
complex: much of it comes from its opponents, including Tertullian, Epiphanius,
Eusebius, and others, and poses all sorts of problems for historical and social
reconstruction. The claim that women founded the New Prophecy and were many
of its subsequent followers and leaders may reflect social reality that itself requires
explanation. Yet, not inconceivably, the gendering of the New Prophecy as female
is part of a rhetoric of opposition that genders orthodoxy as masculine and heresy
as feminine (Kraemer 1992; 1994). Particularly intriguing is the *Debate between a
Montanist and an Orthodox*, a work assigned (in the absence of any real evidence)
to the fourth century. One of the major Orthodox objections to Montanism is not
its appeal to prophecy, but its practice of women authoring books (perhaps of their
own prophecies) in their own names, something the Orthodox speaker sees as a
violation of 1 Timothy 2: 11, which prohibits women from exercising authority over
men. The evidence for the New Prophecy extends beyond these literary references
to inscriptions from ancient Asia Minor (Gibson 1978; Heine 1989; Tabbernee 1997)
that seem to confirm the presence of women leaders and allow scholars some access
to more than just rhetorical debates; but this, too, is rarely straightforward.

23.3.4 The Virgin Mary

Finally, there is the example of the figure of the Virgin Mary. Work on the historical
mother of Jesus lies outside the scope of this essay, although it seems reasonable
to note that the earliest sources for Jesus and his family provide only the most
minimal of evidence. The relationship between subsequent Christian traditions

about Mary and the study of women, gender, and religion is incredibly complex. Later traditions about Mary, whether the *Protevangelium of James*, probably composed in the second century, which contains most of the material for the elaborated birth traditions, or the less frequently cited *Ascension of Isaiah*, or the Byzantine narratives of Mary's dormition, do not necessarily say anything either about women themselves or about issues of particular interest to women. Yet they clearly engage issues of gender construction (Harvey 2005a), if in extraordinarily complex ways that are particularly difficult to analyse given the continued reverence for Mary in contemporary Christian discourse.

Eventual Christian veneration of Mary, whose history is itself thorny, raises other questions. Epiphanius construed women's devotion to Mary as heretical, both because women's offering of some sort of baked goods to Mary constituted an unacceptable exercise of priesthood, and because it made Mary the object of devotion that was appropriate only for God and Christ. In other words, it made Mary a goddess. Some scholars suspect that Epiphanius himself invented these accounts, or at least significant portions of them, but his invective is nevertheless telling. Much of the Marian corpus may reflect only male constructions of gender and divinity. Yet women's devotion to Mary, regardless of the precise form it took, needs to be analysed as such. Further, women's Marian devotion raises questions about what, precisely, women do when denied the opportunities for the kinds of polytheist veneration that Sered argues typifies women's religions in many cultures (Sered 1994). Marian devotion in particular, although certainly not exclusively, points up the possibilities for contact with the study of women's religious practices more broadly.

23.4 PRIMARY ISSUES

Interest in early Christian women is not entirely an outgrowth of what has now come to be called the second wave of feminism in the second half of the twentieth century. Often correlating with prior movements in North America and Europe for women's emancipation, particularly in the late nineteenth and early twentieth centuries, entries in nineteenth-century reference works demonstrate various degrees of interest in the subject (Brown 1846; Hatch 1880; Wilson 1884; LeClercq 1922). In 1900, the intrepid traveller, scholar, and translator Agnes Smith Lewis (Price 1985; Lewis and Gibson 1898) had published a transcription and a translation of an ancient Syriac manuscript entitled *Select Narratives of Holy Women* (Lewis 1900) that contained stories about Saints Eugenia, Barbara, Irene, and others. Monographic treatments of varying lengths and interests appeared from time to time, many by

German authors (Zscharnack 1902; Stöcker 1907; Donaldson 1907; von der Goltz 1914; Braun 1919; Gottlieb 1928; Nugent 1941; Leenhardt 1949).

Yet scholarship of the last 30 years or so unquestionably has its roots in the debates about the ordination of women to ministerial and priestly offices in contemporary Christian communities, themselves fuelled by the resurgence of the women's movement in the last third of the twentieth century. Thus, early scholarship was particularly preoccupied with questions pertaining to ministerial ordination for women (Daniélou 1960; Gryson 1972; Ruether and MacLaughlin 1979; Swidler and Swidler 1977; see also Kraemer 1983), as well as the quest for explanations of the subordination and inferiority of women in Christian teaching and practice (questions which were sometimes themselves deflected by claims that women in Christianity were not inferior, merely 'different').

Many of the initial questions were frequently framed by an ancient Christian discourse about gender and the priesthood explicitly articulated in writers like Tertullian and Epiphanius (and reiterated at length in the 1976 Vatican Declaration denying the ordination of women priests). This claimed that women could not be priests both for 'systemic' reasons, i.e. that priesthood was an inherently masculine prerogative and an inherently masculine practice, and for historical reasons: Jesus could have chosen women apostles (apostles themselves being construed as the forerunners of a Christian priesthood); could have been baptized by a woman (his mother), but did not choose to do so, a choice thus binding on subsequent Christians. These early studies frequently focused first on the New Testament, especially the gospels, to consider the claims both that Jesus intentionally did not choose women apostles (and disciples), and that any such choices on his part were intended to bind subsequent churches. These questions, while in some ways historical, were deeply theological, and rarely (and only accidentally) sociological, anthropological, and so forth. Some scholars began to ask about the historical and political processes in the second century and following that produced particular textual readings of the New Testament, suggesting that at least in some cases, these readings obscure the presence and authority of early Christian women and reflect concerns in subsequent Christian communities (Epp 1966; Witherington 1984; Ehrman 1993). Brooten argues that the Junias of Romans 16: 7 whom Paul called 'prominent among the apostles' was actually a woman named Junia, transformed in antiquity into a male to eliminate evidence for women apostles (Brooten 1977; Epp 2005).

Particularly because no teachings attributed to Jesus himself are definitively misogynist or restrictive of women (and a few are, on the contrary, quite supportive of women—such as the famous story of Martha and Mary in Lk 10: 38–42), it was relatively easy for early Christian feminist scholars to argue for a historical narrative of an initial, pristine, egalitarian 'Christianity' followed by a period of contestation and ultimate subordination of women that begins almost immediately with the writings of Paul, is articulated and developed in the writings of proto-orthodox and then truly orthodox male authorities, and culminates in the eventual exclusion of women from the orthodox priesthood (Otranto 1982; Fiorenza 1983; Rossi 1991; Torjesen 1993; also Ellwood 1921; Daniélou 1960). Unfortunately, it was also relatively easy for some scholars to argue that any apparent discrimination on Jesus' part was due to his upbringing in a gender-asymmetrical, if not misogynist, Jewish culture, while at the same time often arguing that Jesus' own treatment of women was both much more egalitarian and a significant departure from the practices of other Jewish men (Swidler 1976; Witherington 1992; see the critiques of Plaskow 1978; von Kellenbach 1994; Corley 1996, 2002; Kraemer 1999).

This narrative of egalitarian beginnings and subsequent decline prompted considerable scholarship, whose interests lay both in the articulation of this history and in its depiction and explanation as contingent and therefore not binding on later (that is, modern) communities. Understanding just how the original egalitarian intentions of Jesus himself and the original egalitarian nature of the earliest followers of Jesus degenerated became an urgent historical task that had a significant impact on the work of scholars whose expertise lay in the second and subsequent centuries.

This task was spurred on in some ways by the publication of the corpus of texts found near Nag Hammadi in the late 1940s, but not published, either in the original Coptic and Greek or in English translation until the mid-1970s (Robinson 1977; Layton 1987). These texts, with their prominence of female divine or cosmic figures (*Thunder: Perfect Mind*; *Hypostasis of the Archons*; *Pistis Sophia*, the *Thought of Norea*) and their authorization of women as mediators of divine teaching in the *Dialogue of the Saviour* or the *Gospel of Mary*, threw into much sharper relief a diversity of ancient Christian practice and thought regarding women and gender (Pagels 1976, 1979). Still, the problem of paradigms persisted: a conflict between those who would write a history of early Christianity along the lines of Walter Bauer (1934) (one in which Christianity was diverse from its inception, and in which divergent positions concerning women and constructions of gender were part of the diversity) and a far more traditional narrative in which gender restrictions and conformity were always present, in which later Christian teachings had their legitimate authorization in foundational intentions and practices, and divergence from those foundational gender arrangements were unequivocally heretical and thus illegitimate. And still, theological interests dominated the discourse. Very few scholars seemed interested in feminist but non-theological accounts that did not need to argue for a pristine origin followed by a decline that could be remedied in the modern world by a return to those allegedly original egalitarian arrangements.

Concern for the history of Christian teachings about women prompted much early work identifying and attempting to explain the crucial troubling passages in various early Christian texts (e.g. Ruether 1974; Clark and Richardson 1977;

E. Clark 1983). Often, scholars sought to account for hostile language and negative representations of women as products of the larger misogynist culture, or of general male antagonism to women, or of particular psychological or personality traits of individual writers. These explanations were generally consistent in their strategy to detach such views, including opposition to women ministers and leaders, from any authentic core of Christianity.

The interest in contemporary questions about ordination (Ruether and McLaughlin 1979) also spurred inquiry into the actual roles played by women in ancient Christian communities, and the writing of a history of ancient Christianity that more accurately reflected the presence and activity of women. References to seemingly historical persons in the canonical gospels and other New Testament writings, especially Acts and the undisputed letters of Paul, drew extensive scrutiny. The few texts thought to be composed by women, Perpetua in particular, drew new editions and translations and extensive discussion (B. Shaw 1993; Tilley 1994; Perkins 1995: 104–23; Kraemer and Lander 2000; Bremmer 2003), but also Egeria and Thecla, for which female authorship was sometimes proposed. Scholars in the field that was once known as patristics were particularly interested in the extensive correspondence between writers like Jerome and Chrysostom and their female patrons and disciples, as well as the *Lives* of select elite Christian women. The work of Elizabeth A. Clark was path-breaking and formative (Clark 1979, 1981, 1983, 1984, 1986). Often this interest was spurred by a desire both to illuminate the active participation of women in early Christian communities and to argue that their less than completely equal participation was a function of ancient historical, economic, social, and cultural conditions, rather than, again, some essential, immutable aspect of Christianity.

Scholars specifically focused on questions of ancient Christian ministry began to seek evidence for women's exercise of various religious offices: for women presbyters, deacons, teachers, prophets, and other public leaders (Gryson 1972; LaPorte 1982). References in heresiological writers to prominent women were examined for their possible utility as evidence for actual women's practices, stripped of the negative representations in which these descriptions were clothed. Following the lead of Brooten's (1982) work on inscriptional evidence for Jewish women leaders in ancient synagogues, a few scholars began to scrutinize Christian inscriptional and papyrological evidence, material generally neglected by scholars in a field that had long privileged the study of literary texts (but see already Hatch 1880 and, more extensively, Gryson 1972).

Although it may be unwise to impose too much artificial categorization on a fairly diverse field, significant shifts in interest are discernible in the work of the last 15 years or so. Several factors may account for these shifts. First, the ordination debates were largely resolved, one way or another, by the late 1980s, and further research and debate seemed unlikely to effect change, at least in the near future. (This issue is not entirely moot, however (see e.g. Madigan and Osiek 2005), while in 2006, debates over the ordination of women priests and the elevation of women bishops in the Anglican communion continue to make the press, as do accounts of unauthorized ordinations of women as Roman Catholic priests.) Second, research on women and gender in other fields, particularly classics, literature, and history, was beginning to have a substantial effect on the questions and the theoretical perspectives employed by scholars of ancient Christianity. Third, significant numbers of graduate students have come to see research on women and gender in early Christianity no longer as the professional risk that I was warned it was 30 years ago. Rather, they appear to see it as an opportunity to do genuinely new and original work in a field where new data are rare (although some sources are more neglected than others) and new questions and approaches are generally the best we can do.

Thus, more recent work has taken several directions. Some scholars who began their work in the 1970s and early 1980s moved away from earlier reconstructive historical work and delineations of male 'attitudes' toward women in writers such as Tertullian, Jerome, Chrysostom, and Augustine to more sophisticated analysis of gender constructions in these authors: again, the work of Elizabeth Clark (1989, 1998a, b, 1999, 2000, 2004), as well as Burrus (1991, 1994, 1995, 2000, 2001, 2004) has been trail-blazing (see also Brooten 1996). Peter Brown's (1988) massive study of the Christian asceticism of women and men both reflected these newer interests and has been deeply influential on subsequent scholarship. Susan Harvey has almost single-handedly established an entire sub-field of studies on women and gender in the Syrian Orient (Brock and Harvey 1987; Harvey 1990, 1993, 1996, 2001, 2004). Numerous dissertations, influenced or directed by these same scholars, have focused on increasingly specialized areas, in the process often revisiting the work of earlier scholars, both descriptively and theoretically (Krumeich 1993 on Jerome; Cooper 1996 on the discourse of virginity in writings from Thecla to Ambrose; Brakke 1995 on Athanasius; Krawiec 2000 on Shenoute and the women of the White Monastery; Davis 2001 on the cult of Thecla; Leyerle 2001 on Chrysostom's critique of 'spiritual marriage'; Lander 2002 on women's devotion to saints in Roman North Africa; Trevett 1996 on the New Prophecy; see also Castelli 2004 on martyrdom and memory, with particular attention to Thecla and Perpetua).

Numerous studies have focused on both the rhetoric and the practice of early Christian asceticism and celibacy (G. Clark 1993; Elm 1994; Cloke 1995; T. M. Shaw 1998), with many scholars intrigued by ancient Christian deployment of the concept of 'becoming male' in the Gospel of Thomas, the Acts of Thomas, the Acts of Thecla, and elsewhere (Meyer 1985; Castelli 1991; Cloke 1995; Davis 2002). Major ancient authors continue to be the focus of scrutiny, such as John Chrysostom (Broc 1993; Ford 1996; Mayer 1997, 1999b; Hartney 1999; Harrison 2000, 2002; Leyerle 2001) and Augustine (E. Clark 1996, 1999; P. Clark 1998; Hunter 2003).

An excellent example of these shifts may be seen in newer work on the corpus of texts found near Nag Hammadi, as well as related texts known earlier, either independently or through excerpts in anti-Gnostic writers. Early scholarship saw the profusion of female figures in these texts as both positive imagery and consistent with the claims of heresiological writers like Irenaeus, Hippolytus, and Epiphanius that women played central roles in these movements. While the prominence of women mediators of divine revelation in many of these texts continues to pose intriguing questions, further reflection and analysis of these texts has led scholars to be considerably more cautious about the social composition of allegedly gnostic groups, about the gender ideologies of so-called Gnostic texts, and about the complex correlations between the two (Buckley 1986; King 1988, 2003; Hoffman 1995; Marjanen 1996; McGuire 1999).

Much of this more recent work has emphasized the distinction between questions about women and their lives and questions about rhetoric and ancient gender constructions (Allen 1992; Perkins 1995; M. Y. MacDonald 1996). While various known historical Christian women continue to be the focus of research (Holum 1982; Mayer 1999a), the increasing pessimism of Elizabeth Clark that ancient depictions of women provide access to anything more than ancient gender constructions and the diverse ways in which male authors utilized women as devices to explore their own concerns has been increasingly influential (Clark 1994; 1998a, b, c; 1999, 2000, 2004; Lieu 1998; Hunter 1999, 2003). Scholars continue to pursue questions of historical, social, and demographic description (Mayer 1999a, b; Aubin 2000) and reconstruction, but usually with far more attention to the minefields of ancient male rhetoric (although not always: e.g. Stark 1996; see Castelli 1998). The various *Lives* of exemplary Christian women have been analysed more for what they say about their male authors than about their female subjects (Krueger 2000; Laurence 2002a, b; J. W. Smith 2004). Studies have also focused on questions of women's religious practices such as martyrdom (Hall 1993; Jones 1993; Perkins 1995), devotion to saints (Davis 2001), pilgrimage (Dietz 2005), choral performance (Harvey 2005b), Marian devotion (Benko 1993; Shoemaker 2002), and other aspects of women's lives (e.g. Schroeder 2004). Particularly meticulous has been the work of Carolyn Osiek and various collaborators on early Christian families, including attention to domestic architecture (Osiek and Balch 1997; Balch and Osiek 2003; Osiek and MacDonald 2006; also O'Roark 1999; Jacobs 1999, 2003; Jacobs and Krawiec 2003). Some attention has also been paid to representations of women in early Christian catacomb painting (Dückers 1992; Tulloch 2005, forthcoming).

Finally, numerous studies have engaged questions of ancient gender construction and contestation, often focusing particularly on Christian critique of Roman constructions of masculinity and the formulation of new Christian conceptions (Burrus 2000; Cooper and Leyser 2000; Kuefler 2001; Ringrose 2003).

23.5 DIRECTIONS FOR FRUITFUL STUDY IN THE NEAR FUTURE

Research of the last 30 years has made significant progress on a variety of fronts: better editions and translations of texts pertaining to women and gender; better historical analysis and reconstruction; better literary and rhetorical analysis; far more sophisticated investigation into ancient gender constructions, and so forth. Nevertheless, numerous areas for future work exist.

There are still numerous under-analysed texts, such as *The Acts of Xanthippe and Polyxena* (Gorman 2001, 2003); the *Martyrdoms* of Barbara, Irene, and Christine; the *Life of St Eugenia*, and others. Very little has been published on the female characters of the *Acts of Philip*, for which new editions and French translations are now available, although a Brown University dissertation partly on Mariamme is presently in progress. I am unaware of any published work on women in the *Pseudo-Clementines* (or on the other texts often associated with 'Jewish Christianity' that raise fascinating questions both about gender construction and about the possibility of women's involvement).

While individual prosopographic studies exist, much prosopographic work remains. An ambitious if important project would be a catalogue of all known actual ancient Christian women, comparable in some ways to the *PLRE*. Related to this is a need for more demographic work. Stark's (1996) provocative and in many ways misinformed work nevertheless poses important questions that scholars of the field have only partially addressed: what was the gender (and age, and other markers of social status) distribution in early Christian churches: was it any different from the general demographic distribution of the later Roman Empire; and if so, what accounts for such differences? How significant a practice was celibacy? How many Christian families were producing children, at what rates, and with what implications?

Another relatively understudied area is ancient biblical exegesis of texts pertaining to women, whether in homilies or other forms of ancient interpretation. The work that has been done often focuses on later Christian exegesis of the crucial Pauline passages on women, or on Marian interpretation and expansion (Harvey 2005a); but unquestionably, much more could be done. What such exegesis might say, if anything, about the realities of ancient Christian women's lives and experiences remains to be considered, although quite early on, Higgins (1978) pointed to a relatively obscure interpretation of the Adam and Eve story in the writings of Anastasius of Sinai as possible evidence for more egalitarian communities and practices (see also Levison 1989, 2004). Further work on women and gender in early Christian art and architecture is also highly desirable.

Although it is no longer a new issue, Elizabeth Clark's engagement with contemporary literary, historical, and critical theory (especially Clark 2004) poses a substantial challenge to scholars of ancient Christianity that requires significant consideration and that will, I imagine, continue to provoke discussion for some time.

Finally, it continues to be the case that scholars trained in ancient Christianity often have little training (or interest) in religious studies more broadly, and often engage only minimally with discussions about the relationships between religion and gender in other cultural contexts. While Clark's cautions are pertinent here as well, more general and theoretical work in women's religions and in religious studies is relevant for multiple issues: Christian women's interest in particular religious practices such as healings or devotion to saints; Christian women's preference for, or resistance to, particular conceptualizations of divine beings; the correlations between celibacy, autonomy, and women's exercise of communal leadership, and many others. Scholars of ancient Christianity could often profit from the work of scholars of women's religions in other historical and cultural contexts, especially studies that seek to analyse the intersections of women's practices, including their beliefs, with prevailing gender constructions (e.g. Kitch 1989; Wessinger 1993; Sered 1994; 1999; Gutschow 2004).

SUGGESTED READING

Given the extensive nature of the evidence, there is no comprehensive single collection of the sources. Several anthologies, however, contain English translations of a range of relevant texts (E. Clark 1983; Brock and Harvey 1987, 2nd edn. 1998; Kraemer 2004, replacing and expanding Kraemer 1988; Miller 2005; also useful is Ehrman 1999, although texts focusing on women and gender are not identified as such). Despite considerable overlap, scholars and advanced students alike will find it convenient to have at least Brock and Harvey (1998), Kraemer (2004), and Miller (2005) (and E. Clark 1983, if available). Anthologies of texts about the ancient Mediterranean often contain at least some selections pertaining to women and early Christianity (e.g. Lefkowitz and Fant 1992). Following the model of Brooten's work on women leaders in Jewish synagogues (Brooten 1982), epigraphical and literary sources for Christian women's leadership in ancient churches are collected in Eisen (2000) and Madigan and Osiek (2005). Some more specialized collections such as those on Montanism (Heine 1989; Tabbernee 1997) are particularly helpful, as are the many volumes of the series New Documents Illustrating Early Christianity, published by the Ancient History Documentary Research Centre, Macquarie University. In many cases, all these collections also provide useful entry to the major critical editions and translations, as well as secondary bibliography. Still useful for their catalogues of the primary sources and references to early editions are Hatch (1880), LeClercq (1922), and Thraede (1972).

A number of scholarly studies have become an informal canon of sorts, frequently used in courses at various levels and cited regularly (Kraemer 1992; G. Clark 1993; E. Clark 1979, 1994, 1998*a*, *b*, 2000, 2004; Clark and Hatch 1981; Cloke 1995; Cooper 1996; M. Y. MacDonald 1996; Burrus 2000). While Kraemer and D'Angelo (1999) focus more on the first and early second centuries, the essays in the last section are quite germane (Cardman 1999; Streete 1999; McGuire 1999). Similarly, while many entries in Fiorenza (1994) are devoted to New Testament writings, a significant number treat other ancient Christian texts. Scholer (1993) reprints many earlier articles on women in early Christianity, while the recent volume dedicated to Elizabeth Clark (Martin and Miller 2005) and the Festschriften for Elizabeth Schüssler Fiorenza (Segovia 2003; Matthews 2003; Schaberg *et al.* 2004) contain many useful new articles. Among the most recent scholarship particularly valuable are Kuefler (2001), Ringrose (2003), and Osiek and MacDonald (2006).

BIBLIOGRAPHY

ALLEN, P. (1992), 'Contemporary Portrayals of the Byzantine Empress Theodora (A.D. 527–548)', in B. Garlick, S. Dixon, and P. Allen (eds.), *Stereotypes of Women in Power: Historical Perspectives and Revisionist Views* (New York: Greenwood Press), 10–35.

ALT, A. (1921), *Der griechische Inschriften der Palaestina tertia westliche der 'Araba* (Berlin: de Gruyter).

AUBIN, M. (2000), 'More Apparent than Real? Questioning the Difference in Marital Age between Christian and Non-Christian Women of Rome during the Third and Fourth Centuries', *Ancient History Bulletin*, 14: 1–13.

BALCH, D. L., and OSIEK, C. (2003) (eds.), *Early Christian Families in Context: An Interdisciplinary Dialogue* (Grand Rapids, Mich.: W. B. Eerdmans).

BAUER, W. (1934), *Orthodoxy and Heresy in the Early Church*, trans. and ed. R. Kraft and G. Kroedel (Philadelphia: Fortress Press, 1970).

BENKO, S. J. (1993), *The Virgin Goddess: Studies in the Pagan and Christian Roots of Mariology* (Leiden: E. J. Brill).

BOURDIEU, P. (2001), *Masculine Domination* (Palo Alto, Calif.: Stanford University Press).

BOYARIN, D. (1998), 'Gender', in M. C. Taylor (ed.), *Critical Terms for Religious Studies* (Chicago: University of Chicago Press), 117–35.

BRADBURY, S. (1996), *Severus of Minorca: Letter on the Conversion of the Jews*, OECT (Oxford: Oxford University Press).

BRAKKE, D. (1995), *Athanasius and the Politics of Asceticism* (Oxford: Clarendon Press).

BRAUN, W. (1919), *Die Frau in der alten Kirche* (Berlin: E. Runge).

BREMMER, J. N. (1996), 'Magic, Martyrdom and Women's Liberation in the Acts of Paul and Thecla', in J. N. Bremmer (ed.), *The Apocryphal Acts of Paul and Thecla* (Kampen: Kok Pharos), 36–59.

——(2003), 'Perpetua and Her Diary: Authenticity, Family and Visions', in D. Wood (ed.), *Martyrs and Martyrologies: Papers Read at the 1992 Summer Meeting and the 1993 Winter Meeting of the Ecclesiastical History Society* (Oxford: Blackwell), 77–120.

BROC, C. (1993), 'Le rôle des femmes dans l'Église de Constantinope d'après la correspondance de Jean Chrysostome', *StPatr* 27: 150–4.

BROCK, S. P., and HARVEY, S. A. (1987) (eds.), *Holy Women of the Syrian Orient* (Berkeley: University of California Press, 2nd edn. 1998).

BROOTEN, B. J. (1977), 'Junia…Outstanding Among the Apostles (Romans 16:15)', in Swidler and Swidler (1977), 141–4.

—— (1982), *Women Leaders in the Ancient Synagogues: Inscriptional Evidence and Background Issues*, Brown Judaic Studies, 36 (Chico, Calif.: Scholars Press).

—— (1996), *Love Between Women: Early Christian Responses to Female Homoeroticism* (Chicago: University of Chicago Press).

BROWN, J. N. (1846), *Encyclopedia of Religious Knowledge* (Brattleboro, Vt.: Joseph Steen and Co.; Philadelphia: J. B. Lippincott and Co.).

BROWN, P. (1988), *The Body and Society: Men, Women, and Sexual Renunication in Early Christianity* (New York: Columbia University Press).

BUCKLEY, J. J. (1986), *Female Fault and Fulfilment in Gnosticism* (Chapel Hill, NC: University of North Carolina Press).

BURRUS, V. (1987), *Chastity as Autonomy: Women in the Stories of Apocryphal Acts*, Studies in Women and Religions, 23 (Lewiston, NY: Edwin Mellen Press).

—— (1991), 'The Heretical Woman as Symbol in Alexander, Athanasius, Epiphanius, and Jerome', *HTR* 84/ 3: 229–48.

—— (1994), 'Word and Flesh: The Bodies and Sexuality of Ascetic Women in Christian Antiquity', *JFSR* 10: 27–51.

—— (1995), 'Reading Agnes: The Rhetoric of Gender in Ambrose and Prudentius', *JECS* 3: 25–46.

—— (2000), *'Begotten, not made': Conceiving Manhood in Late Antiquity* (Palo Alto, Calif.: Stanford University Press).

—— (2001), 'Is Macrina a Woman? Gregory of Nyssa's Dialogue on the Soul and Resurrection', in G. Ward (ed.), *The Blackwell Companion to Postmodern Theology* (Oxford: Blackwell), 249–64.

—— (2004), *The Sex Lives of Saints: An Erotics of Ancient Hagiography* (Philadelphia: University of Pennsylvania Press).

BUTLER, J. (1993), *Bodies That Matter: On the Discursive Limits of 'Sex'* (New York: Routledge).

—— (2004), *Undoing Gender* (New York: Routledge).

BUTLER, R. D. (2006), *The New Prophecy and 'New Visions': Evidence of Montanism in the Passion of Perpetua and Felicitas* (Washington D.C.: Catholic University of America Press).

BYNUM, C. W., HARRELL, S., and RICHMAN, P. (1986) (eds.), *Gender and Religion: On the Complexity of Symbols* (Boston: Beacon Press.)

CARDMAN, F. (1999), 'Women, Ministry and Church Order in Early Christianity', in Kraemer and D'Angelo (1999), 300–29.

CASTELLI, E. (1991), ' "I Will Make Mary Male": Pieties of the Body and Gender Transformation of Christian Women in Late Antiquity', in J. Epstein and K. Straub (eds.), *Body Guards: The Cultural Politics of Gender Ambiguity* (New York: Routledge), 29–49.

—— (1998), 'Gender, Theory, and the Rise of Christianity: A Response to Rodney Stark', *JECS* 6: 227–57.

—— (2001) (ed.), *Women, Gender, Religion: A Reader* (New York: Palgrave).

—— (2004), *Martyrdom and Memory: Early Christian Culture Making* (New York: Columbia University Press).

CLARK, E. (1979), *Jerome, Chrysostom and Friends: Essays and Translations* (Lewiston, NY: Edwin Mellen, 2nd edn. 1982).

—— (1981), 'Ascetic Renunciation and Feminine Advancement: A Paradox of Late Antique Christianity', *Anglican Theological Review*, 63: 240–57.

—— (1983), *Women in the Early Church*, MFC 13 (Collegeville, Minn.: Liturgical Press).

—— (1984), *The Life of Melania, the Younger: Introduction, Translation, and Commentary* (Lewiston, NY: Edwin Mellen Press).

—— (1986), *Ascetic Piety and Women's Faith: Essays on Late Ancient Christianity* (Lewiston, NY: Edwin Mellen Press).

—— (1989), 'Theory and Practice in Late Ancient Asceticism: Jerome, Chrysostom, and Augustine', *JFSR* 5: 25–46.

—— (1992), 'Eusebius on Women in Early Church History', in H. W. Attridge and G. Hata (eds.), *Eusebius, Christianity and Judaism* (Detroit: Wayne State University Press), 256–69.

—— (1994), 'Ideology, History, and the Construction of "Woman" in Late Ancient Christianity', *JECS* 2: 155–84.

—— (1996) (ed.), *St Augustine on Marriage and Sexuality* (Washington: Catholic University of America Press).

—— (1998a), 'Holy Women, Holy Words: Early Christian Women, Social History, and the Linguistic Turn', *JECS* 6: 413–30.

—— (1998b), 'The Lady Vanishes: Dilemmas of a Feminist Historian after the "Linguistic Turn" ', *CH* 67: 1–31.

—— (1998c), 'Melania the Elder and the Origenist Controversy: The Status of the Body in a Late-Ancient Debate', in J. Petroccione (ed.), *Nova & vetera: Patristic Studies in Honor of Thomas Patrick Halton* (Washington D.C.: Catholic University of America Press), 117–27.

—— (1999), 'Rewriting Early Christian History: Augustine's Representation of Monica', in J. W. Drijvers and J. W. Watt (eds.), *Portraits of Spiritual Authority* (Leiden: E. J. Brill), 3–23.

—— (2000), 'Women, Gender, and the Study of Christian History', *CH* 70: 395–426.

—— (2004), *History, Theory, Text: Historians and the Linguistic Turn* (Cambridge, Mass.: Harvard University Press).

—— and HATCH, D. F. (1981) (eds.), *The Golden Bough, The Oaken Cross: The Virgilian Cento of Faltonia Betitia Proba* (Chico, Calif.: Scholars Press).

—— and RICHARDSON, H. (1977) (eds.), *Women and Religion: A Feminist Sourcebook of Christian Thought*, rev. and expanded, 1996 (San Francisco: HarperSanFrancisco).

CLARK, G. (1993), *Women in Late Antiquity: Pagan and Christian Lifestyles* (Oxford: Clarendon Press).

CLARK, P. (1998), 'Women, Slaves and the Hierarchies of Domestic Violence: The Family of St. Augustine', in S. R. Joshel and S. Murnaghan (eds.), *Women and Slaves in Greco-Roman Culture: Differential Equations* (New York: Routledge), 109–29.

CLOKE, G. (1995), *This Female Man of God: Women and Spiritual Power in the Patristic Age*, 350–450 (London: Routledge).

COOPER, K. (1996), *The Virgin and the Bride: Idealized Womanhood in Late Antiquity* (Cambridge, Mass.: Harvard University Press).

—— and LEYSER, C. (2000), 'The Gender of Grace: Impotence, Servitude and Manliness in the Fifth-century West', *Gender & History*, 12/3: 536–51.

CORLEY, K. E. (1996), 'Feminist Myths of Christian Origins', in E. A. Castelli and H. Taussig (eds.), *Reimagining Christian Origins: A Colloquium Honoring Burton L. Mack* (Valley Forge, Pa.: Trinity Press International), 51–67.

——(2002), *Women and the Historical Jesus: Feminist Myths of Christian Origins* (Santa Rosa, Calif.: Polebridge Press).

DANIÉLOU, J. (1960), 'Le ministère des femmes dans l'Église ancienne', *La Maison Dieu*, 61: 70–96.

DAVIES, S. (1980), *The Revolt of the Widows: The Social World of the Apocryphal Acts* (Carbondale, Ill.: Illinois University Press).

DAVIS, S. J. (2001), *The Cult of Saint Thecla: A Tradition of Women's Piety in Late Antiquity* (Oxford: Oxford University Press).

——(2002), 'Crossed Texts, Crossed Sex: Intertextuality and Gender in Early Christian Legends of Holy Women Disguised as Men', *JECS* 10: 1–36.

DIETZ, M. (2005), *Wandering Monks, Virgins and Pilgrims: Ascetic Travel in the Mediterranean World A.D. 300–800* (Philadelphia: Pennsylvania State University Press).

DONALDSON, J. (1907), *Woman: Her Position and Influence in Ancient Greece and Rome and Among the Early Christians* (London: Longmans, Green).

DOYLE, P. M. (1974), 'Women and Religion: Psychological and Cultural Implications', in Ruether (1974), 15–40.

DRONKE, P. (1984), *Women Writers of the Middle Ages: A Critical Study of Texts from Perpetua († 203) to Marguerite Porete († 1310)* (Cambridge: Cambridge University Press).

DÜCKERS, P, (1992), 'Agape und Irene: Die Frauengestalten der sigmamahlszenen mit antiken Inschriften in der Katakombe der Heiligen Marcellinus und Petrus', *JAC* 35: 147–67.

DUNN, J. D. G. (1991), *The Partings of the Ways: Between Christianity and Judaism and their Significance for the Character of Christianity* (London: SCM Press; Philadelphia: Trinity Press International).

EHRMAN, B. D. (1993), *The Orthodox Corruption of Scripture: The Effect of Early Christological Controversies on the Text of the New Testament* (New York: Oxford University Press).

——(1999) (ed.), *After the New Testament: A Reader in Early Christianity* (New York: Oxford University Press).

EISEN, U. (2000), *Women Officeholders in Early Christianity: Epigraphical and Literary Studies,* trans. L. M. Maloney (Collegeville, Minn.: Michael Glazier, Liturgical Press).

ELLWOOD, C. (1921), 'Woman, Religious and Ethical Status of', in S. Mathews and G. Birney Smith (eds.), *A Dictionary of Religion and Ethics* (New York: MacMillan Company), 475.1–476.1.

ELM, S. (1994), *'Virgins of God': The Making of Asceticism in Late Antiquity* (Oxford: Clarendon Press).

EPP, E. J. (1966), *The Theological Tendency of Codex Bezae Cantabrigensis in Acts* (Cambridge: Cambridge University Press).

——(2005), *Junia: The First Woman Apostle* (Minneapolis: Fortress Press).

FERRUA, A. (1944/5), 'Questioni di Epigrafia Eretica Romana', *Rivista di Archeologia Cristiana*, 21: 185–93.

FIORENZA, E. S. (1983), *In Memory of Her: A Feminist Theological Reconstruction of Christian Origins* (New York: Crossroads).

——(1994) (ed.), *Searching the Scriptures*, 2 vols. (New York: Crossroads).

FORD, D. C. (1996), *Women and Men in the Early Church: The Full Views of St. John Chrysostom* (South Canaan, Pa.: St Tikhon's Seminary Press).

FOUCAULT, M. (1976), *Histoire de la Sexualité*, 3 vols. (Paris: Gallimard).

FRANKFURTER, D. (2001), 'Jews or Not? Reconstructing the "Other" in Rev 2:9 and 3:9', *HTR* 94: 403–25.

GIBSON, E. (1978), *The 'Christians for Christians' Inscriptions of Phrygia: Greek Texts, Translations and Commentary*, HTS 32 (Missoula, Mont.: Scholars Press).

GLANCY, J. A. (2003), 'Protocols of Masculinity in the Pastoral Epistles', in S. D. Moore and J. Capel Anderson (eds.), *New Testament Masculinities*, Semeia Studies, 45 (Atlanta: SBL), 235–64.

GLEASON, M. W. (1990), 'The Semiotics of Gender: Physiognomy and Self-Fashioning in the Second Century C.E.', in D. Halperin, J. Winkler, and F. Zeitlin (eds.), *Before Sexuality: The Construction of Erotic Experience in the Ancient Greek World* (Princeton: Princeton University Press), 389–416.

—— (1999), 'Elite Male Identity in the Roman Empire', in D. S. Potter and D. J. Mattingly (eds.), *Life, Death and Entertainment in the Roman Empire* (Ann Arbor: University of Michigan Press), 67–84.

GORMAN, J. (2001), 'Thinking With and About "Same-Sex Desire": Producing and Policing Female Sexuality in the Acts of Xanthippe and Polyxena', *JHSex* 10/3–4: 416–41.

—— (2003), 'Reading and Theorizing Women's Sexualities: The Representation of Women in the *Acts of Xanthippe and Polyxena*' (Ph.D. dissertation, Temple University).

GOTTLIEB, E. (1928), *Die Frau im frühen Christentum* (Leipzig: A. Klein).

GRANT, R. M. (1985), 'A Woman of Rome: The Matron in Justin, 2 *Apology* 2.1–9', *CH* 54: 461–72.

GRYSON, R. (1972), *Le ministère des femmes dans l'Église ancienne* (Gembloux: J. Duculot).

GUTSCHOW, K. (2004), *Being A Buddhist Nun: The Struggle for Enlightenment in the Himalayas* (Cambridge, Mass.: Harvard University Press).

HALL, S. G. (1993), 'Women Among the Early Martyrs', in D. Wood (ed.), *Martyrs and Martyrologies: Papers Read at the 1992 Summer Meeting and the 1993 Winter Meeting of the Ecclesiastical History Society* (Oxford: Blackwell), 1–21.

HALPERIN, D. M. (1990), 'Why is Diotima a Woman?', in *idem*, J. J. Winkler, and F. I. Zeitlin (eds.), *Before Sexuality: The Construction of Erotic Experience in the Ancient Greek World* (Princeton: Princeton University Press), 257–308.

HANSON, A. E. (1990), 'The Medical Writer's Woman', in D. Halperin, J. J. Winkler, and F. I. Zeitlin (eds.), *Before Sexuality: The Construction of Erotic Experience in the Ancient Greek World* (Princeton: Princeton University Press), 309–38.

—— (1999), 'The Roman Family', in D. S. Potter and D. J. Mattingly (eds.), *Life, Death and Entertainment in the Roman Empire* (Ann Arbor: University of Michigan Press), 19–66.

HARNACK, A. VON (1904–5), *The Expansion of Christianity in the First Three Centuries*, trans. J. Moffat (London: Williams & Norgate; New York: G. P. Putnam's Sons; 2nd enlarged rev. edn., 1908); reprinted as *The Mission and Expansion of Christianity in the First Three Centuries* (Gloucester, Mass.: Peter Smith, 1972).

HARRISON, N. V. (2000), 'The Inevitability of Hermeneutics: David C. Ford on St. John Chrysostom', *St Vladimir's Theological Quarterly*, 44: 195–205.

—— (2002), 'Women and the Image of God according to St. John Chrysostom', in P. M. Blowers *et al.* (eds.), *In Dominico Eloquio/In Lordly Eloquence: Essays on Patristic Exegesis in Honor of Robert Louis Wilken* (Grand Rapids, Mich.: Eerdmans), 259–79.

HARTNEY, A. (1999), 'Manly Women and Womanly Men: The Subintroductae and John Chrysostom', in L. James (ed.), *Desire and Denial in Byzantium: Papers from the Thirty-First Spring Symposium of Byzantine Studies*, Society for the Promotion of Byzantine Studies Publications, 6 (Aldershot: Ashgate), 41–8.

HARVEY, S. A. (1990), 'Women in Early Byzantine Hagiography: Reversing the Story', in L. Coon, K. Haldane, and E. Sommer (eds.), *'That Gentle Strength': Historical Perspectives on Women in Christianity* (Charlottesville, Va.: University Press of Virginia), 36–59.

—— (1993), 'Feminine Imagery for the Divine: The Holy Spirit, the Odes of Solomon and Early Syriac Tradition', *St Vladimir's Theological Quarterly*, 37: 111–39.

—— (1996), 'Sacred Bonding: Mothers and Daughters in Early Syriac Hagiography', *JECS* 4: 27–56.

—— (2001) (ed.), *Women in the Syriac tradition*, Hugoye, 4.2 <http://bethmardutho. cua. edu/hugoye/Vol4No2/index.html>.

—— (2004), 'Women and Words: Texts By and About Women', in L. Ayres, A. Louth, and F. M. Young (eds.), *Cambridge History of Early Christian Literature* (Cambridge: Cambridge University Press), 382–90.

—— (2005a), 'On Mary's Voice: Gendered Words in Syriac Marian Tradition', in D. B. Martin and P. Cox Miller (eds.), *The Cultural Turn in Late Ancient Studies: Gender, Asceticism and Historiography* (Durham, NC: Duke University Press), 63–86.

—— (2005b), 'Revisiting the Daughters of the Covenant: Women's Choirs and Sacred Song in Ancient Syriac Christianity', *Hugoye*, 8.2, <http://bethmardutho.cua.edu/hugoye/Vol8No2/HV8N2Harvey.html>.

HASPELS, C. H. E. (1971), *The Highlands of Phrygia: Sites and Monuments*, 2 vols. (Princeton: Princeton University Press).

HATCH, E. (1880), 'Virgins', and 'Widows', in W. Smith and S. Cheetah (eds.), *A Dictionary of Christian Antiquities, Being a Continuation of 'The Dictionary of the Bible'* (London: John Murray), ii.: 2019–22, 2033–6.

HEFFERNAN, T. (1995), 'Philology and Authorship in the *Passio Sanctarum Perpetuae et Felicitatis*', *Traditio*, 50: 315–25.

HEINE, R. (1989), *Montanist Oracles and Testimonia* (Macon, Ga.: Mercer University Press).

HIGGINS, J. (1978), 'Anastasius Sinaita and the Superiority of Woman', *JBL* 97: 253–56.

HILHORST, A. (1996), 'Tertullian on the Acts of Paul', in J. Bremmer (ed.), *The Acts of Paul and Thecla*, Studies on the Apocryphal Acts of the Apostles, 2 (Kampen: Kok Pharos), 150–63.

HOFFMAN, D. L. (1995), *The Status of Women and Gnosticism in Irenaeus and Tertullian*, Studies in Women and Religion, 36 (Lewiston, NY: Edwin Mellen Press).

HOLUM, K. G. (1982), *Theodosian Empresses: Women and Imperial Dominion in Late Antiquity* (Berkeley: University of California Press).

HUNTER, D. G. (1999), 'Clerical Celibacy and the Veiling of Virgins: New Boundaries in Late Ancient Christianity', in W. E. Klingshirn and M. Vessey (eds.), *Limits of Ancient Christianity: Essays on Late Antique Thought and Culture in Honor of R. A. Markus* (Ann Arbor: University of Michigan Press), 139–52.

—— (2003), 'Augustine and the Making of Marriage in Roman North Africa', *JECS* 11: 63–85.

JACOBS, A. S. (1999), 'A Family Affair: Marriage, Class, and Ethics in the Apocryphal Acts of the Apostles', *JECS* 7: 105–38.

—— (2003), ' "Let Him Guard Pietas": Early Christian Exegesis and the Ascetic Family', *JECS* 11: 265–81.

—— and KRAWIEC, R. (2003), 'Fathers Know Best? Christian Families in the Age of Asceticism', *JECS* 11: 257–63.

JOHNSON, S. F. (2006), *The Life and Miracles of Thekla: A Literary Study* (Washington D.C.: Center for Hellenic Studies; Cambridge, Mass.: Harvard University Press).

JONES, C. (1993), 'Women, Death and the Law during the Christian Persecutions', in D. Wood (ed.), *Martyrs and Martyrologies: Papers Read at the 1992 Summer Meeting and the 1993 Winter Meeting of the Ecclesiastical History Society* (Oxford: Blackwell), 23–34.

KAESTLI, J. D. (1989), 'Les Actes Apocryphes et la reconstitution de l'histoire des femmes dans le christianisme ancien', *Foi et Vie*, 88: 71–9.

——(1990), 'Fiction littéraire et réalité sociale: Que peut-on savoir de la place des femmes dans le milieu du production des Actes apocryphes des apôtres?', *La fable apocryphe*, 1: 279–302.

KELLENBACH, K. VON (1994), *Anti-Judaism in Feminist Religious Writings* (Atlanta: Scholars Press).

KING, K. L. (1988) (ed.), *Images of the Feminine in Gnosticism* (Philadelphia: Fortress Press).

——(2003), *The Gospel of Mary of Magdala: Jesus and the First Woman Apostle* (Santa Rosa, Calif.: Polebridge Press).

KITCH, S. (1989), *Chaste Liberation: Celibacy and Female Cultural Status* (Urbana, Ill.: University of Illinois Press).

KLAWITER, F. C. (1980), 'The Role of Martyrdom and Persecution in Developing the Priestly Authority of Women in Early Christianity: A Case Study of Montanism', *CH* 49/3: 251–61.

KOESTER, H. (1990), *Ancient Christian Gospels: Their History and Development* (Valley Forge, Pa.: Trinity Press International).

KRAEMER, R. S. (1976), 'Ecstatics and Ascetics: Studies in the Functions of Religious Activities for Women in the Greco-Roman World' (Ph.D. dissertation, Princeton University).

——(1980), 'The Conversion of Women to Ascetic Forms of Christianity', *Signs: Journal of Women in Culture and Society*, 6/2: 298–307; repr. in J. M. Bennet, E. A. Clark, J. O'Barr, B. A. Vilen, and S. Westphal-Wihl (eds.), *Sisters and Workers in the Middle Ages* (Chicago: University of Chicago Press), 198–207.

——(1983), 'Women in the Religions of the Greco-Roman World: A Review Essay', *Religious Studies Review*, 9/2: 127–39.

——(1988) (ed.), *Maenads, Martyrs, Matrons, Monastics: A Sourcebook of Women's Religions in the Greco-Roman World* (Minneapolis: Fortress Press.)

——(1991), 'Women's Authorship of Jewish and Christian Literature in the Greco-Roman Period', in A.-J. Levine (ed.), *'Women Like This': New Perspectives on Jewish Women in the Greco-Roman Period*, Early Judaism and its Literature, 1 (Atlanta: Scholars Press), 221–42.

——(1992), *Her Share of the Blessings: Women's Religions among Pagans, Jews and Christians in the Greco-Roman World* (New York: Oxford University Press).

——(1994), 'The Other as Woman: Aspects of Polemic between Pagans, Jews and Christians in Greco-Roman Antiquity', in L. Silberstein (ed.), *The Other In Jewish Thought and History* (New York: New York University Press), 121–44.

——(1999), 'Jewish Women and Christian Origins: Some Caveats', in Kraemer and D'Angelo (1999), 35–49.

——(2004) (ed.), *Women's Religions in the Greco-Roman World: A Sourcebook* (New York: Oxford University Press).

——and D'ANGELO, M. R. (1999) (eds.), *Women and Christian Origins* (New York: Oxford University Press).

——and LANDER, S. L. (2000), 'Perpetua and Felicitas', in P. Esler (ed.), *The Early Christian World* (London: Routledge, 2000), ii. 1048–68.

KRAWIEC, R. (2002), *Shenoute and the Women of the White Monastery: Egyptian Monasticism in Late Antiquity* (New York: Oxford University Press).

KRUEGER, D. (2000), 'Writing and the Liturgy of Memory in Gregory of Nyssa's Life of Macrina', *JECS* 8: 483–510.

KRUMEICH, C. (1993), *Hieronymus und die christlichen feminae clarissimae* (Bonn: R. Habelt).

KUEFLER, M. (2001), *The Manly Eunuch: Masculinity, Gender Ambiguity, and Christian Ideology in Late Antiquity* (Chicago: University of Chicago Press).

LANDER, S. L. (2002), 'Ritual Power in Society: Ritualizing Late Antique North African Martyr Cult Activities and Social Changes in Gender and Status' (Ph.D. dissertation, University of Pennsylvania).

LAPORTE, JEAN (1982), *The Role of Women in Early Christianity* (New York: Edwin Mellen Press).

LAURENCE, P. (2002*a*), 'Helena, mère de Constantin: métamorphoses d'une image', *Aug* 42: 75–96.

—— (2002*b*), 'Proba, Juliana et Démétrias: Le christianisme des femmes de la gens Anicia dans la première moitié de Ve siècle', *REAug* 48: 131–63.

LAYTON, B. (1987), *The Gnostic Scriptures: A New Translation with Annotations and Introductions* (Garden City, NY: Doubleday).

LECLERCQ, H. (1922), 'Femme', in *DACL*, v/i: 1300–54.

LEENHARDT, F. J. (1949), *Die Stellung der Frau im Neuen Testament und in der alten Kirche* (Zürich: Zwingli-Verlag).

LEFKOWITZ, M. R. (1991), 'Did Ancient Women Write Novels?', in A-J. Levine (ed.), *'Women Like This': New Perspectives on Jewish Women in the Greco-Roman Period*, Early Judaism and its Literature, 1 (Atlanta: Scholars Press), 199–219.

—— and FANT, M. B. (1992) (eds.), *Women's Life in Greece and Rome: A Source Book in Translation*, 2nd edn. (Baltimore: Johns Hopkins University Press).

LEVISON, J. R. (1989), 'The Exoneration of Eve in the Apocalypse of Moses 15–30', *Journal for the Study of Judaism in the Persian, Hellenistic and Roman Period*, 20: 135–50.

—— (2004), 'Adam and Eve in Romans 1.18–25 and the Greek *Life of Adam and Eve*', *NTS* 50: 519–34.

LEWIS, A. S. (1900), *Select Narratives of Holy Women: From the Syro-Antiochene or Sinai Palimpsest as Written Above the Old Syriac Gospels by John the Stylite, of Beth-Mar-Qanūn in A.D. 778*, Studia Sinaitica, 9–10 (London: C. J. Clay and Sons).

—— and GIBSON, M. D. (1898), *In the Shadow of Sinai: Stories of Travel and Biblical Research* (Cambridge: Macmillan and Bowes, repr. Brighton: Alpha Press, 1999).

LEYERLE, B. (2001), *Theatrical Shows and Ascetic Lives: John Chrysostom's Attack on Spiritual Marriage* (Berkeley: University of California Press).

LIEU, J. M. (1994), ' "The Parting of the Ways": Theological Construct or Historical Reality?', *JSNT* 56: 101–19.

—— (1998), 'The "Attraction of Women" in/to Early Judaism and Christianity: Gender and the Politics of Conversion', *JSNT* 72: 5–22.

MACDONALD, D. R. (1983), *The Legend and the Apostle: The Battle for Paul in Story and Canon* (Philadelphia: Westminster Press).

MACDONALD, M. Y. (1996), *Early Christian Women and Pagan Opinion: The Power of the Hysterical Woman* (Cambridge: Cambridge University Press).

—— (2003), 'Was Celsus Right? The Role of Women in the Expansion of Early Christianity', in Balch and Osiek (2003), 157–84.

MADIGAN, K., and OSIEK, C. (2005) (eds.), *Ordained Women in the Early Church: A Documentary History* (Baltimore: Johns Hopkins University Press).

MARJANEN, A. (1996), *The Woman Jesus Loved: Mary Magdalene in the Nag Hammadi Library and Related Documents* (Leiden: E. J. Brill).

MARSHALL, J. W. (2001), *Parables of War: Reading John's Jewish Apocalypse* (Waterloo, Ont.: Wilfred Laurier Press).

MARTIN, D., and MILLER, P. C. (2005) (eds.), *The Cultural Turn in Late Ancient Studies: Gender, Asceticism and Historiography* (Durham, NC: Duke University Press).

MATTHEWS, S. (2002), 'Thinking of Thecla: Issues in Feminist Historiography', *JFSR* 17: 39–55.

——*et al.* (2003) (eds.), *Walk in the Ways of Wisdom: Essays in Honor of Elisabeth Schüssler Fiorenza* (Harrisburg, Pa.: Trinity Press International).

MAYER, W. (1997), 'The Dynamics of Liturgical Space: Aspects of the Interaction between St. John Chrysostom and his Audiences', *Ephemerides Liturgicae*, 111: 104–15.

——(1999*a*), 'Constantinopolitan Women in Chrysostom's Circle', *VC* 53: 265–88.

——(1999*b*), 'Female Participation and the Late Fourth-Century Preacher's Audience', *Aug* 39: 139–47.

McGUIRE, A. (1999), 'Women, Gender and Gnosis in Gnostic Texts and Traditions', in Kraemer and D'Angelo, (1999), 257–99.

MEYER, M. (1985), 'Making Mary Male: The Categories of "Male" and "Female" in The Gospel of Thomas', *NTS* 31: 554–70.

MILLER P. C. (2005) (ed.), *Women in Early Christianity: Translations from Greek Texts* (Washington D.C.: Catholic University of America Press).

NUGENT, M. R. (1941), *Portrait of the Consecrated Woman in Greek Christian Literature of the First Four Centuries* (Washington D.C.: Catholic University Press of America).

O'ROARK, D. (1999), 'Parenthood in Late Antiquity: The Evidence of Chrysostom', *GRBS* 40: 53–81.

OSIEK, C., and BALCH, D. L. (1997), *Families in the New Testament World: Households and House Churches* (Louisville, Ky.: Westminster/John Knox).

—— and MACDONALD, M. (2006), with J. H. TULLOCH, *A Woman's Place: House Churches in Earliest Christianity* (Minneapolis: Fortress Press).

OTRANTO, G. (1982), 'Note sul sacerdozio femminile nell'antichia in margine a una testimonianza di Gelasio I', *VetChr* 19: 341–60.

PAGELS, E. H. (1976), 'What Became of God the Mother: Conflicting Images of God in Early Christianity', *Signs: Journal of Women in Culture and Society*, 2: 293–303.

——(1979), 'God the Father/God the Mother', in *The Gnostic Gospels* (New York: Random House), ch. 3.

PARKER, H. N. (1997), 'The Teratogenic Grid', in J. Hallett and M. Skinner (eds.), *Roman Sexualities* (Princeton: Princeton University Press), 47–65.

PERKINS, J. (1995), *The Suffering Self: Pain and Narrative Representation in the Early Christian Era* (London: Routledge).

PLASKOW, J. (1978), 'Christian Feminism and Anti-Judaism', *Cross Currents*, 28: 306–9.

PRICE, A. W. (1985), *The Ladies of Castlebrae* (Gloucester: Alan Sutton).

REED, Y., and BECKER, A. (2004) (eds.), *The Ways That Never Parted: Jews and Christians in Late Antiquity and the Early Middle Ages* (Tübingen: Mohr/Siebeck).

RINGROSE, K. M. (2003), *The Perfect Servant: Eunuchs and the Social Construction of Gender in Byzantium* (Chicago: University of Chicago Press).

ROBINSON, J. (1977) (ed.), *The Nag Hammadi Library in English* (New York: Harper & Row, 3rd edn. 1988).

ROSSI, M. A. (1991), 'Priesthood, Precedent and Prejudice: On Recovering the Women Priests of Early Christianity. G. Otranto's "Notes on the Female Priesthood in Antiquity"', *JFSR* 7: 73–94.

RUETHER, R. R. (1974) (ed.), *Religion and Sexism: Images of Women in Jewish and Christian Tradition* (New York: Simon & Schuster).

——and MCLAUGHLIN, E. (1979) (eds.), *Women of Spirit: Female Leadership in the Jewish and Christian Traditions* (New York: Simon & Schuster).

SALISBURY, J. (1997), *Perpetua's Passion: The Death and Memory of a Young Roman Woman* (New York: Routledge).

SCHABERG, J. C., et al. (2004), *On the Cutting Edge: The Study of Women in Biblical Worlds: Essays in Honor of Elisabeth Schüssler Fiorenza* (New York: Continuum).

SCHOLER, D. A. (1993) (ed.), *Women in Early Christianity* (New York: Garland).

SCHROEDER, J. A. (2004), 'John Chrysostom's Critique of Spousal Violence', *JECS* 12: 413–42.

SCOTT, J. W. (1986), 'Gender: A Useful Category of Historical Analysis', *American Historical Review*, 91: 1053–75.

SEGOVIA, F., et al. (2003) (eds.), *Toward a New Heaven and a New Earth: Essays in Honor of Elisabeth Schüssler Fiorenza* (Maryknoll, NY: Orbis).

SERED, S. L. (1994), *Priestess, Mother, Sacred Sister: Religions Dominated by Women* (New York: Oxford University Press).

——(1999), *Women of the Sacred Groves: Divine Priestesses of Okinawa* (New York: Oxford University Press).

SHAW, B. (1993), 'The Passion of Perpetua', *Past and Present*, 139: 3–45.

——(1996), 'Body/Power/Identity: The Passions of the Martyrs', *JECS* 4: 269–312.

SHAW, T. M. (1998), *The Burden of the Flesh: Fasting and Sexuality in Early Christianity* (Minneapolis: Fortress Press).

SHOEMAKER S. J. (2002), *Ancient Traditions of the Virgin Mary's Dormition and Assumption* (Oxford: Oxford University Press).

SLATER, P. (1968), *The Glory of Hera: Greek Mythology and the Greek Family* (Boston: Beacon; repr. Princeton: Princeton University Press, 1992).

SMITH, J. W. (2004), 'A Just and Reasonable Grief: The Death and Function of a Holy Woman in Gregory of Nyssa's Life of Macrina', *JECS* 12: 57–84.

SNYDER, J. M. (1989), *The Woman and the Lyre: Women Writers in Classical Greece and Rome* (Carbondale, Ill.: Southern Illinois University Press).

STARK, R. (1996), 'The Role of Women in Christian Growth', in *The Rise of Christianity: A Sociologist Reconsiders History* (Princeton: Princeton University Press), ch. 5.

STÖCKER, L. (1907), *Die Frau in der alten Kirche* (Tübingen: J. C. B. Mohr/Paul Siebeck).

STREETE, G. C. (1999), 'Women as Sources of Redemption and Knowledge in Early Christian Traditions', in Kraemer and D'Angelo (1999), 330–54.

SWIDLER, L. J. (1976), *Women in Judaism: The Status of Women in Formative Judaism* (Metuchen, NJ: Scarecrow Press).

——and SWIDLER, A. (1977) (eds.), *Women Priests: A Catholic Commentary on the Vatican Declaration* (New York: Paulist Press).

TABBERNEE, W. (1997), *Montanist Inscriptions and Testimonia: Epigraphic Sources Illustrating the History of Montanism*, PMS, 16 (Macon, Ga.: Mercer University Press).

THRAEDE, K. (1972), 'Frau', in *RAC*, viii. 227–70.

TILLEY, M. (1994), 'The Passion of Perpetua and Felicity', in Fiorenza (1994), ii. 829–58.

TORJESEN, K. J. (1993), *When Women Were Priests: Women's Leadership in the Early Church and the Scandal of Their Subordination in the Rise of Christianity* (San Francisco: Harper-SanFrancisco).

TREVETT, C. (1996), *Montanism: Gender, Authority and the New Prophecy* (Cambridge: Cambridge University Press).

TULLOCH, J. (2006), 'Women Leaders in Family Funerary Banquets', in Osiek and MacDonald (2006): 164–93, 289–96.

—— (forthcoming), *Speaking About Agape and Irene: Women and Hospitality in Roman Christian Funerary Art* (Waterloo, Ont.: Wilfred Laurier University Press).

VON DER GOLTZ, E. A. F. (1914), *Der Dienst der Frau in der christliche Kirche* (Potsdam: Stiftungsverlag).

WESSINGER, C. (1993) (ed.), *Women's Leadership in Marginal Religions: Explorations Outside the Mainstream* (Urbana, Ill.: University of Indiana Press).

WILSON, R. (1884), 'Woman', in A. A. Benton (ed.), *Church Cyclopedia: A Dictionary of Church Doctrine, History, Organization and Ritual* (Philadelphia: L. R. Hamersly and Co.), 794–5.

WILSON-KASTNER, P. (1981) (ed.), *A Lost Tradition: Women Writers of the Early Church* (Lanham, Md.: University Press of America).

WINKLER, J. (1990), *The Constraints of Desire: The Anthropology of Sex and Gender in Ancient Greece* (New York: Routledge).

WITHERINGTON, B., III (1984), 'Anti-feminist Tendencies of the "Western" Acts', *JBL* 103/1: 82–4.

—— (1992), 'Women, in The New Testament', in *ABD*, vi. 957–61.

WYPUSTEK, A. (1997), 'Magic, Montanism, Perpetua, and The Severan Persecution', *VC* 51: 276–97.

ZSCHARNACK, L. (1902), *Der Dienst der Frau in den ersten Jahrhunderten der christliche Kirche* (Göttingen: Vandenhoeck & Ruprecht).

I am grateful to Jeanne-Nicole Saint-Laurent for her assistance with the Bibliography.

CHAPTER 24

···

MONASTICISM

···

J. WILLIAM HARMLESS, SJ

CHRISTIANITY had ascetic commitments from its very foundation, in the words and deeds both of Jesus and of Paul. Praying in deserts, fasting, celibacy, renunciation of family and wealth—these occupy a large place in the narratives and ethical teaching of the New Testament. When Christianity surfaced into legitimacy in the 310s, its deep-seated ascetic impulses surfaced as well, and quickly assumed organized, even institutional contours. The movement we now call monasticism would, over the next millennium, leave an indelible impress upon Christian faith and practice in the medieval West and Byzantine East and beyond. The challenge for scholars of early Christianity is to give an account of this organizing of asceticism, to plot out its practices, map its movements, chart its varieties, probe its motives.

The Greek word for 'monk', *monachos*, meant, in its origins, 'a solitary'. Two classic forms of monasticism emerged early: the anchoritic, or solitary life of the hermit, and the cenobitic, or life within a structured (and often secluded) community. These two organizational patterns, while routinely cited in modern textbooks, do not begin to do justice to the wide-ranging experiments in monastic living that sprouted up across the Empire. Monastic life required, from the outset, stark renunciations: of family, property, marriage, career. There is no early mention of vows, but in Egypt and elsewhere, distinctive garb marked the monk as one set apart. Early monks typically joined ascetical disciplines—fasting, vigils, poverty, lifelong celibacy—with a life of manual labour. Many recited psalms at fixed hours, especially at dawn and sunset. They also took to heart Paul's admonition to 'pray unceasingly' (1 Thess 5: 17), and honed methods of unceasing meditation and contemplation. Egypt has been called the birthplace of Christian monasticism. That is only partially true. Scholars now recognize that other regions—Syria, Palestine,

Cappadocia—had their own traditions, as old as Egypt, if less well documented and perhaps less influential in the long run.

Traditional recitals of the history of early monasticism have, until recently, centred on a handful of purported 'founders' celebrated in ancient accounts. We first need to survey the classic figures and classic texts, since these provide the point of departure for contemporary research, both the deconstruction of received views and the reconstructions opened up by new discoveries and new methods.

24.1 SOURCES FOR THE STUDY OF EARLY MONASTICISM

Among monasticism's purported 'founders', two names appear repeatedly: Antony (c. 254–356) and Pachomius (c. 292–346). The *Life of Antony*, written around 358 by Athanasius, the much-exiled bishop of Alexandria, portrays its hero as an un-educated Egyptian peasant. After hearing the gospel story of Jesus and the rich young man, Antony sold what he had and adopted a life of stern asceticism. After a stint enclosed in a tomb, he moved to an abandoned desert fortress, where he lived as a hermit for 20 years. Disciples sought him out, and Athanasius portrays him emerging from the fortress 'as though from some sanctuary, a mystic initiate, mystery-taught and God-inspired' (*Vit. Ant.* 14). Athanasius had a knack for folk-loric narrative, and casts Antony as a fearless hero who, with equal ease, charmed crocodiles and learned philosophers, and whose preternatural powers enabled him to peer into the future and fend off the fiercest demons. Moderns read this as hagiography, not history, but the *Life's* influence on the history of monasticism was immense and immediate. It popularized monastic ideals and desert spirituality across the Empire, and sparked imitators (e.g. Jerome's *Life of Paul of Thebes*). It also provoked conversions. In the *Confessions*, Augustine reports how Antony's story helped spark his decisive conversion in 386. Modern textbooks routinely—but *inaccurately*—speak of Antony as 'the first monk' and 'the founder of Christian monasticism'. He was neither, as we shall see.

Textbooks routinely contrast Antony the hermit with Pachomius, whom they routinely—and *inaccurately*—describe as the 'founder of cenobitic monasticism'. More precisely, Pachomius was an organizational pioneer who, between 330 and 345, established a remarkable confederation of large monasteries, known as the *koinōnia* ('fellowship'), in Upper Egypt and composed the first known monastic rule. His life was celebrated in a series of biographies, edited in the 390s and preserved in Greek and in dialects of Coptic. We also have letters and addresses attributed to Pachomius and to his successors, Theodore and Horsiesius. Two other monastic pioneers lionized in early sources are Macarius the Egyptian (d. 390), who founded the monastic settlement of Scetis, what is now Wādī al-Natrūn, west of the Nile (and still a major centre of Coptic monasticism); and Amoun (d. 347), founder of the cenobitic monastery of Nitria and its austere offshoot, Kellia, both in Lower Egypt.

A key source is the *Apophthegmata Patrum* (*Sayings of the Fathers*), an anthology of terse anecdotes and memorable sayings from (mostly) Egyptian monastic leaders active from the 330s to the 460s. Its 1000+ stories and sayings illustrate life especially at Scetis, where monks lived as hermits from Monday to Friday and gathered on weekends for the eucharist and common meals. The *Apophthegmata's* anecdotes often portray a young monk approaching an *abba* (monastic elder), begging him for a 'word'—that is, a prophetic insight into his calling or his deepest struggles. One version of the *Apophthegmata* has anecdotes arranged under chapter headings such as 'progress in perfection', 'interior peace' (*hesychia*), 'compunction' (*penthos*), 'fornication', 'discernment', 'hospitality', 'obedience', 'charity', 'unceasing prayer', 'visions'. These headings give clues to what the early monks numbered as the critical issues in monastic living.

Very different in accent are the 'histories'. The anonymous *History of the Monks in Egypt*, composed around 400, is a travelogue recounting a pilgrimage through Egypt taken by seven Palestinian monks in 394. It strings together anecdotes about remarkable hermits, healers, and holy men, accenting their aptitude for miracles. Another compendium is the *Lausiac History*, which has seventy snapshot biographies of (mostly Egyptian) holy men and women. Its author, Palladius (*c.* 363–431), a native of Galatia, travelled to Egypt in the early 390s, settling as a monk in Nitria and Kellia. He left around 400—probably because of the Origenist controversy—and was ordained a bishop by John Chrysostom. These two narratives provide glimpses of the wide-ranging experiments in monastic lifestyle: desert solitaries, of course, but also virgins walled up in tombs, clusters of ascetics dotting the Nile marshes or ringing populous villages, and even whole towns, like Oxyrhynchus, teeming with monks. Both works highlight John of Lycopolis, a hermit-prophet, who, from his cell's window, dispensed oracles to crowds of pilgrims and oversaw a community of attendant monks.

Desert tales and desert spirituality were translated to the Latin West especially by John Cassian (d. 435). Born probably in Scythia, Cassian became a monk in Bethlehem and moved to Egypt in 385, settling in Scetis. Around 400—perhaps because of the Origenist controversy—he left for Constantinople, where Chrysostom ordained him a deacon. Around 415, he settled in Massilia (modern Marseilles), founded two monasteries, and forged close contacts with Gallic bishops and with the monks of the island monastery of Lérins. To these, he dedicated his two major works, the *Institutes* and the *Conferences*. The *Institutes* surveys monastic basics: garb, psalmody, instruction of newcomers, and remedies against the eight vices. The *Conferences* is Cassian's *magnum opus*, nearly 900 pages in modern editions, and claims to record twenty-four conversations with leading Egyptian masters, each centred on a core theme: e.g. purity of heart, discernment, renunciation, unceasing prayer, chastity, biblical interpretation. Because Benedict, in his *Rule*, legislated that his monks read Cassian, Cassian's teachings became a mainstay of western medieval monasticism.

While many famous monks and many early texts are associated with Egypt, monasticism was an international movement from the outset. Cappadocia was an early centre. Its leading figure was Basil of Caesarea (330–79). After studies in Athens, he toured monastic sites in Mesopotamia, Syria, Palestine, and Egypt. In 357, on family estates in Pontus, he began his first monastic venture. After ordination as presbyter and, then, bishop of Caesarea, he brought his ascetic vision to the city, establishing and guiding local monasteries. He sought to harness ascetic currents and integrate them into the wider Church. He was critical of anchorites, insisting that 'nothing is so characteristic of our nature as to associate with one another, to need one another and to love our kind' (*Long Rules*, 3). As bishop, he helped institutionalize Christian charity, founding hospitals for the poor, hospices for pilgrims, soup kitchens for the hungry—creating a sizeable urban sector known as the Basiledios. He called on monks to combine contemplation with a life of service, articulating his vision in the *Asceticon*, whose major sections are the *Long Rules* and the *Short Rules*.

Basil was not alone in blending the roles of bishop and monk, legislator and theologian. They reappear in Augustine (354–430), who pioneered monastic experiments in North Africa, first on his family property in Thagaste and later in his episcopal seat of Hippo Regius. His *Rule* (*Praeceptum*), as well as various letters and treatises, articulated norms for communities under his authority. Nothing captures the spirit of Augustine's monastery better than the *Rule*'s opening: 'The chief motivation for your sharing life together is to live harmoniously in the house and to have one heart and one soul seeking God. Do not call anything your own; possess everything in common' (Lawless 1987: 80–1). Augustine's stated model was the Jerusalem community of Acts 4, and his accent was decidedly communitarian. The lifestyle, while austere, lacked the ascetical athleticism of the East. It was a learned place, with a well-stocked library, and became (though not by design) a training centre for future North African bishops. Centuries later, Augustine's *Rule* was resurrected as the constitutional basis for medieval orders such as the Augustinians and the Dominicans.

In Gaul, an early figure was Martin of Tours (d. 397), an ex-soldier from Pannonia, who established hermitages at Ligugé (near Poitiers) and later near Tours. After election as bishop, he reverted to a monastic lifestyle, setting up a hermitage at nearby Marmoutier, where disciples joined him to create a thriving colony of hermits. Our main source is the hagiographic *Life of Saint Martin* composed by his disciple and defender, Sulpicius Severus (d. 420). Paulinus of Nola (355–431), a friend of Sulpicius and Martin, was prominent in Italy. A native of Aquitaine and ex-governor of Campania, Paulinus renounced politics and spectacular wealth—a gesture that won him international celebrity. Together with his wife Theresia, he established a monastery at the shrine of St Felix in Nola (near Naples), and there composed learned poetry and carried on a Mediterranean-wide correspondence with like-minded ascetics, such as Augustine and Jerome.

Syria had monastic roots as old as Egypt, but its most famous figure, Symeon the Stylite (*c.* 390–459), appears late. His 40-year career atop a pillar has tantalized Christian imaginations, ancient and modern. From ground level, he seemed poised halfway between earth and heaven, arms raised in prayer, a mediator between humankind and God. The best-known account of Symeon appears in Theodoret of Cyrrhus's *Religious History*. This also celebrates other Syrian monastics, wild men in a wild landscape, some grazing on grass like cattle, others chained to rocks or imprisoned in caves.

Other authors compiled similar regional histories to celebrate local holy men. Cyril of Scythopolis (*c.* 525–after 559) put together his *Lives of the Monks of Palestine*, a collection of biographies of seven monastic leaders active in the Judean desert from 400 to 550. Of these, the most famous was Sabas (d. 532), founder of the Great Laura. Another regional history is Pope Gregory the Great's *Dialogues*, which celebrates leading abbots of Italy. Of these, the most famous was Benedict of Nursia (*c.* 480–540). Benedict founded monasteries at Monte Cassino and Subiaco, but his lasting fame rests on his *Rule*. By the tenth century, it became *the* constitution for Western monasticism—though how it achieved its monopoly is a long and winding tale. The *Rule*, a work of legislative genius, is numbered among the oldest constitutions for community living in world history. Benedict set out guidelines that define monastic life to this day: a daily rhythm of chanting psalms (*opus Dei*, 'the work of God'), of meditative reading (*lectio divina*), and of manual labour (*opus manuum*). Moderation and a profound tolerance mark the *Rule* at every turn, and give a better glimpse of Benedict's personality than the extravagant miracle-worker portrayed in Gregory's *Dialogues*.

This is a very wide array of famous figures and famous texts—and, I should emphasize, these are only the best known. There are many, many others. Yet in standard textbooks on western civilization or in glossy one-volume surveys of church history one finds a strangely homogenized reconstruction. Textbook authors typically pick and choose from this stock list of monastic leaders and authors—who range about quite widely in geography, time, language, and culture—and weave an artificially seamless narrative, giving readers the false impression that Antony inaugurated Christian monasticism, that Pachomius concocted its cenobitic organization, that Egypt was monasticism's birthplace, that it spread from there to other parts of the Empire, both East and West, that it received its defining form in the Greek East from Basil and its defining form in the Latin West from Benedict.

Such a reconstruction is—to put it bluntly—wrong, and wrong on many scores. It glosses over the messy unevenness of the data; it presumes that monasticism has nameable founders and known origins; it presumes that sources about purported founders are neutral, unproblematic accounts; and it presumes that as one moves from landmark to landmark, and from region to region, there were clear, easily identifiable stages of development. Historical research is rarely simple, and charting historical developments rarely straightforward. This is certainly true of early monasticism, which, like many grass-roots movements, is full of quirky twists and turns, of frustrating gaps in the historical record, and of colourful figures whose moment of fame tells us little of local or regional realities. Like any movement of real historical significance, monasticism—both its rise and its fits-and-starts dissemination—defies easy generalizations. We must approach monastic sources with great modesty, recognizing that they are rarely interested in what interests us. To chart things, one needs, on the one hand, to dig deep into extant sources, and on the other, to scan widely, gathering the full compass of evidence—textual, archaeological, epigraphic, papyrological—and bring it all under a range of analytic methods and lenses. Then a rather different picture emerges, more subtle, more textured, more human. To get a sense of this, let us survey recent research on two key figures, Antony and Evagrius Ponticus.

24.2 RETHINKING ANTONY

Just as New Testament scholars have quested for the historical Jesus, so scholars of early Christianity have sought out the historical Antony. This century-long quest has been part demolition, part reconstruction. In its wake, textbook pronouncements about Antony as 'first monk' and 'father of Christian monasticism' seem not only out of date, but naive. The quest has made advances on various fronts.

A first set of breakthroughs has come from reading Athanasius's *Life of Antony* with a historical-critical eye. The *Life* is clearly no modern biography. Its fantastical world-view and hearsay anecdotes are far removed from modern biographer's concern with sober facts, verifiable chronology, and critical evaluation of sources. Athanasius's modern counterpart is an action movie like *Raiders of the Lost Ark*, in which viewers enjoy exotic tales of high adventure and pitched battles against supernatural forces. Early twentieth-century classics scholars such as Richard Reitzenstein uncovered how Athanasius drew on motifs from the ancient 'lives' (*bioi*, *vitae*) of philosophers. The scene of Antony stepping out from the desert fort matches nearly word for word a scene in Porphyry's *Life of Pythagoras*. This parallel is not plagiarism, but part of Athanasius's pointed artistic message: Antony too is a philosopher, a 'lover of wisdom', yet more heroic than any pagan; though an unschooled peasant, he is 'God-taught', and enjoys mystical insights from being an adept of the crucified God of the Christians. Athanasius says in the often overlooked epilogue that he wants the work read to pagans; in other words, he consciously crafted it as a tool for evangelization.

A second cluster of discoveries has come through reading the *Life of Antony* as an ecclesiological and a theological document. Athanasius, as bishop of Alexandria, was an astute and unbending ecclesiastical politician who faced a divided church both at home and abroad. At home, he clashed, sometimes violently, with schismatic Melitians. Abroad, he faced strong opposition to his management of the Egyptian church and to his theological commitments to the Council of Nicaea and its creed. These opponents he labelled 'Arians'—even if the anti-Nicene opposition was hardly a united front, and its theologies bore little resemblance to Arius's views. So it comes as no surprise that Athanasius's Antony denounces both Melitians and Arians in the sternest possible language. Nor is it a surprise that Athanasius's Antony expounds summaries of Athanasius's own sophisticated Nicene Christology. The *Life* thus served as propaganda for what David Brakke (1995) has called Athanasius's 'politics of asceticism'.

A third area of research has come from scholars exploring ancient translations of the *Life*. It was translated early, not only into Latin, but also into the languages of the Christian East. In 1980, René Draguet published a critical edition of the Syriac, and noted striking differences from the Greek text. Where the Greek (in a famous passage) says that 'the desert was made a city by monks who left their own people and registered themselves for citizenship in the heavens' (*Vit. Ant.* 14), the Syriac says that 'the life of the solitaries in the desert and the mountains began to multiply and increase in the manner of a tabernacle of the new world' (*Vit. Ant.* Syriac 14). Note the contrast: the Greek speaks of a desert city, an image both attractive and paradoxical to a city-dweller like Athanasius, while the Syriac uses 'tabernacle', a biblical and liturgical image. This and dozens of other discrepancies led Draguet to argue that the Syriac version comes not from Athanasius's Greek version, but from an earlier, cruder Greek version that retained Coptic phraseology, and that, therefore, Athanasius was not the *Life*'s original author, but its redactor. This thesis set off an intriguing scholarly dispute, as to whether or in what sense Athanasius was author. Draguet's views did not, in the long run, win over many, but he and others who argued against Athanasian authorship forced scholars to re-evaluate the question (Lorenz 1989; Brakke 1994). Defenders noted evidence both external and internal. As for external, they cited how soon after its publication other ancient authors—Gregory of Nazianzus, Jerome, the Greek *Life of Pachomius*—attributed it to Athanasius. As for internal evidence, they compared the *Life* with Athanasius's theological works and showed linked themes, even identical phraseology. Few now question Athanasius's authorship, but scholars acknowledge that he drew on oral sources and perhaps written ones, likely from his friend and Antony's one-time disciple Serapion of Thmuis.

These three clusters of studies concentrated on the *Life of Antony* itself. But Antony makes an appearance in many early monastic texts. In the 1930s and 1940s, scholars such as Hermann Dörries (1949) contrasted the sayings of Antony in the *Apophthegmata* with Athanasius's report. In the *Apophthegmata*, Antony denounces neither Melitians nor Arians; he makes no pronouncements on the intricacies of Nicene theology, but teaches a simpler, blunter faith. Where the Antony of the *Life* fearlessly faces down demonic assaults, the Antony of the *Apophthegmata* is more human, more vulnerable. He gets depressed; he struggles with boredom; he anguishes about the justice of God in a world divided between rich and poor. Such contrasts led Dörries and others to argue that the *Apophthegmata* better preserved the teachings of the historical Antony. This view has, in turn, met challenges as scholars recognize that the *Apophthegmata* has its own editorial biases and silences.

Exploration of alternative Antonys has continued. In his *On Illustrious Men*, Jerome mentioned that Antony had written seven letters in Coptic, and that he had seen Greek translations of these. The seven letters that Jerome knew seem to have been preserved. There are fragments in Coptic, one complete letter preserved in Syriac, and a complete, if muddled, version in Latin, but the best text is an ancient translation in Georgian, preserved at Saint Catherine's Monastery in Sinai. This version was published in 1955 by Gérard Garitte, but received scant attention until 1995, when Samuel Rubenson argued not only for the *Letters'* authenticity but also showed how their authenticity radically altered how early monastic history should be read. Rubenson's work is a *tour de force*, deftly moving between a formidable array of ancient languages and intricate manuscript traditions. Rubenson argues that the *Letters*, not Athanasius's *Life* or the *Apophthegmata*, give us the most accurate image of the historical Antony. They show that Antony, far from being illiterate, was conversant with Greek philosophy and favoured Origenist views, including Origen's bold hypotheses on the pre-existence of souls. In other words, Athanasius's portrait of the God-taught illiterate is inaccurate; so too is the *Apophthegmata's* portrait of a theology-free Antony. Rubenson has been criticized for exaggerating the intellectual sophistication of the *Letters*; and in an age in which pseudonymous works proliferated, it is not untenable that the *Letters* came from Origenist circles in the desert who conveniently ascribed them to Antony. Still, most scholars accept Rubenson's basic arguments for the *Letters'* authenticity, and to some extent, his wider conclusions.

One final area of research touches on the common, but inaccurate claim that Antony was the 'founder of Christian monasticism'. Not even Athanasius claimed that Antony was the first. He portrays the young Antony apprenticing himself to an 'old man' who had 'practiced the solitary life from his youth' (*Vit. Ant.* 3). That, if true, pushes back monastic origins to the mid-third century at the very least. But who was this unnamed teacher of Antony, this 'man of zeal', as Athanasius calls him? Or, more to the point, how common were such edge-of-the-village ascetics? Interesting perspectives on this came when a papyrus, *P. Coll. Youtie 77*, was published in 1977. It preserves a legal petition, dated June 324, filed by one Aurelius Isidorus, who complains that, as he led a cow out of his fields, his rival attacked him, beating him with a club, and would have killed him if not for the intervention of 'the deacon Antoninus and the monk Isaac' (Judge 1977). This mundane legal document is extraordinary because it is the oldest surviving text to use the word 'monk' (*monachos*). Edwin Judge, in a path-breaking study, used this papyrus to explore the wider phenomenon of *apotaktikoi* ('renouncers'), so often mentioned in fourth-century papyri. These were ascetic solitaries who, like early Christian virgins and widows, lived in or near villages and towns, and while they may have renounced marriage and practised ascetical routines, remained respected figures within local churches. This casts new light on Antony and the desert movement. Antony's innovation is not renunciation as such, but its desert locale (Goehring 1999: 21–32). I should add that it seems highly unlikely that *all* desert monks took their cue from Antony. The movement is simply too widespread geographically. It is better to speak of Antony neither as founder nor innovator, but as a *symbol* of an innovation.

24.3 REDISCOVERING EVAGRIUS PONTICUS

In my initial survey of famous figures, a notable name was absent: Evagrius Ponticus (345–99). It is a name only slowly making its way into reference works and surveys of church history. The rediscovery of Evagrius is a remarkable tale, and illustrates how scholars are akin to detectives: both question witnesses; both dig up buried clues; both chase down obscure leads. Scholars, like detectives, are in the business of solving mysteries, and the mystery here is a case of a missing person.

Here is the story. If, in 1900, one had asked an erudite church historian who Evagrius was, he would have replied that we know little: a hodge-podge of Evagrius's proverbs survives; Palladius's *Lausiac History* gives snippets of his biography; Socrates' *Ecclesiastical History* lists titles of his books; Evagrius (along with Origen and Didymus the Blind) was posthumously condemned for heresy by the Council of Constantinople in 553. Interesting titbits, but these give little clue to his historical significance. That would soon change. In 1912, Wilhelm Frankenberg published ancient Syriac translations of Evagrius's works, together with a facing retroversion into Greek to piece together what Evagrius's original texts may have looked like. In 1923, Robert Melcher demonstrated that among Basil of Caesarea's writings, *Letter* 8—famous in the development of the doctrine of the Trinity—was authored not by Basil, but Evagrius. In 1930, Maurice Viller proved that the seventh-century theologian Maximus the Confessor was deeply indebted to Evagrius's theology—even though Maximus labelled Evagrius a heretic—and that via Maximus, Evagrius's ideas subtly but profoundly shaped Orthodox mystical theology. In 1936, Salvatore Marsili proved that Evagrius had equally influenced monasticism in the Latin West. He showed that John Cassian, who so powerfully shaped medieval Benedictine spirituality, had lifted, without acknowledgement, his key ideas directly from Evagrius.

Breakthroughs and discoveries kept coming. In 1934, Irénée Hausherr published studies on *De oratione* (*Chapters on Prayer*), a mystical treatise attributed for centuries to Nilus of Ancyra and famously anthologized in the *Philokalia*. Hausherr, drawing on ancient translations into Syriac and Arabic, showed that Evagrius, not Nilus, was the true author. In 1952, Antoine Guillaumont announced the discovery of a manuscript in the British Museum of an unexpurgated Syriac version of Evagrius's *Kephalaia gnostica* (*Gnostic Chapters*). With this he demonstrated that Evagrius held the Origenist views ascribed to him in the conciliar condemnation of 553. By the mid-twentieth century, scholars realized that Evagrius was 'one of the most important names in the history of spirituality' (Bouyer 1963: 381); 'he is the almost absolute ruler of the entire Syriac and Byzantine mystical theology, and ... has influenced in a decisive manner Western ascetical and mystical teaching as well' (von Balthasar 1965: 183).

So who was Evagrius? He grew up in Pontus (northern Turkey, near the Black Sea), the son of a Christian bishop. He was ordained lector by Basil of Caesarea, and deacon by Gregory of Nazianzus. He followed Gregory to Constantinople and earned fame for his skilled defence of the emerging orthodox view on the Trinity. He was almost certainly present when the Council of Constantinople of 381 put together the version of the Nicene Creed recited today. Not long after this, he fell in love with a married woman. After a dream-vision, he broke off the affair and fled the imperial capital for Jerusalem, where he came under the sway of Melania the Elder, an aristocrat who founded a Latin-speaking monastery on the Mount of Olives. Melania convinced him to adopt monastic life, and sent him to friends in Egypt. In 383, Evagrius settled at Amoun's monastery at Nitria. Two years later he moved on to the more austere settlement of Kellia, where he spent the remainder of his life. He did his monastic apprenticeship under two leading desert fathers: Macarius the Egyptian and Macarius the Alexandrian. Evagrius was a natural leader and soon headed a circle of intellectual monks and became renowned for his skills in the discernment of spirits. A long-overlooked *Life of Evagrius*, penned by Palladius and preserved only in Coptic, offers glimpses of his routine at Kellia: 'This was [Evagrius's] practice: The brothers would gather around him on Saturday and Sunday, discussing their thoughts with him throughout the night, listening to his words of encouragement until sunrise. And thus they would leave rejoicing and glorifying God, for Evagrius' teaching was very sweet' (trans. Vivian 2004: 17). He made his living as a copyist and calligrapher—a monastic occupation common in the Middle Ages, but rare in this period. His death in 399 saved him from persecution. Later that year, Theophilus, bishop of Alexandria, turned against Evagrius's friends and followers, branding them as heretical Origenists and chasing them out of Egypt. This crisis, the so-called Origenist controversy, had international repercussions, pitting monks against one another in Egypt, Palestine, and the Latin West, and leading ultimately to the downfall of the monk-bishop of Constantinople, John Chrysostom.

Research on Evagrius's biography led to a major archaeological find. In 1964, Antoine Guillaumont discovered the buried ruins of Kellia, where Evagrius had spent much of his monastic career. Archaeological teams from France and Switzerland eventually uncovered a great sprawl of hermitages scattered over 49 square miles (Guillaumont 1991; Orban 1993). The hermitages are large rectangular compounds, enclosed with mud-brick walls, so that when seen from the air, they form a giant checkerboard across the desert's surface. Within each compound, one finds the abba's personal cell abutting one corner. Typically it had several rooms: an oratory, a kitchen, storage bins, and a bedroom. Interior walls were of mud-brick, covered with a whitewash glaze and often decorated with depictions of lions, camels, or birds, as well as an array of crosses painted in red and gold. In most compounds, one finds remains of a well and irrigation channels, presumably for a garden. Some compounds have a second smaller cell, presumably for a disciple. A gatehouse controlled entrance into individual compounds. Because most hermitages date from the mid-sixth century, it is hard to know how well their design reflects Kellia as Evagrius knew it.

Greater insights have come from excavating Evagrius's complex writings. Here, too, Antoine Guillaumont has been at the forefront of Evagrian studies, producing critical editions, translations, and theological analyses. Scholars now recognize that Evagrius, whose contributions had been forgotten for centuries, was not only one of the earliest, but also one of the most comprehensive theoreticians of monasticism. He divided monastic life into two phases. The first was *praktikē*, the life of ascetic practice. He presumed that his monastic readers were accomplished practitioners of ascetical disciplines—fasting, celibacy, poverty, psalm-singing—and so his reflections focus on the deeper chemistry of these disciplines, on their medicinal power to heal what ails the monk's soul. He stressed that the real task was to gain mastery over passions that distorted both the monk's quest for God and his life in community. Evagrius was an astute psychologist, and developed intricate analyses of eight demon-inspired compulsions (*logismoi*): gluttony, fornication, greed, depression, anger, boredom (*acēdia*), vainglory, and pride. His teachings on these passed to the Latin West via Cassian and became, with slight modification, the famous seven deadly sins. Evagrius argued that diligent monks could, with time, attain a measure of control over compulsions and arrive at a state of passionlessness (*apatheia*), which, in turn, gives birth to selfless loving (*agapē*). This marked one's entrance into a second mature phase of monastic life: *gnostikē*, or life of mystical knowledge. The monk, with both effort and grace, comes to see God's vivid presence both in the cosmos and in history. Evagrius was one of the earliest advocates of unceasing wordless and imageless prayer, and speaks of how, at peak moments, the monk catches glimpses of the sapphire light of the Trinity reflected in the pinnacle of his mind (Harmless and Fitzgerald 2001; Stewart 2001).

The English-speaking world has been surprisingly slow to pick up on these advances. In 1972, John Eudes Bamberger, a disciple of Thomas Merton, published an English translation of Evagrius's *Praktikos* and *Chapters on Prayer*. Recent years have seen an upswing in technical scholarly studies (Casiday 2004), but only in 2003 did a complete English translation of Evagrius's ascetical works become available (Sinkewicz).

24.4 REMAPPING THE LANDSCAPE

These overviews of research on Antony and Evagrius illustrate the ebb and flow of scholarly discovery and insight. Virtually every monastic pioneer and every classic text has undergone similar challenge, rediscovery, and rethinking. In the last 50 years, scholarly excavations have radically reconfigured the landscape of early monasticism. The old landmarks may still be standing, but they look different—on the one hand, restored to more subtle colouration and, on the other, set amid new landmarks and against much more variegated environs. It is difficult to do justice to the extraordinary breadth of contemporary research, but what follow are a few highlights in the redrawn map.

24.4.1 Rewriting the Who's Who

Various biases skewed reconstructions of early monasticism. Sometimes the bias was linguistic. Before the twentieth century, scholars rarely studied sources beyond the traditional Greek and Latin; but as more and more scholars mastered the languages of the Christian East—Syriac, Armenian, Coptic, Ethiopic, Arabic—a vast library of new texts has come to light, and with these, fresh perspectives on the wider world of early monasticism. Some, such as the Coptic *Virtues of Abba Macarius the Great*, offer alternative readings of famous figures; others, such as the Ethiopic *Collectio Monastica* or the Syriac *Asceticon* of Isaiah of Scetis, preserve oral traditions of great antiquity and offer fresh perspectives on the *Apophthegmata* (Harmless 2000); still others, such as the Syriac *Discourses* of Isaac of Nineveh (half the collection was rediscovered in 1983), offer a rich monastic spirituality, rivalling the better-known achievements of Basil and Cassian (Alfeyev 2000).

Few instances reveal this linguistic bias more than the rediscovery of Shenoute of Atripe (*c.* 348–*c.* 464). Shenoute's name never appears in classic Greek and Latin sources, but we now recognize that he was a pivotal figure. He spent decades as abbot of the White Monastery, outside Akhimim in Upper Egypt, and had several thousand monks, both men and women, under his authority. He was a brilliant stylist in Coptic, but only recently has the dishevelled welter of manuscripts that preserve his writings begun to be sorted out (Emmel 2004). Scholars have just begun a thorough study of his many-sided career as abbot and rural evangelist, as heresy-hunter and pagan demolitionist, as exegete and literary artist.

Other little-explored sources in Greek and Latin are still being collated and gradually published in critical editions. One example: between 1997 and 2002, the Sources Chrétiennes published a sprawling correspondence, nearly 850 letters, of two sixth-century leaders of Palestinian monasticism, Barsanuphius and John of Gaza. The two—referred to as 'the Great Old Man' and 'the Other Old Man'—lived as enclosed hermits in Gaza and, from their dark cells, directed a monastic community. The two hermits met the wider world via a single intermediary, Abba Seridos, who passed on brief notes written in response to questions of enquirers. The back and forth of question and answer is so detailed that one can literally chart the spiritual ups and downs of ancient directees and glimpse how ancient masters practised the art of spiritual direction. A selection has been translated into English (trans. Chryssavgis 2003), but analysis of this rich corpus has only begun (Hevelone-Harper 2005).

24.4.2 Recovering Silenced Voices

There were other biases. Often classic texts systematically excised memories of individuals and groups on grounds of orthodoxy. The case of Evagrius illustrates this, but his excision is only one of many. Scholars have worked to undo this historical amnesia, to recover suppressed memories and silenced voices. For example, Jean Gribomont in the 1950s demonstrated that Basil of Caesarea's monastic innovations owe much to Eustathius of Sebaste (*c.* 300–*c.* 377). Eustathius had begun organizing ascetic communities in his native Armenia in the 330s. Study of Basil's letters reveals how he was under Eustathius's sway, and how much he owed him for a conception of monasticism that wedded community life with service to the poor. In the 370s, the bond between disciple and mentor broke down irreparably. The cause was largely theological. Eustathius was a Homoiousian and refused to call the Holy Spirit 'God', while Basil had become a committed Nicene and was forging his famous defence of the Spirit's divinity. As Augustine Holmes has noted, 'Eustathius was thus pushed into a heretical twilight, and official history came to regard Basil as the founder of monasticism in Asia Minor' (2000: 42).

Sometimes whole groups have been excluded. Athanasius's Antony railed bitterly against schismatic Melitians, but it was not until H. I. Bell published a cache of papyri in 1924 that scholars realized that the Melitians too had monks and monasteries. In 1987, another Melitian papyrus archive was published, enabling scholars to reconstruct life in the economically vigorous and spiritually respected Melitian monastic community at Hathor. These finds provided James Goehring with material to argue that the Melitians had created a confederation of monasteries even earlier than the reputed cenobitic 'founder' Pachomius (Goehring 1999: 187–95). Scholars have also recovered teachings of another condemned group, the Messalians, active in Syria in the late fourth century and the source of the influential *Pseudo-Macarian Homilies* (Stewart 1991).

24.4.3 Re-cognizing Women's Monasticisms

Advances in women's studies and feminist theory have helped redress a major historiographic imbalance: the neglect and underestimate of women's contributions to early monasticism. There is a new appreciation of formidable women, such as Melania the Elder, who founded the vibrant Latin-speaking double monastery on the Mount of Olives and whose patronage supported Rufinus's scholarly translation projects; and Paula, who did much the same for Jerome in Bethlehem; and Olympias, whose benefactions were key to Chrysostom's work in Constantinople. At the forefront of these scholarly advances has been Elizabeth Clark, who, for more than 25 years, has combined great erudition with an adventurous willingness to explore cutting-edge sociological and literary methodologies to restore women's contributions to their rightful contours. She has demonstrated (among many matters) how asceticism became a paradoxical vehicle for women's advancement (Clark 1986: 175–208).

Other path-breaking perspectives have come from Susanna Elm, whose *Virgins of God* (1994) explores women's monasticisms in Cappadocia and Egypt. Especially remarkable has been her study of Macrina, Basil of Caesarea's older sister. Elm has reconstructed the evolution of Macrina's community, showing that what began in the 350s as an experiment in family asceticism became by 380 a burgeoning monastic community. In the process, Elm demonstrates that Basil was not even the earliest monastic 'founder' in his own family, let alone in Cappadocia.

Scholars have also explored the way in which women's foundations prospered alongside the better-documented male foundations: e.g. how Pachomius's sister led a large women's community in the Pachomian *Koinonia* and how Shenoute exercised less than complete control over independent-minded superiors of the women's community in the White Monastery (Krawiec 2002). Here, as elsewhere, harvesting neglected texts such as the Pseudo-Athanasian *Life and Activity of Blessed Syncletica* (Castelli, in Wimbush 1990: 266–311) has prompted new assessments while feminist readings have deconstructed old narratives and opened fresh perspectives (Cloke 1995).

24.4.4 Charting Diversities

Taxonomies of monastic lifestyles appeared early: in Jerome's letters, in Cassian's *Conferences*, and most famously in Benedict's *Rule*. 'Acceptable' monks were either anchorites or cenobites. This traditional taxonomy masks the extraordinary diversity of actual monastic practice. It fails to account for organizational patterns of well-known monastic communities: both the monasteries of Scetis and Kellia in Egypt and the Great Laura in Palestine mixed weekday solitude with weekend communal liturgies and meals. Less well known, and much less studied, is the pattern of enclosed hermits like John of Lycopolis and Barsanuphius of Gaza who doubled as prophetic oracles and abbots of attached communities. In Syria, stylites and other eccentrics would get the best publicity, but the local ascetic norm was better represented by the sons/daughters of the Covenant (*bnay/bnāt qyāmā*), who pledged celibacy at baptism, lived in town, and ministered in local churches. Their spirituality would be celebrated in Ephrem the Syrian's poetry. One controversial lifestyle was that of the holy wanderers, whom Benedict labelled 'gyrovagues' and denounced as 'slaves to their own wills and gross appetites' (*Rule* 1. 10–12). Recent studies have rescued them from this *damnatio memoriae*, showing not only how they saw themselves fulfilling Jesus' mandates for the apostolic life, but also how their monasticism threatened political codes and ecclesiastical interests (Caner 2002; Dietz 2005). A lifestyle that seemed odd at the time was that of the bishop-monk. One glimpses its novelty in Ambrose's panegyric on Eusebius of Vercelli, who, he claims, 'was the first one in the west to unite these different disciplines; while living in the city he observed the monastic way of life, and he governed the church while keeping a sober fast' (Ambrose, *Ep.* 66). This double lifestyle later became normative in the Byzantine East and routine in the medieval West, but its normalcy emerged only fitfully and with conscious ideological construction (Sterk 2004).

Recent scholarship has highlighted diversity not only of lifestyle, but of locale. Athanasius's exotic image of monks forging cities in the desert has skewed popular perceptions, both ancient and modern (Goehring 2005). James Goehring has stressed that Pachomius established his *koinōnia* not in the desert, but along the Nile. The Pachomians turned deserted villages into thriving communities and carried on a brisk commerce, sailing ships up and down the Nile (Goehring 1999: 89–109). Sailor-monks is not our typical image, but it is a healthy corrective. Sulpicius Severus claims that Martin of Tours sought a retreat 'equal to the solitude of the desert', but his hermitage was a forested enclave overlooking 'a gentle bend in the river Loire' (*Vita s. Martini*, 10). Other Gallic monks, such as Eucherius of Lyons, wrote glowing panegyrics on desert monasticism, but the heart of Gallic monasticism was the exquisite island of Lérins, just off the French coast near Cannes (Leyser 1999). Much monasticism was urban or suburban, a fact only fitfully acknowledged in traditional sources. The Pachomians set up the monastery of the Metanoia in the heart of downtown Alexandria. Augustine reports stumbling on thriving monastic communities in Milan and Rome (*Mor. eccl.* 1. 33. 70). But urban monasticism took root especially in Constantinople, where it could cause even a monk-bishop like Chrysostom political grief (Dagron 1970).

Scholars now stress the geographical specificity of early monasticism (Clark 1999: 27–33). One still stumbles across out-of-date claims that 'monastic life began in Nitria in the first decades of the 4th century and spread rapidly throughout Egypt, Syria, Palestine, and Asia Minor' (Laboa 2004: 40). Scholars long ago realized that this 'big bang theory' of monastic origins (as Goehring (1999: 13) has aptly called it) is wrong. They have detected complex ascetical undercurrents and experiments at work in various locales in the third century. Once Christianity was legalized in the early fourth century, independent regional monasticisms surfaced simultaneously. There is the old saying that 'all politics is local'; the same could be said of monasticism.

24.4.5 Renegotiating the Social World

Recent years have witnessed a methodological shift, what has been called 'the cultural turn in late ancient studies' (Martin and Miller 2005), in which scholars, drawing on analyses from social history, anthropology, psychology, sociology, and economics, have charted the social moorings of monasticism. Few studies capture this trend better or have been as influential as Peter Brown's 1971 essay 'The Rise and Function of the Holy Man in Late Antiquity'. When first published, it seemed 'a lightning bolt out of the sky' (Elm 1998: 343). Brown focuses on Syria, its holy men, and their extreme gestures. Why, he asks, did they achieve political prominence? The answer, he argues, lay in the patronage system of the late Empire. He details the everyday role of village patrons, who settled lawsuits, won tax relief, got debts cancelled, and mediated feuds with nearby villages. Brown argues that to grasp the sudden rise of the holy man, one must see his 'histrionic feats of self-mortification . . . as a long drawn-out, solemn ritual of dissociation—of becoming a total stranger' (Brown 1982: 131). Holy men—most dramatically Symeon on his pillar—embodied a paradox: that those who had withdrawn from society and its webs of patronage became, in turn, the ultimate patron.

An avalanche of studies have followed Brown's lead, prompting scholars to explore little-read lives of saints and leading them to plot out how miracle-working monks, beneath their pieties and ritual gestures, reveal an intricately coded language of power. There have been shifts and reassessments as new methods have been deployed. Brown himself has shifted, exploring the holy man as 'exemplar' (1983) and as 'arbiter of the holy' (1995). Brown's work has also sparked critique; for all his attention to the social world, he overlooked 'the stylite's defining ritual context': 'the eucharistic liturgy of the gathered body of the church, the collective presentation of the Christian salvation drama' (Harvey 1998: 525).

24.5 FUTURE DIRECTIONS

Some monks, like John of Lycopolis, earned fame for their prophetic foresight. I have no oracular skills, but let me suggest several possible directions for monastic studies. First, I suspect that the most labour-intensive—and most fruitful—work will continue to be textual archaeology, digging up overlooked texts and recovering lost voices. New data are always needed. We also need a new synthesis, a comprehensive history that does better justice to the 'many-ness' of early monasticism, both within regions and between them; that integrates suppressed voices and roads not taken; that roots monks, monasteries, and movements in the intricacies of local politics and local social realities; that charts how chance intersections transmuted local experiments into international convergences.

One urgent issue is a conceptual one: How do asceticism and monasticism fit together? In the last 35 years, scholars of early Christianity have produced brilliant and wide-ranging studies under the nomenclature of 'asceticism'. This has helped uncover a vast array of pre-institutional, uninstitutionalized, and suppressed experiments in monastic living. But this research trend has sometimes, perhaps unconsciously, relegated 'monasticism' to the less exciting, more staid forms. Future scholarship may wish to re-evaluate realities behind the nomenclature, to understand how, within the wider umbrella of Christian asceticism, monasticism finds its proper specificity.

While 'asceticism' has been much studied, sexual renunciation and, to a lesser extent, fasting have received the lion's share of attention. There has been insufficient study of the no less dramatic renunciation of family and dispossession of property. While modern scholars have written much on ascetic bodies, ancient monks stressed that the real struggle was not with the body, but the heart. Yet one sees few studies on asceticism of heart, few studies on humility or obedience or combating anger. Strictly speaking, asceticism was the negative pole of what ancient theorists like Evagrius called *praktikē*; its positive side was the quest for virtue. Early monks worried much about the slow, unswerving, unspectacular routine of cultivating virtues—charity, forgiveness, peace-making. Cultivating virtue may not sound very monastic; it may sound too much like ordinary Christian living. But early Christian monks were in the business of doing ordinary Christianity extraordinarily well. If we do not see this, we do not see them.

Suggested Reading

For a detailed introduction to the literature of early monasticism, see my *Desert Christians* (Harmless 2004), which tries to balance historical, literary, and theological perspectives. Each chapter also includes annotated bibliographies, as well as appendices with excerpts from papyri and from little-known Greek, Latin, Coptic, Syriac, and Ethiopic texts. For a survey of recent research methods and findings, see Clark (1999: 14–42); for a sampling of essays illustrating the diversity of methodological practice and scope of concern, see Wimbush and Valantasis (1995). James Goehring has both charted developments and pioneered new perspectives; see his collected essays (1999). Few scholars combine erudition and lucid prose better than Antoine Guillaumont; see especially the two collections of his wide-ranging essays (1979, 1996). Individual monastic classics, both original texts and English translations, are listed below. Given the lack of a comprehensive, up-to-date history of early monasticism, it is best to work from the many excellent, but more narrowly focused, studies of individual figures, texts, and regions. For a good start on Athanasius and Antony, see Brakke (1995); on the *Apophthegmata Patrum*, see Burton-Christie (1993) and Gould (1993); on Evagrius, see Dysinger (2005); on Cassian, see Stewart (1998); on Basil of Caesarea, see Rousseau (1994) and Holmes (2000); on Augustine of Hippo, see Lawless (1987); on Martin of Tours, see Stancliffe (1983); on Paulinus of Nola, see Lienhard (1977) and Trout (1999); on women's monasticisms, see Clark (1986) and Elm (1994); on Palestine, see Hirschfeld (1992) and Binns (1994); on Syria, see Vööbus (1958, 1988) and Griffith (1994, 1995); on Italy, see Jenal (1995); on the early medieval West, see Dunn (2000).

Bibliography

Primary Sources: Texts and Translations

Antony, *Epistulae*. Georgian text: G. Garitte (ed.), *Lettres de Saint Antoine: version géorgienne et fragments coptes*, CSCO 148–9 (Louvain: Secretariat du Corpus SCO, 1955). Eng. trans.: S. Rubenson, *The Letters of St. Antony: Monasticism and the Making of a Saint*, SAC (Minneapolis: Fortress Press, 1995). Also D. J. Chitty, *The Letters of St. Antony the Great* (Fairacres, Oxford: S.L.G. Press, 1974).

Apophthegmata Patrum. Alphabetical Collection: Greek text: J.-B. Cotelier (ed.) (1647), repr. in PG 65: 71–440. Eng. trans.: B. Ward, *The Sayings of the Desert Fathers: The Alphabetical Collection*, CS 59 (Kalamazoo, Mich.: Cistercian Publications, 1975). Systematic Collection: Greek text and French trans.: J.-C. Guy (ed.), *Les Apophtegmes des Pères, Collection systématique*, SC 387 (Books I–IX), 474 (Books X–XVI), 498 (Books XVII–XXI) (Paris: Éditions du Cerf, 1993, 2003, 2005).

ATHANASIUS, *Vita Antonii.* Greek text and French trans.: G. J. M. Bartelink (ed.), *Athanase d'Alexandrie: Vie d'Antoine*, SC 400 (Paris: Éditions du Cerf, 1994). Eng. trans.: R. C. Gregg, *Athanasius: The Life of Antony and the Letter to Marcellinus*, CWS (Mahwah, NJ: Paulist Press, 1979). Syriac version: R. Draguet (ed.), *La vie primitive de saint Antoine conservée en syriaque*, CSCO 417–18 (Louvain: Secrétariat du Corpus SCO, 1980).

AUGUSTINE, *De opere monachorum.* Latin text: J. Zycha (ed.), CSEL 41 (Vienna: Temsky, 1900). Eng. trans.: S. Muldowney, *The Work of Monks*, in R. J. Deferrari (ed.), *Saint Augustine: Treatises on Various Subjects*, FC 16 (New York: Fathers of the Church, Inc., 1952), 321–94.

—— *Regula.* Latin text: L. Verheijen (ed.), *La Règle de saint Augustin*, i: *Tradition manuscrite* (Paris: L'Institut d'études augustiniennes, 1967). Eng. trans. and comm.: G. Lawless, *Augustine of Hippo and his Monastic Rule* (Oxford: Clarendon Press, 1987).

BARSANUPHIUS and JOHN OF GAZA, *Quaestiones et responsiones.* Greek text and French trans.: F. Neyt, P. de Angelis-Noah, and L. Regnault, *Barsanuphe et Jean de Gaza: Correspondance*, SC 426, 427, 450, 451, 468. (Paris: Éditions du Cerf, 1997–2002). Eng. trans.: J. Chryssavgis, *Letters from the Desert: Barsanuphius and John: A Selection of Questions and Responses* (Crestwood, NY: St Vladimir's Seminary Press, 2003).

BASIL OF CAESAREA, *Regulae Fusius Tractatae et Regulae Brevius Tractatae*, PG 31: 889–1305. Eng. trans.: M. Monica Wagner, *Basil of Caesarea: Ascetical Works*, FC 9 (New York: Fathers of the Church, Inc., 1950).

BENEDICT, *Regula.* Latin text and English trans.: T. Fry (ed.), *RB 1980: The Rule of Benedict* (Collegeville, Minn.: Liturgical Press, 1980).

CYRIL OF SCYTHOPOLIS, *Vitae.* Greek text: E. Schwartz, ed. *Kyrillos von Skythopolis*, TU 49/2 (Leipzig: Heinrichs, 1939). Eng. trans.: R. M. Price, *Cyril of Scythopolis: Lives of the Monks of Palestine*, CS 114 (Kalamazoo, Mich.: Cistercian Publications, 1989).

EVAGRIUS PONTICUS, *De oratione.* Greek text: PG 79: 1165–1200. Eng. trans.: R. E. Sinkewicz, *Evagrius of Pontus: The Greek Ascetic Corpus*, OECS (Oxford: Clarendon Press, 2003), 183–209. Also J. Eudes Bamberger, *Evagrius Ponticus: Praktikos and Chapters on Prayer*, CS 4 (Kalamazoo, Mich.: Cistercian Publications, 1971), 43–80.

—— *Gnostikos.* Greek text and French trans.: A. Guillaumont (ed.), *Évagre Le Pontique: Le Gnostique ou a celui qui est devenu digne de la science*, SC 356 (Paris: Éditions du Cerf, 1989).

—— *Kephalaia gnostica.* Syriac text and French trans.: A. Guillaumont (ed.), *Les six centuries des 'Kephalaia gnostica' d'Evagre le Pontique: édition critique de la version syriaque commune et édition d'une nouvelle version syriaque*, PO 28.2 (Paris: Firmin–Didot, 1958).

—— *Praktikos.* Greek text and French trans.: A. Guillaumont and C. Guillaumont (eds), *Évagre le Pontique, Traité Pratique ou le Moine*, SC 170–1 (Paris: Éditions du Cerf, 1971). Eng. trans.: R. E. Sinkewicz, *Evagrius of Pontus: The Greek Ascetic Corpus*, OECS (Oxford: Clarendon Press, 2003), 91–114. Also J. Eudes Bamberger, *Evagrius Ponticus: Praktikos and Chapters on Prayer*, CS 4 (Kalamazoo, Mich.: Cistercian Publications, 1971), 1–42.

—— *Skemmata.* Greek text: J. Muyldermans, 'Evagriana', *Mus* 44 (1931): 37–68, 369–83. Eng. trans. with commentary: W. Harmless and R. R. Fitzgerald, ' "The Sapphire Light of the Mind": The *Skemmata* of Evagrius Ponticus', *TS* 62 (2001): 498–529.

GREGORY OF NYSSA, *Vita Sanctae Macrinae.* Greek text with French trans.: P. Maraval (ed.), *Grégoire de Nysse: Vie de sainte Macrine*, SC 178 (Paris: Éditions du Cerf, 1971). Eng. trans.:

J. M. Peterson, *Handmaids of the Lord: Contemporary Descriptions of Feminine Asceticism in the First Six Christian Centuries*, CS 143 (Kalamazoo, Mich.: Cistercian Publications, 1996), 51–66.

GREGORY THE GREAT, *Dialogi*. Latin text with French trans.: A. de Vogüé (ed.), *Grégoire le Grand: Dialogues*, SC 251, 260, 265 (Paris: Éditions du Cerf, 1978–80). Eng. trans.: O. J. Zimmerman, *Gregory the Great: Dialogues*, FC 39 (New York: Fathers of the Church, Inc., 1959).

Historia monachorum in Aegypto. Greek text with French trans.: A-J. Festugière (ed.), *Historia Monachorum in Aegypto: Éditions critique du text grec et traduction annotée*, Subsidia Hagiographica (Brussels: Société des Bollandistes, 1971). Eng. trans. N. Russell, *Lives of the Desert Fathers*, CS 34 (Kalamazoo, Mich.: Cistercian Publications, 1981).

ISAAC OF NINEVEH, *Discourses*. Syriac text of Part I: P. Bedjan (ed.), *Mar Isaacus Ninevita: De perfectione religiosa* (Leipzig: Otto Harrassowitz, 1909). Eng. trans.: A. J. Wensinck, *Mystic Treatises of Isaac of Ninevah* (Amsterdam: Koninklijke Akademie van Wetenschappen, 1923); Mary Hansbury, *St. Isaac of Nineveh: On the Ascetical Life* (Crestwood, NY: St Vladimir's Seminary Press, 1989). Syriac text of the newly discovered Part II, with Eng. trans.: S. Brock (ed.), *Isaac of Nineveh: 'The Second Part', Chapters IV–XLI*, CSCO 554–5 (Louvain: Peeters, 1995).

ISAIAH OF SCETIS, *Asceticon*. Syriac text: R. Draguet, *Les cinq recensions de l'Asceticon syriaque d'abba Isaïe*, CSCO 289–90, 293–4 (Louvain: Secrétariat du Corpus SCO, 1968). Eng. trans. of Greek version: J. Chryssavgis and P. Penkett, *Abba Isaiah of Scetis: Ascetic Discourses*, CS 150 (Kalamazoo, Mich.: Cistercian Publications, 2002).

JEROME, *Vita s. Pauli*. PL 23. 17–60. Eng. trans.: C. White, *Early Christian Lives* (London: Penguin, 1998), 75–85.

JOHN CASSIAN, *Collationes*. Latin text and French trans.: E. Pichery (ed.), *Jean Cassien: Conférences*, SC 42, 54, 64 (Paris: Éditions du Cerf, 1955–9). Eng. trans.: B. Ramsey, *John Cassian: The Conferences*, ACW 57 (New York: Paulist Press, 1997).

——*De institutis cenobiorum*. Latin text and French trans.: J-C. Guy (ed.), *Jean Cassien: institutions cénobitiques*, SC 109 (Paris: Éditions du Cerf, 1965). Eng. trans., B. Ramsey, *John Cassian: The Institutes*, ACW 58 (New York: Paulist Press, 2000).

JOHN CHRYSOSTOM, *Adversus oppugnatores vitae monasticae*, PG 47. 319–86. Eng. trans.: David G. Hunter, *A Comparison between a King and a Monk / Against the Opponents of the Monastic Life: Two Treatises by John Chrysostom* (Lewiston, NY: Edwin Mellen, 1988), 77–176.

——*Comparatio regis et monachi*, PG 47. 387–92. Eng. trans.: David G. Hunter, *A Comparison between a King and a Monk / Against the Opponents of the Monastic Life: Two Treatises by John Chrysostom* (Lewiston, NY: Edwin Mellen, 1988), 69–76.

PALLADIUS, *Historia Lausiaca*. Greek text: C. Butler (ed.), *The Lausiac History of Palladius*, TaS 6. 1–2 (1898, 1904). Eng. trans.: R. T. Meyer, *Palladius: Lausiac History*, ACW 34 (New York: Paulist Press, 1964). Coptic text: É. Amélineau, *De Historia Lausiaca, quaenam sit huius ad Monachorum Aegyptiorum historiam scribendam utilitas* (Paris, 1887). Eng. trans.: T. Vivian, *Four Desert Fathers: Pambo, Evagrius, Macarius of Egypt, and Macarius of Alexandria: Coptic Texts Relating to the* Lausiac History *of Palladius* (Crestwood, NY: St Vladimir's Seminary Press, 2004).

PAULINUS OF NOLA, *Epistulae*. Latin text: G. de Hartel, *Sancti Pontii Meropii Paulini Nolani epistulae*, CSEL 29 (Vienna: 1894). Eng. trans.: P. G. Walsh, *The Letters of Paulinus of Nola*, ACW 35–6 (Westminster, Md.: Newman Press, 1966–7).

PSEUDO-ATHANASIUS, *Vita sanctae Syncleticae*. Greek text: PG 28. 1488–1557. Eng. trans.: E. A. Castelli, 'Pseudo-Athanasius, *The Life and Activity of Holy and Blessed Teacher Syncletica*', in V. L. Wimbush, *Ascetic Behavior in Greco-Roman Antiquity*, SAC (Minneapolis: Fortress Press, 1990), 266–311. Also E. Bryson Bongie, *The Life of Blessed Syncletica by Pseudo-Athanasius* (Toronto: Peregrina Publishing Co., 1996).

SULPICIUS SEVERUS, *Vita Martini*. Latin text with French trans. and commentary: J. Fontaine, *Sulpice Sévère: Vie de Saint Martin*. SC 133–5 (Paris: Éditions du Cerf, 1967–9). Eng. trans.: C. White, *Early Christian Lives* (London: Penguin, 1998), 131–59.

THEODORET OF CYRRHUS, *Historia religiosa*. Greek text with French trans.: P. Cavinet and A. Leroy-Molinghen (eds.), *Theodoret de Cyr: Histoire des Moines de Syrie*, SC 234, 257 (Paris: Éditions du Cerf, 1977–9). Eng. trans. R. M. Price, *Theodoret of Cyrrhus: A History of the Monks of Syria*, CS 88 (Kalamazoo, Mich.: Cistercian Publications, 1985). Also R. Doran, *The Lives of Simeon Stylites*, CS 112 (Kalamazoo, Mich.: Cistercian Publications, 1992).

Verba Seniorum. Latin text: H. Rosweyde (ed.) (1615), repr. in PL 73. 855–1022. Eng. trans. B. Ward, *The Desert Fathers: Sayings of the Early Christian Monks* (London: Penguin, 2003).

Vita Pachomii (Bohairic). Coptic text: L-T. Lefort (ed.), *Sancti Pachomii vitae bohairice scripta*, CSCO 89 (Vienna: Sécretariat du Corpus SCO, 1953). Eng. trans.: Armand Veilleux, *Pachomian Koinonia: The Lives, Rules, and Other Writings of Saint Pachomius*, CS 45 (Kalamazoo, Mich.: Cistercian Publications, 1980), 23–295.

Vita Pachomii (Greek). Greek text: F. Halkin (ed.), *Sancti Pachomii Vitae Graecae*, Subsidia Hagiographica, 19 (Brussels: Société des Bollandistes, 1932). Eng. trans.: Armand Veilleux, *Pachomian Koinonia: The Lives, Rules, and Other Writings of Saint Pachomius*, CS 45 (Kalamazoo, Mich.: Cistercian Publications, 1980), 297–423.

Vita Sanctae Olympiadis. Greek text with French trans.: A-M. Malingrey (ed.), *Jean Chrysostom: Léttres à Olympias; Vie anonyme d'Olympias*, SC 13bis (Paris: Éditions du Cerf, 1968). Eng. trans.: E. A. Clarke, *Jerome, Chrysostom, and Friends* (New York: Edwin Mellen Press, 1979), 107–57.

Studies and Collections

ALFEYEV, H. (2000), *The Spiritual World of Isaac the Syrian*, CS 175 (Kalamazoo, Mich.: Cistercian Publications).

BELL, H. I. (1924), *Jews and Christians in Egypt: The Jewish Troubles in Alexandria and the Athanasian Controversy, Illustrated by Texts from Greek Papyri in the British Museum* (London: British Museum).

BINNS, J. (1994), *Ascetics and Ambassadors of Christ: The Monasteries of Palestine, 314–631*, OECS (Oxford: Clarendon Press).

BOUYER, L. (1963), *The Spirituality of the New Testament and the Fathers*. Vol. i of *History of Christian Spirituality* (New York: Desclée Co.).

BRAKKE, D. (1994), 'The Greek and Syriac Versions of the *Life of Antony*', *Mus* 107: 29–53.

—— (1995), *Athanasius and the Politics of Asceticism*, OECS (Oxford: Clarendon Press).

BROCK, S. (1987) (trans.), *The Syriac Fathers on Prayer and the Spiritual Life*, CS 101 (Kalamazoo, Mich.: Cistercian Publications).

BROWN, P. (1971), 'The Rise and Function of the Holy Man in Late Antiquity', *JRS* 61: 80–101; repr. in *Society and the Holy in Late Antiquity* (Berkeley: University of California Press, 1982), 103–52.

BROWN, P. (1983), 'The Saint as Exemplar in Late Antiquity', *Representations*, 1/2: 1–25.

——(1988), *The Body and Society: Men, Women, and Sexual Renunciation in Early Christianity* (New York: Columbia University Press).

——(1995), *Authority and the Sacred: Aspects of the Christianisation of the Roman World* (Cambridge: Cambridge University Press).

——(1998), 'The Rise and Function of the Holy Man in Late Antiquity, 1971–1997', *JECS* 6: 353–76.

BURTON-CHRISTIE, D. (1993), *The Word in the Desert: Scripture and the Quest for Holiness in Early Christian Monasticism* (New York: Oxford University Press).

CANER, D. (2002), *Wandering, Begging Monks: Spiritual Authority and the Promotion of Monasticism in Late Antiquity*, Transformation of the Classical Heritage, 33 (Berkeley: University of California Press).

CANIVET, P. (1977), *Le monachisme syrien selon Théodoret de Cyr*, Théologie historique, 42 (Paris: Beauchesne).

CASIDAY, A. (2004), 'Gabriel Bunge and the Study of Evagrius Ponticus', *St Vladimir's Theological Quarterly*, 48: 249–97.

CHITTY, D. (1966), *The Desert A City: An Introduction to the Study of Egyptian and Palestinian Monasticism under the Christian Empire* (London: Basil Blackwell).

CLARK, E. A. (1986), *Ascetic Piety and Women's Faith: Essays on Late Antique Christianity*, Studies in Women and Christianity, 20 (Lewiston, NY: Edwin Mellen Press).

——(1992), *The Origenist Controversy: The Cultural Construction of an Early Christian Debate* (Princeton: Princeton University Press).

——(1999), *Reading Renunciation: Asceticism and Scripture in Early Christianity* (Princeton: Princeton University Press).

CLOKE, G. (1995), *This Female Man of God: Women and Spiritual Power in the Patristic Age, AD 350–450* (New York: Routledge).

DAGRON, G. (1970), 'Les moines et la ville: Le monachisme à Constantinople jusqu'au Concile de Chalcédon (451)', *Travaux et Mémoires*, 4: 229–76.

DESPREZ, V. (1998), *Le monachisme primitif: Des origines jusqu'au concile d'Éphèse*, Spiritualité orientale, 72. (Bégrolles-en-Mauges: Abbaye de Bellefontaine).

DIETZ, M. (2005), *Wandering Monks, Virgins, and Pilgrims: Ascetic Travel in the Mediterranean World, A.D. 300–800* (University Park, Pa.: Pennsylvania State University Press).

DÖRRIES, H. (1949), 'Die Vita Antonii als Geschichtesquelle', *Nachrichten der Akademie der Wissenschaften in Göttingen*, 14: 357–410; repr. in *Wort und Stunde: Gesammelte Studien zur Kirchengeschichte des vierten Jahrhunderts* (Göttingen: Vandenhoeck & Ruprecht), i. 145–224.

DUNN, M. (2000), *The Emergence of Monasticism: From the Desert Fathers to the Early Middle Ages* (Oxford: Blackwell).

DYSINGER, L. (2005), *Psalmody and Prayer in the Writings of Evagrius Ponticus*, Oxford Theological Monographs (New York: Oxford University Press).

ELM, S. (1994), *'Virgins of God': The Making of Asceticism in Late Antiquity*, Oxford Classical Monographs (New York: Oxford University Press).

——(1998), 'Introduction: The Rise of the Holy Man in Late Antiquity, 1971–1997', *JECS* 6: 343–52.

EMMEL, S. (2004), *Shenoute's Literary Corpus*, CSCO 599–600 (Leuven: Peeters).

FESTUGIÈRE, A. J. (1959), *Antioche païenne et chrétienne: Libanius, Chrysostome et les moines de Syrie*, Bibliothéque des Écoles françaises d'Athènes et de Rome, 194 (Paris: Éditions de Boccard).

GOEHRING, J. (1999), *Ascetics, Society, and the Desert: Studies in Early Egyptian Monasticism* (Harrisburg, Pa.: Trinity Press International).

—— (2005), 'The Dark Side of Landscape: Ideology and Power in the Christian Myth of the Desert', in Martin and Miller (2005), 136–49.

GOULD, G. E. (1993), *The Desert Fathers on Monastic Community*, OECS (Oxford: Clarendon Press).

GRIBOMONT, J. (1953), *Histoire du texte des Ascétiques de s. Basile*, Bibliothèque du Muséon, 32 (Louvain: Publications universitaires).

—— (1984), *Saint Basile: évangile et église*, 2 vols., Spiritualité orientale, 36–7 (Bégrolles-en-Mauges: Abbaye de Bellefontaine).

GRIFFITH, S. H. (1994), 'Julian Saba, "Father of the Monks" of Syria', *JECS* 2: 185–216.

—— (1995), 'Asceticism in the Church of Syria: The Hermeneutics of Early Syrian Monasticism', in V. Wimbush and R. Valantasis (eds.), *Asceticism* (New York: Oxford University Press), 220–45.

GUILLAUMONT, A. (1962), *Les 'Kephalaia gnostica' d'Evagre le Pontique et l'histoire de l'origénisme chez les grecs et chez les syriens*, Patristica Sorbonensia, 5 (Paris: Éditions du Seuil).

—— (1979), *Aux origenes du monachisme chrétien: Pour une phénoménologie du monachisme*, Spiritualité orientale, 30 (Bégrolles-en-Mauges: Abbaye de Bellefontaine).

—— (1991), 'Kellia', in A. S. Atiya (ed.), *The Coptic Encyclopedia* (New York: Macmillan), v. 1396–1410.

—— (1996), *Études sur la spiritualité de l'Orient chrétien*, Spiritualité orientale, 66 (Bégrolles-en-Mauges: Abbaye de Bellefontaine).

HARMLESS, W. (2000), 'Remembering Poemen Remembering: The Desert Fathers and the Spirituality of Memory', *CH* 69: 483–518.

—— (2001), 'Salt for the Impure, Light for the Pure: Reflections on the Pedagogy of Evagrius Ponticus', *StPatr* 37: 514–26.

—— (2004), *Desert Christians: An Introduction to the Literature of Early Monasticism* (New York: Oxford University Press).

—— and FITZGERALD, R. R. (2001), 'The Sapphire Light of the Mind: The *Skemmata* of Evagrius Ponticus', *TS* 62: 493–529.

HARVEY, S. A. (1990), *Asceticism and Society in Crisis: John of Ephesus and the Lives of the Eastern Saints*, Transformation of the Classical Heritage, 18 (Berkeley: University of California Press).

—— (1998), 'The Stylite's Liturgy: Ritual and Religious Identity in Late Antiquity', *JECS* 6: 523–39.

HAUSHERR, I. (1960), *Les leçons d'un contemplatif: Le traité de l'oraison d'Evagre le Pontique* (Paris: Beauchesne).

HEVELONE-HARPER, J. (2005), *Disciples of the Desert: Monks, Laity, and Spiritual Authority in Sixth-Century Gaza* (Baltimore: Johns Hopkins University Press).

HIRSCHFELD, Y. (1992), *The Judean Monasteries in the Byzantine Period.* (New Haven: Yale University Press).

HOLMES, A. (2000), *A Life Pleasing to God: The Spirituality of the Rules of St. Basil*, CS 189 (Kalamazoo, Mich.: Cistercian Publications).

JENAL, G. (1995), *Italia ascetica atque monastica: Das Asketen- und Mönchtum in Italien von den Anfängen bis zur Zeit der Langobarden (ca. 150/250–604)* (Stuttgart: A. Hiersemann).

JOHNSTON, W. W. (2000), *Encyclopedia of Monasticism*, 2 vols. (Chicago: Fitzroy Dearborn).

JUDGE, E. A. (1977), 'The Earliest Use of Monachos for "Monk" (*P. Coll. Youtie 77*) and the Origins of Monasticism', *JAC* 20: 72–89.

KRAWIEC, R. (2002), *Shenoute and the Women of the White Monastery: Egyptian Monasticism in Late Antiquity* (New York: Oxford University Press).

LABOA, J. (2004) (ed.), *The Historical Atlas of Eastern and Western Monasticism* (Collegeville, Minn.: The Liturgical Press).

LAWLESS, G. (1987), *Augustine of Hippo and His Monastic Rule* (New York: Oxford University Press).

LEYSER, C. (1999), ' "This Sainted Isle": Panegyric, Nostalgia, and the Invention of Lerinian Monasticism', in W. E. Klingshirn and M. Vessey (eds.), *The Limits of Ancient Christianity: Essays on Late Antique Thought and Culture in Honor of R. A. Markus* (Ann Arbor: University of Michigan Press), 188–206.

——— (2001), *Authority and Asceticism from Augustine to Gregory the Great*, OHMS (Oxford: Clarendon Press).

LIENHARD, J. T. (1977), *Paulinus of Nola and Early Western Monasticism*, Theophaneia, 28; Beiträge zur Religions- und Kirchengeschischte des Altertums. (Cologne: Peter Hanstein Verlag).

LORENZ, R. (1989), 'Die griechische *Vita Antonii* des Athanasius und ihre syrische Fassung: Bemerkungen zu einer These von R. Draguet', *ZKG* 100: 77–84.

MARTIN, D. B., and MILLER, P. C. (2005) (eds.), *The Cultural Turn in Late Ancient Studies: Gender, Asceticism, and Historiography* (Durham, NC: Duke University Press).

ORBAN, M. (1993) (ed.), *Déserts Chrétiens d'Égypte* (Nice: Culture Sud).

PATRICH, J. (1995), *Sabas, Leader of Palestinian Monasticism: A Comparative Study in Eastern Monasticism* (Washington: Dumbarton Oaks).

ROUSSEAU, P. (1994), *Basil of Caesarea*, Transformation of the Classical Heritage, 20 (Berkeley: University of California Press).

——— (1999), *Pachomius: The Making of a Community in Fourth Century Egypt*, Transformation of the Classical Heritage, 6, rev. edn. (Berkeley: University of California Press).

RUBENSON, S. (1995), *The Letters of St. Antony: Monasticism and the Making of a Saint*, SAC (Minneapolis: Fortress Press).

STANCLIFFE, C. (1983), *St. Martin and His Hagiographer: History and Miracle in Sulpicius Severus* (Oxford: Clarendon Press).

STERK, A. (2004), *Renouncing the World Yet Leading the Church: The Monk-Bishop in Late Antiquity* (Cambridge, Mass.: Harvard University Press).

STEWART, C. (1991), *Working the Earth of the Heart: The Messalian Controversy in History, Texts and Language to A.D. 431* (Oxford: Clarendon Press).

——— (1998), *Cassian the Monk* (New York: Oxford University Press).

——— (2001), 'Imageless Prayer and the Theological Vision of Evagrius Ponticus', *JECS* 9: 173–204.

TROUT, D. E. (1999), *Paulinus of Nola: Life, Letters, and Poems*, Transformation of the Classical Heritage, 27 (Berkeley: University of California Press).

Vogüé, A. de (1991–8), *Histoire littéraire du mouvement monastique dans l'antiquité*, 5 vols. (Paris: Cerf).

——and Bunge, G. (1994), *Quatre Érmites Égyptiens: D'après les fragments coptes de l'Histoire Lausiaque*, Spiritualité orientale, 60 (Bégrolles-en-Mauges: Abbaye de Belle-fontaine).

Von Balthasar, H. U. (1965), 'The Metaphysics and Mystical Theology of Evagrius', *Monastic Studies*, 3: 183–95. Eng. trans. of 'Metaphysik und Mystik des Evagrius Ponticus', *Zeitschrift für Aszeze und Mystik*, 14 (1939): 31–47.

Vööbus, A. (1958–88), *A History of Asceticism in the Syrian Orient*, 3 vols. CSCO 184, 197, 500 (Leuven: Peeters).

Wimbush, V. L. (1990) (ed.), *Ascetic Behavior in Greco-Roman Antiquity: A Sourcebook*, SAC (Minneapolis: Fortress Press).

——and Valantasis, R. (1995) (eds.), *Asceticism* (New York: Oxford University Press).

PART VI

EXPRESSIONS OF
CHRISTIAN
CULTURE

CHAPTER 25

EARLY CHRISTIAN APOCRYPHAL LITERATURE

STEPHEN J. SHOEMAKER

THE apocryphal literature of early Christianity consists primarily (but not exclusively) of narrative traditions about the life and teaching of Jesus, his family, and his apostles, as well as letters, apocalyptic visions, and other-worldly journeys attributed to these individuals that fall outside the biblical canon. These writings, however, do not always (as is often maintained) correspond to the literary genres of the New Testament; nor are they even restricted to 'New Testament' themes. Although some early Christian apocrypha do in fact have generic similarities to the canonical texts, others clearly do not, and apocryphal literature is neither defined by nor limited to the genres of the New Testament. Many apocrypha, it is true, bear titles reflecting the biblical genres—acts, gospels, apocalypses, etc.; but when examined from either a literary or a historical standpoint, it is obvious that these writings do not simply mimic the genres of the New Testament. The apocryphal acts of the apostles, for instance, have more in common from a literary perspective with the canonical gospels than with the canonical Acts, and the so-called *Protevangelium of James* was not in antiquity identified as a gospel but was instead known as the *Birth of Mary* (Bovon and Geoltrain 1997: pp. xliv–xlvi). Consequently, in recent years scholars have laboured to remove the early Christian apocrypha from the shadow of the New Testament writings and to free them from the biblical concepts and categories that have heretofore dominated their study and interpretation.

The production of apocrypha in antiquity was of course not limited to early Christianity or to Christian themes. The various expressions of ancient Judaism also produced a wealth of extra-biblical writings about the many personages of the Hebrew scriptures. These apocrypha, perhaps more commonly known today as the 'pseudepigrapha', were also embraced by various early and medieval Christian groups, who made these writings their own, often redacting them according to Christian interests and concerns. In fact, we owe the preservation of these ancient Jewish 'apocrypha' primarily to the interest of Christians, rather than to rabbinic Judaism, which favoured instead the authority of its own extra-biblical traditions, the oral Torah. But it is also the case that the Christians of antiquity and the Middle Ages continued to develop new stories about the various figures and events of the Hebrew scriptures, and many of the 'pseudepigrapha' are in fact Christian, rather than Jewish, creations. Consequently, these 'Jewish' apocrypha should unquestion-ably be numbered among the apocrypha of the Christian tradition: there is no viable reason to exclude from this category texts such as the *Ascension of Isaiah* and the *Life of Adam and Eve*, which were valued by Christians for the same literary, liturgical, and doctrinal purposes as were the *Acts of John* or the *Gospel of Peter*. Consequently, the apocryphal writings of early Christianity form a rather large and theologically diverse corpus that mirrors the variety of Jewish and Christian groups in late antiquity and the early Middle Ages that produced and used this literature.

25.1 THE PROBLEM OF TERMINOLOGY

Over the last decade, the terminology used to describe 'apocryphal' literature has come under scrutiny from a number of directions. These include the generic com-plexities of certain writings unearthed among the Dead Sea Scrolls, as well as a heightened concern in early Christian studies to radically rethink and interrogate the language deployed within the ancient Christian tradition to establish a discourse of theological truth, including especially the labels 'orthodoxy', 'heresy', and 'gnos-ticism' (e.g. Williams 1996; King 2003b). Inasmuch as the boundaries of the canon (which in part define the corpus of apocrypha) played a fundamental role in the creation of Christian orthodoxy, and, moreover, since many of the early Christian apocrypha are associated in one way or another with various heterodox Christian groups, it is no surprise that that use of term 'apocrypha' has come into question as a part of this effort to re-describe Christian origins.

The first significant moves toward developing new terminology for discussing this extra-biblical literature came primarily from scholars dealing with certain 'apocryphal' writings found among the library of the Jewish community at

Qumran, including the so-called *Genesis Apocryphon* and fragments of various other writings that present a reworking, rewriting, or paraphrase of texts and themes from the Hebrew Bible (Ginsberg 1967; Attridge *et al.* 1994; Broshi *et al.* 1995; Brooke *et al.* 1996; Brooke 2000). Other previously known early Jewish writings, such as the *Book of Jubilees* and Ps.-Philo (the *Liber Antiquitatum Biblicarum*), were also recognized as representing a rather similar phenomenon (Fisk 2001: 13–33), whose precise nature is somewhat misrepresented in identifying these texts as 'apocrypha'. In many instances, these 'rewritings' of the Bible are so closely related to the biblical text that it makes little sense to view them as distinctly separate texts; rather, they present many of the biblical traditions in parallel versions that often appear expanded or revised in comparison with the received text. It is important to note, however, that during the first and second centuries BCE, there was not always and everywhere a standard, normative text of the Hebrew scriptures that these authors would have consciously 'rewritten'. Instead, these traditions appear to represent a 'biblical' literature whose development is to some extent parallel with the traditional text of the Hebrew Bible (Talmon 2000: 157; Anderson 2000; Meier 2003: 57 n. 10). Consequently, the frequent use of the term 'rewritten Bible' to describe this material is in fact not altogether accurate, and has potentially misleading connotations. For this reason, the term 'parabiblical' literature is preferable, since this emphasizes in part the parallel development (and authority?) of these (now) extra-canonical traditions.

Very recently, a few North American scholars have begun to experiment with the possibility of extending the term 'parabiblical' more broadly, to serve as a somewhat less problematic label for discussing early Christian apocrypha as well as the extra-canonical literature of early Judaism.[1] The traditional term 'apocrypha', it has been suggested, is too intimately linked with 'heresy' and forgery in orthodox Christian discourse, and consequently, a new designation is required. Although scholars are just beginning to explore the possibilities and problems of re-describing Christian apocryphal literature as 'parabiblical', Annette Yoshiko Reed (2002) has presented a thoughtful preliminary essay on the subject that considers the applicability of this term for describing early Christian as well as Jewish apocrypha. It is perhaps still too early to pass judgement either favourably or negatively on this new approach, but the extension of the notion 'parabiblical' from the various examples of 'rewritten Bible' in early Judaism to encompass the entire corpus of early Jewish and Christian apocrypha is not without its difficulties.

While 'parabiblical' is a perfectly suitable moniker for a certain type of early Jewish literature—that is, the various 'rewritings' of the Bible mentioned above, such as *Jubilees*, Ps.-Philo, and the *Genesis Apocryphon*—it does not so accurately describe many other kinds of early Jewish apocrypha, let alone the diverse panoply of Christian apocryphal literature. The vast majority of this material is not in fact 'parabiblical' in the same way as the early Jewish 'rewritten Bible' literature; instead, many apocrypha expand considerably on the biblical narratives or fill in various missing pieces, while some Christian apocrypha have only the loosest relationship to the biblical traditions. Only certain early Christian writings, such as the *Gospel of Thomas*, the *Gospel of Peter*, Tatian's *Diatessaron*, and the *Secret Gospel of Mark* (if genuine), for example, represent something more or less equivalent to early Judaism's parabiblical literature (Junod 1992: 39–41; Kaestli 1996: 36–8). Yet, while some Christian apocrypha present traditions that were certainly parallel with the canonical traditions, such as the Nativity traditions of the *Protevangelium of James*, others clearly depend on the canonical writings, whose contents they have expanded and whose gaps they have filled, such as the *Infancy Gospel of Thomas* and 'Paul's' *Third Epistle to the Corinthians*. Still other texts show remarkably little contact with the traditions of the scriptures at all, as in the case of the apocryphal acts of the apostles (Junod 1992: 41–3; Kaestli 1996: 35–6). Thus, the fact that all of the literature classified as 'apocrypha' is not exactly parallel to the biblical writings in time, content, or purpose makes their identification as 'parabiblical' somewhat problematic.[2]

Furthermore, the designation of this literature as parabiblical has the unfortunate consequence of reinscribing the canonical writings as the theological and literary norms to which apocryphal texts must be compared and according to which they should be judged. That result runs counter to the general tendency of most contemporary scholarship on this topic, which has laboured intensively over the past two decades to bring an end to the evaluation of Christian apocrypha according to the 'standards' presented by the writings of the Bible, an orientation that was basic to most earlier scholarship on apocryphal literature (see the following section). The result of this older approach was a general view of apocrypha as both deviant and derivative from the normative texts of the canon, rather than as original literary creations that explore (often quite independently) many of the same events and characters described in the Bible. Only by abandoning this scriptural standard, which appears to be something of a vestige from the 'sola scriptura' mindset, can we begin to appreciate the highly varied purpose and function of many Christian apocrypha. Not everything that fell outside the scriptural canon was disregarded or denigrated by Christian orthodoxy: these writings were not merely 'deviant' scriptures, but often a valued and influential component of ecclesiastical tradition, and the conceptualization of apocrypha literature according to strictly biblical norms obscures this important aspect of their use (Bovon and Geoltrain 1997: pp. xxxiii–xxxiv; Picard 1999*a*; Bovon 1999*a*).

For example, a rather significant obstacle to re-conceiving the early Christian apocrypha as parabiblical literature is the nagging problem of how to distinguish Christian apocrypha from hagiography, especially from the third century on. If 'parabiblical' might in some respects be useful for rethinking the earliest Christian apocrypha in light of certain precedents within Judaism and their relation to the formation of the canon, such terminology becomes rather problematic for discussing this literature as the boundaries between apocrypha and hagiographical texts become quite blurred in late antiquity. In this era, the nature of Christian apocrypha and their relationship to other types of 'extra-canonical' literature is already such that the category 'parabiblical' to some degree obscures the complexities of a literary phenomenon that often is just as much 'parahagiographical'. Indeed, the complex and uncertain relationship between Christian apocryphal literature and hagiography has not yet been fully explored. Although scholars have often noted the difficulty of how to distinguish between the two categories, adequate criteria have not yet been articulated, and in some cases it is almost certainly pointless to try (Junod 1992: 27, 34–6; Markschies 1998: 117–19; Bovon 1999a, 1999b: 3–4; Mimouni 2002: 4–5; but see Schneemelcher 1989–90: i. 44, 48–51; English trans., 1991–2: i. 54, 57–60).

The liturgical use of many early Christian apocrypha further complicates the discrete classification of these writings. While certain apocryphal texts were undoubtedly used in worship by those communities judging them to be canonical, even within 'orthodox' Christianity, which excluded these writings from its Bibles, one finds widespread use of apocryphal materials as liturgical readings (Bovon and Geoltrain 1997: pp. xxviii, lii–liii; Bovon 1999a, 1999b: 3–15; Picard 1999b). Many Christian 'apocrypha' appear to have been composed deliberately for liturgical usage, and in other cases apocryphal texts were adopted for this purpose, often being 'rewritten' in the process. The various narratives of Mary's Dormition, for instance, illustrate the liturgical use of apocrypha, affording examples of both apocrypha specifically designed for liturgical use and the adaptation of earlier narratives for this purpose (Mimouni 1993a, b; Shoemaker 2002a: 32–66). Thus there is a certain irony that many of these 'apocrypha', although excluded from the official list of books authorized for reading in church services as 'scripture', eventually found their voice in Christian worship as liturgical readings. In the apocrypha, then, we have a literature that is not just 'parabiblical' but is often also hagiographical and liturgical all at once. To refer to this material as parabiblical obscures these other important roles of apocryphal literature in the Christian tradition: they are not merely rivals or reworkings of the canonical texts of the scriptures, but they are an important and often authoritative part of ecclesiastical tradition (Picard 1999a).

Furthermore, the designation of texts as 'apocryphal' in antiquity did not *always* connote the negative and heretical associations that certain church fathers sought (with more or less success) to establish. The Greek word ἀπόκρυφος simply means 'hidden' or 'secret', and its use to describe writings in the pre-Christian world generally had a positive sense, identifying their contents with esoteric wisdom. In early Judaism, for instance, the term 'hidden' as applied to books does not always have the pejorative sense that it was given by certain early Christian writers (Mimouni 2002: 13–15). Such 'hidden' writings stood outside of the canon, but this did not always preclude their reading: 4 Ezra (2 Esdras), for example, a Jewish apocryphon from the first century CE that subsequently became a canonical part of many Christian Bibles,[3] advises withholding extra-canonical 'sacred books' from the public, reserving them only for the learned (14: 45–7). Many early Christian groups similarly identified certain of their sacred writings as apocryphal—or 'secret'—books, in order to signify their revered status as works containing 'hidden mysteries' not intended for uninitiated readers. Several of the early church fathers, however, including especially Irenaeus, Tertullian, and Hippolytus, and later on Eusebius, Athanasius, and Augustine, turned this language against their more esoterically inclined rivals, redefining 'apocryphal' as equivalent in meaning to 'false' or 'forged', and thus imbuing it with the negative associations that persist today (Schneemelcher 1991–2: i. 14; Mimouni 2002: 15–17; Bertrand 2002; Le Boulluec 2002).

Yet this negative valence was not universally recognized, even among the church fathers (or the rabbis for that matter (Mimouni 2002: 15)). There were in fact early fathers who took a more accepting attitude toward the apocrypha, including Rufinus, and even Jerome and Athanasius on occasion. These fathers used the designation in a more neutral sense, characterizing apocryphal literature as writings that, while outside the canon of scriptures and therefore not divinely inspired or acceptable for reading in churches, could (and should) be read with profit by orthodox Christians for spiritual instruction (Jacobs 2000: 140–1; Brakke 1994: 397). Likewise, Priscillian of Avila, who is now seen as considerably less heretical than his opponents made him out to be (Burrus 1995), authored a compelling defence of apocrypha in the later fourth century. Although Priscillian's views on apocrypha played a not inconsiderable role in his condemnation, they are reasonably orthodox, in that he unequivocally recognized the boundaries of the established canon and did not seek to add apocryphal works to this authoritative collection. Rather, Priscillian argued for the value of reading apocrypha alongside the established canon, and he appealed to instances where the canonical texts refer to extra-canonical writings as evidence that the scriptures themselves authorized this practice. According to Priscillian, the very canon itself demands the careful and selective use of apocrypha by orthodox Christians (Jacobs 2000: 144–52; trans. Ehrman and Jacobs 2004: 427–33).

Yet, despite the fact that Priscillian's advocacy of apocrypha (or at least his opponents' representation of his position) contributed at least partially to his execution, views similar to his were common among the Christians of early Byzantium (Bovon 1999a).[4] It would appear that the anti-apocryphal rhetoric of certain church fathers did not always correspond with the real status of apocrypha in Christian churches. For instance, John of Thessalonica, bishop of that city during the early seventh century, writes the following about his use of an apocryphon of Mary's Dormition and Assumption as the basis for his homily commemorating this feast:

[A]fter those who had been present then [at the Virgin's Dormition] ... wrote about her consummation, later, some of the wicked heretics, introducing their tares, twisted the writings, and on account of this, our fathers abstained from these as unfit for the catholic church. ... But we do not spit on these truthful writings on account of their God-hated deceits, but cleansing the evil interpolations, we embrace these deeds of the saints as truly to the glory of God (*dorm. BMV A* (G3) 1).

(Jugie 1926: 376–7)

A similar attitude toward apocrypha appears in the seventh-century *Life of the Virgin* attributed to Maximus the Confessor, where the author (Maximus?) explains that in compiling this *vita* he has utilized a number of sources, including 'some things from apocryphal writings, namely, that which is true and without error and which has been accepted and confirmed by the...holy fathers' (Maximus the Confessor, *Life of the Virgin* 2 [van Esbroeck 1986: 4 (Geor) & 3 (Fr)]).[5] Comparable attitudes are present in western Christendom as well, and the Irish church in particular affords numerous examples of continued usage of apocryphal writings in a variety of ecclesiastical contexts (McNamara 1984: 1–12). For these and many other Christians, certain apocryphal writings were (and still are) an important, and even authoritative, part of the Church's tradition that should be consulted alongside the canonical writings.[6]

Altogether, despite the objections of a handful of influential church fathers, the apocryphal literature of early Christianity maintained a popular, if also ambiguous, status throughout history. As a result, the terms 'apocrypha' and 'apocryphal' were not always and only associated with heresy and forgery in Christian discourse. In addition to their early association with esoteric wisdom, these labels were also used in a more neutral sense as technical terms to describe non-biblical literature that could be read with profit by the faithful: it was important only to distinguish between 'heretical' and more 'orthodox' apocrypha and to avoid the former. This less virulent and even engaging attitude toward apocrypha is evident in a continuous tradition stretching from late antiquity to the sixteenth and seventeenth centuries, when both Catholics and Protestants alike were still able to find spiritual value in reading 'apocryphal' writings (Bovon and Geoltrain 1997: p. xxxiv; Backus 1998, 2002; Balley 2002).

Admittedly, 'apocrypha' is not an unproblematic term, but its history of usage in this less pejorative sense is often overlooked. Since this continues *faute de mieux* to be the most appropriate and accepted designation for the literature in question, it is important that we not abandon the label 'apocrypha' to the negative rhetoric of certain church fathers. Rather, their slanders should be countered by bringing to light the frequent non-pejorative use of both the term 'apocrypha' and apocryphal texts in the ancient and medieval Church. We must begin to better appreciate the positive roles that apocryphal texts played in Christian piety and culture, as well as their authoritative status as a part of tradition for many Christians (in the guise of liturgy and hagiography particularly). Only then will we recognize that in reality neither the 'apocrypha' nor their use were universally condemned in orthodox Christian discourse, resulting in a more complex and nuanced understanding of 'apocrypha' that balances some of the negative associations.[7] Nevertheless, it is important that efforts to search out better terminology for this literature should continue: the negative associations of 'apocrypha' and 'apocryphal' in contemporary usage are considerable, and perhaps a better designation remains to be discovered. But for the time being, 'apocrypha', despite its flaws, remains the preferred term for this type of Christian literature.

25.2 DEFINING 'CHRISTIAN APOCRYPHA'

While scholars of early Christianity are largely agreed on the continued use of the term 'apocrypha', the definition of apocrypha has been rather vigorously contested over the past two decades, with the result that the *opinio communis* appears to have settled on a new set of parameters for defining the corpus of Christian apocrypha. For much of the later twentieth century, Wilhelm Schneemelcher's definition of this literature held sway. Schneemelcher defined the 'New Testament Apocrypha' as follows:

The New Testament Apocrypha are writings which have not been received into the canon, but which by title and other statements lay claim to be of equal status (*gleichwertig*) to the writings of the canon, and which from the point of view of Form Criticism further develop and mould the literary genres (*Stilgattungen*) created and received in the NT, whilst foreign elements certainly intrude.

(1959–64: i. 6; English trans., 1963–5: i. 27, slightly modified)

Schneemelcher further limits such texts to the period prior to the closure of the New Testament canon, which he approximates to the fourth century. The 'so-called' apocrypha written after this time are not truly worthy of the name: only texts that were intended to be included in the canon (and thus were written prior to its closure) are, according to Schneemelcher, properly named 'apocrypha' (1959–64: i. 7, 17–18, 32–5; English trans., 1963–5: i. 28, 40–1, 60–4). For many years Schneemelcher's definition was widely accepted, and it was adopted by many other scholars, including Mario Erbetta (1966–81) and Luigi Moraldi (1971) in their Italian collections of apocrypha, as well as by Robert McL. Wilson in his article on Christian apocrypha in *TRE* 316–62.

Yet in 1983 Éric Junod issued an important challenge to this definition, questioning its validity on three main points (1983a: 409–14). First, Junod challenges Schneemelcher's assertion that an apocryphon, in order to be worthy of this title, must have claimed a status equal to the canonical writings, with pretensions to being included in the canon. Junod argues that this quality presents an especially poor criterion for defining the apocrypha, inasmuch as the 'intent' of a particular writing with respect to possible inclusion in the canon is rather difficult to ascertain. Moreover, if this standard were rigorously applied, it would in fact exclude most of the works included by Schneemelcher in his third edition of *Neutestamentliche Apokryphen* (a project that he inherited from Edgar Hennecke). Closely related to this is Junod's second objection: he rejects Schneemelcher's imposition of a chronological limit to the production of apocrypha. Since any text written after the third century could not have had the intention of entering the canon, which was effectively closed by this point, such texts may not, according to Schneemelcher's definition, be counted among the apocrypha. Junod argues instead that production of apocrypha is not bounded by time, but continued in the fourth, fifth, and sixth centuries, and even up until the present day. Finally, Junod criticizes Schneemelcher's limitation of apocrypha only to texts that reflect the literary genres attested in the New Testament. According to Junod, most apocrypha in fact have little or nothing to do with genres of the New Testament: for instance, many so-called gospels hardly reflect the New Testament genre.

Junod completes his challenge to Schneemelcher's definition of 'New Testament Apocrypha' by offering one of his own:

Anonymous or pseudepigraphical texts of Christian origin which maintain a connection with the books of the New Testament as well as the Old Testament because they are devoted to events described or mentioned in these books, or because they are devoted to events that take place in the expansion of events described or mentioned in these books, or because they focus on persons appearing in these books, or because their literary genre is related to those of the biblical writings.

(1983*a*: 412)

One can see from this definition that Junod envisions a much larger corpus of writings than Schneemelcher. Consequently, he advocates abandoning Schneemelcher's more restrictive term 'New Testament Apocrypha' and replacing it with 'early Christian apocrypha', a designation that reflects the more extensive collection of apocryphal literature he has in mind. Several key factors underlie this proposed change in terminology. On the one hand, Junod wants to separate the definition and conceptualization of apocrypha from both the generic restrictions of the New Testament and the historical limitations of the process of canonization imposed by Schneemelcher's definition. Junod calls attention to the fact that many apocrypha are far removed from the genres of the New Testament and also that the relation between individual apocrypha and the closure of the canon is quite varied, with some being more clearly affected by the canon's establishment than others. Furthermore, Junod's new terminology reflects his opening of the category to include writings related to the Hebrew scriptures that either were adopted by Christianity from early Judaism or are original Christian compositions on Old Testament themes. Junod qualifies his definition by explaining that a Christian apocryphon need not possess all these characteristics; nor will they all be found to the same degree in every text. He additionally cautions that the relationship between individual apocrypha and the writings of the Bible can at times be quite distant, and, as we have already noted, that the boundary between apocrypha and hagiography is often very difficult to trace.

Schneemelcher responds to Junod's new definition in the introduction to the fifth edition (as well as the corrected sixth edition) of his *Neutestamentliche Apokryphen* by expanding considerably upon his earlier discussion of the nature of apocrypha in the third (and fourth) edition (1989–90: i. 40–52; English trans., 1991–2: i. 50–61). There is not, however, much that is very new in Schneemelcher's reply. He continues to insist on the process of canon formation as the definitive criterion for identifying apocryphal texts. Although he softens somewhat his earlier views on the importance of New Testament genres and canonical intentions, these features remain essential components of his definition. Nevertheless, he adamantly maintains a limit of 300 CE for the production of apocrypha; only texts produced before this date can rightly be counted among the apocrypha. As Schneemelcher explains, this boundary is necessary to establish a divide between apocryphal literature (written before 300) and hagiography (written after 300). In this regard he additionally suggests the important influence of a new *Sitz im Leben* on the hagiographical writings of the fourth century and later: the emerging cult of the saints and nascent monasticism. He dismisses rather brusquely, however, Junod's proposal that apocrypha related to the traditions of the Hebrew scriptures should be included in this corpus, judging the idea 'not very sensible' (*wenig sinnvoll*). All in all, Schneemelcher's response essentially reiterates his previous views, only with greater verbiage, justifying his position largely through an appeal to the pressing need to distinguish apocrypha clearly from hagiography by maintaining a firm line in the sand at 300 CE.

In a more recent article, Junod responds at some length to Schneemelcher's renewed definition (1992: esp. 35–9; see also Kaestli 1996; Picard 1999b). Here Junod focuses squarely on their main points of difference: the significance of the process of canonization and the related limitation of the production of apocrypha to the period before 300. Perhaps most importantly, Junod rejects almost out of hand Schneemelcher's insistence that these strict criteria are essential for distinguishing between hagiography and apocrypha. Schneemelcher's solution is entirely arbitrary and overly simplistic, according to Junod. Merely establishing a boundary between the two types of literature around 300 is a rather artificial way of dealing with a very complex problem. Not surprisingly, scholarly consensus has moved rather decidedly toward Junod's views on this particular point (as indicated above), and there seems to be widespread acknowledgement among scholars of apocryphal literature that it is extremely difficult—and in many cases, impossible—to distinguish between apocrypha and hagiography. After all, the apostles and many other biblical figures were venerated as saints and martyrs from early on; consequently, it is rather difficult in many instances to explain how the 'acta' of an apostle differs in content and function from the 'vita' of a more recent saint. In some cases the difference is clear: for instance, certain genres, such as a *laudatio* or homily, belong more properly (but not exclusively!) to hagiographical literature. Yet the problem cannot be resolved by simplistically asserting (as does Schneemelcher) a rather arbitrary chronological divide between the two types of literature. Each text must be considered individually, and ultimately we must resign ourselves to the fact that in many cases it simply is not possible to classify a given writing as either strictly hagiographical or apocryphal.[8] Nevertheless, it is undoubtedly worth bearing in mind Schneemelcher's observation that the rise of the cult of saints and of monasticism to prominence in the Christian tradition during the fourth century presents a changed *Sitz im Leben* for the production of literature: the impact of these specific developments on the nature of Christian apocrypha is certainly worth noting.

So, liberated from the need to strictly demarcate apocrypha from hagiography, Junod once again rejects Schneemelcher's insistence on the importance of the literary genres of the New Testament and his chronological limits on the production of apocrypha. He particularly criticizes Schneemelcher's focus on what is essentially an early 'canonical' collection of apocrypha, consisting largely of writings in Greek, to the exclusion of important texts and versions in Near Eastern languages or Irish, as well as more recent Greek and Latin versions. Junod further strengthens his argument by demonstrating just how poorly two of Schneemelcher's 'canonical' early Greek apocrypha, the *Gospel of Peter* and the *Acts of Andrew*, actually fit his criteria (1992: 39–43). Altogether, Junod's definition envisions a much larger and more complex corpus of traditions than Schneemelcher had previously allowed. It refuses to place chronological and generic limits on apocrypha and insists on the importance of examining the full extent of each apocryphal tradition's development and transmission over both time and space.

By and large, Junod's definition of 'early Christian apocrypha' has now become widely accepted in discussions of this literary corpus. It reflects, for instance, the position of the Association pour l'étude de la littérature apocryphe chrétienne (AELAC), the main professional organization for the study of apocrypha, of which Junod is one of the founding members. The Association's many publishing projects are clearly guided by principles very similar to Junod's (Kaestli 1996: 28–9; DuBois 2001: 24–6). A rather telling indication that this viewpoint has come to prevail as the new *status quaestionis* is the announcement that the forthcoming seventh edition of Hennecke and Schneemelcher's collection of apocrypha will drop the title *Neutestamentliche Apokryphen* in favour of *Antike christlichen Apokryphen*. That this involves more than a superficial name change is made clear by Christoph Markschies, who is preparing the new edition: in an article surveying the history and future of this important and influential collection, Markschies (1998) explains that the new edition will adhere to the broader principles articulated by Junod, rather than Schneemelcher's more restrictive corpus of 'New Testament' apocrypha.

While Markschies recognizes the absence of a chronological limit to the production of apocrypha, the collection will—primarily for pragmatic reasons—focus on ancient Christian apocrypha, including only those texts produced before the end of late antiquity (754 CE, according to Markschies). As a result, additional texts will be included in the new edition, and more consideration will be given to traditions and versions transmitted in Near Eastern languages. Only a few of the 'Old Testament' apocrypha or 'pseudepigrapha' will be included, however, again, primarily to keep the collection at a manageable size. Only those texts composed in a Christian context will be incorporated, while pre-Christian Jewish compositions that have been lightly reworked by Christian transmitters will be excluded (Markschies 1998: 128–30).

One especially significant consequence of this new definition of apocrypha is its recognition that the production of apocryphal texts has proceeded uninterrupted until the present, and that these more recent writings are also worthy of serious study as part of an enduring tradition of Christian apocryphal literature. During the last century, two studies were devoted to 'modern' apocrypha: Edgar Goodspeed's *Modern Apocrypha* (1956; see also his 1931) and Per Beskow's *Strange Tales about Jesus* (1983), which examine such diverse recent apocrypha as the *Gospel of Barnabas*, the *Book of Mormon*, and the *Essene Gospel of Peace*. Both scholars, however, while they are to be commended for their efforts to investigate this often overlooked literature, take a rather condescending and dismissive approach to these apocrypha, aiming to expose the fraudulence of such works and to separate them from what is truly ancient and, therefore, 'authentic'.

While some of these works are perhaps deserving of such rough dismissal, others are not, as Pierluigi Piovanelli has recently argued in a pair of insightful articles on the importance of these modern apocrypha for understanding the nature and history of apocryphal literature more generally (2005, 2006). Focusing on Levi H. Dowling's *Aquarian Gospel*, Piovanelli explains how Dowling's gospel, rather than being simply dismissed as a fraud, should instead be understood as the work of a man who believed that he had been commissioned by Visel, the goddess of Wisdom (and the third Person of the Trinity, who appeared to him in visions), to announce the coming of a 'new age'—the Aquarian Age, or the Age of the Spirit. Whether or not one accepts its claims of authenticity, his 'gospel' meets the criteria for classification as an apocryphon, and should not be excluded simply because its author received his 'hidden' knowledge many centuries after the writers of other apocryphal gospels. In a similar vein, Piovanelli further suggests some intriguing connections between early Christian apocrypha and the re-mythologizing of Christian origins that takes place in modern biblical novels such as Kazantzakis's *The Last Temptation of Christ*. Even scholarly biographies of the 'historical figure of Jesus' reflect the apocryphal impulse, inasmuch as they are themselves narrative retellings of the gospel traditions in a modern idiom.

25.3 Major Trends and Developments in the Study of Early Christian Apocrypha

Without question the most important development in the study of Christian apocrypha during the later twentieth century was the discovery of the Nag Hammadi codices in 1945 in Egypt. These thirteen codices, written in Coptic, brought to light several dozen new apocrypha, most of which had been completely unknown previously. Although they are often described collectively as 'Gnostic', these sundry texts present instead an invaluable witness to the diverse heterodox groups of early Christianity. While many of the texts do in fact reflect the beliefs and practices of certain early Christian Gnostic groups, the collection is increasingly seen as theologically diverse: some texts are quite orthodox, and one piece is actually a passage from Plato's *Republic* translated (rather poorly) into Coptic. The entire Nag Hammadi collection has now been published in a set of definitive critical editions with facing English translations, as well as in a single volume of English translations (J. M. Robinson 1988, 2000).

Perhaps the single most important apocryphon discovered at Nag Hammadi was a complete version of the *Gospel of Thomas*, a very early collection of sayings attributed to Jesus that had previously been known only from a few unidentified Greek papyrus fragments (Layton 1989). There is much debate regarding the date of this apocryphon: it was almost certainly written before 150 CE (Schneemelcher 1991–2: i. 110–14), although some scholars believe that it is as early as 50 CE (e.g. Davies 1983). The majority of scholars, however, agree that Thomas is most likely contemporary with the canonical gospels (Layton 1989: i. 38–49). Consequently, the *Gospel of Thomas* is particularly important for study of the historical Jesus, since it preserves early sayings material that has been transmitted independently of the canonical traditions, and thus provides a new source for reconstructing Jesus's teaching (J. M. Robinson 1971; Koester 1971b; 1990: 85–6; Patterson 1993)—although a few scholars continue to maintain Thomas's dependence on the canonical gospels (e.g. Meier 1991: 124–39).

There is much overlap between Thomas and the Synoptic Gospels, especially with Q material; and in some cases it is believed that Thomas has preserved the earliest and most authentic versions of particular sayings of Jesus (Koester 1983; Funk and Hoover 1993). Yet much of Thomas is radically different from the canonical gospels. Most notably, Jesus in Thomas does not preach an apocalyptic message, which has opened up serious discussion among scholars as to whether the historical Jesus was in fact an apocalyptic prophet. Some scholars have used Thomas to reinterpret Jesus as a sort of non-apocalyptic Cynic sage (Downing 1988; Crossan 1991; 1994), although the clear majority of scholars continue to believe that he was an apocalypticist (Sanders 1993; Meier 1994; Ehrman 1999). The *Gospel of Thomas* is also very important for understanding the earliest history of Christianity, since Thomas most likely reflects the gospel as it was preached within the early Christian communities of Edessa and eastern Syria. Thomas thus offers an important confirmation of Walter Bauer's hypothesis concerning the history of 'orthodoxy' and 'heresy' in this region, and is a precious witness to the diversity with which the Christian message was first articulated during Christianity's first century (Koester 1971*a*; Bauer 1971: 1–43).

The Nag Hammadi apocrypha have impacted the study of early Christianity in many other ways over the past 30 years, and while it is not possible to list them all here, some of the most significant issues have been questions that these texts raise about the ideological diversity of earliest Christianity, the nature of 'Gnosticism', the development of the categories 'orthodoxy' and 'heresy', and the origins of Christian monasticism. Yet one area in which the Nag Hammadi apocrypha have been especially influential is in the study of women and gender in early Christianity. Many of the Gnostic apocrypha, for instance, identify among the divine powers of the universe beings that are both male and female, in contrast to the highly masculinized Godhead of orthodox Christianity. Although the images of feminine deities in these cosmologies are not always positive or empowering, they nevertheless present us with varieties of early Christianity that thought about divine realms in terms of both genders in a manner rather foreign to their proto-orthodox rivals (Pagels 1979; Buckley 1986; King 1988).

In addition to revealing Christianities more inclined to conceive of divinity as (at least in part) feminine, the Nag Hammadi and certain other early Christian apocrypha provide evidence that many of these same groups had traditions allowing women to assume positions of religious leadership in their communities. Perhaps the single most important indication of this practice is a figure known as 'Mary', who appears in a number of early Christian apocrypha, most of which are preserved in Coptic, and many of which were discovered only at Nag Hammadi, including the *Gospel of Mary*, the *Pistis Sophia*, and the *Gospel of Philip* in particular. Although this Mary is generally identified with Mary of Magdala by modern scholarship, she is actually a rather complex literary representation, whose identity most likely draws on Mary of Nazareth as well as the Magdalene (Shoemaker 2001, 2002*b*, 2005*a*). In any case, however we conceive of her identity, this apocryphal Mary is depicted as an enlightened teacher, learned in the hidden mysteries of the cosmos, which Jesus himself has revealed to her. Furthermore, Mary instructs the other apostles in this secret knowledge, and she is represented as their equal, although in some cases not all of the apostles appear willing to accept this status. The handful of apostles who occasionally object to Mary's teaching and leadership are thought by many to be literary representations of other early Christian communities who objected to women's leadership in the churches. In responding to these 'outside voices', several of these apocrypha effectively defend the leadership of women through their vindication of this apostle named Mary (Bovon 1984; Marjanen 1996; King 1998; Schaberg 2002; Brock 2003; King 2003a).

Another especially important and active area of research has been the apocryphal acts of the apostles, legendary accounts of the missionary activities of individual apostles that culminate (usually) in the apostle's martyrdom. A driving force behind much of the interest in these apocrypha is a prolific group of Swiss scholars (associated with AELAC) who have been very active in studying these traditions and publishing new critical editions and translations of the *acta*. Although these apocrypha have long been known, until recently they were not available in reliable editions that take into account all of the complex manuscript evidence and transmission history of these popular narratives. Several of these mammoth editions have already appeared (*Acts of John* (Junod and Kaestli 1983), *Acts of Andrew* (Prieur 1989), and *Acts of Philip* (Bovon *et al.* 1999)), and more are in the works, including new editions of later acts (often known as 'secondary acts'), which heretofore have been largely ignored. This editorial activity has done much to stimulate interest in these remarkable apocrypha.

One of the most noteworthy features of the apocryphal acts is their intriguing representation of women, gender, and sexuality, topics that have attracted much recent study. All of these acts prominently feature women, mostly of high social status, whose conversions by an apostle provoke decisions to renounce marriage and sexuality. While this theme is consistent with the highly ascetic, 'encratite' theology of most apocryphal acts, there is no obvious reason why all of these narratives should choose to focus on women, and particularly women of high status, to emphasize the rejection of marriage. These female characters have given rise to a number of different interpretations. Some scholars envision a community of ascetic women behind these stories, who created these tales as reflections of their own experiences and circulated them orally until they finally found their way into written form as a part of the apocryphal acts. Such theories occasionally identify these women with the order of 'widows' in the early church and use methods from folklore studies to reconstruct the history of these 'old wives' tales' (Davies 1980; MacDonald 1983, 1984; Burrus 1987; see 1 Tim 4: 7). Other interpreters, however, do not see any connection between these stories and real, historical women; rather, the authors of the apocryphal acts are understood as merely using women 'to think with' (Kaestli 1986; Brown 1988: 154; see also Clark 1998). These well-to-do female characters represent instead the conflict between the social order of the Graeco-Roman world and the new values of the Christian community with its vision for a transformed society in which the hierarchies of the classical world are dissolved. Viewed in this light, these women represent an early Christian critique of marriage as a basic element of social hierarchy, rather than the experiences of early Christian 'widows' or any other women (Cooper 1996: 45–67; Jacobs 1999). The *Acts of Paul and Thecla*, however, presents a particularly valuable source for understanding the range of early Christian attitudes toward women and gender, inasmuch as its traditions reflect a rival trajectory within Pauline Christianity that rejected the social conservatism of the Pastoral Epistles (MacDonald 1983; Kaestli 1989).

On a rather different front, the apocryphal acts have long been studied for their connections with the literature of classical antiquity. Since the nineteenth century, scholars have explored the complex literary relations between the apocryphal acts and the ancient Greek novel (Rohde 1867; Söder 1932). While earlier scholars attempted to interpret the apocryphal acts simply as expressions of Christianity in the form of this classical genre, it is now recognized that the relationships between the apocryphal acts and the Hellenistic novel are more complex (Kaestli 1981; Junod 1983b). Likewise, older conceptions of the apocryphal acts as a 'popular' literature intended for the masses have come into question: after all, it appears that they were intended for a literate audience (Kaestli 1981: 66; Bovon and Geoltrain 1997: pp. xxxii, i–li). Nevertheless, relations with the classical novel cannot be denied, and these antecedents show the apocryphal acts as prime examples of apocrypha that have been influenced more by classical genres than by biblical ones (*contra* Schneemelcher). Thus, the apocryphal acts can rightly be described as 'Christian novelistic literature', although the authors almost certainly have pieced together their compositions from a variety of pre-existing traditions. Likewise, while the apocryphal acts may not have been written for common folk, it is safe to say that the intended audience for this literature was somewhat broader than the readership of the recondite theological and ascetic treatises of early Christian literature (Junod 1983b; Bovon 2003).

In more recent years, several scholars have interpreted the apocryphal acts as a sort of antitype of the Hellenistic novels that inverts and subverts their ideology, challenging the traditional values of romantic love, marital fidelity, and the civic order of the *polis* that the classical novels persistently advance (Perkins 1995; Cooper 1996: 45–67; Jacobs 1999). Another recent approach has been Dennis Ronald MacDonald's investigation of the relations between the apocryphal *Acts of Andrew* and Homeric literature; it remains to be seen exactly where this avenue of approach might lead (1994; see also his 2003). In any case, it seems likely that the apocryphal acts of the apostles will remain an especially lively area of investigation in early Christian studies for the foreseeable future.

Apocryphal literature in general promises to be a very active field of research in the near future, for a variety of reasons. Insofar as interests in the nature of 'Gnostic' Christianity, the diverse varieties of early Christianity, and the complex relationship between 'orthodoxy' and 'heresy' remain at the forefront of research in early Christian studies, the ancient Christian apocrypha will continue to be valued for the insights they provide into these questions. The apocrypha are one of the most valuable resources for mining the early church for dissonant voices that have otherwise been silenced (e.g. Koester 1995; Kaestli 1996: 33–4; Bovon and Geoltrain 1997: pp. xix–xxix). Many apocrypha, for instance, were contemporary rivals of the canonical texts, whose views of Christianity were later rejected by the guardians of 'orthodoxy', while other more recent texts bear witness to diverse beliefs and practices of Christian communities in various times and places. Furthermore, so long as hagiography and the cult of the saints remain areas of interest, the apocrypha will continue to be studied for their relations with these phenomena. As already seen, the apocrypha have proved very important in discussions of gender and sexuality, and it is likely that these issues will remain at the forefront of research.

There are, however, numerous other aspects of early Christian apocryphal literature that await serious investigation, including very many apocrypha that have not yet received the degree of attention that they merit. Although much still remains to be said about the apocrypha discovered at Nag Hammadi, there is no need to wait for another similar discovery to 'find' new texts: many already known apocrypha await 'discovery'. The long-neglected later apocrypha especially have valuable new perspectives to offer for understanding the diverse varieties of late ancient Christianity, as evidenced in recent studies of the *Acts of Philip* (Bovon *et al.* 1999; Slater 1999; Bovon 2002), the Dormition apocrypha (Shoemaker 2001, 2002*a*, 2003), and the unfortunately obscure Ethiopic *Book of the Cock* (Piovanelli 2003*a*, *b*). Many apocryphal texts await modern, comprehensive editions, and in the near future, this promises to be a major focus of scholarship (Bovon 1983; DuBois 1984; Kaestli 2003). This is of course difficult and often tedious work, made especially challenging by the complicated transmission history of these marginalized texts; but it is fundamental to better understanding both this literature and its many complex roles in the Christian tradition (Kaestli 1996: 31–3; Bovon and Geoltrain 1997: pp. xxv–xxxvi; Bovon 1999*b*; Picard 1999*c*).

NOTES

1. The Philadelphia Seminar on Christian Origins has made the topic of 'parabiblical literature' its subject for the years 2002–3 and 2003–4, and also organized a session at the 2002 SBL meetings on this topic. In both venues scholars have explored the possibility of extending the label 'parabiblical' to apply more generally to early Christian and Jewish apocrypha as a whole.

2. Nevertheless, the practice of metaphrase exemplified in early Jewish parabiblical literature is highly relevant to the interpretation of much early Christian literature: see e.g. Scott Johnson's recent study of the *Life and Miracles of Thekla* (2005: esp. 67–112).

3. 4 Ezra is canonical in Russian Orthodox (but not Greek Orthodox) and Ethiopic Bibles. It is usually present in medieval manuscripts of the Vulgate, but since the Council of Trent it has been published separately in an appendix, although it continues to be printed as a part of the Latin Bible. It has a similar deuterocanonical status in the Armenian Bible (Cowley 1974; Stone 1979: 35–43; Charlesworth 1983: ii. 516–19; Stone 1990: 3–8).

4. Nevertheless, one should also note Photius's rather negative assessment of the apocryphal acts of the apostles, which he condemned as pernicious to Christian faith: *Bibliotheca*, Codex 114 (PG 103, 389); see also Junod 1981.

5. As yet there is no consensus regarding the attribution of this earliest *Life of the Virgin* to Maximus, but on the basis of literary relationships, a seventh-century date seems highly likely (Shoemaker 2005*b*, 2006). Note that while the author of this *Life* is accepting of some apocrypha, he rejects others explicitly, including the *Infancy Gospel of Thomas* in particular: this selectivity is reminiscent of the view advocated by Priscillian. If the attribution to Maximus is in fact authentic, this would be an important endorsement of the use of apocrypha by a revered church father.

6. As an excellent example of this in a modern setting, see *The Life of the Virgin Mary, the Theotokos* written and compiled by the Holy Apostles Convent. This Orthodox biography of Mary openly acknowledges its considerable dependence on 'apocryphal' sources, accounts which the Church—the church fathers, hymnographers, and iconographers—have made 'part of the ancient Tradition' (Holy Apostles Convent 1989: pp. vii–x).

7. It would be best to avoid, however, continued use of the term 'Apocrypha' in reference to those books of the Christian (and Hellenistic Jewish) Bible that were removed by the sixteenth-century Protestant Reformers in order to conform with the canon of the Hebrew version of the Bible. Although this designation enjoys widespread use, it is at its root polemical, having been deployed primarily to reflect the Protestant view that these writings are non-canonical, which is a primary meaning of 'apocrypha' in the Christian tradition. The fact that the designation was first deployed by Jerome because of his insistence on the *Hebraica veritas* does not excuse its usage (nor does it make it any less polemical!). Even though one finds examples from the medieval Church where the term 'Apocrypha' is used for these texts, this does not reflect the fact that for the overwhelming majority of Christians they were (and indeed are) not apocryphal but part of the scriptures. Such usage is therefore neither accurate nor respectful of this view, and these texts are certainly not apocryphal in the sense described in the present chapter. Moreover, suitable terminology already exists for referring to this corpus of texts: 'deuterocanonical'. This term, although it is a sixteenth-century Catholic designation created in response to the Protestant excisions, is (in my opinion) more suited for both academic and ecumenical discourse, since it recognizes both the canonical status of this literature in various historical communities (both Jewish and Christian) but also signals its slightly awkward status in regards to the Hebrew canon by designating it as in some sense 'secondary'.

8. It is revealing, for instance, just how many Christian 'apocrypha' also appear in the *Bibliotheca Hagiographica Graeca*, the *Bibliotheca Hagiographica Latina*, and the *Bibliotheca Hagiographica Orientalis*.

SUGGESTED READING

Perhaps the single best resource for information about research on apocryphal literature is the Association pour l'étude de la littérature apocryphe chrétienne (AELAC), the main professional organization dedicated to the study of Christian apocrypha. The Association's website is a well-organized treasure trove of information <http://www2.unil.ch/aelac/>. Among other things, the website includes an extensive bibliography, organized by author and subject, which has been meticulously compiled over the last 15 years and is updated annually. The bibliography is heavily weighted toward Continental scholarship, which is primarily a reflection of the Association's membership. The website also includes a directory of the Association's members, online copies of its newsletters, and an index of its journal *Apocrypha*, the most important periodical specifically dedicated to the study of Christian apocrypha (whose articles unfortunately are not indexed in the American Theological Libraries Association database). A very useful and comprehensive bibliography of earlier scholarship was compiled by James H. Charlesworth and James R. Mueller (1987).

The two most important collections of early Christian apocrypha in English are the two Schneemelcher volumes (1991–2) and J. K. Elliott's *The Apocryphal New Testament* (1993). Neither of these is ideal, however. The Schneemelcher collection is valuable above all for its extensive introductions to individual texts, which are unmatched by any other collection, translated from the original German version (1990–7; note that the most recent English translation is based on the 6th edn. of vol. i. (1990) and the 5th edn. of vol. ii. (1989). The 6th edn. of vol. ii. (1997) is, like the 6th edn. of vol. i., a corrected reprint of the 5th edn.), but these often reflect older, more 'New Testament'-oriented views of Christian apocrypha. Furthermore, the translations of apocryphal texts in this English collection are unfortunately based on the German translations of the originals, which have been checked 'against the originals in Latin, Greek, or Coptic to insure that they were English versions of the original' (Schneemelcher 1991–2: Preface to the English Edition). Although this is somewhat reassuring, direct translations from the original languages would certainly be preferable. Moreover, this collection is limited by the more restrictive definition of 'New Testament Apocrypha' adopted by Schneemelcher, and therefore many important and interesting texts have been excluded. Elliott's collection includes a slightly broader selection of early Christian apocrypha (including at least a brief appendix on the Dormition and Assumption apocrypha, for instance), although it contains only the *Gospel of Thomas* and the *Apocryphon of James* from the Nag Hammadi collection, whose apocrypha are well (although by no means completely) represented in Schneemelcher. In addition, Elliot's version has the decided advantage that most of the texts were translated directly from the original languages, although several texts, particularly those in 'oriental languages', were simply adopted from M. R. James's earlier collection (1924) with some updating of James's rather stilted 'King James' language, while one translation was imported from the Schneemelcher collection (Elliot 1993: p. xv). Elliott provides a useful bibliography for each item, but his volume does not have the extensive scholarly introductions of Schneemelcher.

The most comprehensive collection of apocrypha in a modern language is Mario Erbetta's Italian collection (1966–81), which alone comes close to representing the full extent of early Christian apocryphal literature: it is the only collection, for instance, that comprehensively presents the Dormition and Assumption apocrypha. Although Erbetta's brief introductions cannot rival those of the Schneemelcher collection, his copious footnotes are extremely helpful, often amounting almost to a commentary. A most welcome new addition is the French collection *Écrits apocryphes chrétiens*, published by the members of AELAC. The 'Pléiade' edition, as it is often called, is an extensive collection of apocrypha that, while not as exhaustive as Erbetta's, includes considerably more texts than do Schneemelcher or Elliott. The first volume appeared in 1997, containing apocrypha on Jesus, Mary, John the

Baptist, and the apostles, and a collection of 'Visions and Revelations' that were written during the 'first centuries of Christianity' (Bovon and Geoltrain 1997). The much anticipated second volume has recently been published (Geoltrain and Kaestli 2005), presenting a broad selection of apocrypha from later centuries, up to and including the Middle Ages (although the Pseudo-Clementine literature, much of which is quite early, accounts for almost half the volume). These translations are well introduced and footnoted, and have the distinct advantage of being made by scholars who have been intimately involved for many years with the texts that they translate. In light of the high quality of this edition, one wonders if the next English translation of a collection of apocrypha will be made from French instead of German.

In all of these collections, the Nag Hammadi apocrypha are only sparsely and very selectively represented (although their exclusion is certainly more a matter of pragmatism than principle. In the case of the 'Pléiade' collection, the Nag Hammadi texts are largely omitted primarily to avoid overlap with an anticipated 'Pléiade' volume dedicated specifically to the Nag Hammadi writings). For these, the reader should consult *The Nag Hammadi Library in English* (J. M. Robinson 1988) and Bentley Layton's *The Gnostic Scriptures* (1987). The latter, which includes only a selection of writings from Nag Hammadi, is superior for its commentary and annotations. Likewise, all of these collections contain very few of the Christian apocrypha dealing with themes and characters from the Hebrew Bible, but most of these can be found in James Charlesworth's *The Old Testament Pseudepigrapha* (1983), which includes well-annotated translations and substantial introductions for each text.

Definitive critical editions of the early Christian apocrypha are currently being produced under the auspices of AELAC in the *Series Apocryphorum* of the *Corpus Christianorum*, published by Brepols (Bovon 1983; DuBois 1984; Kaestli 2003). So far fifteen volumes have appeared in this series, and critical editions of twenty-six more apocryphal traditions are in the works. These editions are quite comprehensive, including multiple versions, extensive introductions, commentary, indices, and complete concordances. As we await the completion of this massive editorial project, other older editions of apocrypha remain useful. Some of the most important collections of Greek and Latin apocrypha include Tischendorf's editions of various apocryphal gospels and apocalypses (1866, 1876), Lipsius and Bonnet's editions of the apocryphal acts of the apostles (1891–1903), and the various apocrypha published by James in his *Apocrypha Anecdota* (1893). An important and often overlooked assortment of Byzantine apocrypha was published by Vassiliev (1893). Wright had published two important collections of Syriac apocrypha (1865, 1871), and several editions of various Coptic apocrypha have been published (F. Robinson 1896; Lacau 1904; Budge 1913). An extensive collection of apocryphal writings in Armenian was prepared by the Mekhitarists of Venice (Yovsep'eanc' 1896; Tayets'i 1898; Č'rak'ean 1904), and editions of Georgian, Arabic, and Ethiopic versions of the apocryphal acts have also been published (Kurcik'ize 1959; Smith Lewis 1904; Budge 1899–1901). An invaluable resource for locating editions and translations of specific texts is the *Clavis apocryphorum Novi Testamenti* (Geerard 1992) and, in the case of Christian apocrypha with Old Testament themes, the *Clavis apocryphorum Veteris Testamenti* (Haelewyck 1998). These recent publications catalogue rather exhaustively the various versions and editions of Christian apocrypha, as well as indicating some of the most important studies. For apocrypha in Church Slavonic, however, one must consult de Santos Otero's catalogue (1978–81). The various Nag Hammadi texts received definitive critical editions during the past few decades, which first appeared in the Nag Hammadi and

Manichaean Studies series published by Brill and have since been republished collectively as a five-volume set (J. M. Robinson 2000).

BIBLIOGRAPHY

ANDERSON, G. A. (2000), 'Law and Lawgiving', in L. H. Schiffman and J. C. VanderKam (eds.), *Encyclopedia of the Dead Sea Scrolls* (New York: Oxford University Press), i. 475–7.

ATTRIDGE, H. W., ELGVIN, T., MILIK, J. T., OLYAN, S., STRUGNALL, J., TOV, E., VANDERKAM, J. C., and WHITE, S. (1994) (eds.), *Qumran Cave 4, Parabiblical Texts, Part I*, Discoveries in the Judaean Desert, 13 (Oxford: Clarendon Press).

BACKUS, I. (1998), 'Christoph Scheurl and His Anthology of "New Testament Apocrypha" (1506, 1513, 1515)', *Apocrypha*, 9: 133–56.

—— (2002), 'Les apocryphes néo-testamentaires et la pédagogie luthérienne des XVIᵉ-XVIIᵉ siècles: les recueils de Michael Neander (1564, 1567) et de Nicolas Glaser (1614)', in S. C. Mimouni (ed.), *Apocryphité: Histoire d'une concept transversal aux religions du livre*, Bibliothèque de l'École des Hautes Études, SR 113 (Turnhout: Brepols), 263–76.

BALLEY, N. (2002), 'Jacques Lefèvre d'Étaples (1450?–1536): un humaniste face aux apocryphes', in S. C. Mimouni (ed.), *Apocryphité: Histoire d'une concept transversal aux religions du livre*, Bibliothèque de l'École des Hautes Études, SR 113, (Turnhout: Brepols), 255–62.

BAUER, W. (1971), *Orthodoxy and Heresy in Earliest Christianity* (Philadelphia: Fortress Press).

BERTRAND, D. A. (2002), 'La notion d'apocryphe dans l'argumentation de la *Réfutation de toutes les hérésies*', in S. C. Mimouni (ed.), *Apocryphité: Histoire d'une concept transversal aux religions du livre*, Bibliothèque de l'École des Hautes Études, SR 113, (Turnhout: Brepols), 131–40.

BESKOW, P. (1983), *Strange Tales about Jesus: A Survey of Unfamiliar Gospels* (Philadelphia: Fortress Press).

BOVON, F. (1983), 'Vers une nouvelle édition de la littérature apocryphe chrétienne', *Aug* 23: 373–8.

—— (1984), 'Le privilège pascal de Marie-Madeleine', *NTS* 30: 50–62.

—— (1999*a*), 'Byzantine Witnesses for the Apocryphal Acts of the Apostles', in F. Bovon, A. G. Brock, and C. R. Matthews (eds.), *The Apocryphal Acts of the Apostles*, Religions of the World (Cambridge, Mass.: Harvard University Center for the Study of World Religions), 87–98.

—— (1999*b*), 'Editing the Apocryphal Acts of the Apostles', in F. Bovon, A. G. Brock, and C. R. Matthews (eds.), *The Apocryphal Acts of the Apostles*, Religions of the World (Cambridge, Mass.: Harvard University Center for the Study of World Religions), 1–35.

—— (2002), 'Mary Magdalene in the *Acts of Philip*', in F. S. Jones (ed.), *Which Mary? The Marys of Early Christian Tradition*, Symposium Series, 19 (Atlanta: SBL), 75–89.

—— (2003), 'Canonical and Apocryphal Acts of the Apostles', *JECS* 11: 165–94.

—— and GEOLTRAIN, P. (1997) (eds.), *Écrits apocryphes chrétiens*, i, Pléiade, 442 (Paris: Gallimard).

BOVON, F., BOUVIER, B., and AMSLER, F. (1999) (eds.), *Acta Philippi*, CCSA 11–12 (Turnhout: Brepols).

BRAKKE, D. (1994), 'Canon Formation and Social Conflict in Fourth-Century Egypt: Athanasius of Alexandria's Thirty-Ninth *Festal Letter*', HTR 87: 395–419.

BROCK, A. G. (2003), *Mary Magdalene, the First Apostle: The Struggle for Authority*, HTS 51 (Cambridge, Mass.: Harvard University Press).

BROOKE, G. (2000), 'Rewritten Bible', in L. H. Schiffman and J. C. VanderKam (eds.), *Encyclopedia of the Dead Sea Scrolls* (New York: Oxford University Press), ii. 777–81.

——COLLINS, J. J., FLINT, P., GREENFIELD, J., LARSON, E., NEWSOM, C., PUECH, É., SCHIFFMAN, L. H., STONE, M., TREBOLLE BARRERA, J., and VANDERKAM, J. C. (1996), *Qumran Cave 4, Parabiblical Texts, Part 3*, Discoveries in the Judean Desert, 22 (Oxford: Clarendon Press).

BROSHI, M., ESHEL, E., FITZMYER, J., LARSON, E., NEWSOM, C., SCHIFFMAN, L., SMITH, M., STONE, M., STRUGNELL, J., YARDENI, A., and VANDERKAM, J. C. (1995), *Qumran Cave 4, Parabiblical Texts, Part 2*, Discoveries in the Judean Desert, 19 (Oxford: Clarendon Press).

BROWN, P. (1988), *The Body and Society*, Lectures on the History of Religions, NS 13 (New York: Columbia University Press).

BUCKLEY, J. J. (1986), *Female Fault and Fulfilment in Gnosticism* (Chapel Hill, NC: University of North Carolina Press).

BUDGE, E. A. W. (1899–1901), *The Contendings of the Apostles; Being the Histories of the Lives and Martyrdoms and Deaths of the Twelve Apostles and Evangelists. The Ethiopic Texts Now First Edited from Manuscripts in the British Museum, with an English Translation* (London: H. Frowde).

—— (1913), *Coptic Apocrypha in the Dialect of Upper Egypt* (London: British Museum).

BURRUS, V. (1987), *Chastity as Autonomy: Women in the Stories of Apocryphal Acts*. Studies in Women and Religion, 23 (Lewiston, NY: Edwin Mellen Press).

—— (1995), *The Making of a Heretic: Gender, Authority, and the Priscillianist Controversy*, The Transformation of the Classical Heritage, 24 (Berkeley: University of California Press).

CHARLESWORTH, J. H. (1983–5) (ed.), *The Old Testament Pseudepigrapha*, 2 vols. (Garden City, NY: Doubleday).

—— and MUELLER, J. R. (1987), *The New Testament Apocrypha and Pseudepigrapha: A Guide to Publications with Excursuses on Apocalypses*, American Theological Libraries Association Bibliography Series, 17 (Metuchen, NJ: Scarecrow Press).

CLARK, E. A. (1998), 'The Lady Vanishes: Dilemmas of a Feminist Historian after the "Linguistic Turn" ', CH 67: 1–31.

COOPER, K. (1996), *The Virgin and the Bride: Idealized Womanhood in Late Antiquity* (Cambridge, Mass.: Harvard University Press).

COWLEY, R. W. (1974), 'The Biblical Canon of the Ethiopian Orthodox Church Today', *Ostkirchliche Studien*, 23: 318–23.

Č'RAK'EAN, K. (1904), *Անկանոն գիրք առաքելականք (Ankanon girk' arak'elakank' [Apocryphal Books of the Apostles])*, T'angaran Haykakan hin ew nor dprut'eants', 3 (Venice: I Tparani S. Łazaru).

CROSSAN, J. D. (1991), *The Historical Jesus: The Life of a Mediterranean Jewish Peasant* (San Francisco: HarperSanFrancisco).

—— (1994), *Jesus: A Revolutionary Biography* (San Francisco: HarperSanFrancisco).

DAVIES, S. L. (1980), *The Revolt of the Widows: The Social World of the Apocryphal Acts* (Carbondale, Ill.: Southern Illinois University Press).

—— (1983), *The Gospel of Thomas and Christian Wisdom* (New York: Seabury).

DE SANTOS OTERO, A. (1978–81), *Die handshriftliche Überlieferung der altslavischen Apokryphen*, PTS 20, & 23 (Berlin: de Gruyter).

DOWNING, F. G. (1988), *Christ and the Cynics: Jesus and Other Radical Preachers in First-Century Tradition* (Sheffield: Journal for the Study of the Old Testament Press).

DUBOIS, J.-D. (1984), 'The New Series Apocryphorum of the Corpus Christianorum', *Second Century*, 4: 29–36.

—— (2001), 'L'AELAC vingt ans après, ou remarques sur l'étude des littératures apocryphes', *Bulletin de l'AELAC*, 11: 24–30.

EHRMAN, B. D. (1999), *Jesus: Apocalyptic Prophet of the New Millenium* (New York: Oxford University Press).

—— and JACOBS, A. S. (2004) (eds.), *Christianity in Late Antiquity: 300–450 C.E.* (New York: Oxford University Press).

ELLIOTT, J. K. (1993), *The Apocryphal New Testament: A Collection of Apocryphal Christian Literature in an English Translation* (Oxford: Clarendon Press).

ERBETTA, M. (1966–81), *Gli Apocrifi del Nuovo Testamento*, 3 vols. (Turin: Marietti).

ESBROECK, M.-J. VAN (1986) (ed.), *Maxime le Confesseur: Vie de la Vierge*, CSCO 478–9, Scriptores Iberici, 21–2 (Louvain: Peeters).

FISK, B. N. (2001), *Do You Not Remember? Scripture, Story and Exegesis in the Rewritten Bible of Pseudo-Philo*, JSPSup 37 (Sheffield: Sheffield Academic Press).

FUNK, R. W., and HOOVER, R. W. (1993), *The Five Gospels: The Search for the Authentic Words of Jesus* (New York: Macmillan).

GEERARD, M. (1992), *Clavis apocryphorum Novi Testamenti*, CCSA (Turnhout: Brepols).

GEOLTRAIN, P., and KAESTLI, J.-D. (2005) (eds.), *Écrits apocryphes chrétiens, ii*, Pléiade, 516 (Paris: Gallimard).

GINSBERG, H. L. (1967), 'Review of Joseph A. Fitzmeyer's *The Genesis Apocryphon of Qumran Cave 1: A Commentary*', *TS* 28: 574.

GOODSPEED, E. J. (1931), *Strange New Gospels* (Chicago: University of Chicago Press).

—— (1956), *Modern Apocrypha* (Boston: Beacon Press).

HAELEWYCK, J. C. (1998), *Clavis apocryphorum Veteris Testamenti*, CCSA (Turnhout: Brepols).

HOLY APOSTLES CONVENT (1989), *The Life of the Virgin Mary, the Theotokos* (Buena Vista, Colo.: Holy Apostles Convent and Dormition Skete).

JACOBS, A. (1999), 'A Family Affair: Marriage, Class, and Ethics in the Apocryphal Acts of the Apostles', *JECS* 7: 105–38.

—— (2000), 'The Disorder of Books: Priscillian's Canonical Defense of Apocrypha', *HTR* 93: 135–59.

JAMES, M. R. (1893–7), *Apocrypha Anecdota: A Collection of Thirteen Apocryphal Books and Fragments Now First Edited from Manuscripts*, TaS 2.3, 5.1 (Cambridge: Cambridge University Press; repr. Nendeln, Liechtenstein: Kraus, 1967).

—— (1924), *The Apocryphal New Testament* (Oxford: Clarendon Press).

JOHNSON, S. F. (1995), *The Life and Miracles of Thekla: A Literary Study*, Hellenic Studies, 13 (Washington D.C.: Center for Hellenic Studies).

Jugie, M. (1926), *Homélies mariales byzantines (II)*, PO 19. 3 (Paris: Librairie de Paris/Firmin-Didot et Cie).

Junod, É (1981), 'Actes apocryphes et hérésie: le jugement de Photius', in F. Bovon (ed.), *Les actes apocryphes des apôtres: Christianisme et monde païen*, Publications de la Faculté de théologre de l'universilé de Genève, 4 (Geneva: Labor et Fides), 11–24.

——(1983a), 'Apocryphes du Nouveau Testament ou apocryphes chrétiens anciens? Remarques sur la désignation d'un corpus et indications bibliographiques sur instruments de travail récents', *Études théologiques et religieuses*, 59: 409–21.

——(1983b), 'Creations romanesques et traditions ecclésiastiques dans les Actes apocryphes des Apôtres', *Aug* 23: 271–85.

——(1992), ' "Apocryphes du Nouveau Testament": un appellation erronée et une collection artificielle', *Apocrypha*, 3: 17–46.

——and Kaestli, J.-D. (1983) (eds.), *Acta Iohannis*, CCSA 1–2 (Turnhout: Brepols).

Kaestli, J.-D. (1981), 'Les principales orientations de la recherche sur les Actes apocryphes des Apôtres', in F. Bovon (ed.), *Les actes apocryphes des apôtres: Christianisme et monde païen*, Publications de la Faculté de théologie de l'Université de Genève, 4 (Geneva: Labor et Fides), 49–67.

——(1986), 'Response [to Virginia Burrus]', *Semeia*, 38: 119–31.

——(1989), 'Les Actes apocryphes et la reconstitution de l'histoire des femmes dans le christianisme ancien', *Foi et Vie*, 88: 71–9.

——(1996), 'Les écrits apocryphes chrétiens: Pour une approche qui valorise leur diversité et leurs attaches bibliques', in J.-D. Kaestli and D. Marguerat (eds.), *Le mystère apocryphe: introduction à une littérature méconnue*, Essais bibliques, 26 (Geneva: Labor et Fides), 27–41.

——(2003), 'Corpus Christianorum *Series Apocryphorum*: une collection au profil original, portée par un projet de recherche collectif', in J. Leemans (ed.), *Corpus Christianorum 1953–2003: Xenium Natalicium: Fifty Years of Scholarly Editing* (Turnhout: Brepols), 174–89.

King, K. L. (1988) (ed.), *Images of the Feminine in Gnosticism*, SAC (Philadelphia: Fortress Press).

——(1998), 'Prophetic Power and Women's Authority: The Case of the Gospel of Mary Magdalene', in B. M. Kienzle and P. J. Walker (eds.), *Women Preachers and Prophets through Two Millennia of Christianity* (Berkeley: University of California Press), 21–41.

——(2003a), *The Gospel of Mary Magdalene: Jesus and the First Woman Apostle* (Santa Rosa, Calif.: Polebridge Press).

——(2003b), *What is Gnosticism?* (Cambridge, Mass.: Harvard University Press).

Koester, H. (1971a), '*GNOMAI DIAPHOROI*: The Origin and Nature of Diversification in the History of Early Christianity', in J. M. Robinson and H. Koester (eds.), *Trajectories through Early Christianity* (Philadelphia: Fortress Press), 114–57.

——(1971b), 'One Jesus and Four Primitive Gospels', in J. M. Robinson and H. Koester (eds.), *Trajectories through Early Christianity* (Philadelphia: Fortress Press), 158–204.

——(1983), 'Three Thomas Parables', in A. H. B. Logan and A. J. M. Wedderburn (eds.), *The New Testament and Gnosis: Essays in Honor of Robert McL. Wilson* (Edinburgh: T & T Clark), 195–203.

—— (1990), *Ancient Christian Gospels: Their History and Development* (Philadelphia: Trinity Press International).

—— (1995), *Introduction to the New Testament* (New York: Walter de Gruyter).

Kurcik'ize, C. I. (1959), ქართული ვერსიები აპოკრიფებისამოციქულოთა შესახებ (*K'art'uli versiebi apokrip'ebisa mocik'ult'a šesaxeb [Georgian Versions of Apocrypha concerning the Apostles]*) (Tbilisi: Sakartvelos SSR mec'nierebat'a akademiis gamomc'emloba).

Lacau, P. (1904), *Fragments d'Apocryphes coptes*, Mémoires publiés par les membres de l'Institut français d'archéologie orientale du Caire, 9 (Cairo: Imprimerie de l'Institut français d'archéologie orientale).

Layton, B. (1987), *The Gnostic Scriptures* (Garden City, NY: Doubleday & Co.).

—— (1989) (ed.), *Nag Hammadi Codex II, 2–7*, NHS 20, 2 vols. (Leiden: E. J. Brill).

Le Boulluec, A. (2002), 'Écrits "contestés," "inauthentiques," ou "impies"? (Eusèbe de Césarée, *Histoire Ecclésiastique*, III, 25)', in S. C. Mimouni (ed.), *Apocryphité: Histoire d'une concept transversal aux religions du livre*, Bibliothèque de l'École des Hautes Études, *SR*, 113 (Turnhout: Brepols), 153–65.

Lipsius, R. A., and Bonnet, M. (1891–1903), *Acta apostolorum apocrypha* (Leipzig: H. Mendelssohn).

MacDonald, D. R. (1983), *The Legend and the Apostle: The Battle for Paul in Story and Canon* (Philadelphia: Fortress Press).

—— (1984), 'The Role of Women in the Production of the Apocryphal Acts of the Apostles', *Iliff Review*, 40: 21–38.

—— (1994), *Christianizing Homer: The Odyssey, Plato, and the Acts of Andrew* (New York: Oxford University Press).

—— (2003), *Does the New Testament Imitate Homer? Four Cases from the Acts of the Apostles* (New Haven: Yale University Press).

Marjanen, A. (1996), *The Woman Jesus Loved: Mary Magdalene in the Nag Hammadi Library and Related Documents*, NHMS 40 (Leiden: E. J. Brill).

Markschies, C. (1998), ' "Neutestamentliche Apokryphen": Bemerkungen zu Geschichte und Zukunft einer von Edgar Hennecke im Jarh 1904 begründeten Quellensammlung', *Apocrypha*, 9: 97–132.

McNamara, M. (1984), *The Apocrypha in the Irish Church* (Dublin: Dublin Institute for Advanced Studies).

Meier, J. P. (1991), *A Marginal Jew: Rethinking the Historical Jesus*, i: *The Roots of the Problem and the Person* (New York: Doubleday).

—— (1994), *A Marginal Jew: Rethinking the Historical Jesus*, ii. *Mentor, Message, and Miracles* (New York: Doubleday).

—— (2003), 'The Historical Jesus and the Historical Law: Some Problems within the Problem', *CBQ* 65: 52–79.

Mimouni, S. C. (1993a), 'La lecture liturgique et les apocryphes du Nouveau Testament: Le cas de la Dormitio grecque du Pseudo-Jean', *OCP* 59: 403–25.

—— (1993b), 'Les Transitus Mariae sont-ils vraiment des apocryphes?', *StPatr* 25: 122–8.

—— (2002), 'Le concept d'apocryphité dans le christianisme ancien et médiéval: Réflexions en guise d'introduction', in S. C. Mimouni (ed.), *Apocryphité: Histoire d'une concept transversal aux religions du livre*. Bibliothèque de l'École des Hautes Études, *SR* 113 (Turnhout: Brepols), 1–21.

MIMOUNI, S. C., and ULLERN-WEITÉ, I. (2006) (eds.), *Pierre Geoltrain, ou, Comment 'faire l'histoire' des religions?: le chantier des 'origines', les méthodes du doute et la conversation contemporaine entre les disciplines*, Histoire et prosopographie de la section des sciences religieuses, 2, Bibliothèque de l'École des Hautes Études, *SR* 128 (Turnhout: Brepols).

MORALDI, L. (1971), *Apocrifi del Nuovo Testamento*, Classici delle religioni, 24, Sezione 5: Le altre confessioni cristiane (Turin: Unione tipografico-editrice torinese).

PAGELS, E. H. (1979), *The Gnostic Gospels* (New York: Random House).

PATTERSON, S. J. (1993), *The Gospel of Thomas and Jesus* (Sonoma, Calif.: Polebridge Press).

PERKINS, J. (1995), *The Suffering Self: Pain and Narrative Representation in the Early Christian Era* (London: Routledge).

PICARD, J.-C. (1999*a*) (ed.), 'Comment découvrir pratiquement l'existence et certains charactères du continent apocryphe', in *Le continent apocryphe: essai sur les littératures apocryphes juive et chrétienne*, Instrumenta Patristica, 36 (Turnhout: Brepols), 7–10.

—— (1999*b*) (ed.), 'Le continent apocryphe', in *Le continent apocryphe: essai sur les littératures apocryphes juive et chrétienne*, Instrumenta Patristica, 36 (Turnhout: Brepols), 3–6.

—— (1999*c*) (ed.), 'Mémoire des origines chrétienne', in *Le continent apocryphe: essai sur les littératures apocryphes juive et chrétienne*, Instrumenta Patristica, 36 (Turnhout: Brepols), 271–87.

PIOVANELLI, P. (2003*a*), 'Exploring the Ethiopic *Book of the Cock*: An Apocryphal Passion Gospel from Late Antiquity', *HTR* 96: 427–54.

—— (2003*b*), 'Pre- and Post-canonical Passion Stories: Insights into the Development of Christian Discourse on the Death of Jesus', *Apocrypha*, 14: 99–128.

—— (2005), 'What Is a Christian Apocryphal Text and How Does It Work? Some Observations on Apocryphal Hermeneutics', *Nederlands Theologisch Tijdschrift*, 59: 31–40.

—— (2006), 'Qu'est-ce qu'un "écrit apocryphe chrétien", et comment ça marche? Quelques suggestions pour une herméneutique apocryphe', in Mimouni and Ullern-Weité (2006), 171–84.

PRIEUR, J.-M. (1989) (ed.), *Acta Andreae*, CCSA 5–6 (Turnhout: Brepols).

REED, A. Y. (2002), 'Apocrypha, "Outside Books," and Pseudepigrapha: Ancient Categories and Modern Perceptions of Parabiblical Literature', <http://ccat.sas.upenn.edu/psco/year40/areed1.html>, 1 October 2006.

ROBINSON, F. (1896), *Coptic Apocryphal Gospels: Translations together with the Texts of Some of Them*, TaS 4 (Cambridge: Cambridge University Press).

ROBINSON, J. M. (1971), 'LOGOI SOPHON: On the Gattung of Q', in J. M. Robinson and H. Koester (eds.), *Trajectories through Early Christianity* (Philadelphia: Fortress Press), 71–113.

—— (1988) (ed.), *The Nag Hammadi Library in English* (San Francisco: Harper & Row).

—— (2000) (ed.), *The Coptic Gnostic Library: A Complete Edition of the Nag Hammadi Codices* (Leiden: E. J. Brill).

ROHDE, E. (1867), *Der griechische Roman und seine Vorläufer* (Leipzig: Breitkopf & Härtel).

SANDERS, E. P. (1993), *The Historical Figure of Jesus* (London: Allen Lane).

SCHABERG, J. (2002), *The Resurrection of Mary Magdalene: Legends, Apocrypha, and the Christian Testament* (New York: Continuum).

SCHNEEMELCHER, W. (1959–64), *Neutestamentliche Apokryphen in deutscher Übersetzung*, 3rd edn., 2 vols. (Tübingen: J. C. B. Mohr/Paul Siebeck).

—— (1989–90) (ed.), *Neutestamentliche Apokryphen in deutscher Übersetzung*, 5th edn., 2 vols. (Tübingen: J. C. B. Mohr/Paul Siebeck).

—— (1990–7) (ed.), *Neutestamentliche Apokryphen in deutscher Übersetzung*, 6th edn., 2 vols. (Tübingen: J. C. B. Mohr/Paul Siebeck).

—— (1963–5) (ed.), *New Testament Apocrypha*, 2 vols. (Philadelphia: Westminster Press).

—— (1991–2) (ed.), *New Testament Apocrypha*, 2 vols. (Louisville, Ky.: Westminster/John Knox Press).

SHOEMAKER, S. J. (2001), 'Rethinking the "Gnostic Mary": Mary of Nazareth and Mary of Magdala in Early Christian Tradition', *JECS* 9: 555–95.

—— (2002*a*), *Ancient Traditions of the Virgin Mary's Dormition and Assumption*, OECS (Oxford: Oxford University Press).

—— (2002*b*), 'A Case of Mistaken Identity? Naming the Gnostic Mary', in F. S. Jones (ed.), *Which Mary? The Marys of Early Christian Tradition*, SBL Symposium Series, 19 (Atlanta: SBL), 5–30.

—— (2003), 'Christmas in the Qur'an: The Qur'anic Account of Jesus' Nativity and Palestinian Local Tradition', *Jerusalem Studies in Arabic and Islam*, 28: 11–39.

—— (2005*a*), 'Jesus' Gnostic Mom: Mary of Nazareth and the Gnostic Mary Traditions', in D. Good (ed.), *Mariam, the Magdalen, and the Mother* (Bloomington, Ind.: Indiana University Press), 153–83.

—— (2005*b*), 'The Virgin Mary in the Ministry of Jesus and the Early Church according to the Earliest *Life of the Virgin*', *HTR* 98: 441–67.

—— (2006), 'The Georgian Life of the Virgin attributed to Maximus the Confessor: Its Authenticity(?) and Importance', in A. Muraviev and B. Lourié (eds.), *Mémorial R.P. Michel van Esbroeck, S. J.*, Scrinium, 2 (St Petersburg: Vizantinorossika), 66–87.

SLATER, R. N. (1999), 'An Inquiry into the Relationship between Community and Text: The Apocryphal *Acts of Philip* 1 and the Encratities of Asia Minor', in F. Bovon, A. G. Brock, and C. R. Matthews (eds.), *The Apocryphal Acts of the Apostles*, Religions of the World (Cambridge, Mass.: Harvard University Press for the Center for the Study of World Religions), 281–306.

SMITH LEWIS, A. (1904), *Acta mythologica apostolorum*, Horae semiticae, 3, 4 (London: C. J. Clay).

SÖDER, R. (1932), *Die apokryphen apostelgeschichten und die romanhafte literatur der antike*, Würzburger studien zur altertumswissenschaft, 3 (Stuttgart: W. Kohlhammer).

STONE, M. E. (1979), *The Armenian Version of IV Ezra*, University of Pennsylvania Armenian Texts and Studies, 1 (Missoula, Mont.: Scholars Press).

—— (1990), *Fourth Ezra: A Commentary on the Book of Fourth Ezra*, Hermeneia (Minneapolis: Fortress Press).

TALMON, S. (2000), 'Textual Criticism: The Ancient Versions', in A. D. H. Mayes (ed.), *Text in Context: Essays by Members of the Society for Old Testament Study* (Oxford: Oxford University Press), 141–70.

TAYETS'I, E. (1898), Անկանոն գիրք Նոր Կտակարանաց (*Ankanon girk' Nor Ktakaranats'* [*Apocryphal Books of the New Testament*]), T'angaran Haykakan hin ew nor dprut'eants', 2 (Venice: I Tparani S. Łazaru).

TISCHENDORF, C. (1866), *Apocalypses apocryphae Mosis, Esdrae, Pauli, Johannis, item Mariae dormito: additis evangeliorum et actuum apocryphorum supplementis. Maiximam partem nunc primum* (Leipzig: H. Mendelssohn; facs. repr. Hildesheim: G. Olms, 1966).

—— (1876), *Evangelia Apocrypha* (Leipzig: H. Mendelssohn).

VASSILIEV, A. (1893) (ed.), *Anecdota Graeco-Byzantina, Pars Prior* (Moscow: Universitas Caesarea).

WILLIAMS, M. A. (1996), *Rethinking Gnosticism: An Argument for Dismantling a Dubious Category* (Princeton NJ: Princeton University Press).

WRIGHT, W. (1865), *Contributions to the Apocryphal Literature of the New Testament* (London: Williams & Norgate).

—— (1871), *Apocryphal Acts of the Apostles* (London: Williams & Norgate).

YOVSEP'EANC', S. (1896), *Անկանոն գիրք Հին Կտակարանաց* (*Ankanon girk' Hin Ktaka-ranats' [Apocryphal Books of the Old Testament]*), T'angaran Haykakan hin ew nor nakhneats', 1 (Venice: I Tparani S. Łazaru).

CHAPTER 26

···

APOLOGETICS

···

MARK EDWARDS

26.1 APOLOGETICS

···

IN Greek forensic usage an 'apology' (*apologia*) is a formal speech on behalf of the defendant. The first surviving works to bear this title professed to be records of the speech delivered by Socrates in reply to a capital charge in 399 BCE. As Plato reports it, this was more than a protestation of innocence: it was a manifesto for the examined life, which turned the argument (though not the trial itself) against his accusers, and required him to dwell at some length on his previous career. The autobiographical element dominates the apologies of Lucian, Apuleius, and Libanius, all conceived in imitation of Plato's Socrates, though none of these erudite sophists seems to have shared his desire to convert the audience to philosophy. Christians, on the other hand, being ambassadors for Christ in court, as elsewhere, could not fulfil the injunction to 'give an apology for the hope that is in you' (1 Pet 3: 15) without pronouncing judgement on their own judges. Testimony on one's own behalf was not forbidden, as we see from Paul's remonstrations with his own countrymen in Acts; but Paul never ends without exhorting his listeners to embrace his own faith, and accounts of later martyrdoms suggest that, when the magistrate was a Gentile, an apology for Christ could easily turn into a polemic against idolatry. No distinction between polemic, protreptic, and apologetic appears to have been observed by the early Christians, least of all by those who consciously aped the rhetoric of the schools.

26.1.1 Observations and Caveats

If the term 'apologetic' has prevailed, it is because Christians gave it currency. The Latin-speaking African Tertullian was the first, so far as our knowledge goes, to entitle a work of his own *Apologeticus*, though the term itself (as the adjective from *apologia*) must surely have a Greek pedigree. His treatise, commonly dated to 197 CE, finds a place, perhaps 120 years later, in the earliest known canon of apologetic writings. Of the writings mentioned by Eusebius, those of Aristides and Justin are extant entire, while fragments at best survive from those of Quadratus, Melito, Apollonius, Miltiades, and Apollinarius (*Hist. eccl.* 4. 3. 1, 4. 3. 3, 4. 8. 3, 4. 26. 1, 5. 17. 5, 5. 21. 2–5; Frede (1999: 227) observes that all are addressed to emperors). The rebuttal of pagan calumnies is the one ubiquitous aim of the surviving texts, which otherwise would hardly have deserved to be called apologies; in most, however, forensic vindication is accompanied by satire on the folly, expense, or lewdness of civic cults. Jews had no opportunity to put Christians on trial after the sack of Jerusalem in 70 CE, and it is no doubt for this reason that the literature against them—consisting largely of testimonia from the Old Testament, interpreted through the spectacles of the New—is not described as apologetic by Eusebius. It is not, however, uncommon for true apologies to support the claims of Christ by appeal to prophecy, or to counter the charge of novelty by arguing that the Gospel was the fulfilment of a Law that antedated the oldest writings of the Greeks (Droge 1989).

Such reasoning would also serve of course to intimidate doubt and restrain apostasy among Christians. It is a common observation today that evangelical literature is most often read by members of the author's own communion, and as no evidence proves that any pagan was acquainted with the apologies that survive from the first three centuries, it is reasonable to suppose that they were more widely known within than outside the Church. Indeed, it may be plausibly surmised that in many cases other Christians were not only the actual but the intended recipients of the discourse. Christianity, as the apologists themselves complain, was a capital offence under pagan rulers, and it is therefore hard to believe that so many speeches, often bearing the name of the author and presupposing an aggravation of hostilities, could have been delivered in public without reprisal. Even a written plea would expose the author; yet no allusion to such a document occurs in the trial of Justin, the one apologist who is known to have been martyred. Heretics, by contrast, were armed only with verbal sorceries, against which there could be no more potent charm than to present one's creed as the faith for which other Christians had died.

While we cannot hope, from internal evidence alone, to overrule an author's statements as to the purpose and destination of his own book, we should remember that the apologists were writing in an age of theatrical oratory, in which audiences demanded not a commentary on affairs of the day but an erudite virtuosity in the juggling of inherited conceits. If we suspect these Christians of purveying a stereotype in their accounts of polytheism, if we look in vain for allusions to any work by a living author, we should not be in too much haste to convict them of ignorance or deception: it was only by such refined anachronism that one could prove oneself a true contemporary of the Second Sophistic. Reality intrudes upon convention in the occasional apostrophes to named magistrates or circumstantial narratives of atrocities against Christians. For all that, no apology is a bulletin, and we cannot (for example) cite the incidence of such writings as a measure of public enmity. A sudden concentration of apologies in a certain decade may, for example, indicate that the authorities were less vigilant, that literacy and leisure were increasing within the Church, or that the talents of Christian writers had been challenged by some pagan ebullition. The gestation of a literary form, which we can easily follow in the extant specimens, is not the same thing as a history of the Church in the Roman world.

26.1.2 The Second Century

The longest surviving text of the *Apology* which the Athenian philosopher Aristides addressed to Hadrian is a Syriac translation from the Greek (Geffcken 1907). In this document humans are divided into four races, each with its characteristic notion of the gods. Whereas Jews had defined themselves against Gentiles, and Greeks against barbarians, the new ethnography is quadratic, dividing polytheists into Greeks and barbarians, and monotheists into Christians and Jews. In a Greek version, preserved as a tutor's homily in the Byzantine novel *Barlaam and Ioasaaph*, a threefold division of peoples into Christians, Jews, and polytheists is ramified by a subsequent division of the last group into Egyptians, Chaldaeans, and Greeks. While it is clear that the novelist truncated and refined the original work, the later chapters of his version, in which libels against the morals of the Christians are refuted, correspond well enough to a Greek papyrus fragment of the fifth century; since, moreover, Christians passed for a third race in antiquity, it seems probable that his distribution of humans into three races is more primitive than the fourfold scheme of the Syriac. Both taxonomies give the lie to modern studies which claim that there was no concept of a plurality of religions in antiquity (W. C. Smith 1978: 15–50). It is truer to say that the work done in English by the term 'religion' is performed in Greek by nouns that we translate as 'race' or 'law'.

This remark is borne out by the *Epistle to Diognetus*, also commonly dated to the reign of Hadrian. Christians, the author declares, are 'another race' set apart not by their dress or a code of manners, but by purity of life. They are the invisible soul of the world: they beget but do not kill their offspring, keep the Law and surpass it, live on earth as citizens of heaven, die in order to live again (*Diogn.* 5). A Jewish prototype has been suggested for this portion of the document; but no Jew would have slighted such external marks of identity as the Sabbath, dietary laws, and circumcision. It was Christians, and they alone in the ancient world, who regarded all distinction of race and custom as provisional; its value, while it obtained, was to furnish a proof that nurture is more powerful than the stars in the determination of character. There are, on the other hand, no peculiar traits of Christianity in such works as the *Exhortation to the Greeks* or the treatise *On Monarchy*, both falsely ascribed to Justin by tradition. These are catenae of passages, purportedly though not always verifiably culled from ancient poets and dramatists to demonstrate that monotheism is neither a novel tenet nor a rare one. That they aim to show nothing more than this is no index of Jewish provenance: the verse most often quoted in the Christian martyrologies is Acts 4: 24, which asseverates not that God is the Father of Jesus, but only that he is the maker of heaven and earth.

Justin seems to have been the first to offer a written defence of the claims of Jesus to the Gentiles. In his First *Apologia*, addressed to the emperor Antoninus Pius and his two colleagues, Justin alludes to some redaction of the canonical gospels (1 *Apol.* 66. 3, 67. 3.; cf. *Dial.* 100. 4, 101. 3, 102. 5, 103. 6, 103. 8, 104. 1, 105. 6, 106. 1, 106. 3, 106. 4, 107. 1; Tatian, *Orat.* 21. 2), argues that the prophecies of the Old Testament are fulfilled in Jesus of Nazareth, and banishes suspicions of obscenity in his candid accounts of baptism and the eucharist (1 *Apol.* 61 and 64–7). At the same time he woos the Greeks by likening Christ to Hermes, the son and emissary of Zeus (22. 2), and anointing Socrates as a Christian before Christ (46. 3; see 5. 3–4, 2 *Apol.* 10. 5). All that is true in philosophy, he declares, is the gift of the Logos—meaning not the abstract force of reason diffused in every mind, but the Word of God, disseminated first in scripture and then in Christ, the author and fruit of all the scriptures. As a mouthpiece of orthodoxy, he takes occasion to censure his fellow Palestinian Simon Magus, an infamous heretic who was now the recipient of divine honours in Rome (26. 1–4). Another work against heretics, to which he refers (26. 8), contained a critique of Marcion (Irenaeus, *Haer.* 4. 6. 2), who denied that the redeemer was the son of the creator, or that the New Testament was prefigured in the Old. Marcionites may also have been one intended audience of the *Dialogue with Trypho*, though its avowed aim is to convince an incredulous Jew that all his prophets spoke of Jesus and that the Church has now inherited the promises made to Israel. At the same time, since a number of his objections go unanswered, it is possible that Trypho is not a wholly imagined character (Horner 2001); the dialogue, which does not end with his conversion, shows an animus which may have arisen from a real encounter. It does not, however, make Trypho a party to the gratuitous calumnies which had made the mere profession of Christianity a capital offence (see *Dial.* 10. 1), and Romans alone are held accountable for the judicial murder which Justin relates in the opening chapters of his Second *Apologia*.

Severe laws were enacted against foreign cults by Marcus Aurelius, whose reign saw the publication of three memorable philippics against the Church. Lucian, in his skit *On the Death of Peregrinus*, insinuates that the worshippers of the 'crucified sophist' are Cynics without a philosophy; Celsus, who may have been his friend, assailed the scriptures knowledgeably in his *True Word (Alēthes Logos)*; Fronto, the Emperor's tutor, embellished the charges of 'Oedipodal mating and Thyestean banquets'. It was not, however, these verbal barbs but the death of his tutor Justin in 165 CE that prompted Tatian's satire on the inanity of Roman cults and the immoralities of Greek philosophy. His *Oration to the Greeks*, while it insists on the chronological priority of the Old Testament to the Greek classics (*Orat.* 36), never names Christ or quotes the Gospels. The Greeks are refuted sufficiently by the turpitude of their gods (chs. 33–4), the childish absurdities of the theatre (chs. 22, 24), and their susceptibility to the arts of demons (chs. 14–17). Falsely preaching the natural immortality of the soul (ch. 13), they have lost that knowledge of God which comes to us only through the Spirit (ch. 12); only through the Logos can we recover the divine image and the promise of immortality which the first humans possessed (ch. 7), because only he was present with the Father from the beginning, when he 'leapt forth' to create the world (ch. 5). A similar doctrine is held by Athenagoras of Athens in his *Embassy*, with the caveat that the Logos is not a contingent being (*genētos*) but the true *gennēma*, or offspring, of the father (*Embassy*, 10). Like his fellow Athenian Aristides, he adopts a philosophical vocabulary in describing God; his epithets—mainly privatives like 'ineffable', 'invisible', 'immortal', and 'immutable'—find parallels in Middle Platonic encomia of the first principle.[1] His treatise is for the most part another defence of monotheism, in which cause he enlists the *Sibylline Oracles*, unaware (as it seems) that they are Jewish or Christian forgeries (*Embassy*, 30. 1). Homer, the tragedians, and Orpheus are also laid under contribution, but only to demonstrate that the Greeks possess only fabulous accounts of the creation and hold their gods in low esteem.

More interesting are the three books *To Autolycus* by Theophilus of Antioch, reputedly a bishop, hence the first cleric among the apologists. The first book is a sluggish vindication of the unity and simplicity of God, eked out by the customary sneers at the folly of pagans. So far, Theophilus stands with the philosophers, but the greater part of his second book is a commentary on the opening chapters of Genesis, the first such exercise in orthodox literature. This record of creation in seven days by omnipotent fiat, he maintains, is more veridical as history and more profitable to the soul than the diverse but jejune cosmogonies of the Greeks. The Bible alone perceives that the beauty and harmony of the world bespeak a rational Creator; for this benign purpose the *logos endiathetos*, or immanent reason of God, came forth as his *logos prophorikos*, or express command, and the *trias*, or Trinity, was completed by his Wisdom—whom we would call the Holy Spirit (*Autol.* 2. 15). To this dogmatic exposition Theophilus adds moral and typological corollaries: the beasts which God created on the fifth day are symbols of the unregenerate in their proper state of servitude to the righteous (*Autol.* 2. 16), while the sun and moon on the fourth day stand for the prophets, and other lights for the people of God (*Autol.* 2. 15). Theophilus recapitulates the biblical account of the corruptions which succeeded the Fall (*Autol.* 2. 31–5), embellishing his attack on the folly of idols with a long quotation from the *Sibylline Oracles* (*Autol.* 2. 36).The third book proves the antiquity of the Mosaic text, and argues that in their conduct Christians realize the virtues which are unanimously, though speculatively, preached in the pagan schools. Epistolary only in its title, this work is longer and more contentious than any letter that is known to have been penned by a Greek philosopher.

26.1.3 The Early Latin Tradition

By contrast, the *Octavius* of Minucius Felix beautifully imitates the form and style of a Ciceronian dialogue. Set in Ostia, it takes for its protagonists two Africans, for whom Fronto is *Cirtensis noster*, a fellow townsman of Cirta in Numidia (*Octavius*, 2. 9). It consists of two reciprocal apologies, for the pagan speaker Caecilian is goaded into invective against the Christians (*Octavius*, 1. 5–3. 15) by his interlocutor's unprovoked assault on his own religion (proem 4). Replying on the behalf of the Church, Octavius never mentions Christ, but argues that the oneness of God is proved by reason, obscure as it may be to our unschooled senses (*Octavius*, 5. 17–19). Error in religion, like disease in the body, is the work of demons (*Octavius*, 8. 26); even they, however, are tools of Providence, for when they are driven out by Christian exorcists, they bear unwilling testimony to the power of God (*Octavius*, 8. 26).

The same arguments are deployed, the same witnesses summoned, in Tertullian's *Apologeticus* of 197 CE (chs. 22–3); Tertullian alone, however, could have scoffed in such a fiery and mordant vein at the decrepitude of pagan shrines and the folly of worshipping deities created in recent memory by the senate (ch. 5). It is clear that he and Minucius are not writing independently, but centuries of debate have failed to demonstrate the priority of either.[2] Tertullian is undoubtedly the more memorable, the more quotable: why, he demands, should Christians be tortured into denying their beliefs, when you torture others to elicit a confession (ch. 2)? Why, when the Tiber floods or the Nile does not, does the populace always raise a shout of 'Christians to the lion'—and why one lion (ch. 40)? Why, for all that, does the earth now groan with the weight of those whose numbers were insignificant the day before yesterday (ch. 39)? Tertullian also improves on Minucius as a dogmatician, explaining that Christ's emergence from the Father to create the world does not impair the unity of the Godhead (ch. 21). He does not elucidate this or other doctrines with the subtlety and minuteness of his later works against heresy and, in contrast to his Greek forebears, he makes little use of the language of philosophy. His reticence is voluntary, for he parades his copious reading in philosophy when he passes from theology to physics in his treatise *On the Soul*.

His two books *Against the Nations* recapitulate the contents of the Apology, though they have more to say on pagan accusations of immorality (1. 7), on the use of the term 'third race' (which he regards as a pagan coinage: 1. 8. 1), and on the spread of biblical customs among the Gentiles (i. 13. 4). An essay *On the*

Witness of the Soul takes up a phrase of his own (*Apol.* 17), contending that in their involuntary exclamations—'God preserve us', 'God be thanked'—the pagans betray a latent knowledge of their Creator. A remonstratory tract to the governor Scapula is of interest to historians because it denies that Christians took up arms for any rival to Septimius Severus in the civil war that commenced in 193. The *Apologeticus* too declares that Christians are invariably loyal to the secular government (*Apol.* 10), provided that it does not attempt to turn their prayers on the Emperor's behalf into an acknowledgement of his divinity. The treatise *On the Shows* deplores atrocities against Christians in the arena, warning the culprits that the martyrs will smile from heaven while they suffer an everlasting retaliation of the same torments. For all his venom, his history of the games remains indispensable to scholars, and he is capable of appealing to the humanity of his persecutors in terms reminiscent of Seneca, who, as he once remarked (*An.* 20. 1), is 'often on our side'.

The showpiece *On the Philosopher's Cloak* may be read as a veiled apology for the robe of faith, which, though their fathers wore it, the Romans ignorantly reject as foreign garb. If that is so, this little work foreshadows the greater apologies of Lactantius and Arnobius, in which Christian values coalesce with those of the ancient Romans. Cyprian of Carthage (d. 258) is the first witness to a libel that was to be invoked as a pretext in a number of Latin apologies: as he tells his correspondent Demetrianus, every natural calamity is now construed by pagans as a punishment sent by jealous gods whose votaries have deserted them for Christ. His rebuttal of this charge is stale enough, and the most formidable defence of Christianity in the corpus of Cyprian's writings is an apocryphal piece, *On the Mountains Sinai and Zion*, which takes for its text the antithesis drawn in Hebrews between the mountain of law and the mountain of redemption; but this, like the *Testimonia* from the Old Testament preserved under Cyprian's name, does not pretend to have been inspired by a persecution, and is merely a polemic against the Jews.

26.2 ALEXANDRIAN APOLOGETIC

Alexandria has a name as the home of Christian philosophy, but even if we forget that Clement (*c.* 150–*c.* 220) is said to have come from Athens and that Origen (185–254) decamped to Caesarea, we should remember that it was in Alexandria, more than in any other Christian centre, that philosophy was put to the test of scripture. Origen held that pagans might be consulted on points of usage or on particulars of natural science, just as an evangelical theologian of our own day might accept the theory of natural selection on authority; but in matters that pertained to God, the self-taught Greek was no more a prophet on his own account than Balaam's ass. The vocabulary came from the schools, the doctrine came from above; the marriage of philosophy with the gospel served to nourish the curiosity and perfect the understanding of believers, while it made their faith intelligible to those (the vast majority still) who were reared in pagan households. It was not, as is often suggested, a device to reconcile the Church to the larger world, for that was not the purpose of philosophy. The philosopher was a dissident by profession, and the creation of an autonomous system gave the Church the right to differ without being liable to the charges of bad citizenship and ignorance that Celsus had hurled against it. Clement looks to philosophy (though not to the living philosopher) as an ally when he mocks the folly and turpitude of the mysteries in his *Exhortation to the Greeks (Protrepticus)*. The alliance is cemented in his *Teacher (Paedagogus)*, the earliest manual of Christian ethics; even here, however, it is clear that the goal of Christian life is service to the incarnate Logos, not the cultivation of an impregnable serenity or the deliverance of the pre-existent soul.

In his *Stromateis*, or eight books of miscellanies, Clement labours to show that Christian thought is congruent with the best in Greek philosophy. By this he means primarily Platonism—not because Plato was more fashionable than any other thinker in Alexandria, but because Christians regarded him as a champion of divine unity, creation in time, and personal immortality entailing reward and punishment after death. It remains true that no doctrine in the *Stromateis* is espoused on the sole authority of any Greek philosopher; that, while he hints that the *logos* is the seat of Platonic ideas (4. 158), Clement never employs the term idea except when quoting Plato; and that the dialogues are cited far less often in the *Stromateis* than the more exiguous writings of St Paul. Clement does not even concede inspiration to the philosophers: only such vessels of prophecy as the Sibyl and Hystaspes are said in the *Stromateis* to have received the truth directly (6. 42–3), and the second half of book 5 is a catalogue of Greek thefts from the Old Testament—none of which, of course, would be recognized as such by a modern scholar. It is not clear whether Clement's object is to impress the pagans, to reconcile Christians to philosophy, or to arm them with new weapons in polemic; it certainly is not to present an encyclopaedic system of dogma, for he gives short weight to such important tenets as the Incarnation and the Resurrection, which were probably treated at greater length in his *Hypotyposes*, or *Outlines of the Faith*.

Origen's *Against Celsus* (*c.* 248 CE), to judge by its title, is unequivocally an apologetic work. It is an answer to a dead man, avowedly written in a time of peace, though usually dated to the eve of the first imperial persecution. It is possible that Origen, already besieged by critics, wrote these eight books as a testament to his own orthodoxy. Here at last he plainly declares that the Fall occurred when Adam and Eve were already clothed in flesh, and that as everyone enters the present world with a body (7.39), not even the saints will be resurrected without one (5. 23). While spurning the accusation that a Christian cannot be loyal to the Empire (8. 73–5), he denies that the one God delegates his authority in the manner of human sovereigns (8. 35), and maintains that the world is under the sway of demons who can be exposed and put to flight by the fortitude of martyrs (8. 44). Christians are not, as Celsus alleges, renegade Jews, but the restorers of the true covenant; for this reason they have a right to seek out and apply to themselves the latent sense of scripture (4. 45). The pagans have established no such right, and in any case even the literal sense of scripture is seldom marred by the obscenities that disfigure the work of Hesiod and Plato (4. 38–9). Solemnity befits the word of God, which is the only source of our knowledge of him, for all that the philosophers try to storm his *incognito* by their syntheses, analyses, and analogies (7. 42). Christ incarnate, revealed to faith in scripture (4. 15), is the plenipotentiary of the hidden Father, one in will, although distinct enough in hypostasis to be called a second God (5. 39).

26.2.1 The Age of the Tetrarchy and Constantine

Porphyry the philosopher sneered that Origen, to justify his defection to Christianity, had applied Stoic palliatives to Hebrew fables (Eusebius, *Hist. eccl.* 6. 19). His attack on Christianity—the existence of which is certain, though its scope and form continue to be debated—elicited from Eusebius (*c.* 260–*c.* 339) the most copious and erudite, and perhaps the last, apology to appear under pagan rulers. Yet he himself plays only an editorial role in his fifteen books of extracts from the literature of paganism and Hellenistic Jewry which make up his *Preparation for the Gospel* (Digeser 2000; see Barnes 1973). But for this compilation, there would scarcely be any material now for editions of the Cynic Oenomaus, the Platonists Atticus and Numenius, Ezekiel the Jewish dramatist, or the mythographer Philo of Byblos; we should have no knowledge of Porphyry's treatise *On Statues* or his dossier of plagiarisms in literature, and only feeble traces of his *Philosophy from Oracles*. Whereas other writers are quoted either to corroborate Christian teaching or to expose the inconsistencies of the Greek tradition, Porphyry is quoted against himself, as an exemplar of the perilous arts by which philosophers reconcile themselves to superstition. His oracles had in fact already been laughed into extinction by Oenomaus (*Hist. eccl.* 5. 21), just as Philo of Byblos had lifted the blanket of allegory from myth (1. 10. 40); the hint that all Greeks are plagiarists (10. 3), however, is not pursued, because Eusebius, alone of the apologists before Constantine, conceded that philosophers might arrive at truth about God by the direct prompting of the Logos (see esp. the *Tricennial Oration*). It is not the antiquity, but the truth, of a thought that gives it value; and since it is more important that a statement should be proved than that it should be elegant, no criterion of stylistic uniformity forbids the transcription of documents in such works as his *Demonstration of the Gospel, Life of Constantine*, and *Ecclesiastical History*. This adoption of a practice more reminiscent of the lawcourts than of classic historiography serves to illustrate the apologetic motive of these writings; the only other composition, however, that is avowedly a defence of Christianity against pagans is the refutation of Sossianus Hierocles, who had argued that the miracles ascribed to the itinerant philosopher Apollonius were superior to those of Christ.[3]

Hierocles is one of two philosophers whom Lactantius (*c.* 260–*c.* 320) accuses of having connived at persecution under Diocletian (*Inst.* 5. 2). The other remains anonymous, but is commonly assumed, for want of another name, to be Porphyry (so Digeser 2000; but cf. Barnes 1973); certainly Lactantius seems to be building a caricature from Porphyry's metaphors, and his appeal to Sibylline prophecies (*Inst.* 7. 13, 16–19, 23–4) may be a calculated rejoinder to Porphyry's compilation of texts from pagan shrines. But, as Lactantius himself informs us (5. 1), his aim in the *Divine Institutes* (seven books in all) is not so much to defend his co-religionists, in the manner of Minucius Felix, Cyprian, and Tertullian, as to bring maturity of understanding to the Christian and to show that his religion is the consummation of all that is best in Roman thought and practice. Seneca, Cicero, Virgil, and Ovid are cited as witnesses to truths that have been more openly revealed and more faithfully honoured in the Church; Christians are in fact the sole practitioners of those virtues which the Romans love to read of, but have ceased to practice under the influence of the conquered Greeks (1. 18). Rome's sovereignty must pass to the East—it troubles even an African to say this (7. 15)—but only in order that the authentic Roman virtues may be immortalized in the new kingdom. The good Christian is a good Roman; conversely, as Lactantius purports to show in his tract *On the Deaths of the Persecutors*, those who oppress the new faith are invariably bad rulers, whom divine providence has marked out for ignominy or painful death.

Both this harsh obituary and the *Institutes* are commonly dated to the second decade of the fourth century. They will therefore have been roughly contemporaneous with Constantine's capture of Rome in 312. This is the last datable event to which he alludes in his *Oration to the Assembly of the Saints* (ch. 22); his language, however, is so arcane that an audience in any other city would have been puzzled to construe it. The detailed appropriation of Virgil's Fourth Eclogue as a messianic prophecy (chs. 19–21) also betokens a Latin audience, as does the absence of the title *Nikētes* (Victor), which was always employed by Constantine in addressing Christians after his seizure of the eastern throne in 324 (Edwards 2003).[4] Whatever its date, this speech will have helped to canonize the argument that a single world requires a single overlord (*Oration*, 3). Lactantius states the same thesis, without the political innuendo (see Digeser 2000); it recurs, with no design to flatter the Emperor, in Athanasius's treatise *Against the Nations* (7. 2; 39), another work of uncertain date, though it can scarcely have been composed before he reached the age of 20 in 318. Athanasius goes on to rehearse familiar objections to idolatry (ch. 22) and to argue that Greek stories of turpitude among the gods must foster public immorality (ch. 26). This work has a more interesting sequel, a defence of the Incarnation against the Platonists, who denied that the transcendent God could unite himself to a portion of the world. In an answer that may be read also as an oblique rejoinder to Arius, Athanasius contends that humans cannot be redeemed by a lesser being than their own archetype, the divine Word who is capable of subsuming his whole creation in one man. Since no death can be natural for such a being, he chose to make a spectacle of his voluntary submission to it, spreading out his arms to embrace humanity (chs. 22–5). Previous apologists, fearing pagan ridicule, had spoken more circumspectly of the passion, but Athanasius was writing when the Cross was already a symbol of Christian triumph and was soon to become the most venerated relic of the Church.

An anomaly of the Constantinian era is the seven-book lucubration of Arnobius, *Against the Nations*. Arnobius was the tutor of Lactantius, reaching his acme, as Jerome tells us, in the reign of Diocletian (*Vir. ill.*). Yet the date assigned to the treatise in Jerome's *Chronicle* is 326/7, and is corroborated not only by the silence of Lactantius but by references in the first book to conversions among the Alamanni and victories over the Scythians (*Nat.* 1. 16). Arnobius's remark that Christianity has been in the world for somewhat less than 300 years (1. 13. 2) is not compatible with an earlier date, and since his references to persecution are vague, generic, and undocumented, we need not doubt Jerome's statement that he wrote this work to demonstrate the sincerity of a late conversion in 326/7 (so Edwards 2004; but cf. Simmons 1995). Porphyry has been plausibly identified as the bell-wether of the 'new men' (*novi viri*) whom he opposes in his second book (2. 13–62); nevertheless, the most original feature of his apology is his argument that, even if Christianity is a novel creed, the new is often better than the old, and all societies, even Rome, have periodically reformed their ancestral customs. This is not to say that Rome has gained by acquiring an empire, since she can now be held accountable for all the barbarous practices at which her pagan rulers have connived. Arnobius's denunciation of sacrifice in book 7 may be a specimen of the Christian agitation against this practice, which led to a general interdict under Constans and Constantius II in 341.

One catalyst to the passing of this decree was the harangue *On the Error of Profane Religions*, addressed to the emperors by Firmicus Maternus. Improving on the remark of Aristides that there are nations who identify their god with one of the elements, Firmicus assigns a deity and an element to each quarter of the barbarian world, so that Egypt is bedevilled by Osiris and water (ch. 2), Phrygia by Attis and air (ch. 3), Assyria and Africa by Venus and air (ch. 4), Persia by Mithras and fire (ch. 5). When the mysteries of these four are suppressed, there will still be others over whom trophies may be erected (20. 7); their shrines should not overawe us, as their weaknesses are freely confessed in Porphyry's *Philosophy from Oracles* (13. 4). Although he is also the author of a treatise on astrology, Firmicus writes in this work not as a philosophical monotheist, but as a Christian, who traces all iniquity to the Fall (ch. 25), maintains that only the blood of Christ can dispel its consequences (28. 1), and damns the pagan mysteries as demonic caricatures of the Christian rites (ch. 27).

26.2.2 Epilogue: Defence without Defendants

The heirs of Constantine did not extinguish paganism, but by securing the ascendancy of the Church, they removed the formal pretext for apologetic. It was no doubt the meteoric reign of Julian (361–3) that prevented it from expiring altogether. If he does not deserve his reputation as persecutor of Christians, he was no friend to the claims of the 'Galilaeans', as he styled them in a long polemic, which spared the Old Testament no more than the New.[5] Where Josephus had boasted that the Jews had a single law and the Gentiles many, Julian held that the multitude of customs refuted Moses, as it showed that all laws are grounded in caprice. Furthermore, he argued, the rejection of any God but the Creator in the Old Testament deprives the latter of any power to act on his creation. Christians cannot adduce this ancient scripture on their own behalf when they flout the laws relating to the Sabbath, sacrifice, and circumcision. The Christ whom they revere is neither God nor an intermediary, but a crucified malefactor who is no better than his votaries. In his rejoinder Gregory of Nazianzus (c. 330–c. 390) mocked the obscenity and folly of the pagan cults for which Julian had sought palliatives in philosophic allegory. Cyril of Alexandria (d. 444) replied in thirty books, of which ten are extant. His defensive expositions of biblical passages are seasoned with invective—hitherto commoner in heresiological literature—against the overweening use of reason in matters known to none but God.

The last of the great apologies is Augustine's *City of God* in twenty-two books. It was conceived as an answer to pagan recriminations against the Christians after Rome was sacked by her own Gothic mercenaries in 410. This event followed hard on the destruction of the pagan Altar of Victory—a measure that had been eloquently commended by Augustine's mentor Ambrose and as eloquently resisted by his former patron Symmachus (see Croke and Harries 1982)—and it was natural that pagans should attribute the reversal of Rome's fortunes to her desertion of the gods. In fact, it was not Augustine who wrote strictly to this brief, but his friend Orosius, whose *Universal History* maintained that the Roman state had been more liable to calamities when it persecuted Christians, and that evils would persist as long as it persevered in error—though there had been some amelioration since the union of church and throne. Augustine replies to the accusation first by pointing out that it was only by posing as Christians that many pagans had eluded death (*Civ.* 1. 1), and then by adumbrating a theological view of history which dethrones every earthly capital. Latin historiography, typified by Cicero's *Republic*, had assumed that Rome's supremacy was fated, and hence an index of divine approval; Augustine holds, by contrast, that from the Fall to the present there have been two cities, one of the reprobate and one of the elect. The first is built by human pomp and artifice, the second gathered secretly by God, to be revealed at the final Judgement. The Church is not identical with the second city, but all who are predestined to salvation in the present world are within her, while the patriarchs and prophets were members by anticipation. Augustine takes occasion to belittle the antiquarian Varro, Cicero's contemporary, whose labours had unearthed a multitude of forgotten deities, each with its petty sphere of action (*Civ.* 6. 4 ff.); he also attacks less obsolete forms of polytheism, urging that omnipotent gods would not rely, as Apuleius imagines, on the mediation of demons (9. 6–8), and that had Porphyry been a Christian, he would have found the universal way to God of which he despairs in his credulous treatise *On the Regression of the Soul* (10. 32). The exposition of God's providential scheme requires him to justify not only the Fall (14. 10–14) but the order of creation (11. 29–34), and to maintain against the Platonists that the world may have an origin in time yet be immortal by divine fiat. Thus we are prepared for the last two books, which prove with sedulous ingenuity that after death our bodies will be able to sustain not only the bliss of heaven but the pains of hell.

It is evident that the project has exceeded its stated purpose, that apologetic has ripened into polemic, which in turn has become the seed for a whole compendium of theology. Augustine may have felt that he had more hope of correcting the errors of believers than of winning over the conscientious pagan who had not already been lured into the Church by worldly interest. After his death, the business of apologists in the West was not to uphold the faith against pagans but to preserve the catholic form of it against German kings who favoured Arian tenets. In the East the Platonists were doughty, but hardly formidable; it was only when the eastern Mediterranean fell to the Arabs that the advocates of Christianity once again had a cause to defend, not merely a case to prove. No doubt it was mere formality when a new caliph or emperor sent his counterpart a reasoned exhortation to conversion (Meyendorff 1982: 104–10), but the *Dialogue of a Saracen and a Christian* by John of Damascus—a Christian in Muslim territory, suspected of idolatry even by his co-religionists—will have been a less perfunctory undertaking. Islam was to him a heresy, the last work of the Antichrist; nevertheless, no Christian apologist before Clement can be shown to have perused the Greek philosophers as closely as this poet and theologian of the eighth century read the Qur'ān.[6]

NOTES

1. Extensively documented by Barnard (1972).
2. Thus Buizen (1915) maintains the priority of Tertullian; Borleffs (1925) argues on the same evidence that Minucius wrote first.
3. The authorship is questioned by Hägg (1992).
4. The hypothesis is proved if, as David Woods suggests, the 'sacred assembly' of the title was initially the senate. Contrast Barnes (2001).
5. On content and purpose see R. Smith (1995: 178–210).
6. See Louth (2002: 76–83) for the dialogue and strictures on Islam in John of Damascus's *On Heresies.*

Suggested Reading

The following four books are recommended: Droge (1989); Daniélou (1973, 1977); and Edwards *et al.* (1999).

Bibliography

Primary texts

ARISTIDES, *Apology*. Trans. and commentary, J. Rendel Harris (Cambridge: Cambridge University Press, 1891); text and commentary, C. Alpigiano (Florence: Nardini Editore, 1988).

ARNOBIUS, *Against the Nations*. Latin text in C. Marchesi (Milan: Paravia, 1953); Eng. trans. in G. McCracken (London: Longmans, 1949).

ATHANASIUS, *Contra Gentes* and *De incarnatione*. Edition, trans. and commentary, R. W. Thomson OECT (Oxford: Clarendon Press, 1971).

ATHENAGORAS, *Legatio*. Text with trans., W. Schoedel OECT (Oxford: Clarendon Press, 1972).

AUGUSTINE, *City of God*, LCL, ed. G. E. McCracken, 7 vols. (Cambridge, Mass.: Harvard University Press, 1931–72).

CLEMENT OF ALEXANDRIA, *Protrepticus*, text, M. Marcovich (Leiden: E. J. Brill, 1995); *Stromateis*, text, ed. O. Staehlin, 4 vols. (Berlin: Akademie-Verlag, 1905–36); translation of Clement's works, ANF 4 and 12.

CONSTANTINE, *Oration to the Saints*. Text, ed. I. A. Heikel (Leipzig: Heinrichs, 1906); trans. M. J. Edwards, *Constantine and Christendom* (Liverpool: Liverpool University Press, 2003).

CYRIL OF ALEXANDRIA, *Against Julian*, PG 76. Critical edition in progress under direction of C. Riedweg (Zurich).

CYPRIAN, *To Demetrianus*. Text, ed. E. Gallicet (Turin: Editrice Torinese, 1976).

Epistle to Diognetus. Text with French trans., ed. H. Marrou (Paris: Éditions du Cerf, 1951). English trans. of this and Justin's corpus in ANF 2.

EUSEBIUS, *Against Hierocles*. Text with trans., as appendix to *Ecclesiastical History*, by J. C. Conybeare (Cambridge, Mass.: Harvard University Press, 1912).

——*Preparation for the Gospel*. Text with trans., ed. E. Gifford, 5 vols. (Oxford: Clarendon Press, 1903).

——*Tricennial Oration*, ed. I. A. Heikel (Leipzig: Hinrichs, 1906 with *Leben Konstantins*); trans. with commentary by H. Drake as *In Praise of Constantine* (Berkeley: University of California Press, 1976).

FIRMICUS MATERNUS, *On the Error of Profane Religions*. Text, ed. A. Pactorini (Florence: Nardini, 1956).

GREGORY OF NAZIANZUS, *Against Julian*. Text, ed. J. Bernardi (Paris: Éditions du Cerf, 1983); Bohn Library trans., C. W. King (London: Bohn, 1888).

JULIAN, *Against the Galilaeans*. LCL, text with trans., ed. W. C. Wright, *Julian*, iii (Cambridge, Mass.: Harvard University Press, 1823), 319–427.

JUSTIN, *Apologies*. Text, A. Wartelle (Paris: L'Institut d'études augustiniennes, 1987); English trans. and commentary, L. W. Barnard (New York: Paulist Press, 1977).

——*Dialogue with Trypho*. Text, M. Marcovich (Berlin: de Gruyter, 1997); trans. T. Falls (Washington D.C.: Catholic University of America Press, 2003).

LACTANTIUS, *Divine Institutes*. Text, ed. S. Brandt *et al.* (Turnhout: Brepols, 1890, 1893). Trans. P. Garnsey (Liverpool: Liverpool University Press, 2003).

——*On the Deaths of the Persecutors*. Text and trans., ed. J. L. Creed (Oxford: Clarendon Press, 1984).

MINUCIUS FELIX, *Octavius*. Text, ed. J. Beaujeu (Paris: Belles Lettres, 1964). English trans. and commentary, G. W. Clarke (New York: Paulist Press, 1974).

ORIGEN, *Against Celsus*. Text, ed. P. Koetschau, 2 vols. (Berlin: Hinrichs, 1899); trans. with introduction, ed. H. Chadwick (Cambridge: Cambridge University Press, 1985).

PSEUDO-JUSTIN. Texts of *On Monarchy* and *Cohortatio*, C. Riedweg (Basle: Reinhardt, 1994).

TATIAN, *Oratio ad Graecos and Fragments*. Text with trans., ed. M. Whittaker OECT (Oxford: Clarendon Press, 1982); text only, M. Marcovich (Berlin: de Gruyter, 1995).

TERTULLIAN. Text of complete works, ed. A. Gerlo, 2 vols. (Turnhout: Brepols, 1950, 1954); trans. ANF 11–13.

THEOPHILUS, *Ad Autolycum*. Text with English trans., ed. R. M. Grant OECT (Oxford: Clarendon Press, 1970); text with Tatian, ed. M. Marcovich (Berlin: de Gruyter, 1995).

Secondary sources

BARNARD, L. W. (1972), *Athenagoras: A Study in Second-Century Apologetic* (Paris: Beauchesne).

BARNES, T. D. (1973), 'Porphyry against the Christians: Date and Attribution of the Fragments', *JTS* 25: 424–42.

——(2001), 'Constantine's Speech to the Assembly of the Saints: Date and Place of Delivery', *JTS* 52: 26–36.

BORLEFFS, J. D. P. (1925), *De Tertulliano et Minucio Felice* (Gröningen: J. B. Wolters).

BUIZEN, C. M. (1915), *Quid Minucius Felix in Dialogo Octavio sibi Proposuerit* (Amsterdam: A. H. Kruyt).

CROKE, B., and HARRIES, J. (1982), *Religious Conflict in Fourth-Century Rome: A Documentary Study* (Sydney: Sydney University Press).

DANIÉLOU, J. (1973), *Gospel Message and Hellenistic Culture*, trans. J. A. Baker (London: Darton, Longman, and Todd).

——(1977), *The Origins of Latin Christianity*, trans. J. A. Baker (London: Darton, Longman, and Todd).

DIGESER, E. (2000), *The Making of a Christian Empire: Lactantius and Rome* (Ithaca, NY: Cornell University Press).

DROGE, A. (1989), *Homer or Moses?* (Tübingen: J. C. B. Mohr).

EDWARDS, M. J. (2003), *Constantine and Christendom* (Liverpool: Liverpool University Press).

——(2004), 'Dating Arnobius: Why Ignore the Evidence of Jerome?', *L'Antiquité Tardive*, 12: 263–72.

——GOODMAN, M. D., and PRICE, S. R. F., with ROWLAND, C. C. (1999), *Apologetics in the Roman Empire* (Oxford: Oxford University Press).

FREDE, M. (1999), 'Eusebius' Apologetic Writings', in Edwards *et al.* (1999), 223–50.

GEFFCKEN, J. (1907), *Zwei Griechischen Apologeten* (Leipzig: B. G. Teubner).

GRANT, R. M. (1988), *Greek Apologists of the Second Century* (Philadelphia: Westminster Press).

Hägg, T. (1992), 'Hierocles the Lover of Truth and Eusebius the Sophist', *SO*, 67: 138–50.

Horner, T. (2001), *Listening to Trypho* (Leuven: Peeters).

Laato, A. M. (1998), *Jew and Christian in the De Duobus Montibus Sina et Sion* (Abo: Abo Akademi University Press).

Louth, A. (2002), *John of Damascus: Tradition and Originality in Byzantine Theology* (Oxford: Oxford University Press).

Meyendorff, J. (1982), *The Byzantine Legacy in the Orthodox Church* (Crestwood, NY: St Vladimir's Seminary Press).

Simmons, M. B. (1995), *Arnobius of Sicca: Religious Conflict and Competition in the Age of Diocletian* (Oxford: Clarendon Press).

Smith, R. (1995), *Julian's Gods: Religion and Philosophy in the Thought and Action of Julian the Apostate* (London: Routledge).

Smith, W. C. (1978), *The Meaning and End of Religion* (London: S.P.C.K.).

CHAPTER 27

···

HOMILETICS

···

WENDY MAYER

UNDERVALUED and largely ignored until the last decade of the twentieth century, the topics of early Christian preaching and the early Christian homily have only recently begun to receive the attention they deserve. What is beginning to emerge from this growing area of research is a realization that the homily and the preaching of it are of far greater interest in their own right and are far more complex than had previously been imagined. That aside, the field itself is a minefield and full of traps for the unwary. If one is to take advantage of the riches offered by early Christian sermons and their preaching, one needs to approach every aspect of this complex field with care.

27.1 EARLIER APPROACHES

···

Scientific study of early Christian preaching can be said to have begun with Joseph Bingham, who treats the subject in book 14, chapter 4, of his ten-volume *Origines Ecclesiasticae* (1708–22, reprinted and re-edited numerous times). Covering topics as varied as who did and did not preach in different parts of the early Christian world, how many homilies were preached at a time and how often, how homilies were preached (whether read, from notes, or spontaneously), what immediately preceded and followed in the liturgy, content and relevance, the length of homilies, audience stance and behaviour, how homilies were delivered, and how they were recorded, so thorough and useful is his survey that it has been superseded only recently. Olivar's monumental *La predicación cristiana antigua* (1991) now offers the most comprehensive treatment of the topic. Prefaced by a brief discussion of the origins and terminus of patristic preaching, the body of this encyclopaedic work divides into two parts: a lengthy survey of individuals who preached in Greek, Latin, Syriac, Armenian, and Coptic; and an equally lengthy discussion of different aspects of preaching. This second half expands on the topics introduced by Bingham, offering a much more developed study of the audience, and in addition including new topics such as the classification of homilies, where homilies were delivered, attendance levels, and textual transmission.

Prior to the 1990s interest in early Christian homilies *per se* and in the act of preaching was limited (Cunningham 1990). Attention tended to focus on a small number of areas: the editing of texts, the associated issues of textual transmission and authenticity, the rhetorical or syntactical analysis of individual corpora (with emphasis on the Second Sophistic (Ameringer 1921; but see Müller 1954 on preaching techniques in Coptic), and consideration of exegetical technique or theological or moral content. Throughout this period there was a tendency to pair hagiography and homiletics (e.g. Ehrhard 1937–52), and the volumes of the *Bibliotheca Hagiographica Latina* (*BHL*) and *Graeca* (*BHG*) remain major sources for locating unedited homilies on saints and martyrs. In publishing diplomatic editions of single homilies and information about inedita that exist in a variety of languages, the journals *Analecta Bollandiana*, *Revue Bénédictine*, and *Le Muséon*, among others, have throughout the twentieth century played a major role. The series Corpus Christianorum (CCSL (Latin): 1953– ; CCSG (Greek): 1976–) and Sources Chrétiennes (SC) (1941–) have also been instrumental in publishing new editions of homilies in the Greek and Latin tradition.

Throughout this period a few isolated scholars displayed interest in other aspects of preaching. As early as 1907 it was recognized that homilies were a significant source of social and cultural information (Vance 1907), which led to the occasional exploration of a particular aspect of popular belief or practice via the corpus of a specific homilist (Politis 1921; Loukatos 1940; Graffin 1978), and later to a small number of articles advocating the investigation of homilies from this perspective (Berthold 1977; Spira 1985). The occasional study of the preacher's audience also appeared. In 1917 Zellinger published a brief article on audience acclamations and applause in early Christian homilies; in 1945 Pontet included a chapter on the audience and where the homilies were preached in his examination of Augustine's homiletical exegesis; and in 1968 Bernardi produced an investigation of the preacher and his audience with a focus on Basil of Caesarea, Gregory of Nazianzus, and Gregory of Nyssa. These were followed more than a decade later by investigations on Maximus of Turin (Devoti 1981), Romanos Melodos (Hunger 1984), Origen (Monaci Castagno 1987), and the Cappadocians, this time expanded to include Chrysostom (MacMullen 1989). Not until Olivar (1991) and the first focused study of the preacher–audience dynamic within the eastern church (Cunningham and Allen 1998), however, did the subject begin to receive treatment across more than a narrow range of preachers in any depth. Aside from the topics of homilies as a source for daily life and for the preacher and his audience, the subject of how homilies were composed, delivered, and recorded has also received brief attention (Wikenhauser 1907; Deferrari 1922).

27.2 REVALUING EARLY CHRISTIAN PREACHING

In the last decade of the twentieth century, early Christian homiletics began to come into its own as a serious field of research. Homiletics, often lumped together in scholars' minds with hagiography, had in the main been viewed prior to that point as 'popular', and therefore trivial. The rise of late antiquity as a separate discipline, with its emphasis on cultural and social history, rather than the history of ideas, and its equal interest in the eastern and western regions of the Mediterranean, has played a significant role in the recent rehabilitation of the homily and its elevation in value. When scholars wish to recover the daily life of a city, to explore villages and the surrounding countryside, or to look at sectors of the population other than the elite, it is to the more 'popular' or bureaucratic literary forms, such as saints' lives, homilies, and letters, that they are obliged to turn. The result has been the greater inclusion of homilies as evidence in recent publications, the change in view being epitomized by Peter Brown in the epilogue to the new edition of his biography of Augustine. 'On looking back', he writes, 'I think…that I had not paid sufficient attention at the time to his sermons and letters' (Brown 2000: 446). He then goes on to show how remedying this oversight now substantially alters his perspective on the Augustine he had come to know.

Homilies have other riches to offer, in addition to access to the daily life of the world in which they played a role. Homilies from Origen onwards, to varying degrees, reflect the rhetorical training of the day. That rhetorical expertise was taken up and transformed in the service of communicating God's word. In the process, the early Christian homily became a new rhetorical and literary form in its own right, albeit not one that sprang forth newly formed. While homilies have been studied piecemeal as works of persuasion, which promote a discourse and construct a reality often quite at odds with that experienced by the audience whom they sought to persuade (Wilken 1983), and while Averil Cameron (1991) does much to locate them among the texts through which the alternative reality of Christian discourse gained its power, what we lack is a serious engagement with the homily as both medium and message in its own right. As part of this, we need to document and analyse the exempla that homilists use and document in greater detail the diverse forms which a homily can take. We need to trace more thoroughly the development of discourse on topics such as authority, poverty, wealth, marriage, and virginity across regions and through time, with an awareness that the choice of exempla or topic has as much to say as the exempla and topic themselves. We need to liberate ourselves from the study of great preachers to focus on the homily itself. This kind of approach is just beginning to emerge (Retzleff 2003) and will gain momentum as traditional approaches to the homily continue to bring their reward.

Homilies have an important role to play, too, as liturgical documents. By the end of the third century, the act of preaching within the Christian assembly had become a culminating moment in the Liturgy of the Word. Delivered variously in response to the date in the local liturgical calendar, the lections of the day, or to novel events (such as the arrival of new relics), and at different locations in a city or its suburbs, the homily can be a rich source of information about regional variation in liturgical practice and about local liturgical practice and developments. The value of the homily in this area has long been recognized (Baumstark 1897–99; 1925; Willis 1962; van de Paverd 1970; Sottocornola 1973), but there is much unexplored that remains, particularly in the domain of what took place liturgically in the streets and public spaces of towns and cities. The acts of preaching and receiving the homily also offer fruit for research. Reception theory, for instance, has scarcely been applied to the field of early Christian homiletics, and is due to receive attention. The effect of preaching on the audience and their subsequent behaviour is another area that is just beginning to receive serious analytical thought in light of Bourdieu's theory of *habitus* (Maxwell 2006: 144–68; Bourdieu 1990), as is the framing of preacher and audience within theories of religious identity and religious interaction drawn from both anthropology and sociology.

27.3 THE ORIGINS AND EARLY DEVELOPMENT OF CHRISTIAN PREACHING

One aspect of early Christian homiletics that received surprisingly little attention before the 1970s is the question of how Christian preaching arises from within the classical Graeco-Roman and Jewish traditions. Initially this question was posed by scholars of the New Testament and post-apostolic era, who were less interested in following it through to the emergence of mature preaching in the third and fourth centuries. Kyrtatas's sociological approach to the question (1988) constitutes one of the few attempts at this early period to explain the full development of the phenomenon. Relying on the analytical concepts of prophets and priests, which always existed side by side within the early church, Kyrtatas traces a transfer of authority over time from prophets to priests, associated with the requirement for radically new techniques for communicating moral instruction to the masses that emerged following the conversion of Constantine. In his schema, as one of the radical new tools, preaching became a powerful underpinning of priestly authority, although elements of prophetic sensitivity were still preserved within the priestly ministry.

Recently, a more nuanced model has been proposed (Stewart-Sykes 2001), in which during the period between the teaching ministry of Jesus and Origen a development from prophecy to preaching in the need to communicate the word of God 'to believers within the Christian assembly' is likewise traced. For Stewart-Sykes the origins lie in the need to test the prophetic message, which saw prophecy becoming increasingly tied up with scripture, as this could be used to provide an external check. In the process, the techniques of scrutinizing prophecy became transferred to scripture itself. All of this took place initially within a household setting, and was quite separate from preaching in the synagogue or from the practice of the Hellenistic philosophical schools. In time, however, and parallel to the development of a growing respect for the written scriptural canon and a growing dominance of scripture over prophecy, the households themselves developed into scholastic social organizations, with the result that the models of communication current in the synagogue, and to a lesser extent in the Hellenistic schools, came to influence how the word of God was communicated. This development occurred unevenly in different regions within the first three centuries, but is seen by Stewart-Sykes essentially to underpin the development of moral exhortation and scriptural exegesis which emerge as normative elements in the preaching of the fourth century. The homily is thus not a 'new creation', as some have claimed (Merkt 1997; Schäublin 1994), but an oral form that has a long evolution from prophetic traditions and which has absorbed influences from Jewish synagogue preaching and Hellenistic philosophical pedagogy along the way.

While this model accords the Hellenistic schools a lesser degree of influence in the first three centuries of Christian preaching, their influence by the fourth century was more considerable. After his ordination to the priesthood, Augustine, for example, maintained his interest in the mode of spiritual guidance adopted by classical philosophical teachers, and this understanding of 'psychagogy' can be traced clearly in his homiletical theory and practice (Kolbet 2002). Again, while Stewart-Sykes shows that one cannot look to the diatribe form for the origins of the early Christian homily, it is undeniably the case that the diatribe style, utilized by classical philosophical teachers, influenced the homiletic techniques employed by some preachers of the later fourth century (Uthemann 1998). Indeed, with the flowering of preaching in both East and West in the later third and fourth centuries, rhetorical techniques, forms, and exempla learnt by the homilists of wealthier background during their secular education were readily appropriated and transformed, becoming an essential and inseparable part of preaching (Hong 2004; Schäublin 1994; Oberhelman 1991).

27.4 PROBLEMS OF DEFINITION

A key problem in dealing with early Christian homiletics is the question of definition. What constitutes a homily? This question has been a particular dilemma for investigators of the origins of Christian preaching, for whom the greatest difficulty has surrounded the task of identifying homilies among early literary remains. For the period prior to Origen, the task involves a great deal of circularity in argument, since what we tend to identify as a homily in the later third and fourth centuries and beyond does not identifiably exist at that earlier time. Scholars who engage with homilies from this later period, on the other hand, have tended not to ask the question at all, on the assumption that the characteristics of a homily are by this later period self-evident. However, if we believe that a norm has developed by the fourth century, or look to the works of the major preachers of the Latin- and Greek-speaking worlds as our models, the idea of what constitutes a homily that results is misleading, since in the Syriac-speaking East, homiletics developed in a more fluid way. Within a liturgical setting, the blurred boundaries that existed between instruction that was spoken and that was chanted, and the development of the *memra* or verse homily, not dissimilar to the *madrasha* or teaching song, both of which served to instruct the audience in the teachings of the church (Griffith 1998: 12–16), negate the effectiveness of a definition of preaching derived from a strictly Graeco-Roman setting. The difficulty with definition is intensified when local practice is transferred to another context, as in the case of Romanos Melodos, a native of Emesa whose works were delivered in the churches of Constantinople. His *kontakia* are usually seen as a category of hymn, so different are they from the Greek homiletic 'norm' of the fourth and fifth centuries, but can also be identified as homiletic (Hunger 1984). At the most basic level, then, all that we can claim is that a homily is something that conforms to a few essential conditions, but whose shape is elastic and changes with regional cultural conditions and with time.

What conditions are essential, however, is a matter of debate. In terms of setting, investigators of the origins of preaching point out that the communication of God's word to believers within the Christian assembly, whether within a house or a church, is only one of three options, which include catechesis and missionary preaching. A broad definition that embraces all three homiletic settings and audiences is required, if it is to describe the full range of what occurs as preaching develops over the first six centuries. Orality, on the other hand, has been put forward as a defining characteristic of the Christian homily (Merkt 1997). The words *homilia* in the Greek tradition and *sermo* in the Latin both indicate a conversation or dialectic, while the verbs *didaskalein* and *praedicare* indicate instruction or teaching, and speaking in front of an audience or proclaiming, respectively. The full range of terms used by homilists of their own activity fall within this general pattern (Olivar 1991: 487–511). Unfortunately, retrieving definitive marks of 'orality' from what has come down to us as a written (and often edited) text can prove difficult, and involves the kinds of circular arguments that are required when one tries to identify a 'homily' in the period prior to Origen, when the 'norm' used to test what one has found itself derives from a later century. In some cases, what are considered characteristic features of orality (direct address, use of the second person, remarks on audience response and behaviour, topical references) have been edited out in the subsequent process of transmission (Merkt 1997: 82 on Augustine and Maximus of Turin). In others, there is evidence that preachers wrote out their homilies beforehand and memorized them before delivering them themselves, or intentionally wrote homilies for dissemination to, and delivery by, others (Deferrari 1922; Olivar 1991: 589–633). When the arguments for 'orality' are carefully scrutinized, it can be seen that what they really seek to identify is spontaneity (evidence that material has been added *ad hoc*, without prior meditation). Yet, when Syrian preaching, with its formal poetic structures, is included, marks of spontaneity fail entirely as a criterion. It is delivery, rather than 'orality', that is in most of the instances adduced the common feature.

That delivery before an assembly of some kind has been considered an important criterion is shown by the development within the literature of categories such as 'desk homily' and 'commentary' (Junod 1994). These are usually used to distinguish between something with homiletic features that was delivered (regardless of whether it was written out beforehand) and something with the same or similar features that was written but not delivered (at least not in a liturgical, catechetical or missionary setting). Here we arrive at much the same problem as before. If what has been passed down to us is in the form of a written text, how do we know whether or not it was ever delivered? At the same time, in a culture of relatively low literacy levels it cannot be assumed that a 'commentary' on scripture was not in fact produced for reading out loud to a Christian assembly of some kind, and can therefore be said to qualify as orally delivered instruction. These questions are brought to the fore by a work such as Augustine's *Enarrationes in psalmos*, a 'commentary' put together by Augustine himself, which contains material which he had written in the style and form of a 'homily', but apparently never delivered, to supplement homilies that he had actually preached (Olivar 1991: 933). In the end, the usefulness of artificial distinctions of this kind needs to be questioned, and we should perhaps accept that the term 'homily' covers a much broader range of possibilities than is usually admitted. In this respect, medieval sermon studies, a field which is more advanced, may have something to offer (e.g. Howard 1995, who introduces the idea of an 'oral artifact').

Criteria based on length, structure, intended audience, and the existence or otherwise of features such as scriptural exegesis and moral exhortation are equally problematic, since some of the features assumed to be homiletic are also characteristic of other early Christian literary forms, and the arguments used to support such criteria are again often circular. That a criterion such as length is dependent on norms based on what survives can be demonstrated by the reappraisal of the length of Augustine's preaching occasioned by the discovery of the Dolbeau sermons. In the case of those sermons that are doublets of ones already known, the previously known sermons on which such assumptions were based have proved to be drastically shortened due to editing, such that Dolbeau 23 is five-sixths longer than Sermon 374, and Dolbeau 26 contains more than 1,500 lines compared to some sixty in Sermon 198 (Hill 2000). This finding has implications for distinctions that have been made between tractates and homilies, which have their basis in large part in assumptions about length.

Even if we restrict ourselves to preaching in the post-Constantinian era, when it is presumed that homiletics has settled down into a set of norms, and focus on preaching in the Latin- and Greek-speaking worlds alone, classification of the homiletic subtypes, too, fails to be straightforward. Of the categories proposed (Olivar 1991: 511–14)—exegetical (continuous series, as well as independent homilies) and thematic (catechesis, homilies following the liturgical cycle, panegyrics of persons both living and dead, moral exhortation, and circumstantial homilies)—these types, based on content, are inadequate for describing every possibility. As a result, Olivar is forced to resort to locating together a range of disparate, nonconforming homilies under 'other'. If study of early Christian homiletics is to continue to progress in a scientific way, a clearer and broader definition of the category 'homily' and an alternative classification of its subtypes are an urgent desideratum. Of equal urgency to early Christian homiletics is a detailed study of how preaching developed in the third to sixth centuries from Origen onwards, with the virtuoso homilists relegated to the background, preaching in languages other than Latin and Greek accorded equal status, and careful attention paid to regional variation and the progressive absorption or loss of different influences. A small step has been taken along this path by Paz (1994), with his study of the development of homiletic discourse in late antique and Visigothic Spain.

27.5 Basic Sources

Two reference works are essential to any study of early Christian homilies within the Latin or Greek tradition. For homilists of the first six centuries who preached in languages other than these, tracking down individual works or gaining a quick overview of their corpora is more problematic. Of the two key works of reference, one, the *Clavis Patrum Latinorum* (*CPL*) can be frustrating, because of the failure to assign individual homilies a unique number and entry. It remains, however, the primary place to look, if one wishes to track down the authorship of a particular homily or to check its authenticity. Of particular use is cross-referencing, where new editions now exist, to earlier editions in Patrologia Latina (PL) and its Supplement (PLS). Information concerning the most recent edition, at the time of the publication of *CPL*, is always supplied. For the Greek homiletic tradition, the more detailed, and more helpfully organized, *Clavis Patrum Graecorum* (*CPG*) is an essential reference, although it is important to constantly cross-check the Supplement with the original volumes in order to ensure the most up-to-date information. *CPG*, in particular, assigns uniquely numbered entries to individual homilies or homiletic series, gives information about the *editio princeps*, inedita, or new editions in progress, and, like *CPL*, provides a cross-reference to older editions in *Patrologia Graeca* (PG), where they exist. It also provides references to versions of homilies in other languages (Syriac, Latin, Coptic, Armenian, Georgian, Slavic, Old Russian, Palestino-Aramaic, Arabic), including cataloguing survivals in other languages when a Greek original is missing. Information about authenticity is an important feature of both *CPL* and *CPG*, since in the process of transmission many homilies were passed down under the names of a variety of authors.

Establishing and finding the best edition of a homily to use can be a difficult process. Despite the assistance of *CPL* and *CPG*, and the steadily increasing number of new editions located in major series such as CCSL, CCSG, SC, and Patrologia Orientalis (PO; 1903–)—occasionally also in Corpus Scriptorum Ecclesiasticorum Latinorum (CSEL)—isolated homilies are just as often edited in locations that are difficult to access, such as doctoral dissertations, articles in journals, and isolated monographs by less well-known academic publishers. The large numbers of manuscripts which can be involved in establishing a reliable stemma, especially for major homiletic authors, has tended to lead to the appearance of new editions of small clusters of homilies or small exegetical series first. With the attention of editors tending to focus on the more major authors, it is often the case that no new edition has been attempted since those that appear in PG and PL, which are themselves simply reprints of editions which were undertaken in the seventeenth and eighteenth centuries. While a few small corpora have been edited in recent decades in a single location (Leontius of Constantinople, Leo I, Asterius of Amasea, Amphilochius of Iconium), in the majority of cases the difficulties just described prevail. In the case of Ephrem, whose works (both authentic and dubious) appear in a variety of languages, the editions by Assemani (1732–46) and Lamy (1882–1902), neither satisfactory, remain the default, while improved editions of some of the homilies and hymns have appeared subsequently in the series Corpus Scriptorum Christianorum Orientalium (CSCO; 1903–) and elsewhere (Griffith 1998: 1–2). In the case of Severus of Antioch, a sixth-century homilist whose output, originally preached in Greek, survives mainly in Syriac and occasionally in Coptic translation, the text available in PO is a diplomatic edition without critical apparatus. In the case of John Chrysostom, not only is less than 20 per cent of his corpus available in new scientifically edited texts, but in the case of his exegetical series on the Pauline letters (a group of 244 homilies), an edition which improves upon that of Montfaucon (reproduced in PG) was published by Field in the mid-1800s, but rapidly went out of print and, due to problems of access and awareness, is only rarely used in preference. The Montfaucon edition itself (1718–38), upon which one is obliged to rely for the bulk of Chrysostom's homilies, is often based on a limited collation of manuscripts, contains lacunae which can now be filled from elsewhere, and on occasion groups homilies together as a series without support of the manuscript tradition. The situation with Augustine is little better, with editions of some homilies in CCSL, some in Dolbeau, some in articles in *Revue Bénédictine* and other journals, and yet others still in PL and PLS. In the majority of cases, consulting *CPL* and *CPG* is indispensable, and immersing oneself in the modern history of the editing of the homilies of the particular author in which one is interested essential.

A final point to be kept in mind is the issue of the clear identification of individual homilies. When homilies are cited by those who do not work intimately with homiletics as a field, this is often done idiosyncratically, which can result in confusion. Because we owe a great deal to European scholarship in this field, Latin was adopted at an early date as the standard for labelling homilies. Even if this protocol is observed, since homilists often preached on the same topic more than once, there often exist in the larger corpora more than one homily with the same or a similar title (such as *In martyres, Hom. in martyres, In martyres omnes*). If clear reference to the *editio princeps* or to *CPG* is not also supplied, it can be difficult to distinguish them. In a corpus such as that of Chrysostom, with more than 820 genuine homilies and some 3,000 dubious or spurious homilies that survive under his name, the necessity for supplying as much detail as possible when citing an individual homily is urgent. This is also the point at which the lack of individually numbered entries for homilies in *CPL* becomes problematic. In the case of Augustine, with editions occurring in a number of different locations, clear reference to the edition along with the sermon number is essential. It is in any case important to be aware that the order in which a group of homilies is presented, or indeed the grouping of a number of homilies together, can be unique to a particular edition, with changes in numbering or grouping occurring between some of the former seventeenth- and eighteenth-century editions that were commonly used and recent modern editions.

27.6 METHODOLOGICAL ISSUES

Aside from problems of definition, the status of editions, and problems of identi-fication, the sheer weight of the methodological issues that face anyone attempting to use an early Christian homily can be overwhelming. This is due in no small part to what happened to a homily after it had been delivered. In the case of Augustine, Origen, Basil of Caesarea, John Chrysostom, Gaudentius of Brescia, and Gregory the Great, we know that *notarii*, or stenographers, were often present in the audience and recorded the homilies verbatim in shorthand as they were delivered (Olivar 1991: 902–22). In some cases, the homilies were subsequently written out in full and published without alteration. Some homilies were written down by the author beforehand and later distributed. In yet other cases, the homilist appears to have collated his own homilies exegeting the same book of scripture, edited them, and published them as a commentary. This might even necessitate the production of new homilies (written, but not delivered) to fill in the gaps. Of Augustine's *Enarrationes in psalmos*, for instance, it is estimated that 119 were actually delivered, while a further 86 were dictated in the form of a homily (Olivar 1991: 933). The editorial process in such cases could also be undertaken by a colleague of the homilist, as the title to Chrysostom's homilies on Hebrews suggests.

The degree to which the homilist had control of what happened to the homily after it was preached could vary considerably. In the case of John Chrysostom, the titles appended to a set of homilies he preached in response to major polit-ical events are clearly not from his own hand, since in some cases the summary of the contents and identification of the individuals involved are mistaken (Alan Cameron 1988: 35–6). This is thought to have occurred early enough that the events were within memory of the author of the titles, but not so early that they were remembered accurately. In the case of Chrysostom's numerous exegetical series, those on Colossians and Hebrews, at least, were not assembled in their final form until long after the homilies that constitute them were preached, since they contain homilies from two separate locations and therefore two different periods in his career (Allen and Mayer 1994; 1995). Homilies could, on the other hand, be edited quite substantially by later copyists, as homilies were reused in later centuries and as needs and audiences changed. The significant differences between some of the Dolbeau sermons of Augustine and previously known versions of the same sermons have already been mentioned. The alteration could be subtle, with the removal of difficult words, technical discussions, and references to events and controver-sies local to the time of Augustine, performed in such a way that the tone was preserved intact, making it difficult to discern their removal (Hill 2000: 16). Such material, of great interest to us, was clearly of little interest to the medieval copyists and their intended audience. In the case of Chrysostom's fifty-five homilies on Acts, Byzantine editors of the eleventh century added material that they thought

Chrysostom should have said, and smoothed out his Greek to suit their taste, with variations between what is thought to be the oldest version (the rough recension) and the later, smooth recension of up to 17 per cent (Gignac 1998). In the case of his homily *De resurrectione*, a long and a short recension survive, which are identical in part but otherwise differ substantially. Determining the authenticity of each, which came first, and their relationship is a difficult and subtle process, and even the most recent conclusions are provisional (Rambault 1999).

The categories of 'dubious' and 'spurious' homilies complicate the picture even further. The category 'dubious' describes those homilies which are a later composite of material original to an earlier author such as Augustine, extracted and linked in ways which suited users of the seventh to ninth centuries and later. Worthy of study in their own right, they also offer a witness to at least fragments of the original compositions. The category 'spurious' describes a much more diverse and complicated body of work. Passed down under another author's name for a variety of reasons, these homilies were usually wholly authored by someone else. The corpora of a number of lesser-known preachers have survived in this manner, such as Leontius of Constantinople (Datema and Allen 1987) and Severian of Gabala (Datema 1988), usually by attribution to the much more famous Chrysostom; while in the case of Caesarius of Arles and Maximus of Turin, survival of many of their homilies depended on the name of Augustine. The case of Ephrem is even more complex. The relationship between the works attributed to him that survive in Greek and those that survive in Syriac is distant, and the biographies demonstrate two distinct personae (Griffith 1998: 5). Identifying an 'author' or even discussing authenticity in this instance is problematic, and so we talk of 'Ephraem Graecus' and 'Ephraem Syrus' to distinguish the two corpora. To further complicate matters, monks of the Graeco-Syrian communities of the sixth century, in addition to transmitting the works of Ephraem Graecus in both Greek and Syriac, composed new *memre* and *madrashe* in his style and under his name (Griffith 1998: 6). Falsification of a quite different and more malicious kind appears to have occurred towards the end of John Chrysostom's career, with at least one homily attributed to him (*Sermo cum iret in exsilium*), of which fragments survive, in which the empress Eudoxia is slandered. This is probably only one of a number of spurious homilies circulated by his enemies with the intent of exacerbating an already difficult situation, among which the famous Herodias homily cited by Socrates (*Hist. eccl.* 6. 18) can probably be numbered (Voicu 2005). From this it can be seen that knowledge of the transmission history of a homily or set of homilies and of the relationship between author and homily is vital, if homilies are to be used with care. It is an unfortunate fact of working with homilies that certainty in either case is not always achievable, although it is a goal always to be pursued.

Translation is another means by which the gap between homilist and the homily handed down to us can widen. We have seen that the corpus attributed to Ephrem has been passed down from an early period in both Greek and Syriac, and we have also seen that the corpus of Severus of Antioch, originally preached in Greek, survives now almost entirely in Syriac, with a few homilies surviving also in Coptic. The reasons for translation, and for the particular languages in which the works of an individual homilist survive, are various. In the case of Severus, the cause is twofold. In regard to the survival of his works in Syriac, he maintained a Mono-physite Christology against the Chalcedonian view which was supported by the eastern emperors and the West. On his exile in 518, his works, now labelled heretical, were at risk, and his supporters moved quickly to preserve them by translating them into Syriac, the local but less widely known language. Two separate translations are known: one by Paul of Callinicus produced within ten years of Severus's departure into exile, and another by Jacob of Edessa, produced in the first half of the seventh century. That the strategy worked is indicated by the survival of 125 homilies in Syriac, while only a few fragments in Greek remain. In the case of their survival in Coptic, Severus fled in exile to Egypt, where the local church embraced his beliefs and thus translated his works into the local language for its own benefit (Allen and Hayward 2004).

While the works of homilists from the Latin-speaking world were rarely trans-lated into anything other than later western languages, those of homilists from the Greek-speaking world were frequently translated into Latin as well as a variety of eastern languages. In the case of John Chrysostom, translations of his homilies and treatises into Latin occurred at a very early date, such that Jerome, Augustine, and others were familiar with them. Of other eastern preachers, both genuine and spuri-ous homilies of the Cappadocians, Amphilochius of Iconium, Asterius of Amasea, Eusebius of Emesa, Athanasius, Theophilus of Alexandria, and many others have been passed down to us variously in Armenian, Syriac, Georgian, Arabic, Ethiopic, and Old Slavic. In some cases the translation occurred at a sufficiently early date that the translation bears witness to a version of the homily older than the Byzantine manuscripts in which the Greek 'original' often survives. Precisely because of this phenomenon, more serious attention needs to be paid to the surviving translations of homilies in languages other than Greek and Latin than has hitherto been the case.

The issues of provenance (in which town or city a homily was delivered) and chronology (sequence and date) are equally critical, and here the peculiarities of the careers of individual preachers, rather than the problem of what happened to the homilies once they were out of the preacher's mouth or hand, play a role. Throughout their careers homilists did not always preach in the one location, with Augustine moving between Hippo and Carthage, Chrysostom from Antioch to Constantinople, and Gregory of Nazianzus from Nazianzus to Constantinople and back again. Even homilists whose preaching career is largely tied to the one location, such as Severus of Antioch, did regular circuits out into surrounding towns and villages, and preached to congregations there, an activity which Basil undertook in the vicinity of Caesarea and Pontus, and which the Dolbeau sermons show that Augustine also undertook in the towns of the Medjerda Valley in the vicinity of

Carthage. Theodoret of Cyrrhus preached at Antioch on several occasions when he visited there, as too did Eusebius of Emesa. We know from Chrysostom's remarks in a homily preached at Constantinople (*In illud: Pater meus usque modo operatur*) that the bishop of Galatia had preached in that city on the previous Sunday. Numerous bishops visited Constantinople during the latter decades of the fourth century, who presumably also took advantage of the opportunity to deliver a guest homily. Severian of Gabala preached the majority of those homilies which survive during his periods of residency in Constantinople, but must also have preached other homilies in Gabala, his own see. John Chrysostom, Palladius implies, even preached in Armenia while in exile (*Dialogue on the Life of John Chrysostom*, 11). The issue of date is thus dependent to a large degree on an accurate map (over space and time) of an individual homilist's movements. This necessitates a careful understanding of the homilist's life and how his preaching career fitted into it, in addition to knowing about the history of an individual homily and understanding how it fits into the corpus.

Because of its dependency on provenance, and because titles to homilies are not always reliable and we are thus thrown on to internal evidence for determining the sequence in which homilies were preached (when a large enough corpus exists to attempt this), the issue of dating homilies is far more complex than has hitherto been appreciated. In the case of the two largest corpora of homilies which survive, those of Augustine and John Chrysostom, publications of only very recent appearance have begun to challenge long-accepted schema for dating these homilies. In the process they have called the fundamentals of the methodology previously employed into question (Drobner 2000, 2003, 2004; Mayer 1999, 2005). What is remarkable in the case of Augustine is that a complete reappraisal of the dating of his homilies, taking the Dolbeau sermons into account, which is itself now brought into question by Drobner, had only just been published (Hombert 2000). So rapid has this overturning of the chronology of Augustine's sermons been that Brown in his epilogue to the new edition of his Augustine biography, penned in 1999, refers to the new advances in chronology not of Hombert, but of La Bonnardière (Brown 2000: 483), which emerged as the new authority after the writing of Brown's original biography in 1961. The major argument in the work of Drobner and Mayer is that the methodology previously applied was insufficiently rigorous, and as a result a completely new methodology for dating homilies needs to be developed. This requires being more honest about how much weight particular kinds of internal evidence can bear, and being more scrupulous about matching internal with external evidence. The reappraisal being undertaken in both these corpora has profound implications for the dating of homilies across the board, and it may prove the case that achieving an accurate date for homilies within much smaller corpora, except in isolated cases, will prove impossible. What this latest upheaval counsels is caution when approaching the conclusions of previous scholars regarding both chronology and provenance, and the acute necessity of reconsidering the evidence for oneself.

The growing utilization of homilies as a historical source leads to a further methodological issue that complicates how we read the evidence. The homily from Origen onwards is in essence a rhetorical medium. At the same time, one of its primary purposes is pedagogical. As a result, whatever data relevant to daily life or to a historical event that a homily contains are often only piecemeal and have been selected and presented in a way that suits the homilist's agenda. Reading such data at face value is ill-advised, and a careful consideration of the context in which the data occur, as well as the rhetorical medium, is essential (Mayer 2005: 480–5; 2001). In addition, distinguishing between an exemplum that is a standard part of the rhetorical repertoire and an exemplum that has a basis in the realia of local conditions can be extremely difficult, while the vagaries of the transmission process (as seen in the case of the Dolbeau sermons, with their restoration of large slabs of information about the local Donatist situation) can mean that information that might otherwise change our interpretation of the evidence that we do have is unfortunately missing.

While the difficulties that attach to utilizing early Christian homilies can be considerable, this should not be seen as a stumbling block, but as a challenge. The study of early Christian homiletics, still in its infancy, has much to yield the sensitive investigator as it is explored in more scientific and novel ways in the years to come.

Suggested Reading

Despite its antiquity, the best starting point on this topic for the English-language reader remains Bingham 1708–22, bk. XIV, ch. iv (in any edition). While some of the specifics are no longer accurate, the wide-ranging topics give the reader a broad awareness of the context of preaching in the early Christian era and of some of the local peculiarities. Olivar (1991, in Spanish) is the most up-to-date reference on the topic, but is not readily accessible. For discussion of the origins of Christian preaching, Stewart-Sykes (2001) provides a useful introduction, now supplemented by Maxwell (2006: ch. 1). Cunningham and Allen (1998) provide the most comprehensive discussion of the relationship between preacher and audience in the East. A comparable study is still awaited for the West.

Bibliography

Works of reference

Bibliotheca Hagiographica Latina Antiquae et Mediae Aetatis, Subsidia Hagiographica, 6 (Brussels: Société des Bollandistes, 1898–1901, repr. 1992).

Bibliotheca Hagiographica Latina Antiquae et Mediae Aetatis: Novum Supplementum, Subsidia Hagiographica, 70 (Brussels: Société des Bollandistes, 1986).

DEKKERS, E. (1995) (ed.), *Clavis Patrum Latinorum*, 3rd edn., CC (Turnhout: Brepols).

EHRHARD, A. (1937–52), *Überlieferung und Bestand der hagiographischen und homiletischen Literatur der griechischen Kirche von den Anfängen bis zum Ende des 16. Jahrhunderts*, TU 50–2 (Leipzig: J. C. Hinrichs).

GEERARD, M. (1974–87) (ed.), *Clavis Patrum Graecorum*, 5 vols., CC (Turnhout: Brepols).

——and NORET, J. (1998) (eds.), *Clavis Patrum Graecorum: Supplementum*, CC (Turnhout: Brepols).

HALKIN, F. (1957) (ed.), *Bibliotheca hagiographica graeca*, Subsidia Hagiographica, 8 (Brussels: Société des Bollandistes; repr. 1985).

——(1984), *Novum Auctarium Bibliothecae hagiographicae graecae*, Subsidia Hagiographica, 65 (Brussels: Société des Bollandistes).

Editions of Homilies

ASSEMANI, J. S. (1732–46), *Sancti Patris nostri Ephraem Syri Opera omnia quae exstant graece, syriace, latine, in sex tomos distributa* (Rome).

DATEMA, C., and ALLEN, P. (1987), *Leontii Presbyteri Constantinopolitani Homiliae*, CCSG 17 (Turnhout: Brepols).

DOLBEAU, F. (1996) (ed.), *Augustin d'Hippo: Vingt-six sermons au peuple d'Afrique*, Collection des Études Augustiniennes, Série Antiquité, 147 (Paris: L'Institut d'études augustiniennes).

FIELD, F. (1854–62), *Joannis Chrysostomi Interpretatio Omnium Epistularum Paulinarum*, 7 vols. (Oxford: Bibliotheca Patrum).

LAMY, T. I. (1882–1902), *Sancti Ephraem Syri Hymni et Sermones*, 4 vols. (Mechlin).

Secondary literature

ALLEN, P., and HAYWARD, C. T. R. (2004), *Severus of Antioch* (London: Routledge).

——and MAYER, W. (1994), 'Chrysostom and the Preaching of Homilies in Series: A New Approach to the Twelve Homilies *In epistulam ad Colossenses* (CPG 4433)', *OCP* 60: 21–39.

————(1995), 'The Thirty-Four Homilies on Hebrews: The Last Series Delivered by Chrysostom in Constantinople?', *Byzantion*, 65: 309–48.

AMERINGER, T. E. (1921), 'The Stylistic Influence of the Second Sophistic on the Panegyrical Sermons of St. John Chrysostom: A Study in Greek Rhetoric' (Ph.D. dissertation, Catholic University of America).

BAUMSTARK, A. (1897–9), 'Das Kirchenjahr in Antiocheia zwischen 512 und 518', *RQ* 11: 31–66; 13: 305–23.

——(1925), 'Der antiochenische Festkalendar des frühen sechsten Jahrhunderts', *Jahrbuch für Liturgiewissenschaft*, 5: 123–35.

BERNARDI, J. (1968), *La prédication des Pères Cappadociens: le prédicateur et son auditoire*, Publications de la Faculté des Lettres et Sciences humaines de l'Université de Montpellier, 30 (Paris: Presses universitaires de France).

BERTHOLD, H. (1977), 'Frühe christliche Literatur als Quelle für Sozialgeschichte', in J. Irmscher and K. Treu (eds.), *Das Korpus der Griechischen Christlichen Schriftsteller: Historie, Gegenwart, Zukunft*, TU 120 (Berlin: Akademie Verlag), 43–63.

BINGHAM, J. (1708–22; new rev. edn. 1834), *Origines Ecclesiasticae; or the Antiquities of the Christian Church*, rev. Bingham, 8 vols. (London: William Straker).

BOURDIEU, P. (1990), *The Logic of Practice*, trans. R. Nice (Palo Alto, Calif.: Stanford University Press).

Brown, P. (2000), *Augustine of Hippo: A Biography*, new edn. with epilogue (Berkeley: University of California Press).

Cameron, Alan (1988), 'A Misidentified Homily of Chrysostom', *Nottingham Mediaeval Studies*, 32: 34–48.

Cameron, Averil (1991), *Christianity and the Rhetoric of Empire: The Development of Christian Discourse* (Berkeley: University of California Press).

Cunningham, M. B. (1990), 'Preaching and the Community', in R. Morris (ed.), *Church and People in Byzantium* (Birmingham: Centre for Byzantine, Ottoman and Modern Greek Studies), 29–47.

——and Allen, P. (1998) (eds.), *Preacher and Audience: Studies in Early Christian and Byzantine Homiletics* (Leiden: E. J. Brill).

Datema, C. (1988), 'Towards a Critical Edition of the Greek Homilies of Severian of Gabala', *Orientalia Lovaniensia Periodica*, 19: 107–15.

Deferrari, R. J. (1922), 'Saint Augustine's Method of Composing and Delivering Sermons', *American Journal of Philology*, 43: 97–123, 193–219.

Devoti, D. (1981), 'Massimo di Torino e il suo pubblico', *Aug* 21: 153–67.

Drobner, H. R. (2000), 'The Chronology of St. Augustine's *Sermones ad populum*', *AugStud* 31: 211–18.

——(2003), 'The Chronology of St. Augustine's *Sermones ad populum* II: Sermons 5 to 8', *AugStud* 34: 49–66.

——(2004), 'The Chronology of Augustine's *Sermones ad populum* III: On Christmas Day', *AugStud* 35: 43–53.

Gignac, F. T. (1998), 'Evidence for Deliberate Scribal Revision in Chrysostom's *Homilies on the Acts of the Apostles*', in J. Petruccione (ed.), *Nova & Vetera: Patristic Studies in Honor of Thomas Patrick Halton* (Washington: The Catholic University of America Press), 209–25.

Graffin, F. (1978), 'La vie à Antioche d'après les homélies de Sévère: Invectives contre les courses de chevaux, le théâtre et les jeux olympiques', in G. Wiessner (ed.), *Erkenntnisse und Meinungen*, ii, Göttinger Orientforschungen: Syriaca, 17 (Wiesbaden: Otto Harrassowitz), 115–30.

Griffith, S. (1998), 'A Spiritual Father for the Whole Church: the Universal Appeal of St. Ephraem the Syrian', *Hugoye*, 1, <syrcom.cua.edu/Hugoye/vol1No2/HV1N2Griffith.html>.

Hill, E. (2000), *Sermons III/11: Newly Discovered Sermons*, in WSA.

Hombert, P.-M. (2000), *Nouvelles recherches de chronologie augustinienne*, Collection des Études Augustiniennes, Série Antiquité, 163 (Paris: L'Institut d'études augustiniennes).

Hong, S. (2004), 'Origen's Rhetoric as a Means to the Formation of the Christian Self' (Ph.D. dissertation, Claremont, California).

Howard, P. (1995), *Beyond the Written Word: Preaching and Theology in the Florence of Archbishop Antoninus, 1427–1459*, Istituto Nazionale di Studi sul Rinascimento, Quaderni di 'Rinascimento' (Florence: Leo S. Olschki).

Hunger, H. (1984), 'Romanos Melodos, Dichter, Prediger, Rhetor—und sein Publikum', *Jahrbuch der Österreichischen Byzantinistik*, 34: 15–42.

Junod, E. (1994), 'Wodurch unterscheiden sich die Homilien des Origenes von seinen Kommentaren?', in J. van Oort and E. Mühlenberg (eds.), *Predigt in der Alten Kirche* (Kampen: Kok Pharos Publishing House), 50–81.

Kolbet, P. (2002), 'The Cure of Souls: St. Augustine's Reception and Transformation of Classical Psychagogy' (Ph.D. dissertation, University of Notre Dame, Indiana).

KYRTATAS, D. (1988), 'Prophets and Priests in Early Christianity: Production and Transmission of Religious Knowledge from Jesus to John Chrysostom', *International Sociology*, 3: 365–83.

LOUKATOS, D. S. (1940), 'Laographikai peri telentes endeixeis para Ioanne to Chrysostomo', *Epeteris tou Laographikou Archeiou*, 2: 30–117.

MACMULLEN, R. (1989), 'The Preacher's Audience (AD 350–400)', *JTS* ns 40: 503–11.

MAXWELL, J. (2006), *Christianization and Communication in Late Antiquity: John Chrysostom and his Congregation in Antioch* (Cambridge: Cambridge University Press, 2006).

MAYER, W. (1999), ' "Les homélies de s. Jean Chrysostome en juillet 399": A Second Look at Pargoire's Sequence and the Chronology of the *Novæ homiliæ* (CPG 4441)', *Byzantinoslavica*, 60: 273–303.

—— (2001), 'The Homily as Historical Document: Some Problems in Relation to John Chrysostom', *Lutheran Theological Journal*, 35: 17–22.

—— (2005), *The Homilies of St John Chrysostom: Provenance: Reshaping the foundations*, OrChrAn 273 (Rome: Institutum Pontificum Orientalium Studiorum).

MERKT, A. (1997), 'Mündlichkeit: Ein Problem der Hermeneutik patristischer Predigten', *StPatr* 31: 76–85.

MONACI CASTAGNO, A. (1987), *Origene predicatore e il suo pubblico* (Milan: Franco Angeli).

MÜLLER, C. D. G. (1954), 'Einige Bemerkungen zur "ars praedicandi" der alten koptischen Kirche', *Mus* 67: 231–70.

OBERHELMAN, S. M. (1991), *Rhetoric and Homiletics in Fourth-Century Christian Literature: Prose Rhythm, Oratorical Style, and Preaching in the Works of Ambrose, Jerome, and Augustine*, American Classical Studies, 26 (Atlanta: Scholars Press).

OLIVAR, A. (1991), *La predicación cristiana antigua*, Sección de teología y filosofía, 189 (Barcelona: Editorial Herder).

PAVERD, F. VAN DE (1970), *Zur Geschichte der Messliturgie in Antiocheia und Konstantinopel gegen Ende des vierten Jahrhunderts*, OrChrAn 187 (Rome: Institutum Pontificum Orientalium Studiorum).

PAZ, F. J. TOVAR, (1994), *Tractatus, sermones atque homiliae: el cultivo del género literario del discurso homilético en la hispania tardoantigua y visigoda*, Anejos del anuario de estudios filologicos, 15 (Cáceres: Universidad de Extrimadura: Servicio de Publicaciones).

POLITIS, N. G. (1921), 'Laographikai endeixeis en to A kai B katechetiko Ioannou tou Chrystostomon', *Laographia*, 8: 5–12.

PONTET, M. (1945), *L'Exégèse de s. Augustin prédicateur*, Théologie, 7 (Aubier: Faculté de Théologie S.J. de Lyon-Fourvière).

RAMBAULT, N. (1999), 'Jean Chrysostome: Homélies pascales (PG 50, 417 ter-442): introduction, texte critique, traduction et notes' (Ph.D. dissertation, Université de Limoges).

RETZLEFF, A. (2003), 'John Chrysostom's Sex Aquarium: Aquatic Metaphors for Theatre in *Homily 7 on Matthew*', *JECS* 11: 195–207.

SCHÄUBLIN, C. (1994), 'Zum paganen Umfeld der christlichen Predigt', in J. van Oort and E. Mühlenberg (eds.), *Predigt in der Alten Kirche* (Kampen: Kok Pharos Publishing House), 25–49.

SOTTOCORNOLA, F. (1973), *L'Anno liturgico nei sermoni di Pietro Crisologo: Ricerca storico-critica sulla liturgia di Ravenna antica* (Cesena: Centro studi e ricerche sulla antica provincia ecclesiastica Ravennate).

SPIRA, A. (1985), 'Volkstümlichkeit und Kunst in der griechischen Väterpredigt des 4. Jahrhunderts', *Jahrbuch für Österreichischen Byzantinistik*, 35: 55–73.

STEWART-SYKES, A. (2001), *From Prophecy to Preaching: A Search for the Origins of the Christian Homily*, Suppl. VC 59 (Leiden: E. J. Brill).

UTHEMANN, K.-H. (1998), 'Forms of Communication in the Homilies of Severian of Gabala: A Contribution to the Reception of the Diatribe as a Method of Exposition', in M. B. Cunningham and P. Allen (eds.), *Preacher and Audience: Studies in Early Christian and Byzantine Homiletics* (Leiden: E. J. Brill), 139–77.

VANCE, J. M. (1907), *Beiträge zur Byzantinischen Kulturgeschichte am Ausgange des IV. Jahrhunderts aus den Schriften des Johannes Chrysostomus* (Jena: Universitäts-buchdruckerei G. Neuenhahn).

VOICU, S. J. (2005), 'La volontà e il caso: La tipologia dei primi spuri di Crisostomo', in *Giovanni Crisostomo: Oriente e Occidente tra IV e V secolo, XXXIII Incontro di Studiosi dell'Antichità Cristiana, Augustinianum 6–8 maggio 2004, Roma*, Studia Ephemeridis Augustinianum, 93 (Rome: Institutum Patristicum Augustinianum), 101–18.

WIKENHAUSER, A. (1907), 'Der hl. Chrysostomus und die Tachygraphie', *Archiv für Stenographie*, 58 NS 3: 268–72.

WILKEN, R. L. (1983), *John Chrysostom and the Jews: Rhetoric and Reality in the Late Fourth Century*, The Transformation of the Classical Heritage, 4 (Berkeley: University of California Press).

WILLIS, G. G. (1962), *St Augustine's Lectionary* (London: S.P.C.K.).

ZELLINGER, J. (1917), 'Der Beifall in der altchristlichen Predigt', in H. M. Geitl (ed.), *Festgabe Alois Knopfler zur vollendung des 70 Lebensjahres* (Freiburg: Herder), 403–15.

CHAPTER 28

EARLY CHRISTIAN HISTORIANS AND HISTORIOGRAPHY

WILLIAM ADLER

A wealth of historical writing survives from the early church: ecclesiastical histories, memoirs, universal histories and chronicles, biographies, historical fiction, and accounts of the acts of martyrs. Even works that are not histories in the strict sense (apologies and heresiologies, for example) sometimes touch on historical subjects. Since it would be neither practical nor profitable to review all of this literature in a single essay, my concern here will be with works that either illustrate basic trends in early Christian historiography or had a lasting impact on its development.

A comparison between two works by Eusebius of Caesarea (260–340) may help to clarify the selection of source material. Eusebius's *Life of Constantine* is a document well deserving of the scholarly attention that it has received. But its influence on Christian historiography was negligible. Socrates, an ecclesiastical historian of the fifth century, dismissed the effusive language of the *Vita* as better suited to encomium than history (*Hist. eccl.* 1. 1. 5). 'Historiographically a blind alley' is the way Momigliano described it (1963: 94). For that reason, it will not fall within the ambit of this study. Eusebius's *Ecclesiastical History* will. Once Eusebius established the model for the writing of church history, numerous works of the same genre followed in its wake (Chesnut 1986). The *Ecclesiastical History*, not the *Life of Constantine*, is the work that has earned Eusebius the title 'father of Christian history'.

28.1 CHRISTIAN HISTORIOGRAPHY
BEFORE EUSEBIUS

A study of Christian historical writing before Eusebius, comparable to Momigliano's programmatic essay on pagan and Christian historiography in the fourth century (1963), remains to be written (but cf. Boer 1961–2; Grant 1972; Milburn 1954: 21–37). Historical material from the early centuries of Christianity's existence is diffuse, and in many cases fragmentary. We would certainly like to know more, for example, about the *Chronographiae* of Julius Africanus, a sprawling five-volume universal chronicle that Eusebius describes as 'a monument of accuracy and diligence', and whose author he praises as 'no ordinary historian' (*Hist. eccl.* 1. 6. 2; 6. 31. 2). Unfortunately, the work survives only as a patchwork of scattered excerpts and references.

In the prologue to the *Ecclesiastical History*, Eusebius salutes those earlier writers who helped to guide the course of his work (*Hist. eccl.* 1. 1. 3). But because no historian before his time had undertaken anything approaching a comprehensive account of the early church, his history would satisfy an urgent need. For the same reason, he urges readers to forgive the shortcomings of a work lacking models and precedent (*Hist. eccl.* 1. 1. 5). To gain sympathy and support for their work, ancient authors often reminded readers of the importance and difficulty of the task facing them. But while making due allowance for the requirements of literary convention, we can still grant the essential accuracy of Eusebius's description of Christian historiography before the fourth century. Sozomen, one of Eusebius's continuators, later identified three writers—Clement, Hegesippus, and Africanus—who in his view met the requirements of the church historian (*Hist. eccl.* 1. 1. 12). None of these writers, however, qualify as ecclesiastical historians of the same cast as Eusebius and Sozomen himself (see below).

The same observation applies to the Acts of the Apostles, Eusebius's principal source for the very early period of the church. A recent study of Acts, noting the work's adherence to classical conventions of historiography, has gone so far as to confer on its author the title 'first Christian historian' (Marguerat 2002: p. xi). While the genre of Acts is far from settled, it would in any case be misleading to regard Acts as a church history in miniature. Acts and the *Ecclesiastical History* do share common features. Both works assume that unity was Christianity's natural state, and both have an optimistic, even triumphalist, view of its prospects in the world. But the differences should not be overlooked. Acts is a record of the 'heroic age of Christianity', the story of its spread by people empowered by God with superhuman courage, perseverance, and boldness in speech (Momigliano 1990: 140). Miracles, theophanies, and dramatic discourses, not the establishment of ecclesiastical institutions, are the main engines of the church's growth. It is hardly remarkable, then, that Acts did not inspire sequels comparable to the continuations of the *Ecclesiastical History*. What it did engender were stories of the wondrous feats of individual apostles, the so-called apocryphal acts. These works are better categorized as 'aretalogies' than as histories.

28.2 Early Christian Historians on Time and the Divine Plan of History

In his account of the unfolding of the apostolic mission, the author of Acts faced a dilemma confounding Christian historiography for a long time thereafter: how to end the narrative. Whether the historian looked forward to the return of Christ or the evangelization of the entire world, neither objective had yet been realized. How, then, could a historian recount the story of a divine plan that in his own day had yet to be fully enacted? The author of Acts developed a unique strategy to resolve the tension. For a work generally triumphant in tone, the ending of Acts is muted. Acts never allows Paul the chance to proclaim the gospel before Caesar. All that we learn is that Paul in Rome 'boldly and without hindrance' continued preaching the kingdom of God and teaching about the Lord Jesus Christ (28: 30). Even so, we are hardly in doubt about the outcome. From an angel of God and from Jesus himself, we know that Paul 'must stand before the emperor' (27: 24), and that the gospel must be preached to the end of the earth (1: 8). The plan of history may be a work in progress, but its result is preordained (Marguerat 2002: 92–8).

In Acts, the 'end' is not the end of time, but the ends of the earth. This distinction is elaborated at the very beginning of the work, with the first commissioning of the apostles. Here Jesus declines to reveal anything to them about the 'times or periods that the Father has set by his own authority' (1: 7). Two centuries later, Eusebius found this admonition valuable enough to cite in the introduction to his chronicle. Jesus' counsel to the apostles, he writes, is a salutary warning about the limitations of the study of dates and times (see below). But that was far from the majority view. At about the same time that Eusebius had completed the first edition of his chronicle, Lactantius boasted in his *Divine Institutes* (7. 14): 'We whom the holy scriptures instruct to the knowledge of the truth know the beginning and the end of the world.' Other historians of the early church could have made the same claim.

Before the appearance of the genre of church history in the fourth century, chronography—that is, the study of 'dates and times'—was the dominant form of Christian historiography. For a long time thereafter, the universal chronicle rivalled the church history for pre-eminence. These were ambitious projects, beginning from Adam or from some other remote point in time, and at least in some cases, looking forward to the end of the age. By contemporary standards, they would barely qualify as history. More interested in scope than in historical analysis, chroniclers allowed long stretches of time to pass with hardly anything more than a nod. For this and other reasons, historians in the classical tradition tended to spurn the writing of chronicles. In a caustic assessment of the chronicle genre, Eunapius, a historian and sophist of the late fourth century, wondered why anyone would waste time chasing after knowledge that contributed nothing of value to the understanding of the character of great figures of the past (1. 207. 19–211. 28, ed. Dindorf).

Why would a Christian historian have taken an interest in a subject that, to his pagan counterparts, might have looked like little more than an unedifying collection of disconnected events? Part of the answer is grounded in apologetics. To answer the charge that Christianity was a religion with no foundation in ancient tradition, defenders of Christianity liked to point to figures from Jewish tradition who had prepared the way for his coming. Moses, a person already familiar to pagan readers, was the name most frequently cited. Jewish historians of the Hellenistic period had already established the chronological priority of Moses to datable events of Greek history (Droge 1989: 45–7). Even his disparagers could not deny that he was a man of the distant past. The study of chronology was thus vital to the defence of the Church against its detractors. Once it is established, writes Tatian in the second century, that Moses is older than Homer and all the other Greeks of recognized antiquity, then readers will find that 'our doctrines are older, not only than those of the Greeks, but than the invention of letters' (*Orat.* 31. 1).

The other reason for Christian interest in the subject of chronology was rooted not in apologetics, but in an understanding of time as an expression of the divine will. The idea that in the orderly flow of time God reveals his plan for the world had a rich older tradition upon which to draw. In the apocalyptic literature of Second Temple Judaism, knowledge about the time of the end was sometimes revealed to the seer in the form of an extended survey of past history. One highly influential example of the genre was the 'apocalypse of 70 weeks of years', revealed to the prophet Daniel by the angel Gabriel (Dan 9: 24–7). Like many apocalyptic historical surveys, the revelation concludes in a crisis during which 'the anointed one is cut off' and the city and the temple sanctuary are made desolate. After the resolution of that crisis, the apocalypse looked forward to the imminent arrival of a new age, and with it an 'end to sin and everlasting righteousness'.

Because of its chronological specificity, Christian chroniclers were fascinated, even obsessed, with Daniel's vision and its correlation to events of their own day (Adler 1996: 218–38). During the reign of Septimius Severus (193–211), a writer named Judas composed a chronicle fashioned in the form of a commentary on these four verses from Daniel. Its purpose, as Eusebius characterizes it, was to prove that the arrival of the Antichrist was imminent. Eusebius, our only witness to this work, cites Judas's chronicle as one more illustration of an age gripped by fantastic notions about the end-times. He also seems to have grasped what modern scholars now see as an essential feature of end-time thinking: it intensifies in periods of crisis. Judas's interpretation of Daniel, Eusebius writes, was the product of a mind unhinged by the ferocity of the persecutions during his time (*Hist. eccl.* 6. 7).

Judas's chronicle was destined for oblivion, overshadowed by the more influential chronicle of Julius Africanus (221). While sharing Judas's view that the course of human history conformed to a divinely ordained plan, Africanus organized his chronicle around a different set of principles. In Africanus's view, the course of world history conformed to the chronology of the creation. Just as God had taken six days to create the world, so too would the world last for 6,000 years, followed by 1,000 years of millennial rest. Numerical patterns and prefigurations of the end-times appear everywhere in his work, as is befitting the divine intelligence guiding the course of history. By Africanus's calculations, Christ's birth occurred in the 5,500th year from Adam: that is, precisely in the middle of the sixth millennium (Gelzer 1967: 24–6). The understated millennialism of his chronicle ensured that it would not suffer the untimely obsolescence of Judas's chronicle. But by deferring the end of history for another 279 years, Africanus's chronicle left contemporary history stranded in a kind of stasis. In treating his own time as the dramatic conclusion of the angelic revelation to Daniel, Judas's chronicle captured the sense of urgency of the apocalyptic text that inspired it. Africanus, on the other hand, seems to have had trouble fitting events of his own day into his grand historical scheme. In a revealing remark that Africanus makes about the same verses from Daniel, he expresses doubt that the passage had any relevance to his own time. With the resurrection, everything predicted in the vision had been fulfilled (frag. 93). True to this understanding of history, Africanus had no choice but to treat events after the resurrection as little more than a postscript (Photius, *Bibliotheca*, 34. 7a. 10–14).

Whether it was to establish the ancient roots of their religion or to demonstrate the unfolding of the divine plan in history, the inclination of the first Christian historians was constantly to extend the exploration of the past into domains that their Greek counterparts would have considered beyond the reach of historical research. In a letter written at the end of the second century, Theophilus, the bishop of Antioch, tried to explain to a pagan detractor why Christian historians felt confident in doing so. Part of his justification is of a piece with apologetic writing of the second century. His chronology of universal history from Adam will demonstrate that our 'doctrine is not recent, nor our tenets mythical and false, as some think, but very ancient and true' (*Autol.* 3. 29). Just as important, it will illustrate the advantage that Christian historians have over their pagan counterparts. For Theophilus, it boiled down to one essential ingredient: source material. In the absence of a securely documented knowledge of the past, even the most able Greek historians could write with confidence only about relatively recent events. By contrast, Christian historians could take in the entire sweep of human history (*Autol.* 3. 26).

This was not an entirely original argument. In the first century, Josephus had already made much the same point in defence of Judaism. Why, Josephus asks, must non-Greek peoples always genuflect to the judgement of Greek historians? Because the Greeks were negligent in maintaining records for their posterity, he writes, their historians could rely only on conjecture and opinion. With access to carefully and continuously maintained documents even from the distant past, historians from the older nations of the East had a much easier task. All they had to do was to represent their sources accurately (*c. Ap.* 1. 6–8). Theophilus now asserts for Christians the same advantage that Josephus had earlier claimed on behalf of the civilizations of the East. Because they were limited by their sources to relatively trifling events of recent history, Greek historians had to cede important questions about the age and origin of the world to the philosophers. Their Christian counterparts, on the other hand, were able to plot the entire arc of human history (*Autol.* 3. 26). While falling short of a philosophy of history, Theophilus's boast encapsulates two features of early Christian historiography: an unquestioning confidence in their sources and a tendency to think about the past on a grand scale (Momigliano 1963: 83).

28.3 EUSEBIUS AND CHRISTIAN HISTORIOGRAPHY IN THE FOURTH CENTURY

Momigliano's claim (1963: 84) that after the third century Christian study of chronology had passed its 'creative stage' overlooks the innovative uses of the chronicle genre after that time. Chroniclers of the fourth century were now experimenting with applications of the genre extending beyond apologetics and millennialist speculation. Works consisting largely of lists and tables were easy to update and well suited for cataloguing and correlating lists of bishops and other leaders of the church. The Christian monk Annianus, an Alexandrian chronographer of the early fifth century, used the tabular format of the chronicle to assist in the much-disputed question of the dating of Easter (Grumel 1958: 92–4). Beginning from the first year of creation, Annianus fashioned his chronicle in the form of an Easter computus, into the margins of which were inserted brief historical notices. The other virtue of the chronicle was its concise and austere style, the embodiment of the Christian ideal of simplicity in expression (Croke and Emmett 1983: 3). Accessible to a wide reading public, chronicles thus made useful tools for instruction. In the preface to Sulpicius Severus's *Chronica*, the author states that his purpose in writing his narrative chronicle of the world from Adam down to the year 400 was 'to instruct the ignorant and convince the learned' (*Praef.* 2).

One indication of the continuing vitality of the genre is Eusebius's own exploration of the subject. Before he published the *Ecclesiastical History*, Eusebius had already completed the first edition of his two-volume universal chronicle. The once conventional view that Eusebius's *Chronicon* did little more than tinker around the edges of Africanus's more original work misrepresents a work that in many ways marked a radical departure from the earlier tradition (Winkelmann 2003: 18–20). This is evident from the disclaimers at the very outset of the work. Broadly understood, Eusebius writes, Jesus's caveat to the apostles in the Acts of the Apostles about 'times and dates' applies to the entire field of chronology, including biblical chronology (*Chronicon*, 1. 25–2. 11, ed. Karst). If we recall the earlier boasts of Theophilus and Africanus, Eusebius's de-privileging of biblical chronology was a daring move.

In his subsequent exploration of the subject, Eusebius sets about dismantling the enshrined conventions of Christian chronography. Traces of the apologetic roots of the genre, albeit still visible, are noticeably understated. In the prologue to the *Canons*, the second book of his chronicle, Eusebius asserts that his own investigations confirm the antiquity of Moses; but he then upends the tradition with his discovery that Moses was not nearly as old as Jewish and Christian historians before him had maintained (*Chronici Canones*, 7. 11–14. 15, ed. Helm). And he is remarkably comfortable with ambiguity and uncertainty. Absent are the neat chronological symmetries that for Africanus were intimations of the mind of God. Eusebius initially makes the expected defence of the authority of the Greek text of the Old Testament, even accusing the Jews of deliberately falsifying their text of the Hebrew Bible (*Chronicon*, 37. 10–36, ed. Karst). But he does not conceal its marked differences from the Hebrew Bible and the Samaritan Pentateuch, especially for the period from Adam up to Abraham (*Chronicon*, 37. 10–40. 20, ed. Karst). Nor does he consistently favour it over competing versions. For the period from Moses to Solomon, he prefers the Hebrew version to both the Septuagint and the apostle Paul himself. Paul's summary of Hebrew chronology in one of his speeches in the Acts of the Apostles, Eusebius writes, was only a reflection of popular tradition, and thus of no real service to the historian (*Chronicon*, 50.3–23, ed. Karst).

For Eusebius's predecessors, the biblical narrative presented a seamless narrative from the birth of Adam. Africanus's millennialism and Theophilus's claim that Christian historians alone knew the age of the world demanded this confidence. But Eusebius retreats from this convention, suggesting that certain parts of the biblical narrative were beyond the reach of the historian. Because the story of Adam and Eve in Paradise is an allegory of the fall of the soul into bodies, and thus outside of the realm of time and space, he writes, no one can reconstruct a chronology of the world from the creation of Adam, much less from the creation of the world (*Chronicon*, 36. 16–37. 9, ed. Karst). In the *Canons*, Eusebius is even more circumspect. To make a claim of universality, Eusebius insists that the Christian chronicle of the world had to look beyond the biblical narrative. His preferred approach is thus to use the era from Abraham, on the grounds that before the birth of Abraham nothing could be known with certainty about Greek or barbarian history (*Chronici Canones*, 14. 20–15. 7, ed. Helm; see Sirinelli 1961: 46–52).

Christian chroniclers before Eusebius would hardly have found this a persuasive argument for slighting pre-Abrahamic history. But for Greek historians accustomed to relegating segments of their own past to 'pre-history', there was little to dispute in Eusebius's decision to apply the same principle to the period before Abraham. And they would have had no trouble identifying the principles underlying the *Canons*. In the Vulgate tradition of Hellenistic historiography, the Assyrian king Ninus was widely understood to be the earliest recorded king of Asia (Drews 1965: 130). Following this convention, the sequence of kingdoms in Eusebius's *Canons* begins with Ninus, during whose reign Eusebius fixed the birth of Abraham. After that, Eusebius organized the *Canons* according to a well-known scheme of a succession of world empires: Assyrians, Medes, Persians, Macedonians, and finally the Romans (Momigliano 1984: 87–92). The overall trend is clear. In adopting a more even-handed approach to his sources, and in combining into one work the traditions of sacred and secular chronology, Eusebius intended to move chronography away from apologetic and millennialist speculation and into the mainstream of Greek historiography.

If dissemination is the measure of a work's influence, then Eusebius's chronicle was far more successful than the fragmentarily preserved work of Africanus. Epitomes, expansions, and corrections of the work testify to the enduring influence of the work in the East (Adler 1992: 481–6; Burgess 1999). But if Eusebius's aim was to redefine the norms of Christian chronography, he was only partially successful (Winkelmann 2003: 20). Millennialist chronography continued to find advocates, among them Quintus Julius Hilarianus, a Latin chronicler of the late fourth century. His *De cursu temporum* was written to settle a dispute about the date of the end of the world (1. 153–74, esp. 171. 5–174. 4). If anything, the tendency in Christian chronography after Eusebius was to broaden the temporal sweep of the universal chronicle. Starting in the early fifth century, the era from creation, not the era from Abraham, became the standard for Christian chronography in the East. In the formulation of this era, dogmatic, not critical, considerations were determinative: namely, to confirm the theological principle that the birthday of the world, Christ's incarnation in the 5,500th year of the world, and his resurrection all occurred on the same day and month of the year (Grumel 1958: 85–97).

28.4 THE *ECCLESIASTICAL HISTORY*

Eusebius's *Chronicon* appeared in two editions, spanning the period before and after the conversion of Constantine in 312. The second edition, and the version of the *Chronicon* that came to be known in the West through Jerome's translation, appeared sometime after the twentieth year of the reign of Constantine (Barnes 1981: 112–13; Burgess 1997). In the intervening period, Eusebius began work on his *Ecclesiastical History*. As he acknowledges, the chronological tables that he had compiled in the *Canons* supplied the raw material for the fuller historical treatment of the *History* (1. 1. 6).

The textual development of the *Ecclesiastical History*, which may have appeared in as many as four, possibly even five, editions, is a notoriously complex and unsettled problem (Barnes 1980; Grant 1980: 10–21; Louth 1990). As outlined in the prologue, the original aims of the *History* were to recount the 'successions of the apostles', the major events of ecclesiastical history, the various leaders, writers, and martyrs of the Church, the names of those who introduced error into the Church, the fate that befell the Jews for their plots against Jesus, and the persecutors and martyrs of the Church (*Hist. eccl.* 1. 1. 1–2). In the first edition of the work, Eusebius was mostly successful in executing this plan. But subsequent events—the great persecution, the fall of Licinius, and the reunification of the Empire under Constantine—required a mid-course correction.

How would an ancient reader have received a work described by its author as unprecedented? One thing they would have noticed is Eusebius's zeal for direct quotation. The scholarship on Eusebius's citation habits is substantial (see e.g. Barnes 1981: 140–3; Gustaffsson 1961). While modern readers accustomed to ample documentation might not find his approach disagreeable, ancient historians generally eschewed the documentary approach to history writing. It disrupted narrative continuity, and made it difficult to achieve the rhetorical elegance to which most historians aspired. Copious citations, a generally unadorned style, and the absence of speeches suggest that the *History* was untouched by these concerns (Markus 1975: 3). The archival quality of the *History* departed so far from classical norms that Eduard Schwartz once questioned whether Eusebius had even planned to write a conventional history. In Schwartz's view, Eusebius's *History* was history only in the more archaic sense of the Greek word: that is, as a collection of raw material to be used by his successors (Schwartz 1938: 114–17; see also Leppin 2003: 249).

We need not reach back into the distant recesses of Greek historiography to find models for this style of composition. Jewish and Christian historians had always placed a premium on documentation. The superiority of their sources was, after all, the singular advantage of eastern historians over their Greeks counterparts. Eusebius, a historian of bookish tastes with the available library resources to satisfy them (Carriker 2003), adopted the documentary style in many of his works. The first book of his *Chronicon* is in the main a collection of excerpts. And in his *Preparation for the Gospel*, a sprawling work of apologetic, Eusebius found that amassing citations from older authorities, especially non-Christian sources, was an effective form of argumentation. One example of the use of the same technique in the *History* is his appeal to the Jewish historian Josephus. From a 'writer sprung from the

Hebrews', Eusebius claims to have proof that the divine judgement on the Jews was sealed from the moment of their 'plot against the saviour' (*Hist. eccl.* 1. 1. 9).

It was more than habit, however, that drew Eusebius to the documentary style in the *History*. Precedent and tradition, as Momigliano has observed, required ecclesiastical historians to 'quote documentary evidence to an extent which is seldom to be found in political historians' (Momigliano 1990: 137). This was also true of the father of the genre. Voluminous citation of older works demonstrated the continuity of the Church's traditions and teachings and the care with which it preserved and transmitted them.

28.5 EUSEBIUS AND THE CONTINUITY OF THE CHURCH

The guiding principle of the *History* is that the Church, despite repeated threats to its survival, never strayed from its original teachings (4. 7. 13). The idea that the Church was from the very outset a unified body is a theme that runs through much early Christian literature. One could hardly tell from reading the Acts of the Apostles, for example, that Paul disagreed with the other apostles on fundamental matters. Apologists of the second century continued to claim that the unity of Christian teachings proved their superiority to Greek philosophy, with all its schools, quarrels, and controversies. But by that time, it was no longer possible to sustain a myth of universal accord. The task for Eusebius was to demonstrate how champions of orthodoxy in the second century faithfully preserved the teachings of Jesus and the apostles in the face of division and conflict.

Most modern studies of 'heresy' in early Christianity tend to view diversity as organic to its growth and development. But this was not Eusebius's perspective. For him, the heresies besetting the Church were one more hardship sent by the devil to harass the Church after it had successfully resisted persecutions from the Jews. Eusebius was not a heresiologist. He is less interested in exposing the errors of heresy than he is in documenting the vigour of the Church's counterattack. As Eusebius represents it, the weapons in the war against heresy were mostly literary. The sources that he cites—according to him, only a fraction of the quantity of material written during that time—proved orthodoxy's overwhelming success in its literary war with heresy and the care with which the Church preserved and transmitted its traditions (*Hist. eccl.* 4. 21).

An unbroken succession of church leadership stretching back to the apostolic period was the other means by which the Church of his day maintained continuity with its past. Already in the late second century, Irenaeus, the bishop of Lyons, had set forth a succession list for the bishops of the church at Rome, thereby establishing its historic link to the apostles Peter and Paul. But Irenaeus was silent about the episcopal succession of the other major Christian communities, on the grounds that it would be 'very tedious to reckon up the successions of all the churches' (*Haer.* 3. 3. 2). Eusebius had a more ambitious goal. Since the various Christian communities were by definition microcosms of the universal church, telling the story of one church was not enough. Our purpose, he writes, is to 'rescue the successions, if not all, at least of the most distinguished of the apostles of our saviour throughout the churches of which the fame is still remembered' (*Hist. eccl.* 1. 1. 4). In this expansive understanding, the 'leaders and the presidents of the church' extended to the principal teachers of the Christian schools at Alexandria and Caesarea and the bishops of the leading churches of the East (Grant 1980: 44–59).

Eusebius's chief source for the Eastern churches was Hegesippus's *Hypomnemata*, a work that can be called a 'history' only in the most generous sense of the word. It seems to have been a loosely structured collection of memoirs, on which Eusebius imposed his own chronological order (Grant 1980: 67–70; Hyldahl 1960). What mainly interested Eusebius in the work was its account of the leadership of the primitive Christian community in Jerusalem and its subsequent corruption by heresies. According to Hegesippus, the authority of James, the first to govern the Jerusalem church, descended both from his kinship with Jesus and his priestly role as intercessor in the Jerusalem Temple. Corruption occurred only after his death, when false prophets and teachers arose, motivated by resentment and bent on poisoning and dividing the Church (in Eusebius, *Hist. eccl.* 2. 23. 6; 4. 22. 4–6). As further evidence that heresy was only a deviation from the teachings of the early church, Hegesippus states that in his meetings with the bishops of Rome and Corinth, he found the same doctrines taught, all in accordance with 'the law, the prophets and the Lord' (*Hypomnemata*, 4. 22. 1–3). It is small wonder that later writers, whose knowledge of Hegesippus was filtered through Eusebius, would regard him as a church historian before Eusebius.

Eusebius's contention that despite repeated assaults on its very existence, the Church always held 'to the same points in the same way' (*Hist. eccl.* 4. 17. 3), was hard to sustain as an organizing principle for the almost 300 years of Christianity's existence. A static vision of the early church that does not allow room for change and development produced in the words of Barnes 'less a coherent narrative than a series of disconnected notes' (Barnes 1981: 132). It also resulted in a history that by classical norms would seem inverted. Unlike most historians of the classical tradition, for whom the subject of origins was usually prolegomena to more recent events, Eusebius devotes most of the first three books of the *History* to the apostolic age, that is, the period ending with the death of John, during which its fundamental, enduring, and eternal traditions were first established (Markus 1975: 2–3).

The difficulties of accommodating ideology to the demands of historiography are equally evident in Eusebius's attempts to define the beginning point of his history.

For the most part, modern scholars assume that Jesus himself did not intend to establish a new religion, and that the process by which Christianity became identifiably different from Judaism was only gradual and uneven. This was not Eusebius's take on the question. While the name 'Christian', he writes, may be only recently known, the practice of Christianity is 'primitive, unique and true' (*Hist. eccl.* 1. 4. 2). Long before Moses instituted the laws for the Jewish people, there was a nation—Eusebius calls them 'Hebrews'—who practised the true religion. The antiquity of this people should thus put to rest the allegation that Christianity was 'new and strange, inasmuch as it was put together by a youth no better than the rest of men' (*Hist. eccl.* 1. 4. 1).

That claim was better suited to apology than history. In two of his other works, the above-mentioned *Preparation for the Gospel* and the *Demonstration of the Gospel*, Eusebius assembled a vast array of older sources in support of his thesis that Christianity was almost as old as the world itself (Barnes 1981: 126–8; Sirinelli 1961: 139–246). As he says in the *Preparation* (1. 2), the purpose of this effort was to answer the charge, still circulating in Eusebius's day, that Christians had fashioned a 'new kind of track in a pathless desert that keeps neither the ways of the Greeks nor those of the Jews'. But in a history of the Church, would it be practical to trace the development of the Christianity from its supposed primordial roots? Eusebius seems to have sensed that it was a poor fit; for he judiciously relegates the story of the 'Hebrews' to a theological preamble, or in his words the 'necessary preliminaries' (*Hist. eccl.* 1. 5. 1).

28.6 THE *ECCLESIASTICAL HISTORY* AND ITS SUCCESSORS

At places in the *History* Eusebius writes as if he were recounting the history not of a religious movement, but rather of a nation with very ancient roots, 'not little or weak, nor founded in some obscure parts of the earth but the most populous of all nation, ... alike innocent and invincible' (*Hist. eccl.* 1. 4. 2). While the language of military and political history helped to call attention to the importance of his topic, Eusebius was also aware that his account of the victories of the Christian 'nation' would disappoint readers accustomed to stories of military conquest and the exploits of generals. His own history would recount a different kind of warfare: not struggles for countries and friends, but wars 'most peaceful waged for the very peace of the soul' and victories over unseen adversaries (*Hist. eccl.* 5. 1. 2–4).

The sentiment expressed by these words is very much in character with the triumphalist and hopeful tone of much of the *History*. When Eusebius later describes the fall of Licinius and the reunification of the Empire under Constantine, his language verges on the messianic (*Hist. eccl.* 10. 9. 9). By the end of the fourth century, events in the western part of the Empire made it difficult to share that optimism. Augustine disliked theories of moral decline that yearned for the lost virtues of Rome. But neither did he share Eusebius's idea that human history had culminated in the convergence of Christianity and Rome (Chesnut 1992: 692–6). Jerome never did follow through on his plan to write a church history. If he had, it would have been far different in tone from Eusebius's *History*: not one of ascent and triumph, but of the Church's decline 'from the apostles down to the excrement of our time, how...it flourished under persecution and after it came to Christian rulers became greater in power and riches but inferior in virtues' (*Vita Malchi*, 1; on which see Grant 1980: 168).

While the ecclesiastical historians who succeeded Eusebius in the Greek-speaking East were not nearly as sanguine as he was about Christianity's political fortunes, they continued to hold to the basic Eusebian principle that divine providence would reward the pious emperor with peace, prosperity, and military conquest. For the most part, they paid tribute to Eusebius by not working ground that he had already ploughed. But for the period that they did cover, his successors did not always hold fast to the norms that he had established for the genre. In the introduction to his *Ecclesiastical History*, for example, Sozomen states that his original plan was to 'trace the course of events from the very commencement'. But once he recognized that Eusebius and others had already done much of that work up to their own time, he begged off from this plan, choosing instead only to epitomize what these earlier writers had already written (*Hist. eccl.* 1. 1. 12). For the period encompassed by his own history (324 to 439), Sozomen followed Eusebius's precedent by avoiding rhetorical speeches. But he does bend to the standards of classical historiography in another way. In the introduction to his *History*, he informs readers that he will transcribe documents for controversial subjects only; otherwise they will have to settle for summaries (1. 1. 14).

Sozomen also chose to treat two subjects that Eusebius had overlooked: monasticism and the Christian communities under Persian and barbarian rule (*Hist. eccl.* 1. 1. 18; Stevenson 2002–3). His decision to broaden the scope of ecclesiastical history underscores a central problem of the Eusebian model of ecclesiastical history: Does a perspective of the early church confined mainly to the succession of its leaders and its various struggles with its enemies do justice to the complexity of the subject? In later editions of the *Ecclesiastical History*, Eusebius himself had to rethink the project. Socrates, a little over a century later, decided that his own continuation of Eusebius (from 305 to 439) would have to treat secular matters in much greater depth (Urbainczyk 1997: 69–79). Worried that his readers might disapprove of his decision, he wryly points out that a record of the wars waged by Roman emperors would at least relieve the monotony of the endless wranglings and plottings of bishops. More importantly, it would recognize what was by his time an inescapable truth. By 'some sort of vital sympathy', Socrates writes, 'the mischiefs of the state and the troubles of the church have been inseparably connected' (*Hist. eccl.* 5 proem.).

While Socrates' decision may have been a necessary concession to the political realities of his own day, the eroding of the boundaries between secular and sacred history threatened to dissolve the whole genre of church history (Markus 1975: 7–17). The effect is more clearly visible in the late fourth-century church history of Philostorgius. Philostorgius's digressions on the extraordinary flora and fauna of places to the east (e.g. *Historia ecclesiastica*, 3. 6–11), while satisfying a popular interest in wondrous stories about remote regions, extended well beyond Eusebius's conception of the genre (Argov 2001: 524). The diffuse history of Philip of Side (*c.* 430) was even more removed from the Eusebian model (Heyden 2006). Comparable in scope to the Christian universal chronicle, it began with the Mosaic cosmogony and ran to thirty-six books. In his summary of the contents of Philip's history, Socrates was quick to point out that Philip had written a history of Christianity, not a history of the Church. But judging from his inventory of the contents of this lost work, it might not merit even that description. According to Socrates (*Hist. eccl.* 7. 27), the mishmash of topics treated in his history included 'geometrical theorems, astronomical speculations, arithmetical calculations, musical principles, geographical delineations of islands, mountains, forests and various other matters of little moment'.

28.7 UNRESOLVED TENSIONS IN CHRISTIAN HISTORIOGRAPHY

In the early fifth century, Paul Orosius, a Christian historian of Spain, composed, at the instance of Augustine, a universal history meant to elaborate the theory of history that his mentor had set out in the *City of God*. One of Orosius's objectives was to demystify the Roman past, demonstrating that the history of Rome, like that of the entire human race, was scarred with corruption, defeats, and misery. To forestall the likely criticism that a project of this magnitude was impracticable, Orosius takes issue with his pagan counterparts for beginning their narratives from the 'middle of time' and thus emptying the past of meaning. If they had taken a longer view, they would have recognized that wars and calamities had existed from the very creation of mankind, and were the way in which God had 'disciplined the world by alternating periods of good and bad' (*Hist. adv. pag.* 1. 1. 10–11). Orosius's opening salvo invites the impression that the ensuing narrative would flout the prevailing norms of classical historiography. But what follows can hardly be described as a Christian 'counter-history'. At best an imperfect embodiment of Augustine's theory of history, his *Seven Books of History against the Pagans* adheres quite closely to classical conventions. Orosius gives but fleeting notice to the 3,184 years that he rebukes pagan historians for neglecting. His subsequent history is not a barebones chronicle, but a fleshed-out treatise on universal history, heavily dependent on pagan sources and written in what G. Zecchini describes as a 'highly rhetorical, mannered, and complex style'. These features of his history reveal Orosius's 'desire to overcome the narrow limits of Christian chronography and return to the grand tradition of classical historiography' (Zecchini 2003: 321).

That description points to a fundamental tension underlying much early Christian historiography: how to make a distinctively Christian conception of the past intelligible to an audience with differing expectations and assumptions. From the outset, millennialism, the demands of apologetic, and a supreme confidence in their sources pitted Christian historians against their pagan counterparts. The long reach of the universal chronicle and its preoccupation with dates and times made it the ideal medium through which to pursue these interests. But millennialist chronicles tend by their very nature to self-invalidation. And when the Christian chronicle began to emerge as an independent genre, its originally apologetic character proved far too confining. In his repudiation of millennialist chronography, his acknowledgement of the imperfections of the whole enterprise, and his openly expressed doubts about even biblical chronology, Eusebius's chronicle represents a watershed event in the evolution of the genre.

By the fourth century, the leading motifs of Eusebius's *History*—the unity of the Church, the primordial roots of Christianity, and the representation of Christians as a 'nation'—were already part of the Christian theological tradition. But Eusebius was the first to subject these ideas to the test of a continuous historical treatment. In doing so, he produced a new style of history. The absence of rhetorical speeches, a heavy layering of documents, and an inverted set of priorities that at least initially placed more emphasis on origins than on contemporary events would have made it barely recognizable as a history to readers brought up in the classical tradition of historiography. There are many ways to measure Eusebius's effectiveness in bringing the idea of 'church history' to fruition. Surely, one of them is his success in erecting 'on a desolate and untrodden way' enduring landmarks for others to follow.

28.8 DIRECTIONS FOR FUTURE STUDY

The preceding discussion has dealt mainly with aspects of early Christian historiography that helped to give it an identifiably Christian character. This approach is true of much modern scholarship on the subject. A feature of a Christian history that is counter to ancient norms of historiography is usually ascribed to some underlying ideological motive. For the same reason, much of the analysis examines how historians integrated into their works ideas about eschatology, divine providence, the miraculous, time, heresy and orthodoxy, and church/state relations. While these are completely valid pursuits, emphasis on Christian authorship runs the risk of inflating the distinctiveness of these works from other ancient historical writing (Liebeschuetz 1993: 161–2). It can also overshadow other factors that contributed to a work's distinctive shape and identity. A single example may help to illustrate the point. The favoured explanation of the documentary style that Eusebius adopted in the *History* holds, quite plausibly, that his preference for written over oral sources and the importance of tradition and precedent in the early church required him to forgo the aesthetic requirements of rhetorical histories. But we need not assume that Eusebius's practice was entirely driven by ideology. Ancient historians who avoided citing older documents did not do so strictly for stylistic reasons. Written resources were not always readily accessible (Urbainczyk 1997: 88). Had the library at Caesarea not been available to him, Eusebius might well have written a very different kind of church history, if he had written one at all. Practical considerations, as much as ideology, have their own role to play in deciding the final outcome of a historical project.

Christian historians were not entirely from the clerical class. The church historians Sozomen, Evagrius, and perhaps Socrates as well, were all trained in law, (Harries 1986). Nor does the writing of Christian chronicles and church histories track a steady and linear trajectory. There are periods of concentrated literary activity, followed by relative quiescence. The cultural and political conditions that encouraged the flourishing industry of ecclesiastical historiography in the late fourth and early fifth centuries, especially during the reign of Theodosius II (406–50), are subjects that might reward further investigation. Regional differences also need to enter into the analysis. This does not just apply to the obvious cultural, linguistic, and political factors helping to differentiate the Latin West from the Greek and Syriac-speaking East. We may assume that a church history or chronicle originating from Alexandria, Antioch, Caesarea, or Constantinople would bear a local stamp. All of this is to say that extending the study of Christian historiography beyond the strictly religious domain can be a useful corrective to an approach that prefers to see an author's 'Christian identity' as determinative.

SUGGESTED READING

For a general orientation to Christian historiography, especially in the fourth century, several older works are still essential reading. These include Momigliano's suggestive and much-cited essay (1963) and Sirinelli's authoritative study of Eusebius's historical method (1961). Barnes's work on Constantine and Eusebius (1981) contains an excellent section on

Eusebius's historical works. Grant (1980) is a good, readable orientation to Eusebius as church historian. For the emergence and development of the genre of church history after Eusebius, Markus's original essay (1975) is indispensable, along with Chestnut (1986, 1992) and Momigliano (1990). For studies of various aspects of the Christian universal chronicle, Mosshammer (1979), Adler (1992), and Burgess (1999) are all recommended.

References

Primary sources

AFRICANUS, SEXTUS JULIUS, *Chronographiae: The Extant Fragments*, ed. M. Wallraff, GCS NF 15 (Berlin: de Gruyter, 2007).

EUNAPIUS, *Fragmenta Historica*, in L. Dindorf (ed.), *Historici Graeci minores* (Leipzig: Teubner, 1870).

EUSEBIUS, *Chronici Canones*, in R. Helm (ed.), *Die Chronik des Hieronymus*, 3rd edn., GCS 47, Eusebius Werke, 7 (Berlin: Akademie Verlag, 1984).

——*Chronicon*, in J. Karst (ed.), *Die Chronik des Eusebius aus dem Armenischen übersetzt*, GCS 20, Eusebius *Werke*, 5 (Leipzig: J. C. Hinrichs, 1911).

——*Historia ecclesiastica*, in E. Schwartz and T. Mommsen (eds.), *Die Kirchengeschichte*, 2nd edn., GCS NF 6 (Leipzig: Akademie Verlag, 1999). English trans. by K. Lake and J. E. L. Oulton, as *Ecclesiastical History*, LCL (Cambridge Mass.: Harvard University Press, 1964–5).

HILARIANUS, QUINTUS JULIUS, *De cursu temporum*, in C. Frick (ed.), *Chronica Minora* (Leipzig: Teubner, 1892), i. 153–74.

OROSIUS, *Historiarum adversum paganos libri I–VII*, 1. 1, 10–11, ed. K. Zangemeister, CSEL 5 (Vienna: C. Gerold, 1882).

PHILOSTORGIUS, *Historia ecclesiastica*, in J. Bidez and F. Winkelmann (eds.), *Philostorgius: Kirchengeschichte*, 3rd edn., GCS 21 (Berlin: Akademie Verlag, 1981).

PHOTIUS, *Bibliotheca*, in R. Henry (ed.), *Photius: Bibliothèque* (Paris: Les Belles Lettres, 1959–77).

SEVERUS, SULPITIUS, *Chronica*, in G. de Senneville-Grave (ed.), *Sulpice Sévère: Chroniques*, SC 441 (Paris: Éditions du Cerf).

SOCRATES, *Historia ecclesiastica*, in G. C. Hansen (ed.), *Sokrates: Kirchengeschichte*, GCS NF 1 (Berlin: Akademie Verlag, 1995).

SOZOMEN, *Historia ecclesiastica*, in J. Bidez and G. C. Hansen (eds.), *Sozomenus: Kirchengeschichte*, GCS 50 (Berlin: Akademie Verlag, 1960).

Secondary literature

ADLER, W. (1992), 'Eusebius' Chronicle and its Legacy', in Attridge and Hata (1992), 467–91.

——(1996), 'The Apocalyptic Survey of History Adapted by Christians: Daniel's Prophecy of 70 Weeks', in J. C. VanderKam and W. Adler (eds.), *The Jewish Apocalyptic Heritage in Early Christianity* (Assen: Van Gorcum; Minneapolis: Fortress Press), 201–38.

ARGOV, E. I. (2001), 'Giving the Heretic a Voice: Philostorgius of Borissus and Greek Ecclesiastical Historiography', *Athenaeum*, 89: 497–524.

ATTRIDGE, H. W., and HATA, G. (1992) (eds.), *Eusebius, Christianity, and Judaism* (Detroit: Wayne State University Press).

BARNES, T. D. (1980), 'The Editions of Eusebius' *Ecclesiastical History*', *GRBS* 21: 191–200.

—— (1981), *Constantine and Eusebius* (Cambridge, Mass.: Harvard University Press).

BOER, W. DEN (1961–2), 'Some Remarks on the Beginnings of Christian Historiography', *StPatr* 3–4: 348–62.

BURGESS, R. W. (1997), 'The Dates and Editions of Eusebius' *Chronici Canones* and *Historia Ecclesiastica*', *JTS* 48: 471–504.

—— (1999), *Studies in Eusebian and post-Eusebian Chronography* (Stuttgart: Franz Steiner).

CARRIKER, A. J. (2003), *The Library of Eusebius of Caesarea* (Leiden: E. J. Brill).

CHESNUT, G. F. (1986), *The First Christian Histories*, 2nd edn. (Macon, Ga.: Mercer University Press).

—— (1992), 'Eusebius, Augustine, Orosius and the Later Patristic and Medieval Christian Historians', in Attridge and Hata (1992), 687–713.

CROKE, B., and EMMETT, A. M. (1983), 'Historiography in Late Antiquity: An Overview', in B. Croke and A. M. Emmett (eds.), *History and Historians in Late Antiquity* (Sydney: Pergamon Press), 1–12.

DREWS, R. J. (1965), 'Assyria in Classical Universal Histories', *Historia*, 14: 129–42.

DROGE, A. (1989), *Homer or Moses?* (Tübingen: J. C. B. Mohr/Paul Siebeck).

GELZER, H. (1967), *Sextus Julius Africanus und die byzantinische Chonographie* (Leipzig, 1885–98; repr. in 1 vol. by Burt Franklin).

GRANT, R. M. (1972), 'The Uses of History in the Church before Nicaea', *StPatr* 11: 166–78.

—— (1980), *Eusebius as Church Historian* (Oxford: Clarendon Press).

GRUMEL, V. (1958), *La chronologie*, Traite d'études Byzantines, 1 (Paris: Presses universitaires de France).

GUSTAFSSON, B. (1961), 'Eusebius' Principles in Handling his Sources, as Found in his Church History, Books I–VII', *StPatr* 4: 429–41.

HARRIES, J. (1986), 'Sozomen and Eusebius: The Lawyer as Church Historian in the Fifth Century', in C. Holdsworth and T. P. Wiseman (eds.), *The Inheritance of Historiography 350–900*, Exeter Studies in History, 12 (Exeter: University of Exeter Press), 45–52.

HEYDEN, K. (2006), 'Die Christliche Geschichte des Philippos von Side', in W. Wallraff (ed.), *Julius Africanus und die Christliche Weltchronistik*, TU 57 (Berlin: de Gruyter), 209–43.

HYLDAHL, N. (1960), 'Hegesippus' *Hypomnemata*', *Studia Theologica*, 14: 70–113.

LEPPIN, H. (2003), 'The Church Historians (I): Socrates, Sozomenus, and Theodoretus', in Marasco (2003), 219–54.

LIEBESCHUETZ, J. H. W. G. (1993), 'Ecclesiastical Historians on their Own times', *StPatr* 24: 151–63.

LOUTH, R. A. (1990), 'The Date of Eusebius' *Historia Ecclesiastica*', *JTS* 41: 111–23.

MARASCO, G. (2003) (ed.), *Greek and Roman Historiography in Late Antiquity* (Leiden: E. J. Brill).

MARGUERAT, D. (2002), *The First Christian Historian: Writing the "Acts of the Apostles"*, Society for New Testament Studies, Monograph Series, 121 (Cambridge: Cambridge University Press).

MARKUS, R. A. (1975), 'Church History and Early Church Historians', in D. Baker (ed.), *The Materials, Sources and Methods of Ecclesiastical History*, SCH (Oxford: Blackwell), 1–17.

MILBURN, R. L. P. (1954), *Early Christian Interpretations of History* (New York: Harper).

Momigliano, A. (1963), 'Pagan and Christian Historiography in the Fourth Century A.D.', in A. Momigliano (ed.), *The Conflict of Paganism and Christianity in the Fourth Century* (Oxford: Clarendon Press), 79–99.

——(1984), 'The Origins of Universal History', in *Settimo contributo alla storia degli Studi Classici e del Mondo Antico*, Storia e letteratura, Raccolta di studi e testi, 161 (Rome: Edizioni di storia e letteratura), 77–103.

——(1990), 'Ecclesiastical Historiography', in A. Momigliano, *The Classical Foundations of Modern Historiography* (Berkeley: University of California Press), 132–52.

Mosshammer, A. A. (1979), *The Chronicle of Eusebius and Greek Chronographic Tradition* (Lewisburg, Pa.: Bucknell University Press).

Schwartz, E. (1938), 'Die Kirchengeschichte', in E. Schwartz, *Vergangene Gegenwärtigkeiten: exoterica inter arma et post cladem dis manibus*, Gesammelte Schriften, 1 (Berlin: de Gruyter), 110–30.

Sirinelli, J. (1961), *Les vues historiques d'Eusèbe de Césarée durant la période prénicéenne*, Faculté des lettres et sciences humaines, Publications de la Section de langues et littératures, 10 (Dakar: Université de Dakar).

Stevenson, W. (2002–3), 'Sozomen, Barbarians, and Early Byzantine Historiography', *GRBS* 43: 51–75.

Urbainczyk, T. (1997), *Socrates of Constantinople: Historian of Church and State* (Ann Arbor: University of Michigan Press).

Winkelmann, F. (2003), 'Historiography in the Age of Constantine', in Marasco (2003), 3–41.

Zecchini, G. (2003), 'Jerome, Orosius and the Western Chronicles', in Marasco (2003), 317–45.

CHAPTER 29

MARTYR PASSIONS AND HAGIOGRAPHY

SUSAN ASHBROOK HARVEY

A large body of literature survives from the early Christian period, devoted first to accounts of martyrdom suffered on behalf of the emerging religion and then to lives of exemplary Christian witness. These texts were part of the rising of saints, which would leap to public importance in the fourth century. They appeared in every language of the early Christian period, establishing literary traditions that would continue to flourish throughout the medieval and Byzantine periods, and even into our own time. These texts have an importance for early Christian studies separate from their role in the cult of saints, and their study has its own scholarly issues. In the present essay, I address these literary concerns, rather than those related to the cult of saints (see Price, Ch. 39 below).

'Hagiography' is an umbrella term covering writings about holy persons (*hagios* = holy one; *graphai* = writings). By the Middle Ages, hagiography was a particular literary form: the 'Life', or *vita*, of a saint, distinct from the martyr's 'passion' (*passio*) or 'acts' (*acta*), the account of a martyr's suffering death. Within the time period covered by this Handbook, hagiography came to be composed following well-developed literary conventions, with a distinct agenda of glorifying the subject at hand. But in the early Christian centuries, variety characterized both the behaviour that might be considered holy, as well as the literary forms

I am grateful to Michelle Oing for research assistance.

through which such behaviour was celebrated. Following the trajectory of early Christianity's development, matters began with the accounts of martyrs.

29.1 MARTYR PASSIONS

The New Testament book of Acts, chapters 6–7, recounts the death of the apostle Stephen, stoned by Jewish persecutors, presenting the first Christian martyrdom. The account is deliberately modelled on the passion narratives of the early gospels, to which Acts was attached as the second part of Luke. The widely circulating apocryphal acts of the apostles generally contained martyr accounts as the culminating event of an apostle's career. The imitation of Christ through an unjust death was a constant theme of Christian literature from the late first century onwards.

At the same time, historically based accounts of martyrdoms were also circulating, beginning in the second century. The *Martyrdom of Polycarp of Smyrna* (*c.*155) is the earliest literary martyr's passion, written in the form of a letter by eyewitnesses and sent to other churches. Eusebius of Caesarea preserved another letter written not long thereafter, again by eyewitnesses, reporting on Christians martyred in Lyons and Vienne in 177. Other testimonies took the forensic form of trial narratives, such as the *Acts of the Scillitan Martyrs*, executed in 180 in Carthage. At the turn of the third century, the extraordinary *Martyrdom of Perpetua and Felicitas* provides an account of a group of Christians martyred in Carthage, including in its report what the anonymous editor claims to be the prison diary of one of the victims, the young noblewoman Perpetua. During the second half of the third century, as persecutions grew harsher, Christian accounts became more elaborate. The *Martyrdom of Pionius* also purports to include a sizeable portion of first-person memoir by the martyr himself. Early in the fourth century, Eusebius of Caesarea composed a work called *The Martyrs of Palestine*, separate from his *Ecclesiastical History*. Its primary contents were included in the *History* as book IX.

The martyr accounts of pre-Constantinian Christianity have been highly influential on modern scholarship. Not only have they preserved moving testimony regarding the persecution and sufferings of early Christians, but they have done so in literary forms which invited historical confidence: letters by eyewitnesses, court records, diaries or memoirs of victims. Historians have often privileged these martyr acts far above those appearing after Christianity's legalization and subsequent rise to power in the Roman Empire. As a result, historical presentations of early Christianity have been strongly coloured by an emphasis on persecution and martyrdom during the first three Christian centuries. Moreover, these accounts have been mined for information on many aspects of early Christian society. Compelling details about women, slavery, children, and family life have been culled from these texts, in addition to references to early relic veneration, burial, memorial and liturgical practices. Such details have been cited repeatedly by scholars as providing 'authentic' glimpses of early Christian—and indeed, Roman—society.

In the past 40 years, however, scholars have become increasingly aware of the literary qualities of these texts. More attention has been paid to the broader literary traditions in which these texts participate. The notion of the 'noble death' was already strongly ingrained in Graeco-Roman society, with a distinguished philosophical lineage that prominently included the model of Socrates' own death in fourth-century BCE Athens (Droge and Tabor 1992). The crucifixion narratives of the gospels were hardly the only biblical texts on which to draw, and were themselves strongly shaped by scriptural allusions to the psalms and prophets of the Hebrew Bible (Deléani-Nigoul 1985a, 1985b; Saxer 1991). Perhaps most influentially for Christians, the stories of the second-century BCE Maccabean martyrs circulated widely. The version given in the extra-canonical book of 4 Maccabees, itself heavily marked by Stoic ideals, was a favourite among early Christians (DeSilva 2006). Its vividly rendered presentation of execution by drawn-out, monstrously cruel torture, endured by the heroically faithful Jews, provided a clear script for early Christian martyr passions, as well as a number of principal motifs (Avemarie and van Henten 2002).

Appreciation for these pre-Christian traditions grew at the same time that scholars working on the apocryphal acts were starting to emphasize the literary links between these early Christian legendary narratives and other imaginative literature of the Hellenistic and Roman eras: the Greek novels, Jewish extra-canonical narratives, Latin romances (Hägg 1983; Pervo 1987, 1996, 1997; Tatum 1994; Wills 1995; Schmeling 1996). Post-structural literary theory was raising awareness of the need to read texts with attention to their authors' rhetoric *as* rhetoric (Cameron 1989a, 1991). For historians of early Christianity, this meant considering the extent to which even so-called eyewitness reports and first-person narratives were constructed narratives, shaped by particular literary conventions, as well as by the agendas and rhetorical strategies of their authors (Ronsse 2006). More nuanced historical-critical method meant modifying significantly the picture of early Christianity as a persecuted religion.

With scholars now in agreement that persecution was far less frequent or extensive than formerly thought, these early martyr accounts have been approached as articulations of ideologies, theologies, identity formation, and other early Christian agendas. As such, they present the scholar with a different kind of historical information than that of reconstructing factual events (Fox 1986; Bowersock 1994, 1995). To be sure, factual information may be found in these texts. Much of what we know about Roman trials, interrogation procedures, prison practices, and routine employment of torture in legal contexts derives from martyr accounts (Bisbee 1988;

Shaw 1993, 1996). The literary conventions of these accounts require fairly detailed descriptions of such activities and contexts, and these leave pronounced marks on the imaginative narratives, nightmares, and visionary literature that Christians produced long after the threat of martyrdom has passed (Miles 1989; Burrus 1995; Shaw 2003).

At the same time, Christians used the presentation of martyrdom as occasion for challenging the existing social order. They presented a crafted narrative of Christian witness that subverted inherited traditions of Graeco-Roman society, by inverting the meaning of what had taken place in the event of the martyr's death. The Romans displayed public death by torture as a spectacle of power and domination. Christian authors utilized a rhetoric of paradox to declare this apparent defeat of Christians a victory for Christ. In doing so, they played out basic New Testament motifs of the divine become human, the Lord of All crucified as a common criminal, life resurrected from death, the illiterate fisherman become the eloquent proclaimer of God's Word (Cameron 1991). The very vocabulary of what counted as virtues and vices in this situation reversed traditionally cherished ideals. Basic social categories were destabilized by the literary celebration of women or slaves as glorious exemplars; or the exaltation of long-suffering endurance as venerable, or the passive reception of active penetration (by sword or other means of execution) as the display of 'manly virtue' rather than feminine weakness (Shaw 1996; Heffernan and Shelton 2006).

Yet Graeco-Roman culture broadly speaking was responding to the changes of empire through the formation of new subjectivities. The 'suffering self' was an identity self-consciously articulated in philosophical discourse, imaginative narratives, medical literature, and personal correspondence, throughout the religious diversity of the early Empire (Perkins 1995). From this perspective, Christian martyr literature contributed to the formation of subjectivities appropriate to larger cultural identities of the Roman Empire (Castelli 2004).

Following legalization in the early fourth-century Roman Empire, accounts of Christian martyrdom began to diverge along two basic literary trajectories. Wherever and whenever persecution against Christians broke out, accounts purporting to narrate the events were published and widely read by Christian communities. Within the Roman Empire, this would happen primarily for groups labelled as 'heretical' by the reigning orthodoxy of the day. For example, a powerful set of Donatist martyr passions was produced in the fifth century, as the conflict between Donatist and Catholic Christianity played out in North Africa (Tilley 1997a, 1997b). More often, such literature now appeared from beyond Roman borders. The fourth and fifth centuries brought extensive persecutions of the Christians in Persia, with a resulting martyr literature produced in both Greek and Syriac (Brock and Harvey 1998). This circulated, translated from Syriac into Greek and from both into Latin, fairly quickly and widely. In the sixth century, accounts of the Christian martyrs of Najran, a small Jewish kingdom in the south Arabian peninsula, appeared in

Syriac, and were again soon translated (Shahid 1971). These 'new' martyrdoms were recounted in literary forms closely modelled on the earlier second- and third-century texts, but especially on the pattern set by Eusebius of Caesarea. Yet the historical circumstances kept a vivid sense of urgency in their narratives, a quality that would recur in Christian history each time persecution arose. The issue of distinguishing historically accurate material from literary conventions and rhetorical traditions is continually in the foreground for scholars working with these texts.

The second trajectory is the emergence of the martyr's *passio* or *acta* as a highly developed literary genre. As distance grew from the historical event, and as Christianity within the Roman Empire gained its unrivalled ascendancy, the memory of early Christian martyrdom took on glorious and elaborate shape. With strong literary influences from epic romance, martyrs' legends proliferated in the fourth through sixth centuries (and well after), producing a huge volume of narratives. These, too, took varying literary forms: not only the prose *acta*, but homilies and hymnography served as vehicles for these thrilling, swashbuckling, gruesome, and often fantastic accounts of extraordinary Christian heroism played out against inhuman Roman savagery. The *Peristephanon*, or *Crown of the Martyrs*, by the fifth-century Spanish poet Prudentius (Ross 1995), is an excellent example, as is the originally Syriac *Life of Febronia* (a martyr's passion in the form of an epic romance) (Brock and Harvey 1998).

As Christianity finally began to grow in sizeable numbers in the fourth and fifth centuries, some communities refashioned their earlier histories, adding in the grandeur of early martyrs when in fact surviving evidence presents a very different story. The development of Christianity became the subject of contested memory. Thus, for example, the great Syrian city of Edessa produced important accounts of the martyrs Shmona, Guria, and Habib, all three of whom died in the Great Persecution, just prior to Constantine's legalization of Christianity in 313. Late in the fourth century a second group of *acta* appear, recounting the magnificent executions of the Edessan Christians Sharbil, Barsamyas, and Babai, said to have occurred under the reign of Trajan around the year 105. These spurious martyrdoms provide a heroic Christian witness from early in Edessa's history (although no martyrdoms took place there prior to those of the Diocletianic persecutions), and add the further element that Sharbil and Barsamyas were said to be born of Edessa's nobility—unlike the villagers Shmona, Guria, and Habib. Edessa—and its aristocracy—gained a grander Christian legacy through these tales, and it was one that gained great popularity in Greek and Latin traditions as well (Brock 1991).

The early Christian martyr narrative lent itself to numerous ideological uses, some local or regional (as with Edessa) and others that served broader traditions of Christian social memory. It functioned with dramatic effect whenever invoked, as indeed remains the case in our own time (Naguib 1994; Castelli 2004).

29.2 SAINTS' LIVES

The legalization of Christianity in the early fourth-century Roman Empire brought an end to the threat of martyrdom for many Christians. Literature about heroic Christians turned to the life, rather than the death, of the saint as its primary focus. Our earliest examples are closely patterned on the literary traditions of Greek biography and panegyric: the *Life of Cyprian of Carthage* by the deacon Pontius, composed soon after Cyprian's death in 258; Eusebius's *Life of Origen*, preserved at least in part in his *Ecclesiastical History*, book 6, as well as his laudatory *Life of Constantine*, were early steps in this direction. Most scholars take the *Life of Antony of Egypt*, written by Athanasius of Alexandria soon after the saint's death in 356, as the real turning point, however, and the start of the literary genre of hagiography proper: the saint's *vita*. Indeed, the *Life of Antony* is arguably the single most influential 'biography' written in Christian history, apart from the gospels themselves—a perspective famously attested in Augustine's account of his own conversion in *Confessions*, book 8 (Harpham 1987).

At virtually the same moment that the *Life of Antony* was published, an explosion of Christian literature took place in Greek, Latin, Syriac, and Coptic, presenting accounts of praiseworthy men and women. Although the *Life of Antony* presented the basic script for the saint's *vita* as it would become formalized in the medieval and Byzantine traditions, it is characteristic of late antiquity that hagiography at first appears in a great variety of literary forms. Laudatory presentations were offered in full-length, ostensibly biographical narratives, or in collections of short cameos of a number of holy figures, beginning with Palladius's *Lausiac History*; or in collections of *Sayings* (*Apophthegmata*, resembling the earlier philosophical *chreia*) (Harmless 2004). Often these narratives took the literary form of letters, as had the *Life of Antony* itself; Gregory of Nyssa's account of his sister, the *Life of Macrina*, is another such example. Funeral orations imitating the classical panegyric were a major genre, such as Gregory of Nazianzus offered for his friend Basil of Caesarea, or for his sister Gorgonia. Homilies and hymns are major sources for hagiographical accounts, and sometimes provide our earliest textual witness to saints who would become extremely popular in subsequent centuries. Already in the fifth century we find highly learned, literarily crafted *vitae*, as the *Life of Antony* surely was, as well as simple didactic tales like that of the anonymous Man of God from Edessa (Doran 2006). Although some scholars have stressed the importance of this distinction (e.g. Browning 1981), the line can be hard to draw. With highly accomplished intellectuals well represented among hagiographical authors—in addition to Athanasius, Gregory of Nazianzus, and Gregory of Nyssa, we might also mention Theodoret of Cyrrhus, Jerome, Sulpicius Severus, Cyril of Scythopolis, John of Ephesus, Gregory of Tours, Gregory the Great, and others—late antique hagiography provides us with a literature in which class distinctions in intended audience can become unclear.

Once begun, however, the popularity of hagiography was immediate. Not only were accounts of known historical figures avidly sought, but stories of legendary persons to an equal degree. The time was ripe for new paradigms of holiness to replace the earlier types favoured in martyr literature or that followed closely on traditions from Greek biography (Cox 1983; Alexandre 1984). There were gaps to be filled: named and unnamed figures from biblical literature gained their own traditions. The Samaritan woman who met Jesus at the well became St Photini; the Roman centurion who had acknowledged the dying Christ as Lord became St Longinus. Developments occurred not only in devotional cults, but also in hagiographical literature that provided stories where there had been none. St Thecla, famed from her appearance in the legendary *Acts of Paul and Thecla*, gained an extensive collection of miracle stories in the fifth century (Johnson 2006), and further elaborations of her legend with localized Egyptian interests at the same time (Davis 2001). Named persons from earlier Christian history, such as the second-century bishop Polycarp of Smyrna and the elusive epigram-writer Abercius of Phrygian Hierapolis, were accorded lengthy *vitae* recounting their careers, where none had existed before (Nissen 1912; Stewart-Sykes 2002).

The penitent harlot motif, rooted in the biblical imagery of Israel's uneven faithfulness to God, yielded some of the most profoundly enduring *vitae* of Christian tradition in the stories of Mary of Egypt, Pelagia the Harlot, the prostitute Thaïs, and Mary the niece of Abraham of Qidun (Ward 1987). Pelagia's *vita* was also part of a series of 'transvestite' women saints, who upon their conversion to a life of faith also took up a life disguised as a monk (Patlagean 1976; Davis 2002). This motif of concealed sanctity would also flourish in the stories of holy fools: the short account of an anonymous nun pretending madness in Palladius's *Lausiac History*; John of Ephesus's sixth-century encounters with deliberate and invented ascetics practising vocations as beggars (Harvey 1990); the anonymous Man of God of Edessa whose simple narrative would become the legend of St Alexius the Man of God and also of St John the Hutdweller; the elaborately literary *Life of Simeon the Holy Fool* of Emesa (Krueger 1996).

Hand in hand with hagiography's flourishing was a veritable industry in translation. Occasionally, we are lucky enough to have multiple versions of a saint's story by different authors, and even in different languages. The contrasting presentations of St Simeon the Stylite found between the Greek *vitae* by Theodoret of Cyrrhus and a writer claiming to be a monk of Simeon's monastery named Antonios, along with the anonymous Syriac *vita*, present the historian with conflicting and even irreconcilable narratives, with all three authors apparently eyewitnesses (Doran 1992). Yet the contrasts are significant for alerting us to different cultural and social contexts, as well as competing ascetic, theological, or ideological claims. In the case of the Merovingian queen St Radegund, we again have three *vitae*, written by three people who knew her personally: the poet Venantius Fortunatus, the bishop Gregory of Tours, and her fellow nun Baudonivia (Petersen 1996). The two men present Radegund with an emphasis on her domestic devotional life, her (private) individual acts of mercy, and her horrifying self-mortification. By contrast, Baudonivia emphasizes Radegund's political and civic involvements, as well as her theological acumen and the spiritual teachings she offered to her nuns—the fruits of her prayer practice and her visions. The difference is arresting and renders vivid the stark absence of women's voices from a literature that provides one of our few spotlights on ancient Christian women (Gäbe 1989).

Differences in accounts are found no less tellingly in the translations that seem often to have been produced quickly, and with wide circulation. In fact, the polylingual nature of early Christianity was both a literary motif within hagiographical texts as well as a major means of cultural cross-fertilization (Peeters 1950). These texts were translated and transmitted back and forth across language barriers, and sometimes retranslated into their original languages from later, secondary versions. Athanasius presented Antony as an illiterate Coptic Christian, unlearned in Greek, yet able to out-argue the great Greek philosophers of his day. The motif echoes the transformation in the New Testament book of Acts of the apostles from illiterate fishermen to philosophically eloquent preachers after the experience of Pentecost. Yet we now know that Antony was highly educated and literate in Greek, as demonstrated by a group of extant letters attributed to him and recently shown to be authentic (Rubenson 1995). Similarly, Theodoret of Cyrrhus presents his Syrian ascetics as incomprehensible to imperial officials who did not speak Syriac (Urbainczyk 2000). In both cases, genuine language differences were used to present an ideological point: that the old, 'pagan' wisdom was now defeated by the 'new' revelation of Christian truth.

Yet, in the textual transmission of hagiography, important exchanges took place across linguistic barriers. The *Life of Antony* in its Coptic, Syriac, and Latin versions shows intriguing differences in word choices. Where the Greek stresses civic imagery, for instance, the Syriac uses liturgical allusions. More concretely, hagiography provided one of the few channels through which Greek and Latin literature could be influenced by the literatures of other languages, notably Syriac and, to a lesser extent, Coptic. *The Life of Pelagia the Harlot of Antioch*, to take one such instance, originated in Syriac, but would eventually be translated into every language of the Christian Middle Ages (Petitmengin *et al.* 1981).

As in the case of martyr *passions*, hagiographical *vitae* could be—and until relatively recently often were—taken as providing empirical evidence for historical developments within Christianity. This was particularly true in scholarship on the development of monasticism, where the romantic aura surrounding the early hagiographies by Athanasius and Palladius, as well as the voluminous tradition of *Sayings* and the rich Pachomian materials, long dominated the work of modern historians (Veilleux 1980–2; Chitty 1966). Among the most significant scholarly shifts of recent decades has been the critical reassessment of even the most 'historically based' hagiographical texts, with a view to deconstructing and challenging the traditional narratives of Christianity's growth (Cameron 1997, 2000). Ironically, the move to treat all hagiography as equally 'textual' (Cameron 1989, 1991; Clark 2004) recalls the earlier admonitions of the Bollandists to suspect every text of pious exaggeration if not outright invention. But the tools of critical theory have offered historians a fertile array of new possibilities for working with hagiography. If an empirical method of historical positivism has been definitively set aside, tremendous vitality has been gained in the process.

29.3 SITUATING THE SCHOLARSHIP

During the first half of the twentieth century, the work of the Bollandist fathers dominated the study of Christian martyrs and saints. After three centuries of devoted yet unstable effort, occasionally derailed by political or ecclesiastical up-heavals, the Bollandists had achieved a notable international status, affirmed by scholars, church hierarchs, and lay people alike for the scientific rigour, intellectual integrity, and historical accuracy of their research. Specific concerns character-ized their efforts. Fundamental to the Bollandist project was the establishment of historical authenticity for the cult of saints. All evidence must be judiciously, meticulously assessed, and none more so than the narratives recounting the lives, legends, glorious feats, and exemplary deaths of the holy men and women compris-ing the Christian company of saints. Despite the staggering scope of the project, the Bollandists had determined to examine every story about every saint and martyr, in every Christian language, for the whole of Christian history (Delehaye 1959; Joassart 2000).

In the course of the twentieth century, the cumulative achievements of their prodigious efforts became clear. In numerous monographs and in the pages of their journal *Analecta Bollandiana*, the Bollandists sifted the wheat from the chaff. Historical persons and events were disentangled from myths and legends; authentic documents from spurious, forged, or falsified accounts. The Bollandist scholars sought positive data: the historical veracity of the saint, of events, places, dates, shrines, churches, relics, memorial festivals. From the bewildering array of manu-scripts preserved unevenly across the Christian world, the Bollandists led the way in establishing critical editions of hagiographical texts, working out the compli-cated transmissions through different recensions and often multiple ancient and medieval languages, in the quest for the original account of each and every saint.

In the process of their work, the Bollandists established careful criteria for iden-tifying the various literary genres of hagiography: the *passio* or *acta* of the martyr, the *vita* of the saint. From the thousands of accounts they had collected, it was possible for the historian to see how such texts were constructed and composed: to see principal leitmotifs and *topoi*, the influences of biblical patterns, or of classical, pre-Christian ('pagan') conventions. In their focused search for the historically accurate, the Bollandists identified numerous elements in the writings about saints that seemed to undermine every claim to authenticity or factual reliability. As in biblical scholarship, historical-critical method destabilized some certainties and raised questions as to how narratives of martyrs and saints should—or could—be studied or used by historians of any academic discipline.

By the middle of the twentieth century, a sea-change was under way, as historians began—slowly at first—to engage the accomplishments of the Bollandists (and of historical criticism more generally) through other methodologies. Narratives about martyrs and saints are among the most plentiful textual remains of ancient, medieval, Byzantine, and oriental Christianity. How might these texts serve the scholar, of various disciplines, in the task of understanding the Christian past? In two influential essays, Byzantinist Norman Baynes urged historians to enter the 'thought world' of the ancient Christian, leaving aside the presuppositions and standards of one's own time (Baynes and Dawes 1948; Baynes 1955). Hagiography provided a vivid entry into the huge burdens of anxiety, fear, and uncertainty surrounding the ancient person in daily life. What made hagiography important was not its capacity to convey historical facts, but rather, its ability to represent the tenor of its times as people felt and experienced them. Hagiography offered a window into the psychology of the ancient or Byzantine Christian; it could thus bring history alive to the discerning and culturally sensitive reader.

In 1968 Evelyne Patlagean took the bold step of publishing an article in which she argued forcefully and eloquently for hagiography as a uniquely powerful source of social history. Herself a student of structuralist Claude Lévi-Strauss, and an active contributor to the *Annales* school of thought, Patlagean challenged the caricature of Bollandist positivism to urge a more intellectually nuanced reading of hagiography. Despite its veneer of timeless, ahistorical, and mythical narrative, hagiography often provided a wealth of historical detail to which the scholar otherwise had little access. Embedded in its miracle accounts were thick descriptions of illness, infertility, mental instability, domestic violence; children, prostitutes, and other social outcasts; spaces normally omitted from the purview of official or mainstream literary documents: the household, the kitchen, the living quarters of women and slaves. With literary ties to the Greek novel, early Christian apocryphal texts, and classical biography and panegyric, hagiography was part of a tradition of imaginative narrative that could work outside the strictures of elite literary forms (whether Greek, Latin, Syriac, or any other of the languages available). Far from being simplistic, 'popular' literature intended merely for uneducated and unsophisticated masses, hagiography in its different forms showed clear concern with the complex whole of the society that produced it. Literacy, reading, transmission, and exchange of knowledge were part of plot lines that presented the study of scripture, chanting of psalms, and epistolary correspondence between even the poorest or most remote of desert hermits and the broader ecclesiastical community of monastery and urban church. Varieties of social classes were invariably included in the stories, as they were also intermixed in the common course of daily life. Hagiographers wanted to show their saints interacting with the whole of society, even as they intended their accounts to be read and heard by all social classes, in order to champion particular values and teachings. Nor was hagiography at any point isolated from other intellectual expressions. It was, for example, closely aligned with contemporary historiography, sharing themes and categories, and often borrowing directly from it.

The historian, then, must seek access to this genuine historical context which underlay hagiography and to which its writers spoke, despite its concealment behind conventionalities of plots and characters. To this end Patlagean proposed a structural analysis that would read a common script underlying every hagiography, a script that presumed the mental categories of the Byzantine hagiographer but which was equally revealing of the larger late antique and medieval world. This script presented the human person in a constantly embattled relation to the world. The saint's story operated according to three essential and superimposed models for that relation: the demonic model, in which the human person was attacked by forces working outside normative moral structures; the scriptural model, in which the terms of the human relationship to the world were played out according to biblical events or characters; and finally, the ascetic or moral model, in which that relationship was consciously transposed onto an ascetic plane of virtue and vice, and thus to a certain extent within human control. The saint was a mediator whose ascetic training enabled the disruption or inversion of a social order operating according to the impaired (embattled) human relation to the world. This mediation allowed a return to divine intention: the healing of physical, civic, or moral suffering. Understanding these models could enable the critical historian to extract valid information from hagiographical texts. Most importantly, because of hagiography's intrinsic interests, that information could prove invaluable for purposes of social history. Gender, class, ethnicity, medicine, and science were all areas where our knowledge could be substantially enhanced through a more sophisticated reading of hagiography, as Patlagean's further scholarship on poverty and on the family amply demonstrated (Patlagean 1977, 1981). Structuralism would pass as an academic fad, but Patlagean's insistence on the importance of hagiography as a crucial source of social history has been more than vindicated in subsequent scholarship.

The watershed moment for contemporary historians was the publication of Peter Brown's essay 'The Rise and Function of the Holy Man in Late Antiquity' (1971). This essay marked a turning point for scholars in a number of areas and disciplines (as is evident from other essays in the present volume). Unlike Patlagean, although drawing on her work, Brown took his interpretive models from cultural anthropology—at this point, notably from Mary Douglas. In the following decades, he engaged a variety of influential methodological currents in critical theory. The results revitalized scholarly debate about and appreciation for a number of larger areas of interest: asceticism and sexuality; religion, society, and politics; intellectual and social history.

For the study of hagiography, 'The Rise and Function of the Holy Man' was decisive on two accounts: first, by its insistence that hagiography offered the historian singular access to the ordinary person and humble concerns of daily life in late antique society; and second, by demonstrating—as had Patlagean—that diverse methodologies from different academic disciplines could provide the tools necessary for opening hagiography as a historically valid source. From this perspective, the achievements of the Bollandists could be justly affirmed. They had brought—and continue to bring—rigorous order to the vast body of hagiographical literature produced over the course of Christian history: separating out the layers of historical, legendary, and fictive material; distinguishing basic elements from later accretions; rendering visible the conventional building blocks by which an author composed a hagiographical narrative. In effect, the Bollandists had made hagiography usable by, and useful for, historians. Baynes, Patlagean, and Brown were among the most effective trail-blazers in showing how rich a treasure store had thus been opened.

Recent decades have brought fresh considerations of hagiography from every direction, but these may be broadly clustered into two primary areas: the treatment of hagiography as a literary genre and its consideration as historical data. The latter, of course, depends significantly on the former. Scholars have given careful consideration to how the hagiographer constructed his text (Derouet 1976). This has included attention to classical models (Heinzelmann 1973; Clark 1984; Momigliano 1987a, 1987b, 1993; Rousseau 2000), and to folklore (Festugière 1960; Heist 1981; Elliott 1987). At the most fundamental level, however, biblical themes, motifs, and stories provided the component pieces out of which the saint's *persona* and story were composed. This was true regardless of the historicity or lack thereof behind the narrative (Lifshitz 1994; Philippart 1998). Historical persons would be fitted into conventions of biblical types, just as those types could be articulated through elaborate imaginative narratives (Saxer 1986; Coon 1997). As the biblical canon became set, hagiography became a literature that conveyed biblical narrative as an ongoing aspect of history: the salvation drama was not confined to the biblical past, but continued to play out in the lives of Christians in their present world. Hagiography by this means proved formative for what would become the distinctively Christian literatures of the Middle Ages (Van Uytfanghe 1985, 1993, 1999).

Just as early hagiography was written in a surprising array of literary forms—almost effervescently—so the notion of sanctity was expressed through a great variety of different life locations. As the ecclesiastical institution began to settle authority definitively in the office of bishop and the person of the monk–holy man, so, too, did the range of possibilities (in life and in text) narrow. Set types emerged: the bishop, the monk, the ascetic virtuoso, the enclosed nun, the young virgin, the penitent harlot, the pious widow. These types were represented textually through *topoi* about clothing, hair, bodily adornment, and work, all based in biblical motifs (Coon 1997). Sanctity was a condition that narrative articulated through carefully chosen conventions, enacting—just as the saint performed—familiar patterns of holiness (Heffernan 1988; Constantinou 2005).

These types had the effect of conforming Christian behaviours and practices to conventional and expected norms (Réal 2001). Ironically, late antique hagiography most often employed a rhetoric of inversion and paradox to present a consistent message of Christian triumph in the cosmos. In this rhetoric, as in its biblical predecessors, the 'old order' was passing away, and a 'new order' coming to be (Delierneaux 1997). Thus, in hagiography, even a woman, a slave, or a street beggar could be a saint (Flusin 2004). The desert became paradise regained. The saint imitated the work of Christ in reversing what had been a distorted natural order of the universe: the sick were healed, the poor fed, the weary comforted (Cameron 1991; Coon 1997). As this rhetoric became conventionalized, so too did it support normative social models (Kitchen 1998; Delierneaux 2002). Hagiography might seem to support the renunciation of family and the rejection of society. But as a mainstream element of the religion, it must also serve to support and sustain the social order.

Even when written about holy women, then, hagiography could carry the agenda of a patriarchal, androcentric society, and it did (Cooper 1996; Constantinou 2005). In fact, hagiography offered a powerful medium through which to negotiate the tensions inherent in Christianizing the Roman Empire and establishing the institutional power of the Church in political, economic, and social terms (Flusin 1981). Athanasius wrote the *Life of Antony* at the very moment that episcopal authority was being stabilized in the Empire's cities. Yet that stability was threatened by the sudden growth of ascetic and monastic communities. Antony and his fellow ascetics, often lay people, carried a viscerally powerful spiritual authority with the public. In the hagiographical scheme that Athanasius fashioned, desert and city articulated polarities of human existence. The ascetic hero fought Satan in a desert world devoid of society's comforts, even as Christ had done in the forty days after his baptism. In turn, the bishop guarded the Church in the world, even as Christ had done during his ministry. Episcopal and ascetic authority were thus differentiated by their very geographical locations, and placed over differing domains (Goehring 1993, 1999; Brakke 1995). The ecclesiastical institution could thereby embrace the ascetic's spiritual power in ways that drew it into the service of the Church, rather than challenging or competing with it (Flusin 1983, 1996; Van Dam 1993; Rapp 2005).

A sizeable number of prominent late antique bishops also wrote hagiography about the holy men and women of their dioceses: Athanasius, Gregory of Nazianzus, Gregory of Nyssa, Palladius of Helenopolis, Theodoret of Cyrrhus, John of Ephesus, Gregory of Tours, and Cyril of Scythopolis all wrote formal hagiographies; Augustine of Hippo, John Chrysostom, Jacob of Serug, and Severus of Antioch all excelled at the hagiographical sermon. In these hagiographical texts, ecclesiastical norms were established and supported: ascetics were unequivocally obedient to their bishops; ascetic women remained enclosed under their bishop's supervision; ascetic men dwelt in communities under their bishop's care or in the desert beyond public reach. The desert landscape, so prominent a literary motif throughout the Bible, became a mythic space in Christian thinking and lore, fantasized in hagiography, visual art, and ascetical literature (Goehring 1993; 2005). Archaeological evidence, by contrast, renders incontrovertible the opposing historical situation already apparent from documentary materials. Monastic history, whether in the native desert landscapes of Egypt, Palestine, or Syria, no less than in the forests of Europe, developed in intimate intersection with urban civic life. The ties were economic, social, familial, ecclesiastical, and political. Desert and city were rarely discrete, delineated spaces of late antique Christian landscapes, except in the mythic universe of Christian imagination (Brakke 1995; Coon 1997).

Scholars have thus looked with increasing interest at what the hagiographical text represents through its constructed narratives (Rubenson 2000; Rousseau 2004; Goehring 2006). Unfailingly didactic, hagiography provided a powerful medium for social control. Precisely through its normative agendas, hagiography offers the historian an entry into the late antique social world (Kazhdan 1990). The challenge lies in determining how, precisely, it does so (Fox 1997; Déroche 2004). For example, as a literature deliberately attentive to domestic contexts, hagiography has been a major source for information about women and families (Giannarelli 1980, 1992, 1993; Harvey 1996). But to what extent do the (invariably?) male authors of these texts preserve anything of women's lives? Is the female saint merely a gendered construction for a 'totalizing discourse' so thoroughly the product of patriarchal culture and society that no 'trace' of women's presence can be confidently reclaimed (Clark 1998a, b; Smith 2004)? Hagiography presented stories remembered and told in the context of the larger Christian public, both male and female. Even if composed in and for monastic audiences (Anson 1974; Miller 2005), the saints it venerated were also part of the larger ecclesiastical life of the Church, commemorated further in hymns and homilies, on feast-days celebrated locally as well as widely, domestically as well as in civic churches. How might the same stories have been heard differently by women than by men (Bynum 1986; Harvey 1993–4)?

Again, how are we to understand hagiography as the representation of embodied holiness (Williams 1999)? Heavily articulated through ascetic discourse and produced predominantly within monastic contexts, even when circulated throughout the lay populace, hagiography often appears to work with dualistic imagery that devalues or denigrates the physical body in its very physicality (mortal and transient, requiring food, shelter, and reproduction), valorizing instead the ascetically disciplined, socially intact body of the celibate saint. Yet both martyr texts and saints' lives must, by their very literary forms, be focused on the bodies of their subjects (Frank 2000). Their task is that of presenting a holy body for their saints, one notably distinct from the body of 'ordinary' society by its location, activities, practices, purposes, functions, and capabilities. Peter Brown's scholarship has set the saint's body as the locus wherein power (social, cultural, political, and economic) could be contested and negotiated most effectively in late antiquity (Brown 1971, 1981, 1982, 1988, 1995). Recent scholarship has been reconsidering the saint's body precisely in its physicality, as embodied experience and as material existence. Scholars are highlighting how hagiography re-construes the physical: whether through emphasis on the senses as a crucial mode of epistemology (Harvey 1998, 2006); or holy embodiment as a condition heightened by a counter-erotics that redirect and redefine the significance of bodily habitation and sensation (Castelli 1992; Burrus 2004, 2005); or materiality as a mode of existence charged with new cultural force (Miller 2000, 2004, 2005). The questions surrounding hagiography, gender, and embodiment have been some of the most vigorously argued matters in recent scholarship, producing some of the most far-reaching changes in our understanding of early Christian history.

The consideration of hagiography as a literature of representation has yielded renewed appreciation of both author and audience as active agents in the production of sacred memory. Recent attention has turned to the author's role as more than the agent crafting the holy subject in terms that would elicit particular responses from the audience who read or heard the text. Scholars now argue that the task of writing hagiography itself produced a particular subjectivity in the author. In the process of fashioning the literary portrait of the saint, the author also fashioned the writing itself as an ascetic discipline through which a changed authorial *persona* emerged. The production of the text could become a liturgical act, sacramental in effect on the author as much as on the reader/listener. From this perspective, the author's production of the text participates in the collective ritual life of the Church as community (Rapp 1998; Kalogeras 2003; Krueger 2004).

Indeed, much hagiography is not the product of a single author, even when we can credit the text to a particular writer. Rather, the narrative voice of hagiography is to some extent always collective. Recent scholarship has highlighted this long neglected aspect of hagiographical literature, arguing that the saint must be recognized as such by the Church as a larger community, even in the most informal terms, or hagiography fails. Hence hagiography is always the product of the community, both in its literary construction by the author and in its enacted reception by the audience. For a saint to be seen as such—for the figure to be perceived and thus acknowledged as holy—the author must present the saint according to the received traditions of the community's collective memory. In turn, the audience must respond to the hagiography in ways that recognize and thereby serve to produce the saint whom the author has represented (Heffernan 1988; Coon 1997; Constantinou

2005). The audience does more than respond to the didactic cues of the narrative; it is arguably inextricable from the authorial process (Kalogeras 2002).

These recent developments in literary and historical analysis are opening new areas for scholarly contribution. Changing trends in critical theory and methodologies from across the humanities provide continually fresh questions, modes of analysis, and perspectives to bring to hagiographical texts. Much is also needed in the comparative study of different versions of hagiography in their ancient translations. Numerous critical editions in the array of ancient Christian languages have appeared in recent decades. Often, these have been considered only in terms of basic questions of historicity. Richer questions of social and cultural history should be brought to bear on this under-utilized body of writings. More work is also needed to place hagiography within its varying contexts of reception: where and how it was read, heard, performed, enacted, in what ritual or performative conditions or spaces, and how these differing contexts contributed to the narrative represented and received (Harvey 1988, 1998).

Late antique hagiography was a literary genre of great variety in its literary forms and in its models of sanctity. As Christianity moved into the medieval and Byzantine periods, a notable impetus to constrain these proliferations of form and type appeared. In Byzantine tradition, the gravitation was towards antiquarianism: to retell the 'old' stories rather than produce new ones, and to narrow the acceptable range of types of saints (Patlagean 1976; Rapp 1995; Talbot 1996; Constantinou 2005). In the medieval West, hagiography helped to form the 'new' literatures of the emerging vernacular languages and the vitality of their cultures (Van Uytfanghe 1999). Perhaps the most important contribution of recent scholarship to the study of hagiographical literature, both of martyrs and of saints, has been to allow the focus on late antiquity to highlight this period of hagiographical production as distinct from the longer history of the genre. Seen as a literature, a task, a choice of authorial or ecclesiastical or gendered voice, through which Christians constructed, contested, performed, and negotiated their religion in its formative centuries, hagiography continues to present the scholar with challenges that bear upon every aspect of early Christianity: history, culture, or belief.

Suggested Reading

Introductions to hagiographical literature that follow Bollandist models remain valuable for student and scholar alike: Delehaye (1961, 1966, 1991) and Aigrain (1953) are classic in this regard. At the same time, Grégoire (1987), Heffernan (1988), and Coon (1997) can also serve as excellent introductions, while drawing on the diverse methodologies and concerns of more recent critical scholarship.

But there is no substitute for the texts themselves, and with this type of literature it is important to read widely among its different forms. A number of excellent anthologies in

English are now easily available: Musurillo (1972), Waddell (1936 repr.), Ward (1978 repr.), Baynes and Dawes (1948 repr.), Veilleux (1980–2), Head and Noble (1995), Brock and Harvey (1998), Talbot (1996), and White (1998). The following bibliography includes a number of important translations of specific works. In every case, the reader will find the necessary information on critical editions included in the volume.

For more in-depth study, scholars will want to check the *Bibliotheca Hagiographica Graeca* (1957, 1984), the *Bibliotheca Hagiographica Latina* (1949, 1986) and the *Bibliotheca Hagiographica Orientalis* (1954) for listings of the known manuscripts for each martyr or saint.

BIBLIOGRAPHY

Manuscript resources

Bibliotheca Hagiographica Graeca, ed. F. Halkin, 3 vols., 3rd edn., Subsidia Hagiographica, 8a (Brussels: Société des Bollandistes, 1957). *Novum auctarium bibliothecae hagiographicae graecae*, ed. F. Halkin, Subsidia Hagiographica, 65 (Brussels: Société des Bollandistes, 1984).

Bibliotheca Hagiographica Latina antiquae et mediae aetatis, ed. Socii Bollandiani, 2 vols., Subsidia Hagiographica, 6 (Brussels: Société des Bollandistes, 1949). *Bibliotheca Hagiographica Latina antiquae et mediae aetatis Novum Supplementum*, ed. H. Fros, Subsidia Hagiographica, 70 (Brussels: Société des Bollandistes, 1986).

Bibliotheca Hagiographica Orientalis, ed. P. Peeters, Subsidia Hagiographica, 10 (Brussels: Société des Bollandistes, 1954).

Secondary literature

AIGRAIN, R. (1953), *L'Hagiographie—Ses sources, ses methods, son histoire* (Paris: Bloud et Gay).

ALEXANDRE, M. (1984), 'Les nouveaux martyrs: Motifs martyrologiques dans la vie des saints et themes hagiographiques dans l'éloge des martyrs chez Grégoire de Nysse', in Spira (1984), 33–70.

ANSON, J. N. (1974), 'The Female Transvestite in Early Monasticism: The Origin and Development of a Motif', *Viator: Medieval and Renaissance Studies*, 5: 1–32.

ATHANASSAKIS, A. N., and VIVIAN, T. (2003), *The Life of Antony by Athanasius of Alexandria: The Coptic Life and the Greek Life*, CS 202 (Kalamazoo, Mich.: Cistercian Publications).

AVEMARIE, F., and VAN HENTEN, J. W. (2002), *Martyrdom and Noble Death: Selected Texts from Graeco-Roman, Jewish, and Christian Antiquity* (London: Routledge).

BAYNES, N. (1955), *Byzantine Studies and Other Essays* (London: Athlone Press).

—— and DAWES, E. (1948), *Three Byzantine Saints: Contemporary Biographies translated from the Greek* (London: Mowbrays; repr. Crestwood, NY: St Vladimir's Seminary Press, 1977).

BIELAWSKI, M., and HOMBERGEN, D. (2004) (eds.), *Il Monachesimo tra Eredità e Aperture: Atti del simposio 'Testi e Temi nella Tradizione del Monachesimo Cristiano', Roma, 28 maggio—1 guigno 2002*, Studia Anselmiana, 140 (Rome: Centro Studi S. Anselmo).

BISBEE, G. A. (1988), *Pre-Decian Acts of Martyrs and Commentarii*, Harvard Dissertations in Religion, 22 (Philadelphia: Fortress Press).

BOWERSOCK, G. (1994), *Fiction as History: Nero to Julian* (Berkeley: University of California Press).

—— (1995), *Martyrdom and Rome* (Cambridge: Cambridge University Press).

BRAKKE, D. (1995), *Athanasius and the Politics of Asceticism* (Oxford: Clarendon Press).

BROCK, S. P. (1991), 'Eusebius and Syriac Christianity', in H. Attridge and G. Hatra (eds.), *Eusebius, Christianity, and Judaism* (Detroit: Wayne State University Press), 212–34.

—— and HARVEY, S. A. (1998), *Holy Women of the Syrian Orient* (Berkeley: University of California Press).

BROWN, P. (1971), 'The Rise and Function of the Holy Man in Late Antiquity', *JRS* 61: 80–101.

—— (1981), *The Cult of the Saints: Its Rise and Function in Latin Christianity* (Chicago: University of Chicago Press).

—— (1982), *Society and the Holy in Late Antiquity* (Berkeley: University of California Press).

—— (1988), *The Body and Society: Men, Women, and Sexual Renunciation in Early Christianity* (New York: Columbia University Press).

—— (1995), *Authority and the Sacred: Aspects of the Christianisation of the Roman World* (Cambridge: Cambridge University Press).

BROWNING, R. (1981), 'The "Low Level" Saint's Life in the Early Byzantine World', in Hackel (1981), 117–27.

BURRUS, V. (1995), 'Reading Agnes: The Rhetoric of Gender in Ambrose and Prudentius', *JECS* 3: 25–46.

—— (2004), *The Sex Lives of Saints: An Erotics of Ancient Hagiography* (Philadelphia: University of Pennsylvania Press).

—— (2005), 'Macrina's Tatoo', in Martin and Miller (2005), 103–16.

BYNUM, C. W. (1986), 'Introduction: The Complexity of Symbols', in *eadem*, S. Harrell, and P. Richman, *Gender and Religion: On the Complexity of Symbols* (Boston: Beacon Press), 1–20.

CAMERON, A. (1989) (ed.), *History as Text: The Writing of Ancient History* (London: Duckworth).

—— (1991), *Christianity and the Rhetoric of Empire: The Development of Christian Discourse* (Berkeley: University of California Press).

—— (1997), 'Eusebius' *Vita Constantini* and the Construction of Constantine', in Edwards and Swain (1997), 145–74.

—— (2000), 'Form and Meaning: The *Vita Constantini* and the *Vita Antonii*', in Hägg and Rousseau (2000), 72–88.

CASTELLI, E. A. (1992), 'Mortifying the Body, Curing the Soul: Beyond Ascetic Dualism in *The Life of Saint Syncletica*', *Differences*, 4: 134–53.

—— (2004), *Martyrdom and Memory: Early Christian Culture Making* (New York: Columbia University Press).

CHITTY, D. (1966, repr. 1995), *The Desert a City: An Introduction to the Study of Egyptian and Palestinian Monasticism under the Christian Empire* (Crestwood, NY: St Vladimir's Seminary Press).

CLARK, E. A. (1984), *The Life of Melania the Younger: Introduction, Translation, and Commentary*, Studies in Women and Religion, 14 (Lewiston, NY: Edwin Mellen Press).

—— (1998a), 'Holy Women, Holy Words: Early Christian Women, Social History, and the "Linguistic Turn"', *JECS* 6: 413–30.

—— (1998b), 'The Lady Vanishes: Dilemmas of a Feminist Historian after the "Linguistic Turn"', *CH* 67: 1–31.

—— (2004), *History, Theory, Text: Historians and the Linguistic Turn* (Cambridge, Mass.: Harvard University Press).

CONSTANTINOU, S. (2005), *Female Corporeal Performances: Reading the Body in Byzantine Passions and Lives of Holy Women*, Studia Byzantina Upsaliensia, 9 (Uppsala: Acta Universitatis Upsaliensis).

COON, L. (1997), *Sacred Fictions: Holy Women and Hagiography in Late Antiquity* (Philadelphia: University of Pennsylvania Press).

COOPER, K. (1996), *The Virgin and the Bride: Idealized Womanhood in Late Antiquity* (Cambridge, Mass.: Harvard University Press).

COX, P. (1983), *Biography in Late Antiquity: A Quest for the Holy Man* (Berkeley: University of California Press).

DAGRON, G. (1978), *Vie et miracles de Sainte Thècle: texte grec, traduction et commentaire*, Subsidia Hagiographica, 62 (Brussels: Société des Bollandistes).

DAVIS, S. J. (2001), *The Cult of St Thecla: A Tradition of Women's Piety in Late Antiquity* (Oxford: Oxford University Press).

—— (2002), 'Crossed Texts, Crossed Sex: Intertexuality and Gender in Early Christian Legends of Holy Women Disguised as Men', *JECS* 10: 1–36.

DELÉANI-NIGOUL, S. (1985a), 'Les *exempla* bibliques du martyre', in Fontaine and Pietri (1985), 261–88.

—— (1985b), 'L'utilisation des modeles bibliques du martyre par les écrivains du IIIe siècle', in Fontaine and Pietri (1985), 315–38.

DELEHAYE, H. (1959), *L'œuvre des Bollandistes à travers trois siècles, 1615–1915*, 2nd edn., Subsidia Hagiographica, 13A (Brussels: Société des Bollandistes).

—— (1961), *The Legends of the Saints: An Introduction to Hagiography*, trans. V. M. Crawford (Notre Dame, Ind.: University of Notre Dame Press).

—— (1966), *Les passions des martyrs et les genres littéraires*, 2nd edn., Subsidia Hagiographica, 13B (Brussels: Société des Bollandistes).

—— (1991), *L'ancienne hagiographie Byzantine: Les sources, les premiers modèles, la formation des genres*, Subsidia Hagiographica, 73 (Brussels: Société des Bollandistes).

DELIERNEAUX, N. (1997), 'Virilité physique et sainteté feminine dans l'hagiographie orientale du IVe au VIIe siècle', *Byzantion*, 67: 179–243.

—— (2002), 'Anne-Euphémianos, l'epouse devenue eunuque: continuité et evolution d'un modèle hagiographique', *Byzantion*, 72: 105–38.

DÉROCHE, V. (2004), 'La forme de l'informe: La Vie de Théodore de Sykéôn et la Vie de Syméon Stylite le Jeune', in Odorico and Agapitos (2004), 367–86.

DEROUET J.-L. (1976), 'Les possibilités d'interpretation sémiologiques des texts hagiographique', *Revue d'histoire de l'Église de France*, 62: 153–62.

DESILVA, D. A. (2006), *4 Maccabees: Introduction and Commentary on the Greek Text in Codex Sinaiticus* (Leiden: E. J. Brill).

DORAN, R. (1992), *The Lives of Simeon Stylites*, CS 112 (Kalamazoo, Mich.: Cistercian Publications).

—— (2006), *Stewards of the Poor: The Man of God, Rabbula, and Hiba in Fifth-Century Edessa*, CS 208 (Kalamazoo, Mich.: Cistercian Publications).

DRIJVERS, J. W., and WATT, J. W. (1999) (eds.), *Portraits of Spiritual Authority: Religious Power in Early Christianity, Byzantium, and the Christian Orient* (Leiden: E. J. Brill).

DROGE, A. J., and TABOR, J. D. (1992), *A Noble Death: Suicide and Martyrdom among the Christians and Jews in Antiquity* (San Francisco: HarperSanFrancisco).

EDWARDS, M. J., and SWAIN, S. (1997) (eds.), *Portraits: Biographical Representation in the Greek and Latin Literature of the Roman Empire* (Oxford: Clarendon Press).

ELLIOTT, A. G. (1987), *Roads to Paradise: Reading the Lives of the Early Saints* (Hanover, NH: University Press of New England).

FESTUGIÈRE, A.-J. (1960), 'Lieux communs littéraires et themes de folk-lore dans l'hagiographie primitive', *Wiener Studien*, 73: 123–52.

FLUSIN, B. (1981), 'Miracle et hiérarchie', in Patlagean and Riché (1981), 299–317.

—— (1983), *Miracle et histoire dans l'oeuvre de Cyrille de Scythopolis* (Paris: L'Institut d'études augustiniennes).

—— (1996), 'L'hagiographie palestinienne et la reception du concile de Chalcédoine', in Rosenquist (1996), 25–47.

—— (2004), 'Le serviteur cache ou le saint sans existence', in Odorico and Agapitos (2004), 59–71.

FONTAINE, J., and PIETRI, C. (1985) (eds.), *Le Monde latin antique et la Bible*, ii: *Bible de tous les temps* (Paris: Beauchesne).

FOX, R. L. (1986), *Pagans and Christians in the Mediterranean World from the Second Century AD to the Conversion of Constantine* (Harmondsworth: Viking).

—— (1997), 'The *Life of Daniel*', in Edwards and Swain (1997), 175–225.

FRANK, G. (2000), 'Macrina's Scar: Homeric Allusion and Heroic Identity in Gregory of Nyssa's *Life of Macrina*', *JECS* 8: 511–30.

FREYBURGER, G., and PERNOT, L. (1997) (eds.), *Du héros païen au saint chrétien* (Paris: L'Institut d'études augustiniennes.

GÄBE, S. (1989), 'Radegundis: sancta, regina, ancilla: zum heiligkeitsideal der Radegundis-viten von Fortunat und Baudonivia', *Francia*, 16: 1–30.

GIANNARELLI, E. (1980), *La tipologia femminile nella biografia e nell' autobiografia cristiana del Ivo secolo* (Rome: Instituto Storico Italiano per il Medio Evo).

—— (1992), 'La biografia femminile: temi e problemi', in C. Anselmelto and U. Mattioli (eds.), *La donna nel pensiero cristiano antico* (Genoa: Merielti), 223–45.

—— (1993), 'Women and Miracles in Christian Biography (IVth–Vth Centuries)', *StPatr* 25: 376–80.

GOEHRING, J. (1993), 'The Encroaching Desert: Literary Production and Ascetic Space in Early Christian Egypt', *JECS* 1: 281–96.

—— (1999), *Ascetics, Society, and the Desert: Studies in Early Egyptian Monasticism* (Harrisburg, Pa.: Trinity Press International).

—— (2005), 'The Dark Side of Landscape: Ideology and Power in the Christian Myth of the Desert', in Martin and Miller (2005), 136–49.

—— (2006), 'Remembering Abraham of Farshut: History, Hagiography, and the Fate of the Pachomian Tradition', *JECS* 14: 1–26.

GREGG, R. C. (1980), *Athanasius: The Life of Antony and the Letter to Marcellinus* (New York: Paulist Press).

GRÉGOIRE, R. (1987), *Manuale di agiologia: Introduzione alla letteratura agiographica* (Fabriano: Monastero San Silvestro Abate).

HACKEL, S. (1981) (ed.), *The Byzantine Saint*, Studies Supplementary to *Sobornost* 5 (London: Fellowship of St Alban and St Sergius; repr. Crestwood, NY: St Vladimir's Seminary Press, 1984).

HÄGG, T. (1983), *The Novel in Antiquity* (Berkeley: University of California Press).

——and ROUSSEAU, P. (2000) (eds.), *Greek Biography and Panegyric in Late Antiquity* (Berkeley: University of California Press).

HARMLESS, W. (2004), *Desert Christians: An Introduction to the Literature of Early Monasticism* (New York: Oxford University Press).

HARPHAM, G. G. (1987), *The Ascetic Imperative in Culture and Criticism* (Chicago: University of Chicago Press).

HARVEY, S. A. (1988), 'The Sense of a Stylite: Perspectives on Simeon the Elder', *VC* 42: 376–94.

——(1990), *Asceticism and Society in Crisis: John of Ephesus and the 'Lives of the Eastern Saints'* (Berkeley: University of California Press).

——(1993–4), 'The Memory and Meaning of a Saint: Two Homilies on Simeon Stylites', in Shafiq Abouzayd (ed.), *Festschrift for Sebastian P. Brock, Aram* 5/6 (Leuven: Peeters), 1–23.

——(1996), 'Sacred Bonding: Mothers and Daughters in Early Syriac Hagiography', *JECS* 4: 27–56.

——(1998), 'The Stylite's Liturgy: Ritual and Religious Identity in Late Antiquity', *JECS* 6: 523–39.

——(2006), *Scenting Salvation: Ancient Christianity and the Olfactory Imagination* (Berkeley: University of California Press).

HEAD, T., and NOBLE, T. F. X. (1995) (eds.), *Soldiers of Christ: Saints and Saints' Lives from Late Antiquity and the Early Middle Ages* (University Park, Pa.: Pennsylvania State University Press).

HEFFERNAN, T. J. (1988), *Sacred Biography: Saints and their Biographers in the Middle Ages* (Oxford: Oxford University Press).

——and SHELTON, J. E. (2006), '*Paradisus in carcere*: The Vocabulary of Imprisonment and the Theology of Martyrdom in the *Passio Sanctarum Perpetuae et Felicitatis*', *JECS* 14: 217–24.

HEINZELMANN, M. (1973), 'Neue Aspeckte der biographischen und hagiographischen Literatur in der lateinischen Welt (1.–6. Jahrhundert)', *Francia*, 1: 27–44.

HEIST, W. H. (1981), 'Hagiography, Chiefly Celtic, and Recent Developments in Folklore', in Patlagean and Riché (1981), 121–41.

HOWARD-JOHNSON, J., and HAYWARD, P. A. (1999) (eds.), *The Cult of Saints in Late Antiquity and the Early Middle Ages* (Oxford: Oxford University Press).

JOASSART, B. (2000), *Hippolyte Delehaye: Hagiographie critique et modernisme*, Subsidia Hagiographica, 81, 2 vols. (Brussels: Société des Bollandistes).

JOHNSON, S. F. (2006), *The Life and Miracles of Thekla: A Literary Study* (Washington D.C.: Center for Hellenic Studies, Harvard University).

KALOGERAS, N. (2002), 'The Role of the Audience in the Construction of Narrative: A Note on Cyril of Scythopolis', *Jahrbuch der österreichischen Byzantinistik*, 52: 149–59.

——(2003), 'The "Rhetoric of Emulation" in the Work of Cyril of Scythopolis and the *Vita Abraamii*', *Byzantinoslavica*, 61: 113–28.

KAZHDAN, A. (1990), 'Byzantine Hagiography and Sex in the Fifth to Twelfth Centuries', *DOP* 44: 131–43.

KITCHEN, J. (1998), *Saints' Lives and the Rhetoric of Gender: Male and Female in Merovingian Hagiography* (Oxford: Oxford University Press).

KRUEGER, D. (1996), *Symeon the Holy Fool: Leontius' Life and the Late Antique City* (Berkeley: University of California Press).

KRUEGER, D. (2004), *Writing and Holiness: The Practice of Authorship in the Early Christian East* (Philadelphia: University of Pennsylvania Press).

LIFSHITZ, F. (1994), 'Beyond Positivism and Genre: Hagiographical Texts as Historical Narrative', *Viator*, 25: 95–113.

MARKUS, R. A. (1996), *Signs and Meanings: World and Text in Ancient Christianity* (Liverpool: Liverpool University Press).

MARTIN, D., and MILLER, P. C. (2005) (eds.), *The Cultural Turn in Late Ancient Studies: Gender, Asceticism, and Historiography* (Durham, NC: Duke University Press).

MAYER, W., with NEIL, B. (2006), *Saint John Chrysostom: The Cult of Saints* (Crestwood, NY: St Vladimir's Seminary Press).

MEYER, R. T. (1964), *Palladius, the Lausiac History*, ACW 34 (New York: Newman Press).

MILES, M. (1989), *Carnal Knowing: Female Nakedness and Religious Meaning in the Christian West* (Boston: Beacon Press).

MILLER, P. C. [see also Cox, P.] (2000), 'Strategies of Representation in Collective Biography: Constructing the Subject as Holy', in Hägg and Rousseau (2000), 209–54.

—— (2004), 'Visceral Seeing: The Holy Body in Late Antiquity', *JECS* 12: 391–411.

—— (2005), 'Is There a Harlot in This Text?: Hagiography and the Grotesque', in Martin and Miller (2005), 87–102.

MITCHELL, S., and GREATREX, G. (2000) (eds.), *Ethnicity and Culture in Late Antiquity* (London: Duckworth and the Classical Press of Wales).

MOMIGLIANO, A. (1987*a*), 'Ancient Biography and the Study of Religion', in Momigliano (1987*c*), 159–77.

—— (1987*b*), 'The *Life of St. Macrina* by Gregory of Nyssa', in Momigliano (1987*c*), 333–47.

—— (1987*c*), *On Pagans, Jews, and Christians* (Middletown, Conn.: Wesleyan University Press).

—— (1993), *The Development of Greek Biography*, 2nd edn. (Cambridge, Mass.: Harvard University Press).

MUSURILLO, H. (1972), *The Acts of the Christian Martyrs* (Oxford: Clarendon Press).

NAGUIB, S.-A. (1994), 'The Martyr as Witness: Coptic and Copto-Arabic Hagiographies as Mediators of Religious Memory', *Numem*, 41: 223–54.

NISSEN, T. (1912), *Abercii vita* (Leipzig: Teubner).

ODORICO, P., and AGAPITOS, P. (2004) (eds.), *Les vies des saints à Byzance: genre literature ou biographie historique?*, *Actes du IIe colloque international philologique Paris 6–7–8 juin 2002* (Paris: Centre d'études Byzantines, néo-helléniques et sud-est européenes, École des Hautes Études en Sciences Sociales).

PATLAGEAN, E. (1968), 'À Byzance: Ancienne hagiographie et histoire sociale', *Annales: e.s.c.* 23: 106–26 [= *Structure sociale, famille, chrétienté à Byzance, IVe–XIe siècle*, ch. V]. English trans. by J. Hodgkin, 'Ancient Byzantine Hagiography and Social History', in Wilson (1983), 101–21.

—— (1976), 'L'histoire de la femme déguisée en moine et l'évolution de la sainteté feminine à Byzance', *Studi medievali*, 17: 597–623 [= *Structure sociale, famille, chrétienté à Byzance, IVe–XIe siècle*, ch. XI].

—— (1977), *Pauvreté économique et pauvreté sociale à Byzance: 4e–7e siècles* (Paris: Mouton).

—— (1981), *Structure sociale, famille, chrétienté à Byzance, IVe–XIe siècle* (London: Variorum).

—— and RICHÉ, P. (1981) (eds.), *Hagiographie Cultures et Sociétés, IVe–XIIe siècles: Actes du Colloque organisé à Nanterre et à Paris, 2–5 mai 1979* (Paris: L'Institut d'études augustiniennes).

PEETERS, P. (1950), *Orient et Byzance: Le tréfonds oriental de l'hagiographie Byzantine*, Subsidia Hagiographica, 26 (Brussels: Société des Bollandistes).

PERKINS, J. (1995), *The Suffering Self: Pain and Narrative Representation in the Early Christian Era* (London: Routledge).

PERVO, R. (1987), *Profit with Delight: The Literary Genre of the Acts of the Apostles* (Philadelphia: Fortress Press).

—— (1996), 'The Ancient Novel Becomes Christian', in Schmeling (1996), 685–712.

—— (1997), 'Rhetoric in the Christian Apocrypha', in Porter (1997), 793–806.

PETERSEN, J. (1996), *Handmaids of the Lord: Contemporary Descriptions of Feminine Asceticism in the First Six Christian Centuries*, CS 143 (Kalamazoo, Mich.: Cistercian Publications).

PETITMENGIN, P. et al. (1981, 1984) (eds.), *Pélagie la Pénitente: metamorphoses d'une légende*, i: *Les textes et leur histoire*; ii: *La survie dans les literatures européennes* (Paris: L'Institut d'études augustiniennes).

PHILIPPART, G. (1998), 'L'hagiographie comme literature: concept recent et nouveaux programmes?', *Revue des sciences humaines*, 251: 11–39.

PORTER, S. (1997) (ed.), *Handbook of Classical Rhetoric in the Hellenistic Period, 330 BC–AD 400* (Leiden: E. J. Brill).

PRICE, R. M. (1985), *Theodoret of Cyrrhus, A History of the Monks of Syria*, CS 88 (Kalamazoo, Mich.: Cistercian Publications).

—— and BINNS, J. (1991), *Cyril of Scythopolis, The Lives of the Monks of Palestine*, CS 114 (Kalamazoo, Mich.: Cistercian Publications).

RAPP, C. (1995), 'Byzantine Hagiographers as Antiquarians, 7th–10th Century', *ByF* 21: 31–44.

—— (1998), 'Storytelling as Spiritual Communication in Early Greek Hagiography: The Use of *Diegesis*', *JECS* 6: 431–48.

—— (2005), *Holy Bishops in Late Antiquity: The Nature of Christian Leadership in an Age of Transition* (Berkeley: University of California Press).

RÉAL, I. (2001), *Vies de saints, vie de famille: Répresentation et système de parenté dans le Royaume mérovingien (481–751) d'après les sources hagiographiques* (Turnhout: Brepols).

REININK, G. J., and KLUGKIST, A. C. (1999) (eds.), *After Bardaisan: Studies on Continuity and Change in Syriac Christianity in Honor of Han J. W. Drijvers* (Leuven: Peeters).

RONSSE, E. (2006), 'Rhetoric of Martyrs: Listening to Saints Perpetua and Felicitas', *JECS* 14: 283–327.

ROSENQVIST, J.-O. (1996) (ed.), *LEIMON: Studies Presented to Lennart Ryden on his 65th Birthday*, Studia Byzantina Upsaliensia, 6 (Uppsala: Acta Universitatis Upsaliensis).

ROSS, J. (1995), 'Dynamic Writing and Martyrs' Bodies in Prudentius' Peristephanon', *JECS* 3: 325–55.

ROUSSEAU, P. (2000), 'Antony as Teacher in the Greek *Life*', in Hägg and Rousseau (2000), 89–109.

—— (2004), 'Moses, Monks, and Mountains in Theodoret's *Historia Religiosa*', in Bielawski and Hombergen (2004), 323–46.

RUBENSON, S. (1995), *The Letters of St. Antony of Egypt: Monasticism and the Making of a Saint* (Minneapolis: Fortress Press).

—— (2000), 'Philosophy and Simplicity: The Problem of Classical Education in Early Christian Biography', in Hägg and Rousseau (2000), 110–39.

RUSSELL, N., and WARD, B. (1980), *The Lives of the Desert Fathers: The Historia Monachorum in Aegypto*, CS 34 (Kalamazoo, Mich.: Cistercian Publications).

SAXER, V. (1986), *Bible et hagographie: texts et thèmes bibliques dans les Actes des martyrs authentiques des premiers siècles* (Bern: Peter Lang).

—— (1991), 'Aspects de la typologie martyriale: Récits, portrait et personnages', in Tilliette (1991), 321–31.

SCHMELING, G. (1996) (ed.), *The Novel in the Ancient World* (Leiden: E. J. Brill).

SHAHID, I. (1971), *The Martyrs of Najran: New Documents*, Subsidia Hagiographica, 49 (Brussels: Société des Bollandistes).

SHAW, B. (1993), 'The Passion of Perpetua', *Past and Present*, 139: 3–45.

—— (1996), 'Body/ Power/ Identity: Passions of the Martyrs', *JECS* 4: 269–312.

—— (2003), 'Judicial Nightmares and Christian Memory', *JECS* 11: 533–63.

SMITH, J. W. (2004), 'A Just and Reasonable Grief: The Death and Function of a Holy Woman in Gregory of Nyssa's *Life of Macrina*', *JECS* 12: 57–84.

SPIRA, A. (1984) (ed.), *The Biographical Works of Gregory of Nyssa* (Philadelphia: Philadelphia Patristic Foundation).

STANCLIFFE, C. (1983), *St. Martin and his Hagiographer: History and Miracle in Sulpicius Severus* (Oxford: Clarendon Press).

STEWART-SYKES, A. (2002), *The Life of Polycarp: An Anonymous Vita from Third Century Smyrna*, Early Christian Studies, 4 (Sydney: St Paul's Publications).

TALBOT, A.-M. (1996) (ed.), *Holy Women of Byzantium: Ten Saints' Lives in English Translation*, Byzantine Saints' Lives in Translation, 1 (Washington D.C.: Dumbarton Oaks Publications).

TATUM, J. (1994), *The Search for the Ancient Novel* (Baltimore: Johns Hopkins University Press).

TILLEY, M. (1997a), *Donatist Martyr Stories: The Church in Conflict in Roman North Africa* (Liverpool: Liverpool University Press).

—— (1997b), 'Sustaining Donatist Self-Identity: From the Church of the Martyrs to the Collecta of the Desert', *JECS* 5: 21–35.

TILLIETTE, J.-Y. (1991) (ed.), *Les fontions des saints dans le monde occidental (IIIᵉ–XIIIᵉ siècle): Actes du colloque organisé par l'École française de Rome avec le concours de l'Université de Rome «La Sapienza», Rome, 27–29 octobre 1988* (Rome: École française de Rome).

URBAINCZYK, T. (2000), ' "The Devil Spoke Syriac to me": Theodoret in Syria', in Mitchell and Greatrex (2000), 253–65.

VAN DAM, R. (1993), *Saints and their Miracles in Late Antique Gaul* (Princeton: Princeton University Press).

VAN UYTFANGHE, M. (1981), 'La controverse biblique et patristique autour du miracle, et ses repercussions sur l'hagiographie dans l'Antiquité tardive et le haut Moyen Âge latin', in Patlagean and Riché (1981), 205–33.

—— (1985), 'L'empreinte biblique sur la plus ancienne hagiographie occidentale', in Fontaine and Pietri (1985), 565–611.

—— (1993), 'L'hagiographie: un «genre» chrétien ou antique tardif?', *AnBoll* 111: 135–88.

—— (1999), 'La formation du langage hagiographique en occident Latin', *Cassiodorus*, 5: 143–69.

VEILLEUX, A. (1980–2), *Pachomian Koinonia*, 3 vols. (Kalamazoo, Mich.: Cistercian Publications).

WADDELL, H. (1936), *The Desert Fathers* (Ann Arbor: University of Michigan Press).

WARD, B. (1987), *Harlots of the Desert: A Study of Repentance in Early Monastic Sources*, CS 106 (Kalamazoo, Mich.: Cistercian Publications).

WHITE, C. (1998), *Early Christian Lives* (London: Penguin Books).

WILLIAMS, R. (1999), 'Troubled Breasts: The Holy Body in Hagiography', in Drijvers and Watt (1999), 73–8.

WILLS, L. M. (1995), *The Jewish Novel in the Ancient World* (Ithaca, NY: Cornell University Press).

WILSON, S. (1983) (ed.), *Saints and their Cults: Studies in Religious Sociology, Folklore, and History* (Cambridge: Cambridge University Press).

WIMBUSH, V. L. (1990) (ed.), *Ascetic Behavoir in Greco-Roman Antiquity: A Sourcebook* (Minneapolis: Fortress Press).

POETRY AND HYMNOGRAPHY (1): CHRISTIAN LATIN POETRY

MICHAEL J. ROBERTS

CHRISTIAN Latin poetry begins in all probability with the unmetrical quasi-hexameters of Commodian, now generally dated to the mid-third century CE. The last important figure still writing in the late Roman tradition is Venantius Fortunatus, most of whose works date to the late 560s and to the 570s. Many poems survive from the intervening years, though not all periods were equally productive. Because of considerations of length, I will concentrate on certain particularly important authors and periods: the beginnings of Christian poetry with Juvencus (early fourth century), the late fourth-century coming of age of Christian poetry with Paulinus of Nola, Prudentius, and, in hymnody, Ambrose, and the fifth- and sixth-century traditions of biblical narrative poetry. These are the periods and authors that have received most attention in the scholarship.

30.1 THE BEGINNINGS: JUVENCUS

The first Christian poetry in classical metres follows closely on epochal events in the history of the Church, the conversion of Constantine and Edict of Milan (313 CE) decreeing toleration throughout the Empire. The new status of Christianity within the Roman Empire, its enjoyment of imperial favour and patronage, will have provided a favourable context for such classicizing poetry. In particular, Juvencus could expect a readership for his ambitious four-book epic the *Evangeliorum libri IV* (c. 330) from among the Roman educated classes, who would be attracted by its Virgilian language as a welcome alternative to the stylistic uncouthness, by conventional standards, of the Old Latin translations. The charm of poetry and the pleasure it gave to readers were a literary commonplace, but one attested by many late Roman writers. For Christians, poetry, and fine writing generally, had long been seen as dangerously seductive. In the first years of the fourth century, Lactantius, in the *Divine Institutes* (*Divinae Institutiones*), laid the groundwork for the reclamation of eloquence in the service of apologetic and catechesis, and at least potentially for the value of the pleasure given by poetry, when employed in praise of God (*Inst.* 1. 1. 10 and 6. 21. 9; Van der Nat 1977: 215–25, 232–4). When Juvencus, at the end of his poem, speaks of the 'glory of the holy law receiv[ing] ... the earthly adornment of language' (4. 804–5) he echoes Lactantius's legitimization of fine writing in the service of the Christian message.

Juvencus's hexameter *Evangelia* presents a gospel harmony, primarily following Matthew. The poem adheres closely, though not slavishly, to the biblical text, applying to it the techniques of the rhetorical exercise of the paraphrase, chief among them procedures of amplification and abbreviation (Roberts 1985). Juvencus naturally brings a strong personal commitment to his narrative. The complementary techniques of abbreviation and amplification frequently throw into relief passages of special devotional importance, and techniques of *ornatus*, whether characterizing epithets, insistent periphrases, or more detailed elaborations, often incorporating the language of classical poetry, serve to intensify the edifying impact of the poem and its emotional force on the reader (Herzog 1975: 106–54).

Juvencus's work is preceded by an important preface that is one of the most discussed of all passages in Christian Latin poetry. It establishes key themes of Christian poetics. He contrasts his epic with those of Homer and Virgil. He, unlike the pagan poets, can aspire to true immortality, and his poem will secure his salvation at the Last Judgement (*Praefatio*, 15–24). For inspiration he appeals to the Holy Spirit and to the pure stream of the Jordan to water his mind (*Praefatio*, 25–7). Such invocations were to become standard elements in subsequent Christian poetry, often accompanied by rejection of Apollo or the Muses (Klopsch 1980: 4–9, 20–35).

The last decades of the fourth century saw the completion of the process by which Christianity became the sole official religion of the Roman state. Imperial legislation gathered pace, culminating in the banning of sacrifice and the closing of temples by Theodosius in 391. Conversions became increasingly common, even among the conservative aristocracy of Rome. This period of increasing Christian confidence and self-assertiveness coincided with developments within the Christian community: the popularity of asceticism and experiments in various forms of monasticism; the growth in the cult of the saints; the coming to maturity of biblical exegesis in the West; and the wide dispersal of basic Christian beliefs and the language in which they were expressed in homiletics and the practice of the liturgy. In this climate Christian Latin poetry reached its high point in the late Roman world in the hymns of Ambrose and the extensive poetic corpora of Paulinus of Nola and Prudentius, most of whose poems date from the last few years of the fourth and the first few years of the fifth century.

30.2 PAULINUS OF NOLA

Paulinus was born in Bordeaux in the early 350s, of a distinguished and wealthy senatorial family. After beginning a traditional senatorial career, in the late 380s he underwent conversion from worldly to ascetic Christianity, withdrawing first to his wife's properties in Spain and then moving in 395 to Nola, near the Bay of Naples, where he owned property and had previously served as governor. Paulinus set up a quasi-monastic community there devoted to the cult of St Felix, who was buried in the cemetery of Cimitile.

The bulk of Paulinus's poetry derives from his devotion to Felix. His corpus contains as its largest component thirteen poems (*Natalicia*) written to celebrate the anniversary of the saint's death on 14 January (*Carm.* 12–16, 18–21, 23, 26–8); the poems extended in continuous sequence from the first, written in anticipation of the poet's journey to Nola in 395, to 407. They are a form of epideictic occasional poetry, designed to be recited on the saint's feast day. Scholars differ on the audience: whether they are intended for performance before an educated elite or for recitation before all those attending the festival (Fontaine 1981: 172 n. 305 argues for the latter). The poems show a tendency to greater elaboration as the time passes, but they all take their immediate impulse from a special day in the religious calendar of the Nolan community.

As the impresario of the cult of St Felix, Paulinus took special pleasure in the architectural improvements he made to the cult site at Cimitile. In poem 27 (ll. 345–647), he gives Nicetas of Remesiana, on his second visit to Nola, a guided tour of the shrine, and he continues his account of the new construction in poem 28. In the latter Paulinus represents the building work as an effort of moral renewal, clearing the accumulated rubble of sin from the building site of the heart to prepare the location for a divine construction (*Carm.*–28. 279–313). In a way that is typical of Christian poetry, particular actions—in this case, building activities at Nola—take on a variety of meanings through the multiple interpretative levels of Christian allegory (here *aedificatio*, 'building', as the moral formation of the soul).

The latest of the surviving *Natalicia*, *Carmen* 21 (407), is the longest and most ambitious of the series. It records the presence of the ascetic couple Melania the Younger and Pinian, along with their entourage, at Felix's festival. Alone of the *Natalicia*, it is polymetric, with sections in iambic trimeters, elegiac couplets, and, most extensively, dactylic hexameter. The variety of metres mimics the multi-coloured flowers of a garden, just as Felix's shrine flowers with the varied brilliance of his guests (*Carm.*–21. 85–9). Summoned to participate in song praising God, in language reminiscent of the Psalms, the distinguished company of ten becomes a ten-stringed lyre that produces a harmonious sound from a variety of notes when plucked with the plectrum of Felix by the lyre-player Christ (ll. 272–7 and 332–43) (Fontaine 1980: 393–413). The poem ends with a third trope for Paulinus's guests: they are now 'springs from the holy river of Christ' which 'bubble up in Felix's bosom' (ll. 845 and 849). The literal provision of water to the shrine, the abundant springs of charity from Melania and Pinian (ll. 841–4), and the font of blessings channelled by Felix from Christ (l. 855) become analogous acts of spiritual and physical quickening.

30.3 PRUDENTIUS

Paulinus's contemporary Prudentius was born in 348; he came from Spain, probably from Calahorra. According to the preface to his poems, he pursued a successful career in the imperial bureaucracy, rising to high office, before retiring to devote himself to the service of God. Fontaine argues persuasively (1981: 145–7) that he withdrew to his own estate, and there devoted himself to the life of the *conversus*, the lay convert to an ascetic way of life (Griffe 1964–6: iii. 128–42). In Prudentius's case, his service to God took the form of a sequence of poems, described in the *Epilogue* as a sacrificial offering (ll. 1–8) and a humble clay vessel, the poet's modest expression of devotion that can yet in some slight way be of use for Christ (ll. 25–34).

The preface to Prudentius's poems contains a catalogue of his works: hymns for the celebration of God by night and day, the *Cathemerinon* ('Daily Round'); poems against heresy and setting forth Catholic orthodoxy, the *Apotheosis* and *Hamartigenia*; a denunciation of Roman paganism, the *Contra Symmachum*; and a poem devoted to the martyrs and to praise of the apostles, the *Peristephanon* ('Crowns of the Martyrs'). Of Prudentius's major poems only the *Psychomachia* receives no unambiguous mention. Prudentius also wrote a collection of four-line biblical epigrams, the *Dittochaeon*, in a form suitable to accompany a visual programme of mosaics or paintings in a church. Although Ludwig's concept of Prudentius's corpus as a sort of 'super-poem' embracing all its individual components in a comprehensive compositional plan is hard to maintain in its fullest form, Prudentius's poetry does show a unity of conception and consistency of purpose (Ludwig 1977). Notwithstanding attempts to date individual poems earlier, it represents a remarkable burst of creative activity over a short period of time, the last few years of the fourth century and the first few of the fifth.

In *Peristephanon* 2, and pre-eminently in the *Contra Symmachum*, Prudentius shows himself a Roman patriot, devoted to the city and the secular traditions of Rome. The Theodosian *Roma Christiana* is the fulfilment of God's providential plan for the city (*Peristephanon*, 2. 413–40; *Contra Symmachum*, 2. 538–633). To express this idea, Prudentius attributes to Theodosius language from the most revered text of Roman patriotism and *Romanitas* generally, the *Aeneid* of Virgil: 'he sets limits neither in space nor time, he teaches of empire without end' (*denique nec metas statuit nec tempora ponit,* | *imperium sine fine docet* (*Contra Symmachum*, 1. 541–2; compare Virgil, *Aeneid*, 1. 278–9). Jupiter's prophecy to Aeneas of Rome's glorious imperial future becomes a confident pronouncement of the Christian emperor. The passage reminds us that traditions of Christian and classical poetry are not directly opposed to each other. For an educated Roman like Prudentius, Virgil is an essential and prestigious constituent of his mental world. There is certainly some element of contrast between the two passages, most obviously between the pagan god Jupiter and the Christian emperor Theodosius, the two speakers. But its force depends largely on the bringing into convergence of Virgilian and Christian worlds, of two Roman traditions. Such Virgilian language is sometimes used programmatically by Christian poets. Prudentius's *Psychomachia* begins, 'Christ, who has always pitied humans' grievous troubles'. The language is adapted from Aeneas's address to Apollo (*Aeneid*, 6. 56), with the substitution of 'Christ' for 'Phoebus' and 'humans' for 'Troy'. Similarly, Juvencus, at the end of his preface, seeks inspiration from the Holy Spirit and the waters of the Jordan 'in order to speak worthily of Christ' (*Praefatio*, 27), just as Virgil had described the holy poets (*pii vates*) in the Elysian Fields as 'having spoken worthily of Phoebus' (*Aen.* 6. 662). In these cases the element of contrast with the classical poet is more pronounced. But in all three passages a dynamic of contrast, convergence, and reorientation is at work.

The language of the classical poets pervades Christian Latin poetry of all periods, and the relationship between the Christian and the classical in these poems remains central to critical discussion. In late antiquity the three main Augustans—Virgil, Horace, and Ovid—and the writers of the first century, especially Lucan, Statius, and Juvenal, are the strongest influences, whether the subject is Christian or secular, with Virgil by far the most important. Such language may be neutral formulae or part of a common literary *koinē* that encode a text as poetic, but it may also evoke

similarities and differences between the source text and the receiving text that contribute significantly to the latter's meaning. Two German scholars, Klaus Thraede
and Reinhart Herzog, have proposed taxonomies of such imitative procedures
(Thraede 1962: 1034–41; Herzog 1975: 185–202). Herzog insists that these procedures
always potentially involve a hermeneutic process, definable simultaneously in terms
of metaphor and exegesis (Herzog 1975: 202; compare 194–5). The play of similarity
and difference in such textual exchanges is analogous to the workings of metaphor.
But also, reuse of language from the *Aeneid*, for instance, in a new Christian context
is inherently exegetical and may prompt an epic reading of the Bible or Christian
belief, as well as a Christian reading of Virgil (Thraede 1962: 1035).

The question of genre is another point of contention when discussing the relation
of Christian poetry to its classical predecessors. In an influential and wide-ranging
article on the poetics of Prudentius, Fontaine invokes the notion of the 'mixing'
or 'crossing' of genres to characterize Prudentian practice (Fontaine 1980: 1–23).
The variations in tone and poetic voice of his work, as well as its variety of generic
inspiration—elements of lyric, satire, pastoral, and epic—support that characterization. But generally the system of genres presupposed in antiquity, however much
qualified in practice, is much less evident in late Roman literature. This generic
indeterminacy, along with the vitality of many poetic subgenres, is characteristic of
late antique poets as a whole, whether sacred or secular. The epideictic sub-genres
are particularly popular in late antiquity (*epithalamium*, consolation, birthday
poem). Paulinus composes, in addition to his *Natalicia*, an *epithalamium*, a poem
of consolation, and a *propemptikon*. But such generic descriptions fail to capture
the particular nature of the poems, which owe more in content and structure
to Christian ways of thinking (Herzog 1977). For instance, much of Paulinus's
Epithalamium (*Carmen* 25) has the quality of an improving sermon addressed to
the young couple, exploiting Christian traditions of exegesis and homiletic.

Of these new developments, perhaps the Christian spiritual imagination and the
concept of allegory played the largest role in defining what is new in Christian
Latin poetry (Herzog 1966). In *Cathemerinon* 1, for instance, a particular everyday
event, the cock-crow at dawn takes on a range of meanings. The event replicates
the gospel story of Peter's denial; the cock is Christ, calling Christians to raise
themselves from sin and bringing the promise of redemption, as daylight follows
the darkness of night. Literal darkness and light figure damnation and salvation,
but also the moral dark and light of the individual's soul. To shake off sloth and raise
oneself becomes a symbolic action, a figure that invites fulfilment in the individual
life of the Christian (Fuhrmann 1971). Such analogies, though analysable in the
literary-theoretical terms of metaphor, are in the Christian scheme of things not
poetic inventions but signs written into the nature of things by God (Gnilka 1980).
Individuals then may interpret their own experiences and actions in similar terms.
Paulinus's building activity takes on spiritual and moral dimensions; Melania and
Pinian become quickening springs, with analogies to Felix and Christ, and with

associations with the built (the fountains of the complex) and cultivated (gardens) environment. At one level this is panegyric of the ascetic couple, but the form it takes depends on Christian ways of thinking.

Perhaps the classic example of the multiple levels of exegesis in Christian poetry is the description of the temple of the soul at the end of Prudentius's *Psychomachia* (Gnilka 1963: 83–128). The temple is a figure of the moral excellence of the individual soul and of the triumph of virtue over vice as dramatized in the first part of the poem. It is a model of the Church triumphant, victorious over heresy, as represented by *Discordia* in the poem, a construction of surpassing brilliance. And, with its apocalyptic language, the description anticipates the eschatological glory that awaits the believer in God's heavenly kingdom. This tendency for the spiritualizing imagination to collapse distinctions of time and place finds special significance in Prudentius's martyr poems. Most astonishingly, in the poem on St Vincent, the time of the poet/devotee and of the passion are collapsed. In a typical authorial intrusion for Christian poetry, the poet protests at the insatiable cruelty of Vincent's persecution: 'Will no way be found to break your purpose?' (*Peristephanon* 5. 432). But far from typically, the persecutor replies to the poet: 'None. I shall never stop' (*Peri.* 5. 433). The collapse of time of narrative and time of narration is complete. This effect mirrors the experience of devotees to the saints, who in their worship at a saint's tomb or in their affective response to an account of the saint's passion, felt the saint present to them in the here and now or the passion re-enacted before their eyes (Roberts 1993: 193–7).

30.4 BIBLICAL NARRATIVE POETRY

Paulinus and Prudentius are the most prolific and substantial of the early Christian Latin poets. Their successors tend to be somewhat less experimental, while exploring a variety of different possibilities for Christian authorial personae and for forms of address to the reader. In the fifth and sixth centuries the biblical epic was the most practised of Christian poetic forms: that is, the continuous narrative poem, written in hexameters, and based on the Bible.

Old Testament Christian poetry begins with a hexameter version of the Heptateuch attributed in the scholarship to a Cyprianus Gallus, though neither the author's name nor his homeland are securely established. Its likely date is the first quarter of the fifth century. Two other Old Testament biblical epics follow the *Heptateuchos*, the *Alethia* ('Truth') of Claudius Marius Victorius (third decade of the fifth century), a teacher of rhetoric in Marseilles, and the *De spiritalis historiae gestis* ('Spiritual History') of Avitus, bishop of Vienne *c.* 494–*c.* 518. The former, in its present state, occupies three books following the account of Genesis up to the destruction of Sodom and Gomorrah. While the *Alethia* follows the sequence of the biblical text, Avitus adopts an organizing theme, the history of salvation. Books 1–3 are continuous—Paradise, the Fall, and the expulsion from Paradise—but book 4 contains the story of the Flood, and book 5 the crossing of the Red Sea. The poet interprets both of the last two books, in accordance with standard Christian exegesis, as figures of salvation through baptism that reverse the consequences of the Fall with which the poem begins. Both Victorius and Avitus have a subtle theological awareness, though the former typically adopts a didactic persona in the manner of a commentator, while Avitus consistently maintains the stance of narrator (Stella 2001: 93–100 and 129–37).

Pride of place in the New Testament epic goes to Sedulius and his *Carmen paschale* ('Poem of the Passion'). Biographical details about the poet are unreliable, but he probably came from Italy; the work dates to the second quarter of the fifth century. Familiar with the work of Juvencus, his predecessor in New Testament biblical poetry, and with the achievements of Prudentius and Paulinus, Sedulius opens up new expressive possibilities for Christian narrative poetry. The poet announces his subject as 'four books of divine miracles' in his dedicatory letter to the bishop Macedonius. These correspond to books 2–5 of the *Carmen paschale*. Book 1 is introductory in nature, and includes a substantial section enumerating God's Old Testament miracles.

Sedulius intensifies a tendency already evident in Juvencus to break up the gospel story into discrete sections of narrative. Most obviously, each miracle is treated as a distinct unit, with little attention to the circumstances of time and place that link it to what precedes and follows. Miracle stories typically pivot on the words or, in the manner of depictions of Christ's miracles on sarcophagi, the gestures of healing. But the simple narrative unit becomes the matrix for a variety of interventions by the poet. To take a particular example, in the account of the raising of Lazarus, Sedulius includes the exegetical detail that Christ 'wept . . . in his body, not in his divinity and grieved for the lifeless frame with that part with which he was to die' (4. 276–8); he addresses directly Lazarus's two sisters in apostrophes that communicate the characteristic involvement of the Christian poet in his narrative and the collapse of the time of narrated event and the devotional present of the narrator: 'Why are you hesitant to believe, Martha? Why do you weep, Mary? Do you doubt that Christ can recall just one man from the caves of the underworld who after death will cause numberless crowds to rise again?' (4. 279–82). The reference to the resurrection in the flesh then inflects Sedulius's introduction to the words that bring about the miracle: 'Then when the *trumpet of the Lord* sounded forth with his shout, saying "Lazarus, come forth . . ."' (4. 283–4; compare 1 Cor 15: 52). The section ends with a meditation on the significance of the miracle that finds in paradox a verbal equivalent to the reversal of rational order that the raising enacts: 'A *living corpse* (*vivus . . . cadaver*) is seen to stand before their eyes and, as if reformed after the office of the tomb, in death *he is his own successor and heir*' (*postumus extat et haeres*) (4. 288–90).

Sedulius is an important figure in the history of Christian Latin poetry, and deserves more attention than he has received hitherto in the scholarship (but see Springer 1988 and Mazzega 1996). He has a claim to be the main influence on the subgenre of hagiographical epic, represented in late antiquity by the poetic *Vitae Sancti Martini* of Paulinus of Périgueux (460s) and Venantius Fortunatus (between 574 and 576). Sedulius was the right model for composing a poetic version of a text like the *Life of St Martin* by Sulpicius Severus, with its episodic narrative structure and emphasis on the saint as wonder-worker. He had shown how the disjunctive structure of such texts could be enabling rather than inhibiting, permitting the development of narrative pericopes that incorporated homiletic and exegetical elements, and constituted meditative commentaries on the individual episodes, while still phrased in the distinctive idiom of Virgilianizing epic.

From the first, Christian narrative poetry, and particularly biblical poetry, had reflected the personal investment of poets in their subject—the style is subjective and empathetic—and the transparency of the historical sense of the narrative to various levels of interpretation. The exegetical and edifying inform the poetic text in a variety of different ways: lexicon, style, structure, thematics, and voice and address to the reader. In the New Testament epic, certain tendencies already evident in the *Carmen paschale* reach a natural conclusion in the last biblical epic of antiquity, Arator's *Historia apostolica* (recited on the steps of St Peter *ad vincula* in Rome in 544). While following the sequence of Acts, the poet elevates to a principle of composition the regular interchange of the historical sense (*historia*, *littera*) of the narrative and its allegorical interpretation (*res...mystica*; *Ep. ad Virg.* 19–22). Each section of the biblical text is followed by its own, often extensive, commentary. He makes the most thoroughgoing use of all the biblical poets of the technical language of biblical exegesis, and lends to his narrative a special density of allegorical and typological reference that transcends the practice of any of his predecessors, while remaining true to the Virgilianizing idiom of the genre.

The Bible and Bible exegesis were central to Christian narrative and didactic poetry from their beginnings. Recent scholarship has emphasized the exegetical knowledge that underlies even Juvencus's biblical epic, though that exegetical subtlety may not immediately be apparent to the less theologically aware reader of the text. At the other end of the tradition of late Roman biblical epic, scholars have studied in some detail the interaction of poetry and exegesis in the epics of Avitus and Arator (Bureau 1997; Arweiler 1999: 12–72; Stella 2001). Christian poetry is suffused from at least the late fourth century with a consciousness on the part of author and reader of Christian doctrines and their biblical foundations, communicated not just in commentaries but by the more commonplace means of the liturgy, homiletics, and catechesis. This shared exegetical competence transforms the writing of poetry at every level, from lexical choice to structure and thematics. Christian poetry develops a spectrum of exegetical forms that communicate the significance of a biblical text, from overt instruction in the manner of Claudius Marius Victorius to lexical substitution that points to a typological or allegorical association.

Christian Latin poets do not directly address the question of style in their poetry. Their poetics is implied in the way they write. Fundamental to much late Latin poetry is an aesthetics of variety that finds positive value in the many disparate parts that make up a single composition and considers them necessary elements of the beauty of the whole. This attitude finds expression in Paulinus of Nola's poetry in his discussion of architecture, music, and even the attractions of Felix's festival. As a consequence, the classical virtues of organic unity and the proper proportion of the part to the whole receive less emphasis. Such attention to the constituent parts of a larger work of literature promotes a focus on small-scale units of composition. Scholars speak of the miniaturization of such poetry and the fragmentation of the textual surface (Roberts 1989).

This is not to say that there is a uniform quality to the style of Christian Latin poetry. As Augustine argues in the fourth book of *De doctrina christiana*, style is subordinated to Christian purpose and will vary, depending on the function of any particular text or portion of text. When the Christian poet adopts the role of teacher, he will write in a simpler style than when he is a preacher exhorting to action. The latter requires the more emotional figures of thought associated with the grand style. Praise and hymnic passages may well accommodate such higher flights as well, though more characteristically they are in the ornamental middle style, with more emphasis on figures of diction. Whatever the style, though, the poets aspire to that characteristic poetic charm (*delectatio*) that has psychagogic and mnemonic functions for their readers. Much of the most important modern work on Christian Latin poetry centres precisely on this intersection between the rhetoric and poetics of such poems and the Christian theological, exegetical, devotional, and edifying motives that inspire them. Reinhart Herzog's book *Die Bibelepik* (1975) and a series of studies that followed it were an important stimulus to this reorientation, while the study of Christian style and poetics owes most to the erudition, literary sensibilities, and wide-ranging sympathies of Jacques Fontaine in a series of articles and books on both prose and poetry.

30.5 AMBROSE AND LATIN HYMNODY

Christian Latin poetry in classical metres is primarily intended for an educated readership or audience. But a second form of poetry, intended for liturgical performance, acquired definitive form in the early years of the western church. This is the Christian hymn, as composed by Ambrose of Milan (bishop of Milan, 374–97). Ambrose had one predecessor in Latin hymnody, Hilary of Poitiers, three of whose hymns survive in a single manuscript, though all three are incomplete. The fourteen hymns with the best claim to Ambrosian authorship are now available in a monumental edition, with detailed introduction to the collection as a whole and to the individual poems, and a full commentary, prepared by leading scholars under the direction of Jacques Fontaine (Fontaine *et al.* 1992). The poems serve as a doctrinal, moral, and spiritual catechesis. Their regular form and concision (eight four-line stanzas of iambic dimeters) give them a ready memorability that is reinforced by their repeated performance in the liturgy.

Stylistically, the very denseness of the poems and the regularity of their structure—recurrent four-line units—promote that play of contrasting elements, the aesthetics of *variatio*, that characterizes much of the literature of the period more broadly (Fontaine 1981: 136–40). In such a spare form, individual words take on special relief. Ambrose is sensitive to the multiple levels of meaning with which the Christian spiritual imagination invests particular words and ideas, and exploits this polysemy in his poetry in a way that prepares the way for Prudentius (Fontaine *et al.* 1992: 74–5). The frequent use of figures of diction, the so-called Gorgianic figures, and the consequent emphasis on verbal patterning and the play of language anticipate some of the characteristics of the hymnic and lyric style of later Christian dactylic poetry. Finally, in a classic article, Fontaine has shown the importance of the traditions of Roman poetry for the formation of Ambrose's lyric imagination (Fontaine 1980: 146–83). By the literary qualities of his hymns, Ambrose is able to combine the sweetness or charm traditionally associated with poetry (compare Augustine, *Conf.* 9. 6. 14) with a form of expression that meets the liturgical needs of the *plebs Christiana* as a whole.

Ambrose's model soon became authoritative. Both Sedulius and Ennodius, deacon of Milan in the early sixth century, adopted the iambic dimeter for their hymns. In the late 560s Venantius Fortunatus composed his two famous hymns *Pange, lingua* and *Vexilla regis* to celebrate the arrival of a fragment of the holy cross at the convent in Poitiers, soon to be named the Convent of the Holy Cross, which his patron, St Radegund, had established. The former is in trochaic tetrameters catalectic, a meter used earlier by Hilary and associated since classical times with marching and processions, but the latter adopts the Ambrosian iambic dimeter. Fortunatus, whose extensive corpus includes poetry on secular and religious themes, concludes a tradition of Christian Latin poetry that had continued unbroken for the better part of three centuries.

Suggested Reading

Primary sources

Ambrose, *Hymnes*, ed. J. Fontaine *et al.* (Paris: Éditions du Cerf, 1992).

Arator, *De Actibus Apostolorum*, ed. A. P. McKinlay, CSEL 72 (Vienna: Hoelder–Pichler–Tempsky, 1951). Eng. trans. by R. J. Schrader, J. L. Roberts III, and J. F. Makowski, *On the Acts of the Apostles* (Atlanta: Scholars Press, 1987).

AVITUS, ALCIMUS ECDICIUS, *Opera*, ed. R. Peiper, Monumenta Germaniae Historica, Auctores Antiquissimi, 6.2 (Berlin: Weidmann, 1883).

—— *Histoire spirituelle*, ed. N. Hecquet- Noti, 2 vols., SC 444, 492 (Paris: Éditions du Cerf, 1999, 2005).

—— *The Poems of Alcimus Ecdicius Avitus*, trans. G. W. Shea. Medieval & Renaissance Texts & Studies, 172 (Tempe, Ariz., 1997).

BULST, W. (ed.), *Hymni latini antiquissimi LXXV, Psalmi III* (Heidelberg: Kerle, 1956).

CYPRIANUS GALLUS, *Heptateuchos*, ed. R. Peiper, CSEL 23 (Vienna: Tempsky, 1881).

JUVENCUS (Gaius Vettius Aquilinus Iuvencus), *Evangeliorum Libri Quattuor*, ed. J. Huemer, CSEL 24 (Vienna: Tempsky, 1891).

PAULINUS OF NOLA (Meropius Pontius Paulinus), *Carmina*, ed. W. de Hartel, CSEL 30 (Vienna: Tempsky, 1894; 2nd edn. Margit Kamptner (Vienna: Österreichische Akademie der Wissenschaften, 1999)). Eng. trans. by P. G. Walsh, *Poems* ACW 40 (New York: Newman Press, 1975).

PRUDENTIUS (Aurelius Prudentius Clemens), *Carmina*, ed. J. Bergman, CSEL 61 (Vienna: Hoelder-Pichler-Tempsky, 1926). Eng. trans. by H. J. Thomson, *Poems*, 2 vols. (Cambridge, Mass.: Harvard University Press, 1949–53).

—— *Carmina*, ed. M. P. Cunningham, CCSL 126 (Turnhout: Brepols, 1966).

SEDULIUS, CAELIUS, *Opera Omnia*, ed. J. Huemer, CSEL 10 (Vienna: Tempsky, 1885).

VICTORIUS, CLAUDIUS MARIUS, *Alethia*, ed. P. F. Hovingh, CCSL 128 (Turnhout: Brepols, 1960), 115–93, 269–97.

Secondary sources

For secondary sources, see Fontaine (1980, 1981); Herzog (1975); Roberts (1985, 1989), and Stella (2001). See also Witke, C. (1971), *The Old and the New in Latin Poetry from Constantine to Gregory the Great* (Leiden: E. J. Brill).

BIBLIOGRAPHY

ARWEILER, A. (1999), *Die Imitation antiker und spätantiker Literatur in der Dichtung 'De spiritalis historiae gestis' des Alcimis Avitus, mit einem Kommentar zu Avit, carm. 4, 429–540 und 5, 526–703* (Berlin: de Gruyter).

BUREAU, B. (1997), *Lettre et sens mystique dans l'Historia apostolica d'Arator: Exégèse et épopée* (Paris: L'Institut d'études augustiniennes).

FONTAINE, J. (1980), *Études sur la poésie latine tardive d'Ausone à Prudence: Recueil de travaux* (Paris: Belles Lettres).

—— (1981), *Naissance de la poésie dans l'occident chrétien: Esquisse d'une histoire de la poésie latine chrétienne du IIIe au VIe siècle* (Paris: L'Institut d'études augustiniennes).

—— et al. (1992), *Ambroise de Milan, Hymnes* (Paris: Éditions du Cerf).

FUHRMANN, M. (1971), 'Ad Galli Cantum: Ein Hymnus des Prudenz als Paradigma christlicher Dichtung', *Der altsprachliche Unterricht*, 14/3: 82–106.

GNILKA, C. (1963), *Studien zu Psychomachie des Prudentius* (Wiesbaden: O. Harassowitz).

—— (1980), 'Die Natursymbolik in den Tagesliedern des Prudentius', in E. Dassmann and K. Suso Frank (eds.), *Pietas: Festschrift für Bernhard Kötting* (Münster: Aschendorff), 411–46.

GRIFFE, É. (1964–6), *La Gaule chrétienne à l'époque romaine*, 3 vols. (Paris: Letouzey et Ané).

HERZOG, R. (1966), *Die allegorische Dichtkunst des Prudentius* (Munich: Beck).

—— (1975), *Die Bibelepik der lateinischen Spätantike: Formgeschichte einer erbaulichen Gattung* (Munich: Fink).

—— (1977), 'Probleme der heidnisch-christlichen Gattungskontinuität am Beispiel des Paulinus von Nola', in *Christianisme et formes littéraires de l'antiquité tardive en occident* (Geneva: Fondation Hardt), 373–423.

KLOPSCH, P. (1980), *Einführung in die Dichtungslehren des lateinischen Mittelalters* (Darmstadt: Wissenschaftliche Buchgesellschaft).

LUDWIG, W. (1977), 'Die christliche Dichtung des Prudentius und die Transformation der klassischen Gattungen', in *Christianisme et formes littéraires de l'antiquité tardive en occident* (Geneva: Fondation Hardt), 303–72.

MAZZEGA, M. (1996), *Sedulius, Carmen paschale, Buch III* (Basel: Schwabe).

ROBERTS, M. (1985), *Biblical Epic and Rhetorical Paraphrase in Late Antiquity* (Liverpool: Cairns).

—— (1989), *The Jeweled Style: Poetry and Poetics in Late Antiquity* (Ithaca, NY: Cornell University Press).

—— (1993), *Poetry and the Cult of the Martyrs: The Liber Peristephanon of Prudentius* (Ann Arbor: University of Michigan Press).

SPRINGER, C. P. E. (1988), *The Gospel as Epic in Late Antiquity: The Paschale Carmen of Sedulius* (Leiden: E. J. Brill).

STELLA, F. (2001), *Poesia e teologia*, i: *L'occidente latino tra IV e VIII secolo* (Milan: Jaca).

THRAEDE, K. (1962), 'Epos', in *RAC* v. 983–1042.

VAN DER NAT, P. G. (1977), 'Zu den Voraussetzungen der christlichen Literatur: Die Zeugnisse von Minucius Felix und Laktanz', in *Christianisme et formes littéraires de l'antiquité tardive en occident* (Geneva: Fondation Hardt), 191–234.

POETRY AND HYMNOGRAPHY (2): THE GREEK WORLD

JOHN A. McGUCKIN

31.1 GREEK HYMNODY—A NEGLECTED DOMAIN

GREEK Christian hymns are a massive part of the surviving literary record of the early church, but have rarely attracted the level of scholarly attention that they deserve. One of the reasons for this is surely the manner in which the genre of hymn had, by the post-Reformation era, been firmly established in the life of the various churches, as one of the most popular levels of common devotion and liturgical 'involvement', and familiarity in this case bred contempt. In Europe, after the eighteenth century, there was a veritable explosion of interest in hymnody, one which was given further impetus by the Oxford High Church movement under such scholars as Keble, Newman, and J. M. Neale (1862), who did much to bring the lyrics of ancient Greek Christian hymns back to a higher level of popular awareness.

It was, however, the very notion of the 'popularity' of the hymn that led many to continue to be its 'cultured despisers'. Victorian writers such as F. W. Faber were responsible for bequeathing much sentimental slush to the hymn books, and it became a kind of supposition among the scholars that 'real theology' ought to be looked for elsewhere; the hymn being merely the levelling down of significant

Christian thought into a form of low-level catechesis. This was a mistaken attitude; how mistaken became clearer only after the late nineteenth century when Christ and Paranikas (1871) brought out what is still the leading collection of ancient Greek hymnal texts. The *editio princeps* of Greek hymns by La Rovière (1614) had marked a milestone in the scholarship, but had no immediate take-up. Joseph Bingham, that pan-epistemic eighteenth-century writer on the early church, had also devoted a chapter of his monumental *Origines Ecclesiasticae* (1845) to hymnody, but of the seven pages he offered there, almost all were concerned with Latin hymnody. It was to fall to the Victorians to breathe life into hymnographic study. In 1867 the French Cardinal Jean Baptiste Pitra issued a critical study of the Greek hymns at Paris and Rome (Pitra 1867). A few years later, the classical scholar and Anglican priest Allen Chatfield (1876) combined his theological and linguistic skills in the first serious publication of Greek hymns in English. A little beforehand he had written an entire prayer book (*Litany*) in Greek verse that won the critical acclaim of university critics, and now he rendered the Greek hymns into English verse.

The scholarly attention led to a slow but sure revival of interest in the following decades. In 1890 E. W. Benson, the archbishop of Canterbury, passed the so-called Lincoln Judgement that allowed the use of hymn singing in Church of England Sunday services, and activity flourished after that point, among Anglicans and Catholics, whose hymnography had a special concern for reviving ancient patterns. In 1892 another learned Anglican priest, John Julian, brought together a team of the leading hymnographic scholars of Europe and North America to issue the very detailed *Dictionary of Hymnology*. It was a most important reference review of the field from antiquity to the contemporary scene, and went through several editions into the Eighties of the twentieth century. The article in that dictionary dealing with Greek hymnology is a monument of precision, and still one of the clearest expositions of the varieties of Byzantine liturgical 'types' of hymns such as troparia, kontakia, idiomela, hirmoi, katavasia, and canons. Chatfield's and Julian's interests were very much in the early period, but the revival in hymnographic studies over which they presided soon turned its main attention to contemporary composing of new hymns for parochial usage; and the study of the ancient hymns continued only slowly, incrementally through to the present.[1]

In most cases the vast corpus of Greek hymnody is only slowly receiving its first serious English renditions. Those that have been rendered before were usually set in Victorian-style verse settings that too often appear insipid to modern taste; indeed, most of the attempts to render the ancient texts in the Victorian anthologies were so paraphrastic that, reviewing them, J. M. Neale once said, caustically, they hardly merited the description of 'translation' (though his own best versions take large liberties with the originals). A generation ago, Trypanis (1971) brought out a very useful (and massively select) bilingual collection of all Greek poetry from Homer to Seferis in a popular Penguin edition, and in it the Christian Greek hymns from the early church as well as from Byzantium received a very honourable showing. More recently, Church and Mulry (1988) composed an anthology of the earliest Christian hymns that also gives a good flavour of the early corpus.

Greek hymns rarely received as much attention as their Latin cousins. This was due in the main to the profound neglect of Byzantine studies in western academies, a state of affairs that only began to receive redress in the present generation (Grosdidier de Matons 1977). Nevertheless, some of the early pioneers in Byzantine musical and liturgical study had an eye on the importance of the hymnic genre, and Wellesz (1961) as well as Skeris (1976) and Conomos (1984) put the study of Greek hymns on a new basis with their analysis of Byzantine music and chant. My own book (McGuckin 1997) tried to present some of the interesting examples of early Greek and Latin hymnody, accurately rendered, along with an apologia for the importance of their renewed study. Modern New Testament scholars had, perhaps, done the most for breaking the reluctance of the 'cultured despisers' by alerting readers to the fact that the hymnic elements of the New Testament were the earliest strata of material after the logia themselves.

Soon significant books were appearing, dedicated entirely to the New Testament Greek hymns (Sanders 1971; Liderbach 1998). Specialist studies of Byzantine hymn-writers followed suit, and though today there are useful studies (and translations) of some of the leading Greek hymn-writers, such as Gregory of Nazianzus (McGuckin 2005a), Romanos the Melodist (Carpenter 1970–3; Schork 1995; Lash 1995), and Symeon the New Theologian (Maloney 1976; McGuckin 2005b), there are still major gaps in the scholarly literature. There is, for example, no collected edition and English translation of the hymns of such fundamentally important writers as Andrew of Crete or John of Damascus. An important collection of the Greek liturgical hymns was made available by the collaborative efforts of Bishop Kallistos Ware and Mother Mary of Whitby (1969; see also Ware 1987). Together they issued volumes devoted to the *Akathistos Hymn* (one of the great Marian hymns of the Byzantine tradition, fifth century) and the whole *Festal Menaion*, the church order book for the great feasts of Orthodoxy. The latter is an important introductory resource for Byzantine hymnody up to the thirteenth century, although the material is organized according to the liturgical calendar, not historically or grouped by author, and has no historical commentary.

31.2 CLASSICAL ORIGINS OF THE GREEK CHRISTIAN HYMNS

Today, therefore, more and more scholars admit the hymn to be a very significant window into Christian antiquity. This might well have been suspected, of course, when one considers that hymnic worship was the bedrock of ancient Greek religion. The earliest surviving collection is the magnificent poetry from the seventh century BCE known as *The Homeric Hymns*, which are dedicated to a number of the Olympian gods. Pindar and Bacchylides later set out the genres of two major types of Greek hymnography: paeans and prosodies. The first were acclamations to the gods sung on religious occasions, while prosodia were processional songs, meant for recitation during the sacrifices. The *Orphic Hymns*, of *circa* second century CE, consisting of eighty-seven Asia Minor temple songs, are the largest extant collection of pre-Christian Greek hymnography. The early establishment of the major forms for hymnal composition by Greek *littérateurs* had an important impact on Christian writers. Modern scholars have marked the distinction by separating hymns that were congregationally designed for liturgical or devotional singing from the finely crafted rhetorical 'poetry' that comes from the hands of some of the leading patristic rhetors and that prefers classical metres. It is unlikely that any of these high-literary hymns were ever conceived for public chanting, though congregational singing seems to have been a practice that was established before the Constantinian peace.

31.3 THE BIBLE AND THE ANCIENT LITURGY

Greek Christians did not need extensive tutoring in the art of hymnody as integral to religious devotion, but hymns that were distinctively Christian took some time, about two centuries, to accumulate their own tradition. Nevertheless, from the very beginning, hymns can be traced in the Christian records. When Pliny the Younger undertook an investigation of the Christian cult, placidly torturing a deaconess to get the story, he was able to report to the emperor Trajan that it was essentially harmless, a meeting on Sundays when devotees 'sang a hymn to Christ as if to a god' (Pliny, *Ep.* 96. 7). The Psalms and Odes of Israel were massively influential on this process of development. Most Christian Greek hymnody, in fact, can be understood as a careful mixing of the ancient literary traditions, with a new 'biblicist' sense of how poetry could be put to service in paraphrasing and retelling scriptural events, and building up extensive church services around a skeleton of Psalms.

Apart from the 150 Psalms (which constituted hymns at the Last Supper itself, according to Mk 14: 26), there were many other hymnic forms within the Old Testament (Ex 15: 1–18; Judg 5: 3–5; Job 5: 9–16; 12: 13–25; Isa 42: 10–12; 52: 9–10; Sir 39: 14–35; 42: 15–43: 33), some of which the Christians designated as 'The Odes'. From Ephesians 5: 19–20, it is clear that hymnody had an established place in Christian prayer; and in Colossians 3: 16, the writer has already identified the three classical forms that should be used: psalms, hymns, and odes. Acts 16: 25 presents Paul himself as a great 'singer'. Fragments and quotations from the earliest Christian hymnody are found in several places within the New Testament (Jn 1: 1–18; Col 1: 15–20; 15: 3–4; 19: 1–8). One famous example is a pre-Pauline hymn which the apostle quotes back to the local church to demonstrate their belief (Phil 2: 5–11). Many of these earliest fragments are Christological in character, and several of them (e.g. 1 Tim 3: 16) are clearly 'credal' in form, thus beginning a very long tradition, for what we today recognize as the great baptismal creeds that began life as catechumenate hymns of faith.

Several of Luke's New Testament hymns are rightly famous. They sit on the borderline between hymn and poetic prose, indebted to the Old Testament, consciously aware of the wider Greek tradition, and rising out of both to become significant works in their own right. One thinks of the Magnificat (Lk 1: 46–55), the Benedictus (Lk 1: 68–79), and the Nunc Dimittis (Lk 2: 29–32). The fact that one can so readily identify them by titles shows how extensively these sections have been used in Christian worship throughout history. The cardinal points of the day, sunset (the beginning of a new day in ancient thought) and sunrise, became focal points around which many Christian hymns would accumulate. One of the earliest (still sung in the Orthodox vespers rite) was the early third-century *Phōs Hilaron* (Christ and Paranikas 1871: 40; trans. McGuckin 1997: 19). The *Phōs Hilaron* is like several other third- and early fourth-century hymns in being essentially non-metrical prose, though there are other equally early examples (Oxyrhynchus Papyrus 15. 1786; Amherst Papyrus 1.2) that show a more generally recognizable *anapaestic* form (metrical 'feet' comprised of two short stresses and one long). It was not a far step to take from the poetic Aramaisms of Jesus to the rolling rhythmic phrases of the Greek New Testament. Even in translation, the Beatitudes cannot be mistaken for mere prose (Mt 5: 2–10; Lk 6: 20–6).

31.4 STAGES OF SYRIAN INFLUENCE ON BYZANTINE HYMNOGRAPHY

Syrian Christian literature always retained this intimate union of poetry and prose, and in four discrete waves it washed over the entire Greek tradition, shaping it profoundly. The first was in the earliest writers such as Melito of Sardis and his second-century prose-poem homily *On the Pasch*. This text is much indebted to Semitic forms. The preferred modality of poetic prose applied to most of the earliest Greek Christian preaching. It can be witnessed in the roughly contemporary *Epistle to Diognetus* and *1 Clement* 59–61. The second wave was the fuller articulation of this Syrian poetic tradition in the fourth century, and especially in the person of Ephrem, a figure who would have massive impact on the fourth wave, which we shall note subsequently. Ephrem set a tone that constituted a norm for Byzantine hymnology in ways comparable to Ambrose's influence in the West.

The third wave was the coalescing of fixed liturgical forms. Again, this was largely centred in the creative cauldron of Antioch, with deep Syrian resonances, but fashioned when Syria was at the height of its Hellenistic sensibility, able to marry Syrian styles with the purest Greek semantic. After this point, all Byzantine liturgical development retained the poetic vision bequeathed to it from its Syro-Antiochene heritage, and in its turn the Byzantine liturgy dominated poetic composition, and gave occasion for most of further hymnic development. Major Greek liturgical songs, known as troparia, such as the 'Only begotten Son' (*Monogenēs Huios*), traditionally ascribed to Justinian, and the 'Cherubic Hymn' (*cherubikon*), exemplify this. The first is a summary of the Nicene Creed, in the light of the Monophysite crisis that was causing problems in the sixth century. It reflects much of the theology of Cyril of Alexandria (the 'Theopaschite' settlement that would be promulgated at the Second Council of Constantinople in 553), insisting on the 'selfsameness' of the heavenly Lord and the Christ who suffered on earth. It is now sung as the second antiphon at the beginning of the Liturgy of St John Chrysostom in Orthodox churches. The *cherubikon* was sung just before the solemn entrance into the cathedral of Hagia Sophia, with the prepared eucharistic gifts (the Great Entrance). It was, in the heyday of Byzantium, chanted by the choir of imperial eunuchs, a massed *castrati* rendering that was reported to be very eerie and atmospheric. The few lines, based around Isaiah 6: 1, when the prophet saw the angels singing the thrice holy, are to this day sung at a high moment of liturgical drama in the eastern liturgy, as the holy gifts are carried into the sanctuary for the consecration.

The fourth and last wave of the Syrian formative influence might be described as the formation of a classical Byzantine poetic canon, after the time of Romanos the Melodist in the sixth century. As conscious heirs to Ephrem and the earlier fathers, such as Gregory of Nazianzus, the liturgical poets of the later Byzantine period were active in adapting, extending, and renovating the hymnic tradition, up until the end of the first millennium, when the vast size of the service books began to signal an end to liturgical creativity and a need for pruning.

31.5 HYMNS OF THE HETERODOX–ORTHODOX STRUGGLES

The second and third centuries that were so formative an era for the development of the Christian hymn were also periods of great flux, an era when common themes of sophic religiosity in the Greek world (also known as 'Gnostic' tendencies) encouraged innovation in forms of worship. It is no surprise to discover that the hymnic genre much interested the Christian teachers Marcion, Valentinus, Bardesanes (Bar Daysan), and his son Harmonius. Only fragments of Christian Gnostic hymns have survived in Greek; but larger elements of the Syriac corpus are extant, such as elements in the *Odes of Solomon* and the two very beautiful hymns in the apocryphal *Acts of Thomas*: namely, the *Hymn of the Pearl* (Klijn 1962: 120–5), which is thought by some to be a surviving piece by Bardesanes himself, and the similarly magnificent *Hymn of the Bride* (sometimes known as the 'Wedding Song of Wisdom'), which comes shortly after it (*Acts of Thomas*, 1. 6–7), with its *initia*: 'Maiden, Daughter of Light'. One of the few Greek examples, coming from the cusp of 'orthodox Gnosis', is the hymn *Christ the Shepherd*, quoted, or perhaps composed, by Clement of Alexandria. It is a hymn of initiates chanting to their heavenly Pedagogue, as if in a mystery cult, and celebrating Christ's redemptive guidance (Christ and Paranikas 1871: 37–8; trans. McGuckin 1997: 15).

The early involvement by writers of hymns that later church tradition would look at askance for heterodoxy has sometimes been taken as evidence that the hymn represented 'popular' religion, while the liturgy represented the clerical elite. The trend has even been carried further into the Nicene era, and the example of the Arian party using hymns and poems to transmit their doctrine is sometimes cited as evidence of why hymns had a bad reputation and only in the fifth century started to develop in the liturgy more obviously. The thesis is exaggerated and uncertain. The concept of the hymn as 'popular' religion is belied by the fact that, in the main, they show highly developed rhetorical powers. Linguistic simplicity is, after all, a sign of great rhetorical skill, not evidence of composition by rustics. Throughout Christian antiquity, the influence of the popular (or secular) song, with its well rehearsed themes of love, or valour, were certainly adapted by church hymnographers (Ephrem's *Hymns on Virginity*, for example, show many signs of reference to contemporary *Erōtikai*, as do the hymns of Symeon the New Theologian, much later). The traffic, surely, was two-way. Hymns, in fact, did not belong to any section, heterodox or orthodox. If Arius had recourse to poetic form in his apologetic *Thalia*, and Athanasius steered away from hymnic form, not too much can be deduced from this, given that in the second generation of Arianism, in the late fourth century, Gregory of Nazianzus was a prolific poet and hymn writer, whereas his neo-Arian opponents Aetius and Eunomius show no interest in verse whatsoever.

31.6 *LITTÉRATEUR* POETS IN GREEK LATE ANTIQUITY

Gregory of Nazianzus (329–90) and Synesios of Cyrene (370–413) are two examples of a rising phenomenon in the ranks of late fourth-century church leaders: the presence of highly educated rhetoricians and literary stylists in the episcopate. The lists could be expanded significantly, including men such as John Chrysostom (*c.* 347–407), whose fluid prose rhythms were outstanding, and who was known to have encouraged hymn singing in the cathedrals where he served (Antioch and Constantinople); or Proclus of Constantinople, an equally gifted rhetor (d. 447), who wrote the first memorable Marian hymns, describing Mary as the new Penelope who 'wove the flesh of Christ' on the loom of her own life. Mary was a magnet who constantly attracted great attention from the Greek hymn writers (Woodward 1919). Gregory of Nazianzus could rightly be described as the most learned man of his generation. In later life he composed a vast body of poetry in almost all the existing Greek metres. Gregory was very conscious of the manner in which Plato had left unresolved a classical debate between Philosophy and Poetry for the right to carry the palm of Greek letters (McGuckin 2005*a*), and his numerous poems in which he invokes the Spirit of God (he was to be one of the chief architects of the doctrine of the consubstantiality of the divine Spirit) show that he deliberately set out to advance a body of Christian literature wherein divine inspiration was closely married to the notion of 'inspired text' (*poiēsis*). In his *Theological Orations* (ch. 27) Gregory set out an important principle for all Greek theology that followed him: that refinement of mind was necessary for the perception of the truth, and that this was produced by careful study as much as by careful living. Gregory was the most quoted of all Christian writers in Byzantium: his poetry stimulated countless others to emulate it, and his theology of aesthetics was never to be challenged in Byzantium.

Synesios was an example of a less consciously 'ecclesiasticized' writer than the ascetical bishop Gregory. When he was elected by Egyptian townsfolk to be their bishop in Pentapolis, the learned aristocrat was less than sure that he wanted the honour. He negotiated with the archbishop of Alexandria, Theophilus, and while agreeing (reluctantly) to leave aside his hunting with hounds, he refused to separate from his wife, or adapt elements of his Neoplatonist philosophy to the strictures of current orthodoxy. He has left behind a corpus of *Nine Hymns*. The tenth in the manuscript collection is not by him. It is the well-known hymn 'Lord Jesus, think on me', and is the product of the tenth-century monk George Hamartolos. The *Nine Hymns* are a strange fusion of Neoplatonism, Christianity, and classical culture. They never caught on in any sense (one presumes) as liturgical pieces, and thus represent the hymn as pure literary construct. Synesios's passion is to evoke the supreme transcendence of God; a popularized form of Neoplatonic discourse. Christ appears in the guise of a divine hero, rising through the spheres, to show the way to immortality to his initiates. The harrowing of hell is told as an account of Christ as the new Hercules who sends Cerberus (Hades) cringing back into his lair. The result is a strikingly beautiful conceit, but better suited, perhaps, to a symposium in the bishop's apartments than to a typical Christian small town *synaxis*.

Gregory of Nazianzus and Synesios, the elite of Christian rhetoricians in the patristic era, had both attempted to write in quantitative Greek metre. They gained few later disciples in this respect. Most subsequent Greek Christian hymnody stayed with accentual metre as its preferred form: an easier genre in which to compose. Much of Byzantine hymnography also adopts a popular style of language, rather than the self-conscious classicism of the rhetors, who loved to use rare forms and archaisms.

31.7 THE FLOWERING OF BYZANTINE HYMNOGRAPHY: SIXTH TO ELEVENTH CENTURIES

It is in the age after Justinian that we see Byzantine hymnography come into its maturity. It comprises a large body of literature that for centuries has remained largely unknown outside the domain of the Orthodox Church, which still uses these hymns in the fabric of its offices of prayer (especially matins and vespers). Even today much remains untranslated, or is available only in poor versions. Some of the great masters, such as the sixth-century Romanos the Melodist, are now available in English; but for others, equally significant, such as Joseph the Hymnographer, Kosmas of Maiouma, and John Damascene, there is still no collected edition to allow popular access. A substantial volume of Byzantine religious poetry in translation is thus urgently needed. The forms of Byzantine hymnography underwent a rapid development in this period.

The first stage was that of single-stanza troparion. The high Byzantine age saw this beginning to be extended significantly in size and scope. This was the birth of the kontakion. As we have noted, this was probably a result of the extensive Syrian influence that was prevalent in the great city in this period. From composers such as Ephrem, who had become 'classical' by the sixth century, the Byzantines saw the potential in drawing out long biblical paraphrases of the readings of the offices. The notion of a 'sung sermon' has been used to describe this development, and it fits the case well. The hymns weave in and out of the biblical passage, taking up small details and amplifying them, supplying a psychological explanation, making their hearers 'enter into' the events being sung about. The kontakion bears the same role to the biblical text as midrash did in Jewish circles.

At first these much longer hymns were sung in the interstices between the various offices, especially in the all-night services led by the monks (the *pannychis* or *agrypnia*), which basically fused together vespers and matins; but soon they grew to become integral to those same offices. An outstanding example of one of the earliest of them, which has unusually remained outside the liturgical vortex (eventually attracting its own special service), was the *Akathist Hymn* (Limberis 1994; Peltomaa 2001). This means 'not sitting down'; in other words, it was a processional. It celebrates the Virgin as the protector of the race of Christians. Once attributed to Romanos, it is now thought to pre-date him, probably from the time of Proclus, and added to (a *proimion* at least) by Patriarch Sergius I (d. 638). Almost all Marian icons in eastern Orthodoxy draw from the Akathist's rich fund of images that retell the story of salvation from Mary's perspective. At later times, when the reading of the scriptures fell out of the vigil services, or were drastically cut back, the hymnic paraphrases of the chanters were left behind to give witness to what was once being proclaimed by the lectors and commented on by the preachers.

The word *kontakion* derives from the term for a 'roll' of parchment, something that was still retained as a deliberate archaism in the Byzantine rite, even though the Church had long gone over to the codex. Kontakia were 'songs on a roll', therefore, though the word soon came to designate simply a liturgical hymn. The kontakion is begun with a preface (*proimion*) sometimes called a 'little hood' (*koukoulion*, after the monastic habit). This states the purpose and theme of the hymn *in nuce*, and ends with what will become the refrain. The refrain occurs throughout the remaining stanzas, sung either by the whole congregation, which would thus have to memorize only one tune for a few lines, or else (in a large cathedral) by the 'Second Choir', led by the *lampadarios*. The 'First Choir', led by the *prōtopsaltēs*, took the melodic line, with the second chorus responding and adding depth through 'sympathetic' notes. In contemporary Byzantine chant the practice survives in what is known as the iso-tone, a strong first cantor taking the lead with a complex melody, while the larger group gives bass resonance by lingering on key notes, and stretching out key words, mirroring the music that is in flight above them.

Romanos the Melodist (fl. 540) was one of the greatest composers of kontakia. He introduces his compositions with the *proimion*, and then binds together a long series of strophes in the same metre (called *oikoi*) with initial letters of the line making up an acrostic when read vertically. The favoured device of Romanos is 'Of the Humble Romanos'. It was a clever habit that prefigured copyright laws, for the watermark of attribution was impossible to hide. It was also a good technique to assist in the correct memorization of the kontakion, for any forgotten lines would glaringly emerge in the text when the acrostic no longer worked. There were traditions that Romanos himself was a Jewish convert. He was most likely a Syrian by birth. Eighty kontakia have come down under his name, though not all are genuine. Some of them are rightly considered literary masterpieces. His kontakia *On the Birth of Christ*, *On the Lamentation of the Virgin for her Dead Son*, and *On the Resurrection* are in this inner circle (Krueger 2004).

In the *Kontakion on the Nativity* Romanos sets the whole piece around the worried musings of the Virgin Mary, who has just given birth and wishes to protect her baby from all the disruption that seems to be coming in from outside: magi, shepherds, and the like. She is the central character 'pondering these things in her heart', and so serving in the role of a guide (*psychopompos*) for the less initiated, as to the essential meanings of these various mysteries. In his *Kontakion on the Resurrection*, the Cross is set up on Golgotha, and its foot pierces the rocky ceiling of Hades. Hearing the noise of the intrusion, Satan and Death (personified) have an alarmed dialogue with each other. Death complains that he feels (mortally) sick, and Satan is bewildered as to why his age-old rights have been trampled in such a way that escapes his comprehension. In the *Kontakion on the Death of Christ*, which is still part of the Great Friday Passion services in Orthodoxy (just as the *Kontakion on the Nativity* forms a large part of Christmas services), the Virgin is depicted as a bleating ewe. The mother sheep runs around the field crying out inconsolably for its lost lamb. The image is more difficult for moderns to empathize with, but was widely taken in antiquity as a moment filled with *pathos*, and one that must have been very familiar even to city-dwellers in paschal springtime, when the lambs were culled from the flock. The imagery, which occurs in both Latin and Greek Great Friday services derives from Romanos's hymns:

> My people, what have I done to you,
> how have I offended you?
> I hung the stars upon the frame of heaven,
> but you hung me upon a cross

Another of his significant devices is to juxtapose strong contrasts and paradoxes. The refrain in the *Nativity* kontakion is typical of this: 'A newborn child who is God before the ages'.

After the seventh century the kontakion was radically cut back in liturgical reforms, and often remains in the Orthodox offices as a tiny remnant of the considerable size it once had. In its place the new genre of the canon (*kanōn*) was jostling for room. This moment in Byzantine history corresponds to a certain shrinking of all the old cities of the late antique Empire. Inflation and military weakness had radically altered the face of what constituted the 'Empire of the Romans'. We are now in the more domestic world of the Middle Ages, not classical antiquity. Architecture starts to become smaller and poorer, less monumental. At this period in Byzantine life, the number of truly great urban centres dwindled considerably. Islam was making rapid advances and taking its own territory from the antique heartlands of East Rome and Persia. Rome itself, Constantinople, and Thessaloniki alone could claim to be continuing centres of cultural activity. But to compensate, as it were, monasticism was more and more securely established as the bearer and preserver of ecclesiastical culture. The monks were mobile, and their international subculture was woven together in complex ways, aware of what was happening in other parts of the Christian world from the Euphrates to Ethiopia. After the loss of Palestine to the Byzantine Empire, the shock made for long-lasting changes to Greek worship, and introduced new elements into hymnography.

Jerusalem had to be ceded to the Islamic caliph in 614. After that, the clergy of the Anastasis Church (Holy Sepulchre), which for centuries had been a world-renowned centre of liturgical development and innovation, tended to fall back onto the nearest bastion of free Christianity, which was the fortress monastery of Mar Saba, near Bethlehem. This had retained its independence by negotiation, and indeed still survives like an isolated outpost of Orthodoxy. The monks of Mar Saba initiated a strong cross-referencing of liturgical practices from the cathedral church and their own community. Formerly, the pattern of liturgy in the eastern Church had been largely based around the civic complex. It has often been called 'cathedral rite'. Now monastic practices, such as were more common in isolated houses of ascetics, began to predominate.

To make a complicated story simple: less stress was placed on processional and ceremonial ritual, and more emphasis was given to psalmody (lots of it), as well as hymns and chants. Offices grew longer, and less importance was assigned to hymnography as a didactic tool (for explaining the faith to large city congregations), while more attention was given to the desire of monks to have texts that would illuminate mysteries and reflections that they were already versed in. In the ranks of these chief Byzantine poets we should note Andrew of Jerusalem (or Andrew of Crete, c. 660–740), John of Damascus (c. 655–750), his kinsman Cosmas of Maiouma (c. 675–751), and Joseph the Hymnographer (c. 810–86). Theodore the Studite (759–826) and Theophanes (800–50) are also noted hymn-writers who have left a mark in the Greek service-books. Christian women were leading sponsors of the writing of hymns. The large collection of *Hymns on Virginity* by Ephrem was sponsored by the community of Syrian virgins for whom he wrote and who (presumably) sang these compositions in their prayer services. Christian women, however, did not have such ready access to the processes of manuscript copying throughout history, and thus manuscript transmission, and so their compositional efforts were always more vulnerable than those of the male, clerical monastics. This is why it is predominantly the compositions of men which feature in the liturgy.

Nevertheless, there are some notable exceptions. Chief among them is the ninth-century female Byzantine aristocrat and monastic Kassia (also known in the manuscripts as Eikasia and Kassiane) (Tripolitis 1992; Topping 1997). Her works passed through the manuscript tradition with great vitality and were highly treasured. Of the forty-nine attributed hymns, at least twenty-three are certainly genuine. In the twelfth century the critic Theodore Prodromos noted that Kassia had originally authored the four-ode Canon for Holy Saturday, but that it was reattributed to Cosmas of Maiouma, on the grounds that it was thought to be unseemly to sing the song of a woman on such a holy day! One of her most powerful compositions, a sticheron turning around the figure of the lamentation of the sinful woman in the Gospel (Lk 7: 36–50), features in the matins of Wednesday of Holy Week. Whereas Romanos (who deals with the same episode in his own poetry) makes much of this woman's 'shame' as a prostitute, Kassia sees the point of the Gospel symbolism, and identifies with the passion of the woman's repentance and the deep love for Christ it exemplifies, which the Lord himself exalts as a model of discipleship. Another canon of her composition (252 verses on the theme of the burial of the dead) is the only piece of Kassia's that did not make its way into the service-books. In the fourteenth century, when Nikephoros Kallistos Xanthopoulos drew up a list of Byzantine hymn-writers, Kassia was entered as the only female poetess of note. Modern scholarship has also drawn attention to several others, though most of them are now known only by name, such as Theodosia, Thecla, and Palaiologina (Topping 1987). Already by the late ninth century, the golden age of Byzantine hymn writing was passing away, with notable exceptions such as the eleventh-century Symeon the New Theologian, whose *Hymns of Divine Eros* surely count among the world classics of mystical literature, yet are more or less entirely unknown (McGuckin 2005*b*).

The Greek Christian hymns have reached the stage, perhaps, where their topography has now been sufficiently sketched out. They still require, from future generations, a sustained theological and literary analysis, which has not yet been accomplished. Their preference for the abstract contemplation of divine action in the world and their (general) avoidance of an easy appeal to the emotions give them a character very different from Latin hymns in the main. They comprise a wonderful body of literature that remains to be worked to the full by future scholars, who will (perhaps) be more attuned to a theology of art than were those of the past. One of the great difficulties, always, is that so many skills are concurrently necessary: those of the historian, the poet, the literary analyst, and the theologian. But those who choose to work here will find the challenge most rewarding, and certainly greatly illuminating of the soul of the Christian movement. In Greek hymnody we can see creed, antiphon, poem, prayer, song, and sacrament welded to form a seamless unity: here Byzantine theology, mysticism, and liturgical chant merge into a profound symbiosis in a programme that already consciously understood itself to be a theology of beauty and of culture. The ancient hymn is thus a potent symbol, still a waiting its full articulation.

Note

1. See e.g. Lingas (2000); McGuckin (1997); McKinnon (1987); Quasten (1983); Strunk (1977).

Suggested Reading

Opportunities for further reading in Greek Christian hymnography abound for those who are interested, especially in relation to the primary materials, though the secondary studies may lag behind somewhat, to the extent that it is still more common to find precise and sharply focused works of scholarship on individual authors than it is to find broader introductions to, or commentaries on, the Greek hymns generically. The earliest materials from the Syrian church—for example, the complete texts of the *Hymn of the Pearl* and the *Hymn of the Bride*—are available on the website of the Gnostic Society: <http://www.webcom.com/gnosis/library/hymnpearl.htm>.

The poetic works of Ephrem and Gregory of Nazianzus are available in good, purchasable modern editions, in the translations of McVey (1989), White (1996), and Gilbert (2001). The poems of Romanos are beautifully rendered in a model translation (that is, one that works poetically and is also accurate textually) by Archimandrite Ephrem Lash (1995). The *Hymns of Divine Love* by Symeon the New Theologian are in a more difficult-to-find translation by G. Maloney (1976). Antonia Tripolitis's (1992) book on Kassia gives the main works from the greatest of the women hymnographers and sets them in an excellent context. The currently out-of-print collection by Trypanis in the *Penguin Book of Greek Verse* (1971) is a marvellous mix of Greek poetry, with English prose translations at the foot of each page, ranging from Homer to George Seferis. The early Christian and Byzantine representations in this volume are quite respectable. The translation of the *Festal Menaion* by Mother Mary and Bishop Kallistos Ware (1969) opens out in one handy volume a treasury of good versions of the major liturgical poetry of the Orthodox Church. The volume by Church and Mulry (1988) can also be highly commended for the early Christian materials. The collection of poetry and hymnography by John Mason Neale (1862) is an important and pioneering work, but, like the versions of Marian hymns assembled by Woodward (1919), the form of English used often gets in the way of contemporary appreciation.

In terms of secondary studies the scholarly discussion by Eva Topping (1997) is a fine place to begin an acquaintance with Byzantine hymnography, and the work of Dimitri Conomos (1984) is also an excellent general introduction to (unfortunately) a still arcane subject. The internet continues to grow in quality, as well as in extent, and 'searches' for the writings of individual authors more and more can render some surprisingly qualitative results (along with much dross). The Ancient and Medieval Web resources gathered by Professor Paul Halsall at Fordham University is only one example of the rich fund of materials that are freely offered by scholars who clearly love their subject, and delight in making it more widely available. His web page at <http://www.fordham.edu/halsall/> also contains links to numerous other relevant sites.

Bibliography

BINGHAM, J. (1845), *Origines Ecclesiasticae: The Antiquities of the Christian Church* (1 edn. 1708–22; repr. London: Bohn & Co.).

CARPENTER, M. (1970–3), *Kontakia of Romanos, Byzantine Melodist*, Eng. trans. and commentary by M. Carpenter, 2 vols. (Columbia, Mo.: University of Missouri Press).

CHATFIELD, A. W. (1876) (trans.), *Songs and Hymns of the Earliest Greek Christian Poets, Bishops, and Others* (London: Rivington Ltd.).

CHRIST, W., and PARANIKAS, M. (1871) (eds.), *Anthologia Graeca Carminum Christianorum* (Leipzig: B. G. Teubner).

CHURCH, F. F., and MULRY, T. J. (1988) (trans.), *The Macmillan Book of Earliest Christian Hymns* (New York: Macmillan).

CONOMOS, D. E. (1984), *Byzantine Hymnography and Byzantine Chant* (Brookline, Mass.: Holy Cross Press).

GILBERT, P. (2001), *On God and Man: The Theological Poetry of St. Gregory of Nazianzus* (Crestwood, NY: St Vladimir's Seminary Press).

GROSDIDIER DE MATONS, J. (1977), *Romanos le Mélode et les origines de la poésie religieuse à Byzance* (Paris: Beauchesne).

JULIAN, J. (1892), A *Dictionary of Hymnology* (London: J. Murray; repr. London, 1907, and Grand Rapids, Mich.: Kregel Press, 1985).

KLIJN, A. E. J. (1962), *The Acts of Thomas* (Leiden: E. J. Brill).

KRUEGER, D. (2004), *Writing and Holiness* (Philadelphia: University of Pennsylvania Press). See esp. ch. 8: 'Textuality and Redemption, the Hymns of Romanos the Melodist'.

LA ROVIÈRE, P. (1614), *Poetae graeci veteres* (Geneva: Typis Petri de la Rouière).

LASH, E. (1995) (trans.), *St. Romanos The Melodist: Kontakia on the Life of Christ* (San Francisco: HarperCollins).

LIDERBACH, D. (1998), *Christ in the Early Christian Hymns* (New York: Paulist Press).

LIMBERIS, V. (1994), *Divine Heiress: The Virgin Mary and the Creation of Christian Constantinople* (New York: Routledge).

LINGAS, A. (2000), 'Hymnography', in G. Speake (ed), *The Encyclopedia of Greece and the Hellenic Tradition* (Chicago: Fitzroy-Dearborn), i. 786–7.

McGUCKIN, J. A. (1986) (trans.), *St. Gregory of Nazianzus: Selected Poems* (Oxford: Oxford University Press).

—— (1997), *At the Lighting of the Lamps: Hymns of the Ancient Church* (Harrisburg, Pa.: Morehouse Press).

—— (2005a), 'Gregory of Nazianzus: The Rhetorician as Poet', in J. Børtnes and T. Hägg (eds.), *Gregory of Nazianzus: Images and Reflections* (Copenhagen: Museum Tusculanum Press), 193–212.

—— (2005b), 'A Neglected Masterpiece of the Christian Mystical Tradition: The Hymns of Divine Eros by the Byzantine Poet Symeon the New Theologian (949–1022)', *Spiritus*, 5/2: 182–202.

McKINNON, J. (1987), *Music in Early Christian Literature* (Cambridge: Cambridge University Press).

McVEY, K. (1989), *Ephrem the Syrian: Hymns* (New York: Paulist Press).

MALONEY, G. (1976), *Symeon the New Theologian: Hymns of Divine Love* (Denville, NJ: Dimension Books).

NEALE, J. M. (1862), *Hymns of the Ancient Eastern Church* (London; repr. New York: AMS Press, 1971).

PELTOMAA, L. M. (2001), *The Image of the Virgin Mary in the Akathist* (Leiden: E. J. Brill).

PITRA, J. B. (1867), *Hymnographie de l'église grecque* (Rome).

QUASTEN, J. (1983), *Music and Worship in Pagan and Christian Antiquity* (Washington D.C.: National Association of Pastoral Musicians).

SANDERS, J. T. (1971), *The New Testament Christological Hymns* (Cambridge: Cambridge University Press).

SCHORK, R. J. (1995), *Sacred Song from the Byzantine Pulpit* (Gainesville, Fla.: University Press of Florida).

SKERIS, R. A. (1977), *Chrōma Theou: On the Origins and Theological Interpretation of the Musical Imagery Used by the Ecclesiastical Writers of the First Three Centuries, with Special Reference to the Image of Orpheus* (Altotting: A. Coppenrath & Co.).

STRUNK, O. (1977), *Essays on Music in the Byzantine World* (New York: Norton).

TAFT, R. (1992), *The Byzantine Rite: A Short History* (Collegeville Minn.: Liturgical Press).

TOPPING, E. CATAFYGIOTOU (1987), 'Theodosia, Melodos and Monastria', *Diptycha*, 4: 384–405.

—— (1997), *Sacred Songs: Studies in Byzantine Hymnography* (Minneapolis: Light and Life Publications).

TRIPOLITIS, A. (1992), *Kassia: The Legend, the Woman, and her Work* (New York: Garland Press).

TRYPANIS, C. (1971) (ed. and trans.), *The Penguin Book of Greek Verse* (Harmondsworth: Penguin).

WARE, K., and MOTHER MARIA (1969) (trans.), *The Festal Menaion* (London: Faber & Co.).

WELLESZ, E. (1961), *A History of Byzantine Music and Hymnography*, 2nd edn. (Oxford: Clarendon Press).

WHITE, C. (1996), *Gregory of Nazianzus: Autobiographical Poems*, Cambridge Medieval Classics (Cambridge: Cambridge University Press).

WOODWARD, G. E. (1919), *The Most Holy Mother of God in the Songs of the Eastern Church* (London: Faith Press).

POETRY AND HYMNOGRAPHY (3): SYRIAC

SEBASTIAN P. BROCK

POETRY has always played a very important role in the history of Syriac literature, and even today collections of poems by contemporary authors continue to appear. Verse can often also serve as the vehicle for instruction, the most notable example of which is the thirteenth-century polymath Bar ʿEbroyo's verse *Grammar*. But it is above all in the writings of some of the great authors of the fourth to sixth centuries, and in the liturgical tradition, that Syriac poetry has found its finest expression (Brock 2005).

32.1 POETIC FORM

Syriac metre is based on syllable count, and not length. Although a number of scholars in the past (notably Hölscher 1932) have tried to argue that stress was also an organizing principle, the evidence produced in support of this has not proved to be convincing (Bergsträsser 1933; a good discussion of earlier theories is given by Sprengling 1915–16: 145–67). Syriac writers on poetry themselves, from

Anton Rhetor in the ninth century (Watt 1986), through Jacob bar Shakko in the thirteenth (Martin 1879), to Yuhanon Dawlabani in the twentieth (Dawlabani 1970), consistently speak of the syllable as constituting the 'material' (hulē) of Syriac metre; no mention is ever made of stress.

Basically there are two categories of poetry, isosyllabic couplets (known as *memre*) for narrative and didactic verse, and stanzaic verse, known above all as *madrashe*. The former can employ a small number of different metres, the most usual being 5 + 5 syllables (designated as the metre of Balai), 7 + 7 (the metre of Ephrem), and 12 + 12 (the metre of Jacob of Serugh). *Madrashe*, by contrast, can employ a very large number of different syllabic patterns, though any single poem will employ the same pattern throughout all its stanzas. Within a single stanza there will be metrical breaks (caesuras) between the various segments, usually corresponding to slight breaks in the sense. These segments are built up of smaller units consisting of two to five syllables. Two examples from Ephrem will illustrate this, the first with a very simple syllable structure, and the second with a more complex one:

(1) *manu mse d-ne'mar*   'al bar kasya   5 + 4
     da-nhet w-et'attap   pagra b-karsa   5 + 4
     'Who is able to tell   about the Son of the Hidden One
     who came down and was wrapped in   a body in a womb?'

(Madrashe on the Nativity, 4. 193)

(2) *kaltak (h)i napsha*   ap pagra gnonak (h)u   5 + 6
     zminayk 'itayhon regshe   'am hushshabe   7 + 4
     w-en had pagra   hlula hwa lak   4 + 4
     meshtutak (h)i   'idta kad shalma   4 + 5
     'The soul is Your bride,   the body, too, is Your bridal chamber,
     your guests are the senses   along with the thoughts;
     and if a single body   has become a wedding feast for You,
     it is a (veritable) banquet   when the church is complete.'

(Madrashe on Faith, 14. 5)

Whereas *memre* were evidently recited, *madrashe* were sung. Since the melody title (qala) employs the opening words of a well-known *madrasha*, it also serves as an indicator of the particular syllabic metre that is being used.

Acrostics, above all alphabetical, but also occasionally with the author's name, are already attested in Ephrem's poetry (e.g. *Madrashe on the Church*, 8, for his name). The use of rhyme as a regular feature is only found from about the ninth century onwards; this was evidently introduced under the influence of Arabic poetry. In verse of the thirteenth century onwards, all manner of artifices, such as lipograms and 'figure-poems', may sometimes be found. A much admired example of this type of writing is to be found in the *Paradise of Eden* by the east Syriac author 'Abdisho' of Nisibis (d. 1318).

32.2 TERMINOLOGY

Much confusion surrounds many of the Syriac terms used. This results from the fact that (1) several different terms may be used for the same phenomenon; (2) the same term often has many different meanings, depending on context. This situation is due to changes over time and to differing developments in the four main liturgical traditions, Syrian Orthodox, Church of the East, Maronite, and Melkite (Antiochene Orthodox). Thus, for example, *memra* can also designate a prose discourse, and *qala* can denote, besides 'melody', also the syllabic metre used, and in a liturgical context it can often refer to a whole stanzaic poem, or a collection of stanzas; later on in time it can also mean (musical) tone. Several further examples will be encountered below.

The term *madrasha*, in particular, has been the subject of discussion: in the case of Ephrem's poems, which are described as *madrashe* in the earliest manuscripts (sixth century), a *madrasha* was a poem sung, either by a soloist, with the refrain ('*onitha*) sung by a choir, or by two choirs in alternating verses with the refrain sung by both. According to Jacob of Serugh in his *memra* on the saint, Ephrem employed women's choirs. The precise meaning of the term *madrasha*, however, is not clear: although cognate to Hebrew *midrash*, 'exposition', the verb *drash* in Syriac has rather different senses, 'to dispute' and 'to tread out'; the former sense would suit Ephrem's *madrashe* against false teachings, but is hardly appropriate for many others. Conventionally, the term has been translated as *hymnus* ('hymn'), but this is problematic, at least for German (Lattke 1989; 1991: 344, 353); Lattke would prefer to reverse the usual definition of *madrasha* as 'a species of hymn', and say instead that a hymn is a species of *madrasha*.

A second problem concerns the origin of the *madrasha*: was it originally a sung stanzaic poem, or was the musical aspect an innovation introduced by Bardaisan (thus McVey 1999)? The matter hangs on the interpretation of a passage in Ephrem's *Madrashe against Heresies*, 53 (stanza 5), where Ephrem states that Bardaisan (d. 222) 'fashioned *madrashe* and mingled them with tunes'. The passage is capable of a number of different interpretations (Beck 1983: 348–59; Palmer 1993a: 392), and has been used in the past to suggest that Bardaisan introduced syllabic poetry into Syriac (this still seems to be the implication of Dihle 1954: 191–4), which is a reversion to the statement of Sozomen in his *Ecclesiastical History* (3. 16), that 'Bardaisan's son Harmonios, who was deeply versed in Greek learning, was the first to subdue his native tongue to metres and musical laws'. Though Sozomen's view has been influential, it should be seen as the product of Greek cultural chauvinism, for it lacks any sound basis (Sprengling 1915–16: 202; Brock 1985).

Ephrem further informs us that Mani, too, wrote *madrashe* (*Madrashe against Heresies*, 1. 4–5). That these were sung is suggested by the fact that the Manichaean hymns preserved in Parthian are provided with melody titles (Brunner 1980: 351–2), and presumably these were modelled on Syriac antecedents. In the case of the two poems in the *Acts of Thomas*, the one on the Bride of Light (sections 6–7) is described as a *zmirta*, 'song', while that on the Pearl (sections 108–13) is called a *madrasha*, and is introduced as being 'spoken'. Both poems, though somewhat corrupted, are in the six-syllable metre which is rarely used later on; according to Anton of Tagrit (Watt 1986: 41), this was the metre used by the early (but otherwise unknown) poet Aswana, whom Dawlabani (1970: 24) further describes as the teacher of Ephrem (though on what basis, is unclear).

Zmirta also happens to be the term used for the *Odes of Solomon*, and the interjection of '*h*(*alleluiah*)' into the middles (as well as the ends) of each Ode in the later manuscript indicates that they were adapted, in the manner of Psalms, to liturgical chant in the Syrian Orthodox community that had preserved them as late as the fifteenth/sixteenth century. Although they are clearly poetry, the Odes are not, however, in syllabic verse, and this poses a problem for the view that they were originally composed in Syriac.

32.3 EPHREM'S *MADRASHE*

The greatest practitioner of the *madrasha* was undoubtedly Ephrem (d. 373). Complete texts of Ephrem's *madrashe* are preserved almost exclusively only in sixth- and seventh-century manuscripts. The preservation of these (three are dated, 519, 551, 552) is fortunate, since his poems were later excerpted, broken up, added to, and even completely reconstituted, for liturgical purposes (some striking examples are given in Brock 1997). In these early manuscripts the *madrashe* are already grouped into cycles of varying sizes (the largest is that *On Faith*, with eighty-six poems), and named after the subject of either the whole cycle (such as that *On Paradise*), or after the subject of a group of *madrashe* within the cycle (as in the case of that *On Virginity*). Whether or not the grouping into cycles goes back to Ephrem himself is uncertain, though this seems likely with at least some of them. In any case, several of the titles of the surviving cycles were already known to Philoxenus, in a florilegium which he placed at the end of his *Discourse against Habbib*, written about 485. That some cycles have been entirely lost is clear from an index of the *qale* employed in Ephrem's *madrashe*, preserved in Sinai Syr. 10 (de Halleux 1972, 1974). Even among the surviving early manuscripts there are lacunae in several of the cycles; occasionally it is possible to fill at least some of the gaps from the printed liturgical texts (some examples are given in Brock 1997). It is quite possible that more could be done in this way once the earlier liturgical manuscripts are properly studied.

Scholars of the nineteenth and earlier part of the twentieth century often showed little appreciation for Ephrem's poetry, describing it as 'prolix' or 'turgid'. More recently, however, there has been a marked change of opinion; this is partly thanks to the provision of a greatly improved edition of his poems by E. Beck (in the CSCO), but also to the fact that Syriac poetry is no longer judged according to the aesthetic criteria that are applicable to classical Greek and Latin poetry. It is now generally recognized that Ephrem was a poet of consummate skill and artistry (Palmer 1993*b*), and at the same time a theologian of considerable profundity, expressing his thought through symbol (*raza*, lit. 'mystery') and paradox (Murray 1975–6; Bou Mansour 1988; Brock 1992).

Among the wide range of topics covered by Ephrem's *madrashe*, two may be singled our here. Near the end of the *Madrashe on Faith* is a famous group of five poems 'On the Pearl', where Ephrem draws out and explores in a highly imaginative way the different aspects of this multivalent symbol. In the second half of the *Nisibene Madrashe*, the main topic dealt with is Christ's descent into Sheol; in quite a number of these the theme is presented in dramatized form, with Death and Satan personified and allocated speeches. Within this larger group are three poems (nos. 52–4) where Death and Satan argue in strictly alternating stanzas. Ephrem is here taking over the ancient Mesopotamian genre of the precedence disputation, where two personifications argue over who is the stronger, or more important. The standard format consists of a brief introduction, followed by the disputation in alternating stanzas, with a brief conclusion at the end. The genre is attested in many different languages of the Middle East over the course of four millennia (Murray 1995; Brock 2001). In Syriac, where it is usually adapted to a specifically Christian (and usually biblical) context, it was to take on a distinctive life of its own (see below).

32.4 METRES

The 400 or so *madrashe* by Ephrem that survive employ some forty-five different syllabic metres. For these, just under 100 different *qale*, or melody titles, are recorded in the manuscript tradition: in some cases the different manuscripts for the same *madrasha* will give differing *qala* titles, and in others, the same syllabic metre will be given one *qala* title in one cycle, but a different one in another. Whether different melodies were involved, or whether the same melody was known under different titles is not clear, though the latter seems quite likely. In some cases the *qala* title can be identified as coming from the first words of one of Ephrem's own *madrashe*. A single example will illustrate the situation. The five poems on the

Pearl (*Madrashe on Faith*, 81–5) have the *qala* title *manu sapeq* ('Who is capable'), which represents the opening words of the thirty-eighth *Madrasha on the Church*; if one turns to *Madrashe on the Church*, 38–42, all in the same metre (4 + 4 + 4 4 + 4 + 4 + 4 4 + 4 + 4), it will be found that the *qala* title there is given as *hanaw yarha* ('This is the month'), which are the opening words of the fifth *Madrasha on the Nativity*. *Madrashe on the Nativity*, 5–20 (all in this same metre), however, have as their *qala* title *manu sapeq la-mmallalu*; by contrast, the list of *qale* in Sinai Syr. 10 gives *hanaw yarha*, and this is the standard *qala* title for the metre in the later liturgical tradition. In the consolidated list of *qale*, the compiler of Sinai Syr. 10 points out that these two *qala*, and a third entitled *marganitha* ('the Pearl', i.e. based on *On Faith*, 81–5), are all the same metre (*rekna*; de Halleux 1972: 187–8). A listing and metrical analysis of the *qale* used by Ephrem is provided by Lamy (1889: pp. xi–xiii. compare also Breydy 1979: iii. 521–50), as well as by E. Beck in the introductions to his editions.[1]

In all the early manuscripts, Ephrem's poems are written out continuously, and not line by line (as they appear in the standard modern editions by Beck). Stanza endings are clearly marked, and the internal metrical units are usually indicated by points (which also serve as sense breaks). While the analysis of the syllabic structure of most of the metres (*qale*) is reasonably straightforward, in the case of some long stanzas it remains problematic.

Ephrem quite often employs alphabetic acrostics, and the imperfect nature of some of these, even in the early manuscripts, suggests that corruptions have entered in. This is a problem that has been studied by Palmer in a number of articles (notably Palmer 1993*b*, 2002, 2003); while his diagnosis and many of his observations are illuminating, some of his explanations of how corruptions and interpolations have come about are very hypothetical in character: in particular, it should be observed that his suggestions concerning the original layout of the poems, written out line by line (notably Palmer 1995), have no support in the surviving sixth-century manuscripts.

32.5 NARRATIVE *MEMRE*

Since 7 + 7 syllable couplets are known as 'the metre of Ephrem', a very large number of *memre* in this metre are falsely attributed to Ephrem. Amongst those which are likely to be genuine is the long narrative concerning Jonah and the repentance of the Ninevites; not only did this come to be used in both east and west Syriac liturgical traditions for the 'Fast of Nineveh' (between Epiphany and Lent), but it was also translated into Greek, Latin, Armenian, Georgian, and Ethiopic

(Brock 1994). Narrative *memre* of this kind, employing speeches by the different characters involved, represent a distinctive genre in early Syriac literature. Ephrem's authorship of two further poems of this nature is uncertain: one of these concerns the sinful woman who anointed the feet of Jesus (Luke 7). This *memra*, which introduces a new character, the seller of the unguent that she buys, was adapted into Greek, and thus had an indirect influence on the handling of the episode in the medieval West (Mahr 1942). The other narrative poem which may or may not be by Ephrem (it is also attributed to Balai, a slightly later poet) is in the form of an epic recounting the history of the patriarch Joseph and his brothers (Genesis 37, 39–48) in twelve books.

A number of other such narrative poems, based on biblical characters, survive. Although these are usually attributed to Ephrem in the manuscripts, their true authors (who probably belong to the fifth century) are unknown. Particularly remarkable are two poems based on Genesis 22, Abraham and the binding of Isaac (edition and translation in Brock 1986). In both of these Sarah, who receives no mention at all in the biblical text, plays a prominent role; and indeed in the later of these two *memre*, it is she, rather than Abraham or Isaac, who emerges as the protagonist, for instead of undergoing only one trial, she is also presented as having to undergo a second as well, thus making her the true heroine of the episode. Other such imaginative retellings of the biblical narrative in dramatic form concern Abraham and Sarah in Egypt (Genesis 12), some further *memre* on the Joseph narrative (wrongly attributed to Narsai), the prophet Elijah and the widow of Sarepta (1 Kings 17), and Mary and Joseph (based in part on the *Protevangelium of James*).

These narrative *memre* are entirely devoid, or almost so, of homiletic asides in the author's voice. This distinguishes them from the much better-known *memre* of Narsai (d. *c.* 500) and Jacob of Serugh (d. 521), the two great practitioners of the distinctively Syriac genre of the verse homily (Brock 1987). In the case of Jacob, a further distinguishing feature is usually present in the form of a doxological preface in the course of which a request for inspiration is often made. In other respects the narrative techniques, the use of direct speech, and sometimes also speeches which the biblical character might instead have made, are very similar to what we find in the anonymous *memre*. Although a few narrative poems on biblical episodes are to be found among the unpublished *memre* attributed to another poet of the same period, Isaac, the published corpus of *memre* under his name is of a rather different character, for many of these deal with moral, doctrinal, and monastic topics. In fact, probably at least three different Isaacs are involved, but at present only a little work has been done on sorting these out (Bou Mansour 2003; a bibliographical guide is provided in Mathews 2002).

The anonymous *memre*, and likewise usually those of Narsai and the Isaacs, employ the seven-syllable couplets. Jacob seems to have been the first person to employ a different metre, with twelve-syllable couplets (where each line consists of

4 + 4 + 4 syllables). This was to prove to be a highly popular metre, and it was already taken up on occasion by Narsai, Jacob's older contemporary, who belonged to the opposite Christological tradition. Jacob's techniques of composition, making use of a number of stock four-syllable phrases, bear some resemblance to oral composition, an aspect that has been studied briefly by Blum (1983) and Papoutsakis (1998).

32.6 DIALOGUE POEMS

The term *soghitha* is used for *madrashe* consisting of short stanzas of four lines with a simple metre, usually 7 + 7 7 + 7 syllables. The term (of uncertain meaning) seems not to have come into use until the fifth century, and is never found in connection with Ephrem's *madrashe* that employ this metre. *Soghyatha* quite often have an alphabetic acrostic, and a distinctive subcategory of them are in the form of dialogues between two persons speaking in alternate stanzas. As was noted above, this genre, whose roots lie in the ancient Mesopotamian precedence dispute, was introduced into Syriac by Ephrem, with Death and Satan as the disputants. In the hands of later—and almost always anonymous—poets, the element of dispute over precedence usually fades into the background, and is replaced by an argument between two biblical figures that is inherently theological in character (e.g. faith versus reason). The starting point is a moment of tension implicit in the biblical text: the rejection of Cain's sacrifice, the appearance of the angel Gabriel to Mary, Joseph's discovery of his fiancée's pregnancy, the different reactions of the two thieves crucified either side of Jesus, etc. Only rarely, as most notably in the case of the dialogue between Abraham and Isaac, is the sequence of the biblical narrative followed through: in that particular *soghitha*, Sarah is also introduced at the point when Abraham and Isaac leave home, and God in person is introduced as a speaker at the moment when Abraham is just about to sacrifice Isaac. In the case of the dialogue between Satan and the sinful woman (Luke 7), Satan represents the exteriorization of the woman's thoughts as she deliberates whether or not to risk going into a stranger's house to anoint the feet of Jesus, since (as Satan stresses) she might very well be thrown out in disgrace. Some forty-five *soghyatha* are known (a list indicating those published is given in Brock 1991: 117–19, with some addenda in the reprint).

A small number of these dialogue *soghyatha* deal with non-biblical persons, such as Queen Helena and the Jews, Cyril and Nestorius, Marina and Satan; or on occasion (and more in line with the examples in Sumerian and Accadian), the participants are personifications, such as the Months of the Year, Gold and Wheat, or Body and Soul (no fewer than four poems on this last topic survive).

The dialogue *soghyatha* survive only in liturgical manuscripts, and the oldest poems, presumably of the fifth century, are to be found in both east and west Syriac liturgical tradition. Their liturgical context seems normally to have been the night office, and their lively character no doubt discouraged drowsiness. Usually the full texts are to be found only in the earliest liturgical manuscripts, and only the *soghitha* on *The Cherub and Thief* (Gen 3: 24 and Lk 23: 43) seems to have survived in use to this day, when it is sometimes acted out.

32.7 THE LATER LITURGICAL TRADITIONS

The various Syriac liturgical traditions are extremely rich in poetry, despite the fact that certain monastic circles in the late sixth and seventh centuries resisted the introduction of hymnody.[2] The main repositories of this poetry are the large festal hymnaries, usually referred to today as the *Fenqitho* ('small(!)' volume, from Greek *pinakidion*) in the Syrian Orthodox/Catholic and Maronite traditions, and as the *Hudra* ('Cycle') in the Church of the East/Chaldean traditions. The printed editions (for these, see the Suggested Reading) provide only a small proportion of what is to be found in the manuscripts, the earliest of which date from about the ninth century. The manuscripts, especially those of Syrian Orthodox provenance, give evidence of a great variety of local usage (Baumstark 1910); indicative of this is the fact that there is very little overlap between the two printed editions (Mosul and Pampakuda) belonging to the west Syriac tradition, whereas the two east Syriac editions have a great deal in common. The contents of liturgical manuscripts are often inadequately described in catalogues (Sachau 1899 is an exception), and only a few beginnings have been made on studying and classifying the materials in a systematic way.

Not surprisingly, the texts in these liturgical collections are of very varied date; it is likely, however, that quite a lot of those in verse go back to at least the sixth century, although hardly any work has yet been done on sorting out the early material from the late. Attributions to specific authors are rare in these collections, but even when an author is named (almost always Ephrem in the case of the *madrashe* which regularly feature in the Syrian Orthodox night office), little weight should be given to such indiscriminate attributions, since in many cases they are manifestly wrong. An exception is provided by some east Syriac *teshbhatha* (lit. 'praises') with named authors, all of whom belong to the sixth and seventh centuries.[3]

Just as in the Greek tradition the kontakion came to be replaced by the Canon, so too in the Syriac, the *madrasha* was largely displaced by verse texts that are simply described as *qale* (Husmann 1979). The melody titles for these (also called *qale*) partly overlap with those known from Ephrem's *madrashe*; in due course these came to be classified for liturgical use in various ways (Husmann 1976) and provided with model stanzas (corresponding to the Greek *hirmoi*), and gathered into the liturgical handbook known as the *Beth Gazo* ('treasury').[4]

32.8 Translation into and out of Greek

Liturgical poetry sometimes crossed language boundaries. Syriac psalm antiphons were already being translated into Greek in the late fourth century, according to Theodore of Mopsuestia (PG 139. 1390C), and several *memre* by Ephrem were likewise translated, in this case sometimes taking over the seven-syllable metre. The possibility that the *madrasha* and *memra* had some influence on the emergence of the *kontakion* seems quite likely (Brock 1985, 1989), and the greatest exponent of the *kontakion*, Romanos, appears to have been aware of the poetic Syriac exegetical tradition of Genesis 22 concerning a positive role for Sarah (Brock 1986: 91–6).

An influential body of Greek liturgical texts which were translated into Syriac in the seventh century were the *ma'nyatha* (responsorial verses), often misleadingly known as the Octoechos of Severus (d. 538). This collection, of disparate origin, came to be very widely used in the Syrian Orthodox tradition, and from about the eighth or ninth century onwards its contents, along with other verse material of indigenous Syriac provenance, came to be adapted to the system of the eight tones (Octoechos; earlier claims that this system goes back to the sixth century have now been shown to be wrong: Cody 1982; Jeffery 2001).[5]

In the course of the eighth and ninth centuries a considerable amount of Greek liturgical poetry in the form of canons by John of Damascus (Sachau 1895; Baumstark 1941), Andrew of Crete, Cosmas of Jerusalem, and others was translated into Syriac in Melkite circles (where Syriac remained a liturgical language, alongside Arabic, until the early eighteenth century). Some of this was taken over in Syrian Orthodox circles as 'Greek canons', and this gave rise to the new Syriac genre of 'Syriac canons' (Husmann 1972b, 1975). Not surprisingly these were largely confined to the more westerly Syrian Orthodox communities. It is interesting to observe that John of Damascus's famous Resurrection canon features in the printed Syrian Catholic Fenqitho (v. 342–5) in almost complete form.[6]

The stanzas of verse texts of whatever sort were often sung alternately by two choirs, and as a result, manuscripts were sometimes written in pairs, each one giving only the verses sung by one of the two choirs (Husmann 1972*a*). Since later liturgical manuscripts also tend to abbreviate through omission of stanzas, it is usually necessary to go to manuscripts of the twelfth century or earlier in order to discover the full text of a particular verse text. A good example of this is provided by a beautiful Epiphany poem, probably of the sixth century, whose full form of twenty-six stanzas is only to be found in a single twelfth-century manuscript, whereas all that is left of the poem in the printed editions is seven stanzas in the Mosul Fenqitho and five in the east Syriac Hudra (Brock 1988–9).

Needless to say, a great deal of basic work still remains to be done in the area of Syriac poetry, above all in making available the very large quantity of unpublished texts, both those by well-known authors such as Narsai, Jacob, and the various Isaacs, and those by the many anonymous authors whose work remains to be recovered from the later liturgical tradition.

Notes

1. The classification of Ephrem's *qale*, which I made in 1978 for *ANRW* has never appeared (it would now need some revision).
2. An early example of this among Syriac writers is Gabriel of Qatar, *c.* 600, in his (unpublished) commentary on the liturgical Hours, in British Library, Or. 3336: on f. 76^r he states that 'the Fathers of old' did not have various types of sung poetry (*'onyatha, qanone* (here in the sense of verse psalm refrains) or *qale d-shahra*), and that the traditional monasteries, such as that of Izla and of Rabban Shabur, still in his day did not use them.
3. Some of these were taken over in the Maronite weekday office (Brock 2004). In the west Syriac tradition, a whole genre of liturgical poetry was named after Shem'un the Potter (Ququyo), who lived in the early sixth century.
4. A metrical classification of Maronite *qale* (which often overlap with Syrian Orthodox) was made by Patriarch Douayhi (d. 1704), published by Hage 1987; compare also Breydy 1979 and Hage 2001.
5. Musical notation is absent, except in the Melkite tradition, where neumes are very occasionally found (Husmann 1978).
6. Only two stanzas (10 and 24) are absent; at the end there are three further stanzas of unknown provenance.

Suggested Reading

For Ephrem's works, an invaluable guide is provided by K. den Biesen, *Bibliography of Ephrem the Syrian* (Giove, in Umbria: the author, 2002). Information concerning editions and translations of Narsai, Isaac of Antioch, and Jacob of Serugh can be found in S. P. Brock,

'The Published Verse Homilies of Isaac of Antioch, Jacob of Serugh and Narsai: Index of Incipits', *Journal of Semitic Studies*, 32 (1987): 279–313.

The standard printed editions of the festal hymnaries in the east and west Syriac liturgical traditions are: (1) P. Bedjan (ed.), *Breviarium iuxta ritum Syrorum Orientalium id es Chaldaeorum*, i–iii (Rome: Pro Ecclesia Orientali, 1938; recently reissued as a single volume, ed. P. Yousif, Rome, 2002) (Chaldean); and T. Darmo (ed.), *Hudra*, i–iii (Trichur: Mar Narsai Press, 1960–2) (Church of the East). (2) *Breviarium iuxta ritum Ecclesiae Antiochenae Syrorum*, i–vii (Mosul: Typis Fratrum Praedicatorum, 1886–96) (Syrian Catholic); and A. Konat, *Fenqitho d-hudro shattonoyo*, i–iii (Pampakuda: Mar Julius Press, 1962–3) (Syrian Orthodox).

Information about editions and translations, along with other relevant bibliography since 1960, can be found in S. P. Brock, *Syriac Studies: A Classified Bibliography (1960–1990)* (Kaslik: Université Saint-Esprit, 1996), with supplements for 1991–5 in *Parole de l'Orient*, 23 (1998), 241–350, and for 1996–2000 in *Parole de l'Orient*, 29 (2004), 263–410.

BIBLIOGRAPHY

BAUMSTARK, A. (1910), *Festbrevier und Kirchenjahr der syrischen Jakobiten*, Studien zur Geschichte und Kultur des Altertums, 3/3–5 (Paderborn: F. Schöningh).

—— (1941), 'Der jambische Pfingstkanon des Johannes von Damaskus in einer alten melchitisch-syrischen Übersetzung veröffentlicht', *Oriens Christianus*, 36: 205–23.

BECK, E. (1983), 'Ephräms des Syrers Hymnik', in H. Becker and R. Kaczynksi (eds.), *Liturgie und Dichtung: Ein interdisziplinäres Kompendium*, i. *Historisches Presentation* (St Ottilien: Eos), 345–79.

BERGSTRÄSSER, G. (1933), review of Hölscher (1932), *Orientalistische Literaturzeitung*, 36: 748–54.

BLUM, J. G. (1983), 'Zum Bau von Abschnitten in Memre von Jakob von Sarug', in R. Lavenant (ed.), *III Symposium Syriacum*, OrChrAn 221 (Rome: Pontificium Institutum Orientalium Studiorum), 307–21.

BOU MANSOUR, T. (1988), *La pensée symbolique de saint Ephrem le syrien*, Bibliothèque de l'Université Saint-Esprit, 16 (Kaslik: Université Saint-Esprit).

—— (2003), 'Une clé pour la distinction des écrits des Isaac d'Antioche', ETL 79: 365–402.

BREYDY, M. (1979), *Kult, Dichtung und Musik im Wochenbrevier der Syro-Maroniten*, i–iii (Kobayath, Lebanon).

BROCK, S. P. (1985), 'Syriac and Greek Hymnography: Problems of Origins', in E. A. Livingstone (ed.), *StPatr* 26 = TU 129 (Berlin: Akademie Verlag), 77–81; repr. in S. Brock, *Studies in Syriac Christianity* (Aldershot: Variorum, 1992), ch. 6.

—— (1986), 'Two Verse Homilies on the Binding of Isaac', *Mus* 99: 61–129; repr. in S. Brock, *From Ephrem to Romanos: Interactions between Syriac and Greek in Late Antiquity* (Aldershot: Variorum, 1999), ch. 6.

—— (1987), 'Dramatic Dialogue Poems', in H. J. W. Drijvers, R. Lavenant, C. Molenberg, and G. J. Reinink (eds.), *IV Symposium Syriacum 1984*, OrChrAn 229, (Rome: Pontificium Institutum Orientalium Studiorum), 135–47.

—— (1988–9), 'An Anonymous Hymn for Epiphany', *Parole de l'Orient*, 15: 169–96.

—— (1989), 'From Ephrem to Romanos', *St Patr* 20: 139–51; repr. in S. Brock, *From Ephrem to Romanos: Interactions between Syriac and Greek in Late Antiquity* (Aldershot: Variorum, 1999), ch. 4.

—— (1991), 'Syriac Dispute Poems: The Various Types', in G. J. Reinink and H. L. J. Vanstiphout (eds.), *Dispute Poems and Dialogues in the Ancient and Mediaeval Near East*, Orientalia Lovaniensia Analecta, 60 (Leuven: Peeters), 109–19; repr. in S. Brock, *From Ephrem to Romanos: Interactions between Syriac and Greek in Late Antiquity* (Aldershot: Variorum, 1999), ch. 7 (with addenda).

—— (1992), *The Luminous Eye: The Spiritual World Vision of St Ephrem the Syrian*, CS 124 (Kalamazoo, Mich.: Cistercian Publications).

—— (1994), 'Ephrem's Verse Homily on Jonah and the Repentance of Nineveh: Notes on the Textual Tradition', in A. Schoors and P. van Deun (eds.), *Philohistor: Miscellanea in honorem Caroli Laga septuagenarii*, Orientalia Lovaniensia Analecta, 60 (Leuven: Peeters), 71–86; repr. in S. Brock, *From Ephrem to Romanos: Interactions between Greek and Syriac in Late Antiquity* (Aldershot: Variorum, 1999), ch. 5.

—— (1997), 'The Transmission of Ephrem's *madrashe* in the Syriac Liturgical Tradition', in E. A. Livingstone (ed.), *StPatr* 33: 490–505.

—— (2001), 'The Dispute Poem: From Sumer to Syriac', *Journal of the Canadian Society for Syriac Studies*, 1: 3–10.

—— (2004), 'Some Early Witnesses of the East Syriac Liturgical Tradition', *Journal of Assyrian Academic Studies*, 18: 9–45.

—— (2005), 'Liturgical Texts', 'Poetry', in Centre d'Études et de Recherches Orientales, *Nos sources: Arts et littérature syriaques*, Sources syriaques, 1 (Antélias: CERO), 291–313, 315–38.

BRUNNER, C. (1980), 'Liturgical Chant and Hymnody among the Manichaeans in Central Asia', *ZDMG* 130: 342–68.

CODY, A. (1982), 'The Early History of the Octoechos in Syria', in N. Garsoian, T. Mathews, and R. W. Thomson (eds.), *East of Byzantium: Syria and Armenia in the Formative Period* (Washington D.C.: Dumbarton Oaks), 89–114.

DAWLABANI, MAR PHILOXENOS Y. (1970), *Pu'itutho* (Aleppo).

DE HALLEUX, A. (1972), 'Une clé pour les hymnes d'Ephrem dans le ms Sinai syr. 10', *Mus* 85: 171–99.

—— (1974), 'La transmission des hymnes d'Ephrem d'après le ms Sinai syr. 10', in *Symposium Syriacum*, OrChrAn 197 (Rome: Pontificium Institutum Orientalium Studiorum), 21–63.

DIHLE, A. (1954), 'Die Anfänge der griechischen Akzentuierenden Verskunst', *Hermes*, 82: 182–99.

HAGE, L. (1987), *The Syriac Model Strophes and their Poetic Meters*, Bibliothèque de l'Université Saint-Esprit, 14 (Kaslik: Université Saint-Esprit).

—— (2001), *Musique Maronite, V–VII: Les Strophes-types Syriaques*. Bibliothèque de l'Université Saint-Esprit, 42–44 (Kaslik: Université Saint-Esprit).

HÖLSCHER, G. (1932), *Syrische Verskunst*, Leipziger semitistische Studien, NS 5 (Leipzig: J. C. Heinrichs).

HUSMANN, H. (1972a), 'Die antiphonale Chorpraxis der syrischen Hymnen nach den Berliner und Pariser Handschriften', *Ostkirchliche Studien*, 21: 281–97.

—— (1972b), 'Die syrische Auferstehungskanones und ihre griechischen Vorlagen', *OCP* 38: 209–42.

HUSMANN, H. (1975), 'Die melkitische Liturgie als Quelle der syrischen Qanune iaonaie: Melitene und Edessa', *OCP* 41: 5–56.

——(1976), 'Madrasche und Seblatha: Repertoireuntersuchungen zu den Hymnen Ephräms des Syrers', *Acta Musicologica*, 48: 113–50.

——(1978), *Ein syro-melkitisches Tropologion*, Göttingen Orientforschungen, Reihe Syriaca, 9 (Wiesbaden: O. Harrassowitz).

——(1979), 'Zur Geschichte des Qala', *OCP* 45: 99–113.

JEFFERY, P. (2001), 'The Earliest Oktoechoi: The Role of Jerusalem and Palestine in the Beginnings of Modal Ordering', in P. Jeffery (ed.), *The Study of Medieval Chant* (Cambridge: Cambridge University Press), 147–209.

LAMY, T. J. (1889), *Sancti Ephraem Syri Hymni et Sermones*, iii (Malines: H. Dessain).

LATTKE, M. (1989), 'Sind Ephraems *Madrashe* Hymnen?', *Oriens Christianus*, 73: 38–43.

——(1991), *Hymnus: Materialien zu einer Geschichte der antiken Hymnologie*, Novum Testamentum et Orbis Antiquus, 19 (Freiburg: Universitätsverlag; Göttingen: Vandenhoeck & Ruprecht).

MAHR, A. C. (1942), *Relations of Passion Plays to St Ephrem the Syrian* (Columbus, Oh.: Wartburg Press).

MARTIN, J. P. P. (1879), *De la métrique chez les Syriens*, Abhandlungen für die Kinde des Morgenlandes, 7/2 (Leipzig: F. A. Brockhaus).

MATHEWS, E. G. (2002), 'A Bibliographical Clavis to the Corpus of Works Attributed to Isaac of Antioch', *Hugoye: Journal of Syriac Studies*, 5/1 <http://syrcom.cua.edu/syrcom/Hugoye>.

McVEY, K. E. (1999), 'Were the Earliest *Madrashe* Songs or Recitations?', in G. J. Reinink and A. C. Klugkist (eds.), *After Bardaisan: Studies on Continuity and Change in Syriac Christianity in Honour of Professor Han J. W. Drijvers*, Orientalia Lovaniensia Analecta, 89 (Leuven: Peeters), 185–99.

MURRAY, R. (1975–6), 'The Theory of Symbolism in St Ephrem's Theology', *Parole de l'Orient*, 6/7: 1–20.

——(1995), 'Aramaic and Syriac Dispute Poems and their Connections', in M. J. Geller, J. C. Greenfield, and M. Weitzman (eds.), *Studia Aramaica*, Journal of Semitic Studies, Supplement 4 (Oxford: Oxford University Press), 157–87.

PALMER, A. N. (1993a), ' "A Lyre without a Voice": The Poetics and the Politics of Ephrem the Syrian', *Aram*, 5: 371–99.

——(1993b), 'The Merchant of Nisibis: Saint Ephrem and his Faithful Quest for Union in Numbers', in J. den Boeft and A. Hilhorst (eds.), *Early Christian Poetry: A Collection of Essays*, Suppl. *VC* 22 (Leiden: E. J. Brill), 167–233.

——(1995), 'Words, Silences, and the Silent Word: Acrostics and Empty Columns in Saint Ephraem's Hymns on Faith', *Parole de l'Orient*, 20: 129–200.

——(2002), 'Akrostich Poems: Restoring Ephrem's *madroshe*', *The Harp: A Journal of Syriac and Oriental Studies*, 15: 275–87.

——(2003), 'Restoring the ABC in Ephraim's Cycles on Faith and Paradise', *JECS*, 55: 147–94.

PAPOUTSAKIS, M. (1998), 'Formulaic Language in the Metrical Homilies of Jacob of Serugh', in R. Lavenant (ed.), *Symposium Syriacum VII*, OrChrAn 256 (Rome: Pontificium Institutum Orientalium Studiorum), 445–51.

SACHAU, E. (1895), 'Studie zur syrischen Kirchenlitteratur der Damascene', *Abhandlungen der Königlichen Akademie der Wissenschaften zu Berlin, Phil.-hist. Kl.*, 1–92.

—— (1899), *Verzeichniss der syrischen Handschriften*, Die Handschriften-Verzeichnisse der Königlichen Bibliothek zu Berlin, 23 (Berlin: A. Asher).

SPRENGLING, M. (1915–16), 'Antonius Rhetor on Versification', *American Journal of Semitic Languages and Literature*, 32: 145–216.

WATT, J. W. (1986), *The Fifth Book of the Rhetoric of Antony of Tagrit*, CSCO 481, Scriptores Syri, 204 (Leuven: Peeters).

CHAPTER 33

CHRISTIAN PHILOSOPHY

HUBERTUS R. DROBNER

'Tis written: In the beginning was the Word (John 1: 1). Here now I'm balked. . . . In the beginning was the Thought!' (Goethe, *Faust*, part I. act 1, scene 3). A philosopher's plight to start thinking resembles the one encountered by Faust in his endeavour to translate John's Gospel. One balks at the first sentence. The reason for this is that reason, logic, and language at the same time serve as both the instruments and the subjects of reflection. As this dilemma cannot be resolved, philosophy cannot help but be aware of it and constantly checking its methods of reflection against the results, and vice versa. Consequently, the starting point for studying Christian philosophy must be the question of what this notion means and what kind of presuppositions it implies.

Obviously, by juxtaposing the adjective 'Christian' one presupposes that the noun 'philosophy' in general represents a wider subject, and that there are other, non-Christian philosophies as well. As far as ancient Christianity is concerned, 'philosophy' refers to various systems of thought in order to interpret the true reality of the world through human reason, which began to develop in Greece in the sixth and fifth centuries BCE. However, even the notion of 'philosophy' and the periodization of its history is a result of later philosophical reflection. The word *philosophia* (love/pursuit of knowledge/wisdom) is not attested before Plato's time (427–347 BCE; e.g. *Phaedo* 61a; *Definitiones* 414b), and Aristotle (384–322 BCE; *Metaphysics* I 3) was the first to consider the Ionian thinkers of the sixth century BCE, such as Heraclitus (*c.* 544—*c.* 483) and Pythagoras (*c.* 540–500), to be the first 'philosophers' (de Vogel 1970). They themselves had called their occupation 'inquiry' (*historia*), and only the nineteenth century introduced for them the current term 'Presocratic philosophers'.

Having reached its fully developed form in Plato and Aristotle, Greek philosophy formed influential schools, such as Stoicism, Middle Platonism, and Neoplatonism, which were to have a major impact on Christianity. When Rome eventually incorporated Greece into its Empire in the second century BCE, Greek language and thought began to pervade the whole Mediterranean culture. When Christ was born, this 'Hellenism' had shaped a new composite Graeco-Roman culture.

33.1 HELLENIZATION OF CHRISTIANITY?

The first major question of Christian philosophy, therefore, is when and how Christianity encountered Hellenistic philosophy, and into what kind of (mutual) relationship they entered. For the longest time the common opinion was that Christianity did not occupy itself with Greek philosophy before the middle of the second century, when the 'Greek Apologists', among them in a most prominent place Justin Martyr (d. 165 in Rome), under the pressure of persecution by an empire that was thoroughly impregnated by philosophy, felt the need to defend their convictions on the grounds of their opponents.

This view ultimately goes back to Reformation times. As a consequence of the humanist return to the ancient sources and the Renaissance view of antiquity as the historical ideal that was lost in the Middle Ages, both Erasmus and Melanchthon also envisaged an original 'simplicity' of the biblical message. According to them, the further, rather complicated, history of doctrine and theology had only developed because the fathers introduced philosophy in order to explain the Christian faith. While the Catholic Church, in accordance with the conviction of her own continuity and the constant truth of her teaching, interpreted this as a valid progress in proclaiming the faith, the Protestant side—also with a view to justifying their return to an exclusively biblical testimony (*sola scriptura*)—eventually saw Christian philosophy in the light of a decline from the original pure and simple truth of the gospel (cf. Arnold 1699–1700).

After some 200 years of further modifications and refinements, incorporating contemporary philosophical ideas, the thesis of a 'Hellenization of Christianity' became most famous and influential through Adolf von Harnack's *Lehrbuch der Dogmengeschichte* (1886–90) and reigned virtually unchallenged until the middle of the twentieth century.

In 1958, Jean Daniélou published a volume on 'Theology of Judeo-Christianity', that started to challenge Harnack's thesis and was to become a classic:

Beginning with the Apologists, Christian theology used the intellectual instruments of Greek philosophy. However, before that there existed an earlier theology of semitic character. The existence of such a theology has hitherto been generally ignored. Harnack's *History of Doctrine*, for instance, has no room for it. According to him, it seems as though theology emerged from the encounter of the message of the gospels with Greek philosophy. However, this thesis actually seems to be highly disputable. We think on the contrary, that theology is as old as revelation, which from the beginning was an object of reflection and further investigation. Harnack's mistake might be explained by the scarcity of testimonies regarding that first period of the history of theology.

(Daniélou 1958: Foreword, 5)

Daniélou thus initiated a whole new line of research, which investigated the Jewish-Semitic, non-philosophical background of Christian theology. However, he did not change the fundamental categories of investigation. He maintained the division of early Christianity into two separate phases, before and after its encounter with Greek philosophy in the second century, and he still investigated only the sources and influences that shaped Christianity, not the impact that Christianity also possibly had on its sources.

It took another decade before scholars started to apply modern hermeneutical criteria to the now twofold theory of both 'Judaization' and 'Hellenization'. They perceived that also in the history of thought every action causes a reaction. Consequently, 'Hellenization of Christianity' will automatically imply a 'Christianization of Hellenism'. In the end, one deals with complex multilateral influences; wherever one element changes, the whole of it readjusts. Thus the particular question of 'Hellenization' became part of the comprehensive question of the general relationship of 'Antike und Christentum': that is, the mutual adaptation of interlocking cultures (or dependency, encounter, influence, integration, merging, reception, transformation, etc., which are now the most current terms for it).

The possibility of a total separation or a merely unilateral influence of two or more cultures existing together at the same time in the same place can be ruled out hermeneutically. Moreover, in connection with the concept of 'Antike und Christentum', it has rightly been pointed out that Christianity and ancient Graeco-Roman culture were not two phenomena that had developed separately and then met. Christianity grew up as part of the Roman Empire right from the start (cf. Thraede 1993: 757 f.).

Consequently, the question arose whether the idea of an original, 'authentic' Christianity, deriving from Semitic Judaism and thus untainted by Hellenism, could really be true. Not only was Judaism forced to coexist with the Hellenized Roman Empire, but even before Christ was born, Judaism itself had been largely Hellenized, especially outside Palestine in the 'Diaspora'. Thus the fact that Christianity originated from Judaism did not separate it from Greek philosophy and culture, but included a certain degree of Hellenization.

This new framework no longer permits popular categories such as 'rise and progress' versus 'decline and fall'. One may only ask to what extent changes were inevitable, and whether they were unconsciously happening or purposefully implemented. Leslie Dewart (1969) maintained that the Hellenization of Christianity was a consequent and inevitable continuation of the development of ancient Greek thought, while Christian Gnilka (1984) showed that early Christianity quite consciously distinguished between right and wrong use of Hellenistic philosophy and culture.

'Inculturation' is the presently preferred term, and it points to where future research might turn. The present-day development of a single multicultured world through worldwide communication and mobility calls for new philosophies, as the development of societies did in the past. Likewise, our new understanding of merging cultures in our own time will most certainly transform our views of history, too.

33.2 *VERISSIMA PHILOSOPHIA*

How, then, does the relationship between Hellenistic philosophy and early Christianity present itself in the light of contemporary research? First of all, there seems to be no indication as to whether or how deeply Jesus was acquainted with Greek philosophy, beyond the fact that he grew up in the confines of the Hellenized Roman Empire. However, Judaism as a whole was certainly not untouched by it. Especially outside Palestine in the Diaspora, particularly in Egyptian Alexandria, it had lost its Hebrew exclusiveness long before, and had embraced Greek language and ideas. The Greek version of the Old Testament, the Septuagint, translated in Egypt in the third century BCE, and the writings of the Alexandrian Jew Philo (20 BCE–42 CE) are the most outstanding testimonies for this. Nor was Palestine completely free from Hellenistic influences. Despite strong Jewish opposition, it was part of the Roman Empire, and with the presence of the Roman military, administration, and trade, Graeco-Roman culture also pervaded Palestine. In general, one can hardly underestimate the omnipresence of philosophical ideas in the Roman sphere of influence, if often in popularized and syncretistic forms.

The fact that Christianity came in touch with Greek philosophy through Hellenized Judaism is suggested by Acts 2, the account of the feast of Pentecost in Jerusalem. There were present 'Parthians and Medes and Elamites, and residents of Mesopotamia, Judea and Cappadocia, Pontus and Asia, Phrygia and Pamphylia, Egypt and the parts of Libya belonging to Cyrene, and visitors from Rome, both Jews and proselytes, Cretans and Arabians' (Acts 2: 9–11)—in short, Hellenized

Jews from all over the Mediterranean and Middle Eastern Diaspora. After Peter had spoken, those became the first converts to the new faith: 'those who received his word were baptized, and there were added that day about three thousand souls' (Acts 2: 41).

Moreover, the oldest literary testimonies of Christianity, St Paul's letters and the gospels, not only point to an implicit influence of Hellenism, but also relate explicit encounters between philosophers and Christians. The Acts of the Apostles presents Paul in Athens meeting with Epicureans and Stoics, members of the two most influential philosophical schools of his age (Acts 17: 18). In the letter to the Colossians 2: 8, Paul (or one of his disciples) expressly warns against the deceit of human philosophy over against Christ's teaching, and in 1 Corinthians 1: 22 he characterizes the Greeks as people 'looking for wisdom (*sophia*)'. Both instances— Paul discussing the faith with philosophers in a traditional public dispute in the marketplace (*agora*), and warning of possibly deceitful philosophical teachings, because they were not based on divine authority—presuppose that he implicitly acknowledged ancient philosophies as competing, if wrong, 'faiths', and that he offered a new 'Christian philosophy'.

This was made possible by two fundamental characteristics of ancient philosophy which modern ones do not necessarily share. First, ancient philosophy was never just a system of thought, a subject-matter for reflection, a theory. It sought truth in order to teach the right way of life; it was a personal conviction that determined the behaviour of the person thinking it. Ancient philosophy and ethics were inseparable (Hadot 1995, 2004). Second, ancient philosophy was never a-religious, let alone anti-religious. God alone is the *sophos*; the philosopher, who is searching for wisdom, only participates in it. Augustine later applied this argument in order to distinguish the uniqueness of Christ, the incarnate Son of God, from all other men: 'it is one thing just to become wise through God's wisdom, and quite another to be God's wisdom in person' (*De agone Christiano* 20. 22; cf. *Expositio epistulae ad Galatas* 27; Drobner 1986: 159–65). Departing from this presupposition, the *sophistēs* knows, since the times of Socrates, that his knowledge amounts to nothing. However, from this starting point the philosopher moves beyond the pure negation of any knowledge towards a (divine) wisdom that he is aware of, but which he knows he can never fully attain. Consequently, ancient philosophers did not distinguish between philosophy and theology; nor did the first two Christian centuries. The Christian apologists of the second century defended the Christian faith with a philosophical discourse, especially when addressed to emperors who were proud of their own philosophical education, like Marcus Aurelius.

Justin Martyr dedicated his life to searching for 'the true philosophy', which, after wanderings to the Stoics, Peripatetics, Pythagoreans, and Platonists, he finally found in the Christian faith. In order to prove it, he donned the distinctive cloak of the ancient itinerant philosopher, the *pallium*. He perceived the Christian faith to be the superior philosophy, because it was proclaimed and lived by the divine

Logos. Nevertheless, for him all other philosophies at least contained germs of the full truth, *logoi spermatikoi*, because the world as God's creation naturally reflects the divine truth in an incipient way.

While there was never a doubt in the mind of Christians that their faith was the only true, and therefore superior, 'philosophy'—that is, way of life—the second century also began to make a marked distinction between pagan philosophy and Christian faith and to define their relationship. Some authors of the second half of the second century judged them to be irreconcilable opponents. The apologist Tatian 'the Syrian', a pupil of Justin's in Rome, wrote an *Oration to the Greeks* (155–170 CE). Therein he condemned all of Hellenistic culture in order to prove the exclusive superiority of Christianity. According to him, the Greeks had no reason to be proud of anything, because all of their supposed achievements they got from the barbarians, and their rhetoric, poetry, and philosophy (including its morals) are completely worthless. Moreover, the truth, as it was proclaimed by the Old Testament and handed down to Christianity, is older than all of Greek culture, because Moses lived before Homer. Consequently, for Tatian, Greek culture and Christian faith have nothing in common.

Differently motivated, and addressing himself to Christian heretics, not pagan philosophers, almost half a century later, the North African Tertullian reiterated the general refusal of philosophy in his tractate *The Prescription of Heretics* (some years before 207/8). Starting from Colossians 2: 8, he suspects that the heretics draw their erroneous doctrines from the teaching of the various philosophical schools. Therefore his verdict is clear:

Heretics and philosophers perpend the same themes and are caught up in the same discussions.... From philosophy come those fables and endless genealogies and fruitless questionings.... To hold us back from such things, the Apostle testifies expressly in his letter to the Colossians that we should beware of philosophy.... What has Jerusalem to do with Athens, the Church with the Academy, the Christian with the heretic?... I have no use for a Stoic or Platonic or a dialectic Christianity. After Jesus Christ we have no need of speculation, after the Gospel no need of research.

(*Praescr.* 7; trans. Greenslade 1956: 35–6)

Tertullian even rejects in general the use of the term 'philosophy' for the Christian faith (*Apol.* 47–8).

Those radical views were not to prevail. At the same time, Clement of Alexandria (*c*. 150–215) attributed to philosophy in the Greek world a similar propaedeutic role as the Mosaic Law had had for the Hebrews:

Before the Lord's coming, philosophy was an essential guide to righteousness for the Greeks. At the present time, it is a useful guide towards the reverence for God. It is a kind of preliminary education for those who are trying to gather faith through demonstration.... For philosophy was to the Greek world what the Law was to the Hebrews, a tutor escorting the Greeks to Christ. So philosophy is a preparatory process; it opens the road for the person whom Christ brings to his final goal.... There is only one truth, but different paths from different places to join it...

(Strom. 1.5)

This attitude continued for the rest of antiquity: in Origen, *Contra Celsum*; Eusebius of Caesarea, *Praeparatio evangelica* and *Demonstratio evangelica*; Basil the Great, *Ad adolescentes*, etc. However, John Chrysostom, in his *Homily on the Kalends* (PG 48. 953–62; *a.* 386/7), was the first to use the term 'Christian philosophy' in contrast to 'Greek philosophy', yet always in the comprehensive sense of 'the Christian way of life'. In the West, Augustine eventually distinguished between the human intelligence, which leads to an understanding of the human word (wisdom), and the faith, which makes us understand the Word (*Logos*) of God (*Sermo* 43. 9: *intellege, ut credas, uerbum meum; crede, ut intellegas, uerbum dei*). Christian faith is the 'absolutely true philosophy' (*verissima philosophia*) (*De Academicis*, 3. 20–2, 42; *Civ.* 10. 32).

33.3 PHILOSOPHICAL VERSUS BIBLICAL EDUCATION

So far it may seem as though, after having overcome some initial, but transient opposition, the reception of philosophy in a supplementary and propaedeutic role to theology and faith was universal. This impression is caused by the fact that the classical school system, the seven 'liberal arts', which led up to philosophy as the crowning art, had no real competition throughout antiquity. All of the famous and influential theologians of early Christianity received this kind of education or were even its teachers. They are the authors of almost all ancient Christian literature, and they acted as the outstanding leaders of their times, whose deeds were recorded.

Because of this, one tends to forget that ancient Christianity did not consist exclusively of this special type of bishops and their communities. Every single little township had its own bishop. The list of participants of the numerous councils name hundreds of otherwise completely unknown bishops. What kind of education had they received, and what role did they play? Sometimes they had no education at all. Some of them were so illiterate that they could not even sign their own name, as is reported from the Council of Ephesus (431). From the third century onwards, others had been raised in monasteries since childhood and received an education exclusively based on the Bible. Very few of them ever wrote a book— Epiphanius of Salamis (*c.* 315–403) is one of the exceptions—but all of them had a vote in the councils, and both their influence and opposition to the philosophical kind of education grew, especially during the controversies from the fourth to the seventh centuries.

Furthermore, one tends to overlook that, despite all mutual transformation of philosophy and theology, since New Testament times fundamental differences persisted. Christ is called both 'Logos' (Jn 1: 1) and 'wisdom' (1 Cor 1: 24), but there always persisted a clear understanding of the differences between the wisdom 'of this world' and the faith: 'For Jews demand signs and Greeks desire wisdom, but we proclaim Christ crucified, a stumbling block to Jews and foolishness to Gentiles, but to those who are the called, both Jews and Greeks, Christ the power of God and the wisdom of God.... Not many of you were wise by human standards ... but God chose what is foolish in the world to shame the wise' (1 Cor 1: 22–7).

However close philosophy and Christianity came, Christ's incarnation, his crucifixion and resurrection, and the consequent willingness of the faithful to follow Christ even unto martyrdom remained the fundamental stumbling block. As long as Paul talked in Athens about God as the highest spiritual being from whom creation descends, the philosophers were prepared to listen to him. The very moment he started on the resurrection of the dead, 'some mocked him, but others said: We will hear you again about this' (Acts 17: 32). Fronto of Cirta, Emperor Marcus Aurelius's teacher, made a public speech in order to point out the absurdity of Christian beliefs. The sophist Lucian of Samosata ridiculed Christians in his satire *On the Death of Peregrinus* (c. 170) for their love of their neighbours and their willingness to sacrifice, suggesting that Peregrinus committed suicide in order to be with his God, and that all Christians had better follow his example. The Alexandrinian Platonist Celsus (c. 178) composed a book entitled *The True Doctrine* (*Alēthes Logos*). Therein he readily acknowledged the Christian teaching of a Logos, which could easily be reconciled with the Platonizing philosophical currents of the times. He acknowledged the high ethical standards of Christianity, which are also a true mark of philosophy. However, the identification of the Logos with the person of Christ could not be true. He could not have been but an impostor and conjuror, and the myth of his resurrection could only be a clumsy invention by his pupils. To a true philosopher it just made no sense.

These fundamental differences between philosophy and the biblical message never ceased to exist, and with the introduction of non-biblical terms like *homoousios* at the Council of Nicaea (325), the 'biblicizing' opposition grew. And while the further councils and influential theologians quarrelled about philosophical terms like *physis, ousia, hypostasis, prosōpon, natura, essentia, substantia, subsistentia, persona,* and what not, the number of monks in Egypt, Palestine, Syria, and Constantinople and their influence in the Church grew as well. And only few of them had received a philosophical education.

Of course, one may argue: 'If they did not know philosophy, why include them in a study of ancient Christian philosophy?' In order to know its limits. Philosophy in ancient Christianity was certainly most influential, but not universally so. Consequently, in order to arrive at a complete picture, one must also ascertain where the influence of philosophy ended and where it met opposition. Hitherto, this aspect has received relatively little attention, because the testimonies of the Christian philosophers are so overwhelmingly voluble in comparison to the 'silent majority'. Nevertheless, the admittedly tedious collection of data from reading the texts under this aspect, combining them with detailed historical, prosopographical, educational, and sociological analyses, seems to open a promising future line of research which might prove very helpful in evaluating the true extent of the impact of ancient Christian philosophy.

33.4 PLATO CHRISTIANUS?

The philosophical school that influenced Christianity most was undoubtedly Platonism. It developed in three distinct phases. Its original author, Plato, lived several centuries before Christ (427–347 BCE); however, his philosophy eventually dominated all of both pagan and Christian philosophy up to the end of antiquity and beyond. It replaced Stoicism as the most popular philosophy of the imperial age, while it adopted quite a number of its doctrines. Plato's works were also translated into Latin, and numerous fathers read and quoted them, especially the dialogues *Phaedo, Phaedrus, Symposium, Theaetetus, Timaeus*, and the *Republic*. Plato was admired as the author of the highest and most inspired philosophy, a genuine theology, the worthiest tool in searching for the divine truth.

The second and third phases, Middle Platonism and Neoplatonism, developed contemporary to and in exchange with Christianity. The term 'Middle Platonism' refers to the first stage of a strongly religious syncretistic form of Platonism in the first and second centuries CE, which regarded Plato as the supreme theologian, mingling his philosophy with elements from Pythagoras, Aristotle, and the Stoics with the intention of creating an 'absolute philosophy'. Middle Platonism proclaimed an absolutely transcendent deity, ineffable and remote from the sensible world. God became identical with the Plato's concept of the Good (*Respublica* 6. 509b), the One of the second hypothesis (*Parmenides*). He was seen as an absolutely immutable being formed by the Ideas and the Beautiful. He is the *nous*, the creator (demiurge), and the good world-soul (*anima mundi*; cf. *Laws* 10). He is the beginning, free from mixture, the first, ungenerate, incorrupt, pure, simple, free from passions. The divine Logos is the sum of all the *logoi*, the rational and spermatic principles, which govern the universe.

It is this form of Platonism that the Christian apologists of the second century encountered and discussed, among them in prominent roles Justin Martyr, Clement of Alexandria, and Origen. And it is not surprising that they were intrigued by a philosophy/theology that corresponded in so many respects with their own ideas of God as the supreme eternal being, the creator, the source of all that is good, and of his Son the Logos leading the way to perfection.

At the beginning of the third century, Middle Platonism developed into Neoplatonism in the cultural melting-pot of Alexandria. Ammonios Sakkas (*c.*175–*c.*242), a Christian and teacher of both Plotinus and Origen, is traditionally considered to be the founder of Neoplatonism. However, as he did not publish any books, the *Enneads* of his pupil Plotinus (*c.*204/5–*c.*269/70) became the cornerstone of this new form of Platonism, followed by Porphyry (*c.*234–*c.*302/5), Iamblichus (*c.*240/50–*c.*325), and Proclus (412–85). The most prominent Christian Neoplatonists were Gregory of Nyssa (*c.*335/40–after 394), Augustine (354–430), and Pseudo-Dionysius the Areopagite (end of fifth/beginning of sixth century), who transmitted it to the Middle Ages.

Plotinus identified the supreme being no longer as the *nous*, but as the One of the first hypothesis in Plato's *Parmenides* and the absolute Good in *Republic* VI 509b (*Enneads* V 1, 8). The One is the first and highest principle of all; it is prior to all and above everything; it is absolutely pure and without quantity or quality; it is completely self-sufficient, unchangeable, infinite, the absolute good; it stands at the summit of all and reigns over it; it is desired by all things; it is the generator of the *nous*, which is light and also shines in the human intellect. The second hypothesis, the *nous*, is generated by the One before all times as an overflowing of its abundant power and an irradiation of its light. Being *nous*, it then turns to its origin and contemplates it. It is the act, image, and imitation of the One, and while it remains below it, it stands above everything else. The third hypothesis is represented by the world-soul (*anima mundi*), which Plato talks about above all in the *Timaeus*, *Philebus*, and book 10 of the *Laws*. In its turn it is born from the *nous* and contemplates it; it participates in both the intelligible and the sensible world; it generates the sensible world and endows it with its reasonable principles (*logoi*); it gives life to the world and guides it.

Regarding the cause of evil, Plotinus takes two different positions. It is either the absence of the Good, a form of non-being, or it is matter. Consequently, the aim of life consists in the 'flight [from the world and] likeness (*homoiōsis*) to God as far as possible', as Plato had defined it in *Theaetetus* 176b. This final unity with the One in ecstasy can be achieved only through the 'contemplative virtues', the *katharsis* of all passions, the total detachment of the soul from the body, which eventually leads to *apatheia*.

Porphyry, and especially Iamblichus, refine this system further in a syncretistic way. They talk of a triad of hypostases; Porphyry even identifies the first triad with the 'Father' of the Chaldaean Oracles. While Plotinus and Porphyry speak only of 'political, cathartic, theoretical and paradigmatic virtues', Iamblichus adds the 'hieratic virtues' (Lilla 1992*b*).

No wonder that this philosophy appealed to Christians in a supreme way, regarding both their theology (Trinity, Christology) and their ethics. Throughout Christian antiquity there was no doubt that this was not only an adequate, but the appropriate way to formulate the faith, while, of course, one had to distinguish thoroughly which details were acceptable or not. 'Platonism' as a problem—that is, whether the incorporation of Platonic philosophy into theology overwhelmed and thus falsified the original Christian doctrine, or whether Christians transformed philosophy into theology by using philosophy adequately—did not arise before the end of the nineteenth century.

The three possible extreme positions are, naturally: (1) Christianity did not receive Platonism at all; it only borrowed its terminology as an outward form, without being substantially influenced by it. This is the opinion prominently defended by Heinrich Dörries (1971; cf. Peroli 1993). (2) Christian theology was overwhelmed by philosophical terminology, which falsified the original biblical message. This is von Harnack's thesis of the 'Hellenization of Christianity' (cf. above). (3) By using philosophical terminology and ideas, the meaning of Christian doctrine did not change at all. Rather, Plato was posthumously made a Christian. This is the basic tenor of Endré von Ivánka's famous book *Plato Christianus* (1964).

In the wider context of 'Antike und Christentum' and modern hermeneutics, the opinion gained ground that both philosophical terminology and the ideas expressed by it were the adequate way both to develop a deeper understanding of Christianity and to proclaim it in an adequate form. This is Cornelia de Vogel's (1985) position. One may even go a step further, as Salvatore Lilla does: 'Neoplatonism is completely christianized. However, at the same time Christianity permits Neoplatonism to penetrate it profoundly, and thus it receives its unmistakable character' (Lilla 2004: 171). This might the stepping stone for further inquiries into this still not definitively resolved problem.

33.5 OTHER PHILOSOPHERS AND THEIR SCHOOLS

Besides Platonism, early Christianity met a number of other popular philosophical systems, in many instances in the form of the prevailing philosophical syncretism of the times. Nevertheless, none of them had a comparable impact, because too often their doctrines could not be reconciled with Christian convictions.

Aristotle excluded divine providence from the lowest part of the universe. He considered the fifth element, the ether, to be God's body, and God was for him virtually identical with the *anima mundi*, the world's soul, which moved the universe. This universe was co-eternal with God, and the human soul was mortal, at least according to Aristotle's later works, because it was an integral part of the body. Only the mind (*nous*) was immortal (cf. Lilla 1992*a*).

On the other hand, before the middle of the second century, when Platonism became predominant, Stoicism seems to have had a major influence on Christianity, which made Cicero and Seneca popular among Christians, while Stoicism, being an eclectic system, was itself impregnated with Aristotelianism and Platonism. Already the writings of the New Testament show traces of it. Doctrines such as the presence of God's reason (*pneuma*) and providence in the world, creation as reflecting the creator by its order and thus serving as a guide towards him, man as *animal rationale*, as the centre of the world and the world at his service, the innate natural goodness of the soul—they all readily coincided with Christian beliefs. The Stoic distinction between the *logos endiathetos* and the *logos prophorikos* could be applied to the eternal Son of God and his incarnation, and the idea that procreation was the sole aim of marriage, which rules out sexual pleasure separated from this aim, is closely resembled in Augustine's theology. Early Christian ethical and moral teaching was profoundly influenced by Stoicism, as is attested, for example, by Tertullian's evaluation of '*Seneca semper noster*' (*An.* 20. 1) and by Ambrose's book *De officiis*, which he modelled on the homonymous treatise by Cicero. Also the Stoic idea of virtue being the goal of life and the threefold category of 'good' (virtue), 'bad' (vice), and 'indifferent' (*adiaphora*) could readily be adapted by Christian ethics. In monasticism, Epictetus was especially popular, because the perfect monk was outlined in the characteristics of a Stoic sage (cf. Tibiletti 1992). However, similar vocabulary could not mask fundamental differences in doctrine. Stoicism was a philosophy for an exclusive circle of the elect, whereas Christianity taught universal salvation. Stoic *apatheia* had little in common with Christian patience and long-suffering, because this is rooted in the love of God and neighbour. And there was certainly no room in Stoicism for divine redemption (cf. Ferguson 1987: 346 f.).

The life of the neo-Pythagorean Apollonius of Tyana (first century CE) as the prototype of a 'godlike man' (*theios anēr*) served as literary background for the portrayal of Jesus in both the canonical and the apocryphal books of the New Testament, and Numenius (late second century CE) did have some influence on Plotinus and contacts with both Jews and Christians. However, in the end, this line of philosophy was assimilated by Neoplatonism (cf. Ferguson 1987: 360–4). Epicureanism, finally, seems to have had no impact on Christianity whatsoever.

Regarding these other philosophers and their schools, there does not exist any major discussion of their relationship to Christianity. Of course, any future analysis of early Christian literature will also have to take this background into account and might render quite different results than attained hitherto.

33.6 TRINITY AND CHRISTOLOGY

Given the general atmosphere of the world in which Christianity developed, which was impregnated by syncretistic philosophical ideas, adding to it the alluring appeal of Platonic ideas and terminology mixed with Stoic and other elements, which seemed so closely related to Christian beliefs, it seems inevitable that theologians took up philosophy for deeper reflection, with the intention not of substituting but of complementing the biblical message by it. Thus the great theological controversies on the Trinity and Christology from the fourth to the seventh centuries were both triggered and moulded by applying philosophical categories and vocabulary to theology.

The controversies started with the Alexandrian priest Arius (*c.* 256–336), who intended to develop and clarify Origen's doctrine on the Trinity by using Platonic categories. Origen had attributed one *hypostasis* to Father, Son, and Spirit each in a subordinating way, in order to vouchsafe both the monarchy (unity) of God and, against Sabellianism, their distinction. Arius now added that the Father is the one (*to hen*), who is the source (*archē*) of everything, and therefore alone the divine nature (*ousia*) and substance (*hypostasis*) in the proper sense, because he alone is without beginning (*anarchos*), that is, unbegotten (*agennētos*) and uncreated (*agenētos*), eternal (*aidios*), unchangeable (*atreptos*), and immutable (*analloiōtos*) The Son is a creature (*ktisma, poiēma*), because he was begotten (*gen[n]ēton*) by the Father; that is, he is not eternal. Once there was a time when he was not (*ēn pote hote ouk ēn*). However, respecting the biblical message of the uniqueness of the Son, Arius admits that he was before all of the rest of creation, that everything else was created through him (cf. Col 1: 16), and that he surpasses all of creation (cf. Prov 8: 22–31). He may also be called 'God, Logos, Sophia, and Dynamis', but this makes him no 'true God' (*alēthinos theos*), because he is all this only through the grace of the Father, not by nature. The Son not only remains subordinate to the Father, but 'in everything alien and foreign to his nature and being' (*allotrios men kai anhomoios kata panta tēs tou patros ousias kai idiotētos*).

The Council of Nicaea (325), which met to solve the problem, did so by introducing the philosophical counter-term *homoousios* (of the same being with the Father). However, many were opposed to this non-biblical term, and the acceptance of the *homoousios* took almost 60 years, until the Second Ecumenical Council in Constantinople (381). The fundamental terminological problem consisted in the fact that, on the one hand, *ousia* and *hypostasis* were used as interchangeable terms, and, on the other hand, *ousia* meant 'nature' or 'being', *hypostasis* 'substance'. Then, logically, Origen's formula of *treis hypostaseis* in God was impossible to accept. God was certainly not 'three substances', as even the great Latin Platonist of the time, Marius Victorinus, translated (*Adversus Arium* 1. 41). Because a distinct term for 'person' was still lacking, *homoousios* bore the danger of being misunderstood in a

Sabellian way: that is, levelling out the distinction between the three—a reproach that was often enough brought up against the Nicene Creed. Only when the Synod of Alexandria (362) first accepted that *hypostasis* could also be used in the sense of 'person', was the way opened to the final distinction the Cappadocian fathers developed: *mia ousia—treis hypostaseis.*

Nevertheless, the problems were far from over. Since the Synod of Alexandria, Apollinarius of Laodicea had begun to reflect further on the person of Christ: that is, on how the unity of God and man could theologically be better understood and expressed. He considered *hypostasis* as the basis for the identity of the Son of God and Christ and the unity of divinity and humanity in him, which, however, he did not distinguish from *ousia*. As this *ousia* carried the power of self-determination (*autokinēton*), of which the one and same subject (*hypokeimenon*) can only have one (*hēgemonikon*), and as it was unimaginable that the Son of God could have lost or given up his *hēgemonikon*, his human body could not have one; that is, the Logos had to have replaced the human *nous*. Christ was for Apollinarius *mia physis tou logou sesarkomenē* (one incarnate nature of the Logos), while the unity of natures, substances, and person all remained on the same level.

Gregory of Nazianzus countered this theology with the famous formula 'what has not been assumed, has not been saved; however, what was united to God, that was also saved' (*Ep.* 101. 20–1), and Apollinarius was condemned. Nevertheless, here too, the problem was far from being definitively solved, because Apollinarius's works were pseudonymously transmitted under the name of the great orthodox patriarch of Alexandria, Athanasius. Convinced to continue on the approved grounds of his famous predecessor, patriarch Cyril of Alexandria unwittingly took up the Apollinarian formula '*mia physis tou logou sesarkomenē*', which the Council of Chalcedon (451) condemned.

For while the problematic terms grew more numerous in the East—to *physis*, *ousia*, and *hypostasis*, was added *prosōpon*—in the West, Augustine, aided by the fact that the Latin language had to cope with fewer terms, had found a solution which was to become final: *una persona in utraque natura*. Pope Leo the Great was convinced by it, and through his *Tomus ad Flavianum*, the Council of Chalcedon decided to say that Christ is made known 'in two natures' (*en duo physesin*), whose distinct properties come together in one 'person' (*prosōpon*).

All the rest of the history of the reception or refusal of the decision made in Chalcedon by the eastern churches remained a (finally unsolved) dispute over philosophical terms introduced into theology. It extended well into the seventh century, included two more ecumenical councils (Constantinople II and III in 553 and 680/1), introduced two more crucial terms, *energeia* (active force) and *thelēma* (will), and ended with the definite breakaway of various eastern churches.

Alois Grillmeier's lifelong research made huge inroads into this field with his monumental, but still unfinished, work *Christ in Christian Tradition*. Nevertheless, the studies are far from being completed. In some respects even, in particular regarding the history of the reception of Chalcedon, and especially the exact meaning of those philosophical terms and the numerous attempted solutions, the surface seems hardly to have been scratched. This field still holds tasks in store for generations to come.

33.7 MAN AND WORLD

The last important field of Christian philosophy is man and the world he lives in. In some respect it is really the first one, because philosophy is done by people in order to understand their existence in the world they live in. On the other hand, the first question of the Christian faith is: 'How are we saved?', and a Christian sees the world from this point of view. Consequently, Christians continue to ask basically the same philosophical questions as before, but now in the horizon of their salvation in Christ:

1. The origin and aim of the universe and everything in it, including the stars, which Christians answer with the new concept of God as its creator from nothing (*creatio ex nihilo*) and the old notion of the beatification/divinization of man (*homoiōsis theou;* cf. Plato, *Theaetetus* 176d), sometimes even with the return of everything, including the devil, to its primeval paradisiacal state (*apokatastasis*; cf. Acts 3: 21; Origen, Gregory of Nyssa).

2. Thus man is referred to God and the question who and how he is. His characteristics are in part philosophical (one, good, beautiful, immaterial, invisible, infinite, etc.), in part exclusively Christian, among them omniscience, omnipotence, and love, that caused God to save the world. A special and hitherto unsolved problem is presented by the question of how to reconcile divine providence and human freedom (theodicy).

3. Man is obviously composed of matter (the body) and something invisible and immaterial, which causes the body to die and decay when it leaves it (the soul). On the basis of humans being God's creatures, Christians explain the soul according to Genesis 2: 7 as God's life-giving and immortal breath (spirit), intelligence (*gnōsis, mens*) as participation in God's presence, and man's individuality as person, the same term as used for God. Moreover, they also confess the resurrection of the flesh, without which man is incomplete—a horrifying thought for any ancient non-Christian philosopher.

4. Birth and death, beginnings, changes, and ends are the marks of the finite world man lives in. The world revolves in yearly cycles. So, what are time and history? In clear distinction to various philosophical schools, which saw time as an eternal cycle, it is for the Christian a linear evolution, purposefully planned by God from creation towards the return of Christ for the Last

Judgement. God himself is present in human history, while the incarnation of the Son of God marks the 'fullness of time' (cf. Gal 4: 4; Eph 1: 10).

5. Finally, what is man to do? Ancient philosophy was, as was said before, inseparable from ethics. Consequently, Christian philosophy continues the ancient reflections on the virtues and duties, good and evil, passions and public life (politics) from a fundamentally new point of view: God as the supreme Good, Satan and the free will of man as the sources of evil, God as the source of the virtues and the aim of duties, and human life (both private and public) governed by God's ordering presence and commandments.

All of these questions and all of the above are dealt with in the writings of the most outstanding Christian philosophers of antiquity, which all represent their own wide field of studies: the Greek authors Justin Martyr (d. 165), Clement of Alexandria (*c.* 150–*c.* 215), Origen (*c.* 185–254), Gregory of Nyssa (*c.* 335/40–after 394), Maximus the Confessor (*c.* 580–662), and Pseudo-Dionysius the Areopagite (end of fifth/beginning of sixth century) in the East; Marius Victorinus (*c.* 282/91— soon after 362), Augustine (354–430), and Boethius (*c.* 475/80–*c.* 580) in the Latin West.

These fields of studies are not as controversially disputed as the former ones. Yet there is still much to explore, especially in order to understand humanity even today. 'Where do we come from? Where do we go to? What shall I do? What is the meaning of life?' These questions will remain basic as long as the human race exists and continues to wonder.

33.8 CONCLUSION

In the end, all studies of Christian philosophy come down to the original question asked at the beginning: What does the juxtaposition of the adjective 'Christian' to the noun 'philosophy' mean? An assimilation of both terms and notions from ancient pre-Christian and contemporary non-Christian philosophy; the continuation of asking the same basic questions that humanity has asked since it began reasoning, in order to make sense of the universe; the search for knowledge and truth. At the same time, the faith in one personal God, his incarnate Son, and salvation made the fundamental difference. It let non-Christian philosophers refuse Christianity, and Christians refuse philosophy or parts of it. And in the same way that philosophy formed the understanding of the Christian faith, faith changed and moulded philosophy.

Therefore, the basic questions of 'Christian philosophy' remain: What did Christians accept from philosophy, and how did this change Christianity? What did

Christians reject of philosophy, because they considered it incompatible with faith? How did Christianity change traditional questions and ideas? And finally, how far did the influence of Christianity on non-Christian philosophies affect them?

This last question might be one of the most fascinating for future research. It is relatively recent, but new discoveries like Augustine's Sermon Dolbeau 26 seem to point more and more in this direction (cf. Dodaro 1998). And it has generally become quite clear that 'inculturation' is never a one-way street. It seems hermeneutically impossible that influence was only exerted from *Antike* to *Christentum*, from philosophy to Christianity; there must have been some kind of backlash. In this complex topic of the multilayered mutual interactions of philosophy and Christian faith consists the future task of studying ancient Christian philosophy.

SUGGESTED READING

ANDRESEN, C. (1978), 'Antike und Christentum', in *TRE* iii. 50–99.

ARMSTRONG, A. H. (1967) (ed.), *The Cambridge History of Later Greek and Early Medieval Philosophy* (Cambridge: Cambridge University Press).

——and MARKUS, ROBERT A. (1960), *Christian Faith and Greek Philosophy* (London: Darton, Longman, and Todd).

BLUMENTHAL, H. J. (1987), 'Plotinus in the Light of Twenty Years' Scholarship, 1951–1971', *ANRW* II, 36. 1: 528–70.

COLISH, M. L. (1985), *The Stoic Tradition from Antiquity to the Early Middle Ages*, 2 vols., Studies in the History of Christian Thought, 34–5 (Leiden: E. J. Brill).

COLPE, C., HONNEFELDER, L., and LUTZ-BACHMANN, M. (1992) (eds.), *Spätantike und Christentum: Beiträge zur Religions- und Geistesgeschichte der griechisch-römischen Kultur und Zivilisation der Kaiserzeit* (Berlin: Akademie Verlag).

CORRIGAN, K., and O'CLEIRIGH, P. (1987), 'The Course of Plotinian Scholarship from 1971 to 1986', *ANRW* II, 36. 1: 571–623.

COURCELLE, P. (1948), *Les lettres grecques en Occident de Macrobe à Cassiodore* (Paris: Éditions de Boccard).

DILLON, J. (1977), *The Middle Platonists: A Study of Platonism 80 B.C. to A.D. 220* (London: Duckworth).

GERSH, S. (1986), *Middle Platonism and Neoplatonism: The Latin Tradition* (Notre Dame, Ind.: University of Notre Dame Press).

GRILLMEIER, A. (1975), *Hellenisierung—Judaisierung des Christentums als Deuteprinzipien der Geschichte des kirchlichen Dogmas: Mit ihm und in ihm. Christologische Forschungen und Perspektiven* (Freiburg: Herder).

HAASE, W. (1987–89) (ed.), *ANRW*, Teil II: *Principat*, Band 36. 1–3: *Philosophie, Wissenschaft, Technik* (Berlin: de Gruyter).

HYLDAHL, N. (1966), *Philosophie und Christentum: Eine Interpretation der Einleitung zum Dialog Justins*, Acta Theologica Danica, 9 (Copenhagen: Prostant apud Munksgaard).

MORESCHINI, C. (2004), *Storia della filosofia patristica* (Brescia: Editrice Morcelliana).

PRESTIGE, G. L. (1952), *God in Patristic Thought* (London: S.P.C.K.)

RAMOS-LISSÓN, D., MERINO, M., and VICIANO, A. (1996) (eds.), *El diálogo fe-cultura en la antigüedad cristiana* (Pamplona: Ediciones Eunate y Servicio de Publicaciones de la Universidad de Navarra).

SPANNEUT, M. (1969), *Le stoïcisme des pères de l'Église de Clément de Rome à Clément d'Aléxandrie*, 2nd edn. (Paris: Éditions du Seuil).

TRESMONTANT, C. (1961), *La métaphysique du christianisme et la naissance de la philosophie chrétienne* (Paris: Éditions du Seuil).

WOLFSON, H. A. (1964), *The Philosophy of the Church Fathers*, i: *Faith, Trinity, Incarnation* (Cambridge, Mass.: Harvard University Press).

BIBLIOGRAPHY

ARNOLD, G. (1699–1700), *Unparteiische Kirchen- und Ketzer-Historie* (Frankfurt am Main: Fritsch).

DANIÉLOU, J. (1961), *Histoire des doctrines chrétiennes avant Nicée*, ii: *Message évangélique et culture hellénistique aux IIe et IIIe siècles* (Tournai: Desclée & Cie).

——(1991), *Histoire des doctrines chrétiennes avant Nicée*, i: *Théologie du Judéo-Christianisme*, 2nd edn. Texte établi sur l'édition italienne de 1974 par Marie-Odile Boulnois; revu et corrigé par Joseph Paramelle et Marie Josèphe Rondeau (Tournai: Desclée/Cerf; 1st edn. 1958).

DEWART, L. (1969), *The Foundations of Belief* (London: Burns & Oates).

DODARO, R. (1998), '*Christus sacerdos*: Augustine's Preaching against Pagan Priests in the Light of *S*. Dolbeau 26 and 23, in Goulven Madec (ed.), *Augustin prédicateur (395–411)*. *Actes du Colloque International de Chantilly (5–7 septembre 1996)*, Collection des Études Augustiniennes, Série Antiquité, 159 (Paris: L'Institut d'études augustinienne), 377–93.

DÖRRIES, H. (1971), 'Was ist "spätantiker Platonismus"? Überlegungen zur Grenzziehung zwischen Platonismus und Christentum', *TRU* 36: 285–302.

DROBNER, H. R. (1986), *Person-Exegese und Christologie bei Augustinus: Zur Herkunft der Formel una persona*, Philosophia Patrum, 8 (Leiden: E. J. Brill).

FERGUSON, E. (1987), *Backgrounds of Early Christianity* (Grand Rapids, Mich.: William B. Eerdmans).

GNILKA, C. (1984), *Chrēsis: Die Methode der Kirchenväter im Umgang mit der antiken Kultur I. Der Begriff des 'rechten Gebrauchs'* (Basel: Schwabe).

GREENSLADE, S. L. (1956), *Early Latin Theology*, LCC (London: SCM Press).

GRILLMEIER, A. (1965–96), *Christ in Christian Tradition*, i–ii/4 (London: Mowbrays).

HADOT, P. (1995), *Philosophy as a Way of Life: Spiritual Exercises from Socrates to Foucault*, trans. Michael Chase (Malden, Mass.: Blackwell).

——(2004), *What is Ancient Philosophy?*, trans. Michael Chase (Cambridge, Mass.: The Belknap Press of Harvard University Press).

HARNACK, A. VON (1886–90), *Lehrbuch der Dogmengeschichte*, 3 vols. (Freiburg: Mohr).

IVÁNKA, E. VON (1964), *Plato Christianus: Übernahme und Umgestaltung des Platonismus durch die Väter* (Einsiedeln: Johannes Verlag; repr. Paris: Presses universitaires de France, 1990).

LILLA, S. (1992a), 'Aristotelianism', in *Encyclopedia of the Early Church*, ed. A. Di Berardino, trans. from the Italian by A. Walford with foreword and bibliographic amendments by W. H. C. Frend (Cambridge: James Clark & Co., 1992), i. 73–6.

——(1992b), 'Neoplatonism', in *Encyclopedia of the Early Church*, ed. A. Di Berardino, trans. from the Italian by A. Walford, with foreword and bibliographic amendments by W. H. C. Frend, Institutum Patristicum Augustinianum (Cambridge: James Clark & Co., 1992), i. 585–93.

——(2004), *Neuplatonisches Gedankengut in den 'Homilien über die Seligpreisungen' Gregors von Nyssa*, ed. H. R. Drobner, Supple. *VC* 68 (Leiden: E. J. Brill).

PEROLI, E. (1993), 'Il conflitto fra Platonismo e Cristianesimo nell'interpretazione di Heinrich Dörrie', in Cornelia de Vogel, *Platonismo e cristianesimo. Antagonismo o comuni fondamenti?*, ed. Giovanni Reale e Enrico Peroli (Milan: Vita e Pensiero), 105–38.

THRAEDE, K. (1993), 'Antike und Christentum', in *LTK* i. 755–9.

TIBILETTI, C. (1992), 'Stoicism and the Fathers', in *Encyclopedia of the Early Church*, ed. A. Di Berardino, trans. from Italian by A. Walford, with foreword and bibliographic amendments by W. H. C. Frend (Cambridge: James Clark & Co., 1992), ii. 795–7.

VOGEL, C. J. DE (1970), 'Some Reflections on the Term Filosofia', in *Philosophia*, i (Assen: Van Gorcum), 3–24.

——(1985), 'Platonism and Christianity: A Mere Antagonism or a Profound Common Ground?', *VC* 39: 1–62, republished as *Platonismo e cristianesimo: Antagonismo o comuni fondamenti?*, ed. Giovanni Reale e Enrico Peroli (Milan: Vita e Pensiero, 1993), 25–104.

PART VII

RITUAL, PIETY,
AND PRACTICE

CHAPTER 34

CHRISTIAN INITIATION

MAXWELL E. JOHNSON

THE study of the rites of Christian initiation (baptism, post-baptismal rites, and first communion) in the first five centuries of the Church's existence, like the study of early liturgy in general, has been called rightly 'a study in diversity' (Bradshaw 2002: 144). That is, to study the rites of Christian initiation in the early church is to encounter not one but several liturgical traditions in development, each with its own unique ritual patterns, structures, and theologies: the early Aramaic or Syriac-speaking Christians centred in Edessa and, later, Nisibis, Syria (modern-day Iraq, Iran, and portions of Turkey); the Greek-speaking Syrian Christians centred in Antioch of Syria and in the Jerusalem of Syro-Palestine, and from the beginning of the fourth century, also in Armenia; the Greek-speaking Christians of Lower Egypt and the Coptic-speaking Christians of Upper Egypt, where already by the third century both liturgy and scripture had been translated into Coptic; the Latin-speaking members of the North African churches; and the, undoubtedly, multi-linguistic groups which made up the Christian communities living in Rome and elsewhere in the West. Further, these distinct ecclesial, linguistic, and cultural traditions will themselves come to be expressed, especially in the centuries immediately after Constantine, in those various families called 'rites', those unique ways of being Christian still existing as Armenian, Byzantine, Coptic, East Syrian, Ethiopic, Maronite, and West Syrian in the Christian East, and Ambrosian (Milanese), Mozarabic (Visigothic), and Roman in the West (Johnson 2007: 1–307).

Given their nature as 'rites of passage', one might legitimately study initiation rites in early Christianity from an anthropological or ritual studies perspective (see van Gennep 1960; V. Turner 1969; Eliade 1958; and, more recently, Bell 1992; Grimes 1992; and Rappaport 1999). This chapter, however, employs the historical-critical methodology of liturgical scholarship called, after the great pioneer in the field, Anton Baumstark, 'comparative liturgy' (Baumstark 1958). And indeed, while a ritual studies method might reveal a common ritual process across several traditions and a way to interpret their meaning(s) in general human, social, and cultural terms, it is a focus precisely on the *diversity* and distinct *variety* of initiation practices in the early churches which has been the great contribution of comparative liturgical scholarship over the past 30 years. Prior to this, liturgical scholarship had inherited several common historical and influential assumptions about the origins and early practice of Christian initiation, which served as unquestioned norms, namely:

1. That there was a single, monolinear, and original unitive pattern of baptism, 'confirmation', and first communion, celebrated from antiquity at the Easter Vigil (interpreted by Romans 6 in death and burial imagery) and prepared for by at least a nascent Lent, which, in the course of the Middle Ages, was disrupted and separated into distinct sacraments and ultimately divorced from their 'original' connection to Easter.

2. That an important document, like the *Apostolic Tradition*, ascribed to Hippolytus of Rome (*c.* 215), thanks to the work of Bernard Botte (1963) and Gregory Dix (1937), was actually composed by the early third-century antipope Hippolytus himself, and thus reflected our earliest and authoritative piece of evidence for reconstructing early initiation practice at Rome.

3. That any variations to this supposed normative pattern (e.g. that of early Syria) were to be viewed precisely as accidental and unimportant 'variations' or idiosyncratic departures from this norm.

Today, however, all of these assumptions, due to a new scholarly and critical reading of the sources, have been, and are increasingly being, revised. Thanks, in large part, to the seminal work of Gabriele Winkler (1982) on the early Syrian and Armenian liturgical traditions, summarized in English in a highly significant article (Winkler 1978), modern liturgical scholars have come to emphasize that what was normative in early Christian initiation practice was precisely liturgical diversity and multiple patterns from the very beginning. In other words, there appears to have been no single common pattern, ritual contents, or theological interpretation that suggested themselves as universally normative, apart from some rather obvious things like catechesis, the water bath, and the profession of faith. Hence, some of what has been viewed as universally normative was but the result of various developments toward liturgical uniformity brought about in the aftermath of Constantine's imperial ascendancy and the various Trinitarian and Christological ecumenical councils of the fourth and fifth centuries.

This chapter seeks to provide students with an introductory overview of the sources, issues, and problems encountered in the development and interpretation of the rites of Christian initiation within early Christianity. It proceeds in two parts: (1) from the first century to the Council of Nicaea; and (2) from the Council of Nicaea to Augustine of Hippo. Augustine of Hippo serves as a fitting conclusion to this focus since, as a result of his controversies with both Donatism and Pelagianism, a new chapter in Christian initiation, especially in the West, begins and continues throughout the medieval and even Reformation periods of church history.

34.1 FROM THE FIRST CENTURY TO THE COUNCIL OF NICAEA

Based on Jesus's baptism by John (Mt 3: 13–17; Mk 1: 9–11, Lk 3: 21–2; and Jn 1: 31–4), possibly on Jesus's own baptismal practice (Jn 3: 22, 26, and 4: 1), and in general continuity with the overall context of ritual washings and bathing customs within first-century Judaism (see Collins 1989; Lathrop 1994), new converts to Christianity, from the earliest times (see Acts 2: 38–42) on (see Johnson 2004), were initiated into Christ and the Church by a ritual process which included some form of 'baptism' with water, a process that would eventually be based in the command of the risen Jesus (Mt 28: 19). Unfortunately, the New Testament itself records little detail about this baptismal practice or what additional ceremonies may have been included. While we might assume that some kind of profession of faith in Jesus as Lord was present, we do not know, for example, if any particular 'formula'— e.g. 'I baptize you in the name of the Father and of the Son and of the Holy Spirit' from the dominical command for baptism in Mt 28: 19, or 'in the name of Jesus' (Acts 3: 6)—was employed. Nor do we do know precisely how baptisms were regularly conferred (by immersion, complete submersion, or pouring; see Stauffer 1994), whether infants were ever candidates for baptism in the first century, what kind of preparation may have preceded adult baptism, whether anointings were already part of the process, or if occasional references to the apostolic conferral of the post-baptismal gift of the Holy Spirit (Acts 8 and 19) were regular features of baptismal practice in some early communities or exceptional cases due to particular circumstances. For that matter, in a recent study of foot washing in the Gospel of John it has even been suggested that among some early 'Johannine' communities it was not baptism at all, but a foot-washing ceremony that constituted the 'rite' of Christian initiation (Connell 1996).

What New Testament texts do provide is a rich mosaic of baptismal images: forgiveness of sins and the gift of the Holy Spirit (Acts 2: 38); new birth through water and the Holy Spirit (Jn 3: 5; Titus 3: 5–7); putting off the 'old nature' and 'putting on the new', that is, 'being clothed in the righteousness of Christ'

(Gal 3: 27; Col 3: 9–10); initiation into the 'one body' of the Christian community (1 Cor 12: 13; see also Acts 2: 42); washing, sanctification, and justification in Christ and the Holy Spirit (1 Cor 6: 11); enlightenment (Heb 6: 4; 10: 32; 1 Pet 2: 9); being 'anointed' and/or 'sealed' by the Holy Spirit (2 Cor 1: 21–2; 1 Jn 2: 20, 27); being 'sealed' or 'marked' as belonging to God and God's people (2 Cor 1: 21–2; Eph 1: 13–14; 4: 30; Rev 7: 3); and of course being joined to Christ through participation in his death, burial, and resurrection (Rom 6: 3–11; Col 2: 12–15). Two of these stand out with particular emphasis: Christian initiation as new birth through water and the Holy Spirit (Jn 3: 5–8) and Christian initiation as being united with Christ in his death, burial, and resurrection (Rom 6: 3–11). Around these, several of the other New Testament images will eventually cluster as specific baptismal 'ceremonies'.

Our next sources for the rites of Christian initiation provide only a few more, albeit important, details. Chapter 7 of the (probably Syrian) late first- or early second-century proto-church order called the *Didache* directs that, after instruction (presumably the kind of ethical formation supplied by chapters 1–6 of the document) and one or two days of fasting on the part of the candidates, baptizers, and community alike, baptism is to be conferred in the following manner:

1. As for baptism, baptize in this way: Having said all this beforehand, baptize in the name of the Father and of the Son and of the Holy Spirit, in running water. Regarding baptism. 2. If you … do not have running water, however, baptize in another kind of water; if you cannot [do so] in cold [water], then [do so] in warm [water]. 3. But if you have neither, pour water on the head thrice in the name of the Father and Son and Holy Spirit. 4. Before the baptism, let the person baptizing and the person being baptized—and others who are able—fast; tell the one being baptized to fast one or two [days] before.

(Whitaker and Johnson 2003: 2)

Only the baptized, we are instructed further in chapter 9, are to receive the eucharist.

There is much, however, that the *Didache* does *not* tell us about the initiation rite: for example, the duration of pre-baptismal catechesis, whether the Trinitarian language is a reference to a baptismal 'formula' (see Milavec 2003: 62), or whether the baptismal rite culminated immediately in the eucharist. Nor does the *Didache* indicate any preferred day or season for baptism: it is silent about what sort of profession of faith may have been expected from the baptismal candidates, offers no information about the 'ministers' of baptism, and makes no reference whatsoever to any sort of additional rites that may have accompanied baptism itself. Equally absent from this document is any definitive theological interpretation of, or reflection on the meaning of baptism. Unfortunately, then, the information provided about the rites of Christian initiation by the *Didache* is only of the most general kind (Niederwimmer 1998; Van de Sandt and Flusser 2002).

In the middle of the second century at Rome, chapters 61 and 65 of the *First Apology* of Justin Martyr not only corroborate the information provided by the *Didache*, but add some other elements:

(*Chapter 61*): ... Those who are convinced and believe what we say and teach is the truth, and pledge themselves to be able to live accordingly, are taught in prayer and fasting to ask God to forgive their past sins, while we pray and fast with them. Then we lead them to a place where there is water, and they are regenerated in the same manner in which we ourselves were regenerated. In the name of God, the Father and Lord of all, and of our Saviour, Jesus Christ, and of the Holy Spirit, they then receive the washing with water. For Christ said: 'Unless you be born again, you shall not enter the kingdom of heaven' (John 3: 5)....In order that we do not continue as children of necessity and ignorance, but of deliberate choice and knowledge, and in order to obtain in the water the forgiveness of past sins, there is invoked over the one who wishes to be regenerated, and who is repentant of his sins, the name of God, the Father and Lord of all....This washing is called illumination, since they who learn these things become illuminated intellectually.

Furthermore, the illuminated one is also baptized in the name of Jesus Christ, who was crucified under Pontius Pilate, and in the name of the Holy Spirit, who predicted through the prophets everything concerning Jesus.

(*Chapter 65*): After thus baptizing the one who has believed and given his assent, we escort him to the place where are assembled those whom we call brethren, to offer up sincere prayers in common for ourselves, for the baptized person, and for all other persons wherever they may be, in order that, since we have found the truth, we may be deemed fit through our actions to be esteemed as good citizens and observers of the law, and thus attain eternal salvation. At the conclusion of prayers we greet one another with a kiss. Then, bread and chalice containing wine mixed with water are presented to the one presiding over the brethren.

(Whitaker and Johnson 2003: 3)

Because Justin refers in the above description to what may be called 'credal' language, it is not clear if a baptismal formula is intended or if he is alluding to an early example of the *western* threefold profession of faith as constituting the 'formula' of baptism. At the same time, while it is often assumed that Justin describes *Roman* liturgical practice, his theology of baptism as 'new birth' and his reference to baptism as *phōtismos* ('enlightenment'), characteristic emphases in the Christian East, may reflect an *eastern* Christian tradition (Justin, after all, was from Flavia Neapolis in Syria) or, possibly, a Syrian community at Rome. Nevertheless, the overall ritual pattern described by him underscores that some kind of pre-baptismal 'catechesis' (instruction) preceded baptism, and that this entire process of becoming a Christian culminated in sharing in the prayers, kiss, and eucharist of the community.

It is only in the early third century that a more complete picture of the variant processes of early Christian initiation begins to emerge. Here, we begin to see detailed evidence of several additional ritual elements. But the extent to which any of these elements are present varies according to liturgical tradition.

In early Syrian documents—the *Didascalia Apostolorum*, the *Acts of Judas Thomas*, and the *Acts of John*—a pattern of initiation appears to exist wherein the baptism of Jesus is seen as the primary paradigm for Christian baptism, and the theology of baptism flows from the 'new birth' focus of John 3. While these documents place minimal stress on catechesis, there is a strong emphasis on a pre-baptismal anointing of the head (and, eventually, the whole body), interpreted as a 'royal' anointing by which the Holy Spirit assimilates the candidate to the kingship and priesthood of Christ, baptism accompanied by the Matthean Trinitarian formula, and the concluding reception of the eucharist (Winkler 1978). There is no question but that it is this pre-baptismal anointing, derived from the anointing of kings and priests in ancient Israel, which was the very high point of the 'baptismal' ritual, a ritual which, during the course of the fourth century, at least in Syro-Palestine and the Graeco-Roman coastland, was transformed to accommodate a *post-baptismal* pneumatic anointing and a reinterpretation of the pre-baptismal anointing as exorcistic, purificatory, and preparatory. It is also possible, but by no means proven, that one of the principal occasions for initiation in the early Syrian tradition was 6 January, the Feast of the Epiphany, interpreted, primarily, as the Feast of Jesus's baptism. Alternatively, based on later Armenian liturgical sources, it is also possible that pre-baptismal catechesis was limited to a three-week period prior to baptism, whenever it was celebrated (Johnson 1990).

Several scholars have also suggested that early Egyptian initiation practice provides a close parallel to that of Syria in this time period (see Kretschmar 1963; Bradshaw 1989; Johnson 1995: 7–16), although in Egypt it appears that candidates for baptism were enrolled *on* Epiphany, when the opening section of Mark's Gospel would have been read, and then baptized forty days later at some point in mid-February, with catechetical instruction given during a fast already associated with Jesus's own 40-day fast in the wilderness (Talley 1986: 194–213). Indeed, later Coptic tradition, primarily through legends about earlier practice, preserves a memory of the fourth century being a time of baptismal innovation, with the adoption of a post-baptismal anointing in Egypt. At the same time, the writings of both Clement of Alexandria and Origen indicate that a central baptismal metaphor in Egyptian Christianity was the crossing of the Red Sea, understood not as baptism but as entrance into the catechumenate, with baptism itself interpreted as the Israelites' crossing of the Jordan under Joshua (Jesus), thus underscoring again Jesus's baptism in the Jordan as the dominant baptismal paradigm (McDonnell 1996: 43–4; Johnson 1995: 7–16).

Western sources of the third century provide alternative patterns to the early Syrian, and possibly Egyptian, practice. In North Africa, Tertullian's *De baptismo* (*c.* 200) describes a ritual process which included 'frequent' pre-baptismal vigils and fasts, a renunciation of Satan, a threefold credal profession of faith in the context of the conferral of baptism, a post-baptismal 'Christic' anointing related to priesthood, a 'blessing' by laying on of hands associated with the gift of the Holy Spirit, and participation in the eucharist, which also included the reception of milk and honey as symbols of entering into the 'promised land' (Whitaker and Johnson 2003: 9–11). Tertullian's description is corroborated generally a bit later in North Africa by Cyprian of Carthage (Whitaker and Johnson 2003: 11–13), and for Rome, presumably, in the *Apostolic Tradition, c.* 215, ascribed to Hippolytus of Rome (Whitaker and Johnson 2003: 4–8).

According to the *Apostolic Tradition*, pre-baptismal catechesis was to last for 3 years, and included frequent prayer, fasting, and exorcism, with entrance into the 'catechumenate' itself accompanied by a detailed interrogation of the motives and lifestyles of those seeking admittance (on the history of the catechumenate see Kreider 1999). For those eventually 'elected' to baptism, the rites themselves took place at a Saturday night vigil, and consisted of a renunciation of Satan, a full body anointing with the 'oil of exorcism', a threefold, credal interrogation accompanied by the three immersions of baptism itself, a post-baptismal anointing by a presbyter with the 'oil of thanksgiving', an entrance into the assembly, where the bishop performed a laying on of hands with prayer and a second anointing, and, after the kiss, the sharing of the eucharist, including the cup(s) of milk and honey referred to by Tertullian. Since authorship, date, provenance, and influence of this church order are all subject to intense scholarly debate today, the details provided by it must be received with due caution. It is possible that several of these elements—for example, the 'three year catechumenate' and the episcopal anointing, reflect later (fourth-century) additions or interpolations (Bradshaw, Johnson, and Phillips 2002: 96–8 and 132–4). With regard to the episcopal hand-laying prayer and anointing, the Latin version of the *Apostolic Tradition* does not interpret these ritual actions in relationship to a 'giving' of the Holy Spirit to the newly baptized, but provides, instead, the following rubrics and texts:

And the bishop shall lay his hands on them and invoke saying: Lord God, you have made them worthy to receive remission of sins through the laver of regeneration of the holy Spirit: *send upon them your grace*, that they may serve you according to your will; for to you is glory, to Father and Son with the holy Spirit in the holy Church, both now and to the ages of ages. Amen.

  Then, pouring the oil of thanksgiving from his hand and placing it on his head, he shall say: I anoint you with holy oil in God the Father almighty and Christ Jesus and the Holy Spirit.

(Whitaker and Johnson 2003: 8)

The subsequent 'oriental' (i.e. Sahidic, Ethiopic, and Arabic) versions of this document transform the hand-laying prayer precisely into an explicit invocation of the Holy Spirit on the newly baptized. Hence, it is not surprising that one of the principal scholarly debates on Christian initiation in the *Apostolic Tradition* has been on the interpretation of these post-baptismal 'episcopal acts' in relation to what would later become in the Roman Rite the separate sacrament called 'confirmation'.

In treating these episcopal rites, Aidan Kavanagh has argued that they reflect only the traditional structure of what may be termed an episcopal *missa* (Kavanagh 1984, 1988). That is, this episcopal unit has the overall structure of a 'dismissal' rite, used to dismiss various categories of people from the liturgical assembly (e.g. catechumens and penitents), a practice known to have been used frequently in Christian antiquity at the close of various liturgies. Different groups of people, before leaving the liturgical assembly, would go before the bishop and receive, often by a hand-laying rite, his blessing. Consequently, just as these neophytes had often been 'dismissed' from both catechetical instruction and from other liturgical gatherings by a rite which included the laying on of hands, so now, after baptism and anointing by the presbyter, they are again dismissed by means of a similar ritual structure. But this time the 'dismissal' is *from* the baptismal bath *to* the eucharistic table. Although this dismissal rite would later develop theologically into a post-baptismal conferral of the Holy Spirit, and ultimately be separated from baptism itself, the origins of what will later become the independent rite called 'confirmation' are thus *structural* rather than theological.

In a response, Paul Turner (1991) questioned Kavanagh's interpretation of these episcopal acts as constituting an actual 'dismissal', and suggested, alternatively, that they should be viewed as 'the first public gesture of ratification for the bishop and the faithful who did not witness the pouring of water', as it is quite clear that both baptism and the presbyteral anointing happened at a place outside the liturgical assembly itself. In other words, this unit of the bishop's hand-laying prayer and anointing constitutes a rite of 'welcome' rather than dismissal, a rite by which those newly born of water *and* the Holy Spirit are now welcomed officially into the eucharistic communion of the Church. And they are welcomed there by the chief pastor of the community, the bishop, who prays for God's grace to guide the neophytes, that they might be faithful to what their baptism has already made them to be. In its origins, therefore, what was to become 'confirmation' may simply have been the way in which the baptismal rite was concluded and the eucharist begun in some communities.

Along with these specific ritual details, third-century sources in both East and West also show that infant baptism, including infant communion, since the question is not simply one of 'baptism' but of full 'initiation', was being practised widely. Tertullian strongly cautions against it, and urges that only those 'competent' should be admitted to it (*Bapt.* 18). Origen calls it an 'apostolic custom' (*Comm. Rom.* 5. 9). The *Apostolic Tradition* makes provision for those 'who cannot answer for themselves' (Whitaker and Johnson 2003: 7). And Cyprian gives a theological defence based on the inheritance of the 'disease of death' from Adam (*Ep.* 64). Similarly, Tertullian is the first author to express a preference for initiation taking place either at Easter or during the fifty days of Easter ('for then was accomplished our Lord's passion, and *into it we are baptized*') (Whitaker and Johnson 2003: 10). It may be that something similar is intended in the *Apostolic Tradition*, but since this document refers only to initiation at a vigil, there is no compelling reason to assume that it is the *Easter* vigil, or even necessarily, a *Saturday* night vigil that is meant (Bradshaw, Johnson, and Phillips 2002: 110–11).

In the middle of the third century the churches of Rome and North Africa found themselves involved in an intense controversy about baptism with special regard to the reconciliation of heretics and schismatics who sought to return to the unity of the Church. This controversy began with the 'Novatianist schism', a split in the church at Rome resulting in the establishment of a rival Christian community called the 'Novatianists', which refused to readmit to communion any who had lapsed (i.e. denied the Christian faith) during the recent Decian persecution of 250. Established in 251 in opposition to the church of Rome and its elected bishop Cornelius, who permitted the reconciliation of those who had lapsed after a period of penance, this community, under the leadership of its own bishop, Novatian, saw itself as the legitimate heir to the tradition of the Church. Excommunicated as 'heretical', the continued existence of a Novatianist church raised the question of the validity of the sacraments administered by those outside the unity of the Church, and it is within this context that the real baptismal controversy arose.

Cyprian of Carthage followed what had been the traditional teaching of the North African church (see Tertullian, *Bapt.* 15; Willis 1950; Burns 1993, 2002), and stressed the invalidity of baptism given by heretics and schismatics alike. So strong, in fact, is Cyprian's insistence on the proper and necessary *ecclesiological* context of baptism that he writes: 'he can no longer have God for his Father, who has not the Church for his mother' (*De unitate ecclesiae*, 5). And since baptism itself did not exist outside the Church, 'those who come thence are not *re-baptized* among us, but are baptized' (*Ep.* 71 to Quintus, 1). But it is on this point that Cyprian and Stephen, the bishop of Rome, enter into a profound disagreement, a disagreement that seriously threatened to break off communion between the churches of North Africa and Rome (Burns 2002). According to Cyprian, baptism administered outside of unity with the Catholic Church was invalid, and so had to be repeated for those seeking to come back into unity (Cyprian, *Ep.* 69 to Magnus, 3, 7, and 11; *Ep.* 73 to Jubaianus, 2 and 21). But at Rome those baptized in schism or heresy were merely received back into communion, as in the reconciliation of apostates and penitents, by the imposition or laying on of hands by the bishop. Stephen, in fact, is so adamant about this as the practice to be followed, a practice based, in his opinion, on the authority of St Peter the Apostle himself, that he threatens to break off communion with the North African church if it continues in this 'innovative' manner. This issue remained unresolved in the lifetimes of Cyprian and Stephen, but it would return with a vengeance in Augustine's controversy with Donatism.

34.2 FROM THE COUNCIL OF NICAEA
TO AUGUSTINE

The various cultural and social shifts in the Constantinian era and beyond brought with them the need for the churches to respond to those changing circumstances. One of those responses was the first of several great periods of liturgical reform and renewal in the history of the Church. And our contemporary knowledge of the process and rites of Christian initiation is due, in large part, to the documentary evidence that exists from this period: namely, the extant catechetical homilies of the great 'mystagogues', Cyril of Jerusalem, John Chrysostom, and Theodore of Mopsuestia for the East, and Ambrose of Milan and Augustine of Hippo for the West (Whitaker and Johnson 2003: 26–33, 40–50, 142–52, 176–83; Yarnold 1994).

As recent liturgical scholarship has demonstrated, however, what we see in this first reform or renewal is the development of what has been called 'liturgical homogeneity', wherein through a process of assimilation to the practices of the great patriarchal and pilgrimage churches of the world—for example, Rome, Jerusalem, Alexandria, Antioch, and Constantinople—and through the cross-fertilization of borrowing and exchange, distinctive local practices and theologies disappear in favour of others becoming copied, adapted, and synthesized (Bradshaw 1996). Therefore, what we often appeal to as *the* early Christian pattern for initiation is but the end result of a process of assimilation, adaptation, and change, wherein some of the distinctive and rich theologies and patterns of an earlier period either disappear or are subordinated to others.

As a result of the shift from a private to a public expression of Christian faith in the wake of Constantine's own 'conversion', the subsequent legalization and eventual adoption of Christianity as the official religion of the Roman Empire, the building of shrines and basilicas in the holy places of Jerusalem associated with Christ's passion, the Trinitarian and Christological decisions of the first ecumenical councils, and the end of the age of the martyrs, on account of which a baptismal theology based on Romans 6 could come to the fore (Jeanes 1993), this fourth- and fifth-century 'homogenization' in liturgical practice is easily demonstrated. And, thanks to the extant catechetical homilies noted above, while some local diversity continued to exist, the following came to characterize the overall ritual pattern of baptism throughout the Christian East, with the notable exception of the east Syrian liturgical traditions, and, to some extent, that of Egyptian practice:

1. the adoption of Paschal baptism and the now 40-day season of Lent as the time of pre-baptismal (daily) catechesis on scripture, Christian life, and, especially, the Nicene Creed for the *phōtizomenoi* (those to be 'enlightened');
2. the use of 'scrutinies' (examinations) and daily exorcisms throughout the period of final baptismal preparation;

3. the development of specific rites called *apotaxis* (renunciation) and *syntaxis* (adherence) as demonstrating a 'change of ownership' for the candidates;

4. the development of ceremonies like the solemn *traditio* and *redditio symboli* (the presentation and 'giving back' of the Nicene Creed);

5. the reinterpretation of the once pneumatic pre-baptismal anointing as a rite of exorcism, purification, and/or preparation for combat with Satan;

6. the rediscovery and use of Romans 6 as the dominant paradigm for interpreting the baptismal immersion or submersion as entrance into the 'tomb' with Christ;

7. the introduction of a post-baptismal anointing associated with the gift and 'seal' of the Holy Spirit; and

8. the use of Easter week as time for 'mystagogical catechesis' (an explanation of the sacramental 'mysteries' which the newly initiated had experienced).

While eventually all of the rites of the Christian East would locate or shift the ritualization of the initiatory Spirit gift to a post-baptismal location, with pre-baptismal rites becoming exorcistic and merely preparatory in nature, it is important to note that evidence of the other pattern and interpretation is still discernible in east Syrian sources (Aphrahat and Ephrem), where the ritual pneumatic focus remains the pre-baptismal anointing, and the theology of new birth and adoption remains normative (Whitaker and Johnson 2003: 51–4).

Although a similar overall pattern also existed in the West, western sources display some significant differences, including the fact that the creed of choice for the *traditio* and *redditio symboli* tended more often to be the credal formulae which would become known as the 'Roman' or 'Apostles' Creed' (Westra 2002). Ambrose of Milan witnesses to a post-baptismal rite of foot washing (*pedilavium*) as an integral component of baptism (Whitaker and Johnson 2003: 181). And it is Ambrose who refers to some kind of post-baptismal rite associated with the Holy Spirit as the 'spiritual seal', although scholars have not been able to determine what this was (Yarnold 1994: 34–8; Johnson 1996; Satterlee 2002: 176–80), especially since there is no trace of it in later Milanese sources (Whitaker and Johnson 2003: 183–203). Some sources from Rome (e.g. the *Letter of John the Deacon to Senarius* (Whitaker and Johnson 2003: 208–12)) and North Africa (Augustine (Whitaker and Johnson 2003: 145)) indicate the presence of three public scrutinies (including even physical examinations) held on the third, fourth, and fifth Sundays of Lent. And, thanks to an important fifth-century letter from Pope Innocent I to Decentius of Gubbio (Whitaker and Johnson 2003: 205–6), it is clear that at Rome itself the pattern of post-baptismal episcopal laying on of hands with prayer and second post-baptismal anointing, noted above in the so-called *Apostolic Tradition*, was understood as an essential component of initiation and now associated explicitly with the bishop's prerogative in 'giving' the Holy Spirit. Some have seen a close parallel here with Ambrose's 'spiritual seal', but scholars are not in agreement on this topic at all (Yarnold 1994: 34–8; Johnson 1996; Satterlee 2002: 176–80).

Away from Rome, however, at least until the Carolingian period, the rites of Christian initiation appear not to have contained this unique Roman post-baptismal ceremony, but were full rites of initiation consisting of baptism, anointing, foot washing, and a concluding prayer without any ritual gesture attached (Levesque 1981). Similarly, within various fifth-century local conciliar decrees from both France and Spain one encounters the terminology of *confirmare* ('to confirm') and *perficere* ('to perfect') to refer to something apparently 'done' by the bishop apart from the baptismal rite, that serves to 'complete' baptism. But anachronism in interpreting this terminology must be avoided. That is, as Gabriele Winkler demonstrated, such practices called *confirmare* and *perficere* in these conciliar decrees do not appear to be regular parts of the rites of Christian initiation, but episcopal actions done in extraordinary or irregular situations (e.g. after 'emergency baptisms', at the reconciliation of heretics, or in those situations where chrism had not been obtained from the bishop by presbyters prior to conferring baptism). In addition, Winkler argued that the reference to '*in confirmatione*' ('at confirmation') in canon 2 of Orange was not necessarily a reference to an episcopal 'rite' at all, but to the bishop 'confirming' the local ministries of presbyters during his pastoral visits (Winkler 1984). Winkler's interpretation, notably, has been followed by Gerard Austin (1985) and Aidan Kavanagh (1988) in their own studies of confirmation.

The adoption of several of these ceremonies for the preparation and baptism of candidates was, undoubtedly, the result of the Church seeking to ensure that its sacramental life would continue to have some kind of integrity when, in a changed social and cultural context, in which Christianity was now favoured by the Emperor, authentic conversion and properly motivated desire to enter the Christian community could no longer be assumed automatically. Defective motivations for 'converting' to Christianity included the desire to marry a Christian, as well as seeking after political or economic gain in a society having become increasingly 'Christianized'. And, since it was thought that the forgiveness of sins which baptism conveyed could be obtained only once, with the exception of the one-time post-baptismal 'canonical penance', there was a widespread tendency to *delay* baptism as long as possible, in order to be more sure of winning ultimate salvation. Even Constantine himself was not baptized until he was on his deathbed. Because entry into the catechumenate assured one's status as a Christian, the postponement of baptism became a common practice in this period, and there were those who, like Constantine, remained catechumens for life. Indeed, as the experience of Augustine himself demonstrates (*Conf.* 1. 11), it became common in some places to enrol infants in the catechumenate and then postpone their baptism until later in life, if ever. Similarly, as the rites themselves take on from a Graeco-Roman mystery religions context (e.g. from the Eleusinian Mysteries and the cults of Isis and Mithras) either ritual elements (e.g. periods of instruction, rites of purification, processions, and an emphasis on secrecy, the *disciplina arcani*) or interpretations (references to initiation as an 'awesome mystery', etc.) of the rites which heightened dramatically the experience of those being initiated, the overall intent was surely to impress upon the catechumens and the elect the overall seriousness of the step they were taking (Yarnold 1994: 59–66). It is especially here, with regard to possible parallels with the mystery religions, that the contributions of a ritual studies or anthropologies of ritual have made their contribution by underscoring common human ritual behaviours and social structures.

It is not only the baptismal candidates, however, who seem to have regularly experienced this process. Egeria, the late fourth-century Spanish pilgrim to Jerusalem near the end of Cyril's episcopate, records in her travel diary that, along with the candidates and their sponsors, members of the faithful also filled the church of the Holy Sepulchre in Jerusalem for the daily catechetical lectures of the bishop. 'At ordinary services when the bishop sits and preaches,' she writes, 'the faithful utter exclamations, but when they come and hear him explaining the catechesis, their exclamations are louder...; and...they ask questions on each point.' Further, during the Easter week of mystagogy, she notes that the applause of the newly baptized and faithful 'is so loud that it can be heard outside the church'. Because of this, she states that 'all the people in these parts are able to follow the Scriptures when they are read in church' (Wilkinson 1971: 144–6).

Designed, of course, with adult converts in mind, the overall ritual process of baptism in these several sources was to be short-lived, due, according to John Baldovin, to its success (Baldovin 1991: 167). In other words, it eventually died out, in part at least, because, apparently, it had worked and, for good or ill, the Empire had become 'Christian'! The North African controversy between 'Pelagianism' and Augustine, resulting in Augustine's theological rationale for infant initiation based on a theology of 'original sin', however, would lead to its further decline, even if, in the case of Rome, it would still be contained in the various liturgical books. Nevertheless, one must be cautious here about assuming that infant initiation all of a sudden became a '*quamprimum*' ('as soon as possible') event immediately after Augustine (Cramer 1993: 131–6). The rubrics in the seventh- or eighth-century *Gelasian Sacramentary* and elsewhere continue to assume that parents are to bring their elect infants to the public Lenten scrutinies, now, by this late date, shifted to weekdays and increased to seven in number, before Easter baptism. Of this process the great historian of the catechumenate Michel Dujarier writes:

we must stress that there was a kind of 'catechumenate' for infants. It is interesting to note that, even for babies, the celebration of baptism was not limited to one single liturgical ceremony. The practice of seven scrutinies on the weekdays of Lent developed when there were many infants among the candidates. The testimony of Caesar of Arles in the sixth century is irrefutable: addressing himself to mothers bringing their babies to the scrutinies, he urged them not to miss these celebrations. This custom was undoubtedly a vestige of the tradition of baptizing infants at the same time as adults. . . . This custom also had the great advantage of having the parents of these infants participate in the preparation for baptism. Since the parents 'answered' for their children, it was normal that they make the catechetical and liturgical journey leading to baptism.

(Dujarier 1979: 133)

At the same time, Augustine's lengthy battle with 'Donatism', over the Donatist practice of 'rebaptizing' Catholics and their insistence on the moral character of the baptizer in assuring the validity of baptism in the aftermath of the Diocletian persecution, would lead also to an 'orthodox' sacramental theology based on the use of proper elements and words, with Christ himself underscored as the true sacramental minister. If Augustine himself knew an initiation rite similar to those summarized above (Harmless 1995: 79 ff.), his own theological emphases, born in the heat of controversy, would set the agenda for what I like to refer to as a later western-medieval 'sacramental minimalism' focused on 'matter' and 'form', the 'quamprimum' baptism of infants, and an objective sacramental validity ensured by an 'ex opere operato' understanding.

In spite of the apparent success of this baptismal process in early Christianity, however, we should be careful not to romanticize it today. We have little to corroborate Egeria's perhaps exaggerated description of the apparently large numbers of catechumens and faithful in late fourth-century Jerusalem who gathered to hear Cyril's lectures and who greeted them with thunderous applause. Jerusalem, after all, was a major pilgrimage centre, whose liturgical practices may or may not have been typical of churches elsewhere or everywhere. In other words, while we know that such a baptismal process clearly existed in the Church of this period, we do not know how many people actually went through such an extended catechumenate in preparation for baptism or what the overall ritual shape of 'baptism' was really like away from these major centres. For that matter, even Easter baptism, notes Paul Bradshaw, appears to have been a 'custom' that lasted for only about 50 years in some places, and there is enough evidence to suggest that, even if it remained on the books as the theoretical 'norm', other occasions besides Easter, such as Epiphany, the feasts of particular local martyrs, and even Christmas remained and continued in some places, even in the West, as baptismal occasions (Bradshaw 1993). Our evidence for this 'Golden Age' of baptism, then, is pretty much limited to the practice of the large patriarchal and pilgrimage centres and to surviving texts from their illustrious bishops. Hence, we should not automatically assume that everyone everywhere was doing this, any more than we should assume that actual parish liturgical practice today can be read from liturgical manuals, the texts of our current worship books, or, from exceptional parishes and university churches.

Finally, it should be noted that the study of the rites of initiation in early Christianity is by no means concluded. In particular, study of the Coptic and Ethiopic rites in the Christian East is only in its beginning stages, and with the Ethiopian rite especially there is need for critical editions of texts. Similarly, work on the rites and theologies of Christian initiation in Cappadocia is also in its beginning stages, with my student Nancy Johnson currently writing her doctoral dissertation on post-baptismal sin in Basil of Caesarea, Gregory of Nazianzus, and Gregory of Nyssa. The rites of initiation in Cappadocia are particularly important in relation both to the rites of early Syria and to the developing rites of Armenia in the early period of its history. It seems likely that the Cappadocian rites, like those of Syria and possibly early Egypt, may well have contained only a pre-baptismal anointing, which was pneumatic in orientation.

For the early West, more studies like the recent doctoral dissertation of my student Christian McConnell on Christian initiation in Visigothic Spain (McConnell 2005) and that of my student Michael Whitehouse on hand-laying rites in early Christianity (in progress) are needed. McConnell, for example, has challenged the long-standing scholarly assumption that the *single* baptismal immersion characteristic of Spain was an anti-Arian development, and has argued that it was simply the traditional practice of Spanish Christianity, which received an anti-Arian interpretation later.

In addition to the areas noted above, attention to the overall cultural and social contexts is also needed to balance approaches that have been primarily textual and philological, though this method known as comparative liturgiology remains absolutely essential and cannot be abandoned in favour of a strict social sciences approach. Future study of New Testament and other early texts by various methods will, undoubtedly, reveal an even more variegated ritual process of initiation among different communities, and greater attention to the literature of sectarian Judaism, including the Qumran materials, will assist in our interpretation of not only Christian initiation but other liturgical rites in this period. Indeed, there is plenty to keep scholars of early Christian initiation rites busy for a long time to come.

Suggested Reading

The following are recommended: Austin (1985); Johnson (2007); Kavanagh (1988); Kreider (1999); Whitaker and Johnson (2003); and Yarnold (1994).

See also:

Johnson, M. (1995) (ed.), *Living Water, Sealing Spirit: Readings on Christian Initiation* (Collegeville, Minn.: Liturgical Press, A Pueblo book).

BIBLIOGRAPHY

AUSTIN, G. (1985), *Confirmation: Anointing with the Spirit* (Collegeville, Minn.: The Liturgical Press, A Pueblo book).

BALDOVIN, J. (1991), 'Christian Worship to the Eve of the Reformation', in P. Bradshaw and L. Hoffman (eds.), *The Making of Jewish and Christian Worship* (Notre Dame, Ind.: University of Notre Dame Press), 156–83.

BAUMSTARK, A. (1958), *Comparative Liturgy*, 3rd edn. (London: Newman Press).

BELL, C. (1992), *Ritual Theory, Ritual Practice* (Oxford: Oxford University Press).

BOTTE, B. (1963), *La Tradition apostolique de saint Hippolyte* (Münster: Aschendorff).

BRADSHAW, P. (1989), 'Baptismal Practice in the Alexandrian Tradition: Eastern or Western?', in *idem* (ed.), *Essays in Early Eastern Initiation*, Alcuin/GROW Liturgical Study, 8 (Bramcote and Nottingham: Grove Books, Ltd.), 5–17 [repr. M. Johnson (ed.), *Living Water, Sealing Spirit: Readings on Christian Initiation* (Collegeville, Minn.: Liturgical Press, A Pueblo book, 1995), 82–100].

—— (1993), ' "Diem baptismo sollemniorem": Initiation and Easter in Christian Antiquity', in E. Carr *et al.* (eds.), *Eulogêma: Studies in Honor of Robert Taft, S. J.*, Studia Anselmiana, 110; Analecta liturgica, 17 (Rome), 41–51; repr. M. Johnson (ed.), *Living Water, Sealing Spirit: Readings on Christian Initiation* (Collegeville, Minn.: Liturgical Press, A Pueblo book, 1995), 137–47.

—— (1996), 'The Homogenization of Christian Liturgy—Ancient and Modern: Presidential Address', *Studia Liturgica*, 26: 1–15.

—— (2002), *The Search for the Origins of Christian Worship*, 2nd, enlarged edn. (London: S.P.C.K.).

—— JOHNSON, M., and PHILLIPS, L. E. (2002), *The Apostolic Tradition: A Commentary*, Hermeneia (Minneapolis: Fortress Press).

BURNS, J. PATOUT (1993), 'On Rebaptism: Social Organization in the Third Century Church', *JECS* 4: 367–403.

—— (2002), *Cyprian the Bishop* (London: Routledge).

COLLINS, A. (1989), 'The Origin of Christian Baptism', *Studia Liturgica*, 19: 28–46; repr. M. Johnson (ed.), *Living Water, Sealing Spirit: Readings on Christian Initiation* (Collegeville, Minn.: Liturgical Press, A Pueblo book, 1995), 35–47.

CONNELL, M. (1996), ' "Nisi Pedes" except for the Feet: Footwashing in the Community of John's Gospel', *Worship*, 70/4: 20–30.

CRAMER, P. (1993), *Baptism and Change in the Early Middle Ages, c.200–c.1150* (Cambridge: Cambridge University Press).

DIX, G. (1937), *The Treatise on the Apostolic Tradition of St. Hippolytus of Rome* (London: Alban Press).

DUJARIER, M. (1979), *A History of the Catechumenate* (New York: Saliers).

ELIADE, M. (1958), *Birth and Rebirth: The Religious Meanings of Initiation in Human Culture* (New York: Harper and Brothers).

GRIMES, R. (1992), *Deeply into the Bone: Re-inventing Rites of Passage* (Berkeley: University of California Press).

HARMLESS, W. (1995), *Augustine and the Catechumenate* (Collegeville, Minn.: Liturgical Press, A Pueblo book).

JEANES, G. (1993), 'Baptism Portrayed as Martyrdom in the Early Church', *Studia Liturgica*, 23: 158–76.

JOHNSON, M. (1990), 'From Three Weeks to Forty Days: Baptismal Preparation and the Origins of Lent', *Studia Liturgica*, 20: 185–200; repr. M. Johnson (ed.), *Living Water, Sealing Spirit: Readings on Christian Initiation* (Collegeville, Minn.: Liturgical Press, A Pueblo book, 1995), 118–36.

—— (1995), *Liturgy in Early Christian Egypt*, Alcuin/GROW Liturgical Study, 33 (Cambridge: Grove Books, Ltd.).

—— (1996), 'The Postchrismational Structure of Apostolic Tradition 21, the Witness of Ambrose of Milan, and a Tentative Hypothesis Regarding the Current Reform of Confirmation in the Roman Rite', *Worship*, 70/1: 16–34; repr. M. Johnson, *Worship: Rites, Feasts, and Reflections* (Portland, Ore.: Pastoral Press, 2004), 63–82.

—— (2004), 'Tertullian's "Diem baptismo sollemniorem" Revisited: A Tentative Hypothesis on Baptism at Pentecost', in *idem* and L. E. Phillips (eds.), *Studia Liturgica Diversa: Essays in Honor of Paul F. Bradshaw* (Portland, Ore.: Pastoral Press), 31–44.

—— (2007), *The Rites of Christian Initiation: Their Evolution and Interpretation*. Revised and expanded edn. (Collegeville, Minn.: Liturgical Press, A Pueblo book).

KAVANAGH, A. (1984), 'Confirmation: A Suggestion from Structure', *Worship*, 58: 386–95; repr. M. Johnson (ed.), *Living Water, Sealing Spirit: Readings on Christian Initiation* (Collegeville, Minn.: Liturgical Press, A Pueblo book, 1995), 148–58.

—— (1988), *Confirmation: Origins and Reform* (Collegeville, Minn.: Liturgical Press, A Pueblo book).

KREIDER, A. (1999), *The Change of Conversion and the Origin of Christendom* (Harrisburg, Pa.: Trinity Press International).

KRETSCHMAR, G. (1963), 'Beiträge zur Geschichte de Liturgie, insbesondere der Taufliturgie, in Ägypten', *Jahrbuch für Liturgik und Hymnologie*, 8: 1–54.

LATHROP, G. (1994), 'Baptism in the New Testament and its Cultural Settings', in S. A. Stauffer (ed.), *Worship and Culture in Dialogue* (Geneva: Lutheran World Federation), 17–38.

LEVESQUE, J. (1981), 'The Theology of the Postbaptismal Rites in the Seventh and Eighth Century Gallican Church', *Ephemerides Liturgicae*, 95: 3–43; repr. M. Johnson (ed.), *Living Water, Sealing Spirit: Readings on Christian Initiation* (Collegeville, Minn.: Liturgical Press, A Pueblo book, 1995), 238–58.

McCONNELL, C. (2005), 'Baptism in Visigothic Spain: Origins, Development, and Interpretation' (Ph.D. dissertation, University of Notre Dame).

McDONNELL, K. (1996), *The Baptism of Jesus in the Jordan: The Trinitarian and Cosmic Order of Salvation* (Collegeville, Minn.: Liturgical Press, Michael Glazier).

MILAVEC, A. (2003), *The Didache: Text, Translation, Analysis, and Commentary* (Collegeville, Minn.: Liturgical Press, Michael Glazier).

NIEDERWIMMER, K. (1998), *The Didache: A Commentary*, Hermeneia (Minneapolis: Fortress Press).

RAPPAPORT, R. (1999), *Religion and Ritual in the Making of Humanity: Ritual in the Making of Religious Life* (Cambridge: Cambridge University Press).

SATTERLEE, C. (2002), *Ambrose of Milan's Method of Mystagogical Preaching* (Collegeville, Minn.: Liturgical Press, A Pueblo book).

STAUFFER, S. A. (1994), 'Cultural Settings of Architecture for Baptism in the Early Church', in *idem* (ed.), *Worship and Culture in Dialogue* (Geneva: Lutheran World Federation), 57–65.

TALLEY, T. (1986), *The Origins of the Liturgical Year*, 2nd edn. (Collegeville, Minn.: Liturgical Press, A Pueblo book).

TURNER, P. (1991), 'The Origins of Confirmation: An Analysis of Aidan Kavanagh's Hypothesis', *Worship*, 65: 320–36; repr. M. Johnson (ed.), *Living Water, Sealing Spirit: Readings on Christian Initiation* (Collegeville, Minn.: Liturgical Press, A. Pueblo book, 1995), 238–58.

TURNER, V. (1969), *The Ritual Process: Structure and Anti-Structure* (Chicago: Aldine Publishing Co.).

VAN DE SANDT, H., and FLUSSER, D. (2002), *The Didache: Its Jewish Sources and its Place in Early Judaism and Christianity*, Compendia Rerum Iudaicarum ad Novum Testamentum, 5 (Minneapolis: Fortress Press).

VAN GENNEP, A. (1960), *The Rites of Passage* (Chicago: University of Chicago Press).

WESTRA, L. H. (2002), *The Apostles' Creed: Origin, History, and Some Early Commentaries*, Instrumenta Patristica et Mediaevalia, 43 (Turnhout: Brepols).

WHITAKER, E. C., and JOHNSON, M. (2003), *Documents of the Baptismal Liturgy*, 3rd edn., Alcuin Club Collections, 79 (London: S.P.C.K.).

WILKINSON, J. (1971), *Egeria's Travels* (London: S.P.C.K.).

WILLIS, G. (1950), *Saint Augustine and the Donatist Controversy* (London: S.P.C.K.).

WINKLER, G. (1978), 'The Original Meaning of the Prebaptismal Anointing and Its Implications', *Worship*, 52: 24–45; repr. M. Johnson (ed.), *Living Water, Sealing Spirit: Readings on Christian Initiation* (Collegeville, Minn.: The Liturgical Press, A Pueblo book, 1995), 58–81.

—— (1982), *Das armenische Initiationsrituale*, OrChrAn 217 (Rome: Pontificium Institutum Orientalium Studiorum).

—— (1984), 'Confirmation or Chrismation? A Study in Comparative Liturgy', *Worship*, 58/1: 2–17; repr. M. Johnson (ed.), *Living Water, Sealing Spirit: Readings on Christian Initiation* (Collegeville, Minn.: The Liturgical Press, A Pueblo book, 1995), 202–18.

YARNOLD, E. (1994), *The Awe-Inspiring Rites of Initiation: The Origins of the R. C. I. A.* (Collegeville, Minn.: Liturgical Press).

CHAPTER 35

EUCHARISTIC LITURGY

DANIEL SHEERIN

35.1 EUCHARISTIC NOMENCLATURE

THE *Didache* (composed perhaps as early as *c.* 60 in Antioch; Slee 2003: 97–8) mentions perennial features of the eucharist that came to stand for the eucharistic liturgy as a whole: 'Assembled (*synachthentes*) on the Lord's day, break bread (*klasate arton*) and give thanks' (*eucharistēsate, Did.* 14. 1). Hence the eucharist is called *synaxis*, the name for the eucharistic assembly, 'breaking of bread' (*klasis tou artou, fractio panis*; also 'Lord's supper', *kyriakon deipnon, dominica cena, dominicum convivium*, sometimes reduced to *dominicum*), and, the name applied to both rite and sacrament, eucharist (*eucharistia*), a term for thanks and praise. Other terms in eucharistic nomenclature describe what is done in the eucharist: along with thanksgiving (*eucharistia*), there is the offering (*prosphora, anaphora, oblatio, actio, agenda*) of a sacrifice that is unbloody (*thysia, anaimaktos tēs prosphoras thysia, incruentum sacrificium, incruentam hostiam*), a spiritual sacrifice (*logikē thysia, rationabilis hostia*). A term commonly employed that revealed nothing of the rite but the awe in which it was held is 'mysteries' (*mystēria*), often embellished as 'heavenly and awesome mysteries' (*epourania kai phrikta mystēria*). Other terms were adopted from civic life: for example, '(divine) service' (*theia* or *mystikē*) *leitourgia / officium* (*divinum*), or the word that became the standard term for the eucharistic liturgy in the West, *missa*, whence *missam / missas agere, missarum sollemnia*, etc. (Isidore of Seville, *Etym.* 6. 19. 4; Mohrmann 1961–77, iii. 351–76).

But the term 'eucharist' designated both the ritual and its object, the consecrated bread and wine. These were named from their scriptural antecedents: 'bread from heaven', 'bread of angels', 'coal', 'pearl', 'intoxicating cup'; from their physical appearances: 'the bread and the cup', or called what they were believed to be: 'the body and blood of Christ'. Their nutritional role was emphasized by the terms 'spiritual nourishment' (*spiritualis alimonia, incarnationis Christi ... alimonia*). Their sacred character and divine origin were indicated by terms like 'the holy thing(s)' (*hagion -a / sanctum -a, sanctum domini*), 'the divine gift' (*theion dōron*), and their sacramental character reinforced by reference to the eucharist as the 'symbol' (*symbolon*; the *archisymbolon* for Pseudo-Dionysius (*E.h.* 3. 2. 1), 'type', 'antitype' (*typos, antitypos*), 'figure', 'image', 'likeness' (*figura, imago, eikōn, similitudo*), and 'sacrament' (*sacramentum*) of the body and blood of Christ.

Verbs for the changing of the elements of bread and wine into the body and blood of Christ include 'consecrate' (*hagiazein, consecrare, sanctificare*) and transform (*metaballein, metapoiein, metastoicheioun, transfigurare, mutare, convertere*), all with associated nominal forms, this change being 'the consummation of the mysteries' (*teleiosis mystēriōn*).

Reception and consumption of the eucharist was designated by the ordinary verb 'approach' (*proserchesthai/accedere*), or by verbs for eating and drinking, as in 1 Corinthians 11: 26–9, even 'eating and drinking Christ' (*esthiōn kai pinōn Christon*), or it is described as a 'receiving' (*hypodochē, perceptio, sumptio*), 'partaking' (*metalēpsis, participatio*), or 'sharing' (*koinōnia, communio*).

The eucharistic liturgy, along with the other rites, generated an extensive vocabulary of technical terms for persons, places, times, events, actions, objects, texts, etc., as a *Fachsprache*, or 'Language for Special Purposes' (LSP). This was used mainly by the clergy, but was known in part to ordinary worshippers as well. Various terms for the eucharist are reviewed by Isidore of Seville in *Etymologiae* 6. 18–19 and John of Damascus in chapter 86 of *Expositio fidei*. A modern treatment of western terms can be found in Jungmann (1951: i. 169–75), and of eastern terms in the glossary in Brightman (1896: 568–603) and discussions in Hanssens (1930: ii. 21–41, iii: 181–2).

35.2 THE PRIMITIVE EUCHARIST

Since there is a relative dearth of evidence from before the fourth century, and materials once thought primitive have been found to contain later strata (see *Bradshaw, Johnson, and Philips* (2002), 37–48, on the eucharistic prayer in *The Apostolic Tradition*), reconstructions of the earlier eucharist have to be informed conjectures. Endeavours to explain the primitive eucharist principally on the basis of Jewish rites and prayers, pagan mystery religions, or Graeco-Roman banquets and symposia have been reductionist, as has the assumption that primitive Christian rites were evolutionary antecedents of later 'canonical' liturgical patterns (sketch history of scholarship in Bradshaw 2002: 118–43). Of course the early eucharist adapted familiar elements, but did so selectively, creatively, and, thus, distinctively in a variety of experimental combinations.

What we know of the earliest eucharist must be deduced from brief and often ambiguous references in early Christian literature: Luke 24: 30, 35; Acts 2: 42, 46; 20: 7, 11; 1 Corinthians 10: 16–17, 11: 17–34; *Didache* 9–10, 14; Ignatius of Antioch, *Epistles*; *Acts of Paul* 7; *Acts of John*, 85–6, 109–10; *Acts of Thomas*, 27, 49–50, 133, 158; Justin Martyr, 1 *Apology* 65–7. Biblical accounts of the Last Supper, the so-called institution narrative (1 Cor 11: 23–6; Mk 14: 17–28; Mt 26: 20–9; Lk 22: 14–20) are a case apart, for contemporary scholars describe the institution narrative variously as a gospel account of the Last Supper amplified by the insertion of liturgical formulae, as an aetiological insertion with formulae from contemporary liturgical practice, or as an insertion drawn from eucharistic catechesis (opinion surveyed in Raffa 1998: 35–9; Johnson 2006: 44–6). There is no evidence for the inclusion of the institution narrative in a eucharistic prayer before the fourth century, and contemporary scholarship regards these accounts as neither determinative nor descriptive in detail of earliest practices in the celebration of the eucharist (Bradshaw 2004: 1–23, but also Yarnold 2001). Even so, from earliest times the institution narratives were routinely cited as the warrant and/or injunction for the celebration of the eucharist and as evidence of its divine origin and sacramental character. The importance assigned to the last/mystical supper and to the eucharist in the economy of salvation is summarized by Cyrus of Edessa's assertion that 'the handing on of the Mysteries is the beginning of the dispensation of immortality' (*Explanation of the Pasch*, 5. 12).

Didache 9–10 provides our first specimen of a eucharistic prayer; section 14 offers directions for a Sunday eucharist, and 9 and 14, along with 1 Corinthians 11, provide the earliest regulations for participation in the eucharist: only the baptized are to be given communion (*Did.* 9); communion is to be preceded by examination of conscience (1 Cor 11: 27–8) and confession, and any quarrels are to be mended (*Did.* 14). At this early stage the eucharist was linked to a community meal (*agapē*). However, tensions created by ethnic and socio-economic diversity in the first Christian communities (Acts 6: 1, Jas 2: 1–9) made what Paul called the 'Lord's Supper' problematic early on (1 Cor 11: 20–34). These tensions combined with various other factors led to the separation of *agapē* from the eucharist in the second half of the third century (Bradshaw 2004: 114–15).

Early references to the eucharist exhibit basic features that endured even as understandings of both rite and sacrament changed to adjust to transformations of the Christian community: the use of the material elements of bread and wine; the complex of concepts conveyed by *eucharistia* and *eucharistein*, at once the act, the vehicle, the occasion, and the cause for thanks and praise; the role of the eucharist as a living, participatory, and instrumental memorial of Jesus and his saving work; its function as both symbol and source of unity in the Church (1 Cor 10: 17; *Did.* 9–10); the dangers of unworthy communion (1 Cor 11: 29–32; *Did.* 14); and fulfilment by the eucharist of ancient prophecies and types (*Did.* 14).

35.3 THE EUCHARISTIC LITURGY: ROME, C.150

Justin Martyr's *First Apology*, composed in Rome *c.* 150, provides our first account of the rite of the eucharist and a clear statement of its meaning. The two rites he described, the one used after baptisms (section 65) and the routine Sunday rite (section 67), are linked by an explanation of the eucharist (section 66). The Sunday eucharist consists of the following stages. The faithful assemble. 'The records of the apostles or the writings of the prophets are read as time allows,' and the presider gives a sermon on the readings. The congregation stands and offers common prayers and 'bread…and wine and water' are presented to the presider. He 'sends up prayers and thanksgivings to the best of his ability', which are concluded by the people's 'Amen'. Next comes communion in 'the things over-which-thanks-has-been-given', and these are also distributed through the deacons to those not present (*1 Apol.* 66).

Justin does not identify the presider by title, but that the usual presider was the bishop is strongly suggested by other sources; see, for example, Ignatius of Antioch's insistence on only one eucharistic celebration, presided over by one bishop assisted by presbyters and deacons, or by a presbyter to whom the bishop delegated the task, as the sovereign cure for factionalism (*Eph.* 20.2; *Phil.* 4; *Smyr.* 8. 1).

Justin says that the Christians' name for this food is *eucharistia*, and that communion is restricted to those who share the beliefs of the Christian community, have been baptized, and live as Christ taught; for this *eucharistia* is not ordinary food and drink, but 'we have been taught that the food over which thanks have been given by a word of prayer which is from him … is both the flesh and blood of that incarnate Jesus'.

35.4 THE 'CLASSIC' EUCHARIST

Multiplex changes in the eucharist were among the adjustments required by the dramatic enlargement of the Christian community and the new popular and public character which Christianity assumed after its emancipation and establishment under Constantine. The single, episcopal eucharistic liturgy insisted on by Ignatius could not accommodate the enlarged community, so the number of eucharists and sites for their celebration were multiplied by an expanded sharing of the role of presider with the presbyters (see esp. De Clerck 2005*a*). The eucharist became a public occasion, even an 'event', and its rites and *mise en scène* were altered accordingly, although the better-documented eucharistic rites of the fourth and fifth centuries retained the basic components and order of the eucharist described by Justin variously elaborated and augmented. Here we can review only selected features of what some have called the 'classic' eucharist and invite the reader to consult the liturgical-historical works listed in the bibliography for thorough treatments of the ensemble and its details.

35.4.1 The 'Liturgy of the Word'

Augustine told his congregation: 'When you assemble in church, put away your idle talk. Pay attention to the scripture. We are your books!' (*Serm.* 227; see Sheerin 1992: 34–43). The inclusion of biblical readings in the eucharist was the universal practice, and although this 'liturgy of the word' has received less attention than other aspects of the early Christian eucharist (but see Kaczynski 1974; Mateos 1971), the readings and psalmody were 'sacraments', too—witness, for example, Origen's analogical application to scripture of language and imagery derived from the eucharist (Lies 1978). Some have claimed that primitive practice was a *lectio continua*, that is, a segmented but continuous reading through entire books of scripture. But by the time solid evidence becomes available (fourth century), what we find is the traditional use of fixed readings and responsorial psalms for particular feasts and seasons along with *ad libitum* selection of readings and psalms for all other occasions. Eventually, increase of the number of days with fixed sets of readings and psalms led to the creation of lectionaries for the liturgical year, with local variations occurring in the number, length, and sources of the readings.

Most historical studies of reading practices focus on the individual reader or a 'reading public', and neglect vicarious forms of reading and literacy like liturgical readings (Sheerin 1992; for liturgical readings outside the eucharist, see Taft 1986). Of course, those who could do so were encouraged to read the scriptures in private devotional study, but the illiterate mass of Christians had their only extended encounter with scripture in liturgical settings that were both the venue and a crucial part of the scriptural passages' exegesis. There the people were presented with texts that had been given heightened prominence through selection and performance, and the attentive could absorb them through careful listening to interpretively presented readings, through participation in responsorial psalmody, and through hearing the texts repeated and explained verse by verse by preachers with whom they interacted visually and audibly.

35.4.2 Eucharistic Prayer

Justin Martyr says that the prayers were improvised, according to the traditional content of *eucharistia*, sc., thanks and praise, by presiders who varied in their ability to compose them (Bouley 1981: 111). In the first centuries the main eucharistic prayer (technical term: *anaphora*) was improvised, not with radical freedom, but with certain common themes (thanks and praise for creation, for redemption, for the eucharist) and standard structures: for example, intercessions, *anamnēsis*, and a conclusion that would invite the people's Amen. Fixed forms like those in the *Didache* and the *Apostolic Tradition* were provided for presiders who wanted guidance in the task of improvisation. But in the fourth century both improvised prayers and prayers fixed through writing and memorization were in use, and shortly, although at rates and in ways varying from region to region, efforts to collect and control written prayers led to the imposition of approved written prayers for some or all of the eucharistic rite.

The eucharistic prayer was pronounced audibly, if not to the entire congregation, then at least to those near the celebrant. An edict of Justinian (*Novellae*, 137. 6) requiring audible recitation provides the first indication of what came to be the common practice of reciting the prayer *sotto voce* or in silence, with only the cues for responses being sung aloud (Trembelas 2001). Consecratory power was considered by some to inhere in the prayer itself, hence the stories in John Moschus's *Pratum spirituale* of consecration of the eucharistic elements by the careless recitation of the prayer (citations in 35. 7. 2 below).

The surviving eastern anaphoras, though by no means uniform (sketch of the various 'families' in Gelsi 1992), usually have the following features: introductory dialogue of celebrant with people; celebrant's prayer of thanks and praise leading into the people's chant of the Sanctus; celebrant's prayer elaborating themes of the Sanctus; an institution narrative ending with command to 'remember'; the *anamnēsis* (i.e. memorial; Beitia 2006) which reviews the redemptive actions of Christ; the *epiklēsis* (invocation) summoning the Holy Spirit upon the gifts; intercessions for the living (and in some cases for the dead); most anaphoras have interspersed cues for responses and acclamations by the people, and culminate in a final doxology, which is concluded by the people's Amen, followed in turn by the common recitation of the Lord's Prayer. Eastern anaphoras do not allow for internal adjustment to liturgical feast or season, that being accomplished for the eucharistic liturgy by the readings and psalmody.

Rome, Milan, and associated communities developed anaphoras (*canon, canon actionis, missa canonica*) that had a variable introduction (*praefatio*, collected in

Corpus praefationum, CCSL 161–161D), but only very limited options for alterations to the rest of the eucharistic prayer to accommodate it to the feast and season, that function being performed by readings and psalmody and by variable prayers at other points of the eucharistic liturgy (collected in *Corpus orationum*, CCSL 160–160M). Gallican, Iberian, and Hibernian communities employed both variable pre-Sanctus prayers and longer variable prayers that were part of the corpus of the anaphora (Smyth 2003).

The prayers of the eucharistic liturgy are highly structured documents composed in what amounted to a euchological dialect that was a fusion of biblical and theological language blended with diction, formulae, and structures borrowed from the language of the imperial court and from pre-Christian prayer patterns (Brightman 1896 prints biblical borrowings in uncial type; see also Antoniadis 1939: 89–117; Blaise 1964; Eizenhofer 1954–66; Giraudo 1981; Liver 1979). The frequent citation of these prayers in later theological literature validates the adage *Lex orandi, lex credendi.*

35.4.3 Participants in Eucharistic Celebration

Clergy. Justin mentions only 'the one presiding' and 'those whom we call 'deacons''; but in later sources we encounter the emergent clerical class in their different ranks: bishops, presbyters, and deacons. The liturgical readings prompted the emergence of the lesser clerical order of readers (Quacquarelli 1959; Shiell 2004), and with the development of eucharistic psalmody, the *psaltēs/cantor* emerged as leader and expert in liturgical chant (Foley 1982). All of these figures needed a set of skills obtained through education and experience: a sophisticated literacy, developed vocal skills, a sense of the liturgy so that they would know what was required, what was *ad libitum*, and how to accommodate the ritual to the unexpected. They needed also an effective 'stage presence' to enable them through word and gesture to win and retain the attention of the congregation, especially on the great feasts when, to use Chrysostom's term, *pasa hē polis*, 'the whole city' filled the church (*Homilia 1 in Actorum principium*, 1; this 'presence' could be placed in a negative light: see Gregory of Nazianzus's portrayal of his fellow bishops as vulgar entertainers, *Carm.* 2. 1. 13). Presiders at the eucharist had to be able to improvise the prayers acceptably, or at least to enunciate memorized prayers clearly and intelligently. Augustine urged special catechesis of educated converts so that they would not snigger at the bad grammar and garbled reading of the clergy (*Cat. rud.* 9. 13. 5; cf. John bar Qursus of Tella, Canon 13).

Congregation. The participation of the laity in the eucharist was extensive and essential (John Chrysostom, *Homily 18 on 2 Cor.* 3). Justin mentions only 'Amen' as the response of the congregation, but we learn from authors from Cyprian onward that ancient congregations knew a series of responses, acclamations, and prayers. They learned the literal and figurative meanings of these words as part of their catechesis, and were probably not above parodying them if *Anthologia graeca* 16. 19 is any indication. They took part in responsorial singing of psalms during the eucharist with skill and enthusiasm, a practice defended by Augustine in the lost *Contra Hilarium* (*Retract.* 2. 11). They either knew the postures and gestures appropriate to the different stages of the eucharist, or imitated the movements of the celebrant, or responded to the deacon's directives to be attentive, to stand, to pay attention, to face east, to bow, to kneel, to rise, and, finally, to depart. They could 'approach' for communion 'in order, with reverence and godly fear' (*Apostolic Constitutions*, 2. 57. 21) and participate in the communion psalmody (Schattauer 1983; see also non-scriptural communion antiphons in the *Antiphonary of Bangor*, and pre- and post-communion hymns by Severus of Antioch and John of Kenneshere). They knew the approved way to receive communion in the hand and from the chalice, and to say their 'Amen' to the minister's declaration, for example, 'The body of Christ', 'The blood of Christ' (Lugmayr 1997; Philoxenus of Mabbug, ed. Cody; Caseau 2002: 80–3).

Infants presumably attended the eucharist with their mothers or nurses (one wonders what was the age at which boys joined their fathers or pedagogues in church). Early evidence of infant communion is very slight, Cyprian in the third century being our first and best witness; but from the fourth century onwards, evidence of infant communion is extensive, Augustine urging it as a necessity (*Pecc. mer.* 1. 24. 34; Dalby 2003).

We learn much of how the people were expected to behave at the eucharist from denunciations of their misbehaviour. We have early examples of this from Clement of Alexandria (*Paed.* 3. 11), and Commodian, who included in his *Instructiones* a poem 'Concerning Gossips and Silence' which criticizes people who talk at the eucharist (CCSL 128, 267–8). Celebrated preachers—for example, John Chrysostom, Caesarius of Arles, Jacob of Serûgh—have left sermons complaining of talking business, joking, gossip, acting out of indifference or impatience, lounging about, displaying oneself, ogling others, etc. Chrysostom was complaining about eucharistic assemblies into which the social, economic, professional, and political networks of the city had been imported and flourished (Natali 1985), eucharistic assemblies at which he also expected the presence of choirs of angels and nothing but 'attentive silence and urgent prayers' (*Hom.* 88 *in Mt.* 4).

Preachers also denounced arriving late and leaving early, or skipping worship to attend spectacles. Perceived abuses led to regulation, and so, for example in the churches of Gaul, skipping Mass on a feast-day to attend spectacles was made grounds for excommunication (*Statuta ecclesiae antiqua*, 33) and early departure from Mass was formally forbidden by, for example, a series of Gallican councils (CCSL 148, 212; 148A, 11, 125) and Canon 17 of John bar Qursus of Tella (CSCO 368, 149).

35.4.4 Class and Gender at the Eucharistic Assembly

The early Christian laity were liturgically subordinated to the ordained clergy and even to the professionally religious, as is suggested by, for example, the order for reception of communion mandated by the *Apostolic Constitutions* (redaction *c.* 380 in region of Antioch): bishop, presbyters, deacons, subdeacons, lectors, cantors, ascetics, deaconesses, consecrated virgins, consecrated widows, 'and then the people, in their order, with reverence and godly fear, without disorder' (8. 13. 14). Nor did socio-economic class distinctions become inoperative at the church doors, and though writers and preachers make much of the equal access to communion of all the baptized, equality of status at the eucharistic assembly was surely more ideal than real.

Women were subordinated liturgically to men (Berger 1999). No women could celebrate the eucharist; when we do find female celebrants, it is in the eucharist of heretics, as in Irenaeus's account of the ecstatic eucharist of the Marcosians (*Haer.* 1. 13. 1–3, in Miller 2005: 32–5; but see Power 1991: 13 n. 5). Women were, in fact, barred from all real clerical ministries so they could not read the lessons, lead the singing, nor administer communion (deaconesses were allowed to administer communion to other females and infant males (Martimort 1986: 140, 154, 167), except during their menstrual periods as in, for example, John bar Qursus of Tella, *Profitable and Good Questions*, 36).

The zealous author of *De singularitate clericorum* reassured his celibate male readers that the eucharist was one place where they were safe in the company of women (paras. 13–16). But even so, women were physically separated in church both from the clergy and from laymen: 'the people gather at church in a chaste throng, with a respectable segregation of the sexes' (Augustine, *Civ.* 2. 28). All prospective communicants were expected to wash their hands in lavabos outside the church doors, but in Gaul women communicants were forbidden to touch the eucharist, but had to receive it on a linen cloth, called a *dominicalis*, spread over their hands (Caesarius of Arles, *Serm.* 229. 4; Council of Auxerre, canons 36 and 42).

35.5 FREQUENCY OF THE EUCHARIST

The *Didache* and Justin mention a Sunday eucharist in their communities in the first and the second centuries, but third-century North African sources report both the routine Sunday eucharist and additional eucharists on fast-days (Wednesdays and Fridays) and the anniversaries of the deaths (feast days) of martyrs. Cyprian also reports *ad hoc* eucharistic celebrations in prisons (*Ep.* 5. 2) and private residences. A wary attitude towards celebration of the eucharist apart from the official church is evident in the restriction of domestic eucharists by Canon 2 of the Council of Antioch (341) and Canon 58 among those ascribed to the Council of Laodicea (end of fourth century). But daily communion is approved in the letter ascribed in canonical collections to Basil the Great (*Ep.* 93), but perhaps the work of Severus of Antioch, and Augustine is quite accepting of local diversity in the frequency of eucharistic celebrations and personal diversity in the frequency of communion (*Ep.* 54. 1–5). Celebrations of the eucharist were multiplied in the West to the point that daily masses are reported *c.* 400 in Milan, Spain, and North Africa.

But frequency of reception of communion seems to have declined even as the number of eucharistic celebrations increased. Reception of communion on major feasts only became a widespread practice, due perhaps to religious awe of what Chrysostom called 'the most awesome sacrifice' (*Sac.* 6. 4; Fittkau 1953: 122–7, 131–6), or to the surfeit of frightening warnings against unworthy reception of the eucharist, or to devotional laxity. Whatever the cause, fourth-century synods sought to reform this behaviour through canons that demanded reception of communion by those who attended the eucharistic liturgy (Canon 2 of the Council of Antioch of 341; *Apostolic Constitutions*, 8. 47. 9; the collection called the *Canons of the Holy Apostles* of *c.* 400; and Canon 13 of the First Council of Toledo of 400). However, Canon 18 of the Council of Agde of 506 probably indicates acceptance of common practice in its requiring reception of communion only at Christmas, Easter, and Pentecost.

35.6 COMMUNION APART FROM THE EUCHARISTIC LITURGY

But the pseudo-Basilian letter warns us to distinguish between the frequency of celebrations of the eucharist and the frequency of communion, for the practice of carrying the eucharist to one's home for self-administered communion during the week or in places where access to a eucharistic celebration was difficult was widespread. In fact, 'home communion' survived even into the seventh and eighth centuries in some places and circumstances, although it was forbidden earlier in some regions; for example, Canon 3 of the Council of Saragossa (380) and Canon 14 of Toledo I (400) anathematize anyone who receives the eucharist in church and fails to consume it there.

Justin reports the delivery by deacons of the eucharist to those who were absent from the liturgy, presumably the infirm and ill. It was, presumably, while on an errand like this that the martyr Tarsicius, memorialized in an epigram by Pope Damasus, met his end (no. 15. 6–9; ed. Ferrua 1942: 117). But it was the dying who were thought to be in particular need of communion. Indeed, the practice of placing the eucharist in the mouth of a corpse if death had intervened before communion could be brought had to be forbidden by a series of synodal and conciliar enactments. Although some rigorists barred those guilty of certain very grave sins permanently from communion (e.g. at the Council of Elvira of *c.* 305), Canon 13 of Nicaea I guaranteed communion to the dying, even sinners not yet reconciled to the Church. This communion *in extremis* was designated by a term that in common usage meant money and/or provisions for a journey, *ephodion* or *viaticum* (Volp 2002). The need of the dying for viaticum was anticipated by reserving the eucharist, first in a suitable container in the sacristy, but later upon the altar of the church. Reservation of the eucharist, whether in a home for home communion or in a church for viaticum, provided the occasion both for use of the eucharist as a medicine or talisman in the early Christian period (see 36. 7. 2) and for the later developing cult of the eucharist outside the liturgical setting (Nussbaum 1979; Mitchell 1999).

35.7 TEACHING THE EUCHARIST

35.7.1 Instruction about the Eucharist: The *disciplina arcani*, 'mystagogical' catechesis, and mystagogy

Didactic and paraenetic passages about the eucharist occur everywhere in early Christian literature, in homilies of all types, epistolography, polemic (Irenaeus, Cyprian, Theodoret), apologetics (Macarius of Magnesia, *Monogenēs* 3. 15, 23), and especially in biblical exegesis, where some of the most important presentations of eucharistic doctrine are found (Origen, John Chrysostom, Cyril of Alexandria, Augustine). References to the eucharist are, however, often guarded, because details of the rites of initiation, baptism, chrismation, and eucharist were not to be disclosed to the uninitiated, part of a practice of 'reserve in communicating religious knowledge' to which the name *disciplina arcani* ('practice of secrecy') was given in the early modern period. The practice was clearly in force in the fourth and fifth centuries, although how widely it was observed earlier is a matter of dispute (account of controversy in Jacob 1990). The eucharistic references in the second-century epitaphs of Pectorius of Autun and Abercius of Hierapolis (Guarducci 1978: 487–94, 377–86; trans. in Hamman 1967: 184–5, 184) are quite obscure, and reserve in speaking of the eucharist is evident in the writings of Tertullian, Origen, and Cyprian. But the practice, whatever one calls it, was clearly in force, or treated as being in force, in the fourth and fifth centuries, and preachers used catechumens' ignorance and curiosity about the eucharist as an enticement to baptism (e.g. Gregory of Nyssa, *Adversus eos qui baptismum differunt*, and Augustine, *Serm.* 132).

In the fourth and fifth centuries the principal venue for instruction about the eucharist was in the series of instructions, often called 'mystagogical' catecheses, which were presented to neophytes after their baptism, chrismation, and first communion (Yarnold 1999). Catecheses on the eucharist survive from Ambrose, Augustine, Cyril of Jerusalem, Gaudentius of Brescia, Gregory of Nyssa, John Chrysostom, Narsai, Theodore of Mopsuestia, and various anonymous figures. Catechesis on the eucharist explained its role in sacred history and in the lives of individuals, described and commented on features of the eucharistic rites, including the people's responses and, in some cases, even described the correct form for receiving communion (Lugmayr 1997, and Philoxenus of Mabbug, ed. Cody).

When formal mystagogical catechesis disappeared as adult baptism became uncommon, the summarizing of eucharistic doctrine was continued in encyclopaedic works like John of Damascus's *Expositio fidei* (para. 86), which was widely read in both East and West. The earlier catechesis on the rites of the eucharist was replaced by aetiological accounts of them like Isidore of Seville's influential *De ecclesiasticis officiis* and by allegorical exegesis of the rites in documents commonly called 'mystagogies'. Origen had envisioned application of allegorical exegesis to the rites of the church (e.g. *Hom. 5 in Num.* 1. 4); such interpretations are alluded to in catecheses generally, and are used extensively in those by Theodore of Mopsuestia. The mystagogies contain more systematic treatments of the rites in the form of detailed descriptions (*historia*, the literal level) followed by a discussion (*theōria*, contemplation) that include, in varying mixtures, typology, moralizing interpretations, rememorative allegories that recall the events of salvation history (Maximus the Confessor), and anagogic interpretations that relate the rites to the mystical life of the soul or to the life to come (Pseudo-Dionysius the Areopagite). The clergy were also informed about eucharistic 'best practices' through the circulation of authoritative opinions in question–answer format (*erōtapokriseis*, by Basil of Caesarea, Anastasius of Sinai, John of Tella).

35.7.2 Eucharistic Doctrine

Ancient Christian authors created a pre-history for the eucharist from the types and prophecies of which it was considered the fulfilment, and from events in Jesus' ministry regarded as propaedeutic to the eucharist. Biblical texts applied to the eucharist were collected in *testimonia* collections, from Cyprian's *Ad Quirinum* 1. 22, 2. 2, 3. 26, 94, to Isidore of Seville's *De fide catholica ex veteri et novo testamento*, *contra Iudaeos*, 2.27. Figures, objects, and actions—for example, the sacrifice of Abel (Gen 4: 4), Noah's grapes (Gen 9: 20–7), the offering of bread and wine by Mechisedek (Gen 14: 18 and Ps 109: 4b), the sacrifice of Abraham (Gen 22: 1–18), the passover meal (Ex 12), the manna (Ex 16), the flour offering (Lev 14: 10), the showbread (Ex 25: 30; 1 Sam 21), and the cluster of grapes (Num 13: 24–7)—are cited or alluded to *passim* as types of the eucharist (see Daniélou 1956). Prophetic texts include many verses from the Psalms, esp. Pss 22, 33: 9, and 77: 20 (and Wis 16: 20), Wisdom's banquet in Prov 9: 1–5, Isaiah's coal (Isa 6: 6), and Malachy's prophecy of a universal sacrifice (Mal 1: 10b–11). Gospel anticipations of the eucharist include the feast at Cana, the multiplication of the loaves, and Jesus's 'bread of life' discourse in John 6: 31–59.

The eucharist did not receive the sort of precise and thorough dogmatic formulation elaborated for other points of doctrine. It does figure significantly in treatments of Christology, soteriology, and ecclesiology, but usually as a firm point of agreement to which controverted matters are referred, although the eucharist is considered to have been the flashpoint in the controversy between Cyril of Alexandria and Nestorius (Chadwick 1951; Welch 1994; Kilmartin 1998: 32–58). Strong assertions about eucharistic doctrine and practice occur in denunciations of the views and rites of non-Christians (e.g. Manichees, Gnostics; Grillmeier 1975, 1997; DuBois 1999) and of non-standard practices of Christians (see 35. 8. 2 below). Differing perceptions of the eucharist manifested themselves as preferences for particular terms and formulations, depending on whether one's emphasis was Christ's historical body, his glorified body, or his ecclesial body, or whether the identity of the eucharist with the body and blood of Christ is simply asserted or expressed variously in terms of sacramental mediation.

But one finds basic unanimity, both diachronic and synchronic, about fundamental eucharistic doctrine. Though baptism incorporated one into the body of Christ, regular communion in the body and blood of Christ through the eucharist was considered necessary to sustain the Christian life, and so the eucharist was the only one of the 'sacraments' of initiation that could be repeated. To live without regular reception of the eucharist, by choice or by prohibition, was to be deprived of 'communion', of membership in the Church, and for that ecclesial community, the eucharist was at once the representation, the manifestation, the fact, and the cause of its unity. Augustine elaborated 1 Corinthians 12: 27 in this way: 'If, then, *you are the body of Christ*, it is your sacrament that has been placed on the altar. You receive your sacrament. You answer, "Amen" to what you are, and by your response you give this fact your endorsement' (*Serm.* 272). Augustine asserted the absolute necessity of both baptism, which, he says, Punic Christians called 'salvation', and communion in the eucharist, which they called 'life', for incorporation into the body of Christ and so for eternal salvation (*Pecc. mer.* 1. 20. 27, 1. 24. 34), but Quodvultdeus of Carthage's corrective that baptism alone was required became the orthodox position and circulated widely under Augustine's name (*Ep.* 12. 26; under Augustine's name in Gratian, *Decretum*, De consec. 2. 136, 4. 131, and in Peter Lombard, *Sententiae* 4. 9. 1. 3).

For the individual, the eucharist was, in the remarkable formulation of Ignatius of Antioch, 'the medicine of immortality and an antidote, that we not die, but live forever in Jesus Christ' (*Eph.* 20. 2). According to Cyril of Jerusalem, the communicant's ingesting the body of Christ made him same-body and same-blood with Christ (*Catech* 4. 3). Through this transformation, the eucharistic flesh of Christ became, as Cyril of Alexandria insisted, at once the instrument and guarantee of eventual immortality. In John of Damascus's doctrinal summary, the benefits conferred by the eucharist are 'the forgiveness of sins...eternal life...the safeguarding of soul and body' (*F.o.* 86).

We may catch a view of unsophisticated attitudes towards the eucharist and eucharistic liturgy in the following anecdotes: the ailing Gorgonia, Gregory of Nazianzus's sister, 'anointed' herself with the eucharist (*Or.* 8. 18) and Ambrose's brother Satyrus used the eucharist as a lifebuoy (*De excessu fratris*, 1. 46); in stories of visions of angels or demons attending the eucharistic liturgy, for example, John Chrysostom, *On the Priesthood*, 6. 4, John Moschus, *Pratum spirituale*, 199, *Historia monachorum*, 25. 2–3, Rufinus, *Historia monachorum*, 29. 4. 14–15, and *Apophthegmata patrum*; in accounts of the unintended consecration of the elements simply through the recitation from memory of the eucharistic prayer, for example, John Moschus, *Pratum spirituale*, 25, 196, but see Augustine, *Contra litteras Petiliani*, 2. 30. 68–9; and in trials by ordeal of the eucharistic as proofs of orthodoxy, for example, John Moschus, *Pratum spirituale* 25, 29, 79, 196.

35.8 REGULATING THE EUCHARIST

35.8.1 Access

Didache 9 denies participation in the eucharist to the unbaptized, citing Matthew 7: 6a: 'But let no one eat or drink of your thanksgiving (*eucharistia*) but those who have been baptized in the name of the Lord. For about this also the Lord has said, "Do not give what is holy to dogs."' But *Didache* 14 demands of the baptized that they confess their transgressions before communicating, and excludes any engaged in public quarrels, and Justin reports similar restrictions of access to communion. Detailed discussions of the correct dispositions for receiving communion were later provided by Basil of Caesarea (*Regula brevius tractata*, 172) and Augustine (*Ep.* 54).

But the non-baptized who were excluded from communion included not only non-Christians, but increasing numbers of Christian catechumens who postponed baptism, and by the third century one finds the division of the eucharistic liturgy into the two parts which eventually came in the West to be called the 'Mass of the Catechumens' and the 'Mass of the Faithful' (sc. the baptized). The initial prayers, readings, and sermon were open to the not-yet-baptized and even to non-believers (Canon 16 of the *Statuta ecclesiae antiqua* of *c.* 475; cf. first canon of the Council of Valencia in 546). But catechumens and strangers were ejected from the church before the community proceeded to the eucharistic prayer and communion, which were accessible only to the baptized.

But the baptized, too, could be barred from communion because of their beliefs (heretics), professions (e.g. charioteers, actors), or scandalous lives (many varieties), and for such as these, conversion, confession, and public penance had to precede readmission to communion. Even Christians in good standing created temporary impediments to their receiving communion if they broke the required pre-communion fast, or if the day for communion fell within their menstrual period (Taft 2001*b*: 74–9), or if they had experienced a nocturnal emission the night before, or, if married, had failed to observe sexual continence immediately before communion.

35.8.2 'Matter and Form'

Later documents in the canonical literature provide an overview of forbidden and, by implication, approved practices affecting the eucharist. Canon 2 of the Third Council of Braga of 675 contains a catalogue of abuses connected with material form and ministration of the eucharist. The Pseudo-Basilian *Sermo ob sacerdotum instructionem* (probably of Alexandrian origin) likewise contains a collection of directives to priests on how and with whom to celebrate the eucharistic liturgy and on care of the eucharist and its vessels, as does the first part of Bishop John bar Qursus of Tella's *Profitable and Good Questions* (Menze 2004: 15–16). The canons of the Council 'in Trullo' of 691 contain accumulated regulations of access and practice.

35.9 THE EUCHARIST IN MATERIAL CULTURE

The eucharist was a sacramental gift for sacramental people. Many ancient authors present the eucharist as an extension of the Incarnation, as a divine condescension to human materiality: for example, John Chrysostom: 'He would have given you incorporeal gifts unclothed, but because the soul is mingled with the body, He gives you things spiritual in things that are sensible' (*Hom 82 in Mt.* 4). Eventually, the eucharistic liturgy, with gospel book, altar, gold and silver ornaments and vessels, and the body and blood of the Lord became a central arguing point in John of Damascus's defence of the material (*Contra imaginum calumniatores*, 1. 16, 2. 14).

Bread and a cup of wine mixed with water came to be the standard—indeed, the required—material of the eucharist, and alternative practices, use of water alone, use of bread and cheese, use of wine alone were declared heretical (Gaïse 2001: 86–93, 130–45). In time, the bread was given special form through the use of eucharistic bread stamps (Galavaris 1970). Vessels for bread and wine, patens and chalices, and associated ritual objects, ewers, flabella, etc., ranged in quality and sophistication from the plain to highly wrought productions in precious metals (Dodd 1973; Mango 1986; Leader-Newby 2004), costly objects that in times of distress could be broken up and coined to relieve the poor (Ambrose, *Off.* 2. 137–43 and Davidson's extensive note *ad loc.*). The liturgy of the word required books, and so the capacity to produce books, whether plain codices or masterpieces of calligraphy and illustration enclosed within precious book-covers (Gamble 1995; Di Berardino 1996; Palazzo 1998). Primitive tables became altars placed on elevated structures, with associated furnishings (Nussbaum 1965). The growth of the worshipping community made the 'house church' obsolete, and brought on the basilica with its grounds and outbuildings as a dedicated site for the eucharist and other liturgical and ecclesiastical events. This space reflected its uses, with places set apart for the church's treasures and stores, for social services, and for worship. Before the doors of the church were basins in which those entering could wash their hands (*DACL* i. 104–5) and space for the poor and handicapped, so that churchgoers' almsgiving could wash the hands of their souls (John Chrysostom, *Poenit.* 4. 2). The forecourt also provided a space where the catechumens could wait after they had been dismissed and the church doors closed. The interior space was subdivided by elevations, curtains, chancel screens, and barriers that facilitated crowd control and provided a physical delineation of the hierarchical distinction between the clergy in their several ranks, laymen, and women.

The church building and the liturgy were considered to be 'types' of heaven, both vertically, as an earthly replica of heaven in which the eucharist was conducted as a participatory imitation of heavenly worship, and horizontally (historically), that is, they had been prefigured by the types in the Law and, in turn, were themselves prefigurations of the good things to come.

All turned out for the eucharist in their prototypical 'Sunday best', the garments of the clergy being for a long time much the same as those of the laity. Tendencies towards the differentiation and aggrandizement of clerical liturgical dress were opposed, for example, by Augustine and Celestine I (*Ep.* 4. 1), but distinctive vestments and their allegorical interpretation are already subjects of Theodore of Mopsuestia's catechetical homilies at the end of the fourth century. Pavan (1992) asserts that liturgical dress became decidedly distinctive when its cut and style became obsolete, but the clergy also elaborated the cut, material, and ornamentation of vestments in keeping with the protocols of splendour, awe, and mystery that were developing around the eucharist (Braun 1907; Papas 1965; Kalamara 2002).

As for layfolk's dress, it seems reasonable to suppose that those who could afford to do so devoted a lot of attention and expense to the costumes they wore for their public appearances at the eucharist, for church was a place to see and be seen, and luxurious dress invited invective against luxury at the expense of the poor (e.g. John Chrysostom, *Hom. in 2 Thess.* 3. 3). The routine clerical censures of the women's elaborate make-up, perfume, coiffure, jewellery, dress, and manners were occasioned principally by their smart appearance in church. Nor were the clergy the only critics: the poet Commodian composed a satiric portrait of a talkative church-goer who, while the celebrant 'is entreating the Most High on behalf of His devoted people, that not any of them be lost', is 'chatting away with a grin on your face or criticizing the appearance of the woman next to you' (CCSL 128, 68).

The eucharistic liturgy became, especially in urban settings, a powerful multi-sensory experience (Howes 2006) in an optimal setting of internal architectural features and furnishings of a quality seen elsewhere only in public buildings and palaces, of splendid paintings and mosaics, lighted appropriately to mystery and display of splendour (Potamianos 2000), and, from the late fourth century onwards, perfumed by incense (Harvey 2006). The churches became spectacular settings for spiritual spectacles that could compete with court and circus, and the allegorical interpretations of mystagogy endowed their splendours and the entire web of material culture in which the eucharist was situated with a sacramental character and meaning.

35.10 AREAS FOR NEW RESEARCH

35.10.1 Eucharistic Discourse

Study of the performative aspects of liturgical language (e.g. Scherman 1987) is only one example of the application of discourse analysis that could be adapted to the ancient Christian eucharist. All the prayers and texts of the eucharist and the context of the eucharistic assembly would benefit from socio-linguistic study. For example, Gregory of Nyssa challenged those who postponed their baptism: 'Be made one with the people of the mystery and learn the unutterable words; join us in singing those words which the six-winged Seraphim, too, sing along with the full-fledged Christians' (*Adversus eos qui baptismum differunt* (GNO 10.2, 362)). We could ask: How did his addressees understand this? Into what socio-linguistic entity was he inviting them? And many questions besides. But to reconstruct early Christian discourse(s) of the eucharist, we really should go beyond liturgical texts and discursive contexts, beyond technical and semi-technical eucharistic language, to include the entire spectrum of discursive modes used in talking about, and in keeping silent about, the eucharist.

35.10.2 Performance Theory

The necessarily loose concatenation of approaches that is performance theory is obviously applicable to the study of the early Christian eucharist (discussions of ritual and performance in Couldry 2003; Grimes 2004, and application of performance theory to medieval rituals in Morrill, Ziegler, and Rodgers 2006). Both congregation and clergy were both audience and performers, and we must ask who were the real arbiters who had to be satisfied with the liturgy. Moreover, if we extend the idea of performance beyond the obvious, we must be ready to consider the eucharistic liturgy as the venue for multiple personal performances of social identities. Consider, for example, the 'performances' described in John Chrysostom's account of the entrances into church of a wealthy woman in her finery and of a wealthy man with his entourage (*Hom. 3 in 2 Thess.* 3; Leyerle 2001: 58–9).

35.10.3 Spectacle Studies

Denunciation of the spectacles, theatre, circus, etc., of contemporary society is a commonplace of early Christian literature. One reason for this was the competition posed by spectacles to liturgical services: 'when they are in the very church', writes Salvian of Marseilles, 'if they hear the games are on, they abandon the church...We leave Christ on the altar to commit adultery of the eyes in the fornication of disgraceful shows' (*Gub.* 6. 6. 38). Modern scholarship (e.g. Pasquato 1976; Hartney 2004) has described virtuoso preaching and the cult of the martyrs as 'alternative' spectacles, and a similar approach could be taken to the eucharistic liturgy. There was splendour in space and its décor, a cultivated aura of mystery and awe, a variety of media: chanting, reading, preaching, praying, and silence (Bruneau 1972); choreographed movements and gestures; varieties of mode of participation from respectful silence, to verbal participation, to actual communion. Indeed, the responses and acclamations of the congregation could be seen as parallel to those of throngs at spectacles and civic occasions (described in Aldrete 1999).

35.10.4 The Composition of the Eucharistic Assembly and Foci of its Attention

An analysis of what the ancient sources tell us about early Christian eucharistic assemblies along lines suggested by contemporary techniques for the analysis of audiences (e.g. McQuail 1997; Ruddock 2001) would be worth the attempt. A related endeavour would be a rigorous application of analyses of attention and distraction (Styles 2005) to ancient liturgical assemblies with their multiple simultaneous claims on individual and collective attention, to see how the ministers went about claiming and holding the attention of the congregation, to see whether that attention corresponds to concepts of attention in later psychologies and spiritualities.

SUGGESTED READING

An orientation can be obtained from solid encyclopaedia articles like those by Dassmann, Duval, Geki, Hamman, and Pavan in Di Berardino (1992); from essays like those by Baldovin, Chaillot, and Johnson in Wainwright and Westerfield Tucker (2006); and articles in Jones *et al.* (1992).

Basic texts have been collected by Quasten (1935–7) and Di Nola (1997–2000, Greek and Latin text with facing-page Italian translations); many of these are available in English in Sheerin (1986). The standard collection of eucharistic prayers (in Greek and Latin, with Latin translations of those in Eastern languages) is Hänggi and Pahl (1998); English translations are available in Jasper and Cuming (1987), 7–173. Texts on liturgical music have been collected and translated by James McKinnon (1987). Study of the ancient texts should be accompanied by careful reading of the essays in Chupungco (1999) and of standard liturgical historical works like Jungmann (1951–5) and the volumes of Taft's *History of the Liturgy of St. John Chrysostom* (1991, 1994, 2000).

Many will wish to develop familiarity with the eucharistic liturgy of particular places and times, and some studies cited in the Bibliography will help with this: Africa: Gutiérrez-Martin (2001), Harmless (1995), Marini (1989), Saxer (1969); Antioch: Baur (1959–60), Cuming (1990), Natali (1985), Slee (2003), van de Paverd (1970); Constantinople: Baur (195–60), Mathews (1971), Taft (1991, 1994, 2000), van de Paverd (1970); Egypt: Giamberardini (1957), Johnson (1995); Gaul: De Clerck (2005*b*) Smyth (2003); Ireland: Evans (1996), Kennedy (2005); Jerusalem: Baldovin (1989), Drijvers (2004); Milan: Schmitz (1975); Rome: Metzger (1999), Nocent (1999), Willis (1994); Spain: Carpin (1993), Godoy Fernández (1995), Ramis (2005); Syria: Maniyattu (1995), Menze (2004), Murray (2006), Yousif (1984).

Bibliography

Primary sources

Collections

Aubreton, R., and Buffière, F. (1980) (eds. and trans.), *Anthologie grecque*, xiii (Paris: Société d'Édition "Les belles lettres").

Brightman, F. E. (1896), *Liturgies Eastern and Western*, i (Oxford: Clarendon Press).

Cabrol, F., and Leclercq, H. (1900–13), *Reliquiae liturgicae vetustissimae: ex Ss. Patrum necnon Scriptorum Ecclesiasticorum*, 2 vols., Monumenta Ecclesiae liturgica (Paris: Firmin-Didot). Extensive general index, ii. 243–72.

Di Nola, G. (1997–2000), Bibliotheca Patristica Eucharistica, 4 vols. (Vatican City: Libreria Editrice Vaticana): i: *La dottrina eucaristica di Giovanni Crisostomo*; ii: *La dottrina eucaristica di Sant'Agostino*; iii: *La dottrina eucaristica dei secoli I–IV: Clemente Romano— Atanasio*; iv: *La dottrina eucaristica dei secoli I–IV: da Afraate il saggio a Didimo il cieco*.

Guarducci, M. (1978), *Epigrafi sacre pagane e cristiane*, Epigrafia greca, 4 (Rome: Istituto poligrafico dello stato).

Hamman, A. (1967), *The Mass: Ancient Liturgies and Patristic Texts* (Staten Island, NY: Alba House).

Hänggi, A., and Pahl, I. (1998) (eds.), *Prex Eucharistica*, Spicilegium Friburgense, 12, 3rd edn. (Freiburg: Universitätsverlag).

Jasper, R. C. D., and Cuming, G. J. (1987) (eds.), *Prayers of the Eucharist, Early and Reformed*, 3rd edn., rev. and enlarged (New York: Pueblo).

Joannou, P. P. (1962–4), *Discipline générale antique*, Fonti / Pontificia commissione per la redazione del codice di diritto canonico orientale [ser. 1] fasc. 9, 4 vols. (Grottaferrata (Rome): Tipografia Italo-Orientale 'S. Nilo').

Madigan, K., and Osiek, C. (2005) (eds.), *Ordained Women in the Early Church: A Documentary History* (Baltimore: Johns Hopkins University Press).

Martinez Diez, G., and Rodriguez, F. (1966) (eds.), *La colección canónica Hispana 4: Concilios Galos, Concilios Hispanos*, Monumenta Hispaniae Sacra, Series canónica, 1. 4 (Madrid: Consejo Superior de Investigaciones Científicas, Instituto Enrique Flórez).

Mansi, G. D. (1759–98), *Sacrorum conciliorum nova et amplissima collectio* (repr. Paris: H. Welter, 1901–27).

McKinnon, J. (1987) (ed.), *Music in Early Christian Literature* (Cambridge: Cambridge University Press).

Miller, P. C. (2005), *Women in Early Christianity: Translations from Greek Texts* (Washington D.C.: Catholic University of America Press).

Munier, C. (1963), *Concilia Galliae*, CCSL 148–148A (Turnhout: Brepols).

—— (1974), *Concilia Africae a.345–a.525*, CCSL 149 (Turnhout: Brepols).

Quasten, J. (1935–7), *Monumenta eucharistica et liturgica vetustissima*, Florilegium Patristicum, 7 (Bonn: Peter Hanstein).

Sheerin, D. (1986), *Eucharist*, MFC 7 (Wilmington, Del.: Michael Glazier).

Stewart-Sykes, A., and Newman, J. H. (2001) (eds.), *Early Jewish Liturgy: A Sourcebook for Use by Students of Early Christian Liturgy*, Joint Liturgical Studies, 51 (Cambridge: Grove Books).

Vives, J., Marín Martínez, T., and Martínez Díez, G. (1963) (eds.), *Concilios visigóticos e hispano-romanos, España cristiana*, Textos i (Barcelona: Consejo Superior de Investigaciones Científicas, Instituto Enrique Flórez).

Yarnold, E. (1994), *The Awe-Inspiring Rites of Initiation: The Origins of the R.C.I.A.*, 2nd edn. (Collegeville, Minn.: Liturgical Press).

Individual authors/texts

Abraham bar Lipeh, *Interpretatio officiorum*, ed. and trans. R. H. Connolly, CSCO 72, (Louvain: Secrétariat du Corpus SCO, 1953), 163–80; 76 (Louvain: Secrétariat du Corpus SCO, 1960), 151–66.

Ambrose, *De officiis*, ed. with intro., trans., and comm. I. J. Davidson (Oxford: Oxford University Press, 2001).

—— *De sacramentis*, ed. B. Botte, 2nd edu., SC 25bis (Paris: Éditions du Cerf, 1980); trans. in Yarnold (1994), 99–153.

Apophthegmata patrum, PG 65.

Anastasius of Sinai, *Quaestiones et responsiones*, ed. M. Richard and J. A. Munitiz, CCSG 59 (Turnhout: Brepols, 2006), esp. nos. 39–41, 64, 67, and App. 10ab, 11–3, 17.

Apostolic Constitutions, ed. M. Metzger, SC 320, 329, 336 (Paris: Éditions du Cerf, 1985–7).

The Apostolic Tradition, ed. P. Bradshaw, M. E. Johnson, and L. E. Phillips, in *The Apostolic Tradition: A Commentary* (Minneapolis: Fortress, 2002).

Augustine, *De catechizandis rudibus*, ed. I. B. Bauer, CCSL 46 (Turnhout: Brepols, 1959), trans. J. P. Christopher, ACW 2 (Westminster, Md.: Newman Press, 1946).

—— *De civitate dei*, ed. B. Bombart and A. Kalb, CCSL 47–8 (Turnhout: Brepols, 1955).

—— *De peccatorum meritis et remissione*, ed. C. F. Urba and J. Zycha, CSEL 60 (Vienna: Tempsky, 1913); trans. R. J. Teske, in WSA I/23 (1967).

—— *Ep. 54 (Ad inquisitiones Ianuarii 1)*, ed. A. Goldbacher, CSEL 34/1 (Vienna: Tempsky, 1895), 158–68; trans. R. J. Teske, in WSA II/1 (2001), 210–14.

—— *Retractationes*, ed. A Mutzenbecher, CCSL 57 (Turnhout: Brepols, 1984).

—— *Sermo* 227, ed. S. Poque, SC 116 (Paris: Éditions du Cerf, 1966), 234–43; trans. in Sheerin (1986), 96–9.

The Antiphonary of Bangor: An Early Irish Manuscript in the Ambrosian Library at Milan, ed. F. E. Warren, Henry Bradshaw Society, 4, 10 (London: Henry Bradshaw Society, 1893, 1895).

Basil of Caesarea, *De spiritu sancto*, ed. B. Pruche, 2nd edn. SC 17bis (Paris: Éditions du Cerf, 2002); *On the Holy Spirit*, trans. D. Anderson (Crestwood, NY: St Vladimir's Seminary Press, 1980).

—— *Regula brevius tractata*, Interr. 172, PG 31. 1196; trans. Rufinus, PL 103: 535–6; trans. in A. M. Silvas, *The Asketikon of St. Basil the Great* (Oxford: Oxford University Press, 2005), 365–6.

Ps-Basil (Severus of Antioch?), *Ep.* 93, ed. P. P. Joannou, in *Discipline générale antique*, iii. 191–3; trans. A. C. Way, *Basil of Caesarea: Letters*, FC 13 (New York: Fathers of the Church, Inc., 1951), 208–9.

Pseudo-Basil, *Sermo ob sacerdotum instructionem*, CPG 2933, ed. P. P. Joannou, in *Discipline générale antique*, iii. 187–91, FC.

Celestine I, *Ep.* 4, PL 50. 430–6.

CLEMENT OF ALEXANDRIA, *Paedagogus*, ed. H.-I. Marrou, SC 50, 108, 158 (Paris: Éditions du Cerf, 1960–70); trans. S. P. Wood FC 23 (New York: Fathers of the Church, Inc., 1954).

COMMODIAN, *Instructiones* 76, ed. J. Martin, CCSL 128 (Turnhout: Brepols, 1960) 267–8; trans. R. E. Wallis ANF 4.

CYPRIAN, *Ad Quirinum*, ed. R. Weber, CCSL 3. 1 (Turnhout: Brepols, 1972); trans. A. F. Wallis, ANF 5.

——*Epistularium*, ed. G. F. Diercks, CCSL 3AB (Turnhout: Brepols, 1994–6); trans. G. W. Clarke, ACW 43, 44, 46, 47 (New York: Newman Press, 1984–9).

PS-CYPRIAN, *De singularitate clericorum*, ed. W. Hartel, CSEL 3. 3 (Turnhout: Brepols, 1871), 274–82.

CYRIL OF JERUSALEM, *Catecheses mystagogicae*, ed. A. Piédagnel, SC 126 (Paris: Éditions du Cerf, 1966); trans. E. Yarnold, in *Cyril of Jerusalem* (London: Routledge, 2000), 169–87.

CYRUS OF EDESSA, *Six Explanations of the Liturgical Feasts: An East Syrian Theologian of the Mid Sixth Century*, ed. and trans. W. J. Macomber, CSCO 355–6, Scriptores Syri, 155–6 (Louvain: Secrétariat du Corpus SCO, 1974).

DAMASUS, *Epigrammata Damasiana*, ed. A. Ferrua, Sussidi allo Studio delle antichità cristiane, 2 (Vatican City: Pontificio Istituto di Archeologia cristiana, 1942).

Didache, ed. W. Rordorf and A. Tuiliei, SC 248bis (Paris: Éditions du Cerf, 1978).

PS.-DIONYSIUS THE AREOPAGITE, *De ecclesiastica hierarchia*, iii, PG 3. 423–46; in *Pseudo-Dionysius: The Complete Works*, trans. C. Luibheid (New York: Paulist Press, 1987), 210–24.

FULGENTIUS OF RUSPE, *Ep.* 12, ed. J. Fraipont, CCSL 91 (Turnhout: Brepols, 1968), 362–81; trans. R. Eno, FC 95 (Washington D.C.: Catholic University of Press, 1997), 476–96.

GABRIEL OF QATAR, *Commentary on the Liturgy*, ed., trans., comm. S. P. Brock, *Hugoye* 6. 2 (July 2003), <http://syrcom.cua.edu/Hugoye/Vol6No2/HV6N2Brock>.

GEORGE, BISHOP OF THE ARABS, *Explanation of the Mysteries of the Church*, in R. H. Connolly and H. W. Codrington (eds. and trans.), *Two Commentaries on the Jacobite Liturgy* (London: Williams & Norgate, 1913).

PS.-GERMANUS OF PARIS, Epistle 1, ed. Ph. Bernard, CCCM 187 (Turnhout: Brepols, 2007), 337–52; trans. in Sheerin (1986), 127–36.

GRATIAN, *Decretum*, ed. Æ. Friedburg, Corpus iuris canonici, 1 (Leipzig: Bernhard Tauchnitz, 1879).

GREGORY OF NYSSA, *Adversus eos qui baptismum differunt*, ed. H. Polack, GNO (Leiden: E. J. Brill, 1996), (10. 2) 355–70.

——*Oratio catechetica magna*, ed. E. Mühlenberg, GNO 3. 4 (Leiden: E. J. Brill, 1996); trans. J. H. Srawley, *The Catechetical Oration of St. Gregory of Nyssa* (London: S.P.C.K., 1917).

Historia monachorum in Aegypto, ed. A. Festugière, Subsidia Hagiographica, 53 (Brussels: Société des Bollandistes, 1971); trans. N. Russell, *The Lives of the Desert Fathers: The Historia monachorum in Aegypto*, CS 34 (Kalamazoo, Mich.: Cistercian Publications, 1981).

IGNATIUS OF ANTIOCH, *Epistulae*, ed. Th. Camelot, 4th edn., SC 10bis (Paris: Éditions du Cerf, 1969); trans. in W. R. Schoedel, *Ignatius of Antioch: A Commentary on the Letters of Ignatius of Antioch* (Philadelphia: Fortress Press, 1985).

INNOCENT I, *La lettre du pape Innocent Ier à Décentius de Gubbio, 19 mars 416*, ed. R. Cabié, with introduction and commentary, Bureau de la R.H.E., 58 (Louvain: Publications universitaires de Louvain, 1973); trans. in M. F. Connell, *Church and Worship in Fifth-Century Rome: The Letter of Innocent I to Decentius of Gubbio*, Liturgical Studies, 52 (Cambridge: Grove Books Ltd., 2002).

IRENAEUS, *Adversus haereses*. Relevant passages in D. N. Power (ed. and trans.), *Irenaeus of Lyons on Baptism and Eucharist: Selected Texts with Introduction, Translation and Annotation*, Alcuin/GROW Liturgical Study, 18 (Bramcote, Nottingham: Grove Books Ltd., 1991).

ISIDORE OF SEVILLE, *De ecclesiasticis officiis*, ed. C. M. Lawson, CCSL 113 (Turnhout: Brepols, 1989), 1. 13–15; trans. in Sheerin (1986), 159–65.

—— *De fide catholica ex veteri et novo testamento contra Iudaeos ad Florentinam sororem suam*, PL 83. 449–538.

—— *Isidori Hispalensis episcopi Etymologiarum sive Originum libri XX*, ed. W. M. Lindsay (Oxford: Clarendon Press, 1911); trans.: *Etymologies of Isidore of Seville*, trans. S. A. Barney, W. J. Lewis, J. A. Beach, and O. Berghof, *Etymologies of Isidore of Seville* (Cambridge: Cambridge University Press, 2006).

JACOB OF SERÛGH, 'On the Reception of the Holy Mysteries', in P. Bedjan (ed.), *Homiliae selectae Mar-Jacobi Sarugensis* (Paris: O. Harrassowitz, 1908–10), iii. 646–63. Eng. trans.: H. Connolly, 'A Homily of Jacob of Serûgh on the Reception of the Holy Mysteries', *Downside Review*, 27 (1908), 278–87.

JOHN BAR QURSUS OF TELLA, *Canons*, ed. and trans. A. Vööbus, CSCO 367 (Louvain: Secrétariat du Corpus CSO, 1975), 145–56; 368 (Louvain: Secrétariat du Corpus SCO, 1975), 142–51.

—— *Profitable and Good Questions which Presbyter Sargis Asked from the Venerable and Holy Bishop Mar Johannan, his Teacher*, ed. and trans. A. Vööbus, CSCO 367 (Louvain: Secrétariat du Corpus SCO, 1975), 211–21; 368 (Louvain: Secrétariat du Corpus SCO, 1975), 197–205.

JOHN CHRYSOSTOM, *Catechetical Homilies*, ed. A. Wenger, SC 50bis (Paris: Éditions du Cerf, 1970); trans. P. Harkins ACW 31 (New York: Newman Press, 1963).

—— *De sacerdotio*, ed. A.-M. Malingrey, SC 272 (Paris: Éditions du Cerf, 1990); trans. G. Neville, *St. John Chrysostom: Six Books on the Priesthood* (London: S.P.C.K., 1964).

—— *Homilia 88 in Matthaeum 82*, PG 58. 775–82.

—— *Homilia 36 in Ep. 1 ad Corinthios*, PG 61. 305–16.

—— *Homilia 18 in Ep. II ad Corinthios*, PG 61. 523–9.

—— *Homilia 3 in Ep. 2 ad Thessalonicenses*, PG 62. 479–86.

JOHN OF DAMASCUS, *Expositio fidei*, ed. B. Kolter, in *Die Schriften des Johannes von Damaskos*, 2, PTS 12 (Berlin: de Gruyter, 1973).

—— *Contra imaginum calumniatores orationes tres*, ed. B. Kolter, in *Die Schriften des Johannes von Damaskos*, 3, PTS 17 (Berlin: de Gruyter, 1975).

JOHN OF KENNESHERE, *Prosphoral Hymns*, ed. and trans. E. W. Books, PO 6. 1 (Turnhout: Brepols, 1971), nos. 220–6 (678–81).

JOHN MOSCHUS, *Pratum spirituale*, PG 87. 3; *The Spiritual Meadow (Pratum Spirituale) by John Moschus*, trans. J. Wortley, CS 139 (Kalamazoo, Mich.: Cistercian Publications, 1992).

JUSTIN MARTYR, *Apologiae*, ed. and trans. A. Wartelle (Paris: L'Institut d'études augustiniennes, 1987); sects. 65–7 on 188–93, 294–8; trans. Jasper and Cuming (1987), 28–30.

JUSTINIAN, *Novellae constitutiones*, ed. W. Kroll and R. Schöll, *Corpus iuris civilis*, iii (Berlin: Weidmann, 1880–95, repr. 1968).

MACARIUS OF MAGNESIA, *Monogenēs (Apocriticus)*, in R. Goulet (ed. and trans.), *Macarios de Magnésie, Le Monogenēs*, Textes et Traditions, 7 (Paris: J. Vrin, 2003); see also R. M. Berchman, *Porphyry Against the Christians*, Ancient and Medieval Texts and Contexts, 1 (Leiden: E. J. Brill, 2005), 202–3.

MAXIMUS THE CONFESSOR, *Mystagogia*, PG 91. 657–717; trans. G. C. Berthold, in *Maximus the Confessor, Selected Writings* (New York: Paulist Press, 1985), 181–225.

NARSAI, *Liturgical Homilies*, trans. R. H. Connolly, in *The Liturgical Homilies of Narsai*, TaS 8. 1 (Cambridge: Cambridge University Press, 1916).

ORIGEN, *Homiliae in Numeros*, ed. L. Doutreleau, SC 415, 442, 461 (Paris: Éditions du Cerf, 1996–2001).

PALLADIUS, *Historia Lausiaca*, in G. J. M. Bartelink (ed.), *Palladio, La Storia Lausiaca*, Vite dei santi, 2 (Verona: Mondadori, 1974); Eng. trans. R. T. Meyer, ACW 34 (New York: Newman Press, 1964).

PETER LOMBARD, *Magistri Petri Lombardi Parisiensis episcopi Sententiae in IV libris distinctae*, 3rd edn. (Grottaferrata: Editiones collegii S. Bonaventurae ad Claras Aquas, 1971–81).

PHILOXENUS OF MABBUG, trans. A. Cody, 'An Instruction of Philoxenus of Mabbug on Gestures and Prayer when One Receives Communion in the Hand, with a History of the Manner of Receiving the Eucharistic Bread in the West Syrian Church', in N. Mitchell and J. F. Baldovin (eds.), *Rule of Prayer, Rule of Faith: Essays in Honor of Aidan Kavanagh, O.S.B.* (Collegeville, Minn.: Liturgical Press, 1996), 56–79.

RUFINUS, *Historia monachorum siue De uita sanctorum patrum*, ed. E. Schulz-Flügel, PTS 34 (Berlin: de Gruyter, 1990); trans. N. Russell, in *The Lives of the Desert Fathers: The Historia monachorum in Aegypto*, CS 34 (Kalamazoo, Mich.: Cistercian Publications, 1981).

SALVIAN, *De gubernatione dei*, ed. G. Lagamgue, SC 220 (Paris: Éditions du Cerf, 1975); trans. J. F. Sullivan, FC 3 (Washington D.C.: Catholic University of America Press, 1947).

SEVERUS OF ANTIOCH, JOHN OF KENNESHERE, *Pre-Communion and Post-Communion Hymns*, ed. and trans. E. W. Books, PO 7. 5 (Turnhout: Brepols, 1971), Nos. 227–34 (674–88, 689–92).

THEODORE OF MOPSUESTIA, *Catechetical Homilies* 15–16, ed. R. Tonneau and R. Devreese in *Homilies catechetiques*, Studi e Testi, 145 (Vatican City: Bibliotheca apostolica Vaticana), 461–605; trans. E. Yarnold, *The Awe-Inspiring Rites of Initiation*, 201–50.

XOSROV ANJEWAC'I, *Commentary on the Divine Liturgy*, trans. S. P. Cowe (New York: St Vartan Press, 1991).

Secondary literature

ALDRETE, G. S. (1999), *Gestures and Acclamations in Ancient Rome* (Baltimore: Johns Hopkins University Press). [Note esp. 'Characteristics of the Acclamations', 128–47.]

ANTONIADIS, S. L. (1939), *Place de la liturgie dans la tradition des lettres grecques* (Leiden: A. W. Sijthoff) [Note sections 'Vocabulaire', 89–117, and repertory of sources from the first through fifteenth centuries, 142–221].

BALDOVIN, J. F. (1987), *The Urban Character of Christian Worship: The Origins, Development, and Meaning of Stational Liturgy*, OrChrAn 228 [See esp. 'Stational Liturgy and the Development of the Eucharist', 238–47].

——(1989), *Liturgy in Ancient Jerusalem*, Alcuin/GROW Liturgical Study, 9 (Bramcote, Nottingham: Grove Books).

——(2006), 'The Empire Baptized', in Wainwright and Westerfield Tucker (2006), 77–130.

Baur, C. (1959–60), *John Chrysostom and His Time*, trans. Sr. M. Gonzaga, 2 vols. (Westminster, Md.: Newman Press). [See esp. 'Chrysostom as Liturgist', i. 190–205, 'The Liturgy and Divine Service', ii. 72–81.]

Beck, E. (1958), 'Symbolum-Mysterium bei Aphraat und Ephräm', *Oriens Christianus*, 42: 19–40, esp. 25–6, 32–3.

Beitia, P. (2006), 'L'Oraison «post pridie» du «Liber Missarum» des Églises d'Espagne: structure et théologie du mémorial', *Ephemerides liturgicae*, 120: 3–23.

Berger, T. (1999), *Women's Ways of Worship: Gender Analysis and Liturgical History* (Collegeville, Minn.: Liturgical Press).

Bernard, P. (2002), 'Les Latins de la Liturgie (Antquité tardive et moyen-âge): Vingt-cinq années de recherches (1978–2002)', *Bulletin du Cange/ALMA* 60: 77–170.

Betz, J. (1979), *Eucharistie: In der Schrift und Patristik*, Handbuch der Dogmengeschichte, 4.4a (Freiburg: Herder).

Bishop, E. (1916), 'Ritual Splendor' and 'The Eucharistic Service as a Subject of Fear and Awe', in his appendices to R. H. Connolly, *The Liturgical Homilies of Narsai*, TaS 8. 1 (Cambridge: Cambridge University Press), 88–97.

Billings, B. S. (2006), *Do This in Remembrance of Me: The Disputed Words in the Lukan Institution Narrative (Luke 22.19b–20): An Historico-Exegetical, Theological and Sociological Analysis*, Library of New Testament Studies, 314 (London: T & T Clark).

Blaise, A. (1964), *Le Vocabulaire latin des principaux thèmes liturgiques*, ouvrage revu par Dom Antoine Dumas (repr. Turnhout: Brepols, 1966).

Bornert, R. (1966), *Les Commentaires byzantins de la divine liturgie du VIIe au XVe siècle*, Archives de l'Orient Chrétienne, 9 (Paris: Institut français d'études byzantines).

Bouley, A. (1981), *From Freedom to Formula: The Evolution of the Eucharistic Prayer from Oral Improvisation to Written Texts*, Studies in Christian Antiquity, 21 (Washington: Catholic University of America Press).

Boulnois, M.-O. (2000), 'L'Eucharistie, mystère d'union chez Cyrille d'Alexandrie: Les modèles d'union trinitaire et christologique', *RSR* 74: 147–72.

Bradshaw, P. F. (1997) (ed.), *Essays on Early Eastern Eucharistic Prayers* (Collegeville, Minn.: Liturgical Press).

—— (2002), *The Search for the Origins of Christian Worship: Sources and Methods for the Study of Early Liturgy*, 2nd edn. (New York: Oxford University Press).

—— (2004), *Eucharistic Origins*, Alcuin Club Collections, 80 (London: S.P.C.K.).

Bradshaw, P., Johnson, M. and Phillips, L. E. (2002), *The Apostolic Tradition: A Commentary*, Hermeneia (Minneapolis: Fortress Press).

Brock, S. (1992), *The Luminous Eye: The Spiritual World of Saint Ephrem*, CS 124 (Kalamazoo, Mich.: Cistercian Publications), esp. ch. 6: 'The Medicine of Life', 99–114.

Bruneau, T. J. (1972), 'Communicative Silences: Forms and Functions', *Journal of Communication*, 23: 17–46.

Cabrol, F., 'Eucharistie 2', in *DACL*, v.1. 686–92.

Callam, D. (1984), 'The Frequency of Mass in the Latin Church ca. 400', *TS* 45: 613–50.

Carpin, A. (1993), *L'Eucaristia in Isidoro di Siviglia*, Collana 'Claustrum', 12 (Bologna: Ed. Studio Domenicano).

Caspers, C., and Schneiders, M. (1990) (eds.), *Omnes circumadstantes: Contributions towards a History of the Role of the People in the Liturgy* (Kampen: J. H. Kok).

Caseau, B. (2002), 'L'Abandon de la communion dans la main (IVe–XIIe siècles)', *Travaux et mémoires*, 14: 79–94.

CHADWICK, H. (1951), 'Eucharist and Christology in the Nestorian Controversy', *JTS*, NS 2: 145–64.

CHAILLOT, C. (2006), 'The Ancient Oriental Churches', in Wainwright and Westerfield Tucker (2006), 131–69.

CHAVASSE, A. (1993), *La liturgie de la ville de Rome du Ve au VIIIe siècle: une liturgie conditionnée par l'organisation de la vie in urbe et extra muros*, Studia Anselmiana, 112 (Rome: Pontificio Ateneo S. Anselmo).

CHUPUNGCO, A. J. (1999) (ed.), *The Eucharist*, Handbook for Liturgical Studies, 4 (Collegeville, Minn.: Liturgical Press).

COULDRY, N. (2003), *Media Rituals: A Critical Approach* (London: Routledge).

CUMING, G. C. (1990), 'The Liturgy of Antioch at the Time of Severus (513–518)', in J. N. Alexander (ed.), *Time and Community: In Honor of Thomas Julian Talley* (Washington D.C.: Pastoral Press), 83–103.

DALBY, M. (2003), *Infant Communion: The New Testament to the Reformation*, Joint Liturgical Studies, 56 (Cambridge: Grove Books).

DANIÉLOU, J. (1956), *The Bible and the Liturgy* (Notre Dame, Ind.: University of Notre Dame Press). [see esp. chapters 'Eucharistic Rites', 'The Figures of the Eucharist', 'The Paschal Lamb', and 'Psalm XXII'].

DASSMANN, E. (1992), 'Eucharist II: Iconography', in *Encyclopedia of the Early Church*, i. 294.

DE CLERCK, P. (2005a), 'Croissance démographique et évolutions théologiques: Eucharistie(s) et ministères à la fin de l'Antiquité chrétienne', *La Maison-Dieu*, 242: 7–32.

—— (2005b), 'Les prières eucharistiques gallicanes', in Gerhards *et al.* (2005), 203–23.

DÉROCHE, V. (2002), 'Représentations de l'eucharistie dans la haute époque byzantine', in *Mélanges Gilbert Dagron, Travaux et Mémoires*, 14: 167–80.

DE VOGÜÉ, A. (2005), 'Le passage de la messe du dimanche à la célébration quotidienne chez les moines (IVe–Xe siècle)', *La Maison-Dieu*, 242: 33–44.

DI BERARDINO, A. (1967–2006) (ed.), *Patrologia*, 5 vols. (Turin: Marietti).

—— (1992) (ed.), *Encyclopedia of the Early Church*, trans. Adrian Walford, 2 vols. (New York: Oxford University Press).

—— (1996) 'Libri liturgici', *Patrologia*, 4: 523–8.

—— and NIN, M. (2006), 'Canonical and Liturgical Literature', in A. Berardino (ed.), *The Eastern Fathers from the Council of Chalcedon (451) to John of Damascus (†750)*, trans. A. Walford, Patrologia, 5 (Cambridge: J. Clarke & Co.), 655–81.

DODD, E. C. (1973), *Byzantine Silver Treasures* (Bern: Abegg-Stiftung).

DRIJVERS, J. W. (2004), *Cyril of Jerusalem: Bishop and City*, Suppl. *VC* 72 (Leiden: E. J. Brill).

DUBOIS, J.-D. (1999), 'Les pratiques eucharistiques des gnostiques valentiniens', in M. Quesnel, Y.-M. Blanchard, and C. Tassin (eds.), *Nourriture et repas dans les milieux juifs et chrétiens de l'antiquité: Mélanges offerts au Professeur Charles Perrot*, Lectio divina, 178 (Paris: Éditions du Cerf), 255–66.

DUHR, J. (1953), 'Communion fréquente', in *DSp* ii. 1. 1234–92.

DUVAL, N. (1992), 'Church Buildings', in Di Berardino (1992), i. 168–75.

EIZENHÖFER, L. (1954–66), *Canon Missae Romanae*, 2 vols. Rerum ecclesiasticanum documenta, Series Minor, Subsidia Studiorum, 7 (Rome: Casa Editrice Herder) [Note collection of parallel passages from pagan and Christian literature in ii].

EVANS, G. R. (1996), 'Ireland: Liturgy', *Patrologia*, 4: 472–4.

FENWICK, J. (1986), *Fourth Century Anaphoral Construction Techniques*, Grove Liturgical Study, 45 (Bramcote, Nottingham: Grove Books Ltd.).

FITTKAU, G. (1953), *Der Begriff des Mysteriums bei Johannes Chrysostomus*, Theophaneia: Beiträge zur Religions- und Kirchengeschichte des Altertums, 9 (Bonn: Peter Hanstein).

FOLEY, E. (1982), 'The Cantor in Historical Perspective', *Worship*, 56: 194–213.

FRANK, G. (2001), ' "Taste and See": The Eucharist and the Eyes of Faith in the Fourth Century', *JECS* 70: 619–43.

GAÏSE, R. (2001), *Les signes sacramentels de l'Eucharistie dans l'Eglise latine: Études théologiques et historiques*, Studia Friburgensia, 89 (Fribourg: Éditions Universitaires Fribourg Suisse).

GALAVARIS, G. (1970), *Bread and the Liturgy: The Symbolism of Early Christian and Byzantine Bread Stamps* (Madison: University of Wisconsin Press).

GAMBLE, H. Y. (1995), *Books and Readers in the Early Church: A History of Early Christian Texts* (New Haven: Yale University Press).

GELSI, D. (1992), 'Anaphora', in Di Berardino (1992), i. 33–5.

GERHARDS, A., BRAKMANN, H., KLÖCKNER, M., and PAHL, I. (2005) (eds.), *Prex Eucharistica*, iii: *Studia, Pars Prima: Ecclesia antiqua et occidentalis*, Spicilegium Friburgense, 43 (Freiburg, Schweiz: Universitätsverlag).

GIAMBERARDINI, G. (1957), *La consecrazione eucharistica nella chiesa copta* (Cairo: Tipografia Mondiale).

GIRAUDO, C. (1981), *La struttura letteraria della preghiera eucaristica: saggio sulla genesi letteraria di una forma: toda veterotestamentaria, beraka giudaica, anafora cristiana*, Analecta Biblica, 92 (Rome: Biblical Institute Press).

GODOY FERNÁNDEZ, C. (1995), *Arqueología y liturgia: Iglesias hispánicas (siglos IV al VIII)* (Barcelona: Universitat de Barcelona).

GOLITZIN, A. (1994), *Et introibo ad altare Dei: The Mystagogy of Dionysius Areopagita: With Special Reference to its Predecessors in the Eastern Christian Tradition*, Avalecta Vlatadōn 59 (Thessalonica: Patriarchikōn Idruma Paterikōn Meletōn).

GRIFFITH, S. H. (1999), ' "Spirit in the Bread; Fire in the Wine": The Eucharist as "Living Medicine" in the Thought of Ephraem the Syrian', *Modern Theology*, 15: 225–46.

GRILLMEIER, A. (1975), *Christ in Christian Tradition*, trans. J. Bowden, 2nd rev. edn. (Atlanta: John Knox Press). [For a discussion of eucharist in Shenoute's *Contra Origenistas*, 203–7.]

—— (1997), 'Verweigerung der Kelchkommunion durch römische Manichäer unter Papst Leo I. (440–461)', in T. Hainthaler (ed.), *Fragmente zur Christologie: Studien zum altkirchlichen Christusbild* (Freiburg: Herder), 389–400.

GRIMES, R. L. (2004), 'Performance Theory and the Study of Ritual', in A. Peter, A. W. Geertz, and R. R. Warne (eds.), *New Approaches to the Study of Religion*, ii: *Textual, Comparative, Sociological, and Cognitive Approaches*, Religion and Reason, 43 (Berlin: de Gruyter), 109–38.

GUTIÉRREZ-MARTIN, J. (2001), *Iglesia y liturgia en el Africa romana del siglo IV: Bautismo y eucaristía en los libros de Optato, obispo de Milevi*, Bibliotheca ⟨⟨Ephemerides liturgicae⟩⟩, Subsidia, 116 (Rome: Edizioni Liturgiche).

HAMMAN, A. (1961), 'Mystère eucharistique', in *DSp* iv. 2. 1553–86.

—— (1992), 'Eucharist. I. In the Fathers', in Di Berardino (1992), i. 292–3.

HANSSENS, I. M. (1930), *Institutiones liturgicae de ritibus orientalibus*, 3 vols. (Rome: Apud Aedes Pontificiae Universitatis Gregorianae) [Each segment of the detailed description of the eucharistic liturgy in iii. 1–535 provides under the heading 'Historia' citations of the sources for ancient practice].

HARMLESS, W. (1995), *Augustine and the Catechumenate* (Collegeville, Minn.: Liturgical Press).

HARTNEY, A. M. (2004), *John Chrysostom and the Transformation of the City* (London: Duckworth).

HARVEY, S. A. (2006), *Scenting Salvation: Ancient Christianity and the Olfactory Imagination*, The Transformation of the Classical Heritage, 42 (Berkeley: University of California Press).

HEIN, K. (1975), *Eucharist and Excommunication: A Study in Early Christian Doctrine and Discipline*, 2nd rev. edn., European University Papers, Series 23: Theology, v. 19 (Bern: Herbert Lang).

HOWES, D. (2006), 'Scent, Sound and Synaesthesia: Intersensability and Material Culture Theory', in C. Tilley *et al.* (eds.), *Handbook of Material Culture* (London: Sage Publications), 161–72.

JACOB, C. (1990), *"Arkandisziplin", Allegorese, Mystagogie: Ein neuer Zugang zur Theologie des Ambrosius von Mailand*, Athenäums Monografien, Theophaneia: Beiträge zur Religions- und Kirchengeschichte des Altertums, 32 (Frankfurt am Main: Hain).

JOHNSON, M. E. (1995), *Liturgy in Early Christian Egypt*, Joint Liturgical Studies / Alcuin Club and the Group for Renewal of Worship, 33 (Cambridge: Grove Books Ltd.).

—— (2006), 'The Apostolic Tradition', in Wainwright and Westerfield Tucker (2006), 32–75.

JONES, C., WAINWRIGHT, G., YARNOLD, E., and BRADSHAW, P. (1992) (eds.), *The Study of Liturgy*, rev. edn. (London: S.P.C.K.).

JUNGMANN, J. A. (1951–5), *The Mass of the Roman Rite: Its Origins and Development*, trans. F. A. Brunner, 2 vols. (New York: Benziger Bros.).

KACZYNSKI, R. (1974), *Das Wort Gottes in Liturgie und Alltag der Gemeinden des Johannes Chrysostomus*, Freiburger theologische Studien, 94 (Freiburg: Herder).

KALAMARA, P. (2002), *Le système vestimentaire à Byzance du IVe jusqu'a la fin du XIe siècle* (Lille: Atelier National de Reproduction des Thèses).

KENNEDY, H. P. (2005), 'The Eucharistic Prayer in Early Irish Practice', in Gerhards *et al.* (2005), 225–41.

KILMARTIN, E. J. (1998), *The Eucharist in the West: History and Theology*, ed. R. J. Daly (Collegeville, Minn.: Liturgical Press, A Pueblo book), 3–60.

KLÖCKENER, M. (2005), 'Das Eucharistische Hochgebet in der nordafrikanischen Liturgie der christlichen Spätantike', in Gerhards *et al.* (2005), 43–128.

LEADER-NEWBY, R. E. (2004), 'Sacred Silver: From *patera* to Paten', in *Silver and Society in Late Antiquity* (Aldershot: Ashgate), 61–122.

LEBRETON, J. (1909), 'Le Dogme de la transsubstantiation et la christologie Antiochienne du Ve siècle', in *Report of the Nineteenth Eucharistic Congress: Held at Westminster from 9th to 13th September 1908* (London: Sands), 326–47.

LECLERCQ, H. (1914), 'Communion', in *DACL* iii. 2. 2427–65. [Includes sections on rite of communion, communion antiphon, communion from the hand of the bishop, communion of the absent and ill and infants, communion of the dead and dying, frequent communion, communion in inscriptions, daily communion, and communion under a single species.]

—— (1922), 'Eucharistie 1', in *DACL* v. 1. 681–6.

LEONARD, J. K., and MITCHELL, N. D. (1994), *The Postures of the Assembly during the Eucharistic Prayer* (Chicago: Liturgy Training Publications).

LEYERLE, B. (2001), *Theatrical Shows and Ascetic Lives: John Chrysostom's Attack on Spiritual Marriage* (Berkeley: University of California Press).

LIES, L. (1978), *Wort und Eucharistie bei Origenes: zur Spiritualisierungstendenz des Eucharistieverständnisses*, Innsbrucker theologische Studien, 1 (Innsbruck: Tyrolia-Verlag).

LIVER, R. (1979), *Das Nachwirkung der antiken Sakralsprache im Christlichen Gebet des lateinischen und italienischen Mittelalters* (Bern: Fraucke).

LODI, E. (1999), 'The Oriental Anaphoras', in Chupungco (1999), 77–102.

LUGMAYR, M. (1997), 'The History of the Rite of Distributing Communion', in *The Veneration and Administration of the Eucharist*, The Proceedings of the Second International Colloquium on the Roman Catholic Liturgy organised by the Centre International d'Études Liturgiques, translated and edited by members of CIEL UK (Southampton: Saint Austin Press), 53–72.

MADEC, G. (1975), '«Panis angelorum» (Selon les Pères de l'Église, surtout s. Augustin)', in *Forma futuri: Studi in onore del Cardinale Michele Pellegrino* (Turin: Bottega d'Erasmo), 818–29.

MANGO, M. M. (1986), *Silver from Early Byzantium: The Kaper Koraon and Related Treasures* (Baltimore: Trustees of the Walters Art Gallery).

MANIYATTU, P. (1995), *Heaven on Earth: The Theology of Liturgical Space-time in the East Syrian Qurbana*, Mar Thoma Yogam Publications, 10 (Rome: Mar Thoma Yogam).

MARINI, A. (1989), *La celebrazione eucaristica presieduta da Sant'Agostino: La partecipazione dei fedeli alla Liturgia della Parola e al Sacrificio Eucaristico* (Brescia: Pavoniana). [Index of Latin terms relative to participation in the eucharist, 173–80].

MARTIMORT, A. G. (1986), *Deaconesses: An Historical Study*, trans. K. D. Whitehead (San Francisco: Ignatius Press).

—— (1991), 'L'Esprit saint dans la liturgie'; 'Fonction de la psalmodie dans la liturgie de la Parole'; 'À propos du nombre des lectures à la messe', in A. G. Martimort (ed.), *Mirabile laudis canticum: Mélanges liturgiques*, Bibliotheca ⟨⟨Ephemerides liturgicae⟩⟩, Subsidia, 60 (Roma: C. L.V.–Edizioni liturgiche), 48–74, 75–96, 125–35 resp.

MATHEWS, T. F. (1971), *The Early Churches of Constantinople: Architecture and Liturgy* (University Park, Pa.: Pennsylvania State University Press).

MATEOS, J. (1971), *La Célèbration de la parole dans la liturgie byzantine*, OrChrAn 191 (Rome: Pontificium Institutum Orientalium Studiorum).

MAYER, C., 'Eucharistia', in *AugL* 2: 1151–7.

MAZZA, E. (1989), *Mystagogy: A Theology of Liturgy in the Patristic Age*, trans. M. J. O'Connell (New York: Pueblo Pub. Co.).

—— (1999*a*), *The Celebration of the Eucharist: The Origin of the Rite of the Development of its Interpretation*, trans. M. J. O'Connell (Collegeville, Minn.: Liturgical Press).

—— (1999*b*), 'The Eucharist in the First Four Centuries', in Chupungco (1999), 9–60.

McGOWAN, A. (1994), 'Eating People: Accusations of Cannibalism against Christians in the Second Century', *JECS* 2: 413–42.

—— (1999), *Ascetic Eucharists: Food and Drink in Early Christian Ritual Meals* (Oxford: Clarendon Press).

—— (2005), 'Food, Ritual, and Power', in V. Burrus (ed.), *Late Ancient Christianity: A People's History of Christianity* (Minneapolis: Fortress Press), ii. 145–64.

McLEOD, F. G. (2002), 'The Christological Ramifications of Theodore of Mopsuestia's Understanding of Baptism and the Eucharist', *JECS* 10: 37–75.

McQUAIL, D. (1997), *Audience Analysis* (Thousand Oaks, Calif.: Sage Publications). [Note 'The Audience in Communication Theory and Research', 12–24, and 'Typologies of Audience', 25–64.]

MENZE, V. (2004), 'Priests, Laity and the Sacrament of the Eucharist in Sixth Century Syria', *Hugoye: Journal of Syriac Studies*, 7/2, <http://syrcom.cua.edu/Hugoye/Vol7No2/HV7N2Menze.html>, 18 July 2007.

MESSNER, R. (1993), 'Zur Hermeneutik allegorischer Liturgieerklärung in Ost und West', *Zeitschrift für katholische Theologie*, 115: 284–319, 415–34.

—— (2005), 'Grundlinien der Entwicklung des eucharistischen Gebets in der frühen Kirche', in Gerhards *et al.* (2005), 3–41.

METZGER, M. (1999), 'The History of the Eucharistic Liturgy in Rome', in Chupungco (1999), 103–31.

—— (2005), 'La prière eucharistique de la prétendue *Tradition Apostolique*', in Gerhards *et al.* (2005), 263–80.

MITCHELL, N. D. (1999), 'Worship of the Eucharist Outside Mass', in Chupungco (1999), 263–75.

MOHRMANN, C. (1961–77), *Études sur le latin des chrétiens*, 4 vols. (Rome: Edizioni di storia e letteratura).

MORRILL, B. T., ZIEGLER, J. E., and RODGERS, S. (2006) (eds.), *Practicing Catholic: Ritual, Body, and Contestation in Catholic Faith* (New York: Palgrave Macmillan).

MURRAY, R. (2004), *Symbols of Church and Kingdom: A Study in Early Syriac Tradition*, 2nd edn. (London: T & T Clark), esp. 76–9 (Ephrem), 271–4 (Balai).

NATALI, A. (1985), 'Tradition ludique et sociabilité dans la pratique religieuse à Antioche d'après Jean Chrysostome', *StPatr* 16. 2; TU 129 (Berlin: Akademie Verlag), 463–70.

NOCENT, A. (1999), 'The Roman Lectionary for Mass', in Chupungco (1999), 177–88.

NUSSBAUM, O. (1965), *Der Standort des Liturgen am christlichen Altar vor dem Jahre 1000: eine archäologische und liturgiegeschichtliche Untersuchung*, 2 vols. (Bonn: Peter Hanstein).

—— (1979), *Die Aufbewahrung der Eucharistie*, Theophaneia: Beiträge zur Religions- und Kirchengeschichte des Altertums, 29 (Bonn: Peter Hanstein).

PAGELS, E. H. (1972), 'A Valentinian Interpretation of Baptism and Eucharist—and its Critique of "Orthodox" Sacramental Theology and Practice', *HTR* 65: 154–69.

PALAZZO, E. (1998), *A History of Liturgical Books: From the Beginning to the Thirteenth Century*, trans. M. Beaumont (Collegeville, Minn.: Liturgical Press).

PAPAS, T. (1965), *Studien zur Geschichte der Messgewänder im byzantinischen Ritus*, Miscellanea Byzantina Monacensia, 3 (Munich: Institut für Byzantinistik und neugriechische Philologie der Universität München).

PARENTI, S. (1999), 'The Eucharistic Liturgy in the East: The Various Orders of Celebration', in Chupungco (1999), 61–75.

PASQUATO, O. (1976), *Gli spettacoli in S. Giovanni Crisostomo: Paganesimo e Cristianesimo ad Antiochia e Costantinopoli nel IV secolo*, OrChrAn 201 (Rome: Pontificium Institutum Orientalium Studiorum).

PAVAN, V. (1992), 'Vestments, Liturgical', in Di Berardino (1992), ii. 864–6.

PETERSON, E. (1927), 'Die Bedeutung von αναδεικνυμι in den griechischen Liturgien', in K. L. Schmidt (ed.), *Festgabe für Adolf Deissmann* (Tübingen: J. C. B. Mohr), 320–6.

POTAMIANOS, I. (2000), *Light in the Byzantine Church* (Thessalonica: University Studio Press).

POWER, D. N. (1991), *Irenaeus of Lyons on Baptism and Eucharist: Selected Texts with Intro-duction, Translation and Annotation*, Alcuin/GROW Liturgical Study, 18; Grave Liturgical Study, 65 (Nottingham: Grove Books Ltd.).

QUACQUARELLI, A. (1959), 'Alle origini del «lector»', in E. Rapisarda (ed.), *Convivium do-minicum: Studi sull'eucarestia nei padri della chiesa antica e miscellanea patristica* (Catania: Centro di studi sull'antico cristianesimo, Università di Catania), 381–406.

RAFFA, V. (1998), *Liturgia eucaristica: Mistogogia della Messa dalla storia e dalla teologia alla pastorale practica*, Bibliotheca «Ephemerides liturgicae», Subsidia, 100 (Rome: C. L. V.- Edizioni liturgiche).

RAINOLDI, F. (2000), *Traditio canendi: Appunti per una storia dei riti cristiani cantati*, Biblio-theca «Ephemerides liturgicae», Subsidia, 106 (Rome: C. L. V.- Edizioni liturgiche).

RAMIS, G. (1999), 'The Eucharistic Celebration in the Non-Roman West', in Chupungco (1999), 245–62.

—— (2005), 'La anáfora eucaristica hispano-mozárabe', in Gerhards *et al.* (2005), 243–80.

RIGHETTI, M. (1966), *La Messa: Commento storico-liturgico alla luce del Concilio Vaticano II*, 3rd edn. (Milan: Editrice Àncora).

ROUILLARD, P. (1999*a*), 'The Eucharist in the First Four Centuries', in Chupungeo (1999), 9–60.

—— (1999*b*), 'The Viaticum', in Chupungco (1999), 287–93.

ROUWHORST, G. (1990), 'La celebration de l'eucharistie selon les Actes de Thomas', in Caspers and Schneiders (1990), 51–77.

—— (2005), 'Didache 9–10: A Litmus Test for the Research on Early Christian Liturgy Eucharist [*sic*]', in H. van de Sandt (ed.), *Matthew and the Didache: Two Documents from the Same Jewish-Christian Milieu?* (Assen: Royal Van Gorcum), 143–56.

RUDDOCK, A. (2001), *Understanding Audiences: Theory and Method* (London: Sage).

RUGGIERI, V. (1991), *Byzantine Religious Architecture (582–867): Its History and Structural Elements*, OrChrAn 237 (Rome: Pontificium Institutum Orientalium Studiorum).

SAXER, V. (1969), *Vie liturgique et quotidienne à Carthage vers le milieu du IIIe siècle: Le té-moinage de saint Cyprien et de ses contemporains d'Afrique*, SAC 29 (Minneapolis: Fortress Press).

—— (1971), 'Figura corporis et sanguinis Domini: Une formule eucharistique des pre-miers siècles chez Tertullien, Hippolyte et Ambroise', *Rivista di archeologia cristiana*, 47: 65–89.

SCHATTAUER, T. H. (1983), 'The Koinonikon of the Byzantine Liturgy', *OCP* 49: 91–129, esp. 113–29.

SCHECHNER, R. (1987), *Performance Theory*, rev. and expanded edn. (New York: Routledge, 1988).

SCHERMAN, J. (1987), 'Die Sprache im Gottesdienst', *Innsbrucker theologische Studien*, 18 (Innsbruck: Tyrolia Verlag).

SCHMITZ, J. (1975), *Gottesdienst im altchristlichen Mailand: Eine liturgiewissenschaftliche Un-tersuchung über Initiation und Messfeier während des Jahres zur Zeit des Bischofs Ambrosius (obit. 397)*, Theophaneia: Beiträge zur Religions- und Kirchengeschichte des Altertums, 25 (Cologne: Peter Hanstein).

—— (1995), 'Canon Romanus', *Aug(L)* 45: 141–75.

SCHRENK, S. (1995), *Typos und Antitypos in der frühchristlicher Kunst*, JAC Ergänzungsband 21 (Münster: Aschendorff Verlagsbuchhandlung).

SHEERIN, D. (1990), 'The Anaphora of the Liturgy of St John Chrysostom: Stylistic Notes', in D. Jasper and R. C. D. Jasper (eds.), *Language and the Worship of the Church* (Basingstoke: Macmillan), 44–81.

—— (1992), 'Sonus and Verba: Varieties of Meaning in the Liturgical Proclamation of the Gospel in the Middle Ages', in M. D. Jordan and K. Emery, Jr. (eds.), *Ad litteram: Authoritative Texts and their Medieval Readers* (Notre Dame, Ind.: University of Notre Dame Press), 29–69.

—— (1996), 'The Liturgy', in F. A. C. Mantello and A. G. Rigg (eds.), *Medieval Latin: An Introduction and Bibliographical Guide* (Washington D.C.: Catholic University of America Press), 157–82.

SHIELL, W. D. (2004), *Reading Acts: The Lector and the Early Christian Audience*, Biblical Interpretation Series, 70 (Boston: Brill Academic Publishers).

SIEBEN, H. J. (2003), 'Koinonia III: Chez les Pères: sens sacramentaire et ecclésiologique', in *DSp* viii. 1750–4.

SLEE, M. (2003), *The Church in Antioch in the First Century CE: Communion and Conflict*, *JSNT* suppl. ser. 244 (London: Sheffield Academic Press).

SMITH, D. E. (2003), *From Symposium to Eucharist: The Banquet in the Early Christian World* (Minneapolis: Fortress Press).

SMYTH, M. (2003), *La liturgie oubliée: La prière eucharistique en Gaule antique et dans l'Occident non romain* (Paris: Éditions du Cerf).

SPINKS, B. D. (2005), 'The Roman Canon Missae', in Gerhards *et al.* (2005), 129–43.

STOHR, J. (1989), 'Eucharistie und Maria', 'Eucharistische Hochgebet', in R. Bäumer and L. Scheffczyk (eds.), *Marienlexikon*, (St. Ottilien: EOS Verlag), ii. 407–9, 410.

STYLES, E. A. (2005), *Attention, Perception and Memory: An Integrated Introduction* (Hove: Psychology Press).

SUNTRUP, R. (1984), 'Präfiguration des Meßopfers in Text und Bild', *Frühmittelalterliche Studien*, 18: 468–528.

TAFT, R. F. (1986), *The Liturgy of the Hours in East and West: The Origins of the Divine Office and its Meaning for Today* (Collegeville, Minn.: Liturgical Press).

—— (1991), *A History of the Liturgy of St. John Chrysostom*, iv: *The Diptychs*, OrChrAn 238 (Rome: Pontificium Institutum Orientalium Studiorum).

—— (1994), *A History of the Liturgy of St. John Chrysostom* ii: *The Great Entrance: A History of the Transfer of Gifts and Other Preanaphoral Rites*, OrChrAn 200, 3rd edn. (Rome: Pontificium Institutum Orientalium Studiorum).

—— (1997), *Beyond East and West: Problems in Liturgical Understanding*, 2nd rev. enlarged edn. (Rome: Edizioni Orientalia Christiana, Pontifical Oriental Institute).

—— (2000), *A History of the Liturgy of St. John Chrysostom*, v: *The Precommunion Rites*. OrChrAn 261 (Rome: Pontificium Institutum Orientalium Studiorum).

—— (2001*a*), 'The Frequency of the Celebration of the Eucharist throughout History', in M. E. Johnson (ed.), *Between Memory and Hope: Readings in the Liturgical Year* (Collegeville, Minn.: Liturgical Press), 77–96.

—— (2001*b*), 'Women at Church in Byzantium: Where, When—and Why?', in *Divine Liturgies—Human Problems in Byzantium, Armenia, Syria and Palestine*, Variorum Collected Studies Series, 716 (Aldershot: Ashgate/Variorum), item 1.

—— (2002), ' "This Saving Command" of the Chrysostom Anamnesis and the "Missing Command to Repeat" ', *Studi sull'Oriente Cristiano*, 6/1: 129–49.

—— (2003*a*), 'Christian Liturgical Psalmody: Origins, Development, Decomposition, Collapse', in H. W. Attridge and M. F. Fassler (eds.), *Psalms in Community: Jewish and Christian Textual, Liturgical, and Artistic Traditions*, SBL Symposium Series, 25 (Atlanta: SBL), 7–32.

—— (2003*b*), 'Home Communion in the Late Antique East', in C. V. Johnson (ed.), *Ars liturgiae: Worship, Aesthetics and Praxis: Essays in Honor of Nathan D. Mitchell* (Chicago: Liturgy Training Publications), 1–25.

—— (2006), 'Was the Eucharistic Anaphora Recited Secretly or Aloud? The Ancient Tradition and What Became of It', in R. R. Ervine (ed.), *Worship Traditions in Armenia and the Neighboring Christian East* (Crestwood, NY: St Vladimir's Seminary Press, St Nerses Armenian Seminary), 15–57.

TETERIATNIKOV, N. B. (1996), *The Liturgical Planning of Byzantine Churches in Cappadocia*, OrChrAn 252 (Rome: Pontificium Institutum Orientalium Studiorum).

TRIACCA, A. M. (2005), 'Le preghiere eucaristiche ambrosiane', in Gerhards *et al.* (2005), 145–202.

TRISTAN, F. (1996), *Les premières images chrétiennes: Du symbole à l'icône: IIe–VIe siècle* (Paris: Fayard).

VAN DE PAVERD, F. (1970), *Zur Geschichte der Messliturgie in Antiocheia und Konstantinopel gegen Ende des vierten Jahrhunderts: Analyse der Quellen bei Johannes Chrysostomus*, OrChrAn 187 (Rome: Pontificium Institutum Orientalium Studiorum).

VOICU, S. J. (2006), 'Patristic Texts in Armenian (5th to 8th Centuries), Liturgy', in Di Berardino (ed.), *The Eastern Fathers from the Council of Chalcedon (451) to John of Damascus (+750)*, trans., A. Walford, Patrology, 5 (Cambridge: J. Clarke, 2006), 575–607.

VOLP, U. (2002), 'Tod und Ritual in den christlichen Gemeinden der Antike', Suppl. *VC* 65 (Leiden: E. J. Brill), 166–72.

WAINWRIGHT, G., and WESTERFIELD TUCKER, K. B. (2006) (eds.), *The Oxford History of Christian Worship* (Oxford: Oxford University Press).

WELCH, L. J. (1994), *Christology and Eucharist in the Early Thought of Cyril of Alexandria* (San Francisco: Catholic Scholars Press).

WHITE, L. M. (1997), *The Social Origins of Christian Architecture*, HTS 42 (Valley Forge, Pa.: Trinity Press).

WICK, P. (2002), *Die urchristlichen Gottesdienste: Entstehung und Entwicklung im Rahmen der frühjüdischen Tempel-, Synagogen-, und Hausfrömmigkeit*, 2nd edn., Beiträge zur Wissenschaft vom Alten (und Neuen) Testament, 8. Folge, Heft 10 (Stuttgart: Kohlhammer).

WILLIS, G. G. (1962), *St. Augustine's Lectionary*, Alcuin Club Collections, 44 (London: S.P.C.K.).

—— (1994), *A History of Early Roman Liturgy to the Death of Pope Gregory the Great*, with a memoir of G. G. Willis by M. Moreton, Henry Bradshaw Society Subsidia, 1 (published for the Henry Bradshaw Society, London: Boydell Press).

YARNOLD, E. (2001), 'The Function of Institution Narratives in Early Liturgies', in R. F. Taft and G. Winkler (eds.), *Comparative Liturgy Fifty Years after Anton Baumstark (1872–1948): Acts of the International Congress, Rome, 25–29 September 1998*, OrChrAn 265 (Rome: Pontificium Institutum Orientalium Studiorum), 997–1004.

YOUSIF, P. (1984), *L'Eucharistie chez Saint Ephrem de Nisibe*, OrChrAn 224 (Rome: Pontificium Institutum Orientalium Studiorum).

CHAPTER 36

....

PRAYER

....

COLUMBA STEWART, OSB

PRAYER is a universal feature of human religious practice. Among early Christians, prayer had two broad and frequently overlapping categories. First, and primordially, there was communal or liturgical prayer, consisting largely of conventional words and actions. Second, there was individual or 'private' prayer, more variable in form. Such personal prayer is the focus of this essay, though the language of private prayer often drew from liturgical prayer, and in any case was rooted in the same biblical and traditional sources. In their personal prayer early Christians also used gestures and postures familiar to them from the liturgical assembly. The manner of performance of both communal and individual prayer was similar: liturgical prayer was spoken aloud, and private prayer also was typically vocalized or at least verbalized. Silent prayer, like silent reading, was rare in antiquity (van der Horst 1994; Chapot and Laurot 2001: 7).

Although ubiquitous in early Christian life, today the personal prayer of early Christians is one of the least-studied aspects of their experience. The liturgy of the period has benefited from superb textual scholarship and, increasingly, from other forms of analysis such as performance theory and ritual studies. The same is true of pious practices such as pilgrimage and other public devotional activity. Because there was considerable overlap between the ways in which early Christians prayed when together and when alone, some of the benefits of ritual and performance studies accrue to the study of personal prayer. Nonetheless, the study of early Christian prayer has tended to focus on textual and theological analysis (e.g. Kiley 1997), following the approach exemplified by the landmark French *Dictionnaire de spiritualité ascétique et mystique, doctrine et histoire* (completed in 1994 after 60 years of work). Even the recent strong interest in early Christian asceticism has focused more on sexuality, diet, gender, and questions of authority than on the devotional practices of ascetic men and women. One can now just begin to see evidence of fresh approaches (Bitton-Ashkelony 2003).

Much of this reticence can be explained by the elusiveness of the subject and the paucity of traditional kinds of scholarly evidence. But there is also the irreducibly spiritual and theological nature of prayer: might it be too narrowly 'religious' to interest much of the modern academy? Ironically, prayer is becoming a significant topic in western medieval studies. The study of mysticism, particularly among medieval women, and of devotional practices of many kinds, has begun to employ a variety of methodologies. There are perhaps particular factors at work: the textual evidence is far more abundant from the Middle Ages, the social terrain is more accessible, and the academic community studying it is larger.

At a time in which virtually everyone prayed to someone or something—after all, Romans defined 'atheism' as not praying to the official gods, for not to pray to *any* god would have been unimaginable to them—what was it to be a praying Christian? In the first instance it meant distinguishing Christian prayer from that of Jews, from whom Christians had inherited so much of their religious practice. Then, in the broader Mediterranean world in which Christianity flourished, Christians had to affirm how their religious practice differed fundamentally from Greek, Roman, and other 'pagan' pieties. The study of prayer in early Christianity highlights the uneasy position of Christian religion in late antiquity. Oriented toward Judaism by their sacred writings and devotional practices, yet culturally and socially of the nations (that is, 'gentile'), Christians found themselves in their early years struggling on two fronts to define their distinctive religious identity and to justify their understanding of God as disclosed in Jesus Christ.

36.1 SOURCES

Liturgical prayer tends to leave written traces, as communities preserve prayer texts and instructions for worship. Various early Christian church orders such as the *Didache*, the *Apostolic Tradition* attributed to Hippolytus, the *Apostolic Constitutions*, and related texts, describe patterns of daily and weekly prayer. These texts were intended to govern the public, liturgical prayer of the Church, though from them one can glean suggestions of private practice, especially with regard to the daily times of prayer.

Generally speaking, personal prayer, being individual and evanescent, is elusive. From the available evidence one can reconstruct the basic elements of the *practice* of early Christian prayer in terms of common verbal formulae, times of prayer, postures and gestures, favoured spaces, and visual aids. The *content* of prayer is less accessible. Written sources can present only a partial view of how individual Christians prayed. Few would have prayed by writing, even if some of them quoted or composed prayers. In any case, texts preserve only words. Words can point to the other dimensions of prayer (how people used their bodies, what they were looking at while they prayed, what they were imagining), but are like the dried rusks eaten by early Christian monks, needing reconstitution to become something more like food.

Written sources, however preserved, are also inherently formal. Early Christian inscriptions, ranging from monumental and formulaic inscriptions on gravestones and stelae, to graffiti preserved on ostraca or plastered walls, often feature prayer (examples in Hamman 1952; 1989a and Griffith 2002). Even seemingly random prayers hurriedly scratched or painted on a readily available surface, however vivid, are still at one remove from an actual prayer in thought or speech (see e.g., Ong 1988). This distance from the live act is mitigated somewhat by the tendency of religious practice towards formalization. Most personal prayer was conditioned by the formal discourse of the liturgy, the psalms and biblical odes, and other conventional patterns into which one's personal needs or requests could be inserted.

Several early Christian writers developed theologies or spiritual interpretations of prayer, typically through commentary on key biblical texts such as the Lord's Prayer. Some are primarily catechetical treatises intended for a general audience (e.g. those by Tertullian and Cyprian), while other texts are directed at a more sophisticated audience (e.g. book 7 of Clement of Alexandria's *Stromateis* or Origen's *On Prayer*). These texts generally included some practical counsel about postures, times, and places for prayer. There are also exhortatory writings associated with ascetical groups, such as the *Discourses* of Aphrahat, a fourth-century Syriac author, and the *Homilies* of Pseudo-Macarius, a late fourth-century Greek author with links to Syriac asceticism.

With the rise of the monastic movement in the fourth century, one finds extensive discussion of the practice of prayer in the stories about famous monks, such as the *Life of Antony* by Athanasius, the *Apophthegmata* ('Sayings' of the elders), and related literature, as well as theological analysis of the nature and forms of prayer in the writings of Evagrius Ponticus, John Cassian, Diadochus of Photike, and others. Although one of the most famous early Christian texts, Augustine's *Confessions*, is written in the form of an extended prayer, this highly refined memoir tells us more about its author's spiritual and intellectual struggles than about early Christian prayer. Monastic rules, common in the Latin West from the fifth century, typically say little about personal prayer apart from specifying particular times for prayerful reading of biblical and other religious texts.

   Although the remainder of this essay will explore the textual sources more closely, the evidence from early Christian art and archaeology is important for corroborating and amplifying the written references to posture, gestures, and visual supports for prayer. A standing posture with raised or outstretched arms was common in Graeco-Roman religion and became the normal stance for Christian prayer in both liturgical and private contexts. Carvings and paintings from the second century onward, most famously those of the Roman catacombs, depict praying figures in a characteristic stance with upraised arms, known commonly as the 'orans' (lit., 'praying') position (see examples in Zibawi 1998). While many of these paintings are obviously depictions of biblical scenes, many portray a veiled female figure with upraised arms whose precise significance remains a matter of controversy, though it is likely that this particular image is a Christianization of a standard Graeco-Roman symbol for *pietas*, or duty (Prigent 1992). Christians used other postures, such as bowing, prostrating, and kneeling, that were less common in Graeco-Roman practice as they were thought to be too 'oriental'. In Christian use they indicated an attitude of penitence and submission, and became central to ascetical prayer practices (on postures, see Hamman 1980: 1212–19; Chapot and Laurot 2001: 13–16; Bunge 2002: 138–86). The opportunity to analyse a trove of skeletal remains at a major monastic site in Jerusalem has revealed evidence of repetitive injuries explainable only by years of frequent genuflection (Driscoll and Sheridan 2000).

   Facing in a particular direction for prayer is another common feature of religious anthropology. Jews faced toward Jerusalem, as Muslims would later face Mecca. Christians were taught to pray facing toward the east, symbol of the risen Christ. The east was also the direction from which Christ was expected to come at his return in glory (Hamman 1980: 1208–12; Bunge 2002: 57–71). Early Christian churches were accordingly 'oriented' so that worshippers faced eastward. Tertullian writes of crosses inscribed on the east wall of a home (*Or.* 3). Archaeological investigation in Egypt, home of the most extensive ancient monastic settlements, has uncovered niches in the east walls of oratories indicating the direction for prayer, as well as painted crosses on the same wall perhaps used as a visual focus for meditation (Stewart, forthcoming).

   The role of images in prayer, whether painted, mosaic, or carved, is very hard to establish with any certainty before the fifth and sixth centuries. Recent scholarship has challenged earlier scholarly consensus that the Christians of the first four centuries were firmly anti-iconic (Finney 1994; Jensen 2005). The wall paintings of catacombs and the mosaics later placed in churches surely inspired reflection and prayer, but evidence for the veneration of images and their direct use in prayer belongs to the very end of the early Christian period. Relics of the martyrs and their burial places would have been a focus of devotion and prayer. The development of pilgrimage to the Holy Land in the fourth century made sacred place, and devotional acts performed there, increasingly important in Christian life.

36.2 THE EVOLUTION OF CHRISTIAN PRAYER

36.2.1 Jesus, Paul, and the Earliest Christians

The early Christian understanding of prayer was shaped most directly by traditions inherited from Judaism, the teaching of Jesus in the gospels, and the writings of Paul, the Jewish persecutor of Christians who became the evangelist to the Gentiles. Both Jesus and Paul were deeply schooled in the religious heritage of Israel, and their teaching on prayer drew from the Hebrew scriptures and contemporary practice (Marshall 2001; Finkel 2001). The presentation by the evangelists of Jesus's teaching on prayer may also reflect conflicts between the followers of Jesus and other Jewish groups (e.g. Pharisees) several decades after Jesus's death, particularly following the destruction of the Temple in Jerusalem in 70 CE.

As a devout Jew who taught in the synagogues of Galilee and the Temple precincts of Jerusalem, Jesus would have observed the daily times of prayer linked to the Temple sacrifices (evening, morning, afternoon) and their associated rituals. His preaching—or the presentation of it in the gospels—likely bears traces of sectarian conflicts within Palestinian Judaism of the first century. He followed the tradition of the Hebrew prophets by reminding his listeners that true religious observance consists not only of publicly observable behaviour, but must extend to one's private devotions and personal intentions. He urged his audiences to pray in secret and to fast without ostentation (Mt 6: 1–18). His parables on prayer used unlikely exemplars of an integrity which he contrasted with the practices of the conventionally religious, normally represented in his preaching by the Pharisees, a sect known for careful observance of the Mosaic Law. For example, Jesus describes a scene in which both a Pharisee and a tax collector enter the Temple to pray. In the Pharisee's (audible) prayer, he thanks God that he is not like other, sinful people. Meanwhile, the tax collector in both posture and words humbly demonstrates his sense of unworthiness and need for God's mercy. Jesus excoriates the Pharisee's inversion of prayer by which he glorifies himself rather than God (Lk 18: 9–14).

The gospels emphasize Jesus's own devotion to prayer, highlighting his withdrawal into solitude for the sake of intense prayer at the outset of his ministry (Mk 1: 12–13), during his preaching tours (Mk 1: 35, 6: 46; Lk 4: 42, 6: 12, 9: 18, 9: 28), and, most powerfully, the night before his death (Mk 14: 32–42). An emphasis on privacy, or at least the avoidance of ostentatious display, became a keynote of Jesus's teaching on prayer (Mt 6: 5–6). He prayed to God as 'Father' (the Aramaic *Abba*) and taught his followers to do the same (Mt 6: 9–13). He used the example of a widow unrelenting in her pursuit of justice as a model of urgent, unceasing prayer (Lk 18: 1–8). Both Jesus and Paul followed the traditional Jewish association of prayer with fasting; Jesus's critique of fasting was directed not against the practice itself but against the temptation to call attention to one's piety by obvious misery (Mt 6: 16–18).

The study of prayer in polytheistic Graeco-Roman religion is fraught with methodological questions and controversies. Some modern scholars, especially those interested in early Christian spirituality, have often detected (or presumed) a kind of pre-Christian piety, while others have emphasized the sharp differences between polytheistic and monotheistic religious practice (Aubriot-Sévin 1992: 6–9, 33–48; Brown 2004: 34–73). In Graeco-Roman polytheism there was certainly a strong emphasis on cult, typically linked to sacred place and sacred object. Cultic practice was based on a transactional pattern of petition for divine favour accompanied by sacrificial offering. The basic form of Greek prayer, an invocation followed by a request, such as 'O Zeus, give me good health,' presumed sacrifice (Pulleyn 1997: 7–15; Aune 2001: 29–31). To the sacrifice and the request might be added an argument as to why the request deserved to be heard, and promise of further offerings if the request were granted (Chapot and Laurot 2001: 12–13). One did not approach a figure of power, localized in a sacred place (temple, grove, statue), informally or with empty hands.

Jesus contrasted his own model prayer (known later as the 'Lord's Prayer') with the 'babbling and long-windedness' of the Gentiles (Mt 6: 7). Paul, preoccupied with establishing the position of his Gentile converts *vis-à-vis* Judaism, was also keenly aware of the religious milieu in which his Gentile converts lived. Paul knew that new Christians would have scruples about the fact that the meat available in the markets typically came from sacrificial offerings in pagan temples (1 Cor 8–10). The refusal of Christians to participate in local cults or to frequent local temples set them apart from their neighbours, and caused turmoil during Paul's ministry in Ephesus (Acts 19: 23–41). Because Christian prayer was not linked to particular sacred places such as temples and shrines, Christians could pray both communally or individually in any convenient location. In this they were akin to the Jews, but lacked the ancient lineage that earned Jews some respect in the Graeco-Roman world. Furthermore, the lack of a tangible object of worship such as a statue or other sacred object contributed to the charge of atheism levied against Christians in the Roman Empire. Not only would they not conform to official veneration of the Emperor, they also refused to acknowledge the various deities of the Graeco-Roman world represented by sacred animals, trees, or rivers (Justin, *1 Apol.* 34).

Much Christian prayer certainly echoed that of devotees of civic cults in asking for good health, prosperity, safety, and attention to other essential needs. Both Jesus and Paul taught that prayer is efficacious, and prayed for their followers (Mt 7: 7–11; Jn 14: 13–14, 17: 6–26; Eph 3: 14–20; Phil 1: 9–11; Col 1: 9–17). The etiquettes of Christian praying found in the principal writings on prayer follow Jewish insistence that requests be situated within a framework of praise and thanksgiving like Jesus's own prayer, the 'Our Father'. The central prayer in the communal celebration of the eucharist had many affinities with Jewish table blessings. Christianity also followed Judaism in seeing religion and morality as a whole. Christian writers on prayer frequently quoted a verse from one of the deutero-Pauline letters urging that Christians 'pray in every place, lifting up holy hands without wrath or dispute' (1 Tim 2: 8; cf. Ps 140 (141): 2).

In the Mediterranean world in which Jews and Christians lived, personal morality or world-view was more likely to be determined by social convention or addressed by philosophical traditions than to be linked explicitly to cultic practice (Hadot 1977, 1987). For Jews and Christians, however, their religion was their philosophy. The difference between the tales of the gods and the comprehensive religious narrative contained in the Jewish scriptures may go some way in explaining the primarily forensic nature of prayer and the emphasis on religious etiquette characteristic of Graeco-Roman polytheism. Christian belief in a single, universal God to be worshipped everywhere and by everyone, whose historical interactions with humans were recorded in sacred writings, required that the Christian worshipper place his or her own prayer within this worldview pervading all aspects of religious practice (Bitton-Ashkelony 2003: 203–8).

Paul understood prayer as a leaning into the new age that would be fully realized when Christ returned (Longenecker 2001). Prayer was communion with God made possible by the Spirit of God acting within the baptized person. The Spirit enabled prayer to the Father (Aramaic *Abba*: Rom 8: 15–17; Gal 4: 6), making real the union with God that Paul characterized as 'adoption'. Such life 'in the Spirit', Paul's comprehensive way of describing Christian existence, was opposed to life 'in the flesh' governed entirely by human desires and worldly concerns. This duality, rooted in atavistic notions of holy and profane, drew more immediately from Jewish religious concepts and the Hellenistic thought pervasive in the Mediterranean world. Paul's exhortations to prayer suggest both urgency and perseverance. One must pray unceasingly (1 Thess 5: 17), 'persevere' in prayer (Rom 12: 12; Col 4: 2), pray 'at all times' and 'keep vigil' (Eph 6: 18; Col 4: 2). Prayer, the means of participation in the 'real', spiritual world, was in the most fundamental sense a matter of life and death.

36.2.2 Early Christian Writings on Prayer

In addition to the so-called 'church orders', which focus on liturgical prayer, several early Christian treatises dealt specifically with personal prayer. They followed a similar format, including both general instruction and a commentary on the Lord's Prayer, which was one of the principal elements of pre-baptismal catechesis. The written commentaries arose from that catechetical tradition and used each clause of the prayer as an opportunity for instruction on theological, moral, and practical issues (Brown 2004). The famous Latin treatises by Tertullian and Cyprian were straightforward and accessible, intended for a broad audience. The surviving Greek examples by Clement of Alexandria (in book 7 of *Stromateis*, though without commentary on the Lord's Prayer) and Origen were much more sophisticated, clearly intended for the highly educated and philosophically inclined readers whom both of them normally addressed. Cyprian built explicitly on Tertullian's treatise. Origen did not name Clement, but clearly used his earlier work as a reference point for his own.

All of these early guides on prayer emphasize moral preparation and the need to place prayer in the context of other practices of the Christian life such as fasting and almsgiving. They follow the tradition of urging prayer at morning, evening, and during the night as well as at the third, sixth, and ninth hours of the day (Hamman 1961). They presume the standard posture of standing for prayer with upraised hands (Clement and Origen refer explicitly to facing the east while praying, a practice certainly familiar to the others). All make abundant use of biblical examples of devotion to prayer, include numerous exhortations from Old and New Testaments, and are concerned that their readers learn to broaden and elevate their prayer by including gratitude and praise along with requests.

Clement and Origen proved the most influential for the course of later Christian spirituality. Their integration of piety with a highly developed cosmology, and their use of Hellenistic philosophy as a hermeneutic for the obligations of Christian life, laid a substantial intellectual and spiritual foundation for subsequent theologians of prayer. In the way of early Christian authors, both Clement and Origen were eclectic in their use of philosophy. Origen expanded Clement's highly Stoic portrait of the Christian 'Gnostic' with the stronger emphasis on spiritual aspiration characteristic of Platonism. Origen also fully employed his skills in philology and biblical interpretation to move beyond the exemplary use of scriptural texts to reading them as multi-layered invitations to deeper contemplation. After an opening terminological discussion and assessment of philosophical arguments against the efficacy of prayer, Origen took in turn the standard topics of moral preparation, forms of prayer, the Lord's Prayer, and practical prescriptions about place and posture. Even there he focuses on the spiritual significance of physical practices, for the posture of prayer has meaning only as an image (*eikōn*) of the soul at prayer (*Or.* 31. 2). Clement had noted that standing to pray (and moving onto tiptoes at the end), with eyes upraised and hands extended, represents the soul's ascent to the 'intelligible essence' (*Strom.* 7. 40. 1–2). Origen develops the point more fully: the goal of prayer is to stretch the soul toward God, to raise the intellect to God, to stand one's 'governing reason' before God.

Origen's greatest contribution was to the theology of prayer. The recognition of his significance in the history of spirituality continues to grow. Indeed, the 'recovery' of Origen by scholars such as Jean Daniélou, Marguerite Harl, and Henri Crouzel was one of the major fruits of twentieth-century study of early Christianity (e.g. Daniélou 1948; Harl 1958; Crouzel 1961). Origen brought Christian teaching on prayer into a manifestly Trinitarian context, with special emphasis on prayer as an experience of revelation through, participation in, and divinization by Christ, the eternal Word of God. He taught a standard grammar of prayer, familiar from the liturgy, in which prayer is directed *to* the Father but *through* the Son, empowered by the Spirit (*Or.* 15). For Origen, however, such a formula was much more than simple etiquette. Although his Christology was later viewed as deficient from the perspective of the Nicene insistence on the consubstantiality of Father and Son, Origen's insistence on the Trinitarian economy of prayer was of great importance in the development of Christian mysticism.

For both linguistic and cultural reasons, the Church in Syriac-speaking areas of Mesopotamia was less obviously engaged with Hellenistic philosophy, and more biblical and poetic in its theology. Fourth-century Syriac Christianity produced three significant writers and inspired a fourth. Aphrahat, Ephrem, and the anonymous author of the *Book of Steps* all manifested the ascetic orientation characteristic of early Syriac Christianity. They appealed particularly to those who have dedicated themselves to live celibately as 'sons and daughters of the covenant' (*bnay and bnāt qyāmā*), or in the *Book of Steps* (often known by its title in Latin, *Liber graduum*), as 'perfect' renunciants rather than as 'righteous' married householders (Brock 1992: 107–17; Murray 2004: 13–17; Kitchen and Parmentier 2004: pp. xxxviii–xlix). In each case, prayer is understood as a means of access to the invisible, spiritual realm 'on high', which is ultimate and eternal. This strongly eschatological spirituality, linked to a vivid pneumatology and, particularly in Ephrem, associated particularly with the sacramental effects of baptism, made its way into the Greek-speaking world by influencing the unknown author of the *Homilies* traditionally, but incorrectly, attributed to the Egyptian monk Macarius the Great. These attractive exhortations employed examples drawn from both the Bible and daily life, and were marked by an emphasis on religious experience felt and perceived through spiritual senses. Though linked in the fifth century to the condemned 'Messalian' sect, these writings circulated widely and had a great impact on the development of Byzantine spirituality (Stewart 1991; Plested 2004).

36.2.3 The Rise of Monasticism

In the fourth and fifth centuries the literature on prayer both echoed the earlier themes (as in Gregory of Nyssa's *Sermons on the Lord's Prayer*) and began to show the influence of the increasingly prominent monastic movement. Athanasius's *Life of Antony*, fantastically successful in both the Greek original and in translation, popularized the model of the Egyptian anchorite devoted almost entirely to prayer, the memorization of scripture, long vigils, and fasting. Most of Athanasius's intriguing *Letter to Marcellinus*, an extended justification for the central place of the Psalms in Christian prayer, is attributed by him to an 'old man', likely a monk. Reading the Psalms intertextually with the rest of the Bible, Athanasius finds in them a compendium of scripture with two added, interrelated qualities. First, their often searing poetry is a particularly apt mirror for the soul, a kind of spiritual diagnostic tool. Second, what is simply narrated elsewhere in the Bible comes alive in the Psalms, expressed as if in one's own words (*Ep. Marcell.* 9–12). Athanasius draws from Pythagorean musical theories as he argues for the calming and integrating effect of psalmody on the singer, who harmonizes body and soul through the act of singing (*Ep. Marcell.* 27–9; Dysinger 2005).

The monastic interpretation of the biblical injunction to 'pray always', while inspiring to many (including the young Augustine), had the effect of shifting both interpretation and fulfilment of the biblical imperative to emergent monasticism. Monastic figures (even the great hermit Antony) interacted regularly with lay people and became recognized as the experts on prayer. The surviving letters to laity from monks such as the Egyptian Isidore of Pelusium (active 400–40) and the Gazan hermits Barsanuphius and John a century later show further evidence of a spiritual ministry with prayer at its centre. In the year 412, Augustine's famous *Epistle* 130 on prayer, addressed to the widow and ascetic Proba, while covering much the same ground as the classic earlier texts on prayer, also contains a reference to the Egyptian monastic custom of using frequent, but brief, prayers to focus attention during long vigils (*Ep.* 130. 20). This reference to monastic prayer practice in a Latin text from outside Egypt provides one of the first indications of broader awareness of a form of prayer that would eventually give rise to the Jesus Prayer so central to later Byzantine spirituality and, less directly, to the Rosary of the medieval Latin West.

From within the monastic movement itself, the first extant treatise on prayer is the knotty *On Prayer* by Evagrius Ponticus, written at the very end of the fourth century. Evagrius actually gave few practical instructions, presuming as he did the customs he learned when he went to Egypt in the 380s. Instead, he probes the psychology and spirituality of prayer, insisting that 'true' or 'pure' prayer consists of a complete transcendence of mental conceptions of God. Evagrius's complex work must be read within his larger *oeuvre*, in which he sketches an entire monastic ascetical theology and cosmology crafted from both Egyptian monastic wisdom and his own extensive knowledge of Origen's works (Stewart 2001). The perennial concern for moral purity as preparation for prayer became for the monks a constant vigilance against obsessive or distracting thoughts, codified by Evagrius into a system of 'eight generic thoughts' that could be used as a psychological inventory for both self-scrutiny and consultation with experienced spiritual guides. Evagrius drew heavily on Origen's analysis of thought and will in book 3 of *On First Principles*, but he placed his system firmly in the context of the standard monastic practices of late fourth century Egypt (Stewart 2003, 2005).

Evagrius's heir and popularizer in the Latin West, John Cassian, recapitulated for his readers in Gaul the earlier catechetical tradition on prayer, reinterpreting it from a monastic and strongly Evagrian perspective. Cassian's *Conferences* 9 and 10 on prayer, the most extensive single treatment of prayer in early monastic literature, are manifestly based on both Origen's and Evagrius's treatises *On Prayer*. Cassian followed the classical model by emphasizing moral preparation for prayer and by commenting on the Lord's Prayer. He also outlined the practices characteristic of monastic prayer: praying psalms at certain times of the day, repeating brief quotations from scripture as an aid to concentration and in resistance (*antirrhēsis*) to distraction, and the alternation of vocalized psalm or other biblical text with brief personal prayer. Cassian includes several references to a kind of ecstatic prayer, which he terms 'fiery prayer', that can arise spontaneously in the midst of the normal monastic routines of psalmody or repeating brief formulae from the Bible (Stewart 1998: 100–32).

John Cassian's curious mix of Evagrian spirituality and ecstatic prayer was not unique. Despite the distinct difference in tone between the cool, apophatic tradition represented by Evagrius and the much warmer, experiential tone of Pseudo-Macarius, the two approaches were often woven together by later authors. Cassian may have been the first, though any formal connection between his writings and those of Pseudo-Macarius, despite striking parallels, remains elusive. More explicitly tributary to Pseudo-Macarius, as well as to Evagrius, were the Greek authors Diadochus of Photike and Mark the Hermit in the fifth century, some portions of the writings attributed to Isaiah of Scetis, Maximus the Confessor in the seventh century, and, via Syriac translations, the seventh-century Syriac writer Isaac of Nineveh (Plested 2004). Many of Isaac's writings were translated into Greek, reinforcing the dual heritage, Evagrian and Pseudo-Macarian, of Byzantine spirituality.

36.3 THE FORMS OF CHRISTIAN PRAYER

36.3.1 Biblical and Liturgical Influence on Individual Prayer

The Bible provided both guidance and content for Christian prayer. Paul's recommendation of 'psalms, hymns, and spiritual songs' (Eph 5: 19; Col 3: 16) underscores the continuing use by Christians of the Psalter and similar 'odes' excerpted from other books of the Jewish Bible. Christians also composed their own canticles, some of which appear in the epistolary literature of the New Testament, as well as in the opening chapters of the Gospel of Luke, which contain three canticles (later known as the *Magnificat*, *Benedictus*, and *Nunc dimittis*, from their Latin incipits) that became staples of Christian prayer. These Christian hymns, composed in Greek, followed the biblical style of poetry rather than classical Greek metrical forms (Hamman 1980: 1228–9). Psalms and canticles, familiar to all Christians from liturgical use, were the first texts memorized by monks for both liturgical and personal prayer (Hamman 1989b; Stewart 1998: 102–3).

Jesus' custom of praying to God as Father (*Abba*), handed on to his disciples in the prayer he taught them, became a standard form of Christian address to God. Christians also followed the Jewish custom of praying to God as 'Lord' (*Adonai*; Gk. *Kyrios*). Christians used *Kyrios* in their manuscripts of the Old Testament to translate the sacred Tetragrammaton YHWH. Jews had left it untranslated in the Greek version of the Hebrew Bible, but used *Kyrios* as a verbal substitute in public reading (Fitzmyer 1979). Jesus was called 'Lord' already in the New Testament period, based on messianic interpretation of Psalm 109 (110) and other texts. Paul cites an Aramaic equivalent in the closing words of 1 Corinthians, *Marana tha*, 'Come, our Lord' (1 Cor 16: 22), and the book of Revelation ends with the similar, 'Amen. Come, Lord Jesus!' (Rev 22: 20). The phrase *Kyrie eleison*, 'Lord have mercy', with roots in the Septuagint version of the Old Testament and the gospel stories of people asking Jesus for healing, became both a liturgical refrain and a formula for private prayer. Many of the early examples of the brief, repeated phrases used by monks for meditation are variants of the *Kyrie eleison*. Normally interpreted by Christians as a prayer to Christ, the *Kyrie eleison* and the similar prayer 'God, have mercy on me, a sinner!' from the story of the tax collector and the Pharisee (Lk 18: 13), were the core of the later 'Jesus Prayer', 'Lord Jesus Christ, Son of God, have mercy on me, a sinner'. The use of the name of Jesus as a repeated invocation in prayer is traceable at least as far back as Diadochus (Stewart 1998: 104).

Various biblical words and phrases became staple elements of Christian prayer, such as 'Amen', used frequently in the Old Testament and in synagogue liturgy as an expression of agreement, and by Jesus to underscore his more solemn sayings. The acclamation 'Alleluia' (Heb. *Halleluyah*, 'praise the Lord'), used as a refrain in some of the Psalms, was part of the heavenly liturgy depicted in the book of Revelation and passed into Christian use.

One of the most common biblically inspired formulae for prayer was the 'doxology', or concluding prayer of praise that names and ascribes glory to God. This form, based on Jewish models and Graeco-Roman epistolary traditions, was common in the New Testament letters, used in the liturgy, and became a standard feature of individual prayer (Rom 11: 36, 16: 25–7, etc.; Werner 1945: 275–323; Neyrey 2005). A common Trinitarian example was 'Glory be to the Father, and to the Son, and to the Holy Spirit, as it was in the beginning, is now, and will be for the ages of ages. Amen'. Other liturgical prayers based on biblical models such as the 'Holy, holy, holy Lord, God of Hosts, heaven and earth are full of your glory, hosanna in the highest' (see Isa 6: 3 and Rev 4: 9) and the kindred late fourth-century prayer 'Holy God, Holy Strong One, Holy Immortal One, have mercy on us' (known as the 'Trisagion') also shaped the rhetoric of individual devotion.

The eucharist strongly influenced individual practices of prayer in both format and formula. The fundamental movement of eucharistic praying, inherited from the Jewish *berakah* ('blessing') tradition, was to begin with praise and thanksgiving for God's blessings past and present, perhaps include confession of sins and unworthiness, and only then turn to petition. The Lord's Prayer, based on Jewish models, was a simple example of this pattern and was the cornerstone of individual prayer. Origen recommended a similar pattern of praising God the Father through Christ and by the Holy Spirit, followed by thanks, confession of sins, and prayer for healing, then the requests for specific things, and finally a closing doxology echoing the opening Trinitarian invocation (*Or.* 33. 1–6). The actual words used would have been largely inspired by rhetorical patterns learned at the celebration of the eucharist and other liturgical celebrations.

Early Christian monks memorized large sections of the Bible (Pachomius required novices to memorize the Psalms and the New Testament) for use in both public and private prayer. In private use the purpose was to occupy the mind with biblical rather than other thoughts, as well as to cultivate deeper intimacy with the text (Stewart 1998: 101–13). Evagrius Ponticus compiled an enormous list of biblical verses, the *Antirrhētikos*, that could be used to resist dangerous thoughts, a practice seen already in the *Life of Antony* (Brakke 2005, 2006). The classic monastic form of individual prayer became alternation of recited (or chanted) biblical passages with a brief period of personal prayer. This pattern was used in the liturgical gatherings for prayer at the appointed times of day and night, as well as for individual devotion while keeping vigil or working (Stewart, forthcoming). In later monastic literature, the emphasis on memorization of scripture became more focused on texts used liturgically, such as the Psalms, and one finds a greater role for private reading, the *lectio divina* so prized by Benedict (e.g. *Rule* 8. 3–5, 48. 4, 48. 13–22). Since reading, even when alone, was vocalized, the experience of the text was closer to hearing it read aloud or recited from memory than would be the case with the purely ocular ('silent') reading which became normative several centuries later.

While the Bible clearly shaped the language of praying, prayer was also closely linked to the reading and interpretation of the sacred text. The preparation and concentration required for prayer clarified insight into the spiritual significance of a biblical passage. Origen was most famously associated with this approach, teaching that apparent obscurities in the Bible pointed to defects in the reader's spiritual acumen rather than to faults in the text, and had been placed there by the Holy Spirit as an encouragement to continued diligence (*Princ.* 4). For Origen and those formed in his thought, such as Evagrius Ponticus and John Cassian, the Bible was their principal contemplative medium, the best access to the ways and intentions of God for humankind in general and oneself in particular (Stewart 1998: 89–95).

36.3.2 Mystical Prayer

The New Testament describes episodes in which both Jesus and Paul experienced a suspension of normal parameters of space and time, visions, and intense prayer. In the stories of Jesus's time in the wilderness, his transfiguration, his prayer at Gethsemane, and his post-resurrection appearances, the border between ordinary existence and the numinous blurs or disappears. Paul spoke of his own ecstatic experience of being 'caught up into the third heaven' where he saw and heard things incapable of expression in human speech (2 Cor 12: 2), and wrote about spiritual gifts (*charismata*) such as prophecy and speaking in tongues as things he himself had experienced (1 Cor 12–14). The disciples gathered at Pentecost received an outpouring of the Holy Spirit evident in speaking new languages and powers of healing (Acts 2). These phenomena had precedents in the ecstasies of the Hebrew prophets (1 Sam 10: 1–13, 19: 18–24). Despite this heritage, such experiences caused anxiety for Paul and for his successors. Paul feared that the acquisition of spiritual gifts could become an end in itself, and that they could become means of self-glorification rather than service to the Church.

Later Christian writers manifest similar concerns. The *Didache* cautions against itinerant false prophets who take advantage of hospitality. As movements centred on prophecy, visions, and charismatic inspiration (such as the Montanists) emerged as rivals to biblically and liturgically oriented communities, suspicion of such phenomena grew among church leaders within the developing 'Catholic' Church. As it moved outside of the Jewish religious ambit, Christianity also became more exposed to influence from esoteric sects and mystery religions. With this exposure came a rising concern among church leaders to demarcate Christians ever more sharply from others in the religious marketplace. This process was protracted, and lines were not always clearly drawn. The ambiguity about the extent of 'Gnostic' influence on early Egyptian Christianity, for example, is a reminder that the landscape of early Christianity was much more complex in the second and third centuries than in the fourth. The definition of the biblical canon during this period was part of the resolution of this complexity. The writings which came to be accepted as mainstream Christian literature tended to avoid prophetic and visionary themes (the *Shepherd of Hermas* is an interesting exception), though hagiographical texts allowed more room for them. The suspicion of unusual or ecstatic spiritual experience makes tracking the early development of what would later be called 'mystical' prayer quite difficult (for an overview, see Stroumsa 1992).

As with other aspects of the history of early Christian prayer, the best evidence for mystical experiences comes from the ascetic and monastic movements that became prominent in the fourth century. Many scholars have suggested that the emergence of organized, officially sanctioned monasticism in the fourth century represented an ecclesiastical 'domestication' of the sectarian tendencies of ascetic groups. Within monasticism and around its edges one finds descriptions of profound spiritual experiences that involved speechless prayer, loss of awareness of time and place, and, sometimes, visions. The Pseudo-Macarian *Homilies* contain such accounts, as do some of the standard monastic writings (Stewart 1998: 114–30). Gregory of Nyssa's *Life of Moses* proved to be a charter text for Christian mysticism, with its descriptions of meeting God in the darkness of spiritual ascent, an approach developed further by the sixth-century author known as Pseudo-Dionysius. Evagrius Ponticus was cautious about describing 'pure' or 'true' prayer in other than negative terms (as beyond form, beyond colour, beyond thought, beyond image). John Cassian, however, analysed a variety of powerful spiritual experiences ranging from sorrow to exuberance that he collected under the heading of 'compunction' (Stewart 1998: 114–29). Cassian's 'fiery prayer' is much closer to Pseudo-Macarius's descriptions of intense experience than to the language of Origen and Evagrius, his normal masters. Isaac the Syrian, deeply indebted to Syriac translations of Evagrius's writings, wrote about an ecstatic 'prayer beyond prayer' in terms reminiscent of Pseudo-Macarius (Alfeyev 2000: 217–68). Such exploration continued despite recurrent complaints about Messalianism or similar spiritualist heresies alleged to prefer charismatic experiences to the normal sacramental practices of the Church (Stewart 1991: 100–69; Plested 2004: 16–27). The inherent difficulties of analysing religious experience, joined to the complex interrelationships among these texts, make this particular aspect of early Christian prayer an intriguing area for further study.

One kind of intense experience in prayer was uncontroversial: tears. The association of weeping with prayer had biblical roots in both Old and New Testaments, and became a marker of Christian asceticism and monasticism. One of the Syriac terms for monk was 'weeper', and many of the Egyptian desert hermits were famous for their tears. While tears might express sorrow for sin, they also indicated sincerity and emotional engagement, and were regarded as a spiritual gift that could not be forced by sheer human effort. Cassian analysed the phenomenon of spiritual tears, a theme which became even more prominent in the writings of Diadochus and, especially, Isaac the Syrian (Stewart 1998: 122–29; Alfeyev 2000: 129–42). Western texts such as the *Moral Commentary on Job* (*Moralia*) of Gregory the Great followed Cassian's lead. Every reference to personal prayer in the *Rule of Benedict* mentions tears (*Rule* 4. 57, 20. 3, 49. 4, 52. 4). The Mediterranean world of late antiquity found such an association perfectly understandable.

Suggested Reading

Primary sources

For an array of examples ranging from inscriptions to liturgical texts, see Adalbert Hamman's *Early Christian Prayers* (1961). His more recent collection, *La prière dans l'Église ancienne* (1989*a*), includes the original Greek and Latin texts along with French translations. The best starting point for theological and practical instruction is to read the classic treatises on prayer by Tertullian, Cyprian, Clement, and Origen. Their monastic counterparts, Evagrius Ponticus and John Cassian, are starting points for that tradition. For the Syriac tradition, see Sebastian Brock's translation of key texts in *Syriac Fathers on Prayer and the Spiritual Life*. The *Homilies* of Ps.-Macarius and the *Chapters on Prayer* of Diadochus are an intriguing counterpoint to the approach of Origen and Evagrius.

Secondary sources

The best general survey is McGinn (1991), the first volume in his study of the Western mystical tradition. Bunge (2001) reviews the evidence for the practical aspects of prayer such as posture, gesture, place. Many of the articles in the *Dictionnaire de Spiritualité* are excellent orientations to the subject: e.g. those on 'Prière', 'Expérience spirituelle', 'Coeur', 'Larmes'. On the monastic tradition, Stewart (1998: chs. 5–7) provides an overview of monastic practice and theology of prayer, and Harmless (2004) is a comprehensive survey of the sources.

BIBLIOGRAPHY

Primary sources

APHRAHAT, *Demonstrations*. Syriac text with Latin trans.: R. Graffin, Patrologia Syriaca, 1–2 (Paris: F. Didot, 1894, 1907). Eng. trans. of selections: J. Gwynn, NPNF[2] 13, 345–412. For *Demonstration 4* on prayer: S. Brock, *The Syriac Fathers on Prayer and the Spiritual Life*, CS 101 (Kalamazoo, Mich.: Cistercian Publications, 1987), 5–25.

Apophthegmata patrum. Alphabetical Collection: Greek text with Latin trans.: PG 65. 76–440. Eng. trans.: B. Ward, *Sayings of the Desert Fathers*, CS 59 (Kalamazoo, Mich.: Cistercian Publications, 1975). Systematic Collection: Greek text and French trans.: J.-C. Guy, *Les Apophthegmes des Pères, Collection systématique*, SC 387, 474, 498 (Paris: Éditions du Cerf, 1993, 2003, 2005). Eng. trans.: B. Ward, *The Wisdom of the Desert Fathers* (Oxford: S.L.G. Press, 1975).

Apostolic Constitutions. Greek text and French trans.: M. Metzger, *Les constitutions apostoliques*, SC 320, 329, 336 (Paris: Éditions du Cerf, 1984–7). Eng. trans.: J. Donaldson, ANF 7 (American edn.), 391–505.

Apostolic Tradition. Latin text and French trans.: B. Botte, *La tradition apostolique d'après les anciennes versions*, SC 11bis (Paris: Éditions du Cerf, 1984). Eng. trans.: A. Stewart-Sykes, *On the Apostolic Tradition* (Crestwood, NY: St Vladimir's Seminary Press, 2001).

ATHANASIUS, *Life of Antony, Vita Antonii*. Greek text and French trans.: G. J. M. Bartelink, *Vie d'Antoine*, SC 400 (Paris: Éditions du Cerf, 1994). Eng. trans.: R. C. Gregg, *The Life of Antony and the Letter to Marcellinus*, CWS (Mahwah, NJ: Paulist Press, 1980).

—— *Letter to Marcellinus*. Greek text: PG 27: 12 ff. Eng. trans. in Gregg, *The Life of Antony and the Letter to Marcellinus*, CWS (Mahwah, NJ: Paulist Press, 1980), 101–29.

AUGUSTINE, *Confessions*. Latin text and English commentary: James O'Donnell (Oxford: Clarendon Press, 1992). Eng. trans.: H. Chadwick (Oxford: Oxford University Press, 1991).

AUGUSTINE, *Letter* 130. Latin text: Al. Goldbacher, CSEL 44 (Vienna: Tempsky, 1904), 40–77. Eng. trans.: R. Teske, WSA xi. 2: *The Letters 100–155* (Hyde Park, NY: New City, 2002), 184–99.

BARSANUPHIUS and JOHN, *Letters*. Greek and French trans.: F. Neyt and P. de Angelis-Noah, *Correspondance*, SC 426–7, 450–1 (Paris: Éditions du Cerf, 1997–2002). Eng. trans.: J. Chryssavgis, Barsanuphius and John, Letters, FC 113–14 (Washington D.C.: Catholic University of America Press, 2006–7).

BENEDICT, *Rule*. Latin text and French trans.: A. de Vogüé and J. de Neufville, *La Règle de Saint Benoît*, SC 181–2 (Paris: Éditions du Cerf, 1971). Eng. trans: and Latin text: T. Fry et al. (eds.), *RB 1980: The Rule of St. Benedict in Latin and English with Notes* (Collegeville, Minn.: Liturgical Press, 1981).

Book of Steps. Syriac text and Latin trans.: M. Kmosko, *Patrologia Syriaca*, 1. 3 (Paris: Firmin-Didot, 1926). Eng. trans.: R. Kitchen, *The Book of Steps: The Syriac Liber Graduum*, CS 196 (Kalamazoo, Mich.: Cistercian Publications, 2004).

CLEMENT, *Stromateis*, book 7. Greek text and French trans.: A. le Boulleuc, SC 428 (Paris: Éditions du Cerf, 1951). Eng. trans.: J. E. L. Oulton, *Alexandrian Christianity: Selected Translations of Clement and Origen*, LCC 2 (London: SCM Press, 1954), 93–165.

CYPRIAN, *On the Lord's Prayer*. Latin text and French trans.: M. Réveillaud, *L'oraison dominicale [par] saint Cyprien*, Études d'histoire et de philosophie religieuses, 58 (Paris: Presses universitaires de France, 1964). Eng. trans.: A. Stewart-Sykes, *On the Lord's Prayer: Tertullian, Cyprian and Origen* (Crestwood, NY: St Vladimir's Seminary Press, 2004), 65–93.

DIADOCHUS OF PHOTIKE, *Chapters on Knowledge*. Greek text and French trans.: É. des Places, *Diadoque de Photicé: Oeuvres spirituelles*, SC 5bis (Paris: Éditions du Cerf, 1966). Eng. trans.: G. E. H. Palmer et al., *The Philokalia* (London: Faber & Faber, 1979), i. 253–96.

Didache. Greek text and Eng. trans.: A. Milavec, *The Didache: Faith, Hope, & Life in the Earliest Christian Communities, 50–70 C.E.* (New York: Newman Press, 2003).

(Ps.-)DIONYSIUS, *Mystical Theology*. Greek text: G. Heil and A. Martin Ritter, *Corpus Dionysiacum*, 2, PTS 36 (Berlin: de Gruyter, 1991), 141–50. Eng. trans.: C. Luibhéid, *Pseudo-Dionysius: The Complete Works*, CWS (Mahwah, NJ: Paulist Press, 1987), 135–41.

EVAGRIUS, *Antirrhētikos*. Syriac version: W. Frankenberg, *Euagrius Ponticus*, Abhandlungen der königlichen Gesellschaft der Wissenschaften zu Göttingen, Philologisch-historische Klasse, NF 13/2 (Berlin: Weidmann, 1912).

—— *On Prayer*. Greek text and Eng. trans.: R. E. Sinkewicz, *Evagrius of Pontus: The Greek Ascetic Corpus*, OECS (Oxford: Oxford University Press, 2003).

GREGORY OF NYSSA, *Life of Moses*. Greek text: H. Musurillo, GNO, 7. 1 (Leiden: E. J. Brill, 1991). Eng. trans.: A. J. Malherbe and E. Ferguson, *The Life of Moses*, CWS (Mahwah, NJ: Paulist Press, 1978).

—— *Sermons on the Lord's Prayer*. Greek text: J. F. Callahan, GNO, 7. 2 (Leiden: E. J. Brill, 1992), 5–74. Eng. trans.: H. Graef, *The Lord's Prayer: The Beatitudes*, ACW 18 (Westminster, Md.: Newman Press, 1954), 21–84.

HAMMAN, A. G. (1952), *Prières des premiers chrétiens* (Paris: Fayard). Eng. trans.: W. Mitchell, *Early Christian Prayers* (Chicago: Regnery; London: Longmans, 1961).

ISIDORE OF PELUSIUM, *Letters*. Greek text and French trans.: P. Évieux, *Lettres*, SC 422, 454 (Paris: Éditions du Cerf, 1997–2000).

JOHN CASSIAN, *Conferences*. Latin text: M. Petschenig, CSEL 13 (Vienna: Tempsky, 1886). Eng. trans.: B. Ramsey, *The Conferences*, ACW 57 (New York: Paulist Press, 1997).

——*Institutes*. Latin text: M. Petschenig, CSEL 17 (Vienna: Tempsky, 1888). Eng. trans.: B. Ramsey, *The Institutes*, ACW 58 (New York: Paulist Press, 2000).

Justin Martyr, *First Apology*. Greek text: E. J. Goodspeed, *Die ältesten Apologeten* (Göttingen: Vandenhoeck & Ruprecht, 1914). Eng. trans.: L. W. Barnard, *The First and Second Apologies*, ACW 56 (New York: Paulist Press, 1997).

(Ps-)Macarius, *Homilies*. Collection II: Greek text, H. Dörries *et al.* (eds.), *Die 50 geistlichen Homilien des Makarios*, PTS 4 (Berlin: de Gruyter, 1964). Eng. trans.: G. Maloney, *The Fifty Spiritual Homilies and the Great Letter*, CWS (Mahwah, NJ: Paulist Press, 1992).

Origen, *On First Principles, De principiis*, books 3 and 4. Greek and Latin text: H. Crouzel and M. Simonetti, *Traité des principes*, SC 268 (Paris: Éditions du Cerf, 1980). Eng. trans.: G. W. Butterworth, *On First Principles* (New York: Harper & Row, 1966).

——*On Prayer*. Greek text: P. Koetschau, E. Klostermann, E. Preuschen, W. A. Baehrens (eds.), *Origenes Werke*, 2, GCS 3 (Leipzig: J. C. Hinrichs, 1899), 297–403. Eng. trans.: R. Greer, *Origen*, CWS (Mahwah, NJ: Paulist Press, 1979), 81–170. Also A. Stewart-Sykes, *On the Lord's Prayer: Tertullian, Cyprian and Origen* (Crestwood, NY: St Vladimir's Seminary Press, 2004), 111–214.

Shepherd of Hermas. Greek and Eng. trans.: K. Lake, *The Apostolic Fathers*, LCL 2 (Cambridge, Mass.: Harvard University Press, 1913).

Tertullian, *On the Lord's Prayer*. Latin text and Eng. trans.: E. Evans, *Q. Septimii Florentis Tertulliani De oratione liber/ Tertullian's Tract on the Prayer* (London: S.P.C.K., 1953). Also see A. Stewart-Sykes, *On the Lord's Prayer: Tertullian, Cyprian and Origen* (Crestwood, NY: St Vladimir's Seminary Press, 2004), 41–64.

Secondary sources

Alfeyev, H. (2000), *The Spiritual World of Isaac the Syrian*, CS 175 (Kalamazoo, Mich.: Cistercian Publications).

Aubriot-Sévin, D. (1992), *Prière et conceptions religieuses en Grèce ancienne jusqu'à la fin du Ve siècle avant Jésus-Christ*, Collection de la Maison de l'Orient, 22, Série littéraire et philosophique, 5 (Lyons: Maison de l'Orient).

Aune, D. E. (2001), 'Prayer in the Greco-Roman World', in R. N. Longenecker (ed.), *Into God's Presence: Prayer in the New Testament* (Grand Rapids, Mich.: Eerdmans), 23–42.

Bitton-Ashkelony, B. (2003), 'Demons and Prayers: Spiritual Exercises in the Monastic Community of Gaza in the Fifth and Sixth Centuries', *VC* 57: 200–21.

Brakke, D. (2005), 'Making Public the Monastic Life: Reading the Self in Evagrius Ponticus' Talking Back', in D. Brakke *et al.* (eds.), *Religion and the Self in Antiquity* (Bloomington, Ind.: Indiana University Press), 222–33.

——(2006), *Demons and the Making of the Monk: Spiritual Combat in Early Christianity* (Cambridge, Mass.: Harvard University Press).

Brock, S. (1992), *The Luminous Eye: The Spiritual World View of Saint Ephrem*, CS 124 (Kalamazoo, Mich.: Cistercian Publications).

Brown, M. J. (2004), *The Lord's Prayer through North African Eyes: A Window into Early Christianity* (New York: T & T Clark).

Bunge, G. (2002), *Earthen Vessels: The Practice of Personal Prayer according to the Patristic Tradition* (San Francisco: Ignatius Press).

Chapot, F., and Laurot, B. (2001), *Corpus de prières grecques et romaines*, Recherches sur les rhétoriques religieuses, 2 (Turnhout: Brepols).

CROUZEL, H. (1961), *Origène et la «connaissance mystique»*, Museum Lessianum, Section théologique, 56 (Paris: Desclée de Brouwer).

DANIÉLOU, J. (1948), *Origène* (Paris: La Table Ronde).

DRISCOLL, M. S., and SHERIDAN, S. G. (2000), 'Every Knee Shall Bend: Liturgical and Ascetical Prayer in V–VII Century Palestine', *Worship*, 74: 130–7.

DYSINGER, L. (2005), *Psalmody and Prayer in the Writings of Evagrius Ponticus* (Oxford: Oxford University Press).

FINKEL, A. (2001), 'Prayer in Jewish Life of the First Century as Background to Early Christianity', in R. N. Longenecker (ed.), *Into God's Presence: Prayer in the New Testament* (Grand Rapids, Mich.: Eerdmans), 43–65.

FINNEY, P. C. (1994), *The Invisible God: The Earliest Christians on Art* (New York: Oxford University Press).

FITZMYER, J. A. (1979), 'The Semitic Background of the New Testament *Kyrios*-Title', in J. A. Fitzmyer, *A Wandering Aramean: Collected Aramaic Essays*, SBL Monograph Series, 25 (Missoula, Mont.: Scholars Press), 115–42.

GRIFFITH, S. H. (2002), 'The Handwriting on the Wall: Graffiti in the Church of St. Antony', in E. S. Bolman (ed.), *Monastic Visions: Wall Paintings in the Monastery of St. Antony at the Red Sea* (Cairo: American Research Center in Egypt; New Haven: Yale University Press), 185–93.

HADOT, P. (1977), 'Exercices spirituels', *Annuaire de la Ve Section de l'École Pratique des Hautes Études*, 84: 25–70.

—— (1987), 'Exercices spirituels et "philosophie chrétienne" ', in *Exercices spirituels et philosophie antique*, 2nd edn. (Paris: L'Institut d'études augustiniennes), 59–76.

HAMMAN, A. (1961), 'Le rythme de la prière chrétienne ancienne', *La Maison-Dieu*, 64 (1961), 6–28; repr. in *Études patristiques: Méthodologie-Liturgie-Histoire-Théologie* (Paris: Beauchesne, 1991), 159–81.

—— (1980), 'La prière chrétienne et la prière païenne, formes et différences', in *Principat: Religion: Vorkonstantinisches Christentum: Verhältnis zu römischem Staat und heidnischer Religion*, ANRW II. 23. 2 (1980), 1190–1247.

—— (1989a), *La prière dans l'Église ancienne* (Berne: Peter Lang).

—— (1989b), 'L'utilisation des psaumes dans les deux premiers siècles chrétiens', *StPatr* 18. 2: 363–74; repr. in *Études patristiques: Méthodologie-Liturgie-Histoire-Théologie* (Paris: Beauchesne, 1991), 147–58.

HARL, M. (1958), *Origène et la fonction révélatrice du verbe incarné* (Paris: Éditions du Seuil).

HARMLESS, W. (2004), *Desert Christians: An Introduction to the Literature of Early Monasticism* (New York: Oxford University Press).

JENSEN, R. M. (2005), *Face to Face: Portraits of the Divine in Early Christianity* (Minneapolis: Fortress Press).

KILEY, M. (1997), *Prayer from Alexander to Constantine: A Critical Anthology* (London: Routledge).

LONGENECKER, R. N. (2001), 'Prayer in the Pauline Letters', in R. N. Longenecker (ed.), *Into God's Presence: Prayer in the New Testament* (Grand Rapids, Mich.: Eerdmans), 203–27.

McGINN, B. (1991), *The Presence of God: A History of Western Christian Mysticism*, i: *The Foundations of Mysticism* (New York: Crossroad; London: SCM Press).

MARSHALL, I. H. (2001), 'Jesus-Example and Teacher of Prayer in the Gospels', in R. N. Longenecker (ed.), *Into God's Presence: Prayer in the New Testament* (Grand Rapids, Mich.: Eerdmans), 113–31.

MURRAY, R. (2004), *Symbols of Church and Kingdom: A Study in Early Syriac Tradition*, rev. edn. (Piscataway, NJ: Gorgias).

NEYREY, J. (2005), ' "First," "Only", "One of a Few", and "No One Else": The Rhetoric of Uniqueness and the Doxologies in 1 Timothy', *Biblica*, 86: 59–87.

ONG, W. J. (1988), 'Before Textuality: Orality and Interpretation', *Oral Tradition*, 3: 259–69; repr. in T. J. Farrell and P. A. Soukup (eds.), *Faith and Contexts* / Walter J. Ong, iii: *Further Essays 1952–90*, South Florida-Rochester-Saint Louis Studies on Religion and the Social Order (Atlanta: Scholars Press, 1992–9).

PLESTED, M. (2004), *The Macarian Legacy: The Place of Macarius-Symeon in the Eastern Christian Tradition* (Oxford: Oxford University Press).

PRIGENT, P. (1992), 'Les orants dans l'art funéraire du christianisme ancien', *Revue d'histoire et de philosophie religieuses*, 72: 143–50, 259–87.

PULLEYN, S. (1997), *Prayer in Greek Religion* (Oxford: Clarendon Press).

STEWART, C. (1991), *Working the Earth of the Heart: The Messalian Controversy in History, Texts, and Language to AD 431*, Oxford Theological Monographs (Oxford: Clarendon Press).

——(1998), *Cassian the Monk*, Oxford Studies in Historical Theology (New York: Oxford University Press).

——(2001), 'Imageless Prayer and the Theological Vision of Evagrius Ponticus', *JECS* 9: 179–210.

——(2003), 'John Cassian's Schema of Eight Principal Faults and his Debt to Origen and Evagrius', in C. Badilita and A. Jakab, with M. Alexandre *et al.* (eds.), *Jean Cassien entre l'orient et l'occident*, Actes du colloque international organisé par le New Europe College en collaboration avec la Ludwig Boltzman Gesellschaft, Bucarest, 27–28 septembre 2001 (Paris: Beauchesne; Iaşi: Polirom).

——(2005), 'Evagrius Ponticus and the "Eight Generic Logismoi" ', in R. Newhauser (ed.), *In the Garden of Evil: The Vices and Culture in the Middle Ages* (Toronto: Pontifical Institute of Medieval Studies), 3–34.

——(forthcoming), 'The Practices of Monastic Prayer: Origins, Evolution, and Tensions', in P. Sellew (ed.), *Living for Eternity: Monasticism in Egypt*, Interdisciplinary Studies in Ancient Culture and Religion (Leuven: Peeters).

STROUMSA, G. G. (1992), '*Paradosis*: Traditions ésotériques dans le christianisme des premiers siècles', in *Savoir et salut* (Paris: Éditions du Cerf), 127–43.

VAN DER HORST, P. W. (1994), 'Silent Prayer in Antiquity', *Numen*, 41: 1–25.

WERNER, E. (1945), 'The Doxology in Synagogue and Church: A Liturgico-Musical Study', *Hebrew Union College Annual*, 19: 275–351.

ZIBAWI, M. (1998), 'Les débuts de l'art chrétien' and 'Le paléochrétien', in M. A. Crippa and M. Zibawi (eds.), *L'art paléochrétien: Des origines à Byzance* (Saint-Léger-Vaubun: Éditions Zodiaque), 69–182.

CHAPTER 37

ASCETICISM

REBECCA KRAWIEC

37.1 INTRODUCTION

UNLIKE most chapters in this Handbook, this one does not explore a concrete historical topic but an abstract concept, 'asceticism'. What is more, 'asceticism', like 'religion', is a modern construct (Fraade 1987: 253), although based on an ancient term, *askēsis* (for which the standard translation is 'training', signalling its association with athletics).[1] Two obstacles immediately present themselves to an overview of the role of asceticism in shaping early Christian studies: the lack of a clear definition of asceticism and, equally problematic, the ubiquity of the topic in both ancient sources and modern scholarship, especially in the past 35 years. There is no standard set of ancient 'ascetic' texts, since asceticism is part of the discourse that Christianity created, especially in the post-Constantinian period (Cameron 1991). Letters, hagiographies, homilies, even acts of councils (Burrus 1992) all participate in the construction of an asceticism that was a central concern of Christians in late antiquity. To chart the shifts in the study of, and indeed definition of, asceticism is to follow as well the major changes in the field from 'patristics' to 'early Christian studies' (Martin 2005: 4–13). No longer a pathology in religion that needs to be explained away, or simply an account of extreme, or even bizarre, behaviours, asceticism is the means by which historians of early Christianity confront central methodological issues in investigating discourses, power, social relations, the body, and all the attendant current concerns of the construction of the self and society.

37.2 THEORIZING ASCETICISM

In recent years there have been several descriptions of the importance of asceticism in shaping the field of early Christian studies, even as scholars continue to debate the meaning and application of the term (Elm 1998; E. A. Clark 1999: 14–42; Martin 2005). These accounts agree on key paradigm shifts as the study of asceticism moved from older, theologically motivated models (accepting or rejecting asceticism as legitimate) to those that have embraced a range of modern critical approaches to analyse the function and construction of asceticism. Throughout these developments there has been a continued effort to hone a definition of asceticism that is broadly applicable to a variety of religions and historical time periods, rather than being specific to one religious tradition (namely, Christianity) in one set of historical circumstances (late antiquity) (Wimbush and Valantasis 1995; Valantasis 1995b; Flood 2004).

In general the search for the 'origins' and 'motivations' (E. A. Clark 1999: 18) of asceticism (distinct from monasticism, which poses its own methodological problems (Rubenson 1995)) reveals a pervasive assumption in scholarship: that asceticism is a stable category that can define a change in Christianity. The basic division in older studies of asceticism followed denominational lines, with Protestant scholars in particular rejecting any notion that asceticism was part of earliest Christianity. These scholars saw 'pure' Christianity as stemming from a presumably anti-ascetic Judaism and later corrupted by Greek influences (see E. A. Clark 1999: 19–20). Many of these mainly German and French nineteenth-century studies examined asceticism as a pathology. Although some later, early twentieth-century works countered this view with a more complex analysis (see Wimbush and Valantasis 1995: pp. xx–xxi for a survey), characterizations of ascetic practices as 'bizarre', 'abnormal', and 'childish and ridiculous' continued (Shaw 1998b: 18, quoting Musurillo). These labels dismiss asceticism as too 'bodily', and thus promote a hierarchy of mind (or soul) over body wherein ascetic practices either must be rejected or, in order to be thought suited to religion, 'spiritualized'.

This line of thinking has been debunked in numerous ways: scholars have questioned whether Judaism in this time period was, in fact, anti-ascetic (Fraade 1987); they have examined ascetic portions of the New Testament (Wimbush 1987; Derrett 1995; Wimbush and Vaage 1999); and they have investigated strains of asceticism in the variety of Christian literature, both orthodox and non-canonical, from the second and third centuries. Another corrective to the earlier view of asceticism has been to recognize that asceticism was a training of the body together with the soul (Brown 1988; Castelli 1992; Shaw 1998b). Asceticism is now seen as a religious impulse to be studied theoretically and often in a comparative framework. In the study of early Christianity, asceticism creates connections between analyses of changes in social relations and of much early Christian theology about the body, creation, salvation, and humanity's new relationship to God through the transformation of the Incarnation.

The catalyst for these new approaches to asceticism was the 1971 publication of Peter Brown's foundational article 'The Rise and Function of the Holy Man in Late Antiquity' (Brown 1971). This essay marked a decisive shift in the study of all early Christianity, including asceticism, since ascetic practice was the source of the holy man's holiness, that is, his status as 'other' and 'stranger'. In this work, Brown introduced functionalist anthropology (mainly the work of Mary Douglas) to the study of asceticism. Later, Brown (1983) would embrace cultural anthropology (mainly the work of Clifford Geertz) to create a 'thick description' of the saint as authority figure who both imitates and is to be imitated. Aline Rousselle's (1988) analysis of ancient expressions of desire and attendant constructions of the body and Michel Foucault's theories of self, power, and knowledge also began to take asceticism seriously, not just as a bodily practice but as a means to construct the self and as an indicator of broader cultural attitudes. Indeed, Brown's next interpretation of the holy man as a negotiator in complex social systems stemmed from Foucault's theories about the relationship between power and knowledge (Brown 1995; for analyses of Brown, see Elm 1998; Harvey 1998; Howard-Johnston and Hayward 1999; Martin 2005). These crucial works introduced particular themes—power and authority, the body, subjectivity, and the self—that have become central to the study of asceticism in early Christianity.

Yet one must still ask: what is asceticism?[2] And should it be studied in relation to particular circumstances, such as one religious tradition, in one specific time period, or even one geographical location within that period and tradition? Asking these questions allowed scholars to 'explode simple notions about asceticism, including the notion that it has to do simply with the negative' (that is, denial, withdrawal, and even hatred of the body) and 'simply with the distant past' (Wimbush and Valantasis 1995: p. xxvi). Rather, scholars began to form a 'cross-cultural, theoretical framework' (Wimbush and Valantasis 1995: p. xxiii) for the study of asceticism that would recognize its role in a variety of religions, and even as a basis for culture itself.

In much of the earlier scholarship, 'asceticism' as a term was accepted uncritically with little or no effort to create a theoretical definition that would apply to its diverse settings. Geoffrey Harpham's *The Ascetic Imperative in Culture and Criticism* (1987), however, suggested that asceticism was not 'merely' religious but the key to culture; it '*raises the issue* of culture by structuring an opposition between culture and its opposite' (Harpham 1987: p. xii). For Harpham, then, asceticism has a broad definition, namely, 'any act of self-denial undertaken as a strategy of empowerment or gratification' (Harpham 1987: p. xiii). More-over, through its ability to balance oppositions without privileging one over the other, asceticism becomes no longer simply an aspect of religious expression throughout history, but an impulse that is as evident in modern critical theory (including the work of Foucault (Harpham 1987: 220–35)) as it is in Athana-sius's *Life of Antony* (Harpham 1987: 3–18). Harpham's arguments had a pro-found effect on the study of early Christian asceticism, as they pushed inves-tigations of asceticism beyond descriptions of fasting, sexual renunciation, and various bodily mortifications to a more theoretical understanding of how as-ceticism functioned as a foundation of culture. Asceticism therefore came to serve as an 'analytical tool' for understanding the cultural shifts and changes evident in the fourth and fifth centuries of the Roman Empire (Elm 1994: 350).

Definitions of asceticism, of which there are a wide variety (see E. A. Clark 1999: 14–17), began to combine a historical outlook (focused on practices) with a theoretical emphasis on asceticism as a cultural system (Valantasis 1995b: 544). Perhaps one of the most oft-cited descriptions suggested that 'asceticism may be defined as performances within a dominant social environment intended to in-augurate a new subjectivity, different social relations, and an alternative symbolic universe' (Valantasis 1995a: 797). This definition highlights another shift in schol-arship, one towards performance theory and analyses of subjectivity, that is, of the relationship between the ascetic and the self. Such an approach allows fresh examination of what constitutes asceticism. For example, Valantasis, using his own definition, argued that the *Gospel of Thomas* is ascetical, not because it has themes of bodily renunciation or self-denial (negative aspects of asceticism), but rather because it argues for a transformation of the self (a positive aspect of asceticism) (Valantasis 1999). While useful, this definition has also been criticized for lacking the 'everyday' meaning of asceticism, since it does not include any clear reference to renunciation. Asceticism necessitates giving up, beyond 'normal' amounts, goods that are recognized as enjoyable in order to be not simply transformed but trans-formed to a higher order of existence (Martin 2005: 14–15). Scholars have agreed that asceticism is performance, but one specifically tied to memory and tradition, and therefore a 'quintessentially religious act' rather than a secular pursuit (Flood 2004: 1–2). In addition, asceticism engages its contemporaneous symbolic universe, rather than creating a completely alternative one (Brakke 2001a: 533–4). These critiques help chart continuing developments in the theorizing of asceticism, in which key themes emerge: it involved bodily performances, but these exist as textual artefacts; ascetics believed that they could transform themselves, both body and self, into something that prefigures the heavenly order; and constructions of asceticism provide an avenue to understanding the broader historical developments of late antiquity.

37.3 SOURCES

There are, unfortunately, no foundational texts for early Christian asceticism, since the concept is not limited either in terms of time period or literary genre. Although the various treatises titled *On Virginity* and monastic rules would seem the most obvious sources, late antique letters, sermons, and especially hagiographies comprise the bulk of the material examined in scholarship. Although the ubiquity of the topic would seem to suggest that asceticism was an ideal embraced by all Christians in late antiquity, the surviving sources' authors are primarily elite, male ascetics, themselves the victors in various ecclesiastical and doctrinal struggles in the period. This raises the question of whether this small group represents the 'norm' of Christianity in this time period. In addition, these sources are now regarded as much as literary texts as historical documents (see E. A. Clark 2001 on this distinction). As such, both texts that explicitly encourage asceticism and those that use ascetic language create an 'ascetic discourse' (Cameron 1995: 150–2). This 'discursive turn' in examining sources allows scholars to investigate the authors of texts in addition to their subjects.

Christian asceticism has its roots in the New Testament, and indeed ascetical passages in scripture have provided an area of historical investigation for earliest Christian asceticism. These same texts, however, were also read and interpreted by late antique authors to support their own ascetic inclinations, thereby shaping scriptural passages to be 'pro-ascetic' even when they might seem completely contrary, especially in the Hebrew Bible (E. A. Clark 1999). To say that earliest Christianity—that is, both the Jesus movement and the Christian communities apparent in the New Testament—is ascetical or not is itself to embrace both a category and a method of reading that are shaped by later commentary. For example, the Gospel of Luke contains the famous passage that to be a follower of Jesus a person must hate his various family members (Lk 14: 26). Late antique writers often used this passage to define not only the ascetic life as one of renunciation of worldly, that is, familial, ties (E. A. Clark 1995, 1999) but also the proper priorities of all Christians (to choose Christ before 'the world'). Yet these same writers, despite their ascetic inclinations, had to make this passage applicable to those Christians who did not embrace the ascetic life in totality, who did not renounce childbearing and familial relationships (Jacobs 2003). Sources for biblical asceticism, then, include both scripture itself, as a historical record of one period of Christianity, and also the vast biblical interpretations of the late antique era that provided support for the cultural changes of the period.

The sources from the second and third centuries show that asceticism was not limited to one variety of Christianity, defined either geographically or doctrinally.[3] Rather, it was a means by which Christians tried to live out their new identity, and so marks the divergent anthropologies of various forms of Christianity. Some authors refer to asceticism positively, such as Athenagoras in his claim that asceticism is one reason why Christians are ethical people (*Plea* 33). Others examine degrees of asceticism to distinguish between acceptable and unacceptable forms of Christianity. Alexandrian theologians had to contend with the challenges of Gnosticism and the different views of the body it presented; the writings of Clement and Origen therefore contribute to a construction of an orthodox asceticism (McGuckin 1985; Hunter 1992; Behr 1999; see also the frequency with which Origen appears in E. A. Clark 1999). Syrian Christianity included a vow of 'singleness' that some Christians (called 'covenanters') took at baptism (see Brock 1973 for an overview). Scholars have scrutinized the meaning of this term. The older view suggested that this vow was quickly abandoned, since it would exclude married Christians (Vööbus 1958), while a modified position argues that it denoted categories for both virgins and chaste marriages (Harvey 1990: 4–6). Although the term is related to the Greek term for monk, *monachos*, the 'singleness' of these ascetics did not stem from living apart from society but rather evoked a singleness of purpose and the singleness of the Only-Begotten Son of God (Murray 1974; Griffith 1995; see Aphrahat, *Demonstration* 6, in Jacobs 2004).

These same early ascetic trends appear in the apocryphal acts of the apostles (Paul and Thecla, Thomas, Andrew, Peter, John). The emphasis on ascetic teaching in these texts stands out in part because of their perceived difference from canonical sources. For example, both the Pastoral Epistles and the *Acts of Paul and Thecla* claim Paul as their authority, but they diverge in their interpretations of his teachings. The canonical Pastorals embrace family, marriage, and childbearing as the means to salvation, which the apocryphal acts locate in asceticism, especially in the Beatitudes with which the story begins (MacDonald 1983). Some of these acts also have as main characters women who embrace asceticism, either against their husbands' wishes or as a catalyst for their spouses' conversion to (ascetic) Christianity as well. This dual focus, asceticism and women, alongside the texts' marginalization (Tertullian specifically denounced the *Acts of Paul and Thecla*), led scholars to argue that asceticism provided a source of liberation for women. These texts now could be understood as representing a lost women's history within Christianity (Davies 1980; Burrus 1987, 1994). As with sources for asceticism in general, however, this view changed with the field's interest in discourse. The stories being told were thus seen to be less about women and their agency, and more about the struggle between various male forms of authority, acted out through the control of women (Cooper 1996). Asceticism remains a crucial factor in the interpretations of these texts, but its function differs.

There have been a number of attempts to explain why asceticism appears more frequently in fourth-century and later texts. The most common include: it replaced martyrdom; it was a move against the increased institutionalization and politicalization of Christianity; it had a special appeal for women. Yet none has offered a fully persuasive explanation of why nearly every writer of this period—from famous leaders such as Athanasius of Alexandria, Jerome, Ambrose of Milan, John Chrysostom, the Cappadocian fathers (Basil of Caesarea, Gregory of Nazianzus, Gregory of Nyssa), and Augustine, to those involved in the monastic movement, to those deemed heretics, to those writing lives of the saints—engages the topic of asceticism (E. A. Clark 1999: 22–7). Monastic literature, from the *Sayings of the Desert Fathers* (*Apophthegmata Patrum*), to the histories, to the ascetical theories of Evagrius of Pontus, not only records the development of monasticism as an institution but also presents the ascetic values that constitute monastic identity. There are also 'documentary' sources such as Egyptian papyri and canons of councils that evidence a diversity of ascetic practices, especially for women (Elm 1994: 227–52; Goehring 1999: 13–38). If we cannot account for this increase fully in terms of motivation, we can nevertheless investigate how this shift in language, and thus ideas and values, contributes to the 'Christianization' of the Roman Empire (Cameron 1995: 148).

All these sources combine to create the 'ascetic discourse' that is characteristic of late antique Christianity, again illustrating that an assessment of 'sources' for asceticism involves an examination of *how* to read particular texts, rather than what to read. The various analyses of the *Lives of Symeon Stylites* (Doran 1992), the collection of three hagiographies that describe the ascetic career of this Syrian figure who represents, to some, the 'wilder' side of asceticism, serve as an example of this point. First, Brown's 'Rise and Function' examines hagiography, with all its rhetorical flourishes and seemingly legendary qualities, as a legitimate source for social history. Symeon becomes an example of the new patron for a Christian milieu, whose status as 'other' and 'stranger'—made possible by the distance created from 'ordinary' Christians by his ascetic practice—was the basis of his authority (Brown 1971). After Brown, hagiography was no longer simply read from a positivist view, as history of the saints, but as recording 'data' that could be interpreted through an anthropological lens.

Apart from numerous critiques of this early rendition of the 'holy man' (Cameron 1999; Rousseau 1997, 1999), the three *Lives* themselves show divergent constructions of Symeon's asceticism, dependent on the individual author's framework (Harvey 1988). Moreover, Harvey also re-examines the *Lives* using ritual theory to argue that Symeon's authority lay not in being 'stranger' but rather in how his asceticism was integrated, through the liturgy, into the life of the community. The holy man was not a lone ascetic figure. Instead, as the hagiographies make clear, charismatic and institutional forms of authority were reconciled through a shared status as part of the Christian body (Harvey 1998: 525, 538–9). Harvey's analysis is as much of how the author constructs the text as it is of the portrait of Symeon that emerges (see Cameron 1999: 35–6 for a critique of Brown on this point). Within that portrait, moreover, the bodily actions of Symeon, such as standing on a pillar with arms outstretched, created new perceptions of the body for the audience, namely, outside the normal dimensions of time and space that define humanity (Miller 1994: 147). Finally, Theodoret of Cyrrhus, in his version of Symeon's *Life*, uses his asceticism and that of his subjects to shape and anchor the text's authority. His subjects' authority lies in their reconfiguration of biblical models, and Theodoret's authority lies in his role as 'evangelist' (Krueger 2004: 15–32). This list is by no means exhaustive of the scholarship on Symeon's hagiographies, but it illustrates the shifts that have occurred in the ways in which scholars examine the sources.

This type of overview could be repeated at length for any number of major sources of asceticism in late antiquity, both as a practice of piety and as part of the emerging monastic movement. This vast array of literature in the fourth century and beyond, in East and West, would seem to support the view that the spread of Christianity and its power led to the 'invasion of the ascetic ideal' (Markus 1990) as the formative religious and cultural shift. Yet, to assume that all ascetic texts, and their authors, share the same view of asceticism—that is, agree on the proper role of ascetic practices within Christianity, both for clergy and for laity—is to flatten the sources. Just as there is no single collection of sources for asceticism, so too there is no one 'asceticism' that is promoted within the diversity of texts available.

37.4 WHAT IS ASCETICISM? THE ANCIENT DEBATE

Defining asceticism in ancient texts is linked with efforts to locate authority, especially within the new social orders created by Christianity. Asceticism, through its 'negative' construction of withdrawal, resistance, and renunciation, calls into question existing social structures, and through its 'positive' element of transformation, suggests new options. Christian writers embraced both aspects of asceticism, even as they sought to control them by setting boundaries, especially between orthodox and heretical forms of ascetic practice and between bishop and ascetic teacher as holders of authority. Debates over asceticism engaged the major theological controversies of the fourth and fifth centuries, and were part of the cultural and societal shifts of the period, as Christian ascetic leaders sought to balance the transformative aspects of asceticism with the social mores that remained important to the elite male leadership. Constructions of asceticism in ancient texts, therefore, are influenced by the social, political, and theological positions of their authors. In the fourth to fifth centuries, despite a general preference for asceticism among major theologians such as Jerome, Ambrose, John Chrysostom, and Augustine, different 'ascetic messages' emerged in their writings and teachings (E. A. Clark 1989: 29). This diversity exposes the paradox inherent in Christian asceticism: asceticism requires bodily denial and renunciation, but that requirement needs to be made compatible with the inherent goodness of a body created by God, divinely commanded to 'be fruitful and multiply', and sanctified by the Incarnation. In creating this balance, ancient authors used different tools, such as biblical exegesis and instruction to female ascetics, that helped support their own theologies and forms of authority during periods of crisis. In these texts, then, asceticism is an ideology as much as it is a set of particular bodily practices or a view of the self shaped by those practices.

Athanasius, the embattled bishop of Alexandria during the Arian and Meletian controversies and the rise of monasticism, illustrates this view of asceticism as ideology. Athanasius used the *Life of Antony* to construct a particular version of the monk Antony as a figure who argued against Athanasius's Arian opponents and supported the bishop (Brakke 1995: 201–65). In addition, his *Letters to Virgins* created a proper female asceticism wherein virgins living in the city of Alexandria were to follow a Marian model of submission and seclusion. This limited women's exposure to non-ecclesial authority figures like the teacher Hieracas (Goehring 1999: 110–33). Athanasius's definition of female virgins as brides of Christ who were to be under the authority of their Groom, and by extension the bishop as Christ's representative, furthered his own authority (Brakke 1995: 17–79). Finally, Athanasius's discourse embraced an asceticism that formed a basis for a Christian 'heavenly civic life' (*politeia*) (Brakke 1995: 164) that included both those Christians who lived ascetically every day and those who limited their asceticism to the liturgical calendar (Lenten fasts and the like) (Brakke 1995: 182–98). Athanasius presented a coherent ascetic ideology, but one constructed in the context of other forms of asceticism flourishing in fourth-century Alexandria and elsewhere in Egypt, especially for women (Elm 1994: 331–72; Goehring 1999: 187–95, 200–7).

Jovinian posed the greatest challenge in the West, with his resistance to the ascetic ideal and its hierarchy that placed ascetic Christians over those who married and had children (Hunter 1987, 2007). All the major ascetic western writers of the period had to counter both Jovinian's teaching in particular and the general resistance to asceticism. Yet how they did so was shaped by their varying ecclesial positions. Ambrose, in *On Virgins* and the later *On Virginity*, taught an asceticism that solidified his own role as bishop in consecrating, and thus controlling, the virgins who were veiled (Hunter 2000: 285–90). This position also agreed with his teaching on Mary's perpetual virginity (Hunter 2005: 123–7; 2007: 197–204). Jerome was ousted from Rome and denied his hoped-for bishopric because of his suspicious relations with aristocratic women whom he encouraged in a strict asceticism. He sought in his *Against Jovinian* to re-establish his authority through his anti-heretical teachings (Hunter 2005: 127–31). His ascetic language, however, in its seeming denigration of the body (Miller 1994), opened him to charges of Manichaeanism (E. A. Clark 1989: 31), accusations also levied at Ambrose for his teaching about Mary (Hunter 2005: 124). Augustine engaged in less strident language in his embrace of asceticism, in part to avoid the label 'Manichaean' (E. A. Clark 1989: 32) and in part to create a unified church wherein ascetics were part of a whole (Leyser 2000: 12–13).

These western debates can highlight differences with their eastern counterparts. John Chrysostom, whose pro-ascetic language does not differ substantially from that of his contemporaries in the East, does not provoke the same reaction that characterizes the ascetic debates in the West (E. A. Clark 1989: 30).

Two topics have emerged in scholarship as a means of distinguishing these an-cient authors' constructions of an asceticism that supports both emerging orthodox theology and various forms of male Christian authority. The first is biblical exegesis. Late antique authors created readings of biblical texts that have to be understood in the context of the ascetic milieu of the period, even as these authors were part of creating that milieu. Analyses of passages such as Genesis 1–3 (Clark 1986b) and Psalm 45 (Hunter 2000) in the exegesis of Jerome, Ambrose, and Augustine provide the contours of debates over heresies. This approach adds a literary dimension to the social and historical investigations of asceticism, showing how readings of the foundational Christian texts supported the general cultural changes of the period (E. A. Clark 1999).

The second topic lies in the ancient writers' creation of proper models of as-ceticism for women. The irony that these men engaged in ascetic discourses that demeaned women as a category, even as they enjoyed close relationships with 'real' individual women, has long been recognized (E. A. Clark 1979). In addition, scholars have noted that these men created ascetic ideologies in their writings to ascetic women. These ideologies reveal less about the women in question and more about a solidification of male ascetic authority. For example, the Roman value of *nobilitas*, rather than being rejected, could be redefined to include ascetic ideals (Jacobs 2000; Salzman 2001). Likewise, a bishop like Ambrose could reconfigure his relationship with the consecrated virgins using the cultural notion of *paterfamilias* (Hunter 2000: 289). Once again, 'asceticism' emerges as a means of legitimating authority, rather than simply a set of religious practices.

Finally, the East had its own arguments about asceticism that also tried to fix a boundary between orthodoxy and heresy, mainly in the Origenist controversy of the later fourth century (E. A. Clark 1992). Once again, all the major figures in this controversy were ascetic practitioners (many in monasteries (Goehring 1999: 208–18)), and like their western counterparts, they differed about how asceticism was pertinent to an understanding of God's creation, the fall of humanity, Christian marriage and procreation, and salvation, especially the resurrected body (E. A. Clark 1992: 5–6). The role of asceticism in this controversy differs from the western examples, however, in that the eastern debate was largely over ascetic theory and the theology that supported that theory. The question of how that theory influenced pietistic practice is present (E. A. Clark 1992: 75), but not central. Another differ-ence is that, while only western writers debate with Jovinian, the eastern Origenist controversy expanded westward when it became part of the larger struggle between Augustine and Pelagius (E. A. Clark 1999: 194–247). A final caution, however: while these various debates can help us to see difference and diversity in asceticism, these categories can also impose expectations on asceticism and ascetic discourse. Not all ancient sources on asceticism need to be read through the lens created by these disputes (Shaw 2005: 228–9).

Within this diversity and debate, there was general agreement on the unacceptability of certain ascetic practices, most notably a living arrangement between celibate men and women. This practice was roundly criticized or condemned (for a list see E. A. Clark 1986c: 266–70), but with the women receiving particular attention (as *subintroductae*) from John Chrysostom (E. A. Clark 1986c) and from Athanasius (Brakke 1995: 31–4). Other ascetic practices were apparently condemned as being too disruptive to social structures, such as the family and proper gender roles, or to emerging clerical authority. Thus forms of ascetic practice in Cappadocia, associated with Eustathius of Sebaste, were rejected as too extreme (e.g. women cutting their hair short, dressing like men, or leaving their marriages (Elm 1994: 108)); Basil and his sister Macrina modified asceticism into a more acceptable form (Elm 1994: 106–36). Similarly, the Acts of the Council of Saragossa, during the controversy over Priscillian in Spain, condemned a variety of practices, not as a stance against asceticism as a whole, but rather to curb those ascetic practices which were perceived as challenging the authority of the episcopacy (Burrus 1992; fuller discussion in Burrus 1995).

The complexity of asceticism is incompatible with the view that its rise was an inevitable development in late antiquity. Those who agreed that asceticism created a 'distinct' class of Christians still created a spectrum of positions to support that distinction theologically (E. A. Clark 1999: 263). In addition, resistance continued in the West not simply to asceticism as a preferred mode of living but especially as a requirement for clerical authority (Hunter 1999). Not all those who argued against Jovinian, such as the bishop of Rome, Siricius, embraced asceticism enthusiastically (Hunter 2005: 120–3). However, the figure of the 'monk-bishop', an advocate and follower of asceticism who was also an ecclesial authority, sometimes against his will, became the ideal in both the West (Rousseau 1978; Leyser 2000) and the East (Sterk 2004), and thereby blurs the distinction between 'charismatic' and 'institutional' authority (Rapp 2005).

37.5 THE ASCETIC BODY: SOCIAL RELATIONS, SYMBOL, AND THE SELF

Asceticism is ultimately located in the body and, through its transformation of that body, creates both a new self and a new social order. For Christianity, asceticism does not negate the body and the goods associated with it, but changes the body from its fallen state to one that anticipates the heavenly state, either of the resurrected body or of the angelic body (a common trope in monastic literature in particular). Yet these bodily performances, for ancient Christianity, are also located in texts, making the practice of writing itself part of asceticism. Both material bodily practices and language about the body recur as themes in ancient Christian authors. Moreover, this 'body symbolism' draws on 'all the central elements in orthodox Christianity', including especially the incarnation, eucharist, and resurrection, making the body 'symbolic of higher truth' (Cameron 1991: 68). Many of the heretical debates of the period include asceticism because of the period's concern with the body (E. A. Clark 1992: 85). Explorations of asceticism, then, necessarily examine ancient descriptions of the body while also drawing on a wide array of modern theoretical investigations of the body. The ascetic body thus functions in several ways in the study of asceticism: as a locus for social relations, as a metaphor within ascetic discourse, as an object for (male) authors to shape, and as a site for a new self and subjectivity to enact its 'symbolic universe' (recalling the definition in Valantasis 1995a).

The body is a major topic in the study of asceticism because of its centrality to ascetic practice and its obvious pertinence to human identity and society (Castelli 1992: 134–6). Part of the shift from a view of asceticism as a devaluing of the body to that of a positive transformation of the body and self arises from the influence of Michel Foucault, who saw in Christianity a series of new 'technologies of the self'. His *History of Sexuality* (Foucault 1978–86) includes an examination of various modes of subjectivity, especially in the areas of desire and sexuality, from ancient Greece to early Christianity.[4] Foucault argues that Christian discourses about asceticism generated a new subjectivity, creating a new self by determining a new relationship between the subject and her desires (Boyarin and Castelli 2001: 360). This view has altered the study of early Christian asceticism and explains the overall shift in scholarship towards issues such as sexuality in particular and abstinence more generally; to the body, 'both as symbol and as reality'; and to questions of the self, and how that self is formed, that is, subjectivity (Cameron 1999: 36). At the same time, Foucault has been criticized for analysing subjectivity only from the perspective of power and knowledge, and not within Christian theological frameworks. Foucault thus imposes the 'modern (sexual) subject' (Behr 1999: p. vii) on the sources rather than examining them from the authors' perspective. The 'distinctive modality of subjectivity' for early Christian asceticism is that the incarnation made all things new (Behr 1993: 15). Secondly, not all sexual activity 'became transformed into sexual discourse' (E. A. Clark 1988: 628). The concerns of ascetic theorists and practitioners in antiquity were not merely self-examination for its own sake, nor did Christian asceticism form a monolithic view of the self.

Foucault's theories, however, brought ancient discourses about the ascetic body to the fore. Nowhere is this more apparent than in Brown's *Body and Society* (Brown 1988: pp. xvii–xviii).[5] Here Brown explores the emphasis on the sexual elements of asceticism from Paul to Augustine, covering both 'orthodox' and 'heretic' (Marcion, Gnostics, Mani) and some non-Christians (though no rabbinic sources (Boyarin 1993)). He links the ascetic body to a shift in society. With the rise of ascetic Christianity, the body was 'no longer set in place, as a link in the great chain of being' (Brown 1988: 434), but 'was thought to have recovered the glory of Adam against a landscape where the benevolent chain of life had snapped' (p. 437). In so doing, the ascetic body was no longer subject to civic control, but needed to be transformed through human action to be readied for the resurrection (p. 442). Such a view of the body moves from a structuralist argument, wherein the body is an analogy, or map, for society (found in Mary Douglas), to a post-structuralist one, wherein the body 'becomes a site for the playing out of complex theological and social ambiguities' (Castelli 1992: 135–6).

Of the myriad ways in which scholars have studied the ascetic body since Brown, three are especially pertinent to current trends: (1) examination of the ascetic body as a metaphor for salvation and social relations in communal monasticism; (2) analysis of the transformation of the ascetic body through ritualized practices; and (3) understanding the ascetic body as a 'written body'. Although interdisciplinary in their use of theory, these approaches have two recurring influences: Catherine Bell's theories on ritual and Pierre Bourdieu's on the creation of culture.

First, the discipline that the ascetic body performs provides a key to understanding the relationship between ascetic practice and institutional monasticism. The asceticism that transforms the individual body can be linked to the communal body of a monastery. The extent to which the ascetic body remains 'pure' from sin, or, conversely, becomes polluted by it, could affect the health of the overall monastic body. This language of purity and pollution evident in the ascetic ideology of Shenoute of Atripe in fourth- and fifth-century Egypt locates the ascetic body, ritualized through monastic rules (Schroeder 2007), as the site on which the very struggle for salvation is played out. The ascetic body is not just a symbol of the community, but rather is equated with the larger social environment of the monastery: what affects the one affects the other (Krawiec 2002: 66–9; Schroeder 2007).

Second, through ascetic practice the body becomes a means of stepping out of time, out of the 'horizontal dimension' that defines much of human existence (Miller 1993). It serves as the means of the 'reversal of flow' (Flood 2004) of human existence, and it does so by literally changing the body. The ascetic body, as Palladius noted in his *Lausiac History*, was proof of the resurrection for all to see (or read about) (Miller 1994: 137). Ascetic practices, however, are not just directed against the body but against how the body is perceived by those witnessing the actions, seeing the transformed body, or reading about these events (and thus visualizing them) (Miller 1994). Moreover, the body's transformation lies not just in sexual renunciation but in all ascetic practices. The idea that the body can represent the future paradisiacal state in the here and now is as much evident in ancient descriptions of fasting as of sexuality (Shaw 1998*b*). The ascetic body, therefore, was not simply a map, but a 'new signifier'; asceticism was the means by which the body, and all the paradoxes it represented, could be reimagined and reread (Miller 1994: 141). Since the ascetic body was poised between two states, within this world and anticipating the next, ancient writers had to use fantastical language—of dreams, for example (Miller 1995)—to express this transgressive mode.

Finally, some scholars have emphasized that the ascetic body is a written body, both in terms of authors writing the bodies of others and of themselves, and in terms of the text as a body. For example, in his *Letter to Eustochium* (*Ep.* 22) Jerome can be understood as writing both her body and his own. This writing creates an 'erotics of asceticism' through which he can express his desire for the textualized, not literal, body (Miller 1993). This shift towards 'writing bodies', especially towards male authors writing female bodies, caused a crisis of sorts, both for the study of asceticism and for the related study of women, since many women who appear in late antique sources were ascetics. These writings about women's bodies, and how the women's embrace of asceticism changed their social status because of the transformation of their bodies, have been the basis of much scholarship on women's history. These texts allow a recovery of women's social role in ascetic Christianity (E. A. Clark 1986*a*; G. Clark 1993: 94–118; 1995; Cloke 1995: 25–81). The texts themselves, although male in authorship, recorded a 'female' view (Castelli 1992) and also served as access to understanding women's sexuality (Castelli 1986). However, Elizabeth Clark, who notes her own efforts in recovering the history of women (1998: 30), nevertheless questions how to study 'traces' of women through these texts (E. A. Clark 1998: 31) and, more broadly, asks whether 'the body' is a legitimate analytical category as it is so enthusiastically embraced especially by feminist historians (E. A. Clark 2001: 409). Although female subjectivity is seemingly lost in this mode of interpretation, construction of gender, what it meant to be female, remains a crucial question. Male authors were creating, through writing, female bodies, and therefore delineating proper femaleness within ascetic practice. Teresa Shaw has demonstrated this process in her examination of how male authors described proper female ascetic bodily appearance generally (Shaw 1998*a*), and the female body transformed by fasting specifically (1998*b*: 220–53). Clark herself turns to the notion of 'social logic' to examine, for example, how Gregory of Nyssa uses 'Macrina', appropriating her voice through his own (male) writing, to work through controversies, to provide examples of his own theological positions, and as a shaming device (E. A. Clark 1998: 27–9). Moreover, Gregory's *Life of Macrina* contains aspects of the female setting for much ascetic practice, namely, the ascetic household, itself a community transformed through ascetic training, and so again pointing to the linkage between asceticism, bodies, social relations, and emerging Christian identity (Elm 1994: 78–105; Krawiec 2003: 296–301; Rousseau 2005).

Yet even so, Macrina's ascetic body, under her control, has seemed to vanish. Virginia Burrus has argued that by teaching Gregory how to write, Macrina has left traces of herself in the *Life* (Burrus 2005: 112–13; see also Burrus 2000: 120–2 for an analysis of both Gregory's and Macrina's presence in *The Life of Macrina*). Although Burrus's approach does not treat asceticism *per se*, it does include a significant focus on 'writing the ascetic body' (Burrus 2005: 111), and so how asceticism is part of this process of writing. Indeed, the process of writing, of constructing the textual ascetic body, can then be seen as part of ascetic practice (Krueger 2004: 94–109), and the texts themselves become 'substitutes for bodies' (Krueger 2004: 133).

But the materiality of ascetic practices themselves should not get lost in this focus on writing and discourse. For example, three male theologians (Jerome, Pelagius, and Augustine) all wrote ascetic instructions to one Demetrias, and in 'this relation between male discourse and female ascetic practice' an 'ascetic logic' appears as a way of theorizing about the woman who is the recipient of so much advice (Jacobs 2000: 722–4; Brakke 2005: 26–7). Likewise, the disappeared female ascetic can (partially) reappear in monastic literature about transvestite monks, wherein a female body 'may actually have been rendered "real" or "materialized" through monastic performance' (Brakke 2005: 28); the 'real "woman" that these stories construct is the detritus of monastic performance, the material body of sexuality, discourse, and the world that the monastic regime rejects' (Brakke 2005: 35). The ascetic body, therefore, as a signifier has come to represent the very paradox that lies at the heart of Christian ascetic discourse and practice: in its transcendence it continues to represent what needs to be transcended, even as it 'makes present and manifest' the 'paradise still to come' (Shaw 1998*b*: 174).

37.6 CONCLUSION: FUTURE TRENDS

To the extent that asceticism does 'raise the issue of culture' (recalling Harpham), we may expect that future scholarship will continue to investigate asceticism through the shifting lens of modern cultural preoccupations. To that end, two recent insights stand out. Halvor Moxnes rereads Paul and his asceticism through Foucault, with an emphasis on identity which he notes is of importance in early twenty-first-century Europe (2003: 3–4). Second, David Brakke has observed that topics which had been rejected as too 'subjective' or 'theological' (such as demonological theory) in favour of the body and asceticism can now be included as part of the construction of monastic identity (Brakke 2001*b*: 19–20; see also Brakke 2006). Future study of this central religious element of early Christianity should thus benefit from scholars' recognition of, and engagement with, emerging cultural concerns and new theoretical approaches.

Notes

1. For an examination of the various translations of the term, and its philosophical importance in non-Christian late antiquity, see Francis (1995).
2. A group of scholars, the Ascetic Behavior in Greco-Roman Antiquity Group, part of the Society of Biblical Literature, formed in the 1980s to ask these questions. For a description of the group, see Wimbush (1990: 1–11, 1992: 1). Their work, influenced by Brown, Rousselle, and Foucault, comprises much of the scholarship on asceticism, which remains a largely Anglophone interest.
3. For a brief overview of the role of asceticism in the historical development of early Christianity, see Goehring (1997).
4. Foucault's proposed volume on Christian monastic texts remains unpublished, but has been a source of scholarly speculation (Boyarin and Castelli 2001). Of equal importance to Foucault's 3-vol. *History of Sexuality* is his work on other modern institutions, such as prisons (*Discipline and Punish*), and his larger theories about the role of discourse and control of knowledge in the construction of power.
5. Behr (1993 and 1999: 5–15) gives as vigorous a theological critique of Brown (1988) as of Foucault.

Suggested Reading

Given the array of sources that fit into the category 'ascetic discourse', there is hardly any text from late antiquity that could not be included in a survey. The best choices to begin, then, are primary text collections. Prime among these remains *Ascetic Behavior in Greco-Roman Antiquity: A Sourcebook* (Wimbush 1990) for its diversity and for the little-known nature of many of the texts. For more standard fare, Miller (2005) contains selections (not full texts) from the variety of discussions of female asceticism, from treatises on virginity, to condemnations of the *subintroductae*, to hagiographies of female ascetics. In addition, certain texts are so central to the study of early Christian asceticism that it seems fair to highlight them in particular: Gregory's portrait of his sister Macrina remains crucial; for another brotherly portrait of a beloved sister, see Gregory of Nazianzus, *Oration 8 (on Gorgonia)*. Of Jerome's vast library, the *Letter to Eustochium* (*Ep.* 22), *Against Jovinian*, and his eulogy of Paula (*Ep.* 108) stand out. One can consult any of the various treatises *On Virginity* (Gregory of Nyssa, John Chrysostom, and Ambrose are the main sources). Athanasius's *Life of Antony* is, of course, the classic ascetic portrait, but his *Letters to Virgins* should not be overlooked (see also the list of primary sources for Ch. 24 above, especially Palladius's *Lausiac History*). Finally, the *Lives of Symeon Stylites* (Doran 1992), Theodoret of Cyrrhus's *Religious History*, and Gerontius's *Life of Melania the Younger* round out the major portrayals from eastern and western asceticism.

Much the same can be said about secondary sources; the list is so long and varied that it seems somewhat arbitrary to select a few, though here certain standards stand out more clearly than among the primary sources. *Asceticism* (Wimbush and Valantasis 1995) remains crucial reading in part because of the diversity of topics and methodologies (and so tensions and disagreements) contained within it, but also for the conversations set up among and between the papers and responses. Both Brown's essays on the holy man (Brown 1971, 1983, 1995) and his *The Body and Society* (1988) remain necessary reading, but should be supplemented by two critiques in particular (Cameron 1999 and Rousseau 1999). A nice counter to Brown's emphasis on sexual renunciation is Shaw's work on fasting (Shaw 1998*b*). The definitive work for understanding how biblical exegesis contributes to the construction of an ascetic discourse and culture is E. A. Clark (1999), though it should be noted that her work is not organized around set passages but around reading techniques. Finally, the essays collected in Martin and Miller (2005) point to the current state of scholarship on asceticism as well as to future trends.

BIBLIOGRAPHY

Primary sources

AMBROSE OF MILAN, *On Virgins*. Latin text and Italian trans. in F. Gori (ed.), *Verginità e vedovanza*, SAEMO 14.1 (Milan: Biblioteca Ambrosiana; Rome: Città nuova, 1989).
——*On Virginity*. Latin text and Italian trans. in F. Gori (ed.), *Verginità e vedovanza*, SAEMO 14.2 (Milan: Biblioteca Ambrosiana; Rome: Città nuova, 1989).
ATHANASIUS OF ALEXANDRIA, *Life of Antony*. Greek text: G. J. M. Bartelink (ed.), *Athanase d'Alexandre: Vie d'Antoine*, SC 400 (Paris: Éditions du Cerf, 1994). Eng. trans. in R. C. Gregg, *Athanasius: The Life of Antony and the Letter to Marcellinus*, CWS (New York: Paulist Press, 1979).
——*First Letter to Virgins*. Coptic text: L. Th. Lefort, S. *Athanase: Lettres festales et pastorales en Copte* (Louvain: Secrétariat du Corpus SCO, 1955). Eng. trans. in D. Brakke, *Athanasius and the Politics of Asceticism*, OECS (Oxford: Oxford University Press, 1995).
——*Second Letter to Virgins*. Syriac text: J. Lebon, 'Athanasiana Syriaca II: Une lettre attribuée à saint Athanase d'Alexandrie', *Mus* 41 (1928): 169–216. Eng. trans. in D. Brakke, *Athanasius and the Politics of Asceticism*, OECS (Oxford: Oxford University Press, 1995).
ATHENAGORAS, *Plea Regarding the Christians*. Greek text: E. Goodspeed, *Die altesten Apologeten* (Gottingen: Vandenhoeck & Ruprecht, 1914). Eng. trans. in C. Richardson, *Early Church Fathers*, LCC, 1 (Philadelphia: Westminster Press, 1970).
DORAN, R. (1992) (trans.), *The Lives of Symeon Stylites*, CS 112 (Kalamazoo, Mich.: Cistercian Publications).
GERONTIUS, *The Life of Melania the Younger*. Greek and Latin texts: Cardinal M. Rampolla del Tindaro (ed.), *Sancta Melania Giuniore, senactrice romana* (Vatican City, 1905). Eng. trans. in E. A. Clark, *The Life of Melania the Younger: Introduction, Translation, and Commentary* (Lewiston, NY: Edwin Mellen Press, 1984).
GREGORY OF NAZIANZUS, *Oration 8*, PG 35. 790–818. Eng. trans. in P. Schaff and H. Wace (eds.), *S. Cyril of Jerusalem, S. Gregory Nazianzen*, NPNF[2] 7.
GREGORY OF NYSSA, *Life of Macrina*. Greek text: P. Maraval (ed.), *Grégoire de Nysse: Vie de saint Macrine*, SC 178 (Paris: Éditions de Cerf, 1971). Eng. trans. in J. M. Peterson, *Handmaids of the Lord: Contemporary Descriptions of Feminine Asceticism in the First Six Christian Centuries*, CS 143 (Kalamazoo, Mich.: Cistercian Publications, 1996).

—— *On Virginity*. Greek text: M. Aubineau, Grégoire de Nysse: *Traité de la virginité*, SC 119 (Paris: Éditions du Cerf, 1961). Eng. trans. in V. W. Callahan, *Gregory of Nyssa: Ascetical Works*, FC 58 (Washington D.C.: Catholic University of America Press, 1967).

JEROME, *Against Jovinian*, PL 23. 221–352. Eng. trans. in P. Schaff and H. Wace (eds.), *St. Jerome: Letters and Select Works*, NPNF² 6.

—— *Letters 22 and* 108, CSEL 54: 143–214, CSEL 55: 306–51 (Vienna: Tempsky, 1910–18). Eng. trans. in J. M. Peterson, *Handmaids of the Lord: Contemporary Descriptions of Feminine Asceticism in the First Six Christian Centuries*, CS 143 (Kalamazoo, Mich.: Cistercian Publication, 1996).

JOHN CHRYSOSTOM, *On Virginity*. Greek text: H. Musurillo and B. Grillet, *Jean Chrysostome: La virginité*, SC 125 (Paris: Éditions de Cerf, 1966), 92–394. Eng. trans. in S. R. Shore, *John Chrysostom: On Virginity, Against Remarriage* (Lewiston, NY: Edwin Mellen Press, 1983).

MILLER, P. Cox (2005) (ed.), *Women in Early Christianity: Translations from Greek texts* (Washington D.C.: Catholic University of America Press).

THEODORET OF CYRRHUS, *Religious History*. Greek text: P. Canivet and A. Leroy-Molinghen, *Theodoret de Cyr: Histoire des moines de Syrie*, SC 234, 257 (Paris: Éditions du Cerf, 1977, 1979). Eng. trans. in R. M. Price, *Theodoret of Cyrrhus's History of the Monks of Syria*, CS 88 (Kalamazoo, Mich.: Cistercian Publications, 1985).

WIMBUSH, V. L. (1990) (ed.), *Ascetic Behavior in Greco-Roman Antiquity: A Sourcebook*, SAC (Minneapolis: Fortress Press).

Secondary sources

BEHR, J. (1993), 'Shifting Sands: Foucault, Brown and the Framework of Christian Asceticism', *Heythrop Journal*, 34: 1–21.

—— (1999), *Asceticism and Anthropology in Irenaeus and Clement* (Oxford: Oxford University Press).

BOYARIN, D. (1993), *Carnal Israel: Reading Sex in Talmudic Culture*, The New Historicism: Studies in Cultural Poetics, 25 (Berkeley: University of California Press).

—— AND CASTELLI, E. A. (2001), 'Introduction: Foucault's *The History of Sexuality*: The Fourth Volume, or, A Field Left Fallow for Others to Till', *JHSex* 10: 357–74.

BRAKKE, D. (1995), *Athanasius and the Politics of Asceticism*, OECS (Oxford: Clarendon Press).

—— (2001*a*), 'Ethiopian Demons: Male Sexuality, the Black-Skinned Other, and the Monastic Self', *JHSex* 10: 501–35.

—— (2001*b*), 'Making of Monastic Demonology: Three Ascetic Teachers on Withdrawal and Resistance', *CH* 70: 19–48.

—— (2005), 'The Lady Appears: Materializations of "Woman" in Early Monastic Literature', in Martin and Miller (2005), 25–39.

—— (2006), *Demons and the Making of the Monk: Spiritual Combat in Early Christianity* (Cambridge, Mass.: Harvard University Press).

BROCK, S. (1973), 'Early Syrian Asceticism', *Numen*, 20: 1–19.

BROWN, P. (1971), 'The Rise and Function of the Holy Man in Late Antiquity', *JRS* 61: 80–101; repr. in *Society and the Holy in Late Antiquity* (Berkeley: University of California Press, 1982), 103–52.

—— (1983), 'The Saint as Exemplar in Late Antiquity', *Representations*, 1: 1–25.

—— (1988), *The Body and Society: Men, Women and Sexual Renunciation in Early Christianity*, Lectures on the History of Religions, 13 (New York: Columbia University Press).

Brown, P. (1995), *Authority and the Sacred: Aspects of the Christianization of the Roman World* (Cambridge: Cambridge University Press).

Burrus, V. (1987), *Chastity as Autonomy: Women in the Stories of Apocryphal Acts*, Studies in Women and Religion, 23 (Lewiston, NY: Edwin Mellen Press).

—— (1992), 'Ascesis, Authority, and Text: *The Acts of the Council of Saragossa*', *Semeia*, 58: 95–108.

—— (1994), 'Word and Flesh: The Bodies and Sexuality of Ascetic Women in Christian Antiquity', *JFSR* 10: 27–51.

—— (1995), *The Making of a Heretic: Gender, Authority, and the Pricillianist Controversy*, Transformation of the Classical Heritage, 24 (Berkeley: University of California Press).

—— (2000), '*Begotten, not Made*': *Conceiving Manhood in Late Antiquity* (Palo Alto, Calif.: Stanford University Press).

—— (2005), 'Macrina's Tattoo', in Martin and Miller (2005), 103–16.

Cameron, A. (1991), *Christianity and the Rhetoric of Empire: The Development of Christian Discourse*, Sather Classical Lectures, 55 (Berkeley: University of California Press).

—— (1995), 'Ascetic Closure and the End of Antiquity', in Wimbush and Valantasis (1995), 147–61.

—— (1999), 'On Defining the Holy Man', in Howard-Johnston and Hayward, 27–44.

Castelli, E. (1986), 'Virginity and Its Meaning for Women's Sexuality in Early Christianity', *JFSR* 2: 61–88.

—— (1992), 'Mortifying the Body, Curing the Soul: Beyond Ascetic Dualisms in the *Life of St. Syncletica*', *differences: A Journal of Feminist Cultural Studies*, 4: 134–53.

Clark, E. A. (1979), *Jerome, Chrysostom, and Friends: Essays and Translations*, Studies in Women and Religion, 1 (Lewiston, NY: Edwin Mellen Press).

—— (1986a), 'Ascetic Renunciation and Feminine Advancement: A Paradox of Late Ancient Christianity', in *Ascetic Piety and Women's Faith: Essays on Late Antique Christianity*, Studies in Women and Christianity, 20 (Lewiston, NY: Edwin Mellen Press), 175–208.

—— (1986b), 'Heresy, Asceticism, Adam and Eve: Interpretations of Gen. 1–3 in the Later Latin Fathers', in *Ascetic Piety and Women's Faith: Essays in Late Antique Christianity*, Studies in Women and Christianity, 20 (Lewiston, NY: Edwin Mellen Press), 353–85.

—— (1986c), 'John Chrysostom and the *Subintroductae*', in *Ascetic Piety and Women's Faith: Essays in Late Antique Christianity*, Studies in Women and Christianity, 20 (Lewiston, NY: Edwin Mellen Press), 265–90.

—— (1988), 'Foucault, the Fathers, and Sex', *JAAR* 56: 619–41.

—— (1989), 'Theory and Practice in Late Ancient Asceticism', *JFSR* 5: 25–46.

—— (1992), *The Origenist Controversy: The Cultural Construction of an Early Christian Debate* (Princeton: Princeton University Press).

—— (1995), 'Antifamilial Tendencies in Ancient Christianity', *JHSex* 5: 356–80.

—— (1998), 'The Lady Vanishes: Dilemmas of a Feminist Historian after the "Linguistic Turn"', *CH* 67: 1–31.

—— (1999), *Reading Renunciation: Asceticism and Scripture in Early Christianity* (Princeton: Princeton University Press).

—— (2001), 'Women, Gender, and the Study of Christian History', *CH* 70: 395–426.

Clark, G. (1993), *Women in Late Antiquity: Pagan and Christian Lifestyles* (Oxford: Oxford University Press).

—— (1995), 'Women and Asceticism in Late Antiquity: The Refusal of Status and Gender', in Wimbush and Valantasis (1995), 33–48.

CLOKE, G. (1995), *'This Female Man of God': Women and Spiritual Power in the Patristic Age, AD 350–450* (London: Routledge).

COOPER, K. (1996), *The Virgin and the Bride: Idealized Womanhood in Late Antiquity* (Cambridge, Mass.: Harvard University Press).

DAVIES, S. L. (1980), *The Revolt of the Widows: The Social World of the Apocryphal Acts* (Carbondale, Ill.: Southern Illinois University Press).

DERRETT, J. D. M. (1995), 'Primitive Christianity as an Ascetic Movement', in Wimbush and Valantasis (1995), 88–107.

ELM, S. (1994), *'Virgins of God': The Making of Asceticism in Late Antiquity*, Oxford Classical Monographs (Oxford: Oxford University Press).

—— (1998), 'Introduction: The Rise of the Holy Man in Late Antiquity, 1971–1997', *JECS* 6: 343–52.

FLOOD, G. (2004), *The Ascetic Self: Subjectivity, Memory and Tradition* (Cambridge: Cambridge University Press).

FOUCAULT, M. (1977), *Discipline and Punish: The Birth of the Prison*, trans. A. Sheridan (New York: Random House).

—— (1978–86), *The History of Sexuality*, i: *An Introduction* (1978); ii: *The Use of Pleasure* (1985); iii: *The Care of the Self* (1986), trans. R. Hurley (New York: Random House).

FRAADE, S. (1987), 'Ascetical Aspects of Ancient Judaism', in A. Green (ed.), *Jewish Spirituality: From the Bible Through the Middle Ages* (New York: Crossroad), 253–88.

FRANCIS, J. (1995), *Subversive Virtue: Asceticism and Authority in the Second-Century Pagan World* (University Park, Pa.: Pennsylvania State University Press).

GOEHRING, J. E. (1997), 'Asceticism', in E. Ferguson (ed.), *Encyclopedia of Early Christianity*, 2nd edn. (New York: Garland), i, 127–30.

—— (1999), *Ascetics, Society, and the Desert: Studies in Early Egyptian Monasticism*, SAC (Harrisburg, Pa.: Trinity Press International).

GRIFFITH, SIDNEY H. (1995), 'Asceticism in the Church of Syria: The Hermeneutics of Early Syrian Monasticism', in Wimbush and Valantasis (1995), 220–45.

HARPHAM, G. (1987), *The Ascetic Imperative in Culture and Criticism* (Chicago: University of Chicago Press).

HARVEY, S. A. (1988), 'The Sense of a Stylite: Perspectives on Simeon the Elder', *VC* 42: 376–94.

—— (1990), *Asceticism and Society in Crisis: John of Ephesus and the Lives of the Eastern Saints*, Transformation of the Classical Heritage, 18 (Berkeley: University of California Press).

—— (1998), 'The Stylite's Liturgy: Ritual and Religious Identity in Late Antiquity', *JECS* 6: 523–39.

HOWARD-JOHNSTON, J. D. and HAYWARD, P. A. (1999) (eds.), *The Cult of the Saints in Late Antiquity and the Middle Ages: Essays on the Contribution of Peter Brown* (Oxford: Oxford University Press).

HUNTER, D. G. (1987), 'Resistance to the Virginal Ideal in Late Fourth-Century Rome: The Case of Jovinian', *TS* 48: 45–64.

—— (1992), 'The Language of Desire: Clement of Alexandria's Transformation of Ascetic Discourse', *Semeia*, 57: 95–112.

HUNTER, D. G. (1999), 'Vigilantius of Calagurris and Victricius of Rouen: Ascetics, Relics, and Clerics in Late Roman Gaul', *JECS* 7: 401–30.

—— (2000), 'The Virgin, the Bride, and the Church: Reading Psalm 45 in Ambrose, Jerome, and Augustine', *CH* 69: 282–303.

—— (2005), 'Rereading the Jovinianist Controversy: Asceticism and Clerical Authority in Late Ancient Christianity', in Martin and Miller (2005), 119–35.

—— (2007), *Marriage, Celibacy, and Heresy in Ancient Christianity: The Jovinianist Controversy*, OECS (Oxford: Oxford University Press).

JACOBS, A. (2000), 'Writing Demetrias: Ascetic Logic in Ancient Christianity', *CH* 69: 719–49.

—— (2003), ' "Let Him Guard *Pietas*": Early Christian Exegesis and the Ascetic Family', *JECS* 11: 265–81.

—— and EHRMAN, B. (2004), *Christianity in Late Antiquity, 300–450 C.E.: A Reader* (New York: Oxford University Press).

KRAWIEC, R. (2002), *Shenoute and the Women of the White Monastery: Egyptian Monasticism in Late Antiquity* (New York: Oxford University Press).

—— (2003), ' "From the Womb of the Church": Monastic Families', *JECS* 11: 283–307.

KRUEGER, D. (2004), *Writing and Holiness: The Practice of Authorship in the Early Christian East* (Philadelphia: University of Pennsylvania Press).

LEYSER, C. (2000), *Authority and Asceticism from Augustine to Gregory the Great*, Oxford Historical Monographs (New York: Oxford University Press).

MACDONALD, D. R. (1983), *The Legend and the Apostle: The Battle for Paul in Story and Canon* (Philadelphia: Westminster Press).

MARKUS, R. (1990), *The End of Ancient Christianity* (Cambridge: Cambridge University Press).

MARTIN, D. B. (2005), 'Introduction', in Martin and Miller (2005), 1–21.

—— and MILLER, P. Cox (2005), *The Cultural Turn in Late Ancient Studies: Gender, Asceticism, and Historiography* (Durham, NC: Duke University Press).

McGUCKIN, J. A. (1985), 'Christian Asceticism and the Early School of Alexandria', in Sheils (1985), 25–39.

MILLER, P. Cox (1993), 'The Blazing Body: Ascetic Desire in Jerome's *Letter to Eustochium*', *JECS* 1: 21–45.

—— (1994), 'Desert Asceticism and "The Body from Nowhere" ', *JECS* 2: 137–53.

—— (1995), 'Dreaming the Body: An Aesthetics of Asceticism', in Wimbush and Valantasis (1995), 281–300.

MOXNES, H. (2003), 'Asceticism and Christian Identity in Antiquity: A Dialogue with Foucault and Paul', *JSNT* 26: 3–29.

MURRAY, R. (1974), 'The Exhortation to Candidates for Ascetical Vows at Baptism in the Ancient Syriac Church', *NTS* 21: 59–80.

RAPP, C. (2005), *Holy Bishops in Late Antiquity: The Nature of Christian Leadership in an Age of Transition*, Transformation of the Classical Heritage, 37 (Berkeley: University of California Press).

ROUSSEAU, P. (1978), *Ascetics, Authority, and the Church in the Age of Jerome and Cassian* (Oxford: Oxford University Press).

—— (1997), 'Eccentrics and Coenobites in the Late Roman East', in L. Garland (ed.), *Conformity and Non-conformity in Byzantium*, ByF 24 (Amesterdam: Adolf M. Hakkert), 35–50.

—— (1999), 'Ascetics as Mediators and as Teachers', Howard-Johnston and Hayward, 45–59.

—— (2005), 'The Pious Household and the Virgin Chorus: Reflections on Gregory of Nyssa's *Life of Macrina*', *JECS* 13: 165–6.

ROUSSELLE, A. (1988), *Porneia: On Desire and the Body in Antiquity*, trans. F. Pheasant (Oxford: Basil Blackwell).

RUBENSON, S. (1995), *The Letters of St. Antony: Monasticism and the Making of a Saint*, SAC (Minneapolis: Fortress Press).

SALZMAN, M. R. (2001), 'Competing Claims to "Nobilitas" in the Western Empire of the Fourth and Fifth Centuries', *JECS* 9: 359–85.

SCHROEDER, C. T. (2007), *Monastic Bodies: Discipline and Salvation in Shenoute of Atripe* (Philadelphia: University of Pennsylvania Press).

SHAW, T. (1998a), 'Askesis and the Appearance of Holiness', *JECS* 6: 485–500.

—— (1998b), *The Burden of the Flesh: Fasting and Sexuality in Early Christianity* (Minneapolis: Fortress Press).

—— (2005), 'Ascetic Practice and the Geneaology of Heresy: Problems in Modern Scholarship and Ancient Textual Representation', in Martin and Miller (2005), 213–36.

SHEILS, W. J. (1985) (ed.), *Monks, Hermits and the Ascetic Tradition*, Papers read at the 1984 Summer Meeting and the 1985 Winter Meeting of the Ecclesiastical History Society, SCH 22 (London: Basil Blackwell).

STERK, ANDREA (2004), *Renouncing the World Yet Leading the Church: The Monk-Bishop in Late Antiquity* (Cambridge, Mass.: Harvard University Press).

VALANTASIS, R. (1995a), 'Constructions of Power in Asceticism', *JAAR* 63: 775–821.

—— (1995b), 'A Theory of the Social Function of Asceticism', in Wimbush and Valantasis (1995), 544–52.

—— (1999), 'Is the Gospel of Thomas Ascetical? Revisiting an Old Problem with a New Theory', *JECS* 7: 55–81.

VÖÖBUS, A. (1958–88), *A History of Asceticism in the Syrian Orient*, 3 vols., CSCO 184 (Louvain: Secrétariat du Corpus SCO, 1958), 197 (Louvain: Secrétariat du Corpus SCO, 1960), 500 (Leuven: Peeters, 1988).

WIMBUSH, V. L. (1987), *Paul the Worldly Ascetic: Response to the World and Self-Understanding according to 1 Corinthians 7* (Macon, Ga.: Mercer University Press).

—— (1992), 'Introduction', *Semeia*, 57: 1–12.

—— and VAAGE, L. E. (1999) (eds.), *Asceticism and the New Testament* (London: Routledge).

—— and VALANTASIS, R. (1995) (eds.), *Asceticism* (New York: Oxford University Press).

CHAPTER 38

PENANCE

ALLAN D. FITZGERALD, OSA

38.1 INTRODUCTION

THE study of penance in the early church can be challenging, not only because of a scarcity of resources, or merely because of the variety of opinions among scholars; it can also be difficult because of the apparent diversity in penitential practices among the Christian communities in the first 600 years and because of the difference between those practices and modern Christian experience. Since the study of penance may emphasize the scriptures, history, theology, liturgy, or practice, some methodological principles, not just in relation to the study of early Christian worship in general (Bradshaw 2002), but specifically for the study of penance, will be useful. In that way, the various approaches to study may each make its own contribution to the profile and practice of penance in the early church.

Studies of penance have often described penance in terms of its severity, rigour, or laxity—terms that issue from polemical comparisons which do not always facilitate unbiased analysis. Hence, the terminology for this period should stay as close to the texts of that time as possible, so as to allow frameworks and descriptions to be the result of careful study. This will also mean that historical and sociological contexts—often found in recent works on penance in the early church—need to be included in an ever more explicit way.

Some interpretations of the history of penance have presumed an individualistic appreciation of the penitential experience—perhaps because the need to communicate meaning to one's own culture was more immediate than the challenge of describing the cultures of the early church. Liturgy, however, was a significant dimension of the earliest Christian experience, and the communitarian and liturgical contexts for Christian penance need to be given greater importance than they have yet received. Issues such as intercession and exclusion should be seen in their ecclesial contexts, i.e. as more than ritual or juridical categories 'imposed' on a given sinner.

Language about admission to (or exclusion from) the eucharist makes it clear that communities had norms for distinguishing who was or was not allowed to participate. Such language asked the faithful to apply the appropriate scriptural norms to their own lives—a kind of communal examination of conscience rather than a way to bear down on individual sinners. Hence, there was a presumed communal, liturgical, rather than merely individual moral, model; the holiness of the Church was primary at the beginning. By recording and preserving examples of exclusion from the community, there is an implicit indication that such cases were not ordinary.[1] Just how one relates exclusion from the community to the return or the hoped-for return to the community will require careful study of what was or was not presumed in any given period.

38.2 GENERAL OVERVIEW

At the beginning of Christianity, penance was not a set of procedures for readmitting the serious sinner to the community. It was, first and foremost, part of a process of conversion from a world described as 'perverse' (Acts 2: 40), learning how to be part of a holy people (Eph 5: 27), forgiven for past sins and thus capable of a different way of living (1 Pet 2: 12). What was learned in that process helped to define Christian identity by forming catechumens in the ordinary means of conversion—prayer, fasting, and almsgiving (see Mt 6: 1–18). These 'building blocks' of Christian living were also the normal means of Christian penance. However, just as almsgiving, which has mercy at its heart, was a way to relate to one's neighbour—and not just a transfer of goods—so prayer and fasting could be categories, rather than tightly defined actions. By the fifth century, the interrelationship of these three facets of Christian life would be made explicit in Lenten preaching. Not too long thereafter, fasting became a kind of shorthand for all things penitential, a first step toward forgetting the prayer–fasting–almsgiving relationship.

The most basic facet of Christianity was a communal listening to the word of God; that word brought the Christian community together for worship; that same word provided the foundation and the structure of Christian penance. Hence, the study of the earliest patristic texts on penance must begin with the study of the biblical text, especially of the New Testament.

Since conversion to Christianity included the reinterpretation of the Old Testament in light of the life, death, and resurrection of Christ, as well as the appropriation of the Word of God by those seeking baptism (see e.g. Acts 2: 41; 8: 30–1), it was neither physical nor spiritual, but both. Penance as *metanoia* or interior conversion required baptized Christians to maintain their baptismal commitment and helped them to manifest its ongoing quality.

Hence, the conversion process was practised rather than discussed; when penance was mentioned in biblical and early Christian texts, the emphasis tended to be placed on the goal of penance: holiness or growth in holiness. To that process, post-baptismal penance owed its origins as well as its meaning. Day-to-day fidelity to the teaching of the apostles, to their common purpose, to the breaking of bread, and to common prayer (see Acts 2: 42) were the means for the formation of an attitude of ongoing conversion. Penance, therefore, was not an 'added extra' for certain sinners, but a normal part of the life of the catechumen and of the baptized Christian.

If, initially, penance was the normal way for Christians to deal with everyday sins, then the development of procedures for serious sinners also took place within that context, not separate from it—an observation which needs more attention than it has generally received. As exchange among local churches increased—especially evident from the beginning of the fourth century—so did the formal quality of Christian penance tend toward greater unity of expression. As Robert Taft has put it:

[The fourth century] is the period of the unification of rites, when worship, like church government, not only evolved new forms, but also let the weaker variants of the species die out, as the Church developed ... Hence, the process of formation of rites is not one of diversification, as is usually held, but of unification. What one finds in extant rites today is not a synthesis of all that went before, but rather the result of a selective evolution: the survival of the fittest, not necessarily of the best.

(Taft 1977: 355)

Throughout the patristic period, the baptismal foundation upon which penance was built remained at least implicit, anchored in the focus of each one as a means for the *remissio peccatorum*. In the study of penance, therefore, that relationship should not be ignored, either in theory or in practice. Note too that, in the West, either by the time of Ambrose of Milan (Fitzgerald 1988) or by that of Augustine (Rebillard 1994), the beginnings of a shift from a predominantly baptismal spirituality toward a penitential spirituality can be observed. Did such a shift exist beforehand? Unfortunately, the documentation from the preceding period that might best help to answer that question—namely, patristic sermons—has not been preserved, either in the East or in the West. A few methodological statements flow from the previous observations:

1. Jesus did not leave an unambiguous set of instructions for Christian penance. Local churches had to appropriate scriptural directives within their own context. Hence, unity of practice—in rite and in law—was a result of historical development, not a point of departure.

2. Penance developed in strict relation to baptism, and the study of penance should pay careful attention to the baptism–penance relationship: their initial connection, their disputed relationship, and, over time, the faded importance of baptism.

3. Just how the scriptures influenced and guided the development of penitential attitudes and structures needs to be a primary concern of the study of penance.

4. In the available patristic texts, the ecclesial, liturgical context for Christian penance is presumed. Teasing out such presumptions, however challenging, needs to be attempted—without limiting the meaning of 'liturgical' to rites. The relation of penance and of repentance to the communal experience has been too often ignored.

5. In general, early documents tend to mention what is problematic or in need of attention, passing over ordinary, everyday practices in silence. Hence, a first mention of some practice does not indicate that it has just come into existence. Silence about a given practice does not signify a lack of importance.

6. Both Tertullian and Ambrose of Milan wrote works called *De paenitentia*— polemical works that dealt with specific aspects of penance and that framed the discussion in terms of those controversies. Others, such as Pacian and Ambrosiaster, also wrote brief pieces on penance. Sermons on penance are available from the fourth century. Many texts that relate to penance and to repentance, however, are scattered among patristic writings (see section 38.3.1). The study of penance, therefore, requires a set of principles which deal explicitly with the interpretation of textual genres.

38.3 BIBLIOGRAPHICAL OVERVIEW

Since the quantity of recent publications on ancient penance is relatively limited, some observations about how to deal with what does exist will be a practical, concrete way to amplify these initial comments. J. A. Favazza has provided a very useful and concise history of the range of interpretations that has accompanied the study of antique Christian penance since the time of Thomas Aquinas (1988: 9– 57). Note that, sometime after the middle of the twentieth century, the polemical quality of writing on penance began to shift toward a more historical focus. Thus did merely 'confessional' emphases begin to recede.

38.3.1 Collections of Texts: Watkins (1920), Palmer (1959), Vogel (1966a), Karpp (1970)

In the past hundred years, a tendency to study the structure or the form of penance was based on the medieval distinction between penance as sacrament and penance as virtue—a distinction which would have made no sense to a patristic author. In addition, a controversy over the sacraments which culminated in the divisions of the Reformation gave discussions of penance a decidedly 'confessional' flavour (Favazza 1988: 9–57). Collections of texts, therefore, tended to emphasize doctrinal and juridical categories (excommunication, power to forgive, public penance, etc.), and to underemphasize the relationship between baptism and penance; they also tended to omit texts which dealt with repentance or penance as virtue (see, however, Hausherr 1944). In general, a preoccupation with the question of the efficacy of penance tends to place the emphasis on serious sin and on the power of the Church to forgive such sin. The collection of texts by Karpp is the least problematic from that point of view. Collecting the various kinds of penitential texts from later centuries will show just how important everyday penance became from the fourth century.

38.3.2 Penance in Scripture: Murphy-O'Connor (1967), Lipinski (1969), Cothenet (1975)

The studies on penance or on sin in the New Testament tend to be done according to a biblical methodology. The above three articles provide a good basis, albeit hardly exhaustive, for the study of penance in the patristic period. What are still lacking, however, are studies with a clearly articulated way of uniting the study of Christian penance in the New Testament with that of the following centuries—both in the shift to Greek culture and beyond, and in the way that shift influenced scriptural interpretation.

38.3.3 Penance and Eastern Christianity: Dalmais (1958), Hausherr (1944), Ligier (1963, 1967a), van de Paverd (1973 to 1981)

It is perhaps the very lack of an adequate focus on the eastern Christian experience of penance that has allowed the study of penance to be more canonical than theological, more confessional than universal, more structural than pastoral. In that regard the study of Hausherr on repentance (*penthos*) in the early church is a part of the remedy.

38.3.4 Theology of Penance: Poschmann (1964), Vorgrimler (1963), Dassmann (1973)

The process of the study of penance has, over the centuries, often been time-bound; that is, successive periods since scholastic times have tended to ask the questions of their own era—or at least to discuss that topic from within a reigning set of theological presuppositions. By explicitly identifying one's presuppositions, however, such bias can be limited, making the results of the study more successful. While an interest in the power of the keys (Mt 16: 19) or in the existence of a private form of penance appears to have dominated much of the discussion of the first half of the last century, today's interests pay attention to the historical and sociological concerns of that time, thus respecting both theological framework and historical context. Yet, in the dialogue between theology and patristics, it is still necessary to avoid the tendency to use early texts merely to prove or to support a modern theological concept or argument.

38.3.5 History of Penance: Jungmann (1932), Gy (1958), Vogel (1966a), Berrouard (1974), Adnès (1984), Dallen (1986), Favazza (1988), Fitzgerald (1988)

The most recent studies of penance have a greater respect for historical context. While each of the studies listed above is limited—both in time frame and in geography—the study of penance must deal with a range of issues. Early penance is local rather than canonical: that is, the result of regional rather than synodal decisions. But later penance cannot be limited to what is described in the conciliar decisions that have been preserved. The history of penance needs to include the beginnings of the season of Lent in the fourth century and its subsequent impact: uniting in some way penance for serious sin and that of every Christian. See Zeno of Verona (*Tractate* 1. 6) for one example of how all Christians took part in the celebration of the eucharist.

38.4 SCRIPTURAL FOUNDATIONS

Since studies of penance in patristic times do not normally seek to integrate biblical texts and patristic experience, the following summary of penance in the New Testament offers a way to do so. The student of penance in the early church may use these pages as a 'foil' against which it may be possible to establish a greater continuity of vision from the scriptural experience to penance in the Church: trying to measure what was or was not a part of ancient Christian penance necessarily has a biblical component: how did the earliest record of Christian experience influence and support the practice of early Christian penance? How did it provide the general inspiration and the initial basis for penitential practice?[2] A few presuppositions about such a framework may be helpful: Christian communities gathered regularly to listen to the word of God and sought to do what they understood that word to require, both in relation to the holiness of the Church and to the admonition/correction of the sinner.

At the beginning, Jewish forms of worship and of penance were no less local than Christian forms. Since universally accepted Jewish forms with which to match early Christian penitential forms are not generally available, it will be better to describe the connections between the Jewish and Christian mind-sets or spiritualities, rather than limit the discussion to specific rituals.

The 'structuring' of Christian penance was accomplished through controversy about the meaning of specific biblical texts. That process begins to be a bit more evident in the time of Tertullian (and afterwards), when division over the meaning of specific biblical texts became evident (see e.g. *De pudicitia*). The process of seeking to reconcile contrasting, or even apparently contradictory, scriptural passages will continue long after Tertullian.

38.5 GENERAL SCRIPTURAL OVERVIEW

Christian communities exercised authority over sin through baptism, celebrating in a local community the power of God in the waters of baptism by living according to its grace (Acts 2: 38–40). Entry into Christian society meant being saved from 'a perverse generation', as well as participating in what happened to Jesus. Hence, the Church not only preached her holiness (Eph 5: 25–7), but she also called her members (1 Cor 3: 16–17; Heb 10: 14) to avoid sin and thus to keep the Christian community in clear contrast with the surrounding society (1 Pet 2: 9–12). By exhortation (1 Thess 5: 11, 14), through mercy (Jude 22), on the basis of fraternal love (Gal 6: 1; 2 Tim 2: 25), in the confession of sin to one another (Jas 5: 16), or by prayerful intercession (1 Jn 5: 16; Jas 5: 20), the Church identified the ideals of Christian living.

Sin was an ever-present reality, but one should not overemphasize the presence of serious sinners in the early history of the church. In the New Testament, Peter's frail, growing fidelity stands out. Implicitly, he summarizes the breadth of the meaning of penance—a reality that will become explicit only in the apocryphal literature near the end of the second century (*Acts of Peter*). In the time after Cyprian, Peter's penance began to be used against those who would deny the possibility or the value of penance for serious sin (Fitzgerald 2001). In Christian art from the end of the third century (Sotomayor 1962), Peter will become an example of Christian life in his penance, his faith, and his leadership.

Personally confronted by Christ's holiness, Peter acknowledged his sinfulness (Lk 5: 8). The scriptures remembered his effort to understand sin (Mt 15: 15–30), forgiveness (Jn 13: 6–9) and growth in face of doubt (Mt 14: 28)—perhaps as examples of what the first-century church also needed. Jesus' words about binding and loosing (Mt 16: 17–19) and about the constant renewal of forgiveness (Mt 18: 21–2) were spoken to Peter. He called all to repentance (Acts 2: 38) and confronted serious sinners (Acts 5: 1–11 (Ananias and Saphira); Acts 8: 21–3 (Simon Magus)), just as he had been rebuked for his failures (Mt 16: 23; Gal 2: 14) and, with a glance (Lk 22: 61–2; Lampe 1973),[3] was called to repentance for having denied his Lord. He received Christ's missionary command (Jn 21: 15–17) and learned that repentance could not be artificially limited (Acts 11: 18). If Peter was part of the stories about sin, penance, and pardon at the beginning, he will later come to represent the Church (Augustine, *Serm.* 229 N. 2; Carola 2001). That experience was received and implemented in three areas: (1) Christian identity or community membership; (2) pardon in the community (Mt 5: 23–4); and (3) exclusion from ecclesial communion.

Since the exercise of penance by baptized Christians was in some way based on their experience of pre-baptismal penance, research into the formation of Christian identity in the earliest period of Christianity is needed. In what ways were Christian penitential practices recommended and learned? Were such practices recommended in relation to avoidance of sin, to healing after sin, or to Christian holiness/perfection? How so? Even when the language of penance is not explicit, such study ought to be able to explain how the baptismal promises were perceived, and by what means they were to be maintained.

Various biblical passages affirmed the exercise of Christ's power in the Church and by the Church (e.g. Mt 6: 12, 14–15; 9: 2–8; 16: 17–19; 18: 15–22; Jn 20: 20–3; 2 Cor 2: 5–11). Several others call for repeated forgiveness (Mt 6: 14–15; 18: 1–14; 21–2; Mk 9: 33–50). Hence, one can rightly ask how the early church decided to emphasize one biblical text rather than another and, even more puzzling, where the 'only once' dimension of penance—modelled on the same limitation as baptism—came from. Apparently, repeated pardon coexisted with the 'only once' constraint, and no one in the early church appears to have noticed any contradiction.

Hence, one challenge for the study of early Christian penance is to explain that fact. Was the relative silence about the relationship between repeated and limited pardon an indicator of ignorance? A sign of its unproblematic integration in everyday living? A sign of the still unsophisticated understanding of sin (serious or not) and of penance (church-regulated or not)? It seems most likely that the requirement of repeated forgiveness was an unproblematic aspect of Christian penance because it was understood as a requirement for every Christian at all times. Hence, it will barely be mentioned in the documents that have been preserved; in fact, only with the beginning of sermon collections or of festal letters will it begin to be documented—namely, in the fourth century.

In the case of serious sin, however, the development of procedures for dealing with serious sinners was so out of the ordinary that it required the personal involvement of church leadership (Mt 16: 16–17). Such forgiveness thus became an ecclesial process: that is, one that was not, in the first place, focused on individual sinners or on church officials, but on the Christian community itself.

Nowhere in the gospels was the reconciliation of the baptized sinner emphasized (Dallen 1986: 11–12). Framed in terms of the relationship between one Christian and another (Mt 5: 23–4) or, doctrinally speaking, as the gift of Christ within the broad sweep of salvation (Eph 2: 14; Col 1: 20), reconciliation—applied to the baptized sinner—may only come to the fore in the third century. To preserve the holiness of the Church, there was a tendency to exclude serious sinners (2 Jn 11; Rev 18: 4; Eph 5: 11; 1 Tim 1: 19–20), thus removing them from the protection of the Christian community. That process was described as handing them over to Satan (1 Cor 5: 1–5; Rom 6: 13–23; 1 Jn 5: 16–17), or as placing them back in the world (see Act 2: 40)—at least until they might be reintegrated into the community through pardon (2 Cor 2: 10–11; 2 Thess 3: 15). When a person showed that penance had verifiably borne fruit (Mt 3: 9), there was a return to the community, i.e. a reconciliation in fact.

Along with the exclusion of the serious sinner, Christians were told to avoid contact with sinners (Titus 3: 10–11; 2 Thess 3: 5)—at least to avoid those whose sins excluded the sinner from the kingdom of God (1 Cor 6: 9–10; Gal 5: 19–21; Eph 5: 5). The judgement of the community was the final appeal.[4] Sin against the Holy Spirit appears to be an exception (Mk 3: 29; Roulin 1959), although the restriction on pardon comes from an individual's refusal to recognize God's desire to save (Cothenet 1975: 88), not from a decision by the Church (Dallen 1986: 15–18).

Most Christians did not need a special framework for bringing about their daily recommitment. Everyday sins were forgiven in various ways, whether by love (1 Pet 4: 8; Lk 7: 57), mercy (Lk 11: 41), mutual pardon (Jas 5: 19–20), or prayer (Mt 6: 12, 14–15). Origen provided a list of several such means (*Hom. in Lev.* 2. 4).

To say that the early experience of repentance or penance was structured by the scripture is, more than anything else, an effort to counter the impression that there was a 'disconnect' between the New Testament and the early church (Rouillard 1999). The primary Christian ritual of penance was baptism; penitential forms either extend that process for everyday penance or develop their own procedures for serious sinners on the basis of texts like Mt 18: 15–18. The Jewish background (Petuchowski 1978; Arranz 1975) is never further away than the Old Testament, but the presumption that Jewish practice was somehow more ritually organized than Christian practice overstretches the available evidence.

38.6 BEYOND THE SCRIPTURES

As one turns to the literature that is not biblical, any fragment relating to penance should be read as if it were the witness to a local experience, rather than an example of general practice. When an experience is described in more than one place or context, or that experience is a clear application of a significant biblical experience, then the discussion may be widened accordingly. Previous studies of penance have tended to focus on serious sin and on the 'birth of the ecclesiastical institution of penance' (Karpp 1970: p. ix).[5] But the determination of which sins were or were not 'serious'—and the appropriate response of the local community—was a matter of time and of discernment.

A few comments on penance in this period are found in the letters of Clement of Rome (*c.* 96) and Ignatius of Antioch (before 105–135), the *Epistle of Barnabas* (prior to 135), the *Letter to the Philippians* of Polycarp of Smyrna (before 155–167?), the *Shepherd of Hermas* (*c.* 140), the *First Apology* of Justin Martyr (before 150–165), a letter of Pseudo-Clement (between 120 and 160), and in the *Didache* (*c.* 50–100; Rordorf 1975; Karpp 1970: nos. 41, 53, 54, 59, 70a, 81–7). Study should notice how the scriptures were—or were not—used as a basis for penitential decisions, rather than trying to define specific penitential forms. Hence, in the case of serious sin, penitential responses were the practical extension of the lessons learned by attentive, communal reading and interpretation of the scriptures. Hence, there was a 'local' quality to most of them.

Repentance, community, and liturgy are closely intertwined. Penance was for everyone (Ps-Clement, *Ep.* 16.1; 8.1–3), a part of the Christian vocation (*1 Clem.* 30) that recognizes all as sinners (Mt 6: 12). Each Christian was to care for the salvation of the neighbour (Ps-Clement, *Ep.* 17.1–2), by interceding for sinners (*1 Clem.* 56.1) and by fraternal correction (*1 Clem.* 56. 2; Polycarp, *Phil.* 11. 4; *Ps-Clement* 15.1). Purification from sin—and by necessity where there was serious sin (*Did.* 10. 6; 15.3)—was to precede the celebration of the eucharist, as required by Mt 5: 23–4 (*Did.* 4.14; 14.1–2). Justin summarizes that requirement concisely: 'This food is, among us, called eucharist; no one may partake if he does not believe that what we teach is true, if he has not been bathed for the remission of sins, and if he does not live according to what Christ has commanded' (*1 Apol.* 56).

Discernment was concerned mostly with a person's relation to the Christian community (see Justin, 1 *Apol.* 16). When that relationship was compromised by serious sin, the sinner was excluded (Ignatius, *Smyr.* 4.1), making penance necessary (Ps-Clement, *Ep.* 15.1; 17.1–2)—a return to the means that had prepared for baptism in the first place. Responsibility for that discernment may have belonged to community leaders (*1 Clem.* 57), but they were hardly isolated in that responsibility. The exercise of mercy was a common responsibility, rather than an episcopal judgement (Ignatius, *Phil.* 6. 1–2). Correction showed that abstention from evil was in view of the preservation of the unity of the community (Ignatius, *Phil.* 11. 1–4).

The exhortation to penance, the invitation to prayerful intercession, and the call for merciful intervention so that sinners might return to the community all suggest that penance was part of living as a Christian community rather than a separately organized discipline. In fact, there is little basis for forming an opinion about whether reconciliation was celebrated, since penance itself may have been the return to the community. Penance also included care for the poor as a means of pardon (*Did.* 4. 6; *Ps-Clement* 16. 4)—a hint of the ongoing role of scriptural interpretation by the churches (cf. Tob 4: 10; 12: 9; Sir 3: 30; 1 Pet 4: 8). Thus intercession by the community was a constant element of penance in the early church, both spiritually and practically.

38.6.1 The *Shepherd of Hermas*

The writings of Hermas on penance are especially significant (Henne 1992: 91–139). In the middle of the second century, he wrote to and about the Roman church; some gave his writing the same authority as the scriptures themselves (see Irenaeus and Clement of Alexandria; Origen, Tertullian,[6] and Athanasius). Even so, the allegorical style has made these writings a tangle of diverse interpretations. It can at least be said that he develops, in image-filled language, the meaning of baptismal faith, its unicity and its relation to penance.

Metanoia is the repentance which opens toward God, a profound conversion to the Christian community or to living one's baptism, although not called a liturgical event. Those who, seduced by the devil after their baptism, had failed to respect the holiness of their baptismal commitment, had the possibility of a new conversion (*Vis.* 3. 5; *Mand.* 4. 3). Hermas insisted that such recognition of human frailty did not diminish the value of the remission of sins already given in baptism, nor did such apparent indulgence encourage further sin. Rather, it provided an effective chance to live for God in a chaste and holy way (*Sim.* 8. 6; Henne 1992: 117).

The 'only once' provision was not so much a matter of legalism as it was an echo of the baptismal process.[7] Although Hermas was the first to speak of that limitation, there is no evidence that he invented it. Hermas explains the meaning of penance for catechumens (*Vis.* 2) and for baptized Christians (*Mand.* 4): one complements the other (Henne 1992: 138 f.). In fact, Hermas is quite traditional in his insistence that repentance assures life, while the lack of it brings death. Thus, his interest is the conversion of the sinner, not the definition of sin[8] or of penance.

Hermas shows the willingness of the Church to forgive serious, post-baptismal sin. The sinner was expelled from the community, but in view of a future repentance. The fact of allowing penance seems to bring the sinner back to the church as penitent, even if no rite of reconciliation is found in Hermas (Favazza 1988: 103 ff.). Hence, the study of penance in Hermas needs to address an important question: was admission to penance the sign of a return to the Church? Was that penance always lifelong? Such an impression might only be reinforced by Irenaeus's language: *exomologēsis* was that confession whereby Cerdon, more than once, 'came to the church and did penance' (Irenaeus, *Haer.* 3. 4. 3; Holstein 1948), and by the fact that Clement of Alexandria will not speak about ecclesial reconciliation (Poschmann 1940: 256 ff.). Doing penance is what makes the sinner part of the tower under construction (*Vis.* 3. 5).

The question about which sins did or did not allow for penance, and about how one's answer could be reconciled with the emphasis on the holiness of the Church, may have remained implicit in Hermas. Shortly, however, interest in that question will turn into controversy. As P. de Clerck (1989: 354) has observed:

In answer to the question about whether it was possible to remain a member of the church after having denied one's baptismal commitment, the response of the second and third centuries was, in the end, affirmative; on the fully logical condition that one return to the life of the baptized. Hence, baptism could, in some way, be renewed, even if only once; for, if baptism were limited to once, the discipline based on it had to be as well.

Although Hermas allowed for post-baptismal penance for serious sin, the danger was that such a position could be understood as encouraging a life of sin rather than a life of holiness. In addition, to preach penance without also preaching the reconciliation of the serious sinner was to insist upon one dimension of the parallel with baptism without paying attention to the other: that is, to bring an end to the time of penance. When the practice of 'second baptism' begins to appear in the North African church, it is possible that this very ambiguity in the discipline of penance was, in some vague or implicit way, a part of the problem. A fuller appreciation of the baptism–penance relationship is one of the unaddressed challenges of the study of penance in this time.

38.6.2 Toward the Third Century

As the third century approached, Christian penance for serious sinners began to 'take shape' through controversy. Texts from this period can be found in Clement of Alexandria (d. 215/16), Tertullian (d. after 220), Hippolytus (d. 235), Novatian (d. c. 250), Origen (d. 254), Cyprian (d. 258), and Gregory Thaumaturgus (d. c. 270). The liturgical texts (Bradshaw 2002: 71–83) include *Didascalia of the Apostles* (Syria, c. 230) and *The Apostolic Tradition* (Rome, 215–25). Polemical documents from the second half of the third century (*De rebaptismate* and *Ad Novatianum*) identify the depth of the problem. By then, Peter's example had become a significant part of the discussion of penance and pardon (Sotomayor 1962; Fitzgerald 1988, 2001).

Much of the understanding of the history of penance depends upon how the controversies over who should be allowed to do penance at the time of Callistus and Aggripinus are interpreted. The nineteenth- and early twentieth-century arguments did not provide an appropriate framework (Favazza 1988: 18–33). To evaluate the information that Hippolytus and Tertullian provide, one can ask whether they were defending existing traditions or criticizing innovation. By the time of Cyprian, limits on who could be accepted as penitent were widened (Burns 2001), and reconciliation by the imposition of hands or by communion was explicit.

The church's primary spiritual instincts were still baptismal. Penance and even martyrdom were defined in relation to baptism.[9] In North Africa, those coming from schismatic groups were treated as if the baptism received was no baptism at all, although that practice may have been recent—initiated in an episcopal gathering in Carthage at the time of Aggripinus (Clarke 1989: 196–9 n. 4).

Tertullian's concern is firmly centred on the proper exercise of penance, especially everyday penance (Krykowski 1998). Thus, in *De paenitentia* he lays out the meaning of true repentance, and in *De pudicitia* he develops the proper interpretation of the scriptures (*Pud.* 2. 10–11) about sin and forgiveness.[10] Hence, the correct exercise and the correct interpretation of penance according to the scriptures required, in the case of certain serious sinners, expulsion (1 Cor 5: 1–5). Tertullian refuses to accept 2 Cor 2: 5–11 as related to the incestuous Christian, thus denying a scriptural basis for his reconciliation. Separating the sinner from the community returned him to the realm of Satan; Tertullian did not allow penance for certain sins, because that would return the sinner to the threshold of the church, i.e. reclaim him from Satan (see *Paen.* 5; *Pud.* 19). Novatian's interpretation (*De bono pudicitiae*, 6.1) also required a definitive expulsion; Origen would interpret 1 Cor 5: 1–5 (*Hom. in Lev.* 14. 4) in a healing context; and Ambrose (*Paen.* 2. 8. 64) would clearly align it with Paul's words about reconciliation in 2 Cor 2: 5–11. Hence, in the time between Tertullian and Ambrose and the Cappadocians (Basil of Caesarea, Gregory of Nazianzus, and Gregory of Nyssa), the emphasis on immediate expulsion diminished significantly.[11]

The concisely expressed positions of Tertullian were apparently about a practice that he perceived as 'traditional' (de Clerck 1989: 353 n. 2), fearful of laxity. Hermas had addressed that issue, and Cyprian would do so as well. Novatian would challenge the effort to bring reasonable balance to the process. Later, the Council of Elvira (*c.* 305) would reaffirm severity, without, however, denying the possibility of penance. Such positions, rather than a growing rigorism, were about existing discipline (Dallen 1986: 30).

After the persecutions of mid-century, Cyprian, in concert with other African bishops, would foster change in penitential discipline (Burns 2001).[12] His efforts were focused on the *lapsi*. The barely outlined difference between Cyprian of Carthage and Stephen of Rome (Dallen 1986: 41) shows that, by mid-century, baptism was the way to reintegrate schismatics and heretics, at least from the time of Aggripinus. Cyprian had to face Stephen's challenge that he was 'innovating' by allowing rebaptism to fulfil that role. 'The fundamental difference between Cyprian and Stephen lies in the way each established the boundary separating the realm of Christ from that of Satan' (Burns 1993: 403).

By late in the fourth century, rebaptism—sharply defined as a substitute for penance by the Donatists (and their imitators in rebaptizing)—would be firmly rejected by the Church and punished in Roman law. The study of how and why rebaptism was transformed from a rite for receiving heretics and schismatics to a practice opposed to any formal penance could benefit from further reflection and study, beginning perhaps with the third-century documents *De rebaptizmate* and *Ad Novatianum*. Such study should also clarify the changes in the baptism–penance relationship from the third to the end of the fourth centuries (Burns 1993; Fitzgerald 2001), exercising more than a little care in describing just what return to the church meant (in some stage of penance or as a communicant?), carefully documenting whether or when pardon or forgiveness can be an explicitly documented result of the penitential process and not merely a logical or implicit presumption.

38.6.3 Into the Fourth Century

Sources for the study of penance in the fourth century are more and more abundant, a simple fact which defies any mere listing of available resources (see Fitzgerald 1988; Favazza 1988). In any case, the 'effects of the penitential controversy became more evident in the fourth and fifth centuries as the institutionalization of second conversion was canonically regulated' (Dallen 1986: 52). In many ways, however, new developments will lead to a clearer expression of what it meant to be baptized, to acknowledge one's sinfulness, to do penance and intercede for sinners as a Christian community, and to celebrate reconciliation. Some significant new developments are the following:

1. The Council of Arles (314) approved baptism in the name of the Trinity, articulating a doctrinal basis for understanding baptism. In reproving Donatist rebaptism, it clarified the role of penance. During the fourth century, rebaptism was progressively more strongly resisted, and penance and pardon were more clearly integrated into preaching and practice. The growing resistance to rebaptism apparently forced Donatists and Novatianists to accept a need for penance (Ambrosiaster, *Comm. in 1 Cor.* 1: 14 f.; *Quaest.* 102. 28, 32), while stubbornly resisting the granting of pardon (Vogt 1968: 218). This can be seen as a sign of how effective the Church's response to Novatian had been.

2. *Confessio fidei*, a prominent aspect of the writings of Tertullian and Cyprian (and even in Hilary)—was an appropriate emphasis in a time of persecution. But that emphasis took second place to *confessio peccati* (Valgiglio 1980; Fitzgerald 2000)

as the shift toward penance became pronounced in the fifth century. Studies of penance are moving slowly from doctrinal/structural issues to doctrinal/pastoral issues.

3. Pope Siricius described the season of Lent in a letter to Himerius of Tarragona (385), thus witnessing to an already formed framework for the Church—for catechumens, penitents, and faithful to celebrate the *remissio peccatorum* together. Its very existence signals a new penitential emphasis, providing a framework for uniting catechumens, penitents, and the faithful (Zeno of Verona, *Tractate* 1, 6; Leo I, *Sermon* 39, 2–3). Begun perhaps in Jerusalem (Lages 1969) or in Alexandria (Camplani 1989: 171–83), Lent became an ecclesial celebration of penance in prayer, fasting, and almsgiving. Its fourth-century articulation is surely the culmination of a longer period of development—at least in passing from 3 weeks to 40 days (Fitzgerald 1999b; Dallen 1986: 85–8). It came to emphasize confession, penance, and reconciliation in parallel with pre-baptismal penance (see Ambrose, *Paen.*). In the end, however, Lent set the stage for the penitential—rather than baptismal—emphases of succeeding centuries (Bradshaw 2002: 211–17).

4. Various groups (Donatists, Novatians, Luciferians, etc.) use rebaptism to affirm their opposition to the Church—thus giving rise to detailed responses on the meaning and importance of penance (Ambrosiaster, *Quaest.* 102; Ambrose, *Paen.*; Fitzgerald 1988).

5. With the recording and preservation of sermons by the end of the fourth century, the close relationship between canonical penance and everyday penance is evident. It is probable that such a union was always implicitly present in the history of the Church, but, in this period, it became clear that penance—in the best and broadest sense—is for every Christian. Canonical legislation would be for exceptional situations.

6. A significant change would be an increasing number of 'conversations' (conciliar jurisprudence) among the churches, thus highlighting, affirming, and codifying some elements of previous experience.

7. While witness to penance can be found in many texts in the fourth century (tractates, sermons, conciliar decrees, letters), physical testimony can also be identified (images, inscriptions; Vogel 1966b; Fitzgerald 1988: 93–130). The appearance of the image of Christ, Peter, and the rooster on Roman sarcophagi (already in the late third century) demonstrates that controversy was not just a clerical matter, but also touched those who thus claimed the benefits of penance for their deceased (Fitzgerald 1988: 93–130). Changes in the way in which the image was commented upon show that the original rationale for that image had changed significantly by mid-century (Fitzgerald 2001).

The preceding paragraphs provide an overview of the issues that need to be taken into account in the study of the penance which was regulated by common decisions by the fourth century (Poschman 1964: 87–99). The bishops who met in councils and synods and who preached in local churches found a need to clarify and to codify Christian penance, both legally and liturgically. The imposition of hands by the bishop appears to become significant (albeit not always in relation to penance). Its place in the penitential process needs further study (Dallen 1977; Cavalli 1999; Vogel 1973). At the same time, the intercessory role (in prayer and in tears) of the Christian community must be given greater attention (Carola 2001). The pastoral difficulty in the choices that a bishop faced with regard to penitents is movingly articulated by Augustine in a letter to Paulinus of Nola (*Ep.* 95).

However, reformulating that experience in a way that does not isolate canonical penance for observation and analysis, but which seeks to appreciate just how penance was a many-sided experience, will be a demanding task. By choosing to study penance in the writings from both the East and the West, the exaggerated emphasis on western legal categories can be turned into a discussion of a Church for which penance was not yet a mere means of discipline, or of punishment, but still a source of life.

38.6.4 Toward Further Change

By the beginning of the fifth century, penance is both an institutional fact, a frequent object of preaching, and a liturgy (Dallen 1986: 56–76). Various pastoral questions continue to be raised: for example, about deathbed communion (Innocent I, *Epistle* 6, 6; Celestine I, *Epistle* 4, 3) or about the open confession of one's sins (Leo I, *Epistle* 168, 2). The abbreviation of penance into a deathbed ritual (Dallen 1986: 78–82) is a sign of the changes in the offing. But reconciliation at the hands of the bishop was normal (Bussini 1967, 1968), at least for a time. By mid-century, clerics—previously forbidden—are allowed to do penance in some places, but not in others (Sant-Roch 1991: 89–103; Crespin 1965).

What surely needs greater attention, however, is the study of exactly how penance in the fourth and fifth centuries—whether regulated by canonical legislation, preached to all the faithful, or celebrated in Lent—was transformed. Did canonical penance simply die out because of its severity, or were the social conditions such that temporary exclusion from the community ceased to be a meaningful way to bring about repentance? With the growth of preaching on penance in the fourth and fifth centuries came a corresponding emphasis on everyday penance for everyday sins. But sinners, even serious sinners, were treated in a more individual way; sin was a matter of individual behaviour, not an affront to the Christian community (Dallen 1986: 77, 101). Just how each of the earlier experiences of penance was affected by this transformation needs further study. But rather than another study of the fate of canonical penance, it would be more useful to pay special attention to everyday penance in the East and the West. The end of chapter 3 and the beginning of chapter 4 in Dallen's (1986) book begin to document the breakdown of canonical penance. But there is room for the study of Lenten preaching as Christians came to feel that everyone needed to participate (p. 88). There is, no doubt, a history yet to be described, a reality that is not adequately expressed by the term 'ceremonial penitents' (p. 88).

38.7 Concluding Comments

The story of penance in the early church appears to be one of gradual movement from severity to mercy at the level of ecclesial structure. The constantly renewed affirmation of the authority of the Church to remit sin is set within the context of sin serious enough to disrupt the life of the Christian community. But the reality of the penance learned in the catechumenal process and lived by those whose actions had a positive impact on the life of the Church was also scriptural and was the very matrix within which Christian reflection on penance took place. Insofar as the study of penance has tended to neglect everyday penance for everyday sin, it has isolated and objectified a specific element of the Church's experience for analysis. Although such study was useful, and even necessary to some extent, a return to the wider perspectives about penance in the early church appears to be the best way to advance the study and the understanding of ancient penance.

Notes

1. Serious sins were those that transgressed faith (e.g. heresy), family (e.g. adultery), and the life of the Christian community (e.g. murder). But lists of sins appear to be local and adaptable. Based on Ex 20: 13, e.g. Tertullian would include apostasy, blasphemy, theft, participation in violent, sexually explicit theatre, false witness, lying (see e.g. *Marc.* 4. 9. 6; *Apol.* 2. 4; 11. 12).
2. Even though every New Testament book may not have been known in every church, and some writings, such as those of Hermas, were accepted by some as if they had scriptural authority.
3. In the earliest Christian experience, no effort appears to have been made to reconcile Peter's experience with texts like Mt 10: 33 which condemn such denial.
4. Note that Heb 6: 4–8 refers to baptism, not to penance (see Proulx and Schokel 1975); i.e. one cannot renew baptism, since that would appear to crucify Christ another time. See Epiphanius of Salamis (*Pan.* 59. 1. 2. 5) and Ambrose of Milan (*Paen.* 2. 2. 6) for similar interpretations.
5. This important collection of texts does not always include those which refer to daily repentance for sin, thus failing to provide a fully biblical context for the institutional forms that did develop. It would be best to presume that the early writers were less concerned with penitential form than with the repentance that baptized Christians—whether seriously sinful or not—were called to live.

6. But Tertullian will come to regard him negatively, because he allowed adulterers pardon after penance.

7. Clement of Alexandria also mentions second repentance: *Strom.* 2. 56–7. 2; cf. *Paed.* 1. 64. 5–65. 2.

8. A detailed history of sin—the vocabulary of sin and of the distinction of sins—still needs to be written. While Christian texts naturally tended to focus on serious sin, precisely because not ordinary, research into the experience of sin in the early church cannot afford to ignore or neglect everyday sin and penance.

9. Tertullian speaks of *secundum lavacrum, paenitentia secunda*, and *secunda subsidia* (*Paen.* 7. 2, 10–12; 9. 1; 12. 5; *Scorpiace* 6. 9. 11; *De patientia* 13. 7; *Bap.* 16. 1. 2; *Pud.* 1. 16–18; 10. 11; 16. 5; 22. 9–10). Hippolytus spoke of second baptism, both to criticize rebaptism and to call it a renewal of baptism (*Haer.* 6. 41. 2–3; 9. 12. 26, 15. 1–3, 13. 15, 120. 56). See Dassmann 1973: 153–82 on martyrdom as second baptism; de Clerck 1989: 360–5.

10. The shift in Tertullian's view, rather than making him a Montanist, was part of a dispute between 'house churches' in Carthage (Tabbernee 2001).

11. Cf. van de Paverd (1981). *Damnatio* in *Pud.* 2. 12–13 refers to expulsion from the community, not eternal damnation. Ambrose discusses the text extensively in *Paen.* 1. 59–96.

12. When Innocent I (*Epistle* 6. 6 to Exsuperius of Toulouse) writes that the Church changed her position from a strict to a more lenient practice, it is likely that his reference is to a third-century shift.

SUGGESTED READINGS

Perhaps the best place to start would be the collections of primary sources on penance edited by Vogel (1966a) or Karpp (1970). Good historical overviews of the development of penance can be found in Gy (1958), Berrouard (1974), Adnès (1984), Dallen (1986), and Favazza (1988). Studies on penance in the western Church have been much more plentiful than those focused on eastern Christianity, though see the important contributions of Hausherr (1944), Ligier (1963, 1967a) and van der Paverd (1973, 1978a, 1978b, 1979, 1981, and 1986) on the Greek Fathers and other oriental sources. Among the Latin writers, scholars have devoted most attention to Tertullian (Munier 1998), Cyprian (Bévenot 1955; Burns 2001), Ambrose (Fitzgerald 1988; Frank 1938; Riga 1973), and Augustine (Berrouard 1964; La Bonnardière 1967, 1968).

BIBLIOGRAPHY

(See also Favazza 1988: 279–97; Karpp 1970: pp. xxxiii–xxxix)

ADNÈS, P. (1984), 'Pénitence (Repentir et Sacrement)', in *DSp* xii. 1. 943–1010.

ARRANZ, M. (1975), 'La liturgie pénitentielle juive après la destruction du Temple', in *Liturgie et Rémission des Péchés* (Rome: Edizioni Liturgiche), 39–56.

BERNHARD, J. (1965), 'Excommunication et pénitence—sacrement aux deux premiers siè-cles de l'église: Contribution canonique', *Revue de Droit Canonique*, 15: 265–81, 318–30.

—— (1966), 'Excommunication et pénitence—sacrement aux deux premiers siècles de l'église: Contribution canonique', *Revue de Droit Canonique*, 16: 41–70.

BERROUARD, M.-F. (1964), Pénitence de tous les jours selon saint Augustine', *Lumière et Vie*, 70: 75–100.

—— (1974), 'La pénitence publique durant les 6 premier siècles: Historie et sociologie', *La Maison-Dieu*, 118: 92–130.

Bévenot, M. (1955), 'The Sacrament of Penance and St. Cyprian's *De Lapsis*', *TS* 16: 175–213; repr. in E. Ferguson, *Christian Life: Ethics, Morality, and Discipline in the Early Church*, Studies in Early Christianity, 16 (New York: Garland), 332–56.

Blanchard, Y.-M. (1998), 'Lavement des pieds et pénitence', *La Maison-Dieu*, 214: 35–50.

BRADSHAW, P. F. (2002), *The Search for the Origins of Christian Worship*, 2nd edn. (New York: Oxford University Press).

BURNS, J. P. (1993), 'On Rebaptism: Social Organization in the Third Century Church', *JECS* 1: 367–403.

—— (2001), 'Confessing the Church: Cyprian on Penance', *StPatr* 36: 338–48.

BUSSINI, F. (1967), 'L'intervention de l'assemblée des fidèles au moment de la réconciliation des pénitents, d'après les trois "postulationes" d'un archidiacre romain du Ve–VIe siècle', *Revue des sciences religieuses de l'Université de Strasbourg*, 41: 29–38.

—— (1968), 'L'intervention de l'évêque dans la réconciliation des pénitents, d'après les trois "postulationes" d'un archidiacre romain du Ve–VIe siècle', *Revue des sciences religieuses de l'Université de Strasbourg*, 42: 326–38.

CAMPLANI, A. (1989), *Le Lettere Festali di Atanasio di Alessandria* (Rome: Unione Accademica Nazionale).

CAROLA, J. (2001), *Solvitis et vos: The Laity and their Exercise of the Power of the Keys according to Saint Augustine of Hippo* (Rome: Institutum Patristicum Augustinianum).

CAVALLI, G. (1999), *L'imposizione delle mani nella tradizione della chiesa latina: Un rito che qualifica il sacramento*, Studia Antoniana, 38 (Rome: Pontificium Athenaeum Antonianum).

CLARKE, G. W. (1989), *The Letters of St. Cyprian of Carthage*, iv, ACW 47 (New York: Newman Press).

COTHENET, E. (1975), 'Sainteté de l'Eglise et péchés des chrétiens: Comment le Nouveau Testament envisage-t-il leur pardon?', in *Liturgie et Rémission des Péchés* (Rome: Edizioni Liturgiche), 69–96.

CRESPIN, R. (1965), *Ministère et sainteté: pastorale du clergé et solution de la crise donatiste dans la vie e la doctrine de Saint Augustin* (Paris: L'Institut d'études augustiniennes).

DALLEN, J. (1977), 'The Imposition of Hands in Penance: A Study in Liturgical Theology', *Worship*, 51: 224–47.

—— (1986), *The Reconciling Community: The Rite of Penance*, Studies in the Reformed Rites of the Catholic Church, 3 (New York: Pueblo Pub. Co.), 1–99.

DALMAIS, H.-I. (1958), 'Le sacrement de pénitence chez les Orientaux', *La Maison-Dieu*, 56: 22–9.

DASSMANN, E. (1973), *Sündenvergebung durch Taufe, Busse und Martryerfürbitte in den Zeugnissen frühchristlicher Frömmigkeit und Kunst*, Münsterische Beiträge zur Theologie, 36 (Münster: Aschendorff).

DE CLERCK, P. (1989), 'Pénitence seconde et conversion quotidienne aux IIIe et IVe siècles', *StPatr* 20: 352–74.

FAVAZZA, J. A. (1988), *The Order of Penitents: Historical Roots and Pastoral Future* (Collegeville, Minn.: Liturgical Press).

FITZGERALD, A. (1988), *Conversion through Penance in the Italian Church of the Fourth and Fifth Centuries* (Lewiston, NY: Edwin Mellen Press).

—— (1999*a*), 'La pénitence dans l'Eglise ancienne', *Connaissance de Pères de l'Eglise*, 75: 17–34.

—— (1999*b*), 'Pénitence et Carême', *Connaissance de Pères de l'Eglise*, 75: 35–42.

—— (2000), 'Ambrose and Augustine: Confessio as initium iustitiae', *Aug* 40: 173–85.

—— (2001), 'Peter and the Rooster', *Aug* 41: 409–23.

FRANK, H. (1938), 'Ambrosius und die Büsseraussöhnung in Mailand', in O. Casel (ed.), *Heilige Überlieferung: Ausschnitte aus der Geschichte des Mönchtums und des heiligen Kultes, dem hochwürdigsten Herrn Abte von Maria Laach dr. theol. et iur. h. c. Idlefons Herwegen zum silbernen Abtsjubiläume*, Beiträge zur Geschichte des alten Mönchtums und des Benediktinerordens, Supplementband (Münster: Aschendorff), 136–73.

GUILLAUME, A. (1954), *Jeûne et charité dans l'Église latine des origines au XIIe siècle en particulier chez Saint Léon le Grand* (Paris: Laboureur).

GY, P.-M. (1958), 'Histoire liturgique du sacrement de Pénitence', *La Maison-Dieu*, 56: 5–21.

HAUSHERR, I. (1944), *Penthos: la doctrine de la componction dans l'Orient chrétien*, OrChrAn 132 (Rome: Pontificium Institutum Orientalium Studiorum).

HENNE, P. (1992), *L'Unité du Pasteur d'Hermas: Tradition et redaction*, Cahiers de la Revue Biblique, 31 (Paris: J. Gabalda).

HOLSTEIN, H. (1948), 'L'exhomologèse dans l'Adversus Haereses de Saint Irénée', *RSR* 35: 282–8.

JUNGMANN, J. (1932), *Die lateinischen Bussriten in ihrer geschichtlichen Entwicklung* (Innsbruck: Rauch).

KARPP, H. (1970), *La pénitence: Textes et commentaires des origines de l'ordre pénitentiel de l'Église ancienne* (Neuchâtel: Delachaux & Niestlé).

KRYKOWSKI, J. (1998), *Il pentimento e la penitenza come atteggiamento di vita cristiana in Tertulliano e in Cipriano*, (unpublished doctoral thesis, Institutum Patristicum Augustinianum, Rome).

—— (1999), *Il pentimento e la penitenza come atteggiamento di vita cristiana in Tertulliano e in Cipriano* (Rome: Pontificia Universita Lateranense, Institutum Patristicum Augustinianum, thesis extract).

LA BONNARDIÈRE, A.-M. (1967), 'Pénitence et réconciliation des Pénitents d'après Saint Augustin', *REAug* 13: 31–53, 249–83.

—— (1968), 'Pénitence et réconciliation des Pénitents d'après Saint Augustin', *REAug* 14: 181–204.

LAGES, M. F. (1969), 'Étapes de l'évolution du carême à Jérusalem avant le Ve siècle', *Revue des Études arméniennes*, 6: 67–102.

LAMPE, G. W. H. (1961), 'Exomologēsis', in *A Patristic Greek Lexicon* (London: Oxford University Press), 499–500.

—— (1973), 'St. Peter's Denial and the Treatment of the Lapsi', in D. Neiman and M. Schatkin (eds.), *The Heritage of the Early Church: Essays in Honor of the Very Reverend Georges Vasilievich Florovsky*, OrChrAn 195 (Rome: Pontificium Institutum Orientalium Studiorum), 113–33.

LAPORTE, J. (1986), 'Forgiveness in Origen', *Worship*, 60: 520–7.

LIGIER, L. (1963), 'Pénitence et eucharistie en Orient: Théologie sur une interférance de prières et de rites', *OCP* 29: 5–78.

—— (1967a), 'Dimension personelle et dimension communautaire de la pénitence en Orient', *La Maison-Dieu*, 90: 155–88.

—— (1967b), 'Le sacrement de pénitence selon la tradition orientale', *Nouvelle Revue Théologique*, 89: 940–67.

LIPINSKI, E. (1969), *La liturgie pénitentille dans la Bible* (Paris: Éditions du Cerf).

MUNIER, C. (1998), 'La discipline pénitentielle d'après Tertullien', *La Connaissance des Pères de l'Eglise*, 71: 37–50.

MURPHY-O'CONNOR, J. (1967), 'Péché et communauté dans le Nouveau Testament', *RB* 74: 161–93.

PALMER, P. (1959), *Sacraments and Forgiveness*, Sources of Christian Theology, 2 (Westminster, Md.: Newman Press).

PÉTRÉ, H. (1948), *Caritas: étude sur le vocabulaire latin de la charité chrétienne* (Louvain: Spicilegium Sacrum Lovaniense).

PELUCHOWSKI, J. (1978), *The Lord's Prayer and Jewish Liturgy* (New York: Seabury Press).

POSCHMANN, B. (1940), *Paenitentia Secunda* (Bonn: Peter Hanstein).

—— (1964), *Penance and the Anointing of the Sick* (New York: Herder & Herder).

PROULX, P., and SCHOKEL, A. (1975), 'Hebrews 6, 4–6: *eis metanoian anastaurounta*', *Biblica*, 56: 193–209.

REBILLARD, É. (1994), *In Hora Mortis: Evolution de la Pastorale Chrétienne de la Mort aux VIe and Ve siècles* (Rome: École française de Rome).

RIGA, P. (1973), 'Penance in Saint Ambrose', *Eglise et Théologie*, 4: 213–26.

RORDORF, W. (1975), 'La remission des péchés selon la *Didaché*', in *Liturgie et Rémission des Péchés* (Rome: Edizioni Liturgiche), 225–38.

ROUILLARD, P. (1999), *Histoire de la pénitence des origines à nos jours* (Paris: Éditions du Cerf).

ROULIN, P. (1959), 'Le péché contre l'Esprit', *Bible et Vie Chrétienne*, 29: 38–45.

SAINT-ROCH, P. (1991), *La pénitence dans les conciles et les lettres des paper des origines à la mort de Gégoire le grand*, Studi de antichità cristiana, 46 (Rome: Pontificio Istituto di Archeologia cristiana).

SAXER, V. (1969), *Vie liturgique et quotidienne à Carthage vers le milieu du IIIe siècle* (Rome: Pontificio Istituto di Archeologia Cristiana).

SOTOMAYOR, M. (1962), *San Pedro en la iconografia paleocristiana* (Granada: Facultad de Teologia).

TABBERNEE, W. (2001), 'To Pardon or Not to Pardon: North African Montanism and the Forgiveness of Sins', *StPatr* 36: 375–86.

TAFT, R. (1977), 'How Liturgies Grow: The Evolution of the Byzantine Divine Liturgy', *OCP* 43: 355–78.

VALGIGLIO, E. (1980), *'Confessio' nella Bibbia e nella letteratura cristiana antica* (Turin: G. Giappichelli).

VAN DE PAVERD, F. (1973), 'La pénitence dans le rite byzantin', *Quaestions Liturgiques*, 54: 191–203.

—— (1978a), '"Confession" (exagoreusis) and "Penance" (exomologesis) in De Lepra of Methodius of Olympus, I', *OCP* 44: 309–41.

—— (1978b), 'Paenitentia secunda in Methodius of Olympus', *Aug* 18: 459–85.

—— (1979), ' "Confession" (exagoreusis) and "Penance" (exomologesis) in De Lepra of Methodius of Olympus, II', *OCP* 45: 45–74.

—— (1981), 'Disciplinarian Procedures in the Early Church', *Aug* 21: 291–316.

—— (1986), 'The Matter of Confession according to Basil of Caesarea and Gregory of Nyssa', in *Studi Albanologi, Balcanici, Bizantini e Orientali in onore di Giuseppe Valentini, S. J.*, Studi albanesi, Studi e Testi, 6 (Florence: Leo S. Olschki Editore), 285–94.

VOGEL, C. (1966*a*), 'La discipline pénitentielle dans les inscriptions paléochrétiennes', *Rivista di Archeologia Cristiana*, 42: 317–25.

—— (1966*b*), *Le pécheur et la pénitence dans l'Eglise ancienne*, Chrétiens de tous les temps, 15 (Paris: Éditions du Cerf).

—— (1973), 'Vulneratum Caput', *Rivista di Archeologia Cristiana*, 49: 375–84.

VOGT, H. J. (1968), *Coetus Sanctorum: der Kirchenbegriff des Novatians und die Geschichte seiner Sonderkirche*, Theophaneia, 20 (Bonn: Peter Hanstein).

VORGRIMLER, H. (1963), 'Mt. 16:18s et le sacrement de pénitence', in *L'homme devant Dieu (Mélanges offerts au Père Henri de Lubac)* (Paris: Aubier), 51–61.

WATKINS, O. (1920), *A History of Penance*, 2 vols. (London: Longmans, Green).

C H A P T E R 39

MARTYRDOM AND THE CULT OF THE SAINTS

RICHARD M. PRICE

39.1 THE ROMAN PERSECUTIONS

IT is a mistake to suppose that scientific history of the Christian church, worthy of continuing use, started only a few decades ago. Arguably, the best work with which to begin a study of the Roman persecutions is chapter 16 of Edward Gibbon's *History of the Decline and Fall of the Roman Empire*, first published in 1776.[1] Gibbon gets a number of important points entirely right. What the Romans required was not the worship of their own gods, but the maintenance of the ancestral cults of the various subject nations: Christians were singled out for persecution because, unlike the Jews, they had abandoned the religion of their ancestors (Gibbon 1897: 74–5). At first there were no general edicts forbidding Christianity, and emperors were concerned to limit the prosecution of Christians. The subsequent general persecutions, initiated by the emperors themselves, were too transient to be effective (pp. 107–35); the total number of victims in the chief of them, at the beginning of the fourth century, was 'somewhat less than two thousand persons' (p. 138). Our notion of Christians as passive victims, moreover, must be qualified by the phenomenon of voluntary martyrdom—Christians who spontaneously defied the pagan authorities out of a desire to be martyred, attracted by the prospect of fame on earth and a glorious future in heaven, by means of a martyrdom that 'supplied every defect and expiated every sin' (p. 103). Some Christians even trusted that the earthly consequence of bearing witness to Christ would be no more than a brief imprisonment, rendered luxurious by the generous alms of the faithful (p. 136). In all, the sufferings of Christians at the hands of pagans pale into insignificance before the sufferings that Christians in later centuries were to inflict on each other (pp. 138–9).

Gibbon's combination of impressive historical knowledge with an unsympathetic attitude towards the martyrs themselves has resurfaced in a number of treatments of the persecutions by his English descendants. A particularly distinguished contribution is that of Ste. Croix (1963). He sums up well the consensus of competent ancient historians on the legal aspects of the persecution. Unlike the first general persecution in 250, there were no formal edicts forbidding Christianity, and provincial governors were guided by rescripts addressed to particular governors by particular emperors, which established a precedent, but were not absolutely binding. Popular hostility to Christianity, intense until about 250, arose not from any positive features of Christian belief or practice, but from fear that Christian abstention from pagan cult threatened the *pax deorum* (the concord between the gods and mankind) and might bring calamity on the whole community. Ste. Croix argues convincingly that until 250 it was local conditions, not imperial policy, that led to persecution, and that Christians were condemned not for refusing to worship the emperor himself but for refusing to worship the pagan gods—two points where writers on the early church still slip into error. Ste. Croix follows Gibbon in laying stress on voluntary martyrdom as 'a factor which both contributed to the outbreak of persecution and tended to intensify it when already in being' (p. 21). In an earlier article (Ste. Croix 1954) he analysed the data in Eusebius's *Martyrs of Palestine*, and concluded that two-thirds of Eusebius's sample had provoked their own arrest and death. We are invited to conclude that martyrdom owed at least as much to Christian fanaticism as to Roman intolerance.

As a final example of the tradition that stems from Gibbon (though reference should also be made to Barnes 1968 and 1985) we may cite Robin Lane Fox (1986), chapter 9: 'Persecution and Martyrdom'. Many themes familiar from Gibbon and Ste. Croix recur, including the 'misguided ideals' (p. 442) of voluntary martyrs. Lane Fox, however, rightly observes that the voluntary martyrdoms of which we are aware were almost always 'secondary martyrdoms, sparked off by the sight or news of fellow Christians who were being tried, abused or sentenced' (ibid.). This conclusion is confirmed by the full analysis of the evidence by Butterweck (1995), who shows that voluntary martyrdom was not a cause of persecution but a reaction to it. Lane Fox treats also, however, themes that earlier historians in the secular tradition had neglected: notably, the ideology of martyrdom and how this shaped not only the literary presentation of martyrdom in the martyr acts but also the experiences of the martyrs themselves, who believed that they were participating in the cosmic battle between Christ and Satan, where the martyr's bold confession and heroic death anticipated, and thereby hastened, the final victory of Christ at the end of the age (pp. 436–41). On this topic Lane Fox rightly draws attention to the letters of confessors contained in the correspondence of Cyprian (for which see the full annotation in Clarke 1984–9), which are free of the editing and sometimes invention that deprive even the most reliable of the martyr acts of total authenticity.

The originality of Christian martyrdom has been much discussed, in particular its debt to Jewish texts on the Maccabean martyrs, notably 2 Maccabees (written in the 70s or 60s BCE) and 4 Maccabees (generally dated to somewhere in the first century CE). The case that the Christian theology of martyrdom was based on the Jewish one was well argued by Frend (1965: ch. 2). The sceptical position has been presented by Bowersock (1995: ch. 1 and app. 2), who argues that the relevant chapters of 2 Maccabees are interpolated, and that 4 Maccabees is more likely to have been influenced by Christian texts than the other way round. The late dating for 4 Maccabees that this implies is not, however, generally accepted.

39.2 THE CULT OF THE MARTYRS

The earliest literary evidence for the cult of martyrs dates to the mid-second century, and relates to the place of burial of the martyred Polycarp of Smyrna: 'Gathering here, so far as we can, in joy and gladness, we will be allowed by the Lord to celebrate the anniversary day of his martyrdom' (*Martyrdom of Polycarp*, 18). The best commentary on this, and indeed on the development of the cult of the martyrs generally, is still Hippolyte Delehaye, *Les origines du culte des martyrs* (1912; 2nd edn. 1933). Delehaye points out that such commemorations were standard practice for all the dead, and that it was far from unusual to invoke their prayers on behalf of the living (pp. 38–40, 120–8). What was new in the cult of martyrs? Principally the fact that the anniversary of a martyr was celebrated not simply by his kin but by the whole Christian community. Delehaye proceeds to describe and illustrate the expansion of the cult in the period after Constantine, with such novel features as the construction of churches over holy tombs, pilgrimage, the commemoration of martyrs in cities other than their own, the translation and division of relics (more in the East than the West), the multiplication of relics through the invention (in both senses) of the remains of hitherto unknown martyrs, the extension of the cult to other saints, such as biblical personages and bishops and ascetics, the adoption of saints' names at baptism, the popularity of burial *ad sanctos* (that is, in the close vicinity of a shrine; see Duval 1988); a later article (Delehaye 1930) treated the dedication of churches to particular saints. In all, Delehaye offers a clear and well-documented account of the development of the cult, which has not been superseded by later studies. His limitation is that he does not attempt to place the cult in a broader social context or analyse the particular needs it served. Writing as a Roman Catholic priest, he finds the development of the cult so natural and inevitable that no particular explanation is called for. He suggests a sensible programme for further research, but with likewise no sense that the boundary posts were going to move:

> The cult of a saint has multiple expressions. Here it is a church that is dedicated to him, there an altar; there is a feast inscribed in the calendar; there are relics preserved with respect; there is an image exposed to the veneration of the faithful, recurring in various forms . . . , there are pilgrimages to the sanctuary of the saint, confraternities established in his honour; there is a corporation which chose him as patron; his name is given in baptism; there is an account of his life and miracles. All of this deserves to be brought to light if one is to give an idea of the saint's popularity.
>
> (Delehaye 1930: 23)

The modern student is likely to take as his starting point not Delehaye, but the celebrated set of lectures by Peter Brown, *The Cult of the Saints* (1981). This short volume brings the cult to life through a rare empathy and some vivid details; it is beyond doubt a literary masterpiece, perhaps the most attractive of all Brown's writings.

Brown pillories as the classic misconception an analysis of the rise of the cult of the saints based on the 'two-tiered' model that contrasts throughout history the religion of the educated and rational elite, with its ethical emphasis and strict monotheism, and the superstition of the vulgar masses, with their addiction to the idolatrous veneration of places and things, and accompanying preference for some version of polytheism. Accordingly, the development of the cult of the saints in the late antique period can be viewed as a capitulation of the educated before the demands of a mass of newly converted pagans, who could accept only a Christianity that, in its multiplication of saints, shrines, and relics, had come to imitate the idolatry and polytheism with which they were already familiar. This was the interpretation of the cult that was proclaimed by the Protestant Reformers of the seventeenth century and reaffirmed in the eighteenth-century Enlightenment.

Brown's own picture could not be more contrasted. He insists, even more strongly than Delehaye, on a discontinuity between pagan and Christian piety, to the extent of neglecting the continuity between traditional respect towards the dead and the cult of the saints. The saints of late antique Christian cult were not substitutes for pagan gods, but human beings who had shared our predicament, and who formed a bridge between heaven and ordinary human experience. Their devotees felt towards them a reverence that combined a sense of the holy with normal human feelings of trust and respect. Like the holy man to whom Brown had dedicated a seminal article (Brown 1971), the saint took on the contours of a late antique patron, who looked after the interests of his clients and was frequently an agent for resolving disputes and maintaining social concord. Brown discusses exorcism at length, as a ritual of social reintegration (Brown 1981: ch. 6). He mentions how the cult could liberate oppressed individuals, who could opt 'for dependence on an ideal *dominus* at his distant shrine, rather than for dependence on the all too palpable wielders of power in their locality' (Brown 1981: 123). But Brown's emphasis is on how the cults were adopted and promoted by the ecclesiastical elite. Bishops were adept at appropriating existent cults, or developing new ones, in such a way as to promote their own authority and upstage the patronage of the lay elite. The saint as invisible patron reinforced the role of visible patron exercised by the bishop himself (p. 39). The cult of the saints was so successful at replicating, in an idealized form, the social experience of the later Roman Empire that it hastened the victory of Christianity over its pagan rivals, and at the same time 'made final the processes by which the indigenous cultures of the western Mediterranean [were] eroded by a slow but sure pressure from on top exercised through the grid of administration and patronage relationships that reached ever outwards from the towns' (p. 121). The centring of authority on urban shrines and the clergy who controlled them turned large stretches of the countryside into a religious desert, and destroyed the link, so strong in paganism, between religion and landscape, between pious practices and the natural cycle of the agricultural year (pp. 124–5).

The most touching and imaginative chapter of the book (ch. 3, 'The Invisible Companion') treats with great sympathy the feelings of intimate friendship that saints could evoke in their devotees, taking as a prime case the devotion of Paulinus of Nola to St Felix, in which the saint is at the same time patron, friend, and better self. No one has written better than Brown on late antique patronage (Brown 1971), but themes of friendship and the *alter ego* (which were closely connected) need to be explored in other literature of the period before their role in this context can be properly understood (Fabre 1949; White 1992). The use of different types of human relationships as models for the relations between saint and devotee is a promising field for exploration of a wider range of primary texts. The dominant model was certainly that of patronage—a relationship of dependence and respectful good manners. But the nuances were more varied and less obvious.

Brown's book has remained the starting point for most students of the early cult of the saints in English-speaking countries, and its merits need no emphasis here. It undoubtedly captures certain aspects of the cult, but the emphasis on refuting the 'two-tiered' model has the unfortunate effect of producing a distortion in the opposite direction. Critics have pointed out that, with his emphasis on the bishops as the 'impresarios' of the cult, Brown did not so much exorcize the two-tiered model as invert it, writing as if the cult was the product of episcopal manipulation. Were the bishops really as dominant an influence as he makes out? Brown's account of the development of the cult of the saints follows episcopal propaganda and describes the development that the bishops would have liked to see. The reality on the ground will often have been very different. Kate Cooper in a recent article (1999) reminds us that as far back as 1877 the archaeologist G. B. de Rossi showed that even within Rome itself cults were often developed by local interests in competition with each other, and she herself argues that the cult of the saints should be seen as 'agonistic' rather than 'hierarchical' (Cooper 1999). The student of hagiographical material produced by bishops must look carefully to apportion the share of initiative between bishops and other actors in the cult, and also to distinguish between cults that echoed and promoted episcopal dominance and cults such that, to secure and maintain his position, the bishop had to contrive a prominent role for himself in a cult that was flourishing without him; Van Dam (1993: 69–81, 128–35) has shown how Gregory of Tours fits into this latter category, and needed St Martin more than St Martin needed him. One must also beware of the temptation to treat such figures as Ambrose of Milan and Gregory of Tours as if they were typical bishops: the aristocratic bishop, carrying into his office the seigniorial role and widespread contacts of his class, dominates in Brown's book, but certainly did not dominate in the ranks of the late Roman episcopate (Pietri 1984: 305–6). Perhaps a useful parallel is the development of the monastic movement. The literature written by bishops to celebrate the movement stresses the perfect accord between bishops and monks; and wily bishops, such as Athanasius and Cyril of Alexandria, strengthened their position by a close alliance with monasteries; but this does not mean that the success of the monastic movement was due to episcopal promotion.

It is the great city shrines, visited by hundreds if not thousands of pilgrims and commemorated by the literary elite, that are best documented. Peter Brown's generalization that the city-based cults of saints emptied the countryside of religious significance neglects the evidence for more scattered shrines promoted by the laity or dissident groups. Note, for example, Stephen Mitchell's comment on Cappadocia: 'The creation of shrines in the countryside is a notable feature of the fourth-century evidence as a whole' (1993: 68). Gregory of Tours (*The Glory of the Confessors*, 7) narrates how in a village in the diocese of Tours there was a tree whose bark was credited with miraculous powers because St Martin had supposedly restored it after it had been uprooted by a storm. The veneration of trees was a survival of paganism which Martin (*Life*, 13), like Caesarius of Arles after him (*Serm.* 54. 5), had tried to eradicate; but here peasants use the cult of St Martin to defend their own traditional practices. Bishops were not the only people who exploited the cult of the saints.

Significant in this context is the importance of martyr cults in African Donatism (for which see Tilley 1996 and 1997), the prime case in which the cult of martyrs became crucial for the self-identity of a group that was itself subject to intermittent persecution. In contrast, the promotion of the cult by the officially favoured Catholic Church constituted a more tendentious claim, that she was herself the true church of the martyrs, and that the transformation of the Church's status under Constantine and his successors had not changed the Church's identity. For Robert Markus (1990: 89–95) this is the most important single aspect of the late antique promotion of the cult of the saints. Perkins (1995) argues that the cult was important for serving as the Church's representation of herself as a suffering body, and for the use of this representation as a claim to power.

To explain the cult of the saints, and remove it from the category of 'primitive superstition', Brown used functional analysis, developed in the context of magical beliefs in tribal Africa, where supposedly primitive practices and beliefs find their rationale in their complex relation to social reality and contribution to sensible social aims (Brown 1998). Two notable French experts on the Christianity of the late antique West criticized him, however, for saying nothing about theology (Fontaine 1982; Pietri 1984). The Christian cult of martyrs cannot be separated from the Christian worship of a crucified God, while the veneration of bodily remains, however decayed or fragmentary, cannot be separated either from the celebration of the eucharist, where the consecrated hosts are (in effect) so many fragments of Christ's body, or from the Christian faith in the resurrection of the flesh at the end of time. Van Dam (1993: 105–15) illustrates the move among English-speaking scholars since Brown's book to pay more attention to theology.

The truth is that Brown's book is an essay that seeks to stimulate and provoke, not a comprehensive or magisterial study. As Jacques Fontaine commented aptly, 'the author is too lucidly on guard against the skill of his handling of ideas to imagine that his view of the problems posed is exclusive or, above all, that the truths, at times hypothetical, which he has chosen to explore and present are the whole truth' (Fontaine 1982: 36).

What has happened in the 25 years since the appearance of Brown's book? His own thoughts have to some extent moved on. In a recent retrospect (Brown 1998), he criticizes himself for treating the advent of the holy man too dramatically, as if it introduced a quite new religious order to match a new style of social relations in late antiquity; this criticism would also apply to his analysis of the development of the cult of the saints. In a more recent article on the cult of saints itself (Brown 2000b), he moves away from an account of the role attributed to the saints that ties them too closely to models of episcopal patronage. What the saints offered was not just a mythical variant of episcopal patronage, but 'a moment of total triumph over pain and death', and the saints' supposed generosity extended well beyond the range of aristocratic beneficence to the healing of bodily needs and infirmities, such as sick animals and infertile women, that had hitherto been set apart as 'the most potentially polluted and polluting levels of daily life' (p. 17). Saints did a lot more than replicate, and thereby glorify, the work of bishops as benefactors and mediators.

Meanwhile, many younger scholars have been inspired by Brown's work, though the living holy man has received more attention than the dead saint. A notable collective volume is Howard-Johnston and Hayward, *The Cult of Saints in Late Antiquity and the Early Middle Ages: Essays on the Contribution of Peter Brown* (1999). Brown's work has also stimulated a new interest in the cult of relics (Miller

1998 and 2000; Clark 1999; Hunter 1999), supplementing earlier studies (such as Saxer 1980).

The current scene may best be represented by setting a series of topics that invite particular attention from a student of the subject: (1) The witness of the martyrs; (2) saints and Christian living; (3) a religion of Sundays or of Saints' days?; (4) miracles; (5) archaeology and art; and (6) the cult of the Virgin Mary.[2]

39.2.1 The Witness of the Martyrs

Tertullian's adage that the blood of the martyrs is the seed of the church (*Apol.* 50. 13) is so over-familiar that you have to be a clergyman to have the courage to cite it. That the heroism of confessors in prison could lead to the conversion of their gaolers is illustrated in the *Martyrdom of Perpetua and Felicity* (9. 1, 16. 4) as well as in the Acts of the Apostles (16: 27–34), and recurs monotonously in fictitious martyrology. Whether the sufferings and heroism of Christians in their place of execution had a similar effect is less clear, for the whole mentality at Roman spectacles was for the crowd to identify with the executioners rather than the victims. Recently, some sensitive studies have suggested that the heroism of the martyrs will have impressed spectators expecting degradation and self-pity (Tilley 1991; Shaw 1996; Potter 1993; Cooper 1998); but since the execution of martyrs bore some relation to remembered rites of human sacrifice, where the victims were expected to die willingly (Rousselle 1988: 116–21), the martyrs to some extent did no more than satisfy pagan expectations. Insofar as the Christian defiance of their persecutors struck pagans as unusual, it may well have excited disgust rather than admiration, as in a well-known comment in Marcus Aurelius's *Meditations* (11. 3). For martyrdom as a public spectacle, see also Young (2001).

The martyr acts raise complex problems of authenticity. Bisbee (1988) uses form-critical methods to determine how close the early acts are to authentic court records. The text that seems to most readers to take us closest to the martyrs themselves is the *Martyrdom of Perpetua and Felicity*, because of its lengthy citation of Perpetua's prison diary. The growth of women's studies has stimulated a vast interest in this text, making it perhaps the most studied of early Christian writings outside the Bible; important contributions include Amat (1996; text, French trans., and commentary), Tilley (1995), and Salisbury (1997, with a useful bibliography). Kraemer and Lander (2000) reasonably point out, however, that, even if the voice of Perpetua as it appears in the text is distinctive, we cannot be certain that her 'diary' is not a literary fiction by a sympathetic impersonator. But its authenticity is supported by comparison with such early authentic accounts as the *Martyrdom of Polycarp* and the Letter from the churches of Lyons and Vienne, which show far more obvious literary elaboration.

39.2.2 Saints and Christian Living

A question that arises in the study of the cult of the saints in any age is whether they served primarily as role models or rather as intercessors and miracle-workers. The most influential study has been Vauchez (1988), who argued that a stress on the saints as role models became dominant only in the thirteenth century. It must be admitted that late antique sermons, such as those of Augustine on St Stephen, often stress the exemplary qualities of the saint, such as his fortitude in following the Christian law, or his spirit of forgiveness towards his persecutors. Beyond doubt, the lives of holy ascetics were read by monks and nuns as a spur for their own endeavours (e.g. Davis 2001: 87–112). But there is widespread agreement among historians that for most Christians till at least the late Middle Ages the chief significance of the saints lay in something that was easier to venerate than imitate: their conquest over the normal limitations of human life through union with the death and resurrection of Christ, in a triumph that was made present and active in the celebration of their cult (Brown 2000b).

More realistic than presenting the saints as models for imitation was the preaching that appealed to the martyrs' witness to the Christian law as an argument for the observance of the rules of the Church. Grig (2004) is contemptuous: 'Bishops narrated these stories of horror, wonder and heroism, and then told their congregations that they could imitate the martyrs by abstaining from sex, or avoiding magical charms. Hyperbole was followed by bathos' (p. 144). But it was reasonable to teach that the patronage of the martyrs was open only to those who followed the basic rules that defined Christian identity; this is the reason for the prominence in the miracle accounts collected by Gregory of Tours of illnesses inflicted as a punishment for non-observance of the Christian calendar. It is here that the cult of the saints had clear implications for daily living.

Finally, visits to saints' shrines could, through the protection and patronage they could supply, lead to a change of life—for example, in escaping from a burdensome marriage or recovering free status (Van Dam 1993: 100–3).

39.2.3 A Religion of Sundays or of Saints' Days?

Peter Brown's account, which sees the cult of the saints as a main agent of Christianization, has been criticized for ignoring the regular eucharistic worship, Sunday by Sunday, which had been a main constituent of Christian identity since the apostolic age (Pietri 1984). Certainly the calendar of saints' feasts built up only gradually (Grig 2004: 34–6). No attempt to determine the importance of the cult of the saints can avoid the question of the relative prominence of different forms of practice and different criteria of belonging in late antique Christianity. Evidence for a range of cities, including Rome, Constantinople, Antioch, and Gerasa, supports the statement of Ramsay MacMullen, 'In no city was the church (or were the churches, plural) able physically to accommodate at one time any large minority of the total resident population, even after several generations of post-Constantinian growth of congregation and ecclesiastical building' (MacMullen 1989: 510). Before infant baptism became normal (in the course of the fifth century), there was a host of long-term catechumens, like Augustine before his conversion, who had renounced paganism but were in no hurry to subject themselves to the full rigours of the Christian law. The official liturgy of the Church treated all who were not baptized and communicant Catholics as at best second-class members of the Christian community. The huge advantage of the saints' feasts that involved vigils, processions, and feasting was that everyone could join in. It is impossible to guess the proportions of fully initiated Christians, catechumens, and sympathetic onlookers in the fourth and fifth centuries, but as a means of Christianization, of drawing in those on or outside the fringes, the cult of the saints may well have made a considerable contribution.

Grig (2004: 37) sets out the main sequence of celebration—pilgrimage, night vigil, eucharist, and feasting on the day; she makes exemplary use of Augustine's sermons on St Stephen to illustrate the way in which, through the translation of relics, a martyr cult could become firmly embedded in a particular community and celebrate 'local time and space, and characters familiar to the congregation' (p. 104). For similar festivals of martyrs in the Greek East, see Leemans *et al.* (2003). The complaints by certain of the fathers that saints' days were a mere excuse for merrymaking may seem insufferably high-minded, but Augustine narrates that the vigils were an opportunity for seduction (Brown 2000*b*), and Theodoret gives the game away when he tells us of a holy man who boasted that as a youth he had managed to preserve his virginity intact despite attending many festivals of martyrs (*H. rel.* 20. 2). The mixing of the sexes and the classes (Liebeschuetz 1990: 167–8) was one of the most attractive and liberating features of the cult, reinforcing social solidarity in the way the great pagan festivals had once done.

39.2.4 Miracles

Lives of holy men and confessors typically include stories of miracles they worked in their lifetime, and in the case of saints long dead, posthumous ones as well. From the latter there began to appear towards the end of our period miracle collections as a separate genre from biography. Most of this material, though far from all, relates to cures of illness or other bodily infirmity. How is the modern historian going to treat this mass of material which cannot but arouse his scepticism? The best discussion in English is currently Van Dam 1993: 82–115. He dismisses as reductionist explanations that appeal to false diagnosis or natural remission or to psychosomatic illness and recovery. Without appeal to such explanations, however, the modern reader cannot regard the material as other than pious fiction. But Van Dam is right to point out that such interpretations miss the broader significance of miracles: the stories all presume a providential world order in which illness or other misfortune is willed by God as a punishment for sin or at least a stimulus to devotion, and in which recovery is not merely a cure of the body but a sign of a restoration of proper relations between God and man and within the human community itself.

A more serious problem arises from the repetitive and formulaic character of the accounts, which do not generally reveal the social context within which miracles need to be interpreted. The reason for this was not indifference to the particular context of illness and cure, but the need for maximum generality if the story was to apply to the needs of a whole host of subsequent aspirants to the saint's favour. A number of recent writers (see Grig 2004) have applied to hagiography the concept of *anamnēsis* as it is widely understood in biblical and liturgical studies: an event in sacred history becomes present when it is celebrated, in such a way that the power it revealed can be active again. When some story of a cure wrought by a saint was remembered on his feast, there was not only assurance that such miracles remained possible, but also a real presence of saving power during the celebration. Concrete details that tied a miracle to a particular context could make a story more vivid, but were essentially dispensable and might even limit its power.

Students of miracle accounts will nevertheless look out for every detail that restores something of the original setting; and every collection of miracle stories is open to the basic analysis that classifies the recipients according to sex, age, social status, country of origin, and the like. The exact nature of the illness is generally less revealing, since illnesses shared a common aetiology, in terms of transgression and punishment. This can conjure up an age of guilt and anxiety, where recourse to the miraculous relates to the particular social problems of the declining Empire of late antiquity. But the frequency of very ordinary human afflictions, from contagion to child mortality, from barren marriages to diseases among livestock, shows that miracles related less to exceptional circumstances than to the universal trials of human life. A few cults specialized in particular forms of affliction: the *Miracles of St Artemios* (Crisafulli and Nesbitt 1997) have attracted particular attention because of their bizarre concentration on the genital organs; but such cults were exceptional.

39.2.5 Archaeology and Art

Brown's discussion of the quite new importance accorded to holy places in late antique Christianity as a result of martyr cults has been followed up by Markus

(1994). For the architecture and iconography of these cults, the fundamental study is Grabar (1946). For Africa, Duval (1982) is indispensable; see too Lamberigts and Van Deun (1995).

Easily the most famous monuments of the martyrs are those in the city of Rome (for the history of their excavation, see Frend 1996). Particularly fascinating is the complex and obscure history of the shrines to Saints Peter and Paul. The second-century memorial to St Peter on the Vatican Hill (Lampe 2003) was soon upstaged by the rival shrine to Saints Peter and Paul on the Appian Way, where graffiti give evidence of a lively cult in the second half of the third century; only with the completion of the great Constantinian basilica on the Vatican Hill, not before the middle of the fourth century, did the Vatican shrine seriously challenge its rival. To account for the existence of two rival shrines, complicated hypotheses of temporary translations of the relics were aired in the fourth century and are still aired today (Leclerq 1939: 853–6; Chadwick 1957; Lampe 2003; Grig 2004). The construction of a whole series of great basilicas in the fourth century and the development of the catacombs as places of pilgrimage by Pope Damasus in around 370 (Ferrua and Carletti 1985; Grig 2004: 127–34) have been exhaustively explored. The plethora of shrines must have led to competition. Kate Cooper (1999) illustrates how the fictitious accounts of Roman martyrs composed in late antiquity can be explored as rival pieces of propaganda promoting particular shrines and the patrons and clergy of those shrines; life in Christian Rome was dominated by competitive factionalism throughout antiquity and beyond. Studies of the cult of the saints in Rome show how archaeology by itself is dumb but, when linked to fragments of history and related literary texts, has a story to tell. For the fourth and fifth centuries the classic study is Pietri (1976). *DACL* contains numerous full and expert articles by Leclerq, e.g. 'Catacombes' (ii. 2376–2450), 'Catacumbas (Cimitière ad)' (ii. 2487–2512), and 'Pierre (Saint)' (xiv: 822–981). For Constantinian churches and shrines in Rome, see Holloway (2004).

Grig (2004: ch. 6, 'Picturing Martyrs') provides a useful discussion of martyrs in Roman art; she records differing views on whether descriptions of artistic representations in literature reflect real works of art, an important question considering the paucity of surviving works of art outside Rome. A fine example of the study of artefacts as revelatory of cult is by Davis (2001: 113–200), who offers a lengthy analysis of the cult of St Thecla in Egypt outside Alexandria, based largely on surviving material remains. As he concludes, 'By handling a clay flask worn smooth by pilgrim hands, by stooping through a doorway of a burial chapel, or by deciphering an ancient gravestone, we are able to enter imaginatively the social world of Egyptian Christians who venerated Saint Thecla' (p. 191). Davis illustrates how much more of the cult of the saints in late antiquity remains to be unveiled by a combination of sensitive reading of the sources, investigation of non-literary evidence, and a grasp of the general situation of Christians and the Church in late antiquity.

39.2.6 The Cult of the Virgin Mary

The cult of the Virgin has been well explored both by Catholic scholars (O'Carroll 1983) and by feminists, but its early history has been comparatively neglected, because of the paucity of material. It is a striking fact that the cult of the Virgin Mary developed only slowly in the early church; at first eclipsed (among cults of female saints) by that of St Thecla (Davis 2001), it reached its apogee only in the sixth century. The virginity of Mary received emphasis in ascetical literature, particularly in the wake of the rapid development of monasticism in the fourth century (see O'Carroll 1983, on Origen, Athanasius, Ambrose, and Jerome with useful bibliographies; also Hunter 1993), but literary and homiletic appeals to Mary as a type of virginity must be distinguished from actual cult, involving recourse to her intercession. Some recent studies have claimed intense Marian devotion at Constantinople early in the fifth century (Holum 1982; Limberis 1994), but the evidence invites a degree of scepticism (Price 2004). The earliest known case of a church dedication to the Virgin is in the Acts of the Council of Ephesus of 431, which regularly describe the church where the bishops assembled as 'the church called Mary'; even if the building dedicated to the Virgin whose ruins impress the visitor today was built later, c. 500 (Karweise 1995), the literary evidence shows that the dedication is older. Although it is a mistake to talk of the Council of Ephesus as formally defining that Mary is *Theotokos* (Mother of God), it appears to have acted as a spur for further dedications, the most famous of which is St Mary Major's in Rome, dedicated to the Virgin by Pope Sixtus a few years afterwards (*DACL* x. 2091–2119). These dedications stimulated the development of the cult of the Virgin, involving invocatory prayer and the celebration of her intercessory power.

The cult was also assisted by the development (particularly in the sixth century) in the veneration paid to icons; this made up for the obvious lack of major relics of the Virgin. A striking sixth-century icon of the Virgin surrounded by angels and saints is still preserved in St Catherine's Monastery on Sinai (reproduced in Cunningham 1988: 57). There are notable references to images of the Virgin and the associated cult in Gregory of Tours (d. 594) and in John Moschus, writing in Palestine c. 600 (Bardy 1938). The development of Marian feasts also continued apace, with the feasts of the Annunciation, Nativity, and Presentation appearing in the mid-sixth century, to which the Dormition was added on direct imperial initiative at the beginning of the seventh century. Meanwhile, Constantinople had come to house notable relics of the Virgin, her veil and her girdle, which increased in prominence throughout the sixth century (Cameron 1978). It was the defeat of the Avar and Persian siege of Constantinople in 626, after an icon of the Virgin had been hung on the gates of the city, which secured her status as the unrivalled protector and patron of the imperial city (Cameron 2004).

There is startlingly early evidence of invocation of the Virgin in Egypt in a papyrus dating to the late third century, which gives the text of the prayer known in its Latin version as *Sub tuum praesidium* (Giamberardini 1975: 69–97). But prayer to the Virgin surfaces in patristic literature (apart from stray references) only at the end of the fifth century, and the papyrus cannot be taken as evidence for piety outside Egypt itself. Cyril of Alexandria, Proclus of Constantinople, and other champions of the full acknowledgement of Mary as *Theotokos* at the time of the Council of Ephesus of 431 took no interest in the intercessory power of Mary in response to particular petitions: what they were concerned to celebrate was Mary's contribution to our redemption by bearing Christ in her womb; it was the miracle of the Incarnation that we owe to Mary, not the cures or exorcisms worked by ordinary saints. Only in the century that followed the Council of Chalcedon (451) did it become normal for Christians to invoke Mary's patronage and intercession, and for the Virgin to descend into the ranks of patron saints (Cunningham 1988).

Notes

1. Gibbon (1776), 519–86. The standard edition is Gibbon (1897); chapter 16 is in vol. ii, 71–139, to which my page references relate. Gibbon nowhere treats the subsequent development of martyr cults.
2. The most useful study is Grig (2004), primarily on the cult of martyrs in Italy and Africa in the fourth and fifth centuries, which has an excellent bibliography.

Suggested Reading

The best introduction to the origin and practice of the early cult of the saints remains Delahaye 1933 (in French). For English readers, however, the natural starting point is Brown (1981), which has the great advantage of being addressed to modern sensibilities. Of more recent studies the most useful is Grig (2004), which, though concentrating primarily on the cult of martyrs in Italy and Africa in the fourth and fifth centuries, gives a good idea of the range of questions that need to be asked in relation to any part of the Roman world; in addition, the work has an excellent and up-to-date bibliography.

On martyrdom and persecution Ste. Croix (1963; repr. in Ste. Croix 2006) is still the best introduction to persecution as conceived and conducted by the authorities; to gain an insight into the mentality and convictions of the martyrs themselves, and the Christians who spread their cult, one could read Frend (1965) or, better still, the early martyr acts in Musurillo (1972). Studies of particular saints and cults, or of the cults in a particular area, have the advantage of relating cult and context more closely, as in Rentinch (1970), Van Dam (1993), Klingshirn (1994), Salisbury (1997), and Davis (2001). On the cult of the Virgin Mary, Cunningham (1988), Cameron (2004), and Shoemaker (2007) are exceptionally insightful.

BIBLIOGRAPHY

AMAT, J. (1996) (ed.), *Passion de Perpetue et Felicité*, SC 417 (Paris: Éditions du Cerf).

BARDY, G. (1938) 'La doctrine de l'intercession de Marie chez les Pères grecs', *La Vie Spirituelle*, 56 Suppl. 1–37.

BARNES, T. D. (1968), 'Legislation against the Christians', *JRS* 58: 32–50.

—— (1985), *Tertullian*, rev. edn. (Oxford: Oxford University Press).

BISBEE, G. A. (1988), *Pre-Decian Acts of Martyrs and Commentarii* (Philadelphia: Fortress Press).

BOWERSOCK, G. W. (1995), *Martyrdom and Rome* (Cambridge: Cambridge University Press).

BROWN, P. (1971), 'The Rise and Function of the Holy Man in Late Antiquity', *JRS* 61: 80–101; repr. in Brown (1982), 103–52.

—— (1976), 'Eastern and Western Christendom in Late Antiquity: A Parting of the Ways', in D. Baker (ed.), *The Orthodox Churches and the West*, SCH, 13: 1–24; repr. in Brown (1982), 166–95.

—— (1981), *The Cult of the Saints: Its Rise and Function in Latin Christianity* (London: SCM Press).

—— (1982) *Society and the Holy in Late Antiquity* (London: Faber & Faber).

—— (1998), 'The Rise and Function of the Holy Man in Late Antiquity, 1971–1997', *JECS* 6: 353–76.

—— (2000a), *Augustine of Hippo*, 2nd edn. (London: Faber & Faber).

—— (2000b), 'Enjoying the Saints in Late Antiquity', *Early Medieval Europe*, 9: 1–24.

BURRUS, V. (1995), 'Reading Agnes: The Rhetoric of Gender in Ambrose and Prudentius', *JECS* 3: 25–46.

BUTTERWECK, C. (1995), *«Martyriumssucht» in der Alten Kirche? Studien zur Darstellung und Deutung frühchristlicher Martyrien* (Tübingen: Mohr).

BYNUM, C. W. (1995), *The Resurrection of the Body in Western Christianity 200–1336* (New York: Columbia University Press).

CAMERON, A. (1978), 'The Theotokos in Sixth-Century Constantinople: A City Finds its Symbol', *JTS* NS 29: 79–108.

—— (2004), 'The Cult of the Virgin in Late Antiquity: Religious Development and Myth-Making', in Swanson (2004), 1–21.

CHADWICK, H. (1957), 'St Peter and St Paul in Rome: The Problem of the Memoria Apostolorum ad Catacumbas', *JTS* NS 8: 31–52; repr. in H. Chadwick, *History and Thought of the Early Church* (London: Variorum, 1982).

CLARK, G. (1999), 'Victricius of Rouen: *Praising the Saints*', *JECS* 7: 365–99.

CLARKE, G. W. (1984–9), *The Letters of St. Cyprian of Carthage*, trans. and annotated, ACW 43–4, 46–7 (New York: Newman Press).

COOPER, K. (1998), 'The Voice of the Victim: Gender, Representation and Early Christian Martyrdom', *Bulletin of the John Rylands University Library of Manchester*, 80/3: 147–57.

—— (1999), 'The Martyr, the *Matrona* and the Bishop: The Matron Lucina and the Politics of Martyr Cult in Fifth- and Sixth-Century Rome', *Early Medieval Europe*, 8: 297–317.

CRISAFULLI, V. S., and NESBITT, J. W. (1997), *The Miracles of St. Artemios: A Collection of Miracle Stories by an Anonymous Author of Seventh-Century Byzantium* (Leiden: E. J. Brill).

CUNNINGHAM, M. B. (1988), 'The Mother of God in Early Byzantine Homilies', *Sobornost*, 10/2: 53–67.

Davis, S. J. (2001), *The Cult of Saint Thecla: A Tradition of Women's Piety in Late Antiquity* (Oxford: Oxford University Press).

Delehaye, Hippolyte (1930), 'Loca Sanctorum', *AnBoll* 48: 5–64, and as separate publication (Brussels: Société des Bollandistes).

—— (1933), *Les origines du culte des martyrs*, 2nd edn., Subsidia hagiographica, 20 (Brussels: Société des Bollandistes).

—— (1966), *Les passions des martyrs et les genres littéraires*, 2nd edn., Subsidia hagiographica, 13B (Brussels: Société des Bollandistes).

Duval, Y. (1982), *Loca sanctorum Africae: le culte des martyres en Afrique du IVe au VIIe siècle*, 2 vols. (Rome: École française de Rome).

—— (1988), *Auprès des saints corps et âme: l'inhumation 'ad sanctos' dans la chrétienté d'Orient et d'Occident du IIIe au VIIe siècle* (Paris: L'Institut d'études augustiniennes).

Fabre, P. (1949), *Saint Paulin de Nole et l'amitié chrétienne* (Paris: Bibliothèque des Écoles Françaises d'Athènes et de Rome).

Ferrua, A., and Carletti, C. (1985), *Damaso e i Martiri di Roma* (Vatican City: Pontificia commissione di archeologia sacra).

Fontaine, J. (1982), 'Le culte des saints et ses implications sociologiques: Réflections sur un recent essai de P. Brown', *AnBoll* 100: 17–41.

Frend, W. H. C. (1965), *Martyrdom and Persecution in the Early Church* (Oxford: Blackwell).

—— (1996), *The Archaeology of Early Christianity: A History* (London: Chapman).

Giamberardini, G. (1975), *Il culto mariano in Egitto*, i: *sec. I–VI*, 2nd edn. (Jerusalem: Franciscan Press).

Gibbon, E. (1776), *The History of the Decline and Fall of the Roman Empire*, i (London: Strahan and Cadell).

—— (1897), *The History of the Decline and Fall of the Roman Empire*, ed. J. B. Bury, ii (London: Methuen).

Grabar, A. (1946), *Martyrium: Recherches sur le culte des reliques et l'art chrétien antique*, 2 vols. (Paris: Collège de France).

Grig, L. (2004), *Making Martyrs in Late Antiquity* (London: Duckworth).

Holloway, R. R. (2004), *Constantine and Rome* (New Haven: Yale University Press).

Holum K. G. (1982), *Theodosian Empresses: Women and Imperial Dominion in Late Antiquity* (Berkeley: University of California Press).

Howard-Johnston, J., and Hayward, P. A. (1999) (eds.), *The Cult of Saints in Late Antiquity and the Early Middle Ages: Essays on the Contribution of Peter Brown* (Oxford: Oxford University Press).

Hunt, E. D. (1981), 'The Traffic in Relics: Some Late Roman Evidence', in Sergei Hackel (ed.), *The Byzantine Saint* (London: Fellowship of St Alban and St Sergius), 171–80.

Hunter, D. G. (1993), 'Helvidius, Jovinian, and the Virginity of Mary in Late Fourth-Century Rome', *JECS* 1: 1–19.

—— (1999), 'Vigilantius of Calagurris and Victricius of Rouen: Ascetics, Relics, and Clerics in late Roman Gaul', *JECS* 7: 401–30.

Karweise, S. (1995), 'The Church of Mary and the Temple of Hadrian Olympus', in H. Koester (ed.), *Ephesos: Metropolis of Asia*, HTS 41 (Valley Forge, Pa.: Trinity Press International), 311–19.

Klingshirn, W. E. (1994), *Caesarius of Arles* (Cambridge: Cambridge University Press).

Kraemer, R. S., and Lander, S. L. (2000), 'Perpetua and Felicitas', in P. F. Esler (ed.), *The Early Christian World* (London: Routledge), ii. 1048–68.

LAMBERIGTS, M., and VAN DEUN, P. (eds.) (1995), *Martyrium in Multidisciplinary Perspective* (Leuven: Leuven University Press).

LAMPE, P. (2003), *From Paul to Valentinus: Christians at Rome in the First Two Centuries* (London: Continuum).

LANE FOX, R. (1986), *Pagans and Christians* (Harmondsworth: Viking; New York: Knopf, 1987).

LECLERQ, H. (1932), 'Martyr', in *DACL* x. 2. 2359–2512.

—— (1939), 'Pierre (saint)', in *DACL* xiv. 1. 822–921.

LEEMANS, J. with MAYER, W., ALLEN, P., and DEHANDSCHUTTER, B. (2003) *'Let us die that we may live': Greek homilies on Christian Martyrs from Asia Minor, Palestine, and Syria (c. AD 350–AD 450)* (London: Routledge).

LIEBESCHUETZ, J. H. W. G. (1990), *Barbarians and Bishops: Army, Church and State in the Age of Arcadius and Chrysostom* (Oxford: Oxford University Press).

LIMBERIS, V. (1994), *Divine Heiress: The Virgin Mary and the Creation of Christian Constantinople* (London: Routledge).

MACMULLEN, R. (1989), 'The Preacher's Audience (AD 350–400)', *JTS* NS 40: 503–11.

MARKUS, R. A. (1990), *The End of Ancient Christianity* (Cambridge: Cambridge University Press).

—— (1994), 'How on Earth Could Places Become Holy? Origins of the Christian Idea of Holy Places', *JECS* 2: 257–71.

MILLER, P. C. (1998), ' "Differential Networks": Relics and Other Fragments in Late Antiquity', *JECS* 6: 113–38.

—— (2000), ' "The Little Blue Flower is Red": Relics and the Poeticizing of the Body', *JECS* 8: 213–36.

MITCHELL, S. (1993), *Anatolia: Land, Men, and Gods in Asia Minor*, ii (Oxford: Oxford University Press).

MUSURILLO, H. (1972), *The Acts of the Christian Martyrs: Texts and Translations* (Oxford: Oxford University Press).

O'CARROLL, M. (1983), *Theotokos: A Theological Encyclopedia of the Blessed Virgin Mary*, rev. edn. (Wilmington, Del.: Michael Glazier).

PERKINS, J. (1995), *The Suffering Self: Pain and Narrative Representation in the Early Christian Era* (London: Routledge).

PIETRI, C. (1976), *Roma Christiana: Recherches sur l'Église de Rome, son organisation, sa politique, son idéologie de Miltiade à Sixte III (311–440)*, 2 vols. (Rome: École française de Rome).

—— (1984), 'Les origines du culte des martyrs (d'après un ouvrage recent)', *Rivista di Archeologia Cristiana*, 60: 293–319.

POTTER, D. (1993), 'Martyrdom as Spectacle', in R. Scodel (ed.), *Theater and Society in the Classical World* (Ann Arbor: University of Michigan Press), 53–88.

PRICE, R. M. (2004), 'Marian Piety and the Nestorian Controversy', in Swanson (2004), 31–8.

RENTINCK, P. (1970), *La cura pastorale in Antiochia nel IV secolo* (Rome: Università Gregoriana).

ROUSSELLE, A. (1988), *Porneia: On Desire and the Body in Antiquity* (Oxford: Blackwell).

STE. CROIX, G. E. M. (1954), 'Aspects of the "Great" Persecution', *HTR* 47: 75–109.

—— (1963), 'Why were the Early Christians Persecuted?', *Past and Present*, 26: 6–38.

—— (2006), *Christian Persecution, Martyrdom and Orthodoxy* (Oxford: Oxford University Press).

SALISBURY, J. E. (1997), *Perpetua's Passion: The Death and Memory of a Young Roman Woman* (London: Routledge).

SAXER, V. (1980), *Morts, martyrs, reliques en Afrique chrétienne aux premiers siècles* (Paris: Beauchesne).

SHAW, B. S. (1996), 'Body/Power/Identity: Passions of the Martyrs', *JECS* 4: 269–312.

SHOEMAKER, S. J. (2007), 'Marian Liturgies and Devotion in Early Christianity', in S. J. Boss (ed.), *Mary: The Complete Resource* (London: Continuum), 130–45.

SWANSON, R. N. (2004) (ed.), *The Church and Mary*, SCH 39 (Woodbridge: Boydell Press).

TILLEY, M. (1991), 'The Ascetic Body and the (Un)Making of the World of the Martyr', *JAAR* 59: 467–79.

—— (1995), 'The Passion of Perpetua and Felicity', in E. Schüssler Fiorenza (ed.), *Searching the Scriptures* (London: SCM Press; New York: Crossroad), ii. 829–58.

—— (1996), *Donatist Martyr Stories: The Church in Conflict in North Africa* (Liverpool: Liverpool University Press).

—— (1997), 'Sustaining Donatist Self-Identity: From the Church of the Martyrs to the *Collecta* of the Desert', *JECS* 5: 21–35.

VAN DAM, R. (1993), *Saints and their Miracles in Late Antique Gaul* (Princeton: Princeton University Press).

VAUCHEZ, A. (1988), *La sainteté en Occident aux derniers siècles du Moyen Age: D'après les procès de canonisation et les documents hagiographiques* (Rome: École française de Rome).

WHITE, C. (1992), *Christian Friendship in the Fourth Century* (Cambridge: Cambridge University Press).

YOUNG R. D. (2001), *In Procession before the World: Martyrdom as Public Liturgy in Early Christianity* (Milwaukee, Wis.: Marquette University Press).

CHAPTER 40

PILGRIMAGE

GEORGIA FRANK

EARLY Christian pilgrimage involved a journey to a place in order to gain access to sacred power, whether manifested in living persons, demarcated spaces, or specific objects. Movement toward the sacred site, as well as ritualized movements once at the destination (such as processions, ascents, descents, and circumambulations), shaped pilgrimage. Neither distance nor duration defined these practices so much as the destination's ability to draw visitors from a broader region than a local site might attract.[1] Places associated with the Bible drew large numbers of pilgrims from throughout the Empire. Yet, local martyrs' shrines and pilgrimage centres with international appeal drew visitors to Italy, Asia Minor, Syria, and Egypt.

The nature and origins of Christian pilgrimage are difficult to pinpoint. Greek and Latin lack a single term for what we call 'pilgrimage'. Nor is 'pilgrim' a native category; that is to say, ancient Christians did not identify themselves as 'pilgrim' or some equivalent term. Its Latin cognate, *peregrinatio*, means to travel or reside abroad (s.v. 'peregrinatio', *Oxford Latin Dictionary*, 1335b), but lacks the sense of purpose that pilgrimage connotes. Whereas the pilgrim, as we define her, is drawn toward the next sacred destination, the *peregrinus* longs for home (G. Clark 2004: 151). Instead, ancient Christians spoke of voyaging *orationis causa* ('for the sake of prayer'), to pray (*euchesthai, proseuchesthai*), to venerate (*proskunein*) the holy places. Their motivations were varied, as pilgrims sought prayer, healing, guidance, intercession, oracles, and visual encounters (Maraval 2004: 137–51). This element of blessings and benefits also sets pilgrims apart from other types of religious travellers, such as itinerant teachers, envoys, prophets, and healers. Like pilgrims, itinerant preachers and healers displace themselves, but with the aim of disseminating benefit rather than acquiring it.

Travel to sacred centres was common in Mediterranean religions. Jewish pilgrimage festivals of Passover, Pentecost, and Tabernacles drew large crowds to Jerusalem until the Temple's destruction in 70 CE (Wilken 1992: 105–8). Outside Palestine, Jews travelled to synagogues (Alexandria) and regional Jewish temples (Elephantine and Heliopolis in Egypt; Kerkeslager 1998). Egyptian temples still bear the traces of pilgrims who scraped walls for sand to carry away with them (Frankfurter 1998*b*: 51). Oracles and healing centres displayed various plaques and offerings left by pilgrims honouring the gods. Such votive offerings and inscriptions bore witness to previous supplicants' gratitude for healing and other interventions (Montserrat 1998).

Early Christians maintained many of these practices. They gathered at the burial places of martyrs for prayers and held funerary banquets there. By the late second century, Palestinian places associated with biblical events drew some Christian leaders from Asia Minor (Hunt 1999). The earliest surviving Christian inscription (*c.* 170/80) records one Abercius's voyage to Rome (Mitchell 2007). Whether these early travellers were 'pilgrims' remains debated. More certain is that the legalization of Christianity in 312 marked a watershed for Christian pilgrimage. The emperor Constantine and his mother promoted Christian holy places by erecting martyria at sites associated with Jesus's life, death, and resurrection. Within a century, a growing network of hostels, hospices, and monasteries emerged to serve pilgrims' needs. In addition, many traditional healing centres attracted Christians, who eventually rededicated the shrines to Christian saints. Menouthis in the Nile Delta was home to an Isis temple that promised healing and fertility, as well as a healing centre dedicated to the physician saints John and Cyrus (Montserrat 1998). At Mamre, a site associated with Abraham's hospitality to angelic visitors, the annual summer fair drew Palestinians, Phoenicians, and Arabians, as well as Jews, pagans, and Christians (Sozomen, *Hist. eccl.* 2. 4. 2–6; see Maraval 2004: 275; Lander 2004). Competition among sanctuaries could be quite intense. At Thecla's centre in Seleucia, pilgrims heard stories about Thecla's powers to out-heal, out-fight, and even out-live the patron heroes and deities at nearby shrines (Davis 2001: 75–9).

40.1 Pilgrims' Writings

Several pilgrims' letters and diaries survive from the fourth through the sixth centuries, including many by and about female pilgrims (Talbot 2002). These records vary in style and length, from schematic lists of place names to detailed reminiscences. Together, they offer many insights into pilgrims' experiences, practices, and motivations. Known as a movement of storytellers, Christianity would eventually become a movement of travel writers, especially among visitors to the Holy Land. One of the earliest records of Holy Land pilgrimage is an itinerary by an unnamed pilgrim from Bordeaux (c. 333). Once regarded as a record of travel and topography, the narrative texture of this seemingly rudimentary list of stopping places and distances has received renewed attention among recent interpreters. Whereas some note how the author's portrayal of Jews reflects Christian imperial ideology (Jacobs 2004), others have observed the disproportionate number of holy places associated with female reproduction, sexuality, and children, prompting speculation that the author was a woman (Douglass 1999). Although the author's identity and gender remain unresolved, scholars have renewed interest in this itinerary's subtle web of telling erasures (Elsner 2000).

A half century later, a pilgrim who was probably named Egeria travelled from Gaul and spent three years (during the 380s or 390s) in Egypt, Palestine, Syria, and Asia Minor.[2] Although portions of her travel account are missing, a seventh-century monk's praise fills some gaps in the itinerary. Written as a letter to her 'sisters' back home in Gaul, this diary is among the earliest extant writings by a Christian woman. Compared to the Bordeaux pilgrim's strict diet of resting places, distances, biblical names, and monuments, Egeria offers a heartier spread. The splendours of late fourth-century church architecture (19. 2) do not escape her attention; nor does she overlook the monks and clergy who aided her along the way. Whether marked by a sumptuous church or a simple stone (e.g. 3. 6, 4. 4), no site failed to impress her. In part, her satisfaction with each holy place derived from hearing the relevant passage from scripture read aloud to her at the very site (ipso loco), a convergence she happily noted (4. 3, 10. 7). Readings were typically accompanied by an 'offering', a eucharist. She notes at which sites she received a 'blessing' (eulogia) from her host, typically local fruit, but occasionally a copy of a sacred text. In addition to visiting places mentioned in the Old Testament and those associated with events from the gospels, Egeria also describes her travels to remote monasteries in Syria and healing centres such as that of Saint Thecla in Isauria. The second half of Egeria's travel diary provides key glimpses into architectural and liturgical developments at Jerusalem.

Beyond Jerusalem and the biblical holy places, pilgrims to wonder-working ascetics have been the topic of recent studies. Specifically, collections of monastic biography have been reinterpreted as travel writing. The *Historia monachorum in Aegypto* traces the group's journey in the 390s from Lycopolis in Upper Egypt to monasteries in the Nile Delta. Although the travelogue rarely mentions holy places associated with the Bible, its author exoticizes Egyptian monks as spectacles of the biblical past (Frank 2000). In addition, Palladius, bishop of Helenopolis, composed a travelogue in the form of monastic biographies, in a collection (c. 420) known today as the *Lausiac History*. Both travelogues reveal how pilgrims sought out the biblical past beyond the holy places.

Perhaps the most detailed of ancient pilgrims' writings from antiquity is a diary by a traveller from Piacenza in Italy. His record of a trip undertaken around 570 describes basilicas, healing hot springs, and various sacred ingestibles, such as dew collected or grapes and dates grown near holy places. Such attention to the material splendours of the holy places, however, cannot hide his quotidian travails, including squabbles with Samaritan merchants, the death of a countryman (presumably a travel companion), and delays due to illness. The patterned devotions typical of Egeria's visits—biblical reading, offering, and blessing—contrast with the variety of devotional practices for this sixth-century pilgrim, who drank from a saint's skull (sect. 20), reclined on each of the benches placed at Gethsemane (sect. 17), pressed an ear to a crack in the rock where Abraham bound Isaac (sect. 19; cf. sect. 22), and held wood from Christ's cross in his hand and kissed it (sect. 20). He notes how he saw implements used in Christ's interrogation and torture, including finger impressions left by the Saviour on the column where he was scourged and footprints in the floor of Pilate's praetorium. Not only has the appearance of the Holy Land changed, as a result of more churches and more relics to venerate. The Piacenza pilgrim also reflects a transformed sensibility toward the land, which, like soft putty, can retain the physical traces of biblical events more permanently. What was once perceived as an adamantine site of biblical events for Egeria, now became more pliant as biblical events left sunken, permanent impressions. The land becomes a repository of memory, now more generative, as the Piacenza pilgrim notes its bounty: souvenirs and substances, including seven pints of water taken from a spring at the tomb of Rachel, five pints of solidified manna received at a Sinai monastery, dirt loaded into Christ's tomb then dispensed in small amounts to pilgrims, 'measures' taken of Christ's footprints. By these objects, the Holy Land both marks and metes out the past.

Another important witness to pilgrimage was the biblical scholar Jerome. In a letter eulogizing his cherished friend, Paula (*Ep.* 108), Jerome described her visits to holy places in Judea as well as to monasteries in Egypt. The power of holy places to evoke biblical episodes led to some visionary experiences for her. He and Paula also composed letters inviting other aristocratic Roman women to come to the Holy Land (e.g. *Ep.* 46). Gerontius's fifth-century sacred biography of Melania the Younger also devoted a significant portion of that *Life* to recounting Melania's travels to monasteries in Egypt and then to holy sites. In Syria, Theodoret, bishop of Cyrrhus, did not overlook pilgrimage in his biographical vignettes of departed and living monastics. According to Theodoret, the holy man Peter the Galatian set out to see the holy places where Christ suffered and to worship God there (*H. rel.* 9. 2; cf. 6. 8). When two Syrian holy women, Marana and Cyra, set out for Jerusalem, they fasted during the entire journey to Jerusalem and throughout their devotions at the holy places. They also fasted during a round-trip journey to the shrine of St Thecla in Isauria (29. 7). Although many famous ascetics never journeyed to Jerusalem (Jerome, *Ep.* 58. 2–3), hagiographers regarded such journeys as milestones in saintliness.

Despite the appeal of pilgrimage for hagiographers, long-distance travel to holy places drew criticism. Jerome, for instance, defended Jerusalem from the taint of Jesus' crucifixion (*Ep.* 46. 6). Yet elsewhere, he advised Paulinus of Nola to stay away from this urban centre, better suited to buffoons, actors, and prostitutes than to an upright monk (*Ep.* 54. 4). Likewise, bishops such as Gregory of Nyssa and Athanasius of Alexandria warned local monks against pilgrimage. In a famous letter, Gregory of Nyssa (*Ep.* 2) advised monks to avoid pilgrimage. He listed several objections: visiting the holy places was not enjoined in the gospels, and travel conditions might compromise a proper separation of the sexes. His most forceful critique of pilgrimage, however, regarded the theological implications of travel. To seek God at a distant place, he warned, confines God to that place. Rather than travel to God, Gregory advised, a virtuous life at home might draw God to the soul.[3] Gregory was not the first to speak of God's journey or a soul's journey as an alternative to physical pilgrimage. Athanasius saw the dangers of pilgrimage in the homecoming. Nostalgia for the holy places, he advised virgins, could be redirected into ascetic pursuits at home (Brakke 1995: 292–302). He recognized pilgrimage's transformative effects, but also reminded the women of the need to return to the routine of ascetic life in the home.

Whereas modern scholars once regarded these criticisms as direct evidence of dangerous travel conditions, more recent studies have explored these criticisms in light of church leaders' efforts to preserve ecclesiastical control and uphold theological agendas (e.g. Walker 1990; Bitton-Ashkelony 2005). These studies of criticisms and prohibitions consider spiritual alternatives proposed by church leaders. For instance, in a letter addressed to female ascetics who had returned from a Jerusalem pilgrimage, Athanasius did not prohibit pilgrimage. Instead, he exhorted the returning female pilgrims to find more stable and respectable devotional practices in the home. As David Brakke and Susanna Elm have noted, Athanasius's ambivalence regarding pilgrimage and the display of martyrs' bodies was part of a larger theological and political effort to consolidate his episcopal authority among various ascetics and heterodox groups (Elm 1987; Brakke 1998).

If pilgrimage had a downside, it is not apparent from pilgrims' diaries. Cyril, bishop of Jerusalem, underscored the value of seeing and touching the holy places to candidates for baptism, some of whom came to Jerusalem as pilgrims (Walker 1990). Yet bishops outside Jerusalem struggled to privilege holy places closer to home. It is also important to note bishops' roles not only in contesting pilgrimage, but also in transforming it. Recently, Maribel Dietz (2004) has proposed that Holy Land pilgrimage grew out of efforts to curb religious wandering. Thus, promoting Holy Land pilgrimage and other locus-centred travel served the interests of religious leaders who feared that decentralized wandering threatened episcopal authority. Thus theological critiques of pilgrimage may be reread in the context of travellers' desire for autonomy and 'freedom of experience' (Dietz 2004: 133), as well as economic concerns that wandering mendicant monks may be competing with local bishops for wealthy, lay patronage (Caner 2002).

Protest turned to prohibition, as the Council of Chalcedon in 451 imposed strict limits on monastic wandering. By the sixth century, monks and nuns in some eastern and western churches were forbidden to travel to the Holy Land and other areas, to avoid coming into contact with doctrinal opponents. Overall, however, some bishops recognized the value of pilgrimage for promoting and consolidating regional religious identity. Theodoret, for instance, stressed Marana and Cyra's extraordinary fasts on the road, to demonstrate their resemblance to Moses, but also to avert criticisms of moral laxity often levied against pilgrims. One also detects an apologia for pilgrimage in his description of Peter the Galatian's adoration for the holy places. This holy man, Theodoret noted, longed to see the holy places. By calling attention to Peter's ability to recognize holy places as repositories of Christ's *absence* more than pockets of divine *presence,* the bishop promoted his native Syria as another holy land, populated by ascetics. Regional pride alone, however, cannot account for the promotion of or ambivalence toward holy places. As recent scholars have demonstrated, competition among pilgrimage centres also prompted some bishops to seek consolidation.

Such prohibitions, it seems, had little impact on pilgrimage centres, which continued to produce a variety of writings that would draw even more pilgrims. By the fifth century, saints' lives and miracle collections enticed would-be pilgrims to seek out living saints or their physical remains. Tales of miraculous healings and other wonders reveal the success of some pilgrimage centres, as well as their growing international appeal.

Thus, in recent decades the parameters of 'pilgrims' literature' have broadened considerably, beyond pilgrims' diaries or their guidebooks, to consider how critics and shrines, hagiographers and travellers, fuelled the imagination of would-be pilgrims. In addition to the literary aspects of pilgrimage, its material culture remains an important area of study.

40.2 MATERIAL CULTURE OF PILGRIMAGE

The material culture of pilgrimage includes the large-scale building projects that housed and attracted pilgrims as well as the minute souvenirs they brought home.[4] Whereas saints' lives and pilgrims' diaries offer momentary 'snapshots' of pilgrimage centres, archaeology reveals the transformation of those centres over several centuries. At the Wondrous Mountain, a pilgrimage complex built between 541 and

591 around the column of Symeon the Younger, pilgrims partnered with masons from Isauria to build the inns, a church, and service buildings at the complex (Mango 1991). A single complex might include several pilgrim destinations, such as the Holy Sepulchre in Jerusalem, which included an atrium, a five-aisled basilica, to permit large groups to move about, and an ample porticoed court where the rock of Calvary was displayed, with a rotunda at the site of the resurrection (Ousterhout 1990*b*). The movement from the atrium to the Anastasis Rotunda allowed the steady flow of pilgrim traffic. It is also possible to gauge the success of a pilgrimage destination by its expansion. At Abu Mina in Egypt, a complex dedicated to the martyr saint Menas, early fifth-century pilgrims would have encountered a small church, to which was added stairs to provide easier access to the underground tomb (Grossmann 1998: 283–7). Like many other pilgrimage centres, Abu Mina was also equipped with a baptistery for pilgrims who wished to undergo initiation at the holy site (Stevens 2000). Further expansions, including a larger basilica and baptistery, along with greater accommodations, reflect the growing needs of pilgrims. Qal'at Sim'an, the Syrian pilgrimage centre built following the death of Symeon Stylites the Elder in 459, reveals much about the management of pilgrim traffic. The martyrium there did not follow the east–west orientation typical of many churches. Instead, it was aligned with the approach of pilgrims from the nearby village to the south. Its inscribed arches also guided pilgrims' movement through increasingly sacred holy places. Pilgrims approached the cruciform martyrium through a sacred way marked off by a series of paired arches and a triple arch at the threshold of the martyrium. For women, the journey ended here, whereas male pilgrims entered the church, the eastern branch of which was slightly askew, perhaps to maximize the sunlight on the saint's annual feast-day (Sodini 2001: 254–5). At several pilgrim churches, the saint's relics were kept separate from the altar, housed in a crypt with two sets of stairs, to allow easier access for pilgrims. If relics remained off limits to pilgrims, some shrines found alternate means of access. The crypt of Saint John in Ephesus, for instance, allowed pilgrims to collect holy dust that was said to emanate from the crypt on the saint's feast-day.

Gifts to the saints, or *ex voto* offerings, were presented by pilgrims, in keeping with a practice found at traditional healing centres. Some pilgrims left precious objects, such as jewellery or animals. The Piacenza pilgrim describes the bracelets, rings, tiaras, plaited girdles, belts, emperors' crowns of gold and precious stones deposited at the Holy Sepulchre (sect. 18). Exotic birds roamed the Thecla complex in Seleucia (*Miracles of St Thecla*, 24), to the delight of children there. Small crosses or decorated plaques made of wood or metal typically depicted the saint or simply the body part healed, such as eyes, feet, or hands. Some bore inscribed messages, such as 'in thanksgiving', 'in fulfilment of a vow', 'Lord, help', or simply the word, *euprosdekta* ('may they be acceptable').[5] Eventually, icons of the saint served as votive offerings, a practice that further restricted pilgrims' physical contact with relics (Hahn 1997: 1090–92).[6]

Beyond votives and souvenirs, the material culture of pilgrimage includes objects consumed at the shrine. Saints' festivals were a time of intense pilgrim traffic for many shrines. In Egypt, papyri include ledgers from one shrine complex listing the various wines, meats, lentils, and special breads ordered for festival days. Unlike the white seamless garment worn by Muslim men on the hajj to Mecca, Christian pilgrims in late antiquity did not don special garments. Yet some carried various travel-size objects. Some forty-seven miniature codices with Christian contents survive. These tiny books would have been read by pilgrims, but also served as amulets for the traveller's protection (Gamble 1995: 237–41; cf. Egeria, Diary, 23. 5–6).

Besides what they consumed and inscribed, pilgrims carried many items home. Egeria mentioned various eulogiai, or 'blessings', received when departing from the holy places. In addition to offering visitors fruits and vegetables grown locally, monks also sent pilgrims home with manuscripts, including a copy of Jesus' legendary correspondence with the Syrian royal convert, King Abgar of Edessa, that Egeria received (Diary, 19. 19). Pilgrims' souvenirs often carried healing or protective properties far from the shrine they commemorated. According to one Syrian hagiographer, workshops in Rome displayed images of the pillar saint Symeon the Elder (Theodoret, H. rel. 26. 11). And in one Alexandrian neighbourhood, roughly a 5-days' walk from Abu Mina, modern archaeologists have unearthed some 150 objects depicting St Menas (Haas 1997: 189–206).

Small flasks, known as ampullae, were available at the holy places for pilgrims to collect and transport sacred substances.[7] At the church of St Stephen outside Jerusalem, oil or water could be poured into reliquaries equipped with funnels. After the liquid came in contact with the relics, it was collected in a basin beneath the reliquary and then distributed to pilgrims (Donceel-Voûte 1995: 191–2). Holy men such as Symeon the Stylite dispensed a paste, or hnana, made out of water and perhaps oil mixed with the dust from a holy place (Syr. V. Sym. Styl. 33, 38, trans. Doran: 120, 123). Most ampullae date from about 600. Mass-produced from unglazed clay, although occasionally available in more luxurious materials, such as silver, these flasks held small amounts of dirt, water, or oil that had come in contact with the holy place. A typical ampulla bore a symbol or image of the saint or the biblical figure remembered at the site. Words from the ritual there or distinctive architectural feature might also adorn these souvenirs.

In addition to ampullae, pilgrims collected tokens (sphragidia) at holy places, small earthen objects stamped with an impression (Vikan 1982; Sodini 1993). Inscribed spoons were also available to 'raise a blessing' from a saint's tomb, such as a spoon from Egypt with the words phage mana (eat manna) with connections to the tomb of John the Evangelist in Ephesus (Papaconstantinou 2001: 351). In Palestine, pilgrims to Solomon's tomb benefited from the healing properties of mandrake grown there. Some *eulogiai* bear the image of that tubular root (Rahmani 1999). Although little is known about their exact place of manufacture or their distribution, their decoration sheds light on pilgrims' perceptions of healing.[8]

Pilgrims sought access to the saints' powers by other means. They wrote their requests for the saint's protection on small tickets (Papini 1998; Papaconstantinou 2001: 336–7; Frankfurter 2000). The pleas for assistance in business, love, pregnancy, future travel, and various ailments were submitted in the form of two answers, one positive and one negative. Thus pilgrims to the shrine of St Collouthus at Antinoë would submit both the positive and the negative answers. After submitting both questions to the shrine attendant, one of the paired tickets was returned as the saint's response.

Once studied by art historians as evidence for the appearance of holy places and iconography of saints, these souvenirs, amulets, and votives also reveal much about pilgrims' access to the power of holy places. Closely related to magical practices, these objects could extend the pilgrim's access to a saint's healing power well beyond the sanctuary. Thus, while some later votives, such as icons, represent a trend toward curtailing pilgrims' tactile contact with relics (Hahn 1997: 1090–2), souvenirs reveal the exportation of that power to domestic spheres (Vikan 1982).

40.3 APPROACHES TO PILGRIMAGE

Much research approaches pilgrimage typologically, focusing on the type of destination. Although early studies of pilgrimage tended to concentrate on Holy Land sites associated with the Bible, more recent work has called attention to the role of pilgrimage in shaping local and regional traditions (e.g. Maraval 2004; Markus 1994; Frankfurter 1998b). As Robert Markus (1994) has demonstrated, local martyria in a post-persecution age redefined the relation to the sacred past, and thereby laid the groundwork for the rise of biblical holy places. Such typologies have illuminated the rich dialectic between local, regional, and international shrines, and the roles of bishops, shrine personnel, and pilgrims in shaping those relations.

The transformative effects of ritual have been the focus of many cross-cultural studies of pilgrimage, in large part due to the work of anthropologists Victor and Edith Turner (1978). The Turners focused on pilgrimage as a rite of passage, which involves separating from home at the outset of the journey, followed by a liminal stage characterized by freedom from social structure and a sense of bonding with fellow travellers, or *communitas*, carried through the duration of the journey and the encounter with the sacred destination. The homecoming, or reaggregation, marked the third phase, as pilgrims return to social structures and class divisions. It is difficult to apply such theories to early Christian pilgrims' accounts, since pilgrims tell us so little about their journey to the destination or their travel companions. Yet, the Turners' model has opened historians of Christianity to a broader understanding of journey that includes the homecoming and impact of the pilgrim on those who stayed home. *Communitas*, for instance, may offer some insight into the appeal (and condemnation) of itinerant monastics and the so-called transvestite saints, who abandoned the structures of household and even monastery to pursue a period of wandering. Recent analyses of Athanasius's letter to the female ascetics who returned from Jerusalem also suggest the value of this transformative model for understanding the virgins' nostalgia for the holy places (Frank 2000: 108–11). Early Christian pilgrimage also helps us see some limitations of the model. For instance, is *communitas* or a similar transformation possible for all pilgrims if centres restrict or forbid women's access to the holiest places?

A third approach to pilgrimage emphasizes the function of pilgrimage in satisfying some need(s). Two questions are central to this approach: 'Why do people go on pilgrimages?' and 'What does pilgrimage *do?*' Pilgrimages serve individual needs, such as the stated desire to pray, for relief from ailments, for prophecy, to gain a blessing, and so on. Drawing on recent work in the sociology of tourism, Blake Leyerle (1996) has noted the overlap between how ancient pilgrims and modern tourists seek contact with something authentic. Pilgrims' descriptions of experiences at the shrine also reveal the role of pilgrimage in reshaping perceptions of biblical time (Baldovin 1987; Papaconstantinou 1996: 156–7), not as a distant past, but as a present reality effected by pilgrims' ritual. In the 1980s and 1990s, scholars began to focus more on the role of pilgrimage centres in shaping larger group and regional identities. Thus, David Frankfurter has called attention to pilgrimage as a means for engaging religious communities in Christianization of the sacred landscape (1998*a*, *b*). He calls attention to the persistence of indigenous pilgrimage centres and Christian strategies for continuing those practices.

The literary nature of pilgrims' writings has been the subject of several studies (e.g. Leyerle 1996; Elsner 2000; Frank 2000; Jacobs 2004). Once read as transparent eyewitness reports about travel conditions, holy places, roads, liturgy, and architecture, pilgrims' descriptions can also reveal much about pilgrims' religious imagination and audiences' expectations. Part of a larger 'linguistic turn' in early Christian studies,[9] the poetics of pilgrims' writings has been the subject of recent studies, which call attention to the work that these rhetorical tropes perform and how they represent the distant 'other'. More focused attention on the authors' role in crafting these travel accounts has uncovered parallels to other genres, including exotic travel writing, miracle collections, biography, and apocalyptic. Thus, what was once regarded as a retrospective genre, describing past events, can also be read as more prospective in effect, as these writings shaped audiences' perceptions of monasticism, the biblical past, Jews, and travel (Frank 2000; Jacobs 2004).

More focused attention on pilgrims' storytelling techniques and tropes has revealed the affinities between pilgrimage and other aspects of piety. Specifically, scholars have noted common ideals and practices in the cult of saints (Hahn 1997), icon veneration (Vikan 2003), monasticism (Frank 2000), and liturgy (Baldovin 1987). Beyond piety, pilgrimage and pilgrims' writings have been recognized as vehicles for the Christianization of space (Frankfurter 1998a), time (Markus 1994; Hunt 1982), imperial rule (Jacobs 2004) and elites (Hunt 1982). More work remains to be done on the relationships between pilgrims' writings and apocalyptic narratives to uncover the relationships between patterns of earthly and other-worldly travel. As scholars explore the legacy of cosmic travel for monasticism (Copeland 2004; Connolly 1999) and for perceptions of post-mortem states (Graf 2004), how pilgrimage practices and writings shaped these devotions merits closer investigation.

While the category 'pilgrim' *sensu stricto* remains unresolved,[10] the study of travel to religious destinations has broadened our understanding of how Christians encountered space, matter, and time in their devotions. Pilgrimage remains a valuable category for examining transformations in Christians' embodied engagement with the material world.

Notes

1. Ewa Wipszycka (1995: 429–31) limits the term 'pilgrimage' to long-distance journeys to sacred sites. Yet she also admits that neither pilgrims nor preachers at the holy places explicitly made such distinctions or called attention to the effects of long-distance travel on their perceptions of holy places.

2. On Egeria, see Maraval's 1982 critical edition, as well as Devos (1967); Hunt (2001); Leyerle (1996); Sivan (1988); Starowieyeski (1979).

3. Cf. Porphyry, *V. Plot.* 10. 37–8 (LCL i. 34).

4. This section expands on a portion of my Frank (2007).

5. Theodoret, *Graecarum affectionum curatio*, 8. 64; cf. Mango, (1986: 240–5); cf. Maguire *et al.* (1989: 25, 132).

6. On similar developments in the 'clericalization' of the eucharist, see Caseau (2002).

7. On *ampullae*: Vikan (1982, 1990); Hahn (1990), Maguire *et al.* (1989: 25, 200–1, 209–10).

8. The provenance of these tokens and *ampullae* remains a matter for further study. Many tokens were presumably manufactured at or near the holy places they commemorated (e.g. Rahmani 1999). Yet nothing rules out the possibility that tokens from famous shrines may also have appealed to armchair pilgrims who never visited the site. Whether the production of pilgrims' souvenirs related to major shrines could have been as decentralized as pilgrimage itself is a matter worth pursuing. Pilgrims showed little concern for verifying the 'authenticity' of a souvenir. Further research

on the origins and uses of pilgrims' souvenirs can shed light on these matters relevant to pilgrims' notions of authenticity and its material culture.

9. A helpful and clear overview is now available in E. A. Clark (2004: esp. 165–76).

10. Wipszycka's (1995: 429–32) efforts to distinguish pilgrims *proprement dits* from local visitors has no basis in the writings of long-distance pilgrims or sermons delivered at pilgrimage centres.

SUGGESTED READING

An important anthology of pilgrims' writings remains the critical edition by P. Geyer and O. Cuntz, *Itineraria et Alia Geographica*, CCSL 175–6 (Turnhout: Brepols, 1965). Egeria's *Diary* is also available in Pierre Maraval (ed. and trans.), *Égérie, Journal de Voyage*, SC 296 (Paris: Éditions du Cerf, 1982). Useful English translations are John Wilkinson, *Egeria's Travels to the Holy Land*, rev. edn. (Jerusalem: Ariel; Warminster: Aris & Phillips, 1981) and Wilkinson (2002). For criticisms of pilgrimage, see Athanasius, *Lettre à des vierges qui étaient allées prier à Jérusalem*, ed. and trans. J. Lebon in 'Athanasiana Syriaca: Une lettre attribuée à saint Athanase d'Alexandrie', *Mus.* 41 (1928: 169–215); and trans. David Brakke in *Athanasius and the Politics of Asceticism*, OECS (Oxford: Clarendon Press, 1995: 292–302). Gregory of Nyssa's letters on pilgrimage appear in Pierre Maraval's critical edn., *Grégoire de Nysse, Lettres*, SC 363 (Paris: Éditions du Cerf, 1990); English translations available in *Select Writings and Letters of Gregory, Bishop of Nyssa*, NPNF[2] (Grand Rapids, Mich.: Eerdmans, 1988: 5). On pilgrimage to people, see the anonymous *Historia monachorum in Aegypto*. Greek ed. by A.-J. Festugière (1961; repr. 1971; as Subsidia Hagiographica, 34; Subsidia Hagiographica, 53). The English translation by Norman Russell (1980) appears as *Lives of the Desert Fathers*, CS 34 (Kalamazoo, Mich.: Cistercian Publications). Also important is Palladius's *Lausiac History* (Palladius, *Historia Lausiaca*), ed. Cuthbert Butler (1904) and *The Lausiac History of Palladius*, TaS 6, 2 vols. (Cambridge: Cambridge University Press). Eng. trans.: R. T. Meyer (1964), *Palladius: The Lausiac History*, ACW 34 (New York: Newman Press).

Secondary works have comprised important monographs in the 1980s and valuable collections in the 1990s. The most comprehensive study of late antique pilgrimage remains Maraval (2004). Among the best English-language studies are Hunt (1982), as well as essay collections edited by Ousterhout (1990*a*) and Frankfurter (1998*a*), also Elsner and Rutherford (2005). For archaeological studies, see the fine collection edited by Engemann and Dassmann (1995).

BIBLIOGRAPHY

BALDOVIN, J. F. (1987), *The Urban Character of Christian Worship: The Origins, Development, and Meaning of Stational Liturgy*, OrChrAn 228 (Rome: Pontificium Institutum Orientalium Studiorum).

BITTON-ASHKELONY, B. (2005), *Encountering the Sacred: The Debate on Christian Pilgrimage in Late Antiquity*, Transformation of the Classical Heritage, 38 (Berkeley: University of California Press).

BOUSTAN, R. S., and REED, A. Y. (2004) (eds.), *Heavenly Realms and Earthly Realities in Late Antique Religions* (Cambridge: Cambridge University Press).

BRAKKE, D. (1998), ' "Outside the Places, Within the Truth": Athanasius of Alexandria on the Localization of the Holy', in Frankfurter (1998*a*), 445–81.

CANER, D. (2002), *Wandering, Begging Monks: Spiritual Authority and the Promotion of Monasticism in Late Antiquity*, Transformation of the Classical Heritage, 33 (Berkeley: University of California Press).

CASEAU, B. (2002), 'L'abandon de la communion dans la main (IVe–XIIe siècles)', *Travaux et mémoires*, 14: 79–94.

CLARK, E. A. (2004), *History, Theory, Text: Historians and the Linguistic Turn* (Cambridge, Mass.: Harvard University Press).

CLARK, G. (2004), 'Pilgrims and Foreigners: Augustine on Travelling Home', in Ellis and Kidner (2004), 149–58.

CONNOLLY, D. K. (1999), 'Imagined Pilgrimage in the Itinerary Maps of Matthew Paris', *Art Bulletin*, 81: 612–22.

COPELAND, K. B. (2004), 'The Earthly Monastery and the Transformation of the Heavenly City in Late Antique Egypt', in Boustan and Reed (2004), 142–58.

DAGRON, G. (1978), *Vie et Miracles de Sainte Thècle*, Subsidia Hagiographica, 62 (Brussels: Société des Bollandistes).

DAVIS, S. J. (2001), *The Cult of St. Thecla: A Tradition of Women's Piety in Late Antiquity*, OECS (Oxford: Oxford University Press).

DEVOS, P. (1967), 'La date du voyage d'Égérie', *AnBoll* 85: 165–94.

DIETZ, M. (2004), 'Itinerant Spirituality and the Late Antique Origins of Christian Pilgrimage', in Ellis and Kidner (2004), 125–34.

DONCEEL-VOÛTE, P. (1995), 'Le rôle des reliquaires dans les pèlerinages', in Engemann and Dassmann (1995), i: 184–205.

DORAN, R. (1992) (ed. and trans.), *The Lives of Symeon Stylites*, CS 112 (Kalamazoo, Mich.: Cistercion Publications).

DOUGLASS, L. (1999), 'A New Look at the *Itinerarium Burdigalense*', *JECS* 4: 313–34.

ELLIS, L., and KIDNER, F. L. (2004) (eds.), *Travel, Communication and Geography in Late Antiquity: Sacred and Profane* (Aldershot: Ashgate).

ELM, S. (1987), 'Perceptions of Jerusalem Pilgrimage as Reflected in Two Early Sources on Female Pilgrimage (3rd and 4th centuries, A.D)', *StPatr* 20: 219–23.

—— (1994), *'Virgins of God': The Making of Asceticism in Late Antiquity* (Oxford: Oxford University Press).

ELSNER, J. (2000), 'The *Itinerarium Burdigalense*: Politics and Salvation in the Geography of Constantine's Empire', *JRS* 90: 181–95.

—— and RUTHERFORD, I. (2005) (eds.), *Pilgrimage in Graeco-Roman and Early Christian Antiquity: Seeing the Gods* (Oxford: Oxford University Press).

ENGEMANN J., and DASSMANN, E. (1995) (eds.), *Akten des XII. Internationalen Kongresses für christliche Archäologie, (Bonn 22–28 September 1991)*; JAC, Ergänzungsbände, 20, 1–2 (Münster: Aschendorffsche Verlagsbuchhandlung).

FRANK, G. (2000), *The Memory of the Eyes: Pilgrimage to Living Saints in Christian Late Antiquity*, Transformations of the Classical Heritage, 30 (Berkeley: University of California Press).

—— (2007), 'From Antioch to Arles: Lay Devotion in Context', in A. Cassidy and F. Norris (eds.), *The Cambridge History of Christianity*, ii: *Constantine to c. 600* (Cambridge: Cambridge University Press), 531–47.

FRANKFURTER, D. (1998*a*) (ed.), *Pilgrimage and Holy Space in Late Antique Egypt*, Religions in the Graeco-Roman World, 134 (Leiden: E. J. Brill).

—— (1998*b*), *Religion in Roman Egypt: Assimiliation and Resistance* (Princeton: Princeton University Press).

—— (2000), 'Christian Oracle Shrines', in R. Valantasis (ed.), *Religions of Late Antiquity in Practice* (Princeton: Princeton University Press), 469–72.

GAMBLE, H. Y. (1995), *Books and Readers in the Early Church: A History of Early Christian Texts* (New Haven: Yale University Press).

GERONTIUS, *Vita Melaniae Iunoris*. Text: D. Gorce, *Vie de Sainte Mélanie*, SC 90 (Paris: Éditions du Cerf, 1962). Eng. trans.: E. A. Clark, *The Life of Melania the Younger*, Studies in Women and Religion, 14 (Lewiston, NY: Edwin Mellen, 1984).

GRAF, F. (2004), 'The Bridge and the Ladder: Narrow Passages in Late Antique Visions', in Boustan and Reed (2004), 19–33.

GROSSMANN, P. (1998), 'The Pilgrimage Center of Abû Mînâ', in Frankfurter (1998), 281–302.

HAAS, C. (1997), *Alexandria in Late Antiquity* (Baltimore: Johns Hopkins University Press).

HAHN, C. (1990), 'Loca Sancta Souvenirs: Sealing the Pilgrim's Experience', in Ousterhout (1990), 85–96.

—— (1997), 'Seeing and Believing: The Construction of Sanctity in Early-Medieval Saints' Shrines', *Speculum*, 72: 1079–1106.

HUNT, E. D. (1982), *Holy Land Pilgrimage in the Later Roman Empire (AD 312–460)* (Oxford: Clarendon Press).

—— (1999), 'Were There Christian Pilgrims before Constantine?', in J. Stopford (ed.), *Pilgrimage Explored* (Woodbridge, Suffolk: York Medieval Press), 25–40.

—— (2001), 'The Date of *Itinerarium Egeriae*', StPatr 38: 410–16.

JACOBS, A. S. (2004), *Remains of the Jews: The Holy Land and Christian Empire in Late Antiquity*, Divinations: Rereading Late Ancient Religion (Stanford, Calif.: Stanford University Press).

KERKESLAGER, A. (1998), 'Jewish Pilgrimage and Jewish Identity in Hellenistic and Early Roman Egypt', in Frankfurter (1998*a*), 99–225.

LANDER, S. (2004), 'The Word Made Flesh: Case Studies of Confluence and Conflict in the Shrines of the Terebinths of Mamre (Palestine) and the Maccabean Martyrs (Syria)', paper presented at the AAR, San Antonio, Texas.

LEYERLE, B. (1996), 'Landscape as Cartography in Early Christian Pilgrimage Narratives', *JAAR* 64: 119–43.

MAGUIRE, H. P., DAUTERMAN, E., and DUNCAN-FLOWERS, M. J. (1989) (eds.), *Art and Holy Powers in the Early Christian House* (Urbana, Ill.: University of Illinois Press).

MANGO, M. M. (1986), *Silver from Early Byzantium: The Kaper Koraon and Related Treasures* (Baltimore: Wallers Art Gallery).

—— (1991), 'Wondrous Mountain', in *Oxford Dictionary of Byzantium* (Oxford: Oxford University Press), iii. 2204.

MARAVAL, P. (2004), *Lieux saints et pèlerinages d'Orient: Histoire et géographie des origines à la conquête arabe*, 2nd edn. (Paris: Éditions du Cerf; 1st edn. 1985).

MARKUS, R. A. (1994), 'How on Earth Could Places Become Holy? Origins of the Christian Idea of Holy Places', *JECS* 2: 257–71.

MITCHELL, M. M. (2007), 'Looking for Abercius: Re-Imagining Contexts of Interpretation of the "Earliest Christian Inscription" ', in L. Brink and D. Green (eds.), *Commemorating the Dead* (Berlin: de Gruyter), 303–35.

MONTSERRAT, D. (1998), 'Pilgrimage to the Shrine of SS. Cyrus and John at Menouthis in Late Antiquity', in Frankfurter (1998), 257–79.

OUSTERHOUT, R. (1990a) (ed.), *The Blessings of Pilgrimage*, Illinois Byzantine Studies, 1 (Urbana, Ill.: University of Illinois Press).

—— (1990b), 'Loca Sancta and the Architectural Response to Pilgrimage', in Ousterhout (1990a), 108–24.

PAPACONSTANTINOU, A. (1996), 'La liturgie stationnale à Oxyrhynchos dans la première moitié du 6e siècle: réédition et commentaire du *P.Oxy.* XI 1357', *Revue des Études Byzantines*, 54: 135–59.

—— (2001), *Le Culte des saints en Égypte des Byzantins aux Abbassides: L'apport des inscriptions et des papyrus grecs et coptes* (Paris: CNRS Editions).

PAPINI, L. (1998), 'Fragments of the Sortes Sanctorum from the Shrine of St. Colluthus', in Frankfurter (1998), 393–401.

PIACENZA PILGRIM, *Ps.-Antonini Placentini Itinerarium*. Text: in P. Geyer and O. Cuntz (eds.), *Itineraria et Alia Geographica*, CCSL 175–6 (Turnhout: Brepols, 1965), 175: 129–53. Eng. trans. in Wilkinson (2002).

RAHMANI, L. Y. (1999), 'The Byzantine Solomon *Eulogia* Tokens in the British Museum', *Israel Exploration Journal*, 49: 92–104.

SIVAN, H. (1988), 'Who Was Egeria? Piety and Pilgrimage in the Age of Gratian', *HTR* 81: 59–72.

SMITH, J. Z. (1987), *To Take Place: Toward Theory in Ritual* (Chicago: University of Chicago Press).

SODINI, J.-P. (1993), 'Nouvelles eulogies de Syméon', in C. Jolivet-Lévy et al. (eds.), *Les saints et leur sanctuaire: textes, images et monuments* (Paris: Publications de la Sorbonne), 25–33.

—— (2001), 'La hiérarchisation des espaces à Qal'at Sem'an', in M. Kaplan (ed.), *Le sacré et son inscription dans l'espace à Byzance et en Occident: Études comparées*, Byzantina Sorbonensia, 18 (Paris: Publications de la Sorbonne), 251–62.

STAROWIEYESKI, M. (1979), 'Bibliografia Egeriana', *Aug* 19: 297–318.

STEVENS, S. T. (2000), 'Excavations of an Early Christian Pilgrimage Complex at Bir Ftouha (Carthage)', *DOP* 54: 271–4.

TALBOT, A.-M. (2002), 'Female Pilgrimage in Late Antiquity and the Byzantine Era', *Acta Byzantina Fennica*, NS 1: 73–88.

TURNER, V., and TURNER, E. (1978), *Image and Pilgrimage in Christian Culture* (New York: Columbia University Press).

VIKAN, G. (1982), *Byzantine Pilgrimage Art* (Washington D.C.: Dumbarton Oaks).

—— (1990), 'Pilgrims in Magi's Clothing: The Impact of Mimesis on Early Byzantine Pilgrimage Art', in Ousterhout (1990), 97–107; repr. in Vikan (2003).

—— (2003), *Sacred Images and Sacred Power in Byzantium*, Variorum Collected Studies Series, 778 (Aldershot: Ashgate).

WALKER, P. W. L. (1990), *Holy City, Holy Places? Christian Attitudes to Jerusalem and the Holy Land in the Fourth Century* (Oxford: Clarendon Press).

WILKEN, R. L. (1992), *The Land Called Holy: Palestine in Christian History and Thought* (New Haven: Yale University Press).

WILKINSON, J. (2002) (ed.), *Jerusalem Pilgrims before the Crusades*, rev. edn. (Warminster: Aris & Phillips; 1st edn. 1977).

WIPSZYCKA, E. (1995), 'Les pèlerinages chrétiens dans l'antiquité tardive: Problèmes de definition et de repères temporels', *Byzantinoslavica*, 56: 429–38.

PART VIII

THEOLOGICAL THEMES

CHAPTER 41

INTERPRETATION OF SCRIPTURE

FRANCES M. YOUNG

Now that 'reception history' has become a significant feature of biblical studies, there is renewed interest in the interpretation of scripture in the period of the so-called fathers of the church; for the topic has relevance beyond the merely historical documentation of supposedly outmoded readings of texts and pre-scientific hermeneutical methods. Indeed, this shift means that, before embarking on a project in this area, the investigator needs to understand the enormous intellectual change that has occurred over the past generation, not least so as to be able to assess material offered in secondary sources against the date and context of the scholarly contribution. This chapter begins, therefore, with a discussion of (1) the most notable studies of the past half-century, in order to plot the shifts in assumptions and models brought to the analysis of exegetical method. It will then provide an outline of (2) the significance of scripture in the life of the early church; (3) the range of primary source material; and (4) potential research topics in this area.

41.1 LITERATURE SURVEY

Studies of patristic exegesis during the 'modern' period were deeply affected by the so-called historical critical method. This was thought to call into question the most fundamental aspects of 'pre-modern' interpretation. No longer did biblical scholars seriously entertain the view that the Old Testament was simply prophetic of the New. In particular, allegory was regarded as intellectually disreputable, and coupled with the apparent lack of a sense of history in the fathers, this meant that most exegetes felt there was little to learn from early interpretation of scripture. As I put it elsewhere, 'the standard English account of Origen's exegesis virtually organizes the material around the view that Origen never really understood the Bible because he sat too loosely to history. Since that book was written, the shift in biblical studies has helped us to recognize that concern about "history" has a very modern ring' (Young 1997a: 3).

This statement referred to R. P. C. Hanson's book on Origen, *Allegory and Event* (1959), and Origen may be regarded as the first Christian scholar of the Bible. This meticulous study of his work has hardly been superseded in English, and its republication (2002), with a critical introduction by Joseph Trigg, has provided students with an indispensable tool for entering this arena. Origen is presented primarily as an allegorist, a fact which is taken to vitiate his interpretation, but which Hanson tries to understand in terms of his historical location. Thus the opening section explores the sources of Christian allegory, and Origen's failure to grasp that the Bible is about salvation history is thus set in explanatory context. The allegory he inherited from his Hellenistic predecessors is unhistorical: 'Its ultimate aim is to empty the text of any particular connection with historical events' (Hanson 1959: 63). So, consistently, Hanson treats Origen's approach as arbitrary and fanciful, and allegory as 'largely a façade or a rationalization whereby he was able to read into the Bible what he wanted to find there' (Hanson 1959: 258). In a chapter on historicity, Hanson brings out what he sees as Origen's great failure: 'In history as event, in history as the field of God's self-revelation *par excellence*, Origen is not the least interested' (Hanson 1959: 276). Indeed, history is meaningless unless some kind of parable can be drawn from it, or it is turned into religious experience. Hanson assumes that exegesis means putting yourself into the minds of the biblical writers, and that for them God's revelation in events of history was self-evident; so he judges that allegory makes it quite impossible for Origen to understand scripture.

Now Hanson's book was to some extent a reply to a more sympathetic approach to the 'spiritualizing' tendencies of Origen's exegesis, that of the French Catholic scholars Henri de Lubac and Jean Daniélou; their books were respectively entitled *Histoire et Esprit: l'intelligence de l'écriture d'après Origène* and *Sacramentum Futuri: Études sur les origines de la typologie biblique*, both published in 1950. They too were haunted by the 'modern' question of history, but both challenged the idea that Origen's basic outlook was Platonic. De Lubac 'minimized or explained away wherever possible Origen's often expressed disdain for the letter of the Bible, which [he] identifies as "history" ... Origen, he argued, "spiritualizes" history "or, if one likes, he interiorizes it, but he by no means destroys it"' (Trigg in Hanson 2002: p. xi). Consistently, de Lubac (1959) defended the idea of multiple senses of scripture, suggesting that the spiritual sense built on the literal or historical sense. Meanwhile,

Daniélou's work (Daniélou 1948, 1950, 1958) raised the question of whether it was possible to make a distinction between typology and allegory by appeal to their differing relationship to history and to their different origins: it was not Hellenistic allegory but Jewish typology which was the starting point of Origen's approach, and this enabled an acceptable spiritual reading of scripture which, even if developed by allegorical symbolism, was grounded in history. Thus, he speaks of

a new kind of symbolism, which is characteristic of the Bible. Its specific difference is historicity, for it denotes a relationship between various events belonging to sacred history. It is called *typology*...This figurative sense of Scripture is grounded in the structural unity of God's design: the same divine characteristics are revealed in successive strata of history.

(Daniélou 1958: 140)

Hanson's book in its very title challenges these optimistic assessments and seeks to demolish them. But meanwhile a couple of essays had appeared in English which took up Daniélou's approach to typology and sought to promulgate it. Lampe and Woollcombe became a minor classic, in which the distinction between typology and allegory was presented as the key to what might be appropriated or repudiated in the exegesis of the fathers. Allegory was defined as ahistorical symbolism, while typology 'seeks to discover and make explicit the *real correspondences in historical events* which have been brought about by the recurring rhythm of the divine activity' (Lampe and Woollcombe 1957: 29; my emphasis). The difficulty, they suggested, is that patristic exegesis so easily slips from one to another, and is characterized by fancies and rhetorical tricks, which distract from this fundamentally sound, *historically based* approach.

This last admission alerts us to the difficulties. The fathers themselves did not make any such distinction. 'Typology' is a modern coinage, not a word that patristic interpreters used of their own practice, though they did speak of 'types' of various sorts (Charity 1966: 171 n.; Louth 1983: 118; Young 1994). Although it appeared to be a useful heuristic tool, not least in characterizing the difference between Alexandrian allegory, as practised by Origen and his successors, and Antiochene methods, pursued by exegetes who reacted against allegory in the fourth century, it now has to be seen as the product of 'modern' attempts to come to terms with what the fathers were doing with scripture, when minds were so profoundly shaped by historical consciousness. The fact that 'postmodern' perspectives have challenged the dominance of the historical critical method with biblical studies has reinforced a major shift in evaluation. Paradoxically, better use of the historical critical method with respect to this material is the result. For, rather than deploring or defending patristic exegesis against modern, supposedly better, methodology, more recent scholars are concerned to explain their approach by more careful reference to the intellectual world in which they were operating. We may characterize these developments as the 'philological turn'.

To some extent this was anticipated in the earlier work of R. M. Grant. In *The Letter and the Spirit* (1957) Grant documented the fact that Origen's allegory had Graeco-Roman sources, an approach exploited by Hanson; later he tackled the question how far patristic exegesis showed interest in the historical Jesus in a work entitled *The Earliest Lives of Jesus* (1961), which until recently has not received the attention it deserves. Here he demonstrated the ways in which Origen actually practised a kind of historical criticism, not of the 'modern' sort, but of a kind which can be paralleled in Graeco-Roman rhetoricians. The earthing of Origen's exegesis in contemporary practice was taken further by Bernhard Neuschäfer in his book *Origenes als Philologe* (1987). Meanwhile my own work led to an article (Young 1989) in which I argued that the difference between the Alexandrian and Antiochene schools was to be found in parallel divergences between the approach to texts taken by the rhetorical and philosophical schools of antiquity. Subsequently it became clear that this was an over-simple analysis; for the age-old contrast between philosophy and rhetoric failed to recognize considerable overlaps, and Origen as well as the Antiochenes used the standard exegetical techniques learned from the *grammaticus* and *rhetor* (Young 1997b). Reflection on hermeneutical issues also directed my attention to the principles which informed the fathers' approach to scripture, their discernment of spiritual truth therein, and their arguments over doctrine. All can be paralleled in the intellectual world to which they belonged: the 'moral' meaning of the Graeco-Roman classics was a concern for schoolmasters in the rhetorical tradition, as they tried to counter Plato's attack on literature, and philosophical teachers likewise focused on the exegesis of texts, seeking truth and ethics not just in philosophical books, such as those of Plato, but also in classics such as Homer (Lamberton 1986). Indeed, one way of looking at what happened in the development of Christian thinking is to see a process whereby the books of scripture were substituted for the Graeco-Roman classics as the basis for Christian education, with the same methods utilized and similar outcomes expected (Droge 1989). The results of this kind of investigation are to be found in my book *Biblical Exegesis and the Formation of Christian Culture* (1997a).

The other aspect of taking the historico-cultural context seriously must, of course, be the legacy from the Jewish matrix within which Christianity began its formation. Studies of the earliest Christian exegesis perforce have focused on the fulfilment of prophecy: oracular and typological reading created a legacy, which later scholars like Origen took up into their more sophisticated commentaries. An important work here is Oskar Skarsaune's *The Proof from Prophecy* (1987). Furthermore, it can be shown that rabbinic exegesis provides parallels to the work of early Christian interpreters, and that Origen probably had contact with contemporary Jewish exegetes. One significant study is Nicholas de Lange's *Origen and the Jews* (1976). But an increasing bibliography on rabbinic methods of exegesis makes this a field where serious and well-informed comparative study is really only beginning.

Meanwhile, significant studies of 'figural reading', often informed by postmodern literary theory, have illuminated early Christian exegesis and preaching. The most significant studies are David Dawson's *Allegorical Readers and Cultural Revision in Ancient Alexandria* (1992) and *Christian Figural Reading and the Fashioning of Identity* (2001). In addition, different perspectives on the material are provided by (i) studies of the patristic exegesis of particular books of scripture, such as the Gospel of John (Wiles 1960) or the Epistle to Romans (Gorday 1983), or of Paul more generally (Wiles 1967; Babcock 1990; Mitchell 2000), or the Epistle to the Hebrews (Greer 1973); or (ii) commentaries written with the idea of focusing on reception history, such as Mark Edwards on John's Gospel (Edwards 2004). The publication dates of these books should be noted and taken seriously, since the analytical categories used will have been affected by the general climate of understanding within which the research was undertaken (i.e. the broader intellectual currents outlined above).

In other words, literature concerned with patristic interpretation of scripture itself needs to be interpreted in the light of its context. Results of research are deeply affected by presuppositions as well as investment in the outcome of the research. The shift from 'modernist' presuppositions to 'postmodern' perspectives on discourse, rhetoric, and literature, including 'reader response' theories, has had a profound effect on the way the topic of scriptural interpretation in the fathers is evaluated. It is important to exercise critical awareness in using such a work as the big compendium edited by Kannengiesser (2004), assessing the extent to which account has been taken of the developments sketched here.

41.2 SCRIPTURE IN THE LIFE OF THE EARLY CHURCH

Scriptural interpretation cannot be studied in isolation from other aspects of the life and culture of early Christianity.[1] If one asks what kind of a social phenomenon the Church was—in other words, what analogies existed in ancient society—then one instructive answer would be the school. Of course, such an answer hardly covers the whole picture; other analogies too, such as *collegia*, throw light on the Church. But in the Graeco-Roman world a group of people gathering to study texts would have appeared much more like a school than like a religious institution. The words 'dogma' and 'doctrine' are associated with schools, being simply the words for 'teaching' in Greek and Latin respectively; the word 'heresy' is associated, before its specific application to false teaching in Christianity, with the various different 'opinions' of the philosophers. In Rome, it seems, there were a number of Christian philosophical schools—those of Justin, Valentinus, Marcion, and later Hippolytus—and the distinction between such schools and house churches may not have been self-evident (Lampe 2003). The fact that apologists answer the charge of 'atheism' in the second century is a further indication that 'religion' would not have seemed the natural category by which to categorize Christianity. Yet the Jewish synagogue provides precedents: Jews too could be treated as 'philosophers', with their particular morals and classic books. Christians were happy to be known as a 'third race', despite not being distinguished ethnically from their neighbours— they self-identified as a 'people' with ancient traditions enshrined in a body of literature which they studied to find truth and the right way of life. Indeed, they saw themselves as the rightful heirs of the promises of scripture, for all the prophecies they could find fulfilled in Christ and the Church. Scripture and issues of identity were intertwined.

Initially, the books at the heart of Christian life were the Jewish scriptures, and only gradually did specifically Christian books join them. The formation of the biblical canon was a fundamental element in the development of scripture's interpretation, as criteria for distinguishing the right books and for judging right interpretation were established at the same time: the so-called rule of faith or canon of truth, used by Irenaeus in opposition to the Gnostics, provided those necessary criteria. Ultimately this 'canon' was expressed in credal form, and scripture and creed were seen as mutually dependent. However, another element in the determination of which books were canonical was usage, and this implies that the development of liturgy and homiletics is essential in the spectrum of subjects necessary in order to get a true sense of the place and meaning of scripture in the developing life of the Church. Lections from the Jewish scriptures and interpretations of such texts were associated with readings from what Justin called 'the memoirs of the apostles' by the mid-second century. Much of Origen's scholarship was published in the form of homilies taken down by dictation, even though he also taught exegesis in a more professional school context and composed more specifically 'academic' commentaries. Extant collections of homilies present much of the fourth-century exegesis of scripture to which we now have access. The context of most interpretative activity was the church's worship.

Nor is it just the societal and liturgical context that must be understood for proper evaluation of early Christian interpretation. The history of Christian doctrine, it is said, could be written as a history of biblical interpretation. Certainly, in the great debates of the early centuries the appeal to scripture had an increasing and fundamental part to play. By the third century the meanings of certain texts, and the implications of them when set in juxtaposition, raised contentious issues— the so-called Monarchian controversies provide an instance: how was the biblical affirmation of one true God to be reconciled with the equally biblical affirmation of Jesus as Lord and God? Careful examination of the key primary documents reveals the extent to which scriptural 'proof-texts' figured in the arguments of both sides. The role of interpretation of scripture is even more evident in the fourth-century struggles over Arianism. Some tried to reach doctrinal definitions using scriptural language alone; others argued that individual proof-texts must be interpreted according to the 'mind' of scripture overall. All alike claimed to trace correct 'teaching' within the canonical books. What we have here is not so much 'development' or 'evolution of doctrine' as arguments about what is the appropriate discourse to articulate unequivocally what is given in scripture.

So it is impossible to study the interpretation of scripture as an isolated topic. Engaging with the whole spectrum of issues raised by the early history of Christianity, and indeed its relationship to the culture in which it developed, is vital. Generally speaking, the pre-Constantinian Church saw its mission as a kind of counter-cultural *paideia*. The pagan classics, and education based on them, were to be replaced by this new canon of literature. All kinds of people could attend this 'school', not just the elite, and its aim was to produce lifelong learners progressing in understanding of the truth and in living according to the way of Christ through the teaching offered on the basis of the scriptures. However, by the time that Gregory of Nazianzus was defending Christians against Julian the Apostate in the fourth century, it was clear to him that classical education constituted a universal value, essential for training people in rhetoric and logic—to exclude Christians from the schools was an attack, an attempt to deprive the Church of educated leadership. Christians could 'secularize' pagan literature for the process of education, while using the skills acquired for interpretation of scripture. Yet Augustine's *De doctrina christiana* develops a specific church *paideia*: this work is a guidebook in which he adapts and spells out standard exegetical techniques, using biblical examples, apparently for teachers in the Church who had not received a 'secular' education. The interpretation of scripture, then, bears upon the whole question of Christianity and culture. It is one of the most important keys to understanding the early church.

41.3 PRIMARY SOURCE MATERIAL

The indispensable handbook for advice on primary sources, together with comprehensive bibliographies of available secondary literature, is now Kannengiesser (2004). This compendium is very similar to a patrology, but is focused specifically on patristic exegesis of the Bible. Part A covers a number of general considerations:

I. Patristic Exegesis: Fifty Years of International Research
II. Judaism and Rhetorical Culture: Two Foundational Contexts for Patristic Exegesis
III. Patristic Hermeneutics
IV. Patristic Exegesis of Books of the Bible

Part B works through the material historically, from the second century to the Venerable Bede, with Greek, Latin, and Syriac sources given extended treatment, and also a chapter covering Armenian, Georgian, Coptic, and Ethiopian literature.

Given the availability of this comprehensive handbook, it seems otiose to do much listing here. Nevertheless, the most obvious bodies of material will be introduced, along with occasional bypaths of interest. Concentrating on explicit exegesis means starting with relatively late material. Earlier material will figure subsequently in a brief glance at other potential sources for researching the interpretation of scripture.

41.3.1 Explicit Exegetical Works: John Chrysostom and the 'Antiochenes'

The sequential homilies of John Chrysostom, recorded as homiletic commentaries on many New Testament texts and some major books of the Old Testament, constitute the largest body of material for observing patristic exegetical practice. Migne's Patrologia Graeca (PG) is the only accessible published version of the texts in bulk, though the Sources Chrétiennes (SC) have begun to fill the gap. This lack of modern critical texts, together with other critical questions concerning date and authenticity, makes this material difficult to handle, but also means that it may provide an excellent introduction to the range of questions with which a budding patristic scholar has to grapple.

There are two series of homilies on Genesis, a group of nine and a collection of sixty-seven covering the whole book. There are homilies on the Psalter, a collection of 'explanations' of fifty-eight Psalms, Psalms 4–12, 43–9, 108–17, 119–50, and various occasional homilies which take Psalm passages as their texts (though a good many are spurious). There are six homilies on Isaiah in Greek, and a complete commentary in Armenian. There are various other odds and ends on parts of the Old Testament, and many fragments of comment on other Old Testament material named as from Chrysostom in the catenae: Jeremiah, Daniel, Proverbs, and Job. (The catenae are commentaries created as compendia of extracts from the patristic writers and an important source of lost material, though verifying the identification of the sources can sometimes be problematic.)

Turning to the New Testament, we have homilies on the gospels of Matthew and John: the collection of ninety on Matthew covers the entire text, and was once widely disseminated—we know of early translations into Latin, Armenian, Syriac, Arabic, and Georgian; the collection of eighty-eight much shorter homilies on John focus principally on the dogmatic misunderstandings of Johannine texts found among heretics, especially the Arians and Anomoeans. Fifty-five homilies on the Acts of the Apostles provide the only complete early commentary on this book, but they were probably taken down by stenographers as Chrysostom spoke, and the printed text in Migne fails to reflect the difficulties of the two recensions in the manuscripts. Exposition of the Pauline epistles constitutes about half of Chrysostom's extant homilies: thirty-two on Romans, forty-four on 1 Corinthians, thirty on 2 Corinthians, a commentary on Galatians which was clearly digested out of homilies, twenty-four on Ephesians, fifteen on Philippians, twelve on Colossians, sixteen on 1 and 2 Thessalonian, thirty-four on the Pastoral Epistles, thirty-four on Hebrews, which at this date was generally taken to be Pauline. In addition there are seven panegyrics on Paul, which illuminate the rest of the material by showing how much and why Chrysostom admired the apostle: his life and letters revealed the true pastor and preacher that Chrysostom himself aimed to be (Mitchell 2000).

Chrysostom is regarded as representing the 'Antiochene school', and a text which provides excellent insight into the methods that he and others assumed is a little treatise by one Adrianos, *Isagoge ad sacras scripturas* (PG 98. 1273–1312). Other Antiochene works of exegesis come from Diodore of Tarsus, Theodore of Mopsuestia, and Theodoret of Cyrrhus. Much is fragmentary because of the later condemnation of Diodore and Theodore for their Christological views. A trawl of journals is needed to identify what remains of Diodore's work, though he is reported to have produced commentaries on the whole Old Testament, the four gospels, Acts, and 1 John. From Theodore we have a commentary on the twelve minor prophets extant in Greek, a commentary on the Gospel of John in Syriac translation, and a commentary on the ten minor epistles of St Paul in a Latin version; reports of work on Genesis, the Psalms, Matthew, Luke, and the major epistles of Paul (Romans, 1 and 2 Corinthians, Hebrews) are tantalizing, and generate searches for fragments. Theodoret is another story. Since he avoided condemnation, his work has generally speaking survived. It distils the approach of the Antiochene school rather than being particularly original; for example, it has been shown that his work on the Pauline epistles used and debated the earlier work of Theodore. His extant exegetical work covers 'questions' on the Pentateuch, together with Joshua, Judges, and Ruth, and on the books of Kings and Chronicles; and interpretation of the Psalms, the Song of Songs, Daniel, Ezekiel, the Twelve Minor Prophets, Isaiah, Jeremiah, and the fourteen epistles of Paul.

Antiochene exegesis has in the past been characterized as 'literal' and 'historical' over against the allegorizing of the Alexandrian school. On actually engaging with the original source material, the student will therefore be surprised at the extent to which the outcome is correct dogma, ethical exhortation, or prophetic typology. The shift in approach outlined earlier in this chapter enables a better understanding and appreciation of Antiochene interpretation (Young 1997*b*, 2003). Fundamentally the Antiochenes approached texts philologically, reacting against the identification of allegory where there was nothing in the text to suggest that that was intended.

Their reaction against allegory is first voiced in Eustathius's treatise *On the Witch of Endor and against Origen*; further methodological criticisms of the allegorical approach are to be found scattered in the fragments of Diodore and the work of his successors. They were basically interested in the narrative logic of particular stories, objecting to methods which turned the text into a kind of code to be cracked; and they were also concerned to preserve the overarching story of the rule of faith (i.e. fall and redemption), criticizing the kind of allegory which emptied of reality the story of Adam and Eve, for example. Yet Diodore was as worried by the problem of the 'talking serpent' as ever allegorizers were: this was not to be taken literally but understood as signifying the devil. And, just like the allegorizers, Adrianos shows anxiety about taking anthropomorphisms literally. All alike were grappling with an appropriate way of understanding the discourse of scripture.

41.3.2 Explicit Exegetical Works: The Alexandrians

The target of the Antiochenes's criticism was the third-century Alexandrian, Origen. He was the first great exegete of scripture who approached the task with real scholarship. If his work were all extant, it would be the most significant body of material available, but very little remains in the original Greek; some has survived in later expurgated translations, but much has simply been destroyed. Origen was a controversial figure in his own day, disputes about his legacy arose in the fourth century, and in the time of Justinian he and his works were condemned.

Origen cannot be regarded as just an allegorizer. An important project of his was the production of the *Hexapla*, which is said to have placed six versions of the Old Testament scriptures side by side in parallel columns.[2] This work must have been physically gigantic, and it is hardly surprising that it has disappeared; probably there was only ever one copy. So lack of evidence vitiates research into this famous work, though its existence alerts us to the fact that Origen took basic philological and textual scholarship very seriously.

Origen's exegetical work took three forms: *scholia*, homilies, and commentaries. (1) The *scholia* were simply annotations on difficult passages or words, the sort of thing produced by Alexandrian grammarians and modern editors of classical texts. None of this material is extant, though some of it is doubtless hidden in the *Philokalia* (an anthology of his writings compiled by Basil of Caesarea and Gregory of Nazianzus) and the catenae. (2) Homilies extant in Greek include the one on the Witch of Endor that Eustathius criticized, and twenty on Jeremiah. More have survived in the Latin translation of Rufinus, a fourth-century apologist for Origen; these include sixteen on Genesis, thirteen on Exodus, sixteen on Leviticus, twenty-eight on Numbers, twenty-six on Joshua, nine on Judges, and nine on the Psalms. Some more homilies are preserved in translations from Jerome's hand: two on the Song of Songs, eight on Isaiah, fourteen on Jeremiah, thirty-nine on Luke. To Hilary of Poitiers we are indebted for fragments of the twenty-two homilies on Job. (3) None of the commentaries survives in full. We have eight out of twenty-five books on Matthew; but also a substantial part in a Latin translation, usually cited as *Commentariorum in Matt. series*. Of the thirty-two books of the commentary on John, eight are extant in Greek. Books 1–4 of the commentary on the Canticle survive in Rufinus's Latin translation, and also a version of the commentary on Romans, reduced from fifteen books to ten. Again, further material is to be found in the *Philokalia* and the catenae.

In addition to this evidence of his actual practice, we have an important discussion of his hermeneutical principles in book IV of *On First Principles*. This, however, poses some classic research problems. In the first place, *On First Principles* survives complete only in Rufinus's translation, though there are some substantial fragments in Greek (Butterworth (1936) sets out side by side an English translation of each version). Then, second, the theoretical principles which Origen sets out here do not seem straightforwardly reflected in his actual practice.

Origen's theory implies that there are three senses of scripture: the literal, the moral, and the spiritual, corresponding to the body, the soul, and the spirit. While scholars once suspected that Origen implied three different classes of believers, corresponding to the different levels of interpretation, now it is accepted that he probably intended progress from one level to another (Torjesen 1985). Many things in scripture are quite straightforward, such as the command not to murder; but there are other things in scripture which are *aporiai*, teasers that do not make obvious sense, and these are there to provoke the listener or reader into seeking deeper, spiritual meanings. Things which cannot be taken literally include metaphors and anthropomorphisms, as well as impossibilities, such as Jesus seeing all the kingdoms of the world, including Persians and Indians, from the top of a high mountain, or a right-handed person striking the right cheek. Scripture itself is deployed to justify this hermeneutic, classic passages being Proverbs 22: 20–1 (for the threefold way of interpretation) and nine Pauline texts: Romans 7: 14; 1 Cor 2: 10; 2: 16, 12 (quoted in that order); 9: 9–10; 10: 11; 2 Cor 3: 6, 15–16; Gal 4: 21–4.

One difficulty that arises in comparing this account with Origen's actual practice is that the 'threefold' sense disappears. In practice, there are two levels of meaning: essentially Origen looks at the 'letter' of the text, and then at multiple possible meanings as he indulges in a welter of prophetic, typological, moral, and spiritual interpretations. Furthermore, his theory does not enunciate the most significant aspect of his practice: namely, that it is philological analysis of the 'letter' which generates the 'under-sense'. The important thing was to find logical moves from the 'letter', of which not a jot or a tittle was to be regarded as insignificant, to the meaning intended by the Holy Spirit. One source of allegorical reading was the vast array of prophetic and typological meanings already discerned by the traditions of the Church, examples of which Origen discusses in *On First Principles*; but in his exegesis these are counterbalanced by his focus on providing spiritual guidance for the individual soul. The relationship between these two aspects of his spiritual interpretation is not very clear: some have tried to differentiate these into his 'moral' and 'spiritual' senses. However, his work on the Song of Songs suggests that this may be misguided; for here, one feels, interpretation in terms of Christ and the Church, on the one hand, and God and the individual soul, on the other, are actually two sides of the same coin, individual members making up the body of Christ (Young 2001).

Origen had enormous influence, but perhaps few followers. One was Didymus the Blind, in the fourth century a legendary figure, nicknamed the 'Seer' because of his spiritual insight, but for later centuries a shadowy one, his works having been condemned along with those of Origen. Yet the chance discovery of a cache of his commentaries on papyri at Tura in wartime has made his work the subject of considerable research in the latter part of the twentieth century. Many of the texts became available in the 1960s and 1970s, including commentaries on Zechariah, Genesis, Job, Psalms, and Ecclesiastes, and some scholars then argued that he gave allegorical interpretation a more systematic methodology (Bienert 1972; Tigcheler 1977). Further research on this material would undoubtedly be fruitful.

The other Alexandrian worth mentioning is Cyril, whose reputation is mainly associated with the fifth-century Christological controversy; yet a substantial amount of his exegetical work survives. Kerrigan (1952) provided a comprehensive study, and there are more recent studies by Wilken (1984, 2003). The intriguing thing is that one would hardly characterize it as in the Origenist allegorical tradition, though there is still a sense of two levels of meaning. Cyril's interpretation of the Old Testament is profoundly typological, while in his commentary on John he deliberately seeks a 'more dogmatic exegesis', confuting the interpretation of those opposed to his view of the incarnate Logos. Ironically, this makes his approach closer in practice to that of the Antiochenes, whose Christological views he was opposing. His exegesis has been characterized as 'eclectic', and it certainly challenges the neat classification into 'schools' beloved of modern scholarship.

41.3.3 Explicit Exegetical Works: Other Greek Material

The exegesis of the Cappadocians has likewise been treated as a kind of 'hybrid' between the two schools of Alexandria and Antioch, hardly the most illuminating way to describe it. There is no doubt that Origen had a profound influence on all three: Basil of Caesarea, Gregory of Nazianzus, and Gregory of Nyssa. On the other hand, it is clear that they take a less allegorical and more 'salvation-history' approach to scripture. But the 'philological turn' allows us to see not only what all 'schools' had in common, but also the fundamental character of the fathers' approach to exegesis in general. Basil's one explicitly exegetical work consists of the nine *Homilies on the Six Days of Creation*, though his scriptural interpretation can also be gleaned from other texts, as can that of Gregory of Nazianzus, despite the absence of any commentaries in his *œuvre*. From Gregory of Nyssa we have supplements to Basil on the creation in his works *On the Hexaemeron* and *On the Creation of Humanity*; his *Life of Moses*, which traces the soul's spiritual journey through the biblical narratives about Moses; a work on the Psalm titles, which makes of them a source for the life of virtue and perfection, while his fifteen *Homilies on the Song of Songs* explore the relationship between the soul and Christ; also eight homilies *On Ecclesiastes*, five *On the Lord's Prayer*, and eight *On the Beatitudes*.

41.3.4 Explicit Exegetical Works: The West and Elsewhere

The first scholarly exegete of the West, roughly contemporary with Origen, was the Roman, Hippolytus, who wrote at a time when Greek was still in use among Christians in the capital. There are complex critical problems in sorting out which extant texts are his work, and even exactly who he was; probably we have to think in terms of a 'school' of Hippolytus. Four books of a *Commentary on Daniel* are attributed to him; a variety of fragments have been preserved in a wide variety of languages. To sort out the contribution of Hippolytus to explicit exegetical scholarship would be a complicated but valuable task.

Full commentaries in Latin are not found until Hilary of Poitiers, who wrote a *Commentary on Matthew* and a treatise on some Psalms. Then Ambrose produced a collection of exegetical works, his largest being ten books on Luke's Gospel. In addition, we have available six books on the *Hexaemeron*; homiletic treatises on paradise, Cain and Abel, Noah, and Abraham; works known as *On Isaac and the Soul* and *On Jacob and the Good Life*; and on Joseph, on the Patriarchs (Genesis 49), and a variety of other biblical topics. He also expounded a number of Psalms, Psalm 118 at some length. Other fourth-century western exegetes of note include Marius Victorinus, whose commentaries on Ephesians, Galatians, and Philippians survive with minor lacunae. Roman interest in the Pauline epistles continued with the work of the mysterious 'Ambrosiaster,' who composed the first complete commentary on the apostle around the year 380. Pauline interpretation remained important in the West, as the later commentaries of Pelagius and Augustine attest.

The doyen of biblical studies in the West, however, was Jerome, the person who produced what would become the Vulgate translation of the Bible and supplanted earlier versions in Latin. It seems that he made use of Origen's *Hexapla*, once he had moved to Palestine, as well as the Hebrew original. Jerome clearly admired the scholars of the East, and prior to the Origenist controversy he rendered a number of their works into Latin, including, from Origen, fourteen homilies on Jeremiah, fourteen on Ezekiel, two on the Song of Songs, thirty-nine on Luke, and eight on Isaiah; from Eusebius, a free version of his treatise on biblical names (*Onomasticon*); from Didymus, his treatise on the Holy Spirit. His own *Commentarioli* were indebted to Origen, covering the Psalms, Ecclesiastes, all the prophets, four Pauline epistles, and Matthew.

The most important exegete of the West, however, was Augustine of Hippo, significant both for his methodological contributions and his actual exegetical work. The former are contained in the four books of his *De doctrina christiana*. Here he makes an important distinction between the *res*, or subject-matter, of scripture and the *signa*, or 'signs' by which that subject matter is articulated, adapting the basic rhetorical distinction between style and content. Content was established by *heuresis* or *inventio*, Augustine undertaking this in book I and arguing that the subject-matter of scripture is 'Love God' and 'Love your Neighbour'. Books II–III then map the philological tools required to explain the 'wording' and deal with difficulties in the text. Book IV deals with the communication of scripture. This treatise is a brilliant adaptation of the 'pagan' rhetorical education that Augustine had himself received and taught to the practicalities of teaching scripture in the Church.

The full range of Augustine's exegetical work is to be found in the huge collection of homilies he preached over his years as bishop. There are some specific exegetical collections, notably the *Enarrationes in Psalmos*, which is double the length of *The City of God*! In many cases, more than one exposition of a particular Psalm is collected here. Invariably Augustine discovers in the Psalms Christ and the Church, using typological and allegorical techniques to uncover this central theme. This massive collection throws a very different light on his approach to scripture from the *De doctrina christiana*.

Augustine repeatedly tried to write on Genesis 1–3, and these attempts reflect his continual wrestling with the problem of literal and figurative reading. First he wrote *On Genesis against the Manichees*, wishing to defend the goodness of creation against his former co-religionists. One of the factors in his conversion had been the recognition that scripture could have a spiritual, not just a literal, meaning; so it is not surprising that here he found symbolism of various kinds in the Genesis text. Later he made two attempts to interpret the creation narratives 'according to the letter', by which he meant discerning 'what actually happened'; given his views on the nature of God and eternity, his exegesis would not be recognized as 'literal' by modern readers. The first attempt was incomplete, the second constitutes the twelve books of the *De Genesi ad litteram*. Meanwhile he produced an extended spiritual interpretation in *Confessions*, books XI–XIII.

As far as the New Testament is concerned, the biggest contribution is the 124 sermons on John's Gospel and ten on I John, though other works such as the four books *De consensu evangelistarum* and bits of Pauline exegesis need to be mentioned for completeness.

Also for completeness one must move back east and mention the exegetical works of Ephrem the Syrian. Commentaries on Genesis and much of Exodus are extant in Syriac, those on Tatian's *Diatesseron*, Acts, and the Pauline epistles in Armenian, the latter sometimes taking the form of homilies. Many of his hymns draw on scripture with a characteristic typological approach, and this alerts us to the fact that much exegesis is not found in explicitly exegetical material. Both Narsai and Jacob of Serugh wrote verse commentaries on the *Hexaemeron*, as well as on important biblical episodes, such as the nativity.

41.3.5 Exegesis in Other Material

The earliest Christian exegesis can be deduced only from letters or other non-exegetical works; for the first commentaries as such are to be found with the scholars of the third century. Among second-century literature the most important sources include the *Epistle of Barnabas*, the *Peri Pascha* of Melito of Sardis, and Justin's *Dialogue with Trypho*, but much else is illuminating. It remains the case that letters, festal and occasional homilies, apologetic and dogmatic, liturgical and ascetical works are further sources for exploring the interpretation of scripture: Athanasius's works against the Arians, for example, map out principles on which texts are to be used in dogmatic argument, appealing to the 'mind' of scripture against over-literal use of proof-texts abstracted from the overall context (Young 1997*a*). There are plenty of avenues to pursue and a rich range of source material to explore.

41.4 POTENTIAL WAYS OF ENGAGING
WITH THE MATERIAL

Which brings us, finally, to consider where one might begin research in this area. The most obvious field demanding further attention is the interface between Jewish (rabbinic) interpretation and that of the early church; but there are others worth considering.

More investigation into how particular books of the Bible were interpreted would be illuminating. A stimulating but sketchy section of Kannengiesser's handbook goes through the scriptures indicating the principal passages of interest to the fathers and the way they approached them. Some things are predictable, like the focus on the narratives of creation and fall in Genesis, the Adam–Christ typology and the sacrifice of Isaac; but less obvious to the uninitiated is the appeal to the story of Noah because of its baptismal associations. The section is useful in alerting the student to key motifs in patristic reading of each book, and, as elsewhere, the bibliography gathers together what secondary material is available. To investigate further one or other particular biblical book is a potentially viable project, not least because, just like modern scholars, ancient scholars sometimes debated the proper interpretation of particular passages, and their different ways of reading particular texts often highlight characteristic approaches and interests.

Such a topic would require ranging over the period and the field. Another approach would be to narrow down the investigation to a particular commentary or a particular author. While the mainstream material outlined earlier has been much investigated, there are many byways which are uncharted, and some new discoveries, such as the exegetical works of Didymus, could still be regarded as fertile ground for further research.

Another approach would be to look at different genres and contexts in which exegesis took place, as hinted in section 41.2 above. The use of scripture in doctrinal debate could do with further analysis; likewise its use in the development of 'church orders' such as *The Apostolic Constitutions*. The emergence of lectionaries and the place of scripture in the liturgy is a grey area, and maybe there is insufficient hard evidence to solve the problems, but an investigation of this could spin off into some fruitful avenues.

Thus, the interpretation of scripture in the fathers has become a lively field in recent decades, and remains an area in which research and discussion are likely to continue to be stimulating and also to bear fruit.

Notes

1. In this section references are eschewed, since the scope is so broad, and bibliography suggested elsewhere in this volume will doubtless provide the necessary leads.
2. However, even Eusebius's description is not entirely consistent with this, and its exact nature is a matter of discussion. See Nautin (1977).

Suggested Reading

Augustine (1996), *Teaching Christianity* (*De doctrina christiana*). Eng. trans. and notes by E. Hill, OP (New York: New City Press).
—— (1997), *On Christian Teaching* (*De doctrina christiana*). Eng. trans. by R. P. H. Green, Oxford World Classics (Oxford: Oxford University Press).

CLARK, E. A. (1999), *Reading Renunciation: Asceticism and Scripture in Early Christianity* (Princeton: Princeton University Press).

FRISHMAN, J., and VAN ROMPAY, L. (1997), *The Book of Genesis in Jewish and Oriental Christian Interpretation: A Collection of Essays*, Traditio Exegetica Graeca, 5 (Louvain: Peeters).

FROEHLICH, K. (1984), *Biblical Interpretation in the Early Church*, Sources of Early Christian Thought (Philadelphia: Fortress Press).

GAMBLE, H. Y. (1995), *Books and Readers in the Early Church* (New Haven: Yale University Press).

GRANT, R. M. with TRACY, D. (1984), *A Short History of the Interpretation of the Bible*, 2nd edn., revised and enlarged (London: SCM Press).

HAUSER, A. J., and WATSON, D. F. (2003) (eds.), *A History of Interpretation*, i: *The Ancient Period* (Grand Rapids, Mich.: Eerdmans).

SIMONETTI, M. (1994), *Biblical Interpretation in the Early Church: An Historical Introduction to Patristic Exegesis*, trans. J. A. Hughes, ed. A. Bergquist and M. Bockmuehl, with W. Horbury as Consultant Editor (Edinburgh: T & T Clark).

See also BUTTERWORTH (1936); Daniélou (1960); Dawson (1992, 2001); Grant (1957); Hanson (2002); Kannengiesser (2004); Torjesen (1985); and Young (1997).

BIBLIOGRAPHY

BABCOCK, W. S. (ed.) (1990), *Paul and the Legacies of Paul* (Dallas: Southern Methodist University Press).

BIENERT, W. A. (1972), *'Allegoria' und 'Anagoge' bei Didymos der Blinden von Alexandria*, PTS 13 (Berlin: de Gruyter).

BUTTERWORTH, G. W. (1936), *Origen: On First Principles* (London: S.P.C.K.; repr. Gloucester, Mass.: Peter Smith, 1973).

CHARITY, A. C. (1966), *Events and their Afterlife: The Dialectics of Christian Typology in the Bible and Dante* (Cambridge: Cambridge University Press).

DANIÉLOU, J. (1955), *Origène* (Paris: La Table Ronde, 1948); Eng. trans. by W. Mitchell (New York: Sheed and Ward.

—— (1958), *The Lord of History*, trans. N. Abercrombie (London: Longmans).

—— (1960), *From Shadows to Reality: Studies in the Biblical Typology of the Fathers* (London: Burns & Oates, 1960).

DAWSON, D. (1992), *Allegorical Readers and Cultural Revision in Ancient Alexandria* (Berkeley: University of California Press).

—— (2001), *Christian Figural Reading and the Fashioning of Identity* (Berkeley: University of California Press).

DE LANGE, N. (1976), *Origen and the Jews* (Cambridge: Cambridge University Press).

DE LUBAC, H. (1950), *Histoire et Esprit: l'intelligence de l'écriture d'après Origène* (Paris: Aubier).

—— (1959–64), *Exégèse Mediévale: Les quatre sens de l'Ecriture*, 4 vols. (Paris: Aubier).

DROGE, A. J. (1989), *Homer or Moses? Early Christian Interpretations of the History of Culture*, Hermeneutische Untersuchungen zur Theologie, 26 (Tübingen: J. C. B. Mohr/Paul Siebeck).

EDWARDS, M. (2004), *John*, Blackwell Bible Commentaries (Oxford: Blackwell).

GORDAY, P. (1983), *Principles of Patristic Exegesis: Romans 9–11 in Origen, John Chrysostom and Augustine* (Lewiston, NY: Edwin Mellen Press).

GRANT, R. M. (1957), *The Letter and the Spirit* (London: S.P.C.K.).

—— (1961), *The Earliest Lives of Jesus* (London: S.P.C.K.).

GREER, R. (1973), *The Captain of our Salvation: A Study in the Patristic Exegesis of Hebrews* (Tübingen: J. C. B. Mohr/Paul Siebeck).

HANSON, R. P. C. (1959), *Allegory and Event: A Study of the Sources and Significance of Origen's Interpretation of Scripture* (London: SCM Press; repr. with an Introduction by Joseph W. Trigg (Louisville, Ky.: Westminster/John Knox Press, 2002).

KANNENGIESSER, C. (2004), *Handbook of Patristic Exegesis: The Bible in Ancient Christianity*, with special contributions by various scholars, 2 vols. (Leiden: E. J. Brill).

KERRIGAN, A. (1952), *St. Cyril of Alexandria: Interpreter of the Old Testament*, Analecta Biblica, 2 (Rome: Pontificium Institutum Biblicum).

LAMBERTON, R. (1986), *Homer the Theologian: Neoplatonist Allegorical Reading and the Growth of the Epic Tradition* (Berkeley: University of California Press).

LAMPE, G. W. H. (2003), *From Paul to Valentinus: Christians at Rome in the First Two Centuries*, trans. M. Steinhauser (Minneapolis: Fortress Press).

—— and WOOLLCOMBE, K. J. (1957), *Essays on Typology*, Studies in Biblical Theology, 22 (London: SCM Press).

LOUTH, A. (1983), *Discerning the Mystery: An Essay on the Nature of Theology* (Oxford: Clarendon Press).

MITCHELL, M. M. (2000), *The Heavenly Trumpet: John Chrysostom and the Art of Pauline Interpretation* (Tübingen: J. C. B. Mohr/Paul Siebeck).

NAUTIN, P. (1977), *Origène: sa vie et son oeuvre* (Paris: Beauchesne).

NEUSCHÄFER, B. (1987), *Origenes als Philologe* (Basel: Friedrich Reinhardt Verlag).

SKARSAUNE, O. (1987), *The Proof from Prophecy: A Study in Justin Martyr's Proof-Text Tradition: Text-Type, Provenance, Theological Profile* (Leiden E. J.: Brill).

TIGCHELER, J. H. (1977), *Didyme l'Aveugle et l'exégèse allegorique, son commentaire sur Zacharie* (Nijmegen: Dekker & van der Wegt).

TORJESEN, K. J. (1985), *Hermeneutical Procedure and Theological Method in Origen's Exegesis* (Berlin: de Gruyter).

WILES, M. (1960), *The Spiritual Gospel* (Cambridge: Cambridge University Press).

—— (1967), *The Divine Apostle* (Cambridge: Cambridge University Press).

WILKEN, R. L. (1984), *Judaism and the Early Christian Mind: A Study of Cyril of Alexandria's Exegesis and Theology* (New Haven: Yale University Press).

—— (2003), 'Cyril of Alexandria as Interpreter of the Old Testament', in Thomas G. Weinandy and Daneil A. Keating (eds.), *The Theology of St. Cyril of Alexandria: A Critical Appreciation* (London T & T Clark; New York: Continuum).

YOUNG, F. M. (1989), 'The Rhetorical Schools and their Influence on Patristic Exegesis', in R. Williams (ed.), *The Making of Orthodoxy: Essays in Honour of Henry Chadwick* (Cambridge: Cambridge University Press), 182–99.

—— (1994), 'Typology', in S. E. Porter, P. Joyce, and D. E. Orton (eds.), *Crossing the Boundaries: Essays in Biblical Interpretation in Honour of Michael D. Goulder* (Leiden: E. J. Brill), 29–48.

—— (1997a), *Biblical Exegesis and the Formation of Christian Culture* (Cambridge: Cambridge University Press).

—— (1997*b*), 'The Fourth Century Reaction against Allegory', *StPatr* 30: 120–5.

—— (2001), 'Sexuality and Devotion: Mystical Readings of the Song of Songs', *Theology and Sexuality: The Journal of the Centre for the Study of Christianity and Sexuality*, 14: 80–96.

—— (2003), 'Alexandrian and Antiochene Exegesis', in Alan J. Hauser and Duane F. Watson (eds.) *A History of Interpretation*, i: *The Ancient Period* (Grand Rapids, Mich.: Eerdmans), 334–54.

CHAPTER 42

DOCTRINE OF GOD

LEWIS AYRES

ANDREW RADDE-GALLWITZ

42.1 INTRODUCTION: THE SHAPE OF MODERN SCHOLARSHIP

RECENT scholarship on early Christian doctrines of God may be understood as shaped by reaction against two earlier figures, Adolf von Harnack (1851–1930) and Walter Bauer (1877–1960). Understanding a little of their thought and the main lines of reaction against them will enable us to frame some of the central questions that face scholars in this area of early Christian studies.

Harnack argued that their gradual break with the Jewish community and the universal concern of the Christian gospel drew the earliest Christians to recognize its natural home in the cultural and philosophical world shaped by Hellenism (Harnack 1958). The adoption of this new 'home' radically conditioned the way in which Christians would use and interpret their Jewish and Old Testament heritage. Harnack does not see this process as a passive falling of the Church into Greek hands: it is the result of the Christian community searching for ways to articulate a universal message beyond the boundaries that were the inevitable consequence of its particular birth. In many ways Harnack sees this shift as positive: for example, the adoption from Greek philosophy of the idea of the Logos gives the gospel a new coherence and reveals that Christianity implicitly finds its truest expression in a philosophical and universal form. Harnack understood the production of Christian dogma as a result of Hellenization, but also as a stage through which Christianity had to pass as awareness of its universal character grew and grows. The existence of dogma both reflects the philosophical universality of Christianity and, at the same time, easily becomes part of a hierarchical ritualistic system of superstition (most fully realized for Harnack in the development of Catholicism). With this last sentence it becomes clear that Harnack's account is highly teleological: the culmination of the process of Hellenization in its best sense is reached with the work of the Liberal Protestant theologian who is able to penetrate to the core of the gospel in its universal character and move beyond the need for dogma (for a good summary, see Rowe 1994).

While aspects of this understanding of Hellenization are still repeated, the theory as a whole has been increasingly discredited in recent scholarship. Two reasons may be given for this shift. First, although Harnack rightly sees the Judaism of Jesus's time as already shaped by Hellenistic culture, he operates with a strongly essentialist notion of 'Jewishness' and assumes that Hellenism can never truly intermingle with Judaism as such. This understanding of discrete cultural dynamics, and of the history of Jewish thought in particular, is no longer sustainable. Second, the complex evolution of early Christian doctrine has been the subject of much study in recent decades. Scholars have argued with increasing subtlety that developments in Christian belief are both continually exegetical yet simultaneously involve the piecemeal adoption and adaptation of ideas from a variety of non-Christian philosophical and religious traditions. In this context, scholars have become suspicious of using any one monolithic narrative to summarize the cultural engagements that occurred, especially one inattentive to the continuing centrality of scriptural texts and imagery to Christian thought.

There can be little doubt that the appearance of Walter Bauer's *Orthodoxy and Heresy in Early Christianity* in 1934 marked a significant step in the development of modern critical scholarship on the formation of orthodoxy within early Christianity (Bauer 1971). Bauer argued that the emergence of orthodoxy after the second century involved not the fighting off of 'heresies' that threatened the apostolic faith, but in many significant cases the overturning and labelling as heresy of previously accepted beliefs. For Bauer, narratives of orthodoxy's historical continuity are later constructions aimed at legitimating that which is newly established. Bauer's thesis was controversial in its use of evidence as soon as it was published. Over the decades that have followed, it is probably fair to say that Bauer's thesis has been rejected in two distinct ways. First, most of his examples have turned out to be unconvincing as scholarship on the second and third centuries has progressed (e.g. Hill 2004: 14 ff.). Second, most significant scholarship on the development of Christian belief has rejected the idea that we can narrate a monolithic story of heresy becoming orthodoxy.

This second rejection has not, however, seen scholars return to a picture of simple continuity in early Christian orthodoxy: instead, they have shaped accounts of the emergence of defined orthodoxies from more pluralistic situations which preceded them and frequently from situations of exegetical uncertainty and undecidability (e.g. Le Boulluec 1985; R. D. Williams 1989). Orthodoxy is constructed from a range of possibilities, some more prominent than others, some already seemingly marginal. Scholars working from a variety of perspectives and commitments also now tend to take for granted that the emergence of orthodoxy involves a concomitant definition of heresy as that which is excluded (e.g. Lyman 1993, 2003). In such contexts questions about the legitimacy of claims to continuity involve complex judgements about the relationships between new doctrinal formulations and the language and possibilities that preceded them. Before we can turn to the specific shape of the most significant and influential patristic doctrines of God stemming from the late fourth century, we need to see how the scholarly questions and methods that have emerged in the wake of Harnack and Bauer have shaped modern understanding of those doctrines.

42.2 POLEMIC AND DEVELOPMENT

Criticism of Bauer and Harnack has led scholars to reconsider the relationship between development in the doctrine of God and polemical dispute. Students of the period have explored with increasing sophistication how the doctrine of God emerged out of contexts within which hotly contested common texts and images sustained a number of traditions of thought. In particular, scholars have become wary of using later categories to describe earlier thought. Debate over Origen and his legacy offers an important example. Origen's *Commentary on John* combines a matrix of texts (e.g. bringing together for the first time Wis 7: 25 ff. and Heb 1: 3) as a hermeneutic for interpreting the significance of the divine Word, or Wisdom. This development demonstrates both a close style of exegesis shaped by techniques learnt at the hands of the *grammatikos* (Young 1997) and an adaptation of earlier (Christian and non-Christian) discussion of *epinoia* (a term which describes both a mode of knowing by abstraction and the concepts which result from such knowing). Origen's texts combine anti-modalist and anti-'Gnostic' concerns to argue that the Word/Wisdom/Son is truly distinct, yet stands in a unique relationship to the Father. The resultant picture appears, from the hindsight provided by the fourth century, to look 'subordinationist'; but insofar as this term tries to describe intent, it fails. Origen's intent, when understood in polemical context, is to shape a picture of a Son who is distinct, yet in a unique relationship to the one whose Word he is. Particular circumstances shape developments that, in turn, are recast when new polemical contexts emerge.

42.3 THE FOURTH-CENTURY CONTROVERSIES

In the case of the Trinitarian controversies of the fourth century, we see many further examples of the relationship between polemic and development. Thinking in a little detail about these disputes is particularly important, because of the influential nature of the accounts of the Trinity that became the core of Christian orthodoxy in the last decades of the century. These accounts became the basis for medieval Latin and Greek theology, as well as providing the cornerstone of Protestant theologies in western Europe in the sixteenth century.

Rather than seeing Arius as the starting point and eponymous anti-hero of these controversies, recent scholarship has seen his views as the flashpoint for a battle between pre-existing and already divergent traditions of thought. Such scholarship has suggested that we need to get behind the label 'Arian', which was itself the product of fourth-century attempts to identify particular sets of ideas as 'other' and heretical (Ayres 2004; Barnes 1998; Hanson 1988; R. D. Williams 2002). Trying to move beyond such terms, however, involves the scholar in a series of complex choices about where to begin narrating the story. Virtually all recent accounts have tried to suggest the shape of the tensions within which the dispute between Arius and his bishop Alexander could lead to such a widespread controversy. Within these wider conflicts, disputes over particular formulae that later become important (such as *homoousios*) must be considered against the background of two other concerns. First, such formulae frequently become prominent for purposes of polemic or compromise, and are not deeply rooted in the imagery and language of a particular tradition. Richard Vaggione has helpfully explored the distinction between the 'primary dogmatic formulae' which members of a given tradition may treat as central markers of true Christian faith and the terminology used to negotiate agreements between traditions. Only gradually do the formulae that later become defining markers of orthodoxy take on the density of meaning and strong adherence that are accorded traditional local formulae (Vaggione 1982).

Second, disputes such as that between Origen and his opponents and between the various parties of the fourth century are best understood as disputes about the 'grammar' of divinity:

The use of the term 'grammar' in theological and philosophical discussions has become both frequent and at times confusing: when I use the term, I mean a set of rules or principles intrinsic to theological discourse, whether or not they are formally articulated. If, for instance, a theologian argues that the Son is 'God' but not 'true God', that argument implies the possibility of degrees of deity and a rule that will allow a flexible application of 'God'. Similarly, questions about whether or not the Logos was 'breathed forth' for interaction with the creation or just breathed forth eternally also imply principles about whether the rules for speaking about God will allow some sort of semi-temporal change in God's being.

(Ayres 2004: 14)

The clear articulation of an absolute distinction between Creator and creation (and also between 'creating' and 'begetting') on the part of Nicene and pro-Nicene theologians in the fourth century certainly marks a significant development in Christian thought. In particular, it pushes theologians to find new ways of articulating distinctions between God and Word that might previously have been negotiated by suggesting differences in ontological status. Similarly, clarity about this distinction formed significant background to late fourth-century polemic over the Spirit. It was no longer possible to distinguish Father, Son, and Spirit by according them degrees of divinity and highly distinct roles. The emergence of Nicene theologies sharing such beliefs also shaped the theology of their opponents. Non-Nicenes of various stripes were now forced to articulate with more clarity how they envisaged the distinctions between the 'true' God, Son, and Spirit. Once again, polemical context was the context for development.

We will eventually offer a summary account of the key principles that recent scholarship has seen as constituting late-fourth century Nicene theology. But before doing so, it is important to take a step back and consider three themes of early Christian discussion about the nature of God that have been the subject of much recent scholarship.

42.4 GNOSTICISM

Scholars working on the early Christian doctrine of God will inevitably encounter a relatively amorphous group of texts and ideas that go under the label 'Gnosticism'. While debate continues to rage about the nature and origins of this group or set of groups, there is little question but that the debates of the early Christian centuries surrounding them played a key role in the development of Christian doctrine. Even after they had stopped writing direct polemical treatises against Gnostics, Christians of all persuasions continued to try to associate new enemies with discredited Gnostic ideas. For example, scholarship on the fourth-century Trinitarian controversies has consistently noted the continuing influence of second- and third-century anti-Gnostic polemic, coupled with new concerns with Manichaeism (e.g. R. D. Williams 1983). Anti-Gnostic authors were bewildered by the Gnostic tendency to multiply layers of divine reality, cascading downwards from a supreme God to lower beings sometimes called *aeons*, which are often hypostasized abstractions, such as 'Life', 'Wisdom', 'Church', and 'Thought'. To heresiologists, this scheme of emanation appeared irreducibly materialistic, and hence unbefitting to the divine. The reaction against this provoked anti-Gnostic Christians to articulate with greater clarity their own account of how, for instance, God gives rise to his Son or Word or Wisdom, without falling into materialistic explanations. Gnosticism provoked a wide range of authors, including Irenaeus, Hippolytus, Origen, and Arius, to clarify the distinction between God and the material world.

Understanding of Gnosticism itself has advanced considerably from Harnack's description of it as an instance of the 'acute Hellenization' of the gospel. Scholars have reconsidered the origins of Gnosticism and now suggest that it arose from varieties of Hellenistic Judaism or from within Christianity itself. In addition to this attention to general issues dealing with Gnosticism's origins, there has been a series of critical reassessments of individual figures traditionally associated with Gnosticism. These studies have led us to question the extent to which the ancient heresiological distinctions between 'orthodox' and 'Gnostic' were as rigid and obvious in the second century CE as earlier scholars had assumed. This reassessment allows us to reread certain allegedly 'Gnostic' authors within intellectual traditions that are more 'mainstream'. For instance, Christoph Markschies (2000b) has reconstructed the theology of Valentinus and Ptolemy, two second-century teachers in Rome who have, since the second century, been lumped in with the elaborate mythological forms of Gnosticism such as one finds in some Nag Hammadi texts. Ptolemy's theology appears to bear the imprint of contemporary Platonism, but does not recklessly multiply levels of divine being. Markschies proposes that Ptolemy's doctrine of God may actually have been motivated by a desire to refute what he took to be the extreme position of Marcion (or someone like him). Ptolemy argues that a divine intermediary, identified with Christ, is the agent who gave the Law and who saves Christians. Ptolemy, who had so long been considered a heresiarch of mythological Gnosticism, with its proliferation of levels of divine being, begins to appear a little closer to those contemporaries such as Justin Martyr who have traditionally been labelled 'catholic'. Only with caution should one assume extensive links between authors like Ptolemy and the anonymous texts found at Nag Hammadi. That being said, even for the latter, a number of links have been observed between Gnostic theology and the theology prevalent in contemporary Platonism, especially in the area of negative theology (M. A. Williams 2000). The notion of Gnostic theology as wholly 'other'—whether this be considered external to Christianity, as for Harnack, or outside classical Mediterranean culture generally, as for the 'history-of-religions school'—has faded.

42.5 JUDAISM AND CHRISTIANITY

The demise of the Harnack and Bauer theses has also enabled significant new work on both the separation of Judaism and Christianity (and the developments in both that this involved) and the ongoing presence within Christianity of ex-egetical themes going back to Jewish material from the time of Christ. A variety of scholars loosely associated with what has become known as the 'new history of religions school' have also argued that New Testament accounts of Christ are parasitic on contemporary Jewish notions of a quasi-divine entity who stands in a unique relationship to God and may be described as his glory, image, or power and as containing his 'name' (Segal 1977, 1999; Hurtado 2003). This reappraisal may also be seen in recent discussion of the second-century writers known as the 'apologists', and particularly in discussion of the 'Logos' theology that they have frequently been taken to exhibit. In older standard accounts, this theology involves the adaptation from Stoic and Middle Platonic resources of the idea of a divine reason that comes forth from God before the creation of the world in order to act within it. Such a theology forces upon its adherents, so the standard account assumes, a 'subordinationist' theology in which the Logos stands between creation and Creator. Recent work has emphasized both the variety of theologies which use this terminology, the importance of seeing how it is combined with other themes, and its exegetical bases in contemporary Jewish thought (see Edwards 1995, 2000; Barnes 2001).

Recent scholarship has seen some significant attempts to argue that we speak far too easily about the distinctness of Christianity and Judaism even as late as the fourth century, though these proposals remain very controversial (Boyarin 2004). Whether or not Boyarin's account is sustained in future scholarship, a num-ber of other scholars have also argued that Jewish theological traditions persist within later Christian traditions far more than is acknowledged within scholar-ship indebted to Harnackian perspectives. Particularly significantly, later traditions in which the Word or Christ is seen in glowing form (i.e. as 'glory' or 'light') and traditions of what is loosely termed 'anthropomorphite' theology may well represent the continuing presence within Christianity of ancient Jewish material (Golitzin 2002, 2003). Seeing the continuing interaction of Christianity and Judaism in this way is very different from earlier scholarly models within which 'Jewish Christianity' was imagined as a small, discrete sect within developing Christianity remaining faithful to Jewish food laws and exegetical patterns but largely with-out influence on the broader shape of Christian thought. This way of imagining the continuing influence of Jewish traditions on Christianity may also help us to understand *some* of the controversy provoked among Nicene theologians in the late fourth century. Traditions that went along with Nicene developments in refusing a clear ontological hierarchy between Father, Son, and Spirit may still have made use of imagery of the Word as having a discernible form and visi-ble existence. When such thinkers came into contact with mainstream insistence on the divine invisibility and simplicity, the language of glory and light would need either to be read as metaphorical or there might be conflict among parties who had previously seen themselves as allies (and this may have been a factor in

Egyptian controversies over the divine form and visibility at the end of the fourth century).

42.6 THE INFLUENCE OF POST-CLASSICAL PHILOSOPHICAL TRADITIONS

Scholarship on the doctrine of God has progressed beyond the view that there was a monolithic 'Greek' or 'philosophical' way of talking about God, which early Christian authors appropriated more or less uncritically. The best scholarship in this area is now highly attuned to the complexities both within the philosophical traditions and in their appropriation by Christians, and are much less inclined to see these traditions' views of God as somehow inherently opposed to a 'pure', 'biblical' view. The idea of a fundamental opposition between 'philosophical' and 'biblical' traditions has been discredited, in part, because of a more nuanced understanding of the nature of philosophy in the post-classical period (roughly the period following the death of Aristotle and including both the 'Hellenistic' schools and late ancient philosophy). In particular, two related, problematic assumptions that once commanded scholarly consensus have begun to unravel.

First, many scholars in previous generations assumed that early Christian authors drew directly on philosophers from the so-called classical period, specifically Plato and Aristotle. This assumption led scholars to neglect the importance of intervening developments in philosophy during the Hellenistic and late ancient periods. Second, there was a widespread interpretation of post-classical philosophy as a 'dark age' in which superstition and dogmatism clouded the 'pure' rationalism of Plato and Aristotle. This way of reading late ancient philosophy still rears its ugly head in some accounts of late Platonism as 'mystical' and 'religious' *rather than* 'rational' and 'philosophical'. Hellenistic and late ancient philosophers are viewed as philosophically interesting in their own right (the work of Dillon and Sorabji has been central in showing the complex developments that occurred in the Platonic tradition and in commentary on the available corpus of Aristotle: e.g. Dillon 1996; Sorabji 1990). Influential work by Pierre Hadot and Martha Nussbaum, among others, has argued that philosophical schools were dedicated to developing a 'way of life' and cultivating the self through a form of 'therapy', aspects that we might more commonly associate with religious movements (Hadot 1995; Nussbaum 1994). Against this background, scholars interested in identifying philosophical influence on early Christian thinkers now focus not primarily on parallels in Plato and Aristotle themselves, but on the more proximate engagements of Christians with Hellenistic and late antique philosophers.

A central aspect of the now-discredited reading of late ancient philosophy was the evaluation of it as 'eclectic', where this referred to attempts to mix together doctrines that are in fact incompatible (Zeller 1883). The notion that a weak-minded 'eclecticism' or 'syncretism' was central to late ancient philosophy (particularly to Platonism) has been by and large abandoned, especially in its evaluative component (Donini 1988). To be sure, there was mutual influence among the philosophical schools, especially cross-pollinization between the followers of Plato and Aristotle in late antiquity. A key reason for this, which may seem shocking to students who cut their philosophical teeth on modern textbook accounts of ancient philosophy, was the Neoplatonist thesis that the two were in fundamental agreement. For many Platonists, Aristotle was the greatest commentator on Plato. Yet, none of these extramural influences, including the influences of non-Christian schools on Christians, necessarily implies that this was a sub-philosophical period; to label doctrines from different schools as a priori incompatible is surely to beg the question. For instance, the Bible speaks of God as powerful and of Christ as the power of God. Philosophers of the period also developed technical accounts of the concept of 'power'. As Michel Barnes has demonstrated, Christians like Gregory of Nyssa found such accounts quite useful in interpreting the scriptural language about God (Barnes 2001). It is unclear why we should view this as eclecticism in the negative sense.

One crucial insight that has arisen in recent scholarship is the distinction between a philosophical school's doctrines and its methodology, including the sources it finds authoritative (Boys-Stones 2001). What held 'Platonism' together was less a set of doctrines and more a common attribution of authority to Plato (Sedley 1997). A similar account could be given for early Christianity: the various, sometimes conflicting ideas of God held by early Christians can be seen as presupposing a common ascription of authority to Christian scripture. This commitment to Christian authorities also shaped Christian uses of non-Christian philosophical materials. Older scholarship presupposed an equation between being Christian and holding the pure biblical doctrine of God, and consequently took the borrowing by early Christians of philosophical doctrines, such as Platonist views about divine simplicity, as evidence of eclectic mixing of incompatible views (e.g. Stead 1989). However, in light of the distinction between doctrines and method, the inference to eclecticism no longer follows: it is conceivable that one can use another school's doctrines to explicate the texts and traditions to which one is more fundamentally committed. One can now view such instances of borrowing as attempts to clarify issues raised by Christian authorities, such as troublesome biblical passages and traditions of debate about and commentary on them.

Whether they are explicitly drawing on this distinction or not, scholars generally no longer seek to 'explain' central Christian doctrines like the Trinity solely by reference to some purported non-Christian source. Augustine's Trinitarian doctrine, for instance, is no longer viewed as a mildly Christianized version of a Neoplatonic triad. Yet this does not imply that Augustine was uninfluenced by Neoplatonism. Rather, it means that scholars are looking for more precise influences, rather than reductionistic pseudo-explanations (Manchester 1992; Ayres forthcoming). In sum, better overall understanding of the nature of post-classical philosophy has allowed patristic scholars to be more precise about the question of philosophical influence on early Christian theology.

42.7 THE SHAPE OF TRINITARIAN ORTHODOXY

We are now in a position to consider the classical Christian doctrine of God as it emerged by the end of the fourth century. It is, of course, difficult to summarize principles found in a variety of theologians and theological traditions, but recent scholarship enables an attempt. It should also be noted that this summary identifies both shared themes *and* shared points of continuing controversy and argument. The emergence of pro-Nicene orthodoxy certainly involved the rejection of certain options that were previously part of Christian traditions, but this was itself also a reshaping of the boundaries of ongoing argument and debate. This ongoing debate can be seen, for example, in the 'tri-theist' controversy of the sixth century, and can also be seen a little more indirectly as a factor in the Christological controversies of the fifth century (discussed briefly in the last section of the chapter).

The first key theme is that God is a trinity constituted by Father, Son, and Spirit, or God, Word, and Spirit. During the fifth and sixth centuries the terminology of *hypostasis* and *ousia* in Greek and *persona* and *natura* in Latin became standard terminologies to identify what in God is three and what one, but during the late fourth century itself a wide variety of terms were used. For both Greek and Latin theologians, the Father is the source of Son and Spirit, and thus this summary follows much recent scholarship in denying a fundamental division between Latin and Greek Trinitarian theology in this period (Ayres 2004; Barnes 1995, 1997). Pre-fourth-century accounts frequently used the particular and immediate dependence of Son and Spirit on the Father as a way of arguing either for the unique status of those two over against all other heavenly and earthly realities, or for demonstrating the superiority of the Father. One central principle of pro-Nicene theology is that the three work inseparably. The doctrine of inseparable operations argues not only that all three divine Persons undertake the same operations (particularly those that are assumed to be the prerogative of God, such as creating and saving) but that in each activity all three are inseparably at work. For example, both Gregory of Nyssa and Augustine describe each divine action as being an activity of the Father through the Son in the Spirit.

In pro-Nicene theology the eternal generation of the Son and the eternal breathing of the Spirit are frequently taken as demonstrating the eternally generative and creative nature of God. The divine activities of creating and saving mirror the fact that the Father eternally gives life itself to the Son (and to the Spirit). For Gregory of Nazianzus the threeness of the divine existence is itself an expression of perfection in the Godhead. A fear of quasi-modalist theologies (primarily those of Marcellus of Ancyra and Photinus of Sirmium) seems to have made Nicene theologians wary of using late Platonist accounts of outward flow and return to characterize generation, procession, and the life of God (such accounts begin to make an appearance with the Pseudo-Dionysian corpus and become important long after our period in such medieval Latin theologians as Jan van Ruusbroec).

The second key theme of pro-Nicene theology is that the divine Persons are understood as together constituting the divine nature or essence or power as a simple reality, both absolutely distinct from the creation and yet immanently present in, sustaining, and guiding the creation (God is usually presented as Being itself, rather than as beyond being). God is also understood to be immaterial and invisible. For God to be simple implies that God is incomposite and indivisible, but for late fourth-century theologians it also implies that God's being is unique and in some sense unknowable (as we discuss below). By the time pro-Nicene theology emerged, Christians had for centuries been speaking of God as simple. Not *all* early Christians believed that God was immaterial and simple. The occasional early Christian, such as Tertullian in the second century and Philoxenus of Mabburg in the fifth, espoused a more 'Stoic' understanding of God and the soul as material. This is a position distinct from those of late fourth-century monastic figures labelled 'anthropomorphites', who held that the Second Person of the Trinity was not only material, but had a human form. Neither position should be seen as the more basic or earlier view, which was replaced by the more 'Platonist' understanding of God as immaterial. Christians were able to articulate many positions in the pre-Nicene period, and while a view of immaterial simplicity came to dominate Christian thought in the late fourth century, exceptions could still be found.

Those who held God to be simple put the idea to multiple, indeed mutually incompatible, uses. A range of early theologians—from Clement of Alexandria and Origen to some Nag Hammadi authors—had used the doctrine of simplicity to distinguish the simple Father from the Son, who was viewed as an intermediary between God's simple unity and the complex multiplicity of the world. Often this tradition had associated the Father's simplicity with his utter unknowability. By contrast, others like Irenaeus of Lyons held that since God causes all things, God contains all things in himself, and that this is compatible with divine simplicity. For Irenaeus, the way this works is that God is immaterial mind (*nous* in Greek), which contains its objects in an indivisible manner.

Both of these traditions drew on contemporary philosophical theology. Taken together, they raise important questions: if God is simple, does this mean (a) that he is beyond all multiplicity or (b) that he somehow contains apparent multiplicity, but indivisibly? One radically subordinationist tradition of the late fourth century, whose principal protagonist was Eunomius of Cyzicus, took the first of these options, (a). However, unlike Clement, who took God's transcendence of multiplicity to imply that God has *no* inherent properties, Eunomius took it to imply that God has but *one*, with which he is identical. The late fourth-century pro-Nicenes can be seen as taking the second option, (b). Father, Son, and Spirit are somehow the one, simple God. Clearly, we are dealing here with a unique reality, and it is not surprising that these same theologians came to stress the incomprehensibility of God to human minds. But we should not overlook the fact that they did attempt to articulate what force the concept of simplicity retained in such a context.

Gregory of Nyssa described God's simplicity in terms of purity and perfection. According to Gregory, to say God is simple is to say that any attribute he possesses he possesses by nature or essentially, rather than by participation (Balás 1966). God is essentially goodness, power, wisdom, life, light, justice, and so forth. The (apparent) multiplicity of these attributes did not bother Gregory, since each names God's essence or nature 'as a whole' (though, being simple, God is of course not a whole). This matters, because where a property belongs essentially, according to Gregory, there cannot be degrees of it: perfect goodness, for instance, cannot be more or less than itself. Now, Father, Son, and Holy Spirit all are essentially good, wise, etc. This is Gregory's way of preserving the doctrine of simplicity without excluding the Son and Spirit from true divinity. Other pro-Nicenes like Augustine developed somewhat different accounts of simplicity: for Augustine, the basic implication of simplicity is that whatever we say God 'has', God just is (Ayres 2000). In line with one of the key principles of pro-Nicene theology, both Gregory of Nyssa and Augustine—and others—took simplicity to imply further that the three Persons don't just share 'attributes', but in fact act inseparably.

We have noted that older scholarship tended to associate the doctrine of simplicity with 'Hellenization'. However, more recent scholarship tends to look at it as part of the set of concepts that Christians used to deal with problems and tensions involved in reading scripture as a coherent whole. For instance, how is one to relate the claim in 1 Timothy 6: 16 that God (the Father) 'dwells in unapproachable light' to the many claims in John's Gospel and elsewhere that the Son is the 'true light'? For the pro-Nicenes, the doctrine of simplicity addressed this—and other—exegetical puzzles directly: light is one of the properties that God just is essentially, and there is no variation between the light of the Father and that of the Son. To be sure, the Father and Son are distinct, but not insofar as they share the simple, perfect light or goodness or power that characterize the very essence of God. To be sure, this essence remains incomprehensible to humans. But pro-Nicenes generally did not resort to speaking of divine simplicity as implying that God is beyond essence or being (though the language does occasionally appear in passing remarks). Rather, they tended to speak of God's being as something that we can describe with terms like goodness and light, albeit incompletely and in a manner proportionate to our progress in likeness to God.

The third key theme is that growing in knowledge of God involves the gradual purification of the soul from its obsessions with material imagery. This can be seen in thinkers as diverse as Gregory of Nazianzus and Augustine of Hippo. The term 'purification' here is intended to indicate that this process is not understood as a purely intellectual task achieved by developing skill in dialectic and abstraction. Rather the soul's purification involves growth in humility and virtuous living, the conforming of oneself to the model laid out by Christ and by the descent of the Word into Christ.

Pro-Nicene theologians struggle to describe the character of human knowledge of God. They frequently assert that the divine being or essence is unknowable even while they also assert that the particularities of the divine Persons can be known through the divine action in the world (clear and consistent division between the divine 'essence' and 'energies', a division important in Byzantine theology, is not a feature of pro-Nicene theological epistemology). At this point we should also note that pro-Nicenes use analogies when speaking of God in a variety of ways. Some are happy to speak of the possibility of analogy (based on the participation of all created things in the Creator), but insist on the importance of not deploying analogies in ways that might lead us to think that we have comprehended the nature of divinity; others deny that any analogy (understood basically as analogy of proportion) is possible. While many early Christian authors seem to have been familiar with technical philosophical and rhetorical discussion of analogy (and especially in the fourth century occasionally discuss the specific question of how one should use analogies of God), the character of analogy was not yet the topic of an extensive technical debate within theology itself (such as we find in medieval theology after Boethius. For an introduction to these later discussions, see Ashworth 2004). Two of the most significant attempts to resolve tensions between asserting God's knowablity and unknowability are to be found in Gregory of Nyssa and Augustine. Gregory develops a complex account of the possibility of an endless progress in knowledge of God (Daniélou 1944; Balthasar 1995; Heine 1975). Augustine makes a significant contribution through his account of faith as standing in for vision until after the Judgement. Both treat the divine being as fundamentally intelligible and the possibility of growth in knowledge both now and in the final vision.

42.8 NEGATIVE THEOLOGY AND MYSTICISM

It might seem odd to include a discussion of negative theology in a section on knowledge of God, since negative theology is precisely the denial that one has such knowledge. However, early Christian accounts of how one knows God and what one knows of God often included significant negative components. Negative theology is often summarized with curt phrases like, 'We don't know what God is, only what God is not'. Such simplifications tend to flatten the complex landscape of ancient negative theology. There was not simply one method of negative theology, but several. Most simply, many theologians could say, for instance, that 'God is not bodily', implying a positive affirmation that God has a spiritual mode of existence. More strongly, one could deny that God falls under any category of human thought: 'God is neither whole nor part, neither good nor bad', and so forth. Linked with this, though sometimes distinguished from it, was the method of abstraction (*aphairesis* or *analusis*), originally a geometrical notion whereby one conceived of the geometrical point by mentally taking away shapes, then lines, then length, breadth, and depth (Macleod 1983). Finally, in late Platonism and Christians such as Pseudo-Dionysius, the notion of a 'hypernegation'—that is, a negation even of one's negation—developed. One could accept one or more of these, while refusing others.

Scholarship on negative theology has been profoundly influenced by the work of E. R. Dodds. Before Dodds, it was widely held that the theme of an 'unknown God' in Neoplatonism and Christianity resulted from 'oriental' influence, darkening the pure waters of Greek rationalism. However, Dodds argued that philosophical tradition was indebted on this point to none other than Plato, especially the First Hypothesis of the second part of his dialogue the *Parmenides*. Dodds argued that a theological reading of this dialogue was present in neo-Pythagorean authors of the first century CE and was highly influential on subsequent authors like Plotinus (Dodds 1928, 1963). Dodds's work has opened the door to a new reading of such influential Christian authors as Clement of Alexandria, who was demonstrably influenced by the commentary tradition on the *Parmenides* (see Lilla 1971).

In recent years, 'postmodern' interest in deconstruction and increasing interest in comparative religion have fuelled increasing attention to the negative in Christian theology generally, and early Christian studies particularly. Whatever the motivation, all work in this area is indebted to Raoul Mortley (1986). Mortley offers a historical overview of late ancient negative theology, delineating a range of methods and overturning some scholarly assumptions. For instance, while many have held Gregory of Nyssa to be a pioneer of Christian negative theology (e.g. McGinn 1991), Mortley argues that it was Gregory's doctrinal opponents, Aetius and Eunomius, who were more closely engaged with technical methods of negation. Like much of Mortley's book, this argument remains controversial.

Linked with negative theology is the issue of mysticism. Though we have a number of helpful monographs on the topic in English (Louth 1983; McGinn 1991), we still lack a clear definition of mysticism. At times, it appears to cover any theology that involves an affective and/or spiritual component. More specifically, it refers to theologies wherein there is some account of a union with God that transcends intellectual capacities. However, many issues remain controversial: for instance, it has been argued that language that appears 'mystical' to today's readers played a specific polemical role in its original historical context (Heine 1975).

Recently, historians of doctrine have turned their attention to the theme of divine incomprehensibility. To say that God is incomprehensible does not by itself imply any technical negative theology; it may refer to one's inability to grasp why a certain action of God (e.g. limited election) is just or how God can be Trinity. As we saw in the previous section, divine incomprehensibility came to the forefront of Christian discourse in the late fourth century among pro-Nicene authors (Ayres 2004). Often these theologians were concerned with denying the possibility of *katalēpsis*, a technical Stoic term referring to comprehensive, infallible knowledge, in the case of God. It may well be that pro-Nicene theologians may be understood as wanting to find a technical language in which to define what can and cannot be understood, even as they also define what can and cannot be known by reference to the character of our attitude to knowledge: we can know enough for correctly formed faith, but not enough that we can rest in our knowledge before the *eschaton*. With incomprehensibility, as with more technical negative theologies, recent scholarship has stressed the importance of looking both to immediate polemical/theological context and to Hellenistic and late ancient philosophical epistemology for background.

The theology of the Pseudo-Dionysian corpus makes a significant contribution to the development of patristic thought on divine incomprehensibility. The language of 'apophatic' and 'kataphatic' theology has frequently been applied to early Christian texts whether or not it is actually appropriate to their context, but it first receives significant discussion in the fifth-century texts attributed to Dionysius the Areopagite. Denys Turner (1995) has offered an influential account of this terminology. Turner suggests that Dionysius sees kataphatic theology as making affirmative statements about the divine on the basis of scriptural revelation. Apophatic theology then insists, first, that because God transcends the positive categories as we understand them, God can be said not to be captured by such categories. Turner argues that apophatic theology then posits a second denial: because God truly transcends our categories, one must learn to deny both affirmation and denial. Some scholars have been at pains to suggest the importance of reading Pseudo-Dionysian dynamics as rooted in the experience of early Christian ascetic and liturgical performance (Golitzin 1993, 1994; Louth 1986).

42.9 Feminist Scholarship

While many theologians and scholars of religion writing with feminist agendas have criticized the classical Christian tradition as projecting an image of the ideal rational man onto God, and thus at least implied a critique of patristic accounts, the body of feminist scholarship discussing early Christian doctrines of God in detail is not great. Scholars with explicitly feminist concerns have tended to focus on questions about the role and characterization of women within early Christian texts and institutions. We can, however, identify two streams of feminist scholarship. The first explores and critiques early Christian notions of God as implicitly projecting male ideals onto God. Rosemary Radford Ruether is a central figure here (Ruether 1993, 1998). In recent early Christian scholarship Virginia Burrus has offered a different, and more complex, critique of early Christian Trinitarianism. Burrus argues that the establishment of pro-Nicene orthodoxy also involved and served the establishment by ascetic (and episcopal) writers of an abstract ideal of male existence for all humanity (Burrus 2000).

Ruether's work already participates in a second trajectory of feminist scholarship on early Christian doctrines of God, by suggesting ways in which one can recover a specific tradition of feminist concerns embedded in western religious discourse (see esp. Ruether 2005). Catherine LaCugna's *God For Us* spends considerably more time with the details of early Christian texts, and is more sympathetic to mainstream Christian tradition. She argues an agenda that is initially not specifically feminist in intention. LaCugna charges that Nicene Trinitarian theology creates an artificial and abstract discourse about God in Godself that is inattentive to the drama of redemption as given in the New Testament and in the experience of Christians. In an attempt to recover an 'authentic' Trinitarian theology, LaCugna turns to the 'relational' accounts of person that have been popular among many strands of modern theology, but she does so with a version explicitly driven by feminist and liberationist ends (LaCugna 1991: 267 ff.).

Elizabeth Johnson (1997) offers a perspective considerably more sympathetic to the shape of classical Christian Trinitarian theology, although less engaged with its details. Johnson proceeds by way of subversion and supplementation, arguing that the western Christian tradition already contains a wealth of subversive imagery that can serve feminist ends, and that traditionally male language and speech can be supplemented by the use of language revolving around the term *sophia*. Lastly, Sarah Coakley's work offers a very different example of how early Christian texts may be used within a feminist project. Coakley does not offer an overall synopsis of the direction of Christian tradition, but engages particular texts with the resources of modern feminist theory, exploring how pre-modern Christian discussion of desire, gender, and theological practice may aid the Christian feminist (e.g. Coakley 2002: 55–68, 153–67).

42.10 DIVINE SUFFERING

One significant theme in reconsideration of the doctrine of God in recent scholarship has been debate over the idea of divine suffering. In the first part of the century, under the pressure of modern Protestant theological developments, debate over the idea of divine suffering was shaped by debates over Hellenization. Many scholars felt that early Christian adherence to the doctrine of divine immutability was actually an adoption of a doctrine fundamentally non-biblical and destructive of the centrality of God's love and of Christ's suffering. The shifts in scholarly approaches that this chapter has documented have cleared the way for a range of more complex treatments of the issue. As an example we will offer some remarks on the significance of accounts of divine suffering and mutability in the Christological controversies of the fifth, sixth, and seventh centuries.

One consistent theme of scholarship on this question in recent decades is that debates over the constitution of Christ's person were deeply shaped by pro-Nicene accounts of divine existence. Once it was foundational to orthodoxy to describe the three Persons as constituting an immutable, simple, and transcendent Godhead, to what extent could one talk about the Word forming a real union with humanity in the person of Jesus (Weinandy 2000; Gavrilyuk 2004)? How far did this involve predicating change and suffering of the divine? One solution was to suggest a form of union in Christ that carefully ruled out any mixture of the divine and the human. Such an approach is to be seen particularly clearly in those theologians in the tradition of Nestorius, Diodore, and Theodoret (although it is important to remark that recent scholarship has suggested the importance of not projecting their particular emphases on to all associated with them; O'Keefe 1997). On the other hand, the approach of theologians such as Cyril of Alexandria was to insist both that God does not suffer and yet that we must say that 'the Word became flesh' and that in Christ God suffers, even if not as we do. The gradual evolution of the doctrine of the communication of idioms (*communicatio idiomatum*) represents not only a central feature of the reading of Cyril that gradually came to define how Chalcedon was to be interpreted, but also one of the central places where theologians have attempted to define precisely what remains mysterious about Christian accounts of God's action in Christ. In the first place (for theologians who developed this theology), because of the true union that occurs when the Word takes on an individual human nature, it is essential that Christians confess that in Christ the Word suffers and dies, and that in Christ a human being is creator and saviour. In the second place, because the mode and manner of this union remain incomprehensible, human beings cannot grasp how God both suffers and yet does not (Smith 2001).

42.11 CONCLUSION

Just as every author must come to realize that her or his book sits on the library shelf next to many others, and that no authors control the reception of their own work, so modern scholars should be wary of assuming that their particular concerns and questions represent the final word on a topic. Harnack and Bauer profoundly shaped the scholarly study of the early Christian doctrine of God, even though, as we have seen, their views no longer carry the day. The trends in recent scholarship that we have outlined represent in broad strokes the current state of the question; but just as the pro-Nicene figures discussed above believed that one never stops growing in knowledge of God, so too will scholarship on their contributions in this area continue to evolve. As will be clear from the beginning of the chapter, current scholarship on the early Christian doctrine of God occurs in a context in which many older narratives about the development of doctrine—both its course and its character—have come under significant question. For the foreseeable future, perhaps, students of the period will find themselves focused on detailed study of particular shifts and engagements, looking towards grand narratives with some hesitation.

SUGGESTED READING

References provided in the body of this chapter indicate key pieces of secondary literature. Throughout the bibliography we have tried, where possible, to restrict ourselves to literature in English. For a general introduction to the development of the doctrine of God throughout this period, see Studer (1993). The older text of Kelly (1977) provides little information on the wider cultural and philosophical influences on early Christian thinkers, but much useful information on doctrinal positions. For the use of philosophical traditions by Christians, see Stead (1994). The primary sources relevant to the topic of this article are obviously too numerous to be listed here. A useful collection of primary sources for the Trinitarian debates can be found in Rusch (1980).

BIBLIOGRAPHY

ASHWORTH, E. J. (2004), 'Medieval Theories of Analogy', in E. N. Zalta (ed.), *The Stanford Encyclopedia of Philosophy*, <http://plato.stanford.edu/entries/analogy-medieval>.

ATHANASSIADI, P., and FREDE, M. (1999) (eds.), *Pagan Monotheism in Late Antiquity* (Oxford: Clarendon Press).

AYRES, L. (2000), 'The Fundamental Grammar of Augustine's Trinitarian Theology', in R. Dodaro and G. Lawless (eds.), *Augustine and his Critics* (London: Routledge), 51–76.

AYRES, L. (2004), *Nicaea and Its Legacy: An Approach to Fourth Century Theology* (Oxford: Clarendon Press).

—— (forthcoming), *Augustine and the Trinity* (Cambridge: Cambridge University Press).

BALÁS, D. (1966), *Metousia Theou: Man's Participation in God's Perfections According to Saint Gregory of Nyssa* (Rome: I. B. C. Libreria Herder).

BALTHASAR, H. U. VON (1995), *Presence and Thought: An Essay on the Religious Philosophy of Gregory of Nyssa*, trans. M. Sebanc (San Francisco: Ignatius Press).

BARNES, M. R. (1995), 'De Régnon Reconsidered', *AugStud* 26: 51–79.

—— (1997), ' "One Nature, One Power": Consensus Doctrine in Pro-Nicene Polemic', *StPatr* 29: 205–23.

—— (1998), 'The Fourth Century as Trinitarian Canon', in L. Ayres and G. Jones (eds.), *Christian Origins: Theology, Rhetoric and Community* (London: Routledge), 47–67.

—— (2001), *The Power of God*: Δύναμις *in Gregory of Nyssa's Trinitarian Theology* (Washington D.C.: Catholic University of America Press).

—— and Williams, D. H. (1993), *Arianism after Arius* (Edinburgh: T & T Clark).

BAUER, W. (1971), *Orthodoxy and Heresy in Earliest Christianity* (Philadelphia: Fortress Press; 1st pub. 1934).

BEHR, J. (2001), *The Way to Nicaea* (Crestwood, NY: St Vladimir's Seminary Press).

—— (2004), *The Nicene Faith*, 2 vols. (Crestwood, NY: St Vladimir's Seminary Press).

BOYARIN, D. (2004), *Border Lines: The Partition of Judaeo-Christianity* (Philadelphia: University of Pennsylvania Press).

BOYS-STONES, G. R. (2001), *Post-Hellenistic Philosophy: A Study of its Development from the Stoics to Origen* (Oxford: Oxford University Press).

BURRUS, V. (2000), *'Begotten, not made': Conceiving Manhood in Late Antiquity* (Palo, Alto Calif.: Stanford University Press).

COAKLEY, S. (2002), *Powers and Submissions* (Oxford: Blackwell).

DANIÉLOU, J. (1944), *Platonisme et théologie mystique: Doctrine spirituelle de Saint Grégoire de Nysse*, 2nd edn. (Paris: Aubier).

—— (1964), *History of Early Christian Doctrine before the Council of Nicaea*, i: *The Theology of Jewish Christianity* (London: Darton, Longman, and Todd).

DILLON, J. (1996), *The Middle Platonists, 80 B.C. to A.D. 220*, rev. edn. (Ithaca, NY: Cornell University Press).

DODDS, E. R. (1928), 'The Parmenides of Plato and the Origin of the Neoplatonic "One" ', *CQ* 22: 129–42.

—— (1963), *Proclus: The Elements of Theology*, 2nd edn. (Oxford: Clarendon Press).

DONINI, P. (1988), 'The History of the Concept of Eclecticism', in J. M. Dillon and A. A. Long (eds.), *The Question of 'Eclecticism: Studies in Later Greek Philosophy* (Berkeley: University of California Press), 15–33.

EDWARDS, M. J. (1995), 'Justin's Logos and the Word of God', *JECS* 3: 261–80.

—— (2000), 'Clement of Alexandria and his Doctrine of the Logos', *VC* 54: 159–77.

GAVRILYUK, P. L. (2004), *The Suffering of the Impassible God: The Dialectics of Patristic Thought* (Oxford: Clarendon Press).

GOLITZIN, A. (1993), 'The Mysticism of Dionysius Areopagita: Platonist or Christian?', *Mystics Quarterly*, 19: 98–114.

—— (1994), *Et introibo ad altare dei: The Mystagogy of Dionysius Areopagita* (Thessalonica: Patriarchikon Idruma Paterikon Meleton).

—— (2002), ' "The Demons suggest an illusion of God's glory in a form": Controversy over the Divine Body and Vision of Glory in Some Late Fourth, Early Fifth Century Monastic Literature', *Studia Monastica*, 44: 13–43.

—— (2003), 'The Vision of God and Form of Glory: More Reflections on the Anthropomorphite Controversy of A.D. 399', in J. Behr and A. Louth (eds.), *Abba: The Tradition of Orthodoxy in the West: Festschrift for Bishop Kallistos (Ware) of Diokleia* (Crestwood, NY: St Vladimir's Seminary Press), 273–97.

HADOT, P. (1995), *Philosophy as a Way of Life: Spiritual Exercises from Socrates to Foucault*, ed. A. I. Davidson, trans. M. Chase (Oxford: Blackwell).

HANSON, R. P. C. (1988), *The Search for the Christian Doctrine of God: The Arian Controversy 318–381 AD* (Edinburgh: T & T Clark).

HARNACK, A. VON (1958), *The History of Dogma*, iv, trans. N. Buchanan (New York: Russell & Russell).

HEINE, R. E. (1975), *Perfection in the Virtuous Life* (Philadelphia: Philadelphia Patristic Foundation).

HILL, C. (2004), *The Johannine Corpus in the Early Church* (Oxford: Oxford University Press).

HÜBNER, R. M. (1999), *Der Paradox Eine: Antignostischer Monarchianismus im Zweiten Jahrhundert* (Leiden: E. J. Brill).

HURTADO, L. (2003), *Lord Jesus Christ: Devotion to Jesus in Earliest Christianity* (Grand Rapids, Mich.: Eerdmans).

JOHNSON, E. (1997), *She Who Is: The Mystery of God in Feminist Discourse* (New York: Crossroad).

KELLY, J. N. D. (1972), *Early Christian Creeds*, 3rd edn. (London: Longman).

—— (1977), *Early Christian Doctrines*, 5th edn. (London: A. C. Black).

LACUGNA, C. M. (1991), *God For Us: The Trinity and Christian Life* (New York: Harper-Collins).

LE BOULLUEC, A. (1985), *La notion d'hérésie dans la littérature grecque IIe–IIIe siècles*, 2 vols. (Paris: L'Institut d' études augustiniennes).

LILLA, S. (1971), *Clement of Alexandria: A Study in Christian Platonism and Gnosticism* (Oxford: Oxford University Press).

LOUTH, A. (1983), *The Origins of the Christian Mystical Tradition: From Plato to Denys* (Oxford: Clarendon Press).

—— (1986), 'Pagan Theurgy and Christian Sacramentalism in Denys the Areopagite', *JTS* NS 37: 432–38.

LYMAN, R. (1993), 'Topography of Heresy: Mapping the Rhetorical Creation of Arianism', in Barnes and Williams (1993), 45–62.

—— (1994), *Christology and Cosmology: Models of Divine Activity in Origen, Eusebius, and Athanasius* (Oxford: Clarendon Press).

—— (2003), 'Hellenism and Heresy', *JECS* 11: 209–22.

MACLEOD, C. (1983), 'Analusis: A Study in Ancient Mysticism', in *Collected Studies* (Oxford: Clarendon Press), 292–305.

MANCHESTER, D. (1992), 'The Noetic Triad in Plotinus, Marius Victorinus, and Augustine', in R. T. Wallis (ed.), *Neoplatonism and Gnosticism* (Albany, NY: State University of New York Press), 207–22.

MARKSCHIES, C. (2000a), *Alta Trinita Beata: Gesammelte Studien zur altchristlichen Trinität-stheologie* (Tübingen: Mohr/Siebeck).

MARKSCHIES, C. (2000b), 'New Research on Ptolemaeus Gnosticus', *ZAC* 4: 225–54.

—— (2003), *Gnosis: An Introduction*, trans. J. Bowden (London: T & T Clark).

McGINN, B. (1991), *The Foundations of Mysticism* (New York: Crossroad; London: SCM Press).

MORTLEY, R. (1986), *From Word to Silence*, 2 vols. (Bonn: Peter Hanstein).

NUSSBAUM, M. (1994), *The Therapy of Desire: Theory and Practice in Hellenistic Ethics* (Princeton: Princeton University Press).

O'KEEFE, J. (1997), 'Impassible Suffering? Divine Passion and Fifth-Century Christology', *TS* 58: 39–60.

PRESTIGE, L. (1936), *God in Patristic Thought* (London: Heinemann).

ROWE, W. V. (1994), 'Adolf von Harnack and the Concept of Hellenization', in W. Hellman (ed.), *Hellenization Revisited* (Lanham, Md.: University Press of America), 69–98.

RUETHER, R. R. (1993), *Sexism and God-talk: Toward a Feminist Theology*, with a new introduction (Boston: Beacon Press).

—— (1998), *Women and Redemption: A Theological History* (Minneapolis: Fortress Press).

—— (2005), *Goddesses and the Divine Feminine: A Western Religious History* (Berkeley: University of California Press).

RUSCH, W. G. (1980) (ed.), *The Trinitarian Controversy* (Philadelphia: Fortress Press).

SEDLEY, D. (1997), 'Plato's *Auctoritas* and the Rebirth of the Commentary Tradition', in J. Barnes and M. Griffin (eds.), *Philosophia Togata II: Plato and Aristotle at Rome* (Oxford: Clarendon Press), 110–29.

SEGAL, A. F. (1977), *Two Powers in Heaven: Early Rabbinic Reports about Christianity and Gnosticism* (Leiden: E. J. Brill).

—— (1999), ' "Two Powers in Heaven" and Early Christian Trinitarian Thinking', in S. Davis *et al.* (eds.), *The Trinity: An Interdisciplinary Study of the Doctrine of the Trinity* (Oxford: Clarendon Press), 73–95.

SMITH, J. W. (2001), 'Suffering Impassibly: Christ's Passion in Cyril of Alexandria's Soteriology', *Pro Ecclesia*, 11: 463–83.

SORABJI, R. (1990), *Aristotle Transformed: The Ancient Commentators and their Influence* (London: Duckworth).

STEAD, C. (1977), *Divine Substance* (Oxford: Clarendon Press).

—— (1989), 'Divine Simplicity as a Problem for Orthodoxy', in R. Williams (ed.), *The Making of Orthodoxy: Essays in Honour of Henry Chadwick* (Cambridge: Cambridge University Press), 255–96.

—— (1994), *Philosophy in Christian Antiquity* (Cambridge: Cambridge University Press).

STUDER, B. (1993), *Trinity and Incarnation: The Faith of the Early Church*, trans. M. Westerhoff (Collegeville, Minn.: Liturgical Press).

—— (1999), *Mysterium Caritatis: Studien zur Exegese und zur Trinitätslehre in der Alten Kirche* (Rome: Pontificio Ateneo S. Anselmo).

TURNER, D. (1995), *The Darkness of God: Negativity in Christian Mysticism* (Cambridge: Cambridge University Press).

VAGGIONE, R. P. C. (1982), '*Ouk hos hen ton gennematon*: Some Aspects of Dogmatic Formulae in the Arian Controversy', *StPatr* 17: 181–7.

WEINANDY, T. (2000), *Does God Suffer?* (Edinburgh: T & T Clark).

WIDDICOMBE, P. (1994), *The Fatherhood of God from Origen to Athanasius* (Oxford: Clarendon Press).

WILKEN, R. (2003), *The Spirit of Early Christian Thought: Seeking the Face of God* (New Haven: Yale University Press).

WILLIAMS, M. A. (1996), *Rethinking 'Gnosticism': An Argument for Dismantling a Dubious Category* (Princeton: Princeton University Press).

—— (2000), 'Negative Theologies and Demiurgical Myths in Late Antiquity', in J. D. Turner and R. Majercik (eds.), *Gnosticism and Later Platonism: Themes, Figures, and Texts* (Atlanta: Scholars Press), 272–302.

WILLIAMS, R. D. (1983), 'The Logic of Arianism', *JTS* NS 34: 56–81.

—— (1989), 'Does it Make Sense to Speak of Pre-Nicene Orthodoxy?', in R. Williams (ed.), *The Making of Orthodoxy: Essays in Honour of Henry Chadwick* (Cambridge: Cambridge University Press), 1–23.

—— (2002), *Arius: Heresy and Tradition*, rev. edn. (Grand Rapids, Mich.: Eerdmans).

YOUNG, F. (1997), *Biblical Exegesis and the Formation of Christian Culture* (Cambridge: Cambridge University Press).

ZELLER, E. (1883), *A History of Eclecticism in Greek Philosophy*, trans. S. F. Alleyne (London: Longman).

CHAPTER 43

CHRIST AND CHRISTOLOGIES

BRIAN E. DALEY, SJ

IT seems a truism to say that Christology—the interpretation of the person of Jesus in the light of the Christian canon of scripture, and of the tradition which receives it—is what early Christianity, at its heart, is all about. To recognize in Jesus, on the basis of his crucifixion and resurrection, the unexpected fulfilment of Israel's hopes for a messianic king, a 'Christ'; to understand Jesus's language about his 'Father in heaven' as expressing his sense of a unique relationship to Israel's single God, and to take him as literally God's 'only Son'; to see in him the final revealer of God's secrets and plans, the human embodiment of God's creative Wisdom, God's eternal Word of self-communication now made humanly present in time—all of this was clearly involved in the transformation of memories that led his disciples to proclaim a gospel centred on him: to proclaim that God's kingdom had begun to be real for all humanity in Jesus's death and resurrection. It was because of their understanding of who and what Jesus was (and is) that the first few generations of Christians gradually came to see themselves as forming a distinct body within the religious tradition of Israel; and it was because of their understanding of Jesus, too, that they believed they had a new message of freedom and fulfilment, as well as a new call to moral uprightness and transforming love, to offer to the pagan world.

Christology, then—to use a term originating in post-Reformation academic theology[1]—lay always at the heart of the developing worship, life, and thought of the early church, even as its vocabulary and concepts grew and changed. Our own understanding of that growth, however, has gone through a number of important changes in recent decades. This has been driven less by new archaeological or historical discoveries about late antiquity than by the publication of newly discovered texts from the early church, on the one hand, and by changes in our commonly accepted assumptions about the history of culture and ideas—including those of religion—on the other. At the same time, the development of new theological perspectives and interests has prompted modern interpreters of the history of Christian faith to ask different questions, and to look for different answers, from those their teachers had proposed in the early decades of the twentieth century.

43.1 NEW PERSPECTIVES IN CHRISTOLOGY

Christology, in fact, has moved in the last century from being a theological topic which seemed safe and uncontroversial to an area of bitter controversy and uncertainty. As late as 1954, the Catholic theologian Karl Rahner observed that for theologians of his tradition, at least, Christology was understood to be one of those areas in which all possible problems had been solved by the dense and paradoxical dogmatic formula of the Council of Chalcedon (451), which asserted that 'one and the same Lord Jesus Christ, the only begotten Son, must be acknowledged in two natures, without confusion or change, without division or separation' (Neuner and Dupuis 1981: 154, no. 615). In Rahner's view, the Christological complacency of modern Catholic thinkers suggested a surprising unawareness of the far-reaching implications of even the language of Chalcedon itself, and a failure to keep 'acquiring anew', at a deeper level of contemplative awareness, an intellectual grasp of the vision of Jesus that the community of faith already possesses (Rahner 1954, trans. 1961: 152–3).

It was precisely the discovery of the need to repossess the content and meaning of classical Christology, it seems, that led, in the middle of the twentieth century, to a questioning of some aspects of what most believers thought had been settled permanently by the Chalcedonian formula. The intrusion of modern historical consciousness—an awareness of the relativizing influence of context on ideas, a sense that all theories and dogmas are bound to the language and assumptions of a particular time and place—on the understanding of Christian doctrine and scripture, has led, in the nineteenth and twentieth centuries, to the growing realization, first among 'liberal' Protestants but eventually in more traditional branches of Reformed, Anglican, and Catholic theology, that if Jesus is, as Chalcedon proclaims, 'complete in divinity and complete in humanity, fully God and fully a human being', then some aspects of the portrait of Jesus traditionally drawn by Christian dogma needed to be seriously questioned.

Rahner, in the same article, alludes to a fundamentally mythical conception of the incarnation, according to which 'the "human" element [in Jesus] is merely the clothing, the livery, of which the god makes use in order to draw attention to his presence here with us', and adds that this conception, which can be met in the Apollinarian and 'Monophysite' conceptions of the person of Christ in the patristic period, 'probably lives on in the picture which countless Christians have of the "Incarnation", whether they give it their faith—or reject it' (Rahner 1954, trans. 1961: 156). The Scottish theologian Donald Baillie, writing in 1947 from a Protestant perspective, also points to an earlier unwillingness on the part of Christians of all the Churches to take the humanity of Christ seriously:

> Theologians shrank from admitting human growth, human ignorance, human mutability, human struggle and temptation, into their conception of the Incarnate Life, and treated it as simply a divine life lived in a human body (and sometimes even this was conceived as essentially different from our bodies) rather than a truly human life lived under the psychical conditions of humanity.

(Baillie 1956: 11)

In contrast to this tendency, modern scriptural scholarship, with its emphasis on historical setting and development, had prompted a new engagement on the part of theologians with the historicity of the humanity of Jesus emphasized, in theory at least, by the Chalcedonian dogma. Although Roman Catholic theology, in its officially sponsored form, initially resisted the introduction of historically conditioned thinking to biblical interpretation and the understanding of dogma during the Modernist controversy, by the middle of the twentieth century its perspective had begun to change radically. A gradual dissatisfaction with the deductive, curiously rationalistic character of the scholastic theological manuals used in seminary instruction drew new attention to the patristic and medieval sources of the theological tradition, and to its organic but unpredictable growth. In what came to be known as the *ressourcement* of Catholic theology, context and a sense of coherent development were given primary emphasis (Daley 2005*a*).

In the realm of Christology, this meant paying new attention to the authors and controversies of the early church, in which the classical Christian understanding of Christ's person, underlying both scholastic theology and most forms of Christian piety, was debated and formed. The object of such renewed historical study was originally to uncover lines of logical development: to see an underlying direction in the apparent twists and turns of early Christological debate, a providentially guided movement towards a final formulation 'which like a hidden entelechy had accompanied the wearisome struggles of centuries to interpret the *mysterium Christi*' (Grillmeier 1975: 548). This inner goal, coming gradually and by a kind of common intuition towards full articulation throughout the early debates, was for most students of Christology the formula of the Council of Chalcedon.

The Anglican scholar J. N. D. Kelly, for instance, in his influential handbook *Early Christian Doctrines*, sees 'the problem of Christology, in the narrow sense of the word', as 'to define the relation of the divine and the human in Christ'. Implied in New Testament confessions, and reflected in an unformed way in second- and third-century Christian documents, this issue of Jesus's personal identity as Son of God was brought to the centre of debate, Kelly argues, in 'the decision, promulgated at Nicaea (325) that the Word shared the same divine nature as the Father'; but the balanced enunciation of the central paradox of Christian faith in Jesus—that he is, as a single subject, both fully divine and fully human—awaited the final 'settlement' of the definition of Chalcedon (Kelly 1978: 138; see also pp. 280, 340–2). The much more detailed surveys of early Christology by the German Catholic scholar (later Cardinal) Aloys Grillmeier also begin from the assumption that Chalcedon's formulation is Christianity's most complete expression of the apostolic faith in the person of Christ, the norm by which the adequacy of all earlier or later attempts to express who and what Jesus is must ultimately be judged. Grillmeier writes:

If we look backwards from the year 451, the definition of the Council doubtless appears as the culmination of the development that had gone before it. If we look ahead to the centuries of Christological controversies which followed, the understanding of the Church's faith in Christ, as expressed in 451, constitutes the firm norm, as well as the great source of discord, which occupied and divided spirits. In any case, it was at Chalcedon that the decisive formulation of the Church's faith in the person of Jesus was forged.

(Grillmeier and Bacht 1952: 5)

43.2 DEVELOPMENTS IN EARLY CHRISTOLOGY

43.2.1 Second and Third Centuries

The way to this Chalcedonian formulation and beyond it—however one evaluates its role as norm for the orthodox understanding of Jesus today—was a long and twisted one. The earliest post-New Testament Christian documents that survive tend to present Jesus as a divine revealer, who had taken on human form. For instance, the Syriac hymns known as the *Odes of Solomon*, which probably date from shortly before or shortly after the year 100, invite the hearer to rejoice in the salvation that God's 'Beloved' has brought humanity through becoming like us:

> For there is a Helper for me, the Lord ...
> He became like me, that I might receive Him.
> In form he was considered like me, that I might put him on ...

> Like my nature he became, that I might understand Him.
> And like my form, that I might not turn away from him.
>
> (Ode 7. 3–6)

Ignatius of Antioch (d. *c.* 115), who may have been bishop of the very community for which the *Odes* were composed, also speaks of Jesus unhesitatingly in his letters as 'my God' (see e.g. *Eph.* 18. 2; *Rom. Inscr*; *Rom.* 3. 3; *Smyr.* 1. 1), but emphasizes even more clearly than the *Odes* do—as a point apparently contested at the time—that his flesh and his human experiences were all real (*Trall.* 9; *Eph.* 18. 2; *Smyr.* 2–3. 5). For Ignatius, the reality of Jesus's human body is the link between his divine origin and his historical role as healer and saviour for fleshly creatures.

The long debate between mainstream Christian leaders and Gnostic teachers, which began in the second century and continued, in various forms, at least through the Middle Ages, was to a large degree focused on a debate about the reality of the Saviour's flesh. For Gnostic Christianity, it was axiomatic that the moral and ritual prescriptions of Jewish scripture were given by a lesser god than the God of redemption, and that the created, material world, in which other forms of religion flourished, was in reality hostile and illusory. Understandably, then— at least according to early Christian critics of Gnosticism—the divine Saviour, Jesus, who brought to spirits imprisoned in matter a message of redemption and freedom, was thought by most Gnostic sects not to have had a real body, or to have experienced real human need or suffering (Layton 1987: 162, 198, 211, 239, 267, 293– 6, 423). For Jesus and for those who believe in him, suggests the Valentinian *Epistle to Rheginus*, 'resurrection' does not involve the material human body, even in a transformed state, but is a way of describing the spiritual enlightenment in which the soul lays aside its fleshly concerns like an old garment (see Layton 1987: 320–4).

The most articulate critic of Gnostic forms of Christianity in the second century was Irenaeus of Lyon, a native of Smyrna in Asia Minor, who travelled west and became bishop of that Roman frontier town around 185. In his massive anti-Gnostic elaboration of apostolic tradition, known as *Against Heresies*,[2] Irenaeus makes an elaborate defence of the ordinary ingredients of Christian life in the world, as the place of God's presence and salvation: the Church and its structures of authority; the Jewish scriptures and the Christian writings on which the Church's faith was based; baptism and the eucharist; the fleshly body; the Christian hope of bodily resurrection and judgement; and at the centre of all, the person of Jesus the Saviour, who can transform human life because he shares at once in God's transcendent reality and in our own. Irenaeus writes:

Just as through the disobedience of the one human being, who was shaped first from unformed earth, many became sinners and lost life, so it was right that many should be made just and receive salvation through the obedience of one human being, who was born first from a virgin (cf. Rom 5: 12–17)... But if he had not been made flesh but only appeared as flesh, his work was not truthful. What he appeared to be, then, he also was; God, summing up the ancient formation of humanity in himself in order to put sin to death, made death an empty thing and gave humanity life. Therefore his works are true...For this reason, then, the Word of God became a human being, and the one who is Son of God became Son of Man, so that the human being might receive the Word, and by accepting adoption might become a child of God.[3]

Perhaps the most influential thinker of early Christianity, at least before Augustine, was Origen of Alexandria (c. 185–253), who was also the first Christian to devote his life to scriptural interpretation. Origen's theology and exegesis are always centred on the Church's understanding of the person and work of Jesus (see e.g. *Princ.* 4. 1. 6), and his homilies often demonstrate a deep Christocentric piety (Bertrand 1951). He makes it clear that he understands Christ, at the core of his identity, to be the divine Wisdom, the Word of creation and revelation, begotten of the Father 'beyond the limits of any beginning that we can speak of or understand' (*Princ.* 1. 2. 2); it is he who grants to created intellects the share in the life and wisdom of God that is their salvation (*Princ.* 2. 6. 3). The incarnation of the Word in Jesus, therefore, implies an irreducibly twofold reality in his person (see *Princ.* 1. 2. 1), even though the agent of salvation is the Word himself—a paradox, as Origen acknowledges, that must strike the contemplative mind with utter amazement (*Princ.* 2. 6. 2).

43.2.2 Arius and Athanasius

In the fourth century, Athanasius of Alexandria made new and decisive contributions to the articulation of the Church's understanding of Jesus's personal identity. Athanasius is mainly remembered for his defence—beginning in the early 340s—of the credal formula of the Council of Nicaea (325), which he may have helped draft as a young theological advisor to Alexander, then bishop of Alexandria. The issue now was not so much the denial of Christ's flesh as the continuing influence on the conception of Christ's person of Platonic and earlier Christian ideas, which saw God's action in the world as mediated in steps. In this view, God, utterly unknowable and transcendent, created, redeemed, and sanctified his creatures through the Son and the Holy Spirit as intermediaries, who were themselves produced or created in order to accomplish the Father's will. By standing nearer to the Father in the order of creation, by participating in God's qualities and powers and carrying out his purposes, Son and Spirit could themselves be called divine, and were not of the same creaturely status as the rest of creation. Yet, according to this position, popularized by the Alexandrian priest Arius and (in a more moderate way) by the scholarly bishop Eusebius of Caesarea, the Son or Word of God, who became enfleshed in Jesus to reveal God's saving mystery, still belonged entirely to the created realm, and had a beginning in some age of time. As Arius himself pointedly observed, 'There was a point when he was not.'

For Athanasius, by contrast, the universe is brought into being and held in dynamic order by the presence within it of the eternal, transcendent Word of God, who is fully divine, or (in the phrase of Nicaea) 'of the same substance' as the one God of Israel. Wholly 'other' than the created order because he is God, the Word—as God—is also immediately present to creation, actively involved in forming it and in re-forming it when it becomes destructively alienated from its creator (Anatolios 1998). In the incarnation, the Word takes on a passible, mortal body, in order to reconstruct and reorder fallen humanity from within, and to communicate the incorruptible life that comes only from contact with God (*Inc.* 9).

For reasons that are probably as much connected to modern perceptions of his authoritarian personality and combative style as to his theological works, Athanasius has been more than a little unpopular with patristic scholars for most of the twentieth century. The main theological objection to his portrait of Christ has been that it represents an extreme form of what Grillmeier has labelled a *logos–sarx* or 'Word–flesh' (rather than a 'Word–human being') model of Christ's person: like his opponent Arius, like virtually all Greek theologians of the first three quarters of the fourth century—although unlike Origen—Athanasius has almost nothing to say about the soul or the interior human qualities and experiences of Christ, as playing a decisive role in his actions as Saviour. R. P. C. Hanson quipped that Christ's relation to the 'instrument' of his body is, for Athanasius, 'no closer than that of an astronaut to his space-suit' (Hanson 1988: 448; in response, see Anatolios 1997). As Grillmeier more moderately observed, in Athanasius's work 'the soul of Christ retreats well into the background, even if it does not disappear completely'; it is certainly not a 'theological factor' in his Christology, even if he may regard it as a 'physical factor' in Jesus's life and actions (Grillmeier 1975: 308, 325). It is the Word of God, present in the flesh of Jesus and through it to all of humanity, which communicates a vital and transforming energy that leads to the salvation of all his human brothers and sisters.

This critique of Athanasius's understanding of the person of Christ, however, distorts his intentions by judging them in light of fifth-century issues, standards he never intended to meet. His concern throughout his works is to emphasize that Jesus, the Word incarnate, embodies in his person the paradox of a transcendent, immaterial God making his own the limited, unstable realm of matter, in order to communicate to creatures the Creator's healing power and life. Athanasius's language of the Word and his bodily 'instrument' seems intended not so much as an ontological analysis of Christ's person as a way of emphasizing the contrast between God and the world of flesh, which provides the background for the astonishing proclamation of the Word's incarnation (Petterson 1995; Anatolios 1998).

43.2.3 Apollinarius and his Critics

In the standard modern narrative of the development of early Christology, however, the debates that swirled around Arius's conception of Christ as creature, and the Nicene assertion that the Son is 'of the same substance' as the Father, were essentially theological rather than Christological: arguments about the internal structure of God's transcendent being. It was only in the 360s and 370s, it is usually argued, that the focus of debate shifted from the Person or Persons of God to the personal unity of the incarnate Word—how the eternal Son and the man Jesus can be a single individual—and that the real issues of Christology as such came into focus (Studer 1993: 193–4). The key figure at this new stage of controversy was Apollinarius of Laodicea, a gifted and energetic writer and teacher in the church of Antioch during the second half of the fourth century.

Apollinarius is usually identified with the position that in the person of Christ, the eternal Word of God had simply assumed human flesh—perhaps flesh enlivened by a lower, vegetative soul, or life principle; the Word itself, Apollinarius insisted, took the place occupied in human creatures by the higher, self-determining intellectual soul, or *nous*. This version of what Grillmeier calls *logos–sarx* or Word–flesh Christology is simply a more explicit form of an understanding of Christ's person that had been assumed by most Greek theologians for the preceding century. Apollinarius emerged to prominence in the Antiochene church of the 360s: an enterprising Christian humanist and a leading voice in the Nicene movement, who was also highly critical of the 'modalist' form of anti-Arian theology, which minimized any lasting distinction between Father, Son, and Holy Spirit within the mystery of God. This position, represented in the mid-fourth century by Marcellus of Ancyra, interpreted the Nicene confession of 'one substance' in God as implying that Trinitarian language refers only to the way in which God has been experienced within salvation history. This position seems to have raised at least as much alarm in orthodox circles as Arius's theology of created mediators. Apollinarius's response was to emphasize the eternal, distinct existence of the person of Christ, and to refer to that existence, in some of his writings at least, not only in terms of the divine Word, but also in Paul's language of 'the man from heaven', in whose image we are all being renewed (1 Cor 15: 45–9; Greer 1990). Although Apollinarius clearly accepted the material reality of Christ's living body, as the instrument by which the Word acts in the world, he emphasized, in many passages of his works, that 'the Lordly human being' is substantially different from the ordinary, fallen human beings he has come to save, in that the Word himself is Christ's sole source of energy, thought, and will.

Persuasive and politically well connected in Syria and Asia Minor, Apollinarius seems at first to have won a number of admirers among Nicene churchmen opposed to a modalist theology. When he began to promote his Christological theories as normative for orthodoxy, however, and even ordained like-minded bishops to make this version of Nicene faith a new basis for ecclesial communion, former friends became increasingly resistant to his views. Another leading bishop-theologian of the Syrian church, Diodore of Tarsus, seems to have raised the alarm against Apollinarius, and he was listed among the leaders of heresies at the Council of Constantinople in 381. By the mid-380s, both Gregory of Nyssa and Gregory of Nazianzus had written strong polemics against Apollinarius's understanding of Christ, because it deprived Christ of a human intellectual soul and because it seemed to suggest that even Jesus's flesh was of a different substance from our own. In his first letter to the priest Cledonius, Gregory of Nazianzus quotes an earlier maxim of Origen to sum up his objection:

That which [Christ] has not assumed he has not healed; but that which is united to his Godhead is also saved.[4] If only half Adam fell, then that which Christ assumes and saves may be half also; but if the whole of his nature fell, it must be united to the whole nature of Him that was begotten, and so be saved as a whole.

(*Ep.* 101)

Precisely because the intellectual part of our humanity is what first needs healing, Gregory insisted, the incarnate Word must have a human intellect as well as human flesh. Salvation comes to us by Jesus' identity with us, as God fully sharing in our humanity, not by his merely providing us with an example of moral perfection to imitate.

The Christology developed by the two Cappadocian Gregories, largely in response to Apollinarius, is not, however, simply an affirmation that two wholly different realities coexist in a single agent. Both bishops tend to speak of Christ as a 'double' yet radically unified reality in which the flesh, with all its weakness and 'through the mediation of a mind', is 'mixed together with God' (Gregory of Nazianzus, *Or.* 29. 19). Both emphasize that this 'blending' of two infinitely unequal ingredients results in the transformation of what is weaker by its assimilation to what is stronger, the 'divinization' of the human element in Christ, and through him of all humanity (Gregory of Nazianzus, *Or.* 38. 13). God the Word is clearly the agent, the personal centre of Christ's actions, the source of his ability to heal our fallen state. To meditate on the person and activities of Jesus, to 'walk through' the events of his life as presented in scripture, enables the believer to 'ascend with his Godhead and no longer remain among visible things' (Gregory of Nazianzus, *Or.* 29. 18).

For Gregory of Nyssa, the assumption by the infinite and unchangeable Son of God of a full human nature—that is, as a creature always capable of change—brings about in Jesus, and through him in us, a graded transformation of the negative or limiting properties of humanity into divine qualities: the corruptible into the incorruptible, the mortal into the immortal. In the glorified Jesus, one sees the effects of the process begun in the incarnation of the Word, which eventually results in his sharing his divine qualities with us all:

He who is always in the Father, and who always has the Father in himself and is united with him, is and will be as he was for all ages.... But the first-fruits of human nature which he has taken up, absorbed—one might say figuratively—by the omnipotent divinity like a drop of vinegar mingled in the boundless sea, exists in the Godhead, but not in its own proper characteristics.

(Gregory of Nyssa, *To Theophilus against the Apollinarists*, GNO iii/1, 126. 14–21)

What has only gradually been revealed in Jesus, as his latent divinity, is promised to the rest of humanity through the refashioning of our nature (see also *Eun.* 3. 3. 68; *Or. catech.* 37).

43.2.4 The Nestorian Controversy

Perhaps the most celebrated stage in the development of early Christology came in the first half of the fifth century, in the controversy between representatives of the so-called Antiochene school of exegesis and theological interpretation, such as Theodore of Mopsuestia, Nestorius of Constantinople, and Theodoret of Cyrrhus, and the Alexandrian school, principally represented by Cyril of Alexandria. The usual way of understanding their differences is to see the Antiochene theologians as maintaining a 'Word–human being' (*Logos–anthrōpos*) model of the person of Christ, in which the eternal Word or Son of God, fully divine in nature, has taken up a complete human being to be his 'temple' (Theodore, fragments 1–2, 9; Nestorius, *Sermon*: Norris 1980, 113–17, 121, 123–31). So the Word dwells in Jesus and bestows his favour on him in such a unique way that Jesus can be seen as revealing the 'face' (*prosōpon*) of the Son in the world, while the Son provides Jesus with a divine 'face' (Nestorius, *The Bazaar of Heracleides*, 239–45, 264–8; see Scipioni 1956). The result is that while God the Son and Jesus are never to be confused into a single subject or agent, they reveal each other in a single common form. Along with this approach to understanding Christ, these authors were also known for their distinctive way of interpreting the message of scripture, in which God is understood to reveal his will and our future through human events but, as God, remains independent of history, transcendent, and uncircumscribed.

The Alexandrian school of the late fourth and fifth centuries, on the other hand, took the inspiration for its Christology from Athanasius, and for its biblical interpretation from Origen. Jesus, in Cyril of Alexandria's understanding, always remained God the Word, subsisting personally in the full humanity that he had made his own—a single divine subject acting and suffering in his own soul and flesh. To those spiritually gifted enough to seek the Bible's deeper meaning, the whole canon of scripture told his story, as well as that of the people united with him by faith and the sacraments. The active, personal presence of God in the world, which has reached its climax in Christ and the Church, is the central message of the gospel.

Conflict between these two centres of Christian study began simmering in the middle of the fourth century, doubtless from political and ecclesiastical as well as theological motives. It burst into the open, however, in the winter of 428–9, when the newly appointed bishop of Constantinople, Nestorius—a gifted preacher from Antioch, adamantly opposed to any suggestion that the Word was a creature—openly attacked the popular tradition of using the title 'God-bearer' (*Theotokos*) for Mary, the mother of Jesus, since it seemed to contradict God's transcendence:

Mary, my friend, did not give birth to the Godhead, for 'what is born of the flesh is flesh' (John 3: 6). A creature did not produce him who is uncreatable. The Father has not just recently generated God the Logos from the Virgin. . . . Rather, he formed out of the Virgin a temple for God the Logos, a temple in which he dwelt.

(Norris 1980: 124–5)

Cyril of Alexandria, an accomplished and prolific exegete and a subtle theologian, saw in Nestorius's distinctions an implied denial of the direct involvement of God in the world's history. Although the language for distinguishing between *what* God is—God's *substance* or *nature*—and *who* the Saviour is—God the Son as an individual (*hypostasis*) or 'person' (*prosōpon*)[5]—was still in its early stages of development, and the terminology applied to Father, Son, and Holy Spirit in the Trinity by the Cappadocians was not yet uniformly extended to the complex reality of Christ, Cyril—like Athanasius and Gregory of Nazianzus—stressed the single subject of the acts that have saved us: it is God the Word, God the Son, who is born of a Virgin, who receives the Holy Spirit for us in baptism, who heals the sick and raises the dead by his human touch, who dies in his passible body on the cross and reunites that body with his soul on the morning of resurrection. In an early letter criticizing Nestorius for his rejection of Mary's title *Theotokos*, Cyril sketches out what would be his basic position throughout the debate:

We do not say that the Logos became flesh by having his nature changed, nor for that matter that he was transformed into a complete human being composed out of soul and body. On the contrary, we say that in an unspeakable and incomprehensible way, the Logos united to himself, in his hypostasis, flesh enlivened by a rational soul, and in this way became a human being and has been designated 'Son of man'. . . Furthermore, we say that while the natures which were brought together into a true unity were different, there is, nevertheless, because of the unspeakable and unutterable convergence into unity, one Christ and one Son out of the two. This is the sense in which it is said that, although he existed and was born from the Father before the ages, he was also born of a woman in his flesh. . . . We assert that this is the way in which he suffered and rose from the dead. It is not that the Logos of God suffered in his own nature, being overcome by stripes or nail-piercing or any of the other injuries; for the divine, since it is incorporeal, is impassible. Since, however, the body that had become his own underwent suffering, he is—once again—said to have suffered these things for our sakes, for the impassible one was within the suffering body.

(Norris 1980: 132–3)

Here and throughout his later letters and essays, Cyril is mainly concerned to emphasize that the story of the gospels, of the birth and death and resurrection of Jesus, is not about the formal relationship of divinity and humanity, but about what the Son of God did in history for our sakes. Cyril is careful to respect the narrative sequence in the story of salvation: 'the natures which *were* brought together into a true unity *were* different', yet there *is* now 'convergence into unity, one Son out of the two'. As he insists here and in later letters, the unity of subject in the story of Jesus is 'union in *hypostasis*'—union in the concreteness of an individual existence, which, as the lived-out operation of a single organic being, can also be spoken of as 'union in nature', without ever implying by that a blurring of the infinite ontological distinction between God's uncreated being and the being of creatures (*Third Letter to Nestorius*, 4–7, trans. Wickham 1983: 18–23).

43.2.5 The Controversy around Chalcedon

The Christological differences between Nestorius and Cyril, and their respective colleagues, grew into a major church controversy in the late 420s, involving heated discussion among all the major sees. Emperor Theodosius II summoned a council at Ephesus in the early summer of 431, but the representatives of the opposing sides never met to discuss the issues, and the council members dispersed without coming to a common resolution. Only in 433, after Nestorius had been deposed from episcopal power and sent into exile, was agreement reached between the Antiochenes and the Alexandrians: a negotiated statement accepted by both sides and affirmed in a letter from Cyril to John, patriarch of Antioch, carefully crafted to include the positions that each side considered essential.

Less than 20 years later, when the principal participants in that debate had died, controversy broke out again among their followers, most of whom—on both sides—were now less willing to compromise. At issue was the degree to which Cyril's picture of the person of Christ, and some key terms and phrases from Cyril's later letters (characterizing the one Christ as 'one nature of the Word, made flesh', or speaking of the union of the divine and human in him as a 'union in hypostasis', or as a union 'from two natures' rather than 'of two natures'), should be regarded as norms for Christian confession. After a series of manifestos and excommunications, and the abortive attempt to resolve the discord at another council at Ephesus in 449, Emperor Marcian eventually succeeded in bringing a synod of bishops together at Chalcedon, across the Bosporus from Constantinople, in the autumn of 451— a gathering at which virtually all the Christian churches were to some degree represented. It was there that the famous statement of the Church's understanding of Christ was formulated—including language from both sides of the dispute, as well as from the joint statement of 433—now appended to the Creeds of Nicaea (325) and Constantinople (381) as a kind of hermeneutical norm for interpreting them in their full Christological implications.

It is important to remember, however, that the dogmatic statement of Chalcedon was not a 'settlement' of the Christological controversies that then divided the Church, as historians in the past have suggested. Partisan debate, in fact, was even more heated after the council. Several emperors in the late fifth and sixth centuries sought to downplay or even annul Chalcedon's statement of unity, in the unsuccessful hope of healing the major schisms that followed the council before they became permanent. For a large number of bishops, monks, and lay people in the eastern empire, particularly in Syria, Palestine, and Egypt, the Christology formulated at Chalcedon was an abandonment of centuries of devotion to the person of Christ, as God present in our midst in the full concreteness of a historical human being—an abandonment of the paradoxes sustained so passionately by Athanasius and Cyril, and a victory for the humanistic, overly analytical thinking of Nestorius and his Antiochene supporters. The fact that Pope Leo, and the Latin sources on which he drew, had played an influential part in the council's discussions was also not a positive recommendation to many eastern Christians. As a result, eastern Christians broke communion with the imperially sponsored Church in increasing numbers; in the 70 years after Chalcedon, a number of major theologians opposed to the council's Christology—among them Philoxenus of Mabboug in Syria, patriarch Timothy 'Ailouros' in Egypt, and Severus, a learned monk of Gaza who later became patriarch of Antioch—wrote polemical works arguing that nothing short of the Christological language of Cyril could do justice to the Church's authentic tradition of faith and practice. These writers, and the earlier sources to which they appealed, were to remain the normative 'fathers' of the Oriental Orthodox or non-Chalcedonian churches.

43.2.6 Late Patristic Developments

The Second Council of Constantinople (553), sponsored by the emperor Justinian as part of a larger programme of rebuilding church unity, issued a new set of doctrinal canons, reaffirming the formal validity, essential content, and terminology of the Chalcedonian Definition, and seeking to clarify its intent by emphasizing that the 'one *hypostasis*...acknowledged in two natures' by Christian faith is in fact none other than the eternal *hypostasis* of God the Word (canon 5), 'one of the holy Trinity' (canon 10). The council's statement also recognized legitimate and illegitimate ways of understanding the unconfused but united realities in Christ, both as 'two natures' and also—in the preferred phrase of Cyril's later letters—as 'one nature, made flesh' (canons 7–8).

Despite Justinian's goal of reconciling a fragmented eastern Christendom, the divisions that followed Chalcedon remained largely unaffected by the council of 553. While the Latin West tended to regard these new canons, along with the council's explicit condemnation of the three main doctors of the Antiochene tradition, as an implicit abandonment of the Christological balance of the Chalcedonian Definition, those eastern communities that insisted on the 'miaphysite' (one nature, made flesh) model developed by Cyril of Alexandria did not find the council's position unambiguous enough to lure them back into communion with Constantinople, and continued to maintain independent ecclesiastical structures.

In the seventh century, the Christological debate was recast in ostensibly new terms: this time due to the attempt of the patriarch Sergius of Constantinople, and his successor, Pyrrhus, to craft an official interpretation of Chalcedonian terminology in a way more acceptable to dissident eastern Christians, by affirming the single 'activity' or 'theandric operation' of the two united natures in Christ. This conception could be expressed in psychological terms by speaking of those natures—as Pyrrhus would eventually do—as possessing a single *will*: that of the divine Logos. It was Maximus the Confessor, a learned monk from Constantinople, living for more than two decades as an exile in Latin North Africa, who led the opposition to what he saw here as simply a new form of the Apollinarian hybridization of Christ. In a number of letters and essays written during the 640s, Maximus pointed out some of the further implications of the Chalcedonian picture of a single concrete individual existing in, and fully possessing, two natures—implications intuitively grasped by Augustine two centuries earlier. Every substance or nature, Maximus insisted, operates in a way characteristic of itself; if the human and the divine are distinct natures possessed by the one person of Jesus, as the Church's doctrine teaches they are, then each must have its own distinctive and integral operation, and Jesus must possess, as his own, both a limited human will and the eternal will of God the Son. The marvel of the incarnation, for Maximus, is precisely that Jesus's natures, including their wholly asymmetrical wills, operate distinctly, but in a manner that results not in conflict but in perfect harmony: 'He is divine in a human way, and human in a divine way'.[6] This further refinement of Chalcedonian Christology was confirmed in Rome at the Lateran Synod of 649, attended by Maximus and presided over by Pope Martin I—both of whom were later imprisoned and fatally mistreated, by order of the emperor Constans II, as a result of their position. It was later confirmed by Pope Agatho in a Roman synod of 680, and officially received in the East by the Third Council of Constantinople (680–1), a gathering now recognized by Orthodox and Western Christians as the Sixth Ecumenical Council of the whole Church.

43.3 CONCLUDING REFLECTIONS

Even this brief survey of the development of early Christology reveals how complex that development actually was, how many issues about God and the world lay beneath the surface of verbal formulations. The Christian understanding of the identity and role of Jesus is not the content of a proposition, which emerged slowly but steadily through a centuries-long process of conflict and debate. It is the glimpse of the central reality of the gospel, a vision of God's healing and transforming presence in the world that yokes together two incommensurables in a single paradox, 'God with us'. One factor that has led to a change of modern perspective in the understanding of that development, over the past 50 years, has been theology's growing appreciation of the historical reality of the man Jesus: this has made modern theologians more sympathetic to those ancient voices that seem to have articulated a clear sense of the operative human fullness of Jesus's being, and of the cultural and psychological limitations in which, and through which, he acted. In the 1940s and 1950s, for instance, renewed interest in the Antiochene Christology, because of its recognition of Jesus as a complete human being indwelt by the Word, led to new, positive readings of Theodore of Mopsuestia (Greer 1961; Norris 1963) and even of Nestorius (Scipioni 1956; Grillmeier 1975), despite their rejection by Chalcedon and Constantinople II. At the same time, and even through the 1980s, many historical theologians showed questioning, even hostile attitudes towards Athanasius and Cyril of Alexandria, largely because of what was thought to be their over-emphasis on the divine centre of Jesus's actions and consciousness. On the other hand, historians of theology also began to recognize, early in the twentieth century, that the Christology actually professed by the 'miaphysite' or anti-Chalcedonian theologians of the fifth and sixth centuries, such as Severus and Timothy Ailouros, and by the churches nourished on their works, was much less radical in its picture of the divine unity of Jesus's person than had been previously supposed. Their Christology, seen now as 'verbal monophysism', differed from the Chalcedonian model mainly in the unyielding insistence of these authors that orthodox faith could be expressed accurately only in the language of Cyril (Lebon 1909, 1951).

More recently, renewed emphasis on the distinctively scriptural, rather than cultural or philosophical, basis of Christian doctrine has been one of the main factors in a renewed sympathy for the work of Athanasius (Torrance 1995; Petterson 1995; Anatolios 1998) and Cyril of Alexandria (McGuckin 1994; Weinandy and Keating 2003). Interest in Cyril's Christology has probably also been aided by renewed openness among theologians to the idea of God's participation in human suffering (O'Keefe 1997; Smith 2002; Gavrilyuk 2004). Growing interest in the distinctive Christological emphases of Gregory of Nyssa (Daley 1997, 2002), Augustine of Hippo (Geerlings 1978; Drobner 1986; Daley 2005b), and Maximus the Confessor (Balthasar 1988; Bathrellos 2004), has also led to a deeper understanding of the symphony of voices interpreting the person of Christ in the early church. We now realize more clearly than we did 50 years ago that the formula of Chalcedon, its antecedents and its ultimate reception, is only one strand in a much richer and more complex theological fabric. To understand the full range of ancient Christology, we need to listen more attentively to the whole chorus, and to read individual authors not simply in the light of Chalcedon, but as Christological sources in their own right.

NOTES

1. As subjects within the discourse of faith, early Christians tended to distinguish only between *theologia*, 'language about God', which came to mean language about God as Trinity, and *oikonomia*, the narrative of God's 'management' of history, God's plan of redemption, which would of course include the story of Jesus. Christian *theologia*, however, clearly found its starting point in the Christian story of the *oikonomia*. See Eusebius of Caesarea, *Hist. eccl.* 1. 1. 7; Gregory of Nazianzus, *Or.* 38. 8.
2. A better translation might be: 'Against the Sects'. The word *hairesis*, in the Greek of the time, meant first of all a voluntary organization, and thus the set of beliefs or practices that characterized that organization—all taken in contrast with the wider body of the city or world and generally accepted beliefs.
3. This translation is based on both the ancient Latin version, which is the only complete text we now have of Irenaeus's work, and a Greek fragment of this passage.
4. This idea, expressed in slightly different terms, had already been proposed by Origen, *Dialogue with Heraclides* (SC 67. 70, ll. 17–19). Gregory's phrase is later quoted by Maximus the Confessor, *Opusculum* 9, 'To the Faithful in Sicily' (PG 91. 128D–129A). For further references, see A. Grillmeier, 'Quod non assumptum—non sanatum', in *LTK* viii. 954–5.
5. I have put 'person' in quotation marks here because the modern understanding of the person, characterized by interior self-awareness, freedom, and the ability to form relationships with other persons, was far from being fully developed in the ancient world. *Prosōpon* (originally 'face' or 'mask') suggested the role played by an actor on the stage, or by a human individual in the drama of life: an externally perceived form, what we still call a *persona*. *Hypostasis*, the other common word used in the Christological debates for an individual, simply meant a single instance of some universal substance, a logical subject of attribution.
6. Maximus repeats this maxim several times in his works; see e.g. *Ep.* 15 to Cosmas (PG 91. 573B2–9); *Ep.* 19 to Pyrrhus (PG 91. 593A2–9); *Opusculum* 4 to the Higoumen George (PG 91. 61B1–C11); *Opusc.* 7 to Marinus (PG 91. 84B11–D3); *Dialogue with Pyrrhus* (PG 91. 297D13–298A4).

SUGGESTED READING

Primary sources

The most extensive collection of English translations of early Christian theological texts (second to eighth centuries) remains the nineteenth-century series, Ante-Nicene Fathers and Nicene and Post-Nicene Fathers, which has been reprinted many times by many publishers. For texts specifically representing the Christological controversies, two useful single-volume collections stand out: Edward R. Hardy (ed.), *Christology of the Later Fathers*, LCC (Philadelphia: Westminster Press, 1954); and Richard A. Norris, Jr. (ed. and trans.), *The Christological Controversy*, Sources of Early Christian Thought (Philadelphia: Fortress Press, 1980). For more recent translations of Christological works of important authors, see Frederick Norris and Lionel Williams (trans.), *On God and Christ: St. Gregory of Nazianzus, The Five Theological Orations and Two Letters to Cledonius* (Crestwood, NY: St Vladimir's Seminary Press, 2002); Brian E. Daley, *Gregory of Nazianzus* (Abingdon: Routledge, 2006) (including Orations 38–9); John A. McGuckin (trans.), *St Cyril of Alexandria on the Unity of Christ* (Crestwood, NY: St Vladimir's Seminary Press, 1995); and Paul M. Blowers and Robert L. Wilken (trans.), *On the Cosmic Mystery of Jesus Christ: Selected Writings from St. Maximus the Confessor* (Crestwood, NY: St Vladimir's Seminary Press, 2003).

Secondary literature

The most detailed modern history of patristic discussion of the person of Christ remains that of the German Jesuit, later Cardinal, Aloys Grillmeier: first in the three-volume collection of historical studies published for the 1,500th anniversary of the Council of Chalcedon: A. Grillmeier and H. Bacht (eds.), *Das Konzil von Chalkedon: Geschichte und Gegenwart* (Würzburg: Echter, 1951–4); then in Grillmeier's own unfinished narrative, *Christ in Christian Tradition*, i (up to Chalcedon) (London: Mowbray, 1975); ii/1 (review of sources; history of Christology, 451–527) (London: Mowbray, 1986); ii/2 (Church of Constantinople, sixth century) (London: Mowbray, 1995); ii/4 (Church of Alexandria and Ethiopia) (London: Mowbray, 1996). Vol. ii/3, on the Church of Antioch and Syria, is yet to appear. Foundational essays by Grillmeier, mainly on ancient Christology, are also collected in *Mit Ihm und in Ihm* (Freiburg: Herder, 1975) and *Fragmente zur Christologie* (Freiburg: Herder, 1997). A standard, brief, clearly written survey of the development of ancient Christology is Kelly (1978), 109–37, 280–343. Important studies of the development of Christology after Chalcedon include W. H. C. Frend, *The Rise of the Monophysite Movement* (Cambridge: Cambridge University Press, 1972); and Patrick T. R. Gray, *The Defence of Chalcedon in the East (451–553)* (Leiden: E. J. Brill, 1979). A more recent and more detailed history of the growth of early theology, centred on the person of Christ, is John Behr, *The Formation of Christian Theology*; i: *The Way to Nicaea* ii: *The Nicene Faith* (Crestwood, NY: St Vladimir's Seminary Press, 2001, 2004). For an important new theological perspective on the fourth-century debates over God and Christ, see also Lewis Ayres, *Nicaea and its Legacy: An Approach to Fourth-Century Trinitarian Theology* (Oxford: Oxford University Press, 2004). An excellent general introduction to Christology, which includes discussion of patristic and medieval doctrine, is Gerald O'Collins, *Christology: A Biblical, Historical, and Systematic Study of Jesus* (Oxford: Oxford University Press, 1995).

Important recent studies of particular authors and issues include Roberta C. Chesnut, *Three Monophysite Christologies: Severus of Antioch, Philoxenus of Mabbug, and Jacob of Sarug* (Oxford: Oxford University Press, 1976); Iain R. Torrance, *Christology after Chalcedon: Severus of Antioch and Sergius the Monophysite* (Norwich: Canterbury Press, 1988); Marie-Odile Boulnois, *Le paradoxe Trinitaire chez Cyrille d'Alexandrie* (Paris: L'Institute d'études augustiniennes, 1994); Frederick G; McLeod, SJ, *The Image of God in the Antiochene Tradition* (Washington: Catholic University of America Press, 1999); Uwe Michael Lang, *John Philoponus and the Controversies over Chalcedon in the Sixth Century* (Leuven: Spicilegium

Sacrum Lovaniense, 2001); Susan Wessel, *Cyril of Alexandria and the Nestorian Controversy: The Making of a Saint and of a Heretic* (Oxford: Oxford University Press, 2004); and Paul B. Clayton, jun., *The Christology of Theodoret of Cyrus: Antiochene Christology from the Council of Ephesus (431) to the Council of Chalcedon (451)* (Oxford: Oxford University Press, 2006).

REFERENCES

Primary sources

APOLLINARIUS OF LAODICAEA, *Works and Fragments*. H. Lietzmann (ed.), *Apollinaris von Laodicaea und seine Schule* (Tübingen: J. C. B. Mohr/Paul Siebeck, 1904; photo-offset of Tübingen edn.: Hildesheim; G. Olms, 1970). Eng. trans. and edn.: Norris (1980).

ATHANASIUS, *On the Incarnation*, SC 199 (Paris: Éditions du Cerf, 1973). Eng. trans.: A. Robertson, NPNF[2] 4, 36–67.

CYRIL OF ALEXANDRIA, *Letters 2 and 3 to Nestorius, Letter to John of Antioch*, ed. and trans. L. R. Wickham, in *Cyril of Alexandria: Select Letters* (Oxford: Clarendon Press, 1983), 2–32. Also Eng. trans. and edn.: Norris (1980), 135–45.

GREGORY OF NAZIANZUS, *Oration 29*, SC 250 (Paris: Éditions du Cerf, 1978). Eng. trans.: L. Wickham, *On God and Christ* (Crestwood, NY: St Vladimir's Seminary Press, 2002), 69–92.

—— *Oration 38*, SC 358 (Paris: Éditions du Cerf, 1990). Eng. trans.: B. E. Daley, *Gregory of Nazianzus* (Abingdon: Routledge, 2006), 117–27.

—— *Letter 101*, SC 208 (Paris: Éditions du Cerf, 1974). Eng. trans.: C. G. Browne and J. E. Swallow, NPNF[2] 7, 439–43.

IGNATIUS OF ANTIOCH, *Letters*. Eng. trans. and edn.: M. W. Holmes (Grand Rapids, Mich.: Baker Books, 1992).

IRENAEUS OF LYONS, *Against Heresies*, SC 100, 152–3, 210–11, 263–4, 293–4 (Paris: Éditions du Cerf, 1965–82). Eng. trans.: A. Roberts and J. Donaldson, ANF 5 and 9.

NESTORIUS, *The Bazaar of Heracleides* [= *Liber Heraclidis*] (only in Syriac translation, P. Bedjan (ed.), *Livre d'Héraclide de Damas* (Leipzig: O. Harrassowitz, 1910); Eng. trans.: G. R. Drive and L. Hodgson (Oxford: Oxford University Press, 1925; repr. Eugene, Ore.: Wipf and Stock, 2002)).

Odes of Solomon, ed. and trans. J. H. Charlesworth (Missoula, Mont.: Scholar's Press, 1977); also in J. H. Charlesworth (ed.), *The Old Testament Pseudepigrapha*, ii (New York: Doubleday, 1985), 725–71.

NEUNER, J., and DUPUIS, J. (1981) (eds.), *The Christian Faith, in the Doctrinal Documents of the Catholic Church* (New York: Alba House).

ORIGEN, *On First Principles*, H. Görgemanns and H. Karpp (eds.), *Vier Bücher von den Prinzipien / Origenes* (Darmstadt: Wissenschaftliche Buchgesellschaft, 1976, 2nd edn. Darmstadt, 1985). Eng. trans.: G. W. Butterworth (New York: Harper & Row, 1966).

Secondary works

ANATOLIOS, K. (1997), ' "The Body as Instrument": A Reevaluation of Athanasius' Logos–Sarx Christology', *Coptic Church Review*, 18: 78–84.

—— (1998), *Athanasius: The Coherence of his Thought* (London: Routledge).

BAILLIE, D. M. (1956), *God was in Christ: An Essay on Incarnation and Atonement* (London: Faber & Faber).

BALTHASAR, H. URS VON (1998), *Cosmic Liturgy: The Universe according to Maximus the Confessor* (San Francisco: Ignatius Press). German edition: *Kosmische Liturgie: das Weltbild Maximus' des Bekenners* (Einsiedeln: Johannes Verlag, 1988).

BATHRELLOS, D. (2004), *The Byzantine Christ: Person, Nature, and Will in the Christology of St. Maximus the Confessor* (Oxford: Oxford University Press).

BEHR, J. (2001), *The Formation of Christian Theology*, i: *The Way to Nicaea.* (Crestwood, NY: St Vladimir's Seminary Press).

BERTRAND, F. (1951), *Mystique de Jésus chez Origène* (Paris: Aubier).

DALEY, B. E. (1987), 'A Humble Mediator: The Distinctive Elements in Saint Augustine's Christology', *Word and Spirit*, 9: 100–17.

—— (1997), 'Divine Transcendence and Human Transformation: Gregory of Nyssa's Anti-Apollinarian Christology', *StPatr* 32: 87–95.

—— (2002), ' "Heavenly Man" and "Eternal Christ": Apollinarius and Gregory of Nyssa on the Personal Identity of the Savior', *JECS* 10: 469–88.

—— (2004), ' "He Himself is our Peace" (Eph 2.14): Early Christian Views of Redemption in Christ', in S. T. Davis, D. Kendall, and G. O'Collins (eds.), *The Redemption: An Interdisciplinary Symposium on Christ as Redeemer* (Oxford: Oxford University Press), 149–76.

—— (2005a), 'The *Nouvelle Théologie* and the Patristic Revival: Sources, Symbols, and the Science of Theology', *International Journal of Systematic Theology*, 7: 362–82.

—— (2005b), 'Word, Soul and Flesh: Origen and Augustine on the Person of Christ', *AugStud* 36: 299–326.

—— (2006), ' "One Thing and Another": The Persons in God and the Person of Christ in Patristic Theology', *Pro Ecclesia*, 15: 17–46.

DROBNER, H. (1986), *Person-Exegese und Christologie bei Augustinus: zur Herkunft der Formel Una Persona* (Leiden: E. J. Brill).

GAVRILYUK, P. L. (2004), *The Suffering of the Impassible God: The Dialectics of Patristic Thought* (Oxford: Oxford University Press).

GEERLINGS, W. (1978), *Christus Exemplum: Studien zur Christologie und Christusverkündigung Augustins* (Mainz: Grünewald).

GREER, R. A. (1961), *Theodore of Mopsuestia, Exegete and Theologian* (London: Faith Press).

—— (1990), 'The Man from Heaven: Paul's Last Adam and Apollinaris's Christ', in W. S. Babcock (ed.), *Paul and the Legacies of Paul* (Dallas: Southern Methodist University Press), 165–82.

GRILLMEIER, A. (1969), 'Christology', in K. Rahner *et al.*, *Sacramentum Mundi* (New York: Herder & Herder), iii. 186–92.

—— (1975), *Christ in Christian Tradition*, i, rev. edn. (London: Mowbray).

HANSON, R. P. C. (1988), *The Search for the Christian Doctrine of God* (Edinburgh: T & T Clark).

KELLY, J. N. D. (1978), *Early Christian Doctrines* (San Francisco: Harper & Row).

LAYTON, B. (1987), *The Gnostic Scriptures: Ancient Wisdom for the New Age* (New York: Doubleday).

LEBON, J. (1909), *Le monophysisme sévérien* (Leuven: Van Linthout).

—— (1951), 'La christologie du monophysisme syrien', in A. Grillmeier and H. Bacht (eds.), *Das Konzil von Chalkedon: Geschichte und Gegenwart* (Würzburg: Echter), i. 423–580.

McGuckin, J. A. (1994), *Saint Cyril of Alexandria and the Christological Controversy* (Leiden: E. J. Brill).

Norris, R. A., Jun. (1963), *Manhood and Christ: A Study in the Christology of Theodore of Mopsuestia* (Oxford: Clarendon Press).

——(1980), *The Christological Controversy*, Sources of Early Christian Thought (Philadelphia: Fortress Press).

O'Keefe, J. J. (1997), 'Impassible Suffering? Divine Passion and Fifth-Century Christology', *TS* 58: 39–60.

Petterson, A. (1995), *Athanasius* (Ridgefield, Conn.: Morehouse).

Rahner, K. (1961), 'Current Problems in Christology', trans. C. Ernstinin, in *Theological Investigations* (Baltimore: Helicon), i. 149–200.

Scipioni, L. (1956), *Ricerche sulla cristologia del 'Libro di Ericlide' di Nestorio*, Par 11 (Fribourg: Edizione universitarie).

Smith, J. W. (2002), 'Suffering Impassibly: Christ's Passion in Cyril of Alexandria's Soteriology', *Pro Ecclesia*, 11: 463–83.

Studer, B. (1993), *Trinity and Incarnation*, ed. A. Louth (Edinburgh: T & T Clark).

Torrance, T. F. (1995), 'Athanasius: A Study in the Foundations of Classical Theology', in *Divine Meaning: Studies in Patristic Hermeneutics* (Edinburgh: T & T Clark), 179–228.

Weinandy, T. G., and Keating, D. A. (2003) (eds.), *The Theology of St. Cyril of Alexandria* (London: T & T Clark).

CHAPTER 44

....

DOCTRINE OF CREATION

....

PAUL M. BLOWERS

44.1 INTRODUCTION

....

THE Bible, needless to say, scarcely aspires to a scientific cosmology, a developed theory of cosmic origins, or a comprehensive account of the complexity of the universe. Genesis 1 and 2 inaugurate a long saga of the Creator's resourcefulness and faithfulness wherein creation is both a divine *fait accompli* and the theatre of God's continuing action. The sovereign Creator orders and reorders 'chaos' in its resurgent manifestations, be it the primeval formlessness (Gen 1: 2) and untamed forces of the world (Isa 51: 9–10; Pss 74: 12–17, 89: 9–13, 93: 3–4, 104: 2b–9; Job 38: 8–11, 41: 1–34), the dereliction of humanity (Gen 3–6; 11: 1–9; 2 Pet 3: 5–7), the enemies threatening God's people from without (e.g. Ex 15: 1–21), or the sin and idolatry that pervert the covenant community from within (e.g. Ex 32: 9–10; Deut 8: 11–20; Hos 2: 8–9). Hence creation and redemption are thoroughly intertwined, just as Yahweh's care for the universe and relationship with his covenant people are inevitably of a piece (compare Hos 2: 18–23; Ezek 34: 25–31; Isa 40; 42: 10–12; 44: 24; 45: 18–19; 54: 9–10; Jer 31: 35–7; Hab 3: 2–19; Job 5: 23; Pss 19, 114; Wis 19: 6–12).

In the ancient Jewish faith, Yahweh's creative activity culminates precisely in the election and salvation of Israel. For the early church, however, the story has its climax in Jesus Christ, who pioneers a way of salvation for all the Gentiles in anticipation of a whole *new* creation (Gal 6: 15; 2 Cor 5: 17; Rom 6: 1–14, 8: 18–25; Rev 21: 1), an eschatological reality in which believers have already begun to participate. Paul identifies this as God's pre-creation plan, 'the mystery hidden for ages and generations but now made manifest to his saints' (Col 1: 26; cf. Eph 3: 9). The Christian doctrine of creation thus develops within the framework of a universalizing gospel that has as its very centre the cosmic Christ (Eph 1: 3–23; Col 1: 15–23) *through whom* all created things exist (1 Cor 8: 6; Col 1: 15–23) and under whose rule all creation will be subdued (Acts 2: 34–5; 1 Cor 15: 24–8; Eph 1: 22; Heb 1: 1–13, 2: 5–9).

Accordingly, much of the discourse concerning creation in the New Testament and sub-apostolic sources is confessional and doxological. It is the language of worship, as in John's majestic vision of Christ the enthroned Lamb of God, worthy of praise not only because of his redemptive death but because he has created all things and because they exist solely by his will (Rev 4: 1–5: 14). Acclamations of the Creator, the Father of all, or of Christ as the mediator and redeemer of creation, permeate the works of the late first- and second-century Apostolic Fathers (e.g. *1 Clem.* 19–20, 33, 60; *Did.* 10; *Diogn.* 7) and Christian apologists (e.g. Justin Martyr, 1 *Apol.* 13; *Dial.* 41; Theophilus of Antioch, *Autol.* 1. 6–7) and later regularly appear in the narrated testimonials of early Christian martyrs before their Roman persecutors.[1]

The ever-deepening encounter with the rival religious and philosophical worldviews of Graeco-Roman antiquity, however, raised the stakes of Christian doctrinal self-definition respecting the origins and destiny of the cosmos. While doxological language remained embedded in Christian liturgy and literature, a more prescriptive discourse concerning Creator and creation also took shape. The opening mandate of the *Shepherd of Hermas* signals this trend:

First of all, believe that God is one, who created and completed all things (cf. Eph 3: 9) and made all that is from that which is not (compare 2 Macc 7: 28) and contains all things, and who alone is uncontained.[2] So have faith in him and fear him, and fearing him be self-controlled. Keep these things and you will cast away all evil from yourself, and you will put on every virtue of righteousness and you will live to God, if you keep his commandment.

(Hermas, *Mand.* 1; trans. Snyder 1968: 63–5)

Belief in a personal Creator, utterly transcendent, who 'contains' but is not 'contained' (Schoedel 1979; Torrance 1995), became normative for Christian faith and ethics alike (Scheffczyk 1970: 37–46). Most renditions of the rule of faith (*regula fidei*), the variably worded but thematically consistent epitomes of apostolic teaching used in second- and third-century Christian catechesis, declare the work of the Creator, the Almighty, Maker of heaven and earth, as the foundation of the economy of salvation (Irenaeus of Lyons, *Haer.* 1. 10. 1; 3. 4. 2; *Epideixis* 6; Tertullian, *Virg.* 1; Origen of Alexandria, *Comm. Jo.* 22.15.16). Some versions of the rule specifically affirm the creation of the world through the agency of the Son of God (*Logos*), thereby opposing Plato's myth of the cosmic craftsman and Gnostic and Marcionite teachings ascribing the material world to an ignorant or pernicious demiurge (Irenaeus, *Haer*. 1. 22. 1, 3. 4. 2; Tertullian, *Praescr*. 13. 1–6; *Prax*. 2. 1–2; Origen, *Princ*. 1, pref. 4; *Comm. ser.* 3 *in Mt.*).

44.2 THE INTERPLAY OF CHRISTIAN, GNOSTIC, AND PLATONIC COSMOLOGIES

Recent scholarship on the early Christian doctrine of creation has concentrated significantly on the interrelations between Jewish, Christian, Gnostic, and Graeco-Roman philosophical traditions at a time when boundaries were still being fixed and there was considerable fluidity of cosmological ideas. Complicating the picture is the fact that, within a period roughly coinciding with the development of a canon of holy scripture within catholic Christianity, Jewish, Gnostic, and Christian interpreters were appropriating a shared set of creation texts, most importantly the Genesis cosmogony; and in that same era Gnostic communities were producing a literature rich in cosmological perspectives that drew upon Jewish and Christian scripture reread through their own highly developed symbolic systems (Pearson 1988; Layton 1987: pp. xvii–xxii).

Discovery of the Nag Hammadi corpus not only alleviated over-dependence on patristic accounts of Gnosticism but revealed the profound diversity of Gnostic schools and opened an enduring debate on whether there ever was a 'normative' Gnostic religion or cosmology (M. Williams 1999). There is still wide agreement, however, that in Gnostic traditions metaphysics and cosmology were less a pre-occupation in their own right than a corollary of doctrines of redemption and heavenly gnosis that connected the origins of evil, or more basically *ignorance*, with the origins of the material world itself (May 1994: 43; Rudolph 1987: 58, 65–72, 113). Gnostic cosmology was constructed out of a deep sense of alienation between the eternal spiritual world and the present world, which need not be explained by reference to sinful disobedience (Perkins 1985). Gnostic mythology thus competed strongly with Genesis (Layton 1987: p. xxii) while simultaneously exploring the book's spiritual and ascetical possibilities.[3] Indeed, Gnostic exegesis of the Genesis creation accounts indicates that cosmology was tied up with practical and ethical issues (e.g. sexuality, procreation, marriage, celibacy), not merely speculative concerns (Pagels 1986).

The ancient heresiologists' accusations that Gnostics simply spun cosmic myths (e.g. Irenaeus, *Haer*. 1. 15. 5) now seem overdrawn as historians highlight the many nuances of Gnostic thought; but contemporary research has validated their perception that Gnosticism cultivated various forms of cosmic dualism, whether a metaphysical dualism (rather atypical, and best represented in the Manichaeism known to Augustine), a soteriological dualism polarizing creation and redemption, or an extreme Platonizing dualism elevating the transcendent God far beyond the material world and its creator (Vallée 1980: 179–80; Pétrement 1990: 171–80; Rudolph 1987: 59–67). The allegedly 'classic' Gnostic myth, evidenced in a work like the *Apocryphon of John* (Layton 1987: 12–18, 23–51; Pearson 2004: 202–7, 216–18) conceived the corporeal world as a terrible accident, the upshot of a degenerative process that actually started within the spiritual realm but precipitated a disastrous alienation from the divine *plerōma*, the fullness of being (Layton 1987: 14–16; Rudolph 1987: 70–88; Pearson 2004: 204).

The common themes in Gnostic and Platonic worldviews did not go unnoticed by Irenaeus, whose substantial refutation of Gnostic cosmology in his treatise *Against Heresies* actually weaves together anti-Gnostic and anti-Platonic philosophical rhetoric, at once refuting Plato's vision of the Demiurge who creates the world according to eternal ideas outside himself and the Gnostic vision of an ignorant creator or of a whole series of emanations or angels involved in the creative process (Norris 1965: 81–92; Perkins 1986; May 1994: 166–7). For Irenaeus—and for the later Christian tradition dependent on him—Platonists and Gnostics shared the same fate, since, whatever their differences, both contrived theories that denigrated creation: Platonism by viewing the material creation as a perennially failed image of the eternal, Gnosticism by seeing it as the very unmaking of the divine plan.

Specialists in Gnosticism and Platonism challenge the simplistic caricatures of these traditions by patristic critics, but historical theologians acknowledge how these foils factored into the shape of the doctrine of creation in catholic Christianity. Polemical interests do not, however, exhaustively explain Irenaeus's own deep investment in the theological interpretation of biblical salvation history (Bengsch 1957: 51–163; Vallée 1980: 177–80; May 1994: 164–5; Gunton 1998: 52–6, 61–4), which integrally relates creation and redemption in the unfolding providential plan (*oikonomia*) of the triune God. Like his Gnostic counterparts, Irenaeus's principal motivation is not to articulate a cosmogony or cosmology. Instead, he privileges and augments the cosmic drama of Pauline and Johannine Christology, with God resourcefully and strategically guiding the fledgling creation—most importantly humanity—through the experience of evil to full perfection and transformation. The origin and destiny of the world is bound up with Jesus Christ as the 'recapitulation' (compare Eph 1: 10) of the whole economy (*Haer.* 3. 16. 6; 3. 18. 1–7). Rather than Christ's advent being an episode in the history of creation, creation *ex nihilo*, achieved through Christ, is God's first mighty act *en route* to his full disclosure in the incarnation and passion. The 'lamb who was slain' (and New Adam), says Irenaeus, was alone worthy in the beginning 'to open the book of the Father', revealing the mysteries of heaven and earth (*Haer.* 4. 20. 2–4; see also Behr 2000: 34–85; 2001: 118–26).

Origen of Alexandria shared Irenaeus's insistence on the providential ordering of the material world and its history (Le Boulluec 1977), but proposed a novel explanation of cosmic origins that constructively engaged Platonism, even Valentinian Gnosticism by some accounts (Strutwolf 1993). Newer scholarship on Middle Platonism (esp. Dillon 1977) has illuminated Origen's intellectual context and role as a philosophical and theological 'researcher' (Crouzel 1962: 179–215; 1989: 163; Chadwick 1966: 72). Origen knew firsthand the Middle Platonic discussions of how God, as pure Unity (Monad), gives rise to Duality (Dyad) and thus to plurality and diversity. By Origen's time, Platonists increasingly understood the mythic Demiurge in Plato's *Timaeus* to be the immediate subordinate of the One, the 'second God', the divine Mind (*nous*) and agent of divine reason (*logos*) informing the world (Dillon 1977: 3–7). In Origen's mind, such views were not entirely inconsistent with the biblical understanding of the Godhead, and furthermore corroborated the Christian repudiation of Gnostic and Marcionite notions of an 'alien' creator.

In his classic treatise *On First Principles*, now viewed as the first Christian foray into philosophical physics (Harl 1975: 20–4), but one in which the economy of salvation is still the primary framework (Lies 1992: 68–121), Origen conceives God's Son, the Logos and Wisdom of God, as the bridge between the pure oneness of the incorporeal God and the diversity of corporeal creation.[4] He also postulates a double creation (Tzamalikos 2006: 39–164; Bostock 1992). In the first phase, because God's creativity, sovereignty, and benevolence could never have been inoperative (*Princ.* 1. 2. 10; 1. 4. 3) and because he preconceived the universe in his eternal Wisdom or Word, God created a perfect communion of spiritual beings, not his equals but ontologically subordinate, contingent, and morally mutable (1. 4. 4–5; 1. 5. 1–5; 1. 8. 1–4), sustained through contemplation of the Logos. Having fallen because of spiritual negligence (1. 4. 1), God in a second phase created the material, corporeal world *ex nihilo* as their remedial housing (2. 1. 1–5), with differentiated bodies (angelic, human, demonic, etc.) based on the severity of the creatures' lapse (1. 6. 2; 2. 9. 1–8). The history of material creation in turn becomes the history of the providential rehabilitation of free spiritual beings and their eventual universal restoration (*apokatastasis*) to original unity and beatitude (1. 6. 1–4; 3. 1. 1–24; 3. 5. 1–3. 6. 9).

Origen's speculations dramatized how creation was both estranged from God and longing for reunion—a leitmotif actually shared with Gnosticism but stripped of Gnostic determinism. Indeed, Origen's cosmology in his *On First Principles* and related texts appears as a grand apology for providence and for the interconnected freedoms of Creator and creatures (Koch 1932; Le Boulluec 1975; Lyman 1993: 47–69; Benjamins 1994), and, most importantly for Evagrius of Pontus and Origen's other monastic devotees later on, as the groundwork for a highly developed ascetical theology. Like Irenaeus, moreover, he vindicated materiality and corporeality as inherently good, even if only provisionally so (Chadwick 1966: 85–9). Origen's cosmology was nonetheless destined to foment substantial controversy since, despite his caveats, spiritual beings still appeared to his critics to be 'generated' rather than created *ex nihilo*, to enjoy an intrinsic, albeit derivative share in God's eternity, and to pre-exist their bodies both ontologically *and temporally*. Methodius of Olympus was particularly influential in caricaturing Origen for teaching an 'eternal creation' that necessarily implied the coexistence of matter with the Creator—though, as recent scholars have shown, the stereotype is unfair to Origen's actual analysis, in which God alone is uncreated and self-subsistent.[5]

44.3 Two Formative Interpretive Issues in the Early Christian Doctrine of Creation

Origen's adventurous cosmology in his *On First Principles* set in relief the underlying dilemma of the reconcilability of biblical creation texts with contemporary philosophical insights. Is the transcendent God and Father alone Creator? If so, how can creation be *within time*? If creation is an eternal act outside time, does not matter itself become co-eternal with God? Genesis never directly addresses these and other enduring questions, and long before Augustine penned his highly analytical *Literal Commentary on Genesis*, Christian writers grappled with the theologically 'literal' sense of the creation narratives. The challenge for modern scholarship has been not just to identify the philosophical theories in the background, but specifically to ascertain how patristic exegetes' close reading of scriptural texts both shaped, and was shaped by, their judgements of those theories, and how they understood scripture to be revealing whole new cosmological perspectives.

44.3.1 'In the Beginning...'

Richard Sorabji has observed that the suggestion that the universe had a beginning would have been to everyone in antiquity outside the Jewish and Christian traditions an absurdity. Some Greeks could believe that the present orderly universe might have a beginning, but matter itself had none. Platonists came to see matter as *eternally* created and thus 'beginningless'—that is, as emanating from the eternal God who needed no independent substance from which to create the world (Sorabji 1983: 193–252, 307–18).[6]

Yet the Bible sacred to Jews and Christians opened with the very words, '*In the beginning (en archē)* God created....' At least as early as Theophilus of Antioch (Nautin 1973: 71–3), Christian writers circumvented the issue of temporality by connecting these words both with John 1: 1 ('*In the beginning* was the Word...') and Proverbs 8: 22 ('God created me [Wisdom] the *beginning* of his works...') so as to indicate the identity and priority of the Logos (Christ) as the divine agent of creation (*Autol.* 2.10; Tertullian, *Herm.* 20; Origen, *Hom. 1 in Gen.*; Eusebius, *Vit. Const.* 12. 4–16). As J. C. M. Van Winden has demonstrated, patristic interpreters were countering philosophical traditions that already rendered *archē* as 'principle' or 'causal origin', rather than temporal 'beginning' (1997: 80–2). Platonists had accordingly viewed reality as grounded in three eternal *archai*: God, the transcendent Ideas, and matter itself (Ps. Plutarch, *Plac. phil.* 1. 3; compare Hippolytus, *Haer.* 16; Ambrose, *Hex.* 1. 1; see also Pépin 1964: 21–45).

Embracing a Christocentric interpretation, however, patristic exegetes explored multiple possible meanings for a scriptural text that they believed outstripped the philosophers. Origen and Ambrose connect Genesis 1: 1 not only with John's prologue and Proverbs 8: 22 but with Revelation 22: 13 ('I am … the *beginning* and the end'), and discuss other senses of *archē* from a montage of biblical texts (Origen, *Comm. Jo.* 1. 16. 90–20. 124; cf. Ambrose, *Hex.* 1.4; see also Pépin 1976). For Origen, Christ, as divine Wisdom, was *archē* even before the temporal 'beginning',[7] but as Word was '*in the* beginning' commencing the divine self-revelation and his multiple salvific manifestations (*epinoiai*), of which *archē* was simply the first (*Comm. Jo.* 1. 19. 113–20. 119; see also Tzamalikos 2006: 31–5). Didymus the Blind, imitating Origen's meticulous attention to the preposition 'in', understands Wisdom's (or the Word's) being '*in* the beginning' (Gen 1: 1; Jn 1: 1) as exactly paralleled in Colossians 1: 16: '*in him* all things were created, in heaven and on earth' (*Comm. Gen.* 1B–2A).

But what of a 'beginning' *in time*? And could such be affirmed alongside the Christocentric reading? Tertullian entertains a simple temporal sense of *archē* in Genesis 1: 1: namely, the appearance of 'heaven and earth' first in the sequence of creation (*Herm.* 19). Methodius, once again examining the Word's status 'in the beginning', described the Father as the utter 'unbeginning beginning' of the Son, who is himself, in turn, the 'beginning' of created things that are 'more recent' than him. The Word thus acts 'in' a quasi-temporal 'interval' between Creator and creation (*Creat.* 9, 11; see Patterson 1997: 214–20; Behr 2004: 45–8). Later, however, Basil of Caesarea pursues a more sublime temporal meaning. The 'beginning' is precisely the atemporal, instantaneous moment of creation, the utter immediacy of the divine will in creating (*Hex.* 1. 6)—a position echoed by Gregory of Nyssa, who points to the irreducibility and timelessness of God's will, wisdom, and action in creating (*Hex.*, PG 44. 69A; see Van Winden 1997: 85–8).

Here again one must notice the commanding role of the scriptural text itself. Patristic exegetes pondered the precise sequence of the Genesis cosmogony, which declares that God 'created heaven and earth' (1: 1)—a *fait accompli*—before mentioning the 'formless' earth (1: 2), the 'firmament' (1: 6–8), and the 'dry land' called earth (1: 9–10). The ancients also recognized, like modern commentators, that there are actually two creation narratives, the hexaemeral (six-day) account (1: 1–2: 4a) and the anthropocentric one (2: 4b–3: 24). Philo had set an important precedent by arguing that in a simultaneous moment God created 'heaven and earth', that is, the intelligible world which is the model of the sensible or material one (*Opif.* 15–16, 36, 134 f.), and both Clement (*Strom.* 5. 14. 93) and Origen (*Princ.* 2. 9. 1; 3. 6. 8) in their respective ways appropriated this interpretation (Nautin 1973: 86–91). Basil proposes that there was a pre-temporal condition of things befitting the supernatural powers in their eternity, but that 'heaven and earth' refers to the actual appearance of the universe as we know it, the higher and lower levels of creation (*Hex.* 1. 5–7; see Van Winden 1997: 138–9). Gregory of Nyssa, on the other hand, takes 'heaven and earth' (Gen. 1: 1) together with the invisibility and formlessness of the world (1: 2) as an indication that God *simultaneously* created the 'beginnings', 'causes', and 'powers' both of the noetic and the sensible worlds *in potency*, before their actual appearance (*Hex.*, PG 44. 72–7; see Robbins 1912: 17–18, 54–5; Rousselet 1973; Alexandre 1976: 166–7; Van Winden 1997: 96–9, 139–41).

For Augustine, who affirms with Ambrose, Jerome (*Qu. Heb. Gen.* 1. 1),[8] and earlier exegetes the Christocentric meaning of 'beginning' (*Conf.* 11. 7–9; *Gen. Man.* 1. 2. 3; *Gen. imp.* 1. 3. 6; *Gen. litt.* 1. 4. 9), the relation between timelessness and temporality in the moment of creation is theologically crucial, since it points to the whole providential ordering and 'history' of creation. Citing Sirach 18: 1 ('He created all things *simultaneously* (*simul*) . . .'), Augustine avers, like Gregory of Nyssa, that the 'six days' bespeak an instantaneous creation (*conditio*) of the fullness of 'heaven and earth' *in their potentiality*; more specifically, it is the implanting of their seminal or causal principles (*rationes*), the patterns that will guide creatures' actual emergence in time and space (*Gen. litt.* 4. 33. 51–34. 53; 5. 1. 1 ff.; 5. 5. 12; 6. 11. 18; 6. 14. 25–18. 29; see Solignac 1973). The *rationes* function less as determining 'natural development' than as grounding creatures' stability 'in God' and their openness to the interventions of a Creator who remains utterly free in relation to the cosmos. Indeed, Augustine views the simultaneous creation in the light of the ultimate beauty and perfected love toward which the Creator has projected all things. It is the original 'potentiality' that is established by God and that cannot be actualized save through the concrete history of creation, a complex process of creatures—in their own movements and desires—realizing potential goods (R. Williams 1994: 14–19; 1999: 251–2).

44.3.2 Creation *ex nihilo*

A prima facie reading of the opening verses of Genesis seems to suggest that in the beginning a substance already existed, if only a watery abyss or chaos (1: 2; cf. 2 Pet 3: 5), from which God fashioned the cosmos. At least two prominent patristic theologians, Justin (1 *Apol.* 59) and Clement of Alexandria (*Strom.* 5. 90. 1), deduced that at creation there was a prior material substratum to which the Creator added qualities—a view they recognized as congenial with Plato's Demiurge filling up the 'receptacle' with forms (*Tim.* 50c–51b). In time there appeared remarkably divergent Christian accounts of the eternity of matter, from Marcion's view that matter was the intrinsically evil principle befitting the degraded creator-god Yahweh (Tertullian, *Marc.* 1. 15; May 1994: 53–61), to the Christian Platonist Hermogenes's claim that matter was an eternally subordinate and subservient instrument of the Creator: negatively, as a 'chaos' to be tamed, but positively as the raw resource of the orderly universe (Hippolytus, *Haer.* 8.10; Tertullian, *Herm.*; also May 1994: 140–7). In fourth-century Syria, Ephrem was still refuting followers of the second-century teacher Bardaisan, who held that five elements constituted the original substratum of creation (Ephrem, *Commentary on Genesis*, 1.2).

The notion of the eternity of matter—variously manifested in pagan thought[9] and recast in these and other Christian or Gnostic adaptations—was nonetheless destined to rejection in favour of a doctrine of creation 'out of nothing' (*ex nihilo*) (cf. Tatian, *Orat.* 5; Hippolytus, *Haer.* 1. 1–23; Origen, *Hom. in Gen.* frag. in Eusebius, *Praep.* 7. 20; Athanasius, *Inc.* 2; Basil, *Hex.* 1.2; Ambrose, *Hex.* 1. 2–4; Gregory of Nyssa, *Hom. opif.* 24). Recent studies (Sorabji 1983; Young 1991; May 1994) have shown that this was far from an uncomplicated case of doctrinal development. Multiple contextual factors militated against a uniform understanding of creation *ex nihilo*—a doctrine that has lately returned to controversy among theologians, exegetes, and physicists (Copan and Craig 2004).

First, for early Christian exponents of creation *ex nihilo*, there was neither a ready corpus of extensive biblical *testimonia* nor a secure interpretative tradition via Hellenistic Judaism (May 1994: 6–26). Indeed, Philo himself was a model of ambivalence on the issue (Sorabji 1983: 203–9; May 1994: 9–21). Genesis 1: 2 was certainly the *locus classicus* in mentioning an invisible and unformed 'void' (*abyssos*, LXX; cf. Symmachus: 'idleness', *argon*; Theodotion and Aquila: 'emptiness', *kenōma*) preceding the created order; but the text by itself left open the question of whether this void was itself the 'nothing' from which order arose or else the primitive raw material that God had produced 'from nothing' to fashion the universe.[10] Wisdom 11: 17 adheres closely to Genesis 1: 2 in declaring that God created the world from 'formless matter', and was found useful by Hermogenes. Still another text, 2 Maccabees 7: 28, pointing to the God who created heaven and earth 'from what was not' (*ouk ex ontōn*), though useful for describing the contingency of matter (Origen, *Princ.* 2.1.5), was also understandable simply as extolling the novelty of the ordered cosmos (May 1994: 6–8, 16). From the New Testament, moreover, Romans 4: 17 and Hebrews 11: 3 said less about a theory of matter than about the resourcefulness of the Creator and Redeemer (May 1994: 27–8; Young 1991: 144).

Second, the concept of a pre-existent 'nothing' out of which matter and the universe were created was philosophically a very hard sell. Pagan writers respected Parmenides' axiom, repeated by Aristotle (*Phys.* 1. 8), that no entity could truly 'come into being' unless it had *pre*-existed, and that it would be absurd to say that an entity could be created from non-being (Sorabji 1983: 245–7). They certainly remembered the Epicurean poet Lucretius's catch-phrase *ab nihilo nihil*, 'nothing comes from nothing'.

Some early Christian apologists, such as Theophilus of Antioch and Tertullian, both of whom wrote works against Hermogenes and vilified attempts to render matter co-eternal with the Creator, ostensibly ignored the philosophical incoherence of pure nothingness, advocating creation *ex nihilo* simply as expressing the sheer freedom and independence of the Creator. Against Hermogenes, for example, Tertullian quotes Isaiah 44: 24 ('I am the Lord who made all things, who stretched out the heavens *alone…*') to prove that matter was not an eternally attendant substratum (*Herm.* 6).

Other writers, however, acknowledged that creation from nothing must mean creation from 'something'. One solution, as already observed, was to focus on the nothing from which God created the world as that formlessness or inchoate character of the world instantiated at the moment of the divine will to create. Athanasius identifies it with the original vulnerability and corruptibility of creation in need of the constant nurture of divine grace (*Inc.* 3–5), such that the Creator is in some sense always re-creating the world from nothing. For Augustine, refusing the Manichaean equation of matter with evil, formless matter is 'practically nothing' (*prope nihil*) unless and until invested with forms (*Conf.* 12. 6. 6). But the original formless matter, since it constitutes the potentiality of the actualized fullness of creation, must have already had some inherent intelligibility, which Augustine finds in the *rationes seminales* (R. Williams 1999: 252). Augustine was clearly engaging the Neoplatonic teaching that matter on its own is 'non-existent', a deprivation of true being. Basil of Caesarea for his part unabashedly dismisses the reality of matter without the qualities or forms bestowed by God (*Hex.* 1.8; see Armstrong 1959).

There remained another, seemingly more controversial solution, that the 'nothing' behind creation *ex nihilo* is God himself. It appears in two very different contexts. As Gerhard May has demonstrated, the second-century Gnostic teacher Basilides asserts that the nothing whence sprung the 'cosmic seed' is God's own radically transcendent being, predicable only as 'non-being' by the standards of human *theologia negativa*. The seed of creation, itself in a state of 'non-being' now defined as pure potentiality, unfolds as the world by a strictly predetermined and ineffable process (May 1994: 62–84).

Basilides' teaching, though dismissed by orthodox polemicists, nonetheless anticipated the problem faced by later writers who, spurning the eternity of matter, saw virtues in the Neoplatonic view—a relative *creatio ex nihilo* as 'creation *not from matter*' (Sorabji 1983: 313–15)—whereby God, needing no independent matter, formed the world *from himself*. Gregory of Nyssa, who, paralleling Basil, proposes that matter is 'non-existent' save as the conjunction of intelligible 'ideas' or 'qualities' (*Hex.*, PG 44. 69B–C; *Anim. et res.*, PG 46. 124B–D; *Hom. opif.* 24) even goes so far as to identify *creatio ex nihilo* with creation 'from God' (*Hom. opif.* 23). He also, while confessing the sheer mystery of how created things were originally 'in God', positively mentions a 'substratum' (*hypokeimenon*) (*Hom. opif.* 23–4), prompting considerable scholarly debate on its meaning and status. On one interpretation, Gregory is an idealist whose substratum must be immaterial, referring back to the 'bundling' of the ideas of creatures within the mind of God (Sorabji 1983: 292–3).[11] On another account, Gregory is promoting a kind of divinely *willed* 'emanation', with the substratum (or 'nothing') being an 'intelligible matter' within God from which he generates creatures (Wolfson 1970). Monique Alexandre has instead proposed that Gregory is aligning two distinctive perspectives, one philosophical and one exegetical: first, matter as the conjunction of ideas or qualities, with the substratum logically pre-existing in the qualities themselves; second, matter-as-substratum in its yet unformed state (Gen 1: 2). The two, while difficult to reconcile, both work in the same direction to support Gregory's emphasis on the Creator's utter power to create, the simultaneity in him of thought and act, and the consequent completeness of the material creation in its original potentiality (Alexandre 1976; compare Gregorios 1988: 104–8).

44.4 THE DOCTRINE OF CREATION IN THE LIFE OF THE CHURCH IN THE FOURTH CENTURY AND BEYOND

Reconstruction of the early Christian doctrine of creation cannot be limited to the technical theological and philosophical debates surrounding the Genesis creation accounts. It entailed much more than a nuanced cosmology answering Gnostic or Graeco-Roman theories. Especially from the fourth century on, it found expression simultaneously in multiple contexts in the life of the Church: in erudite theology, to be sure, but also in preaching and catechesis, in the devotional expressions of liturgy and sacrament, and in emerging forms of ascetical theology and practice.

44.4.1 Trinitarian Underpinnings of the Doctrine of Creation

Developments in the extended Trinitarian controversies of the fourth century reinforced certain clarifications of Christian cosmology that effectively dismissed the view that creation was generated or emanated from God. We have already discussed the theologically complex notion of creation *ex nihilo*. Arians and pro-Nicene constituencies alike affirmed this principle, but famously disagreed on the Son of God's status as creature—later Arians believing that, as the one God alone is uncreated, the Son, 'firstborn of creation' (Col 1: 15), was already the highest and greatest of God's creatures and the agent through whom God created all other beings. Athanasius of Alexandria, in confuting Arianism, articulated another key principle: the distinction between the 'eternal generation' of the Son of God, as a reality within God's transcendent *nature*, and the 'creation' of the world, as an act of God's *will* (*Ar.* 3. 62–7; compare Gregory of Nyssa, *Eun.* 8; Gregory of Nazianzus, *Or.* 29. 17–18; Ambrose, *Fid.* 1. 16; John of Damascus, *F.o.* 1. 3; see also Lyman 1993: 132–40; Richard 2003: 401–8). Furthermore, with the Nicene Creed's affirmation that God made 'all that is, seen *and unseen*', subsequent interpreters of the Nicene faith obviated the possibility that the intelligible world enjoyed the Creator's own pure eternity. All the invisible powers, including the highest of heavenly hosts, were, like their subsequent, lower-ranking counterparts, created *ex nihilo* (Gregory of Nazianus, *Or.* 38. 8–10; see also Richard 2003: 25–8, 181–223; Bergmann 2005: 93–5).

The Nicene-Constantinopolitan Creed (381 CE) in time assured regular liturgical confession of the fact that only the Son, 'through whom all things were made', and the Holy Spirit, 'the Lord, the Giver of life' who 'with the Father and the Son is worshipped and glorified', shared the eternal, infinite, uncreated being of the Father. Biblical commentary on the opening verses of Genesis celebrated the Trinitarian co-operation in creation 'in the beginning'. The Father created directly by his Word (Son). And though the influential apologist Theophilus of Antioch (*Autol.* 2. 13) denied that it was the Holy Spirit who hovered over the watery abyss (Gen 1: 2), lest he be confused with Plato's World Soul or the Stoic *pneuma* that pervades matter, an emerging consensus affirmed that this was indeed the Spirit, poised to sanctify and perfect the world as he likewise presides over the re-creative waters of baptism (compare Tertullian, *Bapt.* 4; Origen, *Princ.* 1. 3. 3; Basil, *Spir.* 16. 38; *Hex.* 2. 6; Augustine, *Gen. litt.* 1. 6. 12).

44.4.2 Creation as an Object of Contemplation

From the outset, the early Christian doctrine of creation entailed the imitation of biblical doxology and the cultivation of a spiritual vision (*theōria*) of creation as the theatre of God's redemptive action in advance of the final judgement and consummation. After the Peace of Constantine, the Church's increasing sense— however tentative—of being at home in the world, called not just to transcend the cosmos but to participate in its transformation, stimulated deeper reverence for the complexity and beauty of the created world. Both in churchly devotion and in the burgeoning traditions of monastic piety, there was markedly greater focus on the contemplation of nature (*theōria physikē*) as a formative Christian discipline.

This trend is observable in representative patristic writers of the fourth century. Lactantius, a transitional Latin Christian apologist who, at the dawn of the Constantinian era, vilified pagan culture's fixation on the material and projected a sobering millenarian eschatology, nonetheless positively depicts creation itself as a magnificent, albeit severe, ascetic training ground wherein human beings learn through pain and moral testing to honour the Creator:

The world was made in order for us to be born; we get born in order to acknowledge its maker and our God; we acknowledge him to worship him; we worship him to receive immortality as the reward of our labours (worship of God requires huge labours); we are granted the prize of immortality to become like the angels, to serve our father and lord most high for ever and to be God's eternal kingdom. That is the sum of it all: that is God's secret and the mystery of the world.

(*Inst.* 7. 6. 1–2; trans. Bowen and Garnsey 2003: 404–5)

Lactantius, however, was still fighting old battles with pagan philosophy over the wisdom and providence of the Creator (Groh 2005: 7–13). With the Cappadocian fathers, Ambrose, and others in the next generation, the universe truly becomes an object of sustained contemplation (*theōria*), a revelatory 'book' in its own right, paralleling the Bible and giving alternative witness to the history of salvation (Basil, *Hex.* 11. 4; cf. Evagrius, *Cap. pract.* 92; *Schol.* 8 *on Ps.* 138. 16; Ephrem, *Hymns on Paradise*, 5. 2). Recovering insights from Clement and Origen, they depict the created cosmos as the grand stage on which the drama of divine grace and creaturely freedom and growth is being played out as a progressive spiritual *paideia*. Basil invites his listeners to consider the cosmos an 'amphitheater' in which they must be not only spectators but athletes, struggling along with him to contemplate creation's own testimony to the beginning, the Fall, the human vocation of worship, and the glory yet to come (*Hex.* 6. 1). Creation is 'the school where reasonable souls exercise themselves, the training ground where they learn to know God' (Basil, *Hex.* 1. 6, NPNF² 8, 55), with the provident Christ as the 'shepherd of the entire rational creation' (Gregory of Nyssa, *Eun.* 12). From grass seed to the gratitude of dogs (*Hex.* 5. 1–3; 9. 4), and especially in the intricate mysteries of human nature itself as a microcosm of the reciprocity of spiritual and material creation (Basil, *Hex.* 11. 14; Gregory of Nyssa, *Or. catech.* 6; Gregory of Nazianzus, *Or.* 28. 22; cf. Nemesius of Emesa, *Nat. hom.* 9), the universe proves a treasury of moral and spiritual exempla (Callahan 1958: 48–53). To contemplate it is to discover 'a translucent overlay of different planes of perception, the self, the world, and the drama of God's action' (Rousseau 1994: 325).

The challenge—dialectically, rhetorically, devotionally—was to strike a balance between the biblical images of creation as a fading flower, implicated in the tragedy of the human fall, and creation as the matrix of the eschatologically transformed order of things. For Gregory of Nyssa, the 'vanity' (Eccl 1: 2) of the monotonous cycles of nature, the vanity of human culture and striving, and the splendid order of creation as a vector toward intelligible beauty are dimensions of the same mystery (e.g. *Hom. 1 in Eccl.*). Gregory of Nazianzus likewise intermingles portraits of creation as a model of harmony and as a source of terror (*Or.* 6. 14–17), and extols the inscrutable providence operative amid the intrinsic chaos and vulnerability of material existence (*Or.* 14. 30; *Poem. Ar.* 4–5; *Carm.* 1. 2. 11, 13–16; see also Richard 2003: 237–48). As Sigurd Bergmann has demonstrated, Gregory envisions the whole Trinity at work in the struggle to liberate and transform the created cosmos (2005: 71–171). Indeed, this 'teleological' perspective on creation, as Dieter Groh has termed it (2005: 13–27), found expression in an entire literature interrelating the themes of creation, providence, evil, and rehabilitative suffering (Gregory of Nazianzus, *Carm.* 1. 1. 5; John Chrysostom, *Scand.*; Theodoret, *Provid.*). Especially in the West, amid the collapse of the Roman regime, the cultural shifts attending barbarian occupation, and a series of natural disasters, these themes assumed a new urgency, inaugurated by Augustine's classic *City of God* and climaxing in Prosper of Aquitaine's eloquent poem *On Providence*, Salvian of Marseilles's *On the Government of God*, and Boethius's *Consolation of Philosophy*.[12]

However, as John Chrysostom assures his late fourth-century audience, God subjected the creation *in hope*, a creation which groans to leave behind its vanity (Rom 8: 18–25), and which, like a nursemaid destined to enjoy the crown prince's glory, aspires to be transfigured right alongside restored humanity (*Hom. in Rom.* 14. 4–5). Creation's multifaceted participation in this transformation was an object of contemplation especially in liturgical, homiletical, and sacramental contexts.

The enduring symbolism of Sunday itself as the Lord's day—as first day (creation day), as the true Sabbath, and as the eschatological 'eighth day'—already established a crucial continuity between the completion of the old creation and the breaking in of the new (Carroll and Halton 1988: 17–76; Daniélou 1956: 222–86). In preaching for another liturgical mainstay, the Paschal feast, Gregory of Nyssa portrays the cross as the ultimate intersection of creation's divided extremities (*Sanct. Pascha*; compare *Or. catech.* 32), and with other preachers envisions the restored creation sharing in the resurrection mystery (*Sanct. Pascha*; *De tridui spatio homilia*; compare Proclus of Constantinople, *Oratio 13 in sanctum Pascha* 13. 2; Basil of Seleucia, *Pasch.* 1–2; Chromatius of Aquileia, *Sermo* 16. 1–3). In the Nativity–Epiphany cycle as well, creation becomes a veritable *dramatis persona*, as in the portrait of creation's dark winter vigil preparing for the advent of Christ the Sun of Righteousness (Mal 4: 2), the true *Sol Invictus* (anon., *De Solstitiis*; Maximus of Turin, *Serm.* 61–2), or in Ephrem the Syrian's eloquent sermonic poems celebrating creation's liberation through Christ's incarnation (*Nativity Hymns*, 4, 9, 10, 22, 26).

Such interpretation carried over into the sacraments. Tertullian early on explored the primordial role of water in the creation of the world (Gen 1: 2) and its sanctified role in the new creation incipient in baptism (*Bapt.* 2). Later writers drew a correspondence between those primordial waters and the waters of the Jordan in which Christ was baptized, a truly cosmic event (Cyril of Jerusalem, *Catech.* 3. 5; Ambrose, *Sacr.* 3. 1; see also McDonnell 1996: 50–68, 101–70). Ephrem drew an additional correspondence to the waters of the Virgin's womb, through which, like

Jordan's waters, the incarnate Saviour reopened an access to paradise (*Hymns on the Church*, 36; *Epiphany Hymns*, 12).

44.4.3 The Monastic Vision of Creation

What was true of the Church's liturgical, homiletical, and sacramental contemplation of creation—enhancing the paradox of creation as transitory yet capable of transfiguration—was doubly true of the kaleidoscopic vision of created nature in monastic theology and practice. The desert habitat into which monks flooded in the fourth and fifth centuries itself epitomized the material world—at once a harbour of demons and, in its simplicity and stark beauty, an adumbration of the sanctity of the new creation, a 'book' in its own way disclosing the 'words' of God (Chitty 1966: 6).

Pivotally important here is Evagrius of Pontus, disciple of the Cappadocian fathers and the subject of abundant recent scholarship. Appropriating Origen's grand vision of the fall, embodiment, and restoration of spiritual beings (*logikoi*) as the dramatic backdrop of material reality (Guillaumont 1962: 103–17), Evagrius develops a sophisticated multi-levelled model of 'natural contemplation' (*theōria physikē*), a corollary of the contemplation of scripture, especially of the Psalms, Proverbs, and Ecclesiastes.[13] Monks must intellectually penetrate the diversity of corporeal phenomena in order to grasp the instructive and elevating 'logoi of divine providence and judgment' (*Schol.* 8 *in Ps.* 138. 16; *Keph. gnost.* 48; *Schol.* 1 *in Eccl.*; see also Dysinger 2005: 171–95; Géhin 1993: 23–7), and beyond these the mystery of the Trinity (*Keph. gnost.* 1. 27, 70, 74). The *logoi* of 'judgement' signal the discretion of the cosmic Christ in differentiating and healing the corporeal creation; those of 'providence' reveal the immanent and unitive process whereby Christ is instructing creatures in ascetic virtue and in contemplation leading to higher knowledge (*gnōsis*) of God. For Evagrius, moreover, these *logoi* are deeply concealed; the universe is by no means transparent. Divine grace and diligent asceticism are indispensable in order to discern the meaning and destiny of the universe and thereby advance in the spiritual life.

Since he accepted controversial notions such as the pre-existence of spiritual beings, the 'double creation', and the universal *apokatastasis*, Evagrius was implicated in the later conciliar condemnations of Origenism in 553 (Guillaumont 1962: 133–70). But his attempt to work out a model of cosmic differentiation and re-unification was not in vain. Others in the monastic tradition later took up this challenge, most notably the prolific Byzantine theologian Maximus the Confessor. Maximus's cosmic theology is from one angle a sweeping critique of the Origenist system (*Amb.* 7; Sherwood 1955); from another angle it is a rehabilitation, stripping away the doctrine of pre-existence but maintaining the crucial interplay between the freedom of the Creator and the freedom of creatures, in a diversified world that has a definite temporal beginning (*archē*) and end (*telos*) in God (*Cap. theol.* 1. 1–10; see also Tollefsen 2000: 118–74; Balthasar 2003: 137–71). Creation is truly a 'bible' thoroughly interchangeable with scripture in narrating the history of created beings (*Amb.* 10), and the contemplation jointly of nature and scripture serves to discern the progressive drama wherein particular beings are being drawn toward universal reintegration and deification, their common purpose (*logos*), by a kind of cosmic *mimēsis*, the lower imitating the higher, with the universal virtue of *agapē* conditioning all growth in grace (*Thal.* 2; *Amb.* 7, 37; see also Blowers 2003). As with Evagrius, the Logos, Christ himself, educates the world through the immanent *logoi* of providence and judgement, but more profoundly for Maximus, the *logoi*—constituting God's very 'intentions' (*thelēmata*) for creation (*Thal.* 13; cf. Ps-Dionysius the Areopagite, *D. n.* 5. 8)—unveil the mystery of the incarnation as the secret underlying the whole cosmic order (*Amb.* 7, 33; *Thal.* 22, 60; see also Dalmais 1952; Lossky 1957: 95–101; Thunberg 1995: 64–83, 343–55; Blowers and Wilken 2003). Maximus projects the eschatological correlation between the incarnation of the Logos in Jesus Christ and his mysterious 'embodiment' in the *logoi* of all creatures (*Amb.* 7), thereby enfolding the history of creation into the 'destiny' of the crucified, risen, and glorified Creator:

The mystery of the incarnation of the Logos holds the power of all the hidden *logoi* and figures (*typoi*) of scripture as well as the knowledge of visible and intelligible creatures. Whoever knows the mystery of the cross and the tomb knows the *logoi* of these creatures. And whoever has been initiated into the ineffable power of the Resurrection knows the purpose (*logos*) for which God originally made all things.

(*Cap. theol.* 1. 66)

44.5 CONCLUSION

As with other classic themes in early Christian thought, the doctrine of creation did not have a tidy conceptual evolution. It was a complex construction. It drew broadly and deeply from the language and imagery of the Bible. It took serious account of the challenges of allegedly premature or deviant perspectives. It engaged relevant notions of cosmic 'first principles' in the Graeco-Roman philosophical traditions. Yet its ultimate contours and coherence were shaped primarily in relation to other major aspects of the catholic Christian faith: the Trinity, the nature and vocation of the human 'microcosm', the Fall, the economy of salvation, the mission of Jesus Christ to usher in the new creation, the final consummation of the world, and so on. It was a doctrine about 'origins', to be sure; but it was also a doctrine about grace and nature, about history, about providence and evil, about tragedy and beauty, about corporeality and incarnation, about time and eternity, and about eschatological judgement and perfection.

Creation had to be read like a book or witnessed like a drama, its true plot being discernible only in co-ordination with the interpretation of the biblical narratives.[14] Creation was destined to be, like holy scripture, an object of contemplation (*theōria*) rather than mere conceptual definition because the universe, once more like the contents of the Bible, was not capable of being grasped in a single impression or concept. Early Christians, moreover, envisioned in it something more than an objective body of evidences of the Creator or an 'intelligent design' holding its own against sceptics. To recall Basil of Caesarea's analogy, they beheld the world as an amphitheatre in which the divine *oikonomia*, the strategy of God's creative and redemptive purposes, was playing out toward its mysterious end. The story of the incarnation and the passion of Jesus Christ insinuated itself into the very fabric of the material world. The *logoi* of creation, like the *logoi* of scripture, pointed not merely to the transcendent Logos-Mediator who maintains order and harmony in the cosmos, but to the crucified, resurrected, and glorified Christ.

The rule of faith and the ecumenical creeds provided the epitome of this creative and redemptive economy. But the connecting links and enduring emphases in the doctrine of creation—for example, the pure freedom and resourcefulness of the Creator; creation *ex nihilo*; God's continuing nurture of created nature; salvation as *re*-creation, etc.—must be reconstructed through careful analysis of the patristic exegesis of Genesis and other biblical texts, manifested in discourses of theoretical cosmology, in prose commentaries, and in preaching, poetry, and hymnody that guided believers in the contemplation of the Creator's activity. Those links and emphases appeared as well, implicitly and explicitly, in liturgical and sacramental rituals in which the faithful encountered rich images of the completion of the original creation and the breaking in of the new. Overall, therefore, the challenge in the study of the early Christian doctrine of creation, amid the diverse contexts and literary genres in which it found expression, is not to restrict the search for its many matrices and dimensions. Herein lay the chemistry for centuries of Christian reflection on the mystery of a God who created out of 'the pure desire for the joy of another' (R. Williams 1994: 20; compare Fiddes 2001), out of the 'nothing' of a love incapable of human comprehension.

NOTES

1. For some exemplary cases in various *Acta martyrum*, see Musurillo (1972), esp. 12, 22–4, 42, 90, 102, 156, 288, 304.
2. Compare Philo, *Conf.* 27, who states: 'But all places are filled at once by God, who surrounds them all and is not surrounded by any of them, to whom alone it is possible to be everywhere and also nowhere.'

3. Birger Pearson (1988: 636) notes that of the 600 identifiable Old Testament references in the Nag Hammadi and related literature, there are 230 references to Genesis, 200 of which cite Genesis 1–11.

4. Panayiotis Tzamalikos (2006: 8–13, 30–8, 165–75) has lately argued that Origen's Logos should not be understood at all in terms of a Platonic hierarchy of divinity, as if holding a second place ontologically in the Godhead. Recommending a cautious use of the treatise *On First Principles*, with its complicated textual history and sometimes ambiguous passages, and asserting greater reliance on other works in Origen's corpus, he suggests that for Origen the Logos, *qua* divine Wisdom, is utterly 'beginningless' and enjoys the Father's transcendence absolutely, not derivatively. Nevertheless, the Logos is 'both "in" wisdom, that is into timelessness, and within the world, that is, "outside" of the Trinity' (p. 166). Only in this sense can he be called *mediator* between Creator and creation.

5. L. Patterson (1997: 35–63, 200–14; compare Behr 2004: 38–48) has demonstrated how, early on, in his treatise *On Free Will*, Methodius actually sympathized with important aspects of Origen's focusing of cosmic origins on theodicy and the defence of human free will, but in his later dialogue *Xeno: On Created Things* (extant only in Photius's fragments), he targeted Origen as failing to affirm the Creator alone as 'uncreated' and free of dependence on co-eternal matter.

6. For a concentrated study of the problem of a 'beginning' in pre-Christian Greek philosophy, see Ehrhardt (1966).

7. Compare Augustine's later Trinitarian definition in *Gen. imp.* 1. 3. 6: 'There is, you see, a beginning without beginning, and there is a beginning with another beginning. The beginning without a beginning only the Father is; and that is why we believe that all things come from one beginning. The Son however is the beginning in such a way that he is from the Father' (trans. Hill 2002: 116–17).

8. Jerome did not, however, acknowledge the Christocentric definition as the narrowly 'literal' (i.e. historical) sense, but only as its larger 'intention' (Hayward 1995: 30).

9. For example, atomism; doctrines of one or more primal elements; Aristotle's 'infinite regress' of matter; the Platonic 'receptacle', etc. For a good concise review, see Bouyer 1988: 72–85.

10. The classic version of creation *ex nihilo* ultimately demanded two stages: God's creating primal matter from nothing and his fashioning (and prospective refashioning) of that matter into a cosmic order (e.g. Augustine, *Gen. Man.* 1. 6. 10).

11. A variation of the 'idealist' interpretation is that of Hans Urs von Balthasar (1995: 27–35, 47–55), who, citing *Eun.* 1 (PG 45. 365D), argues that Gregory's substratum (*hypokeimenon*) is none other than the 'space' (*diastēma*) between Creator and creation, which becomes a kind of 'receptacle' for the divine ideas.

12. For an excellent selection of representative texts, see Walsh and Walsh (1985).

13. Like Origen, Evagrius considered Ecclesiastes a book of 'physics', not in the sense of natural science or secular wisdom, but as giving testimony to the spiritual saga of creation (Géhin 1993: 20–7). Christ himself is the true 'Preacher' giving instruction on the secrets of the world.

14. Among contemporary theologians, Oliver Davies (2004: 10–11, 104–8) has attempted a critical appropriation of this early Christian perspective on the world as a mysterious 'text' embodying the 'voice' of the Trinity.

Suggested Reading

The following are recommended: Balthasar (2003); Bostock (1992); Bouyer (1988); Centre d'études des religions du livre (1973); Gregorios (1988); Gunton (1998); Layton (1987); Lyman (1993); May (1994); Norris (1965); Richard (2003); Robbins (1912); Sorabji (1983); Tzamalikos (2006); Williams (1994); Young (1991).

Also:

Chadwick, H. (1983), 'Freedom and Necessity in Early Christian Thought about God', in D. Tracy and N. Lash (eds.), *Cosmology and Theology*, Concilium, (166) 6 (Edinburgh: T & T Clark), 8–13.

Bibliography

Primary sources

Amar, J., and Matthews, E. (1994), *St. Ephrem the Syrian: Selected Prose Works*, FC 91 (Washington: Catholic University America Press).

Ambrose of Milan, *De fide*, ed. O. Faller CSEL 78 (Vienna: Tempsky, 1962).

—— *De sacramentis*, ed. O. Faller CSEL 73 (Vienna: Tempsky, 1955); ed with French trans., B. Botte SC 25bis (Paris: Éditions du Cerf, 1994).

—— *Hexaemeron*, ed. K. Schenkl, CSEL 32 (Vienna: Tempsky, 1897).

Athanasius of Alexandria, *De incarnatione*, Greek text with Eng. trans. in R. Thomson, OECT (Oxford: Oxford University Press, 1971).

—— *Orationes tres contra Arianos*, PG 26. 12–468.

Augustine of Hippo, *Confessiones*, ed. L. M. J. Verheijen, CCSL 27 (Turnhout: Brepols, 1981).

—— *De civitate Dei*, ed. B. Dombart and A. Kalb, CCSL 47–8 (Turnhout: Brepols, 1955).

—— *De Genesi ad litteram*, ed. J. Zycha, CSEL 28.1 (Vienna: Tempsky, 1894) 3–435; trans. E. Hill, in WSA I/13 (2002), 153–506.

—— *De Genesi ad litteram liber imperfectus*, ed. J. Zycha, CSEL 28.1 (Vienna: Tempsky, 1894), 457–503; trans. E. Hill, in WSA I/13 (2002), 103–51.

—— *De Genesi contra Manichaeos*, ed. D. Weber, CSEL 91 (Vienna: Verlag der österreichischen Akademie der Wissenschaften, 1998); in trans. E. Hill WSA I/13 (2002), 23–102.

Basil of Caesarea, *De Spiritu Sancto*, ed. with French trans., B. Pruche SC 17 (Paris: Éditions du Cerf, 1968); Eng. trans. NPNF[2] 8.

—— *In Hexaemeron homiliae*, 1–9, ed. with French trans., S. Giet SC 26 (Paris: Éditions du Cerf, 1949).

—— *In Hexaemeron homiliae*, 10–11 (On the Creation of Humanity), ed. with French trans. A. Smets and M. Van Esbroeck SC 160 (Paris: Éditions du Cerf, 1970).

Basil of Seleucia, *In sanctum Pascha homilia*, ed. with French trans., M. Aubineau, SC 187 (Paris: Éditions du Cerf, 1972), 206–14.

Bowen, A., and Garnsey, P. (2003) (eds. and trans.), *Lactantius: Divine Institutes* (Liverpool: Liverpool University Press).

Carroll, T., and Halton, T. (1988) (eds. and trans.), *Liturgical Practice in the Fathers*. MFC 21 (Wilmington, Del.: Michael Glazier).

CHROMATIUS OF AQUILEIA, *Sermo* 16 (*In nocte magna*), ed. J. Lemarié SC 154 (Paris: Éditions du Cerf, 1969), 258–66.

CLEMENT OF ALEXANDRIA, *Stromateis*, v, ed. A. le Boulluec; French trans., P. Voulet, SC 278 (Paris: Éditions du Cerf, 1981).

DIDYMUS THE BLIND, *Commentarius in Genesim*, ed. with French trans., P. Nautin and L. Doutreleau, SC 233 (Paris: Éditions du Cerf, 1976).

EPHREM THE SYRIAN, *Carmina de Nativitate*, ed. E. Beck, CSCO 186–7 (Louvain: Secrétariat du Corpus SCO, 1959); trans. K. McVey, CWS (Mahwah, NJ: Paulist Press, 1989).

—— *Carmina de Paradiso*, ed. E. Beck, CSCO 174–5 (Louvain: Secrétariat du Corpus SCO, 1957); trans. S. Brock, *St. Ephrem the Syrian: Hymns on Paradise* (Crestwood, NY: St Vladimirs Seminary Press, 1990).

—— *In Genesim et in Exodum commentarii*, ed. R. M. Tonneau, CSCO 152–3 (Louvain: L. Durbecq, 1955); trans. E. G. Matthews and J. Amar, FC 91 (Washington D.C.: Catholic University of America Press, 1994).

EUSEBIUS OF CAESAREA, *De laudibus Constantini*, PG 20. 1316–1440.

—— *Preparatio evangelica*, PG 21. 21–1408.

EVAGRIUS OF PONTUS, *Capita practica* (*Praktikos*), ed. with French trans., A. Guillaumont and C. Guillaumont SC 171 (Paris: Éditions du Cerf, 1971).

—— *Kephalaia gnostica*, ed. with French trans., A. Guillaumont, PO 28. 1 (Paris: Firmin-Didot, 1958).

—— *Scholia in Ecclesiasten*, ed. P. Géhin, SC 397 (Paris: Éditions du Cerf, 1993).

—— *Scholia in Psalmos*. As identified from the *Selecta in Psalmos* attributed to Origen *et al.*, M.-J. Rondeau, 'Le commentaire sur les Psaumes d'Évagre le Pontique', *OCP* 26 (1960): 307–48 (more recently, L. Dysinger, *v. infra*).

GREGORY OF NAZIANZUS, *Carmina moralia*, PG 37. 521–968.

—— *Poemata Arcana*. Greek text ed. C. Moreschini, trans. D. Sykes (Oxford: Oxford University Press, 1997).

—— *Orationes* 6–12, ed. with French trans., M.-A. Calvet-Sébasti, SC (Paris: Éditions du Cerf, 1995) 405.

—— *Orationes* 27–31, ed. with French trans., P. Gallay and M. Jourjon, SC (Paris: Éditions du Cerf, 1978) 250.

—— *Orationes* 38–41, ed. C. Moreschini with French trans., P. Gallay, SC (Paris: Éditions du Cerf, 1990) 358.

GREGORY OF NYSSA, *Apologia in Hexaemeron*, PG 44. 61–124.

—— *Contra Eunomium*, ed. W. Jaeger, in GNO i and ii (Leiden: E. J. Brill, 1960).

—— *De anima et resurrectione*, PG 46. 12–160.

—— *De hominis opificio*, PG 44. 125–256.

—— *De tridui spatio homilia*, ed. G. Heil, A. van Heck, E. Gebhardt, and A. Spira, in GNO ix (Leiden: E. J. Brill, 1992), 273–306; English trans. A., Spira, and C. Klock (1981) (eds.), *The Easter Sermons of Gregory of Nyssa: Translation and Commentary*, trans. S. Hall (Cambridge, Mass.: Philadelphia Patristic Foundation).

—— *In Ecclesiasten homiliae*, ed. J. McDonough and P. Alexander, in GNO v (Leiden: E. J. Brill, 1962), 277–442; Eng. trans. S. Hall and R. Moriarity (Berlin: de Gruyter, 1993).

—— *In Sanctum Pascha homilia*, ed. J. McDonough and P. Alexander, in GNO ix (Leiden: E. J. Brill, 1992), 245–70.

GREGORY OF NYSSA, *Oratio catechetica*, ed. E. Mühlenberg, in GNO iii. 4; (Leiden: E. J. Brill, 1996); ed. with French trans., R. Winling, SC 453 (Paris: Éditions du Cerf, 2000).

HALL, S. (1993) (ed.), *Gregory of Nyssa: Homilies on Ecclesiastes: An English Version with Supporting Studies* (Berlin: de Gruyter).

HIPPOLYTUS OF ROME, *Refutatio omnium haeresium*. Greek text with Eng., M. Marcovich, PTS 25 (Berlin: de Gruyter, 1986).

IRENAEUS OF LYONS, *Adversus haereses* I, ed. with French trans., A. Rousseau and L. Doutreleau, 264 (Paris: Éditions du Cerf, 1979).

——*Adversus haereses* III, ed. with French trans., A. Rousseau and L. Doutreleau, SC 211 (Paris: Éditions du Cerf, 1974).

——*Adversus haereses* IV, ed. with French trans., A. Rousseau and L. Doutreleau, SC 100 (Paris: Éditions du Cerf, 1954).

JEROME, *Quaestiones hebraicae in Genesim*, ed. P. de Lagarde, CCSL 72, (Turnhout: Brepols, 1959). 1–56.

JOHN CHRYSOSTOM, *Ad eos qui scandalizati sunt ob adversitates*, (= *De providentia*), ed. with French trans., A.-M. Malingrey, SC 79 (Paris: Éditions du Cerf, 1961).

——*In epistolam ad Romanos homilia*, PG 60. 523–40.

JOHN OF DAMASCUS, *De fide orthodoxa*, PG 94. 789–1228.

JUSTIN MARTYR, *Apologiae*, ed. M. Marcovich, PTS 38 (Berlin: de Gruyter, 1994).

LACTANTIUS, *Divinarum institutionum libri VII*, ed. S. Brandt CSEL 19 (Vienna: Tempsky, 1890); trans. A. Bowen and P. Garnsey (Liverpool: Liverpool University Press, 1993).

LAYTON, B. (1987) (ed. and trans.), *The Gnostic Scriptures* (New York: Doubleday).

MAXIMUS OF TURIN, *Sermones*, ed. A. Mulzenbecher, CCSL 23 (Turnhout: Brepols, 1962).

MAXIMUS THE CONFESSOR, *Ambiguorum liber*, PG 91. 1032–1417.

——*Capita theologica et oikonomica*, PG 90. 1084–1173.

——*On the Cosmic Mystery of Jesus Christ: Selected Writings of St Maximus the Confessor*, trans. P. M. Blowers and R. L. Wilken (Crestwood, NY: St Vladimir's Seminary Press, 2003).

——*Quaestiones ad Thalassium*, i: *Quaestiones I–LV*, ed. C. Laga and C. Steel, CCSG 7 (Turnhout: Brepols, 1980).

——*Quaestiones ad Thalassium*, ii: *Quaestiones LVI–LXV*, ed. C. Laga and C. Steel, CCSG 22 (Turnhout: Brepols, 1990).

METHODIUS OF OLYMPUS, *De creatis* (fragments), ed. G. N. Bonwetsch, GCS 27 (Leipzig: J. C. Hinrichs, 1917), 493–500.

——*De libero arbitrio*, ed. G. N. Bonwetsch, GCS 27 (Leipzig: J. C. Hinrichs, 1971), 145–206.

MUSURILLO, H. (1972) (ed. and trans.), *The Acts of the Christian Martyrs* (Oxford: Oxford University Press).

NEMESIUS OF EMESA, *De natura hominis*, PG 40. 504–817.

ORIGEN, *Commentarius in Joannem* i, ed. C. Blanc, SC 120 (Paris: Éditions du Cerf, 1966).

——*De principiis* i–ii, ed. with French trans., H. Crouzel and M. Simonetti, SC 252 (Paris: Éditions du Cerf, 1978).

——*De principiis* iii–iv, ed. with French trans., H. Crouzel and M. Simonetti, SC 268 (Paris: Éditions du Cerf, 1980).

——*Homilia in Genesim*, ed. H. Baehrens; French trans., L. Doutreleau, SC 7 (Paris: Éditions du Cerf, 1944).

PHILO OF ALEXANDRIA, *De opificio mundi.* Greek text with Eng. trans., F. Colson and G. Whitaker, *Works of Philo*, i, LCL (Cambridge, Mass.: Harvard University Press, 1929).

PROSPER OF AQUITAINE, *De providentia Dei.* Latin text with Eng. trans. M. Marcovich, Suppl. *VC* 10 (Leiden: E. J. Brill, 1989).

PSEUDO-DIONYSIUS THE AREOPAGITE, *De divinis nominibus*, ed. B. Suchla, *Corpus Dionysiacum*, i (Berlin: de Gruyter, 1990).

SALVIAN OF MARSEILLES, *De guberatione Dei*, ed. G. Lagarrigue, SC 220 (Paris: Éditions du Cerf, 1971).

SNYDER, G. (1968) (trans.), *The Apostolic Fathers: A New Translation and Commentary*, vi (London: Thomas Nelson).

TATIAN, *Oratio ad Graecos.* Greek text and Eng. trans., M. Whittaker, OECT (Oxford: Clarendon, 1982).

TERTULLIAN, *Adversus Hermogenem*, ed. F. Chapot, SC 439 (Paris: Éditions du Cerf, 1999).

——*Adversus Marcionem.* Latin text and Eng. trans., E. Evans, OECT (Oxford: Clarendon Press, 1972).

——*De baptismo*, ed. R. Refanlé SC 35, 2nd edn. (Paris: Éditions du Cerf, 2002).

——*De virginibus velandis*, ed. with French trans., E. Schulz-Flügel and P. Mattei SC 424 (Paris: Éditions du Cerf, 1997).

THEODORET OF CYRRHUS, *De providentia orationes*, PG 83. 556–773.

THEOPHILUS OF ANTIOCH, *Ad Autolycum.* Greek text and Eng. trans., R. Grant OECT (Oxford: Clarendon Press, 1970).

WALSH, J., and WALSH, P. G. (1985) (eds. and trans.), *Divine Providence and Human Suffering*, MFC 17 (Wilmington, Del.: Michael Glazier).

Secondary sources

ALEXANDRE, M. (1976), 'L'exégèse de Gen.1, 1–2a dans l' *In Hexaemeron* de Grégoire de Nysse: Deux approaches du problème de la matière', in H. Dörries *et al.* (eds.), *Gregor von Nyssa und die Philosophie* (Leiden: E. J. Brill), 159–92.

ARMSTRONG, A. (1959), 'The Theory of the Non-Existence of Matter in Plotinus and the Cappadocians', *StPatr* 5: 427–9.

BALTHASAR, H. URS VON. (1995), *Presence and Thought: An Essay on the Religious Philosophy of Gregory of Nyssa*, trans. M. Sebanc (San Francisco: Ignatius Press).

——(2003), *Cosmic Liturgy: The Universe according to Maximus the Confessor*, trans., B. E. Daley (San Francisco: Ignatius Press).

BEHR, J. (2000), *Asceticism and Anthropology in Irenaeus and Clement* (Oxford: Oxford University Press).

——(2001), *The Formation of Christian Theology*, i: *The Way to Nicaea* (Crestwood, NY: St Vladimir's Seminary Press).

——(2004), *The Formation of Christian Theology*, ii: *The Nicene Faith* (Crestwood, NY: St Vladimir's Seminary Press).

BENGSCH, A. (1957), *Heilsgeschichte und Heilswissen: Eine Untersuchung zur Struktur und Entfaltung des theologischen Denkens im Werk 'Adversus Haereses' des Hl. Irenäus von Lyon* (Leipzig: St. Benno Verlag).

BENJAMINS, H. (1994), *Eingeordnete Freiheit: Freiheit und Vorsehung bei Origenes* (Leiden: E. J. Brill).

BERGMANN, S. (2005), *Creation Set Free: The Spirit as Liberator of Nature*, trans. D. Scott (Grand Rapids, Mich.: Eerdmans).

BLOWERS, P. (2003), 'The World in the Mirror of Holy Scripture: Maximus the Confessor's Short Hermeneutical Treatise in *Ambiguum ad Joannem 37*', in P. Blowers *et al.* (eds.), *In Dominico Eloquio / In Lordly Eloquence: Essays on Patristic Exegesis in Honor of Robert Louis Wilken* (Grand Rapids, Mich.: Eerdmans), 408–26.

BOSTOCK, G. (1992), 'Origen's Philosophy of Creation', in R. Daly (ed.), *Origeniana Sexta: Papers of the Fifth International Congress, Boston College, 14–18 August 1989* (Leuven: Leuven University Press), 253–69.

BOUYER, L. (1988), *Cosmos: The World and the Glory of God*, trans. P. de Fontnouvelle (Petersham, Mass.: St. Bede's Publications).

CALLAHAN, J. (1958), 'Greek Philosophy and the Cappadocian Cosmology', *DOP* 12: 29–57.

Centre d'études des religions du livre (1973), *In principio: interprétations des premiers versets de la Genèse* (Paris: L'Institut d'études augustiniennes).

CHADWICK, H. (1966), *Early Christian Thought and the Classical Tradition* (Oxford: Oxford University Press).

CHITTY, D. (1966), *The Desert a City* (Crestwood, NY: St Vladimir's Seminary Press).

COPAN, P., and CRAIG, W. (2004), *Creation out of Nothing: A Biblical, Philosophical, and Scientific Exploration* (Grand Rapids, Mich.: Baker Academic).

CROUZEL, H. (1962), *Origène et la philosophie* (Paris: Anbier).

—— (1989), *Origen: The Life and Thought of the First Great Theologian*, trans. A. S. Worrall, (San Francisco: Harper & Row).

DALMAIS, I. (1952), 'La théorie des 'logoi' des creatures chez saint Maxime le Confesseur', *RSPT* 36: 244–9.

DANIÉLOU, J. (1956), *The Bible and the Liturgy* (Notre Dame, Ind.: University of Notre Dame Press).

DAVIES, O. (2004), *The Creativity of God: Word, Eucharist, Reason* (Cambridge: Cambridge University Press).

DILLON, J. (1977), *The Middle Platonists* (London: Duckworth).

DYSINGER, L. (2005), *Psalmody and Prayer in the Writings of Evagrius Ponticus* (Oxford: Oxford University Press).

EHRHARDT, A. (1966), *The Beginning: A Study in the Greek Philosophical Approach to the Concept of Creation from Anaximander to St. John* (Manchester: Manchester University Press).

FIDDES, P. (2001), 'Creation out of Love', in J. Polkinghorne (ed.), *The Work of Love: Creation as Kenosis* (Grand Rapids, Mich.: Eerdmans), 167–91.

GÉHIN, P. (1993), 'Introduction', in *Évagre le Pontique: Scholies à Ecclésiastique*, SC 397 (Paris: Éditions du Cerf), 9–47.

GREGORIOS, P. (1988), *Cosmic Man: The Divine Presence: The Theology of St. Gregory of Nyssa* (New York: Paragon House).

GROH, D. (2005), 'Creation Theology, Biblical Hermeneutics and Natural Philosophy in Western Christianity', for the symposium *Interpreting Nature and Scripture: History of a Dialogue*, Pascal Centre for Advanced Studies in Faith and Science, Redeemer University College, Ancaster, Ontario, 18 July 2005.

GUILLAUMONT, A. (1962), *Les 'Kephalaia Gnostica' d'Évagre le Pontique et l'histoire d'origénisme chez les grecs et chez les syriens* (Paris: Éditions du Seuil).

GUNTON, C. (1998), *The Triune Creator: A Historical and Systematic Study* (Edinburgh: T & T Clark).

HARL, M. (1975), 'Structure et Cohérence du *Peri Archôn*', in *Origeniana: Premier colloque international des etudes origéniennes, Montserrat, 18–21 septembre 1973* (Bari: Instituto di Letteratura Christiana Antica), 11–32.

HAYWARD, C. (1995), *Saint Jerome's Hebrew Questions on Genesis* (Oxford: Oxford University Press).

KOCH, H. (1932), *Pronoia und Paideusis: Studien über Origenes und sein Verhältnis zum Platonismus* (Berlin: de Gruyter).

LE BOULLUEC, A. (1975), 'La place de la polémique antignostique dans le *Peri Archôn*', in *Origeniana: Premier colloque international des études origéniennes, Montserrat, 18–21 septembre,1973* (Bari: Instituto di Letteratura Christiana Antica), 47–61.

—— (1977), 'A-t-il des traces de la polémique antignostique d'Irénée dans le *Péri Archôn* d'Origène?, in M. Krause (ed.), *Gnosis and Gnosticism: Papers Read at the Seventh International Conference on Patristic Studies, Oxford, September 8–13 1975* (Leiden: E. J. Brill), 138–47.

LIES, L. (1992), *Origenes' 'Peri Archôn': Eine Undogmatische Dogmatik* (Darmstadt: Wissenschaftliche Buchgesellschaft).

LOSSKY, V. (1957), *The Mystical Theology of the Eastern Church* (Cambridge: James Clarke).

LYMAN, J. R. (1993), *Christology and Cosmology: Models of Divine Activity in Origen, Eusebius, and Athanasius* (Oxford: Oxford University Press).

MAY, G. (1994), *Creatio ex Nihilo: The Doctrine of 'Creation out of Nothing' in Early Christian Thought*, trans. A. S. Worrall (Edinburgh: T & T Clark).

MCDONNELL, K. (1996), *The Baptism of Jesus in the Jordan: The Trinitarian and Cosmic Order of Salvation* (Collegeville, Minn.: Liturgical Press).

NAUTIN, P. (1973), 'Genèse 1, 1–2, de Justin à Origène', in *In principio: Interprétations des premiers versets de la Genèse* (Paris: L'Institut d'études augustiniennes), 61–94.

NORRIS, R. (1965), *God and World in Early Christian Theology: A Study in Justin Martyr, Irenaeus, Tertullian, and Origen* (New York: Seabury).

PAGELS, E. (1986), 'Exegesis and Exposition of the Genesis Creation Accounts in Selected Texts from Nag Hammadi', in C. Hedrick and R. Hodgson (eds.), *Nag Hammadi, Gnosticism, and Early Christianity* (Peabody, Mass.: Hendrickson), 257–85.

PATTERSON, L. (1997), *Methodius of Olympus: Divine Sovereignty, Human Freedom, and Life in Christ* (Washington D.C.: Catholic University of America Press).

PEARSON, B. (1988), 'Use, Authority and Exegesis of Mikra in Gnostic Literature', in M. Mulder (ed.), *Mikra: Text, Translation, Reading and Interpretation of the Hebrew Bible in Ancient Judaism and Early Christianity* (Assen: Van Gorcum), 635–52.

—— (2004), *Gnosticism and Christianity in Roman and Coptic Egypt* (New York: T & T Clark).

PÉPIN, J. (1964), *Théologie cosmique et théologie chrétienne* (Paris: Presses universitaires de France).

—— (1976), 'Exégèse de *In Principio* et théorie des principes dans l'*Exameron* (I 4,12–16)', in *Ambrosius Episcopus: Atti del Congresso internazionale di studi ambrosiani di Milano, 1974*, (Milan: Vita e Pensiero), i. 427–82.

PERKINS, P. (1985), 'Sophia and the Mother-Father: The Gnostic Goddess', in C. Olsen (ed.), *The Book of the Goddess Past and Present: An Introduction to Her Religion* (New York: Crossroad), 97–109.

PERKINS, P. (1986), 'Ordering the Cosmos: Irenaeus and the Gnostics', in C. Hedrick and R. Hodgson (eds.), *Nag Hammadi, Gnosticism, and Early Christianity* (Peabody, Mass.: Hendrickson), 221–55.

PÉTREMENT, S. (1990), *The Separate God: The Christian Origins of Gnosticism*, trans. C. Harrison (San Francisco: Harper & Row).

RICHARD, A. (2003), *Cosmologie et théologie chez Grégoire de Nazianze* (Paris: L'Institut d'études augustiniennes).

ROBBINS, F. (1912), *The Hexaemeral Literature: A Study of the Greek and Latin Commentaries on Genesis* (Chicago: University of Chicago Press).

ROUSSEAU, P. (1994), *Basil of Caesarea* (Berkeley: University of California Press).

ROUSSELET, J. (1973), 'Grégoire de Nysse, avocat de…Moïse', in *In principio: Interprétations des premiers versets de la Genèse* (Paris: Études Augustiniennes), 95–113.

RUDOLPH, K. (1987), *Gnosis: The Nature and History of Gnosticism*, trans. R. M. Wilson (San Francisco: Harper & Row).

SCHEFFCZYK, L. (1970), *Creation and Providence*, trans. R. Strachan (New York: Herder & Herder).

SCHOEDEL, W. (1979), 'Enclosing, not Enclosed: The Early Christian Doctrine of God', in W. Schoedel and R. Wilken (eds.), *Early Christian Literature and the Classical Intellectual Tradition* (Paris: Beauchesne), 75–86.

SHERWOOD, P. (1955), *The Earlier Ambigua of St. Maximus the Confessor and His Refutation of Origenism* (Rome: Herder).

SORABJI, R. (1983), *Time, Creation, and the Continuum: Theories in Antiquity and the Early Middle Ages* (Ithaca, NY: Cornell University Press).

SOLIGNAC, A. (1973), 'Éxegèse et métaphysique: Genèse 1, 1–3 chez saint Augustin', in *In principio: Interprétations des premiers versets de la Genèse* (Paris: L'Institut d'études augustiniennes), 153–71.

STRUTWOLF, H. (1993), *Gnosis als System: Zur Rezeption der valentinianischen Gnosis bei Origenes* (Göttingen: Vandenhoeck & Ruprecht).

THUNBERG, L. (1995), *Microcosm and Mediator: The Theological Anthropology of Maximus the Confessor*, 2nd edn. (Chicago: Open Court).

TOLLEFSEN, T. (2000), *The Christocentric Cosmology of St. Maximus the Confessor: A Study of His Metaphysical Principles* (Oslo: Unipub Forlag).

TORRANCE, T. (1995), 'The Greek Conception of Space in Early Christian Theology', in *Divine Meaning: Essays in Patristic Hermeneutics* (Edinburgh: T & T Clark), 289–342.

TZAMALIKOS, P. (2006), *Origen: Cosmology and Ontology of Time* (Leiden: E. J. Brill).

VALLÉE, G. (1980), 'Theological and Non-Theological Motives in Irenaeus's Refutation of the Gnostics', in E. P. Sanders (ed.), *Jewish and Christian Self-Definition*, i: *The Shaping of Christianity in the Second and Third Centuries* (Philadelphia: Fortress Press), 174–85.

VAN WINDEN, J. C. M. (1997), *Archē: A Collection of Patristic Studies*, ed. J. den Boeft and D. Runia (Leiden: E. J. Brill).

WILLIAMS, M. (1999), *Rethinking 'Gnosticism': An Argument for Dismantling a Dubious Category* (Princeton: Princeton University Press).

WILLIAMS, R. (1994), ' "Good for Nothing"? Augustine on Creation', *AugStud* 25: 9–24.

—— (1999), 'Creation', in A. Fitzgerald (ed.), *Augustine through the Ages: An Encyclopedia* (Grand Rapids, Mich.: Eerdmans), 251–4.

WOLFSON, H. (1970), 'The Identification of *Ex Nihilo* with Emanation in Gregory of Nyssa', *HTR* 63: 53–60.

YOUNG, F. (1991), ' "*Creatio Ex Nihilo*": A Context for the Emergence of the Christian Doctrine of Creation', *Scottish Journal of Theology*, 44: 139–51.

CHAPTER 45

EARLY CHRISTIAN ETHICS

FRANCINE CARDMAN

EARLY Christian ethics is only beginning to constitute itself as an area of early Christian studies. Its sources, methods, purposes, and parameters are fluid and shifting, the disciplinary and ideological allegiances of its practitioners multiple and at times refractory. Theologians and ethicists, sociologists of religion, historians of late antiquity, church historians, proponents of cultural studies, gender studies, post-colonial studies, queer studies—all approach this protean terrain with particular interests and insights, commitments and conflicts. As a result, what was once regarded as distant background for Christian ethics (when it was regarded at all) has become a rich matrix for exploring the practice of Christianity in the late ancient world. In this context the study of early Christian ethics is subject to the same transformative pressures and heuristic concerns as early Christian studies as a whole.

Early Christianity was pluralistic, as were the worlds that constituted its context; of necessity the perspectives or methodologies and interpretative frameworks for studying early Christian ethics will be also. Because text does not equal world, practices and material culture must be interrogated along with textual evidence. Theology, doctrine, and ethical teachings are not closed systems that can be understood solely through their own internal logic, but must be viewed in their larger social, cultural, and political contexts and interactions. The study of early Christian

Research for this essay was funded in part by a Henry Luce III Fellowship in Theology from the Association of Theological Schools in 2002–3.

ethics does not belong solely to ethicists or even to Christians, but to a much more diverse community of inquirers than in the past.

45.1 THE STUDY OF EARLY CHRISTIAN ETHICS

One way to see the significance of the shifting terrain and its new explorers is to consider where the study of early Christian ethics has been located for most of the twentieth century—who has pursued the subject, to what purposes, and with what methods—and then to examine a pivotal change in approach that has marked out new directions of inquiry.

45.1.1 Theological Ethics and History

Historians, theologians, ethicists, and sociologists who studied aspects of early Christian ethics in the first half of the twentieth century tended to concentrate on elucidating central ethical themes in a normative construct drawn from the New Testament, and then tracing developments and deformities in their appropriation through various periods. The great syntheses of Adolf von Harnack and Ernst Troeltsch from early in the century were driven by a concern with the relationship of the gospel or the 'Christian religion' (Harnack) or 'Christian ethos' (Troeltsch) to modern life and its religious and social questions, which the authors attempted to address by studying the history of Christianity, especially its early centuries.

In his effort to identify the 'essence of Christianity', Harnack specified three central elements of Jesus' preaching—the kingdom of God, God the Father and the infinite value of the human soul, and higher righteousness and the love commandment (Harnack 1957; original German 1893)—and then examined particular questions about ethics (the relationship of the gospel and the world, the poor, law, and work) and doctrine (Christology and the Creed). Similarly, in *The Mission and Expansion of Christianity in the First Three Centuries* he regarded the 'gospel of love and charity' and its practical implications as a key factor in Christianity's appeal and growth (Harnack 1961b; original German 1905). Troeltsch investigated the 'social problem' of the relationship of Church and world, 'the Christian ethos', and western civilization in *The Social Teaching of the Christian Churches* (Troeltsch 1960; original German 1911). Central to his description of that ethos is the message of the infinite worth of the human soul and the love of God manifested in love of neighbour. Under the now-dated rubric of 'early Catholicism' he examined asceticism and the resultant separation of Church and world, then social teachings on possessions, work, callings and classes, trade, the family, slavery, and charity that partially bridged that gap. Troeltsch's sociological method led him to observe developments often ignored by theologians and ethicists: 'the rise of a new class' constituted by bishops and clergy, the development of a theology of imperial authority, and the influence of Stoicism on Christian ideas of natural law and the functions of the state, thus anticipating issues that would come to the foreground of contemporary studies of early Christian ethics.

Explicitly theological concerns about the foundations of Christian ethics and the relationship between ethics and spirituality drove the historical interpretations of early Christian texts and Graeco-Roman philosophy in the decades after the First World War by Kenneth Kirk (*The Vision of God*, 1931) and Anders Nygren (*Agape and Eros*, 1953). Following the Second World War, H. Richard Niebuhr grappled with 'the enduring problem' of the relationship of Christianity and civilization through his five typologies of *Christ and Culture* (1951).

With the exception of Harnack, these authors were not primarily scholars of early Christian history and theology. All of them read the sources and conceptualized the history of early Christian ethics in light of explicit theological and confessional interests, employing 'types' to interpret previous developments and to elucidate if not direct the course of contemporary Christian ethics. Niebuhr's typologies have influenced the ways in which a generation or more of Christian ethicists has understood early Christianity.

Contemporary ethicists and moral theologians who have dealt with the history of Christian ethics have done so largely for the purposes of constructive theological ethics within the traditions of the Christian churches. Their surveys or analyses give a relatively small amount of attention to the early church, for the most part concentrating on some aspects of Augustine's thought (e.g. sexual ethics or just war), perhaps noting the development of the penitential system in the western church, then leaping to Thomas Aquinas or the Reformation (Pinckaers 1995; Wogaman 1993; to some extent Mahoney 1987[1]). Documentary collections reflect a similar approach (Wogaman and Strong 1996; Forell 1966; Beach and Niebuhr 1973, 2nd edn.).[2]

45.1.2 Changing Patterns

Eric Osborn's *Ethical Patterns in Early Christian Thought* (1976) represented a change in some important respects. His scholarly work was in New Testament and early Christianity, and he made no claims to identify the essence of Christian faith or ethics. Osborn isolated four major ethical patterns in the New Testament (righteousness, discipleship, faith, and love) and analysed the way in which major figures (Clement of Alexandria, Basil of Caesarea, John Chrysostom, and Augustine) employed them. Where his work has more in common with some earlier studies is in focusing almost exclusively on philosophy and theology, leaving readers without a sense of the larger contexts beyond the history of ideas that shaped both authors and audiences in the period. Nevertheless, Osborn's book clearly marks the beginning of a transition in the study of early Christian ethics.

That transition came into full view with the publication of Wayne Meeks's ground-breaking work on *The Origins of Christian Morality* (1993). Preceded by his *Moral World of the First Christians* (1986) and presupposing the methodologies he employed to striking effect in *The First Urban Christians: The Social World of the Apostle Paul* (1983), the new study located the beginnings of Christian ethics in the contexts and communities, the 'social practices and cultural webs of meaning that together constitute "early Christianity"' (1993: 11). Relying on the 'usual suspects' (New Testament and extra-canonical texts, second-century Christian texts, and related Jewish, Greek, and Roman sources), Meeks traced multiple narrative lines—from 'turning' to Christian faith, constructing 'the grammar of Christian practice', and, with intervening stories, moving toward 'senses of an ending'—that emerged from the evolving life of Christian communities in the first and second centuries and shaped their moral sensibilities. The 'ethnography of morals' that he delineated is historical and descriptive, and points the way toward further study of the development of Christian ethics in late antiquity.

Meeks's work inspired sociologist Rodney Stark to apply methodologies and insights from the sociology of religion and the study of new religious movements to early Christianity. *The Rise of Christianity* (1996) has garnered attention for its account of the 'success' of Christianity, which Stark attributes to the 'attractive, liberating, effective social relations and organizations' that were 'prompted and sustained' by Christianity's central doctrines, especially its emphasis on mercy and love of neighbour as necessary corollaries of love of God, which Stark identifies as 'entirely new' in the ancient world (pp. 211–12). Many scholars of late antiquity, on the other hand, have been critical of Stark's methodology and conclusions (e.g. Castelli 1998; Hopkins 1998; Klutz 1998; see also Stark 1998), which in the end sound surprisingly like Harnack's. Yet the wide readership that the book attracted attests to a growing cultural interest in Christian origins and early Christian ethics that is only in part religious or theological in nature and that inquires about the ways in which Christian belief translated (or not) into practice.[3]

45.1.3 Locating Early Christian Ethics

As Osborn (1976) at times suggests, and Meeks (1993) has shown, the sources and subjects of early Christian ethics are broader than treatises that deal explicitly with questions of conflict or discipline, broader than paraenetic and homiletic texts, theological and apologetic works, even than texts themselves. Sources for the reflexive activity that constitutes early Christian ethics are found in the first instance in the practices and rituals of Christian communities, in the memories they privilege and the narratives they construct. Consequently, much of the foundational development of early Christian ethics can be discerned only indirectly, through the emerging outlines of Christian communities and identities as shaped by rituals of initiation, prayer, preaching, prophecy, and the rudiments of church order. These outlines are revealed—and to some extent concealed—in texts that witness to ritual and other communal practices. But neither texts alone, however various, nor the internal logic of theological claims can adequately delineate early Christian ethics. 'When we speak of morality or ethics, we are talking about people. Texts do not have an ethic; people do' (Meeks 1993: 4). Understanding who these people are, what they say and believe, what they *do*, how they relate to each other, what they hope for, and how this shapes their lives, is essential to the study of early Christian ethics. Integrally connected to the social formations (Kile 2005: 227–32) constructed by the way in which such questions are lived is another set of ethical markers. How Christians interact with people outside their religious and social networks, how they regard and relate to religious and cultural practices not their own, how they conceive the political order, and the degree to which they participate in or resist it, mark not simply the 'context' of early Christian ethics but a significant part of its content.

Viewing early Christian ethics from this wider perspective suggests that 'everything is ethics', and in a sense this is true. All the major topics of early church history and historical theology (e.g. martyrdom, apology, asceticism, Church, and empire) are ethical sources, as are more obvious subjects such as social welfare, war and peace, sexual morality, and church order and discipline. A majority of the surviving texts, regardless of their canonicity or their 'orthodoxy', are pertinent to the study of early Christian ethics. Explicitly moral or disciplinary works are a relatively small proportion of these sources. Few, if any, offer what we would recognize as theoretical or second-level reflections on matters of ethics. Rather, early Christian texts relevant to ethics are primarily paraenetic and practical. They are intended to draw their hearers or readers into a world- and character-constructing narrative and move them to act, at times by informing or reminding them of that narrative, at times by delighting them with it, at other times by exhorting, threatening, shaming, or cajoling. The common characteristic of such texts is that they are *rhetorical* in their nature and aims. Persuasion is their primary mode, rather than instruction, explanation, or analysis. Attending to rhetoric, to the changing patterns and content of Christian discourses, is a critically important means of delineating early Christian ethics.

It would be impossible to survey all relevant practices or discourses here or to note every area of ethical concern in early Christianity. Rather, by considering three major patterns—body, social economy, and empire—and some of the ethical issues central to each, my intention is to trace some of the major contour lines of the emerging field of early Christian ethics, point out key methodological and interpretative issues in each area, and identify promising scholarly approaches and directions for further study.

45.2 BODY

For much of the twentieth century theologians and ethicists dealt with the early Christian body primarily in biblical and doctrinal terms, frequently asserting the difference of Christian conceptions from 'Greek' or 'pagan' ideas of the body. Scholarly assessments of the body in early Christianity have undergone a sea-change since the publication of Peter Brown's provocative and influential work, *The Body and Society*, in 1988. By locating the early Christian body in a wider cultural context, Brown was able to make stronger connections, as well as sharper distinctions, between Christian and Roman attitudes and practices. He shows that Graeco-Roman concern for 'care of the self' dictated a sexual ethic that strictly regulated passion and greatly limited sexual expression, even encouraging its disavowal among upper-class Roman males, an outlook which makes Christian sexual renunciation appear less a novelty than a development that stands in some continuity with cultural trends. At the same time, Brown argues that Christian motivations for embracing such an ethic differ in important ways and have a different end in view: Christians directed their bodily performance of single-heartedness towards participation in Christ's resurrection and the end of the cycle of marriage, birth, and death. In each case, however, bodily discipline served to define both the human person and society. Continence and self-control on the part of the Roman elite reinforced social order and distance, while Christian practice, particularly among those men and—an important difference—women dedicated to permanent virginity, anticipated the end of that order entirely.

To see the body, as Brown proposes, as a site of social and symbolic meaning is to see it in greater dimensionality than a good deal of Christian ethics and theology has tended to regard it. Theology and ethics in a Christian context presuppose a beginning and an ending, creation and eschatology in some form, thereby pointing to realities beyond themselves and, ultimately, beyond history. This symbolic strength is also a historical weakness: it is often difficult to correlate theological assertions and ethical imperatives with actual practice, personal or communal behaviour. The more fully incarnated body that Brown and others call for also has a signifying potential that reaches beyond itself, but does so *within* history, suggesting ways of seeing and making connections with practice that can help to illuminate meanings and motivations and perhaps to measure the valence of more formal claims.

From this newer perspective, the body is at once powerful and problematic, a source of early Christian ethics and simultaneously a site of theological and social struggle. What early Christians *do* with their bodies in the multiple and overlapping contexts of their lives is as much the subject-matter of ethics as what they *say* about bodies, and now requires at least as much scholarly attention. The range of questions is extensive: how early Christians treat their own bodies; how they treat the bodies of others, whether sexual partners or spouses, children or slaves, women and men in church communities; how they treat the bodies of their pagan or Jewish neighbours; how the treatment of these and other bodies changed once Christians began to acquire social and political power. Here it is only possible to suggest the outlines of some aspects of these questions as they appear in current scholarship.

45.2.1 Constructing the Christian Body

In the late second and early third centuries, Irenaeus, Tertullian, and, somewhat differently, Clement of Alexandria aimed to mark the boundaries of the Christian social body and at the same time to construct an 'orthodox' stance for the physical body by charging 'heretics' with either libertinism or contempt for the body (and sometimes both). Conflicts over these and related issues were often conceptualized by ancient teachers and many modern scholars under the rubrics of countering 'Gnosticism' (and, by association, Marcionism) and limiting or abetting 'Hellenization' (Harnack 1961a; Chadwick 2001: 127, but see 1980[4]). Scholars now emphasize the limitations of using anti-heretical writings, particularly accusations of sexual immorality, as sources of information about Gnostic teachings and ethics (Knust 2006: 15–50, 89–112; King 2003: 123–4, 190–3, 201–8; E. A. Clark 1999: 28–9) or about actual Christian behaviour in contrast to that attributed to Gnostics. Persistent efforts to counter ascetic rejection of sexuality and marriage or zeal for voluntary martyrdom, however, may suggest that these practices and beliefs appealed to many Christians, 'Gnostic' or not. Estimates of the influence that these debates had on early Christian ethics and practices regarding the body will necessarily undergo revision as scholarship continues to explore the fluidity rather than fixity of 'heresy' and 'orthodoxy' as theological and social categories.

45.2.2 Sexuality, Asceticism, and Care of the Self

A long-standing question about the distinctiveness of Christian ethics in this period has been partially recast by recent scholarship as a debate over the aptness and accuracy of the analyses proffered by Brown (1988) and Foucault (1986) about the meanings of early Christian rhetoric and practice in regard to the body, sexuality, and asceticism. Many scholars see significant continuity between Roman 'technologies of the self' and early Christian practices of sexual asceticism even when allowances are made for differences in their final ends (Perkins 1995: 5–7 and the book as a whole; E. A. Clark 1988, 1990; Corrington 1992; Rousselle 1988; differently, Francis 1995).[5] Others argue that the divergence of ends negates any meaningful similarity or, when continuity can be demonstrated, find that it has compromised the Christian position (Behr 2000: 5–22, on Irenaeus and Clement of Alexandria respectively). Cameron is appreciative but cautious in an early essay (1986); Cooper (1999: 2–4) takes exception to Foucault's lack of attention to the negotiations of social status inherent in self-representation; and Gaca (2003) argues for Christian discontinuity with Greek philosophy and sexual ethics. Nevertheless, as Cameron (1986) suggests, the map of early Christian territory has changed.

It remains to be shown whether and how Christian theological narratives might contextualize apparently similar ethical practices in such a way as to make them radically discontinuous in meaning from their pagan embodiments. Yet it would be difficult, at best, to demonstrate that most early Christians were significantly different from their pagan counterparts in terms of care of the self, sexual morality, marriage and household, corporal punishment, or even exposure of children (Meeks 1993: 147–9; Osiek and MacDonald 2006: 50–3; Corbier 2001: 59–60, 66–72; Bakke 2005: 110–51, 280–6).[6]

Fourth-century controversies about asceticism, virginity, and marriage are dealt with elsewhere in this volume. Here it is important to note the confluence of those debates and the trends preceding them in Augustine's articulation of a theology of original sin and its consequences that tied its transmission to the act of sexual intercourse. Augustine thus guaranteed that the Stoic ethic of procreation as the justification for sex as well as its limit, already appropriated by Clement of Alexandria, would live on in western Christianity for more than a millennium. Unlike Clement, however, he seems to have excepted payment of the 'conjugal debt' from the procreative justification in circumstances when it preserves the fidelity of an immoderately demanding spouse (Hunter 2002). Despite a stricter application of the procreative ethic, Clement had resolved the contrast between asceticism and marriage in favour of marriage, which he saw (for the male) as 'an image of divine providence' (Brown 1988: 122–39, at 135). Later eastern theology would be more reserved. Influenced by Origen's ambivalence about the body[7] and his enthusiasm for virginity, Gregory of Nyssa would propose that sexuality was a necessary post-Fall modification to human bodiliness (but see Behr 1999); his praise of virginity was so extravagant that some interpreters hold that his apparent denigration of marriage is an ironic device (Hart 1990, 1992).

Although eastern Christianity did not make the Augustinian connection between original sin and sex (or entertain doctrinal disputes about original sin), both East and West recognized in practice, if not theology, a sexual hierarchy among Christians in which virginity and continence were superior to marriage, ascetics and celibate clerics to laity. The status that accrued to virginity and continence combined with increasing clerical power in the late fourth century and the force of the procreative ethic to assert clerical control over the laity, particularly in the West (Hunter 2005, 2007). In time, acceptance of the power relations that structure the communal Christian body into a sexual hierarchy itself became a matter of ecclesial ethics.

45.2.3 Martyrdom and Suffering

Persecution and martyrdom created a nexus for the making of ethics, disciplining the personal and communal Christian body. They demanded witness to the faith (confession, suffering, death), created another status hierarchy, occasioned an interpretative crisis over the nature of acceptable witness (voluntary martyrdom, flight or avoidance, co-operation with Roman authorities), and necessitated a means of mitigating an ethical demand that in reality only a small number of Christians actually confronted or were able to meet (Frend 1967: 307–8, 393–4).[8] Controversies about the forgiveness of apostasy led to increased episcopal authority, greater distance between clergy and laity, and further development of penance as a discipline of church order and communal identity.

Despite the religious and political divide represented by the public executions of martyrs, certain commonalities made Christian behaviour intelligible to pagan observers and, perhaps, attractive to some. A cultural discourse of the self as sufferer that was taking root in the early empire provided an opening for Christian narratives of power engendered by martyrdom (Perkins 1995: 15–40, 104–23). Roman 'glorification of suicide' (Bowersock 1995: 72), as well as Jewish and Roman attitudes toward dying for 'noble causes' (Droge and Tabor 1992), offered analogies if not models for Christian martyrdom, though scholars disagree on the extent of such influence (Bowersock 1995: 7–13; Boyarin 1999: 93–126; Young 2005: 76–80; 2001: 5; Rajak 1997). Whether martyrdom was a form of suicide and ethically unacceptable was debated by Christian apologists and their cultural critics; among Christian groups, 'catholic' bishops and theologians seeking to deny the status of martyrs to those regarded as heretical or schismatic (Marcionites, Montanists, Donatists) depicted them as suicides rushing to their religiously meaningless deaths outside the 'true' ecclesial body.

Early Christian martyrdom established a pattern of meaning and behaviour in relation to Roman authority and imperial values that was honoured even in its breach during the period of persecution, but would undergo great revision during and after the reign of Constantine. Yet the significance of state-sponsored violence as an arena for forging Christian identity, the performative dimensions of martyrdom as spectacle, and the way in which Christians turned these public and violent deaths to their own ends would all leave their mark on Christian ethics, particularly beliefs and practices related to suffering, sacrifice, and violence

(Castelli 2004; Salisbury 2004; Harrill 2006: 157–63, on the slave body and spectacle; Young 2001,[9] 2005). Martyrdom's reversal of the most basic bodily experiences—birth and death, pain and joy (even ecstasy), birthing and nurturing, as gendered actions that are transgendered among the martyrs and translocated from physical to spiritual relationships—made the martyr's body both glorious and evanescent, and other Christian bodies more easily subject to martyrdoms' unintended consequences.

45.3 SOCIAL ECONOMY

Personal and group relationships in public and private spheres formed a matrix for early Christian morality. Interactions between rich and poor, slaves and masters, patrons and clients, holy persons and those in need of healing, instruction, forgiveness, or other favours, to name some key relationships, constituted a social economy in which patronage, power, and piety were driving forces. Christian constructions of this social economy created moral demands, helped shape communal identity, and at times sharpened distinctions between believers and their neighbours.

Study of social and economic history in classical antiquity, particularly the culture of patronage that characterized the Roman world (Garnsey 1988, 1999; Veyne 1990), has transformed the way in which scholars of Christian antiquity approach what used to be termed 'social issues' in early Christianity or the 'social teachings of the church fathers'. The introduction of power and its social sources and meanings as a category of analysis appropriate to Christian practices and beliefs has allowed scholars to see early Christianity as embedded in its wider culture even when critiquing it or attempting to separate itself from it (Brown 1995). The effectiveness of early Christian social ethics depended at least in part on continuities with cultural assumptions and expectations; conversely, it was these same shared values that at times limited the range of Christian vision. Consequently, social critique was at once less radical than some interpreters of this period might like and, when it departed from or revised cultural assumptions, more political than others might care to acknowledge. Poverty and slavery are two areas in which attention to the social economy and its relationships of power and patronage is creating a much more complex picture of early Christian ethics and practice.

45.3.1 Poverty

Poverty as a subject independent of its contrast with riches is a new direction in early Christian studies that goes beyond the problematic of the relationship of rich and poor in Christian communities or the rubric of charity as a Christian virtue. New Testament scholars have long laboured over such topics as Paul's collection for the saints, redemptive almsgiving, and the salvation of the rich young man in the synoptic gospels. They began to take a social history approach to economic issues in the early churches rather more recently with studies of property and riches (Hengel 1974, German original 1973) and the relationship of rich and poor Christians (Countryman 1980; Osiek 1983), carrying the discussion into the later second century. Despite the appeal of Latin American liberation theologians since the 1970s to the 'power of the poor in history', late twentieth-century church historians paid little attention to either poor or rich believers and the use of money before Justo Gonzalez's *Faith and Wealth* (1990), which he intentionally limited to a focus on theological and ethical ideas of social and economic relations in the early church, rather than practice.

Recent scholarship, however, has begun to look more closely at the social and economic contexts of poverty, hunger, and famine in late antiquity and Christian practices of poverty relief as these developed in the fourth century (Holman 1999*a*, 1999*b*, 2001; Brown 1992: 71–113; 2002).[10] Prior to Constantine, almsgiving and other forms of charity were mainly personal acts within the life of church communities. With the new privileges granted to Christian clergy by the Emperor, the bishop's office took on increasingly public dimensions. The bishop became 'lover of the poor' and 'governor of the poor', roles that increased his power not only in his church but in his city (Brown 2002). Care of the poor became a public ministry, most visibly in a new institution, the *xenodocheion*, a combination of hostel for strangers and hospice or hospital for the poor; Basil of Caesarea is famously associated with one named for him (the *Basileias*) that he established outside that city when still a priest during the Cappadocian famine *c.* 368/370. The bishop looked and acted like a classical *euergetēs*, a public benefactor, who in Graeco-Roman culture made his gifts for the good of the city and his own honour; but the bishop gave publicly for relief of the poor not because they were citizens, but because they were in need; not for his own honour, but in imitation of God's *philanthrōpia* (Brown 2002; Daley 1999).

This new scholarly approach is most fully realized in Susan Holman's careful study of poverty relief in late fourth-century Roman Cappadocia (2001). Relating the theology of the poverty sermons of Basil of Caesarea, Gregory of Nyssa, and Gregory of Nazianzus to the social and economic conditions of Cappadocia around 370, her analysis models the integration of theology, rhetoric, cultural practices (the 'gift economy'), and poverty studies. Both Holman and Brown note the cultural continuities and discontinuities in the practice of poverty relief, as well as the emergence of a new Christian discourse on poverty (Holman 2001: 179; Brown 2002: 41, 64). Sermons are a major source of this discourse—the Cappadocians and John Chrysostom in the East, Ambrose of Milan and Augustine in the West—and, along with biblical commentaries, are only beginning to be tapped (Mayer and Allen 2000; Allen and Mayer 1993; Brändle 1979). More studies like Holman's would help to fill in the public terrain of early Christian ethics; more attention to Syriac Christianity in this and other areas would extend its geographical range (e.g. Harvey 1993). Further analysis of the rhetoric of exchange in almsgiving, the Christian appropriation of Stoic ideas about poverty and slavery, and the relationship of material to spiritual poverty is also needed (Ramsey 1982: 251–9; Cardman 2008; Buell 2003).

45.3.2 Slavery

Slavery in the ancient world, particularly the Roman Empire, has received considerable attention from classical scholars in the past 40 years (Hopkins 1978; Finley 1980; Wiedemann 1981; Bradley 1987, 1994; Garnsey 1996; DuBois 2003). Central questions in their work concern the economics of slavery (Hopkins 1978), the harshness of slavery and the means by which masters maintained control of their slaves (Bradley 1987), and, more recently, the conjunction of women, slavery, gender, sexuality, violence, and sexual ethics (Saller 1998, 2003; P. Clark 1998; Connolly 1998; Parker 1998). Scholars of Christian origins have begun to carry the analysis of ancient slavery into the New Testament period and second century (Harrill 1995, 2006; Glancy 2002). Responding to Martin's (1990) benign interpretation of slavery as a social reality and as a key theological metaphor for salvation in the Pauline letters, they emphasize the physical and sexual violation of the 'enslaved body' (Glancy 2002), the ideological construction of slaves and slavery as symbolizing weakness, subjugation, immorality, and 'womanish-ness' in contrast to true manhood (Glancy 2002; Harrill 2006), and possible limits on female Christian slaves' obedience to the sexual demands of their masters (Osiek 2003). In reproducing much of the Roman rhetoric of slavery, the New Testament and early Christian writings 'participate in and promote' the 'ideology of mastery' undergirding Roman *auctoritas* (Harrill 2006: 2). Early Christian martyrdom and apologetic literature viewed pagan slaves both as faithful witnesses to the morality of their Christian owners and as their betrayers; Christian slaves among the martyrs (Blandina, Felicity) are depicted as equalling or surpassing their owners or other Christians in suffering and courage, thereby simultaneously elevating their status and recalling the Roman *exemplum* of the faithful slave (Harrill 2006: 145–63, 161–2).

Classicists have shown that interrogating early Christian texts about aspects of slavery and familial relationships yields insight into representation and social history and raises methodological challenges. One critical question is the degree to which sermons and other Christian texts can be taken as evidence for actual practice. Shaw, for instance, considers descriptions or prescriptions of punishments meted out to sons in the sermons of Augustine to be reliable evidence of the 'servile' relationship of sons to fathers in the late empire (1987: 17–28, at 28), while Garnsey (1997: 104, 121) is far more cautious about the move from text to practice, yet unwilling to reject Augustine's sermons or other writings entirely as a source for social history.[11] Patricia Clark takes Augustine's accounts in the *Confessions* of his parents' relationship, Monica's advice to abused wives, and her dealings with her own slaves as evidence for the reality of violence or the threat of violence as a means of domestic control by husbands over wives and mistresses over household slaves, finding little difference between Christians and Romans of similar social status (1998). Brown's brief discussion of slaves and domestic violence reflects a similar perspective (1992: 51–3).

Students of ancient Christianity and ethics have given relatively little consideration to attitudes and practices of slavery and slaveholding among Christians or to theoretical perspectives and critiques such as Glancy's and Harrill's. Meeks (1993) and Brown (2002) refer to Christian slaveholding only in passing, and Gonzalez (1990) describes the economics of Roman slaveholding but does not mention Christian slaves or slaveholders. In the past 40 years, scholarship in English has been slight: a few articles address slavery in the church fathers (Corcoran 1984; Hofbeck 1993), and a short monograph surveys Augustine's views on slavery (Corcoran 1985). German scholarship has been more attentive, with notable studies by Richard Klein (1988, 2000). Nevertheless, the continued lack of attention to slavery among most 'patristic' scholars is startling. Bernadette Brooten raises challenging questions about the legacy of slaveholding culture on Christian sexual ethics, particularly in regard to the ways in which the sexual dynamics of slavery are reflected and repeated in early Christian teachings about marriage, sexuality, and gender relations (1996: 328–9; 2003: 190–1, 193; 2004; forthcoming). Other issues waiting to be addressed include slavery understood as a consequence of the Fall; the interconnections of slavery, domestic violence, corporal punishment, sexual violation of slaves, women, and children, and torture as a legal tool; the dynamics of Christian acceptance of slavery and increased integration into the Empire; ethical strictures on the treatment of slaves by Christians and the extent to which these might imply a broader social critique of slavery.

Some reckoning must also be made of the fact that nearly all Christian writers of the third through fifth centuries take slavery and Christian slaveholding for granted. Classical scholars do not find that Christianity made any positive difference in the lives of slaves, despite declarations of the spiritual equality of slave and free or the elevation as 'sons' of those who were once 'slaves' to sin (MacMullen 1990: 143–4, 154; Garnsey 1997: 102–3, 120–1). Keith Bradley's judgement is more severe, and students of early Christian ethics cannot escape dealing with it: 'Christianity did not humanise or otherwise improve the life of the slave; it destroyed it' by viewing slavery as a consequence of sin, and salvation as found in submission to the master/Master (1994: 151).

45.4 EMPIRE AND ETHICS

Christianizing the Roman Empire went hand in hand with imperializing the Church in the fourth century, and theological and ethical rationales emerged to legitimate both. If power had remained a largely hidden dynamic in Christianity's progress to this point, it came into the open after Constantine's victory at the Milvian Bridge (312) and his deepening identification with the Christian God and Church. As both parties learned to negotiate this evolving relationship, tendencies that had been in the background came to the fore (e.g. associating political and divine authority), while stances that had commanded attention and defined identity (e.g. martyrdom) began to recede, and others (e.g. the burgeoning ascetic movement) took their place. Shifting attitudes and behaviour contributed to reshaping Christian moral discourse in the fourth century: increased interaction of the Emperor and imperial officials with bishops, a providential interpretation of recent history, emergence of Christian religious intolerance supported by the state, a model of episcopal leadership that drew heavily on Roman civic ideals and reflected the style of imperial officials. In this process, as Averil Cameron and others have observed, a new Christian rhetoric of Empire emerged, and with it a new practice of Christian *imperium* (Cameron 1991; Brown 1981, 1988, 2002; Digeser 2000).

45.4.1 Providence and History

With the end of persecution, the inclusion of Christianity under the umbrella of religious toleration raised by Constantine and Licinius, and Constantine's growing interest in the Christian God and the affairs of the Church, fourth-century believers found it necessary to revise their estimates of the Roman Empire and, ultimately, of history. Other chapters of this handbook discuss the changing relationship of Church and Empire and the development of early Christian historiography; this section focuses on the ethical issues and implications of the re-evaluation of providence, history, and Empire by apologists, theologians, and a new kind of writer, the Christian church historian.

Fourth-century Christians sought to account for both the Great Persecution that had brought an end to 40 years of relative peace for the Church and for Constantine's great reversal. They developed ideas of divine providence already familiar from early apologies, distinguished them from pagan notions of providence or fate, and asserted that divine care and wrath could be discerned in contemporary events. God's wrath was evident in the ghastly deaths of persecuting emperors (Lactantius), but also in the persecutions by which God disciplined believers who had grown lax (Eusebius). God's providence was made known by the end of persecution and the rule of the wise and religious 'Christian emperor' Constantine, whose praises Eusebius wove into an imperial theology (Drake 1976; Cameron 1997). Near the beginning of the century Lactantius and Eusebius were enthusiastic proponents of this triumphal view of history and empire; just into the next, following the sack of Rome by the Visigoths in 410, Augustine began to write his negative reassessment in the *City of God* (Garnsey 2002).

The intervening century saw not only the writing but the making of Christian history in an increasingly Christian empire. The providential interpretation of history gave Christians the license to make history and empire their own. That some resisted these changes (e.g. among desert ascetics) did little to prevent them. The imperialization of Christianity and, in important areas, Christian ethics went hand in hand with this sense of the providential disposition of political events in the fourth century.

45.4.2 Religious Intolerance

Christians were the immediate beneficiaries of the policy of religious toleration after 313; by the end of the century 'orthodox' Christianity (i.e. that defined by the Councils of Nicaea and Constantinople) would become the established religion of the Empire. Scholars argue that prior to Diocletian's persecution Lactantius and Eusebius were proponents of religious toleration in an empire they imagined would remain pluralistic (Digeser 2000; Chesnut 1986: 111–40). Under Constantine, however, as Christian bishops learned to exercise political power for religious ends, they also learned the politics of religious intolerance and developed ethical rationales for engaging in it. If, as Drake proposes, intolerance was not a quality inherent in Christian monotheism, but an 'unintended consequence' of the alliance that Constantine had struck with the bishops as he forged a policy of religious inclusivity, there is more than a little irony in the outcome (Drake 2000: 463–70, 479–81).

Christian intolerance of pagans and Jews grew markedly after the brief reign of the emperor Julian (361–3) and his abortive efforts to rebuild the Temple in Jerusalem. The rhetoric of the rejected other was revived in regard to Jews and easily turned against pagans as power was added to the religious equation (MacMullen 1997: 1–73; but see Brown 2002: 29–54 for a less dramatic interpretation). Christian violence against pagan religious sites was lauded in some hagiographical works and generally tolerated by Roman authorities. Ambrose famously outmanœuvred Theodosius I, compelling him to rescind an order that Christians rebuild a synagogue they had burned in the garrison town of Callinicum on the Euphrates in 388 (McLynn 1994: 291–360; Drake 2000: 441–83). The bishop cast his political victory over the Emperor as a victory of the gospel over its enemies, the Jews, who were also endangering the Emperor's salvation. About the same time in Antioch John Chrysostom railed against Jews and Judaizers (Wilken 1983: 95–128; Kelly 1995: 63–6). The theological anti-Judaism and personal invective of these great preachers contributed to politicizing the relationship of Christians and Jews, leaving a troubling ethical legacy.

Intolerance of heresy and schism kept pace with these developments. The execution, by imperial order, of the Spanish bishop Priscillian on charges of sexual immorality and magic (c. 388) was opposed by few bishops (Chadwick 1976; Burrus 1996). The civil proscription of heresy under Theodosius I in the 380s completed a process set in motion by Constantine, thereby reinforcing the Christian rhetoric of otherness and redirecting it against 'others' within the Church (Hunt 1993). Initially reluctant to use coercion against the Donatists, Augustine justified his turn to the use of civil power after 411 to compel them to join catholic churches by appealing to the corrective disciplinary power of God, human fathers, and kings, Nebuchadnezzar being a favourite example of the latter (Frend 1952: 244–99; Brown 1964; Russell 1999; Cardman 1999). Further investigation into the roots of Christian religious intolerance, coercion, and violence is a critical task in the study of early Christian ethics.

45.4.3 Leadership

As bishops, particularly those of major cities, became more powerful ecclesial and political figures, they began to resemble the Roman elite, modelling or striving for the values and virtues that classical *paideia* cultivated (Brown 1992: 35–70). This evolution was abetted by the gradual incorporation of elite women and men into the Church and its leadership ranks, creating a 'Christian aristocracy' by the end of the fourth century who brought the concepts and expectations of aristocratic status culture to the Church (Salzman 2000, 2002). Monks who became bishops (some, like Basil of Caesarea, from elite families) provided a different but basically complementary model of leadership (Sterk 2004) and made asceticism an ideal for episcopal office (Rapp 2005). Rapp examines the leadership of less prominent bishops from the fourth through the seventh centuries, focusing on their public roles in relation to their cities and to imperial authority. The detailed picture that is emerging of the closely related religious and secular responsibilities of late antique bishops makes it possible to relate treatises on the nature of clerical office and the character of office-holders (e.g. Ambrose, *Off.*;[12] John Chrysostom, *Sac.*) to practice and to reassess their ethical injunctions and implications.

45.5 CONCLUSION

This survey of early Christian ethics as an emerging field of study with multiple investigators, interests, methodologies, and subjects has pointed out significant developments that are shaping the field and suggested some of the directions that future study might take. As scholars launch new explorations of this old terrain, perspectives broaden, lost features or forgotten routes of interconnection are rediscovered, familiar landmarks no longer loom as large as they once did, and boundaries begin to fade. In this process, the necessity of self-conscious reflection on the ethics of studying early Christian ethics becomes manifest. The decentring of Christian theology as the orienting point for this field demands a new kind of scholarly, personal, and communal accountability on the part of its students, whatever their relationship to Christianity. Being accountable for the scholarly endeavour is a three-step process. The first step applies to the way in which the field is framed and particular subjects are constructed in relation to the interpreters' (both individuals and academic disciplines) social location and commitments (Buell 2005: 33; DuBois 2003: p. xii); the second applies to examining the rhetoric and practices that constitute early Christian ethics and their relationship to the multiple cultural contexts and communities of late antiquity (Buell 2005; Knust 2006: 11; Lyman 2003; Kile 2005); the third to the social, religious, and political consequences of both previous steps (Drake 2000; E. A. Clark 1991). In the end, the rhetoric and practice of studying early Christian ethics must themselves be ethical.

NOTES

1. Mahoney's explicit intent was *not* to write a comprehensive history but to critique reductionist distinctions that had narrowed Roman Catholic moral theology.
2. Selections from early Christian texts average about one-sixth of the total in these collections; Augustine is a strong favourite here, as in the survey histories.
3. Popular fascination with the entirely fictional *Da Vinci Code* and the historical documents from the Coptic-Gnostic library found at Nag Hammadi reflects the general public's discovery of the multiplicity of early Christianities and its attempts to come to terms with this reality; perhaps at the same time suggesting discontent with a monolithic, dominant Christian narrative and its perceived unsatisfactory present results. A different popular audience may be attracted to Stark's narrative, which can connect with a growing interest in practice without having to attend to the reality of early Christian multiplicity and competing narratives.
4. Chadwick (2001) refers, without editorial comment or qualification, to Clement of Alexandria's characterization of licentious gnostic sects in *Strom.* 3 (on marriage); but in 1980 comments explicitly on the rarity of sexual excess among Gnostics represented in the Nag Hammadi texts.

5. Rouselle's book pre-dates Brown's *Body and Society* (1988) and is contemporary with much of Foucault's work; its methodology has strong affinities to both scholars. Chs. 8–12 deal with early Christian texts, primarily from the fourth century.

6. Bakke (2005) makes stronger distinctions, but some rest on conjecture: Christian condemnations of abortion and exposure presumably led to a reduction in both (pp. 135–9, 149–50, 284); similarly in regard to pederasty (pp. 140–9, 151, 284–5); but he's more certain about an increase in Christian use of corporal punishment of children (pp. 190–1, 219–20, 285).

7. Origen's views (actual or imagined) on the resurrection body were the theological catalyst for a wider controversy over 'Origenism' at the end of the fourth century and again in the mid-sixth century. E. A. Clark (1990, 1992) is essential for the earlier conflict.

8. The number of known martyrs before 250 is small, perhaps fewer than a hundred (my estimate). Frend estimates those who died under Decius and Valerian in the mid-third century as perhaps several hundred, including several bishops; they were vastly outnumbered by those who apostasized; those martyred in the Great Persecution from 303 to 311 might, expansively, number 3,000–3,500.

9. Young views Christian martyrdoms as 'public liturgy' and 'ritual exaltation', anti-spectacles that serve their own purposes, not Rome's; emphasizing their eucharistic and sacrificial dimensions, she does not consider the spectacular way in which these deaths are portrayed in martyr accounts.

10. Patlagean (1977) remains an essential resource for these studies.

11. On whipping, see also Bruyn (1999) and Saller (1991).

12. Colish (2005) argues that Ambrose's treatises on the Old Testament patriarchs, often taken as lesser instances of the ethics expounded in *Off.*, constitute an 'ethics for the common man', and were originally delivered as catechetical sermons for those preparing for baptism.

SUGGESTED READING

As a way into current study of early Christian ethics, Meeks (1993) is an excellent starting point for content, method, and context. Peter Brown (1988) is also essential. Two smaller studies by Brown are important for the way they reorient vision: Brown (1992 and 2002). Works that address cultural continuities in specific areas related to ethics in the New Testament period and second century provide a foundation and model for inquiry into subsequent centuries. These include Perkins (1995) in regard to bodily practices and expectations in caring for the self; Knust (2006) and Buell (2005) on sexual slander and ethnic reasoning respectively as forms of ethical argument with deep cultural roots and profound social and political implications; and Glancy (2002) and Harrill (2006). Studies that embody new methods and perspectives on fourth-century topics are Holman (2001) in regard to poverty relief and Drake (2000) in regard to religious intolerance. Osborn (1976) is helpful in guiding the reader to primary sources and to the previous generation of biblical, philosophical, and theological scholarship.

BIBLIOGRAPHY

ALLEN, P., and MAYER, W. (1993), 'Computer and Homily: Accessing the Everyday Life of Early Christians', *VC* 47: 260–80.

BAKKE, O. M. (2005), *When Children Became People: The Birth of Childhood in Early Christianity* (Minneapolis: Fortress Press).

BEACH, W., and NIEBUHR, H. R. (1973) (eds.), *Christian Ethics: Sources of the Living Tradition* (New York: Ronald Press).

BEHR, JOHN (1999), 'The Rational Animal: A Rereading of Gregory of Nyssa's *De hominis opificio*', *JECS* 7: 219–47.

—— (2000), *Asceticism and Anthropology in Irenaeus and Clement* (Oxford: Oxford University Press).

BOWERSOCK, G. W. (1995), *Martyrdom and Rome* (Cambridge: Cambridge University Press).

BOYARIN, D. (1999), *Dying For God: Martyrdom and the Making of Christianity and Judaism* (Palo Alto, Calif.: Stanford University Press).

BRADLEY, K. R. (1987), *Slaves and Masters in the Roman Empire: A Study in Social Control* (New York: Oxford University Press; Tournai: Editions Latomus, 1984).

—— (1994), *Slavery and Society at Rome* (Cambridge: Cambridge University Press).

BRÄNDLE, R. (1979), *Matth. 25, 31–46 im Werk des Johannes Chrysostomos* (Tübingen: J. C. B. Mohr/Paul Siebeck).

BROOTEN, B. (1996), *Love Between Women: Early Christian Responses to Female Homoeroticism* (Chicago: University of Chicago Press).

—— (2003), 'Nature, Law, and Custom in Augustine's *On the Good of Marriage*', in S. Matthews, C. Briggs Kittredge, and M. Johnson-DeBaufre (eds.), *Walk in the Ways of Wisdom: Essays in Honor of Elisabeth Schüssler Fiorenza* (Harrisburg, Pa.: Trinity Press International), 181–93.

—— (2004), 'Der lange Schatten der Sklaverei im Leben von Frauen und Mädchen', in F. Crüsemann, M. Crüsemann, C. Janssen, R. Kessler, and B. Wehn (eds.), *Dem Tod nicht glauben: Sozialgeschichte der Bibel: Festschrift für Luise Schottroff zum 70. Geburtstag* (Gütersloh: Gütersloher Verlaghaus GmbH), 488–503.

—— (forthcoming), 'What Is Slavery's Religious and Sexual Legacy?'.

BROWN, P. (1964), 'St. Augustine's Attitude toward Religious Coercion', *JRS* 54: 107–16; repr. in Brown, *Religion and Society in the Age of St. Augustine* (London: Faber & Faber, 1982), 80–101.

—— (1981), *The Cult of the Saints: Its Rise and Function in Latin Christianity*, The Haskell Lectures on History of Religions, NS 2 (Chicago: University of Chicago Press).

—— (1988), *The Body and Society: Men, Women and Sexual Renunciation in Early Christianity*, Lectures on the History of Religions, 13 (New York: Columbia University Press).

—— (1992), *Power and Persuasion in Late Antiquity: Towards a Christian Empire* (Madison: University of Wisconsin Press).

—— (1995), *Authority and the Sacred: Aspects of the Christianisation of the Roman World* (Cambridge: Cambridge University Press).

—— (2002), *Poverty and Leadership in the Later Roman Empire*, The Menahem Stern Jerusalem Lectures, Historical Society of Israel (Hanover, NH: University Press of New England for Brandeis University Press).

BRUYN, T. S. DE (1999), 'Flogging a Son: The Emergence of the Pater Flagellans in Latin Christian Discourse', *JECS* 7: 249–90.

BUELL, D. K. (2003), ' "Sell What You Have and Give to the Poor": A Feminist Interpretation of Clement of Alexandria's *Who Is the Rich Person Who Is Saved?*', in S. Matthews, C. Briggs Kittredge, and M. Johnson-DeBaufre (eds.), *Walk in the Ways of Wisdom: Essays in Honor of Elisabeth Schüssler Fiorenza* (Harrisburg, Pa.: Trinity Press International), 194–213.

—— (2005), *Why This New Race? Ethnic Reasoning in Early Christianity* (New York: Columbia University Press).

BURRUS. V. (1996), *The Making of a Henetic: Gender, Authority, and the Priscillianist Controversy* (Berkeley: University of California Press).

CAMERON, A. (1986), 'Redrawing the Map: Early Christian Territory after Foucault', *JRS* 76: 266–71.

—— (1991), *Christianity and the Rhetoric of Empire: The Development of Christian Discourse* (Berkeley: University of California Press).

—— (1997), 'Eusebius' *Vita Constantini* and the Construction of Constantine', in M. J. Edwards and S. Swain (eds.), *Portraits: Biographical Representation in the Greek and Latin Literature of the Roman Empire* (Oxford: Clarendon Press), 145–75.

CARDMAN, F. (1999), 'The Praxis of Ecclesiology: Learning from the Donatist Controversy', Catholic Theological Society of America, *Proceedings*, 54: 25–37.

—— (2008), 'Poverty and Wealth as Theater: John Chrysostom's Homilies on Lazarus and the Rich Man', in S. Holman (ed.), *Wealth and Poverty in Early Church and Society*, Holy Cross Studies in Patristic Theology and History (Grand Rapids, Mich.: Baker Academic), 159–75.

CASTELLI, E. (1998), 'Gender, Theory, and the Rise of Christianity: A Response to Rodney Stark', *JECS* 6: 227–57.

—— (2004), *Martyrdom and Memory: Early Christian Culture Making* (New York: Columbia University Press).

CHADWICK, H. (1976), *Priscillian of Avila: The Occult and the Charismatic in the Early Church* (Oxford: Clarendon Press).

—— (1980), 'The Domestication of Gnosis', in B. Layton (ed.), *The Rediscovery of Gnosticism: Proceedings of the International Conference on Gnosticism at Yale, New Haven, Connecticut, March 28–31, 1978* (Leiden: E. J. Brill), i. 3–16.

—— (2001), *The Church in Ancient Society: From Galilee to Gregory the Great* (Oxford: Oxford University Press).

CHESNUT, G. (1986), *The First Christian Histories: Eusebius, Socrates, Sozomen, Theodoret, and Evagrius*, 2nd edn., rev. and enlarged (Macon, Ga.: Mercer University Press).

CLARK, E. A. (1988), 'Foucault, the Fathers, and Sex', *JAAR* 56: 619–61.

—— (1990), 'New Perspectives on the Origenist Controversy: Human Embodiment and Ascetic Strategies', *CH* 59: 145–62.

—— (1991), 'Sex, Shame, and Rhetoric: En-gendering Early Christian Ethics', *JAAR* 59: 221–45.

—— (1992), *The Origenist Controversy: The Cultural Construction of an Early Christian Debate* (Princeton: Princeton University Press).

—— (1999), *Reading Renunciation: Asceticism and Scripture in Early Christianity* (Princeton: Princeton University Press).

CLARK, P. (1998), 'Women, Slaves, and the Hierarchies of Domestic Violence: The Family of St. Augustine', in S. R. Joshel and S. Murnaghan (eds.), *Women and Slaves in Greco-Roman Culture: Differential Equations* (London: Routledge), 109–29.

COLISH, M. (2005), *Ambrose's Patriarchs: Ethics for the Common Man* (Notre Dame, Ind.: University of Notre Dame Press).

CONNOLLY, J. (1998), 'Mastering Corruption: Constructions of Identity in Roman Oratory', in S. R. Joshel and S. Murnaghan (eds.), *Women and Slaves in Greco-Roman Culture: Differential Equations* (London: Routledge), 130–51.

COOPER, K. (1999), *The Virgin and the Bride: Idealized Womanhood in Late Antiquity* (Cambridge, Mass.: Harvard University Press; first pub. 1996).

CORBIER, M. (2001), 'Child Exposure and Abandonment', in S. Dixon (ed.), *Childhood, Class, and Kin in the Roman World* (London: Routledge), 52–73.

CORCORAN, G. (1984), 'The Christian Attitude to Slavery in the Early Church', *Milltown Studies*, 13: 1–36; 14: 19–36.

——(1985), *Saint Augustine on Slavery*, Studia Ephemeridis «Augustinianum», 22 (Rome: Institutum Patristicum Augustinianum), 40–6.

CORRINGTON, G. P. (1992), 'The Defense of the Body and the Discourse of Appetite: Continence and Control in the Greco-Roman World', in V. L. Wimbush (ed.), *Discursive Formations, Ascetic Piety and the Interpretation of Early Christian Literature*, Semeia, 57 (Atlanta: SBL), part I, 65–74.

COUNTRYMAN, W. (1980), *The Rich Christian in the Church of the Early Empire: Contradictions and Accommodations* (New York: Edwin Mellen Press).

DALEY, B. (1999), 'Building a New City: The Cappadocian Fathers and the Rhetoric of Philanthropy', 1998 NAPS Presidential Address, *JECS* 7: 431–61.

DIGESER, E. DEPALMA (2000), *The Making of a Christian Empire: Lactantius and Rome* (Ithaca, NY: Cornell University Press).

DRAKE, H. A. (1976), *In Praise of Constantine: A Historical Study and New Translation of Eusebius' Tricennial Orations* (Berkeley: University of California Press).

——(2000), *Constantine and the Bishops: The Politics of Intolerance* (Baltimore: Johns Hopkins University Press).

DROGE, A. J., and TABOR, J. D. (1992), *A Noble Death: Suicide and Martyrdom among Christians and Jews in Antiquity* (San Francisco: HarperSanFrancisco).

DUBOIS, P. (2003), *Slaves and Other Objects* (Chicago: University of Chicago Press).

FINLEY, M. (1980), *Ancient Slavery and Modern Ideology* (New York: Viking Press).

FORELL, G. W. (1966) (ed.), *Christian Social Teachings: A Reader in Christian Social Ethics from the Bible to the Present*, 2nd edn. (Garden City, NY: Anchor Books).

FOUCAULT, M. (1986), *The History of Sexuality*, iii: *The Care of the Self*, trans. R. Hurley (New York: Pantheon Books; French original 1984).

FRANCIS, J. A. (1995), *Subversive Virtue: Asceticism and Authority in the Second-Century Pagan World* (University Park, Pa.: Pennsylvania State University Press).

FREND, W. H. C. (1952), *The Donatist Church* (Oxford: Clarendon Press; repr. 1985).

——(1967), *Martyrdom and Persecution in the Early Church* (Garden City, NY: Anchor Books).

GACA, K. L. (2003), *The Making of Fornication: Eros, Ethics, and Political Reform in Greek Philosophy and Early Christianity* (Berkeley: University of California Press).

GARNSEY, P. (1988), *Famine and Food Supply in the Graeco-Roman World: Responses to Risk and Crisis* (New York: Cambridge University Press).

——(1996), *Ideas of Slavery from Aristotle to Augustine* (Cambridge: Cambridge University Press).

——(1997), 'Sons, Slaves—and Christians', in B. Rawson and P. Weaver (eds.), *The Roman Family in Italy: Status, Sentiment, Space* (Oxford: Clarendon Press), 101–21.

——(1999), *Food and Society in Classical Antiquity* (Cambridge: Cambridge University Press).

——(2002), 'Lactantius and Augustine', in A. K. Bowman, H. M. Cotton, M. Goodman, and S. Price (eds.), *Representations of Empire: Rome and the Mediterranean World*, Proceedings of the British Academy, 114 (Oxford: Oxford University Press), 153–79.

GLANCY, J. A. (2002), *Slavery in Early Christianity* (New York: Oxford University Press).

GONZALEZ, J. L. (1990), *Faith and Wealth: A History of Early Christian Ideas on the Origin, Significance, and Use of Money* (San Francisco: Harper & Row).

HARNACK, A. VON (1957), *What Is Christianity?*, trans. T. Saunders, with an introduction by R. Bultmann (New York: Harper; German original 1900).

——(1961*a*), *History of Dogma*, i–ii, trans. N. Buchanan (New York: Dover Publications; repr. of 1899 English trans. of 1893 German 3rd edn.).

——(1961*b*), *The Mission and Expansion of Christianity in the First Three Centuries*, trans. J. Moffatt (New York: Harper; repr. of 1908 English trans. of vol. i of 1905 German 2nd edn.).

HARRILL, J. A. (1995), *The Manumission of Slaves in Early Christianity*, Hermeneutische Untersuchungen zur Theologie, 32 (Tübingen: J. C. B. Mohr/(Paul Siebeck)).

——(2006), *Slaves in the New Testament* (Minneapolis: Fortress Press).

HART, M. D. (1990), 'Reconciliation of Body and Soul: Gregory of Nyssa's Deeper Theology of Marriage', *TS* 51: 450–78.

——(1992), 'Gregory of Nyssa's Ironic Praise of the Celibate Life', *Heythrop Journal*, 33: 1–19.

HARVEY, S. A. (1993), 'The Holy and the Poor: Models from Early Syriac Christianity', in E. A. Hanawalt and C. Lindberg (eds.), *Through the Eye of a Needle: Judeo-Christian Roots of Social Welfare* (Kirksville, Mo.: The Thomas Jefferson University Press), 43–66.

HENGEL, M. (1974), *Property and Riches in the Early Church*, trans. J. Bowden (Philadelphia: Fortress Press).

HOFBECK, J. (1993), 'Ethics and Mysticism of Slavery in Church Fathers', *StPatr* 24: 102–7.

HOLMAN, S. R. (1999*a*), 'Healing the Social Leper in Gregory of Nyssa's and Gregory of Nazianzus's 'περιφιλοπτωχίας', *HTR* 92: 283–309.

——(1999*b*), 'The Hungry Body: Famine, Poverty and Identity in Basil's *Hom. 8*', *JECS* 7: 338–63.

——(2001), *The Hungry Are Dying: Beggars and Bishops in Roman Cappadocia*, Oxford Studies in Historical Theology (Oxford: Oxford University Press).

HOPKINS, K. (1978), *Conquerors and Slaves*, Sociological Studies in Roman History, 1 (Cambridge: Cambridge University Press).

——(1998), 'Christian Number and its Implications', *JECS* 6: 185–226.

HUNT, D. (1993), 'Christianising the Roman Empire: The Evidence of the Code', in J. Harries and I. Wood (eds.), *The Theodosian Code* (Ithaca, NY: Cornell University Press), 143–58.

HUNTER, D. G. (2002), 'Augustine, Sermon 354A: Its Place in His Thought on Marriage and Sexuality', *AugStud* 33: 39–60.

——(2005), 'Rereading the Jovinianist Controversy: Asceticism and Clerical Authority in Late Ancient Christianity', in D. B. Martin and P. Cox Miller (eds.), *The Cultural Turn in Late Ancient Studies: Gender, Asceticism, and Historiography* (Durham, NC: Duke University Press), 119–35.

HUNTER, D. G. (2007), *Marriage, Celibacy, and Heresy in Ancient Christianity: The Jovinianist Controvery*, OECS (Oxford: Oxford University Press).

KELLY, J. N. D. (1995), *Golden Mouth: The Story of John Chrysostom, Ascetic, Preacher, Bishop* (Grand Rapids, Mich.: Baker Books).

KILE, C. (2005), 'Feeling Persuaded: Christianization as Social Formation', in W. Braun (ed.), *Rhetoric and Reality in Early Christianities*, Studies in Christianity and Judaism, 16, Canadian Corporation for the Study of Religion (Waterloo, Ont.: Wilfred Laurier University Press), 219–48.

KING, K. (2003), *What Is Gnosticism?* (Cambridge, Mass.: Belknap Press of Harvard University Press).

KIRK, K. E. (1931), *The Vision of God: The Christian Doctrine of the Summum Bonum* (New York: Harper & Row; repr. 1966).

KLEIN, R. (1988), *Die Sklaverei in der Bischöfe Ambrosius und Augustinus* (Stuttgart: F. Steiner).

—— (2000), *Die Haltung der kappadokischen Bischöfe Basilius Caesarea, Gregor von Nazianz, und Gregor von Nyssa sur Sklaverei* (Stuttgart: F. Steiner).

KLUTZ, T. E. (1998), 'The Rhetoric of Science in the Rise of Christianity: A Response to Rodney Stark's Sociological Account of Christianization', *JECS* 6: 162–84.

KNUST, J. W. (2006), *Abandoned to Lust: Sexual Slander and Ancient Christianity* (New York: Columbia University Press).

LYMAN, R. (2003), 'Hellenism and Heresy', *JECS* 11: 209–22.

MacMULLEN, R. (1990), 'What Difference Did Christianity Make?', in *Changes in the Roman Empire: Essays in the Ordinary* (Princeton: Princeton University Press), 142–55.

—— (1997), *Christianity and Paganism in the Fourth to Eighth Centuries* (New Haven: Yale University Press).

MAHONEY, J. (1987), *The Making of Moral Theology: A Study of the Roman Catholic Tradition* (Oxford: Clarendon Press).

MARTIN, D. B. (1990), *Slavery as Salvation: The Metaphor of Slavery in Pauline Christianity* (New Haven: Yale University Press).

MAYER, W., and ALLEN, P. (2000), *John Chrysostom*, ECF (London: Routledge).

McLYNN, N. (1994), *Ambrose of Milan: Church and Court in a Christian Capital* (Berkeley: University of California Press).

MEEKS, W. A. (1983), *The First Urban Christians: The Social World of the Apostle Paul* (New Haven: Yale University Press).

—— (1986), *The Moral World of the First Christians* (Philadelphia: Westminster Press).

—— (1993), *The Origins of Christian Morality: The First Two Centuries* (New Haven: Yale University Press).

NIEBUHR, H. R. (1951), *Christ and Culture* (New York: Harper).

NYGREN, A. (1953), *Agape and Eros*, trans. P. Watson (Philadelphia: Westminster Press; Swedish original 1930).

OSBORN, E. (1976), *Ethical Patterns in Early Christian Thought* (Cambridge: Cambridge University Press).

OSIEK, C. (1983), *Rich and Poor in the Shepherd of Hermas: An Exegetical-Social Investigation*, CBQ Monograph Series, 15 (Washington D.C.: Catholic Biblical Association of America).

—— (2003), 'Female Slaves, Porneia, and the Limits of Obedience', in D. L. Balch and C. Osiek (eds.), *Early Christian Families in Context: An Interdisciplinary Dialogue* (Grand Rapids, Mich.: William B. Eerdman's Publishing Co.), 255–74.

——MacDonald, M. Y., with Tulloch, J. (2006), *A Woman's Place: House Churches in Earliest Christianity* (Minneapolis: Fortress Press).

Parker, H. (1998), 'Loyal Slaves and Loyal Wives: The Crisis of the Outsider-Within and Roman *Exemplum* Literature', in S. R. Joshel and S. Murnaghan (eds.), *Women and Slaves in Greco-Roman Culture: Differential Equations* (London: Routledge), 152–73.

Patlagean, E. (1977), *Pauvreté économique et pauvreté sociale à Byzance, 4e–7e siècles* (Paris: Mouton; La Haye: EHESS).

Perkins, J. (1995), *The Suffering Self: Pain and Narrative Representation in the Early Christian Era* (London: Routledge).

Pinckaers, S. (1995), *The Sources of Christian Ethics*, trans. M. T. Noble, from French 3rd edn. (Washington D.C.: Catholic University of America Press).

Rajak, T. (1997), 'Dying for the Law: The Martyr's Portrait in Jewish-Greek Literature', in M. J. Edwards and S. Swain (eds.), *Portraits: Biographical Representation in the Greek and Latin Literature of the Roman Empire* (Oxford: Clarendon Press), 39–67.

Ramsey, B. (1982), 'Almsgiving in the Latin Church: The Late Fourth and Early Fifth Centuries', *TS* 43: 226–59.

Rapp, C. (2005), *Holy Bishops in Late Antiquity: The Nature of Christian Leadership in an Age of Transition* (Berkeley: University of California Press).

Rousselle, A. (1988), *Porneia: On Desire and the Body in Antiquity*, trans. F. Pheasant (Oxford: Blackwell; French original 1983).

Russell, F. H. (1999), 'Persuading the Donatists: Augustine's Coercion by Words', in W. E. Klingshirn and M. Vessey (eds.), *The Limits of Ancient Christianity: Essays on Late Antique Thought and Culture in Honor of R. A. Markus* (Ann Arbor: University of Michigan Press), 115–30.

Salisbury, J. (2004), *The Blood of Martyrs: Unintended Consequences of Ancient Violence* (New York: Routledge).

Saller, R. (1991), 'Corporal Punishment, Authority, and Obedience in the Roman Household', in B. Rawson (ed.), *Marriage, Divorce and Children in Ancient Rome* (Oxford: Oxford University Press), 144–65.

——(1998), 'Symbols of Gender and Status Hierarchies in the Roman Household', in S. R. Joshel and S. Murnaghan (eds.), *Women and Slaves in Greco-Roman Culture: Differential Equations* (London: Routledge), 85–91.

——(2003), 'Women, Slaves, and the Economy of the Roman Household', in D. L. Balch and C. Osiek (eds.), *Early Christian Families in Context: An Interdisciplinary Dialogue* (Grand Rapids, Mich.: William B. Eerdman's Publishing Co.), 185–204.

Salzman, M. R. (2000), 'Elite Realities and *Mentalités*: The Making of a Western Christian Aristocracy', *Arethusa*, 33: 347–62.

——(2002), *The Making of a Christian Aristocracy: Social and Religious Change in the Western Roman Empire* (Cambridge, Mass.: Harvard University Press).

Shaw, B. (1987), 'The Family in Late Antiquity: The Experience of Augustine', *Past and Present*, 115: 3–51.

Stark, R. (1996), *The Rise of Christianity: A Sociologist Reconsiders History* (Princeton: Princeton University Press).

——(1998), 'E Contrario' [responding to T. Klutz, K. Hopkins, and E. Castelli], *JECS* 6: 259–67.

Sterk, A. (2004), *Renouncing the World Yet Leading the Church: The Monk-Bishop in Late Antiquity* (Cambridge, Mass.: Harvard University Press).

TROELTSCH, ERNST (1960), *The Social Teaching of the Christian Churches*, i, trans. O. Wyon (New York: Harper & Row; repr. of 1931 English trans. of 1911 German edn.).

VEYNE, P. (1990), *Bread and Circuses: Historical Sociology and Political Pluralism*, trans. B. Pearce (London: Penguin).

WIEDEMANN, T. (1981), *Greek and Roman Slavery* (Baltimore: Johns Hopkins University Press).

WILKEN, R. L. (1983), *John Chrysostom and the Jews: Rhetoric and Reality in the Late Fourth Century* (Berkeley: University of California Press).

WOGAMAN, J. P. (1993), *Christian Ethics: A Historical Introduction* (Louisville, Ky.: Westminster/John Knox Press).

—— and STRONG, D. (1996) (eds.), *Readings in Christian Ethics: A Historical Sourcebook* (Louisville, Ky.: Westminster/John Knox Press).

YOUNG, R. (2001), *In Procession before the World: Martyrdom as Public Liturgy in Early Christianity* (Milwaukee, Wis.: Marquette University Press).

—— (2005), 'Martyrdom as Exaltation', in V. Burrus (ed.), *Late Ancient Christianity*, A People's History of Christianity, 2 (Minneapolis: Fortress Press), 70–92.

CHAPTER 46

....

INSTRUMENTA STUDIORUM: TOOLS OF THE TRADE

....

JOSEPH F. KELLY
JEANNE-NICOLE SAINT-LAURENT

I. GENERAL INTRODUCTION

....

THIS chapter will introduce scholars and students to the study of early Christianity by acquainting them with some of the more important tools of research. We do not claim that we have touched all bases; inevitably we have omitted certain items which some readers may consider important. We have left out items partly because of limitations of space but also for the sake of feasibility. We believe that a seriatim list of an enormous number of titles will not be as useful as a more restricted list of valuable and proven titles. Since our primary reading audience is anglophone, English-language titles will predominate, but we will include essential and significant titles in all relevant scholarly languages. We will focus on general areas and not on specific topics (Nicaea, catacombs) or persons (Perpetua, Constantine), even in cases (Origen, Augustine) where those persons have journals and/or societies devoted to them.

The study of early Christianity presumes that the word 'early' is clear; it also presumes that one can distinguish 'early' Christianity from other forms. By this phrase, we mean Christianity from the first century CE to the sixth because, in general, scholars in western Europe and the Americas have seen the sixth and seventh centuries as a transition period from early to medieval, as the Roman Empire faded into history and the barbarian kingdoms replaced it. But this reflects a western view of the period, because the eastern half of the Roman Empire did not succumb to the barbarians, and what westerners call the 'Byzantine' Empire in fact continued the Roman Empire in the East. Indeed, in the twelfth century, the Turks spoke of the Byzantines as the Romans. Some scholars, especially of Christianity in the eastern Mediterranean, would take 'early' into the seventh and eighth centuries. Even specialists in Latin Christianity may wish to include the Spaniard Isidore of Seville (d. 636) and the Anglo-Saxon Bede the Venerable (d. 735) as 'early' Christians. We cannot solve this historiographical problem. For a working definition, we will accept the general western designation and work mostly in the period from the first to the sixth centuries, but we will not be bound by it.

Another factor defines early Christianity. From the mid-first to the mid-second century, the New Testament books came into being, along with a number of other texts. Study of the New Testament has become a discipline separate from the study of early Christianity, and we will honour that distinction. Thus we will consider tools that deal with writers contemporary with the NT, such as Clement of Rome and Ignatius of Antioch, but not with the NT itself, except where NT questions relate directly to early Christianity—for example, the establishment of the NT text and canon in the early Christian period.

Finally, for centuries, the study of early Christianity actually meant patristics, the study of theologians whose authority earned them the honorific title of 'fathers of the church'. Patristics produced studies of immense value, but it often overlooked topics like art and archaeology, and often patronized those writers whose 'heretical' views, usually determined by later standards, disqualified them from being 'fathers'. Here we understand early Christianity to encompass anything related to the history of Christianity in the first six centuries.

II. READINGS

To understand how 'early' Christianity earned that title, the scholar must have some sense of how this period fits into the larger history of Christianity. A good one-volume history of Christianity is *The Oxford Illustrated History of Christianity*, edited by John McManners (Oxford: Oxford University Press, 1990), with essays by leading scholars and very helpful illustrations. Multi-volume histories include *The Oxford History of the Christian Church*, still being produced, edited by Henry and Owen Chadwick, and the new nine-volume *Cambridge History of Christianity*, with multiple editors, initial volumes published in 2005.

Early Christian writers had their greatest impact on medieval writers. One good general history of medieval Christianity is *The Medieval Church: A Brief History* (London: Longman, 1992) by Joseph Lynch.

What can be said of Christian history can also be said of Christian theology. A good one-volume history that situates early Christian theology in the larger scheme is *A Short History of Christian Thought* by Linwood Urban (Oxford: Oxford University Press, 1995). An older work, Jaroslav Pelikan's *The Christian Tradition*, in 5 vols. (Chicago: University of Chicago Press, 1971–89), has great value.

III. General Reference Works which Include Articles on Early Christianity

1. Assfalg, J. (ed.), *Dictionnaire de l'orient chrétien* (Turnhout: Brepols, 1991).
2. Atiya, A. Z. (ed.), *Coptic Encyclopedia*, 8 vols. (New York: Macmillan, 1991).
3. Balz, H. R., *et al.* (eds.), *Theologische Realenzyklopädie* (Berlin: de Gruyter, 1976).
4. Baudrillart, A., *et al.* (eds.), *Dictionnaire d'histoire et de géographie ecclésiastiques* (Paris: Letouzey et Ané, 1912–), 28 vols. published to date; misleading title—topics are very wide-ranging; bibliographies are dependable in recent volumes; excellent help with primary sources and with links among and between figures and issues.
5. Bautz, F. W., and Bautz, T. (eds.), *Biographisch-bibliographisches Kirchenlexikon*, 18 vols. (Hamm: Bautz, 1975–).
6. Buchberger, M. *et al.* (eds.), *Lexikon für Theologie und Kirche*, 3rd edn. (Freiburg-im-Breisgau: Herder, 1993–).
7. Cabrol, F. (ed.), *Dictionnaire d'archéologie chrétienne et de liturgie*, 15 vols. (Paris: Letouzy et Ané, 1907–53).
8. Carey, P., and Lienhard, J. (eds.), *Biographical Dictionary of Christian Theologians* (Peabody, Mass.: Hendrickson, 2002).
9. Cross F. L., and Livingstone, E. (eds.), *The Oxford Dictionary of the Christian Church*, 3rd edn. rev. (Oxford: Oxford University Press, 2005).

10. Farrugia, E. G. (ed.), *Dizionario enciclopedico dell'Oriente cristiano* (Rome: Pontifical Oriental Institute, 2000).

11. Hart, T. A. (ed.), *Dictionary of Historical Theology* (Grand Rapids, Mich.: Eerdmans, 2000).

12. Parry, K., and Hinnells, J. (eds.), *Blackwell Dictionary of Eastern Christianity* (Oxford: Blackwell, 2000).

13. Vacant, A. *et al.* (eds.), *Dictionnaire de théologie catholique*, 15 vols. (Paris: Letouzy et Ané, 1923–50). This is outdated in some respects, but essential in others. It has the longest articles on minor historical figures of any reference work, excellent theological analyses of historical figures and themes, and guidance to primary source material.

14. Viller, M. *et al.* (eds.), *Dictionnaire de spiritualité, ascétique et mystique, histoire et doctrine*, 16 vols. (Paris: Beauchesne et ses fils, 1932–95).

15. Walsh, M. J. (ed.), *Dictionary of Christian Biography* (Collegeville, Minn.: Liturgical Press, 2001).

IV. Reference Works for the Classical World

Because early Christianity was coterminous with the Roman Empire, many classical reference works provide valuable information. The study of Classics is a separate discipline with an enormous literature. Here we list a few reference works.

1. Cancik, H., and Schneider, H. (eds.), *Brill's New Pauly: Encyclopaedia of the Ancient World* (Leiden: E. J. Brill, 2002). Originally published in German as *Der Neue Pauly: Enzyklopädie der Antike* (Stuttgart: J. B. Metzler, 1996).

2. Grant, M., *The Roman Emperors: A Biographical Guide to the Rulers of the Imperial Rome 31 BC–AD 476* (New York: Scribner's, 1985).

3. Grant, M., and Kitzinger, R. (eds.), *Civilization of the Ancient Mediterranean: Greece and Rome*, 3 vols. (New York: Scribner's, 1988).

4. Hornblower, S., and Spawforth, A. (eds.), *The Oxford Classical Dictionary*, 3rd edn. (Oxford: Oxford University Press, 1996). Also available online through *InteLex*, which publishes the Past Masters® series of full-text humanities databases. See <http://www.nlx.com/pstm/index.htm>, 9 June 2006.

5. Hornblower, S., and Spawforth, A. (eds.), *The Oxford Companion to Classical Civilization* (Oxford: Oxford University Press, 1998). Shortened version of 3rd (1996) edn. of the *Oxford Classical Dictionary*.

V. Historical Introductions to Early Christianity

Before getting into specific questions, the reader should consult a general introduction to the period. Many exist, and we recommend the following:

1. Atiya, A. S., *A History of Eastern Christianity* (Notre Dame, Ind.: University of Notre Dame Press, 1968; Millwood, NY: Kraus Reprint, 1980).
2. Bowerstock, G. W., Brown, P., and Grabar, O. (eds.), *Late Antiquity: A Guide to the Postclassical World* (Cambridge, Mass.: Harvard University Press, 1999).
3. Burrus, V., *Late Ancient Christianity: A People's History of Christianity*, ii (Minneapolis: Fortress Press, 2005).
4. Casiday, A., and Norris, F. (eds.), *Cambridge History of Christianity*, ii: *Constantine to 600* (Cambridge: Cambridge University Press, 2007).
5. Chadwick, H., *The Early Church* (Harmondsworth: Penguin, 1967; rev. 1993).
6. Chadwick, H., *The Church in Ancient Society: From Galilee to Gregory the Great* (Oxford: Oxford University Press, 2001).
7. Daniélou, J., and Marrou, H., *The Christian Centuries*, i: *The First Six Hundred Years*, trans. V. Cronin (New York: McGraw-Hill, 1964).
8. Davies, J. G., *The Early Christian Church: A History of its First Five Centuries* (London: Weidenfeld & Nicolson, 1965).
9. Frend, W. H. C., *The Rise of Christianity* (Philadelphia: Fortress Press, 1983).
10. Grant, R., *Augustus to Constantine: The Rise and Triumph of Christianity in the Roman World* (New York: Harper & Row, 1970; repr. 1990).
11. Hazlett, I. (ed.), *Early Christianity: Origins and Evolution to AD 600* (London: S.P.C.K., 1991).
12. Horsley, R. (ed.), *Christian Origins: A People's History of Christianity*, i (Minneapolis: Fortress Press, 2005).
13. Kelly, J., *The World of the Early Christians* (Collegeville, Minn.: Liturgical Press, 1997).
14. Labourt, J., *Le Christianisme dans l'Empire Perse sous la Dynastie Sassanide (224–632)* (Paris: Lecoffre, 1904).
15. MacMullen, R., and Lane, E. N. (eds.), *Paganism and Christianity, 100–425 CE: A Sourcebook* (Minneapolis: Fortress Press, 1992).
16. Markus, R. A., *Christianity in the Roman World* (London: Thames & Hudson, 1974).
17. Mitchell, M., and Young, F. (eds.), *Cambridge History of Christianity*, i: *Origins to Constantine* (Cambridge: Cambridge University Press, 2005).

18. Ramsey, B., *Beginning to Read the Fathers* (New York: Paulist Press, 1985).
19. Rousseau, P., *The Early Christian Centuries* (London: Longman, 2002).
20. Vallée, G. (1999), *The Shaping of Christianity: The History and Literature of Its Formative Centuries (100–800)* (New York: Paulist Press, 1999).

VI. Reference Works for Early Christianity

1. Dassmann, E. (ed.), *Das Reallexikon für Antike und Christentum und das F.J. Dölger-Institut in Bonn: mit Registern der Stichwörter A bis Ianus sowie Autoren, Bände 1–16* (Stuttgart: Hiersemann, 1994).
2. Di Berardino, A. (ed.), *Encyclopedia of the Early Church*, 2 vols., trans. A. Walford with bibliographical amendments by W. H. C. Frend from *Dizionario patristico e di antichitá cristane* (New York: Oxford University Press, 1992).
3. Ferguson, E. (ed.), McHugh, M., and Norris, F. (associate eds.), *Encyclopedia of Early Christianity*, 2nd edn. (New York: Garland Publishers, 1997).
4. Van der Meer, F., and Mohrmann, C., *Atlas of the Early Christian World* (London: Nelson, 1959).
5. Marrou, H.-I., and Palanque, J. R. (eds.), *Prosopographie chrétienne du Bas-Empire*, i: *Prosopographie de l'Afrique chrétienne (303–533)*, ed. A. Mandouze (Paris: Éditions du CNRS, 1982); ii: *Prosopographie de l'Italie chrétienne (313–604)*, ed. C. Pietri *et al.* (Rome: École française de Rome, 1999–2000).

As noted above, many general reference works, especially the French *dictionnaires*, have fine articles on early Christianity.

VII. Critical Editions of Early Christian Works

One must become acquainted with primary texts in order to begin a field of study. Almost all major early Christian texts have been edited, most of them critically. Some appear in individual editions; most appear in ongoing series. Normally these editions include an introduction by the editor(s), a guide to the manuscripts used, an explanation of the editorial precepts used, the text itself with scholarly apparatus and notes, a bibliography, and sometimes a translation into the vernacular. Often the series consist of texts in a single language, such as Latin or Greek, while others include texts in several languages. Migne was the basic source for research into early Christianity well into the mid-twentieth century, when better editions replaced his. Yet Migne remains the only source for some texts. It is common for scholars to patronize Migne, yet as one of his defenders put it, 'Migne—always abused, always used'.

1. Biblioteca de Autores Cristianos (Madrid: various imprints, 1945–).
2. Biblioteca Patristica (Bologna: various imprints, 1981–).
3. Corpus Christianorum, Series Apocrypha (Turnhout: Brepols, 1983–). The series published by Corpus Christianorum are widely thought to be the most reliable texts because of the employment of modern editorial techniques.
4. Corpus Christianorum, Series Graeca (Turnhout: Brepols, 1977–).
5. Corpus Christianorum, Series Latina (Turnhout: Brepols, 1954–).
6. Corpus Scriptorum Christianorum Orientalium (Louvain: various imprints, 1903–).

This series of oriental Christian writers contains the following sub-series listed below:

7. CSCO: Scriptores Aethiopici (Paris, etc., 1903–12; Louvain, 1926–).
8. CSCO: Scriptores Arabici (Paris, etc., 1903–12; Rome, 1922; Louvain, 1926–).
9. CSCO: Scriptores Armeniaci (Louvain, 1953–).
10. CSCO: Scriptores Coptici (Paris, etc., 1906–49; Louvain, 1949–).
11. CSCO: Scriptores Iberici (Louvain, 1950–).
12. CSCO: Scriptores Syri (Paris, etc., 1907–19; Louvain, 1919–).
13. CSCO: Subsidia (Louvain, 1950–).
14. Corpus Scriptorum Ecclesiasticorum Latinorum (Vienna: various imprints, 1866–). Often called simply 'the Vienna corpus', a reliable and widely used series.
15. Die griechischen christlichen Schriftsteller der ersten drei Jahrhunderts (Leipzig: Hinrich, 1897–1941; Berlin and Leipzig: Akademie Verlag, 1953; Berlin: Akademie Verlag, 1954–). This is known as 'the Berlin corpus'; it is a reliable and widely used series.
16. Döpp, S. *et al.* (eds.), Fontes Christiani (Freiburg: Herder, 1990). Texts and translations from ancient and medieval authors.
17. Graffin, R., Nau, F., *et al.* (eds.), Patrologia Orientalis (Paris: Firmin-Didot, 1903–66; Turnhout: Brepols, 1968–).
18. Migne, J.-P. (ed.), Patrologia Cursus Completus Series Graeca, 162 vols. (Paris: Garnier, 1857–66). As the name says, complete, although drawn from editions existing in the nineteenth century, some of which dated to the Renaissance. The electronic form of *Patrologia Græca* (Electronic PG) has been digitized in image format. Available at <http://rosetta.reltech.org/reltech/PG/>.

19. Migne, J.-P. (ed.), Patrologia Cursus Completus Series Latina, 224 vols. (Paris: Garnier, 1844–64). Hamman, A. (ed.), *Patrologiae Latinae Supplementum*, 5 vols. (Paris: Garnier, 1958–70). As with the PG, PL is complete but dependent upon old editions. Electronic database: Patrologia Latina (Ann Arbor: Proquest Information and Learning Company, New York, 1996). A complete electronic version of Migne's first edition available at <http://pld.chadwyck.co.uk/>.

20. Oxford Early Christian Texts (Oxford: Oxford University Press, 1971–). These appear from time to time. Edition of text with English translation and valuable notes.

21. Patristische Texte und Studien (Berlin: de Gruyter, 1964–).

22. Scrittori Greci et Latini (Milan: A. Mondadori, 1974–).

23. Sources Chrétiennes (Paris: Éditions du Cerf, 1942–); published in paperback with French translation and valuable notes.

24. Texte und Untersuchung zur Geschichte der altchristlichen Literatur (Leipzig: J. C. Hinrich, 1882–1943; Berlin: Akademie Verlag, 1951–). Founded by the great Adolph von Harnack, this series includes texts but also studies on early Christian writers.

25. Traditio Christiana: Texte und Kommentare zur patristischen Theologie (Bern: Peter Lang, 1969–).

Many texts have been edited outside of a series, such as James O'Donnell's 3-vol. edn. with commentary of Augustine's *Confessions* (Oxford: Clarendon Press, 1992), electronic edition from The Stoa Consortium (Medford, Mass., 1999); see <http://www.stoa.org/>, 9 June 2006. There are simply too many independent editions to be listed here.

VIII. GUIDES TO EARLY CHRISTIAN WRITERS

The writers of this period have dominated much of the scholarship, and introductions to them are essential. Often these works carry the title 'patrology': that is, the study of the church fathers. Into the early twentieth century, these introductions would include doctrinal concerns, usually proof that the fathers support the doctrinal position of the author's church. Recent works, however, take more ecumenical and scholarly approaches. They usually provide introductions to the writers' lives and works with a guide to the works in the original languages and to translations as well, along with bibliographies of secondary works. Some guides, such as the *Clavis Patrum Latinorum* (1995) and *Clavis Patrum Graecorum* (1974–) do not offer biographies or recommend translations, but just list the primary sources. Thus they should be used by those already well acquainted with the writer.

As this chapter progresses, we cover numerous works that impact other areas besides the one under which they are listed. For example, the entries in the encyclopedias of early Christianity (Ferguson 1997; di Berardino 1992) often include guides to their subjects' writings. Here we list only those specifically intended to introduce the writings.

1. Albert, M. (ed.), *Christianismes Orientaux: Introduction à l'Étude des Langues et des Littératures* (Paris: Éditions du Cerf, 1993).
2. Altaner, B., and Stuiber, A., *Patrologie: Leben, Schriften u. Lehre d. Kirchenväter*, 9th rev. edn. (Freiburg: Herder, 1980).
3. Cayré, F., *Manual of Patrology and History of Theology* (Paris: Desclée, 1940).
4. Campenhausen, H. von, *The Fathers of the Greek Church* (London: Adam and Charles Black, 1963).
5. Campenhausen, H. von, *The Fathers of the Latin Church* (London: Adam and Charles Black, 1964).
6. Chryssavgis, J., *The Way of the Fathers: Exploring the Patristic Mind.* (Thessalonica: Patriarchikon Hidryma Paterikon Meleton, 1998).
7. Dekkers, E., and Gaar, A. (eds.), *Clavis Patrum Latinorum*, 3rd edn. (Turnhout: Brepols, 1995). The *Library of Latin Texts (CLCLT)* is a database of the Corpus Christianorum available through CD-rom that includes *Clavis Patrum Latinorum* entries: <http://www.brepolis.net/>, 9 June 2006.
8. Drobner, H., *The Fathers of the Church: A Comprehensive Introduction* (Peabody, Mass.: Hendrickson, 2007).
9. Geerard, M., and Florie, F. (eds.), *Clavis Patrum Graecorum*, 3rd edn., 5 vols. (Turnhout: Brepols, 1974–87); *Supplementum*, ed. M. Geerard and J. Noret (Turnhout: Brepols, 1998).
10. Kannengiesser, C., *Handbook of Patristic Exegesis: The Bible in Ancient Christianity*, 2 vols. (Leiden: E. J. Brill, 2004).
11. McGuckin, J., *The Westminster Handbook to Patristic Theology* (Louisville, Ky.: Westminster/John Knox Press, 2004).
12. Quasten, J., *Patrology*, i–iv (Westminster, Md.: Newman Press, 1950–86); vol. iv, A. di Berardino (ed.) Early volumes now dated for secondary sources and some methodological approaches, but still a basic work.
13. Urbina, O. de, *Patrologia Syriaca*, rev. edn. (Rome: Pontificium Institutum Orientalium Studorium, 1965).
14. Young, F., Ayres, L., and Louth, A. (eds.), *The Cambridge History of Early Christian Literature* (Cambridge: Cambridge University Press, 2004).
15. Young, F. M., *From Nicaea to Chalcedon: A Guide to the Literature and Its Background* (Philadelphia: Fortress Press, 1983).

IX. DICTIONARIES

The study of ancient texts requires technical dictionaries. Following are some basic ones:

1. Arndt, W. (ed.), *A Greek–English Lexicon of the New Testament and Other Early Christian Literature,* rev. by F. W. Danker, 3rd edn. (Chicago: University of Chicago Press, 2000).

2. Bedrossian, M., *New Dictionary: Armenian–English* (Beirut: Librairie du Liban, 1974).

3. Blaise, A., and Chirat, H., *Dictionnaire latin-français des auteurs chrétiens: Revu spécialement pour le vocabulaire théologique* (Turnhout: Brepols, 1967).

4. Costaz, L., *Syriac–French–Arabic–English Dictionary* (Beirut: Dar el-Machreq, 1986; repr. Piscataway, NJ: Gorgias Press, 2006).

5. Crane, G., *The Perseus Digital Library,* Tufts University, <http://www.perseus.tufts.edu>, 9 June 2006. Contains Greek and Latin dictionaries and morphological analysis of words.

6. Crum, W. E. (ed.), *A Coptic Dictionary* (Oxford: Clarendon Press, 1939).

7. Dillman, A., *Lexicon Linguae Aethiopicae: cum indice Latino* (New York: F. Ungar Pub. Co., 1955).

8. Glare, P. D. W. (ed.), *Oxford Latin Dictionary* (Oxford: Oxford University Press, 1982).

9. Lampe, G. W. H. (ed.), *A Patristic Greek Lexicon* (Oxford: Oxford University Press, 1961).

10. Leslau, W., *Comparative Dictionary of Ge'ez (Classical Ethiopic)* (Wiesbaden: O. Harrassowitz, 1989).

11. Lewis, C. T., and Short, C. (eds.), *A Latin Dictionary* (Oxford: Oxford University Press, 1963).

12. Liddell, H. G., and Scott, R. (eds.) *A Greek–English Lexicon,* 9th edn. (Oxford: Oxford University Press, 1996).

13. Manzanares, C. (ed.), *Dizionario sintetico di patristica* (Vatican City: Libreria Editrice Vaticana, 1995).

14. Prinz, O. (ed.), *Mittellateinisches Wörterbuch bis zum Ausgehenden 13. Jahrhundert* (Munich: Beck, 1996).

15. Smith, R. P., *A Compendious Syriac Dictionary, founded upon the Thesaurus Syriacus of R. Payne Smith, edited by J. P. Smith (Mrs. Margoliouth)* (Oxford: Oxford University Press, 1957; repr. 1985). For a gateway into the Syriac digital world, consult <www.bethmardutho.org>, 10 June 2006. One can download a Syriac dictionary from this website.

16. Sophocles, E. A. (ed.), *Greek Lexicon of the Roman and Byzantine Periods, from B.C. 146 to A.D. 1100* (Cambridge, Mass.: Harvard University Press, 1914).

17. Souter, A. (ed.), *A Glossary of Later Latin to 600 A.D.* (Oxford: Oxford University Press, 1949).

18. *Thesaurus Linguae Latinae* (Leipzig: Teubner, 1900–).

19. Woodward, Roger (ed.), *Cambridge Encyclopedia of the World's Ancient Languages* (Cambridge: Cambridge University Press, 2004).

20. While there is no dictionary specifically for Christian Arabic, scholars may wish to consult G. Graf's *Verzeichnis arabischer kirchlicher Termini*, CSCO 147 (1954) for a helpful glossary.

X. MANUSCRIPTS

Following is a limited list with some links to manuscript sources:

1. *Bibliotheca Hagiographica Graeca*, 3rd edn., ed. F. Halkin, Subsidia Hagiographica, 8a, 3 vols. (Brussels: Société des Bollandistes, 1957). *Novum Auctarium Bibliothecae Hagiographicae Graecae*, ed. Halkin, F. Subsidia Hagiographica, 65 (Brussels: Société des Bollandistes, 1984).

2. *Bibliotheca Hagiographica Latina Antiquae et Mediae Aetatis*, ed. Socii Bollandiani, Subsidia Hagiographica, 6, 2 vols. (Brussels: Société des Bollandistes, 1898–1901). *Bibliotheca Hagiographica Latina Antiquae et Mediae Aetatis*, (*Novum supplementum*, ed. H. Fros, Subsidia Hagiographica, 70 Brussels: Société des Bollandistes, 1986).

3. *Bibliotheca Hagiographica Orientalis*, ed. P. Peeters, Subsidia Hagiographica, 10 (Brussels: Société des Bollandistes, 1954).

4. *Catalogue de Manuscrits Arabes Chrétiens Conservés au Caire* (Città del Vaticano: Biblioteca apostolica vaticana, 1934).

5. Coulie, B., *Répertoire des Bibliothèques et des Catalogues de Manuscrits Arméniens* (Turnhout: Brepols, 1992).

6. Olivier, J., *Répertoire des Bibliothèques et des Catalogues de Manuscrits Grecs de Marcel Richard*, 3rd edn. (Turnhout: Brepols, 1995).

There are many lists of manuscripts of the works of individual early Christian writers, and critical editions, such as those in the Corpus Christianorum series, that discuss the manuscripts and earlier editions of texts. There is also access to Syriac manuscripts through eBeth Arké: large collection of books, journal articles, pictures, and musical recordings in an eLibrary, to be accessible over the Internet: <www.bethmardutho.org>, 10 June 2006. Several universities have digitalized their manuscript holdings. See e.g. the Digital Scriptorium at Berkeley, <http://sunsite.berkeley.edu/Scriptorium/>, 10 June 2006; Brigham Young University, <http://www.byu.edu/~hurlbut/dscriptorium/>, 10 June 2006;

the Hill Museum and Monastic Library at St John's University, <http://www.hmml.org/index.asp>, 10 June 2006, and the Early Manuscript Collection at Oxford University, <http://image.ox.ac.uk/>, 10 June 2006.

XI. TRANSLATIONS IN SERIES

1. Ancient Christian Writers (Westminster, Md.: Newman Press, 1946–70; now Paulist Press has the imprint)—in general the best translation series because of the extensive footnotes. The earliest volumes are now almost 60 years old, and scholarship has moved past them in many ways. The citations of primary sources, however, especially classical ones, remain valuable, especially since at the time the series was initiated, many patristic scholars were also classicists.

2. The Apostolic Fathers: A New Translation and Commentary, 6 vols. (New York: Thomas Nelson & Sons, 1964).

3. Bibliotheca Armeniaca (Venice: Casa Editrice Armena, 1975–).

4. Cistercian Studies Series (Kalamazoo, Mich.: Cistercian Publications, 1969–)—in spite of the title, this series has many early Christian works, such as the *Pachomian Koinonia*, and with helpful notes.

5. Clark, G. (ed.), Translated Texts for Historians (Liverpool: Liverpool University Press, 1985–)—often publishes texts not found in other collections.

6. Classics of Western Spirituality (Mahwah, NJ: Paulist Press, 1946–)—goes up to the modern era, but many early Christian works are included.

7. Early Church Fathers (London: Routledge, 1996–).

8. Fathers of the Church (New York: Fathers of the Church, Inc., 1949–60; now Washington D.C.: Catholic University of America Press, 1962–)—large, growing series with reliable translations but not the notes available in ACW.

9. Göttinger Orientforschungen (Wiesbaden: O. Harrassowitz, 1971–).

10. Harvard Armenian Texts and Studies (Cambridge, Mass.: Harvard University Press, 1965–).

11. Horae Semiticae, 11 numbers (Cambridge: University Press, 1903–16).

12. Khoury, A. Th., and Glei, R. (eds.), Corpus Islamo-Christianum, Series Coptica (Altenberge: Oros, 2004–); Series Graeca (Altenberge: Telos, 1988); and Series Latina (Würzburg: Echter Verlag, 1990–). Texts with translation.

13. Library of Christian Classics (London: SCM Press; Philadelphia: Westminster Press, 1953–66)—many periods, but several useful early Christian works included.

14. Message of the Fathers of the Church, 22 vols. (Collegeville, Minn.: Liturgical Press, 1983–97)—titles organized topically.

15. Oxford Early Christian Texts (Oxford: Oxford University Press, 1971–). These appear from time to time. Edition of text with English translation and valuable notes.

16. Popular Patristics Series (Crestwood, NY: St Vladimir's Seminary Press, 1977–)—focuses mainly on Greek writers.

17. Selections from the Fathers of the Church (Washington: Catholic University of America Press, 1996–).

18. The Ante-Nicene Fathers: Translations of the Writings of the Fathers, down to A. D. 325. (Edinburgh: T & T Clark, 1867–72). A revised American edition was published by A. Cleveland Coxe (Buffalo, NY: Christian Literature Pub. Co.; 1885–96). Recents reprints have appeared from W. B. Eerdmans, Hendrickson Publishers, and online at Christian Classics Ethereal Library.

19. The Nicene and Post-Nicene Fathers (Edinburgh: T & T Clark, 1867–72). A Victorian collection edited by first-rate scholars of that era; valuable for its completeness and reprinted in 38 vols. Recent reprints have appeared from W. B. Eerdmans, Hendrickson Publishers, and online at Christian Classics Ethereal Library.

20. Sources of Early Christian Thought (Philadelphia: Fortress Press, 1980–). Short English translations of early Christian texts without critical notes or indices.

21. Studia Sinaitica, 12 vols. (Cambridge: Cambridge University Press, 1894–1907).

22. Texts and Studies: Contributions to Biblical and Patristic Literature (Cambridge: Cambridge University Press, 1891–1963; repr. Nendeln, Liechtenstein: Kraus Reprint, 1967).

23. Texts from Christian Late Antiquity (Piscataway, NJ: Gorgias Press).

24. Woodbrooke Studies, 7 vols. (Cambridge: Cambridge University Press, 1927–33).

25. Writings From the Greco-Roman World (Atlanta: SBL; Leiden: E. J. Brill).

XII. Collections of Documents in Individual Volumes

There are many of these, and the number keeps growing. This is a select list.

1. Arnold, E. (ed.), *The Early Christians: A Sourcebook on the Witness of the Early Church,* trans. and ed. by the Society of Brothers at Rifton, New York (Rifton, NY: Plough Publishing Series, 1972).

2. Bettenson, H. (ed. and trans.), *The Early Christian Fathers: A Selection from the Writings of the Fathers from St. Clement of Rome to St. Athanasius* (London: Oxford University Press, 1969).

3. Bettenson, H. (ed. and trans.), *The Later Christian Fathers: A Selection from the Writings of the Fathers from St. Cyril of Jerusalem to St. Leo the Great* (London: Oxford University Press, 1970)—with the previous entry, a basic collection, helpful for the classroom.

4. Brock, S. P., and Harvey, S. A. (eds. and trans.), *Holy Women of the Christian Orient* (Berkeley: University California Press, 1998)—women's hagiographies from the Syrian Orient.

5. Ehrman, B., and Jacobs, A., *Christianity in Late Antiquity, 300–450: A Reader* (New York: Oxford University Press, 2004). Outstanding collection, useful in the classroom, with helpful introductions.

6. Elliott, J. K. (ed.), *The Apocryphal New Testament* (Oxford: Oxford University Press, 1993); abridged version: *The Apocryphal Jesus: Legends of the Early Church* (Oxford: Oxford University Press, 1996).

7. Ferguson, E. (ed.), *Early Christians Speak: Faith and Life in the First Three Centuries*, 3rd edn. (Abilene, Tex.: Abilene Christian University Press, 1999).

8. Grant, R. (ed. and trans.), *Second-Century Christianity: A Collection of Fragments* (London: S.P.C.K., 1957; rev. edn. Louisville, Ky.: Westminster/John Knox Press, 2003). As the title suggests, it contains fragmentary, but important, passages from second-century Christian literature assembled in a convenient volume.

9. Hoare, F. R. (ed.), *The Western Fathers* (New York: Harper & Row, 1965).

10. Layton, B. (ed.), *The Gnostic Scriptures*, Anchor Bible Reference Library (New York: Doubleday, 1987)—despite the subtitle 'Ancient Wisdom for a New Age', this is a sizeable, useful collection.

11. Lee, A. D., *Pagans and Christians in Late Antiquity: A Sourcebook* (London: Routledge, 2000).

12. Maas, M., *Readings in Late Antiquity: A Sourcebook* (London: Routledge, 2000).

13. Madigan, K., and Osiek, C. (eds. and trans.), *Ordained Women in the Early Church: A Documentary History* (Baltimore: Johns Hopkins University Press, 2005).

14. Miller, P. (ed.), *Women in Early Christianity: Translations from Greek Texts* (Washington: Catholic University of America Press, 2005).

15. Robinson, J. (ed.), *The Nag Hammadi Library*, rev. edn. (San Francisco: Harper & Row, 1990)—basic collection of Gnostic texts.

16. Schneemelcher, W. (ed.), *New Testament Apocrypha*, trans. R. McL. Wilson, 2 vols. (Cambridge: James Clark & Co. Ltd., 1991; Louisville, Ky.: Westminster/John Knox Press, 1991)—basic collection with good introductions, notes, and references to other primary sources.

17. Sparks, H. F. D. (ed.), *The Apocryphal Old Testament* (Oxford: Oxford University Press, 1984)—sizeable (990 pp.) collection with notes.

18. Stevenson, J. (ed.), *A New Eusebius*, rev. W. H. C. Frend (London: S.P.C.K., 1966; rev. edn. 1987)—valuable collection of excerpts from early Christian writers and pagan sources about Christians up to Constantine and Nicaea—should be used with its companion volume, *Creeds, Councils, and Controversies* (London: S.P.C.K., 1966; rev. edn. 1987), which takes the story of Christianity down to 451 CE.

19. Valantasis, R. (ed.), *Religions of Late Antiquity in Practice* (Princeton: Princeton University Press, 2000).

XIII. STUDIES IN SERIES

1. Äthiopistische Forschungen (Wiesbaden: Harrassowitz).
2. Ancient Commentary on Scripture (Downers Grove, Ill.: InterVarsity Press).
3. Christianity and Judaism in Antiquity Series (Notre Dame, Ind.: University of Notre Dame Press).
4. The Church's Bible (Grand Rapids, Mich.: Eerdmans).
5. La Collection des Études Augustiniennes (Paris: L'Institut d'études augustiniennes).
6. Early Christian Studies (Brisbane: Centre for Early Christian Studies).
7. Eastern Christian Studies Series, and Texts and Studies Series (Piscataway, NJ: Gorgias Press).
8. Études sur le Christianisme et le Judaïsme (Waterloo, Ont.: Wilfrid Laurier University Press).
9. Handbuch der Orientalistik, Erste Abteilung, Nahe und der Mittlere Osten (Leiden: E. J. Brill).
10. Hermeneia (Minneapolis: Fortress Press).
11. Key Themes in Ancient History (Cambridge: Cambridge University Press).
12. Message of the Fathers of the Church, 22 vols. (Collegeville, Minn.: Liturgical Press).
13. Nag Hammadi and Manichaean Studies (Leiden: E. J. Brill).
14. Orientalia Christiana Analecta (Rome: Pontificium Institutum Orientalium Studorium).
15. Oxford Early Christian Studies (Oxford: Oxford University Press).
16. Patrimoine Chrétien Arabe (Lyon: Librairie Saint-Paul; Rome: Pontificium Institutum Orientalium Studorium).
17. Patristic Monograph Series, North American Patristic Society (Washington D.C.: Catholic University of America Press).

18. Patristic Studies (New York: Peter Lang).
19. Religion in the First Christian Centuries (New York: Routledge).
20. Religions in the Graeco-Roman World (Leiden: E. J. Brill).
21. Religionswissenschaftliche Studien (Attenberge: Oros and Echter).
22. Routledge Early Christian Monographs (New York: Routledge).
23. Studia Ephemeridis Augustinianum (Rome: Institutum Patristicum Augustinianum).
24. Studien und Texte zu Antike und Christentum (Tübingen: Paul Siebeck).
25. Studies in Church History (Woodbridge, Suffolk: Boydell Press; Ecclesiastical History Society, UK).
26. Studies in Early Christianity, 18 vols. (New York: Garland Press).
27. Studies in the History of Christian Thought (Leiden: E. J. Brill).
28. Supplements to *Vigiliae Christianae* (Leiden: E. J. Brill).
29. Transformation of the Classical Heritage (Berkeley: University of California Press).
30. Variorum Reprints (London: Variorum).
31. Wahrheitsanspruch in den ersten Jahrhunderten (Paderborn: Sohöninigh).
32. Wissenschaft und die Kunde der älteren Kirche (Berlin: de Gruyter).

XIV. JOURNALS

1. *Aethiopica* (Hamburg)
2. *American Benedictine Review*
3. *American Journal of Ancient History*
4. *American Journal of Philology*
5. *Analecta Bollandiana*
6. *Anglican Theological Review*
7. *Annales d' Èthiopie* (Paris)
8. *Annual of the American Schools of Oriental Research*
9. *Annual of Armenian Linguistics* (Cleveland)
10. *L'antiquité classique*
11. *Aram* (Peeters)
12. *Aramaic Studies* (electronic journal)
13. *Archaeological Journal*
14. *Augustinian Studies*
15. *Augustinianum*
16. *Bazmavêp: Revue des Êtudes Armêniennes* (San Lazzaro)
17. *Biblical Archaeologist*

18. *Biblische Zeitschrift*
19. *Bulletin d'ancienne littérature et d'archéologie chrétienne*
20. *Byzantinische Zeitschrift*
21. *Byzantion*
22. *Catholic Biblical Quarterly* (journal of the Catholic Biblical Association)
23. *Catholic Historical Review* (journal of the American Catholic Historical Association)
24. *Church History* (journal of the American Society of Church History)
25. *Classical Journal*
26. *Classical Quarterly*
27. *Classical World*
28. *Coptic Church Review*
29. *Dumbarton Oaks Papers*
30. *Eastern Christian Art* (Peeters)
31. *Enchoria*
32. *Ephemerides Theologicae Lovanienses*
33. *Greek Orthodox Theological Review*
34. *The Harp* (a review of Syriac and Oriental Studies, Kottayam)
35. *Harvard Studies in Classical Philology*
36. *Harvard Theological Review*
37. *Hugoye: Journal of Syriac Studies*, <http://bethmardutho.cua.edu/hugoye/>
38. *Islamochristiana* (Rome)
39. *Journal asiatiqe*
40. *Journal of the American Academy of Religion*
41. *Journal of Biblical Literature* (journal of the Society of Biblical Literature)
42. *Journal of Coptic Studies* (Peeters)
43. *Journal of Early Christian Studies* (Johns Hopkins University Press; journal of the North American Patristic Society)
44. *Journal of Eastern Christian Studies* (Peeters)
45. *Journal of Ecclesiastical History*
46. *Journal of Ethiopian Studies* (Addis-Ababa)
47. *Journal of Hellenic Studies*
48. *Journal of Jewish Studies*
49. *Journal of Religion*
50. *Journal of Religious History*
51. *Journal of Roman Studies*
52. *Journal of Semitic Studies*
53. *Journal of Theological Studies* (Oxford)
54. *Le Muséon: Revue d'études Orientales* (Louvain)
55. *Numen*
56. *Oriens Christianus*
57. *L'Orient syrien*

58. *Orientalia Lovaniensia Periodica* (Peeters)
59. *Parole de l'Orient* (Kaslik)
60. *Revue de l'orient chrétien*
61. *Revue d'histoire ecclésiastique*
62. *Revue des études augustiniennes*
63. *Revue des études byzantines*
64. *Sobornost*
65. *Studia Liturgica*
66. *Studia Monastica*
67. *Studia Patristica* (not technically a journal, but publishes papers from the quadrennial International Conference on Patristic Studies held at Oxford University)
68. *St Vladimir's Theological Quarterly*
69. *Syria: Revue de l'art oriental et d' archéologie* (Paris)
70. *Theological Studies*
71. *Vigiliae Christianae*
72. *Worship* (Collegeville, Minn.: Benedictines of St John's Abbey)
73. *Zeitschrift der Deutschen Morgenländischen Gesellschaft*
74. *Zeitschrift für Antike und Christentum* (Berlin: de Gruyter)
75. *Zeitschrift für Kirchengeschichte*

XV. INDICES AND BIBLIOGRAPHIES

1. Aland, K. (ed.), *Repertorium der griechischen christlichen Papyri* (Berlin: de Gruyter, 1976–).
2. Centre D'Analyse et de Documentation Patristiques (eds.), *Biblia Patristica: Index des citations et allusions bibliques dans la littérature patristique* (Paris: Éditions du Centre national de la recherche scientifique, 1975– <2000>).
3. Patristische Kommission der Akademien der Wissenschaften zu Göttingen, Heidelberg, Mainz, und München (eds.), *Bibliographia patristica: Internationale patristische Bibliographie*, i– (1959–); lists annually in helpful organization all of the books, dissertations, and articles published in patristics.
4. Kadel, A., *Matrology: A Bibliography of Writings by Christian Women from the First to the Fifteenth Centuries* (New York: Continuum, 1995). Contains a strong section on early Christianity and late antiquity.

5. Robinson, T., *The Early Church: An Annotated Bibliography of Literature in English* (Metuchen, NJ: American Theological Library Association and Scarecrow Press, Inc., 1993). This is a helpful and detailed source, although more than 10 years old.

XVI. Full Text Databases and Electronic Indices

1. *Academic Jewish Studies Internet Directory*: <http://www.jewish-studies. com/> 9 June 2006. An important discussion forum in the Internet on Judaism in the Greco-Roman world is *Ioudaios*: <http://ccat.sas.upenn. edu/ioudaios/> 1 October 2006. As of 31 December 2004, this website is no longer being updated.

2. *L'Annee Philologique*: 1959–2002; an on-line version of international, multilingual bibliography of all aspects of classical studies. <http://www.annee-philologique.com> 9 June 2006.

3. *Anthropology Plus*. This combines Anthropological Index Online and Anthropological Literature. <http://www.rlg.org/en/page.php?Page_ID=165>, 13 June 2006.

4. *Archival Resources*. Provides finding aids for archives. <http://www.rlg.org/ arr/index.html >, 13 June 2006.

5. Arts and Humanities Citation Index. This provides access to current and retrospective bibliographic information. <http://scientific.thomson.com/ products/ahci/>, 13 June 2006.

6. *ATLA* database and indexing tool for articles, book reviews and collections of essays in Religious Studies: <http://www.atla.com/products/ catalogs/catalogs_rdb.html> 9 June 2006.

7. The *Bibliographic Information Base in Patristics* (BIBP) is a documentary system highly specialized in patristics. <http://www.bibl.ulaval. ca/bd/bibp/english.html> 1 October 2006.

8. Catalog de l'École Biblique et Archéologique Française de Jérusalem: the *Catalogue de l'École Biblique et Archéologique Française* (Catalogue of the French Biblical and Archaeological School of Jerusalem). Electronic edition of the card catalogue database of the École Biblique's library. <http://www.brill.nl/>, 9 June 2006.

9. CETEDOC (Corpus Christianorum, Series Latina): The CETEDOC Library of Christian Latin Texts (CLCLT) is a CD-rom of Christian Latin texts (late

second-century through fifteenth-century texts). Conciliar documents also included. It is located at the Université Catholique de Louvain. The database includes almost all works in the Corpus Christianorum and ancient literature from Bibliotheca scriptorum Romanorum Teubneriana. Some works are from the Corpus Scriptorum Ecclesiasticorum Latinorum, Sources Chrétiennes, Migne's *Patrologia*, Acta Sanctorum, and *Analecta Hymnica Medii Aevi*. The Centre *Traditio Litterarum Occidentalium* (CTLO) is the 'human sciences computer laboratory' for the study of Latin texts and continues the activities of CETEDOC; see <http://www.brepols.net/publishers/ctlo.htm>, 1 October 2006. Also from Brepols are the *Vetus Latina Database* [Bible Versions of the Latin Fathers], *Archive of Celtic–Latin Literature* (ACLL)/ Royal Irish Academy [Corpus of Latin literature produced in Celtic-speaking Europe]. *Lexikon des Mittelalters* (LexMass.): Encyclopedia for medievalists and scholars of various other disciplines covering the period from 300 to 1500, for Europe and parts of the Middle East and North Africa. Gateway to all on-line projects of Brepols Publishers and its partners: <http://www.brepolis.net>, 1 October 2006.

10. FRANCIS database: 1984 to present; through an international perspective, FRANCIS provides citations to interdisciplinary materials for the humanities and social sciences. Citations include journal articles, conference papers, books, reports, and doctoral dissertations. See <http://www.inist.fr/en/PRODUITS/francis.php>, 9 June 2006.

11. Available through *ERL WebSPIRS: History of Art Bibliography, Art Abstracts*, and *Art Index Retrospective* contain bibliographies of articles on all periods of art history, including ancient, late antique, and Byzantine. See SilverPlatter Platform, available through Ovid, <http://www.ovid.com/site/products/tools/silverplatter/>, 9 June 2006.

12. *Index Islamicus.* Published by Brill, guide to new books, reviews, and articles on the Muslim world. <http://www.brill.nl/m_catalogue_sub6_id10433.htm>, 9 June 2006.

13. *In Principio*: Incipit Index of Latin Texts (INPR) Institut de Recherche et d'Histoire des Textes (Paris) and the Hill Monastic Manuscript Library (Collegeville, Minn.). CD-ROM <http://www.hmml.org/>, 1 October 2006.

14. The *International Repertory of the Literature of Art* (RILA) includes art from late Antiquity (fourth century). All types of publication are covered, published by the Getty Institute. <http://www.bcr.org/reference/csa/bhaindex.html>, 9 June 2006.

15. *Thesaurus Linguae Graecae* (TLG): <http://www.tlg.uci.edu>., 13 January 2008. The *Thesaurus Linguae Graecae* (TLG®) has digitized most literary texts written in Greek from Homer to the fall of Byzantium in 1453 CE.

XVII. ELECTRONIC SERIES AND HYPERTEXTS IN EARLY CHRISTIAN STUDIES

1. *Christian Classics Ethereal Library*. Collection of the Ante-Nicene, Nicene and Post-Nicene Fathers in translation. <http://www.ccel.org />, 1 October 2006.

2. *Early Christian Writings* is a collection of texts, translations, and commentary from the first three centuries CE. It contains the New Testament, Apocrypha, Gnostics, and Church Fathers. <http://www.earlychristianwritings.com/>, 1 October 2006.

3. *The École Initiative* [Early Church On-line Encyclopedia]. The École Initiative is an excellent resource that works to compile as a hypertext all of the links to internet resources concerning the early church. It contains translations of Jewish, Christian, and Islamic primary sources, short and long essays, and a geographical timeline with a geographical cross-index. <http://www2.evansville.edu/ecoleweb/>, 1 October 2006.

4. *Guide to Early Church Documents*. The Institute for Christian Leadership manages this hypertext index with pointers to (1) New Testament Canonical Information; (2) Writings of the Apostolic Fathers; (3) Patristic Texts; (4) Creeds and Canons; (5) Later Documents and Miscellaneous Texts; and (6) Relevant Internet Sites. <http://www.iclnet.org/pub/resources/christian-history.html>, 1 October 2006.

5. *Internet Medieval Sourcebook*: This is a good starting point for information on the Middle Ages on the Internet and contains resources on a wide array of topics from late antiquity up through the Middle Ages. <http://www.fordham.edu/halsall/sbook.html>, 1 October 2006.

6. *New Advent*: Collection of the Ante-Nicene, Nicene and Post-Nicene Fathers in translation. It includes the lives of the saints and a wide range of general information about Christian History. <http://www.newadvent.com>, 1 October 2006.

7. *A Social Lens: Late Antiquity in the Sermons of John Chrysostom*. <http://www.cecs.acu.edu.au/chrysostom/history.php>, 1 October 2006. Database directed by Pauline Allen and Wendy Mayer on the homilies of John Chrysostom.

General Subject Index

Index of Persons
(Ancient and Modern)

Index of Biblical Citations

....